CLASSICAL
AND MEDIEVAL
LITERATURE
CRITICISM

Guide to Gale Literary Criticism Series

For criticism on	Consult these Gale series
Authors now living or who died after December 31, 1959	*CONTEMPORARY LITERARY CRITICISM (CLC)*
Authors who died between 1900 and 1959	*TWENTIETH-CENTURY LITERARY CRITICISM (TCLC)*
Authors who died between 1800 and 1899	*NINETEENTH-CENTURY LITERATURE CRITICISM (NCLC)*
Authors who died between 1400 and 1799	*LITERATURE CRITICISM FROM 1400 TO 1800 (LC)* *SHAKESPEAREAN CRITICISM (SC)*
Authors who died before 1400	*CLASSICAL AND MEDIEVAL LITERATURE CRITICISM (CMLC)*
Black writers of the past two hundred years	*BLACK LITERATURE CRITICISM (BLC)*
Authors of books for children and young adults	*CHILDREN'S LITERATURE REVIEW (CLR)*
Dramatists	*DRAMA CRITICISM (DC)*
Hispanic writers of the late nineteenth and twentieth centuries	*HISPANIC LITERATURE CRITICISM (HLC)*
Native North American writers and orators of the eighteenth, nineteenth, and twentieth centuries	*NATIVE NORTH AMERICAN LITERATURE (NNAL)*
Poets	*POETRY CRITICISM (PC)*
Short story writers	*SHORT STORY CRITICISM (SSC)*
Major authors from the Renaissance to the present	*WORLD LITERATURE CRITICISM, 1500 TO THE PRESENT (WLC)*

ISSN 0896-0011

Volume 20

CLASSICAL AND MEDIEVAL LITERATURE CRITICISM

Excerpts from Criticism of the Works of World
Authors from Classical Antiquity through the
Fourteenth Century, from the First Appraisals
to Current Evaluations

Jelena O. Krstović
Daniel G. Marowski
Editors

GALE

DETROIT • NEW YORK • TORONTO • LONDON

STAFF

Daniel G. Marowski, *Editor*
Jelena Krstović, *Contributing Editor*
Gerald Barterian, *Associate Editor*
Michelle Lee, *Assistant Editor*
Aarti D. Stephens, *Managing Editor*

Susan M. Trosky, *Permissions Manager*
Kimberly F. Smilay, *Permissions Specialist*
Maureen Puhl, *Permissions Associate*
Sarah Chesney, *Permissions Assistant*
Kelly A. Quin, *Permissions Assistant Co-Op*

Victoria B. Cariappa, *Research Manager*
Laura C. Bissey, Julia Daniel, Tamara C. Nott, Michele P. Le Meau,
Tracie A. Richardson, Cheryl Warnock, *Research Associates*
Alfred Gardner, *Research Assistant*

Mary Beth Trimper, *Production Director*
Deborah Milliken, *Production Assistant*

Sherrell Hobbs, *Macintosh Artist*
Pamela A. Reed, *Photography Coordinator*
Randy Bassett, *Image Database Supervisor*
Mikal Ansari, Robert Duncan, *Imaging Specialists*

™

This book is printed on acid-free paper that meets the minimum requirements of American National Standard for Information Sciences—Permanence Paper for Printed Library Materials, ANSI Z39.48-1984.

Library of Congress Catalog Card Number 88-658021
ISBN 0-7876-1126-3
ISSN 0896-0011
Printed in the United States of America

10 9 8 7 6 5 4 3 2 1

Contents

Preface   vii

Acknowledgments   xi

Preface

Since its inception in 1988, *Classical and Medieval Literature Criticism* has been a valuable resource for students and librarians seeking critical commentary on the writers and works of these periods in world history. Major reviewing sources have assessed *CMLC* as "useful" and "extremely convenient," noting that it "adds to our understanding of the rich legacy left by the ancient period and the Middle Ages," and praising its "general excellence in the presentation of an inherently interesting subject." No other single reference source has surveyed the critical reaction to classical and medieval literature as thoroughly as *CMLC*.

Scope of the Series

CMLC is designed to serve as an introduction for students and advanced readers of the works and authors of antiquity through the fourteenth century. The great poets, prose writers, dramatists, and philosophers of this period form the basis of most humanities curricula, so that virtually every student will encounter many of these works during the course of a high school and college education. By organizing and reprinting an enormous amount of commentary written on classical and medieval authors and works, *CMLC* helps students develop valuable insight into literary history, promotes a better understanding of the texts, and sparks ideas for papers and assignments. Each entry in *CMLC* presents a comprehensive survey of an author's career, an individual work of literature, or a literary topic, and provides the user with a multiplicity of interpretations and assessments. Such variety allows students to pursue their own interests; furthermore, it fosters an awareness that literature is dynamic and responsive to many different opinions.

CMLC continues the survey of criticism of world literature begun by Gale's *Contemporary Literary Criticism (CLC)*, *Twentieth-Century Literary Criticism (TCLC)*, *Nineteenth-Century Literature Criticism (NCLC)*, *Literature Criticism from 1400 to 1800 (LC)*, and *Shakespearean Criticism (SC)*. For additional information about these and Gale's other criticism series, users should consult the Guide to Gale Literary Criticism Series preceding the title page in this volume.

Coverage

Each volume of *CMLC* is carefully compiled to present:

- criticism of authors and works which represent a variety of genres, time periods, and nationalities

- both major and lesser-known writers and works of the period (such as non-Western authors and literature, increasingly read by today's students)

- 4-6 authors or works per volume

- individual entries that survey the critical response to each author, work, or topic, including early criticism, later criticism (to represent any rise or decline in the author's reputation), and current retrospective analyses. The length of each author or work entry also indicates relative importance, reflecting the amount of critical attention the author, work, or topic has received from critics writing in English, and from foreign criticism in translation.

An author may appear more than once in the series if his or her writings have been the subject of a substantial amount of criticism; in these instances, specific works or groups of works by the author will be covered in separate entries. For example, Homer will be represented by three entries, one devoted to the *Iliad*, one to the *Odyssey*, and one to the Homeric Hymns.

Starting with Volume 10, *CMLC* will also occasionally include entries devoted to literary topics. For example, *CMLC-10* focuses on Arthurian Legend and includes general criticism on that subject as well as individual entries on writers or works central to that topic—Chrétien de Troyes, Gottfried von Strassburg, Layamon, and the Alliterative *Morte Arthure*.

Organization of the Book

An author entry consists of the following elements: author heading, biographical and critical introduction, principal English translations or editions, excerpts of criticism (each preceded by a bibliographic citation and an annotation), and a bibliography of further reading.

- The **Author Heading** consists of the author's most commonly used name, followed by birth and death dates. If the entry is devoted to a work, the heading will consist of the most common form of the title in English translation (if applicable), and the original date of composition. Located at the beginning of the introduction are any name or title variations.

- A **Portrait** of the author is included when available. Many entries also feature illustrations of materials pertinent to the author or work, including manuscript pages, book illustrations, and representations of people, places, and events important to a study of the author or work.

- The **Biographical and Critical Introduction** contains background information that concisely introduces the reader to the author, work, or topic.

- The list of **Principal Works** and **English Translations** or **Editions** is chronological by date of first publication and is included as an aid to the student seeking translated versions or editions of these works for study. The list will focus primarily on twentieth-century translations, selecting those works most commonly considered the best by critics.

- **Criticism** is arranged chronologically in each entry to provide a useful perspective on changes in critical evaluation over the years. All titles by the author featured in the critical entry are printed in boldface type to enable the user to ascertain without difficulty the works being discussed. Also for purposes of easier identification, the critic's name and the publication date of the essay are given at the beginning of each piece of criticism. Anonymous criticism is preceded by the title of the journal in which it appeared. Publication information (such as publisher names and book prices) and parenthetical numerical references (such as footnotes or page and line references to specific editions of works) have been deleted at the editors' discretion to provide smoother reading of the text. Many critical entries in *CMLC* also contain translations to aid the users.

- A complete **Bibliographic Citation** provides original publication information for each piece of criticism.

- Critical excerpts are also prefaced by **Annotations** providing the reader with information about both the critic and the criticism, the scope of the excerpt, the growth of critical controversy, or changes in critical trends regarding an author or work. In some cases, these notes include cross-references to excerpts by critics who discuss each other's commentary. Dates in parentheses within the annotation refer to a book publication date when they follow a book title, and to an essay date when they follow a critic's name.

- An annotated bibliography of **Further Reading** appears at the end of each entry and lists additional secondary sources on the author or work. In some cases it includes essays for which the editors could not obtain reprint rights. When applicable, the Further Reading is followed by references to additional entries on the author in other literary reference series published by Gale.

Topic Entries are subdivided into several thematic rubrics in which criticism appears in order of descending scope.

Cumulative Indexes

Each volume of *CMLC* includes a cumulative **author index** listing all authors who have appeared in Gale's Literary Criticism Series, along with cross references to such biographical series as *Contemporary Authors* and *Dictionary of Literary Biography*. For readers' convenience, a complete list of Gale titles included appears on the page prior to the author index. Useful for locating an author within the various series, this index is particularly valuable for those authors who are identified with a certain period but who, because of their death date, are placed in another, or for those authors whose careers span two periods. For example, Geoffrey Chaucer, who is usually considered a medieval author, is found in *Literature Criticism from 1400 to 1800* because he died after 1399.

Beginning with the tenth volume, *CMLC* includes a cumulative index listing all topic entries that have appeared in the Gale Literary Criticism Series *Classical and Medieval Literature Criticism, Contemporary Literary Criticism, Literature Criticism from 1400 to 1800, Nineteenth-Century Literature Criticism,* and *Twentieth-Century Literary Criticism.*

Beginning with the second volume, *CMLC* also includes a cumulative nationality index. Authors and/or works are grouped by nationality, and the volume in which criticism on them may be found is indicated.

Title Index

Each volume of *CMLC* also includes an index listing the titles of all literary works discussed in the series. Foreign language titles that have been translated are followed by the titles of the translations—for example, *Slovo o polku Igorove (The Song of Igor's Campaign)*. Page numbers following these translated titles refer to all pages on which any form of the title, either foreign language or translated, appears. Titles of novels, dramas, nonfiction books, and poetry, short story, or essay collections are printed in italics, while those of all individual poems, short stories, and essays are printed in roman type within quotation marks. In cases where the same title is used by different authors, the author's name or surname is given in parentheses after the title, e.g. *Collected Poems* (Horace) and *Collected Poems* (Sappho).

Critic Index

An index to critics, which cumulates with the second volume, is another useful feature of *CMLC*. Under each critic's name are listed the authors and/or works on whom the critic has written and the volume and page number where criticism may be found.

A Note to the Reader

When writing papers, students who quote directly from any volume in the Literary Criticism Series may use the following general forms to footnote reprinted criticism. The first example pertains to material drawn from a periodical, the second to material reprinted from books.

Rollo May, "The Therapist and the Journey into Hell," *Michigan Quarterly Review,* XXV, No. 4 (Fall 1986), 629-41; excerpted and reprinted in *Classical and Medieval Literature Criticism,* Vol. 3, ed. Jelena O. Krstović (Detroit: Gale Research, 1989), pp. 154-58.

Dana Ferrin Sutton, *Self and Society in Aristophanes* (University of Press of America, 1980); excerpted and reprinted in *Classical and Medieval Literature Criticism,* Vol. 4, ed. Jelena O. Krstović (Detroit: Gale Research, 1990), pp. 162-69.

Suggestions Are Welcome

Readers who wish to make suggestions for future volumes, or who have other comments regarding the series, are cordially invited to write or call the editors (1-800-347-GALE, Fax: (313) 961-6815).

Acknowledgments

The editors wish to thank the copyright holders of the excerpted criticism included in this volume and the permissions managers of many book and magazine publishing companies for assisting us in securing reproduction rights. We are also grateful to the staffs of the Detroit Public Library, the Library of Congress, the University of Detroit Mercy Library, Wayne State University Purdy/Kresge Library Complex, and the University of Michigan Libraries for making their resources available to us. Following is a list of the copyright holders who have granted us permission to reproduce material in this volume of *CMLC*. Every effort has been made to trace copyright, but if omissions have been made, please let us know.

COPYRIGHTED EXCERPTS IN *CMLC*, VOLUME 20, WERE REPRODUCED FROM THE FOLLOWING PERIODICALS:

Anglo-Saxon England, v. 2, 1973 for "Bede and Medieval Civilization" by Gerald Bonner. © Cambridge University Press 1973. Reproduced by permission of the publisher and the author.—*History: The Journal of the Historical Association,* n.s. v. 62, February, 1977. © The Historical Association 1977. Reproduced by permission.—*The Journal of Narrative Technique,* v. 19, Fall, 1989. Copyright © 1989 by The Journal of Narrative Technique. Reproduced by permission.—*The Listener,* v. 71, February 13, 1964 for "Bede, the Monk of Jarrow" by R. W. Southern. © British Broadcasting Corp. Reproduced by permission of the author.—*Medievalia et Humanistica,* n. IV, 1946 for "Bede as Early Medieval Historian" by Charles W. Jones. © The Medieval and Renaissance Society 1946. Reproduced by permission.—*Proceedings of the British Academy,* v. XXII, 1936. Copyright The British Academy 1936. Reproduced by permission.—*Settimane di studio del Centro italiano di studi sull'alto medioevo,* v. XII, 1969 for "The Historical Writings of Bede" by Peter Hunter Blair. Reproduced by permission.—*Studies in Philology,* v. LXXI, April, 1974 for "The Calendrical Structure of Petrarch's 'Canzoniere'" by Thomas R. Roche, Jr. © 1974 by The University of North Carolina Press. Used by permission of the publisher.—*Traditio,* v. XXXI, 1975. Reproduced by permission.

COPYRIGHTED EXCERPTS IN *CMLC*, VOLUME 20, WERE REPRODUCED FROM THE FOLLOWING BOOKS:

Arberry, A. J. From *Tales from the Masnavi.* George Allen and Unwin, 1961. © George Allen & Unwin Ltd, 1961. Reproduced by permission.—Beer, Frances. From *Women and Mystical Experience in the Middle Ages.* The Boydell Press, 1992. © Frances Beer 1992. All rights reserved. Reproduced by permission.—Braden, Gordon. From "Love and Fame: The Petrarchan Career," in *Pragmatism's Freud: The Moral Disposition of Psychoanalysis.* Edited by Joseph K. Smith and William Kerrigan. The Johns Hopkins University Press, 1986. © Forum on Psychiatry and the Humanities of the Washington School of Psychiatry. All rights reserved. Reproduced by permission.—Brown, George Hardin. From *Bede the Venerable.* Twayne, 1987. Copyright © 1987 by G. K. Hall & Co. All rights reserved. Reproduced with the permission of Twayne Publishers, a division of Simon & Schuster, Inc.—Campbell, James. From an introduction to *Bede: The Ecclesiastical History of the English People and Other Selections.* Edited by James Campbell. Washington Square Press, 1968. Copyright ©, 1968 by Washington Square Press, Inc. All rights reserved. Reproduced by permission of Washington Square Press, Inc., a division of Simon & Schuster, Inc.—Campbell, J. From "Bede," in *Latin Historians.* Edited by T. A. Dorey. Basic Books, 1966. © T. A. Dorey 1966. Reproduced by permission of Routledge. In North America and the Philippines by permission of Basic Books, a division of HarperCollins Publishers, Inc.—Colgrave, Bertram. From "Bede's Miracle Stories," in *Bede: His Life, Times, and Writings.* Edited by A. Hamilton Thompson. Oxford at the Clarendon Press, 1935. Reproduced by permission of Oxford University Press.—Colgrave, Bertram. From "Historical Introduction," in *Bede's Ecclesiastical History of the English People.* Edited by Bertram Colgrave and R. A. B. Mynors. Oxford at the Clarendon Press, 1969. © Oxford University Press, 1969. All rights reserved. Reproduced by permission of Oxford University Press.—Dronke, Peter. From *Women Writers of the Middle Ages.* Cambridge University Press, 1984. © Cambridge University Press 1984. Reproduced with the permission of the publisher and the author.—Duckett, Eleanor Shipley. From *Anglo-Saxon Saints and Scholars.* The Macmillan Company, 1947. Copyright, 1947, renewed 1975 by Eleanor Shipley Duckett. All rights reserved. Reproduced with the permission of Macmillan Publishing Company, a division of Simon & Schuster,

PHOTOGRAPHS AND ILLUSTRATIONS APPEARING IN *CMLC*, VOLUME 20, WERE RECEIVED FROM THE FOLLOWING SOURCES:

Bede

c. 673-735

(Also transliterated as Baeda) English historian, scholar, biographer, scientist, poet, and composer.

INTRODUCTION

Acclaimed as the father of English history, Bede provided the single most important source of information about England prior to 731 with his *Historia ecclesiastica gentis Anglorum* (731; *Ecclesiastical History of the English People*). The work is considered the first great history written in western Europe. There was no English nation as we know it when Bede wrote his *Ecclesiastical History*, but through this work, he popularized the idea that the assorted peoples of the land—including those originated from the Angles, Saxons, and Jutes—were a united people, the English. Well over twelve hundred years later, the work continues to be an important source book for early English history from the Roman invasion of England through 731. In his own lifetime, Bede was known mostly for his exegetical works on the Old and New Testaments. His stated purpose in life was to teach and spread Christianity, and at this he was overwhelmingly successful. Bede wrote for his fellow monks but also for the layfolk, with his goal to inspire his readers to follow the Christian life. Many of his writings on the Bible became handbooks used by missionaries in foreign lands to convert non-Christians. Bede was regarded as a great scholar by most of his contemporaries, and today he is considered a scholar without parallel of Europe during the Middle Ages. His works became standards of the Church and were used for centuries, even beyond the Middle Ages. Bede was also renowned as an expert on chronology; his use of reckoning times from the Incarnation that popularized the practice and brought forth the Western calendar as we use it today.

Biographical Information

Bede was born in Northumbria about 673. Nothing is known of his parents other than that they were Christians of English descent. Possibly an orphan by the age of seven, Bede was placed in the monastery of Saint Peter at Wearmouth, where he became an oblate to Benedict Biscop. Bede soon transferred to the sister monastery of Saint Paul at Jarrow, a few miles away, where he would remain until his death. He never left Northumbria and traveled little; the only trips he is known to have taken were to monasteries in Lindisfarne

and York. In 686, when Bede was about thirteen years old, the plague decimated Bede's monastery, killing all except Abbot Ceolfrid and his student, Bede. Ordained a deacon at age nineteen, six years earlier than is typical, Bede became a priest in 703. During this time Bede the monk worked tirelessly on his studies. The library at the monastery contained volumes numbering only in the low hundreds, but perhaps no library in Europe at the time was its superior. Bede said he worked "to compile extracts from the works of the venerable Fathers on holy scripture, and to make commentaries on their meaning and interpretation," and this is how he devoted most of his life. Bede did not speak out against the decadence of his age until his final year, when he criticized bogus monasteries and their pseudo-monks who joined to avoid military service and who did not understand Latin. Bede worked until the last

1

days of his life, when he finished dictating a vernacular translation of the Fourth Gospel, a work that is now lost. On his deathbed he explained, "I do not want my boys to read a lie, or to labour in vain after I am gone." Bede died on May 25, 735.

Major Works

Although Bede spoke English, all of his works were written in Latin, the dominant language for writing during the Middle Ages. Bede's scientific works came naturally from his study of God's created order. *De natura rerum liber* (circa 703; *On the Nature of Things*) examines phenomena on earth, in the heavens, and in the ocean, and is mostly compiled from others' writings. Calculating the date of Easter was considered of great importance, and it was both a controversial and extremely difficult task. Designed to help solve the problems of the ecclesiastical calendar, *De temporibus liber includens chronica minora* (703; *on Times Including a Short Chronology*) was a treatise on the chronology of minutes, hours, days, months, years, centuries, and epochs. Bede's fellow monks urged him to write a more detailed book, and *De temporum ratione liber includens chronica maiora* (725; *On the Reckoning of Times, Including a Long Chronicle*) was the result. Its effect is still felt today, as it established in England the custom of reckoning years from the era of the Incarnation, rather than from the creation of the world. Bede did not originate this system, but there is no proof of its use in English documents before *On the Reckoning of Times*. Bede appended to this volume an outline of world histories with important dates since the creation of the world. Latin grammar was vital to those men who devoted much of their lives to reading, interpreting, and copying by hand the Bible and other Christian texts, and Bede wrote textbooks on grammar and poetry for his fellow monks. Until recently it was thought that these were Bede's earliest works, but scholars have found evidence supporting later dates for their creation, or at least their revision. *De orthographia* (circa 710-731; *On Orthography*) is an alphabetical arrangement of forms which would likely cause difficultly for students as to spelling or meaning. *De arte metrica et de schematibus tropis* (circa 710-731; *On the Art of Metrics and On Figures and Tropes*) introduces various types of Latin poetry, and its appendix is a study of stylistic figures of speech and allegory. Bede concentrated his efforts on the exegesis of biblical texts. Although much of his writing was not original and some was copied verbatim from other sources, Bede exercised impeccable judgment in his selections and arrangements. Since he wanted to be clearly understood, Bede wrote grammatically, shunning stylistic flourishes. Most of his commentaries were verse-by-verse analyses of a particular passage which detailed the literal meaning and then offered a spiritual meaning. Bede's hagiographies were designed to dem-

onstrate through example the example of a good Christian life. Bede's matter-of-fact and frequent recording of miracles has caused great concern for many modern readers who wonder if he can thus be trusted as an historian, but Bede was following a tradition from which inspiration would result from indications of God's graciousness. Bede wrote two lives of the Northumbrian saint Cuthbert, one in prose circa 706-707, and one in poetry circa 721. Five other lives are the subjects of the *Historia abbatum* (circa 725-731; *History of the Abbots*), which gives a full picture of the life of monks at the beginning of the eighth century. Bede's greatest achievement, the *Ecclesiastical History of the English People*, relates the developments of the Church but focuses on the history of the English nation. Bede's last surviving work, *Epistola ad Ecgbertum Episcopum* (November 5, 734; *Letter to Egbert*), angrily denounces the many false monasteries founded by the nobility to avoid their military duties and bemoans the fact that Bede had found himself having to provide English translations of liturgical texts even for the clergy.

Critical Reception

During his lifetime Bede was highly popular and respected; from at least the ninth century on he has usually been referred to as the Venerable Bede. Such was his acclaim that many works were credited to him that were written by others in order to capitalize on Bede's reputation. At the end of the ninth century, Alfred the Great, almost forty years old, learned Latin himself so that he could translate and supervise the translation of books from Latin into English and educate his people. The *Ecclesiastical History,* one of the books "most necessary for all men to know," was included in King Alfred's project, and thus England was the first nation in Western Europe to have a great history written in the vernacular. Much of the *Ecclesiastical History* also appeared in *The Anglo-Saxon Chronicle*, and his commentaries were used widely by the church until the twelfth century. No author of his time was more respected; this can be seen in the large number of his early manuscripts, including more than one hundred and fifty complete copies of the *Ecclesiastical History,* which survive in spite of massive destruction wrought by Vikings and others. Bede is also highly praised for his accuracy; very few errors in his writings have been found by modern scholars.

PRINCIPAL WORKS

De temporibus liber includens chronica minora [*On Times Including a Short Chronology*] (essay) 703

De natura rerum liber [*On the Nature of Things*] (essay) circa 703

Explanatio Apocalypsis [*On the Apocalypse*] (essay) circa 703-709

Liber hymnorum, rhythmi, variae preces [*Hymns*] (songs) circa 703-731

Vita sancti Cuthberti metrica [*Life of Saint Cuthbert, In Verse*] (biography) circa 706-707

Expositio Actuum Apostolorum [*On the Acts of the Apostles*] (essay) circa 709

De orthographia [*On Orthography*] (essay) circa 710-731

De arte metrica et de schematibus tropis [*On the Art of Metrics and On Figures and Tropes*] (essay) circa 710-731

Homeliarum evangelii libri II [*Homilies on the Gospels*] (essay) circa 720-731

Vita sancti Cuthberti prosaica [*Life of Saint Cuthbert, In Prose*] (biography) circa 721

De temporum ratione liber includens chronica maiora [*On the Reckoning of Times, Including a Long Chronicle*] (essay) 725

Retractatio in Actus Apostolorum [*Retraction on Acts*] (essay) circa 725-731

Historia abbatum [*History of the Abbots*] (history) circa 725-731

Historia ecclesiastica gentis Anglorum [*Ecclesiastical History of the English People*] (history) 731

Aliquot quaestionum liber [*On Eight Questions*] (essay) circa 731-735

Epistola ad Ecgbertum Episcopum [*Letter to Egbert*] (letter) 734

CRITICISM

Rev. G. F. Browne (essay date 1887)

SOURCE: G. F. Browne, "The Homilies of Bede," in *The Venerable Bede*, E. & J. B. Young & Co., 1887, pp. 127-47.

[*In the following excerpt, Browne examines the homilies of Bede, finding them devoid of rhetorical devices, helpful on problematic Latin translations of biblical passages, but characterized by "far-fetched figurative interpretation."*]

The **Homilies** of Bede which have been preserved are in one sense disappointing; they throw little or no light upon the state of society in his time. There is no approach to anything at all resembling the personal interest of which the sermons of Chrysostom are so full. There is no rebuking of notorious sinners, no sarcastic scourging of fashionable follies and vices. The reason of this is obvious, even if we overlook the difference between the two men. Chrysostom preached in a great metropolis, full of luxury and dissipation. Bede read theological lectures in a quiet monastery, where he seems to have had no vices to rebuke, or where, if vices there were, he rebuked them tenderly in private. His **Homilies** reflect the quietness and confidence of the faithful Christian student, addressing a body of his brethren in good works and in a God-fearing life.

Like others of the early preachers, he supports his statements with texts of Scripture more often than is usual in the present time. The Bible was less familiar to ordinary people then than it is now. There was instruction in Christianity to be found in the quotation of texts possibly novel to some hearers. Many points of doctrine were much less assured then; they needed support from every quarter where it could be found, and no support was so good as that which was derived from apposite texts of Scripture.

There is a singular absence of rhetorical attempts in these **Homilies**. It would seem never to have been Bede's intention to work upon the feelings of his hearers by impassioned words. He said what he meant to say clearly and simply, and he left it to its own inherent force to make its way. It would be difficult to find, in the sermons of Bede, passages dwelling in vehement terms upon the horrors of hell and the happiness of heaven. Threats and profuse promises are no more parts of his teaching than are invective and sarcasm parts of his style.

As a rule, Bede took a passage of some considerable length,—one of the lessons for the day, for example, and went through it verse by verse, expounding rather than preaching. He frequently insisted upon the special doctrines which centre round the Incarnation, such as the two natures of Christ, and upon the relation of the Persons in the Blessed Trinity. Such themes suited him better than the more practical subjects which are fitted for those who are conversant with the world and have a mixed and secular congregation to address. It is to be feared that many of Bede's sermons would be stigmatized in these days as "doctrinal," or, by those who say more distinctly what they mean, as "dull."

There is very little indeed of criticism of the text in Bede's sermons. He takes it as he finds it, and he expounds it. This is only what might be expected in those early days; but from a theological student and scholar like Bede we might, perhaps, have expected more reference to the Greek text and to the manner in which the Latin text in use represented it. In some cases where the Greek has a special emphasis which the Latin has not, Bede's remarks take no account of the emphasis in the original. As an example of his textual criticism—there are very few indeed to be found in his sermons—the passage "He came into the parts of Dalmanutha" may be cited. On this Bede remarks that St. Matthew has "Magdala." He thinks that the same place is intended by both evangelists, for "many codices" have "Magedan" in St. Mark instead of "Dalmanutha." It may be noticed as typical of Bede's method of preaching that he makes no point of the emphatic *ye* in John iii. 7, "Marvel not that I said unto thee, *ye* must be born again," though the emphasis of the word is brought out in the Latin text as well as in the Greek original.

Bede's method as a commentator[1] was very different from his method as a preacher. In these days of critical study of the Holy Scriptures in the original languages, it is interesting to observe the manner in which he used the Greek of the New Testament in writing his commentaries. The Bible which was in the hands of his readers and hearers was of course the Latin Bible. Bede did not treat this as later writers treated it, as being sufficient in itself. He was careful to point out omissions, and to warn his readers against mistranslations into which the Latin might lead them if they were not warned. Thus, to take half a chapter as an example, on Acts ii. 20,[2] "the sun shall be turned into darkness," he tells them that though the Latin might suggest "darknesses," it was only because the Latin word had no proper singular; the Greek word, which he gives in his commentary, shows that the correct translation is "darkness." On Acts ii. 23, "Him, being delivered by the determinate counsel and foreknowledge of God, ye have taken," where the Latin omits "ye have taken," he informs his readers that a very important word is omitted in their Latin version, very important because the Jews had the choice between the robber and Jesus, and they *took* Him. Again, in the 30th verse of the same chapter, "that of the fruit of his loins, according to the flesh, He would raise up Christ to sit on his throne," where the Latin omits "according to the flesh, He would raise up Christ," he points out that there is more in the Greek than in the Latin, and tells them what should be added. Similarly in verses 33 and 34 he notes differences between the Latin and the Greek. On verse 41 he remarks that while the Latin text on which he was commenting seemed to say that all who gladly received the word were baptized, another manuscript gave more correctly the true force of the Greek, limiting the statement to the particular individuals who heard the word on that occasion.

On one point Bede was very careful to warn the readers of his commentaries, as careful as a member of the New Testament Revision Company could be. He constantly pointed out the ambiguities caused by the want of an article in the Latin. Thus on Acts i. 6, "Wilt thou at this time restore again the kingdom to Israel?" the Latin gives no hint to enable a reader to determine whether he shall translate it "restore the kingdom of Israel," or "restore the kingdom to Israel." Bede tells

his readers that the Greek article decides the question in favour of the latter. Similarly in the 14th verse of the same chapter, "Mary, the mother of Jesus, and His brethren," the Latin leaves it open to any one to translate, "and her brethren," against which translation Bede gives a warning. And so, too, to take one more example from the same part of the Scripture, in Acts ii. 3, "there appeared unto them cloven tongues, as of fire," the Latin may be rendered "cloven tongues, as it were fire," where Bede informs them that in the Greek there is no ambiguity, the form of the genitive being different from that of the nominative, whereas in the Latin they are the same. An instance of another kind is found in the next verse, "began to speak in other tongues"; here the Latin has "in various tongues," but Bede corrects the translation, and says that it should be "other." From these numerous examples, taken from so small a portion of Scripture, it may be imagined how careful and close was Bede's study of his manuscripts. We feel that we are in the hands of a man who, at least so far as the desire to be accurate is concerned, may be trusted either as a commentator or as a historian.

He speaks in terms of the highest respect of the Virgin Mary, as blessed above all women. But he goes no further than that. His manner of speaking of her may be gathered from a remark which he makes in preaching on one of the festivals in her honour. A most excellent and salutary practice, he says, has long been established in the Church, that her hymn (he is speaking of the *Magnificat*) is sung by all every day at vespers. The object and use of this practice he believes to be that the continual commemoration of our Lord's Incarnation may incite us to deeper devotion, and the recollection of the example set by His mother may strengthen us in virtue. He is careful to explain that the expression "first-born son"—"she brought forth her first-born son"—in no way implies that there were other children born later; and he maintains the theory of the perpetual virginity of the Virgin Mary so strenuously that he prays God to avert from his hearers the blasphemy of holding otherwise. Of "Mariolatry" there is no sign in Bede's *Homilies*. In the *Ecclesiastical History,* Bede relates that Bishop Wilfrid was told by the archangel Michael, in a vision, that the prayers of his disciples and the intercession of the Virgin Mary had moved the Lord to grant Wilfrid a recovery from a dangerous illness.

There are frequent references to the two great Sacraments of Christ, Baptism and the Supper of the Lord. But there is a rather marked absence of any homily on one or other of these subjects specially. It would have been very interesting, and it might have been instructive, to read what Bede thought and taught in detail on these cardinal points of Christian faith and practice. His method of homiletic exposition was such that his views were stated rather incidentally and in passing, than in any very full and formal manner: we find nothing like an elaborate treatise on these and similar points. His mention of the validity of Baptism in the name of the Holy Trinity, by whomsoever administered, is a good example of this. He is preaching on the visit of Nicodemus to Christ, and in commenting on the words of the master in Israel, "How can a man be born when he is old?" he remarks that the same is true of spiritual birth, a man cannot be born again. "No one who has been baptized in the name of the Holy Trinity, even though by a heretic, a schismatic, or an evil person, may be rebaptized by good Catholics, lest the invocation of so great a name be annulled."[3] Passing allusions to the necessity of Baptism will be mentioned when we come to speak of Bede's figurative interpretation of the parable of the Good Samaritan, and of the miracle of the Four Thousand. In another place, speaking on the words of St. Mark vii. 33, "He spit, and touched his tongue," &c., Bede says that from this passage a custom prevalent in his time grew up, the priests touching in like manner the nostrils and ears of those whom they were about to present for Baptism, saying at the same time the word Ephphatha. The touching of the nostrils he understood to be a sign that thenceforward they should be a "sweet savour of Christ" (2 Cor. ii. 15); and he urges all who had received the rite of consecration by Baptism, and all who were about to receive it at the forthcoming season of Easter, to avoid all occasion of falling back into that from which Baptism washed them. In this passage he speaks at some length on the subject of Baptism, and its cleansing power, and it is perhaps rather remarkable that he makes no reference to the question of original sin. In another homily he repeats his reference to the practice of baptizing at Easter; "rightly do we on this night"—the commencement of the festival of Easter—"hallow to the one true God in the font of regeneration the new people of His adoption brought out of the spiritual Egypt."

To the Sacrament of the Supper of the Lord the references in the *Homilies* are frequent and most reverential. English readers not familiar with the early names of things must not be surprised to find that Bede uses the ordinary name *Missa,* the Latin word for *Mass,* to describe the celebration of this Sacrament. In King Alfred's time, "mass-priest" was the accepted designation of officiating clergy in Priests' Orders. In speaking of this Sacrament, Bede uses stronger expressions than he might have done had he known what controversies would rage round almost every word that could be used in connection with it. He uses words well known in Eucharistic controversy, to a greater extent than he uses controversial words in speaking of Baptism. And the reason for this is clear. Our Lord Himself used words as strong as any that can be used when He said, "This is My Body," "This is My Blood," and any language framed on these two statements must seem strong, however free it may be in fact and in

intention from any element of superstition. This is not true of the language used in baptismal controversy. But while it is true that Bede uses words which a cautious writer of the present day might avoid using in public utterances, because of the misconceptions to which his use of them might possibly give rise, it is at least as true that we search in vain for any sign of a belief on Bede's part in the doctrine of transubstantiation. It is so well known that transubstantiation did not appear as a doctrine till long after Bede's time, that it may seem unnecessary to remark that no sign of it is found in Bede. Since, however, some of his expressions have a recognised force in modern controversy, it is not out of place to preface a mention of them by some such caution.

In the passage quoted above from Bede's **"Homily on the Eve of the Resurrection,"** after mentioning the Easter rite of baptism, he proceeds as follows:— "and rightly we celebrate the solemn mass, we offer to God for the advance of our salvation the holy Body and precious Blood of our Lamb, by whom we have been redeemed from our sins." And in another place, speaking of the "manger" of Bethlehem, he says, "He chose the manger, to which animals came to feed, as His resting-place, foreshadowing the refreshing of all the faithful, by the mysteries of His Incarnation, on the table of the holy altar." These are the words of a man who had not been taught by sad experience what mischief may be supposed to lurk under harmless expressions when once they have been appropriated by one side or another in a controversy. Against them we may set such words of his as the following, words which no one who held the views afterwards known as the doctrine of transubstantiation could have used:

> The time of our Passover is at hand. Let us come holy to the Altar of the Lord, not to eat the flesh of a lamb, but to receive the sacred mysteries of our Redeemer. Let no one who abides still in death presume to receive the mysteries of life. Let us pray that He may deign to come to our feast, to illumine us with His presence, to hallow His own gifts to us.

And in another passage he tells his hearers that the sacrifices under the new covenant are spiritual:

> The two altars in the Temple signify the two covenants. The first was the altar of burnt-offerings, covered with brass, for offering victims and sacrifices. This was the Old Covenant. The second was at the entrance of the Holy of Holies, covered with gold, for burning incense. This was the inward and more perfect grace of the New Covenant.

Something to the same effect is a passage on the priesthood after the order of Melchisedech:

Melchisedech, a priest of the most high God, offered to God bread and wine long before the times of the priesthood of the Law. And our Redeemer is called a Priest after the order of Melchisedech, because after the priesthood of the Law had come to an end, He established a similar sacrifice by offering the mystery of His Body and Blood.

Again, in preaching on the words, *"Behold the Lamb of God that taketh away the sins of the world,"* in conjunction with the verse from the Apocalypse, *"Who hath loved us and washed us from our sins in His blood,"* Bede speaks in words which set his views before us in a clear and satisfactory manner.

> He washed us from our sins in His blood, not only when He gave His blood on the cross for us, or when each one of us by the mystery of His holy Passion was washed clean by baptism of water, but He also daily takes away the sins of the world. He washes us from our sins daily in His Blood, when the memory of the same blessed Passion is renewed at the altar, when the creature of bread and wine is transferred into the sacrament of His flesh and blood by the ineffable sanctification of the Spirit; and thus His Flesh and Blood is not poured and slain by the hands of unbelievers to their own destruction, but is taken by the mouth of believers to their own salvation. The paschal lamb in the Law rightly shows forth the figure of this, the lamb which once freed the people from their Egyptian slavery, and in memory of that freeing was wont year by year to sanctify by its offering the same people, until He should come to whom such a victim bare witness; and being offered to the Father for us as a victim and a sweet-smelling savour, after He had offered the lamb, He transferred to the creature of bread and wine the mystery of His Passion, being made a priest for ever after the order of Melchisedech.

It may be worth while to quote on this point the words of a learned divine who presided over the Anglo-Saxon Church two centuries and a half after Bede's death, Ælfric, Archbishop of Canterbury. "When the Lord said, *He that eateth My flesh and drinketh My blood hath everlasting life,* He bade not His disciples to eat the Body wherewith He was enclosed nor to drink that Blood which He shed for us; but He meant that holy morsel which is in a ghostly way His Body and Blood; and he that tasteth it with believing heart hath everlasting life." Thus it would appear that neither early nor late in the history of the Church of England in Saxon times were erroneous views held by the chief divines on this cardinal point of Christian doctrine.

It has already been remarked that there is very little indeed of personal allusion in Bede's sermons. There is not, however, an entire absence of such allusion. In a remarkable sermon on the text, "Every one that hath forsaken houses, . . . shall receive an hundredfold," Bede refers to the high esteem in which those who professed the religious life were held by those who remained in the world, so that they actually did receive much more than they surrendered when they gave up their property and worldly prospects. The "hundred" he takes to be not a mere numeral but the symbol of perfection. He who gives up human possessions and affections will find an abundance of the faithful eager to receive him, to put their houses and goods at his disposal, to love him with a more perfect affection than wife or mother or child. He reminded those whom he addressed that they had practical proof of this. When they passed on rare occasions beyond the bounds of the monastery, they found welcome and support wherever they went. In another homily he speaks of the use of the intellect in a manner which shows how highly he estimated intellectual gifts, and how seriously he felt that he himself devoted to God the hours of study. The text was, "Wist ye not that I must be about my Father's business," or, as Bede completed the expression left indefinite in the Greek, "in my Father's house." This, Bede says, refers not only to the material temple in which Christ was, but also to that temple of the intellect in which He was exercising Himself when He heard the doctors and asked them questions, a temple constructed for the eternal praise of God.

We find Bede's views on what was afterwards changed into the doctrine of Extreme Unction, in his remarks on the Epistle of James, v. 14-20. The Gospels, he says, show us that the Apostles acted as Christians are there bidden to act. In his own time, the custom prevailed that sick men were anointed with oil by the priests, with prayer accompanying, that they might be healed. As Pope Innocent had written, not priests only but any Christians might use the oil for this purpose, in their own or their relations' need. But only bishops might make the oil, for the words "anointing him with oil in the name of the Lord" implied two things, the one that the name of the Lord was to be invoked when the oil was used, the other that the oil was to be "oil in the name of the Lord," *i.e.* made and consecrated in the name of the Lord. Of Confession he proceeds to say that many are in sickness and near death because of their sins. If such confess to the priests of the Church, and earnestly set about to amend, their sins shall be dismissed.

The views of Bede's time, and of Bede himself, on Purgatory, are clearly given in the account of a vision in the Fifth Book of the *Ecclesiastical History.* We have already seen in the life of Benedict Biscop some parts of this vision, but we have not seen all. In addition to the valley one side whereof was burning heat and the other was piercing cold, and to the flaming pit, the place of torment, the man to whom the vision or trance was vouchsafed saw also the abodes of blessedness of two degrees. After passing the place of utmost torment, his guide and he came to a wall whose height and length were infinite. Presently, by what means he knew not, they were on the top of the wall. At their feet lay a vast and joyous plain, full of so sweet a fragrance of vernal flowers as drove away the vile odours of the pit with which his senses had been impregnated. The light was clearer than the day, more splendid than the sun. On the plain were innumerable congregations of white-robed men, and crowds seated by companies rejoicing. Not unnaturally he thought within himself that these were the plains of Heaven. But his companion, knowing his thoughts, answered him, "Not this is the Kingdom of Heaven."

And then, as he moved on, there dawned upon him a yet fairer and more splendid effulgence, from out of which proceeded the sweetest strains of singers and a fragrancy so marvellous as far to transcend the exquisite fragrance of the former abode. His guide allowed him but to perceive these heavenly delights and then led him back to the lesser degree of bliss. Standing there, he expounded to him what he had seen. The valley of overpowering heat and cold was the place where the souls of those were tried and punished who had delayed to confess their sins and amend their lives, but who, having at the last moment confessed and repented, should enter into the kingdom of heaven at the day of judgment. Many of these, the guide declared, were so aided by the prayers and alms and fastings of living men, and especially by masses, that they would be released even before the day of judgment. The flowery plain on which he had seen the happy bands of youth bright and fair, this was the place to which the souls of those were sent, who, dying in good works, were yet not sufficiently perfect to pass at once to the plains of Heaven. At the day of judgment, they would pass to the higher glory.

It will be seen that while the latter class of souls represented men whose lives had been almost perfect, even those who were tormented in the valley had repented before death. For those who died without repentance, there was no hope from prayers or alms or fasting, not even from masses. A similar lesson is taught by another striking vision of which Bede tells. When Bede was about thirty years of age, there was in Mercia a man high in the military service of King Coenred, but he was a man of evil life. When he was very ill, indeed on his death-bed, the king came to exhort him to repent. The unhappy man said that he would amend his life if he recovered, but his companions should never have it to say that he repented under the fear of death. The king came to him again when he was much worse, and again exhorted him. It was too late, the dying man cried; he had seen a vision, and it was too late. There had come into his room two youths very fair to look upon; the one sat down at his head, the other at his feet. They produced a little book, very beautiful, but exceedingly small, and gave it him to read. He found written therein all the good deeds he had done; and behold they were very few and inconsiderable. They

took back the book, and spake never a word. Then on a sudden there rushed in an army of malignant spirits, horrid to see, and they filled the whole house where he was. One among them, who seemed to be chief in horror and in place, brought out a book of terrible appearance and intolerable heaviness, and bade a satellite give it to the dying man to read. Therein was written, alas, all that ever he had done ill, in word or deed or thought. Then the prince of the demons said to the white-robed youths who sat at the head and the foot of the victim, "Why do ye sit here, whereas ye know of a surety that the man is ours?" And they said, "It is true; take him and cast him on to the heap of your damnation"; and having so said, they departed. Then there arose two of the worst spirits, having forks in their hands, and they struck him, the one in the head and the other in the feet. Such was the vision, but the wounds, the desperate man said, were real; they were spreading to meet one another in the midst of his body; and so soon as they should meet he would die, and the demons were at hand to drag him to hell. On which Bede, writing five-and-twenty years after, remarks, that the sinner was now suffering without avail in eternal torments that penance which he had refused to suffer for a brief period with its fruit unto forgiveness of sins.

The feature in Bede's *Homilies* which would probably seem the most prominent to a reader not very familiar with early compositions of the kind, is the somewhat far-fetched figurative interpretation in which he constantly indulges his imagination. To take first an instance of such interpretation which bears on a singular charge of heresy brought against him. The six waterpots at the marriage in Cana of Galilee were the six ages of the world down to the first showing forth of our Lord's divinity. The first was the age of Abel; the second commenced with the Flood; the third with the call of Abraham; the fourth with David; the fifth was the Captivity; the sixth was the birth of our Lord, His circumcision, presentation, and subjection to His parents. In connection with this subject Bede wrote a treatise, **"On the Ages of the World."** In an epistle to Plegwin, he refers to the charge of heresy of which mention has been made. Plegwin's messenger had come to him with pleasant greetings, but he had reported one dreadful thing, namely, that Plegwin had heard that Bede was sung among heretics by wanton rustics in their cups. Bede confesses that he was horrorstruck on hearing this. He turned pale. He asked, of what heresy was he thus accused. The messenger replied, "that Christ had not come in the flesh in the sixth age of the world." He breathed again. That Christ had come in the flesh no priest of Christ's Church could be supposed to have denied. That He came in the sixth age was another matter, and Bede traced the report to one of Plegwin's monks to whom he had shown his book, **"On the Ages of the World."** In this book he made it clear that the fifth age ended with the Incarnation, with which also the sixth began. Thus the question to which of the two ages the Incarnation was to be assigned might be resolved in either way. He had himself assigned it to the sixth age, both in the book and in a homily, so that the report was a calumny. What a curious picture of the age is this singing of heretics by rustics in their cups. It may remind us of the use made of popular songs by Arius in spreading his views and discrediting his orthodox opponents. That conjugal chastity is good, widowed continence better, virgin perfection best of all, Bede proves as follows, apparently on the assumption that those things which are symbolized by the earliest parts of our Lord's life on earth are more holy than those symbolized by parts more remote from His birth.

> Jesus was born of a virgin; therefore virgin perfection is best of all. He was soon afterwards blessed by a widow; therefore widowed continence is next after virgin perfection. Later in His life He was present at a marriage feast; therefore conjugal chastity comes third only in order of merit.

In his **"Homily on the Feeding the Four Thousand,"** he remarks that the seven baskets signified the sevenfold gifts of the Spirit. And he proceeds to say that baskets made of rushes and palm-leaves were employed, to signify that as the rush has its roots in water, so the Christian is rooted in the fountain of life; and as the palm-leaf is the symbol of a conqueror, so the Christian is a conqueror, and more than a conqueror. The two fishes were added to show by means of these creatures of the water that without the water of Baptism man cannot live.

The parable of the good Samaritan affords as good an example as any of Bede's figurative interpretations. The "certain man" is the human race in Adam. "Jerusalem" is the heavenly city of peace, from which Adam went down to "Jericho," that word (meaning "the moon," according to some early commentators) signifying the world with its changes and its wanderings. The "thieves" were the devil and his angels, who stripped him by taking from him the glory of immortality and the garb of innocence. His wounds were the blows of sin. He was left only "half dead," because while man was deprived of the gift of eternal life, there yet was left him sense to discern God. The Priest and Levite were the priesthood and ministry of the Old Covenant. The Samaritan, or "guardian"— Samaria is supposed to have taken its name from its admirable position as a place of observation, or watchtower—was the Lord Jesus. Binding up the wounds was restraining the sins of men. Pouring in oil was saying, "The kingdom of heaven is at hand"; pouring in wine was saying "Every tree that bringeth not forth good fruit is hewn down." The beast of burden was the flesh in which He deigned to come to us. The inn was the Church on earth, where pilgrims are refreshed on their way to heaven; the bringing to the inn is

Baptism. The "next day" is after the resurrection of the Lord. The two pence are the two Testaments, said to be given to the innkeeper then, because then it was that He opened their eyes that they understood the Scriptures. The innkeeper had something over—"whatsoever thou spendest more"—which he did not receive in the two pence, something beyond the requirements of the two Testaments. This Bede illustrates by such passages as "Now concerning virgins I have no commandment of the Lord, yet I give my judgment"; and again, "The Lord hath ordained that they which preach the Gospel should live of the Gospel; but I have used none of these things." To those who obeyed these "counsels of perfection," who did more in such matters than the Scriptures actually required them to do, the debtor would come again, and would pay them, when the Lord came and said, "Because thou hast been faithful over a few things, I will make thee ruler over many things; enter thou into the joy of thy Lord."

The *Homilies* contain incidental allusions which throw light upon some of the ceremonies of the time. In this way, for example, we learn that for the anniversary of the dedication day of the church of Jarrow, they adorned the walls of the church, increased the number of lights and of lections and the amount of singing, and passed the previous night in joyful vigils.

The best means of giving the English reader an idea of a sermon to an educated audience in England in Bede's time, will be to reproduce one of his *Homilies* entire in an English dress.

Notes

[1] His commentaries on the Old Testament fill 1338 octavo pages, and those on the New Testament 1250.

[2] The uncial MS. of the Acts known as E is believed to have been the actual manuscript used by Bede. It has a Latin rendering (not the Vulgate) in addition to the Greek text. It was given to the University of Oxford by Archbishop Laud, whence its name *Laudiensis*.

[3] See Bede's account of Bishop John of Hexham rebaptizing a man who had been catechised and baptized by an ignorant priest, p. 174.

Bertram Colgrave (essay date 1932)

SOURCE: Bertram Colgrave, "Bede's Miracle Stories," in *Bede: His Life, Times, and Writings*, edited by A. Hamilton Thompson, 1935. Reprint by Russell & Russell, 1966, pp. 201-29.

[*In the following excerpt, Colgrave summarizes many of Bede's miracle stories, contending that Bede did not write of miracles as a strict historian, but to satisfy the demand of popular taste, to venerate saints, to inspire, and to tell a vivid story.*]

It probably comes as a shock to the reader unacquainted with medieval literature who approaches Bede's *Ecclesiastical History* for the first time, to find that a miracle occurs on almost every page. What reliance can be placed on the historian who tells us in his very first chapter that 'scrapings of leaves of books that had been brought out of Ireland being put into water have cured persons bitten by serpents',[1] who goes on to deal with the life of Alban and to describe how the river dries up to allow the holy man the more rapidly to receive his martyr's crown, while the executioner's eyes drop out at the same moment as the martyr's head drops off.[2] We read of saints who heal the blind and raise the dead, who quell storms and quench fires, who visit the lower regions and return to tell their story, who see visions of angels prophesying their death and whose bodies after their death remain uncorrupt while heavenly lights tell the faithful where they lie; and the miracles performed by the saint are even more numerous after his death than during his life.

And yet a fuller study of contemporary literature shows us that if there were none of these strange and incredible tales in Bede's History we should have had every reason for astonishment. The only cause for surprise, to the student of the ecclesiastical literature of the times, is that there are not more of them. It was as natural for Bede to relate these marvels as it is for the modern historian to avoid them. As Dill says, dealing with the same aspect in the works of Gregory of Tours, 'had he not done so, he would have done violence to his own deepest beliefs, and he would have given a maimed and misleading picture of his age'.[3] Science had not yet given men a conception of a universe ruled by unchanging laws. It was left for the eighteenth and nineteenth centuries to do that, and perhaps it is the natural reaction of the twentieth century to ask whether after all it may not be possible that there is something more in these strange stories than the earlier editors of Bede believed, and that these holy men, living lives of incredible hardships and asceticism, actually reached a state of being in which they possessed powers—hypnotism, clairvoyance, telepathy—call them what you choose—which are not perhaps miraculous in the strict sense of the term but would certainly be considered so in the early middle ages. The age of Bede was primitive in its outlook; it was naturally credulous, and the nature of evidence was but vaguely understood. All around them men saw inexplicable phenomena, and the most marvellous explanation was always the easiest and the most readily accepted; the pious and the simple-minded were naturally ready to explain a phenomenon as the direct interposition of God on their behalf or on behalf of those who were

especially dear to Him, such as the saints and martyrs. The immediate forefathers of Bede and his contemporaries had imagined themselves to be surrounded by multitudes of unseen powers: every bush held its demon and every grove its god. There was in their minds an elasticity about the order of nature which made it seem probable to them that certain chosen people, magicians and medicine-men, should be able to alter events. When the Western lands accepted Christianity these popular beliefs were too deeply rooted to be lost all in a minute. Gregory the Great recognized this in his letter to Mellitus which Bede himself quotes: Gregory recommends that the people who had until recently slaughtered oxen and built themselves huts of the boughs of trees about their heathen temples, shall now celebrate the nativities of the holy martyrs and other feasts with like ceremonies—so that whilst some outward and visible joys are permitted them, they may more easily learn to appreciate inward and spiritual joys. 'For undoubtedly it is impossible to efface everything at once from their obdurate hearts, because he who seeks to climb the highest peak ascends step by step and not by leaps.[4] Bede himself provides us with other evidence that the change from paganism to Christianity was a slow and often painful process. There is, for instance, an illuminating story in the Life of Cuthbert.[5] A party of monks from the monastery near the mouth of the Tyne were fetching home some wood on rafts, when the wind changed and drove them out to sea. A crowd of people watched them from the shore, jeering at their plight. When the youthful Cuthbert who stood among them, rebuked them for their brutality, they answered, 'May God have no mercy on any one of those who have robbed men of their old ways of worship; and how the new worship is to be conducted, nobody knows.' And again in the same work[6] we read that when Cuthbert was at Melrose, he used to take journeys into the neighbourhood, teaching the common people, who, in times of plague, 'forgetting the sacrament of the Gospel which they had received, took to the delusive cures of idolatry, as though, by incantations or amulets or any other mysteries of devilish art, they could ward off a stroke sent by God their maker'. Another curious instance related by Bede is the story of Redwald, king of the East Saxons, who in the same temple had an altar to Christ and another one on which to offer sacrifices to devils.[7] But perhaps one of the most striking proofs of the mixture of paganism and Christianity is to be found, not in any literary work, but in an artistic production of the period. The famous Franks casket which is usually attributed to this period has, on the same panel, carvings representing on one half the horrible heathen tale of Wayland the Smith and his vengeance on King Nithhad, and, on the other half, one of the most beautiful of the Gospel stories, the Adoration of the Magi.[8] We need only refer to the penitential literature or to the charms and leechdoms of the Anglo-Saxon period to show how long the earlier pagan faith continued to hold sway in this country.

And what is true of England is equally true of the whole of western Europe.

It is clear then that the peoples of western Europe who accepted Christianity, very often under compulsion, would expect of their new Master and His saints powers no less than they had previously associated with their gods and heroes. A naïve illustration of this is found in the story of the conversion of Iceland in the year A.D. 1000. Thrangbrand the Saxon priest in his missionary journey through that island was opposed by an old woman who made a long speech on behalf of the heathen faith. 'Have you heard', she said, 'how Thor challenged Christ to single combat and how He was afraid to fight with Thor?' 'I have heard', answered Thrangbrand, 'that Thor would have been only dust and ashes, if God had not permitted him to live.'[9] The miracle stories of the Bible partly provided them with the satisfaction they sought and miraculous stories very soon came to be told of the saints as well. At first indeed the Fathers of the Church were inclined to answer this demand for miracles in much the same terms as their Lord used to those who sought for a sign. Origen, for instance, affirms that there are wonders comparable to those of past days, but nevertheless declares that they are only the vestiges of a power that has disappeared: instead of the material interventions of past days we have now the spiritual miracles worked in the souls of men.[10] It was the lives of the founders of monasticism which gave the miraculous such an important place in the stories of the saints. These stories seem to have arisen first of all in Egypt, to be repeated in the East and very soon in the West, to satisfy the craving for tales of marvels, a craving which grew rather than diminished all through the Middle Ages. In this way it came about that the *legenda,* the histories to be read on the feast of a saint, gave to the word 'legend' its modern meaning of 'any unhistoric or unauthentic story'. But it is important to notice that these stories are, from the first, popular creations and the editor of the life is no more than the transmitter of the story: for, as we shall see, even though he claims to be an eyewitness of the events he relates, or, as is more often the case, to have received the account from dependable witnesses, his claims need not be taken too seriously.

The first Latin life to attain to any considerable popularity in the West seems to have been Evagrius' Latin translation of Athanasius' Life of St. Antony, which appeared some time before 374. Somewhere about the beginning of the fifth century appeared the Life of St. Martin by Sulpicius Severus. Both these works became models for a vast number of later lives of saints, and passages were often lifted from them bodily.[11] The whole arrangement of many of them is on the model of the Life of St. Antony; beginning with a prologue in which the editor humbly declares his lack of eloquence and his inability for the task set him by his superior,

they go on to describe the youth and vocation of the saint, his virtues, his search for solitude, his asceticism, his stout defence against the attacks of the devil and his satellites, his miracles and prophecies, and finish with a fairly full account of the last exhortations of the saint to his followers, his death and the miracles performed at his tomb.[12] It will be seen that Bede's Life of Cuthbert follows this model fairly closely. But we must remember that all these writers of saints' lives, including Bede, were merely the people who put into writing the floating traditions. As Delehaye points out, there are two main sources in all hagiographical literature. First of all we get the people, whose imagination perpetually creates fresh products of its fancy and attaches wonders drawn from the most diverse sources to the name of its favourite saints, and secondly we get the writer whose function it is to put these floating traditions into literary shape; he has to take the material that is given him, but his ideas and standards determine its permanent form.[13] And it is here that the earlier models such as the Life of St. Antony and the Life of St. Martin show their influence.

Let us now consider in more detail the miracles described by Bede and endeavour to see how he is influenced by the hagiographical interests of his age. In the first place we notice that his miracle stories are almost confined to the *Ecclesiastical History,* the Prose and Verse Lives of Cuthbert, and of course the *Martyrology.* It is very noticeable that the Lives of the Abbots contain no miracle whatever, but recount ordinary and everyday occurrences throughout. We know indeed from the Anonymous Lives of the Abbots, which contain a contemporary account of Ceolfrid, that miracles came to be associated with that abbot after his death.[14] Bede must have known about these stories, but he refrains from mentioning them.

In the *Ecclesiastical History* the miracles related are chiefly grouped round the accounts of Alban, Germanus, Oswald, Aidan, Chad, the nuns of Barking, Hild, Cuthbert, John of Beverley. To these must be added a somewhat special form of miracle, the visions of the other world which are associated with the names of Dryhthelm and Fursey, and two other similar visions. There are a few separate miracles associated with other saints (such as Æthelthryth), but these are the chief groups. In every group except that of Hild we either know his authority independently or he informs us himself. Thus the Alban group is borrowed from an ancient life of St. Albanus, of which only a few traces have come down to us.[15] The miracles of St. Germanus are taken from Constantius' Life of St. Germanus; and, as a glance at Plummer's edition of the text will show,[16] he has borrowed in a wholesale way from the earlier life. The account of the miracles at Barking is borrowed, as he himself tells us twice,[17] from an earlier authority, probably a life of Æthilburg. For the miracles connected with Hild he suggests no authority and we know of none. As he mentions no names of informants, it is possible that he was depending upon some life of the saint which would almost certainly exist at Whitby and might well be known to many of his northern readers. For the miracles connected with Oswald, Aidan, Chad, and John of Beverley, he mentions the names of various authorities like Bothelm, Acca, Cynimund, Trumberht, Egbert, Berhthun, and others, nearly always insisting that their authority is unimpeachable. For the vision of Fursey, he acknowledges his source to be the 'book of his life'[18] while Dryhthelm's vision was learned from one Haemgils, a monk who was still living when Bede wrote. Of the other two visions of the beyond, one was vouched for by Pehthelm the first Anglian bishop of Whithorn, while Bede himself vouches for the other one. It is worth noting in connexion with these groups of miracles, that only one is related of Wilfrid of York. It is very clear, as Raine points out,[19] that there was little sympathy between Wilfrid and Bede, hence it is interesting to note that of all the miracles described by Eddius, the only one he relates is that with which Bede's friend Acca, bishop of Hexham, is associated. It almost looks as though Bede refrained deliberately from relating any miracles about a man who had been the bitter opponent of so many of his heroes.

Bede's account of the miracles attributed to Cuthbert is worth careful study. They occur both in the *Ecclesiastical History* and also in his Prose and Metrical Lives of the Saint. In the *History* he gives two of which he learned after the other two lives had been written.[20] His chief authority was the Life of Cuthbert written by an anonymous monk of Lindisfarne. He has given us a fairly elaborate account of his methods in the prologue to his life of the saint.

> 'I decided', he says, 'to remind you (Eadfrith) who know and to inform those readers who perchance do not know, that I have not presumed to write down anything concerning so great a man without the most rigorous investigation of the facts, nor to hand on what I had written, to be copied for general use, without the most scrupulous investigation of credible witnesses. Nay rather it was only after diligently investigating the beginning, the progress and the end of his glorious life and activity with the help of those who knew him, that I began to set about making notes; and I have decided occasionally to place the names of my authorities in the book itself, to shew clearly how my knowledge of the truth has been gained.'

He goes on to say further how he had shown the notes to Herefrid and others for their judgement, and when all this was done, he had sent the book to Lindisfarne to be read before the elders and teachers of the community there for a final revision, though such had been his care that no changes were made. Curiously enough he does not in this introduction mention the fact that he had all through depended very fully upon the earlier and smaller life written by the anonymous monk of Lindisfarne. In the preface to the *Ecclesiastical History,* however, he states that he had used the earlier life 'yielding simple faith to the narrative'. Of the forty miracles he records of Cuthbert in his Prose Life, only eight are not found in the Anonymous Life, and of these eight, two are mentioned by the earlier writer but passed over.[21] In every instance except one where he introduces a fresh miracle, he adds the name of his authority, such as Herefrid, Cynimund, or unnamed monks from Wearmouth and Jarrow. The two Cuthbert miracles added to the *Ecclesiastical History*[22] are vouched for by the authority of the two brethren on whom the miracles were wrought. In the metrical Life no authorities are given, but as it contains only the miracles found also in the Prose Life, we need not consider it further.

Here then is an imposing array of testimony: let us next consider what is the nature of the miracles which he so abundantly vouches for. In the first place a large proportion of them are obviously based upon scriptural precedents. One of the early miracles in the *Ecclesiastical History* describes how the river dried up to allow Alban to reach his place of martyrdom quickly.[23] A blind girl is healed by Germanus[24] a blind man by Augustine,[25] a dumb and scurvy youth by John of Beverley;[26] evil spirits are cast out[27] and various other cures are performed, sometimes with the aid of holy water[28] or oil,[29] sometimes with consecrated bread,[30] and once with the saint's girdle.[31] In addition, there are the stories of the calming of a storm by Lupus,[32] by Aidan,[33] and by Æthelwald.[34] Springs of water are miraculously produced from a hill or a rock by Alban,[35] and by Cuthbert;[36] food is miraculously provided on four occasions for Cuthbert,[37] and on one occasion water is turned into wine for his benefit.[38] These scriptural miracles abound in the legends of the saints: for instance, there are, quite literally, hundreds of saints to whom the miracle of turning water into wine has been attributed. In fact, if one were to take any single volume of the *Acta Sanctorum* at random, it would be possible to find analogues of practically every one of the miracles related above. But it is worth noting that Bede nowhere relates the miracle of a dead person being restored to life, an extremely common miracle in other lives of saints.[39]

These scriptural miracles found in the legends naturally became standardized and usually preserved certain features of the biblical miracles on which they were based. Thus in the account of the cure of the sick maiden by John of Beverley,[40] we learn that the saint on arriving at a 'monastery of virgins' learns that the abbess's daughter is at the point of death. After much entreaty she persuades the apparently unwilling saint to see the maiden. He goes in, taking his disciple Berhthun with him, blesses her and leaves her. In due course the maiden recovers and asks to see the disciple. 'Do you desire that I should ask for something to drink?' she said to Berhthun. 'Yes,' he replied, 'and I am delighted that you are able to drink.' The story has clearly preserved most of the details of the miracle of the healing of Jairus's daughter though the main thread is different.[41] The ruler of the synagogue becomes the abbess of a monastery; the daughter in one case is dead, in the other, dying: it is only after entreaty that our Lord goes to the maiden. Peter, James, and John go in with him just as Berhthun goes in with John; and refreshment is duly given to the healed maiden just as to the daughter of Jairus. In precisely the same way the thane's servant who is healed by John of Beverley asks for refreshment to be brought to him. Many other instances could be brought of the standardization of the miracle stories. But perhaps the most striking illustration is the comparison between the story of the healing of the thane's wife related of John of Beverley by Berhthun,[42] and the stories of the healing of the thane's wife and the thane's servant in the Prose Life of Cuthbert.[43] In the first account we learn that when John of Beverley, as bishop of Hexham, was consecrating a church in the neighbourhood of a certain thane, the latter begged him to dine in his house after the ceremony. This the bishop refused to do, but after many entreaties, he finally consented. Now this thane had a wife who had long been ill and, before going to the house, the bishop sent some consecrated water by one of the brethren. This he commanded them to give her to drink and with it to wash the parts which were most painful. The woman recovered and served the bishop and his followers with drink till the meal was over, thus following, as Bede points out, the example of Peter's mother-in-law. In the Prose Life, Bede describes how Cuthbert while bishop of Lindisfarne was attending a meeting at Melrose. On his way home a certain thane met him and earnestly sought him to return home with him. On his arrival at the thane's house, he was told that a servant of his had long been ill. Cuthbert consecrated some water and gave it to a servant, namely, the priest Baldhelm, bidding him give it to the sick man to drink. The messenger poured the water into the mouth of the patient, who forthwith fell into a tranquil sleep and was cured by the next morning. The second story in the Life describes how Bishop Cuthbert was preaching in his diocese when he called at the dwelling of a certain thane, who eagerly welcomed him in. After a hospitable greeting he told him of his wife's grave illness and besought him to bless some water wherewith to sprinkle her. The bishop did so and gave it to a priest who sprinkled her and her bed and poured some of the water into her mouth. She was immediately cured and went in to the bishop, offering him a cup of wine, and like Peter's mother-in-law she ministered to him and to his followers. For purposes of comparison it is worth while to add a similar story related of Wilfrid, bishop of York, by

Eddius.[44] While Wilfrid was in prison by the command of Ecgfrith, king of Northumbria, the wife of the reeve of the town in which he lay, was suddenly overtaken with a palsy. The reeve went in to the bishop, and, falling on his knees, implored his help, for she was dying. The bishop was led forth from prison and taking some consecrated water sprinkled it drop by drop upon the woman's face. She was promptly cured and like Peter's mother-in-law she ministered to the bishop. It is not always clear how far these miracle stories, which are apparently imitations of scriptural miracles, may not also be influenced by Jewish or classical sources. Thus the miraculous provision of food for St. Cuthbert and his followers by an eagle,[45] or by the timely arrival of the porpoises,[46] or by the angel in the monastery at Ripon[47] or by the fortunate discovery made by his horse of the bread and meat in the thatch of the shepherd's hut,[48] are most likely reminiscences of the food provided for Elijah by the ravens, of Elijah under the juniper-tree, of the miraculous draught of fishes, or of the angels ministering to our Lord in the desert, but we must not forget classical stories of miraculous feeding such as the nourishment provided by Dionysus for the Maenads, described by Euripides,[49] or Hebrew stories such as that of the poor man who had no food to prepare for the sabbath, but whose wife used to heat the oven on the eve of the sabbath and put something in to make it smoke so as to hide their poverty from their neighbours. But a suspicious neighbour peered into the oven to see what was inside, and lo! a miracle— it was full of bread.[50] Or again when we read of springs of water miraculously produced by the saints, the source may be not merely such texts as Bede quotes in connexion with the spring which Cuthbert miraculously produced in his cell upon Farne:[51] 'God . . . turned the rock into a pool of water, the flint into a fountain of waters' and 'thou shall make them to drink of the river of thy pleasures'; it may be that the stories of Hippocrene and Helicon, of Peirene and the spring behind the temple of the Acrocorinthus[52] also played their part in the development of this miracle so often repeated in the legends of the saints.

Closely connected with the biblical miracles are the many visions and instances of prophetic foresight which Bede relates. Aidan foretells the storm which is going to overtake Utta on his way to fetch Eanfled, daughter of Edwin, to be the wife of King Oswiu and gives him holy oil to pour upon the troubled waters when it occurs. This he does and the storm is calmed.[53] A certain monk called Adamnan prophesies the destruction of the double monastery at Coldingham over which Æbba ruled, as a punishment for the careless life of the inmates.[54] A series of prophecies are connected with various kings and rulers. Thus Aidan predicts the death of King Oswald[55] and Cedd predicts the death of King Sigeberht of Essex.[56] A whole chapter in the Prose Life of Cuthbert is devoted to an interview between Cuthbert and Ælfflæd, the successor of Hild as abbess of Whitby. The saint and the abbess met on Coquet Island and the abbess put him through a sort of cross-examination in the course of which she elicited the facts that her brother Ecgfrith was to die the following year, that Aldfrith was to be his successor and that Cuthbert himself was to be made a bishop, to hold the office for two years and then was to return to his retreat in Farne.[57] A year afterwards, having become bishop, he was being taken round the walls of Carlisle; as he reached a certain fountain, a relic of Roman times, he suddenly stopped and became sorrowful. His followers ascertained that at that very moment Ecgfrith had been slain in his disastrous fight against the Picts at Nechtansmere in 685.[58]

Another type of prophetic vision very commonly met with in the lives of the saints, and one of which Bede is very fond, is the vision granted to the saints or to their followers, foretelling the day on which the saint was to pass away. Sometimes the day was prophesied by the appearance of angels in a vision. An example of this is the long and charming story told of the vision of the heavenly choir which appeared to Chad, a vision which was also seen by Owini, one of the brethren of the monastery, who was working in the fields. Owini learned from Chad that the 'loving guest who was wont to visit our brethren'[59] had appeared to him also and had summoned him to come with him seven days afterwards. A vision of men in white was seen by Earcongota, the daughter of Earconberht, king of Kent, a nun in a double monastery in Brie; they announced to her that they were to take with them 'that golden coin which had come from Kent';[60] Sebbi, king of Essex, was also visited by three men in bright garments, one of whom informed him that he was to depart from the body after three days:[61] the only miracle Bede records of Wilfrid is the story of how when he was at Meaux, he lay four days and nights in a trance, and, on awaking, told his companion Acca, afterwards bishop of Hexham, Bede's close friend, that Michael the archangel had visited him and promised him four further years of life through the intercession of the Blessed Virgin Mary.[62] Eddius[63] adds that in return he was to build a church in honour of St. Mary ever Virgin. Sometimes it was a well-known friend who came in a vision to give the warning—as in the case of Chad mentioned above. Thus one of the nuns at the monastery of Barking on her death-bed told how a certain man of God, who had died that same year, had appeared to her, to tell her she was to depart at daybreak. Another of the sisters named Torhtgyth was heard conversing with an unseen visitor. A curious conversation took place of which only Torhtgyth's part was heard and recorded. Evidently the nun was urging her unseen visitor that she might be taken from the body as soon as possible; when she had finished talking to her heavenly visitant, she told those who sat around that she had been talking to her 'beloved mother Æthilburg'. This was the abbess of the Barking monas-

tery who had died three years before.[64] In other instances Bede infers that the saints knew of the day of their death even though we hear of no prophetic vision. Thus in the beautiful account of Boisil's death we learn how he proposed to read the Gospel of St. John, of which he had a copy, with his disciple Cuthbert. The manuscript[65] had seven gatherings, one of which was to be read every day, for Boisil declared that he had only seven days in which he could teach him. After the seven readings were ended Boisil passed away.[66] Cuthbert, too, was warned by a divine oracle[67] that his death was approaching, though we are not definitely told that he knew the exact date. It is interesting to note that the author of the Anonymous Life knows nothing of this prophetic knowledge.

This particular form of prophecy is of course a commonplace in the lives of the saints from the Life of St. Antony onwards. It was possibly based on the story of Hezekiah who was promised fifteen more years of life by the word of the Lord through the mouth of Isaiah.[68] The idea underlying this widespread tradition was that the saint was thus granted time to prepare himself for the great change and to be fortified by receiving the Communion. The dread of sudden death was very widely spread throughout the middle ages in Christian lands, so that it was not unnatural that the saints should be granted this special grace. So far as the martyrs were concerned, the very fact of their dying for the faith was a sufficient proof of their eternal welfare. Even though a martyr were unbaptized, as was the soldier who was slain for refusing to execute Alban, he was 'cleansed by being baptized in his own blood'.[69] So they needed no divine admonition. One might even suggest that this is why the anonymous writer of Cuthbert's Life relates no such vision about his saint. For him he is a martyr because of his ascetic life and in one place he calls him such, while he frequently refers to him as confessor.[70]

Many of the visions in Bede refer to the departure of the soul of a saint. Thus a priest in Ireland saw the soul of Cedd with a company of angels, taking the soul of Chad to heaven.[71] A nun Bega, in the monastery at Hackness, thirteen miles from Whitby, heard the passing bell tolling and saw Hild's soul being carried to heaven by angels,[72] while a young novice in the remotest part of the Whitby monastery itself saw an identical vision.[73] The brethren of the men's part of the double monastery of Brie saw a similar vision of angels when Earcongota died,[74] and Cuthbert when keeping sheep near the river Leader saw a vision of Aidan's soul being taken to heaven by angels. This vision led to his decision to take up the monastic life.[75] A similar vision came to Cuthbert one day, when he was dining with Ælfflæd, of the soul of a shepherd attached to one of Ælfflæd's lesser monasteries, being carried to heaven by angels. He had been climbing a tree to get food for his flock.[76] It will be seen that all these visions are of exactly the same type. The soul of the dying person is surrounded by a band of angels and the person to whom the vision is granted is invariably absent from the death-bed. A whole series of such visions is related in Adamnan's Life of St. Columba and in every case these two traits appear. Such visions were commonly related of the saints and these two features are almost invariably present. The vision related of Torhtgyth clearly belongs to a different type. She saw a body wrapped in a sheet being drawn up to heaven by golden cords; the body was that of Æthilburg who shortly afterwards died.[77]

One type of vision has more obviously didactic intention. It is that of the future life. Bede relates no less than four of these. One of them, at least, was more than a vision, for Dryhthelm actually died and saw the joys of the blessed and the tortures of the damned before he was restored to life.[78] Fursey's vision of the other world is the best known of all.[79] The third vision is related of a dying layman in Mercia who saw a very small and beautiful book brought to him by two beautiful youths, which contained an account of all his good deeds, and another prodigiously large book containing all his evil deeds, borne to him by a host of devils, who claimed him as their own and struck him with ploughshares.[80] The last vision is related by Bede himself of a brother whose name he will not mention, who resided in Bernicia in a 'noble monastery but himself lived ignobly'. On his death-bed he saw hell open and Satan and Caiaphas and the others who slew the Lord being consigned to everlasting perdition;[81] he also saw the place in their midst which had been appointed for himself. He died soon afterwards without receiving the viaticum and none dared to pray for him.

These visions and stories of journeys to the other world are extremely ancient and widespread. They are found in ancient Egypt and amongst the Greeks and Romans. Odysseus, Theseus, Pollux and Orpheus all visited the lower world, while Plato[82] tells the story of Er, son of Armenius, who was killed in battle, and after visiting the abodes of the dead was restored to life on his funeral pyre. Latin writers, too, notably Virgil, deal with the same theme. Saintyves has collected similar modern stories from a variety of sources from the Algonquin and Ojibway Indians, from northern Asia and Greenland, from Zululand and Oceania.[83] The literary tradition of these stories is preserved in the apocalyptic literature of the pre-Christian and early Christian period. It is found in the Book of Enoch, in the Apocalypse of Abraham and elsewhere in Jewish literature, while in the Apocalypse of Peter, a second-century work, we get the first Christian adaptation of the theme and at the end of the fourth century we get the Apocalypse of Paul which had a great influence on this branch of medieval literature. The tradition is carried on in the visions especially of the African martyrs. For our pur-

pose it is important to notice that similar legends are told in Sulpicius Severus' Life of St. Martin[84] and in Gregory the Great's *Dialogues*. In these dialogues Gregory relates a whole series of these visions, most of which to some extent resemble the visions of Fursey and Dryhthelm. The didactic nature of these visions in Christian times is strongly marked. 'It is plain', says Gregory, after telling the vision about the priest Stephanus, 'that these punishments of hell are revealed so that they may be an encouragement to some and a testimony against others.'[85] Dryhthelm, Bede tells us, only told the story of his experiences 'to those who being either terrified by the fear of torment or delighted by the hope of everlasting joys, desired to win from his words advancement in piety'.[86]

One more vision is worth relating, because of the possible light it throws on Bede's methods. He relates in his second book of his *Ecclesiastical History*[87] the well-known story of the attempt on Edwin's life by the hand of an assassin sent by Cwichelm, king of Wessex. The king promised Paulinus that if he recovered from the wound he had received and succeeded in avenging himself upon the people of Wessex, he would accept Christianity. The conditions were fulfilled and Edwin renounced his heathenism, and allowed his daughter to be baptized, but refused to accept Christianity until he had had further teaching and had consulted his immediate followers. He was further encouraged by a letter from Pope Boniface. The conference with his counsellors is one of the best-known incidents in the *History,* containing the famous simile of the sparrow.[88] The king and his followers as a result of the conference were all baptized together. All this seems natural and has the appearance of strict history. But meanwhile Bede interpolates somewhat awkwardly a long account of a vision which Edwin had had when he was an exile at the court of Redwald, king of the East Angles, and in great danger. An unknown stranger had come to him and promised him safety if he would accept the teaching of one who, as a sign, was to lay his right hand on his head. The king accepted the condition. Paulinus, coming upon the king in meditation, had placed his right hand on his head, asking him if he knew the sign. The king tremblingly accepted the sign and thereupon hesitated no more. What was Bede's object in adding this story? Perhaps he felt that the conversion of his own land to Christianity was an event of such importance that it could hardly have happened without an accompanying sign from heaven: more probably it was a piece of popular tradition which was well known in Northumbria and which Bede, writing, as he acknowledges in his preface, a history that was to be 'pleasing to the inhabitants', dared not omit. Beyond all this, it was a picturesque story, and appealed to Bede's artistic sense. [This incident also occurs in the Life of Gregory the Great, written by an anonymous monk of Whitby. It is just possible that Bede did not see this until after he had written his own account of Edwin's life. Hence the awkwardness of the interpolated incident. This theory might also account for Bede's remarkable omission of the miracles associated with the relics of Edwin which are related in the Whitby Life of Gregory.]

A very considerable number of the miracles in Bede are associated with the bodies and relics of the saints. Bede relates how on one occasion Cuthbert's girdle healed the Abbess Ælfflæd and one of her nuns[89] just as the handkerchiefs and aprons carried from Paul's body healed the sick.[90] But from the earliest period of Christianity, the tomb, after the death of the saint, became a place of the greatest sanctity and anything which had been in contact with it acquired holiness and miraculous power. At first, in western Europe, the strict Roman laws protected the actual bodies of the saints themselves from the many translations and dismemberments which they afterwards suffered, and these representative relics sufficed; but by the middle of the fourth century translation of the bodies of the saints had become frequent. Later on grew up the miracles associated with the finding of the tomb of a martyr or saint and gradually there arose the habit of sending abroad bones and fragments of the body. The extent to which the rage for possession of relics grew is illustrated by the history of the bones of Bede himself and by the story of how Ælfred Westou during the eleventh century stole them from Jarrow in order to add to the collection he had already made around the incorruptible body of his patron.[91] But most of the miracles in Bede are associated with relics of the less gruesome type. Germanus, we read, had with him the limbs of saints brought together from several countries.[92] Benedict Biscop, Acca, Wilfrid, and others who travelled to Rome frequently, never failed to bring relics home to England. Occasionally a visiting prelate like Germanus brought some or else they were sent as presents from Rome. The relics of the Apostles Peter and Paul—of the holy martyrs Laurentius, John, Paul, Gregory and Pancratius were sent by Gregory the Great to St. Augustine,[93] others were sent by Pope Vitalian to King Oswiu.[94] It was customary to deposit relics in a church at its dedication, and the underground crypts at Ripon and Hexham, both of them almost the only remains left of the original churches built by Wilfrid, were intended specially for the exhibition of such relics. Pope Gregory in his letter to Mellitus bids him not destroy the temples of the idols; but, having destroyed the idols, he is to sprinkle the temples with holy water, erect altars, and place relics therein.[95] Whether these relics and the many other relics he mentions were portions of the bodies of the saints or merely some article connected with their tomb, Bede does not say.

There is sufficient testimony then to show the great reverence paid to the relics of the saints by Bede and his contemporaries, and miracles performed by these relics are very frequently related. Bede relates the story of how Germanus healed a girl of blindness by taking a reliquary from his neck and placing it on the girl's eyes. But generally the relics with which miracles were associated by Bede were those of English saints or saints connected closely with England such as Oswald, Aidan, Cuthbert, Fursey, Earconwald and Æthilburg. It may be helpful to consider in detail the miracles which were associated with the body of Oswald. Oswald was slain fighting against Penda, king of the Mercians, at the battle of Maserfeld[96] in 642. The place where he had fallen in battle was discovered in the following way: a man shortly after the king's death was travelling on horseback near the site, when his horse was suddenly taken ill and began to roll about in anguish. By chance it rolled over the very place where Oswald fell, and arose cured. Shortly afterwards the rider came to an inn where the daughter of the house lay stricken with paralysis. She was placed upon a cart, put down on the exact spot which the traveller had previously noted, and was speedily cured.[97] A Briton, travelling near the same spot and noting its unusual greenness, took some of the dust of the place and put it in a linen cloth. Proceeding on his journey he came to a certain village, and entered a house where the villagers were feasting; he hung up the cloth with the dust in it on one of the wall posts. The feasting and drinking went on merrily until the huge fire in the middle of the room set the roof alight, which, being made of wattles and thatch, speedily blazed up. The whole house was burnt except for the post on which the dust was hanging.[98] As a result of the fame of these cures, earth was taken from this place and being put into water produced a healing drink for many; so famous did the place become that a hole as deep as a man's height remained there. His niece Osthryth, queen of Mercia, then decided to transfer his bones to the monastery of Bardney in the province of Lindsey. Did she take the body from the place where he fell? It would seem so, though Bede does not state clearly whence the remains were translated; but the miracles already described correspond with the usual miracles in the passions and legends associated with the invention of the body of the saint. The bones were taken on a wagon to the monastery, but the brethren did not care to receive the remains of their late enemy, and left the relics outside, spreading a tent over them. But all through the night a pillar of light, reaching to heaven and seen all over the province, stood above the wagon and convinced them.[99] The bones were washed in water and placed in a shrine. This water was thrown in a corner of the sacrarium. The earth on which it was thrown acquired the power of curing people possessed of devils.[100] Soon after this a boy was cured of fever at Oswald's tomb. At this point Bede tells us that the head, arms, and hands had been cut off the body by Penda and hung upon stakes. The head was taken to Lindisfarne[101] and the hands to Bamburgh.[102] In fact we are told in another place[103] by Bede that his right hand and arm, in accordance with a prophecy of Aidan, remained uncorrupt and were kept in a silver shrine in St. Peter's Church. A chip of the stake on which his head was placed was put in water by Willibrord when he was a priest in Ireland, and given to a man suffering from the plague. He was cured.[104] Stories are also told of how chips from the cross which he set up at the battle of Heavenfield, when put into water, healed both man and beast.

Now there is not a single detail in all these stories of Oswald's relics which is not met with time and time again in the *Acta Sanctorum*. In fact we need not go further than Bede himself to find analogues of most of them. Thus the burial-place of Peter, first abbot of the monastery of St. Peter and St. Paul at Canterbury, who had been drowned, was revealed by a heavenly light at Ambleteuse and his relics were translated to a church in Boulogne.[105] A heavenly light also revealed the place where the nuns of Barking, who died of the pestilence, were to be buried.[106] A heavenly light together with a vision revealed the whereabouts of the bodies of the martyrs Hewald the White and Hewald the Black after their bodies had been miraculously carried up stream for forty miles.[107] The post against which Aidan was leaning when he died, twice remained unharmed when the rest of the building was burnt down.[108] The water in which the body of Cuthbert was washed was poured into a pit on the south side of the church. A little of the dust from this pit, placed in water, cured a boy possessed of devils.[109] Chips from the post against which Aidan died, placed in water, cured many people and their friends.[110] Chips from the horse-litter used by Earconwald were also responsible for many cures.[111] Dust from Hæddi's tomb wrought many cures and so much of the holy earth was carried away that a great hole was left.[112] Dust from Chad's sepulchre put in water cured both man and beast.[113]

Various other cures at the tombs of saints and martyrs or by their relics, are also related by Bede. Thus the wife of a certain thane was cured of blindness by the relics of the saints at Barking;[114] the linen clothes which wrapped the body of Æthelthryth cured people possessed of devils, and the wooden coffin in which she was first buried healed the eye-diseases of those who prayed with their heads touching it. A white marble coffin was miraculously found near the ruined Roman site of Grantchester;[115] it exactly fitted her and in this she was placed at her translation.[116] A somewhat similar story is told of the coffin which had been provided for Sebbi, king of the East Saxons; when they came to bury him, it proved to be too long; but after various vain efforts to make the coffin fit Sebbi, or Sebbi fit the coffin, it was found to have miraculously adapted itself to the size of the body.[117] Several cures, besides those mentioned above, were effected by the relics of Cuthbert; some of Cuthbert's hair, removed from the uncorrupt body when it was translated, cured a boy of

a disease of the eye;[118] a brother called Baduthegn was healed of paralysis at his tomb;[119] Clement, bishop of Frisia, prayed at his tomb and was cured of a hopeless malady whose nature is not stated.[120] Felgeld, the anchorite who inhabited Cuthbert's cell at Farne after Cuthbert's successor Æthelwald was dead, had to reconstruct the cell which had fallen into decay; while doing so, he cut up a calf's hide which Æthelwald had placed there to protect him against the weather: pieces of this he gave to the numerous people who asked for relics of his predecessors. He placed a piece of this calf's hide in water, and washing his face with the liquid, he was cured of an inflamed swelling of the face which had long troubled him. 'But whether this ought to be ascribed to the merits of Father Cuthbert or of his successor Æthelwald . . . he alone knows who judges the heart. Nor does any reason forbid us to believe that it was wrought by the merits of both accompanied also by the faith of Felgeld.'[121] Bede gives only one example of a widespread type of relic miracle, in which, other relics having proved ineffective, the relic of the particular saint whose virtues are being extolled is successful in working the cure. This occurs in the story of the boy possessed with a devil who was cured by the dust gathered from the place where the monks had thrown water in which Cuthbert's body had been washed. He had first vainly tried those relics of the martyrs which were at Lindisfarne, but the holy martyrs of God would not grant the cure that was sought, in order that they might show what a high place Cuthbert held amongst them.[122]

We have already referred several times to the uncorrupt body of St. Cuthbert and the uncorrupt right hand and arm of Oswald. The phenomenon of the undecayed corpse is a fairly common one and has been known in all lands from the earliest times. The body of Alexander, for instance, according to Quintus Curtius, was found seven days after his death as fresh as though he were still alive.[123] Pausanias also refers to the same phenomenon[124] and there are many examples to-day of corpses preserved in a mummified form such as those still to be seen in the crypt of St. Michel at Bordeaux or in the catacomb of the Capuchins at Palermo. The preservation of the body may be due to various natural causes and sometimes just to embalming, a fact which might possibly explain the perfume so often associated with the disinterment of the uncorrupt bodies of the saints as Bede relates in connexion with the translation of the body of Earcongota.[125] The incorruptibility of the body was usually attributed, at least by the Church, to previous holiness of life. Bede tells us about Fursey's body in order that 'the sublimity of this man may be better known to my readers'.[126] He tells us of the discovery of Cuthbert's body after eleven years 'in order to show still further in what glory the holy man lived after his death'.[127] Occasionally the saints were canonized on the testimony of their undecayed remains,[128] but the Church has never made the incorruptibility of a body a certain sign of sanctity, though it is recorded of a very large number of saints and martyrs that their bodies were found uncorrupt after periods varying from a few days to hundreds of years. There are about forty examples in the first twelve volumes alone of the *Acta Sanctorum*. In popular belief, this very phenomenon was sometimes regarded with the greatest suspicion. There was a long and lingering tradition that the bodies of excommunicated people would not perish in the grave.[129] Witches and wizards too were popularly supposed to be preserved in the same way. When William of Deloraine and the monk of Melrose opened the grave of the Scottish wizard Michael Scott

> Before their eyes the wizard lay
> As if he had not been dead a day.[130]

Bede mentioned four instances of saints whose bodies were found undecayed: Æthilburg,[131] Fursey,[132] Æthelthryth,[133] and Cuthbert.[134] The tradition concerning the body of the latter lingered on until modern times. Eleven years after his burial the brethren found his body uncorrupt: 'Nay his very funeral weeds', as Hegge says in his delightful description of this event, 'were as fresh as if putrefaction had not dared to take him by the coat'.[135] Ælfred Westou, the eleventh-century sacrist at Durham, often used to open the coffin of the saint, and in 1104, when it was translated to its historic shrine in the Cathedral, the body was again found whole. In 1538 Henry VIII's commissioners visiting the monastery at Durham found the body in just the same condition. But when the tomb was opened in 1827 the mere bones were found. There are some, however, who maintain that the bones found on that occasion were not those of Cuthbert and that the incorruptible body still remains in the Cathedral in a secret spot known only to three Benedictines.

On the whole there are comparatively few examples in Bede of what one could call mere fairy-tale wonders, such as the stories of saints hanging their cloaks on sunbeams, or being miraculously protected from a shower of rain, of having their forgotten belongings, such as staves and cloaks and books, marvellously discovered for them, often by being transported through the air to where the saint was. But there are certain miracles which perhaps may not unfairly be classed under this head. There is the story of St. Alban's executioner whose eyes dropped out as the saint's head fell to the ground.[136] There is the story of the Northumbrian captive whose fetters continually fell from him as often as they were put on him; this was due to the intercession of his brother, a priest, who, thinking he was dead, was saying masses for him.[137] There is the story of Hewald the White and Hewald the Black whose bodies were carried for forty miles against the current of the stream.[138] Apart from these,

most of the more extravagant miracles are related about Cuthbert and are due to the influence of the Anonymous Life of which Bede made use. The animal and bird stories so popular in Irish hagiography are represented here and nowhere else. There is the account of how Cuthbert drove away the birds from the barley he had sown on his island, by reproving them:[139] there is the amusing and picturesque tale of the two crows who began to tear the thatch from off the roof of the guesthouse he had built on Farne; these, too, he reproved and soon after one of the crows returned and alighted at his feet, spreading out its wings and uttering humble notes in token of asking forgiveness. The saint forgave the crow and gave it permission to come back with its mate. In return they brought him the half of a piece of swine's fat with which to grease his shoes.[140] Another story relates that, after he had spent the night in prayer, up to his neck in the sea, at Coldingham, seals came and dried him with their fur and warmed his feet with their breath. He blessed them and they returned to the sea.[141] Other fairy-tale stories are the provision of some building wood of exactly the right length, which was washed up by the sea on the Farne when the brethren forgot to get him the wood he had asked for;[142] the marvellous crop of barley produced out of season;[143] the story of the huge stones he carried unaided to build his cell;[144] and the interesting story of how he gave a goose to some of the brethren who came to visit him on Farne and told them to cook it; having already enough food of their own, the brethren did not do so; but a fierce storm arose and kept them in the island for seven days. At the end of this period the saint visited the dwelling in which they were living and saw the goose still uncooked; thereupon he reproved their disobedience very gently but told them that the sea would not become calm until the goose was eaten. This incident does not appear in the Anonymous Life, but Bede learned it 'not from any chance source but from one of those who were present, namely from Cynimund, a monk and priest of reverend life, who is still alive and well'. The story, although it may seem at first sight somewhat childish, throws light on Bede's view of the religious life and on the didactic nature of his miracle stories. The incident is, from our point of view, a simple ordinary occurence and no more than a coincidence is involved. It is a common enough happening nowadays for Farne Island to be cut off by storms for days at a time. But there could be no doubt in the mind of Bede that the two events, the eating of the goose and the calming of the sea, were intimately connected. Nor would it seem to him in any way disproportionate that the elements should rage for seven days merely because a few brethren had forgotten to eat a goose. The question of holy obedience was involved and even nature herself was at one with the saint in impressing the heinousness of their offence in disobeying even his simplest command. The story provided Bede with an opportunity of exalting the saint and of teaching a vital lesson which he was not slow to take advantage of.

And his love of a picturesque incident may have played no little part in inducing him to include it: for it is abundantly clear that Bede did not fail to realize the value of miracle stories as picturesque additions to his narrative.

Such then are some of the miracles of which Bede tells us, backing them up as we have seen by appeals to numerous authorities—books which he had read or trustworthy witnesses—often eyewitnesses of the events, as in the story just related. But when we turn to the other lives of the saints we find the most extraordinary miracles related with precisely the same asseverations of truth. This feature goes back to Athanasius' Life of St. Antony, where in the preface Athanasius declares that he is writing what he himself knows and has learned from Antony himself. Then follow the stories of Antony's combats with devils, of miraculous springs, of visions of souls being carried to heaven, and of many miracles of healings. The sixth-century life of Samson of Dol is, we are told, written in a 'catholic and truthful manner' and yet we read how the saint learned to read in a day, how a dove rested upon him all through the ceremony of his ordination as deacon, how he drank poison with impunity, how a well sprang from the rock for his benefit.[145] Adamnan prefaces his Life of St. Columba with a warning that credence should be given to the stories, and very often names the witness as in the story of the pestiferous rain which the saint foresaw would destory both men and cattle in Ireland. He sent Silnan at once to Ireland, who took some bread blessed by the saint and, putting it in water, used the infusion to heal both man and beast. 'That in all respects these things are most true, the above mentioned Silnan . . . bore witness in the presence of Seghine, the abbot, and of other aged men.' Bishop Jonas of Orleans, in the first half of the ninth century, wrote a life of St. Hubert, in the preface of which he professes to give the account as an eyewitness. But St. Hubert died in 727—Jonas in 843! It is clear then that when Bede produces his witnesses, he is acting in accordance with the hagiographical tradition of his times. This does not of course necessarily mean that he did not get the evidence as he said he did. Some of the miracles he relates, such as those connected with the life of Fursey, or of Germanus or of Cuthbert or of the nuns of Barking, are, as we have seen, based upon the lives in his possession. The stories had been written down and it is too much to expect of a historian of his age that the should have refused to give them credence. Speaking of the Anonymous Life of Cuthbert in his preface to the *Ecclesiastical History,* he tells us how he has 'yielded simple faith to the narrative'. It would almost have been an act of heresy if he had refused to believe these stories. And Bede was, as we know, particularly sensitive to any aspersion of this kind. But having the authority of tradition for finding his eyewitnesses, he would willingly accept their stories, coming as they did from the mouths of men of weight: nor need we expect that he would examine them after the manner of a modern barrister in a court of law to assure himself that the stories told by the eyewitnesses were not coloured by their imagination, or heightened in the retelling. We have learned nowadays how difficult it is to get the truth from perfectly trustworthy eyewitnesses and how often two such people, describing the same incident a few hours after its occurrence, will contradict one another flatly. How much more difficult was it to describe an incident which had happened years before: when the public opinion of the time demanded that a saint when alive, and his relics, when he was dead, should perform miracles: when, above all, there was the incentive to honour one's own patron saint above all other saints, and consequently to make him more glorious in his miracles! Bede has in fact done no less than he claimed to do, namely to 'labour to commit to writing with sincerity such things as we have gathered from common report, which is the true law of history'.[146]

What, we may ask ourselves, was his object in describing these miracles in his works? In the first place he has attempted to put down those things which 'were most worthy of note concerning the separate provinces or the more distinguished places, and pleasing to the inhabitants'. Popular opinion demanded that the traditions concerning the more famous saints should be duly recorded. Then the miracles of the saints were the means of testifying to the trustworthiness of the Gospel they preached. Æthilberht, for instance, was led to put his trust in the 'most pleasing promises' made by St. Augustine and his followers by the miracles they performed, as well as by the example of their lives.[147] St. Augustine healed a blind man to prove that he was a preacher of the divine truth, as opposed to the British party who were unable to cure the man.[148] Another reason was to extol the glory of the saint. For this reason he tells the story of the uncorrupt body of Fursey[149] and the miracles of Cuthbert;[150] for the same reason Gregory had collected the miracles of the saints in his *Dialogues.*[151] We have already seen that the visions of the underworld were intended to warn sinners and strengthen the faithful; so also the vision of Adamnan about Coldingham served, for a few days at any rate, to lead the inhabitants of the monastery to a better way of life.[152] We may look upon many of the miracles Bede relates in much the same light as the illustrative anecdotes with which preachers nowadays sometimes brighten their sermons; and how many of these stories, which, in all sincerity, are put forward as true, would bear a close investigation? Another, and perhaps by no means the least potent, reason was because of Bede's love for a picturesque story. His miracle stories provide some of the most famous passages in his *Ecclesiastical History,* such as the account of the death of Chad or the vision of Fursey. The Prose Life of Cuthbert is full of these picturesque narratives and although it cannot compare in historical importance with Eddius' Life of Wilfrid, it is much more readable. Few who have once read them could forget the stories about the birds on Farne Island or the vivid story of the angels who visited Ripon on a snowy day, or the account of Cuthbert's visit to the Roman ruins at Carlisle. Bede does not merely describe the incidents in threadbare language like many of the writers of legends of the saints. He so evidently takes pleasure in recounting the story with vivid details, that his pleasure transfers itself to the reader. And his skill as a literary artist makes the dry bones of many a traditional tale live again.

It has been pointed out that many of the miracles related by Bede need not necessarily be miraculous at all but merely 'coincidences brought about by perfectly natural means, though a devout mind will gladly believe that they have been divinely ordered'.[153] Such is the miracle which Bede describes as having happened to himself, when, singing the praises of Cuthbert, he was healed of an affection of the tongue,[154] or again the occasion when the young Cuthbert was cured of a swelling of the knee by applying a poultice according to the instruction of an angelic visitor on horseback.[155] Bede seems to feel a little compunction about this miracle, for he goes on to refute from scripture those who would doubt that an angel could appear on horseback. Poulticing is the remedy which the modern physician would prescribe for what he would probably diagnose as synovitis. Another similar miracle is the divine provision of wood from the sea for the building which Cuthbert was engaged upon on Farne.[156] And even Bede himself sometimes heightens the miraculous element in his stories as may be seen by comparing some of the incidents in Bede's Life of Cuthbert with the corresponding incidents in the Anonymous Life.[157]

There can be no doubt that Bede himself sincerely believed that the miracles he described really happened, but his views on the miraculous as set out in other parts of his writings seem to be hardly in keeping with his work as a hagiographer. He seems to have taken up much the same position as Gregory the Great whose works he knew so well. In one passage in the *Ecclesiastical History* he quotes at length a letter in which Gregory exhorts Augustine not to be puffed up by the miracles which he was performing. He was to remember the Master's answer to those who rejoiced in their power to cast out devils. 'In this rejoice not. . . . But rather rejoice because your names are written in heaven'.[158] They placed their joys in private and temporal affairs when they rejoiced in miracles, but these words recall them from private to public, from temporal to spiritual joys. For all the elect do not work miracles and yet all their names are written in heaven. And those who follow in the truth ought to have no joy except that which is common to all, a joy which knows no end.[159]

In another place Bede, borrowing from Gregory,[160] declares that miracles were necessary at the beginning of the church, just as when we put in a plant, we water it until we see that it has taken root: then we need no longer water it. And yet Gregory filled his *Dialogues* with the marvellous and Bede wrote his two Lives of Cuthbert. And further, neither Gregory nor Bede makes any references to these stories of marvels in their sermons and commentaries. It is true, Bede further declares that the cessation of miracles is largely due to man's sin and that some men by special holiness gain a power over creation which we have lost, because we neglect to serve the creator as we should.[161] But there seems to be in Bede as in most of the doctors of the Church, as Delehaye points out,[162] the voice of two men in each of them on the subject of miracles. Perhaps we ought to recognize three men in Bede, the theologian, the hagiographer, and the historian. To some extent the three were not altogether in harmony. When he was writing his homilies and commentaries, he was the theologian who accepted the general theory that the day of miracles was past, or at any rate that contemporary miracles were not altogether on the same footing as those of the days of Christ; when he wrote his Lives of Cuthbert he wrote as a hagiographer; when he was writing the Lives of the Abbots he wrote as a historian; but in the writing of the *Ecclesiastical History* both Bede the hagiographer and Bede the historian took part.[163] To exalt his heroes, to teach his lessons, and perhaps also for the sake of adding picturesque incident, he wrote down the miraculous stories which tradition provided and which he was not too careful to submit to close examination, and by quoting his authorities he cast the responsibility upon others. So, to some extent, the historian was satisfied. And when, as we have seen, his stories grew in the telling, it may well have been that the legend had grown even under his hands, for the saint's legend is essentially a popular growth: it is the people who make it and the hagiographer who writes it down. Bede the hagiographer was only a little in advance of his times. Bede the historian was far in advance of them. But how far the historical fact lies behind his hagiography is a difficult matter to decide.

We live in a time when the rapid advance in knowledge, both of the external world and of the human mind, has overwhelmed the self-confident materialism of the recent past, which, with its rigid principles, relegated most things for which it could not account to the realm of mere fiction. We can now afford to admit that there is a substantial basis of fact embedded in the stories we have considered. We may not regard the underlying facts in precisely the same light as did Bede and his contemporaries; but we are bound to treat with reverent sympathy the forms in which they embodied those facts and thus projected their own faith and hope upon the external world.

Notes

[1] *H.E.* [*Baedae Historia Ecclesiastica gentis Anglorum*] i. 1.

[2] *Ibid.* i. 7.

[3] Dill, *Roman Society in Gaul in the Merovingian Age,* 1926, p. 395.

[4] *H.E.* i. 30.

[5] *Vit. Cuth* [*Vita Cuthberti auctore Baeda*], iii.

[6] *Ibid.* ix.

[7] *H.E.* ii. 15.

[8] See *B.M. Guide to Anglo-Saxon Antiquities,* 1923, Pl. VIII.

[9] *Saga of the Burnt Njal,* xcviii.

[10] See H. Delehaye, *Saint Martin et Sulpice Sévère,* Anal. Boll. xxxviii. 73.

[11] Thus the prologue to the Anonymous Life of St. Cuthbert consists entirely of a patchwork of borrowings from Evagrius' Live of St. Antony, Sulpicius Severus' Life of St. Martin, the Life of St. Silvester, and an epistle of Victor of Aquitaine to Hilarius, the proper names being changed to suit the context.

[12] See B. P. Kurtz, *From St. Antony to St. Guthlac,* California, 1926, *passim.*

[13] H. Delehaye, *Les Légendes hagiographiques,* Brussels, 3rd ed., 1927, p. 11.

[14] See Plummer [*Venerabilis Baedae opera historica,* ed. C. Plummer. 2 vols. Oxford, 1896] 1. 403 ff. Though there are several verbal likenesses between the two accounts it does not seem to be quite clear whether Bede made use of the Anonymous Lives or vice versa.

[15] See H. Delehaye, *Origines du culte des martyres,* 1933, p. 362.

[16] Plummer, 1. 34 ff.

[17] *H.E.* iv. 10, 11.

[18] *Ibid,* iii. 19.

[19] *H.C.Y.* [*The Historians of the Church of York and its Archbishops,* ed. J. Raine. 3 vols., 1879-94] 1. xxxiv. See also Plummer, 11. 315 ff.

[20] These two miracles were usually added by the scribes to the various manuscripts of the Prose Life.

[21] See Stevenson [J. Stevenson, *Ven. Baedae opera historica Minora.* 2 vols. 1841] ii. 284.

[22] *H.E.* iv. 30, 31.

[23] *Ibid.* i. 7.

[24] *Ibid.* i. 18.

[25] *Ibid.* ii. 2.

[26] *H.E.* v. 2.

[27] *Vit. Cuth.* xxx.

[28] *Ibid.* xxv, xxix.

[29] *Ibid.* xxx.

[30] *Ibid.* xxxi.

[31] *Ibid.* xxiii.

[32] *H.E.* i. 17.

[33] *Ibid.* iii. 15.

[34] *Ibid.* v. 1.

[35] *Ibid.* i. 7.

[36] *Vit. Cuth.* xviii.

[37] *Ibid.* v, vii, xi, xii.

[38] *Ibid.* xxxv.

[39] It is true that he described Dryhthelm as having been restored to life, but this was without the intervention of a saint and necessarily precedes the account of his vision of the life beyond.

[40] *H.E.* v. 3.

[41] St. Luke viii.

[42] *H.E.* v. 4.

[43] *Vit. Cuth.* xxv, xxix.

[44] Eddius, [*The Life of Bishop Wilfrid by Eddius Stephanus*: text, translation and notes by B. Colgrave. Cambridge, 1927] xxxvii.

[45] *Vit. Cuth.* xii.

[46] *Ibid.* xi.

[47] *Ibid.* vii.

[48] *Ibid.* v.

[49] Euripides, *Bacchae,* 704-11.

[50] Quoted by H. Günter, *Die christliche Legende des Abendlandes,* Heidelberg, 1910, p. 96.

[51] *Vit. Cuth.* xviii.

[52] See Günter, *op. cit.,* p. 58.

[53] *H.E.* iii. 15. The phrase 'to cast oil on troubled waters' can scarcely be derived from this incident as is usually asserted. The idea was widespread and goes back as far as Aristotle. See Plutarch, *Moralia (De primo frigido),* xiii. 5.

[54] *H.E.* iv. 23.

[55] *Ibid.* iii. 14.

[56] *Ibid.* iii. 22.

[57] *Vit. Cuth.* xxiv, and compare ch. viii.

[58] *Ibid.* xxiv.

[59] *H.E.* iv. 3. The 'loving guest' was his brother Cedd, as is explained in the latter part of the same chapter.

[60] *Ibid.* iii. 8.

[61] *Ibid.* iv. 11.

[62] *Ibid.* v. 19.

[63] Eddius, lvi.

[64] *H.E.* iv. 8, 9.

[65] The Stonyhurst Gospel was once supposed to be this very manuscript; but Baldwin Brown (vi. 8) pointed out that the Stonyhurst MS. has not seven but twelve gatherings.

[66] *Vit. Cuth.* viii.

[67] *H.E.* iv. 26.

[68] Isaiah xxxviii. The passage is actually quoted by Eddius (c. lvi) in his account of Wilfrid's vision at Meaux. Possibly Ps. xxxix. 4 and similar passages may have influenced the belief.

[69] *H.E.* i. 7.

[70] Stevenson, ii. 282, 283 (chaps. 44, 45). For the whole subject of the equivalents of martyrdom cf. H. Delehaye, *Sanctus,* Brussels, 1927, pp. 109 ff.; L.

Gougaud, *Devotional and Ascetic Practices,* London, 1927, pp. 205-23.

[71] *H.E.* iv. 3.

[72] *Ibid.* iv. 23.

[73] *Ibid.* Plummer (ii. 248) sees an apparent contradiction between this story and the account in the same chapter of how Hild called the nuns together to deliver her dying exhortation. But surely the explanation is that the nun who saw the vision was a novice and would therefore be separated from the others present at the death of the abbess.

[74] *H.E.* iii. 8.

[75] *Vit. Cuth.* iv.

[76] *Ibid.* xxxiv; *Vit. Metr.* xxxi.

[77] *H.E.* iv. 9.

[78] *Ibid.* v. 12.

[79] *Ibid.* iii. 19.

[80] *Ibid.* v. 13.

[81] *Ibid.* v. 14.

[82] *Republic,* Book 10, 614 B.

[83] P. Saintyves, *En Marge de la Légende Dorée,* Paris, 1930, ch. iv. See the whole chapter on which the above account is based. See also Plummer, ii. 294.

[84] Sulpicius Severus, *Vita Martini,* vii.

[85] Gregory, *Dialogues,* iv. 36.

[86] *H.E.* v. 12.

[87] *Ibid.* ii. 9.

[88] *H.E.* ii. 13.

[89] *Vit. Cuth.* xxiii.

[90] Acts xix. 12.

[91] See p. 37 above.

[92] *H.E.* i. 18.

[93] *Ibid.* i. 29.

[94] *Ibid.* iii. 29.

[95] *Ibid.* i. 30.

[96] Usually identified with Oswestry. See Plummer, ii. 152.

[97] *H.E.* iii. 9.

[98] *Ibid.* iii. 10.

[99] The monks of Bardney never afterwards closed their doors to any stranger. Hence the Lincolnshire proverbial saying to a person who leaves the door open: 'You come from Bardney, do you?'

[100] *H.E.* iii. 12.

[101] This head was afterwards transferred to Durham with Cuthbert's body and is probably the skull that was found within the innermost coffin when the tomb was opened up in 1827. See Raine, *St. Cuthbert,* 187.

[102] The body, however, was translated about 909 from Bardney, which had been laid waste by the Danes in 876, to St. Oswald's at Gloucester. See *Trans. Bris. and Glouc. Archaeol.* Soc. xliii. 89.

[103] *H.E.* iii. 6.

[104] *Ibid.* iii. 13.

[105] *Ibid.* i. 33.

[106] *Ibid.* iv. 7.

[107] *Ibid.* v. 10.

[108] *Ibid.* iii. 17.

[109] *Vit. Cuth.* xli.

[110] *H.E.* iii. 17.

[111] *Ibid.* iv. 6.

[112] *Ibid.* v. 18.

[113] *Ibid.* iv. 3.

[114] *Ibid.* iv. 10.

[115] The coffin was probably a Roman one. Compare the white marble sarcophagus found in Clapton and now in the Guildhall Museum: see Royal Commission on Historical Monuments, *Roman London,* p. 164 and pl. 57.

[116] *H.E.* iv. 19.

[117] *Ibid.* iv. 11.

[118] *Ibid.* iv. 30.

[119] *Ibid.* iv. 31.

[120] *Vit. Cuth.* xliv.

[121] *Vit. Cuth.* xlvi.

[122] *Ibid.* xli.

[123] Quintus Curtius, x. 10. Quoted by Saintyves, *op. cit.* 284.

[124] Pausanias, v. 20.

[125] *H.E.* iii. 8. For a discussion of the natural causes which may lead to the uncorruptness of the body see Saintyves, *op. cit.* 284 ff.

[126] *H.E.* iii. 19.

[127] *Vit. Cuth.* xlii.

[128] Saintyves, *op. cit.* 306 ff.

[129] *Ibid.* 286.

[130] Scott, *Lay of the Last Minstrel,* canto ii. 19.

[131] *H.E.* iii. 8.

[132] *Ibid.* iii. 19.

[133] *Ibid.* iv. 19.

[134] *Ibid.* iv. 30.

[135] Quoted in Raine, *St. Cuthbert,* 38.

[136] *H.E.* i. 7.

[137] *Ibid.* iv. 22.

[138] *Ibid.* v. 10.

[139] *Vit. Cuth,* xix.

[140] *Ibid.* xx.

[141] *Ibid.* x.

[142] *Ibid.* xxi.

[143] *Ibid.* xix.

[144] *Ibid.* xvii.

[145] Quoted by Günter, *op. cit.* 171.

[146] *H.E.* preface, *ad fin.*

[147] *Ibid.* i. 26.

[148] *Ibid.* ii. 2.

[149] *Ibid.* iii. 19.

[150] *Ibid.* iv. 30.

[151] *Ibid.* ii. I.

[152] *Ibid.* iv. 25.

[153] Cf. Plummer, i, p. lxiv.

[154] *Vit. Metr.* pref.

[155] *Vit. Cuth.* ii.

[156] *Ibid.* xxi.

[157] Cf. for instance ch. iv, v with the corresponding chapters in the Anonymous Life.

[158] St. Luke x. 20.

[159] *H.E.* i. 31.

[160] Giles [*Opera Ven. Baedae quae supersunt,* ed. J. A. Giles. 12 vols. 1843-4] x. 261; Gregory, *Hom. in Evang.* xxix, *P.L.* lxxvi. 1215.

[161] Giles, vii. 27, *Vit. Cuth.* xxi.

[162] *Analecta Bollandiana,* xxxviii. 77.

[163] We have to remember, too, that Bede knew and used Eusebius' *Ecclesiastical History* and Rufinus' translation and continuation of it. So he may have been deliberately modelling his own history upon these works, in which the hagiographical element is kept in the background.

R. W. Chambers (lecture date 1936)

SOURCE: R. W. Chambers, "Bede," in *Proceedings of the British Academy*, Vol. XXII, 1936, pp. 129-56.

[*In the following lecture, Chambers presents Bede in historical context and asserts that, in the* Ecclesiastical History, *Bede captures two traditions: loyalty to Christ and loyalty to the chief.*]

Ours is an age in which those who delight in such things delight to take a 'master mind' and to throw him down from his pedestal. My friend and predecessor in this series, Tenney Frank, speaking of Cicero as a master mind, had to vindicate against cavillers his hero's claim to that title. Indeed, said Professor Frank, 'the first poet of Greece is perhaps the only human being who has attained an undisputed place of honour'. Yet even here he was too optimistic. I was brought up on Mahaffy's *History of Greek Literature,* and Mahaffy and Sayce between them taught me that Homer was *not* a human being, but a collection of inter-polations, 'fitted together', which is what the name *Homêros* means, so that 'with a closer insight into the structure of the epic poems' we must depose him from his pedestal and give the first place to Aeschylus.[1] All my lifetime Homer has been slowly climbing back on to his pedestal again. But he has not yet been selected for the 'master mind' lecture. He lacks one important qualification for public recognition as a master mind: a fixed date of death, which will ensure his merits being officially brought under the notice of the Academy at least once every century.

Bede is more fortunate. We can say with fair certainty that he died at the hour of Vespers, on Wednesday, 25 May 735, the eve of Ascension Day. Quite certainly he did not die before that date, so we are on the safe side in keeping his celebration a little late. To-day, the 27th of May, is, of course, his day in the Church's calendar.

In a broader sense, it is to his date that Bede owes his supreme position. His life was preceded, and it was followed, by a period of great darkness. The seventh century, in which Bede was born, has been called 'the nadir of the human mind'; or at least a great historian of to-day, George Sarton, has censured a great historian of a century ago, Henry Hallam, for so calling it.[2] Sarton has pointed out that, though things were bad in Europe, the early seventh century was a golden age in Arabia, in Tibet, in China, and in Japan. Hallam hardly deserves the censure of his critic, for what he really said was that the seventh century was the nadir of the human mind in Europe. Two pages later on, however, Hallam does so far abandon caution as to say that 'the Venerable Bede may perhaps be reckoned superior to any man *the world* then possessed'. Hallam would have been on safer ground if here also he had said 'Europe'. To-day, as we pass through any great museum, the marvels of the T'ang dynasty warn the most careless of us not to suppose that 'Europe' and 'the world' are synonymous. But of these things Hallam could know nothing; they were hidden in recesses of China and Japan then inaccessible to Westerners.

Amid the European darkness of the seventh and eighth centuries Bede's life 'throws its beams' far; it shines, as Bede's editor, Charles Plummer, has said, like

a good deed in a naughty world.

Or rather, *we* will say, 'like a good deed in a naughty Europe'.

Bede is the most striking example of the truth which Oderisi of Gubbio[3] uttered to Dante, as they paced, crouching together, round the first circle of Purgatory, the circle of the Proud:

Oh vain glory of human powers! How short a time does it remain green upon the top, *if it be not followed by ages of darkness.* Cimabue thought to hold the field in painting; now Giotto has the cry. . . . And for thee, if thou livest to be old, how will thy fame be more than if thou hadst died a babe, ere a thousand years be passed; which yet, to eternity, is a shorter space than the twinkling of an eye.

Which shows, incidentally, how much Dante underestimated his own fame. The six hundred years following Dante's death have been no ages of darkness, yet, so far as anything can be predicted, it seems safe to predict that, a thousand years after his birth, Dante's glory will remain undimmed. Dante tells us how he was burdened by thinking of the heavy load of penance which he would have to carry in Purgatory for his pride.[4] For my part, I find myself amazed at his modesty.

But Bede had a humbler mind than Dante. He was an expert in Chronology, and he knew that he was living in the Sixth, and Last, Age of the World. For the first Five Ages, those before Christ, Bede's reckoning did not differ materially from the results arrived at by Archbishop Usher, which are still in the margins of our bibles. These Ages, according to Bede, together covered 3,952 years, only 52 less than Usher allowed. The last of these five pre-Christian Ages (from the destruction of Solomon's Temple at Jerusalem by Nebuchadnezzar to the Coming of our Lord in the flesh) was the epoch in which, Bede asserted, the world had grown old. The Sixth Age was to stretch from the Incarnation of Christ to the Day of Doom: it was, according to Bede, the age of complete decrepitude, as befitted the epoch which was to end in the destruction of all.[5] Bede deprecated inquiry as to how long this last age of decrepitude would continue; but assuredly he would not, like Dante, have thought in terms of thousands of years. Dante's idea of successive painters, poets, scholars, each surpassing and obscuring the fame of his predecessor, shows how much the outlook of the human spirit had grown since the Dark Age of Bede. The Dark Age continued for many centuries after Bede, and so Bede, as generation followed generation, had few rivals to fear in the West. George Sarton, in the first volume of his mighty *Introduction to the History of Science,* gives the name of one great man to each half-century of his survey, and, with some hesitation, he names the first half of the eighth century after Bede. 'This was my last chance', he says, 'in this volume, of giving a Christian title to a chapter.' Not till the great revival which took place after the year 1100 does the West again begin to take the lead. The two half-centuries before Bede Sarton names after two Chinese travellers. The seven half-centuries after Bede he names from seven sages of the Moslem world. So that, during a period of 500 years, from A.D. 600 to A.D. 1100, Bede is the only master mind of Christendom whom Sarton thinks worthy of a supreme place.

But though Bede lived in what was, so far as Europe was concerned, a dark age, there is nothing dark about *him.* In the words of W. P. Ker:

> He did not, in his reading or writing, go beyond the sources or the models that were commonly accessible. For all that, the impression he leaves is that of something different from his age, an exceptional talent escaping from limitations and hindrances. There is no period in the history of Britain or of the English Church in which Bede is antiquated; in every generation he speaks familiarly. The seventeenth century is less intelligible to the eighteenth, the eighteenth century more in opposition to the nineteenth, than Bede to any one of them; his good sense is everywhere at home. . . . The reputation of Bede seems always to have been exempt from the common rationalist criticism, and this although his books are full of the things a Voltairian student objects to.[6]

Ker goes on to speak of matters where Bede is intolerant. Yet, he says,

> Like Dr. Johnson's refusal to countenance a Presbyterian church in Scotland, the severity of Bede has been taken lightly by the most sensitive, and has failed to make him enemies, even among the fiercest advocates of Christian charity and impartial toleration It appears to be felt that he is a great man. The volume of his book is too much for carpers and cavillers.

Or, if we may translate the classic periods of 'W. P.' into the vulgarisms of to-day, we may say that even Lytton Strachey would have found it difficult to debunk the Venerable Bede. True, there *is* a volume entitled *The Venerable Bede expurgated, expounded, and exposed,* but the satire of that moderately amusing book is aimed, not at Bede, but at Anglican clergy who dare to claim him as their own.

Therefore, when the Academy did me the honour of asking me to give a lecture on the Master Mind Foundation, and chose Bede as the subject, I could only obey, although with many doubts as to my ability to deal with him. There is something which overawes us, in the contemplation of this unchanging reputation, in a world where everything else seems to be open to challenge and dispute, a challenge of which I, at least, am reminded every time I enter the British Museum Reading Room. All my life, when overcome by the atmosphere of that Reading Room, I have been accustomed to get up and walk along the Roman gallery, where the long line of Roman Emperors stood on their polished pedestals, till I finished opposite the bust of Julius Caesar. There, I said to myself, are the features of the foremost man of all this world, fashioned from the life by some master-craftsman of the first century B.C. And I returned refreshed to my work. In accordance with the spirit of our age, the polished pedestals have all been swept away; a sadly diminished line of Emperors now stands, in the Roman gallery, on a shelf reminiscent of a cocktail bar. Julius Caesar has been expelled. He now faces us, as we enter the Reading Room, with an inscription, *Julius Caesar, Ideal portrait of the 18th Century. Rome, bought 1818.* And so he, who insisted that his wife must be above suspicion, now only serves to warn the unsuspicious Englishman against buying sham antiques aboard. There is change and decay in all the galleries of the Museum. No longer does the Etruscan lady deliver, with uplifted finger, an everlasting curtain-lecture to her recumbent spouse. I believe that after the night watchman has done his rounds, from one monument of Antiquity to another there passes

> A timid voice, that asks in whispers
> 'Who next will drop and disappear?'

Yet there *are* works of art in the Museum which have nothing to fear from any hostile critic; and two supreme ones have a special bearing on the Age of Bede. The Chinese pottery statue of a Buddhist apostle sits in the centre of the King Edward VII Gallery, rather more than life-size. In his grand simplicity, utterly remote from all earthly affairs, the apostle gazes into eternity. If our art-critics are right in their dates, he shows us what the East could do in the Age of Bede. He serves as a symbol to remind us that the darkest period of Western civilization coincides with the glories of the T'ang dynasty in China. Dynasties might have changed, and empires fallen, and the meditations of the Chinese sage, from whom that portrait was modelled (for a portrait it must assuredly be), would have been as little disturbed thereby as have been the features of his porcelain image. Like the sage of Bacon's New Atlantis, he has an aspect as though he pitied men. He belongs, we are told, to an age when inspiration was fresh, and Chinese Buddhist art young and virile.

The other great monument of the Age of Bede in the British Museum we can date exactly. It, again, is a monument of a young and virile art. It is the Lindisfarne Book, made on Holy Island by Bede's friend Eadfirth. The Lindisfarne Book is apparently the first great surviving masterpiece of the school to which it belongs. Its perfection is, at that date, so surprising that at least one eminent Celtic expert[7] has persuaded himself that the book was really written about 120 years later (and, of course, in Ireland), shortly after which it fell into English hands, 'doubtless by some nefarious means'. But the Celtic expert forgot that the Lindisfarne Book is not only a masterpiece of design. It is a text of the Latin gospels, and, as such, has a very definite textual history; it has a liturgical history likewise, and these make it clear that the inscription which the Lindisfarne Book bears is not to be disputed when it says that the

book was written by Eadfirth, Bishop of Lindisfarne, in honour of God and St. Cuthbert. Eadfirth also showed his veneration for St. Cuthbert by causing a Latin life to be made by some anonymous writer. Not satisfied with this, he asked Bede to write a second *Life*. Bede did so, and revised it carefully, after conference with those who had known the Saint. He then so far departed from his usual custom of seclusion within his own monasteries of Monkwearmouth and Jarrow, that he took it himself to Lindisfarne, some fifty miles away. There, for two days, it was diligently scrutinized by the brethren. They could find no fault in it, and Bede dedicated it to Eadfirth.

At the time when Bede visited Holy Island, Bishop Eadfirth had probably finished his long task of writing and illuminating the Lindisfarne Book.[8] It seems unlikely that, when Bede brought to Lindisfarne his tribute to St. Cuthbert, the Bishop in return would have failed to show Bede *his* tribute. So we may think that Bede and the Bishop bent their tonsured heads over the leaves of the Lindisfarne Book, and followed the intricate subtleties of the ornamentation, so delicate that the eye can scarcely trace them, and that we wonder how any brain devised them.

The figure of the Buddhist apostle and the designs of the Lindisfarne Book are both, in their way, as near perfection as work of man can be. Compared with the Chinese apostle the Lindisfarne Book belongs to a primitive—almost barbaric—culture. But it is the most beautiful thing the West could do in that age, just as Bede is the greatest product of the West in knowledge. When we think of this meeting, in a humble shack on Holy Island, of the greatest scholar and the greatest artist of the West, we may ask, How did it come that one small English district produced both?

Bede, the scholar, following knowledge, Eadfirth, the craftsman, creating beauty, Cuthbert, the saint, seeking God, were all alive together, pursuing their quest in one remote corner of England.

How did it come, that just when learning and civilization seemed to be dying out on the continent of Western Europe, they flourished among the Celts of Ireland and the Angles, Saxons, and Jutes of England—tribes who had never before known Roman discipline or Greek learning? Whilst Bede as Chronologist was conscious of living in the last, final age of the world, Bede as Geographer was equally conscious of living in the last, uttermost regions. He speaks of Ireland and Britain as the two remotest isles of the ocean.[9] His abbot, Ceolfrid, addressing the Pope, spoke of himself as living 'in the extreme limits'. How did it come that this monastery on the outskirts was the refuge, not only of the English, but also of the European spirit in the eighth century?

Two centuries before, under the magnanimous rule of Theodoric, Italy had still been the centre of Western culture. It was in Italy that Boethius, Cassiodorus, and St. Benedict had planted, amid the ruins of the Roman world, the beginnings of a new world which was to exceed the old in glory. These Italians were the Founders of the Middle Ages. And even in Britain there had been a temporary rally of Christian and Roman civilization; at Mount Badon the harassed Roman-Britons enjoyed that brief taste of victory, the distant reverberations of which have echoed through the ages in the stories of King Arthur and his knights. But the sixth century, despite its fair beginning, closed in disaster for the Roman world. Gregory the Great had to watch bands of 'unspeakable' Lombards, as he called them, plundering up to the very walls of Rome. Yet Pope Gregory had such pity for the barbarian world outside those walls that he dispatched St. Augustine on his mission to England. Like Columbus later, Gregory little realized what he was doing. Gregory merely hoped to snatch a few more souls from perdition before the Coming of Antichrist and the Day of Doom ended an unfortunate business which, thanks to Adam and Eve, the Serpent and the apple, had gone wrong from the first. For, as he explained in his letter to King Ethelbert of Kent, the end of the world was approaching, and would shortly be upon us.[10]

Yet, in reality, Pope Gregory was 'calling in a new world to redress the balance of the old'.

For civilization at the moment had little chance in Romanized Western Europe. The conquering barbarians were quarrelling over the loot of the Roman Empire till they lost whatever barbaric virtues they had formerly possessed, when they lived in the more austere surroundings of their native forests and swamps. A good idea of life in Western Europe can be drawn from the two historians who are nearest in date to Bede, Gregory of Tours for the *History of the Franks,* and Paul the Deacon for the *History of the Lombards.*

What the ruling Frankish kings and queens were like we may gather from the way in which Queen Fredegund suppressed her naughty daughter Rigunth. Growing tired of the impertinences of her daughter, Fredegund invited her to share the crown jewels, which were kept in a huge chest. She handed out one after another, and at length, pretending to be tired, she said, 'Take them out for yourself, my dear.' The daughter put her arm into the chest, and the mother brought down the lid with all her might upon the head of her unruly offspring, and pressed her throat against the edge of the chest, till her daughter's eyes were starting out of her head. The murder was prevented by a handmaid calling for help: 'Her Royal Highness the Queen is suffocating Her Royal Highness the Princess.'[11] This is not an unfair example of the manners and morals of the reigning house in Merovingian France, though there

were exceptions like the worthy King Guntram, 'whose memory is stained by only one or two murders'.

Paul's *History of the Lombards* is not as sordid as Gregory's *History of the Franks*. The Lombards had a certain rough chivalry, but they were utterly barbarous. Alboin, their king, slew the king of a rival Teutonic tribe, the Gepids, and made a drinking-cup of his skull. With typical inconsequence he also wedded Rosamund, the daughter of the king he had slain. The queen managed to avert her eyes from the gruesome table ornament, and all went well for a time. But it befell on a day that Alboin sat at the banquet longer than was proper, and filling the cup with wine, bade his cup-bearer carry it to the queen and tell her to drink with her father.[12] That was more than Queen Rosamund could stand, and Alboin's reign ended suddenly in 572 or 573. He was succeeded by other Lombard rulers, equally barbarous and less picturesque.

Even before the barbarians had gained such complete mastery, the Roman world had been oppressed by a sense of its age. A fifth-century historian tells us that 'Rome is falling more from the weakness of age than from external violence'.[13] What must the depression have become when Romans had to flatter masters like Alboin and mistresses like Fredegund? The only way of escape was the way of complete renunciation. Gregory of Tours[14] tells of a recluse who ate nothing but bread (upon which he condescended to put a little salt), who drank only water (which, however, he allowed himself to sweeten with a little honey), who never slept, ceasing from prayer only to read or write, and who perpetually wore a hair shirt. Such a man was likely to get the reputation of working miracles. And, miracles or no, he dominated his surroundings: he was respected, and feared, by Roman and barbarian, by good and bad alike. Yet the path of complete renunciation is too difficult for many men and women to follow, and the barbarians who overran the Roman Empire found that most Christians were not like that. Therefore the mixture of barbarian and Roman within the Roman Empire resulted in that degradation which often follows when two different cultures and languages are violently brought together. Each nation finds that the task of learning from the others their irregular manners is easier than that of learning their irregular verbs, and generations pass before either morality or grammar becomes stabilized again.

That accounts for the superiority, both in its grammar and its subject matter, of Bede's ***Ecclesiastical History of the English People*** over Gregory's *History of the Franks*. For when Romanized Christians went forth to convert Irish or English in their own homes, they found conditions very different from those within the decaying Roman world. The missionaries found the barbarians living according to the standards which their ancestors had followed for hundreds, perhaps thousands, of years. It is true that there were in England some small remains of Roman civilization, and that those remains were useful to the missionaries. But the point is that the Christian evangelists found the native Teutonic culture intact. And on their side the missionaries who came among the heathen English were chosen men, trained in saintliness or obedience. No others would have undertaken so thankless a task. Also, they were often men of learning. Here, then, Roman, Celt, and Teuton, Christian and Heathen, met, each at his best. And there were things in the new Christian teaching which harmonized with the Germanic heroic traditions.

The essential virtue of the Old Germanic system was loyalty. The chieftain surrounded himself with a band of young companions who were pledged to live and die with him. It was a lifelong disgrace, Tacitus tells us, for the companion to return alive from the field on which his lord had fallen. This loyalty to a person was the bond of Germanic civilization; not the Roman or Greek conception of loyalty to a community: not 'The Republic', but 'My Chief'.

Abstract conceptions of Theology or Philosophy would have been difficult for the primitive English to grasp. But they were ready to listen to the story of 'the young hero, that was God Almighty, strong and stout of heart'. Let us remember the deep words of St. Augustine in the *Confessions,* where he tells how he found certain books of the Platonists, 'and therein I read, not indeed in those words, but with that meaning: "In the beginning was the Word, and the Word was with God, and the Word was God." . . . *But that the Word was made Flesh, and dwelt among us, that I read not there.*'[15]

Whilst all traditions in Western Europe seemed in danger of breaking down, these two traditions of loyalty to Christ and loyalty to the chief fortified each other, whenever the chief became a true Christian convert.

It was the great good fortune of Bede to be born into a society, in the first freshness of its conversion, which understood those two personal loyalties. The glory of it lasted only for a generation—but Bede caught it before it perished, and enshrined it in his *Ecclesiastical History,* to endure as long as the story of England endures. The *Ecclesiastical History* is the greatest, but not the only, expression of it. In the Old English poem, *The Dream of the Rood* (which certainly belongs to the age of Bede), we have a perfect fusion of the loyalty of the Germanic companion to his lord, and the loyalty of the Christian to Christ, and the mystery of a creation groaning and travailing in pain at the foot of the Cross: not the historic cross of Calvary, but a marvel beyond man's understanding. And all this in the style, phraseology, and metre of Germanic heathen heroic poetry, familiar to the companions as they drank beer

in the lord's hall at night. We know that Bede was skilled in English poetry, and the English verses which he composed on his death-bed have survived. Bede tells in the *Ecclesiastical History* how Cædmon first combined Christian teaching with the style of the old heathen lays; Bede's elder contemporary and fellow scholar, Aldhelm, was doing the same in the south of England; and *Beowulf,* with many another Old English poem, remains as a monument of the fusion.

It was the same combination of loyalties which had led, some years after Bede's birth, to the foundation of the monastery in which he was to work, and without which he would not have been the man he was. There was among the retinue of King Oswy of Bernicia a certain young noble named Biscop. Biscop must have seen a good deal of hard fighting in the early days of his king. When Biscop was twenty-five, Oswy offered him an estate on which he might marry and settle down—just as Hygelac did to Beowulf after he had slain Grendel. It was the usual reward to a young warrior who had proved his worth, and was entitled to pass from the . . . young companions, to the . . . veterans. But, instead, Biscop abandoned the world, went on the pilgrimage to Rome, and set himself to learn all that a monk should know. He sojourned altogether in seventeen monasteries at different times of his life, 'committing to memory whatever he found most profitable in each'. Biscop, who had taken the name Benedict after the founder of the monastic rule which he followed, at length returned to Northumbria, and King Ecgfrid (son of Oswy) gave him a large estate upon which he founded the monastery of Monkwearmouth. The monastery was about five years old when Bede, a boy of seven, entered it. For a dozen years Biscop was Bede's teacher and master. When Ecgfrid gave Biscop a further grant of land, upon which he founded the monastery of Jarrow, the young Bede was transferred there.

Biscop made his monasteries centres of art and learning. He made altogether five journeys from England to Rome, every time bringing back many books and works of art. Biscop brought builders and glaziers from France, but, as any one realizes who examines what is left to-day, his buildings were minute if compared with the great structures of later monasticism. In their simplicity, the remains of Biscop's building remind us of the beginnings of the Franciscan movement. A small church was surrounded by the small huts or cells of the brethren. There were many brethren: by the middle of Bede's life he tells us that there were about six hundred in the two monasteries. The terrible mortality when the plague fell on these communities shows how unhealthy they must have been. But treasures like the Codex Amiatinus and the Lindisfarne Book survive to show that no labour was spared in order to make their equipment beautiful.

All this helps us to understand how, in the seventh century, Christian civilization found a refuge in Northumbria. There was the background of the primitive warrior life, not much altered from what it had been in the days of the *Germania* of Tacitus. That was the soldierly education which men like Biscop or Eostorwine received till they were twenty-four or twenty-five. To these still uncorrupted barbarians came Celtic missionaries of the type of the saintly Aidan. Most important of all, the Roman missionaries brought the ordered life of the Benedictine rule.

And so the tone of Bede's *Ecclesiastical History* is altogether different from that of Gregory's *History of the Franks* or Paul's *History of the Lombards*. The tale of Oswin of Deira, which I am going to read from Bede, is typical of Bede's *History,* just as the tales of Fredegund half-strangling her daughter Rigunth, or Rosamund contriving the death of her husband Alboin, are typical of the continental histories.

> King Oswin was of countenance beautiful, of stature high, in talk courteous and gentle, in all points civil and amiable: no less honourable and bountiful to the noble, than free and liberal to persons of low degree. Whereby it happened, that for his outward personage, inward heart, and princely port, he had the love of all men. Especially the nobility of all countries frequented his court, and coveted to be received in his service.

> Among other his rare virtues, and princely qualities, his humility and passing lowliness excelled. Whereof we will be contented to recite one most worthy example.

> He had given to Bishop Aidan a very fair and proper gelding, which that virtuous bishop (though he used most to travel on foot) might use to pass over waters and ditches, or when any other necessity constrained. I fortuned shortly after, a certain poor weak man met the bishop, and craved an alms of him. The bishop, as he was a passing pitiful man, and a very father to needy persons, lighted off, and gave the poor man the gelding, gorgeously trapped as it was.

> The king hearing after hereof, talked of it with the bishop, as they were entering the palace to dinner, and said, 'What meant you, my lord, to give away to the beggar that fair gelding, which we gave you for your own use? Have we no other horses of less price, and other kind of rewards to bestow upon the poor, but that you must give away that princely horse, which we gave you for your own riding?' To whom the bishop answered, 'Why talketh your grace thus? Is that son of a mare dearer in your sight than that son of God?'

> Which being said, they entered for to dine. The bishop took his place appointed, but the king,

coming then from hunting, would stand a while by the fire to warm him. Where standing, and musing with himself upon the words which the bishop had spoken unto him, suddenly he put off his sword, giving it to his servant, and came in great haste to the bishop: falling down at his feet, and beseeching him not to be displeased with him for the words he had spoken unto him, saying he would never more speak of it, nor measure any more hereafter what or how much the bishop should bestow of his goods upon the sons of God.

> At which sight the bishop, being much astonied, arose suddenly and lifted up the king, telling him that he should quickly be pleased, if it would please him to sit down, and cast away all heaviness.

> Afterward, the king being at the bishop's request merry, the bishop contrariwise began to be heavy and sorry; in such sort, that the tears trickled down by his cheeks. Of whom, when his chaplain in his mother tongue[16] (which the king and his court understood not) had demanded why he wept: 'I know,' said he, 'that the king shall not live long. For never before this time have I seen an humble king. Whereby I perceive, that he shall speedily be taken out of this life: for this people is not worthy to have such a prince and governor.'

> Shortly after, the bishop's dreadful abodement was fulfilled, with the king's cruel death, as we have before declared. Bishop Aidan himself also was taken away out of this world, and received of God the everlasting rewards of his labours, even on the twelfth day after the king, whom he so much loved, was slain.[17]

Bede's life shows what a fine thing Benedictine monasticism could be in early eighth-century England. But the words which Dante puts into the mouth of St. Benedict in Paradise were to prove true: 'So easily seduced is mortal flesh, that a good beginning on earth lasts not so long, as the time between the first springing up of an oak, and its bearing an acorn.'[18] When Bede was a boy of twelve or thirteen the reckless aggression of King Ecgfrid ruined the Northumbrian kingdom. The anonymous *Life of St. Cuthbert* tells how Ecgfrid was ravaging the land of the Picts in the far north, and his queen, attended by St. Cuthbert, was awaiting the issue of the war in the city of Carlisle. The governor of the city was showing them an old Roman fountain constructed in wondrous wise, when Cuthbert exclaimed, 'Oh, Oh, Oh, I deem that the war is finished, and that judgement has been pronounced against our soliders in their warfare. Oh my children, consider how beyond scrutiny are the judgements of God.' In a few days came the news of the death of Ecgfrid and all his army at Nechtansmere. From this defeat Bede at a later period dated Northumbrian decay: 'The prowess of the dominion of the English began to decay and go backwards.' The year after the death of Ecgfrid came the visitation of plague, which carried away from the monastery of Jarrow all who could read, or preach, or recite the antiphons, except Ceolfrid the abbot, and one small lad, nourished and taught by him. In the anonymous *History of the Abbots* the moving story is told of how the abbot and the lad carried on the services unaided. The small lad was certainly[19] Bede himself. I mention these anonymous historical works because, with Eddi's *Life of Wilfrid,* they show us that there was already a school of historical writing in Northumbria before Bede produced his masterpiece.

It has been said that, 'some day, scandal mongers and disintegrating critics may become aware that they have produced most accurate autobiographies'.[20] In his ***History*** and in his ***Lives of the Abbots*** Bede has, unconsciously, written his own autobiography. But it adds to our understanding of his character when we realize that Bede's world had already begun to decay when he was a boy of thirteen. Although for another twenty years King Aldfrid ruled the defeated Northumbrian realm competently within its narrower boundaries, after his death, which took place when Bede was about thirty-three, the state of Northumbria became deplorable. Bede's enormous labours were carried on amid a general decline of Northumbrian civilization. Yet Bede only occasionally refers to the decadence of his age. It was not till the last year of his life that Bede spoke out. A young man of royal birth, probably a pupil of his own, Egbert, had just been appointed Archbishop of York. In a letter of advice to him, Bede deals fully with the abuses which had grown in the thirty troubled years since the death of Aldfrid. He is particularly shocked at the bogus monasteries which were everywhere springing up, filled by pseudo-monks whose only object was to avoid military duties and to live in idleness. Bede is for drastic remedies. Even monasteries of professed monks ought to be dissolved or converted if the monks do not live according to their vows:

> And because there are very many places of this kind which, as the common saying is, are useful to neither God nor man, because neither is the religious life observed in them, according to the law of God, nor do they have in them soldiers or thanes of the secular powers to defend our people from the barbarians; if any one were to turn such monasteries into bishoprics, he would be doing a virtuous act. Your Holiness, with the help of the devout king of our nation, ought to tear in pieces the unrighteous charters of former princes, and to provide things useful to our country, lest either religion die out in our day, or else the number of our armed men diminishes, so that there are none left to defend our borders from barbarian invasion.

Bede complains that monasteries have grown so numerous that there are no lands upon which time-expired soldiers can be settled. Such soldiers are compelled either to emigrate oversea, leaving their native land unprotected, or else to live idle and unmarried, growing more and more demoralized.

But, even worse than these many monasteries of unworthy monks, says Bede, are the sham monasteries of laymen, who escape their secular duties without even making any attempt to live the monastic life.[21] The young archbishop was not able to carry through all the reforms which Bede desired; but he founded the Cathedral school at York and taught in it. It was an epoch-making act—for thereby he passed on the learning of his friend and master, Bede, to his friend and scholar, Alcuin, and through him to the Carolingians and the Middle Ages.

Bede was already ill when he wrote the letter to Egbert—it has been called his swan-song. But, as we know, he went on labouring to the day of his death. 'I do not want my boys to read a lie, or to labour in vain after I am gone,' he said on his death-bed.

If the lifetime of Bede was one of downfall and decay throughout his own Northumbria, it was even more so throughout Christendom. At the time of Bede's birth, although the Mohammedan power had established itself in Syria and Egypt, nevertheless the Mediterranean was still the central sea of the Christian world. But during Bede's lifetime the whole of Africa, and almost all Spain, was lost to Christendom. When Bede was writing his ***History,*** the Saracens had reached the centre of France. Then came the turn of the tide. The year after Bede finished his ***History*** Charles Martel won the great victory over the Saracens which saved France from utter devastation. Bede slipped a reference to it into his ***History***. He could not know how epoch-making the victory was to be. Yet we can imagine his satisfaction as he told how, after their terrible devastation of Gaul, the Saracens had incurred the just judgement of God.

There is something very appropriate in this final reference. Bede instructed Egbert, and Egbert taught Alcuin, so we may regard Alcuin as Bede's spiritual grandson. Bede's spiritual grandson was destined to serve Charles the Great, the grandson of Charles Martel, in the re-establishment of learning in Europe. For, contemporary with all this decay within the borders of Christendom had been the amazing missionary efforts of the Englishmen, Willibrord and Boniface and their companions, among the heathen German tribes of the Continent, which first changed the face of Germany, and then had such repercussions upon Gaul as to make possible the Carolingian Renaissance. It is remarkable how constantly the missionaries write back to England for the works of Bede:

> We, labouring to plant the seeds of the Gospel among the wild and ignorant Germans, beg you to

send us something of the writings of Bede the monk, who of late was shining among you like a lantern, with knowledge of the Scriptures. And if you could send us a bell also, it would be a great comfort to us in our exile.[22]

Or

> We beg that you will comfort us by doing as you have done before, by sending us some ray from that lantern of the Church enlightened by the Holy Spirit in your land—Bede. And we are sending by the bearer two small vats of wine, that you may have a day of joy with your monks.[23]

Or

> I beg that you will send us, for a comfort in our exile, any one of these works, which Bede the priest of blessed memory wrote. [A list follows.] I am asking much, but it will not seem much to your charity.[24]

Or

> I am sick, and like to leave this vale of tears. I beg, as a consolation both of my exile and my illness, for the books of Bede of blessed memory on the building of the Temple, or on the Song of Songs, or his epigrams in heroic or elegiac verse— all, if possible, but, if not, the three books on the building of the Temple. Perhaps what I ask is difficult, but I think nothing will be difficult to your charity.[25]

Such is the constant appeal of the missionaries, Boniface, Lull, and the rest, writing home to the abbots of Monkwearmouth and to Egbert at York. The English ecclesiastics do what they can to supply the need—the abbot of Monkwearmouth laments that he cannot send more of Bede's writings: he has put his boys to work, but it has been a horrible winter, with cold and frost and storms, which have numbed the hand of the writer.[26]

It is thanks to the labours of Boniface and Alcuin, and the inspiration of Bede, that discipline and learning were re-established on the Continent. In England the worst time had still to come, when the whole country was harried by the Vikings, but on the Continent learning, however depressed, never sank again as low as it had done before Bede and those whom he inspired began their labours.

When, at the end of the ninth century, King Alfred had at last checked the Viking raids in England, one of the works he promoted was the translation of Bede's *History* into English. England, therefore, was the first of the nations of Western Europe to have a great history written in the vernacular. But the book was multiplied

much more frequently in Latin, and William of Malmesbury looked back to the *Ecclesiastical History* as a model when, four centuries after Bede's time, he re-established in England Bede's tradition of Latin historiography.

How great had been the popularity of Bede's *History,* during the period which intervenes between Bede and William of Malmesbury, is proved by the large number of early manuscripts which have survived, despite all the destruction wrought by Vikings and others. Two of these earliest manuscripts contain chronological notes, which enable us to date them. The oldest, which was written on the Continent, though it is now at Cambridge, was made within some two years of Bede's death. The second oldest, written within eleven years of Bede's death, was once at Corbie, and is now in Leningrad.[27] It has been generally overlooked, and is not mentioned either by Plummer or by Dr. James. Yet it would seem to be of great importance.

Nowadays the medieval veneration of saints' relics is being revived, and the uncorrupted body of Lenin is worshipped by crowds of pilgrims in Moscow, just as that of Cuthbert was of old revered in Lindisfarne and Durham. Could not the trade in relics also be resuscitated? Our Government might then acquire the Leningrad manuscript for the British Museum, in exchange for the bones of Karl Marx, now resting in Highgate Cemetery.

The Durham library claimed, in the Middle Ages, to have four manuscripts written by the hand of Bede. Three of these are still extant, in whole or in part. They are early, but the writing shows too much variation to permit of their being all from the same hand.[28]

In time, Bede's reputation grew mythical. He was supposed to have visited Rome in order to give the *Curia* the benefit of his scholarship. The University of Paris was convulsed by a dispute between Picard and English students, the Englishmen claiming priority on the ground that Bede had founded the University. Pope Martin V is alleged to have sent a legate to allay the quarrel. The legate is alleged to have allowed the English claim, agreeing that Bede, on his way to Rome, *had* stopped at Paris and founded the University there.[29] The University of Cambridge also claimed Bede, and Fuller, though he obviously did not believe the claim, did not like to contradict it.

> Some report [he says] that Bede never went out of his cell, but lived and died therein. If so, the scholars of Cambridge will be very sorry, because thereby deprived of their honour, by Bede's living once in their University, whose house they still show, between St. John's College and the Round Church

or St. Sepulchre's. Surely Bede was not fixed to his cell, as the cockle to his shell.[30]

Dante saw Bede in Heaven;[31] he also reproached the Cardinals for not studying their Bede as they should. When printing was introduced, the rapidity with which Bede's *History* was printed testifies to its continued popularity. At the Reformation Bede continued in favour with both sides. As an early translator of the Bible, he was applauded by the Wycliffites: and his knowledge of the Scriptures won him the praise of John Foxe, the martyrologist. Bede's characteristic apology for his writings, that at least they had kept him from doing worse things, is reproduced by Foxe:

> As touching the holiness and integrity of his life, it is not to be doubted: for how could it be, that he should attend to any vicious idleness, or had any leisure to the same, who, in reading and digesting so many volumes, consumed all his whole cogitations in writing upon the Scriptures? For so he testifieth of himself in the third book of Samuel, saying in these words: 'If my treatises and expositions', saith he, 'bring with them no other utility to the readers thereof, yet to myself they conduce not a little thus: that while all my study and cogitation was set upon them, in the meanwhile, of slippery enticements and vain cogitations of this world I had little mind.'[32]

On the other hand, Bede, as a strenuous defender of the Roman allegiance and practice, was applauded by the Catholics. Thomas Stapleton, the Roman Catholic controversialist, translated the *Ecclesiastical History* into English, and dedicated it to Elizabeth, in the pathetic hope that it might convert her. Stapleton's translation, revised, is the one I have used in this lecture. It needs revision. Bede, for example, had recorded how Edwin of Northumbria provided for the needs of his subjects: where there were springs by the highway, he planted wooden stakes with metal cups attached to them, for the refreshing of wayfarers. In Stapleton the cups become great brazen basons to bathe in, and the stakes become quick-set bowers, planted around in the interests of propriety.[33]

To be simultaneously applauded by Foxe and Stapleton was a triumph, and is characteristic of Bede's wide appeal. We are driven back to the judgement of W. P. Ker: Bede's good sense is everywhere at home.

Bede is an ascetic, but with good sense: his asceticism was unlike that of the Egyptian hermit of whom St. Jerome tells us, who lived in an old cistern upon five rush-stalks a day.[34] Bede's life of self-denial allowed him to keep a few treasures in his casket—some pepper, some napkins, and some incense. That was all which the greatest scholar of his age had been able to accumulate in a lifetime. But still, he could distribute these things to his friends on his death-bed: 'such gifts as God has given me', in his own words.

Self-denial and heroism are sacred things to Bede—whether in a King Oswald fighting for justice and righteousness, or in a soldier like Lilla throwing his body between his king and the sword of the enemy, or in monks like Cuthbert or Chad.

But it is characteristic of Bede that he, the historian of the earliest English monasticism and its great example, is also the earliest great advocate of the dissolution of monasteries. For those who entered monasteries in order to escape their civil or military duties, yet without submitting to the even more rigorous discipline incumbent upon the good monk, Bede, as we have seen, has complete contempt. 'The result of this', he wrote, 'the next age will see.'[35] The next age *did* see it, amid the complete downfall of Northumbrian civilization. Bede's influence continued, a link between ancient and modern times. But it continued outside the limits of his beloved Northumbria, which lay in ruins.

Yet although Bede's main function was to connect Classical times with the Middle Ages, to help to bridge the gap between the end of the sixth century and the beginning of the twelfth, we must remember that what he passed on was not information, but the spirit of freshness in worship, in learning, and in teaching. 'Spending all my life in my monastery,' he says, 'and observing the regular discipline and the daily singing of God's service in the church, the rest of my time I *was delighted* always to learn, to teach, or to write.' Bede placed the *opus Dei* first, as every true monk must; he would not allow either study or sickness to keep him from it. Alcuin, in a letter to the monks of Wearmouth, records the tradition that Bede believed that the angels were present at the canonical hours: 'Will they not say, Where is Bede? Why comes he not to the services with his brethern?' Only the residue of his time was given to learning and teaching, but he did that with gusto and originality. A few examples will suffice.

In the sixth century a certain Scythian monk at Rome, known as Dionysius Exiguus, in compiling his Easter Tables, had reckoned from the Incarnation.[36] The exact measure of Bede's originality here we shall never know: but Bede was certainly the first scholar and historian to make the reckoning by the year of our Lord the standard reckoning. Every time we date a letter we should render homage to the Venerable Bede.

His *Ecclesiastical History* was not only a pattern for all future historians; not only has it been praised by Mommsen for its accuracy, but in many ways it spread through Western Europe a new conception of history, and of other things. I may mention one detail. Bede wrote the *Ecclesiastical History of the English People* before there was any English nation in existence. He might have adopted the political unit and have written an Ecclesiastical History of Northumbria; he might have taken the geographical unit and have written an Ecclesiastical History of the British Isles. He did neither. He preferred to consider all the Germanic-speaking inhabitants of the British Isles, despite their different origins, Angles, Saxons, and Jutes, as one nation—English. It was not an individual conception of Bede's: the correspondence of Boniface and his fellow missionaries shows that they think of themselves, and of the people they have left at home, not as Northumbrians, West Saxons, or Mercians, but as English. Yet it was Bede who gave world-wide currency to this conception. It is time we abandoned the fallacy that the Norman Conquest first hammered Englishmen into unity. Bede's *Ecclesiastical History of the English People* was one of the many forces which had made England into a nation, long before Normans and Angevins formed the impossible idea of creating one nation out of England and so much of France as they could hold: an idea which led to the Hundred Years' War, that 'tissue of calamitous follies' which put back the clock in Western Europe for generations.

Yet Bede's title to our gratitude is not that he spread this or that idea, but that he made it his business 'to maintain a standard of learning, and to preserve the continuity of civilization'. The words are those which our President used, in his address last year,[37] to define the objects of this Academy, and of its members, individually or conjointly.

I suppose that it would be possible to demonstrate an apostolic succession, from teacher to pupil, from Bede in his cell at Jarrow to our President in his chair this evening.[38] Don't be alarmed; at this hour I am not going to attempt it. I have pointed out how Bede instructed Egbert, Egbert Alcuin. Alcuin was not so great a master as Bede, but he was master of a greater school. All Europe was his school, and his influence stretched to Fulda, to Tours, to Rheims, to many other places, till the streams came together in the University of Paris, and so flowed on to the University of Oxford.

Omitting intermediate stages, I will pass to three Oxford men of our own day who knew intimately their Dark Ages and their Bede. W. P. Ker, S. J. Crawford, and Charles Plummer all possessed that 'plain heroic magnitude of mind' which marked Bede himself. If you have followed this lecture carefully, you will have realized that anything of value in it I have learnt from those three men, through whom alone, if at all, I must claim to be in touch with the Venerable Bede.

S. J. Crawford, cut off before his time ('Alas, too little and too lately known'), was a man whose scholarship Ker would have deeply admired. A colleague wrote Crawford's epitaph:

For him books were no dead things; through their pages
He passed into a happy country, where
He held communion with saints and sages,
Heroes and prophets, spirits wise and rare.

He has left his books now; those great souls he knew
Called him from this small world of time and space:
This is not death; he has gone to share the true,
The glorious life of that immortal race.[39]

Charles Plummer seemed the reincarnation of Bede, if ever one man seemed the reincarnation of another—in his vast learning, his humility, his piety, his care for the young. Elected a Fellow of Corpus at a time when celibacy was still imposed, Plummer never broke his monastic vow, remaining single during the fifty-eight years of his Fellowship. Gibbon spoke scornfully of the 'monks of Magdalen' and their unproductiveness. I wish he had lived to see the production of the monks of Corpus, and above all, Plummer's edition of Bede's *Historical Works*.

Plummer was born within a few miles of the spot where Bede was born, lived, and died; and Plummer was not altogether satisfied with the way in which collieries and furnaces had transformed what in Bede's day had been the wooded banks of the Tyne. I myself remember standing on the roof of the North Eastern Hotel at Newcastle, and thinking that, if Bede could have seen the circles of smoke with which I was surrounded, he would have had no doubt where he was, though he might have wondered what he had done to be put there. When Plummer wrote, forty years ago, it was less common than it is in these days to doubt the value of such industrial over-development; and it is with the words of Charles Plummer, rather than any of my own, that I wish to close this lecture. 'Even rating these things at the very highest value that has ever been put upon them by the most zealous votary of material progress, we have not, it seems to me, amid all our discoveries, invented as yet anything better than the Christian life which Bede lived, and the Christian death which he died.'

Notes

[1] *History of Classical Greek Literature,* 3rd edit., 1891, I. i. 284, I. ii. 51.

[2] George Sarton, *Introduction to the History of Science,* i, p. 460, 1927. Compare Hallam, *Literature of Europe,* i, p. 5, footnote, 1837.

[3] *Purgatorio,* xi.

[4] *Purgatorio,* xiii. 136-8.

[5] Mon. Germ. Hist., *Chronica Minora,* ed. Th. Mommsen, iii, p. 248, Berlin, 1898.

[6] W. P. Ker, *The Dark Ages,* 1904, p. 141.

[7] Prof. R. A. S. Macalister, in *Essays and Studies presented to William Ridgeway,* Cambridge, 1913.

[8] In the *De temporum ratione* (725) Bede speaks of having written the prose *Life of St. Cuthbert* recently (*nuper*). This seems to preclude a date much earlier than 720 for Bede's visit to Holy Island. And Eadfirth died in 721.

[9] *Ecclesiastical History,* iii. 25. (A speech placed in the mouth of Wilfrid, at the Council of Whitby.)

[10] *Ecclesiastical History,* i. 32.

[11] *History of the Franks,* ix. 34.

[12] *History of the Lombards,* ii. 28.

[13] Orosius, ed. Zangemeister, II. vi. 14.

[14] *History of the Franks,* v. 5 (10).

[15] vii. 9.

[16] They were both, of course, of Irish stock.

[17] From the translation of the *Ecclesiastical History,* by Thomas Stapleton, 1565, Book III, cap. 14, revised.

[18] *Paradiso,* xxii. 85-7.

[19] Bede was nourished and taught at Jarrow by Ceolfrid. If only one trained lad was left there, it can only have been Bede.

[20] Rand, *Founders of the Middle Ages,* p. 73. Prof. Rand's book places under a great debt all who are interested in the continuity of civilization, and more particularly the transition from Classical times to the Dark Ages.

[21] *Epistle to Egbert,* 11, 12.

[22] Boniface to Huetberht, Abbot of Wearmouth and Jarrow; Jaffé, *Monumenta Moguntina,* 180.

[23] Boniface to Egbert, Archbishop of York; Jaffé, *Mon. Mog.,* 250.

[24] Lull to the Archbishop of York; Jaffé, *Mon. Mog.,* 288.

[25] Lull to Cuthbert, Abbot of Wearmouth and Jarrow; Jaffé, *Mon. Mog.,* 289.

[26] Cuthbert to Lull, Jaffé, *Mon. Mog.,* 300. Cuthbert is, of course, the man who, at an earlier date, had been present at Bede's death, and has left us an account of it.

[27] See O. D. Rojdestvensky in *Speculum,* iii. 314-21; E. A. Lowe, *English Historical Review,* xli. 244-6.

[28] See article by Dr. Montague R. James in *Bede: Essays in Commemoration, edited by A. Hamilton Thompson,* 1935, p. 235. Dr. James enumerates the following as extant in whole or in part:

(1) *The Gospels*; Durham, A. ii. 16: there is also a small slip in the Pepysian library, Magdalene College, Camb.

(2) *Epistles of Paul, glossed*; Trin. Coll., Camb., B. 10. 5: there is also a fragment in the British Museum, Cotton Vitellius C. viii.

(3) Cassiodorus *On the Psalter*; Durham, B. ii. 33. Dr. James thinks (2) and (3) better claimants than (1).

[29] César Égasse du Boulay, *Historia Universitatis Parisiensis,* Parisiis, 1665, i. 113. Rashdall has described Du Boulay as 'perhaps the stupidest man who ever wrote a valuable book' (*Universities of Europe,* 1895, i, p. 271).

[30] *Church History,* 1655, Cent. viii, p. 98.

[31] *Paradiso,* xxii. 85.

[32] *Act and Monuments,* ed. Townsend and Cattley, i. 364-5.

[33] ii. 16.

[34] Rand, *Founders of the Middle Ages,* p. 122. But *was* it rush-stalks? The text in Migne's *Patrologia,* xxiii. 5, runs *quinque caricis per singulos dies sustentabatur.* This would make it five dried figs per day—a meagre diet, to be sure, but, considering the rations of Egyptian hermits, too nutritious, one would think, to justify Jerome's expressions of extreme amazement. So I think Jerome may have written (or at any rate meant to write) *quinque caricis stipulis,* or something of that sort.

[35] *Ecclesiastical History,* v. 23.

[36] Poole, *Chronicles and Annals,* 1926, p. 22.

[37] Mackail, *Presidential Address,* July 1935, p. 9.

[38] Some earlier stages are given in the *History* of Ademar (Pertz, iv. 119).

[39] In Memoriam S. J. Crawford in *The Invisible Sun,* by V. de S. Pinto.

F. M. Stenton (essay date 1943)

SOURCE: F. M. Stenton, "Learning and Literature in Early England," in *Anglo-Saxon England*, Oxford at the Clarendon Press, 1943, pp. 177-200.

[In the following excerpt, Stenton asserts that Bede's greatest talent was his ability to coordinate fragments of information from assorted sources.]

Among the men who brought Northumbrian learning out of isolation, Benedict Biscop, the founder of Wearmouth and Jarrow, deserves to be regarded as the leader. In the history of his time he is overshadowed by his younger contemporary Wilfrid. But Wilfrid's contribution to the enlightenment of the north was made in the spheres of ecclesiastical observance and regulation; he was too impatient to create a great monastic school, and his churches of Hexham and Ripon were not remarkable for their learning. Benedict devoted the knowledge and experience of half a lifetime to the establishment of two monasteries. By 674, when Ecgfrith, king of Northumbria, gave him land for the foundation of his house at Wearmouth, he had made three separate journeys from England to Rome, lived for two years in retirement on the island of Lerins, guided the newly consecrated Archbishop Theodore from Rome to England, and spent two more years as abbot of the monastery of St. Peter and St. Paul outside Canterbury. His importance in the history of English learning is due to the libraries which his knowledge of southern cities enabled him to bring together at Wearmouth and Jarrow. Before there was any prospect of the foundation of Wearmouth he had accumulated a large collection of purchased books at Vienne. Transported to England, these books became the nucleus of the library at Wearmouth, which was increased as a result of a fourth journey to Rome in 679. Two years later a new grant of land from Ecgfrith enabled Benedict to found a second monastery at Jarrow on Tyne, seven miles north-west of Wearmouth, and in 684 he undertook the last of his journeys to Rome in order to obtain books and relics for the new house. When he died, in 689, he had brought into being two neighbouring monasteries, governed as a single community, which possessed an endowment in relics, religious ornaments, and books unparalleled in England.

The books collected by Benedict made possible the work of Bede. The commentaries on scripture and the scientific works, through which he first became famous, prove his acquaintance with a singularly wide range of patristic and historical literature.[1] Only a small proportion of his work has been edited in such a way as to show the exact extent of his debt to his predecessors. Like other ancient scholars, Bede often quotes or refers to authors whose work he only knew through epitomes, or through isolated sentences embedded in later texts. His knowledge of classical literature, for example, was much narrower than has sometimes been inferred from the extent to which classical reminiscence enters into his writing. Even so, his work could never have been done without recourse to libraries of wholly exceptional size and quality. From his admission as a child of seven until his death at the age of sixty-three he was a member of the monastery which Benedict had founded at Jarrow. There is no evidence that he travelled widely in search of books; he never refers to distant libraries which he has visited, and the range of his recorded travel does not extend beyond York and Lindisfarne. Apart from occasional books which he may have obtained through the favour of learned correspondents, it is probable that his work rested on the collections of books made by Benedict, and increased by Bede's own master Ceolfrith, Benedict's successor in the rule of both his monasteries.

Later generations, considering the long series of Bede's commentaries, placed him in the succession of the great fathers of the church.[2] He himself would certainly have wished to be remembered by these works of exposition. His scientific treatises, which form a link between his commentaries and his *Ecclesiastical History,* arose naturally from his conception of his responsibilities as a teacher. Some scheme of chronology was necessary to the understanding of scripture, and the date of Easter was fixed by astronomical calculation. In 703, early in his literary course, he produced the elementary manual of chronology known under the title *De Temporibus*. It is a meagre work, and it involved Bede for once in a charge of heresy, brought by certain individuals whom he describes as rustics wallowing in their cups. The work through which he ranks as a master of technical chronology, the treatise *De Temporum Ratione,* was written in 725. Its influence is not yet spent, for it established in England the custom of reckoning years from the era of the Incarnation. Bede was in no sense the originator of this system, which formed part of a calculus for determining the date of Easter devised by the computist Dionysius Exiguus early in the sixth century. It was ignored by the Roman church and indeed by all ecclesiastical authorities until 663, when Wilfrid, who had probably become acquainted with it during his first Italian journey, brought it forward at the council of Whitby. There is no unequivocal proof of its employment in English documents before the appearance of the *De Temporum Ratione,* and its rapid adoption thereafter was undoubtedly due to the influence of Bede's historical work.

Through this work Bede emerges at last from the atmosphere of ancient science and exegesis to prove himself the master of a living art. As a historian Bede was singularly fortunate in his environment. An interest in history was one of the features which distinguished the northern from the southern scholarship of the eighth century. Between 698 and 705 a monk of

Lindisfarne had described the life and personality of St. Cuthbert in writing which moves stiffly but rises at times to a curious and sinister power. [See *Two Lives of St. Cuthbert*, edited by B. Colgrave. Cambridge, 1940.] Bede himself never surpassed this nameless writer's description of the sudden sense of disaster which came to Cuthbert as he stood in Carlisle with the queen of Northumbria on the day of the battle of Nechtanesmere. A monk of Whitby had attempted the hopeless task of writing the life of Gregory the Great on the basis of the materials supplied by Northumbrian tradition. Eddi's tendentious life of Wilfrid had been written at the request of Acca, bishop of Hexham, and Tatberht, abbot of Ripon. Within Bede's immediate circle, a monk of Wearmouth had written a life of his master, Abbot Ceolfrith. It is remarkable as a piece of pure biography, without any hagiographical admixture, and it received the compliment of imitation from Bede himself in his Lives of the Abbots of Wearmouth and Jarrow. By 731, when Bede put forth his *Ecclesiastical History,* there plainly existed in Northumbria an audience for a work of erudition devoted to the growth of the English church. Bede's *Ecclesiastical History,* which King Ceolwulf of Northumbria read and criticized in draft, is the response of a great scholar to a great opportunity.

Nevertheless, its essential quality carries it into the small class of books which transcend all but the most fundamental conditions of time and place. Bede was a monk to whom the miraculous seemed a manifestation of the divine government of the world. But his critical faculty was always alert; his narrative never degenerates into a tissue of ill-attested wonders, and in regard to all the normal substance of history his work can be judged as strictly as any historical writing of any time. His preface, in which he acknowledges the help received from learned friends, reads like the introduction to a modern work of scholarship. But the quality which makes his work great is not his scholarship, nor the faculty of narrative which he shared with many contemporaries, but his astonishing power of co-ordinating the fragments of information which came to him through tradition, the relation of friends, or documentary evidence. In an age when little was attempted beyond the registration of fact, he had reached the conception of history. It is in virtue of this conception that the *Historia Ecclesiastica* still lives after twelve hundred years. . . .

Notes

[1] On the character of Bede's literary equipment see M. L. W. Laistner, 'Bede as a Classical and Patristic Scholar', *Trans. R. Hist. Soc.*, 4th Series, xvi. 69-94.

[2] Bede's reputation abroad in the Carolingian age is proved by many copies of individual works written on the Continent in hands of this period.

Charles W. Jones (essay date 1946)

SOURCE: Charles W. Jones, "Bede as Early Medieval Historian," in *Bede, the Schools and the Computus*, edited by Wesley M. Stevens, Variorum, 1994, pp. 26-36.

[*In the following excerpt originally published in 1946, Jones provides background and argues that Bede's historiography, which links chronography with hagiography, was typical of historians of his time.*]

Although many believe, considering his archetypal position in English thought and letters, that Bede's contributions to medieval and modern thought have been unduly neglected, his historiography has been scrutinized by two outstanding scholars, Charles Plummer[1] and Wilhelm Levison.[2] I shall not attempt to reproduce the picture they have painted. Rather, I want to generalize their detail by marking structural lines, showing how Bede, exceptional though he was, typifies the historiography of his age. In doing so, I shall pay particular attention to three literary forms of the period, calendar, saint's life, and chronicle—indicating their unity in trinity. Time forbids my citing proof and cogent detail, which must be left for another occasion.[3] We have only begun to study the medieval calendar, which is the motive force of chronicle and martyrology and through them of medieval history. If I speak of the calendar, then, it is of the essence.

A characteristic of the early Middle Ages is poverty—economic and political disorganization and rustic isolation. We note it in the roads, in coinage, in the return to the farm. But most of all we note it in books. From the library of Alexandria, with possibly 600,000 volumes, we descend to the library of Cassiodorus, with possibly two or three thousand. Bede, who lived in an English renaissance and was the most widely-read man of his time, is known to have used some 175 titles, many of them short poems or pamphlets; his library may have been two or three times that size. Because of this dearth of books, the calendar became a primary source for historians. It also shaped the methods of historians, and even determined who the historians would be.

Today the calendar is essential; like salt it is no less necessary because it is cheap. In the Romanesque period it was equally essential, but not cheap. People had to appear in court, pay their debts, plant their crops, go to church, and honor their dead just as much as we. Our calendar is standardized and has been cheapened through mass production. But then one learned clerk had to know the caprices of a score of different calendars and keep a single one for his entire neighborhood. After the Bible it was the most necessary book—even more necessary than the ordinal, with which it was sometimes bound.

Whatever the variations in detail, all calendars of the period were alike in consisting of two parts—a solar calendar marking the days of the year, or anniversaries, which the medieval world inherited from the Rome of Julius Caesar, and a lunar calendar, inherited from the Hebrews, which marked the movable feasts for a succession of years.[4] Either calendar consisted of only a few columns of numbers, parallel down a page. The solar calendar needed only two columns: the day of the month and the Dominical Letter or ferial number; the lunar calendar needed only the number of the year in a chosen era and the date of Easter or of the Easter moon.

The luxurious margins stimulated annotation; so did the fact that the keeper of the calendar had to remind people of necessary duties and important events. The unique event, the one that occurred but once, was recorded opposite the proper year in the lunar calendar; the anniversary, the yearly recurrence, was entered opposite the proper day in the solar calendar. The notations on the lunar calendar are *annals;* the notations on the solar calendar are *martyrology.*

Two essentials escape that host of authors who have written on the relation of annals and Easter-tables. The first is that the annalistic process begins as soon as the calendar becomes the main book in a rustic library. Such a commonplace as that of James Westfall Thompson, drawn from Poole, is clearly erroneous: "Early English monasticism invented one type of medieval historiography of a unique nature. This was the monastic annals."[5] On the contrary, the *Paschale Campanum* shows Paschal annals written on Victorian tables in Italy as early as A.D. 464. The only surviving manuscript of the complete Victorian tables has an entry for A.D. 501 that must have been contemporaneous. There is evidence that the sixth-century Victor of Tonnenna used Easter-annals in composing his chronicle; there is no doubt that such annals underlie the chronicle of Prosper of Aquitaine, just as they underlie the great *Paschal Chronicle.* The historiography of Julius Africanus, Hippolytus, and other early chronographers can only fully be explained by assuming a basic Paschal table. In fact, as much evidence survives as could be expected that the process of Paschal notation was continuous from the scribes of Palestine. Long before the English heard of monasticism, the Irish, Gauls, Spaniards, Italians, and Greeks were entering annals on Easter-tables, and chroniclers and historians were using those entries as sources.

This erroneous commonplace, which is a product of our century, unknown to Mommsen or De Rossi, arises from the fact that, once having used the simple word "Easter-table," historians have avoided its complexities. They have paid little or no attention to the diversity in Easter-tables, to the constant supplanting of one by another in the same province, and to the difficulty of making a concordance of annals written on two different tables. To this problem the medieval historian—Bede, for instance—was keenly alive. To equate one Easter-table with another, when each used a different era, a different beginning of the year, a different cycle of intercalations, is not easy for the modern historian, with an enormous library and a great deal of time at his disposal. It was a challenge that practically no medieval chronicler could meet, as the failures of Victorius and the oscillating dates of the Irish annals clearly indicate. Bede was the single computist in the West after A.D. 450 capable of making such equations, and he avoided doing so whenever possible. Moreover, he made mistakes occasionally when he tried.

Except for the Victorian tables in a few provinces in Gaul, no Easter-table was used consecutively for longer than fifty years in any Latin province until the Dionysiac table was accepted in that province. Moreover, because of the uncyclical construction of the Dionysiac table, it had to be discarded after ninety-five years. When these tables were discarded, the annals too were likely to be discarded.

That is the reason why there is so little direct evidence of annalistic entries on Easter-tables before the seventh century in England, when the cyclical Dionysiac table, used thereafter until the Gregorian reform, was invented. Its users could copy entries from previous Dionysiac tables, but from no others, without error. Nevertheless, as I have said, the annalistic process was operating and the calendar-keeper was perforce an historian.

The second essential that has been overlooked is that the annalist is *ipso facto* a martyrologist and therefore fundamentally a hagiographer. As he keeps the Easter-table, so does he keep the Julian calendar. The difficulty of using annals as an historical base contrasts with the ease of using martyrological items.

The anniversaries were entered on the Julian calendar. It was the only calendar in use in the West, and it never changed. Entries could be transferred freely from one calendar to another; selections and combinations could be made at will. Here was not paucity but wealth of material, which accumulated over the centuries. An archivist at St. Gall even created a "bibliographic calendar," in which, besides the day of the month, he noted the shelf numbers and page references to material about the commemorated saint.

Our historian, then, entered an exacting profession. He was first a scribe, second a librarian or archivist, third an astronomer, fourth an annalist, fifth a hagiographer, and sixth a teacher and probably a priest. He was almost automatically qualified for the group which Manitius calls *universale Schriftsteller.* If we look at the group of chronographers, we see a common pattern in them all: Hippolytus, Julius Africanus, Eusebius, Jerome, Prosper, Sulpicius Severus, and Bede. Isidore was in the tradition, though he lacked the chronographic skill, and Gennadius shows many of the traits though we have little writing from him.

This profession, of which historiography is only a part, changed the form of history written.

I. I have said that the historian or annalist was *ipso facto* a hagiographer. Levison says of Bede, "Chronology was one starting-point of Bede's historiography, the literary expression of the cult of the saints, was the second." These are not two starting-points, but one. Let us look at the simple hagiological process, without its innumerable complications.

A saint dies. The priest is required in succeeding years to hold a mass for the saint. As a reminder for him, our historian jots down the anniversary in the Julian calendar. For the lection, the priest delivers a tributary biography, culled from the flagging memories of the neighborhood. To preserve its essentials for another year, the historian adds the details to his memoranda written on the calendar.

The parish prospers with the growing fame of the saint, and the single mass turns into a cult of a week's or a season's duration. More lavish lections are needed. The very prosperity which the saint has generated allows our historian to expand his library. Some of the new parchment bought in this prosperous era is dedicated to a voluminous life of the saint. The calendar-jottings and appended notes form the basis or outline for the new work.

Yet the number of authentic biographical details preserved is few, partly because of the strictures of marginal notation. Since expansion is needed and the material must be suited to ethical instruction, our historian adds some abstract saintly pictures—such commonplaces and little miracles as might reasonably be attributed to any saint.

Reginald of Canterbury, in the Preface to his *Life of St. Malchus,* clearly advises his readers to compare his story with Jerome's. Where the two agree, he says, the reader finds history; where the two disagree, the reader is to believe Jerome, not Reginald. ("Ubi discordare, non cogitur ut credat nostro; cogitur ut semper credat Hieronimo.") "If I ran across a good story anywhere," says Reginald, "I included it! for *all things are common in the communion of saints.* Since Malchus was just, saintly, loved by Christ, and full of the very essence of righteousness, I do not deviate from the truth, no matter what virtues I ascribe to Malchus, even though they were manifested only in some other saint."[6]

I have quoted Reginald, who lived four centuries after Bede, to show how solidly implanted was the tradition which was active in Bede's day. For the author of the oldest *Life of St. Gregory,* written at Whitby when Bede was a young student, makes an even stronger statement. In fact, we might believe that Reginald was paraphrasing if the limited circulation of the Life of Gregory did not make such an act improbable.

> No one should take offence if any of these deeds were done by some other saint, since the holy apostle, through the mystery of the member saints united in one body, has so brought them into union that, by a comparison with the living body, we may harmonize the members, one with another, in turn (I Cor. xii, 12-14. 19-20). The function of eyes and ears, for instance, will thus serve the hands and feet quite as much as themselves. In this sense all "do not have the same office" in all things (Rom. xii, 4). Yet we know that all the saints are through charity of the body of Christ, whose members are one. Hence if any of those acts which we have written down were not of that man (for indeed we learned them orally and not from any one who had seen and heard—so much do we have it from common report), nevertheless we should little doubt that they too belong to so great a man. For that holy man himself, in his aforesaid wisdom, clearly teaches that, of all living things, there should always be attributed to one what is discovered in others. He (Gregory) declares this to be as nothing in that community of all the angels above of which, as we said before, he secretly attained a full conception, saying that there should be found anew in each and every one what is seen in another no less than what is manifest in him.[7]

This difference between ethical truth and manifestation is implicit in most of the hagiological writing of the period. Apparently it is less clear to us. Colgrave, the excellent editor of Bede and Eddius, can only account for the recurrent miracle stories by saying, "The age of Bede was primitive in its outlook; it was naturally credulous, and the nature of evidence was but vaguely understood."

As chronicler and annalist our historian records only phenomena and follows the normal rules of evidence about phenomena. His annals are remarkably factual, in conformity with those rules, though they are often under the same cover and in the same hand as the martyrology, which is ethical not factual. Bede's *Lives of the Abbots* is a chronicle, drawn from chronicles and annals. We need no further proof of that fact than the appearance of year-dates, drawn from the Easter-annals: "In the 674th year of Our Lord's Incarnation, in the second Indiction, in the fourth year of King Egfrid's reign," says Bede of Benedict Biscop's departure. This is a straight reading across the columns of the Easter-table. In that work he is as factual as are his sources.

If we turn to Bede's prose *Life of St. Cuthbert,* which is based on the solar calendar, or martyrology, we find that he mentions seasons, but not years. The two exceptions only make the case more convincing: he mentions Cuthbert's two years of episcopacy because it is bound up in the miracle of anticipation of death, and he mentions boyhood at eight years of age, which is the generalized formula for the age of purity.[8] The work is as timeless as the solar calendar, which recurs year in, year out, like the rising and setting of the sun. The only time-references within the body of the work are such phrases as "once upon a time," "when he had remained some years," or "at about the same time." In this way the deeds of the hero are removed from this temporal world. Plummer, Levison, and Colgrave, among others, have remarked how much specific detail Bede eliminated in composing his *Life of St. Cuthbert;* but they have not realized that he was employing a professional author's conventions for achieving a specific result.

But where, as in the *Ecclesiastical History,* Bede writes long passages of continuous narrative, the power of the annalist and the power of the hagiographer are met in combination. If what he is writing is didactic, the hagiographical power will predominate. Recent scholars have been at some pains to overlook the miraculous element in the *History* and are thereby doing it a disservice. Bede plainly states his didactic purpose in the Preface:

> For if history relates good things of good men, the attentive hearer is excited to imitate that which is good; or if it mentions evil things of wicked persons, nevertheless the religious and pious hearer or reader, shunning that which is hurtful and perverse, is the more earnestly excited to perform those things which he knows to be good, and worthy of God. *Of which you are deeply sensible.*

Bede's citation of authority has been used as a proof of his struggle for factual accuracy, but readers have not looked to see under what conditions he quotes authority. He never mentions Isidore, Orosius, etc., from whom he drew factual detail. The greater the miracle, the more the authority quoted—a guarantee, not of factual, but of ethical truth. What Dudden said of Gregory applies even more to Bede: "He looked, not to the mental, but to the moral qualities as the guarantee of truth." The computist who wrote his long chronicle of the world only as an illustration of a principle was bound to regard occurrences as secondary to principles; and the traditional mode of illustrating principles was the miraculous anecdote.

I do not mean that Bede was consciously as loose with fact as was Reginald of Canterbury. But he was clearly not interested in it as we are. Such a remark as, "Whether the miracle was effected by the merits of the same blessed Father Cuthbert or by his successor Aethilwald, the Searcher of the Heart knows best. There is no reason why it may not be attributed to either of the two," indicates that Bede was unconcerned about the facts when he was writing didactic works.

II. Our historian was not only a hagiographer, but a chronologist and astronomer. Hence he was a school teacher as well. By profession he was a theorist, though he taught in a professional school. He was in the neo-Platonic tradition of macrocosm and microcosm; he saw all things in terms of principles and types. God was a geometer, to be revealed in numbers and diagrams.

There is a special attribute of teaching in poverty-stricken areas where books are scarce: mnemonic devices are emphasized. There are other reasons why number-symbolism flourished, but above all they were useful to the teacher. The threes and fours and sevens of medieval art and thought took their shape in the years between Prudentius and Bede. Plummer and Levison emphasize Bede's concern with the Six Ages of the World, though a close reading of Bede's works shows that it was fundamentally a teaching-device with him, as it was with St. Augustine. It was Julian of Toledo and Ildefonsus who attached notions of reality to it and disseminated millenial doctrine that Bede found hard to combat. Nevertheless, this kind of dealing with abstraction is a part of the chronographic tradition, and Hippolytus and Julius Africanus, who fathered the tradition, were milleniarists.

The traditional textbooks consisted of two parts: the theoretical (or rules of the game) and the practical (or their application). From Hippolytus on, the chronicles that were written formed only the practical, or less important, part of the basic text. With the Eusebian Chronicle, the theoretical text is missing, as is all the text of Africanus and the theoretical parts of Jerome and Prosper; for later ages chose what they wanted. But both parts are there in pseudo-Cyprian, the Cologne Prologue, the Carthaginian and Irish *computi,* and in Bede.

The selection of items for the chronicle, or practical half of the volume, was therefore controlled in two ways: (1) In the main the author limited himself to what previous teachers of the subject had written—that is, chronicles, brought up to date by the annalistic entries on Easter-tables. The two were bound together in the same computistical volumes. We note, for instance, that from the point where Isidore's continuation of Jerome stops, Bede uses primarily material from the *Pontifical Book* (itself chronographic) or else from Easter-annals, largely English. (2) The author selected items for his chronicle which illustrated the generalizations about time recorded in the theoretical part of the volume.

Bede's great Chronicle is Chapter 66 of his work on Times; the first 65 chapters move progressively through the theory of time from atoms to eras, and Chapters 67-72 treat of the nature of eternity. Bede's statements in the Preface, amplified in the last chapters, show that his interest lay primarily in theory—for instance, the theory of Six Ages (or eras) and their relation to eternity. His selection of events in the chronicle is haphazard so long as it fulfills the desires of the computist or teacher for illustration of the theory. Levison's remark about the shorter chronicle can be applied equally well to the longer: "He gives us a survey which is rather poor in design and performance; the time of single events is not settled distinctly, and the duration of generations and reigns is given only to make out the length of the ages."

I shall pause to indicate the influence of professional bent upon literary selection in only two particulars. As computist, our historian is an astronomer. His history contains an abnormal number of astronomical items, but not because he is superstitious. As annalist he constantly thinks about astronomy, and as naturally footnotes with astronomical items as we footnote with statistics. Why not? Is not that same book the textbook in astronomy? Bede is by no means unique. Idatius is a case in point. Using annals compiled in the flux of the Iberian invasions and living at a time when controversies over the calendar were at their height in the early years of Leo's episcopate, he reflects the interests and concern, not so much of the people, as of himself and the annalist-astronomers on whom he drew.

The other detail is Bede's employment of the Christian Era. We commonly trace the use of our Incarnation era to his *Ecclesiastical History*. It was the first true history to date according to the Year of Our Lord. But we have not asked why. It is a difficult process to adjust dates to another era, especially when the beginnings of the year differ. The wise author will choose to adjust the fewest. Bede's primary source for his Chronicle was Eusebius-Jerome and their continuators; hence he adopted as his pattern their mundane era and adjusted other dates to it. But when he came to write his *History,* his primary source for dated matter was the Dionysiac Easter-table. Inevitably he changed his chronological pattern to the era of Dionysius.

III. That content determines style may be a clouded concept in our own day, but not in Bede's. Here I can but suggest the overwhelming evidence. Delehaye points to the amazing difference in style between Eusebius' *Life of Constantine* and his *Ecclesiastical History*. One was in the panegyric tradition, the other in the historical. The fourth book of Augustine's *Christian Doctrine,* which was Bede's handbook as it was the handbook for every *doctor ecclesiasticus,* devotes

itself to instructing teachers how to shift from one style to another.

Those who have pointed out Bede's debt to Eusebius and Gregory of Tours have had some difficulty developing their case. To be sure, Bede used and venerated the works of each, but his own composition arises naturally from another tradition. Fundamentally his *History* is not that of an English Eusebius, but a hagiography imposed upon the outline provided by a chronicle or assemblage of annals. His was a unique but natural enough invention. The separate "styles" of the two literary forms shine out from its pages.[9]

As an archivist or annalist, Bede writes succinctly. The archivist and reporter are antithetical in style as well as point of view. The margins of calendars, which were our historian's creative sphere, are not so ample as to allow detail and surmise. The prolixity of normal reporting was automatically eliminated. But as hagiographer he not only was diffuse but followed myriad conventions that arose from the tradition I have already dealt with: the elimination of the particular, the relevant (or irrelevant) Biblical quotation, the type or ancient analogy, the superlative good and bad. These two styles are manifest in the *History* though Bede may have meant to fuse them.

How much of each Bede copied *verbatim* from others and how much is his own is a question that has not seriously been examined. Here I can look at but one phase, his time-references,—and that sketchily.

According to Mommsen, Bede was

> first and foremost a man of integrity and a faithful witness. He calls himself a *verax historicus* and he has a right to the title; all who have followed his track will testify that few writers have treated matters of fact with such, and often such laborious, accuracy.[10]

"Witness" is not meant in the sense of eye-witness. Bede quoted Vegetius about the construction of the Roman Wall rather than walk two miles to look for himself. Mommsen had traced Bede's sources and knew how faithfully he repeated them, not necessarily to the letter (if that did not fit his purpose or syntax) but to the spirit. Above all, Bede seldom, if ever, made a surmise; he was far more apt to omit because he was not sure of himself than he was to guess. This quality shines out particularly in his chronological references. We may be sure that those references come directly from Bede's archives, unless there is such an expression as *circiter* to accompany them.

It is surprising how little historians have questioned where Bede got his dates. The Old English Chronicle, the Irish Annals, the British Annals, and Nennius have all been subjected to scrutiny, with Bede's chronology used as a standard of judgment. But seldom has anyone asked where or how Bede got his information.

Nothing is more impossible to transmit orally than a date; and, as I have said, nothing was harder for an historian of Bede's time to translate from one of the numerous chronological systems to another. Hence we can analyze the *History* and learn with some clarity what Bede's sources of information were; for we can assume: (1) that Bede copied his material, if not *verbatim,* at least so as to hold onto the factual content of the original document, and (2) that the method of dating employed by Bede will, barring necessary changes, be that of the document on which he was working.

That remarkable student of diplomatics, Reginald Lane Poole, employed this method in a series of papers that were published about the time of his death in *Studies in Chronology and History.* That certain erroneous assumptions, largely centering in the history of the Dionysiac table, kept his studies from being as fruitful as they might have been only indicates how much study and care are yet necessary and does not vitiate the method, or many of his results.

Seven principles apply in the analysis of Bede's time-references:

    1. Items containing an *annus Domini* without days come from a Dionysiac annal. If the days are given, the item may have come from such an annal.

    2. Days of the month without a year come from a Julian calendar or martyrology.

    3. Indictions without days of the month come from a Dionysiac annal.

    4. Indications with days of the month come from a letter or charter written under the supervision of a Romanist.

    5. The length of a reign given in years, or in years, months, and days, comes from a native regnal list. If the length is given in years, months, and days, the archivist was a Christian. The length of a bishop's tenure comes from an episcopal list.

    6. Verbal formulas that are unquestionably annalistic but lack the era come from non-Dionysiac Paschal annals, probably Victorian or Irish.

    7. Items which give an erroneous *annus Domini* probably originated in a non-Dionysiac table.

As I said at the beginning, the occasion prevents my citing details or more than a few results. I select here four different results of such analysis:

1. Though Poole was right in asserting that Bede's annalistic year began September 1, Bede copied from his sources without adjustment, and other dates for beginning the year were used by other English archivists. Therefore, to adjust the dates given in Bede's *History* without reference to his source is erroneous. The Council of Hertford was, as Poole and Stenton would have it, in 672, not 673. On the other hand, Stenton's assertion[11] that the Council of Whitby occurred in 663 has no justification, and to shift the accepted date of the Battle of Hatfield to 632 is to go beyond the evidence.

2. In the main, the records kept at Canterbury during the mission were few—fewer than would reasonably be expected. Hence Nothelm was forced to derive most of the history of the mission from Rome. The records grew in number and quality under Deusdedit and took on some oriental patterns under Theodore. Kentish regnal lists were less developed before Christianity than were those of Northumbria, the one kingdom that may have had a pre-Christian group of scholars of some importance. Paulinus introduced annalistic notation in Northumbria, but it was carried on after he fled, possibly by the deacon James. There is no indication of a Mercian regnal list or genealogy or of annalistic notation as late as the death of Coinred.

3. Bede simply did not have satisfactory information about Wessex. Bishop Daniel, who seems in his correspondence with Boniface to have been somewhat loose about detail, supplied Bede with far less than was obviously extant, to judge by the writings of Aldhelm alone. Therefore, to use Bede as a standard for judging the reliability of the Parker Chronicle is not satisfactory.

4. Bede had not read Eddius' *Life of Wilfrid* when he wrote the *History.* H.E. v, 19, was, like i, 34 and iv, 14-15, an insertion after the first draft was written. What may have happened is that Bede sent his draft to Acca to read. Acca sent back some notes based on his own memory (iv, 14-15) and ordered a copy of Eddius for Bede, which he digested and inserted as *H.E.* v. 19. The anomaly of Bede's treatment of Wilfrid, which has long puzzled historians, is intelligible on these grounds, which are consistent with Bede's practice and the book-making practices of the age.

These are details of medieval history. But in bulk they teach us Bede's methods in composing his *History.* Plummer and others have said that he "wrote his History by subjects rather than by order of time."

Quite the contrary. He was simply limited in his all-important time-references. Any exact time-references, taken from an Easter-table, appear in their proper order; only where modern scholarship knows more than Bede about the sequence of events is error apparent. Moreover, Bede had neither the time nor the scratch paper to polish his product as could be done in other ages.

His method seems to have been this: Inspired by the concept of a didactic work on a chronographical outline, he created a list of his several Easter-annals and earlier chronological notices. This list he eventually transcribed as his *recapitulatio.* With this outline he tried to place the entries of the regnal and bishops' lists, the Irish and Victorian records, and the letters and acts. Then he wrote in between the dated events the vast amount of undated material—the saints' lives, the accounts of battle, the biographies, and the few legends that he thought purposeful. For Canterbury, the East Saxons, and Northumbria he could place events with fair accuracy, though his annals hardly gave him a sufficient skeleton to bear the mass of material he had on Northumbria. For Wessex, Mercia, Britain, and Ireland, the chronological pattern is confused, and the dates which he gives are often suspect.

The purpose of this paper is to show how Bede's authorship is consistent with the culture of his time. I hope that I have shown not only that the audience had certain predilections which are not our own, but that the author, as a professional man, was controlled by his professional training and interests. I have consciously spoken against a prevalent notion that Bede was phenomenal—that he stands apart from the historians of his time. Yet, now that the paper is over, I grant that he was phenomenal—in his balanced good sense, his vigorous, penetrating prose, in his love of true scholarship and the unremitting study which he took as his portion in life. Even more, he is phenomenal in his optimistic view of the world. He could praise virtue without being trite, and he condemned evil sharply only because he knew it could be corrected. His mind naturally dwelt on the good in this world, not on the bad.

In current literature the pendulum has swung from praise of progress to cries of chaos; Jeremiah has the floor. Our generation is like Bede's, except that for him it was not a generation but an era; the whole age, from Cyprian on, howled calamity. Gregory, who was one of Bede's favorite authors, pointed endlessly the descent into the pit. But not Bede. As we read his words we see him, slightly regretful that the Second Advent will come, he knows not when, to wipe away this shining earth that has so many potentialities for good.

Notes

[1] *Baedae Opera Historica* (Oxford, 1894), 2 vols. Plummer's rare combination of good sense and erudition will always be remarkable and any criticism of detail only accents the monumental quality of the work. Nevertheless, his insularity (see esp. M. L. W. Laistner, *Hand-List of Bede MSS,* p. 93) encouraged an even greater insularity in certain *discipuli Oxonienses* (cf., for example, R. W. Chambers' centenary lecture on Bede before the British Academy, *Proceedings* XXII [1936], 129-156; reprinted in his *Man's Unconquerable Mind* [London, 1939], pp. 23-52). And his neglect of chronicles and martyrology distorted the picture of Bede's historiography, a distortion that Levison has done much to correct.

[2] "Bede as Historian," *Bede: His Life, Times, and Writings,* ed., A. H. Thompson, (Oxford, 1935), 111-151. Very recently Dr. Levison has surveyed the editing of Bede's works in an essay which should be very useful for interested readers: "Modern Editions of Bede," *The Durham University Journal,* N.S. VI (1945), 78-85.

[3] The reader will find such detail in my forthcoming volume, *Saints Lives and Chronicles in Early England (Romanesque Literature,* I).

[4] The reader will do well to remind himself of the construction of the medieval calendars by consulting facsimiles. For instance, the solar calendar, showing the accretion of martyrology, can be seen in a reproduction of *mensis November* of the Calendar of Willibrord in the edition of H. A. Wilson (Henry Bradshaw Society Publications) or in Cabrol and Leclercq's *Dictionnaire* III (1914), 2604. For the lunar calendar or Paschal table, showing the accretion of annals, see facsimiles in R. L. Poole's *Chronicles and Anuals.*

[5] *A History of Historical Writing* I, 158.

[6] Levi R. Lind, *The Vita Sancti Malchi of Reginald of Canterbury,* pp. 40-1.

[7] F. A. Gasquet, *A Life of Pope St. Gregory the Great,* pp. 40-1. A translation of the complete work will be published in *Saints' Lives and Chronicles.*

[8] Cf. Isidore, *Etymologiae* xi, 2, 3.

[9] Such a change of style, for instance, as that at the end of the first paragraph of *H. E.* iii, 8.

[10] *Neues Archiv,* XVII (1892), 389; quoted Poole, *Studies,* p. 57.

[11] *Anglo-Saxon England,* p. 129.

Eleanor Shipley Duckett (essay date 1947)

SOURCE: Eleanor Shipley Duckett, "Bede of Jarrow," in *Anglo-Saxon Saints and Scholars*, The Macmillan Company, 1947, pp. 217-338.

[*In the following excerpt, Duckett examines several textbooks written by Bede on grammar, writing, and chronology, and asserts they were composed before he was a mature writer.*]

The bishop who ordained Bede deacon was that John of Beverley who was just then causing Wilfrid anguish of spirit in holding the see of Hexham; the same John advanced him to the priesthood in his thirtieth year.[1]

Shortly after he entered the diaconate we may imagine him as not only teaching in Jarrow but also as writing manuals that would aid his instruction. His first efforts would naturally be concerned with text-books, and of these we have three from this earlier time. One of them describes itself as *On Orthography;*[2] but its matter scarcely deserves the name. It is simply a list of words arranged alphabetically, with notes on grammar applied to each: details such as derivations from the Greek, correct spellings, conjugations and usages with verbs, whether of case or of preposition, declensions and genders of nouns. In fact, it resembles notes which a modern teacher might use in quizzing his Latin class. The whole is very informally put together and seems to be a number of jottings used by Bede in drilling his students at Jarrow, written down more or less at random as they occurred to him. He did not take the trouble, for instance, to arrange words in alphabetical order within the selection allotted to each letter. There are many sentences for purposes of illustration, taken from both pagan and christian sources. As has been indicated, examples from Cicero, Plautus, Terence, and so on, probably came from the Latin grammarians and from Isidore, the compilers upon whom Bede drew so freely here and elsewhere. Vergil is much in evidence, also the Bible and the Latin Fathers. The standard is not high; evidently the book was used for pupils at an elementary stage. Occasionally a more interesting example strikes the reader:

> *Stranger:* often followed by a noun in the dative case, as saints are said to be strangers "to this world."
>
> Nouns in -*ius* have vocative in -*i;* so the Latin Bible has "Corneli," spoken by the angel to the centurion Cornelius in Acts X, 3.
>
> It is correct to say "I drank half *a* glass," not "half *the* glass." For you don't drink the glass, but what is in it.[3]

The little book had the distinction of being used by Alcuin and by William of Malmesbury in their trea-

tises on orthography; William maintained "that Alcuin simply plucked Bede's material, adding nothing of his own."[4] This is not literally true, for Alcuin's work is of a rather more advanced type.

The two other text-books, *On the Art of Metre* and *On the Figures and Tropes of Holy Scripture,* were dedicated to "Cuthbert, my fellow-deacon" from which it appears that they were written before 702, or perhaps 703; in one or the other year we know that Bede was ordained priest.[5] They, also, contain instruction for his students in Jarrow, among whom Cuthbert seems to have been numbered. Here Bede has diligently gathered from the same sources passages and paragraphs and examples for the explaining of form in poetry and in prose. The discussion on metric starts with the letters of the Latin alphabet, goes on to deal with scansion of syllables, then with the various kinds of feet and of feet combined to make the different varieties of line, with a section on verse that, although rhythmic, is bound by no exact rule. Examples of this last form, we are told by Bede, occur in the well-known volume of the poet Porphyry which won for him from the Emperor Constantine his return from exile. "But since his verses are pagan I did not care to touch them." Bede was not drawn, as was Aldhelm, by the beauty of classical Latin verse; he used it only to further his direct Christian aim. On the other hand, the far inferior Christian poetry of the earliest Middle Ages was freely represented in his work.[6]

In these treatises he wanted, above all, to show that the charm of rhythm and of metre abounded in Biblical literature long before Greek classical days. His aim was practical, and he did not linger by the way to indulge in the curiosities of acrostics and strange shapes in verse. Some have said, he affirms, that the song of Moses in the thirty-second chapter of Deuteronomy and the alphabetical Psalms 118 and 144 were written in elegiacs, and that the Book of Job was written in hexameter verse.[7]

For him, likewise, all pagan classical figures of rhetoric had their prototype in the Bible, with the reasoning that holy Scripture is older, is of Divine inspiration and, hence, of paramount utility as guide of mortal men toward eternal life. Away, then, with the vain boastings of the Greeks! And, therefore, as he describes these figures one after another, he explains them by Biblical illustrations.[8] The fact that he wrote Hebrew words in one passage of his *On the Figures,* in explaining *paronomasia,* yields no proof that he could read Hebrew; he could easily have quoted the words from Jerome, his source.[9]

To the period of Bede's diaconate belong the twin questions: Did he visit Rome? Was he invited by the Pope to do so? These are complicated matters, depending on the evidence of uncertain manuscript readings and the equally uncertain interpreting of human psychology.[10] The answer to the first may be given in the words of a modern authority: "As far as we know, Bede never left his native shores."[11] For the second, it is possible, but not proved, that he received an invitation from Pope Sergius and that he did not use it, perhaps because the Pope died in 701. In this year, shortly before his death, Sergius certainly wrote to Abbot Ceolfrid requesting that he send one of his monks to confer with him on important business of the Church; we cannot now be sure whether he actually mentioned Bede in this letter or left the choice to Ceolfrid's discretion. We do know that some monks from Wearmouth Abbey were in Rome in 701 and that they brought back with them from Pope Sergius a privilege for the protection of their monastic freedom similar in content to that granted Benedict Biscop by Pope Agatho. As Egfrid had done for Biscop, so King Aldfrid, also, by assent confirmed this second charter. Bede, however, was not of their company.[12]

His own evidence concerning himself, written toward the end of his life, shows that he was no traveller from home:

> I, Bede, servant of Christ and priest of the monastery of the blessed apostles Peter and Paul at Wearmouth and Jarrow, born on the estate of this same monastery, was given by my relatives when I was seven years old to the care of the most reverend abbot Benedict, and afterward of Ceolfrid. From that time I have spent my entire life in the dwelling of this same monastery, devoting myself wholly to study of the Scriptures, to following the regular discipline and the round of daily chant within the church. I have always held it my joy to learn, to teach, and to write.

He tells us, also, that for nearly thirty years, from the time he received the priesthood until he was approaching old age, he devoted his time and energy to gathering material, mostly upon the Bible, from the Fathers of the Church in preparation of commentaries upon the same, "for the need of me and mine."[13]

Bede might be called a Christian Cicero in his intense desire to hand on knowledge. Although he does show originality, in criticism, in selection, in adaptation, this was not his primary aim. He wanted, above all, to teach, whether by his own thought or, primarily, in his humility and reverence, by that which he so freely borrowed and made available for less well-provided readers.[14] The words of Seneca the philosopher might have been written by him:

> *Gaudeo discere, ut doceam. Nec me ulla res delectabit, licet sit eximia et salutaris, quam mihi uni sciturus sum;*[15]

"I rejoice to learn, that I may teach. Nor will anything delight me, no matter how excellent, how good for me, if I am to know it for myself alone."

As priest, then, Bede continued to teach and to write. From work on the rules of prose and poetry, belonging to the elementary course of liberal arts, the *trivium,* he now turned to write for his students a little manual, ***De Temporibus, On Times,*** based on the study of one of the subjects of the more advanced *quadrivium,* that of chronology.[16] The primary reason for this was the perennial dispute concerning the date of Easter. Although in practice this had been settled for Northumbria, home of Bede and his monastery, some forty years before this time by the synod held at Whitby in 664, yet many of the Celts still persevered in their own way of dating. It was, therefore, of great concern to Bede that the young monks of Wearmouth should full understand the true doctrine on this matter. It may be of interest to note here Bede's use in this work of the word *sacramentum,* "sacrament," for the mystical meaning lying behind external facts. As the Feast of Easter moves from day to day, year by year, in the calendar, so the soul of man must move, year by year, from death to life.

The progress of the book leads from the consideration of smaller divisions of time and of their names to the greater, from minutes and hours to days and nights, weeks, months, and years. Weeks are ascribed to Divine ruling, months to human custom, years to natural order. Bede's sources here were, of course, the various writings on the Paschal calculation then current in England and Ireland;[17] he borrowed also from Pliny, from Macrobius, and from Isidore, that bishop of Seville in Spain from about 600 to 636, whose compilations contained vast learning and were of immense influence in the Middle Ages.[18] Throughout his literary life he used Isidore so much, albeit with scholarly independence, that it is no marvel to note that Dante placed the two side by side among the scholars who dwell in the sun of Paradise, radiant with a light no words can describe.[19] From Isidore, supported by the teaching of Augustine,[20] he derived the chronology on which he loved to dwell, of the six ages of the world; it recurs again and again in his books. The six ages run:

1. From the Creation to Noah and the Flood:
2. From Noah to Abraham:
3. From Abraham to David:
4. From David to the Captivity of the Jews:
5. From the Captivity to the Birth of Christ:
6. From the Birth of Christ to an indeterminate date, the end of the world, known to God alone.[21]

The time already passed is reckoned here as far as the fifth year of the rule of Tiberius III, Emperor of the East in Constantinople; and this gives the date of 703 for Bede's writing of his book.[22] To these six ages of the world correspond in mystical interpretation the six periods of the life of each individual man: infancy, boyhood, youth, middle age, old age, last years, which are destined to end, like our present world, by death.

Five years later Bede heard that this little book had brought on him an unspeakable charge. A messenger arrived one day at Jarrow, bearing friendly greetings from Plegwin, a monk of the same diocese of Hexham in whihc Jarrow lay. Less welcome words followed. Certain "rustics" at a feast, so Plegwin was informed, had drunkenly shouted that Bede was a heretic, and this, too, in the presence of his and their bishop, Wilfrid, who held the see of Hexham from 706 to 709. It seems that those who thus jeered at Bede's views on theology must have been monks; we shall find other evidence of looseness of monastic living in this age. On the other hand, that monks commonly read and discussed such books as this is to the credit of the time.

Bede turned pale with horror and asked what could the heresy be? "According to them," was the answer, "you denied that the Lord came in the flesh during the sixth age of the world."

For two days he pondered. Then he poured out his indignation in a long letter to Plegwin.[23] As a priest of the Church of Christ, he wrote, he could not possibly have denied His Incarnation; as a student of the Bible, he could not deny that the Lord had come as very Man in the sixth age of the world. This most false slander had arisen from a misunderstanding of his description of the successive eras in the *De Temporibus*. It was, he said, purely a question of the number of years assigned to each of the five ages preceding the sixth. In his calculating Bede had considered the authority of the Vulgate, translated from the Hebrew, to be better than that of the Greek Septuagint, followed by Isidore and the writers, including Jerome, from whom Isidore had drawn. Thus, although he had certainly placed the Incarnation in what he himself held to be the sixth age according to the Hebrew-Vulgate calculation, yet he had dated it at a considerably earlier time after the Creation than the Septuagint reckoning had done, the reckoning followed by Isidore and his sources; in fact, Bede's date for it lay within their fifth age of the world. Hence all the trouble. We may note that Bede showed scholarly independence of judgment in differing thus from Isidore and Jerome.[24]

While he was on the subject, it would be good, he decided, to warn Plegwin not to let himself be deceived, like so many people, by the idea that this present age of the world was to last six thousand years, or, "as I remember reading in some heretic's book when I was

a boy," that the year of the Last Judgment could be foretold by men. No, indeed! When the Lord said, "But of that day and hour knoweth no man," He did not mean that we could tell the year.

> I get really sad and even more angry than sad when the country people round here ask me how many years still remain to this world. The Lord never has told us whether His coming is near or far off; He only bids us watch and wait with loins girded and with lamps burning until He shall come.

His letter ended with an admonition that it be read in the presence of "our reverend Lord and Father, Wilfrid, our bishop, in order that, since in his presence and his hearing I was stupidly insulted, he may now hear and know how wrongly I have been used."

The relation of Bede toward Wilfrid is of interest. He met and talked with him, and he wrote of him at a later time with that courtesy which was his unfailing characteristic. He praised Wilfrid's work among the people of Sussex, a work that had rescued them "not only from the bitterness of everlasting damnation, but also from the unspeakable disaster of temporal death." He called him "a man most learned," "a man most reverend," who first among the bishops that were of the English people learned to pass on the Catholic manner of living to the churches of the English," a statement which was certainly in error. He repeatedly referred to him after his death as "of blessed memory."[25] Yet "it is evident that there was but little sympathy between Wilfrid and the great scholar."[26] In writing of the Church history of his time Bede deliberately omitted much that was of importance in Wilfrid's life. He himself was devoted to John of Hexham, the bishop who ordained him deacon and priest, and to Cuthbert of Lindisfarne; yet both of these held their sees contrary to Wilfrid's will. He admired greatly Egfrid and Aldfrid, those kings of Northumbria who were Wilfrid's enemies. Finally and chiefly, we may reasonably surmise that Bede wholly sympathized with Archbishop Theodore's desire to divide responsibility in the greater English dioceses, and that Bede, the monk of simple life and intellectual interests, found little to attract him in the relatively worldly ambitions of this bishop of York.

With his *On Times* Bede on three occasions couples another treatise of his, *On the Nature of Things*.[27] As he does not give us its date, we only know that it was written before 725.[28] But as it also seems to have been intended for the use of his students in elementary science, there is some ground for supposing its date to have been near that of *On Times,* in or about the year 703. Here he deals with cosmography, teaching his monks what Pliny in his *Natural History* and Isidore in his *Etymologies* had told concerning Nature.[29] They read of the heavens and the waters above the firmament; of the sun and the moon and the stars of heaven; of showers and winds, of hail and snow, of lightnings and clouds; of why the sea is salt and why the Red Sea is red; of the earth and its shape, its inner fires and quakings, its divisions and their placing.

Notes

¹ *HE* [Bede; *Historia Ecclesiastica Gentis Anglorum*] V, c. 24.

² Ed. Keil [Keil; H.: *Grammatici Latini;* vol. VII, 1880] 261ff.; Giles [*Patres Ecclesiae Anglicanae;* ed. J. A. Giles: *Bede, Opera,* 1843-1844] VI, 1ff.

³ Keil, *ibid.,* 269, 278, 286.

⁴ *William of Malmesbury: De Gestis Regum Anglorum,* ed. W. Stubbs, vol. I, cxli, 1887-1889. For the light which the *De Orthographia* throws upon the MSS. of Bede see Laistner, *American Historical Review,* XLVI, New York 1941, 380.

⁵ Ed. Keil, *ibid.,* 227ff.; Halm, *Rhet. lat. min.* 607ff.; Giles VI, 40ff., 80ff.

⁶ See Laistner, *TRHS* [*Transactions of the Royal Historical Society,* London] 72ff.; *Thought and Letters,* 122f.; also in Thompson [Alexander Hamilton Thompson: ed. *Bede, his Life, Times, and Writings,* 1935], 241f. He points out that quotations from ancient authors in Bede may have been borrowed from grammarians or from Isidore, *Etymologies. Cf.* E. F. Sutcliffe, "The Venerable Bede's Knowledge of Hebrew," *Biblica* XVI, 1935, 300ff.: "a few scraps . . . from the writings of St. Jerome."

⁷ Keil VII, 243, 252.

⁸ See J. W. H. Atkins, *English Literary Criticism: The Medieval Phase,* 1943, 46ff. He points out that here is the first reference of an English scholar to the literary "kinds" (i.e., dramatic, narrative, and mixed); that Bede "is the first to attempt an appreciation of Biblical literature"; that he "enlisted grammar in the service of religion."

⁹ Jenkins, in Thompson, 163.

¹⁰ Stubbs, *Dictionary of Christian Biography (to about A. D. 800),* ed. Smith and Wace, I, 300f.; Hunt, *Dictionary of National Biography,* ed. Leslie Stephen and Sidney Lee, IV, 98f.; Haddan, A. W., and Stubbs, W.: ed. *Councils and Ecclesiastical Documents Relating to Great Britain and Ireland,* 1869-1878, III, 248ff.; Whiting, in Thompson, 11ff.

¹¹ Whiting, 13.

¹² *Bede, Vita beatorum abbatum Benedicti, Ceolfridi, Eosterwini, Sigfridi atque Hwaetberhti: Plummer* I, pp. 364ff. c. 15; *De temp. rat.* c. 47; Jones, C.W.: ed. *ODT* [*Bedae Opera de Temporibus: Publications, Medieval Academy of America,* XLI, 1943] p. 267.

¹³ *HE* V, c. 24.

¹⁴ Jenkins, in Thompson, 170; *cf.* Jones, "Bede and Vegetius," *Classical Review* XLVI, London, 1932, 249: "It is dangerous to assert that any words in Bede's works were his own; it is less dangerous to say that, if we had all the materials with which Bede worked, we should find very few statements originating with him."

¹⁵ *Epp. Morales* I, 6.

¹⁶ Jones, *ODT* 130f., 295ff.; Manitius, Max: *Geschichte der lateinischen Literatur des Mittelalters,* vol. I, 1911, p. 77.

¹⁷ Jones, *ODT* 105ff.

¹⁸ *Etymologiae,* ed. Lindsay V, 38f.; *De nat. rerum, PL* [*Patrologia Latina,* ed. J. Migne] LXXXIII, coll. 963ff.; *Chronicon, PL ibid.,* coll. 1017ff.

¹⁹ *Paradiso* X, 130f. For Bede's independence see Laistner, in Thompson, 256; Jones, *ODT* 131.

²⁰ *De civ. Dei* XXII, 30.

²¹ *De temp.* 16: Jones, *ODT* 303.

²² Plummer, Charles: *Bedae Opera Historica;* vol. I, 1896, cxlvi.

²³ Ed. Jones, *ODT* 132ff., 307ff.

²⁴ Levison, in Thompson, 116f.

²⁵ *HE* IV, c. 19; III, c. 25; IV, c. 2; Plummer II, 206.

²⁶ Raine, James, Jr.: ed. *The Historians of the Church of York and its Archbishops,* vol. I, 1879, xxxiv; W. Bright, *Waymarks in Church History,* 1894, 285: "In fact, if one could be angry with Bede, it would be for his leaving us so much to depend on Eddi for information about Wilfrid." On Bede's account of Wilfrid see Plummer II, 315ff., 325, 327; Colgrave, Bertram: ed. *Eddius Stephanus, Life of Bishop Wilfrid,* 1927, xiif.

²⁷ Giles VI, 99ff.

²⁸ *Ibid.,* 139; *HE* V, 24. The mention of the *De nat. rerum* in the *De temp. rat.,* written in 725, shows its earlier date.

[29] On Bede's sources here see Karl Werner: *Beda der Ehrwürdige und seine Zeit,* 1881, 107ff.; Manitius, *Gesch.,* 77f. . . .

R. W. Southern (essay date 1964)

SOURCE: R. W. Southern, "Bede, the Monk of Jarrow," in *The Listener*, Vol. 71, No. 1820, February 13, 1964, pp. 267-69.

[*In the following excerpt, Southern examines the significance and impact of Jarrow, the site of Bede's monastery, on Bede's works.*]

One of the first things to recognize about the Middle Ages is that, far from being a period of substantial uniformity in which men thought and fought, prayed and expressed their beliefs in much the same way from beginning to end, the diversity of experience is immense.

All cats are grey in the dark and it was the darkness of the Middle Ages, now largely dispelled, which encouraged the belief that all men were more or less alike. The diversity of experience in the 1,000 years known rather absurdly as the Middle Ages is immense, and some of the revolutions in thought and feeling which took place at different moments in this long period of change are as important as any that have happened in our history. The men I am going to discuss in these talks illustrate some of the most decisive moments of change in the development of our civilization, and none more so than the Northumbrian monk, Bede, who was born about 672 and died in 735. As a personality he is perhaps the least stimulating of our three subjects, but the importance of his work is in inverse ratio to the noise he made in doing it.

Few men can have spent more years or worked more hours on the same spot than Bede did; and to me at least the site of the monastery at Jarrow, where he lived and died, is one of the most moving things in England. It is a small and undistinguished spit of land about ten or fifteen feet above the waters of the Tyne; across the river are the cranes of the modern docks; at one's feet lie the mud-flats of Bede's day, now partly reclaimed to form timber yards; on the site itself the blackened ruins of monastic buildings surround a small, somewhat dingy, church with a thin Anglo-Saxon tower. The dedication stone in the church gives a date which can be referred to the year 685. But the stone marks more than a ceremony of dedication—it marks nothing less than a new beginning in English civilization. It may seem an odd place for such a beginning, and to many visitors it will suggest the grave of civilization rather than the cradle. It has no grace or comeliness, and whatever beauty there may be is distinctly austere. But in fact the setting is not an inappropriate one for

the work that was done here in Bede's day. Even in the seventh century there were more interesting places than Jarrow, probably more interesting men than Bede, and certainly more immediately exciting works than his: but no one did work which lasted better, and into the foundations of his work he put an energy and originality of mind which are hidden behind the modest exterior.

It would be wrong to think of him as a lonely worker in a barbarous age. During his lifetime England was going through one of the great creative periods in her history. Indeed it has been rightly said that the age of Bede and the age of Gladstone stand out as the only two periods in our history when the ideas and energy which emanated from England were the dominant force in Europe. The manifestations of that energy which survive are mere fragments, but the variety of excellence they display is astonishing: the stone crosses of Bewcastle and Ruthwell which stand for all to see; the Lindisfarne Gospels; the books written at Jarrow; the laws, biographies, poems, in Latin and in Anglo-Saxon; the varied expressions of pagan and Christian, of Celtic and Anglo-Saxon sentiment which these works contain; the careers of men who transformed not only the face of England but of Europe—all tell the same story of intense activity. It was a time when the traditional stock of pagan Germanic ideas was making its last appearance, and new influences were flooding in from all sides—from Ireland, Gaul, Italy and the eastern Mediterranean. As sometimes happens in such circumstances, both the old and the new seem to have inspired enough faith and confidence to produce some of their finest works. There was a struggle for the mind of a people not yet committed to any settled frame of thought or imagination. Some of the protagonists were conscious propagandists for one or other set of ideas; others were artists or ascetics who simply expressed in the most forcible way at their command the ideas and images which had captured their imagination. Whatever the degree of conscious campaigning, the result was a variety of activity which in quality of achievement has never been surpassed.

In all this activity the work of Bede and of the community at Jarrow has a sombre, not to say dull, appearance. If you compare the manuscripts from Jarrow with the famous Gospel book from Lindisfarne you will at once see the difference. The Jarrow books are sober and unadorned, written without frills by craftsmen who have recovered the finest proportions of ancient script. The Lindisfarne book, on the other hand, is an extravagant artistic masterpiece in which the forms of Irish imagination are adapted to a somewhat more restrained, but still luxuriant, pattern of visual images. And there is a similar contrast in the religious life. Bede's life seems to have been one of steady discipline without extravagance. But for the qualities that made Christianity seem a religion of convincing power to Anglo-Saxon minds we must look elsewhere—for instance to Crowland in the Fens, where the hermit Guthlac was living one of those lives of heroic warfare against evil spirits dear to a people who lived for war. The contemporary account of Guthlac's visions and struggles with the forces arrayed against him in his distracted mind and fever-racked body gives us a more vivid insight into the springs of Anglo-Saxon religion than anything in Bede's experience.

In this exciting and tumultuous scene Bede is essentially calm. His gifts and habits were those of a scholar: a capacious mind seldom swayed by prejudice, clear in judgment, well fitted to deal with a large mass of disorderly material and to present it systematically and succinctly. Like many men of this stamp, he never obtrudes his own personality, seldom mentions his own experience, keeps his eye steadily on the material before him, and expresses his condemnation more often by silence than by strictures. His piety was exact and unwavering, and his diligence unremitting. His last hours, spent in translating the Bible and abbreviating a learned work, dividing his few belongings among his friends, breaking out unexpectedly at one moment into the poetic idiom of his ancestors, perfectly reflect the range of his activity and the unruffled temper of his life and death.

Throughout the whole range of our history this combination of temperament and talent is not so very uncommon. The University of Oxford produces perhaps one such scholar in a hundred years. But Oxford University has long existed to do this, and it would be surprising if it did not sometimes succeed. Bede was a pioneer: the first Englishman of his type, the first scientific intellect produced by the Germanic peoples of Europe. Some of his English contemporaries were gifted men, but none had gifts like his. Among the artists, statesmen, missionaries, athletes of the spiritual life, who proliferated in England in the late seventh and eighth centuries, he was that most unexpected of all products of a primitive age, a really great scholar, and the circumstances of the time gave him a great opportunity.

To understand the nature of his opportunity we must turn our eyes once more to Jarrow. Physically it lay on the very edge of the old Roman world: the wall's end which marked the boundary was within an afternoon's excursion from the monastery, and Bede had certainly inspected it. But in Bede's lifetime the foresight of one man had made Jarrow the chief centre of Roman civilization in Europe. Rome itself was falling into ruins; the economy of Italy was being stifled by the collapse of Mediterranean trade; the west everywhere had fallen into a deep disorder. But from the ruins of civilization in the south, the founder of Jarrow, Benedict Biscop, had brought a choice collection of books. By modern standards they were not many—perhaps 200 or 300—

but they brought together in his Northumbrian outpost most of the best works of Christian scholarship in the later Roman empire. From these books it was possible to get a fairly complete and coherent view of the work of the Latin Fathers of the Church, together with a great deal of ancient history, technical chronology, and miscellaneous biblical scholarship. Benedict Biscop must be reckoned the first collector to use the wealth of a new aristocracy, to which he belonged, to appropriate the fruits of civilization from a people who could no longer afford to preserve them; he is the prototype of the great American collectors of our century.

What England lacked in the seventh century was a tradition. No one could say for certain which of the traditions of Anglo-Saxon, Roman, and Celtic origin, which were struggling for the mastery, would have the power to survive. What Benedict Biscop brought to Jarrow was the learning of the Patristic age, and in doing this he picked the future winner. That is to say he extracted from the welter of conflicting materials the most important element for the growth of a new European civilization. But all he could provide were the tools; it was still necessary to find someone to use them. A library is an act of faith, and no one can tell what will come of it. There were no doubt plenty of other libraries in Europe as well equipped as that at Jarrow, but on most of them the dust was gathering ever more thickly and the damp penetrating ever more deeply. This might easily have happened at Jarrow where dust and damp are in plentiful supply. To utilize a collection of materials which no English mind had yet mastered required a genius and determination of the highest order. A great gulf separated the late Anglo-Saxon heroic age of the seventh century from the sophisticated society of the later Roman empire. The two societies were bound together by the thin thread of a common Christianity, but in every external condition of life and habit of thought the gap was immense.

The greatness of Bede lay in this, that apparently without an effort he bridged the gap between the ancient world and his own day. Perhaps it is wrong to say 'without an effort', for among the few things he tells us about himself is an avowal of ceaseless labour. He was obsessed by the fear that inertia might lead to the loss of that which could, as he says, be ours; and this was the mainspring of his energy. Never did a man work with a more distinct idea of what he was aiming at, which was to make the new nation to which he belonged at home in the past—not the past of pagan genealogies, folk-tales, and heroic legend that he could see all round him, but the past of the Latin learning of the Christian Church.

Bede wrote many works with this general aim. His most famous, the ***Ecclesiastical History of the English People*** is in one way the least typical in that it told a story which for the most part lay not in books but in the memories of men who were Bede's contemporaries. But in a larger sense the great history grew out of his task of restoring ancient learning. It linked the earliest history of the Romans in Britain with the present, and applied the rules of ancient historical writing and the methods of historical inquiry of an earlier age to a new field, which was the field of Bede's own day and people. No doubt it was the greatest, as it was also the last, of his works. But if we want to see his plan more clearly, to appreciate the extent of his labours, and to see where his main influence lay, we shall look not to his *History* but to his biblical commentaries.

Bede's commentaries have not had many readers for the last 400 years, and they are not likely to whet many appetites today. They are books which we should be glad to read if we had nothing else; they would provide plenty of subjects for reflection, a stream of good sense, and (through their quotations) a daily contact with some of the greatest minds of the past. The fact remains that anyone who has other books will probably read these other books. But it was precisely for men who had few other books that Bede wrote, and no author of the early Middle Ages had a greater success. His books were the handbooks of the English missionaries who converted Germany in the eighth century; they were among the foundation works of the Carolingian renaissance; and they continued as a main source of monastic learning until the twelfth century.

It is often said that Bede lacked originality, and he would doubtless have agreed. It was his task to make the past accessible to the barbarian present, and this required not primarily originality but judgment and patience. No one would deny that he possessed these qualities in a high degree, but we may also think that to conceive such a plan, to see how it could be carried out, and to carry it out just in the way he did, required a powerful imagination and independence of mind. The Christian learning of the past lay scattered in many volumes by many hands. Even to those who had access to these volumes, they were not easily usable or even intelligible. Bede reduced a great mass of material to the single, simple, and usable form of continuous biblical exposition. Even today a preacher might well do worse than take his material from Bede's rational and lucid summary.

But though his main aim was to digest for others what they could not digest for themselves, he also aimed at adding to the learning of the past. He chose to explain those books of the Bible which had not been expounded before, or which offered scope for his own special interests in history and allegory. At first we are rather surprised to find that, among so many commentaries, he omitted the Gospels of Matthew and John, but chose those of Mark and Luke; that he devoted much attention to the Acts of the Apostles and little to the Pauline Epistles; much to the books of Exodus and Kings and

little to the Psalms; much to the minor prophets, and little or nothing to Ezekiel or Job. Beneath the surface appearance of plodding compilation there was in fact a highly selective and sensitive scholar who aimed not only at bringing the past to the notice of the present, but also at showing that the present—even in the shape of an obscure writer in an obscure monastery in a far corner of Europe—could make an original contribution to the body of ancient learning.

It is astonishing when we think of it that a man of the newest of the new nations of Europe could move with such confidence among ancient learning. As a master of technical chronology and as a historical writer he is among the greatest; as a theologian and exegete he had, if not the highest qualities—he is no Augustine or Jerome—at least the qualities most necessary for his plan. He had no known master. He was the first Englishman who understood the past and could view it as a whole. In the exciting England of his day, which was neither fully pagan nor fully Christian, neither Roman nor Celtic nor Teutonic but something of all of them, a country of dead ends and new beginnings, Bede stood for sobriety and order in thought, common sense in politics, and moderation in the religious life. He was the first Englishman who could look back over the chasm which the collapse of the Roman empire had opened in the history of thought, and see clearly the landscape on the other side; the first, therefore, whose religion was wholly articulate and whose thoughts are entirely intelligible to us today.

In the main square of Jarrow there is a recent monument on which two large figures are prominently displayed. They are not as a matter of fact the figures of the two greatest men of Jarrow. Benedict Biscop and Bede, preservers of the old and chief builders of a new civilization, but of two Vikings, the destroyers who in 796 erased Jarrow from the map of Europe for 1,000 years. It is a strange perspective which gives these destroyers the chief monument in modern Jarrow; but perhaps like everything else in this strange story it has a certain appropriateness. Whatever happened to Jarrow after Bede's death was irrelevant to the spread of his influence throughout Europe, and with it the influence of the community to which he belonged. Like the ships from the yards up the river, Bede's works were not made to stay in port, but for a long future in distant parts.

J. Campbell (essay date 1966)

SOURCE: J. Campbell, "Bede," in *Latin Historians*, edited by T. A. Dorey, Basic Books, Inc., Publishers, 1966, pp. 159-90.

[*In the following excerpt, Campbell emphasizes that Bede's main intention was to promote Christianity through his writings. He also considers Bede's sources and his occasional discrepancies on dates.*]

Bede was not only, or even primarily, a historian. He finished the ***Historia Ecclesiastica Gentis Anglorum*** only three or four years before his death in 735. He may have known that it would be the last of his major works, for he ended it with an almost elegiac sketch of his own life and a list of his writings. These were numerous. Bede devoted a fairly long life—he was born in 672 or 673—and formidable powers to become probably the most learned and certainly the most productive of the European scholars of his day. His works include treatises on grammar, metric and chronology, lives of saints, homilies and, above all, commentaries on the Bible. Much that he wrote was unoriginal, in so far as it consisted of the views—often the words—of his predecessors pieced together with some rearrangement, clarification and amendment. He set out to master and pass on a large part of the learning of the Christian Church; and succeeded in this. Many of his works became standard and remained so through the Middle Ages and sometimes beyond. His historical works comprise, if hagiography is excluded, only the ***Ecclesiastical History,*** the ***Lives*** of the abbots of his abbey of Monkwearmouth-Jarrow and the chronicles—lists of the principal events in the history of the world—appended to ***Liber de Temporibus*** (703) and ***De Temporum Ratione*** (725). They are merely a part, though an important one, of what Bede wrote and what he was valued for through many centuries. His history has to be interpreted in relation to the rest of his work, that of a man whose dominant intention was to expound, spread and defend and Christian faith by all the means in his power.[1]

The ***Ecclesiastical History*** shows how great these means were. That which is first apparent to its readers is Bede's command of Latin. He writes grammatically and very clearly. Unlike some of his contemporaries, who wrote to impress by a florid style and an outré vocabulary, he intended to be understood by an audience the capacities of some of whom he did not value highly. He writes in his commentary on the Apocalypse, 'Anglorum gentis inertiae consulendum ratus . . . non solum dilucidare sensus verum sententias quoque stringere disposui'.[2] Bede knew very well how to be both simple and moving. The style in which he tells many of his stories recalls that of the gospels in its brevity, concentration on essentials, and use of direct speech. What he says is even more remarkable than the skill with which he says it. He sets out to give the history of the Church in his own land in about 85,000 words. Having begun with a short geographical and historical introduction, he gives some account of Christianity in Roman Britain, but devotes much of the first book and the whole of the remaining four to its progress in England from St Augustine's arrival in 597 until 731. The numerous sources which

Bede collected and the skill with which he handled them make the ***Ecclesiastical History*** the masterpiece of Dark Age historiography. No history that can rival it appeared in Western Europe until the twelfth century.[3]

The ***Ecclesiastical History*** itself does much to explain how so remarkable a work could be undertaken. It shows the progress of Christianity in England to have been feeble and flickering until the generation following 635. But by 660 it was established in all the major kingdoms and began to flourish. Many monasteries were founded and many monks became learned. Theodore, archbishop of Canterbury 668-690, established a school at Canterbury where most subjects relevant to Christian learning, including Greek, could be studied. Benedict Biscop founded the twin monasteries of Monkwearmouth (674) and Jarrow (681-2) and collected abroad a library for them which must have been among the best in Europe. There were other important libraries and many monasteries owned books and contained more or less learned men, although only Aldhelm (?640-709) among Bede's English contemporaries approached him in eminence.[4] Although Bede lived on the edge of the civilized world he did not work in intellectual isolation. His reputation and his correspondence spread far beyond the borders of Northumbria. There were others in his own house who could write as well as he: perhaps the finest example of the Bedan style is the description of Bede's death by Cuthbert, his fellow-monk.[5] Bede's works were not only in great demand, but also occasionally criticized.[6] He was not alone in the production of hagiography and biography. We have biographical works by five of his English contemporaries and the fewness of the manuscripts of some of these makes it likely that there were other such works, now lost.[7] Bede would not have been able to accomplish what he did had he not been a member of a learned world with considerable intellectual resources. The achievements of his contemporaries hardly rivalled his, but we know them to have been considerable and may suspect them to have been more considerable than we know.

English learning was fed by that of other countries.[8] The chief debts were naturally to the sources of conversion, Italy and Ireland. Bede's scholarship depended largely on access to Italian manuscripts, the education of many of his contemporaries on access to Irish schools. Something was owed to Gaul, which gave England three bishops in the seventh century and with which some English ecclesiastics, especially Wilfred, had close connections. The cosmopolitan nature of the Church and the willingness to clerics to move to countries other than their own brought influences from further afield and created multiple opportunities for the diffusion of ideas. Archbishop Theodore came from Cilicia; his companion Hadrian was an African. The Irish founded monasteries in Gaul, Germany and Italy

besides England; Ireland had access to the learning of contemporary Spain and indirect communication with the Near East. Between 690 and Bede's death Englishmen converted much of western Germany. Irish missionaries and perhaps a Spaniard were active there at the same time. One of Bede's English contemporaries went to Jerusalem and then settled at Monte Cassino. The Christian world stretched from Scotland and Ireland to Asia Minor and Spain. It was being reduced by the 'gravissima Sarracenorum lues', as Bede well knew, but it was still, if hardly united, much interconnected. The international connections of the Church were partly paralleled by those of the laity. The Anglo-Saxons had left kinsmen in Germany whom they recognized as such and sought to convert. Others had moved with the Lombards, to whom they were related, into Italy: this may have had something to do with the willingness of Englishmen to visit Italy and even to settle there.[9] Saxons had settled in Gaul as Franks may have settled in England. The coming and going of brides and exiles to and from Gaul accompanied and was connected with that of bishops and missionaries. The accumulation of instances may deceive. Many of the contacts between England and the Continent in the seventh century and the early eighth were episodic or tenuous. But there was enough communication to enable Bede to write as the heir to much of the learning of the Church and for an audience which was not entirely insular in its knowledge and interests.

In his historical works Bede was able to draw on many models and sources.[10] He made no use of the classical historians, though he could perhaps have done so— texts of some of their works which were available in Germany in the eighth century may have arrived there via England. His attitude towards most pagan authors was one of cautious reserve. The chief models and foundations for his work were, apart from the Bible, the works of Christian authors from the fourth century on. Perhaps the most important such author was Eusebius. His *Ecclesiastical History* set the standard for historians of the church.[11] It left secular affairs for the attention of the carnally minded. The wars it described were those against heresy and persecution; its heroes were the martyrs; the successions it recorded those not of emperors but of bishops. Distinguished from pagan historiography in technique as in content it included many documents and gave references to sources. Eusebius's *Chronicle* had a different function, to summarize universal history from a Christian point of view, correlating Biblical history with that of the rest of the world and showing the hand of God at work across millennia. Bede did not have either work in the original Greek; he used Rufinus's Latin translation and continuation of the *Ecclesiastical History* and Jerome's of the *Chronicle*. They provided models for his own work in either genre. He knew at least two other Christian histories, the *Adversus Paganos* of Orosius and Gregory of Tours's *Historia Francorum*. His view of

history as the demonstration of the power of God, of orthodoxy and of sanctity, much resembles theirs and he owed a more direct debt to Orosius, whose geographical introduction he imitates and borrows from.[12] His aim seems to have been to do for the history of the Church in England what Eusebius had done for the whole and he follows him in choice of subject-matter and in technique. Nevertheless there are important differences between Bede's *Ecclesiastical History* and its predecessor, which make his work in some respects more like that of Gregory of Tours. Although, like Eusebius and unlike Gregory, Bede rarely recorded secular affairs for their own sake he had to devote considerable attention to them. Eusebius, writing under Constantine, had only one Christian emperor to deal with and so was concerned with the Church as opposed to the State. Bede had to describe a Church very much involved with the State and to show how Providence had affected the affairs of kings many of whom were Christian, some even saints. Secondly, while Eusebius had incorporated accounts of martyrs in his work much more of Bede's is devoted to the lives and particularly the miracles of saints. Belief in the miraculous had increased greatly between the fourth century and the eighth. The demand for it had been fed by hagiographies in the tradition which began with the life of Anthony by Athanasius (*c.* 296-373). Such lives were prominent among Bede's sources and he wrote some himself. Writing with a largely didactic purpose and for an audience which needed vivid and concrete demonstration of the power of God and of virtue Bede made his *Ecclesiastical History* a chronological hagiography as well as a record in the manner of Eusebius.[13] He is distinguished from most hagiographers of his time by his using miracle-stories only to reinforce religious teachings rather than to advertise the merits of a particular shrine.[14]

The works of earlier writers provided Bede not only with models, but with much of the information used in the first book of the *Ecclesiastical History*.[15] His account of the Romans in Britain came largely from Orosius and the pagan historian Eutropius. The interest taken by Gaulish historians in the Pelagian heresy enabled him to gain valuable information from the *Vita Sancti Germani* of Constantius. These, with an important British source—Gildas's *De Excidio*—a *Passio Sancti Albani,* some English tradition and a certain amount of misinformation from the *Liber Pontificalis* largely saw him through the twenty-two chapters devoted to the period before Augustine's mission.[16] His task in compiling his much fuller account of subsequent events was more difficult. Much is known of his sources for this since he describes some of them in his introduction and mentions others later. He obtained a considerable number of documents, especially papal letters, from Rome and Canterbury. Like a true successor to Eusebius he inserted many of them into his text; they comprise about a fifth of it and provide the backbone of his account of the conversion and of subsequent relations with Rome. His contacts with Rome were good enough to allow him access not only to such letters but also to the official history of the popes, the *Liber Pontificalis;* he used its account of Gregory II even while that pope was still alive. Otherwise his chief written sources were biographical—mainly hagiographical. He had *Vitae* of Fursey, Cuthbert, Wilfred, Ceolfrith, Aethelburh and perhaps of others. Some annals, regnal lists and genealogies were available to him but they seem to have afforded little information on events outside Kent and Northumbria or, for the earlier part of the seventh century, within them.[17] He was, for example, unable to record even the year in which Augustine died.

The written sources of which we know leave the origins of much of the *Ecclesiastical History* unaccounted for. Bede tells us that much of his information came from oral tradition, either directly or through correspondents.[18] To determine, or guess, the value of such information it is necessary to consider the forms in which it may have been preserved. Mrs Chadwick has recently suggested that many of Bede's sources were 'ecclesiastical sagas'. These were, she thinks, sometimes transmitted orally, sometimes at some stage written down, but retaining the characteristics of oral saga style—'leisurely, detailed, circumstantial and dramatic', often divided into three parts, recording proper names and retailing conversations verbatim.[19] In the extreme form in which she presents this theory—for example, maintaining that Bede's account of the Synod of Whitby is 'certainly an elaborate form of ecclesiastical saga'—it does not seem altogether helpful.[20] Her criteria appear to be capable of including very diverse works and hardly enable one to distinguish an 'ecclesiastical saga' from a *Vita* of a saint. Nevertheless, it is very likely that many of the traditions used by Bede had been transmitted in fairly defined and constant forms and this may have made them more reliable. How reliable is a matter for conjecture. Certainly even detail could be preserved from the fairly remote past. Bede was able to give a detailed description of the appearance of Paulinus from an oral tradition a century old.[21] Oral tradition can, however, be as false as it is circumstantial and if it is accurate in details may be so in nothing else. We cannot verify many of the traditions Bede records. He must himself have often lacked the means to do so, and sometimes, it may be, the inclination.

There is no doubt that Bede was exceptionally fitted to deal with such diverse and often bad sources. More learned in chronology and computation than any other scholar of his day he was well qualified to correlate chronological data which, although often scanty, were in diverse forms. His Biblical studies had involved the use of many of the techniques of the historian. He had taken particular care in the comparison of different texts of the scriptures. His preference of Jerome's more recent Latin translation of the Old Testament to the Greek of the Septuagint led him radically to revise Eusebius's chronology.[22] His Biblical work naturally involved chronological problems and the comparison of divergent texts describing the same events.[23] The compilation of commentaries required, *inter alia,* the exposition of the literal meaning of scripture and so enquiry into topographical and other facts; this may help to account for the interest in imparting topographical information apparent in parts of the *Ecclesiastical History*. Spurious texts required the attention of a Biblical scholar. Bede showed himself able to expose at least one such, the *De Transitu Beatae Virginis,* partly on historical grounds.[24] In writing the *Ecclesiastical History* at the end of such a scholarly career Bede might have been expected to produce a work of more than ordinary reliability and it is agreed that he did.

This is not to say that the *Ecclesiastical History* is technically flawless within the limits of Bede's intentions. The most conspicuous faults are chronological; the dates he gives are not always mutually consistent. Although Bede was the most expert chronologist of his day his task in dating events in England was very difficult. He had to correlate dates given according to the regnal years of the kings of different kingdoms with one another and with dates from ecclesiastical sources expressed in imperial or consular years or in terms of the position of the year in a nineteen-year cycle, the indiction. He gives dates according to several systems, frequently as years A.D.—it was largely through him that this system became current. The correlation of different dates which Bede gives according to different systems reveals discrepancies. Various attempts have been made to explain and correct these but many of the problems involved remain controversial. There is disagreement on when Bede began the year and on how he calculated regnal years. Thus cases have been put for the battle on the Winwaed's having taken place in 655, which is the year Bede gives, in 654 and in 656. All the theories advanced require the assumption that Bede made some mistakes. It is doubtful whether some of the problems will ever be completely solved. We have little evidence beyond what Bede himself provides. For many secular events he was dependent on dates expressed in regnal years. These may have often been inaccurate or expressed in complete years only. Different systems of calculation may have been used in different kingdoms at different times and Bede may not have been well informed about them. He may have made corrections or alterations on the basis of information unknown to us.[25]

Other errors can be detected in Bede's work which are due to slips, or to the difficulties of his material. Mr D. P. Kirby has shown recently that although Bede clearly implies that the marriage of Edwin of Northumbria to a Kentish princess took place in 625 he provides other evidence which makes it very likely that the marriage took place in or very near to 619. Either Bede made a false assumption—that Paulinus was consecrated before he left for Northumbria—or else he wrote the passage concerned rather carelessly.[26] Arch-Abbot Brechter in an elaborate study of Bede's account of St Augustine's mission to Kent has alleged that Bede knowingly falsified its chronology, ante-dating Ethelbert's baptism, post-dating Augustine's episcopal consecration, reversing their order and discarding a papal letter which showed him to be wrong.[27] This is too dramatic. Brechter's arguments for what the course of events really was are not conclusive, though neither are they implausible, especially on the date of Ethelbert's baptism. The evidence he offers for Bede's dishonesty is unconvincing. Bede may have erred through carelessness in saying that Ethelbert received the faith in 597, if he meant by this that he was baptized then.[28] He may have been wrong about the time at which Augustine was consecrated and certainly confused the archbishop of Lyons with the bishop of Arles and misdated a journey to Rome.[29] He had difficult sources to deal with, could slip, and did not write in an age in which it was thought necessary to distinguish between known facts and deductions or assumptions.[30] There is no need to assume more.

Some of the discrepancies and awkwardnesses in Bede's text may be attributable to the method and circumstances of his writing. He does not seem to have gathered all his evidence before he began to write, but rather to have made insertions in what he had already written as new material reached him. The type of text which Plummer calls C appears to preserve one recension slightly earlier than the last, differing from it chiefly in not including chapter XIV of the fourth book: traces of other insertions into an earlier version or versions appear in the text as we have it.[31] It may well be that Bede had to write under difficulties. He was fairly old by the time he wrote the *Ecclesiastical History*; the tone and nature of the last chapter suggest that he may have been ill. He may have been hindered by liturgical duties and shortages of writing materials and copyists. It was not perhaps easy for him to find his way about his own text or materials; indexes have been invented since his day. One may fancy the *Ecclesiastical History* as the last great work of an elderly and ailing scholar compelled to great labours by a sense of religious duty. It is surprising, not that there are inconsistencies, ambiguities, or loose ends in the *Ecclesiastical History*, but that they are so few. It is to Bede's credit rather than his discredit that it is possible to criticize him largely on a basis of evidence he himself provides. The quantity of the information he records and the care with which he uses it are such that he may be regarded almost as if he were a modern historian. Almost and sometimes, but it is wrong to judge his work, or to use it, as if he really were one.

It is not Bede's competence which marks him as the product of a distant age, but his purpose. His general aim is explicit and inevitable, to describe men and their deeds so that the *religious et pius auditor* may be excited to imitate good and to shun evil.[32] Much of the *Ecclesiastical History* is devoted to inculcating through stories about the past the virtues and the dogmas which Bede had spent most of his life expounding, probably to a narrower and more learned audience, in his commentaries. For example, in the commentaries Bede says that there are two kinds of compunction with the same outward manifestations. One came from the fear of hell and could develop into the other which came from the love of heaven. The story of Adamnan of Coldingham in the *Ecclesiastical History* gives an instance of this. Adamnan, thanks to an accident and his own scrupulousness, continued throughout his life a regime of mortification which had been intended to last for a shorter time and

> quod causa divini timoris semel ob reatum compunctus coeperat, iam causa divini amoris delectatus praemiis indefessus agebat.[33]

Most of the doctrines which Bede dramatizes and makes memorable in the *Ecclesiastical History* are naturally of more general application than this. Thus his accounts of visions of the other world, which are perhaps the most obvious demonstrations of his homilectic intentions, drive home such points as the folly of depending on the chance of being able to make a death-bed repentance, the certainty that even the least thought or action will be taken into account after death, the purpose and frightfulness of purgatory and the much greater frightfulness and eternity of hell.[34] The value of such instruction remains, no doubt, *semper, ubique et pro omnibus*. But much of what Bede seeks to teach by giving examples in the *Ecclesiastical History* is directed towards the particular circumstances of England in his own day and the nature of his work can be fully understood only in relation to these.

The *Ecclesiastical History* was intended to reach a lay as well as a clerical audience. It is the only one of Bede's works to be dedicated to a layman, Ceolwulf, king of Northumbria 729-37 or 38; he had been sent a draft to comment upon. It is not known whether he or other laymen were capable of reading it.[35] A few may have been, but in any case Bede's references to those who were either to read or to hear it suggest that he did not expect knowledge of it to be confined to the literate but rather that it would be read out and, presumably, translated.[36] Offa, king of Mercia 756-97, had a copy of the *Ecclesiastical History* and it was the only one of Bede's works which Alfred had translated.[37] No doubt Bede knew and intended that its main audience would be clerical. But the English Church contained too many nobles and was too dependent upon kings to be indifferent to the needs and interests of secular rulers. Much of the *Ecclesiastical History* was intended to show how the needs of kings could best be fulfilled and where their true interests lay.

England in Bede's day was divided into a number of kingdoms whose relative power fluctuated and whose rulers lacked security. In the course of the seventh century the dynasties of Kent, East Anglia, Mercia, Northumbria and Wessex had in turn been the most powerful in England. All at some stage fell from greatness, some to recover it later, others not. All kings had enemies inside as well as outside their kingdoms. Aethelbald of Mercia, whose superiority south of the Humber was recognized at the time when Bede completed the *Ecclesiastical History,* was to die at the hands of his own bodyguard. A major theme of the probably near-contemporary poem *Beowulf* is that the wages of greatness and heroism is death. The poet constantly reminds his audience that the great kings and kingdoms with which he is concerned all came to disaster.[38] English kings had to struggle hard to stay successful, and alive, in a very dangerous world. It is a question what part the Church and Christianity played in this struggle and it was a question then what part they could and should play. The acceptance of Christianity in the seventh century was part of the process by which England grew more civilized under the influence of those parts of the Continent where the wreck of Roman civilization had been less complete than it had been in Britain. The Church was successful in England partly because it suited the needs and aspirations of kings. It made some contribution to royal government, which may have had to face new problems in the seventh century as some dynasties built up kingdoms of a size unprecedented since the Anglo-Saxon conquest of England. It must in some degree have changed kings' views of themselves and of their functions. But if kings owed something to the Church, the Church was very dependent upon kings and by the time that Bede wrote some kings were seeing their interest in exploiting rather than in protecting it. Although the English Church had a unity which transcended the boundaries of individual kingdoms and although it always in some degree acted in accordance with its own principles rather than with royal demands it was, nevertheless, very much subject to royal power. Bishops were often or usually appointed in accordance with the will of a king. A monastery which lacked royal favour could hardly hope to prosper.[39] Kings were becoming covetous of the wealth of the Church and demanding a share of it. According to St Boniface, Ceolred of Mercia (709-716) and Osred of Northumbria (705-716) were the first kings to violate the 'privilegia ecclesiarum in regno Anglorum'.[40]

The *Ecclesiastical History* is in part an attempt to demonstrate the role of a Christian king, what the Church did for him and what he ought to do for the Church. Bede repeatedly emphasizes the connection between Christianity and success. His account of the

career of Cenwalh, king of Wessex 643-674, is a good example. When Cenwalh succeeded his Christian father he rejected the 'fidem et sacramenta regni caelestis' and not long after 'etiam regni terrestris potentiam perdidit'. While in exile he became converted and then regained his kingdom. But when he expelled his bishop his kingdom became subjected to severe and frequent attacks by his enemies.

> tandem ad memoriam reduxit, quod eum pridem perfidia regno pulerit, fides agnita Christi in regnum revocaverit; intellexitque, quod etiam tunc destituta pontifice provincia recte pariter divino fuerit destituta praesidio.[41]

When Oswy of Northumbria was hard-pressed by his enemy Penda and was unable to buy him off he turned to God. ' "Si paganus", inquit; "nescit accipere nostra donaria, offeramus ei qui novit, Domino Deo nostro . . .".'[42] And so he won a great battle. This campaign is one of the rare events described by Bede of which we have an account in another source. The *Historia Brittonum* attributed to Nennius, a compilation made in Wales probably in the early ninth century, tells a rather different story. It too mentions an offer of treasure to Penda, but one which was accepted. Nennius is later than Bede and the value of his work a matter for speculation. But in this instance he seems to have had information which Bede did not have or use and his employment of the apparently archaic Welsh phrase *atbret Iudeu,* 'the restitution of Iudeu' (? Stirling), to describe the incident suggests that it did take place and was well known in Welsh tradition.[43] The whole truth of the matter will never be known. It is conceivable that there were two offers of treasure, one accepted and one rejected. The suspicion remains, however, that Nennius and Bede were describing the same incident and that Bede was retailing an inaccurate version which suited his didactic purpose. Here and constantly he is insistent that the benefits which the Church can confer come in this world as well as in the next.

The king to whom Bede gives most attention is St Oswald and his account of him is an excellent instance of how Christianity could be presented to suit the needs and feelings of the rulers of England. If the Church deprived the kings of Northumbria of the gods whom they had regarded as their ancestors it soon provided their dynasty with a royal saint, a hero of exactly the kind most appreciated by the Anglo-Saxons, a great and famous man who met disaster nobly. It has been said that the greatest of heroic German themes was that of the inevitable death of the great, the theme of *Beowulf* itself in which 'as in a little circle of light about their halls men with courage as their stay went forward to that battle with the hostile world and the offspring of the dark which ends for all, even the kings and champions, in defeat'.[44] Oswald was an improved version of this type of hero. He came to greatness through being a Christian:

non solum incognita progenitoribus suis regna caelorum sperare didicit; sed et regna terrarum plus quam ulli maiorum suorum, ab eodem uno Deo, qui fecit caelum et terram consecutus est.[45]

Although he met his inevitable fate and died fighting bravely far from home he lived elsewhere and retained power, which was demonstrated in a concrete way by miracles. As a Christian saint he is a somewhat curious figure. No miracles performed during his lifetime were attributed to him (unless his victory at Heavenfield be counted such); he died fighting an army which, though Bede does not tell us so, may well have included Christians; as he died he was popularly thought to have prayed, not for his enemies, but for the souls of his own men.[46] As the product of the interaction between Christianity and the needs of a dynasty in a certain climate of thought and belief his cult is perfectly intelligible. Oswald was not the only type of Christian king. A surprising number of others in the seventh and eighth centuries abandoned their kingdoms in order to enter a monastery or to go to Rome. Christianity was by no means always to a king's earthly advantage. Aidan's remark when Oswine of Deira humbled himself before him was a pregnant one. ' "Scio", inquit, "quia non multo tempore victurus est rex; nunquam enim ante haec vidi humilem regem".'[47] Bede recognized that there was more than one way in which a king could be virtuous. But he makes the duty of a king while reigning clear. It is to protect the Church, to observe its teaching and to defend his people in battle. The happiest times since the English came to Britain were, he says, those 'dum et fortissimos Christianosque habentes reges cunctis barbaris nationibus essent terrori'.[48] In the period of which he is writing here, the last generation of the seventh century, the 'barbari nationes'—he was probably thinking chiefly of the Picts—were all more or less Christian. There is a point where his admiration for the leader and defender of a Christian people meets a less specifically devout delight in the *strenuitas* of a warrior king.[49] It was not that Bede was committed in a simple way to the interests of the kings of Northumbria: he approved of a Mercian rebellion against Oswy and disapproved of a raid made by Ecgfrith on Ireland. It was rather that he was writing for an audience which saw Christianity in heroic terms and which may have believed in a more than rational connection between the virtue of a king and the prosperity of his people.

Bede's account of secular affairs is nearly always intended to show how virtue and vice were rewarded in this world as well as hereafter, or to present models of Christian kingship, or is simply incidental. For example, we learn from him of one of Penda's attacks on Northumbria only because it was involved with a miracle of Aidan's. He does not even tell us the names of the British kingdoms against which the kings of Northumbria fought. He says very little indeed about the political events of the early eighth century, which were those about which he must have known most. Indeed, he gives less space to his own times than he does to any other period after 597; of the four books and twelve chapters devoted to the period 596-731 the years from 687 to 731 receive one book only.[50] The contrast with Gregory of Tours is striking. Gregory devotes six of the ten books of his history to the period of his own greatness, *c.* 573-591. The more he knew the more he wrote. It seems with Bede the more he knew the less he wrote. A clue to the reason for this may be given by his remark on the reign of Ceolwulf—that it was so troubled that 'quid de his scribi debeat quemve sint finem singula, necdum sciri valeat'.[51] This is partly, no doubt, an expression of his usual discretion, but also an intimation that he was waiting for the pattern of God's judgments on the past to emerge. Until it had done so he would not write.

If much of the *Ecclesiastical History* is directed towards the laity, more is directed towards the clergy. The English Church in Bede's day enjoyed a status within the universal Church which it was never to reach again. Bede's own work indicates its learning. During his lifetime Englishmen converted much of Germany and they were soon to reform the Church in Gaul. Bede was proud of English achievements and devoted much of his fifth book to describing the work of English missionaries on the Continent, though he strangely says nothing of St Boniface, who was becoming the greatest of them.[52] But it is not for nothing that much of the rest of the book consists of accounts of visions of hell. Bede felt that much was amiss with the Church and in particular in his own kingdom of Northumbria. We have the letter which he wrote at very nearly the end of his life to Bishop Egbert, of York, lamenting the ills which plagued the church.[53] His criticisms were, briefly, these. There were not enough bishops to ensure that pastoral duties (which then fell largely on the bishop in person) were properly discharged. Large dioceses were maintained because bishops were anxious to exact all the dues they could. Some bishops were surrounded by men given to laughter, jokes, tales, feasting and drink. Many priests were ignorant, many monks ill-conducted. Monasteries were often such in name only, being in fact the property of laymen who sought chiefly the rights and exemptions associated with the monastic tenure of land. The kingdom had become so demented with this 'mad error' since the death of Aldfrith that its security was threatened since there was not enough land left to support the young men who should have defended it. . . .

Thus much of the *Ecclesiastical History* is by implication a criticism of the Church in Bede's own day and expresses his longing for a return to a primitive simplicity which he thought had existed only a short time before. He may well have realized that if the Church was to survive it had to involve itself more with the world than he would wish. He remarks of Putta, Bishop of Rochester, who after his church and its possessions had been ravaged by Aethelred of Mercia, retired elsewhere,

> nihil omnino de restaurando episcopatu suo agens; quia, sicut et supra diximus, magis in ecclesiasticis quam in mundanis rebus erat industrius.[54]

It is a slightly curious but a revealing way of putting it. His sympathies clearly lay with Putta; he thought the world was bad and the Church too much part of it. He wanted a poverty, simplicity and devotion which, if they had ever characterized the English Church, were never to do so again.

Bede's account of the Church in the *Ecclesiastical History* is distinguished by great discretion. While his commentaries contain numerous references to the shortcomings of the Church and in his letter to Egbert he is open and violent in denunciation he has very little to say directly about the sins of the clergy in his history. A few sinful clerics are mentioned, but, Britons apart, almost always incidentally. His account even of Ceolred and Osred, kings who, so we learn elsewhere, oppressed the Church, is limited to the dates of their respective accessions and deaths. The nearest he comes in the *Ecclesiastical History* to the long account and denunciation of fictitious monasteries in the letter to Egbert is the cryptic statement that so peaceful are the times that many Northumbrians have preferred to enter monasteries rather than to exercise the arts of war. 'Quae res quem sit habitura finem, posterior aetas videbit.'[55] Similarly in his *Lives* of the abbots of Monkwearmouth-Jarrow Bede makes no reference to the incident described in the anonymous biography of Ceolfrid—which he used—of Ceolfrid's leaving the abbey partly because of the behaviour of certain nobles, who could not endure his regular discipline.[56] Had we to rely on the *Ecclesiastical History* for our knowledge of the Church in the first generation of the eighth century we should know little of it, and still less of Bede's severe judgment on it. There can be little doubt that Bede's failure to describe the conduct of those of his contemporaries of whom he disapproved was deliberate. In his commentary on the Book of Samuel he is explicit that it is wrong publicly to denounce even evil priests. . . . He clearly did not think it appropriate to enlarge on the deficiencies of the clergy in a work such as the *Ecclesiastical History* which was intended for a fairly wide audience. A letter to another cleric such as that to Egbert was another matter, though even there he mentions no names. Others of his day were not so backward, like the monk who wrote to a friend describing a vision of hell where many named sinners had appeared in torment, among them 'your abbot'.[57] . . .

A theme which stands out above all others in Bede's attempt to instruct and edify through the *Ecclesiastical History* is that of the struggle for the unity and orthodoxy of the Church. To record the nature and fate of heresy was one of the most important functions of an ecclesiastical historian. Eusebius had given much attention to so doing. As a theologian Bede was concerned to refute many heretics and heresies—Plummer collected references to twenty-nine.[58] As a historian he was concerned with one heresy, Pelagianism, and one group of errors, those of the Celtic Churches which departed from orthodox custom, especially in the calculation of the date of Easter. Pelagius's heresy of the denial of the necessity of grace for salvation may have originated in the British Isles. Bede thought that it had been imported in the fifth century, and in his first book describes at some length two visits made by St Germanus to extirpate it. Pelagian views seem to have continued to be held in Ireland in the seventh and eighth centuries and it may well have been from Ireland that there came the two works of the Pelagian Julian of Eclana and the one of Pelagius himself to which Bede had access.[59] The first book of his commentary on the Song of Songs was devoted to the refutation of Julian. His account of Pelagianism and its defeat in the fifth century was then of more than historical significance; the evidence he gives of God's condemnation of it in the past was a useful lesson for his own day.

The errors which received most attention from Bede were those of the Celtic Churches which diverged from Roman customs. The most important difference was that on the calculation of the date of Easter.[60] It was regarded not as a minor point of discipline, but as a rift in the unity of the Church with serious doctrinal implications. For such a theologian as Bede, always seeking mystical interpretations, the movement of Easter and its proper calculation—and no one knew the proper calculation better than he—was loaded with the weightiest significance. Consider, for example, the words Bede attributes to the dying Cuthbert who warns his companions to have no communion with those who depart from the unity of Catholic peace 'vel pascha non suo tempore celebrando, vel perverse vivendo'.[61] A considerable part of the *Ecclesiastical History* is devoted to the subject. In the second book we are told how Augustine attempted to induce the Britons to accept the Roman usages or to assist the evangelization of the English. He failed and prophesied that the recalcitrant Britons would perish at the hands of the English. Bede records with some relish the fulfilment of this prophesy when Aethelfrith massacred the monks of Bangor. Here, as in his use of Gildas's account of the Anglo-Saxon invasions in the fifth century, Bede is able to reconcile two loyalties by showing his pagan ancestors to have been the instrument of God's revenge. He goes on to describe later attempts to persuade the Britons to accept the Roman Easter. The climax of the third book is his famous account of the synod of Whitby at which

Oswy agreed that Roman usages should prevail in Northumbria, while those who did not accept them left. In the fifth book Bede now explains how Iona, northern Ireland and the king of the Picts were converted to a proper view—southern Ireland had become orthodox long since. The emphasis given to the Easter controversy throughout the *Ecclesiastical History* is clear. It receives the longest chapter in the third book and the longest in the fifth. The chapter which describes the conversion of Iona is the last in the whole except for that which gives a final survey of the general state of Britain. It must have given particular satisfaction to Bede to record the acceptance of Catholic unity by the house whence had come Aidan and the Irish missionaries whom he so much admired, but whose adherence to unorthodox usages he so much deplored. The battle for Roman uniformity was still not completely won at the time when he wrote. The Britons remained 'inveterati et claudicantes'.[62] As with Pelagianism, so with the Easter controversy, Bede was writing not only an account of the past, but a tract for his own times.

Bede's preoccupation with the defence of orthodoxy and his distrust of the Britons who had erred, and in his own day still and alone continued to err, may have influenced his selection of subject-matter and coloured his account of what he selected. As always the lack of other sources prevents reasonable certainty as to how far this was so. Thus Nennius gives an account of the conversion of Northumbria quite at variance with that of Bede; it was accomplished, he says, by the British Church, Edwin being baptized by Rhun, son of Urien, a member of the royal dynasty of the northern British kingdom of Rheged. Until recently most scholars have rejected this story. Nennius is later than Bede, less scholarly, and recounts much that is fabulous. A considerable part of Bede's account of the conversion of Northumbria must be broadly true; he can hardly have fabricated the letters of Pope Honorius to Edwin and his queen which help to confirm his account. But Professor Jackson and Mrs Chadwick have recently argued that Nennius's tale should be taken more seriously.[63] It is consistent with the fragments of knowledge which we have about the rulers of Rheged and about Edwin's relations with the Britons. Much of this information inspires more interest than confidence, but it is not negligible. In particular Nennius gives another piece of information about the relations between the royal houses of Rheged and Northumbria, namely that King Oswy had two wives, *Riemmelth,* whose descent is given and who seems to have been a member of the royal house of Rheged, and Eanfled, daughter of Edwin. Bede mentions the second, but not the first. That Nennius's information on this was accurate is suggested by the occurrence of what seems to be an Anglo-Saxon version of the first wife's name at about the right place in the 'list of the names of the queens and abbesses of Northumbria' in the, presumably independent, *Liber*

Vitae of Durham.[64] This fragment of evidence by no means proves Nennius's account of the conversion of Northumbria to have been true. But it does suggest relationships between Northumbria and its British neighbours of which Bede tells us, through ignorance or design, nothing; and it raises the suspicion that the British Church did play a more important part in the conversion of Northumbria than his account, which allows it none, indicates.

The problems involved in assessing Bede's account of the conversion of Northumbria are characteristic of those which arise in connection with the *Ecclesiastical History*. Bede was very learned and very intelligent. His aim was partly simply to describe the history of the Church in England and his care in collecting evidence and the methods, derived from those of Eusebius, with which he handled it enabled him to perform this task in a manner which makes this work more scholarly, in the modern sense, than that of any other Dark Age historian. This aspect of his work has always and rightly attracted attention and praise. But his principal intention was not just to record the past, but to use it to teach lessons to the present, mainly by treating seventh-century England as a gallery of good examples. Excellent instances of the reaction he sought are to be found in the work of Victorian historians, for example W. Bright—'We think not only of the noble earnestness of Ethelbert, of the heroic sanctity of Oswald, of the sweet humility of Oswin but of the genuine conversions of Eadbald and Kenwalch . . .', etc.[65] The differences in the historiographical fortunes of seventh-century England and seventh-century Gaul, the one often being regarded as moving and edifying, the other as repellent and vicious, are attributable not so much to one society's being nobler, or nicer, than the other as to Bede's aims and tastes being different from those of Frankish historians.[66]

Bede wrote then not only in the Eusebian tradition but also in that of hagiography. The principles of hagiographers were largely contrary to those of scholarship, though they sometimes adopted a misleadingly scholarly air, setting store by citing evidence for things which did not happen or which did not happen at the time or to the persons they alleged. They wrote in the attitude of mind with which the Bible is now often interpreted. Moral truth, not literal truth, was what mattered.[67] Emphasis was placed on the need for belief, not on the advantages of doubt. 'Vera lex historiae' is, says Bede, 'simpliciter ea quae fama vulgante collegimus ad instructionem posteritatis litteris mandare.' He prides himself that he has used an earlier life of Cuthbert 'simpliciter fidem historiae quam legebam accomodans'.[68] Hagiographers tended to turn the men and events they described into types. 'Vous lui demandez un portrait', says Fr. Delehaye of the hagiographer, 'il vous répond par un programme'.[69] Bede's account in the *Ecclesiastical History* of such saints as Aidan and Cuthbert is almost purely hagiographical and contrasts with the more factual and sober treatment of other biographies in his *Lives of the Abbots*.[70] It is a question how far what appear to be the more purely historical parts of the *Ecclesiastical History* are affected by his didactic purposes. These purposes certainly determined his selection of subject-matter; it can hardly be doubted that he was very discreet and sometimes suppressed that which could not edify. But one must wonder how far his account of the course of events is affected by his believing that he ought to give the version which best demonstrated the truth of his faith rather than that which best corresponded with the truth, and how far his judgment of what was likely was affected by his conviction of what was appropriate. He is so far our only source for so much of what he describes that no firm judgment on these matters is possible. But a comparison of Bede with such other sources as Eddius and Nennius, questionable though they are, suggests that the veneration which he has so long and so rightly been accorded ought to be tempered by some mistrust. Historians have sometimes been too ready to assume Bede's reliability as axiomatic when it is the point at issue. It is not even safe to assume that the attitudes and emphases of the *Ecclesiastical History* fully reflect Bede's personal views. He thought it the duty of a teacher to suit his teaching to his audience.[71] Some of the apparent crudities in his approach to Christianity, for example the repeated emphasis on its connection with worldly success and on the importance of miracles, may indicate not so much his own view of his faith as his judgment of the limitations of his audience.[72]

Clear, almost simple, though the *Ecclesiastical History* is it is the product of a complex mind working under difficult circumstances. On the one hand Bede was concerned for the truth, interested in hard facts, excellently equipped technically and writing with the good model of Eusebius before him. On the other hand he was using history to teach lessons which he felt to be badly needed; he was writing partly not as a historian but as a hagiographer; he had to suit his work to his audience and present it in such a way that it moved men less learned and less subtle than he. He was a barbarian, one of the first handful of his people to have become literate, yet very learned in a tradition which sprang from the remote world of the Roman empire. He was very devoutly, indeed sternly, Christian and writing in and for a Church which had accommodated itself to the ways of its world. He sought to recall it to what he thought to have been its primitive simplicity while treating it with the respect and discretion which any Church deserved. Many of the difficulties in assessing the *Ecclesiastical History* derive from those inherent in Bede's intellectual position and in the nature of his task.

Whatever the difficulties, few of those who read his book and even fewer of those who work on it fail to come to admire it. Bede had and has the power to seize the imagination of his reader and to transport him to a strange world; strange because it is so distant in time and circumstances, even stranger because it is a world so directly dominated by God, where ordinary historical causality hardly applies. Most Dark Age historians provoke a sense, usually an overwhelming sense, of superiority. We know better, we are cleverer than they. Bede defies patronage. Remote, almost bizarre, though his view of history is he expounds it in the manner, and it is more than just the manner, of an educated, rational and moderate man. The *Ecclesiastical History* is not only the record of most of what we shall ever know of a century or more of English history, but a monument to the extraordinary skill and power of Bede.

Notes

[1] The chronicles are best edited by T. Mommsen, *M.G.H. Scriptores Antiquissimi*, XIII (1898), 223-354, and the other historical works by C. Plummer, *Baedae Opera Historica* (2 vols., Oxford, 1896); references below are to Plummer's edition unless otherwise stated. For editions of Bede's other works see M. L. W. Laistner and H. H. King, *Handlist of Bede Manuscripts* (Ithaca, N.Y., 1943) and M. T. A. Carroll, *The Venerable Bede: his Spiritual Teachings* (Catholic University of America, Studies in Mediaeval History, new ser., IX (Washington, 1946)). The poems, homilies and some of the commentaries have been re-edited in *Corpus Christianorum Series Latine*, CXIX and CXX, ed. D. Hurst, and CXXII, ed. D. Hurst and J. Fraipont (Turnhout, 1962, 1960 and 1955 respectively). For general accounts of Bede see *Bede, his Life, Times and Writings*, ed. A. Hamilton Thompson (Oxford, 1935), E. S. Duckett, *Anglo-Saxon Saints and Scholars* (New York, 1947), pp. 217-338, W. F. Bolton, 'A Bede Bibliography: 1935-60' *Traditio*, xviii (1962), 436-45.

[2] *Venerabilis Bedae Opera*, ed. J. A. Giles, XII (1844), 341.

[3] For Bede as a historian see e.g. W. Levison, 'Bede as Historian', in *Bede, his Life, Times and Writings, op. cit.*, pp. 111-51; C. W. Jones, *Saints' Lives and Chronicles in Early England* (Ithaca, N.Y., 1947) and 'Bede as Early Medieval Historian', *Medievalia et Humanistica*, fasc. IV (1946), 26-36; P. Hunter Blair, *Bede's Ecclesiastical History . . . and its Importance Today* (Jarrow Lecture 1959, Jarrow-on-Tyne, n.d.).

[4] For the history of the church see e.g. M. Deanesly, *The Pre-Conquest Church in England* (1961).

[5] Ed. Plummer, *Baedae Opera Historica* I, clx-clxiv.

[6] Carroll, *The Venerable Bede . . . , op. cit.*, pp. 43-6; M. L. W. Laistner, 'Bede as a Classical and Patristic

Scholar', *Transactions of the Royal Historical Society,* 4th ser., XVI (1933), 83.

[7] The anonymous life of Ceolfrith and Eddius Stephanus's life of Wilfred survive in only two manuscripts each, the Whitby life of Gregory the Great in only one (*Baedae Opera Historica,* ed. Plummer, I, cxl-cxli; *The Life of Bishop Wilfred by Eddius Stephanus,* ed. and trans. B. Colgrave (Cambridge, 1927), pp. xiii-xvi; B. Colgrave, 'The Earliest Life of Gregory the Great', in K. Jackson, N. K. Chadwick and others, *Celt and Saxon: Studies in the Early British Border* (Cambridge, 1963), pp. 119-21). So much damage seems to have been done by the Scandinavian invasions to English libraries that works which were not popular, and in particular not popular on the Continent, must have had only a limited chance of survival.

[8] For this paragraph, W. Levison, *England and the Continent in the Eighth Century* (Oxford, 1946); K. C. King, *The Earliest German Monasteries* (Nottingham, 1961); J. M. Wallace-Hadrill, 'Rome and the Early English Church', *Settimane di studio del centro italiano di studi sull'alto medioevo,* VII (Spoleto, 1960), 519-48; *Bede's Europe* (Jarrow Lecture 1962, Jarrow-on-Tyne, n.d.); K. Hughes, 'Irish Monks and Learning', *Los monjes y los estudios* (Abadia de Poblet, 1963), pp. 61-86, and H. Farmer, 'The Studies of Anglo-Saxon Monks A.D. 600-800', *ibid.,* pp. 87-103; J. N. Hillgarth, 'Visigothic Spain and Early Christian Ireland', *Proceedings of the Royal Irish Academy* LXII, C (1961-3), 167-94.

[9] Levison, *England and the Continent,* p. 40; C. E. Blunt, 'Four Italian Coins Imitating Anglo-Saxon Types', *British Numismatic Journal,* 3rd ser., V (1945-8), 285.

[10] M. L. W. Laistner, 'Bede as a Classical and Patristic Scholar', *op. cit.;* 'The Library of the Venerable Bede', *Bede, his Life, Times and Writings, op. cit.,* pp. 237-266; both articles are reprinted in *The Intellectual Heritage of the Early Middle Ages* (Ithaca, N.Y., 1957).

[11] A. Momigliano, 'Pagan and Christian Historiography in the Fourth Century A.D.', *The Conflict between Paganism and Christianity in the Fourth Century,* ed. A. Momigliano (Oxford, 1963), pp. 79-99.

[12] J. M. Wallace-hadrill, 'The Work of Gregory of Tours in the Light of Modern Research', *The Long-Haired Kings* (1962), pp. 49-70.

[13] Jones, *Saints' Lives and Chronicles, op. cit.,* pp. 82-5.

[14] Bede thought wonder-working shrines could diminish rather than increase faith when the unworthy were not healed (Carroll, p. 197) and he attributes to Cuthbert the view that when such a shrine became a sanctuary for evildoers it also became a nuisance to its keepers, *Two Lives of St. Cuthbert,* ed. and trans. B. Colgrave (Cambridge, 1940), p. 278.

[15] The best accounts of Bede's sources are those of Plummer, Levison and Laistner in the works cited in notes 1, 3 and 10 above.

[16] For the *Passio Sancti Albani,* W. Levison, 'St. Alban and St. Alban's', *Antiquity,* XV (1941), 337-59. Discussion of the possibility of at least part of the *De Excidio* being of a date later than the mid-sixth century one usually accepted has recently been revived: P. Grosjean, 'Remarques sur le *De Excidio* attribué a Gildas', *Archivum Latinitatis Medii Aevi,* XXV (1955), 155-87; 'Notes de hagiographie celtique', *Analecta Bollandia,* LXXV (1957), 185-226.

[17] English sources of an annalistic nature possibly used by Bede are discussed by Jones, *Saints' Lives and Chronicles, op. cit.;* P. Hunter Blair, 'The *Moore Memoranda* on Northumbrian History', *The Early Cultures of North-West Europe,* ed. C. Fox and B. Dickins (Cambridge, 1950), pp. 245-57; 'The Northumbrians and their Southern Frontier', *Archaeologia Aeliana,* 4th ser., XXVI (1948), 98-126; and P. Grosjean 'La date du Colloque de Whitby', *Analecta Bollandia,* LXXVIII (1960), 255-60. Some information may have come to him from inscriptions, C. Peers and C. A. Ralegh Radford, 'The Saxon Monastery at Whitby', *Archaeologia,* LXXXIX (1943), 40-6.

[18] *H.E.* pp. 6-7.

[19] N. K. Chadwick, in *Celt and Saxon, op. cit.,* pp. 138-85, esp. pp. 169, 177.

[20] Jones is equally confident that Bede's account of the synod is in a different genre, modelled on *Acta Synodi Caesareae, Saints' Lives and Chronicles, op. cit.,* 181.

[21] *H.E.* II, 16, 117.

[22] Levison, 'Bede as Historian', *op. cit.,* p. 117.

[23] C. Jenkins, 'Bede as Exegete and Theologian', *Bede, his Life, Times and Writings, op. cit.,* pp. 196-9.

[24] Laistner, 'Bede as a Classical and Patristic Scholar', *op. cit.,* pp. 84-5; cf. Jenkins, *op. cit.,* pp. 160-1.

[25] For the literature on Bede's chronology, D. P. Kirby, 'Bede and Northumbrian Chronology', *English Historical Review,* LXXVIII (1963), 514-27.

[26] Kirby, 518, 522-3.

[27] (H.) S. Brechter, *Die Quellen zur Angelsachsenmission Gregors des Grossen* (Beitr. zur Gesch. d. Alten

Mönchtums u.d. Benediktinerordens, Heft 22), Münster i. W., 1941, pp. 228-52, critically discussed by F. A. Markus, 'The Chronology of the Gregorian Mission: Bede's Narrative and Gregory's Correspondence', *Journal of Ecclesiastical History,* XIV (1963), 16-30.

[28] It is likely that Bede did not know when Ethelbert was baptised. The use of *interea* with the perfect tense to introduce his account of Augustine's journey to be consecrated abroad suggests that when he wrote I, 26 and 27, he was uncertain of the relationship of this event to the baptism of Ethelbert (cf. III, 20, 169; III, 28, 194; IV, 4, 213). The absence of a date for the baptism from the chronological summary in V, 24, strongly suggests that his sources did not give him one. The phrase 'post XX et unum annos acceptae fidei' in II, 5 (p. 90), is not entirely unambiguous. It probably refers to the baptism or conversion of Ethelbert which Bede would therefore here place in 597. If so this may well be a slip on his part. There is other evidence that II, 5, was carelessly written (Kirby, *op. cit.,* p. 521).

[29] The dating of this journey is connected with the vexed question of the authenticity of the *Responsiones* to Augustine attributed to Gregory, for which see M. Deanesly and P. Grosjean 'The Canterbury Edition of the Answers of Pope Gregory I to St. Augustine', *Journal of Ecclesiastical History,* X (1959), 1-49; P. Meyvaert, 'Les "responsiones" de S. Grégoire le Grand a S. Augustin de Cantorbéry', *Revue d'Histoire Ecclesiastique,* LIV (1959), 879-94; 'Bede and the *Libellus Synodicus* of Gregory the Great', *Journal of Theological Studies,* new ser., XII (1961), 298 n.; M. Deanesly, 'The Capitular Text of the *Responsiones* of Pope Gregory I to St. Augustine', *Journal of Ecclesiastical History,* XLI (1961), 231-4.

[30] It is not altogether clear that Bede's well-known account of the co-operation of Oswy of Northumbria and Egbert of Kent in choosing an archbishop of Canterbury is not a mere deduction based on the conflation of a letter from Pope Vitalian to Oswy and some account of Egbert's sending a candidate for the see to Rome, *H.E.* III, 29, 196-9; IV, 1, 201; *Hist. Abb.,* ed. Plummer, *Baedae Opera Historica,* I, 366; cf. Plummer's note, II, 200-1.

[31] For textual questions see Plummer, pp. lxxx-cxliv, *The Leningrad Bede,* ed. O. Arngart (Copenhagen, 1952), pp. 13-35; *The Moore Bede,* ed. P. Hunter Blair and R. A. B. Mynors (Copenhagen, 1959), pp. 11-37.

[32] *H.E.,* p. 5.

[33] *H.E.* IV, 23 (25), 264; Carroll, *The Venerable Bede . . . , op. cit.,* pp. 162-3, 234.

[34] *Ibid.,* chapter IV; *H.E.* V, 12-14.

[35] Aldfrith, Ceolwulf's predecessor, was literate; laymen brought up in such a household as Wilfred's might have become so, *Eddius,* ed. Colgrave, *op. cit.,* p. 44. Wilfred himself was literate well before he was ordained priest and could have gone on to a secular career, as others perhaps did after a similar beginning, *Eddius,* pp. 8, 10, 18.

[36] E.g. *H.E.,* p. 6; V, 13, 313.

[37] D. Whitelock, *After Bede* (Jarrow Lecture 1960, n.p., n.d.), p. 11.

[38] A. G. Brodeur, *The Art of Beowulf* (Berkeley, 1959), pp. 76-85, 103, 116, 119.

[39] *S. Bonifatii et Lulli Epistolae* (*M.G.H. Epistolae Selectae* I), ed. M. Tangl (Berlin, 1916), no. 14.

[40] *Ibid.,* nos. 73, 78, 115; cf. E. John, *Land Tenure in Early England* (Leicester, 1960), pp. 70-3.

[41] *H.E.* III, 7.

[42] *H.E.* III, 24, 177.

[43] K. Jackson, 'On the Northern British Section in Nennius', *Celt and Saxon, op. cit.,* pp. 35-9. Jackson argues convincingly that the *Historia* is partly derived from written sources embodying annals recorded during the seventh century.

[44] J. R. R. Tolkien, 'Beowulf, the Monsters and the Critics', *Proceedings of the British Academy,* XXII (1936), p. 18 of the offprint.

[45] *H.E.* III, 6, 137-8.

[46] *H.E.* III, 12, 151.

[47] *H.E.* III, 14, 157; cf. Sigbert, king of Essex, said to have been murdered because he would forgive his enemies, III, 22, 173.

[48] *H.E.* IV, 2, 205.

[49] Wallace-Hadrill, 'The Work of Gregory of Tours in the Light of Modern Research', *op. cit.,* pp. 60-2.

[50] The period 596-687 occupies 239 pages of Plummer's edition, that after 687, 71.

[51] *H.E.* V, 23, 349.

[52] Wallace-Hadrill, *Bede's Europe, op. cit.,* pp. 11-12.

[53] Ed. Plummer, *Baedae Opera Historica* I, 405-23. . . .

[54] *H.E.* IV, 12, 228.

[55] *H.E.* V, 23, 351.

[56] *Baedae Opera Historica,* ed. Plummer, I, 390. . . .

[57] *S. Bonifatii et Lulli Epistolae, op. cit.,* no. 115. . . .

[58] Plummer, pp. lxii-lxiii n.

[59] Hughes, 'Irish Monks and Learning', *op. cit.,* pp. 62, 72; *H.E.* II, 19, 122-4; Laistner, 'The Library of the Venerable Bede', *op. cit.,* pp. 252, 265.

[60] For what was at issue see e.g. J. K. Kenney, *Sources for the Early History of Ireland* I (New York, 1929), pp. 210-17.

[61] *Two Lives of St. Cuthbert, op. cit.,* p. 284.

[62] *H.E.* V, 22, 347.

[63] K. Jackson, 'On the Northern British Section of Nennius', N. K. Chadwick, 'The Conversion of Northumbria: a Comparison of Sources' in *Celt and Saxon, op. cit.,* pp. 20-62, 138-66.

[64] Jackson, pp. 41-2.

[65] *Chapters of Early English Church History* (Oxford, 1878), p. 435.

[66] If Grosjean is right in identifying Agilbert, bishop of Dorchester 650-60, with the Agilbert who helped to lure an enemy of Ebroin's to his death by swearing an oath on an empty reliqary ('La date du Colloque de Whitby,' *op. cit.,* p. 251) a Frankish historian could reveal other qualities in this man than the *eruditio* and the *industria* to which Bede refers (*H.E.* III, 7, 140).

[67] E.g. Jones, *Saints' Lives and Chronicles, op. cit.,* chapter 4; B. Colgrave, 'The Earliest Saints' Lives Written in England', *Proceedings of the British Academy* XLIV (1958), 35-60; and in general H. Delehaye, *Les légendes bagiographiques,* 4th ed. (Brussels, 1955).

[68] *H.E.,* pp. 7-8; Jones, *Saints' Lives and Chronicles,* pp. 82-3.

[69] Delehaye, p. 24.

[70] Jones, *Saints' Lives and Chronicles,* pp. 29, 54.

[71] Carroll, p. 245; *H.E.* III, 5, 137.

[72] The attitude towards physical miracles of some of the Fathers, including even Gregory the Great, who records so many of them, was one of some reserve, e.g. Jones, *Saints' Lives and Chronicles,* pp. 76-7, Carroll, pp. 196 ff. . . .

Leo Sherley-Price (essay date 1968)

SOURCE: Leo Sherley-Price, in an introduction to *Bede: A History of the English Church and People,* translated by Leo Sherley-Price, revised edition, Penguin Books, 1968, pp. 15-32.

[*In the following excerpt, Sherley-Price explores the background of Bede's historical writings and describes his chief merits as a historian.*]

The centuries on which Bede concentrates are a crucial and formative period in our island history, during which the future shape and pattern of the English Church and nation were beginning to emerge. Once the shield of Roman protection was withdrawn, the Celtic peoples of Britain were steadily forced to yield ground before the ever increasing pressure of the incoming Angles, Saxons, and Jutes, and were driven westward into the remote and inaccessible regions along the storm-swept Atlantic coast. Even here they enjoyed little security, and were harried by raiding parties of Irish pirates, as Saint Patrick, himself a victim, describes in his *Confessions.* Here in Devon and Cornwall, Wales, Cumberland, and south-west Scotland the Romano-Britons clung desperately to the shreds of their native independence and customs. Many were sustained by the Christian faith, brought to this island centuries before Augustine (A.D. 597) in the more peaceful days when Britain enjoyed the protection and administration of Rome as an integral *Provincia* of the Empire. Rallied by such contrasting leaders as Ambrosius, 'last of the Romans' (I. 16), Saint Germanus (I. 20) and the semi-legendary King Arthur, the Britons won sufficient successes against the Saxons to maintain a constantly menaced independence, but were isolated from the remainder of Christendom by their heathen enemies, for whom they felt nothing but bitterness and contempt. Meanwhile the Picts and Scots in their northern fastnesses remained as hostile to Briton and Saxon as they had to the legions of Rome. Bede traces the gradual conversion of all these mutually antipathetic peoples to the religion of Christ, and illustrates the enriching influence of the Catholic Church, which brought them into contact with the rest of Christendom, and, in so doing, brought to these semi-barbaric peoples the wisdom, art, and civilization of Christian Rome. During these vital centuries we see Columba and Aidan bring the Gospel to the north; Ninian to the Picts; Patrick to the Irish; David and his contemporaries to the Celts of Wales and Cornwall; and Augustine to the newly established Saxon peoples.

In Bede's pages we trace the gradual decay of the Celtic tribal and monastic systems, and their supersession by the highly developed and centralized system of the Roman Church. As Dom Louis Gougaud shows in his *Christianity in Celtic Lands,* the principal difference between the Celtic and Roman system of church administration was that the former was monastic, while the latter was diocesan. In the Celtic churches the highest administrative officer was the Abbot, who might or might not be in episcopal orders, and who, as in the case of the Abbot of Iona, ruled the churches over a considerable *provincia.* A striking example of this is Saint Columba, who never received episcopal consecration, but who exercised a wide and unquestioned authority. The Celtic bishop, as a member of a monastic community, was subject to his abbot, and exercised his spiritual functions at the latter's request and direction (see III. 4). It was the abbot who chose and presented candidates for ordination or consecration to the bishop (IV. 24), and appointed members of the community to their various tasks inside or outside the monastery. The duties of the Celtic bishop, therefore, were wholly spiritual, in contrast to those of the Roman prelate, who gradually acquired or had thrust upon him onerous administrative responsibilities, not only in ecclesiastical but in national and provincial affairs. This Celtic emphasis on the spiritual and apostolic nature of the episcopal office might well be borne in mind in these days when bishops are overburdened by countless financial and administrative details, and their true function obscured. However, although one can readily appreciate that the free-lance methods of the learned and saintly Celtic missionaries were supremely effective in breaking new ground and winning converts for Christ, they were not such as would develop and administer a growing Christian community of nation-wide extent. None will deny the holiness of the wandering Celtic saints or their appeal to the imagination, but they were bound to give place to the more regular, stable, and disciplined ways of life introduced and practised by the monks of Saint Benedict. And while much was lost as Celtic Christianity and culture declined, even more was gained. For although the leaders of the British Church rejected Augustine's claim to jurisdiction and refused their cooperation in evangelizing the pagan Saxons, contacts between the Roman and Celtic Churches increased as time went on. Mutual appreciation began to heal the wounds of suspicion and controversy, and a common belief in Christ gradually drew together the peoples of Britain into the English nation.

A decisive step towards this national and spiritual unity was taken in A.D. 664 at the Council of Whitby (IV. 25), described by R. H. Hodgkin in his *History of the Anglo-Saxons* as 'one of the great turning-points in the history of the race. . . . The Synod turned the scales, and decided that the English should take their religion and their civilization from the Roman world rather than from what Wilfrid called "one remote corner of the

most remote island".' From that day the Celtic cause was doomed to gradual extinction. These bonds of national unity were to be greatly tempered and strengthened in the fiery trials of the Danish invasions that began sixty years after Bede's death, when under the devoted leadership of Alfred, noblest of England's kings, one may fairly say that the spirit of England was born. This unification of many races into one people is the imperishable memorial of this great king, who said: 'I have always striven to live worthily, and at my death to leave to those who follow me a worthy memorial of my deeds.' And in Bede we see how Christian leaders and scholars such as Aidan, Cuthbert, and Augustine became the pastors and counsellors of king and peasant alike, laying the foundations of that close alliance between the power spiritual and the power temporal which was to bring such strength and stability to the English nation in centuries to come.

It is almost certain that the first (partial) translation of Bede's *History* from Latin into the vernacular was made by King Alfred himself, who, despite his countless pressing problems and responsibeilities, made time for this task in order to inform and inspire his English subjects. This high tribute is evidence that the ***History*** quickly established itself as a unique and authoritative record of our national history. Even during his lifetime Bede's reputation for learning extended far into Europe, and for generations after his death his ***Commentaries, Martyrology,*** and other works were recognized as standard works of reference in the West. That a new translation of his ***History*** is published in the Penguin Classics today testifies that the work which he complied with such skill and labour over twelve centuries ago still retains its value and freshness for readers of this age.

There should be few in these islands to whom the name of Bede is unknown, but there are perhaps many who do not realize the greatness of our debt to him. Nevertheless, were it not for the rich fund of information that he gathered and sifted with such care, our knowledge of the vital and stirring centuries that he describes would be scanty, while a treasury of tales loved by every English child would have been lost for ever. So any readers who take up this book for the first time can rest assured that they will not find it a dreary chronicle of events and dates; on the contrary, a rich living tapestry will unfold before them, and they will discover a source of interest and enjoyment that may well be lifelong, and stimulate them to learn more about the storied past on which our present and future is built. Such is the interest of the subject-matter and the vividness of Bede's characteristic style that the scenes and folk of long ago live again. We are transported back into the fens and forests, highlands and islands of Celtic Britain and Saxon England, and we feel strangely 'at home'. These are our own people and our own land, and with a little imagination and historical sense we have little difficulty in picturing the contemporary scene, or in appreciating the viewpoint, plans, and problems of the kings, saints, and lesser folk whom Bede describes so well. We can understand Augustine's sense of inadequacy when summoned from his quiet Roman cloister and directed to the tremendous task of converting the heathen Saxons about whom he had heard such grim rumours (I. 23). We can visualize the tense scene as the heathen high-priest Coifi rides out before King Edwin and his thanes to defy his gods and defile their temple (II. 13). We can stand beside the gallant King Oswald at Heavenfield as he sets up a great oaken cross with his own hands, and summons his army to prayer before engaging the heathen hordes in desperate battle (III. 2). Above all, we cannot but be impressed and deeply moved by the selfless Christ-like lives of the northern Celtic saints—Columba, Cuthbert, and Aidan—and their disciples. Men of great personal gifts and radiant faith, they fearlessly carried the Gospel alone among alien peoples, gladly accepting lifelong 'exile for Christ' as his apostles. Redoubtable travellers by sea and land, able scholars, scribes, and craftsmen, the loveliness of their hard and holy lives has won the admiration and captured the imagination of all succeeding centuries. When we read Bede's account of such men and their doings, we realize ever more clearly that the past is not dead and done with, but a force to be reckoned with, silently moulding the present and the future.

As already mentioned, Bede's *History* belongs to his latter years, when he had already won a wide reputation by his many other works, a list of which he appends to the closing chapter of the *History*. But it is by the latter that he is best known today, and by which he has richly earned the title of 'Father of English History'. For Bede was not content to compile a bare chronicle of events and dates, or to restrict himself to hagiography as his predecessors had done. He set himself to examine all available records, to secure verbal or written accounts from reliable living authorities, to record local traditions and stories, to interpret significant events, and, in short, to compile as complete and continuous a history of the English Church and people as lay within his power. He was the first to conceive or attempt such a formidable project, and posterity acknowledges his pioneer work as a remarkably successful achievement.

In order to accomplish his purpose, Bede sets out his *History* in five convenient periods or 'books'. In the first Book, after a preliminary geographical survey of Britain drawn entirely from earlier authorities such as Pliny, Orosius, and Gildas, and a brief account of the Roman occupation, Bede proceeds to tell the story of Christianity in Britain up to the period immediately preceding the death of its great apostle Gregory the Great. The second Book continues the story from his death up to the death of King Edwin and the overthrow of the Northumbrian kingdom by the pagan chieftain Penda. The third Book recounts the Church's struggle against heathenism in the North, and the planting of the Faith among the Mercians and East Saxons. The fourth Book records the appointment of Theodore the Greek to the Archbishopric of Canterbury and his reform and reorganization of the English Church; the lives of Cuthbert and Wilfrid; and the progress of the Church in the south-eastern provinces. The fifth Book carries on the story from the time of Bishop John of Beverley up to the date of the work's completion in A.D. 731.

As he mentions in his Preface, Bede was encouraged to undertake the writing of a history by 'the learned and reverend Abbot Albinus', who succeeded Archbishop Theodore's colleague Hadrian as abbot of the monastery of Saint Peter and Saint Paul at Canterbury in the year A.D. 709. Abbot Albinus was a close and valued friend of Bede, who addresses him elsewhere as his 'best and most beloved father in Christ', and who received great assistance from the latter's researches into the history of the Church in Kent and the adjoining provinces. Bede's Preface affords concise information on his sources, and testifies to his careful treatment of all material, whether written or verbal. He tells how Nothelm, 'a devout priest of the Church in London' (later Archbishop of Canterbury, A.D. 735-40), had made a journey to Rome and obtained permission from Pope Gregory II to examine the papal archives, and to make copies of all letters relevant to the mission of Augustine and the subsequent progress of the Church in England. Doubtless a considerable number of documents were also available at Canterbury. Bede also mentions that he had sought and obtained assistance from various provincial bishops. He mentions in particular Bishop Daniel of the West Saxons, who had provided information about that province and the Isle of Wight; Abbot Esius, who gave facts about East Anglia; and the monks of Lastingham, who did the same for Mercia. And while Bede is naturally best acquainted with events in his own Northumbria, he is careful to supplement and check his facts by recourse to 'innumerable witnesses', such as his friend Bishop Acca and the monks of Lindisfarne, to whom he submitted the draft of his *Life of Saint Cuthbert* for their comment and approval.

Bede's industry and scholarship are generally acknowledged, but his most significant achievement lies in his inspired ability to select and integrate the vast mass of facts and traditions that he had gathered into a single framework. He doubtless rejected much material as unreliable or irrelevant, but all that he retained he welded together into a coherent and eminently readable unity. Even a modern historian, with the advantage of greatly superior facilities and assisted by the researches of many generations of experts, faces a formidable task when compiling a history covering several centuries. And when we consider Bede's limited facilities and resources, it is clear that his achievement is unique. For although Bede's monastery at Jarrow possessed a library, it would seem insignificant by modern standards, and while it contained theological works of the Greek and Latin Fathers, there was little material useful for Bede's purpose except Gildas' *History* and a number of individual *Lives,* such as Constantius' *Life of Saint Germanus* and Possidius' *Life of Saint Augustine.* Furthermore, in addition to the slowness and uncertainty of communications, the physical conditions under which the writers of that day had to work were extremely inconvenient and austere during the long northern winters. Writing to Lullus, Archbishop of Mainz, not long after Bede's death, Abbot Cuthbert of Wearmouth apologizes for the delay in sending copies of Bede's works for which the Archbishop had asked, and explains that the hands of the scribes had been so numbed by the bitter winter weather that they had been forced to discontinue their work for considerable periods. And it is easy to visualize the ageing Bede himself, wrapped in a sheepskin cloak, busily working away under such conditions with a pile of documents on his desk, and rising from time to time to beat his frozen limbs into restored circulation. But it is noteworthy that despite the many difficulties under which it was written, Bede's *History* contains relatively few errors, and modern research has confirmed the accuracy of most of his statements. In his Preface Bede himself concedes that there may be unintentional inaccuracies in his pages, and begs the reader not to blame him too severely since, 'as the laws of history demand, I have laboured honestly to transmit whatever I could learn from common report for the instruction of posterity.' And although he is remarkably accurate and well informed on events in his own north country where he is able to check facts and interrogate responsible persons, he is naturally on less sure ground when dealing with happenings in far distant provinces. Nevertheless he makes every attempt to verify facts and present them in an orderly sequence, and to give us an accurate insight into the beliefs, customs, and everyday life of the times.

Like all writers, Bede is influenced by the circumstances and outlook of his own day, and some of his personal convictions are clearly indicated in his interpretations of events. The modern reader may find it difficult to envisage the intensity of feeling aroused by such matters as the paschal controversy, or he may consider Bede unduly prejudiced when he describes the Britons as *perfida gens*—a faithless race—because of their refusal to admit Augustine's jurisdiction (II. 2). In such matters Bede reflects the viewpoint of his race and generation as we of our own, but he is free from all pettiness and personal rancour, and never stoops to misrepresent the actions of those whose convictions he cannot share. For instance, although a convinced up-holder of Roman customs as against Celtic,

he records the lives and holiness of the Celtic saints with unstinted admiration, and writes of the Roman and Celtic leaders with equal justice and appreciation. An eloquent tribute to these noble qualities in Bede was paid by Bishop Hensley Henson of Durham in 1935 on the twelve hundredth anniversary of the former's death: 'The more closely Bede's career is studied, the more amazing it appears. In him two streams of spiritual influence seemed to meet and blend—the evangelistic passion of the Celtic missionaries, and the disciplined devotion of the Benedictine monks. He was near enough to the original conversion to have personal links with those who had companied with the missionaries from Iona, and to feel the thrill of their triumphant enthusiasm: and yet he was remote enough to have grown up in another atmophere, and to have been shaped by the system which disallowed and replaced theirs. He was too near not to know their merits; too generous not to recognize them; too religious not to revere their sanctity; too wise not to perceive their defects. So he stood at the point of a new departure—a Benedictine monk in the yet living tradition of Celtic piety, an English student in the rich treasury of Celtic learning, a disciple of Rome inspired by the intellectual passion of Ireland.' . . .

James Campbell (essay date 1968)

SOURCE: James Campbell, in an introduction to *Bede: The Ecclesiastical History of the English People and Other Selections,* edited by James Campbell, Washington Square Press, Inc., 1968, pp. vii-xxxiv.

[*In the following excerpt, Campbell provides an overview of Bede's work and concludes that, at least in part, Bede transmuted the past into his own creation which reflected mainly his own values.*]

Bede was born about 673 and died in 735. He entered the monastery of Monkwearmouth (Wearmouth), in Northumbria, at the age of seven, and the remainder of his life was spent there and in the sister monastery of Jarrow.[1] Today he is famous chiefly as the historian of the conversion of England. But he also wrote on almost every other branch of Christian learning; in his own day, and for long afterwards, his commentaries on the Bible and his treatises on chronology and other subjects were as much valued as his history.

It is remarkable that the most notable scholar the Western Church produced at that time should have lived in Northumbria, nearly at the extremity of the known world, and that he should have sprung from a people who had very recently been pagan and illiterate. In Bede's day, although most of the churches of Europe were very old, the English church was very new. In Gaul, Italy, and Spain Christianity survived the fall of the Roman Empire and won over the barbarian conquerors. But the English (Anglo-Saxon) people who, after the departure of the Romans in the early fifth century, occupied the southern and eastern parts of Britain, for long remained pagan and little affected by Roman civilization.

Christianity had been quite strongly established in Britain while the Romans ruled there. It survived the Roman evacuation in those areas of the west and north where the native British population remained free from Anglo-Saxon rule. The Christian Britons seem to have made little attempt to convert the invaders. Christianity was brought to the Anglo-Saxons by missionaries from overseas, most of them Italians or Irishmen.

The first mission of which we know is that of Augustine, who arrived from Rome in 597. He established Christianity in Kent, and he and his Italian followers attempted to convert other kingdoms. Their success was limited and insecure. For a generation the fate of Christianity among the Anglo-Saxons hung in the balance. Thereafter the faith spread quickly and prospered. By 660 it was established in nearly every kingdom.[2] This success was due largely to the efforts of Irish missionaries. Christianity had flourished in Ireland from the fifth century, and by the end of the sixth the Irish church was becoming notable both for its learning and for its missionary enterprise. The most important Irish mission to England was that led by Aidan, who came to Northumbria in 635 from the Irish monastery of Iona, off the west coast of Scotland. Aidan founded the monastery of Lindisfarne in Northumbria. From this base the Irish evangelized Northumbria and much of the English Midlands. At the same time the Roman missionaries based in Canterbury remained active in the southeast; a few years previously they had even made an attempt to convert Northumbria, though with only temporary success. Meanwhile other missionaries, owing allegiance neither to Canterbury nor to Iona, appeared elsewhere in England.

Thus by 660 Christianity had been very successful in England; but English Christians were not united in recognizing a common ecclesiastical authority. Some acknowledged the authority of the archbishop of Canterbury in England and that of the Pope over the whole church. Others looked to Lindisfarne and to Iona. It may well be that some elements in the church recognized no superior authority at all. Before long, all were to recognize the supremacy of Canterbury and of Rome.

In 664 the Irish church in Northumbria accepted the Roman mode of calculating Easter, and an important cause of disunity was thus removed. Even more significant in the unification of the English church was the influence of the pontificate of Theodore, archbishop of Canterbury from 668 to 690. Theodore was a native of Asia Minor and about sixty-seven years old when he arrived in England. Despite these disadvantages he established the authority of Canterbury over all the other English sees. Other great changes came about at the same time. Centers of learning grew up at Canterbury and elsewhere, and many new monasteries were founded. The English church, which had been largely directed by foreign missionaries, became a native one, nearly all of whose bishops were English. By the end of the century the English were themselves sending missionaries to western Germany.

Bede's own monastery of Monkwearmouth-Jarrow played an important part in this prosperous and revolutionary period. Founded in 674 by Benedict Biscop, a Northumbrian nobleman, it was distinguished by its learning, its close connections with Rome and Canterbury, and its size. Its founder endowed it with a great library. A frequent visitor to Rome, he was closely associated with Theodore and was for a time abbot of the monastery of St. Peter and St. Paul in Canterbury. By 716 his foundation held six hundred or more monks. Monkwearmouth-Jarrow was outstanding among the monasteries of Northumbria, and there were few which could rival it in the whole of England.

Bede's work reflects the exceptional circumstances of his house. Its library enabled him to become very learned. The study of the literature of pagan Greece and Rome was unimportant for him, although he had access to at least a few of the Latin classics. His learning was in Christian Latin literature, whose core was the works of the Latin Fathers: Ambrose, Jerome, Augustine, Gregory. This literature presented an account of God, of man, and of the universe which was complete, unified, and satisfying. Thanks to its double inheritance from Judaism and from Greece and Rome, Christianity had developed an intricate and sophisticated intellectual system. Centered on the elaborate interpretation of the Bible to reveal many layers of meaning, it established relationships between every kind of knowledge and showed how all proclaimed the same divine truths. By Bede's time few could read this literature with full understanding. Literacy was rare and unbroken traditions of learning much rarer. There were learned men in the seventh century, especially in Spain and Ireland, but they were not numerous—though it is true that we can learn much more easily of the minority of scholars who wrote than of the majority who simply read. During the Dark Ages Christianity might have lost its theology and have become for all what it became for nearly all: a collection of rituals, precepts, and crude arguments. That it survived as more than the barbarized detritus of a religion is thanks to the preservation of the Christian learning of the later Roman Empire and its continued study, however faltering and by however few. The continuance of that tradition was much more important in the intellectual history of Europe than the incidental preservation of the classics. Bede played an important part in continuing it. His

Page from late eighth-century transcription of Bede's Historia ecclesiastica gentis Anglorum.

wide range of works rested heavily upon, and were intended to transmit, the learning of his predecessors.

As a historian Bede found his models and sources in the histories written by Christians in and after the fourth century. Three features of Christian historiography should be noticed First, it owed very little to the great historians of Greece and Rome. As Arnaldo Momigliano has written, "No real Christian historiography founded upon the political experience of Herodotus, Thucydides, Livy and Tacitus was transmitted to the Middle Ages." The Christian historians made a fresh start in new genres, and the change was not necessarily for the worse. Second, there was no clear division between history and theology. All knowledge was knowledge of God. Few, if any, learned men specialized in history and certainly Bede did not. Most histories were written by men who also wrote on other aspects of divine learning. Third, there were several kinds of Christian history, and the different genres were kept fairly distinct from one another. One author writing in two different genres can give very different impressions of himself.

Bede wrote in most of the historical genres known to him. The contrast between two of them may be seen by comparing his chronicles with his *Life of St. Cuthbert*. His work in one genre is terse, packed with facts, and dry; in the other it is discursive, not containing so much as a date, and very readable. Bede wrote two chronicles, a short one which formed part of his book *On the Measurements of Time* (703) and a longer and better one which was included in *On the Computation of Time* (725).[3] Chronicles were little more than lists of dates and events. Bede's short chronicle is an extreme example. A typical passage is this:

> The third age contains 942 years. Abraham came into Canaan at the age of 75. At the age of 100 Abraham begat Isaac. For he first begat Ishmael, from whom the Ishmaelites. Isaac at the age of 60 begat Jacob. The kingdom of the Argives begins. Jacob begat Joseph at the age of 90. Memphis in Egypt is founded. Joseph lived for ninety years. Greece began to have crops under Argos. The captivity of the Hebrews for 147 years. Cecrops founded Athens. Moses ruled Israel for forty years. Sparta is founded. . . .[4]

Such works seem neither enlightening nor agreeable to the modern reader. Nevertheless they were very important in Christian historiography. The genre was established by Eusebius, bishop of Cæsarea (*c*.260-*c*.340), and thereafter numerous chronicles were compiled. They indicate one of the consequences of the spread of Christianity in the Roman world. Educated Christians knew two traditions of world history, one pagan and the other Christian and Jewish. Chronicles correlated the two so that the reader might learn, for example, what was happening to the Jews at the time

of the foundation of Rome. One of the great distinctions between pagan and Christian scholars in history, as in much else, was that the Christians knew more, or thought they did; and they had a philosophy which enabled them to interpret all they knew. For example, the Bible afforded data which made it possible to calculate the date of the Creation.

More important, a chronicle, in summarizing the whole history of the world, made it possible to display it as a Providential design. This could be done in various ways, but Bede was chiefly attracted by the doctrine of the Ages of the World. Each of his two chronicles was written as part of the chapter on Ages in a treatise on chronology. The history of the world so far was divided into six ages. Each corresponded to one of the six ages of a man's life and also to one of the days of Creation as described in Genesis. The sixth age had begun with the birth of Christ, and its termination would mark the end of the world. Bizarre though this theory now sounds, its comprehensiveness in establishing connections between the life of man, the course of history, creation, and judgment made it a very powerful one. Bede's concern with the exact length of each of the ages made him very careful about dates, and he was the first to correct the biblical chronology of Eusebius. The purpose of such a chronicle as Bede's first one was simply to sketch the history of the world in accordance with a Providential interpretation. His much fuller second chronicle shows how easily such a work could do more than this by serving as a vehicle for almost any kind of historical information.

The Life of St. Cuthbert, which Bede wrote in about 720, is in a very different genre, that of hagiography. It consists almost entirely of beautifully told miracle stories and does not reveal even when its hero was born or when he died. Books of this kind were numerous and more influential than any other kind of history, if they can be called history. They derive from great changes which came about in the Christian church in and after the fourth century. In the third century, belief in contemporary, as opposed to biblical, miracles was not widespread, at least among the sophisticated. Belief in the frequent intervention of God to produce physical miracles and in the omnipresence of devils and angels became much more common from the fourth century. It seems to have been associated with the spread of monasticism from the east. Monks and miracles (which together may have changed the Church as much as the Reformation did when it sought to expel them) came in together. One book, *The Life of St. Anthony* by Athanasius, was of great importance in their proliferation. Written in about 360 (in Greek, but soon translated into Latin), it described the life of Anthony, who lived as a hermit in Egypt until his death in 356. It is simply an account of virtues and marvels, vividly told. As the kind of Christianity which Athanasius described spread, so did imitations of his book. Such lives of the saints differed from one another in various respects but in general conformed to type. They record in some detail the circumstances of their subject's early life, his conversion to religion, his godly conduct, and the manner in which he died. Their main concern is not mundane details, but spiritual triumphs: the cures the saint wrought, the devils he put to flight. Hagiographers were often careful to state their evidence, as Bede does. The more remarkable the story, the more desirable it was that it should be supported. Such statements are not necessarily evidence of scholarly care, but went with this genre of writing. Saints' lives were for edification rather than for record (they were often read out, in whole or in part, on the saint's day), and their authors looked more to the effect they would have in the future than to what had actually happened in the past. Bede's *Life of St. Cuthbert* is a typical and very skillful piece of hagiography. He took a previous "Life of Cuthbert" by an anonymous monk, rewrote it, and modified it in certain respects, inserting additional miracles and giving a much longer account of Cuthbert's death. When he wrote in other genres he displayed great interest in facts and in detailed information. In writing this life he gave fewer facts, particularly topographical facts, than did his source.

Bede's greatest work, *The Ecclesiastical History of the English People,* completed in 731 or 732, represents yet another genre of Christian historiography. Its title recalls that of its model, *The Ecclesiastical History* of Eusebius. In this work Eusebius described the history of the Church from apostolic times until about 325. He sought to relate all the main events in the life of the Church, saying something of the outstanding Christians of each generation. Particular care was taken to record the succession of bishops in the principal sees, the details of heretics and heresies, persecutions and the passions of martyrs. As in his *Chronicle* so in his *History,* Eusebius was the father of a new kind of historiography. His work was distinguished from those of pagan historians not only by its content but also by its methods, in particular by his extensive citation of sources and his inclusion of many original documents. Here, too, Christian scholarship broke new ground. Bede sought to do for the church of England what Eusebius had done for the whole, and his *Ecclesiastical History* much resembles his predecessor's in content and in method.

Bede knew at least two other Christian histories of importance—*The Seven Books Against the Pagans* by Orosius and *The History of the Franks* by Gregory of Tours. They have to be considered beside his *Ecclesiastical History* not so much because of their contribution to it as because of their contrast with it. Orosius wrote his book in 417 to 418; it described and interpreted the history of mankind from the Creation to his own day and was intended as a riposte to those who accounted for the fall of Rome by pointing to the rise of Christianity. Orosius collected catastrophes and misfortunes to show that God had smitten the pagans hard, often, and deservedly.[5] His own times he argued to be better. For him, history fell into a pattern, that of the Four Empires: Babylon, Macedonia, Carthage, and Rome. The history of each of them had followed a similar course; Rome and Babylon were especially alike, and "the number seven by which all things are decided" was demonstrated to have been very important for both. The last empire, that of Rome, was shown to have been established by God in preparation for the advent of Christ. Orosius's scheme of explanation was crude, if elaborate. But his work was orthodox and popular, and his large store of information was drawn on by many, including Bede. Bede also followed him in beginning his work with a geographical introduction. He did not follow him in imposing a pattern upon history. For Orosius, Providence worked like a machine. Bede shows God's purpose and judgment always at work, but makes little attempt to schematize them.

Bede was not the first Christian historian to write on the history of one people. The only such national historian whose work was certainly known to him was Gregory of Tours (*c.* 540-594). Gregory's history was in a sense an ecclesiastical history and has resemblances to Bede's. But it is his contrast with Bede which impresses. Gregory's work is very much that of a bishop of Tours, a great man who participated in great events. He provides a detailed, scandalous, and vivid account of affairs in his own lifetime. He recounts many miracles, often to indicate the power of St. Martin and how he watched over his own see of Tours. Bede was very much more detached. His concern was to omit secular affairs and any kind of scandal. His descriptions of the miraculous are not intended to exalt his own monastery, and he makes no attempt to demonstrate that saints protect their shrines and followers in secular affairs. The temper of his work is entirely different from Gregory's, and the comparison brings home to us that one of the most remarkable things about *The Ecclesiastical History* is the number of things which one would expect an eighth century historian to say which Bede does *not* say.

In writing *The Ecclesiastical History* Bede looked back then to Eusebius and to the beginnings of Christian historiography. There are, indeed, important differences between his work and that of his predecessor. There is nothing in Eusebius to correspond with the geographical and historical introduction to his subject which Bede provides in the first book of *The Ecclesiastical History.* Bede's continual concern with the miraculous reflects a religious climate unlike that in which Eusebius wrote. Bede had to pay more attention to secular affairs, partly because the fortunes of Christianity were more closely involved with those of secular powers than they had been in the early days of the Church, and partly because Bede, and his sources, were more concerned than was Eusebius to emphasize the judgments of God on good and bad rulers. Furthermore, Bede is more concerned to be directly edifying, to use history to teach particular moral lessons. Nevertheless, Bede's history is, as its title implies, modeled on that of Eusebius. Its dominant concern is the same: to describe the principal events in the history of the Church, the succession of its bishops, its heresies, and its saints. His technique, in particular his extensive use of documents, often cited verbatim, also derives from Eusebius. Many of his virtues are those of his model.

Bede's account of the history of his church often leaves the reader admiring, but baffled. It is not hard to understand why *The Ecclesiastical History* should have become famous. Important and interesting events are described, and often made moving, by an extremely accomplished storyteller. Bede's citation of sources, his care with dates, and his inclusion of many documents argue his reliability. The impression is reinforced by his calm and moderate tone. Bede seems both pious and sound and has to a high degree the power of conviction. Nevertheless, *The Ecclesiastical History* seems oddly diverse and incomplete. The narrative of events is constantly broken by accounts of miracles and visions. Sometimes Bede rambles, as in the fifth book where, having mentioned Adamnan, abbot of Iona, he proceeds to devote two chapters to extracts from Adamnan's book on the Holy Places. Disproportionate space seems to be given to controversy over the date of Easter. Surprisingly little is said about Bede's own time, about which one would suppose him to have known most. His book seems a disjointed series of stories and documents held together by an accomplished style.

The unevenness of Bede's narrative is partly to be explained by the nature of his sources and by the way in which he used them. He was able to use the work of earlier historians for the first book, which describes the history of Britain from the time of Julius Cæsar until the coming of Augustine. In spite of the active search for materials, which he describes in his Preface, it was not easy for him to find them for more recent times. It was not normal in the seventh century for churches, let alone kingdoms, to keep records of their doings. Bede probably had some scanty annals from Kent and Northumbria, and a few royal genealogies and lists recording the lengths of the reigns of kings. For the most part, he was dependent on letters, chiefly from Rome, on a handful of saints' lives, and on numerous but doubtfully reliable oral traditions. He did not feel it to be his duty to criticize his sources as a modern historian would (although his theological work shows that he could have been acute in such criticism). The true law of history is, he says, simply to gather and record for the benefit of posterity such stories as are in circulation. It was a new experience for Bede to

write a book on a subject about which no one had written before. His inclination was to follow what others had written, and the result was patchwork. Where we know what his sources were, and they have survived, he can be seen often to have followed them word for word, or very nearly so. This is the case in, for example, I, xvii-xx, which comes from a life of St. Germanus by Constantius, and in III, xix, which comes from an anonymous life of Fursey. One wonders how far Bede treated in the same way those of his sources which are unknown to us, and whether *The Ecclesiastical History* was not written by first establishing a chronological framework and then hanging to it by such verbal hooks as "At that time," "In the meantime," such materials as came to hand, frequently in the form in which they came to hand.

Nevertheless, it will not do to dismiss *The Ecclesiastical History* as no more than a collection of materials. Bede was both selective and subtle. His principles of selection were largely those of Eusebius. For example, like Eusebius he gave particular attention to heresy. But while Eusebius had had numerous heresies to record, Bede had to deal with only one heresy, Pelagianism, and one error, the adherence of some of the Celtic churches to the wrong mode of calculating the date of Easter.

Bede has a long account of the Easter controversy in each of the last four books of his history. It is at first sight not easy to understand why he should have given so much attention to what appears to us as a merely technical issue; for the practice of the Celts seems to have been simply that which had been used elsewhere in the past but which had become superseded. But Bede makes it very clear that the calculation of the date of Easter was not a merely technical or isolated issue. The movement of Easter was one of many things which argument in terms of symbols (as we would say, but *symbol* is for us a limiting word, *mysteries* they would say) showed to be loaded with significance. Easter had to be just at the equinox, for the lengthening days represented Christ's triumph over the powers of darkness. It had to be in the first month of the lunar year, for this was the month in which the world had been created and in which it ought to be newly created. It had to be as the moon was about to wane, for the moon turns from earth toward the sun as it wanes, just as we should turn from earthly to heavenly things. It was appropriate that Easter should always fall within a space of seven days, for seven was a number of divine significance. Considered from another point of view, Easter was to be calculated in such a way as to fulfill both the Old Law of the Jews and the New Law of Christ. If it was celebrated at exactly the right time, then all was in harmony. Nothing can illustrate the gulf between Bede's thought-world and ours more vividly than his views on Easter. Such views were not simple popular piety. They formed part of an elaborate and not unsophisticated system of thought, which brought all knowledge into unity and to divine ends, and whose power depended on the capacity to see an allegory as a mysterious truth rather than as an illustration or a coincidence. Divergence between churches on such a matter as Easter was not a trivial matter. It was a rent in the seamless garment, and it is not surprising that Bede, who was by far the most learned man of his day on computation, should have devoted much of his history to this issue.

Bede's concern was not just to record certain kinds of information and to refute certain kinds of error. His Preface emphasizes that his concern is to edify, to describe the good so that it may be followed and the bad so that it may be shunned. *The Ecclesiastical History* was probably intended for a wider audience than were most of Bede's works, and is dedicated to a king. In his account of good kings (and no laymen other than kings have more than an incidental role), Bede shows how virtue was rewarded here and now as well as hereafter. It was not only heavenly but also earthly kingdoms which Oswald and Edwin gained. There are passages in which he makes his point in a way that is forceful to the point of crudity. He shows that just as those who adhered to the faith did well, so did those who abandoned it fail. Edwin, who brought Christianity to Northumbria, lived in unexampled peace and prosperity. His apostate successors perished miserably and soon. Nevertheless, Bede prefers to dwell upon the rewards of the good rather than on the punishments of the bad. Cadwallon, king of the Britons, is condemned in strong language, but briefly, and his violent and merited death is not dwelt upon. Even Penda, the pagan terror of England in the middle of the seventh century, is treated only incidentally, and Bede attributes worthy sentiments to him. There is no long account of any bad Christian king; indeed, no Christian English kings are said to have been bad, though one or two royal crimes are mentioned.

It is remarkable of Bede's picture of Providence at work in politics that, while he is clear that a causal connection between virtue and success was easy to observe, he makes little effort to explain the whole course of English history in Providential terms and to show God's rewards and punishments to whole peoples. He might, in the manner of Orosius, have chosen to show the pagan Saxon period as one of disaster and misery. In fact, he has almost nothing to say about it— though perhaps he did not know enough to say more. On only two occasions does he elaborate on the punishment visited in this world upon a sinful nation: in his account of Britain after the departure of the Romans and in the story of how the Britons were punished for not yielding to Augustine. In the first instance, his account and its emphasis came straight from the sixth century British historian Gildas, in the second, from some lost source.[6] Although he adopted such

views when they occurred in his sources, he makes almost no independent attempt to show that the Britons suffered for their persistence in the errors he detested. The opportunity was there. He could have described the great conquests made in the late seventh century by the West Saxons at the expense of the Britons, and have presented them as those of God's chosen people, accurate in their Easter reckonings. Instead, he merely mentions the subjugation of some of the Britons and associates it with their errors, very briefly, in V, xxiii. Similarly, although, as we know from his *Letter to Egbert,* he disapproved of much that went on in the Church in his own day, he does not elaborate on this in his history and draw the moral that punishment was at hand, as some historians would have done. Instead, Bede says nothing at all in his history about the sins of the Church, but emphasizes the peacefulness of his own times in England. Even so, he does not say that the acceptance of Christianity and orthodoxy have brought peace and prosperity. If the connection is made it is by implication, and there are undertones of disquiet. Unlike many of his predecessors, he found it hard to see a clear pattern in God's judgments except where individuals were concerned. He is more reserved, less vehement, perhaps more troubled.

If *The Ecclesiastical History* has many lessons for the laity, it has more for the clergy. One of its principal functions is to set them good examples. Bede's account of what the church of England had been in the past is affected by his judgment of what it was and what it ought to have been in his own day. In *The Ecclesiastical History* Bede has very little to say about events in England after 690, and he does not make his views on the contemporary church explicit. But, thanks to the preservation of his *Letter to Egbert,* written to the bishop of York in 734, we know that some of them were unfavorable. The conduct of bishops, monks, priests, and laity all left much to be desired. Avarice, neglect, and ignorance were all too prevalent. His biblical commentaries shed further light on his attitudes. They showed him to have held strict views on the proper conduct of the clergy, and in particular on clerical poverty. How rich the clergy may properly be was, and remains, a subject for argument. Bede was adamant that they ought to be poor. Granted Bede's preference for praising the good rather than denouncing the bad, and his belief, made quite clear in his commentaries, that it is wrong publicly to denounce the clergy, be they never so wicked, it seems that his reticence in his history on the recent past of his church is largely to be explained by his disapproval of some of its members and their acts.

Modern knowledge of the early eighth century church is very incomplete, but the sources suffice to give some idea of those aspects of its life to which Bede objected. Some bishops had become powerful in the things of this world. Such a bishop as Wilfrid was wealthy in land, in treasure, and in followers. Bede says bishops levied dues from every village in their dioceses, and there is other evidence indicating that the church had significant power to tax. There is some reason to suppose that bishops exercised considerable jurisdiction over laymen. When Bede says that Wine bought the see of London in about 666 (III, vii) it is a fair deduction that episcopal office was already remunerative. Such examples of clerical power can easily be paralleled on the Continent. But there bishops had been established for centuries, had inherited power from the days of the Empire, and had added to it as the Empire collapsed. In England some bishops seemed to have gained a comparable position for themselves, having started with nothing. From Bede's point of view much was amiss with monasteries also. Monasteries were numerous, but were often treated as the hereditary property of the founder's family, and the fiscal advantages of monastic tenure seem to have led to the foundation of monasteries which were such in name only. This is not to say that Bede disapproved of all that went on in the church in his day, and we can see that if some elements in it were worldly others were rigidly pious, as he was. The codes of penances and secular laws of the period indicate a desire (there is no means of telling how far it was fulfilled) to make the Christian English observe the letter of a strict law. For example, "If a freeman works on Sunday without his lord's command he is to lose his freedom." Piety is not inconsistent with wealth, nor indeed are strict laws inconsistent with avarice, but it is likely that there were many like Bede who were both pious and unworldly. The English church was not only prosperous but diverse, containing Christians at very different levels of sophistication and, one may guess, sophisticated Christians whose views varied widely. It was faced with the opportunities and problems which occur when an erstwhile missionary church becomes part of society and changes its nature as it changes that of society.

If *The Ecclesiastical History* is read in the light of Bede's views on the church in his own day, it can be seen to be (among other things) an implicit commentary on it. In setting good examples from the past, Bede is especially concerned with bishops. Monks and monasteries are not neglected, but his long accounts are nearly all of bishops, and he has surprisingly little to say even of his own monastery. Bede's first account of a model bishop is that of Augustine in I, xxvi. Augustine is said to have lived in accordance with the mode of the Primitive Church in devotion, in poverty, in steadfastness, in practicing what he preached. Emphasis on the same virtues recurs in Bede's accounts of later bishops such as Aidan, Chad, and Cuthbert. He lays particular stress on poverty. Pope Gregory[7] told Augustine that he ought to live with his followers with all things in common as in the Primitive Church, and

Bede later adopts this statement in describing Hilda. He admired a humble way of life, and points out that the bishops of the Celtic church preferred to walk rather than to ride—though Theodore made Chad ride in order to get about his diocese. The virtues of such men were in obvious contrast to the grasping bishops of his own day, to whose jolly parties he refers in *The Letter to Egbert*. Aidan's way of life was, he says, very different from the idleness of our days. In describing Cuthbert's reception when he went about preaching, he says that in those days people flocked to the preacher. The implication is that in his own day they did not.

Bede treats different bishops in different ways. For Aidan we have some account of the events of his life, a eulogy of the way in which he lived it, and a collection of miracles; for John of Hexham, miracles and almost nothing else; for Theodore a long account of his deeds, nothing of his way of life, and no miracles at all. It is possible to explain these striking differences as the reflection of the differences between Bede's sources and of Bede's deference to his sources. Bede was not concerned, one may think, to give a methodical account of the lives of each of these men, but simply inserted such useful and edifying material as he could find. Such an explanation is valid but not complete. Bede compiled where a modern historian would have edited, but he edited where a modern historian would have compiled.

The extent to which Bede was capable of editing his material in such a way as to exclude the unedifying may be seen from his treatment of Wilfrid. Most of what Bede says in *The Ecclesiastical History* is beyond criticism insofar as we have no other source describing the same events. But a contemporary biography of Wilfrid, probably by his follower Eddius, has survived, and it affords a rare opportunity of comparing Bede's treatment of a subject with that of another man, less able but also less discreet. An early supporter of Roman orthodoxy in Northumbria, Wilfrid was an active founder of monasteries, a successful missionary and, from 669, a bishop in Northumbria. His career was stormy. He seems to have hoped to make himself supreme over the church in the north, and so fell out with successive kings of Northumbria and archbishops of Canterbury. In spite of several periods of exile and one of imprisonment, he survived and prospered. Eddius was a very dutiful biographer and shows the great bishop in all his glory: ascetic, brave, and always right. His holiness was made evident by miracles. At the same time it is made clear that Wilfrid was rich and determined to preserve his riches, and his style of life seems to have been much like that of a great secular lord. His deathbed as described by Eddius is extremely instructive and very different from anything Bede tells us of a bishop. He divided his property into several shares. One of these was to reward the men who had followed him into exile and to whom he had not given land; they sound very like a *comitatus,* a band of warriors who followed a great lord. Part of his treasure was to go to his monasteries to purchase the favor of kings and bishops. Never in his history does Bede give us to understand that a bishop might have a *comitatus* or a treasure, still less that there were bishops whose favor might be bought. His *Letter to Egbert* suggests that he knew perfectly well that such things happened, and two passages in the *Life of St. Cuthbert* associate being made a bishop with becoming wealthy.[8] But he did not regard such matters as a subject for history. It is nearly certain that Bede had Eddius's *Life of Wilfrid,* at least by the time he came to write V, xix; but he uses Eddius with discretion, and his survey of Wilfrid's career is very carefully edited. Nothing is said of Wilfrid's wealth and style of life. His quarrels are treated very discreetly; his imprisonment is not mentioned; his conflicts with other bishops are barely touched upon; a whole council is omitted. In describing such an edifying episode as the conversion of Sussex, Bede attributes near-miraculous powers to Wilfrid, but he relates none of the miracles which Eddius describes to show how God fought on Wilfrid's side in his struggle for episcopal power.

In the light of Bede's treatment of Wilfrid one begins to wonder about his account of Archbishop Theodore. He gives just a hint that he may not have approved of all Theodore's doings when he praises a bishop whom Theodore deposed (IV, vi). Although he usually refers to Theodore as "of blessed memory," he has nothing to say of his personal holiness or of his way of life. No miracles are attributed to him. It is slightly surprising that Bede, who is willing to supply fifty-four lines of verse on an abbess about whom he has already had a good deal to say (IV, xx), should abbreviate the epitaph of so important a man as Theodore (V, viii). Can it be that he did not think well of all that Theodore did, and did the middle of the epitaph describe something of which he disapproved? The problem is typical of those which arise when Bede's history is analyzed. Three kinds of answer are possible. First, it may be that the contrast between his treatment of Theodore and that of some other bishops simply reflects differences between his sources. In particular, the absence of miracles seems characteristic of Bede's Canterbury sources. He describes very few miracles performed by the archbishops or by other members of the Roman church in Kent. Second, it may be that the selection of material for his book was partly determined by incidental reasons of space, time, or chance. Either of these explanations could account for the nature of his treatment of Theodore. But they do not exclude the third, which is that he may have edited his sources, suppressing or abbreviating that which he found unedifying.

For all the superficial simplicity of *The Ecclesiastical History* it is not a simple book. Bede was a very intelligent, learned, and devout man, dealing with subjects which were very difficult (difficult not only because of deficiency of information, but because of the religious problems involved) and according to strongly held principles which were not always quite consistent with one another. The nature of his difficulties and some of the explanation of his power to move may be seen in his treatment of miracles. *The Ecclesiastical History* is full of miracles and visions. Their number may surprise the modern reader, but it is not hard to explain. They may be considered as the equivalent of Eusebius's account of the passions of martyrs. Bede sometimes tells us why he puts a particular story in; it will, he says, be useful (meaning spiritually useful) to his readers. A large part of what sources he had consisted of miracle stories. For all these reasons much of *The Ecclesiastical History* is hagiographical in style, content, and method. Wonder follows wonder. Now recent and contemporary (as opposed to biblical) miracles had for long raised severe difficulties for the thinking Christian. In sophisticated milieux there was the problem of incredulity. On the other side there was the danger (perhaps a worse one) of an endless hunger for the miraculous. Pope Gregory the Great warned more than once (for example, in the letter copied out in I, xxi) that not all saints performed miracles, that miracles could be performed by the wicked, that virtues were more important than wonders. Bede repeats his warnings. Yet both Gregory and Bede retail endless miracles. "They seem to speak with two voices." The difficulty may have been greater for Bede than it was for Gregory, for Bede lived among barbarian Christians and barbarized Christianity was largely a matter of wonders.

Although Bede was a devout believer in miracles and an assiduous collector of miracle stories, nevertheless he seems to have been selective in what he included in *The Ecclesiastical History*. A high proportion of the miracles recorded there are the kind which are susceptible of a natural explanation, particularly miracles of healing. Clearly, he was not at all concerned to explain miracles away; but he does seem to have preferred to avoid the more flabbergasting of them. There are several analogues of scriptural miracles, but he never gives an instance of the raising of the dead. His miracles are usually to demonstrate the saintliness of a particular person or to reinforce some teaching. They are not random wonders. None have any political force; they do not demonstrate how God defended the rights of a particular shrine or of a particular man in a worldly struggle. In all these respects Bede is in sharp contrast to most of those who described miracles.

Perhaps the most influential collection of miracle stories was Gregory the Great's *Dialogues.* Bede knew this book and his style of narration may well owe something to it. But the differences between Bede and

Gregory are more instructive than the similarities. Some of Gregory's miracles are brutal. For example, he tells of an unfortunate man who was struck dead because his playing on the cymbals disturbed a bishop at prayer. Others are trumpery, as in the case of Bishop Boniface's clearing his garden, by Divine aid, of caterpillars: "I adjure you in the name of Our Lord Christ, depart and stop eating those vegetables." It is fair to say that some of the animal miracles which Bede relates of Cuthbert, but only of Cuthbert, are not very different from this tale, though much more impressively told. But his miracles are never brutal and rarely have the anecdotal triviality of many of Gregory's.

Bede's stories contrast even more strongly with those of Gregory of Tours and other Frankish writers. A recurrent theme in Gregory of Tours is the defense of the interests of Tours by God and St. Martin. There is nothing of this kind in Bede. In *The Ecclesiastical History* we never meet such common incidents of life in the Dark Ages as the alleged intervention of saints to protect their shrines and followers against all comers, or violent struggles for the possession of the body of a saint and the useful protection which was thought to come with it. It could be that such things did not happen in England. But this is unlikely and there is some evidence to the contrary. It is much more likely that Bede belonged to a school of thought which was uneasy about such aspects of Christianity among the barbarians and did not think it appropriate to record them. He tended to omit just the kinds of miracle and just the kinds of incident which most jar modern taste. There are exceptions to this. In particular, his accounts of visions of the next world indicate a harshness in his religion, which his preference for describing the good rather than the base generally conceals.

Selective though Bede was, his deference to his sources sometimes led him to introduce material which differs considerably in tone and emphasis from anything he himself wrote. This is most obvious in a comparison of the doctrinal disputes which he records in *The Ecclesiastical History*. His description of the repulse of Pelagianism by Germanus comes almost verbatim from Constantius's *Life of Germanus*.[9] This is a fine example of a hagiographer's view of a theological dispute. Nothing is said of the arguments on either side. We are informed simply that the heretics filled the air with empty words, whereupon the venerable prelates poured forth the flood of their apostolical and evengelical discourse and made them confess their errors to the cheers of the audience. Reasoning was of little significance to Constantius. What mattered most was divine demonstrations that Germanus was right: he could vanquish demons, work cures, and win victories. The account in Bede of Augustine's meeting with the Britons (II, ii) is in a similar vein. The power to cure is used as the touchstone of orthodoxy—"Let some sick man be brought." This account probably

came straight to Bede from a source lost to us. Very different indeed is Bede's account of the later progress of the Easter controversy, which is almost certainly much more his own work, and where we do not find miracles, devils, and cures, but solid and lucid arguments.

Thus Germanus, as described by Constantius, appears as a thaumaturge, not much above the level of a witch doctor; while Wilfrid, in his defense, as Bede describes it, of the Roman Easter, and Ceolfrith, in his letter to Nechtan, appear as the intellectual heirs of the Fathers and ultimately of the civilized learning of Greece and Rome. Germanus was debating subjects which are still thought important and probably always will be: the problems of sin and grace. Constantius's account disregards the issues and debases the subject. The protagonists of the Roman Easter were fighting for a cause which not even Rome now cares about. Bede's account of the case is so skillful that he exalts it to a point where one can almost believe it matters. Bede could, had he wished to do so, have put able arguments against Pelagianism into Germanus's mouth. He chose simply to take over Constantius's account: it was edifying, unexceptionable, and he was bound to give it simple faith. The unevenness of *The Ecclesiastical History* is partly due to Bede's devout acceptance of Christianity as it was expressed at different levels of sophistication.

If *The Ecclesiastical History* is much affected by the nature of Bede's sources it should be possible to see him more by himself in his account of the abbots of his own monastery, *The Lives of the Abbots*. This did not belong, as did most of his other works, to a more or less established genre, though another monk of Bede's monastery had written a *Life of Ceolfrith* which Bede used and which much resembles his own work in style and in content. It is the style of *The Lives of the Abbots* which first impresses the reader. Bede's extreme skill in emotive description can nowhere be better seen than in his accounts of the deaths of Benedict and Eosterwine, and of the departure of Ceolfrith. In using the work of his anonymous predecessor, he sometimes made an addition to heighten the pathos as, for example, when in saying that some of Ceolfrith's followers stayed beside his tomb at Langres, he adds that they were among a people not even whose language they knew. The book is in strong contrast with the *Life of St. Cuthbert* in including numerous facts and no miracles. Bede supplies a remarkable amount of information about the property and buildings of the abbey, and much chronological detail. There are many edifying stories, but not a single miracle. What little there is of the miraculous in the anonymous life of Ceolfrith is excluded. Bede does not say, as the Anonymous does, that his body remained uncorrupted and a light shone above it, and that miracles were reported at his tomb.

It may be that Bede did not regard this as the kind of book in which miracles were to be recorded. But no abbot or monk of Monkwearmouth-Jarrow is credited with miraculous powers in *The Ecclesiastical History* either; perhaps the religious atmosphere there was different from that at Lindisfarne or at Barking. As in *The Ecclesiastical History* Bede's purpose in *The Lives of the Abbots* is continuously didactic: only here he is showing the way to monks and abbots rather than to bishops and kings. Humbleness and simplicity are again emphasized. He is very concerned that it should be understood that the abbacy was not to descend by hereditary succession (as was common in other abbeys). There is just enough evidence to suggest that, for all the lavish detail of *The Lives of the Abbots,* it is edited to give the right impression. The anonymous life of Ceolfrith says that he once left Jarrow "because of the jealousies and most violent attacks of certain nobles, who could not endure his regular discipline." Bede says nothing of this, but it is to be observed that in his account of Eosterwine he is careful to emphasize that he did not expect unusual privileges because he was noble. *The Lives of the Abbots* is unlike *The Ecclesiastical History* in its consistency in style and content and in its exclusion of the miraculous. It is very like it insofar as its purpose is to teach lessons and to do so by dwelling upon the good and saying nothing of the bad.

Any judgment on Bede as a historian must be tempered. We do not know enough about his sources to be able to say even how much of *The Ecclesiastical History* is his in the sense of being more than a selection of stories incorporated much as they came to him. It is impossible to be certain how far there is an element of randomness in its composition. Above all, there are too few other authorities with which to compare him. There is no means of telling whether most of what he says about English history is right or wrong. Our relative ignorance of what the church was like in his own day makes it difficult to assess his attitude and purposes.

Despite the reservations which such difficulties impose, Bede can be seen to be a great historian. Modern historians often praise him because he seems much as they themselves are. Interested in his work mainly as a source, they value those qualities which are thought to vouch for his reliability. Such praise is justified only in part. Bede's greatness comes not only from qualities which would have made him a good historian by modern professional standards, but also from others which would have made him an extremely bad one. Certainly his extensive collection of material and his care for documents and dates make him more reliable than most Dark Age historians. Few, if any, brought such ability and expertise to their task. But to ability and expertise was added high moral purpose and the task Bede set himself was not to describe the history of the English church just as it had happened. It was to describe it in such a way as to illustrate and support the principles of faith and conduct in which he believed. As a consequence *The Ecclesiastical History* is in part an ably constructed record and in part a history idealized to the point of becoming visionary.

Bede was the first important Christian historian to have been a monk. Most of his predecessors had been great men in the secular church. Bede considered events with more detachment or with a different commitment than theirs. His demand for humbleness and poverty among the clergy stands in a tradition which, although always present in the church, had gained new strength with the advent of monasticism from the fourth century. Eusebius had not placed so strong an emphasis on the simple way of life of model bishops. A bishop himself, and basking in the favor of the Emperor Constantine, he had not, perhaps, seen the need so clearly. Bede's views on episcopacy are much more like those of the monk-bishop St. Martin of Tours, who, ascetic, devoted, and disheveled, was until his death in 397 an example and something of a threat to the prelates of Gaul. Bede's views on the proper conduct of the clergy made him opposed to much that went on around him. He stood for episcopal poverty and elected abbots at a time when at least some bishops were rich and powerful and some, perhaps many, abbots had inherited their offices. Soaked in the learning of the Fathers, who were very civilized, he lived among barbarian Christians whose beliefs and practices were often crude. Like Gregory the Great, he was both a devout believer in the frequent manifestation of miracles and mistrusted the consequences of that belief in others.

His history of his own church reflects the complications of his position. Characteristically, he looked a long way back for his model. Just as he had written a chronicle when that genre had been disused for nearly a century, so he wrote a history, not in the manner of his more immediate predecessors, but in that of Eusebius. He was too judicious to impose a simple Providential scheme as Orosius had done, and too reserved and discreet to make his work like that of Gregory of Tours, largely an account of recent events with moralizing commentary. He chose to infuse his record with his beliefs not in these obvious ways, but by emphasis and selection. He dwelt upon the good and passed lightly over the bad, in particular omitting almost everything that might be to the discredit of the church. Bede's views on the miracles, their importance and their dangers, appear by his insertion of numerous miracle stories and also, I think it fair to assume, by his omission of others of kinds popular with other believers and writers, but distasteful to him. His work is so full of awareness of God that it gives a very strange picture of man. Bede seems to lack almost all interest in human character except insofar as it could be represented in religious stereotypes. He had no taste for idiosyncrasy. While *The Ecclesiastical History* is full of very memorable incidents, there is hardly a character in it who appears in any degree individual. Events are typified in much the same way. Bede's principles and his caution led him to sheer away from his own times and from the complications and ambiguities of men and events as they really were and are.

These qualities are not those of a good historian in the modern sense. His history reflects not so much the nature of the past he described as his own nature. The impression which his work gives of calm, moderation, and judiciousness is justified. But, while these virtues led him to write history which was more accurate and technically more sophisticated than that of lesser men, they also made it less real and less revealing than theirs. Bede's power of mind, his narrative skill and, one might almost say, his good taste are employed to transmute the past and to carry the reader into a world which was partly of his own creation. Bede's greatness derives partly from the competence and usefulness of his history as record. Even more impressive is the learning, power of mind, and skill with which he made his account of the past a testament to his beliefs and a lesson to his church. . . .

Notes

1 Almost nothing is known of Bede's life apart from what he himself tells us in *The Ecclesiastical History,* p. 3. For his monastery see *The Lives of the Abbots.*

2 For the political geography of Britain see the note on pp. xxxii-xxxiv.

3 *De Temporibus* and *De Temporum Ratione.*

4 Ed. Mommsen, p. 255.

5 Considerable passages of the first book of Bede's *Ecclesiastical History* are taken directly from Orosius. For example, the second and sixth chapters are almost entirely in Orosius's words and give a fair impression of his terse style and of his gloomy view of the pagan past. . . .

6 Gildas, *c.* 500-*c.* 570, was a British monk whose rhetorical account of the overthrow of the Britons by the Anglo-Saxons, *On the Downfall of Britain,* was used by Bede, often extensively and verbatim, in *The Ecclesiastical History,* I, xii-xvi and xxii.

7 Gregory I, *c.* 540-604, Pope from 590. For an account of his life see *The Ecclesiastical History,* I, xxiii-xxxii and especially II, i.

8 Chapters viii and xxiv.

9 Germanus, *c.* 376-448, bishop of Auxerre. His biography was written by Constantius, *c.* 480. Chapters xvii-xxi of the first book of *The Ecclesiastical History* derive from this work and are, for the most part, in Constantius's words.

Peter Hunter Blair (lecture date 1969)

SOURCE: Peter Hunter Blair, "The Historical Writings of Bede," in *Anglo-Saxon Northumbria,* edited by M. Lapidge and P. Hunter Blair, Variorum Reprints, 1984, pp. 197-221.

[*In the following lecture originally presented in 1969, Blair defends Bede's historical writings against some modern-day critics who impugn the accuracy of his chronologies, accuse him of prejudice against the Celtic and Welsh churches, and suggest that he was fooled by forgeries and suppressed evidence.*]

Bede was born c. 671, about 260 years after the end of the Roman occupation of Britain, and about 225 years after what came to be regarded as the year in which the English first came to Britain. He died on 25 May 735, aged about 64. At the end of the *Historia Ecclesiastica Gentis Anglorum* he records that he had spent the whole of his life from the age of seven within the walls of the monastery at Wearmouth and Jarrow. Although the two places were physically separated from one another by a few miles, he regarded them as comprising only one single monastery dedicated to St. Peter and St. Paul. He writes that "amid the observance of monastic discipline and the daily charge of singing in the church, my delight has always been in learning, teaching or writing"[1]. We do not know the exact date of his earliest piece of writing, but it was about or soon after the year 700, and between that date and his death he wrote in all a total of some 60 volumes. When we read his works we must not forget that he was born, passed his whole life and died close to what had once been the uttermost north-western limit of the Roman Empire. He would have agreed with William of Malmesbury who described his birthplace as lying on the furthest shore of an island which some called *alter orbis,* because it was so remote that not many geographers had discovered its existence[2]. Many years before Bede's birth, Gregory the Great, in a letter to Eulogius, bishop of Alexandria, described the English as a people who lived in a corner of the world and who until recently had put their trust in sticks and stones[3]. Bede was well aware himself of his remoteness from the centres of antiquity and in one of his commentaries he asked his readers not to complain because he had written so much about what he had learnt from ancient authors about trees and herbs. He had not done so out of conceit, but there was no other way for those who lived in a remote island of the Ocean far outside the world to learn about what happened in Arabia, India,

Judaea and Egypt, except through the writings of those who had been there[4]. When we read Bede's works we must always remember that Bede's birthright was not the birthright of classical antiquity, not even the *Romanitas* of Gaul, but the birthright of pagan barbarism which he inherited from his father and grandfather.

Those inclined to take a strict view might argue that out of the total of some 60 volumes only one, the *Historia Ecclesiastica Gentis Anglorum,* whose narrative runs to midsummer of 731 and which probably received some revision in 732, can be regarded as a work of history. Yet it would be an excessively narrow view which rejected as not being historical works, the *Historia Abbatum,* the prose *Vita Sancti Cuthberti* and the chronicles at the end of his two works concerned primarily with chronology—the *de Temporibus* of 703 and the *de Temporum Ratione* of 725. There are indeed passages in his exegetical works which are relevant to an appreciation of his historical interests.

Scholars of an earlier age were mostly content to regard Bede as "the father of English learning" and to treat what he tells us about the history of the English in Britain with the veneration which some may think it still deserves. The current fashion is to dissect the completed work in an attempt to evaluate the different materials of which the *Historia Ecclesiastica* is composed and to determine the way in which these materials reached Jarrow. It is a measure of Bede's originality, in an age when historical writing was at a low ebb, that he foresaw that others with minds as critical as his own would want to know with what authority, and for what purpose, he wrote the *Historia*. Prompted by his sense of historical foresight and his regard for historical authority he answered both questions in the long *Preface* to the *Historia,* showing incidentally a more generous recognition of his debt to others than some modern historians are wont to do. Even on his deathbed his concern was for accuracy. Engaged in translating extracts from the works of Isidore of Seville, he wrote: "I do not want my children to read what is false or to labour at this in vain after my death". This was not a disparaging reference to the unreliability of Isidore, but the expression of a concern lest the pupils of his school at Jarrow might be misled by faulty translations[5].

Bede is currently enjoying what is called in popular jargon a bad press. His skill and accuracy as a chronologist have been attacked. He has been accused of distorting history by a display of prejudice against the Celtic, and particularly the Welsh, church. He has been represented as the dupe of a forger. He has been regarded as treating northern English folk-tales as though they were a reliable source of information about events occurring in distant Rome. Finally, he has been accused of committing that greatest of crimes in a historian—the suppression of evidence which does not accord with a preconceived historical theory. These several charges amount to an assault on Bede's intellectual honesty.

It would be a sad reflection on the work of modern historians who have access to material, written as well as archaeological, which was unknown to Bede, if they were unable to point to the probability of error committed by him in some details. Yet if we know a little that Bede did not know, we do well to remember how much he knew that we can never know. It is unquestionably our duty to be no less critical of Bede's writings than he was himself in his attitude towards his own sources. He, too, was charged with heresy in his own day. Yet ought we not to make our critical approach with at least something of the intellectual humility which his writings reveal as one of Bede's endearing characteristics? We can still take to heart the rebuke which he administered to himself and to others in one of the homilies which reflect the mature thought of his later years:

> When we notice, while we are talking, that some of the less learned brethren cannot understand those mysteries of the Scriptures which we have not always known, but which we have gradually learnt to know with God's help, we are apt to be immediately puffed up. We despise them and boast about our learning as if it were uniquely profound and as if there were not a great many others much more learned than ourselves. We who do not like to be despised by those more learned than ourselves, delight in despising, or even ridiculing, those who are less learned than us[6].

In the very first paragraph of the *Preface* to the *Historia,* addressed to his king, Bede set forth in plain terms his own view of the purpose which this *Historia* was intended to serve. He believed that if history related good things of good men, the attentive hearer would be incited to imitate what was good, and that if it recounted evil things of wicked men, the godly hearer or reader would nevertheless shun what was wrong and become the more eager to do what he knew to be good and worthy of God. And at the end of this same *Preface* he begged his readers that if, in what he had written, they were to find anything set down otherwise than in accordance with truth, they would not impute it to him who, according to the true law of history—*quod vera lex historiae est*—had laboured sincerely to commit to writing for the instruction of posterity such things as he had been able to gather from common report.

Bede wrote, then, *ad instructionem posteritatis,* and the instruction which he left for posterity was not in order that it might be better informed about the course of the Anglo-Saxon invasions of Britain, but that, reading about the way in which those invaders had abandoned heathenism and embraced the only true faith, they might themselves be moved to a more Godly way of life.

We ought not to view Bede's historical writings in complete isolation from his other writings, since all were devoted to the same end, and we can find the phrase *vera lex historiae* in his commentary on St. Luke's Gospel. Commenting on Luke 2, 33, *et erat pater ejus et mater mirantes super his quae dicebantur de illo,* Bede remarks that the evangelist does not call Joseph the father of the Saviour because he was so in very truth, but because it was believed by all that he was so. In calling Joseph the father of Christ, Bede continues, the evangelist was not denying the virginity of Mary but expressing the belief of common people which is the true law of history—*opinionem vulgi exprimens, quae vera historiae lex est*[7]. There is a distinction here between revealed truth and what was held to be true among common people, but of course the phrase *vera historiae lex* is not original in Bede. He would find it in a work of Jerome's which we know that he used, the tract *Adversus Helvidium.* Jerome writes that save for Joseph, Elisabeth and Mary herself, everyone thought that Jesus was the son of Mary, "so much so that even the Evangelists, voicing the opinion of the common people which is the true law of history—*opinionem vulgi exprimentes, quae vera historiae lex est*—said that he was the father of the Saviour"[8]. Bede had good precedent for adopting the view that it was the function of history to record what ordinary people believed, and we are not bound to suppose that he himself believed everything that he chose to record. When he chose to record a Northumbrian legend about a meeting between Gregory (not yet Pope) and some Northumbrian boys in the market place in Rome, he did so because the story was widely believed by the faithful in Northumbria, not necessarily because he himself believed the event to have happened. He introduced the story with the words *nec silentio praetereunda opinio, quae de beato Gregorio traditione maiorum ad nos usque perlata est,* and as though to emphasis his belief that the story was no more than a tradition he added at the end of the tale the words *haec iuxta opinionem, quam ab antiquis accepimus, historiae nostrae ecclesiasticae inserere oportunum duximus*[9].

The dismemberment of an articulated skeleton may be necessary for the detailed study of its individual bones. It is not difficult to apply this process to Bede's historical writings, particularly to the *Historia* itself, but if, after the process has been completed we find ourselves with a lot of seemingly unrelated pieces of information, we must remember that all that we have achieved is the dismemberment of what was Bede's creation. Bede did not view history as a series of isolated events unrelated to one another, but as an orderly chronological development extending over several millenia from the first creation of man, and when we

argue about whether the year which Bede called 670 was the year which we would have called 671, we should not lose sight of this wider view.

Bede was deeply interested in number, not only as a vehicle of mystical symbolism, but also as a science which had practical application to the problems of daily life, as well as the problems of those who wrote history. In Bede's sight, the central fact of past history whose significance over-rode all other past events, was the Resurrection of Christ. Both his homilies and his biblical commentaries contain passages, some of them sublimely moving, in which he expounds the symbolical significance of darkness and light, and sets out his view that through the Resurrection the whole order of time had been reversed. From the moment of creation, with man fallen from the light of paradise into the tribulations of the world, the light of day had been followed by the darkness of night, but with the Resurrection of Christ during the darkness of the night the whole order of time had been so changed that man moved away from the darkness of night towards the light of the following day[10].

Bede accepted the common view which recognised the superiority of the contemplative over the active life within the monastic community[11], yet his was indeed the active life, and his own essentially practical view of daily living raised a number of questions which were of the essence of his faith. On what day in each passing year was the Resurrection to be celebrated? The kingdom of Northumbria lay on the frontier of differing theological views. Before his birth the monastery at Whitby, and during his own lifetime, his own monastery at Wearmouth and Jarrow, played a leading part in keeping the *Ecclesia Anglicana* in conformity with Rome, and in leading at least the more northerly parts of the Celtic church in Ireland and Scotland towards a similar conformity. His interest in chronology, perhaps first acquired from his teacher and abbot, Ceolfrith, would be greatly stimulated by the arguments which he would hear, and in which he would participate, during the later years of the seventh century when he was still a young man. He became sufficiently expert in all the mysteries of Easter Tables to be able himself to compile a double set of the great Paschal cycle of 532 years, one running from the Incarnation to 532, and the other looking ahead as far as 1063.

There were two other questions scarcely less important than the date of the Resurrection—when was Christ himself born and how old when he died? Bede's interest in the first of these questions is reflected in his account of information brought to him by some monks from Wearmouth and Jarrow who had been in Rome in the year 701 of the Incarnation according to Dionysius. The monks had observed the practice of attaching inscribed labels to candles which were lit in the church at Rome at Christmas in honour of the Virgin Mary. The labels which they saw read: "From the Passion of Our Lord Jesus Christ there are 668 years". Bede remarks how in this way the Roman church professed its belief that Christ had lived in the flesh for a little more than 33 years, because the labels on its Christmas candles recorded a number which was less by 33 years than the number which Dionysius gave from the time of His Incarnation[12].

As a historian and as a member of what he called the *Ecclesia Catholica* Bede recorded and accepted the belief which his fellow-monks had witnessed in Rome. The Incarnation had been followed 33 years later by the Passion. But now there was a third question. What was the date of Creation itself? The doctrine of the Six Ages of the World, with the beginning of the Sixth Age marked by the Incarnation, was of course a commonplace of Bede's time. He accepted the doctrine itself, but he was not prepared to accept at third or fourth had opinions about the duration of the Five Ages preceding the Incarnation. He challenged the opinion of Isidore whose figures were derived from Jerome through Eusebius and rested ultimately on the Greek Septuagint. Using knowledge won from the years of Biblical study at Wearmouth and Jarrow which had culminated in the production of Abbot Ceolfrith's Bible, now represented by the *Codex Amiatinus* in the Biblioteca Laurenziano in Florence, he made his own independent calculations from what he regarded as the most authoritative source—what he called the *Hebraica Veritas,* that is to say Jerome's own translation from the Hebrew which we know as the Vulgate. Using this source, and with some help from Josephus, he challenged the long-established tradition which had given a figure of upwards of 5,000 years from the Creation to the Incarnation, and arrived at a figure of 3953 years as covering the whole of the first Five Ages. It was alleged by those who had not troubled to read carefully what he wrote, that he had stated that Christ was born not at the beginning of the Sixth Age, but in the middle of the Fifth, and, like other historians who have challenged accepted views by returning to primary sources of evidence, he was charged with heresy[13].

Given the chronology of the first Five Ages derived from the *Hebraica Veritas* and given the traditional dates for Christ's Incarnation and Passion as they were accepted in Rome, how was it possible to relate the events of the current Sixth Age, as they happened year by year, to events which had occurred at earlier times and in other countries? We must not say that Bede was the first to use the Christian era as an infinitely cumulative method of reckoning the passage of time past and to come. The *Annus Incarnationis* or *Annus Domini* had been used by Dionysius Exiguus in his Easter tables in the sixth century. But Bede's **Historia Ecclesiastica** was the first major historical work in which this era was consistently used as the chronological framework,

and it is not the least of his claims to originality that he set a fashion which subsequently became, and still remains, the universal practice of historians in the western world. Moreover, when Bede borrowed a passage from Orosius in which Orosius gives the *Annus ab Urbe Condita* as marking the consulship of Julius Caesar and Lucius Bibulus, he equated this year with the 60th year *ante Incarnationis Dominicae Tempus*[14].

We cannot tell who it was that equated past events in the history of the English in Britain with the successive *Anni Incarnationis,* and since there are no surviving Easter tables from Bede's own monastery, we cannot tell whether their margins had been used for this purpose. Surviving continental fragments suggest that this may well have been so but there were other chronological systems in use in Bede's age in Northumbria. The inscription which records the dedication of the church at Jarrow to St. Paul makes no reference to the *Annus Incarnationis* but dates the event to the 15th year of King Ecgfrith and the 4th year of Abbot Ceolfrith[15]. A primitive chronicle found on folio 128*b* of the Moore Manuscript of Bede's **Historia Ecclesiastica** dates a short series of events by recording the number of years elapsed since the occurrence of each of them, e.g. *angli in britanniam ante annos ccxcii*[16]. While Bede may well have derived some of his dates from marginal entries in Easter Tables, we ought not to suppose that these were his only source of chronological information. When we reflect that Bede had to take account of the regnal years of seven or eight Anglo-Saxon kings who reigned contemporaneously and had succeeded to their several kingdoms at different, and usually unknown, dates of the month within a calendar year which may not have had a uniform beginning even within England itself—to say nothing of episcopal or abbatial years—we can have no cause for surprise if we should find signs of inconsistency or minor error. In such a situation we should turn to Bede's commentary on the First Book of Kings. Bede knew from Scripture that Solomon began to build the temple in the 480th year after the children of Israel came out of the land of Egypt, and he could account for 423 of them from the Book of Judges. There remained 57 years to be distributed between Joshua, Samuel and Saul, but when he turned to Josephus he found the total ascribed to these three was 58. "We are not to worry", he wrote, "that there is one superfluous year beyond the 480, for either Scripture, giving a round number in its usual way did not trouble to add in the extra year, or else, as is much easier to believe, through lack of care over a long period, the Chronicle of Josephus has somewhere added an extra year, as often happens"[17]. All of us who have struggled with chronological problems will feel grateful to Bede for allowing us this escape.

We shall never be able to trace the growth of Bede's interest in history, and particularly in English history, in any close detail, but we may fairly surmise that it would be stimulated by reading those historical works which reached the libraries of Jarrow and Wearmouth—for example the *Historia Ecclesiastica* of Eusebius both in Jerome's translation and in the version made by Rufinus, the *De Viris Illustribus* of Jerome, with the continuation by Gennadius, as well as some of the writings of Orosius, Eutropius and Isidore of Seville. Touching the history of Britain in particular, he knew the *De Excidio et Conquestu Britanniae* written by the British monk Gildas, and he used it extensively for his own *Historia Ecclesiastica*. Writing in a context of c. 720, and with a backward glance over several years, he remarks how in those times many Englishmen used to go to Rome, noblemen and common people, men and women, officers of government and ordinary citizens[18]. Some of these many travellers doubtless brought back books or information—such as the epitaph on the tomb of Gregory the Great in Rome[19]—which would ultimately reach Bede at Jarrow.

We can discern a little of Bede's growing knowledge of English history by comparing the chronicles of the Sixth Age which he appended to each of his two works on chronology. Most of the material in these chronicles[20] is of course derived from earlier works. In the chronicle at the end of the *De Temporibus* written in 703, there is only one entry which is specific to Britain. It reads: *Saxones in Britannia fidem Christi suscipiunt.* Since this event is assigned by Bede to the reign of the Emperor Phocas 602-10, we may perhaps infer that at this date, i.e. 703, Bede knew nothing about the mission sent by Gregory the Great to Britain under the leadership of Augustine in 596. But when we turn to the corresponding chronicle at the end of the *De Temporum Ratione,* completed 22 years later in 725, we find a very different situation. Not only did Bede include some quite detailed information about the activities of Augustine and his companions in Kent and of Paulinus in Northumbria, but he also referred to the arrival of Theodore and Hadrian, to St. Audrey, the foundress of the double monastery at Ely, to Willibrord who was preaching to the Frisians, and to St. Cuthbert whose *Vita* (says Bede) we have recently written in prose, and some years previously in hexameter verse.

Two significant points emerge from the contrast between these two chronicles of the Sixth Age. First, Bede's account of the Gregorian mission in the later of the two shows a knowledge of some of the works of Gregory the Great—the *Moralia* and the *Dialogi,* as well as a knowledge of the *Liber Pontificalis* and of a letter written by Gregory the Great to Augustine on 22 June 601[21]. And we know from his prose *Vita Cuthberti* that Bede had also received before this date a copy of the *Libellus Responsionum*[22]. This newly-acquired knowledge enabled Bede to correct his earlier error about the date of the arrival of Christianity among the English by putting it back to the reign of Maurice, the

predecessor of Phocas, but it is not clear whether Bede yet knew the exact date of Augustine's arrival in England or whether he knew that the missioners arrived in two separate groups, one headed by Augustine in 597 and the other by Mellitus in 601. Whether or not Bede had already begun to plan the *Historia Ecclesiastica* by 725, I think we may infer that some at least of the material which he would use was now being gathered at Jarrow.

The second significant point arising from the later Chronicle is the interest which it shows in the lives of saints—of Gregory himself, Paulinus, Theodore, Audrey and particularly Cuthbert. Bede's own *Historia Ecclesiastica Gentis Anglorum,* to give it its full title, is at bottom a history of the deeds done by individual men and women in the conversion of the English from paganism to Christianity and in the subsequent development of the Church in England. It is concerned with individual monks and nuns, rather than with the Monastic Order, with particular men who were bishops rather than with ecclesiastical government, with individual teachers of singing rather than with the chant and the liturgy in general, with particular kings who won or lost battles rather than with warfare between kingdoms. This is as much as to say that when we look at the *Historia* as a whole we find that it is in fact precisely what Bede tells us in the *Preface* that it is going to be—a work telling of the good deeds done by good men, and of the evil deeds done by wicked men. But who, in Bede's sight, were the wicked men?

If we look at Bede's account of the history of Britain between the sack of Rome in 410 and the arrival of St. Augustine at Canterbury in 597, we find that it is based mainly upon two sources—the *Vita Germani* of Constantius and the *de Excidio et Conquestu Britanniae* of Gildas who is generally thought to have been writing c. 550. The amount of material which Bede borrowed from Gildas seems to show that he saw the conquest of Britain in much the same light as Gildas had seen it—the vengeance of God upon a people who had fallen from Christian virtues into every kind of corrupt and evil living. To the list of unspeakable crimes attributed to the Britons by their own historian, Gildas, Bede could add the further crime that the Britons never preached the Christian faith to the Angles and Saxons living among them in Britain. He repeated this charge near the end of the *Historia*[23], remarking that as the British had formerly been unwilling to teach the Christian faith to the heathen English, so now when the English were fully instructed *in regula fidei catholicae,* the British still stubbornly persisted in their old errors. Bede well knew that the purpose of the visit paid by Germanus to Britain in 429 was to combat the Pelagian heresy and to call the British church back to the orthodox fold. In using the Constantius *Vita Germani,* representing the victory of Catholicism over Pelagianism, and the work of Gildas which bitterly attacked the

British clergy as well as the laity, Bede was certainly influenced by his passionate devotion to the catholic faith. It may also be that he looked upon the continuance of the British church in error as Divine retribution for the failure of their clergy to preach to the English[24].

In his attitude towards the British clergy Bede expresses himself with an uncompromising vigour which may seem distasteful to those who prefer that measure of tolerance which is ready to admit that there may be more than one point of view. We must not forget that, when the monastery at Jarrow was founded, only half a century had elapsed from that *infaustus annus* of apostasy following the death of Edwin, Northumbria's first Christian king, at the hands of Cadwallon, the British, and Christian, king of Gwynedd[25]. We must not forget that, as Eddius tells us, British clergy had been driven out of their churches and monasteries by the sword of pagan English invaders[26]. Yet we cannot dismiss Bede's remarks as the mere prejudice of an Englishman against all Celts. Those who incline to do so should first read what he wrote of Aidan of Lindisfarne[27], and then take note of one of the most vigorous condemnations in the *Historia*—the condemnation of the English king Ecgfrith for his attack on the Irish and the representation of Ecgfrith's death in battle against the Picts as Divine punishment for his sin[28]—and this was the same English king who gave their first endowments to Wearmouth and Jarrow.

Nor must we forget that when Bede wrote the *Historia,* of all the Christian communities in Britain only the British church had failed to conform to Roman usage in the observance of Easter. We do not need to read very deeply in Bede's Biblical commentaries to realise how much store he set by the maintenance of catholic orthodoxy. Departure from such orthodoxy was in his sight a grave sin upon which there could be no compromise. Our judgment about Bede's attitude towards the British church ought not to be based upon his failure to conform to our prejudices, but upon the extent to which he was true to his own beliefs, and we shall not understand the depth of those beliefs if we confine our reading to his historical works. Yet when we have taken all this into account, we are left with the impression that there may have been other factors operating during Bede's own lifetime of which we know nothing, but which contributed to the hardness of his attitude.

It is in his account of the Gregorian mission, at work first in the south-east of England and later in Northumbria, that Bede's *Historia Ecclesiastica* has come under heavy attack in recent years, an attack which in total seems to impugn the stature of his intellect and, perhaps even worse, his intellectual honesty. It has been said that he was wrong about the place of St. Augustine's consecration as archbishop, that he

accepted as a genuine document a Canterbury forgery foisted upon him by Nothhelm, that he implied a false date for the conversion of King Ethelbert of Kent and that he deliberately suppressed the evidence which he knew would have shown him to be wrong[29], and that he was wrong about the date at which the mission extended its activities to Northumbria under Paulinus[30].

Bede's account of the Augustinian mission in Kent comprises eleven consecutive chapters in the first Book of the *Historia Ecclesiastica*[31]. A little more than two-thirds of the content of those eleven chapters consists of the direct reproduction of letters written by Gregory the Great. The remainder derives from Canterbury tradition which reached Bede from Albinus, abbot of what we now know as St. Augustine's monastery. Albinus himself had been educated in the school established by Theodore and Hadrian, and Bede says of him that he knew not a little Greek, and was as familiar with Latin as he was with English. Both Gregory the Great and Augustine were still alive when Theodore was born. With this background we may suppose that unwritten traditional information coming to Jarrow from Canterbury would be well-founded. And we know from Bede himself of two separate occasions when material was conveyed to him from Canterbury. The account which Bede gives of the church dedicated to St. Martin in which Bertha worshipped, and of the monastery founded by St. Augustine in which there were churches dedicated the one to SS Peter and Paul, and the other to St. Mary, is abundantly confirmed by surviving architectural remains, as well as by the discoveries made in the detailed excavation of the churches of St. Augustine's monastery[32]. We have found the burial places of the early archbishops of Canterbury precisely where Bede, on the strength of his Canterbury informants, describes them as lying. But the reason why Bede could be both detailed and accurate on this heading was because the churches themselves were still in use and the archbishops' tombs could still be seen.

What was the strength of Canterbury tradition touching matters of which no visible evidence remained when Bede was writing? So far as we can tell no documents relating to the mission survived in Canterbury itself. Bede would naturally want to know the answer to a number of questions—when exactly did Augustine land in Kent?—when and where was he consecrated bishop?—when was King Ethelbert of Kent converted to Christianity? It looks very much as if the answers to these questions were not to be found in Canterbury tradition as it reached Bede, and that he was dependent for his knowledge of the mission's chronology on the dating clauses of Gregory the Great's letters, copies of which were brought to him by Nothhelm who had travelled to Rome for the particular purpose of examining the papal register and bringing back copies of such documents as he thought would be of interest to Bede.

Bede knew that when Augustine set out from Rome for the second time, in or after July 596, he did so as an abbot. He also knew that when Gregory wrote to Brunhild in September 597 he referred to Augustine as *co-episcopus*. He derived these facts from Gregory's letters. What then was the source of Bede's statement that at some unspecified date after his arrival in Britain Augustine went to Gaul and was consecrated bishop by Aetherius, archbishop of Arles[33]? We know that in one detail, Bede here fell into error, since the archbishop of Arles was Vergilius, and not Aetherius who was bishop of Lyons. One of our great difficulties is that we do not know for certain how many of Gregory's letters Bede did in fact see. He knew that Gregory had told the archbishop of Arles to give Augustine any help that he might need. We know that Gregory had written to Vergilius of Arles to the effect that if Augustine should come to visit him about the delinquencies of priests or others, the two were to discuss the cases together[34]. Yet there was one particular letter of Gregory's which we can feel certain that Bede did not see. It was written on 29 July 598 to Eulogius patriarch of Alexandria[35]. In this letter Gregory tells how Augustine, who was with his permission made a bishop of the Germanies, has reached England and how 10,000 Englishmen are reported to have been baptised on Christmas Day in 597. If we read Gregory's letter objectively, it is difficult not to infer that Augustine's consecration as bishop had preceded his arrival in England. If this letter had been known either in Canterbury or to Bede, it seems scarcely credible that the scene of the mass baptisms on Christmas Day, authenticated by none other than Gregory the Great himself, would not have had its dramatic potentialities exploited to the full. The failure of any memory of this incident to have become enshrined in Canterbury tradition is most remarkable, as also is the seeming fact that Canterbury tradition did not even know the date of Augustine's death. It remains possible that Bede was right in saying that Augustine was consecrated bishop in Arles, but even if he was wrong, it is not difficult to see how either he or his Canterbury informant may have made a faulty inference from inadequate evidence[36].

Gregory's correspondence, our only contemporary source for Augustine's mission to the English, does not give the date of King Ethelbert's conversion. Bede himself makes no explicit statement about it either in the body of the *Historia* or in the chronological summary, but he implies that it occurred in 597 soon after the arrival of the missioners. It has been alleged that Ethelbert was still pagan in 601, that Bede became aware of this alleged fact c. 731 when he had already written his account of the mission and that he deliberately suppressed the inconvenient evidence which did not accord with the opinion which he had previously reached[37]. The charge has, to my mind, been effectively refuted by Dr. Markus[38], but its nature is so serious, and the refutation perhaps not so widely known, that no apology is needed for presenting a summary of the arguments first advanced by Dr. Markus.

The case against Bede's integrity rests on three legs. The first argument is that if Ethelbert had been converted by 598 Gregory would have mentioned the fact in the letter to Eulogius in July of that year. But why should the Pope in Rome writing to a patriarch in Alexandria have mentioned the name of an obscure king ruling a minute area of land lying on the very edge of the world? The purpose of the letter was to give Eulogius the joyful news that a mission had set out from Rome, that it had reached England and that it had met with success. The second argument rests on a letter which Gregory wrote to King Ethelbert himself on 22 June 601. The relevant passage reads:

> . . . and therefore illustrious son give earnest
> heed to keep the grace which has been given
> you by God; be eager to spread the Christian
> faith among the peoples whom you rule; redouble
> your upright zeal in their conversion; drive out
> the worship of the idols; overthrow the temple
> buildings[39].

I can see no force in the argument that in this passage "grace" need not here refer to the grace of baptism, but may only refer to the grace of faith which the missioners themselves have brought to England. Hitherto successive generations of historians have thought that a letter written in such terms as these could only have been written to one who had already been converted, and I can see no ground for departing from this view.

The third leg of the argument rests upon a letter which Gregory wrote to Bertha, Ethelbert's queen, also in June 601, or rests rather upon a part of the letter which reads thus:

> And indeed it was your duty this long time past by
> the excellence of your prudence like a true Christian
> to have predisposed the mind of our illustrious son,
> your consort, to follow the faith which you cherish[40].

I think we must all agree that in this passage Gregory was blaming Bertha for not having secured Ethelbert's conversion, but let us note the words "this long time past", and consider how the letter goes on:

> And now that by God's good pleasure a fitting
> moment is come, be sure that you repair past neglect
> with interest by the help of divine grace. Confirm
> therefore the mind of your illustrious consort in his
> attachment to the Christian faith by constant
> exhortation; let your care pour into him an increased
> love of God, and inflame his soul for the complete
> conversion of the race of his subjects.

Bertha was a Christian Frankish princess who brought a bishop with her from Gaul and who attended services in St. Martin's church in Canterbury—all this before the Gregorian mission reached Kent. We do not know how how long Bertha had been in Kent before Augustine arrived, but surely we can only interpret the letter—if we read all of it—as a rebuke to Bertha for not having used her past opportunities to convert her husband, and as an exhortation to confirm him in his attachment to the Christian faith. We have no proof that Bede ever saw this letter to Bertha and even if he did, would he not have interpreted it precisely in this way? How can it be said that Bede suppressed the letter because it showed that Ethelbert was still pagan in 601, whilst he had already written his *Historia* with its implication that Ethelbert was converted in 597?

The charge that Bede was deceived by a forgery foisted upon him by Nothhelm concerns the authenticity of the *Libellus Responsionum* which was reproduced by Bede as Book I, chapter 27 of the *Historia.* It springs in part from a letter which Boniface wrote to Nothhelm[41], then archbishop of Canterbury, in 736, asking for an assurance that what we now call the *Libellus* was a genuine Gregorian work since, when the archives of the Roman church were searched, no copy of it could be found among the other writings of Gregory. In its most extreme form the charge represents this document as a forgery perpetrated by Nothhelm himself and first taken to Bede in 731. Part at least of the charge can be easily refuted, since Bede quotes a passage from the *Libellus* in his *Vita Cuthberti* which was written not later than 721, ten years or more before its inclusion in the *Historia Ecclesiastica*. This was time enough for Bede to be able to consider the document and to satisfy himself of its authenticity. Moreover such a forgery could scarcely have been perpetrated in Canterbury without the knowledge of Albinus, abbot of St. Augustine's monastery. From what we know of their personal relationships it is not easy to envisage Albinus and Nothhelm deliberately setting out to deceive Bede in this way, nor is it any easier to envisage Bede being deceived so readily. That the *Libellus* could not then, and cannot now, be found in the Register of Gregory's letters is not a decisive argument since the *Libellus* is not in fact a letter. The *Libellus* enjoyed a very wide circulation as a complete document in itself apart from its inclusion in the *Historia Ecclesiastica*. It survives in a large number of manuscripts and much further work remains to be done on it before any final decision can be reached, but such as has been done lends no support to the belief that it was a Canterbury forgery first taken to Bede c. 731[43].

The ***Historia Ecclesiastica Gentis Anglorum*** has now been read for more than twelve centuries and therein perhaps we may see adequate proof of its qualities. Although we cannot prove that any of the surviving manuscripts were written before Bede's death, there are several eighth-century copies and there is abundant evidence of the great interest which it aroused in France and Germany. It was prized by two famous English kings, Offa of Mercia and Alfred the Great. Alcuin had a copy and it was used also by Paul the Lombard. By the ninth century it was known at Würzburg, St. Gall, Lorsch and Murbach[44]. In all, more than 150 complete manuscripts of the work still survive and it was still being copied by hand in the 15th century when the first printed edition appeared at Strasbourg in about 1475. Some may read it as professional historians, finding in it the prime source of information about the early history of Christianity among the English. Others may be attracted by the lucid style of its Latin which formed an excellent vehicle for the remarkable narrative powers of its author, so little removed in time from his pagan forebears. Others may remember Bede's hope that his account of the past might encourage men to imitate the good and shun the evil. However much we may criticise in detail, we are left in the end with a sense of wonder and admiration that a man who lived in that *alter orbis* so far removed from the ancient centres of civilisation, was yet able to acquire a sense of historical vision which enabled him to see how much was to be gained *ad instructionem posteritatis* from a book which told of the conversion of a people from paganism to Christianity.

Notes

[1] *Historia Ecclesiastica*, ed. C. Plummer, 1896, V. 24.

[2] *Gesta Regum*, ed. W. Stubbs, *Rolls Series* 1887-9, I, 62-3.

[3] *Ep.*, ed. P. Ewald and L. Hartmann, *Mon. Ger. Hist.*, VIII, 29.

[4] *In Cant. Cant.*, ed. Migne, *Pat. Lat.*, 91, 1077.

[5] I agree with J. Fontaine, *Isidore de Seville, Traité de la Nature*, 79, n. 1, in interpreting the passage in this way, rather than with C. W. Jones, *Bedae Opera de Temporibus*, p. 131, who thought that Bede's concern was lest his pupils might find *mendacium* in Isidore's works.

[6] *Bedae Opera Homiletica*, I, 19, ed. D. Hurst, *C.C.S.L.* CXXII, 138.

[7] *In Lucam*, ed. D. Hurst, *C.S.S.L.* CXX, 67.

[8] Ed. Migne, *Pat. Lat.*, 23, 197.

[9] *Hist. Ecc.*, II, 1.

[10] See, for example, *Opera Homiletica*, II, 7, ed. Hurst, 226-7.

[11] See *Op. Hom.,* I, 9, ed. Hurst, 64-5.

[12] *De Temporum Ratione,* c. xlvii, ed. C. W. Jones, *Bedae Opera de Temporibus,* 266-7.

[13] C. W. Jones, op. cit. 132-3. For the *Epistola ad Pleguinam* in which Bede replied to the charge, see *ibid.* 307-15.

[14] *Hist. Ecc.* I, 2 and V, 24.

[15] P. Hunter Blair, *An Introduction to Anglo-Saxon England,* 156 and Pl. VI.

[16] P. Hunter Blair, "The *Moore Memoranda* on Northumbrian History", in *The Early Cultures of North-West Europe,* ed. C. Fox and B. Dickins, 245-57.

[17] *Bedae Opera Exegetica, In I Samuelem,* ed. D. Hurst, *C.C.S.L.,* CXIX, 69.

[18] *Chron. Majora,* ed. Mommsen, *Mon. Ger. Hist., Auct. Ant.,* XIII, 320.

[19] Recorded by Bede in the *Hist. Ecc.* II, 1.

[20] Ed. Mommsen, *Mon. Ger. Hist., Auct. Ant.,* XIII, 247-327.

[21] *Ep.* XI, 39, reproduced by Bede in *Hist. Ecc.* I, 29.

[22] *C.* xvi, ed. B. Colgrave, *Two Lives of Saint Cuthbert,* 208.

[23] *Hist. Ecc.* V, 22.

[24] I am indebted to Professor Whitelock for this point.

[25] *Hist. Ecc.* II, 20, III, 1.

[26] *The Life of Bishop Wilfrid by Eddius Stephanus,* ed. B. Colgrave, c. XVII, 36.

[27] *Hist. Ecc.* III, 5.

[28] *Hist. Ecc.* IV, 26.

[29] On these points see the detailed arguments expressed by S. Brechter, *Die Quellen zur Angelsachsenmission Gregors des Grossen.* See also Brechter's "Zur Bekehrungsgeschichte der Angelsachsen", *Settimane* XIV, Spoleto 1967, 191-215.

[30] See D. P. Kirby, "Bede's Northumbrian Chronology", *English Historical Review,* LXXVIII (1963), 514-27. I hope to discuss this problem more fully elsewhere.

[31] *Hist. Ecc.* V, 20.

[32] H. M. and J. Taylor, *Anglo-Saxon Architecture,* I, 134-45.

[33] *Hist. Ecc.* I, 27.

[34] *Ep.* XI, 45.

[35] *Ep.* VIII, 29.

[36] See P. Meyvaert, *Bede and Gregory the Great,* Jarrow Lecture 1964, 12-13.

[37] S. Brechter, *op. cit.* 240-48.

[38] R. A. Markus, "The Chronology of the Gregorian Mission to England: Bede's Narrative and Gregory's Correspondence", *Journal of Ecclesiastical History* XIV (1963), 16-30. I have used Markus's translations of the relevant documents.

[39] *Ep.,* XI, 37.

[40] *Ep.,* XI, 35.

[41] Ed. M. Tangl, *Mon. Ger. Hist., Ep. Sel.* I, No. 33.

[42] *C.* XVI.

[43] See further M. Deanesly and P. Grosjean, "The Canterbury Edition of the Answers of Pope Gregory I to St. Augustine", *Journal of Ecclesiastical History,* 10 (1959), 1-49; P. Meyvaert, "Les Responsiones de S. Grégoire le Grand le Grand à S. Augustin de Cantorbery", *Revue d'Histoire ecclésiastique,* 54 (1959), 879-94; M. Deanesly, "The Capitular Text of the *Responsiones* of Pope Gregory I to St. Augustine", *Journal of Ecclesiastical History,* 12 (1961), 231-4.

[44] See D. Whitelock, *After Bede,* Jarrow Lecture 1960.

Bertram Colgrave (essay date 1969)

SOURCE: Bertram Colgrave, "Historical Introduction," in *Bede's Ecclesiastical History of the English People,* edited by Bertram Colgrave and R. A. B. Mynors, 1969. Reprint by Oxford at the Clarendon Press, 1992, pp. xvii-xxxviii.

[*In the following excerpt written in 1969, Colgrave discusses the historical sources for Bede's* Ecclesiastical History.]

As Professor Levison has pointed out,[1] when Bede was writing his ***History,*** saints' Lives were being written everywhere, but other forms of historical writing were in decay. Bede was familiar with two histories, both of which may have served him as models, namely Rufinus' translation and adaptation of the *Ecclesiastical History* of Eusebius and Gregory of Tours' *History of the Franks*. But though Bede may have gained hints from both of these and possibly other works, he had one great aim. It was to tell the story of the development of God's plan for the conversion of the English people and the building up of one united Church in the land. He began by painting a background, geographical and historical, picturing the British inhabitants as feeble in time of war and, though Christian in name, vicious in time of peace, easily falling into heresies; but, worst of all, refusing to co-operate in the conversion of the 'heathen Saxons'. Then he plunges straight into the story of the mission of St. Augustine and its arrival in England. From this basis the other books spring directly. Bede shows how the gospel passed the bounds of the petty kingdoms and united the whole land under the aegis of the great catholic Church over which the bishops of the 'apostolic see', as he loved to call Rome, exercised a paternal and benevolent rule. The Irish Church is led into the same fold but the Britons, who refused to help in God's great task of the conversion of the English, meet their due reward and in the last chapter of the Fifth Book we find them partly subject to their English masters and wholly powerless. All other minor aims are subservient to this one. He had at his disposal fairly complete lists of the bishops of each kingdom and thereby he was able to emphasize the continuity of the Church and its close contact with the Church universal. This is only one of the many methods he employed to throw into relief the unity of the whole English race; and it is not for nothing that he ends his first book with the final and utter defeat of the British and Irish people and the firm establishment of the English people in their new land. Bede was perhaps the first to lay stress on the unity of all the smaller kingdoms in the one great English nation.

But, as Bede explains in his Preface, his motive in writing is also didactic; history tells of good men and bad, and the thoughtful listener is spurred on to follow the good and eschew the bad. Further he sees the deep spiritual significance which underlies the events of history and the lives of men and women. Nor is he unaware that what he has to say will also be welcome and give pleasure especially to the inhabitants of the various towns and districts he mentions; his desire to produce matter of special interest to some of the 'more important places' led him to insert some of the biographies and delightful stories with which his *History* is sprinkled. In fact there can be no doubt whatever that Bede was not only hoping to give pleasure to other people but was definitely giving himself the pleasure which every artist finds in producing a genuine work of art.

Let us consider briefly some of the historical sources on which Bede relies. His first book where he is preparing the scene for the coming of Augustine's mis-

sion is based largely upon older material and there is little that is original. His first chapter, for instance, is a mosaic of quotations from Pliny, Gildas, Solinus, and Orosius, together with a sentence from the *Hexaemeron* of St. Basil.[2] In the next few chapters he continues to use Orosius principally, with a few additions from Eutropius and Vegetius as well as from the *Liber Pontificalis,* the official collection of the lives of the popes which he was to use considerably in later books. When he reaches the Diocletian persecutions he is able to use the first saint's Life which had any reference to Britain, that of St. Alban. So he continues mostly from Orosius with occasional insertions from Eutropius, Gildas, and a poem of Prosper. But with the end of the Roman rule, Bede is dependent on Gildas, though with many additions and explanatory notes of his own and occasional facts drawn from other historians. The Gildas borrowings continue to the end of chapter 16 with his own important insertion about the origin of the Angles, Saxons, and Jutes in chapter 15. In chapter 17 he turns to another Life, that of St. Germanus written by Constantius, and this he follows almost verbally to the end of chapter 21 when the Gildas extracts begin again. Then, at the end of chapter 22, with something like a sigh of relief, he turns to his papal and other sources.

It is at this point that he begins to use the chief sources of his information concerning Augustine's mission, namely the material collected by Abbot Albinus gathered both from tradition and from the written records which at that time existed in Kent; besides this there were the letters of Gregory transcribed by Nothhelm from the papal registers and brought to him by the latter. He also had the copy of Gregory's *Responsiones*[3] which he had used ten years before when writing the **Life of St. Cuthbert**[4] and a copy of the second recension of the *Liber Pontificalis.* Of the twenty-nine letters which are still extant referring to the mission of Augustine he uses sixteen, eight from Gregory and eight from other popes, all those from Gregory appearing in the first book. These he quotes verbally, though not always in full, which makes the first book seem heavy and overweighted to the modern reader. But for Bede it is an assurance of accuracy; though he uses oral tradition freely in this and the other books, yet he likes to rely on written documents and his great reverence for Gregory made him choose, when possible, to use the words of the saint himself. The last chapter of the first book reminds us that he had some Northumbrian annals at his disposal which he was to use later on. In spite of all this mosaic the book serves its purpose and moves steadily on through the course of the early history, leaving the English nation firmly settled in their new land and the Christian mission well under way.

At the end of his *History* Bede describes how he 'put together this account of the church of Britain and of the English people in particular, gleaned either from ancient documents, or from tradition or from my own knowledge'.[5] This is an exact description of his sources for the rest of the *History*. The ancient documents are there in the form of more letters from the popes, from Boniface V to Vitalian, seven in book two and one in book three:[6] there are the proceedings of the first two synods of the English church, that of Hertford in 672 and Hatfield in 679.[7] He makes plenty of use of saints' Lives, some of which are still extant, like the Lives of Fursa, Wilfrid, and Cuthbert, while he also uses a lost Life of Æthelburh for the miracles of the nuns of Barking.[8] Other sources which come under the same heading are genealogies, regnal lists, annals and lists of bishops, and records which he obtained from his various friends and helpers such as those referred to in the Preface—from Kent, Wessex, East Anglia, Lastingham, and Lindsey and perhaps some Celtic sources too, though these are uncertain. Then of course there was still much information to be gained from the floating traditions, preserved possibly in the form of a saga, such as Bede brings together in the differing accounts of Edwin's conversion, which he attempts to make, not altogether convincingly, into one whole.[9]

As Bede reaches his own times he is dependent to a much greater extent on what he calls in the Preface 'the faithful testimony of innumerable witnesses'; these he usually names and at the same time attempts to distinguish between first-hand and second-hand information.[10] Though Bede himself, so far as we know, travelled but little, yet he was living in a monastery which was very much in touch with the outside world, and much information from all parts of England, from Ireland, and the Continent would quickly reach them. Thus he is aware of the Moslem invasions; some Roman pilgrim has given him a copy of the epitaphs on Gregory the Great and on Cædwalla in Rome. It is the miscellaneous nature of his information which makes his last book less of an integrated whole than the other books.

The five books into which the *History* is divided differ slightly in length, the first two being slightly shorter than the other three. The first book, as we have already seen, builds up a background and sees the English people firmly planted in their own land and the mission begun. The second book begins with a brief biography of Gregory and an account of his works, emphasizing the important part played by Gregory in English tradition; it goes on to describe the conversion of the north and reaches up to the fall of Edwin and the temporary destruction of the Northumbrian Church. It covers a period of twenty-seven years. The third book deals very largely with the spread of the Celtic Church chiefly in Northumbria but in other parts of the country too. The book reaches a climax with the Council of Whitby after which there follows an uneasy period of reaction and decline in the Church all through the

midlands and the south and ends up with the events which led to the appointment of Theodore. The fourth book describes the great revival of Church life which followed the coming of Theodore, all over the country. It finishes with the death of Cuthbert in 687, a saint whom Bede regarded with special veneration. It may well have been that to Bede Cuthbert symbolized the union of the Celtic and Roman churches, the establishment of good relations with Rome again while all that was best of the Irish tradition remained. The two miracles of Cuthbert which form the last two chapters are no more than an appendix to his own earlier Life of the saint and were always so treated in the manuscripts of the Life which have survived. Finally the fifth book covers the rest of the period from 687 to 731. It is, as we have seen, the most miscellaneous of all the books and the weakest in construction. It contains the biographies of John of Beverley, Willibrord, Wilfrid, and Dryhthelm, while Bede's friend Egbert hovers vaguely in the background as a sort of champion of the Roman way of reckoning Easter in Ireland and Iona. It is possible that Bede felt some hesitation about going into the history of his own times and discussing his own contemporaries in quite the same way as he had dealt with the preceding period. But it is difficult to justify the section on the holy places on any count. The very long letter to the king of the Picts on the date of Easter seems tiresome and unnecessary to modern readers but for Bede it sums up the controversy which occupies much space in the *History* and forms one of its central themes: could the English Church accept her position as the true and loyal offspring of the Roman Church, free from any taint of heresy or particularist error? Or was she to slip back into insular withdrawal and cut herself off from all the spiritual inheritance and cultural influences which Rome stood for? The letter is, in fact, one of the clearest accounts of the Easter controversy to be found anywhere in writers ancient or modern and forms a fitting and final summary of this all-pervasive topic. If Ceolfrith actually wrote it, then he must have been a very able chronologer and master of a clear incisive style. But there are echoes of Bede's style in it so that it is likely that Bede edited the letter freely if he did not actually write it. At the end of the *History,* Bede, like Gregory of Tours in his *History of the Franks,* gives a brief epitome of his life and works.

Bede's very considerable use of saints' Lives, of the sagas associated with them in tradition, together with the stories supplied by friends and contemporaries, is responsible for one of the chief difficulties which faces a modern reader of the *History*. How is it that one who is supposed to be our greatest medieval historian can spend so much time telling wonder tales? It seems strange too when we remember that Bede, borrowing from Gregory the Great, declares that miracles are necessary at the beginning of the history of the Church, just as water is necessary for a plant until it has taken root: then it need be watered no longer.[11] It may be that they felt that the new Church in England needed this help. Yet, even so, Gregory and Bede both fill their writings with every kind of miracle story, some of them being little more than fairy tales. How can a historian expect to be taken seriously who tells a fantastic tale about a bishop being violently beaten by St. Peter at his shrine in Canterbury, so that the bishop when he leaves the saint's shrine is black and blue?[12] or in what sense are we to take the story of the Northumbrian captive whose fetters fall from him whenever his brother, who is a priest, says a mass on his behalf?[13]

The answer to this question seems to stem from the historic association in the Graeco-Roman culture of the second and third centuries between a belief in the marvellous and true devotion. The truly pious person naturally believed strongly in the miraculous element in his religion. Apostolic Christianity took its own line on this question and maintained that only such marvels as were done in Christ's name were true miracles; and that a belief in the miraculous did not necessarily imply true faith and devotion. But this was difficult for the ordinary man to accept and so, although the theologians, such as Bede, knew well the difference between true faith and mere faith in the marvellous, yet they seem to have felt that the latter might be a stepping-stone to the former. Not to have believed in miracles performed by the saints might well seem to the ordinary man to be equivalent to having no faith at all. And Bede, whatever his opinion of the importance of miracles, freely accepted the stories of the marvels wrought by the saints if related by credible witnesses. Yet to him as to Gregory this faith in the marvellous did not seem to be the highest form of faith nor was the gift of working miracles the only sign of sanctity. Indeed, Gregory in a letter which Bede preserves in his *History* warns Augustine against the dangers which may assail the worker of miracles. But Bede and Gregory and their contemporaries took it for granted that God could and did work miracles through and on behalf of those who were very near and devoted to Him. Those who heard these stories were both delighted and edified. They learned from them that God was still ruling in spite of the many troubles that harassed the lives of ordinary men, and that from time to time He could still intervene on their behalf. Nowadays we may not regard the miracle stories in precisely the same light as did Bede and his contemporaries; but we ought to treat them with reverent sympathy, for it was in such ways that they projected their own faith and hope upon the external world. Furthermore, even when the stories seem fantastic and incredible to the modern reader, there is often to be found in them a certain background of historical information which has its value; besides, many of these stories are delightful for their own sake as every reader of Bede's *History* knows.

In the *Lives of the Abbots,* which is mainly a portrait of Benedict Biscop, Bede is pure historian. He deals with the life of Benedict Biscop just as a modern biographer would, bringing in much material about the lives of other abbots of the monastery at Wearmouth and Jarrow. However much he was tempted to add stories of miracles, and there was already a saga growing up about Ceolfrith, who was dearest of all the abbots to him, yet Bede does nothing else but recite sober history as any modern biographer would do. In the *History,* however, Bede is both historian and relater of saints' Lives. We must remember that the *History* was appealing to a much wider audience and so Bede did not refrain from telling the sagas of the saints wherever they seemed appropriate; but in spite of all this his story is firmly based on historical materials, and when we read it in the light of contemporary literature we are not surprised that this miraculous element is present, for it is a true reflection of the mind of the people of his day; we are only surprised that there is not more of it. He was living in an age very different from our own in its attitude to the laws of nature. Yet compared with Gregory of Tours's *History of the Franks,* Bede seems to keep the miraculous element in check, possibly because he was modelling himself on Rufinus who also keeps the wonder element in the background.

Many scholars have praised Bede's Latin style for its straightforwardness and simplicity but it has more than that. Few writers, before or since, have produced so many vivid incidents so dramatically told, in one single work. Many of these, as we have seen, are now part and parcel of our literature; but there are a few which have not received the praise they deserve. One such is the healing of the dumb youth by St. John of Beverley, which is not without its touch of humour: others are the pair of stories of the two men who, each in his own way, discovered the virtues of the soil where Oswald fell.[14] The experiences of Dryhthelm in the other world must surely be one of the most striking examples of a literary genre which was very popular in the Middle Ages.[15] Bede is in fact a master of dramatic effect and his incidents are built up with the skill of a practised writer. He was also familiar with the arts of the rhetoricians and had written a book on the subject himself. He frequently makes use of figures of speech, epigrammatic contrasts, plays upon the meanings of words with implied secondary allusions, all of which are extremely difficult to reproduce in translation. To make Bede's *History* read in translation like any modern history book is not impossible, but it is only done at the cost of losing most of his overtones and producing a result which may be highly readable but is emphatically not Bede.

Bede's respect for Irish scholarship was high,[16] but fortunately he never gave way to the popular *Hisperica Famina* type of Latin with its alliteration, periphrasis, and exotic vocabulary, consisting of a strange combination of new formations based on other Latin or Greek or Hebrew words and rare expressions borrowed from the glosses of grammarians. His contemporary Aldhelm used this form of writing largely and Bede refers to him politely as being 'sermone nitidus';[17] if Bede had followed in his footsteps he could certainly have been more 'nitidus' than Aldhelm, but the result would have been fatal and the *History* would have been something very different from what we know today. It is true that there are obscurities in the course of the work, but these are found mostly either in the documents which he inserts verbatim into his text or in passages where he borrows phrases from other sources. The occasional difficulties which arise elsewhere are generally due to a faulty text or to his habit of bringing in remote scriptural references which were familiar enough in his day but are less familiar nowadays; such for instance is his description of Cædmon ruminating over the scripture stories 'like a clean beast';[18] but taken as a whole Bede's Latin was worthy of the story he had to tell and worthy of the simple, pious, learned scholar who wrote it; and that is perhaps the highest praise we can give it.

Notes

[1] *BLTW* [*Bede, his Life, Times, and Writings*, ed. A. Hamilton Thompson. Oxford, 1935.], p. III.

[2] See also footnotes to the various chapters especially in Books i and ii, and Index of Quotations.

[3] See notes on the *Libellus Responsionum* at i. 27.

[4] *BLTW*, p. 128 n. 2.

[5] v. 24.

[6] ii. 8, 10, 11, 17, 18, 19 (two); iii. 29.

[7] iv. 5; iv. 17. Cf. W. Levison, *England and the Continent in the Eighth Century*, p. 275.

[8] iii. 19; iv. 7-10, 27-33; v. 19.

[9] See ii. 13 and note.

[10] There is an important note on the subject at Plummer [*Baedae Historia Ecclesiastica gentis Anglorum: Venerabilis Baedae opera historica*, 2 vols. Oxford, 1896], I. xliv, n. 3.

[11] *Opp.* x. 261.

[12] ii. 6.

[13] iv. 22.

[14] iii. 9, 10; v. 2.

[15] v. 12 and note; also *BLTW*, pp. 214-15.

[16] iii. 27.

[17] v. 18.

[18] iv. 24.

Gerald Bonner (essay date 1973)

SOURCE: Gerald Bonner, "Bede and Medieval Civilization," in *Anglo-Saxon England*, Vol. 2, 1973, pp. 71-90. [*In the following essay, Bonner discusses the limitations of Bede's library and the subsequent ramifications for his writings.*]

The mortal remains of the Venerable Bede rest today in the cathedral church of Christ and Blessed Mary the Virgin, Durham. They were brought there in the early eleventh century by one Ælfred Westou, priest and sacrist of Durham and an enthusiastic amateur of that characteristically medieval form of devotion expressed in the acquisition, by fair means or foul, of the relics of the saints to the greater glory of God. The removal of Bede's remains to Durham, involving as it did considerable preliminary planning and solitary nocturnal vigil before the final successful snatch, was one of his more brilliant coups, upon which he seems especially to have preened himself. The bones were first kept in the coffin of St Cuthbert, being subsequently removed to a reliquary near the saint's tomb. In 1370 they were placed in the Galilee Chapel, where they now lie under a plain table-tomb of blue marble, made in 1542 after the medieval shrine had been defaced. Bede himself would certainly have preferred that his body should have been left in its grave among his brethren at Jarrow, there to await the coming of Christ which he so ardently desired to see; but if a removal had to be made, we need not doubt that he would have been content to lie at Durham, near but not too near the shrine of St Cuthbert, the great saint and patron of the north, under a modest tombstone, so much more in keeping with his nature than the earlier and richer shrine, despoiled by the commissioners of Henry VIII.

Bede in his writings gives many accounts of miraculous happenings; but no cult of miracles was associated with his name. Rather, there was a spontaneous recognition of his quality, expressed in St Boniface's phrase: 'a candle of the church'. In him may be seen an outstanding example of that flowering of Christian culture in Northumbria produced by the encounter between the Irish tradition of Iona and Lindisfarne and the Latin order of Wearmouth and Jarrow in the seventh and eighth centuries. This flowering is an astonishing phenomenon, inviting exaggerated comparisons with Periclean Athens or the renaissance of the twelfth century in western Europe. But when all qualifications have been made and all proportions duly guarded, there remains an extraordinary cultural achievement, accomplished within a few generations from the time of the conversion to Christianity. Works of art like the Codex Amiatinus and the Lindisfarne Gospels and the Ruthwell and Bewcastle crosses; vernacular poems like those of Cædmon and *The Dream of the Rood;* and Latin compositions like the anonymous lives of Gregory the Great and Cuthbert and Eddius Stephanus's biography of Wilfrid—all these are a testimony to a genius latent in the Northumbrians and brought into being by the inspiration of Christianity. To these must be added the work of Bede. Bede cannot, of course, be regarded simply as a Northumbrian, nor even as an English, figure. He is a European, writing in the international—or supranational—tradition of the Fathers of the Church; but even in this he may be said to exemplify Northumbrian tradition. After all, the uncial hand of the Codex Amiatinus and the inhabited vine-scroll ornamentation of the Ruthwell cross are themselves a reminder of continental associations.

The character of Bede—'vir maxime doctus et minime superbus' as William of Malmesbury called him[1]—presents something of an historical anomaly. Our biographical information is scanty in the extreme, so that our knowledge of his personality has to be formed from his writings—and Bede is one of the least egotistical of authors. Yet in a strange fashion Bede reveals himself through his pages, disarming criticism and making his reader feel that he knows the writer as a man.[2] One may indeed believe that it is Bede himself, as well as his writings, who has attracted many of the scholars who have studied them. In Charles Plummer, one of the greatest of Bede's editors, whose personal life in no small measure resembled that of his author,[3] Sir Roger Mynors has noted 'qualities of heart as well as head',[4] and one may observe similar qualities in more recent students of Bede, like Max Ludwig Wolfram Laistner and Bertram Colgrave.

There is an historical cliché to the effect that St Augustine of Hippo resembles a man standing on the frontiers of two worlds: the ancient world that was passing away, and the medieval world that was coming into being. In a certain sense the same is true of Bede. In the circumstances of his life he was a man of the early Middle Ages, as surely as Augustine was a man of the later Roman Empire; but as a Christian teacher—and this would seem, from the circumstance of Bede's life and from his own words[5] to have been his own view of his vocation—he stood in an unbroken tradition, descending from the Fathers of the Church. Indeed, as everyone knows who attempts to work on the text of Bede's scriptural commentaries, he has so thoroughly assimilated the patristic idiom and the patristic fashion of thought that it is often difficult to decide whether he

is quoting from another author or expressing himself in his own words. There is no question here of conscious plagiarism, for Bede, more than most medieval authors, is anxious to acknowledge his indebtedness to other.[6] Rather, he regarded his commentaries as elementary text-books for those unable or unwilling to read more distinguished authors and his own contributions as little more than glosses on what had already been said authoritatively by those greater than he. A good example of this is provided by his treatment of the verse: '[Ishmael] shall be a wild man, his hand against all and the hands of all against him; and he shall pitch his tents over against all his brethren' (Genesis XVI.12). To explain this passage, Bede first quotes Jerome, without naming him: 'He declares that his seed will dwell in the wilderness—that is, the wandering Saracens with no fixed abode, who harry all the peoples dwelling on the borders of the desert and are assailed by them.'[7] Bede then adds his own observation: 'But these things are of the past. For now is *his hand against all and the hands of all against him* to such a degree that they oppress with their domination the whole of Africa throughout its length and hold the greatest part of Asia too, and some part of Europe, hateful and hostile to all.'[8] In this comment Bede makes no mention of the period of more than three centuries which had elapsed between Jerome's day and his own. He does not question the identification of the Saracens with the descendants of Ishmael, or with the Arab invaders of Syria, Egypt and Spain. He accepts the tradition and merely brings it up to date.[9]

Bede's sense of writing within the patristic tradition is exemplified in another way, in his detestation of heresy and schism. He denounces the 'Arian madness' which corrupted the whole world and even invaded Britain[10] and sees it prefigured in the Pale Horse of the Apocalypse;[11] declares that the precepts and promises of Holy Scripture overturn both the Adoptionism of the Photinians and the Dualism of the Manichees;[12] and warns his readers that Donatists and all others who separate themselves from the unity of the Catholic Church will have their place with the goats at the left hand of Christ on the Day of Judgement.[13] The menace of Pelagianism is recognized and its teaching denounced.[14] Julian of Eclanum, the ablest of the Pelagian apologists, had written a commentary on the Songs of Songs which was apparently still extant in Bede's time and Bede, when writing his own commentary explaining the canticle as an allegory of Christ and his church, devoted the first book to a refutation of Julian's teaching.[15] This concern with doctrinal error of the past seems to the modern reader somewhat surprising. Pelagianism, it is true, is often said to be a heresy to which the English are prone and Pelagian writings were still in circulation in Bede's day; but none of Bede's contemporaries was likely ever to see a Manichee,[16] while Donatism had never had much appeal outside Roman Africa and by Bede's day was as dead as Arianism. But such considerations probably never entered Bede's mind. For him the faith of the Fathers was as his own and their enemies were to be regarded as his.

It is, therefore, difficult to exaggerate the extent of patristic influence on Bede and misleading to confine it to the Latin tradition or even to those among the Greek Fathers whose works we know to have existed in Latin translation. Two examples of occasions on which Bede draws on an unexpected Greek tradition are provided by his sermon on the Decollation of St John Baptist. In this, Bede remarks that we ought not to celebrate our birthdays with feasts or at any time indulge in carnal delights but rather anticipate the day of our death with tears, prayers, and frequent fastings.[17] This rather depressing exhortation appears at first sight to be no more than a typical expression of claustral asceticism, and when a patristic source is discovered it comes as no surprise to find that Bede's immediate inspiration appears to be St Jerome who, with characteristic erudition, points out that the only persons recorded in scripture as having celebrated their birthdays were Pharaoh, who hanged his butler, and Herod, who beheaded John the Baptist.[18] But behind Jerome, and the source upon which he drew, is Origen;[19] and Bede here stands in a tradition of thought going back to the great Alexandrian exegete of the third century. Whether Bede had actually read Origen's homily for himself is not clear. It was available in Latin translation, and we know that the Latin version of another of Origen's homilies in the same series was used by Bede in his commentary on Samuel.[20] More than this we cannot say.

The second example is even more interesting. In the same sermon Bede refers to Herod's fatal promise to the daughter of Herodias, remarking that if we perceive that the performance of an incautious oath will entail a greater crime than its violation we should not hesitate to perjure ourselves and so avoid committing the worse offence—a piece of advice which directly contradicted the ethical assumptions of Bede's society, in which oath-breaking was one of the most shameful crimes that a man could commit.[21] Now in this case, as in the preceding instance, Bede's obvious source of inspiration is Jerome who, however, merely says that he will not excuse Herod for keeping his oath, since if the girl had demanded the murder of his father or mother he would certainly have refused.[22] It is Origen, in his commentary on Matthew, who says that the guilt of oath-keeping which led to the killing of the prophet was greater than the guilt of oath-breaking would have been.[23] Had Bede read Origen on Matthew? No Latin translation survives and the problem arises: is it possible that Bede had actually read the original Greek? Dom Hurst appears to think that he may have done so, judging from the reference in his edition of Bede's sermons.[24]

I am not fully convinced of either Bede's ability or the availability of a Greek manuscript. Perhaps we should assume a Latin translation which has perished, or some reference in a florilegium? The problem remains; but the essential point is that Bede was drawing on a tradition which looks back to the third-century school of Alexandria. Dom Leclercq has emphasized the importance of the influence of Origen in determining the character of biblical exegesis in the west during the Middle Ages.[25] These examples, in indicating Bede's utilization of the past, also reveal his anticipation of the future.

It is not necessary to labour the theme of Bede's devotion to the Fathers, in view of his declared desire to walk 'iuxta vestigia patrum'[26] Nevertheless, it should be added that his attitude to patristic authority was in no way servile, and he was prepared to disregard patristic exegesis if it seemed to him unreasonable. Thus, in discussing why Cain's offering was rejected by God and Abel's accepted, he is concerned to defend the calling of the husbandman, and to see Cain's sin, not in his offering but in the mind in which he made the offering: 'Cain was not rejected on account of the humble nature of his offering, seeing that he offered to God from his habitual livelihood. It was rather on account of the impious mind of the man who offered that he was rejected together with his gifts by him who searches all hearts.'[27] The significance of this exegesis lies in the fact that it ignores the view of Ambrose, whose treatise *De Cain et Abel* Bede had used in composing his commentary, that Abel's sacrifice was preferred to Cain's because it consisted of living animals and not insensate vegetables.[28] Ambrose was, for Bede, a great authority. He had, indeed, for a time been deterred from writing his own commentary on Luke because of the existence of Ambrose's;[29] but when the need arose, he was prepared to maintain his own opinion.

Indeed, when full justice has been done to the influence of the Fathers upon Bede, it remains true that his life was lived in another world than theirs, and that his learning and culture, however profound, were not those of a man of the later Roman Empire but of the Middle Ages. Bede's very scholarship is of a different character from that of Ambrose, Jerome and Augustine and, more important, his outlook is different. One obvious distinction is, of course, that they were all Latin speakers by birth, while Bede was not. For him Latin could never have the flavour and nuances of a mother tongue. This may explain why his Latin verses have never aroused much enthusiasm, even in the kindest critics[30]— few men can hope to write poetry in a foreign tongue.[31] Nevertheless, as we shall see, there are reasons for not laying too much stress on the alien character of Bede's Latin. Rather, the essential difference between Bede's Latin culture and that of the Fathers is that Bede had no foundation of classical literature such as they enjoyed. M. L. W. Laistner in a brilliant paper drew attention to Bede's limitations, and demonstrated how many of his citations from the classical authors were probably at second-hand, in contrast to those from Christian poets.[32] Here is the great cultural change; and if we are to understand Bede, we must try to discover how it came about.

Some clue to the problem is provided by Dom Jean Leclercq in a beautiful and learned study of monastic culture in the west during the early Middle Ages[33] which, although concentrating upon the period from the Caroline reform to the rise of Scholasticism, also throws light on the earlier period from the lifetime of St Benedict onwards and makes several references to Bede. Reading this work one is constantly carried into the world of Wearmouth and Jarrow. First, Leclercq emphasizes the significance of the Benedictine tradition in early medieval western monasticism.[34] Here, at first sight, some difficulty appears to arise. Was Bede in fact a Benedictine? We have been warned not to give too much credence to the belief that Wearmouth and Jarrow were centres of Benedictine monasticism or that Bede, from his earliest profession, was a Benedictine monk. 'Although the influence of the Benedictine Rule may have been considerable, especially as the eighth century advanced, the composite or mixed rule was probably characteristic of much of Anglo-Saxon monasticism during Bede's lifetime'[35]— such is the judgement of one expert. For our purposes, however, the question is not whether the rule occupied 'a preponderant though not an exclusive position'[36] in Benedict Biscop's foundations, but rather to what degree Bede's mind and thought were shaped by it. It is generally agreed that there is only one direct citation from the Rule in Bede—that from ch. 7 in the commentary on Ezra and Nehemiah;[37] but Dom Justin McCann has identified two unmistakable citations in the *History of the Abbots*[38] and to these may be added the 'dura et aspera' of ch. 58, cited in the commentary on the First Epistle of John,[39] while the 'compunctione lacrimarum' of ch. 20 is quoted in Bede's sermon on St John the Evangelist and echoed in the *De Tabernaculo*.[40] There is, indeed, an opportunity for a detailed study of the influence of the Rule on the thought of Bede by some competent scholar. For the present we need only observe that Bede was plainly within the Benedictine tradition in the broad sense of the term, and it is easy to imagine him thoroughly at home in the company of Benedictine scholars like Jean Mabillon and Bernard de Montfaucon. Now the attitude of the Rule to monastic scholarship, as interpreted by Dom Leclercq, is that while a knowledge of letters is regarded as being necessary and normally part of a monk's life, such knowledge forms no part of his vocation, his ideal, or of his monastery's ideal. For the monk the only values are those of eternal life, the only evil sin.[41] Any approach to Bede as a scholar must be conditioned by this view. His concern with the study of scripture—the aspect of his work which most impressed his contemporaries—was determined by pastoral rather than academic considerations. Bede is a literary artist by nature rather than by intention.

Reading Leclercq's study one is made aware how remarkably Bede's writings fit into the pattern of monastic culture as there described. Besides the bible and the Rule, those twin bases of early western monasticism, Leclercq points to St Gregory as the great doctor of monastic spirituality[42]—and we remember Bede's devotion to the greatest of popes. He speaks of the desire for celestial contemplation as being characteristic of the medieval religious life[43]—and we recall how often the theme of contemplation appears in Bede's writings. He tells of the importance of the Song of Songs as an influence on the theology of the medieval cloister[44]—and Bede's commentary comes to mind. He refers to the debt owed by medieval monasticism to Latin patristic tradition[45]—and we recall Bede's frequent quotation from Ambrose, Jerome and Augustine. He speaks of the importance of history as a monastic literary genre[46]—and one remembers that the *Ecclesiastical History* is, in a sense, Bede's crowning achievement. In all these details, and in many others, Bede is wholly within the monastic culture described by Dom Leclercq.

It is in the light of these considerations that we can discuss the problem of how, and why, Bede differs from his predecessors the Latin Fathers. It has been remarked above that his Latin differed from theirs in being an acquired tongue and one that was not, like theirs, formed by a profound study of the pagan classics. Nevertheless, there are two considerations which suggest that too much stress should not be laid on the alien character of Bede's Latinity. First, the position of Wearmouth and Jarrow in Northumbrian monasticism was peculiar, in that they represented a sophisticated and cosmopolitan community constantly in touch with the outside world in general, and with Rome and Italy in particular. In such a society the study and use of Latin was more than a mere liturgical, or even theological, exercise; and the presence of an Italian like John the Archchanter, brought to Northumbria to ensure the correct singing of the Roman chant, would require the use of Latin for the purpose of oral communication. The Latinity of Wearmouth and Jarrow was therefore influenced by the living tradition of the Roman church. But there is another, deeper reason why Bede's Latin should not be regarded as a foreign language, as we commonly use the term today. For a man like Bede, as for Alcuin, Anselm and Bernard of Clairvaux, Latin was not a foreign tongue at all; it was the tongue of the church. Dom Leclercq[47] refers to the question raised by Wolfram von den Steinen in his book *Notker der Dichter und seine geistige Welt* as to why Notker wrote his famous sequences in Latin and not in his German mother-tongue, to which von den

Steinen replies that for Notker and for others like him—among whom he specifically mentions Bede—there was no choice. Their native language was inadequate to express their thoughts.[48] Latin was the language of the bible, the liturgy, and of Christian culture; and there was no other literary culture available to Bede in Northumbria.

Thus Bede learned Latin in order to be a monk and a priest. He learned it accurately enough from the standard grammars and, inevitably, read Vergil; but once he was trained it was to the study of the bible and the Fathers that he directed his attention. He had, of course, a number of stock quotations from classical authors at second hand, which he was prepared to employ for the purposes of literary embellishment or illustration;[49] but he had little inclination to add to this store and even less opportunity, in view of the resources available to him in the library of Wearmouth and Jarrow.

One of the most valuable of the many contributions made by the late Max Laistner to Bedan studies was the famous article on the library of the Venerable Bede.[50] Lacking as we do any contemporary catalogue of the library of Benedict Biscop's foundations, it is possible to estimate its resources only by reference to citations, either avowed or unacknowledged, in Bede's writings, and here Laistner's pioneering work is of fundamental importance. In the very nature of things it could not be definitive, and since its publication some additional works have been identified. For example, it would seem that we can add St Cyprian's *De Unitate Ecclesiae* and his fifty-sixth letter to Laistner's list, together with Jerome's Letter 22.[51] Furthermore, as we have seen, Bede may have had access to Origen's commentary on Matthew, either in the original Greek or in Latin translation. Further research will no doubt add more volumes to the total, though it is difficult to believe that Laistner's list will be enormously enlarged, so thoroughly did he do his work. It is, of course, impossible to be certain that any particular citation is necessarily given by Bede at first hand; but when due allowance has been made for intermediate sources, we are entitled to use Laistner's list with some confidence.

Now from this list it appears that the authors used by Bede are predominantly ecclesiastical, with the writings of the greater Latin Fathers being most abundant. Furthermore, the titles of the works identified lend support to Leclercq's view that monastic readers primarily looked in the Fathers for what would be most helpful in leading the monastic life.[52] Overwhelmingly, Bede's library consists of commentaries on scripture, patristic treatises, or secular works like Pliny's *Natural History,* which would be of value in biblical exegesis. The standard grammaraians are there of course—Donatus, Charisius, Diomedes, Pompeius and the rest—but their function is to train men to read the bible and the Fathers; and if Vergil is present—and no one could

have kept him out—he is balanced and indeed overwhelmed by Christian poets like Ambrose, Prudentius, Paulinus, Sedulius and Arator. This is understandable; Benedict Biscop and Ceolfrith had not faced laborious and dangerous journeys to Rome to build up a classical institute. As a result, Bede's is a theological library, designed for a monastery inspired by the spirit of the Benedictine Rule rather than by the principles for study laid down by Cassiodorus for his monastery at Vivarium in the middle of the sixth century;[53] for Cassiodorus, although a sincere Christian, made far greater provision for the liberal arts in his programme of monastic studies than did St Benedict. In the second book of the *Institutes* Cassiodorus provides for a course of study which anticipates the later medieval *trivium* and *quadrivium*: first grammar, rhetoric, and dialectic; then arithmetic, music geometry and astronomy. There is no hint in Bede of any such programme.[54] He knows Cassiodorus indeed; but he knows him as the former senator suddenly transformed into a teacher of the church and the author of a commentary on the psalms and not as an educational theorist.[55]

It may therefore be said that the cultural activities of Wearmouth and Jarrow were, in the last resort, determined by utilitarian motives; the highest utilitarianism, it is true—the salvation of souls—but utilitarian nevertheless. In the long run this utilitarianism was to have important cultural consequences, as is clearly seen by G. P. Fedotov, in his classic study *The Russian Religious Mind,* when he comes to discuss the problem of why there was no flowering of culture in medieval Russia as there was in France, Germany and England, finding the answer, rather unexpectedly, in the fact that in the ninth century the Slavs received the bible and the liturgy in Slavonic translations, to which were later added some works of theological and scientific content. As a result, there was no intellectual stimulus for the Slavs similar to that supplied in the west by the study of Latin, and the Slavonic bible and liturgy, priceless endowment as they undoubtedly were for Russia's spiritual life, were also an ambiguous gift, in that the Russian intellect was for a long time stunted by the absence of external occasions for exercise. On the other hand, says Fedotov:

> The western barbarians, before they were able to think their own thoughts and to speak their own words—about 1100 AD—had been sitting for five or six centuries on the school bench, struggling with the foreign Latin language, learning by heart the Latin Bible and the Latin grammar with Virgil as the introduction to the Bible. Men of the dark ages had no independent interest in culture. They were interested only in the salvation of their souls. But Latin gave them the key to salvation. As the language of the Church, Latin was a sacred tongue and everything written in it became invested with a sacred halo. Hence the popularity of Ovid in medieval monasteries, and the Latin versifying of

Irish saints, such as Columban, who in their severe asceticism and primitive rudeness of life did not yield to the anchorites of Egypt and Syria. For the Irish the *Trivium* and *Quadrivium* were the way to the Latin Bible.[56]

Fedotov's judgement agrees very well with the estimate which has just been attempted of the character of study at Wearmouth and Jarrow, and it may be remarked in passing that, in the light of what he says about the effect of a vernacular literature on medieval Russia, it may be counted fortunate that the development of an Old English literature went hand-in-hand with, and not to the exclusion of, the study of the universal Latin. Bede, we know, was familiar with the poems of his own English tongue, and enthusiastically praised the poetry of his fellow-countryman Cædmon, and it is certainly a matter for regret that no examples of his own vernacular writing survive;[57] but we may be thankful that his legacy to posterity was written in the international language of the medieval west.

The monastic and utilitarian character of the library available to Bede explains the character of his work. His great contribution to computistical studies—a contribution of such importance that as late as 1537 it was possible to publish his writings for their practical, and not for their historical, value[58]—was inspired by the practical issues of his day. This does not mean that Bede was lacking in scientific curiosity. A modern historian of science has said of the **De Temporum Ratione** that 'it contains the basic elements of natural science', pointing out that Bede, in his discussion of tides, was the first writer to enunciate the principle known as 'the establishment of a port';[59] but while computistical arithmetic, astronomy and cosmography engaged Bede's attention, he was not concerned with the more abstract discipline of geometry.[60]

Furthermore, the nature of Bede's education and the character of the literature available to him helps to shed some light on his attitude to the pagan classics. Notoriously, he is hostile, more hostile than his master, Gregory the Great. An often cited example is his comparison of those who leave the heights of the word of God to listen to worldly fables and the teachings of the demons to the men of Israel who went down to the Philistines unarmed to have their agricultural implements sharpened (I Samuel XIII.20), and another is his identification of the honey which Jonathan ate, in ignorance of his father's orders (I Samuel XIV.27), with pagan literature.[61] These are in marked contrast to Gregory, who considered both passages as furnishing a justification for secular studies.[62] It should however be observed that when Bede comes to expound the significance of the episode of Jonathan, the great warrior who climbed the rocky crag and smote the Philistine, he wishes to use it as an example of how a teacher of the church may be led astray by the enticements of

pagan literature, citing the famous story of how St Jerome was scourged in a vision before the judgement seat of God for having been a Ciceronian rather than a Christian.[63] Bede's object, however, is less to condemn pagan literature than to demonstrate that even great Christian saints continue to be tempted to small sins in order that they may be reminded that their virtues are a gift of God.[64] Pagan eloquence may legitimately be employed to support and sweeten authority;[65] and Bede is aware that neither Moses nor Daniel nor St Paul utterly eschewed pagan learnings or letters.[66] Bede's recognition that the reading of the pagan classics may be of value is clear, if grudging, and was in full accord with the teaching of the Fathers of the Church. Like them, however, he was in his heart doubtful about the reading of the pagan authors by a Christian; and his basic hesitation and suspicion could only be confirmed by the fact that he was unable to take the vision of Jerome other than seriously. Indeed, from the theological viewpoint it taught an unquestionable truth. The demands of Christ are absolute, and if a concern for Cicero leads a man to neglect them, then Cicero must be rejected as giving occasion for sin.

There is, however, one important difference between Bede and the Fathers. For them, the temptation offered by the pagan classics was a very real one. As children their minds had been formed by Vergil and Cicero, Plautus and Terence, and however hard they might try they could never entirely break the spell. Bede's education, on the other hand, had been a progress from the grammarians directly to the bible, without any intervening stage of concentrated literary study. Indeed, apart from Vergil and Pliny, his classical reading seems to have been slight, and his learning mostly from other men's quotations. In describing the dangers of the classics he was denouncing a peril to which he had never been exposed. And this held true, not only in respect of the danger of distraction from the heavenly to the temporal, but also in respect of a reversion to paganism. For the Fathers the classics were, in a very obvious fashion, a temptation to apostasy. For Bede and his age they could never be that. The classical deities might be demons, masquerading as gods; but fundamentally they were literary fictions, without any power to move to adoration. The paganism of Bede's world was German heathenism, not the literary paganism of classical antiquity. This fact may help to explain the revival of classical studies in the Carolingian period. They were no longer, in themselves, a danger to a man's soul.

We have, then, suggested a way in which Bede, although inspired by and thinking within the tradition of the Fathers, nevertheless inhabits another intellectual world from theirs, even within the confines of his monastery of Jarrow. The world of Bede is a monastic world, his culture a monastic culture, designed to bring men to heaven. Of course, the Fathers were equally concerned to bring men to heaven, and many of them were monks; but the majority of them received their education not in the cloister but in the secular schools. Thus Bede's world, although not a narrow one, was narrower than theirs.

But Bede's world differs from that of the Fathers in another way which is more difficult to describe. Put briefly and misleadingly, it is a world in which Christianity has triumphed. Clearly, in the most literal sense of the words this statement is untrue, for the Fathers, after the legal suppression of paganism had begun in earnest at the end of the fourth century, were accustomed to think of themselves as living in Christian times, while the age of Bede was a harsh and barbarous one, as appears all too clearly in the atrocities of nominally Christian kings like Cædwalla of Wessex on the Isle of Wight or Egbert of Northumbria in Ireland;[67] while across the Channel, in the Low Countries and Germany, paganism flourished and the work of the English mission to the continent, begun in Bede's lifetime, was ultimately to be accomplished only by the ruthless extirpation of heathenism wherever the Frankish armies got the upper hand. Yet in spite of this, and in spite of the alarm for the future of Northumbria expressed at the end of the *Ecclesiastical History* and the *Letter to Egbert,* there is in Bede a note of optimism. The night of infidelity has been dispersed by the Sun of Righteousness,[68] and now Christ and his bride the church go forth to the vineyards: *'In the morning,* therefore, he says, *let us go forth to the vineyards,* as though he should say openly: Because the night of ancient unbelief has passed, because the light of the bright gospel already begins to appear, *let us,* I pray, *go forth to the vineyards,* that is, let us labour in establishing churches for God throughout the world.'[69]

It is in the spirit of this passage that we should, I think, understand St Boniface's famous reference to Bede as a candle of the church in the letter sent to Archbishop Egbert of York in 746-7, asking him to send copies of Bede's scriptural commentaries.[70] It is easy when we read it today to impose our own preconceptions upon it, and to think of Bede's life shining with a small but clear flame in a waste of great darkness, the early Middle Ages; but such a romantic image was surely far from Boniface's thought. Rather, our image should be of some great basilica ablaze with brightness, with the great candles of the apostles and the saints and the lesser lights of humbler Christians, all afire with the love of God; and among them Bede, shining with a light hardly less than that of the apostles, a great candle in the house of God. What we somewhat condescendingly call the Dark Ages did not necessarily seem so dark to those who lived in them. Rather, they seemed the age of the triumph of Christ and his church.

Such an interpretation of the mood of the age will explain certain features of Bede's thought which are

otherwise puzzling. Let us consider first the *Ecclesiastical History*. It has been observed of this work:

> No single term will describe Bede's book. It includes a great deal of material quoted from papal and episcopal letters, *concilia,* epigraphic and verbal accounts; it ignores and thus condemns to oblivion, the greater part of the history of the period with which it deals, yet it repeats in detail the lives of monks who took no part in the public affairs of their day . . . As an *ecclesiastical* history—and no event without ecclesiastical relevance is mentioned in the book—Bede's work is an adjunct to scriptural study, that study which he elsewhere described as his life's occupation.[71]

With all this we may agree, except the first sentence. The work is, as Bede says, an ecclesiastical history, composed in the tradition of Eusebius of Caesarea, whom Bede knew in the Latin version of Rufinus. Eusebius was aware, when he embarked upon his *History,* that he was in effect creating a new type of historiography, unknown to the pagan,[72] and the novelty of his enterprise is reflected by his lengthy citations from his authorities. Professor Momigliano, in an important article, has drawn attention to this particular feature of Christian history, destined to make a peculiar contribution to the technique of scientific historiography, though without actually abolishing the style of the classical historians. 'We have learnt', he says, 'to check our references from Eusebius . . .'[73]— though we have contrived to secularize him by the use of footnotes. Bede, in the *Ecclesiastical History,* followed the Eusebian tradition. Where he differs from Eusebius is not in his method but in his ability to exploit his materials—Sir Frank Stenton's comment that 'in an age when little was attempted beyond the registration of fact, he had reached the conception of history'[74] is not likely to be applied to the Father of Church History. Yet so far as the philosophy which underlies their work is concerned, Eusebius and Bede are in agreement. Both saw ecclesiastical history as a struggle between the new nation, the Christians, and the devil.[75] Both wrote to record the victory of the church: Eusebius in the conversion of Constantine, Bede in the conversion of the English. The difference between them—a difference fraught with portentous consequences—is that while Eusebius took for his field the Roman Empire, Bede confined his to a particular race within a limited locality. In so doing he was, of course, only following a trail already blazed by Gregory of Tours and Cassiodorus in his lost work on Gothic history; but the very fact that he did is significant. Here, as in his biblical commentaries, Bede stands in the tradition of the Fathers but points the way to another age.

Let us consider another aspect of this idea of the triumph of Christianity. Perhaps the most significant, and certainly the most distinctive, contrast between the culture of Bede and that of the Fathers—and one which also helps to explain his attitude to the pagan classics—is to be found in the fact that he had at his disposal a corpus of Christian poetry, as distinct from the literature of theological works composed according to the rules of literary composition, which he shared with the Fathers. In this respect the two treatises *De Arte Metrica* and *De Schematibus et Tropis,* regarded by Bede as constituting a single treatise and dated by Laistner to 701 or 702,[76] are instructive. In the *De Arte Metrica* not only are Bede's examples taken overwhelmingly from Christian poets—this, after all, was determined by the resources of his library—but when he lists the three types of poetry, dramatic, narrative, and mixed, he gives examples both from pagan authors and from the Old Testament. Vergil's ninth eclogue is matched by the Song of Songs; to the *Georgics* and the *De Rerum Natura* of Lucretius are opposed Proverbs and Ecclesiastes; the *Odyssey* and the *Aeneid* have the book of Job as their Christian equivalent. *Apud nos*—'our authors'—is Bede's theme.[77] The Christians have their own literature and do not need the pagans any more. Similarly in the *De Schematibus et Tropis* Bede observes that Holy Scripture surpasses all other writings, not only by authority, because it is divine, or by utility, because it leads to eternal life, 'sed et antiquitate et ipsa positione dicendi'—by age and style.[78] We have come a long way from the days when Jerome found the language of the prophets barbarous, or the young Augustine, excited to the pursuit of philosophy by reading the *Hortensius,* found himself repelled by the style of the bible, so inferior to that of Cicero.[79] Some three centuries before Bede's lifetime Augustine of Hippo had produced, in the *De Doctrina Christiana,* a theory of a Christian culture in which the scriptures would take the place of the pagan classics and secular studies would be pursued insofar as they provided material for the Christian exegete. At about the same time Prudentius, the first great Christian poet, and Paulinus of Nola were beginning to provide the church with a corpus of poetry in addition to the liturgical hymns which had already been composed by Hilary of Poitiers and Ambrose of Milan, and Prudentius and Paulinus would be supplemented by the works of Sedulius, Arator and Venantius Fortunatus, all known to Bede. The question whether these writers were, in respect of literary quality, the peers of the great pagan poets is for our purposes irrelevant. So far as Bede was concerned, both the resources of his library and his own writings represent the embodiment of the programme of study proposed by Augustine, even to the extent of his warning expressed—ironically enough in a phrase of Terence!—against any excessive pursuit of learning beyond the bounds of the church of Christ: 'Ne quid nimis!'[80] Thus Bede's attitude to the classics was not simply determined by the consideration that they might be harmful; rather they had, in a certain sense, become unnecessary, in view of the existence of a specifically Christian literature.

This particular assumption of Bede was not shared by the scholars of the Caroline renaissance, who decided that Christian writings alone could not provide the norms of the Latinity which they desired. Few will doubt that they were right in their decision; but Bede's position, granting his premises, was unassailable, and most of us, it may be added, would be well content if we could emulate Bede's Latin style, formed as it was on the grammarians and the Fathers.

We have hitherto considered Bede as a writer who is a key figure in the transmission of patristic tradition and who also modifies that tradition and adapts it to the conditions of his own age. In this respect no one could have been better fitted to be one of the great teachers of the early Middle Ages, in which his influence was immense, as is demonstrated in the most obvious way by the great quantity of manuscripts of his writings which have survived.[81] A few examples of the range of his influence may be given, without any claim to be comprehensive. His *De Arte Metrica* was still in use at the cathedral school of Fulbert of Chartres in the eleventh century,[82] while the *De Temporum Ratione* (described by a leading modern authority as being still 'the best introduction to the ecclesiastical calendar')[83] was, as we have seen, published in the sixteenth century for practical, and not historical, reasons. Again, the *Ecclesiastical History* enjoyed a popularity which was not confined to England[84] where, in the twelfth century, it was to be a source of inspiration to the historian William of Malmesbury.[85] Yet again, Bede's biblical commentaries, the part of his work which his contemporaries most highly valued, enjoyed a remarkable renaissance of popularity during the fifteenth century, if the number of manuscript copies which have survived is any indication.[86] We are not here concerned to give a description of the diffusion of Bede's writings[87] or to give a detailed account of his influence in any particular field. Rather, if we are to regard Bede as an outstanding representative of early medieval culture and a teacher who exercised a decisive influence on the development of the civilization of the Middle Ages, it would be well to conclude this paper by a consideration of what he did not contribute, to note his deficiencies as well as his achievements, and to establish what was lacking in the Christian culture of Northumbria, of which he was the outstanding representative, which later thinkers and scholars would have to supply.

In the *Ecclesiastical History* when he comes to describe the Council of Hatfield of 679, Bede gives part of its confession of faith, declaring its adhesion to the doctrine of the first five ecumenical councils and of the council 'which was held in the city of Rome in the time of the blessed Pope Martin, in the eighth indiction, in the ninth year of the reign of the most religious Emperor Constantine',[88] that is, the Lateran Synod of 649, convened by Pope Martin I under the influence of

St Maximus the Confessor, who was probably present at it, to condemn the Monothelite heresy. Now Bede in his writings makes very little mention of Monothelitism, and none at all of St Maximus, one of the greatest of the later Greek theologians, who had lived in exile in the west, at Carthage from 632 onwards, and then at Rome from about 646 until about 655. It seems curious that Bede should know nothing about this great theologian and catholic Confessor, whose teaching was later to influence the thought of St Bernard,[89] but such is apparently the case. Now if one turns from the thought of Bede to that of Maximus, one enters another world,[90] the sophisticated world of Greek patristic theology in which all the resources of Greek philosophy and Christian experience were applied to the solution of the mystery of the union of the two natures, divine and human, in Christ. To this world, Bede is a stranger. This is not to say that he was intellectually inferior to Maximus—one cannot fairly compare the biblical scholar and historian with the dogmatic and philosophical theologian—but rather, that there was a department of Christian theology which was unfamiliar to Bede as it would not be, for example, to St Anselm at a later date.

How did this come about? Here again, an examination of Bede's library as established by Laistner is revealing, always allowing for the omissions and errors of such a reconstruction. If one looks at the titles of the works available to Bede, one is struck by the absence of books of philosophical theology or of a metaphysical content. Bede did not, apparently, have access to Augustine's early philosophical writings, the *Contra Academicos,* the *De Beata Vita* or the *De Ordine,* nor did he have the *De Trinitate,* perhaps the greatest of Augustine's theological works, nor any of the treatises of the fourth-century Latin Christian Platonist Marius Victorinus. Again, he did not have a copy of Chalcidius's commentary on part of the *Timaeus,* one of the very few Platonic sources available in the Latin west in the early Middle Ages, or of a work like that of Apuleius, *De Deo Socratis.* One can understand the absence of such works from a monastic library; but what is surprising is the lack of any work of Boethius, either the *Consolatio*—an omission so remarkable as to cause Laistner to remark upon it in his article on Bede's library[91]—or of the theological tractates and translations.

The implications of this deficiency in his library are clear: Bede was deprived, through no fault of his own, of precisely the sort of works needed by a Latin divine to whom the writings of the Greek Fathers were not available, if he aspired to be in any sense of the term a dogmatic theologian. To suggest that, had such works been available, Bede would have produced great works on dogmatic theology would be wholly unwarranted; and in any case such an achievement, however admirable and desirable in itself, would have been of less

value to the church of his day in England or on the continent of Europe than what he actually achieved. The process by which the barbarian kingdoms, established after the ending of Roman rule in the west, were turned into the civilized states of the Middle Ages was a gradual one, requiring several centuries of diligent scholarship to prepare the way for the renaissance of the twelfth century. To that renaissance Bede contributed much; but there are some things—its philosophy and its humanism—in which he had no share. The cultural achievement of Northumbria was a limited one, the work of a small élite of monks and clerics and a few cultured laymen within a restricted field, and it was within that field that Bede made his great contribution to medieval civilization. Bede was, without question, a great intellect, a great teacher, and a great Christian; but it is important in any evaluation of his work to maintain a sense of proportion. Bede served later generations as a commentator, a grammarian, an historiographer and a computist. This is his achievement, and it is enough to establish his greatness.

Yet having said this, it does not seem enough; for a man's performance is, after all, dependent upon his opportunities, and when all reservations have been made it is astonishing that Bede, a 'grandchild of pagans' and a 'child of barbarians' [92] should have become a Doctor of the Church and provide, in Plummer's words, 'the very model of the saintly scholar-priest' [93] In attempting to determine the place of Bede in medieval civilization, it would be well to remember the words of Fedotov previously quoted, that 'the western barbarians, before they were able to think their own thought and to speak their own words . . . had been sitting for five or six centuries on the school bench'. It is a measure of his greatness that for more than three of those centuries they sat under the instruction of the Venerable Bede.

Notes

[1] William of Malmesbury, *De Gestis Regum Anglorum,* ed. W. Stubbs, Rolls Series (1887-9) 1, 1.

[2] W. P. Ker, *The Dark Ages* (Edinburgh and London, 1923): 'The reputation of Bede seems always to have been exempt from the common rationalist criticism, and this although his books are full of the things a Voltairian student objects to' (pp. 141-2).

[3] See the memoir by P. S. A[llen], 'Charles Plummer 1851-1927', *Proc. of the Brit. Acad.* 15 (1929), 463-76 (pub. sep. 1931): 'The keynote of his life was to take as little as possible for himself in order to have the more to give to others' (p. 466).

[4] *Bede's Ecclesiastical History,* ed. B. Colgrave and R. A. B. Mynors (Oxford, 1969), p. lxxiii.

[5] *HE* v. 24.

[6] See E. F. Sutcliffe, 'Quotations in the Venerable Bede's Commentary on St Mark', *Biblica* 7 (1926), 428-39 and M. L. W. Laistner, 'Source-Marks in Bede Manuscripts', *JTS* 34 (1933), 350-4.

[7] Hieronymus, *Hebraicae Questiones in Libro Geneseos* XVI. 12, ed. P. Antin, Corpus Christianorum Series Latina 72, 21, lines 1-4.

[8] Bede, *Libri Quatuor in Principium Genesis* IV (XVI. 12), ed. C. W. Jones, CCSL 118A, 201, lines 250-6.

[9] On this, see R. W. Southern, *Western Views of Islam in the Middle Ages* (Cambridge, Mass., 1962), pp. 16-18; but note the qualification by C. W. Jones, CCSL 118A, ix, n. 19.

[10] *HE* 1. 8.

[11] Bede, *Explanatio Apocalypsis* VI. 7, ed. Migne, Patrologia Latina 93, col. 147 C and D.

[12] Bede, *In Cantica Canticorum Allegorica Expositio* VI (PL 91, col. 1205 A and B).

[13] *In Cant.* V (PL 91, col. 1183 B); cf. *In Primam Epistolam S. Iohannis* (PL 93, col. 90 A and B).

[14] Bede, *In Ep. I Ioh.* (PL 93, cols. 88B, 98B and C and 100A).

[15] Bede, *In Cant.* 1 (PL 91, cols. 1065 C-77B).

[16] I assume the virtual extinction of Manichaeism in western Europe between the end of Roman rule and its reintroduction from the east in the eleventh century; see Steven Runciman, *The Medieval Manichee* (Cambridge, 1955), p. 118.

[17] Bede, *Homeliarum Evangelii Libri II* II. 23, ed. D. Hurst, CCSL 122, 351, lines 92-5.

[18] Hieronymus, *Commentariorum in Evangelium Matthei Libri Quatuor* II (XIV. 7) (PL 26, col. 97 B and C).

[19] Origen, *In Leviticum Homilia* VIII. 3, ed. W. A. Baehrens, Die Griechischen Christlichen Schriftsteller, Origenes Werke VI, 396, line 20-397, line 4.

[20] Bede, *In Priman Partem Samuhelis* Libri IIII I (I Reg. IV. 18; CCSL 119, 45, lines 1420-3), citing Origen, *In Lev. Hom.* II. 2-4 (GCS, Origenes Werke VI, 292, line 4-296, line 22).

[21] I am grateful to Mr Christopher Ball of Lincoln College, Oxford, for pointing this out to me.

[22] Hieron., *In Matt.* II (XIV. 7) (PL 26, col. 97 C).

[23] Origen, *Matthäuserklärung* X. 22, ed. E. Klostermann, GCS, Origenes Werke X, 30, lines 20-3).

[24] Bede, *Hom.* II. 23 (CCSL 122, 352, lines 108-15).

[25] *The West from the Fathers to the Reformation, The Cambridge History of the Bible* II, ed. G. W. H. Lampe (Cambridge, 1969), pp. 194-6.

[26] Bede, *Expositio Actuum Apostolorum,* ed. M. L. W. Laistner (Cambridge, Mass., 1939), p. 3, line 9; *In Regum Librum XXX Quaestiones, Prolog.* (CCSL 119, 293, line 23); and *In Cant.* VII (PL 91, col. 1223 A).

[27] Bede, *In Gen.* IV (IV. 3-4; CCSL 118A, 74, lines 42-6 and 49-52).

[28] Ambrose, *De Cain et Abel,* IV, IV. 3-4 (PL 14, col. 337B).

[29] Acca, *Epistola ad Bedam, apud* Bede, *In Lucae Evangelium Expositio* (CCSL 120, 5, lines 5-18).

[30] Helen Waddell, *The Wandering Scholars,* 7th ed. (London, 1934): 'He is a greater critic than craftsman; there are cadences in his prose lovelier than anything in his poetry' (pp. 38-9); and F.J.E. Raby, *A History of Christian-Latin Poetry,* 2nd ed. (Oxford, 1953): 'His was not a poetic nature' (p. 146).

[31] A fact of which Bede was aware. See his remark on Cædmon's hymn: 'Neque enim possunt carmina, quamvis optime composita, ex alia in aliam linguam ad verbum sine detrimento sui decoris ac dignitatis transferri' (*HE* IV. 24).

[32] M.L.W. Laistner, 'Bede as a Classical and a Patristic Scholar', *TRHS* 4th ser. 16 (1933), 69-94, repr. *The Intellectual Heritage of the Early Middle Ages: Selected Essays by M.L.W. Laistner,* ed. Chester G. Starr (Ithaca, N.Y., 1957), pp. 93-116 (to which all references are made); see esp. pp. 95-9.

[33] J. Leclercq, *The Love of Learning and the Desire for God: a Study of Monastic Culture,* trans. C. Misrahi (New York, 1962).

[34] *Ibid.* pp. 19ff.

[35] Peter Hunter Blair, *The World of Bede* (London, 1970), pp. 197 and 199.

[36] Justin McCann, *Saint Benedict* (London, 1938), p. 233. Dom McCann notes that not only were abbatial elections governed by the Rule (Bede, *Historia Abbatum,* chapters 11 and 16, ed. C. Plummer, *Venerabilis Baedae Opera Historica* (Oxford, 1896) 1, 375 and 381; and

Vita Ceolfridi auctore Anonymo, ch. 16, ed. Plummer, *Bede* 1, 393) but also Bede, *Hist. Abbat.* contains unacknowledged borrowings from the Rule: 'vero regi militans' (Ch. 1 (Plummer, *Bede,* p. 365) from *Benedicti Regula, Prolog.,* 3, ed. R. Hanslik, Corpus Scriptorum Ecclesiasticorum Latinorum 75, 2) and 'in pistrino, in orto, in coquina' (Ch. 8 (Plummer, *Bede,* p. 371) from *Reg.* XLVI. I (CSEL 75, 112-13)).

[37] Bede, *In Ezram et Neemiam Libri III* III (CCSL 119A, 350, line 466-351, line 473); *Reg.* VII. 6 and 7 (CSEL 75, 40-1).

[38] See above, n. 4.

[39] Bede, *In Ep. I Ioh.*: "Quae enim natura dura sunt et aspera, spes coelestium praemiorum et amor Christi facit esse levia' (PL 93, col. 113 C); *Reg.* LVIII. 8: 'Praedicentur ei omnia dura et aspera, per quae itur ad deum' (CSEL 75, 134).

[40] Bede, *Hom.* 1. 9: 'Contemplativa autem vita est cum longo quis bonae actionis exercitio edoctus diutinae orationis dulcedine instructus crebra lacrimarum conpunctione adsuefactus a cunctis mundi negotiis vacare et in sola dilectione oculum intendere didicerit' (CCSL 122, 64, lines 163-7), and *De Tabernaculo* III: 'Duobus namque modis lacrimarum et compunctionis status distinguitur' (CCSL 119 A, 137, lines 1700-2); *Reg.* XX. 3: 'Et non in multiloquio, sed in puritate cordis et conpunctione lacrimarum nos exaudiri sciamus' (CSEL 75, 75). It is, however, to be noted that this expression is to be found in Cassian, *Collationes,* IX. 28 (CSEL 13, 274, line 18), which was available in Bede's library, and cannot therefore constitute a decisive argument.

[41] Leclercq, *Love of Learning,* p. 31.

[42] *Ibid.* pp. 33-43.

[43] *Ibid.* pp. 57-75.

[44] *Ibid.* pp. 90-3.

[45] *Ibid.* pp. 103-5.

[46] *Ibid.* pp. 156-60.

[47] *Ibid.* p. 57.

[48] Steinen, *Notker der Dichter und seine geistige Welt* (Berne, 1948) I, 76-80, esp. 79-80.

[49] Ruby Davis, 'Bede's Early Reading', *Speculum* 8 (1933), 179-95 and Laistner, 'Bede as a Classical and a Patristic Scholar', pp. 93-8.

[50] 'The Library of the Venerable Bede', *Bede: his Life, Times and Writings,* ed. A.H. Hamilton Thompson (Oxford, 1935), pp. 237-66; repr. *Intellectual Heritage of the Early Middle Ages,* pp. 117-49.

[51] Bede, *Hom.* 11. 22 (CCSL 122, 347, lines 205-9) citing Cyprian, *De Unitate,* 4 (on which see Maurice Bévenot, *The Tradition of Manuscripts* (Oxford, 1961), pp. 53 and 89, n. 7); and *In Apoc.* 11. 9: 'sicut Beatus Cyprianus sub Deciana contigisse conquestus: "volentibus," inquit, "mori non permittebatur occidi" ' (PL 93, col. 158 B) citing Cyprianus, *Epistulae,* LVI. 2; 'maxime cum cupientibus mori non permitteretur occidi' (CSEL 3(2), 649, line 20). I am indebted to Fr Bévenot for this reference.

[52] Leclercq, *Love of Learning,* p. 104. His remark that Augustine's 'polemics against the Manichaeans or the Neoplatonists had lost all timeliness for the medieval monks and therefore did not claim their attention' is only partly true of Wearmouth and Jarrow, since there were a number of Augustine's anti-Manichaean treatises in Bede's library. It is however significant that they were all concerned with scriptural exegesis and not with a direct attack on Manichaean doctrines.

[53] *Ibid.* pp. 28-31.

[54] See Pierre Riché, *Éducation et Culture dans l'Occident Barbare, 6e-8e Siècle,* Patristica Sorbonensia 4 (Paris, 1962), 434 ff.

[55] Bede, *In Ez. et Neem.* II (CCSL 119A, 295, lines 283-5).

[56] Fedotov, *The Russian Religious Mind* (New York, 1960), p. 39. For a more reserved comment on Irish classical studies see Riché, *Education et Culture,* pp. 371-83.

[57] I can see no safe grounds for regarding the Death Song as Bede's own composition. Only a small and late group of the manuscripts of the *Epistola de Obitu Bedae* assigns the poem to Bede himself, and so the evidence for his authorship is at best weak. See Colgrave and Mynors, p. 580, n. 4.

[58] The Cologne ed. of Noviomagus, 1537. See C. W. Jones, *Bedae Pseudepigrapha: Scientific Writings Falsely Attributed to Bede* (Ithaca, N.Y., 1939), pp. 1 and 7.

[59] A. C. Crombie, *Augustine to Galileo,* 2nd ed. (London, 1969) 1, 41.

[60] Riché, *Éducation et Culture,* pp. 434-6.

[61] Bede, *In I Samuhelem* II (I Reg. XIII. 20 (CCSL 119, 112, lines 1853-9) and XIV. 27 (*ibid.* p. 120, lines 2169-96).

[62] Gregory, *In Librum Primum Regum,* ed. P. Verbraken, CCSL 144, 470-2.

[63] Bede, *In I Samuhelem* II (I *Reg.* XIV. 27): 'Ionathan igitur qui prius scopulorum dentes et ictus devicerat ensium qui hostis audacia compressa suis victoriae salutisque praebuerat improvisa subito blandientis gastrimargiae culpa consternitur. Et nobiles saepe magistri ecclesiae magnorumque victores certaminum ardentiore quam decet oblectatione libros gentilium lectitantes culpam quam non praevidere contrahebant adeo ut quidam eorum se pro hoc ipso scribat in visione castigatum obiectumque sibi a domino inter verbera ferientia quod non christianus sed Ciceronianus potius esset habendus' (CCSL 119, 120, lines 2170-9); Hieronymus, *Epistulae,* XXII. 30, ed. I. Hilberg, CSEL 54, 189-91.

[64] *Ibid.*: 'Sed et auditorum fidelium non pauci magna virtutum gratia pollentes minoribus vitiis temptari non desinunt quod divina geri dispensatione non latet ut qui minora certamina per se superare nequeunt in magnis quae habent non sibi aliquid tribuere sed solo patri luminum gratias agere discant' (CCSL 119, 120, lines 2179-84).

[65] *Ibid.* (lines 2186-94).

[66] *Ibid.* (XIV. 28-9; CCSL 119, 121, lines 2209-16).

[67] Bede, *HE* IV. 16 [14] and 26 [24].

[68] Bede, *In Cant.* II: 'Sicut enim tenebras noctis, sic etiam recte per austeritatem hiemis et imbrium, tempestas exprimitur infidelitatis, quae totum orbem usque ad tempus regebat Dominicae incarnationis. At ubi Sol iustitiae mundo illuxit, abscedente mox ac depulsa prisca brumalis infidelitatis perfidia, flores apparuerunt in terra, quia initia iam nascentis Ecclesiae in sanctorum fideli ac pia devotione claruerunt' (PL 91, col. 1110 C and D).

[69] *Ibid.* IV (col. 1202A).

[70] Boniface, *Ep.* 91, ed. M. Tangl, *Die Briefe des heiligen Bonifatius und Lullus,* Monumenta Germaniae Historica, Epistolae Selectae 1, 207, line 17; cf. *Ep.* 75 *ibid.* p. 158, lines 8-11) and 76: 'quem nuper in domo Dei apud vos vice candellae ecclesiasticae scientia scripturarum fulsisse audivimus' (*ibid.* p. 159, lines 13 and 14).

[71] W. F. Bolton, *A History of Anglo-Latin Literature* (Princeton, New Jersey, 1967) 1, 171 and 172.

[72] Eusebius, *Ecclesiastica Historia,* 1.i.5 (GCS, Eusebius Werke II (I), 8, lines 17-21). On this see Arnaldo Momigliano, 'Pagan and Christian Historiography in the Forth Century A.D.', *The Conflict between Paganism and Christianity in the Fourth Century,* ed. A. Momigliano (Oxford, 1963), p. 90.

[73] *Ibid.* p. 99.

[74] Stenton, *Anglo-Saxon England,* 2nd ed. (Oxford, 1947), p. 187.

[75] Momigliano, 'Pagan and Christian Historiography', p. 90.

[76] Laistener, *A Hand-List of Bede Manuscripts* (Ithaca, N.Y., 1943), pp. 131-2.

[77] Bede, *De Arte Metrica,* 25, ed. H. Keil, *Grammatici Latini* VII (Leipzig, 1880), 259-60.

[78] Bede, *De Schematis et Tropis* (PL 90, col. 175 B).

[79] Hieron., *Ep.* XXII. 30: 'si . . . prophetam legere coepissem, sermo horrebat incultus' (CSEL 54, 189, lines 17-18); and Augustine, *Confessiones,* III. 9 (CSEL 33, 50, lines 4-14). Both these works were apparently available to Bede.

[80] Augustine, *De Doctrina Christiana,* II. XXXIX 58 (CSEL 80, 74, line 12). On all this, see H.-I. Marrou *Saint Augustin et la Fin de la Culture Antique,* 4th ed. (Paris, 1958) and esp. pt 3, ch. 3: 'La Formation de l'Intellectuel Chrétien'.

[81] For which see Laistner, *Hand-List.*

[82] See H. O. Taylor, *The Medieval Mind,* 4th ed. (London, 1925) 1, 300.

[83] C. W. Jones, *Bedae Opera de Temporibus* (Cambridge, Mass., 1943), p. 4.

[84] Laistner, *Hand-List,* p. 94.

[85] *De Gest. Reg. Angl.,* ed. Stubbs 1, 1 and 59.

[86] Laistner, *Hand-List,* p. 7.

[87] For which, see Dorothy Whitelock, *After Bede,* Jarrow Lecture 1960.

[88] Bede, *HE* IV. 17 [15].

[89] See E. Gilson, *The Mystical Theology of St Bernard,* trans. A. H. C. Downes (London, 1940), pp. 25 ff.

[90] See the excellent study by Lars Thunberg, *Microcosm and Mediator: the Theological Anthropology of Maximus the Confessor* (Lund, 1965).

[91] Laistner, 'The Library of the Venerable Bede', p. 264.

[92] Leclercq, *Love of Learning,* p. 45.

[93] Plummer, *Bede* I, lxxviii-lxxix.

Joel T. Rosenthal (essay date 1975)

SOURCE: Joel T. Rosenthal, "Bede's Use of Miracles in Ecclesiastical History," in *Traditio,* Vol. XXXI, 1975, pp. 328-35.

[*In the following essay, Rosenthal examines Bede's descriptions of miracles . . . in the* Ecclesiastical History, *contending that Bede used them carefully and for specific purposes, often to honor particular individuals.*]

Bede believed in miracles. They were basic to him, both as a practicing Christian and as a working historian. Without accepting this we can understand him neither as a man of the seventh and eighth centuries nor as the author who carefully constructed the *Ecclesiastical History*.

One of Bede's warmest admirers, the late Bertram Colgrave, was rather embarrassed by what seemed to be the naïveté of his hero. To rescue Bede from the charge of being either overly credulous or simply simple-minded, Colgrave did a useful study of the use of miracle stories in Bede's works, particularly in the *Ecclesiastical History*.[1] And yet, despite himself, he always remained a little uneasy. His comments to the British Academy reflect a continuing ambivalence, and his last words on the subject were still apologetic in tone.[2]

Colgrave need not have worried about this rationalist dilemma. It no longer seems a serious problem. Largely through the recent labors of such scholars as Colgrave himself, Laistner, Levison, and Jones we quickly come to feel more at home in the world of early English Christianity than were readers of a generation or two ago.[3] Accordingly we can readily digest episodes which once gave pause to even the most sympathetic reader. From students of myth we have learned to take many strange utterances with a new seriousness, and if we cannot 'get behind' the miracles we can at least stop wondering at their inclusion and proceed to an analysis of their use or role.

When examining the use of miracle tales in the *Ecclesiastical History* there are two points worthy of elaboration. One is that in a very large number of instances Bede gives us the specific source for his knowledge of the miracle when he recounts it. The other is that though miracles appear frequently on his pages, Bede's presentation of the conversion—perhaps the basic motif of the history—is accomplished almost wholly without the use of or the resort to miracles. These are two significant characteristics of the *History*. They rein-

force our ideas about the skill of Bede's workmanship. They also reveal the degree to which his religion was a combination of sobriety and sensitivity, of unquestioning faith and of sharp-minded realism. Do these two points make it possible to argue that Bede carefully separated the rational and the miraculous? Or, perversely, do they make it possible to uphold the contrary view?

Colgrave says, with slight exaggeration, that 'a miracle occurs on almost every page' of the *Ecclesiastical History*.[4] Actually there are about 51 different accounts of miracles and the miraculous: cures, visions, dreams, the calming of storms, the quenching of fires, the foreknowledge of death, etc. These 51 accounts reflect many more than that number of miracles, for in many instances a number of tales, usually about the same hero, are strung together and Bede simply says that now 'it is not irrelevant to narrate *one of the many* miracles which have taken place.'[5] The story then chosen, Bede assures us, is but one of the many he could relate if he were so inclined or if he thought it useful for his larger purpose.

The overwhelming majority of the miracle tales come from the later pages of the *Ecclesiastical History*. It is only with the beginning of Book 4, set after the synod of Whitby and the conversion of virtually all the English people, that the miracle tales begin to appear in real profusion. Now Bede 'has in a sense taken a step backward,' if we feel that the miracles represent a lower standard of history or of rational treatment of the world.[6] We can say that the last two books of the *History* comprise about one-third of its total length but that they contain about 28 of the 51 miracles tales, or 55 per cent of the total number. There are several reasons for this change, which was an important one in both narrative style and in theological approach. They are bound up with Bede's whole purpose in writing as well as with his view of what miracles were for and about. They were not to *prove* God's dispensation. They were rather to enrich it, to revitalize it for those who had *already* received it. As Bede says, after relating a marvelous tale: through this 'many . . . were inspired to greater faith and devotion, to prayer and alms giving, and to the offering up of sacrifice . . . for the deliverance of their kinfolk.'[7]

Since this was the role assigned to the miraculous, we can see why Bede waited until he got to Book 4, when all were believers, to begin using the supernatural with great frequency. Now he could relax and tell 'in group' stories around the fire to an audience which would share his confidence in the great theme that had just been unfolded. The tension between the demons of paganism, heresy, and schism on the one hand and the true faith on the other was finally over. It was time to reward the hearers (and readers) with an elevating form of gossip.[8]

When Bede wrote the *Ecclesiastical History* the synod of Whitby was still on the edges of living memory. The tales of miracles from more recent days were probably seen by all as being distinct from those of the time of St. Alban or Germanus of Auxerre. Bede knew that his own audience was no longer living in the days of battle-line Christianity. The miracles of more recent days were granted by divine providence in order to show that while the heroic days may have been over, there was still a need for Christian heroism. Recent miracles must not be allowed to degenerate into vulgar bits of rural folklore. They were to be as serious as, if different from, those of the great days which were gone; current faith was no less valuable than the faith of the seventh century. The faith that one imbibed from Christian parents must be shown as no whit inferior to that newly acquired by recent converts.

It was in keeping with this scope accorded the later miracles that Bede took care to identify the source for so many of the recent marvels. It was not that his veracity would be doubted by his audience, but rather fear lest the unique dispensation of each separate miracle be forgot and the suspension of the natural law be taken for granted. This had not been a danger when he was recounting great tales of the 'good old days,' since no one would take the wonders of 200 years before as a matter of course. But it could happen with an extraordinary event of a mere generation ago. So Bede, believer and psychologist, added a special dimension to most of his more recent miracles tales, i.e., an identification of the source. Of the 23 miraculous tales recorded in Books 1-3 of the *Ecclesiastical History,* only seven (or 30 per cent of the total) have a source mentioned in the text. Of the 28 miracles which appear in Books 4 and 5, 19 (or 67 percent) have a source given with greater or lesser precision.

When Bede did give a source, the style of the identification was much the same for the earlier and later books. Nor is there any qualitative difference between miracles recounted with a source and those without. Only the chronological boundary posed by the synod of Whitby (in 664) seems to make a difference. The earliest miracle Bede fully cites with a source reference was unexceptional. It concerned the way in which Earcongota, daughter of Earconbert of Kent and his wife Sexberga, learned of her own imminent death while abbess of the house at Brie in France.[9] In a similar fashion some of king Oswald's miracles had become known to Bede. The monk Fursa, who had the wondrous vision of the rewards of the just and the punishments of the wicked, told about Oswald to all and sundry, and so it reached the author: 'an aged brother is still living in our monastery who is wont to relate that a most truthful and pious [veracem ac religiosum] man told him that he had seen Fursa him-

self . . . and had heard these visions from his own mouth.'[10]

But if these mid-seventh-century miracles were passed on with a proper citation, this was not the case for many of the earlier ones. After Whitby such identification of the chain of (usually oral) transmission became Bede's customary *modus operandi,* and more often than not he includes a phrase to the effect of: 'This brother's acount . . . agrees with the story of a vision related by the most reverend father Egbert . . . who had lived the monastic life with Chad.'[11] Some accounts of miracles did reach Bede through sources, though these were few in number compared to those he chose to pick out of the grab-bag of oral tradition.[12]

It is often said that to the early medieval mind the line between the natural and the supernatural was a fuzzy one. For Bede at least it was a clear and fast one, judging by the distinction we have been discussing. Bede may have believed in miracles as surely as he knew his own name, in the sense that when he was told they had happened and his source was reliable he was metaphysically and theologically convinced, but he never confused them with ordinary happenings.[13] There was no reason why God could not work both within the ordinary rules and beyond them as well when He chose. Bede himself never claims to have seen a suspension of the natural law, nor was he ever personally touched by a direct dispensation. He knew how unusual these occurences were, and he accepted that their frequency would continue to diminish. One miracle he singles out as being *like* those of the good old days, now passing from this earth.[14] But if men of holy life and good repute told him of wonderful happenings, he had no hesitation in including such tales in his major piece of historical synthesis.

Bede did not identify his sources simply to protect himself against charges of credulity or outright falsehood. The *Ecclesiastical History* is generally replete with references to and quotations from the sources. This was a standard part of the author's methodology. Bede worked in keeping with the best professional canons of the day: 'he checked and sifted his witnesses, but he did not criticize the evidence they produced and the stories they related.'[15] In his preface he not only lists his resource men for the different kingdoms of the English, but he explicitly says that for the north he pulled many threads together: 'What happened in the Church in various parts of the kingdom of Northumbria . . . apart from those matters of which I had personal knowledge, I have learned not from any one source but from the faithful testimony of innumerable witnesses, who either knew or remembered these things.'[16]

The *Anonymous Life of St. Cuthbert,* which Bede knew and used for his own life of Cuthbert before he wrote the *Ecclesiastical History,* was well steeped in this same methodological tradition.[17] While many hagiographic works began with a brief mention of their sources,[18] the *Anonymous Life* gave citations for many of the miracles as they were related through the course of the text. By way of contrast the Life of Wilfrid only identifies the sources of the innumerable miracles on a few occasions, e.g., the woman cured of mortal palsy.[19] But Eddius Stephanus did include the text of various documents in his work, so if he was less scrupulous or acute as an historian, he was not a completely casual hagiographer.[20] Gregory the Great's *Dialogues* did give sources, much as Bede did: 'That which I intend now to tell you, I learned by the relation of one of my fellow bishops, who lived in monk's weeds many years in the city of Ancona, and led there a good and religious life. Many also of mine own friends, who be now of good years and live in the same parts, affirm it to be most true.'[21] So Bede had different examples before him when he worked, and he chose to follow the most exacting practice. The citation of the sources represents a deliberate decision, and its results are seen with such frequency on the pages of the last two books of the **History**.

The other striking point about Bede's use of miracle tales is a negative one. It is that almost none of his accounts of conversion were dependent upon the occurence of a miracle. Bede recognized a sharp cleavage between God suspending natural law so as to honor a holy man or to testify to his special merit and the performance of religious prestidigitation in order to win over the hearts and minds of men. Conversion was for Bede a rational or a spiritual process, whereas miracles were wonders to be savored by those who had *already* joined the élite. Though there are exceptions or qualification to this, it is valid if we look at the bulk of those episodes which relate the process or experience of conversion from paganism.

There are approximately 24 different accounts of conversion in the **Ecclesiastical History**. They are the main points of the book, and if they do not occupy the majority of the pages, without their witness there would be neither Church nor body of believers in England to receive the miracles. Only in a few of the earliest accounts of conversion are miracles seen as representing an instrumental part of the process. In the story of St. Alban the saint's miraculous effect upon the stream seems to have been crucial in winning over a large number of the spectators to Christianity. Even here, however, the wording of the text is ambiguous.[22] And this was the proto-miracle of the British Church; traditional lore, not malleable in Bede's hands. A century later the work of Germanus of Auxerre against the island's Pelagians was accomplished first by words and only subsequently, when the Pelagians had already been discredited, by a miracle. The heretics were already on the road to defeat *before* the blind daughter was cured: 'falsehood was overcome, deceit unmasked.'[23] This sequential order is indicative of Bede's sense of priorities. It was best for Christianity to prevail in 'torrents of eloquence,' not in tricks, even if they were worked with direct divine aid.[24]

The most important conversion in the history of the English Church was that of Ethelbert of Kent. It is almost anticlimactic as laconically related by Bede. Softened by his queen's faith, Ethelbert was won over by the words and, even more importantly, by the example of the missionaries: 'at last the king, as well as others, believed and was baptized, being attracted by the pure life of the saints and by their most precious promises, whose truth they confirmed by performing many miracles.'[25] The miracles were in confirmation, i.e., to verify what the missionaries *had already* exemplified; to use the terminology of the social sciences they were no more than a 'dependant variable.' Through the course of the seventh century other conversions related by Bede were wrought in this same low-key fashion. King Edward came over to the faith after a victory, but it was not a victory like those of Constantine or Clovis where divine help was called for upon conditional terms.[26] Edward's celestial visions certainly helped bring him over to Christ, but even after he was personally convinced his council had the right of free discussion.[27] If Edward had been moved by his own spiritual light he did not expect that by itself to be sufficient to determine the fate of his kingdom. Public debate and assent (if only by the great men) had a role, and as the miracles had just been visited upon the ruler they were not directly responsible for the conversion of Edward's people.

The Anglo-Saxon missionaries as portrayed by Bede were primarily teachers, rather than priests or magicians. Paulinus 'spent 36 days there occupied in the task of catechizing and baptizing.'[28] Edward himself 'persuaded' Eorpwold of the East Saxons to accept the new faith.[29] Paulinus 'preached' the good news.[30] It was by 'instruction' and 'ministry' that the faith was carried, time after time.[31] The East Saxons were saved from damnation by Fursey in this same fashion: 'he converted many both by the example of his virtue and the persuasiveness of his teaching.'[32] These are but typical examples of Bede's accounts of conversion.

In some instances the use of miracles was introduced *after* the actual conversion, showing quite clearly the order of the factors. *After* Oswald's people had become Christian, *then* miracles occurred at Heavenfield, where they had prayed before joining battle with the pagan enemy.[33] Bishop Wilfrid was successful with the South Saxons and *then* the rain came down: 'on the very day on which the people received the baptism of faith a gentle but ample rain fell.'[34] And when the missionaries tried to carry the faith back to the Germanic peoples on the continent before the time was ripe, miracles attested to their personal holiness but offered them no help in their abortive efforts toward conversion. God recognized their efforts and blessed them for their zeal, but He did not intervene to give them success.[35]

In these references to episodes of conversion, drawn almost at random from the *Ecclesiastical History,* we can see how carefully Bede controlled his use of miracle tales. They were an integral part of his great work, but they were neither a literary seasoning to be scattered indiscriminately for their novel flavor, nor were they mechanical levers to be tripped whenever a heavy spiritual task had to be performed. Miracles were specialized and focused. They usually came to honor the individual who worked them or upon whom they centered, as when 'the divine providence wished to show still further in what glory St. Cuthbert lived after his death.'[36] They were the specific indications of divine pleasure.
Conversely, the absence of miracles was not to be seen as indicating any absence of divine favor, whether toward individuals or their endeavors. The closest Bede ever came to having a personal hero (except for the northern saints) was Pope Gregory. Yet in his account of Gregory's life there are no miracle tales. The closest Gregory came to enjoying such a direct dispensation was through the large measure of success his mission to England enjoyed almost immediately. But even here the manifest indication of divine favor was confined to events explicable through the natural laws of causation. Gregory, like Bede, knew little of miracles from personal experience, at least insofar as Bede portrayed him. Both men were soldiers of the Church who had to draw their personal comfort from the words with which Gregory himself exhorted Augustine of Canterbury not to glory overmuch in his miracles, 'for not all the elect work miracles, but nevertheless all their names are written in heaven.'[37]

Notes

[1] Bertram Colgrave, 'Bede's Miracle Stories' in A. Hamilton Thompson, ed., *Bede. His Life, Times, and Writings* (Oxford 1935) 201-29.

[2] B. Colgrave, 'The Earliest Saints' Lives Written in England,' *Proceedings of the British Academy,* 44 (1958) 35-60. B. Colgrave and R. A. B. Mynors, editors, *Bede's Ecclesiastical History* (Oxford 1969) xxxiv-xxxvi. The editors ask 'How is it that one who is supposed to be our greatest medieval historian can spend so much time telling wonder stories?' (xxxv). David Knowles is also defensive about Bede's 'manifest belief in the miraculous,' p. x of the Everyman Library edition of the *Ecclesiastical History.* The concern is not only with Bede, for in B. Colgrave's

edition of *The Life of Bishop Wilfrid,* by Eddius Stephanus (Cambridge 1927) xi-xii, the editor is again concerned with whether the author is 'credulous' as well as partisan.

[3] Among the works that elucidate the thought and faith of early medieval Europe, the following are particularly relevant: B. Colgrave, *Two Lives of St. Cuthbert* (Cambridge 1940); C. W. Jones, *Saints' Lives and Chronicles in Early England* (Ithaca 1947); M. L. W. Laistner, *Thought and Letters in Western Europe, 500-900* revised edition (London 1957); W. Levision, *England and the Continent in the Eighth Century* (Oxford 1946). A recent book with a good bibliography is P. H. Blair, *The World of Bede* (London 1970).

[4] A. H. Thompson, *Bede,* 201.

[5] *Ec. History,* 3. 2 (216). The emphasis is mine.

[6] Colgrave, 'Earliest Saints' Lives,' 59. The tales are a methodological and intellectual regression, since Bede had reached the 'realm of pure history' in his introduction to the *History.*

[7] *Ec. History,* 4.22 (409).

[8] Thompson, *Bede,* 226-27.

[9] *Ec. History,* 3. 8 (238).

[10] *Ec. History,* 3. 19 (274).

[11] *Ec. History,* 4. 3 (344). Other examples are readily found: *Ec. History,* 4.10 (364); 4.19 (390-96), etc.

[12] *Ec. History,* 4.7 (356): 'many signs and miracles were performed which were set down by those acquainted with them as an edifying memorial for succeeding generations and copies are in possession of many people.'

[13] Colgrave, 'Earliest Saints' Lives,' 40.

[14] *Ec. History,* 5. 12 (488). A Northumbrian rose from the dead, 'a memorable miracle . . . like those of ancient days' (antiquorum simile). Colgrave, 'Earliest Saints' Lives,' 41: Along with Gregory Nazianzen, John Chrysostom, Augustine, and Pope Gregory, Bede accepted that miracles belonged to a 'past dispensation.'

[15] Knowles, *op. cit.* x, and Jones, *op. cit.* 76, for the distinction in Bede between 'historical truth' and 'ethical truth.' The latter, naturally, depended in large part on the piety and character of the transmitter of the information.

[16] *Ec. History,* Praefatio (7).

[17] Colgrave, ed., *Two Lives of St. Cuthbert* 65, for an incident of Cuthbert's youth which came to the author from Bishop Tumma, 'of holy memory, who learnt from St. Cuthbert's own lips . . . and Elias also, a priest of our church. These tell the story thus . . .' There are numerous other source-identifications of this type.

[18] For a piece of hagiography which names the sources in the prefatory bit but not miracle-by-miracle, see B. Colgrave, editor, *Felix's Life of St. Guthlac* (Cambridge 1956). The introduction professes great methodological concern: 62-63, 'just as I learned it from the words of competent witnesses whom you know . . .' and, 65, 'I would not write anything about so great a man without an exact inquiry into the facts.'

[19] *Life of Bishop Wilfrid,* 77: A woman was cured of palsy, and now, 'like Peter's wife's mother, she ministered to our holy bishop in all honour; she is still living and is now a holy abbess named Aebbe, and is wont to tell this story with tears' (cum lacrimis hoc narrare consuevit). There are other examples on 129 and 147, where a story 'is proved by the witness of many' (quod multorum testimonio comprobatur). . . .

[20] *Op. cit.* 61-67, 89, 105, 117.

[21] The quotation is from Edmund Gardner, translator, *Gregory the Great's Dialogues* (London 1911) 23-24. The text is found in *Gregorii Magni Dialogi,* libri v, edited U. Moricca, Fonti per la Storia d'Italia 57 (Rome 1924) 39: (21). 'Cuiusdam coepiscopi mei didici relatione quod narro, qui in Anchonitanam orbem per annos multos in monachio habitu deguit, ibique vitam non mediocriter religiosam duxit; cui etiam quidam nostri iam provectioris aetatis, qui ex eisdem sunt partibus adtestantur. . . .' There is another such citation on page 38: 'Ea etiam quae subiungo praedicti venerabilis viri Fortunati, qui valde mihi aetate, opere et simplicitate placet, relatione cognovi.'

[22] *Ec. History,* 1. 7 (33). The persecution does not seem to have ceased because of the miracle, *Ec. History,* 1. 7 (35): 'iudex, tanta miraculorum caelestium novitate perculsus, cessari mox a persecutione praecepit.' But Alban's own conversion was the result of his desire to emulate a confessor whose purity of life had greatly impressed him: page 11.

[23] *Ec. History,* 1. 18 (58-60). Bede concluded this episode by saying, 61: 'After these incidents a countless number of men turned to the Lord on the same day.' But his 'quibus ita gestis' does not quite force us to conclude that the miracles were responsible.

[24] *Ec. History,* 1. 17 (58).

[25] *Ec. History,* 1. 26 (76).

[26] *Ec. History,* 2. 9 (80). For Constantine's conversion, see J. Culfon and H. Lawler, editors, *Eusebius: The Ecclesiastical History* (London 1932) 2. 359-65, and Norman Baynes, 'Constantine the Great and the Christian Church,' *Proceedings of the British Academy* 15 (1929) 341-442. For Clovis' decision to come over, O. M. Dalton, trans., *Gregory of Tours: History of the Franks* (Oxford 1927) 67-70. It was almost a commonplace that miracles and conversion went together: E. A. Thompson, *The Visigoths in the Time of Ulfila* (Oxford 1966) 80.

[27] *Ec. History,* 2. 12 (174-82), and 2. 13 (182-86).

[28] *Ec. History,* 2. 14 (188).

[29] *Ec. History,* 2. 15 (188).

[30] *Ec. History,* 2. 16, 17 (190).

[31] *Ec. History,* 3. 3 (218-20): ' . . . preaching the word of faith with great devotion . . . ,' 'administering the grace of baptism to those who believed . . . ,' 'people flocked together with joy to hear the word,' 'monks who came to preach. . . .'

[32] *Ec. History,* 3. 19 (268).

[33] *Ec. History,* 3. 2 (p. 216).

[34] *Ec. History,* 4. 13 (374). The bishop showed men how to improve their fishing techniques, and this is referred to as a 'good turn' (beneficio) rather than as a repetition of the miracle of the loaves and fishes. It seems like a deliberate attempt to play down the marvelous aspects of the incident.

[35] *Ec. History,* 5. 9 (480).

[36] *Ec. History,* 4. 30 (442).

[37] *Ec. History,* 1. 31 (110). Colgrave, 'Earliest Saints' Lives,' 49: The author of the *Anonymous Life of St. Gregory* 'points out how the gift of performing miracles, as Gregory himself taught, is sometimes of less importance than the gift of teaching.'

Benedicta Ward (essay date 1976)

SOURCE: Benedicta Ward, "Miracles and History: A Reconsideration of the Miracle Stories Used by Bede," in *Famulus Christi: Essays in Commemoration of the Thirteenth Centenary of the Birth of the Venerable Bede,* edited by Gerald Bonner, SPCK, 1976, pp. 70-6.

[*In the following essay, Ward addresses Bede's miracle stories and argues that, for Bede, the emphasis was on the significance of the miracle, not the miracle itself.*]

There is still a question mark against that part of the material in Bede's writings that concerns miracles. This has caused them to be either ignored by historians or treated to a cautious defusing so that they become safe to handle; at best they are considered as primitive survivals of white magic[1] or as a different kind of truth.[2] In Mr Colgrave's introduction to his edition of the *Ecclesiastical History*[3] he expresses the doubts felt about miracles in the query, 'How is it that one who is supposed to be our greatest medieval historian can spend so much time telling wonder-tales?'[4]

It seems to me that the answer to this question is not to be found only in seeing miracle stories in the light of anthropology and folklore, or even in terms of theological definition, but by looking also at the miracles recorded by Bede in relation to miracle material used by other medieval writers, particularly historians. Miracle stories are not the perquisite of the simple-minded and uneducated; they are there in the writings of some of the most sophisticated men of the Middle Ages: even Abailard has them.[5] Miracle stories were told and retold in the circle that included Anselm of Canterbury, Hugh of Cluny, Hugh of Lyons; John of Salisbury was as concerned with miracles as the more credulous Herbert of Bosham; there is hardly a medieval chronicler who does not have miracles to record. Accounts of miracles were part of the material available to all writers in the Middle Ages. It is useful for theologians to see how this was understood and integrated into the Christian scheme of things; it is useful for others with different concerns to discover the sources, conscious or unconscious, of this way of understanding reality. But for the historians there are two more important questions: first, how far is a miracle story an account of events and facts? and second, what use did medieval writers make of this material when it became articulate in their writings?

It is clear, first of all, that Bede and other writers who record miracles believed they were recording facts about events. People believed they had witnessed these events, and they told Bede what they believed had happened; there is no question of deliberate fraud or falsehood. But to believe that what you write about actually happened is not in itself a guarantee that it did, and with miracle material it is peculiarly difficult to find any valid way of checking the personal affirmation. The essence of a miracle is in itself unverifiable, especially after a lapse of time; all that can be said is: here was an event that caused wonder, that was said by sincere and truthful men to be the direct intervention of God in human affairs. Certainly, something was thought to have happened; the rest is interpretation.

In considering this interpretation of the material the first thing to take into account is a world-view very different from our own. In a pre-scientific world which did not depend on the modern notion of causation, what distinguished a miracle from other events? For us, the interesting question about a miracle is 'how?': how was this effect caused, how did it work, what were the mechanics of this event? In the sixth century exegetes had asked that question, too:[6] how did Peter walk on the water? did the water solidify or did Peter become light? It was not asked again until Robert of Melun and Robert Pullen took it up. For Bede and his contemporaries, the important question was not 'how?' but 'what?' and 'why?' It was not the mechanics of the miracle that mattered, but its significance. For Bede the world was shot through with divinity, and a miracle was not just any inexplicable event but an event that was also a sign of God's relationship with man. Bede himself records the extreme of this view when he sets down what Trumbert, 'one of those who taught me the Scriptures', had told him. Chad had said: 'The Lord moves the air, raises the wind, hurls the lightnings and thunders forth from heaven so as to arouse the inhabitants of the world to fear him.'[7] Here the external world is seen as an extension of man, inextricably bound up with his relationship to God. It was not until the twelfth century that miracles were seen in a different context with nature as an entity in itself; and significantly it is only then that miracles can properly be described as 'wonder-tales'.

Bede certainly believed that miracles happened; it was an integral part of his understanding of reality; but what is remarkable is the way in which he controls and uses this material. He was not primarily interested in the external marvellousness of miracles. His most usual word for miracles is not *miracula* but *signa*. It was what was signified that mattered; the wonder itself was secondary. Like St Gregory the Great he saw that 'it is a greater miracle . . . to convert a sinner than to raise up a dead man'.[8] In his account of the only instance of this, the supreme miracle, in the *Ecclesiastical History,* Bede follows just that presumption: Drythelm returned from the dead, but upon that fact Bede spends no time at all. This happened, he says, *namque ad excitationem viventium de morte animae,*[9] and the other importance that it has for Bede is that it happened in Britain, *in Brittania factum est*. There are few if any instances in Bede's works where he tells a story simply for the sake of causing wonder: the wonder is always subservient to the main issue, which is salvation. This is a use of miracles which comes from inside; they are events made integral to his main theme, a part of his deepest convictions about the dealings of God with man. This integral use of miracles has an appearance of simplicity but, to quote Mr Mayr-Harting, 'the appearance of naïveté here is very deceptive indeed'.[10] Bede understood the material he was using from the inside and was not concerned to assert or emphasize the marvellous elements in the traditions he received.

As with his other material, Bede verified very carefully just what the best traditions were about a holy man or miraculous event. With St Cuthbert, he submitted his account to the brethren at Lindisfarne, for instance, and they could find no fault in it. He had recorded the consensus of opinion about the meaning of the life and miracles of St Cuthbert as it was seen by those who still lived in that tradition. They agreed that he was right about what happened and why: the significance of Cuthbert's life was to be seen through the details of events rather than in isolated facts devoid of significance.

Bede was careful also to name the people who were witnesses to miracles, as well as giving his written sources, which he does not do when relating political or military events. This is because the miracle is for Bede part of a living tradition, and its interpretation is vital. The witnesses are 'true and religious men', those in fact who can be relied upon to judge events rightly and see what is significant about them, rather than the most accurate observers of facts. This oral tradition of good men, *ex traditione maiorum,* is a source no longer available for historians; it belongs to the close-knit society of another age, where what is agreed to have happened is held to be a stronger guide than the observations of individuals. The fact that this source is not available now does not invalidate Bede in his use of it.

Bede is concerned primarily with the moral truth and inner meaning of miracle stories, and secondarily with their significance within the story he is writing, whether it is the life of Cuthbert or the missionary saga of the conversion of the English people. He does not leave the miracles as marvellous anecdotes, though, incidentally, he uses the dramatic implications of the material to the full simply as a story-teller. But beyond this moral and missionary bias, Bede uses miracle material from within in yet a third way. I would like to look briefly at a few of Bede's miracle stories and show how an unprejudiced attention to the points Bede is making leads right away from an obsession with wonder-details and gives at least three dimensions to the material used.

First, there is one of Bede's most famous stories: Cædmon's gift of song.[11] Bede is certainly saying what a wonderful thing it is that this unlettered man learnt to sing; he is also saying what a splendid instance this is of God's goodness towards the English nation; and he is also concerned with the moral edification of Cædmon's death. But the story is far more than that; it is also a piece of literary criticism. Bede introduces the story by contrasting Caedmon's poetry with that of other writers; none of them equal him, he says, *nullus eum aequiperare potuit,*[12] and he asks what makes Cædmon a better poet than the rest. The answer is given in vivid and dramatic form based on the traditions at Whitby about the poet and used by Bede in a subtle and sophisticated way. First, he makes it clear that Cædmon had always been a frustrated poet, not someone who had never wanted to sing; and it was with this unresolved tension uppermost in his mind that Bede pictures Cædmon going to sleep one night. Then, in the long tradition of poets and prophets, Cædmon dreams. He does not dream of a saint or an angel, as in a miracle story, but of *quidam,* 'someone', who stands beside him. And what does he tell Cædmon to sing? *Canta,* he says, *principium creaturarum,*[13] the basic subject of all poetry. Cædmon wakes with the tension of his life resolved; he adds more verses, turning the *principium creaturarum* theme into its Christian dimension, 'praising God in fitting style'. Next day he is examined about his experience, not by the 'reverend and holy men' who would judge a miracle, but by *multis doctoribus viris,* men of skill and technical ability. From then on, Cædmon was subject to the ordinary disciplines of a poet—metrical form, style, melodious verse—his gift was not simply a wonder, unconnected with abilities and skills. Significantly, too, the subjects he wrote about were history and moral instruction; the subjects proper to a Christian poet are those Bede himself wrote about. Bede is of course writing about a divine gift of language, and his main point is that God has acted towards the poor and simple; but Bede is also talking about literature and the essence of poetry. Cædmon, he says, was inspired by God and therefore in the mainstream of inspiration that runs through great poetry; he chose subjects within the Christian economy which improved his verse, and he developed a technique to express his inspiration. But Bede asserts that it is the divine gift of poetry that made Cædmon supreme; the others just did not have what it takes.

There is here no dwelling on a wonder for its own sake, and it is revealing to contrast this with other miracle stories about the gift of language. For instance, Roger of Hoveden tells how at the funeral of St Hugh of Lincoln a thief tried to ply his trade; he was rooted to the spot, 'impelled to compose rather inferior Latin verses whether he would or no'.[14] Walter, a lay-brother at Clairvaux, was visited in his sleep by a saint who taught him the mass of the Holy Spirit; when he woke up, he remembered it, but had the ability neither to learn more nor to use what he had learnt.[15] Or there is the story of the dumb lay-brother, William of Ford, who had his speech restored at the prayers of a saint, only to find to his disgust that he spoke low-class English rather than aristocratic French.[16] These are indeed ornamental 'wonder-tales', and the contrast with Bede need not be stressed further.

Another instance of this subtle use of the miracle story is in Bede's account of the dream of Bishop Laurence.[17] Laurence, faced with a crisis in the affairs of the English Church, spent the night in the church of St Peter and St Paul. He dreamed of St Peter, who chided and whipped him; next day he could show the king his wounds. A story of primitive incubation, no doubt; also a story about God's concern for the English people; but for Bede it is far more than this. It is the chief of the apostles who chides Laurence, asserting his own responsibility for the Church in Britain and the responsibility of Laurence as his representative in the line of the Apostles. Bede's theme here is authority in the Christian Church; through the story he says that authority derives from Christ through the Apostles to the bishops, that it centres on the see of St Peter, that it is a matter not of domination but of a responsibility that cannot be evaded or abandoned, and that it is exercised in service and suffering after the pattern of Christ crucified. This is a serious and indeed vital theme, presented under dramatic images; it resolved an otherwise insoluble conflict. Mellitus and Justus returned to England and the king received baptism; he was 'greatly alarmed' (*extimuit multum*) by the dream of Bishop Laurence—and well he might be.

A third instance of this contrast between Bede's use of miracles and that of other writers is to be found in the matter of cures. To take only one example: Roger of Hoveden describes the cure of a woman of Wye[18] by that dubious person Abbot Eustace of Flay, as follows: 'She drank the water from the fountain he had blessed and at once vomited two large black toads, which at once turned into two huge black dogs and then into asses.' The keeper of the fountain sprinkled her with water, and 'at once the creatures ascended into the sky, leaving behind a bad smell'. It is perhaps unfair to take such an extreme example, which is only a wonder-tale—unless perhaps it is used in a study of delusions—but it is the wonder-tale in its extreme form. In Bede there is no such thing. Take, for instance, the story of the cure of Herebald by Bishop John of Beverley.[19] It is an immensely interesting story, with its interaction of spiritual healing by the bishop and physical cure by the infirmarian. And it was Herebald himself who decided it was a miracle, not the onlookers: it was a miracle for him not because it was unusual but because it was significant. He was, he said, cured in order to make good deficiencies in his baptism; and this cure of the soul was to him and to Bede the true miracle.

It is clear that we are misled if we class Bede's accounts of miracles as 'mere wonder-tales'; it is to place an emphasis on the wonder that is not there in Bede himself. There is a use of miracle material that can be called merely decorative, external, concerned chiefly with the element of the unusual, even if for a moral purpose. In Florence of Worcester, for instance, miracles are prodigies, like the movements of the stars or an eclipse of the sun; in Ordericus Vitalis, miracle material is recorded in lumps, taken whole from the shrine of a saint or a saint's life; in William of Malmesbury, who is in some ways closer to Bede,

miracles are often mere wonders. In the *Gesta Regum*, for instance, in one section the miracles at the death of Pope Gregory are put alongside the story of the witch of Berkely *non superno miraculo sed inferno praestigio*,[20] a story of a magical statue of Venus in Rome, a *portenta* of Siamese twins, and the miracle of the uncorrupt bodies of the royal English saints, in such a way that what they have in common is simply their sensational value.

Bede is not, then, concerned with facts for themselves in the miracles; and indeed as his use of the anonymous *Life of Cuthbert* shows, he could alter facts to suit his theme if necessary. Do we then err if we look for factual information in the miracles recorded by Bede? I think there is historical information there, and that it is as great as in the rest of his work, but it is subject to more layers of use and interpretation than the other material. It is essential, therefore, to be aware of the use Bede makes of this material, his preconceptions about it as well as the aims and purposes he has in using it, and to realize that the events reach us essentially through interpretations. Bede is using his miracle material from the inside, and he shapes it according to his purposes. If we try to see the miracles as a simple record of facts we show ourselves more credulous and naive than Bede himself; perhaps it is not only in Bede's miracle material but in all his material that we should exercise some degree of this gift of discernment.

Notes

[1] Cf. Loomis, 'The Miracle Traditions of the Venerable Bede', *Speculum* xxi (1946), pp. 404ff.

[2] Cf. C. W. Jones, *Saints' Lives and Chronicles in Early England*. Ithaca, N.Y. 1947.

[3] Bede, *Ecclesiastical History,* ed. B. Colgrave and R. A. B. Mynors. Oxford 1969. (All quotations here form the *Ecclesiastical History* are from that edition.)

[4] *HE* [*Historia Ecclesiastica*] p. xxxv.

[5] E.g. Abailard *Sic et Non. PL* [Migne, *Patrologia Latina*] clxxviii, 1525-6.

[6] Cf. *De Mirabilibus, PL* xxxv, 2147ff.

[7] *HE* iv.3 (p. 343).

[8] Gregory the Great, *Dialogus* (*PL* lxxvii, 264-5).

[9] *HE* v.12 (p. 489).

[10] H. Mayr-Harting, *The Coming of Christianity to Anglo-Saxon England* (London 1972), p. 50.

[11] *HE* iv.24 (pp. 414-21).

[12] Ibid., p. 414.

[13] Ibid., p. 416.

[14] Roger of Hoveden, ed. W. Stubbs. Vol. IV (*Rolls Series* 51d, 1871), p. 143.

[15] *Exordium Magnum Cisterciense,* ed. B. Griesser (Rome 1961), p. 240.

[16] *Wulfric of Haselmere* by John, Abbot of Ford, Book I, c.14, ed. Dom Maurice Bell (Somerset Record Society, vol. XLVII, 1933), pp. 28-9.

[17] *HE* ii.6 (pp. 154-5).

[18] Roger of Hoveden, vol. IV, p. 123.

[19] *HE* v.6, pp. 464-9.

[20] William of Malmesbury, *Gesta Regum* (*PL* clxxix, 1187-93).

J. N. Stephens (essay date 1977)

SOURCE: J. N. Stephens, "Bede's Ecclesiastical History," in *History: The Journal of the Historical Association*, n. s. Vol. 62, No. 204, February, 1977, pp. 1-14.

[*In the following essay, Stephens explains that Bede differed from other historians in that the proper focus of the* Ecclesiastical History *is the English people, for it was Bede's intent to provide them with a new and fuller history.*]

Bede called his History **'The Ecclesiastical History of the English people'** (*Historia ecclesiastica gentis Anglorum*). It is usually said to be a history of the church. According to Levison, Bede takes 'the history of the English Church as a united whole'[1]; according to Stenton, it is 'devoted to the growth of the English Church'[2]; according to Campbell, 'his aim seems to have been to do for the history of the Church in England what Eusebius had done for the whole and he follows him in choice of subject-matter and in technique'[3]. Other writers say the same: for Mayr-Harting, 'first of all Bede wanted to write about the way in which the order and unity of the English Church had been achieved', while another aim was to give moral examples[4]. According to Colgrave, Bede's History deals 'with the history of the Christian Church'[5]. The emphasis of Hunter Blair and Wallace-Hadrill is slightly different. For the former, it 'is at bottom a history of the deeds done by individual men and women in the conversion of the English from paganism to Christian-

ity and in the subsequent development of the Church in England'[6]. For the latter, '*Historia Ecclesiastica* can be translated 'History of the Church'; and this, at its lowest level, is what it is. Thus we may speak of Bede's 'History of the Church of the English', meaning the story of . . bishoprics and to a lesser extent of monasteries . . . But there was another level and a subtler sense of ecclesiastical history, familiar since the time of Eusebius: history, that is, as a record of salvation'[7].

Although much of this may be true, there are certain difficulties, for if Bede's History is a history of the Church, there are the early chapters to be explained since they do not deal with the Church at all, but describe Britain and its Roman history. They are commonly disposed of as a clumsy introduction to the work which properly begins in cap. 23[8], but this is a very cavalier assumption. Then there is the problem of Bede's models and his peers. We are told that first and foremost Bede's History was modelled on that of Eusebius of Caesarea[9]. We learn that another model was Gildas[10], or that Bede may have drawn his design from Gregory of Tours[11] and generally that he may best be compared, not with Roman or Celtic historians, but with Gregory, Cassiodorus and Jordanes, Isidore, Fredegar and Paul the Deacon[12]. Yet if there are difficulties in conceiving of Bede's History as a history of the Church, this may affect our search for his models and we may wonder what these models can explain. C. W. Jones was surely right to say that Bede's History would have been much what it is without any models and that he 'was far more interested in working in a living tradition than in imitating an ancient model'[13].

Perhaps we may see this by glancing briefly at the surface of such histories. Eusebius, for all his emphasis upon the Empire, writes ecclesiastical history for the Church and from the point of view of the Church. He tells the history of Christianity or the history of churches within the Empire, where Bede is an intermediary between, as we might say, the Church and the State. If anything, Bede's viewpoint lies within the 'State'. He is concerned to explain the Church; to set forth ecclesiastical history not to Christians who were sectaries in a pagan empire or society, but to people who were, or had till recently been, pagans themselves. His is not 'sectarian' history in a sense that Eusebian history is, for Christianity is no longer sectarian in Bede's day, as it was even in the time of Constantine. Bede's emphasis is upon the *gens Anglorum,* whereas that of Eusebius had been upon the apostolic succession of the churches and upon the nature, the antiquity and the spread of the truth.

Bede's History has more in common with the histories of Gregory of Tours, Fredegar and Paul the Deacon, for all of them concern the story of the barbarian *gentes* who settled in the Roman provinces of northern and western Europe[14]. It means more to say that he is related to these writers than to say that he is descended from Eusebius, because he is like them in being unlike Eusebius. But this is too low a common denominator to help our understanding, since he can also be unlike them. Gregory's History, like that of Eusebius, begins in the Bible, in his case with the Creation. It is a rambling and disorganized chronicle of happenings in Francia both to churches and to kings and, as he says at the start, of 'the wars of kings with enemy peoples, of the martyr with the pagan and of churches with heretics'.[15] It is, as he implies in the Preface, more a record than a lesson, and certainly it is not, in the way that Bede's History may be, a lesson in the faith. Gregory is one 'who can promulgate the deeds of the present for a remembrance of things past' amongst future generations,[16] not, like Bede, for their 'instruction', or less clearly and consciously so. The proportions of Bede's book might indicate that his History is carefully, purposefully and differently designed. Fredegar's chronicle, or its original parts, continue where Gregory had stopped, to relate the deeds of later times, 'the acts of kings and the wars of peoples'.[17] Paul the Deacon simply writes the history of the Lombards. As with Gregory and Fredegar, his is not an ecclesiastical history.

Like Eusebius then, Bede writes about the spread of the faith. He writes, but not in the same way, about conversion and salvation. Like Gregory and Paul the Deacon, he makes his History a 'national' history. But these similarities do not reach the heart of the matter. Bede is interesting for what he does not owe to Eusebius and what he does not share in common with his barbarian peers. It is very drastic summarily to condemn the early chapters as a clumsy introduction, or to assume that Bede's intentions are fully explained by mentioning earlier models. Are there not, according to the usual idea of the work, disproportions in its dimensions? The space given to miracles and to the Easter question is often noticed, classified as a minor imperfection or explained away. But this space may have a bearing on Bede's intentions and upon whether, or in what sense, his work is a history of the Church, that is, in what sense Bede's understanding of 'an ecclesiastical history' is what we mean by a history of the Church.

Bede's work is not just a history of the Church; it is a history of the *gens Anglorum*. What relationship do the things ecclesiastical have to the *gens Anglorum*? It may seem that this is easily answered: Bede's book is simply a history of the English Church—or, the ecclesiastical history of the English people, for what is the difference? I would like to suggest that there lies a great difference and that only by grasping it may we fully understand what Bede's History is: what he sought to do and what he achieved; how he went about it and what his work may have meant to his contemporaries. In antiquity there was the ecclesiastical history (as with Eusebius) and there was the history of a people

(as with Livy). The originality of Bede was to write the ecclesiastical history of a people. An original title may reveal an original purpose.[18]

Like a new reader, having examined the title-page, let us turn to the table of contents and describe them so far as possible in Bede's own words. We may take the contents of Book III and let them stand for the whole. These contents are fairly easily described. We find advances and retreats from the faith: *gesta erga fidem Christi*.[19] We see the defenders of the faith and the apostates. We hear of saints and the 'signs' of Almighty God; *ostensio caelestium signorum*.[20] We are instructed in the succession of bishops (*successio sacerdotalis*)[21] and in the custom of the universal Church: *mos uniuersalis ecclesiae*.[22] Already we have materials by means of which we may determine something of the nature of Bede's History—and that something is, more or less, what he draws, even literally, from Eusebius.[23]

We can find many things that concern, as we would say, the history of the Church. We can find the history of the faith: of conversion and relapse, of vice and virtue. We have eminent Christians and apostates. We have the dignitaries of the Church, or more especially, the apostolic succession of the bishops. We have human merit, the judgement of God and orthodoxy on earth. Here perhaps is the history of the Church. However Bede does not tell us much about the clergy, unless about bishops and saints and usually saintly bishops. He does not tell us about the relations, as we would say, of Church and State, except in the story of kings and bishops. Nor does he tell us about ecclesiastical institutions. All these things would bulk very large in a modern work on the history of the 'Church'.

There would be one more large part of such a modern work, which might be called 'popular' piety: the system of religious practices and beliefs (as distinct from theories and doctrines, laws and institutions), which are accepted by a people. Is this not more nearly the stuff of Bede's History? Do we not approach nearer to the mark in calling it a history of the faith: of its beginnings, its successes, its setbacks and its present position?[24] It tells the story of the men who kindled it and those who kept it alight. We hear of its defenders and its enemies and we are constantly reminded that it all takes place under the watchful arbitration of God.[25] More than all this, it tells the story of what the faith should be: of *fideles catholici* against *perfidi* and *pagani*; of the *rex christianissimus* against the *rex iniustus*[26]; of the Roman against the Irish church; of Oswald against Penda; of Aidan (as we may assume) versus Wilfrid: 'on the one hand divine faith, on the other, human presumption; here piety, there pride'.[27]

This is certainly an important part of what Bede's History is, but surely it does not fully explain what

Bede was trying to do or how significant it may have seemed to his first readers? It does not explain the early chapters, nor the number of miracles, nor the weight that attaches to the *gens Anglorum* in the title and throughout the book. Perhaps if we turn back to the Preface we may find a clue from what Bede tells us there about the interests of King Ceolwulf, to whom the history is dedicated.

Does this Preface not suggest that Bede's History was an attempt to provide for King Ceolwulf, not just a Christian history or a Latin history or a universal history, but a Christian replacement for the epic; the heroic saga of pagan ancestry he loved so well—the *gestis siue dictis priorum, et maxime nostrae gentis uirorum inlustrium?*[28] Perhaps we may say that Bede sought to show the *gens Anglorum* that they had a new history; to endow them with a new history. He showed them that they belonged first to the history of Britain, or rather to Roman history, and then to the catholic history of the Church. He showed them that their history began not with the annals of Saxon settlement or with Hengest and Horsa, but with the British landscape and Roman Britain. He showed them that they belonged to Britain as much as Britain belonged to them, so that Bede's History properly ends, as it was begun, with Britain and the *status uniuersae Brittaniae*.[29] Surely Bede did not describe the periods relatively remote from his own in greater detail than those nearer to him because he was waiting for the 'pattern of God's judgement on the past to emerge',[30] but because he was instructing the *gens Anglorum* in its past—and that meant the relatively distant past.

The early chapters of Bede (however conventional their information or approach) are not an awkward introduction to his History 'proper', which begins in chapter 23. Britain is the essential beginning, as it is the essential ending of the book. Bede is introducing the English, and especially English kings, to a larger world. He is showing his race (*nostra gens*) that their history, like their genealogy, is longer than they thought. He is saying that their history is a part of British history, just as their pagan descents from Woden[31] were not the whole story—that they were descended, like all mankind, through innumerable progeny from God.

> Almighty God has established your kin to spring up from the first man whom he formed, after numberless generations had been drawn out through the ages.[32]

Then he wished, more particularly, to show or reveal the Christian history of the *gens Anglorum*. We may suggest that this, rather than the desire for 'chronological unity', was why it was so important to show how the times of English kings might be counted as years of, or even from, the Lord. Thereby the Anglo-Saxons might understand how they did not live only under the reign of a pagan king, but in the reign of

Christ and grasp how the two reigns were related. As pagan history and pagan genealogy is not abandoned, but absorbed by the Christian; so likewise the new virtue does not exclude the old.

Oswald was at once an old and a new sort of hero[33] and while the greatest of Oswine's many virtues was humility, those virtues included the 'royal dignity', which attracted nobles to his thegnage from every province of the *gens Anglorum*.[34] Nevertheless the emphasis is upon the new virtues and their glorious prospect. Did they not open up a new history of glory and fame? To set against the deeds framed by the pagan brave in a world where 'for earl whosoever, it is afterword, the praise of livers-on, that, lasting, is best'[35], he offered the miracles of saintly heroes, which brought them greater fame. Those who fought for their earthly kingdoms like Æthelfrith, might 'strongly yearn for glory'[36], but the old religion lacked *uirtus*[37], whereas the 'virtues' of the new might bring glory:

> This was in the likeness of the Apostles: with both glory and authority from conscience, doctrine through scripture, divine powers (*uirtutes*) from merit.[38]

Bede's History is itself the proof (or as a History it offers the proof) that Christian fame is greater than pagan fame. This must have had a powerful appeal for how could northern earls resist a religion that brought fame even across the seas? In the case of Oswald, not only did his fame

> encircle all the confines of Britain, but the rays of his healing light were also strewn far across the Ocean and reached at once to Germany and Ireland.[39]

'Divine dispensation' exerted itself to show that Cuthbert lived in glory after death,[40] while the name of the archbishops of Canterbury 'liveth to all generations'.[41]

Bede's great purpose and perhaps his achievement was to give the English a longer and a larger history than they thought. This may be easily overlooked. It is because Bede succeeded that we take Britain for granted and make it the backbone of Anglo-Saxon England. Bede's contemporaries did not do so—and for him to convert the barbarian and the pagan meant not just a plunging in the river, but baptism into the secrets, the traditions and the learning,—Romano-Christian history whole.[42]

Bede made the English belong to Britain and to Rome. They could count the years of their lives not from the accession of their kings but from Christ and count their regnal years as Christian years. There were also consequences that followed from this larger history. Christian history and Roman history might include 'English' history and equally they altered its interpretation. In order to see how great the consequences of this might be, we must remember what it was that in those days the historian and the singer of song did, and how different it is from what historians do now. In Dark-Age England what they sang and what they wrote was history and there was none other. An individual history is now merely a point of view, which may be checked, confirmed and corrected from a dozen other histories and a thousand other sources that record the past. Then, what the singer sang was history. To be forgotten or remembered in the song was nearly to be forgotten or remembered forever. This was true not so much because of the paucity of 'histories', but because there was only one sort of history or one view of history, until Bede showed that there was room for two, or redefined the first.

This gave the singer power and it gave Bede even greater power to decide who might afterwards be remembered— 'quae memoratu digna' and what was more dreadful in the North than to be forgotten after death? Bede, like other monastic annalists, did not hesitate to use that power, but unlike them he did not write only for monks. With a clear voice, he told the others that there was more than one sort of history and more than one view of who might be remembered in after-time; more than one list of kings:

> Hence it has pleased all who compute the chronology of kings, that having destroyed the intervening memory of those perfidious kings, the same year might be assigned to the reign of the following king, that is to Oswald, a man beloved of God.[43]

By a new and frightening standard, the memory of kings might be abolished, or else preserved, as by God, more glorious than ever:

> He may also repay your glorious name more gloriously still among posterity.[44]

We have seen that Bede lengthened and widened the Anglo-Saxon conception of history. He showed that Anglo-Saxon history was a part of British history and that both were Roman. He altered its interpretation and its very character. This he did less by replacing pagan history by christian history, but by doing what is to use a more subtle, and to his contemporaries a more controversial thing: by writing about good and not about evil.

Bede's History does not tell the story of a struggle against evil in England. It tells us about the correction of error—about a gens correcta (as Bede says of the Picts).[45] It celebrates and it demonstrates the power of 'Almighty' God and the powerful effects of a faith in a powerful God:

> Now let us praise the maker of the Heavenly kingdom, [as Bede paraphrased the song of Caedmon], the power of the Creator and his counsel, the deeds of the Father of glory: and how he, since he is the eternal God, is the author of all miracles.[46]

This may seem obvious. But is this very obviousness not something to be explained? Would it not have been still more striking and peculiar to Bede's contemporaries? We know from Beowulf,[47] and from what must have been its audience, something of the beliefs of kings and thegns, in and out of monasteries in 8th century England. They conceived of history as an heroic struggle against evil, perhaps on behalf of the Christian God, or with his help, but it was still a struggle and not a miracle hand-made by God. Did Bede seek to show them that they had another history commanded by God, and one where fame might be won not by struggling heroically against evil, but by humbly entrusting their 'faith' to God?

Once again did not the breadth of Bede's vision encompass an older or a narrower view? Pope gregory rescued 'our people' (gens) 'from the teeth of the old enemy'[48] while James the Deacon 'saved much prey from the old enemy'.[49] Sigeberht of Essex was murdered, 'at the instigation of the enemy of all good men'[50] and one afflicted man, after he had received a portion of the soil soaked by the water which had washed Oswald's bones, suffered no terrors or vexations by night 'from the old enemy'.[51] Let us recall Beowulf:

> with the coming of Grendel; grief sprang from joy when the old enemy entered our hall![52]

Beowulf is all about the Old Enemy, while Bede's History is all about the True God.

This slight welcoming of evil within Bede's larger vision would perhaps have helped all the more forcefully to direct his readers' attentions from the old conceptions to the new: from the Old Enemy to Almighty God; from heroic evil to trust; from loftiness to lowliness;[53] from the 'presumption' of man to 'faith' in God, so that (as by Caedmon's songs):

> the minds of many were frequently inflamed to despisement of the world and to an appetite for heavenly life.[54]

Bede may have been seeking to pass on to the gens Anglorum, and especially to their kings and thegns, a new conception of 'divine knowledge'—a less heroic and a more apostolic notion. It is perhaps this purpose which explains the large number of miracles that Bede reports in his History. They were not 'crudities' designed by a higher mind for a lower audience.[55] They were the proofs of God's might and proofs that man might only partake of the almightiness and the glory of

God through humble submission to His grace, as opposed to proud strife on His behalf. This conception is conveyed even by the use of the word *virtus* which meant both a virtue and a miracle. In the Gospel sense it meant divine virtue, hence divine power. It could be used both of divinity and its 'sign'; both of virtue and the 'works' of virtue. It reveals and it allows man's access to God.

In the miraculous parts of his History, Bede may have been imitating and adapting the work of Augustine and Gregory the Great. Those parts may be seen as a sort of *libellus miraculorum* designed (if we may bend Augustine's words to Bede's task) to establish the faith and by the faith to make them better known—to show that miracles are still done and by the same God who had done them in the past.[56] The Acts had preserved the 'glorious' miracles of the Apostles in the East; Augustine had done his bit for Africa in cap. 8 of the twenty-second book of the *City of God.* Gregory the Great had spoken for Italy in his *Dialogues;* now Bede, not perhaps without some pride, would do the same for England.

Bede's wide use of miracles has been explained by reference to a great increase of belief in them in the preceding centuries,[57] but there is no evidence that belief in the miraculous was less widespread in the 4th century than in the 8th century—unless amongst the half-pagan aristocracy of Rome. For Augustine, Gregory and Bede alike it was not widespread enough. What may have changed is the exegetical purpose and its effect. Pope Gregory began his *Dialogues* in order to tell his Deacon Peter about the Italian saints after he had denied knowing the life of anyone in Italy with divine powers (*virtutibus*). The Deacon did not doubt that there had been good men in Italy, but no *signa atque virtutes* had been done by them.[58] Bede glosses Gregory's task by saying that he recorded his miracles *ad exemplum uiuendi posteris.*[59]

As Gregory had written to supply the wishes of his Deacon for information about the Italian saints and (as Bede would have it) as an example to posterity, Bede himself writes to supply the liking of King Ceolwulf for the deeds of his ancestors. The miracles of Bede's History form a substantial part of the record of those deeds that he will offer. As such, they become a very new history of glory and fame. Where Ceolwulf would doubtless have liked the heroic deed, Bede will offer him the apostolic *ad instructionem posteritatis.*[60]

Bede imitates the purposes of Augustine and Gregory (and the *Acts*) and he adapts them. Augustine and Gregory seem more concerned with miracles as works of God—works of the living God. Bede may have been not only concerned to emphasize that God was alive (and alive to the English), but that he was of a particular sort. He wishes to reinterpret the sayings and deeds

of the forbears of the Anglo-Saxons 'as an example of life to posterity' (as Bede revealingly describes and subtly alters Gregory's purpose). This may be the profile of Bede's History as he once carved it himself, though the head has long been buried and forgotten. There are also particular embellishments to uncover.

Bede is not only concerned with British history and Christian history, but with Roman history and 'catholic' history and with the role played in them by the *gens Anglorum*. We have been told that Bede adopted Gildas's emphasis upon the sinfulness of the Britons and was able to develop this into a theme of his History. He could show that the fate of the British was deserved by sin and imposed by God as vengeance, so that the Anglo-Saxons could emerge as a chosen people: as a new Israel.[61] But may this not have been only a shattered fragment of a larger or abandoned theme which decorates or litters Bede's History? We have seen that the History ends, as it was begun, with Britain. May we not suppose that Bede would also have wished for it to end with the *gens Anglorum* triumphant in all Britain, perhaps by arms and certainly by religion? He might then have been able simply to describe the work at its close as an *Historia ecclesiastica Brittaniarum* and not, as he was forced, perhaps reluctantly, to add, *et maxime gentis Anglorum.*[62]

He might then have been able to draw his work to a nice conclusion of matchng proportions. He had begun with Britain. He continued with the departure of the Romans and the arrival of the *Anglorum siue Saxonum gens.*[63] He proceeded thereafter in two ways: with the return of the Romans 'to preach the word of God to the *gens Anglorum*'[64] and with the Irish bringing that grace to the 'whole' English people.[65] He brought it to completion with the successive pilgrimages of English kings to Rome (balancing perhaps the visits of Roman bishops to English kings) and 'with a wonderful dispensation of divine compassion, since that *gens,* which had willingly and without envy taken care to communicate to the English peoples the grasp of divine knowledge which it had possessed, was itself presently brought by the *gens Anglorum* to a perfect way of life, which it had lacked'.[66]

It would have been more perfect still if the 'English' people had succeeded to the whole of the Roman *Britannia* so as to hand it back intact to Rome as a complete member of the Roman faith—that faith, 'which all the churches throughout the world' (i.e. throughout the Roman world) 'agree in Christ'.[67] Thus was Bede anxious to bear testimony to the adhesion of the English to the universal church: *exemplum catholicae fidei Anglorum*[68] and, as he says of the Picts, to the subjection of a 'corrected' people to the guardianship of St. Peter.[69] His History is nearly brought to an end with the proud boast:

The English peoples are now believing and instructed in every way in the rule of the catholic faith.[70]

It is surely this—and not the traditional preoccupation of the ecclesiastical historian with error[71]—which explains Bede's emphasis on the Paschal controversy.[72] His preoccupation is not with error as such, but with the 'catholicism' of the *orbis Romanus,* of which *Britannia* was one part.

At moments in writing his History Bede seems to have felt that he might yet write that full story. May not such momentary feelings explain those Bedan 'prejudices', which historians have, according to inclination, been fond of noticing or blushing to admit? Might this not dispose at once (or dispose in terms of a larger or less meaningless prejudice) of Bede's so-called approval of *strenuitas* in kings, his account of Æthelfrith, his prejudice against the British monks at Chester, his 'incomplete' list of kings holding *imperium* over the southern English peoples and his appetite for 'brave christian kings terrorizing barbarian nations'?

Is it not odd that Bede found apparent relish for Æthelfrith, who 'wasted the British more than any other English leader'; making 'more land habitable or tributary to the English', than any other king or tribune, having first 'exterminated or subjected the inhabitants'? Why does Bede compare him to Saul 'with this only excepted, that he was ignorant of divine religion'? What are we to make of Bede's proud announcement, that after Æthelfrith no 'king of the Scots in Britain has dared until this day to come in battle against the *gens Anglorum*'?[73] Although this may seem odd, do we need to introduce Bernician sympathies or inadequately assimilated heroic poems in order to explain it? Although Bede may have drawn on local Bernician sources, (including perhaps such poems) was not Æthelfrith merely a convenient example of the Old Testament of the *gens Anglorum*? This was their age of kings—Hebrew kings, when they were 'foreknown' to God.[74] It was one stage in their conquest of the promised land, and perhaps one stage in their conquest of *Britannia*.[75]

As for Bede's list of kings, those who held *imperium* over the southern English peoples were followed by kings who ruled the Britons too.[76] Perhaps Bede may have hoped that they would become, or would be succeeded by, kings who would be truly *reges Britanniae*. Hence the often mentioned exclusion of later Mercian kings from this list, not from Northumbrian prejudice, but since they ruled again only the English peoples south of the Humber. Hence also, it may be, Bede's habit of calling the English kingdoms, not 'kingdoms', but 'provinces': a Roman name for a Roman conception, for were these not dismembered parts of the Roman 'province' of Britain? Reassembled, the *provincia Anglorum* might become again *Britannia*. English kings, now catholic and Roman, might become the hammer of barbarian kings. It was not to be.

'From that time', says Bede of Ecgfrith's reign, 'the hope and valour of the *regnum Anglorum* began to ebb and fall away. For the Picts recovered possession of their land which the English had held, and the Irish who lived in Britain and some part of the British nation recovered their liberty'.[77] In the end, Bede had to be content with a lesser symmetry: that the English brought the Picts to the customs of the universal church[78] (perhaps thereby continuing to repay the English debt to the Irish, since it was the Irish who had once converted the Picts) and the British were left in error, just as they themselves had failed to bring knowledge of the Christian faith to the English.[79]

Whether or not Bede would have wished (even haltingly, confusedly and with some contrary feeling) for English kings to become the kings of Britain or for the *gens Anglorum* to triumph over Britain by force or by religion, he may certainly have prepared them as its heirs. He may have done this by telling them their British, Roman history and in doing so by creating them as one *gens* with the traditions to succeed to it. Is it not Bede more than anyone else, who was responsible for creating or at least for propagating, the notion that the various Anglo-Saxon peoples were one 'English' *gens, the gens Anglorum*[80]? To what purpose or effect, did he do it, but to make them capable, like a Roman *gens,* of succeeding at least in spirit to the Roman province?

So much for the themes. Let us now try to draw the threads together and see how far light may have been cast on Bede's intentions and on the disproportions of his History: the early chapters, the space devoted to miracles and to the Easter question. Bede's History is not a history of the Church in our sense of the term. Nor does it merely follow classical or more nearly contemporary Latin 'models'. Bede was not doing what Eusebius or Gregory of Tours did, as the contents and even the title of his work may show. He should be compared not to the Greek history but to the German. His History, if we can grasp what it is by calling it any one thing is, as Bede himself also called it in the Preface, a 'history of our nation' (*historia nostrae nationis*), in the sense that an epic like *Beowulf* is such a history. However much Bede was influenced by his reading of the Church Fathers and Latin histories and *synodalia,* a similar spirit animates and unifies both his work and *Beowulf*. That is why there is a great difference between calling Bede's History a history of the Church and calling it the ***Ecclesiastical history of the English people*** and why we may only understand what he was doing by grasping what it is.

Bede's History does not concern the English 'Church', but the *gens Anglorum*. Nor is it an ecclesiastical history, if we understand thereby that it concerns only one part of the life of the *gens*—its ecclesiastical part. It is a history of that life itself, interpreted from a particular point of view, which was not so much 'ecclesiastical' as based upon a particular conception of God. In the same way *Beowulf* is such a history informed by another conception of God. Bede's History is a Christian replacement for the epic. It is a saga of the doings of the *gens Anglorum* under the power of God.

It may be harder for us to think of Bede's History as an epic (except as a metaphor) than it is to recall the proximity of Greek history and Greek epic. They are in the same language. Yet language can mislead and, stark as they may have been, we may exaggerate the cultural differences between Bede's monastery and the native world outside. We may make them so stark that we cannot explain at all the sudden flowering of the so-called Northumbrian Renaissance or the writing of Bede's History, its greatest work.

A consideration of Bede's 'models' may help us to understand that Renaissance. At the same time, will not his purpose do as much for the Carolingian revival? Bede is usually said to have been the father of its literature or scholarship, but may he not have been also behind its method and its purpose? Was his History not designed to transmit, interpret and refashion the classical tradition (in its loosest sense) for the conversion of his own kind, and was not that also the essential purpose of the Carolingian revival? Did not Bede, more than anyone else, directly pass on that conception through Alcuin and the school of York to the 'intellectuals' of Carolingian Francia? Similar circumstances certainly helped to define the purpose, but Bede had already been there to express and hence to form it.

Bede's History, as an apostolic saga or a Germanic *Acts*, may have been his greatest piece of teaching. He gave the Anglo-Saxons a new name, or gave it currency: that they were one 'English' *gens*. He gave them a new history and a much longer and larger one than they knew. He gave them a British history and a Roman history. He showed them that they belonged to Britain and to Rome. To adapt Bury's old remark, he showed them that their minds need no longer linger 'in the forests of Germany'. He showed them a new home. That was one ancestry. Another was Christian. He showed the Anglo-Saxons that their history began earlier than Hengest and Horsa, and differently. He showed that they were descended from God and not from Woden. This new ancestry opened up a new history of glory and fame, with new things to look for in the history of the *gens Anglorum* and new things to find. Above all, there were the deeds of the English saints or deeds done by their relics, and the fame they won.

In all these ways may Bede not have been anxious to reveal the 'allegorical' meaning of English history, as

he had already done for Scripture? In his Commentary on the Book of Samuel he had referred to drawing out the allegorical meaning of Biblical sayings 'which revives us inwardly, correcting, teaching, consoling', and such commentaries were what St. Boniface sent for to help him in his missions to the Germans.[81] Was Bede perhaps not similarly concerned, as a lesson in conversion, to draw out the allegorical meaning of 'English' history, that is, to draw out its Christian meaning as a story of conversion, so that for him, as one recent writer has said, the divine becomes 'the dynamic element of history'?[82]

This, like some of the other things that we may glimpse in Bede,[83] is a forgotten theme and justly so, for it was without a future. But what Bede says about the *gens Anglorum;* what he did for it; the history he created for it and the emphasis which he placed upon it is more important, for its consequences endured. If we wish to play the games that literary critics play, and call things 'good' and 'bad' (though if that should be anyone's task at all, it is not the historian's), Bede may be called a great historian, or at least a great English historian. It is not that he is the first English historian or the first great English historian. He is not great for his moderation (Campbell), for his co-ordination of information (Stenton) or because he so nearly fails to be one of the moderns. He is great by comparison with those who came after. We could say that he is greater than Matthew Paris, Clarendon, Hume or Macaulay and greater than all those who have written the history of the *gens Anglorum* until historians gave up writing that history altogether. He succeeded in doing what none of them were able even to attempt: he gave his audience a new history. He gave the Anglo-Saxons first a British history; then by turns a Roman, a Catholic and a Christian history. Finally he showed them that all this meant that they had a new history of their own, English history. Thereby he created it.

Notes

[1] W. Levison, 'Bede as historian', in *Bede: his life, times and writings* ed. A. Hamilton Thompson (Oxford, 1935), 143.

[2] F. M. Stenton, *Anglo-Saxon England* (Oxford, 1943; 1971), 187.

[3] J. Campbell, 'Bede' in *Latin Historians* ed. T. A. Dorey (London, 1966), 162-3.

[4] H. Mayr-Harting, *The Coming of Christianity to Anglo-Saxon England* (London, 1972), 42-3.

[5] *Bede's Ecclesiastical History of the English People*, ed. B. Colgrave, R. A. B. Mynors (Oxford Medieval Texts, 1969), xix.

[6] P. Hunter Blair, 'The Historical writings of Bede', in *La Storiografia altomedievale* (Settimane di studio del centro ital. di studi sull'alto Medioevo, xvii, 1970), 210-11.

[7] J. M. Wallace-Hadrill, *Early Medieval History* (Oxford, 1975), 79.

[8] *Venerabilis Baedae Opera Historica* ed. C. Plummer (Oxford, 1896), ii, 36; M. L. W. Laistner, *Thought and Letters in western Europe AD. 500-900* (London, 1957), 165; W. Levison, *ubi supra*, p. 141; G. Musca, *Il Venerabile Beda, storico dell'alto Medioevo* (Bari, 1973), 171.

[9] e.g. W. Levison, *ubi supra*, p. 133 (but recognizing later on that page that he may not have needed one); cf. the view of J. Campbell, quoted above.

[10] see below, p. 9 & references there.

[11] J. M. Wallace-Hadrill, 'The work of Gregory of Tours in the light of modern research', *Trans. roy. hist. soc.*, 5th ser., i (1951), 45.

[12] *idem*, 'Gregory of Tours and Bede: their views on the personal qualities of kings', *Frühmittelalterliche studien*, ii (1968), 31.

[13] *Saints' Lives and chronicles in early England* (Ithaca, 1947), 89-90; cf. G. Musca, *ubi supra*, pp. 146-7, 180.

[14] J. M. Wallace-Hadrill, 'Gregory of Tours and Bede', p. 31; cf. G. Musca, *ubi supra*, pp. 145-6.

[15] Gregory of Tours, *Opera* ed. W. Arndt (Monumenta Germaniae Historica, scriptorum rerum Merovingicarum, i, 1884), 33.

[16] *ibid.*, p. 31.

[17] Fredegar, *Chronica* ed. B. Krusch (M.G.H., script. rer. Mer., ii, 1889), 123.

[18] I owe this point to Mr. C. W. Macleod.

[19] *H. E., Praef.* (ed. Colgrave & Mynors, p. 6: all page references are to this edition).

[20] *ibid.*, ii, 1 (p. 130).

[21] *ibid., Praef.* (p. 6).

[22] *ibid.*, iii, 25 (p. 294).

[23] W. Levison, *ubi supra*, p. 143 & n.

[24] cf. G. Musca, *Il Venerabile Beda*, pp. 128-9, 176, 179-80.

[25] *H. E.*, iii, 15 (p. 260): 'Qui cuius meriti fuerit, etiam miraculorum signis internus arbiter edocuit.'

[26] to use a phrase other than Bede's own.

[27] *H. E.*, i, 17 (pp. 56-8), based on Constantius' *Life of St. Germanus*.

[28] *ibid.*, Praef. (p. 2).

[29] *ibid.*, v, 23 (p. 560)

[30] J. Campbell, *ubi supra*, p. 172.

[31] *H. E.*, i, 15 (p. 50).

[32] *ibid.*, ii, 10 (p. 170), quoting Pope Boniface.

[33] J. Campbell, *ubi supra*, pp. 170-1.

[34] *H. E.*, iii, 14 (pp. 256-8).

[35] *The Seafarer* (tr. of M. Alexander).

[36] *H. E.*, i, 34 (p. 116).

[37] *ibid.*, ii, 13 (p. 182).

[38] *ibid.*, i, 17 (p. 56), quoting Constantius' *Life of St. Germanus*.

[39] *ibid.*, iii, 13 (p. 252).

[40] *ibid.*, iv, 30 (p. 442): 'volens autem latius demonstrare diuina dispensatio, quanta in gloria uir Domini Cudberct post mortem uiueret.'

[41] *ibid.*, v, 8 (pp. 472-4), quoting *Ecclesiasticus* 44. 14.

[42] cf. R. W. Southern, 'Bede' in his *Medieval humanism and other studies* (Oxford, 1970), 5.

[43] *H.E.*, iii, 1 (p. 214); cf. iii, 9 (p. 240).

[44] *ibid.*, i, 32 (p. 112), quoting Gregory the Great.

[45] *ibid.*, v, 21 (p. 552).

[46] *ibid.*, iv, 24 (p. 416).

[47] or, for that matter, from Felix's *Life of Guthlac:* cf. R. W. Southern, *ubi supra*, pp. 2-3.

[48] *H.E.*, ii, 1 (p. 130).

[49] *ibid.*, ii, 20 (p. 206).

[50] *ibid.*, iii, 22 (p. 284).

[51] *ibid.,* iii, 11 (p. 250).

[52] *Beowulf,* 1775-6 (tr. of M. Alexander): this is a loose translation, but 'old enemy' itself is literally translated from *eald-gewinna,* which in turn may have been a literal translation of *antiquus hostis.*

[53] cf. *H.E.,* ii. 12 (p. 176).

[54] *ibid.,* iv, 24 (p. 414).

[55] J. Campbell, *ubi supra,* p. 183.

[56] *De Civitate Dei,* Bk. xxii, cap. 8 (ed. Welldon, ii, 589, 599); cf. H. Delehaye, 'Les Premiers "Libelli Miraculorum" ', *Analecta Bollandiana,* xxix (1910) pp. 427-34.

[57] J. Campbell, *ubi supra,* p. 163.

[58] Gregory the Great, *Dialogi* ed. U. Moricca (Fonti per la storia d'Italia, 1924), 15.

[59] *H.E.,* ii, 1 (p. 128).

[60] *ibid., Praef.* (p. 6).

[61] E. Faral, *La Légende Arthurienne* (Bibl. de l'Éc. des hautes études, 255-7, 1929), i, esp. 50-5; followed in various ways and degrees by R. W. Hanning, *The Vision of history in early Britain* (New York-London, 1966), 69-70; P. Hunter Blair, 'The Historical writings of Bede', pp. 211-12; J. M. Wallace-Hadrill, *Early Germanic kingship in England and on the Continent* (Oxford, 1971), 74, 97; H. Mayr-Harting, *ubi supra,* p. 44; C. Leonardi, 'Il Venerabile Beda e la cultra del secolo viii', in *I Problemi dell' Occidente nel secolo viii* (Settimane di studi del centro italiano di studi sull' alto Medioevo, xx, 1973), 636-8.

[62] *H.E.,* v, 24 (p. 566).

[63] *ibid.,* i, 15 (p. 50).

[64] *ibid.,* i, 23 (p. 68).

[65] *ibid.,* iii, 3: here, when Bede refers to Oswald's anxiety to convert the *tota gens* over which he ruled, it might be thought that he is referring simply to the conversion of Bernicia as well as Deira—the *tota gens Nordanhymbrorum* (cf. iii, 2—p. 216). But shortly afterwards Bede refers to Oswald ruling over the *gens Anglorum* and over *provinciae Anglorum,* so it seems as reasonable to conclude that the *'tota gens'* is the *gens Anglorum.*

[66] *ibid.,* v, 22 (p. 554).

[67] *ibid.,* ii, 2 (p. 136).

[68] *ibid.,* iv, 18 (p. 390). On this theme, cf. L. Torretta, 'Coscienza nazionale e ideale d'universalita nella "Historia Ecclesiastica" del Venerabile Beda', *Atti del v congresso nazionale di studi Romani,* iii (1942).

[69] *H.E.,* v, 21 (p. 552).

[70] *ibid.,* v, 22 (p. 554).

[71] J. Campbell, *ubi supra,* p. 179.

[72] cf. M.T.A. Carroll, *The Venerable Bede: his spiritual teachings* (The Catholic University of America, studies in med. hist., n.s., ix, 1946), 79.

[73] *H.E.,* i, 34 (p. 116).

[74] *ibid.,* i, 22 (p. 68).

[75] Alternatively it has been suggested that Æthelfrith was called Saul because he would soon be replaced by a 'David' more pleasing to God. One might further elaborate that he was a Bernician Saul to Edwin's Deiran David or that Æthelfrith and Oswald were two chapters in the Bernician Book of Kings. The story of Æthelfrith also helps to introduce Northumbrian affairs to the reader.

[76] *H.E.,* ii, 5 (pp. 148-50).

[77] *ibid.,* iv, 26 (p. 428).

[78] *ibid.,* v, 21.

[79] *ibid.,* v, 22 (p. 554).

[80] R. W. Chambers, 'Bede', *Proc. Brit. Acad.,* (1936), 153-4.

[81] B. Smalley, *The Study of the Bible in the Middle Ages* (Oxford, 1952), 36.

[82] C. Leonardi, 'Il Venerabile Beda e la cultura del secolo viii', pp. 636-7.

[83] It is noticeable that the emphasis on Britain tends to be suppressed in the Old English Bede: cf. D. Whitelock, 'The Old English Bede', *Proc. Brit. Acad.,* (1962), 62.

George Hardin Brown (essay date 1987)

SOURCE: George Hardin Brown, "Homilies, Hagiography, Poems, Letters," in *Bede the Venerable,* Twayne Publishers, 1987, pp. 62-80.

[In the following excerpt, Brown examines stylistic differences among the four different genres in which Bede composed: homilies, hagiography, poems, and letters.]

These popular medieval genres, once dismissed as dull or derivative, have peculiar qualities that have elicited a good deal of interest and study in recent years. But, despite Bede's important contributions and fame in each of these categories, his own creations have received little theological, historical, or literary attention. Bede's writing was often praised in his age and is esteemed in ours for its clarity, cleanness, straightforwardness, and force.[1] Yet there has not yet been any comprehensive investigation into the sources of his style or any extensive study of the style itself.[2] Similarly, the other literary qualities the works possess have with few exceptions only been alluded to. At present relatively few students learn and become competent in Latin and particularly in postclassical Latin, so the laborers in this fruitful vineyard are scarce. Still, now that we have better editions of Bede, we may hope the literary neglect of his work, so immensely popular and influential in the early Middle Ages, will be remedied by dedicated and intelligent scholars.

The Homilies

"Homilies on the Gospel: two books" (*HE* V. 24, pp. 568-69). For Bede, preaching as a form of teaching the meaning of Scripture, correct theological understanding, and moral rectitude had a special, even sacramental, significance. According to his view, preachers are the successors of the prophets and apostles.[3] Bede considered preaching the primary function of a priest: "spiritual pastors are especially ordained for this, that they preach the mysteries of the word of God, and the wonders that they have learned in the Scriptures they should display to their hearers to be wondered at" (I.7, CCSL 122, p. 49, ll. 100-4; see also p. 281). As a priest Bede took that function seriously indeed, as his collection of sermons on the Gospels, renowned and used widely throughout the Middle Ages, demonstrates. Many more sermons were attributed to Bede over the course of the Middle Ages than he authored. Further, many sermons were made by simply excerpting sections from his commentaries, especially on Mark and Luke, and assigning them to the Sundays when the gospel texts occur in the liturgy. Finally, the homilies that were his were transferred to different days to accommodate them to the later liturgy. The fact is, Bede composed fifty homilies, in two books of twenty-five each, ordered in the sequence of major feasts and Sundays of the liturgical year according to the Romano-Neapolitan use.[4] Since they are designed for general use (except for one that commemorates Benedict Biscop (*Homelia* I.13, CCSL 122, pp. 88-94), they provide few personal or local details about Bede and his immediate world; but they are clear indicators of Bede's religious attitudes and mature artistry. Although individual pieces may have come from an earlier period, he most likely assembled the collection between 730 and 735.

Bede's method of preaching is not greatly different from his exegetical procedure; that is, he takes the assigned gospel text for the day's feast and probingly comments on its verses, extracting its meanings, for the edification of the attentive Christian. It is a meditative process of rumination, savoring the spiritual content.[5] Since his sermons are essentially reflective, with the purpose of meditation on the divine mysteries, interior compunction, and quiet attainment of virtue, they differ from the public sermons of the Fathers. As usual he borrows pertinent parts from their works,[6] but he transforms them all into his monastic modality. His homilies do not display the rhetorical and oratorical flights of Ambrose's sermons to his Milanese church. They do not exhibit the pyrotechnics and rhetorical verve of Augustine's *Enarrationes in Psalmos,* preached to a noisy African congregation. They do not even directly resemble the papal sermons of Gregory the Great, though Gregory's attitudes and spirituality Bede greatly admired and imitated. They do posses their own splendid qualities of clarity, sincerity, and sobriety; they are also inventive. They remind one of the complex simplicity of Gregorian chant, in contrast to the bravura of a polyphonic orchestrated chorale.

Granted that Bede's homilies resemble the commentaries in general tone and technique, within the limits set for them they show a considerable range of artful diversity.[7] Sermons for the great high feast days of joy—Christmas, Easter, Pentecost—display more overall shape, structural symmetry, figures of speech, cadenced endings, liturgical formulae, and a higher style. Homilies for vigils, Advent, and Lent display a simpler mode, and a more verse-by-verse approach.

Even for the more austere occasions, however, there is no lack of artistry. Take, for a random example, homily II. 14 for Rogation Days (or Greater Litanies), *In litaniis maioribus* (pp. 273-79). The Gospel for the day is Luke 11:9-13, in which Jesus says:

> I tell you, Ask, and it will be given you; seek, and you will find; knock, and it will be opened to you. For every one who asks receives, and he who seeks finds, and to him who knocks it will be opened. What father among you, if his son asks for a fish, will instead of a fish give him a serpent; or if he asks for an egg, will give him a scorpion? If you then, who are evil, know how to give good gifts to your children, how much more will the heavenly Father give the Holy Spirit to those who ask him?

After introducing the general intention of the text, Bede explains that "asking" refers to our praying, "seeking" describes right living, and "knocking" means our persevering. He develops the semantic fields of asking, seeking, and knocking for thirty lines. Then with a series of *ipselnos* phrases, he contrasts the healing power of the Lord with our diseased condition (ll. 46-64). Next he turns to the reliability of God's response to those "calling upon him in truth" (Ps. 144:18): "They call upon the Lord in truth who say in their praying what they do not contradict in their living" (ll. 71-73). (Surely that phrasing is worthy of Augustine.) He moves from the concept of those seeking the Lord in truth to their opposites, those who seek badly (James 4:3; p. 274, ll. 88-89). He succinctly describes the four types of those seeking badly with a phrase beginning *male petunt* followed by a slightly but pleasingly varied clause (*qui* 89, *qui* 97, *quia* 104, *et illi qui* 107), all neatly turned to exhortation and giving the section closure: "It is true that all these kinds of seekers in so far as they seek badly (*male petunt*) will not merit to receive; let us strive, beloved, to seek well and to be worthy of obtaining what we seek" (p. 275, ll. 123-25). He proceeds to the next verses in Luke (11-12): At the literal level he stresses the comparison between an earthly father and the heavenly Father, emphasizing the sublimer qualities of the latter. Then he takes up the figural meanings (*iuxta typican intelligentiam*, 149) of bread (charity, as the principal spiritual food), of fish in the water (faith in the element of God and surrounded by the pressures of adverse surroundings), and of the egg (hope for the future). These are the goods we are to ask for of the Father (186). God will not give us hardness of heart (stone), allow the poison of infidelity (serpent), or encourage backsliding (the sting in the scorpion's rear). Bede concludes the homily by identifying the "good spirit" given by God in verse 13 with the Holy Spirit who comes with the seven gifts prophesied by Isaiah (11:2-3). The sermon ends on a confident note of encouragement and promise (ll. 258-69). The homily is not elaborately rhetorical, but it does use a number of tropes and figures in a quietly effective way; it is not structured like a classical oration but it does move forward effectively and cumulatively to a strong conclusion; it does not move the emotions wildly, but it exhorts warmly; it pleases.

Hagiography

"Also the histories of the saints: a book on the life and passion of St. Felix the confessor, which I put into prose from the metrical version of Paulinus; a book on the life and passion of St. Anastasius which was badly translated from the Greek by some ignorant person, which I have corrected as best I could, to clarify the meaning. I have also described the life of the holy father Cuthbert, monk and bishop, first in heroic verse and then in prose" (*HE* V.24, pp. 568-71).

Bede composed these pieces with the conviction shared by all Christians, that God has conferred virtues and superior gifts on certain men and women who have responded courageously to his special call. With Augustine, Bede believed that their lives were signs of the wonderful rule and love God exercised in his world. The miracles they performed in life and after death were revelations of God's power and his intervention in history. God's justice, blessing the good through the saint and punishing the wicked who have oppressed him or her, is manifest in a fallen world in which injustice and suffering are the usual human experience.

Bede also understood well and carefully incorporated the literary conventions that had been established traditionally for the description of those saints' lives.[8] In this genre, the saint's career had to conform to accepted essential patterns and be characterized by a set of standard deeds that served as credentials and proof of divinely inspired life. Moral qualities, not individual characteristics, were paramount.

The story could be expressed in prose or poetry, or transferred from prose into poetry or vice versa. Bede exercised his talents in both forms. While discussing Aldhelm's works he calls the dual format *opus geminatum* (*HE* V.18).[9] It represents a development of the classical training program of *conversio*, paraphrase, an exercise of turning prose into poetry and vice versa. Prudentius, Juvencus, Caelius Sedulius, Arator, and Venantius Fortunatus developed the practice in Christian Latin literature. Although Aldhelm's prose version of *De virginitate* is more difficult than his poetic rendition, Bede and Alcuin used prose to provide accessibility and clarity, poetry to provide artifice and grandeur. A straightforward prose account could be read aloud to the community and be more or less understood at a first reading. It served to edify the simple as well as the learned. A simple style, with the use of direct quotation and unobtrusive rhetoric, was the norm. But a higher style, in poetic form, was used as panegyric for the saint.

For the *Vita Felicis* Bede paraphrased in chaste prose the ornate poetic version of the life and miracles of the third-century saint, Felix of Nola.[10] Writing quite early in his career, probably before 709, Bede explains what he has done to his source, the series of panegyrics by Paulinus of Nola (353-431) celebrating the *Natalicia* (that is, the birthday into heaven, 14 January) of Felix: "The most felicitous triumph of blessed Felix, which he merited with God's help in the Campanian city of Nola, the bishop Paulinus of that same city has described most beautifully and fully in hexameter verses. Because they are fitting for those versed in metrics rather than for simple readers, for the benefit of the many it has pleased me to elucidate the account with plainer words and to imitate the industry of the author who translated the martyrdom of blessed Cassian from the metrical work of Prudentius into common and suitable speech" (PL 94.789B).

Comparing Bede's clean, short, easily readable prose version with the elaborately florid poetic panegyrics of Paulinus is very instructive.[11] Although Bede picks up some of Paulinus's wordplay, especially at the beginning and end on the name Felix, the relatively simple structure, short sentences, uncomplicated syntax, and prosaic vocabulary of his text make it suitable for reading aloud to the monks in chapter or refectory.[12]

Why did Bede take the trouble to rewrite a life of this particular southern Italian saint? First, the cult of Saint Felix is part of the southern Italian influence on the Anglo-Saxon liturgy, much of it under the aegis of Hadrian when he became prior of Saint Peter's (later, Saint Augustine's) at Canterbury.[13] Other evidence of this influence includes Bede's ordering his homilies according to the Roman-Neapolitan tradition, the southern Italian features of books produced in the Wearmouth-Jarrow scriptorium, particularly its Bibles (the pandects), and the Bedan testimonies to the cultural influences of Theodore and Hadrian in the ***Ecclesiastical History***. Second, as with his educational tracts and his exegetical commentaries, Bede is filling another gap in the Northumbrian Christian cultural void. Finally, this little life, a successful exercise in transfer from poetry to prose, is a charming and entertaining narrative, with its tale of Felix's using physical and verbal stratagems to elude the pursuing Romans, of stolen cattle finding their way home to a grieving old man by the intervention of Felix, of uncooperative tenants refusing to move their shabby dwellings and belongings from the immediate vicinity of Paulinus's elegant chapel for Felix.

Bede reworked a badly written life and passion of Saint Anastasius, the Persian monk martyred in 628 by Chosroes II. His relics were honored in Rome, and his cult was probably brought to England by Theodore and Hadrian (again that southern Italian connection). Until recently, Bede's version of the life of Saint Anastasius was considered lost. Now it seems that we possess not only the version "badly translated from the Greek by some ignorant person" but perhaps also Bede's own revision of it.[14] We have editions of the original Greek version of Anastasius's life and martyrdom. The slavish and awkward Latin translation, which Bede justifiably but rather peevishly criticizes (Bede was a man of standards), has come down to us in a single tenth-century manuscript witness, MS F.III.16 of the Biblioteca Nazionale of Turin, from the monastery of Bobbio. Most remarkably, according to the preliminary but painstaking analysis by Carmela Franklin and Paul Meyvaert, the version of BHL 408 may very likely be Bede's: the careful revision with respect for the integrity of the text, the aim to make sense of everything in the original, and the clean and orderly prose, all suggest Bede's work. On the other hand, the manuscript tradition does not attribute BHL 408 to Bede, and there are a few minor discrepancies between the wording of his ***Chronicle*** and that of BHL

408. Since his version was only a correction and not a total recasting of the life and passion of Saint Anastasius, Bede may not have claimed or been assigned authorship; moreover, the discrepancies between the life and chronicle entry are minor enough to be argued away.[15] Still, only more research can lead to a firmer decision about the identity of the reviser.

Bede's most important hagiographic writing is an *opus geminatum* on the life of Northumbria's great ascetic, Saint Cuthbert (ca. 634-87), successively monk, recluse, and bishop of Lindisfarne. Both Bede's versions represent a thorough reworking of an earlier (between 699 and 705) anonymous prose life by a brother or "brothers of the church of Lindisfarne" (*HE* prologue, pp. 6-7). The anonymous life is not without its virtues; as a matter of fact, some eminent Bedan admirers—Plummer, Colgrave, Levison, Jones—have preferred it in some major ways to his versions.[16] Despite its wholesale borrowings from the *Epistola Victorii Aquitani ad Hilarium,* Athanasius's *Vita Antonii,* Sulpicius Severus's *Vita sancti Martini,* and the *Actus Silvestri* in the first sections, and despite its obvious use of motifs from hagiographic lore, specifically Celtic, the four books of the anonymous *vita* present a fairly detailed but quick-moving narrative of Cuthbert's life.[17] It possesses simplicity and spriteliness; its strained attempts to relate the saint's actions to those of prominent types in the Bible are winsome. Indeed, its unsophisticated freshness and spareness does contrast both with Bede's artifical and learned poetic panegyric and with his carefully structured, stylistically superior, and generically more suitable prose account. The criticism directed against Bede's versions seems to stem from a misunderstanding of medieval literary genre and Bede's objective for these works. The metrical version represents the same kind of literary exercise that Juvencus and Sedulius performed on the Gospels by transforming the humble prose account into highly stylized hexameter verse, the same kind of artistic heightening that hymnists did for the liturgy, and that Christian men of letters such as Augustine sanctioned as a means of glorifying God.[18] The prose version, on the other hand, served another purpose. Bede's words in the preface to Bishop Eadfrith and the congregation of monks at Lindisfarne clearly intimate that he has been commissioned by them to write an official life of the recent saint whose fame and cult, no longer only familiarly local, had become widespread. As the best writer around, he accepted the task of writing the life and miracles of the saint in a form acceptable for *lectio divina,* for perusing not only in private devotion but also for annual public reading on the feast of the saint. He therefore took the anonymous Lindisfarne life as the most reliable textual history of Cuthbert's life and added to that his own findings from witnesses, particularly Herefrith. In order to improve the style of his source, he completely rewrote the life in his own lucid fashion, rearranging the sequence of events, smoothing transitions, adding quotations and augmenting plot to form a continuous narrative. By drawing out the spiritual and moral lessons to be derived from hagiographic reading, he observed the requirements of the genre. As J. F. Webb points out, "His main aim was not historical accuracy but imaginative truth within the framework of a conventional literary form, the saint's life."[19]

Bede wrote the metrical version of 979 competent hexameter lines between 705 and 716, according to the reference to Osred's reign in verses 552-55.[20] In the dedicatory preface Bede tells the priest John that he was unable to include all Cuthbert's wondrous deeds because new ones were daily being done through his relics and old ones were newly being brought to light. He then adds the striking comment: "One of those wondrous deeds I myself experienced by a guidance [or: curing] of the tongue (*per linguae curationem*), as I have already told you, while I was singing his miracles" (*Vita Cuthberti*, ed. Jaager, p. 57, ll. 17-19). Whether this means that Bede received direction and guidance through Cuthbert's inspiration as a saintly muse or whether he was cured of some lingual affliction is unclear because the Latin bears both meanings, "administration, attention, treatment, guidance," or "cure, healing," but modern critics favor the former.[21]

As the *apparatus criticus* of Jaager's edition makes clear, Bede's metrical version owes very little to the wording of the anonymous life, but it does remain closer to the order and arrangment of that source than does the prose version. Bede includes all miracles of the anonymous life except those only summarily mentioned without detail. And Bede adds a dozen chapters' worth of material.[22] But his poetic version provides less historical detail than the anonymous and certainly less than his prose version; in the former he placed greater emphasis on Cuthbert's wonders. Stylistically the poem follows the late antique classical tradition of Juvencus, Sedulius, and Arator, from whom Bede takes phrases and vocabulary; but he also uses Virgil copiously, and (according to the editor Jaager's conservative reckoning) in descending order of frequency, Cyprianus Gallus, Venantius Fortunatus, Paulinus of Nola, Dracontius, Prudentius, Aldhelm, Paulinus of Périgueux, Alcimus Avitus, Damasus, Serenus Sammonicus, Ovid, Horace, Prosper, Orientius, Augustine, and Persius. His metrics and prosody are enviably correct despite an occasional variation from classical usage; he uses rhyme and alliteration sparingly (indicating how little Bede carries over the Anglo-Saxon poetic verse tradition into his Latin). For anyone familiar with early medieval poetry the poem offers no great difficulty and considerable pleasure.

The poem is nicely constructed, moving from the general view of the Lord's numerous and various saints as lights of the Church to examples of individuals, who shine particularly for their own locale—e.g., Peter and Paul for Rome, Cyprian for Africa, John Chrysostom for Constantinople, and finally Cuthbert for the English. Thus, at the outset Bede places Cuthbert in a cosmic setting as the patron of the English but honored universally. In the spirit and with the world as audience, Bede presents in studied and solemn verse the glorified Cuthbert. In contrast to the solemnity of the proem and the gravity of the prophetic warning of the destruction of the monastery (chap. 37), some of the account is charming, mock-pastoral and mock-heroic. The amusing mixture of Virgilian bucolic and epic verse in the following passage reveals not only Bede's command of classical verse but also his sense of humor:[23]

XVII

Quique suis cupiens victum conquiere palmis
Incultum pertemptat humum proscindere ferro
Et sator edomitis anni spem credere glebis.
Dumque seges modico de semine surgeret
    ampla,
Tempus adest messis; rapidae sed forte
    volucres
Flaventes praedare senis nituntur aristas.
Talia qui placidus saevis praedonibus infit:
"Quid precor inlicito messem contingitis ausu,
Quae vestro sulcis non est inserta labore?
Pauperies an vestra meam transcendit, ut istud
Incurvam merito falcem mittatis in aequor?
Quod si forte deus iubet his instare rapinis,
Non veto; sin alias, vos finibus indite vestris."
Dixerat, et cessit mox plumea turba nec ultra
Militis audebat domini iam leadere iura.
Quin potius dulci pacis quasi foedere nexum
Unanimemque sui generis redamabat amicum,
Nam teneras ceu pastor oves hanc ipse
    regebat.

                    (ll. 413-30)

(Desiring to get food by means of his own hands, he works to cut through the uncultivated soil with iron tool; and as a sower he entrusts the hope of the year in the tamed glebe. After an ample crop results from the bit of seed, it is time for the reaping. However, by chance quick birds strive to plunder the old man's golden ears of grain. Placid, he begins to speak to the savage thieves: "Why, I beg you, do you reach with illicit daring for the harvest, which was not planted in the rows by your labor? Or does your poverty exceed mine, that you should send your curved scythe justly into that plain? If perhaps God orders you to press on with this rapine, I do not forbid. If otherwise, put yourselves in your own territories." He had spoken, and immediately the plumed mob ceased and dared not further violate now the laws of the soldier lord. Rather, it formed a bond with him as by a sweet pact of peace, and loved him as a united friend of its race, for he ruled this group as a pastor his tender sheep.)

The prose life owes very little to the metrical life but a great deal to the anonymous. Forty miracles are related in this version; only eight are not in the anonymous (Colgrave, *Two Lives,* p. 14). Bede points out in the preface that he showed his notes to the monks of Lindisfarne for their criticism. Additional fine material, such as chapter 33, and his beautiful account of Cuthbert's death, related in chapters 37-39, he owes as he says to Herefrith. In Bede's hands the life displays a skillful blend of the Roman and Celtic ideal ways of monastic life. This is fitting not only because the writer himself owes so much to both traditions but because the hero Cuthbert was according to both biographers an interlocking cornerstone for the two modes of life. In many respects Cuthbert resembles the enterprising Irish ascetics and pilgrim monks in his heroic penitential practices, his search for solitude, and his missionary activity. The arrangements of his Lindisfarne discipline and the relationship of bishop, abbot, and community reveal elements of both Irish and continental monasticism, which Bede feels obliged to explain ("ne aliquis miretur" ["lest anyone should marvel"], chap. 16, p. 206).[24] Bede does not include the detail from the anonymous life, that as prior Cuthbert instituted a rule "which we observe even to this day along with the rule of St. Benedict" (III. 1, pp. 95-97). In the death scene, however, which is totally absent in the anonymous life, Bede has Cuthbert command: "Have no communion with those who depart from the unity of the Catholic peace, either in not celebrating Easter at the proper time or in evil living" (chap. 39, pp. 284-85).

Each of the three versions of Cuthbert's life has its literary and hagiographic merits, but these attributes differ greatly. It is clear from manuscript history that Bede's prose life won the palm in the Middle Ages: extant are seven manuscripts of the anonymous version, nineteen of Bede's metrical version, and thirty-six complete manuscripts of the prose version, not counting two containing extracts only and evidence for many more lost ones.[25] Just as it would prove enlightening to compare the entirety of one of Bede's biblical commentaries with its major source or sources, so a comparison of the three lives tells a student much about Bede's qualities as an author of hagiography.[26] His works invite a closer comparative analysis.

"A martyrology of the festivals of the holy matryrs, in which I have diligently tried to note down all that I could find out about them, not only on what day, but also by what sort of combat and under what judge they overcame the world" (*HE* V. 24, p. 571). Besides the four saints' lives, Bede made another major contribution to hagiography. Using the pseudo-Jerome martyrology, a simple liturgical calendar naming the martyrs and the places of their martyrdom, Bede composed between 725 and 731 what is termed an historical martyrology, which includes a brief account of each saint's life and death. As the above quotation suggests,

Bede did a great deal of research for this project, and, once again, the work is witness to an impressive number of sources, including some fifty lives of saints, ecclesiastical histories, writings of Fathers of the Church, and the *Liber pontificalis.*[27] A typical entry is that for Saint Cassian (the martyr, not the monk) on 13 August:

> On the Ides of August. The birthday [into heaven] of St. Cassian, at Rome. When he had refused to adore idols, the persecutor demanded to know what his profession was. He answered that he taught students grammar (*notas*). Then, stripped of his clothes and bound with his hands behind his back, he was placed in the center. The boys to whom by his teaching he had become hateful were called, and permission was given them to destroy him. In so far as they suffered while learning, to that degree they enjoyed vengeance. Some beat him with their tablets and boards, others wounded him with their pens. In as much as their hands were weak, so much heavier, by an extended death, was the pain of his martyrdom. Prudentius the poet has written the life. (Quentin, p. 68; Dubois and Renaud, p. 149)

Bede's martyrology contained 114 notices. This left a number of calendrical spaces open. With the medieval *horror vacui,* later less careful, more sensational-minded editors encrusted Bede's work beyond recognition with their supplemental entries.[28]

Poems

> A book of hymns in various meters and rhythms. A book of epigrams in heroic and elegiac meter.
>
> (*HE,* V. 24, pp. 570-71)

It seems that these two books did not survive the Middle Ages,[29] although a number of individual poems have come down to us. Besides the metrical life of Saint Cuthbert in almost a thousand lines of skillfully wrought hexameters, we have approximately two dozen poems of varying length and meter, some certainly by Bede and the rest quite probably so.

One poem, in honor of Saint Æthelthryth, we know is genuine because Bede includes it in the *Ecclesiastical History* (IV.20, pp. 396-401), with the introductory remark: "It seems fitting to insert in this history a hymn on the subject of virginity which I composed many years ago in elegiac meter in honor of this queen and bride of Christ, and therefore truly a queen because the bride of Christ; imitating the method of holy Scripture in which many songs are inserted into the account and, as is well known, these are composed in meter and verse."

> Alma Deus Trinitas, quae saecula cuncta gubernas
> adnue iam coeptis, alma Deus Trinitas.

Bella Maro resonet; nos pacis dona canamus,
   munera nos Christi; bella Maro resonet.
Carmina casta mihi, fedae non raptus Helenae
   luxus erit lubricis, carmina casta mihi.

(All-bounteous Three in One, Lord of all time,
   Bless mine emprise, all-bounteous Three in
   One.
Battle be Maro's theme, sweet peace be mine;
   Christ's gifts for me, battle be Maro's
   theme.
Chaste is my song, not wanton Helen's rape.
   Leave lewdness to the lewd! Chaste is my
   song.)

From this sample of the beginning lines, which bravely restate the topos of the "contrast between pagan and Christian poetry," it is evident that the poem is something of a tour de force; it is not only alphabetic (twenty-three distichs each beginning with another letter, plus four for AMEN) but also epanaleptic (that is, the last quarter of the distich repeats the first; termed in the Middle Ages reciprocal, echoic, or serpentine).[30]

Unfortunately, the most recent edition by J. Fraipont in CCSL 122 of most of the rest of the poetry attributed to Bede has serious defects.[31] Fraipont's edition goes by the title "Bedae Venerabilis liber hymnorum, rhythmi, variae preces" (p. 405). This is misleading, since there are no "rhythmi" in the collection that accord with Bede's definition from late Latin grammarians in his *De arte metrica* 1.24, where rhythmic poetry in contrast to metrical means accentual verse.

Thirteen of the fifteen hymns taken by Fraipont from Dreves 1907 edition are probably by Bede; two, IV and V, are most probably not, since they were never even attributed to him in the Middle Ages.[32] Hymns I through XIII are in traditional Ambrosian hymn meter, iambic dimeter.[33] Hymn I, *Primo Deus caeli globum,* is on a topic dear to Bede's heart, as we have seen in his other works: the six days of creation and the six ages of the world. After two introductory stanzas, the first line of one stanza becomes the last line of the next, up to stanza 19, which, after the sabbath rest of souls on the seventh day, deals with the extra-temporal eighth day of eternal bliss. On that day and age,

Vultumque Christi perpetim
Iusti cernent amabilem
Eruntque sicut angeli
Caelesti in arce fulgidi.

(The just behold forever the lovable countenance of Christ; they will be as shining angels in the celestial citadel.)

Stanza 28 ends the poem with a praise to the Trinity. Fraipont unaccountably includes the spurious stanzas 29 to 33, metrically defective and anticlimatic (pp. 410-11).

Hymn II, *Hymnum canentes martyrum,* is for the Feast of the Holy Innocents (28 December). Bede again uses the echoic stanza form, but here throughout the entire sixteen stanzas of the poem. Hymn IX, *In natali SS. Petri et Pauli,* another alphabetic poem, honors the two patron saints of Wearmouth and Jarrow.

Judging from the number of manuscripts extant, Hymn VI, *Hymnos canamus gloriae,* on the Ascension, was Bede's most popular.[34] The poem, with its emphasis on Christ's harrowing of hell and royal entrance into heaven, is an epitome of the early medieval theology of glory. It contains many of the scriptural and patristic motifs that will be used by Cynewulf in his Old English poem, *Christ II* or *The Ascension.*[35] After the beauty and regular meter of the first seventeen stanzas, the interpolated and defective stanza 17a spoils the flow, but 18 through 32 restores the reader's equilibrium.

Another hymn interesting because of its use of a device also found in Old English vernacular literature is the second hymn in honor of Saint Andrew, XIII, *Salue, tropaeum gloriae* (pp. 437-38). In this poem, the first seven stanzas are Andrew's address to the personified cross; they manifest Bede's literary debt to *The Passion of Saint Andrew the Apostle* and suggest some similarities to the prosopopoeia of *The Dream of the Rood.*[36]

A third poem, *De die iudicii* (XIV, pp. 439-44), is still more closely linked with the vernacular, since the fine Old English poem of the late tenth century, *Judgment Day II,* formerly called *Be Domes Dæge,* is a 304-line paraphrase of it.[37] The dactylic hexameter Latin poem, thought to have been composed between 716 and 731, is not in a usual sense a hymn, though it has been included in hymn collections, but a 163-line poem of meditation. Although the poem's authenticity has been questioned in the past, the evidence overwhelmingly supports Bedan authorship. Thirty of the thirty-nine extant manuscripts ascribe it to him; and it has been assigned to no other writer. In Northumbrian manuscripts the poem has a personal epilogue in lines 156 to 163 (p. 144) addressed to Bede's patron, Bishop Acca, and his monks at Hexham. The theme of doomsday is consonant with Bede's other writings, such as *De temporum ratione* (68-70) and Dryhthelm's account of his trip to the otherworld in *HE* V. 12 (pp. 488-99). Nevertheless, Jean Mabillon's impression "it does not seem to follow Bede's vein" still finds adherents, especially since Bede does not elsewhere dwell so on physical pain and torment as depicted in lines 72 to 122 of the poem; in the commentary on Revelation he prefers to transfer such descriptions to an allegorical plane.[38] Still, in addition to the other evidence, it must be admitted that the competent hexameters, poetic but restrained diction, and clean style point to Bede as author. The subject matter of the poem, the separation of the just and unjust according to their merits, their rewards and punishment, naturally prompts a contrastive treatment, but this is done quite effectively. The poem starts out with a line describing a pleasant glade, using the classical and medieval topos of the *locus amoenus,* but immediately wheels about in the second line with a description of a powerful wind that brings on melancholy in line four. The earthly flowery scene in the first line parallels the rosy aspect of heaven in 146-47; the list of hell's sufferings, 93-97 (beginning "Nec uox ulla") contrasts exactly with heaven's joys, 124-28 (echoing with "Nox ubi nulla"). A careful reading of the poem renders F.J.E. Raby's dismissal of it highly contestable: "Its merits are small and it displays nothing half so well as the piety of its author."[39]

Poem XV, *Oratio Bedae Presbyteri,* is a twenty-six line prayer in elegiac couplets. XVI, XVII, and XVIII are poems based on Psalms 41, 83, and 112.

Occasionally Bede inserted a brief poem, epigram, or epitaph before, in, or after a prose work.[40] We apparently also now have some remnants of his lost *Liber epigrammatum.* John Leland, commissioned by Henry VIII to search out British antiquities in ecclesiastical libraries, relates in his *Collectanea* that he inspected a very old collection of epigrams (the manuscript is now lost) belonging to Milred (bishop of Worcester from 745-75), five of which were attributed to Bede apparently on good grounds; Leland transcribed two of them, which Michael Lapidge has recently published and discussed.[41] The last, acephalous epigram in Milred's collection may also be from the concluding lines of Bede's book.[42]

We have Bede's own authority and that of his contemporary Cuthbert that he translated Latin into Old English (Letter to Cuthbert, *EHD* I, p. 801; Letter on the Death of Bede, *HE,* pp. 582-83), and Cuthbert also says that Bede was versed in Old English poetry (Letter, pp. 580-81). Furthermore, from his account of Cædmon's poetic gift and career in *HE* IV.24, (pp. 414-21), we know that Bede was sensitive to the beauty and uniqueness of Old English verse and acknowledged it as a medium for translating and embellishing the sacred text. But there is no compelling evidence that he composed the five-line poem called "Bede's Death Song." The evidence of the early and best manuscripts of Cuthbert's letter indicates only that Bede repeated the little poem as a favorite during his last days. Cuthbert's words are: "In nostra quoque lingua, ut erat doctus in nostris carminibus, dicens de terribili exitu animarum et corpore" ("And in our own language,—for he was familiar with English poetry,—speaking of the soul's dread departure from the body, he would repeat: . . .

(Facing that enforced journey, no man can be
More prudent than he has good call to be,
If he consider, before his going hence,
What for his spirit of good hap or of evil
After his day of death shall be determined.)
                                        (*HE,* pp. 580-83)[43]

Letters

"Also a book of letters to various people: one of these is on the six ages of the world; one on the resting-places of the children of Israel; one on the words of Isaiah, 'And they shall be shut up in the prison, and after many days shall they be visited'; one on the reason for leap year; and one on the equinox, after Anatolius" (*HE* V.24, pp. 568-69).

From this epistolary catalogue it is obvious that Bede did not will to posterity a collection of warm and familiar letters. Although the book itself has not come down to us as such, we have all the five letters listed, in addition to two others, written after the *Ecclesiastical History* was finished.

The first letter (CCSL 123C, pp. 617-26), on the six ages, was discussed in connection with the *De temporibus.* . . . Addressed to Plegwin, monk of Hexham, Bede responds heatedly to the charge of heresy for his reckonings concerning the time span of the ages and Christ's birth in the sixth age; he refutes the accusations laid against him at Bishop Wilfrid's feast and asks that "the most learned brother David" set things straight.[44]

The last two letters listed (four and five) also deal with computation questions put to Bede by colleagues, but in less controversial areas. After removing the paragraph of salutation addressed to Helmwald (printed in CCSL 123C, p. 629), Bede makes the verbatim text of the fourth letter serve as chapters 38-39 of *De temporum ratione* (CCSL 123B, pp. 399-404) to explain bissextile (leap year) intercalation (see above, Chap. 2). The fifth, the letter to Wicthed (CCSL 123C, pp. 633-42), wrestles with problems about the vernal equinox for the dating of Easter in the Anatolian *Canon* and serves as sort of an appendix to the treatment of equinoxes in *De temporum ratione.* . . .

The second and third letters respond to questions of exegesis asked by Bede's patron, Bishop Acca, for whom he wrote so much. Bede interrupted his commentary on 1 Samuel to compose the letters (PL 94.699A and 702B). They are like the *Eight Questions* . . . in that they take a particular biblical topic and discuss it discursively rather than by Bede's usual method of verse-by-verse commentary. *De mansionibus* enumerates and describes the Israelites' stopping places in Exodus and then, following Jerome's interpretation, explains the allegorical, moral meaning of those resting areas (701C-D). The third letter deals with a harder nut, Isaiah 24:22, which seems to prophesy a punishment in hell that will end, since the Vulgate texts says, "they will be visited" (not "they will be punished" [RSV]). The latter part of this long letter discusses the apocalyptic visitation of the Antichrist.

Along with a copy of the recently completed *Ecclesiastical History,* Bede sent a short letter of appreciation to Albinus, abbot of the monastery of Saints Peter and Paul at Canterbury (Plummer I, p. 3).[45] In the preface to the *Ecclesiastical History* Bede recognizes Albinus as "the principal authority and helper" in the historical enterprise by his generous provision of documents from Canterbury and Rome (*HE,* pp. 3-4). In conjunction with the information contained in the preface to the *History* and in the prologue to the life of Saint Cuthbert, this letter tells us something of Bede's publishing procedures: he sent out drafts (*schedulae*) for verification and correction, then a fair copy (*membranulae*) for final approval and copying. Since the manuscript was publicized and copied in various degrees of revision, different versions, or editions, naturally ensured.[46]

The last letter and the last surviving work of Bede is also the most critical of church and state. It is a letter calling for reform. Although all the principal works of his late years deal to some extent with reform of church, to be brought about by a rejuvenated monasticism and episcopate, and reform of society, to be brought about by a well-counseled king and advisors, Bede spells out in detail what a program should entail.[47] On 5 November 734 Bede writes to Ecgbert, who would be elevated as the first archbishop of York in 735, and whose brother Eadbert would become king of Northumbria in 737 (*EHD* I, pp. 799-810; Plummer I, pp. 405-23; II, pp. 378-88). Though in weakened condition physically, Bede energetically admonishes the prelate to carry out much-needed reforms. The tone is that of a prophet exhorting a high priest, and may remind us of another monk, Bernard of Clairvaux, reproving the pope. Actually, this seems to be an early instance of a traditional Christian genre called the *sermo ad clerum,* an admonition to the hierarchy by a respected but lesser ranking member of the clerical club, a convention familiar to students of the English Renaissance in the sermons of Colet and Latimer.

Bede had complained of ecclesiastical abuses of his day in his commentaries and history,[48] but nowhere is he as detailed as he is in this outspoken letter. After calling attention to reports about bishops associating with "those who are given to laughter, jests, tales, feasting and drunkenness, and the other attractions of the lax life" (reminiscent of his censure of Bishop Wilfrid's court in his letter to Plegwin), he points out that the distances are too great in the diocese to serve all the people (p. 801). He notes with some bitterness

"that many villages and hamlets of our people are situated on inaccessible mountains and dense woodlands, where there is never seen for many years at a time a bishop to exhibit any ministry or celestial grace; not one man of which, however, is immune from rendering dues to the bishop" (p. 802). He therefore recommends that new bishoprics be established, with sees established and financed at wealthy monsteries. Pseudo-monasteries, set up as personal familial institutions to acquire lands held by hereditary title by royal indult, to evade taxes, and to avoid public service, he entreats be abolished.[49]

> For—what indeed is disgraceful to tell—those who are totally ignorant of the monastic life have received under their control so many places in the name of monasteries, as you yourself know better than I, that there is a complete lack of places where the sons of nobles or of veteran thegns can receive an estate. . . . But others give money to kings, and under the pretext of founding monasties buy lands on which they may more freely devote themselves to lust, and in addition cause them to be ascribed to them by hereditary right by royal edicts, and even get those same documents of their privileges confirmed, as if in truth worthy of God, by the subscription of bishops, abbots and secular persons. (p. 805)

This sour complaint serves as an interesting complement to the description in the *Historia ecclesiastica* (V.23): "In these favorable times of peace and prosperity, many of the Northumbrian race, both noble and simple, have laid aside their weapons and taken the tonsure, preferring that they and their children should take monastic vows rather than train themselves in the art of war. What the result will be, a later generation will discover" (pp. 560-61).

Although this statement seems either contradictory or ironically cynical when placed against the text of his letter to Ecgbert, Bede is actually expressing the complex state of affairs in contemporary Northumbria, where the presence of the church is hearteningly affirmed by dedication of lives and land to its service, but also where the quality of the church is seriously vitiated by greed, subterfuge, and fraud. What saves the letter from querulousness are its positive recommendations with a true hope of improvement.[50]

After pleading for adequate spiritual teachers for the laity, Bede ends the letter with a fervent appeal that Ecgbert avoid avarice, remembering its effects on religious leaders in the Old and New Testaments (pp. 809-10). Bede's swan song is a strong and urgent cry.[51]

Notes

[1] These two quotations may serve as a just sample of the praise accorded Bede's style:

Bede's command of Latin is excellent, and his style is clear and limpid, and it is very seldom that we have to pause to think of the meaning of a sentence. There is no affectation of a false classicality, and no touch of the puerile pomposity of his contemporary Aldhelm, for whom, however, he cannot help feeling a kind of admiration. Alcuin rightly praises Bede for his unpretending style. (Plummer I, pp. liii-liv)

But such is the pleasing simplicity, clarity, and grammatical superiority of his prose style that at least his narrative and historical works can be read with some aesthetic satisfaction. He habitually spoke, wrote, and taught in Latin all his life, so that there is a natural ease and directness in his prose which contrasts markedly with the rather 'showing-off style of St Aldhelm, who perhaps wished to demonstrate that he could equal the Irish Latinists in stylistic learning. On the other hand, Bede's interest in metre, which produced his treatise *De Arte Metrica*, was due mainly to the value he set on the study of Latin metre as a necessary aid to the discipline of the effective use of that language. (C. L. Wrenn, *A Study of Old English Literature* [New York: Norton, 1967], p. 63)

2 Winthrop Weatherbee, "Some Implications of Bede's Latin Style," in *Bede and Anglo-Saxon England,* ed. Robert T. Farrell, British Archaeological Reports 46 (Oxford: British Archeological Reports, 1978), pp. 23-31, shows that Bede's style with its ease, purity, and freedom from self-consciousness contributed to the development of a medieval Christian humanism.

3 See Alan Thacker, "Bede's Ideal of Reform," in *Ideal and Reality,* ed. Wormald, pp. 130-31.

4 For the summary results of Dom Germain Morin's researches into the original Bedan collection and of his own findings, consult Laistner, *Hand-List,* pp. 114-16. Reflecting the medieval accretions to Bede's collection and its confused order, the editions of Giles and Migne present a muddle. Indeed, one homily is printed twice as I.17 and II.24 in PL 94.89-96 and 262-67. Only the modern edition of Dom David Hurst, CCSL 120, is reliable for authenticity and order. For a list of the factitious homilies extracted from Bede's commentaries on Mark and Luke, see Hurst's appendix, pp. 381-84. For the dating of the collection, see his preface, p. vii.

5 On Bede's elaborate use of the metaphor of rumination, see Gernot Wieland, "Caedmon, the Clean Animal," *American Benedictine Review* 35 (1984): 194-203, and the bibliography cited.

6 For a conspectus of his homiletic use of Scripture and the Fathers, see CCSL 120, Index Scriptorum, pp. 387-99 and 401-3.

7 See the two valuable but uneven articles on Bede's homiletic art by Philip J. West, "Liturgical Style and Structure in Bede's Homily for the Easter Vigil" and "Liturgical Style and Structure in Bede's Christmas Homilies," *American Benedictine Review* 23 (1972): 1-8, 424-38. These are important because they are among the very few specific treatments of Bede's style. In making his point in the second article about the artistry of the sermon for midnight on Christmas (I.6), however, West belittles the form and treatment of the Vigil homily that precedes it (I.5), calling it "almost impoverished" (p. 425). West did not recognize that Bede is using two different methods, both artistic, for two different occasions: the one a simple reflection on the verses of the Gospel, echoing the simplicity of the mass text and spirit; the other, an elaborately structured and linguistically brilliant exposition for a brilliant night. West blames Bede for his procedure in the homily for the second mass, in which Bede "builds his sermon around allegorical interpretation of the Gospel's six main verbs: *transeamus, uideamus, uenerunt festinantes, uidentes, cognouerunt,* and *reuersi.* The sermon's limitation seems [sic] that this arbitrary organizational principal [sic] forced Bede to subordinate unity and continuity to ingenuity" (p. 432). West then praises Bede for holding allegory "to a minimum" in his sermon for Christmas Day (I.8). The arbitrariness is on the part of West, not Bede. If one appreciates Bede's (and the Fathers') allegorical art, then West's literary criticism appears perverse.

8 For a comprehensive survey of hagiography see René Aigrain, *L'hagiographie: ses sources, ses méthodes, son histoire* (Paris: Bloud & Gay, 1953). For an understanding of the literary conventions used by hagiographers, see the studies by Hippolyte Delehaye, such as *The Legends of the Saints,* trans. Donald Attwater (New York: Fordham University Press, 1962), and *Les passions des martyrs et les genres littéraires,* 2d ed. (Brussels: Société des Bollandistes, 1966). For a still stimulating essay on hagiography, see chapter 4 in Charles W. Jones's *Saints' Lives and Chronicles in Early England* (Ithaca, N. Y.: Cornell University Press, 1947), pp. 51-79. For a summary of the influential Augustinian view of the miraculous, see Benedicta Ward, *Miracles and the Medieval Mind* (Philadelphia: University of Pennsylvania Press, 1982), introduction and chap. 1, pp. 1-4.

9 On the development of the *opus geminatum* see, with the attendant bibliography, Peter Godman, "The Anglo-Latin *opus geminatum:* from Aldhelm to Alcuin," *Medium Aevum* 50, no. 2 (1981): 215-29, and his edition of Alcuin, *The Bishops, Kings, and Saints of York,* pp. lxxviii-lxxxviii; and Gernot Wieland, "*Geminus Stilus:* Studies in Anglo-Latin Hagiography," in *Insular Latin Studies,* ed. Michael Herren (Toronto: Pon-

tifical Institute of Medieval Studies, 1981), pp. 113-33. Wieland's study is particularly profitable for its explorations into the purposes and uses of the geminated format: "The conclusion to be drawn from this is not that the *gemina opera* were written to exemplify 'the interchangeability of metrical and non-metrical discourse,' but that the prose was written to complement the verse and the verse was written to complement the prose" (p. 125).

[10] Thomas W. Mackay has furnished us with an analysis of the work in his "A Critical Edition of Bede's Vita Felicis" (Ph.D. diss., Stanford University, 1971; Ann Arbor, Mich.: University Microfilms International, 1972), and in his article, "Bede's Hagiographical Method: His Knowledge and Use of Paulinus of Nola," in *Famulus Christi,* ed. Bonner, pp. 77-92. The factual details about the *Vita* and its source are drawn mainly from his introduction and article. Although I have studied his edition, my references will be to the text in Migne, since Mackay's edition is not yet available in CCSL.

[11] The best edition of the poems of Paulinus is *Sancti Pontii Meropii Paulini Nolani Carmina,* ed. Wilhelm von Hartel, CSEL 30 (Vienna: F. Tempsky, 1894). The *Natalicia* celebrating Felix are poems 12 to 29; the biography used by Bede is found in poems 15 and 16, the *Nachleben* especially in 18, and the buildings of Nola in 28. For a description and translation of the poems, see P. G. Walsh, *The Poems of St. Paulinus of Nola* (New York: Newman Press, 1975).

[12] In the preface to the prose life of St. Willibrord, Alcuin describes the purpose of the *opus geminatum* thus: "At your behest I have put together two small books, one moving along in prose, which could be read publicly to the brothers in church, if it seems worthy to your wisdom; the other, running along with Pierian feet, which ought only to be ruminated by your students in the private room" (*Vita Willibrordi archiepiscopi Traiectensis,* ed. W. Levinson, MGH, Scriptores rerum Merowingicarum VII. 113).

[13] See Mackay, Introduction to his critical edition, pp. xxv-lxi, esp. liii-liv, and "Bede's Hagiographical Method," p. 78; Hunter Blair, *World of Bede,* pp. 119-20.

[14] Carmelo V. Franklin and Paul Meyvaert, "Has Bede's Version of the 'Passio S. Anastasii' Come Down to Us in 'BHL' 408?" *Analecta Bollandiana* 100 (1982):373-400. BHL 408 refers to *Bibliotheca hagiographica latina,* ed. Socii Bollandiani (Bruxelles, Belgium: Bollandists, 1898-99)1:68, no. 408.

[15] Franklin and Meyvaert, "Bede's Version," 394-95.

[16] The most damning censure was leveled by Bede's ablest and kindest critic, Charles Plummer:

In the case of Cuthbert's Life it cannot, I think, be said that Bede has bettered his original. He has improved the Latinity no doubt, and made the whole thing run more smoothly. In fact he seems to take delight in altering the language for the mere sake of alteration, while keeping closely to the sense. But he has obliterated many interesting details of time and place, he shows a marked tendency to exaggerate the ascetic and miraculous element, he amplifies the narrative with rhetorical matter which can only be called padding, inserts as facts explanations of his own, and has greatly spoiled one beautiful anecdote. On the other hand, his account of Cuthbert's death, derived from an eye-witness, is of real and independent value. (p. xlvi)

For the others, see the remarks and documentation in Lenore Abraham, "Bede's *Life of Cuthbert:* A Reassessment," *Proceedings of the Patristic, Medieval, and Renaissance Conference* 1 (1976): 23-24.

[17] On the narrative qualities of the anonymous *Vita Cuthberti* see Theodor Wolpers, *Die englische Heiligenlegende des Mittelalters,* Buchreihe der *Anglia,* no. 10 (Tübingen, Germany: Max Niemeyer, 1964), pp. 74-75.

[18] Augustine, *On Christian Doctrine* IV. 19.38, p. 146. Cf. Wieland, "*Geminus stilus,*" pp. 124-26.

[19] J. F. Webb, ed. and trans. *Lives of the Saints* (Harmondsworth, England, and Baltimore: Penguin, 1981), p. 23. Webb's introduction to Bede's prose life is an excellent rebuttal to Plummer's opinion quoted in n. 6 above.

[20] On the dating from this reference, see Max Manitius, *Geschichte der lateinischen Literatur des Mittelalters,* Handbuch der Altertumswissenschaft, ed. Walter Otto, sec. 9, part 2 (Munich, Germany: C. H. Beck, 1911; rpt. 1965), 1:84; and Werner Jaager, *Bedas metrische vita sancti Cuthberti,* Palaestra 198 (Leipzig, Germany: Mayer and Müller, 1935), p. 4.

[21] On the word *curatio* see *Thesaurus linguae latinae,* IV. 1476-77. For a discussion of the various understandings of Bede's gift in both the medieval and modern periods, see Whitelock, "Bede and his Teachers and Friends," p. 21 and nn. 15-21.

[22] See Jaager's introduction and statistics, pp. 2-3, and B. Colgrave's concordance of the three lives, in *Two Lives of St. Cuthbert,* ed. and trans. Colgrave (Cambridge: Cambridge University Press, 1940), p. 375.

[23] Jaager's three brief references to Virgil's *Georgics* in this passage, I.244 (should read I.224) and II.14 for lines 415 and 16 and I.509 for 423 do not at all convey

the amount of Virgilian imitation in the passage. Cf., for example, *Georgics* I.50 and 111; I.219-24; II.237; IV. 158; *Aeneid* VII. 721; XI.301. As for the mock-epic quality, note that *dixerat,* l. 426, is used by Virgil for epic discourse twenty-five times in the *Aeneid,* but never in the *Eclogues* or *Georgics.* For Bede's use of Virgil in the metrical life, see further Neil Wright, "Bede and Vergil," *Romanobarbarica* 6 (1981): 363, 367-71.

[24] For a discussion of the peculiarities of this monachism see A. Hamilton Thompson, "Northumbrian Monasticism," in *Bede: His Life, Times, and Writings,* pp. 60-101, esp. p. 72; and Colgrave's n., p. 347.

[25] See Jaager, *Bedas metrische Vita,* pp. 24-32; Colgrave, *Two Lives,* pp. 17-50; Laistner, *Hand-List,* pp. 88-90.

[26] For text and translation, unfortunately without commentary, of three accounts of the two sea otters wiping and warming Cuthbert's feet, see Bolton, *Anglo-Latin Literature,* pp. 136-38.

[27] Dom Henri Quentin, *Les martyrologes historiques du moyen âge,* 2d ed. (Paris: Lecoffre, 1908), in a brilliant scholarly enterprise in chap. 2 (pp. 17-119) presents Bede's contribution to the martyrological genre. The martyrology itself is now in a convenient form, *Edition practique des martyrologes de Bède, de l'anonyme lyonnais, et de Florus,* ed. Dom Jacques DuBois and Geneviève Renaud (Paris: CNRS, 1976).

[28] The main contributors before the fixing of the *Roman Martyrology* were the ninth-century writers Florus of Lyons, Hrabanus, Ado, and Usuard. The composite jumble is represented by the martyrology printed with Bede's works in PL 94.799-1148. Until a new edition appears, only Quentin's is reliable.

[29] The usually careful Laistner has misled a number of later scholars about the history of these books. In the *Hand-List* he avers: "Neither of these collections of poems has survived as such, but, according to John Boston of Bury, the library of Bury St Edmunds early in the fifteenth century had a *Liber Hymnorum* and a *Liber Epigrammatum* bearing Bede's name" (p. 122). Richard H. Rouse, "Bostonus Buriensis and the Author of the *Catalogus Scriptorum Ecclesiae,*" *Speculum* 41 (1966): 471-99, demonstrated that Bostonus Buriensis was only the scribe of the catalogue and Henry of Kirkestede, subprior and librarian, was the author; but Rouse also made clear that Kirkestede's catalogue was not an actual catalogue of library holdings but a bio-bibliographic union catalogue which comprised a list of all the books by authoritative and approved authors that Kirkestede knew of and wished to get if they were not yet available (pp. 471-72, 493-94). It is clear that Kirkestede learned about Bede's

works from Bede's own bibliography, which he copied in the same order and wording as found in *HE* V.24 (pp. 566-71). That neither Bury St. Edmunds nor the Franciscan convents or neighboring monasteries possessed Bede's poems is manifest from the fact that Kirkestede was unable to supply an incipit and explicit for the works nor a reference number for the location (see p. 496, items 40 and 41). Laistner's misunderstanding of the nature of the list has been repeated by recent, also usually careful, scholars. Michael Lapidge, for instance, in "Some Remnants of Bede's Lost *Liber Epigrammatum,*" *English Historical Review* 90 (1975): 798, states that a copy of the book of epigrams "was known to Henry of Kirkestede."

[30] On the alphabetic and reciprocal form, see Plummer II, 241. Bede cites the well-known accentual alphabetic poem, *Apparebit repentina* in *De arte metrica* I.24, p. 139. Ernst Robert Curtius, *European Literature and the Latin Middle Ages,* trans. Willard R. Trask (New York: Pantheon, 1953), pp. 235-36, identifies and describes the use of the topos, which he labeled "contrast between pagan and Christian poetry." Bede would be familiar with it from his reading in Juvencus, Paulinus of Nola, and Paulinus of Périgueux.

[31] Anyone using the Fraipont edition should pay attention to Walther Bulst's learned, scathing critique of it, "Bedae Opera Rhythmica?" *Zeitschrift für deutsches Altertum und deutsche Literatur* 89 (1958-59): 83-91. My remarks on the form and contents of the CCSL edition draw on his expertise, as well as on the learning of Josef Szövériffy, *Die Annalen der lateinischen Hymnendichtung* (Berlin: Erich Schmidt, 1966), 1:168-76.

[32] G. M. Dreves, *Lateinische Hymnendichter des Mittelalters,* Analecta hymnica medii aevi, 50 (Leipzig, Germany, 1907, reprint ed. New York: Johnson Reprint, 1961), p. 98, takes over eleven hymns attributed to Bede in George Cassander's Renaissance collection from a tenth-century manuscript but adds another four, including the two hymns, from manuscript Bamberg B.II.10, among the hymn fragments without authorial ascription, found next to hymns attributed to Bede. As Bulst expostulates, that is no good reason to ascribe these two to Bede, which are, moreover, "dürftig, plump und mühselig zusammengestückt"; they could be by any of a dozen hymn writers (Bulst, "Bedae Opera Rhythmica?" pp. 88-89).

[33] For a description of the *hymni Ambrosiani,* see F. J. E. Raby, *A History of Christian-Latin Poetry, from the Beginnings to the Close of the Middle Ages,* 2d ed. (Oxford: Clarendon Press, 1966), pp. 28-41, esp. p. 33.

[34] See A. S. Walpole, *Early Latin Hymns* (Cambridge: Cambridge University Press, 1922; reprint ed., 1966),

pp. 371-76. Walpole's book with its excellent introduction and notes remains the best introductory text for the early hymns.

[35] See Daniel G. Calder, *Cynewulf,* (Boston: G. K. Hall, 1981), chap. 3, pp. 42-74; and George H. Brown, "The Descent-Ascent Motif in *Christ II* of Cynewulf," *Journal of English and Germanic Philology* 73 (1974):1-12. A. S. Cook suggested a relationship between Bede's and Cynewulf's poems in his edition of *The Christ of Cynewulf* (Boston: Ginn & Co., 1909), pp. 116-18.

[36] M. Bonnet, ed., *Acta Apostolorum Apocrypha* II.1 (Leipzig, Germany: Hermann Mendelssohn, 1898), pp. 24-26. See the notes, particularly to verses 39a, 42a, 87-89a, of *The Dream of the Rood* in *Bright's Old English Grammar & Reader,* ed. Frederick G. Cassidy and Richard N. Ringler, 3d ed. (New York: Holt, Rinehart, & Winston, 1971), pp. 309-17; also *The Dream of the Rood,* ed. Michael Swanton (Manchester, England: University Press; New York: Barnes & Noble, 1970), pp. 42-78.

[37] The poem was edited with an English translation by J. Rawson Lumby as *Be Domes Dæge, De Die Judicii,* Early English Text Society Original Series, no. 65 (London: Trübner, 1876). The best edition of the poem, titled *Judgment Day II,* is in the *Anglo-Saxon Poetic Records,* ed. E. V. K. Dobbie, Vol. 6 (New York: Columbia University Press, 1942); the most recent English translation is that by S. A. J. Bradley, *Anglo-Saxon Poetry* (London: Dent, 1982), pp. 528-35. An Old English prose adaptation of *Judgment Day II* appears as part of sermon xxix in *Wulfstan, Sammlung der ihm zugeschriebenen Homilien nebst Untersuchungen über ihre Echtheit,* ed. A. S. Napier, (Berlin, 1883; reprint ed. with bibliographic appendix by Klaus Ostheeren, Zürich: Weidmann, 1967), 1:vi, 136-40. Both Bede's Latin text and the Old English versions have been the subject of extensive investigation over the years by Leslie Whitbread, in preparation for a new, needed (but unfortunately not forthcoming) edition. All Bedan and Old English research is indebted to his research, reported in a series of articles, of which the following pertain to the Latin poem: "A Study of Bede's *Versus De Die ludicii,*" *Philological Quarterly* 23 (1944):194-221; "Note on a Bede Fragment," *Scriptorium* 12 (1958): 280-81; "The Sources and Literary Qualities of Bede's Doomsday Verses," *Zeitschrift für deutsches Altertum und deutsche Literatur* 95 (1966): 258-66; "The Old English Poem *Judgment Day II* and its Latin Source," *Philological Quarterly* 45 (1966): 635-56; "Bede's Verses on Doomsday: A Supplemental Note," *Philological Quarterly* 51 (1972): 485-86; "After Bede: The Influence and Dissemination of His Doomsday Verses," *Archiv* 204 (1967): 250-66. For further information about the Old English versions one should consult Stanley B. Greenfield and Daniel

G. Calder, *A New Critical History of Old English Literature* (New York: New York University Press, 1986), pp. 238-40, and for bibliography on the OE poem, see *A Bibliography of Publications on Old English to the End of 1972,* ed. Greenfield and Fred C. Robinson (Toronto: Toronto University Press, 1979); thereafter, the annual bibliographies in *Anglo-Saxon England* and the *PMLA.*

[38] For Whitbread's final and best argued grounds for attributing the poem to Bede, see his "After Bede," 251-54. Mabillon's remark, "nec Bedae venam assequi mihi videtur" ("this does not seem to me to follow the vein of Bede") found in PL 120.22, is cited in Whitbread's n. 4, along with the opinions of most critics for and against Bede's authorship. The attribution of the poem to Alcuin, often repeated in OE scholarship from Lumby's remark in the preface, pp. v-vi, is due to a chance juxtapostion of the poem next to one attributed to Alcuin in Vienna, MS 89 (See Whitbread, "After Bede," p. 251 and n. 3).

[39] Raby, *Christian-Latin Poetry,* p. 148. In his and James L. Rosier's edition of Aldhelm, *The Poetic Works* (Cambridge, England: D.S. Brewer, 1985), p. 31, Michael Lapidge boldly brands Raby's hitherto revered study "a tissue of errors and wrong-headed opinions."

[40] For a list and location of most of the poems atributed to Bede, see Bolton, *Anglo-Latin Literature,* pp. 167-68. To this should be added the two epigrams from John Leland's *De rebus brittanicis collectanea,* ed. Thomas Hearne, 2d ed. (London: Benjamin White, 1774), 3: 114-15, printed by Lapidge, "Some Remanants," as nos. 2 and 10 (pp. 802, 805); and an eleven-line epigram assocated with the preface to Bede's commentary on the Apocalypse (see Laistner, *Hand-List,* p. 129).

[41] See Michael Lapidge, "Some Remnants of Bede's Lost *Liber Epigrammatum,*" pp. 798-820, with transcript of the epigrams on pp. 802-6. A notation by Leland about *Enigmata Bedae* as part of this manuscript suggests that Bede like Aldhelm and Tatwin authored *aenigmata* (learned riddles) (*Collectanea,* 3:114; Lapidge, "Remnants," p. 803).

[42] Patrick Sims-Williams, "Milred of Worcester's Collection of Latin Epigrams and its Continental Counterparts," *Anglo-Saxon England* 10 (1982): 38.

[43] On this text Colgrave remarks, *HE,* pp. 580-81, n. 4, "Only a comparatively small group of the MSS. of the Letter attribute the composition of the poem to Bede himself, and those the later ones." See Dobbie, *The Manuscripts of Cædmon's Hymn and Bede's Death Song.* A. H. Smith's statement in his edition of *Three Northumbrian Poems,* rev. ed. (Exeter, England:

University of Exeter Press, 1978), p. 17, "On Cuthbert's testimony the Death Song is Bede's," is certainly not valid without qualification. He includes the Latin phrases of the earlier and later manuscript recensions on pp. 41-43. See also Michael W. Twomey, "On Reading 'Bede's Death Song': Translation, Typology, and Penance in Symeon of Durham's Text of the 'Epistola Cuthberti de Obitu Bedae,'" *Neuphilologische Mitteilungen* 84 (1983): 171-81.

[44] Concerning the content of the letter, see *Bedae opera de temporibus,* ed. Jones, pp. 132-35. Both Jones and Bolton (in *Anglo-Latin Literature,* p. 151) mistranslate a portion of the letter, so that the David whom he asks to come to his aid becomes the original perpetrator of the accusation against Bede. See Dieter Schaller, "Der verleumdete David: zum Schlusskapitel von Bedas 'Epistola ad Pleguinam,'" *Literatur und Sprache im europäischen Mittelalter: Festschrift für Karl Langosch,* ed. Alf Önnerfors, Johannes Rathofer, Fritz Wagner (Darmstadt, Germany: Wissenschaftliche Buchgesellschaft, 1973), pp. 39-43.

[45] This letter exists only in a printed version transcribed from a now lost manuscript of the monastery of St. Vincent in Metz, published by Jean Mabillon in *Vetera analecta* (Paris: Montalant, 1723; reprint ed., Farnborough, England: Gregg, 1967), p. 398. No known manuscript contains it. See Laistner, *Hand-List,* p. 119.

[46] See Plummer II, pp. 1-2; Levison, "Bede as Historian," p. 128.

[47] See Thacker, "Bede's Ideal of Reform," pp. 130-53.

[48] For a summary of Bede's protests against clerical abuses, see the texts cited by Plummer I, p. xxxv, and II, pp. 381-86.

[49] The abusive system of founding familial *monasteriola* under the rule and control of a family members as abbot or abbess was, according to Bede, already in existence for thirty years, since King Aldfrith's days. It was also widespread on the Continent. When Ecgbert and Eadbert attempted to put Bede's recommendation into effect, they incurred papal displeasure (see *EHD* I, no. 184). The abuse was again attacked by the tenth-century Benedictine reformers.

[50] See Jan Davidse's thoughtful analysis in "The Sense of History in the Works of the Venerable Bede," *Studi medievali,* 3d ser., 23 (1982): 668-70.

[51] Davidse, "Sense of History," p. 670, justifiably calls in question the tone of Bede's swan song as interpreted by John Smith (1722), Plummer II, p. 378, and Musca, *Il venerabile Beda,* p. 345.

FURTHER READING

Biography

Price, Mary R. "Bede." In *Bede and Dunstan,* pp. 7-32. Oxford: Oxford University Press, 1968.
    Short, heavily illustrated biography of Bede.

Criticism

Blair, Peter Hunter. *An Introduction to Anglo-Saxon England.* Cambridge: Cambridge University Press, 1970, 381 p.
    Provides general introduction to seven centuries of English history, from the latter part of the Roman occupation to the Norman Age.

———. *The World of Bede.* Cambridge: Cambridge University Press, 1990, 342 p.
    Historical examination of Britain's transformation from illiterate paganism to the kind of primitive Christian world which enabled Bede "to . . . delight in learning, teaching, and writing."

Cowdrey, H. E. J. "Bede and the 'English People.'" *The Journal of Religious History* 11, No. 4 (December 1981): 501-23.
    Investigation of the contribution the *Ecclesiastical History* made to the formation of the English as a self-consciously unified people.

Davidse, Jan. "The Sense of History in the Works of the Venerable Beda." *Stvdi Medievali* XXIII (1982): 647-95.
    Considers the importance of the Christian conceptions of time and eternity in Bede's historical writings.

Henderson, George. *Bede and the Visual Arts.* Newcastle-upon-Tyne: J. & P. Bealls, 1980, 32 p.
    Assesses the significance of some of Bede's references to the visual arts.

Kendall, Calvin B. "Bede's Historia Ecclesiastica: The Rhetoric of Faith." In *Medieval Eloquence: Studies in the Theory and Practice of Medieval Rhetoric,* edited by James J. Murphy, pp. 145-72. Berkeley and Los Angeles: University of California Press, 1978.
    Scholarly attempt to reconcile "the sober, reliable historian" and the "credulous, if engaging, storyteller" in Bede's *Ecclesiastical History of the English People.*

Laistner, M. L. W. "Irish and English Scholars and Missionaries to the Death of Bede." In his *Thought and Letters in Western Europe: A.D. 500-900,* pp. 136-66. New York: Cornell University Press, 1957.

Describes the qualities and interests that made Bede a successful writer and praises his ability to select from and adapt the teachings of the great Church Fathers.

Whitelock, Dorothy. *After Bede*. Newcastle-upon-Tyne: J. & P. Bealls, 1960, 16 p.
    Systematic discussion of the early growth of Bede's reputation.

Additional coverage of Bede's life and career is contained in the following source published by Gale Research: *Dictionary of Literary Biography,* Vol. 146.

Hildegard von Bingen

1098-1179

German composer, poet, musician, natural historian, and playwright.

INTRODUCTION

Hildegard was recognized by the twelfth-century Church as a visionary who possessed a divine gift for perceiving images and messages directly from God. Hildegard documented her elaborate visions in several important works, including the *Scivias* (c. 1151) and the *Liber divinorum operum* (c. 1170). She is also noted for her medical and scientific writings and musical compositions. Famed for her prophesies and wisdom, Hildegard's reputation as a source of advice led many people to seek her opinion on a variety of matters, a quality evidenced by her extensive surviving correspondence. Critics have even referred to Hildegard as the "Dear Abby" of the twelfth century. Hildegard's oeuvre has been of increasing interest to twentieth-century scholars, who have praised the diversity and vastness of her works as well as her inventive depiction of images and ideas.

Biographical Information

What is known about Hildegard is derived from numerous surviving letters from her extensive correspondence and from a biography—*Vita* (c. 1179)—completed by Theodoric of Echternach, which incorporates memoirs dictated by Hildegard. Born into a noble family, Hildegard was the tenth child of Hildebert von Bermersheim and his wife, Mechthild. At the age of eight, Hildegard was entered by her parents into the hermitage attached to the isolated Benedictine monastery of Disibodenberg, where she demonstrated a talent for leadership and theology. In 1136, when the abbess Jutta von Spanheim died, the nuns unanimously elected Hildegard as her successor. Although Hildegard possessed a gift for prophetic visions from an early age, it was not until she was in her forties that she revealed her visionary gifts to others. Kent Kraft comments: "[She] experienced an astonishing series of revelations that caused her to break a self-imposed silence concerning her visionary gifts. Above all she found herself subject to a divine command to `write what you see and hear!'" During the next ten years, Hildegard worked toward the completion of the *Scivias* while her fame as a prophet, healer, and visionary grew. In 1148 Hildegard informed the abbot of Disibodenberg that she wished to establish her own convent near Bingen. When the abbot was reluctant to let her depart, Hildegard was stricken with a sudden illness that witnesses claim was a divine punishment for the rejection of Hildegard's request. The abbot capitulated shortly thereafter, and Hildegard moved with her nuns into a new convent at Rupertsberg, near Bingen, in 1150. Throughout the next decade, the convent flourished and Hildegard began to write works on medicine and natural philosophy, along with another visionary treatise, the *Liber vitae meritorum* (c. 1163; *The Book of Life's Rewards*). Between 1158 and 1161 she embarked upon a series of preaching tours, and in 1163 she began the last of her visionary writings, the *Liber divinorum operum* (*Book of the Divine Works*). The later years of Hildegard's life were marked by her controversial yet successful defiance church decrees when they were contrary to her own impulses and beliefs. For example, when Hildegard permitted an excommunicated nobleman to be buried in the convent cemetery (since he had been reconciled to the Church before his death), officials judged the atonement invalid and ordered Hildegard to have the body exhumed. The entire Rupertsberg convent was excommunicated when Hildegard refused to comply. Hildegard wrote an impassioned appeal to Archbishop Christian in Rome, and in March 1179 the convent was restored into the Church. Shortly thereafter, Hildegard became ill; she died on September 17, 1179. The title of "saint" is commonly given to Hildegard despite the fact that she was not in fact canonized, although attempts to establish her sainthood were made under the popes Gregory IX, Innocent IV, and John XXII.

Major Works

Generally considered to be Hildegard's most remarkable literary efforts, the *Scivias* and the *Liber divinorum operum* contain some of her most significant visionary revelations. Composed in three parts, the *Scivias* records Hildegard's visionary account of the Creation through the Apocalypse. The first six visions of the work depict the composition of the universe and the evolution of the relationship of God to humanity, while the next seven visions illustrate the process of human redemption—the coming of the Savior, and the battle between the Church and Satan. The final book contains thirteen visions in which Hildegard describes an elaborate edifice containing the various divine virtues and concludes with her account of the final days of the apocalypse. In her 1985 essay "Hildegard of Bingen: Visions and Validation," Barbara Newman commented: "[In the

Scivias], Hildegard ranged over the themes of divine majesty, the Trinity, creation, the fall of Lucifer and of Adam, the stages of salvation history, the Church and its sacraments, the Last Judgment and the world to come. She lingered long over he subjects of priesthood, the Eucharist, and marriage . . . and she returned time and again to two of her favorite themes, the centrality of the Incarnation and the necessity of spiritual combat." Often considered the most difficult of Hildegard's mystical writings, the visions recounted in *Liber divinorum operum* reveal Hildegard's scientific interest, depicting humanity's place in the scheme of the cosmos and emphasizing a sense of reason and harmony in nature. Also presenting Hildegard's visions is the *Liber vitae meritorum* (1163; *The Book of Life's Rewards*), in which she portrays dialogues between the various human vices and their corresponding virtues interspersed with Biblical glosses and theological commentary.

Hildegard has also been regarded by several scholars as Germany's first woman doctor and scientist. The *Physica* (1158), for example, is a pharmacopoeia and an encyclopedia denoting the characteristic medicinal properties of various plants, animals, and minerals, while the *Causae et curae* (1158) also contains discussion of the origin and treatment of disease. Peter Dronke comments: "After a description of the constitution of the world, we find chapters [in *Causae et curae*] on topics ranging from nutrition and metabolism to gynecology and emotional hygiene."

Music was a fundamental aspect of daily life in the Benedictine convents, and musical compositions are an important part of Hildegard's diverse oeuvre. Scholars have noted the innovation of such musical works as the *Symphonia armonie celestium revelationum* (1158; *Symphony of the Harmony of Heavenly Revelations*), which is distinguished from standard Gregorian chant by Hildegard's unique approach to melody and musical structure. The poetry that accompanies her musical sequences employs a method strikingly similar to modern free verse. Using unrhymed lines and an uneven meter, her poetry is characterized by a freedom from the strict metrical conventions of most twelfth-century compositions.

Critical Reception

Hildegard's works have attracted increasing interest from the academic community in the areas of literature, women's studies, theology, the history of science, and music history and performance. Peter Dronke, for example, has contributed substantially to the awakening of current interest in Hildegard; his 1970 essay "Hildegard of Bingen as Poetess and Dramatist" pointed to her vivid and original use of imagery as "some of the most unusual, subtle, and exciting poetry of the twelfth century." A feminist impulse has characterized much Hildegard commentary, with some critics observing that divine visions served Hildegard by imbuing her ideas with an accepted voice of ecclesiastical authority. Samuel Lyndon Gladden has argued against the notion of Hildegard as a passive agent of the voice of God, suggesting that she "knowingly and willfully encodes a feminine voice in the midst of what appears to be the message of an obviously male-identified God." Also relevant to feminist and historical concerns is Frances Beer's examination of Hildegard's career in the context of twelfth-century life within the Benedictine convents. Beer discusses the abbess's overt challenges to the policies of several male figures in positions of power and authority and her "effective imperviousness to the potent medieval tradition of antifeminism." A physiological interest in the specific source of Hildegard's inspiration has also characterized modern scholarship, with such commentators as Charles Singer suggesting that the images and voices she witnessed may have been in part the by-product of a migraine condition. With the rise of the performance art movement during the 1970s and 1980s, Hildegard's musical compositions have also become the subject of popular performance and recording as well as scholarly attention.

PRINCIPAL WORKS

Scivias [Scito vias Domini; or, Know the Ways of the Lord] (visions/theology) c. 1151
***Liber subtilitatum diversarum naturarum creaturarum libri novum* [Nine Books on the Subtleties of Different Kinds of Creatures] c.1158
Ordo virtutum (liturgical drama) 1158
Symphonia armonie celestium revelationum [The Symphony of the Harmony of Heavenly Revelations] (songs) 1158
Liber vitae meritorum [The Book of Life's Rewards] (visions/theology) 1163
Liber divinorum operum [The Book of the Divine Works] (visions/theology) c. 1170
Vita (completed by Theodoric of Echternach) c. 1179

*Works are listed in order of approximate date of completion.

**Comprises the *Physica* and the *Causae et curae*.

PRINCIPAL ENGLISH TRANSLATIONS

Hildegard of Bingen's Book of Divine Works [translated by Robert Cunningham, Jerry Dybdal, and Ron Miller; edited by Matthew Fox] 1987
Symphonia: A Critical Edition of the Symphonia Armonie Celestium Revelationum [translated by Barbara Newman] 1988

Hildegard of Bingen: An Anthology [translated by Robert Carver; edited by Fiona Bowie and Oliver Davies] 1990

Mystical Writings [translated by Robert Carver; edited by Fiona Bowie] 1990

Scivias [translated by Columba Hart and Jane Bishop] 1990

Hildegard of Bingen: The Book of the Rewards of Life (*Liber vitae meritorum*) [translated by Bruce W. Hozeski] 1994

Holistic Healing [translated by Manfred Pawlik] 1994

The Letters of Hildegard of Bingen [translated by Joseph L. Baird and Radd K. Ehrman] 1994

Secrets of God: Writings of Hildegard of Bingen [translated by Sabina Flanagan] 1996

CRITICISM

Charles Singer (essay date 1917)

SOURCE: Charles Singer, "The Scientific Views and Visions of Saint Hildegard (1098-1180)," in *Studies in the History and Method of Science*, edited by Charles Singer, Oxford at the Clarendon Press, 1917, pp. 1-58.

[*In the following excerpt, Singer focuses on Hildegard's scientific thought, examining the sources of her scientific ideas, her conception of the structure of the material universe, and her theological interpretation of nature and the human body.*]

In attempting to interpret the views of Hildegard on scientific subjects, certain special difficulties present themselves. First is the confusion arising from the writings to which her name has been erroneously attached. To obtain a true view of the scope of her work, it is necessary to discuss the authenticity of some of the material before us. A second difficulty is due to the receptivity of her mind, so that views and theories that she accepts in her earlier works become modified, altered, and developed in her later writings. A third difficulty, perhaps less real than the others, is the visionary and involved form in which her thoughts are cast.

But a fourth and more vital difficulty is the attitude that she adopts towards phenomena in general. To her mind there is no distinction between physical events, moral truths, and spiritual experiences. This view, which our children share with their mediaeval ancestors, was developed but not transformed by the virile power of her intellect. Her fusion of internal and external universe links Hildegard indeed to a whole series of mediaeval visionaries, culminating with Dante. In Hildegard, as in her fellow mystics, we find that ideas on Nature and Man, the Moral World and the Material Universe, the Spheres, the Winds, and the Humours, Birth and Death, and even on the Soul, the Resurrection of the Dead, and the Nature of God, are not only interdependent, but closely interwoven. Nowadays we are well accustomed to separate our ideas into categories, scientific, ethical, theological, philosophical, and so forth, and we even esteem it a virtue to retain and restrain our thoughts within limits that we deliberately set for them. To Hildegard such classification would have been impossible and probably incomprehensible. Nor do such terms as *parallelism* or *allegory* adequately cover her view of the relation of the material and spiritual. In her mind they are really interfused, or rather they have not yet been separated.

Therefore, although in the following pages an attempt is made to estimate her scientific views, yet the writer is conscious that such a method must needs interpret her thought in a partial manner. Hildegard, indeed, presents to us scientific thought as an undifferentiated factor, and an attempt is here made to separate it by the artificial but not unscientific process of dissection from the organic matrix in which it is embedded.

The extensive literature that has risen around the life and works of Hildegard has come from the hands of writers who have shown no interest in natural knowledge, while those who have occupied themselves with the history of science have, on their side, largely neglected the period to which Hildegard belongs, allured by the richer harvest of the full scholastic age which followed. This essay is an attempt to fill in a small part of the lacuna. . . .

SOURCES OF HILDEGARD'S SCIENTIFIC KNOWLEDGE

In the works of Hildegard we are dealing with the products of a peculiarly original intellect, and her imaginative power and mystical tendency make an exhaustive search into the origin of her ideas by no means an easy task. With her theological standpoint, as such, we are not here concerned, and unfortunately she does not herself refer to any of her sources other than the Biblical books; to have cited profane writers would indeed have involved the abandonment of her claim that her knowledge was derived by immediate inspiration from on high. Nevertheless it is possible to form some idea, on internal evidence, of the origin of many of her scientific conceptions.

The most striking point concerning the sources of Hildegard is negative. There is no German linguistic element distinguishable in her writings, and they show little or no trace of native German folk-lore.[1] It is true that Trithemius of Sponheim (1462-1516), who is often a very inaccurate chronicler, tells us that Hildegard 'composed works in German as well as in Latin, although she had neither learned nor used the latter tongue except for simple psalmody'.[2] But with the testimony before us of the writings themselves and of her skilful use of Latin, the statement of Trithemius and even the hints of Hildegard[3] may be safely discounted and set down to the wish to magnify the element of inspiration.[4] So far from her having been illiterate, we shall show that the structure and details of her works betray a considerable degree of learning and much painstaking study of the works of others. Thus, for instance, she skilfully manipulates the Hippocratic doctrines of miasma and the humours, and elaborates a theory of the interrelation of the two which, though developed on a plan of her own, is yet clearly borrowed in its broad outline from such a writer as Isidore of Seville. Again, as we shall see, some of her ideas on anatomy seem to have been derived from Constantine the African, who belonged to the Benedictine monastery of Monte Cassino.[5]

Hildegard lived at rather too early a date to drink from the broad stream of new knowledge that was soon to flow into Europe through Paris from its reservoir in Moslem Spain. Such drops from that source as may have reached her must have trickled in either from the earlier Italian translators or from the Jews who had settled in the Upper Rhineland, for it is very unlikely that she was influenced by the earlier twelfth-century translations of Averroes, Avicenna, Avicebron, and Avempace, that passed into France from the Jews of Marseilles, Montpellier, and Andalusia.[6] Her intellectual field was thus far more patristic than would have been the case had her life-course been even a quarter of a century later.

Her science is primarily of the usual degenerate Greek type, disintegrated fragments of Aristotle and Galen coloured and altered by the customary mediaeval attempts to bring theory into line with scriptural phraseology, though a high degree of independence is obtained by the visionary form in which her views are set. She exhibits, like all mediaeval writers on science, the Aristotelian theory of the elements, but her statement of the doctrine is illuminated by flashes of her own thoughts and is coloured by suggestions from St. Augustine, Isidore Hispalensis, Bernard Sylvestris of Tours, and perhaps from writings attributed to Boethius.

The translator Gerard of Cremona (1114-87) was her contemporary, and his labours made available for western readers a number of scientific works which had previously circulated only among Arabic-speaking peoples.[7] Several of these works, notably Ptolemy's *Almagest,* Messahalah's *De Orbe,* and the Aristotelian *De Caelo et Mundo,* contain material on the form of the universe and on the nature of the elements, and some of them probably reached the Rhineland in time to be used by Hildegard. The *Almagest,* however, was not translated until 1175, and was thus inaccessible to Hildegard.[8] Moreover, as she never uses an Arabic medical term, it is reasonably certain that she did not

consult Gerard's translation of Avicenna, which is crowded with Arabisms.

On the other hand, the influence of the Salernitan school may be discerned in several of her scientific ideas. The *Regimen Sanitatis* of Salerno, written about 1101, was rapidly diffused throughout Europe, and must have reached the Rhineland at least a generation before the *Liber Divinorum Operum* was composed. This cycle of verses may well have reinforced some of her microcosmic ideas,[9] and suggested also her views on the generation of man,[10] on the effects of wind on health,[11] and on the influence of the stars.[12]

On the subject of the form of the earth Hildegard expressed herself definitely as a spherist,[13] a point of view more widely accepted in the earlier Middle Ages than is perhaps generally supposed. She considers in the usual mediaeval fashion that this globe is surrounded by celestial spheres that influence terrestrial events.[14] But while she claims that human affairs, and especially human diseases, are controlled, under God, by the heavenly cosmos, she yet commits herself to none of that more detailed astrological doctrine that was developing in her time, and came to efflorescence in the following centuries. In this respect she follows the earlier and somewhat more scientific spirit of such writers as Messahalah, rather than the wilder theories of her own age. The shortness and simplicity of Messahalah's tract on the sphere made it very popular. It was probably one of the earliest to be translated into Latin; and its contents would account for the change which, as we shall see, came over Hildegard's scientific views in her later years.

The general conception of the universe as a series of concentric elemental spheres had certainly penetrated to Western Europe centuries before Hildegard's time. Nevertheless the prophetess presents it to her audience as a new and striking revelation. We may thus suppose that translations of Messahalah, or of whatever other work she drew upon for the purpose, did not reach the Upper Rhineland, or rather did not become accepted by the circles in which Hildegard moved, until about the decade 1141-50, during which she was occupied in the composition of her *Scivias.*

There is another cosmic theory, the advent of which to her country, or at least to her circle, can be approximately dated from her work. Hildegard exhibits in a pronounced but peculiar and original form the doctrine of the macrocosm and microcosm. Hardly distinguishable in the *Scivias* (1141-50), it appears definitely in the *Liber Vitae Meritorum* (1158-62),[15] in which work, however, it takes no very prominent place, and is largely overlaid and concealed by other lines of thought. But in the *Liber Divinorum Operum* (1163-70) this belief is the main theme. The book is indeed an elaborate attempt to demonstrate a similarity and relationship between the nature of the Godhead, the constitution of the universe, and the structure of man, and it thus forms a valuable compendium of the science of the day viewed from the standpoint of this theory.

From whence did she derive the theory of macrocosm and microcosm? In outline its elements were easily accessible to her in Isidore's *De Rerum Natura* as well as in the Salernitan poems. But the work of Bernard Sylvestris of Tours, *De mundi universitate sive megacosmus et microcosmus,*[16] corresponds so closely both in form, in spirit, and sometimes even in phraseology, to the **Liber Divinorum Operum** that it appears to us certain that Hildegard must have had access to it also. Bernard's work can be dated between the years 1145-53 from his reference to the papacy of Eugenius III. This would correspond well with the appearance of his doctrines in the **Liber Vitae Meritorum** (1158-62) and their full development in the **Liber Divinorum Operum** (1163-70).

Another contemporary writer with whom Hildegard presents points of contact is Hugh of St. Victor (1095-1141).[17] In his writings the doctrine of the relation of macrocosm and microcosm is more veiled than with Bernard Sylvestris. Nevertheless, his symbolic universe is on the lines of Hildegard's belief, and the plan of his *De arca Noe mystica* presents many parallels both to the **Scivias** and to the **Liber Divinorum Operum**. If these do not owe anything directly to Hugh, they are at least products of the same mystical movement as were his works.

We may also recall that at Hildegard's date very complex cabalistic systems involving the doctrine of macrocosm and microcosm were being elaborated by the Jews, and that she lived in a district where Rabbinic mysticism specially flourished.[18] Benjamin of Tudela, who visited Bingen during Hildegard's lifetime, tells us that he found there a congregation of his people. Since we know, moreover, that she was familiar with the Jews,[19] it is possible that she may have derived some of the very complex macrocosmic conceptions with which her last work is crowded from local Jewish students.

The Alsatian Herrade de Landsberg (died 1195), a contemporary of Hildegard, developed the microcosm theory along lines similar to those of our abbess, and it is probable that the theory, in the form in which these writers present it, reached the Upper Rhineland somewhere about the middle or latter half of the twelfth century.

Apart from the Biblical books, the work which made the deepest impression on Hildegard was probably Augustine's *De Civitate Dei,* which seems to form the background of a large part of the **Scivias**. The books of Ezekiel and of Daniel, the Gospel of Nicodemus, the Shepherd of Hermas, and the Apocalypse, all contain a lurid type of vision which her own spiritual experiences would enable her to utilize, and which fit in well with her microcosmic doctrines. Ideas on the harmony and disharmony of the elements she may have picked up from such works as the Wisdom of Solomon and the Pauline writings, though it is obvious that Isidore of Seville and the *Regimen Sanitatis Salerni* were also drawn upon by her.

Her figure of the Church in the **Scivias** reminds us irresistibly of Boethius' vision of the gracious feminine form of Philosophy. Again, the visions of the punishments of Hell which Hildegard recounts in the **Liber Vitae Meritorum**[20] bear resemblance to the work of her contemporary Benedictine, the monk Alberic the younger of Monte Cassino, to whom Dante also became indebted.[21]

Hildegard repeatedly assures us that most of her knowledge was revealed to her in waking visions. Some of these . . . had a pathological basis, probably of a migrainous character, and she was a sufferer from a condition that would nowadays probably be classified as hystero-epilepsy. Too much stress, however, can easily be laid on the ecstatic presentment of her scientific views. Visions, it must be remembered, were 'the fashion' at the period, and were a common literary device. Her contemporary Benedictine sister, Elizabeth of Schönau, as well as numerous successors, as for example Gertrude of Robersdorf, adopted the same mechanism. The use of the vision for this purpose remained popular for centuries, and we may say of these writers, as Ampère says of Dante, that 'the visions gave not the genius nor the poetic inspiration, but the form merely in which they were realized'.

The contemporaries of Hildegard who provide the closest analogy to her are Elizabeth of Schönau (died 1165), whose visions are recounted in her life by Eckbertus;[22] and Herrade de Landsberg, Abbess of Hohenburg in Alsace, the priceless MS. of whose *Hortus Deliciarum* was destroyed by the Germans in the siege of Strasbourg in 1870.[23] With Elizabeth of Schönau, who lived in her neighbourhood, Hildegard was in frequent correspondence. With Herrade she had, so far as is known, no direct communication; but the two were contemporary, lived not very far apart, and under similar political and cultural conditions. Elizabeth's visions present some striking analogies to those of Hildegard, while the figures of Herrade, of which copies have fortunately survived, often suggest the illustrations of the Wiesbaden or of the Lucca MSS.

THE STRUCTURE OF THE MATERIAL UNIVERSE

To the student of the history of science, Hildegard's beliefs as to the nature and structure of the universe are among the most interesting that she has to impart.

Her earlier theories are in some respects unique among mediaeval writers, and we possess in the Wiesbaden Codex B a diagram enabling us to interpret her views with a definiteness and certainty that would otherwise be impossible.

Hildegard's universe is geocentric, and consists of a spherical earth,[24] around which are arranged a number of concentric shells or zones. The inner zones are spherical, the outer oval, and the outermost of all egg-shaped, with one end prolonged and more pointed than the other. The concentric structure is a commonplace of mediaeval science, and is encountered, for instance, in the works of Bede, Isidore, Alexander of Neckam, Roger Bacon, Albertus Magnus, and Dante. To all these writers, however, the universe is spherical. The egg-shape is peculiar to Hildegard. Many of the *Mappaemundi* of the Beatus and other types exhibit the *surface* of the habitable earth itself as oval, and it was from such charts that Hildegard probably gained her conception of an oval universe. In her method of orientation also she follows these maps, placing the east at the top of the page where we are accustomed to place the north.[25]

It is unfortunate that she does not deal with geography in the restricted sense, and so we are not in full possession of her views on the antipodes, a subject of frequent derision to patristic and of misconception to scholastic writers. She does, however, vaguely refer to the inversion of seasons and climates in the opposite hemisphere,[26] though she confuses the issue by the adoption of a theory widespread in the Middle Ages and reproduced in the *Divina Commedia,* that the antipodean surface of the earth is uninhabitable, since it is either beneath the ocean or in the mouth of the Dragon.[27] The nature of the antipodean inversion of climates was clearly grasped by her contemporary, Herrade de Landsberg.

Hildegard's views as to the internal structure of the terrestrial sphere are also somewhat difficult to follow. Her obscure and confused doctrine of Purgatory and Hell has puzzled other writers besides ourselves,[28] nor need we consider it here, but she held that the interior of the earth contained two vast spaces shaped like truncated cones, where punishment was meted out and whence many evil things had issue.[29] Her whole scheme presents analogies as well as contrasts to that of her kindred spirit Dante.[30] Hildegard, however, who died before the thirteenth century had dawned, presents us with a scheme far less definite and elaborated than that of her great successor, who had all the stores of the golden age of scholasticism on which to draw.

In Hildegard's first diagram of the universe, which is of the nature of an 'optical section', the world, the *sphaera elementorum* of Johannes Sacro Bosco and other mediaeval writers, is diagrammatically represented as compounded of earth, air, fire, and water confusedly mixed in what her younger contemporary, Alexander of Neckam (1157-1217), calls 'a certain concordant discord of the elements'. In the illustrations to the Wiesbaden Codex B the four elements have each a conventional method of representation, which appears again and again in the different miniatures.

Around this world with its four elements is spread the atmosphere, the *aer lucidus* or *alba pellis,* diagrammatically represented, like the earth which it enwraps, as circular. Through this *alba pellis* no creature of earth can penetrate. Beyond are ranged in order four further shells or zones. Each zone contains one of the cardinal winds, and each cardinal wind is accompanied by two accessory winds, represented in the traditional fashion by the breath of supernatural beings.

Of the four outer zones the first is the *aer aquosus,* also round, from which blows the east wind. In the outer part of the *aer aquosus* float the clouds, and according as they contract or expand or are blown aside, the heavenly bodies above are revealed or concealed.

Enwrapping the *aer aquosus* is the *purus aether,* the widest of all the zones. The long axis of this, as of the remaining outer shells, is in the direction from east to west, thus determining the path of movement of the heavenly bodies. Scattered through the *purus aether* are the constellations of the fixed stars, and arranged along the long axis are the moon and the two inner planets. From this zone blows the west wind. The position and constitution of this *purus aether* is evidently the result of some misinterpretation of Aristotelian writings.

The next zone, the *umbrosa pellis* or *ignis niger,* is a narrow dark shell, whence proceed the more dramatic meteorological events. Here, following on the hints of the Wisdom of Solomon (chap. v) and the Book of Job (chap. xxxviii), are situated the diagrammatically portrayed treasuries of lightning and of hail. From here the tempestuous north wind bursts forth. This *ignis niger* is clearly comparable to the *dry earthy exhalation* that works of the Peripatetic school regard as given off by the outer fiery zone. The presence of the *ignis niger* thus suggests some contact on the part of the authoress with the teaching of the *Meteorologica* of Aristotle.[31]

The outermost layer of all is a mass of flames, the *lucidus ignis.* Here are the sun and the three outer planets, and from here the south wind pours its scorching breath.

The movements of the four outer zones around each other, carrying the heavenly bodies with them, are attributed to the winds in each zone. The seasonal variations in the movements of the heavenly bodies, along with the recurring seasons themselves, are also determined by the prevalent winds, which, acting as the motive power upon the various zones, form a celestial parallelogram of forces. In this way is ingeniously explained also why in spring the days lengthen and in autumn they shorten until in either case an equinox is reached.

> 'I looked and behold the east and the south wind with their collaterals, moving the firmament by the power of their breath, caused it to revolve over the earth from east to west; and in the same way the west and north winds and their collaterals, receiving the impulse and projecting their blast, thrust it back again from west to east. . . .

> 'I saw also that as the days began to lengthen, the south wind and his collaterals gradually raised the firmament in the southern zone upwards towards the north, until the days ceased to grow longer. Then when the days began to shorten, the north wind with his collaterals, shrinking from the brightness of the sun, drove the firmament back gradually southward until by reason of the lengthening days the south wind began yet again to raise it up'.[32]

Intimately bound up not only with her theory of the nature and structure of the universe but also with her eschatological beliefs is Hildegard's doctrine of the elements. Before the fall of man these were arranged in a harmony,[33] which was disturbed by that catastrophe,[34] so that they have since remained in the state of mingled confusion in which we always encounter them on the terrestrial globe. This *mistio*, to use the mediaeval Aristotelian term, is symbolized by the irregular manner in which the elements are represented in the central sphere of the diagram of the universe. Thus mingled they will remain until subjected to the melting-pot of the Last Judgement,[35] when they will emerge in a new and eternal harmony, no longer mixed as matter, but separate and pure, parts of the new heaven and the new earth.[36]

> 'But the heavens and the earth, which are now, . . . are kept in store and reserved unto fire against the day of judgment and perdition of ungodly men. . . . But the day of the Lord will come . . . in the which the heavens shall pass away with a great noise, and the elements shall melt with fervent heat, the earth also and the works that are therein shall be burned up. . . . Nevertheless we, according to his promise, look for new heavens and a new earth, wherein dwelleth righteousness' (2 Peter iii. 7, 10, and 13).

So Hildegard, acting on a scriptural hint, is enabled to dematerialize her doctrine of the after-things.

But although since man's fall the elements have lost their order and their harmony on this terrestrial orb,

yet is that harmony still in part preserved in the celestial spheres that encircle and surround our globe; and water, air, earth, and fire have each their respective representatives in the four concentric zones, the *aer aquosus*, the *purus aether*, the *umbrosa pellis*, and the *lucidus ignis*. These are the 'superior elements' which still retain some at least of their individuality and primal purity. From each of their spheres blows, as we have seen, one of the cardinal winds, and each wind partakes of the elemental character of the zone whence it issues, and has a corresponding influence on man's body, since each of the four humours is specifically affected by the element to which it corresponds.

> 'Then I saw that by the diverse quality of the winds, and of the atmosphere as they in turn sweep through it, the humours in man are agitated and altered. For in each of the superior elements there is a breath of corresponding quality by which, through the power of the winds, the corresponding element [below] is forced to revolve in the atmosphere, and in no other way is it moved. And by one of those winds, with the agency of sun, moon, and stars, the atmosphere which tempers the world is breathed forth'.[37]

This doctrine of the relation of the various winds to the four elements and through them to the four humours is found in the *De Rerum Natura* of Isidore of Seville, and is occasionally illustrated in European MSS. from the ninth century onward,[38] but we meet it set forth with special definiteness in the twelfth century in the translations from Messahalah. It is encountered also in the work of Herrade de Landsberg. In and after the thirteenth century it had become a commonplace.

The description we have given of the universe was in the main set forth by Hildegard in her first work, the *Scivias* (1141-50).[39] Subsequently she became dissatisfied with the account she had given, and while not withdrawing it, she sought in the **Liber Divinorum Operum** (1163-70) so to modify the original presentment as to bring it more into line with accepted views. Thus she writes: 'There appeared to me in vision a *disk* very like that object which I saw twenty-eight years ago of the form of an *egg*, in the third vision of my book **Scivias**. In the outer part of the disk there was as it were the *lucidus ignis*, and beneath it the circle of the *ignis niger* was portrayed . . . and these two circles were so joined as to be one circle.' There was thus one outer zone representing the fire. 'Under the circle of the *ignis niger* there was another circle in the likeness of the *purus aether* which was of the same width as the two conjoined [outer] fiery circles. And below this circle again was the circle of the *aer aquosus* as wide as the *lucidus ignis*. And below this circle was yet another circle, the *fortis et albus lucidusque aer* . . . the width whereof was as the width of the *ignis niger*, and these circles were joined to make one circle which was thus again of width equal to the outer two. Again, under this last circle yet another circle, the *aer tenuis,* was distinguishable, which could be seen to raise itself as a cloud, sometimes high and light, sometimes depressed and dark, and to diffuse itself as it were throughout the whole disk. . . . The outermost fiery circle perfuses the other circles with its fire, while the watery circle saturates them with its moisture. [cp. Wisdom of Solomon, xix. 18-20]. And from the extreme eastern part of the disk to the extreme west a line is stretched out [i.e. the equator] which separates the northern zones from the others'.[40]

The earth lies concentrically with the *aer tenuis,* and its measurements are given thus: 'In the midst of the *aer tenuis* a globe was indicated, the circumference of which was everywhere equidistant from the *fortis et albus lucidusque aer,* and it was as far across as the depth of the space from the top of the highest circle to the extremity of the clouds, or from the extremity of 'the clouds to the circumference of the inner globe'.

In her earlier work, the **Scivias,** Hildegard had not apparently realized the need of accounting for the independent movements of the planets other than the sun and moon. She had thus placed the moon and two of the moving stars in the *purus aether,* and the sun and the three remaining moving stars in the *lucidus ignis.* Since these spheres were moved by the winds, their contained planets would be subject to the same influences. In the **Liber Divinorum Operum,** however, she has come to realize how independent the movements of the planets really are, and she invokes a special cause for their vagaries. 'I looked and behold in the outer fire (*lucidus ignis*) there appeared a circle which girt about the whole firmament from the east westward. From it a blast produced a movement from west to east in the opposite direction to the movement of the firmament. But this blast did not give forth his breath earthward as did the other winds, but instead thereof it governed the course of the planets.'[41] The source of the blast is represented in the Lucca MS. as the head of a supernatural being with a human face.

These curious passages were written at some date after 1163, when Hildegard was at least 65 years old. They reveal our prophetess attempting to revise much of her earlier theory of the universe, and while seeking to justify her earlier views, endeavouring also to bring them into line with the new science that was now just beginning to reach her world. Note that (*a*) the universe has become round; (*b*) there is an attempt to arrange the zones according to their density, i. e. from without inwards, fire, air (ether), water, earth; (*c*) exact measurements are given; (*d*) the watery zone is continued earthward so as to mingle with the central circle. In all these and other respects she is joining the general current of mediaeval science then beginning to be moulded by works translated from the Arabic. Her knowledge of the movements of the heavenly bodies is

entirely innocent of the doctrine of epicycles, but in other respects her views have come to resemble those, for instance, of Messahalah, one of the simplest and easiest writers on the sphere available in her day. Furthermore, her conceptions have developed so as to fit in with the macrocosm-microcosm scheme which she grasped about the year 1158. Even in her latest work, however, her theory of the universe exhibits differences from that adopted by the schoolmen, as may be seen by comparing her diagram with, for example, the scheme of Dante.

Like many mediaeval writers, Hildegard would have liked to imagine an ideal state of the elemental spheres in which the rarest, fire, was uppermost, and the densest, earth, undermost. Such a scheme was, in fact, purveyed by Bernard Sylvestris and by Messahalah. Her conceptions were however disturbed by the awkward facts that water penetrated below the earth, and indeed sought the lowest level, while air and not water lay immediately above the earth's surface. Mediaeval writers adopted various devices and expended a great amount of ingenuity in dealing with this discrepancy, which was a constant source of obscurity and confusion. Hildegard devotes much space and some highly involved allegory both in the **Scivias** and in the **Liber Divinorum Operum** to the explanation of the difficulty, while Dante himself wrote a treatise in high scholastic style on this very subject.[42]

Macrocosm and Microcosm

The winds and elements of the outer universe, the macrocosm, become in Hildegard's later schemes intimately related to structures and events within the body of man himself, the microcosm, the being around whom the universe centres. The terms *macrocosm* and *microcosm* are not employed by her, but in her last great work, the **Liber Divinorum Operum,** she succeeds in most eloquent and able fashion in synthesizing into one great whole, centred around this doctrine, her theological beliefs and her physiological knowledge, together with her conceptions of the working of the human mind and of the structure of the universe. The work is thus an epitome of the science of the time viewed through the distorting medium of this theory. In studying it the modern reader is necessarily hampered by the bizarre and visionary form into which the whole subject is cast. Nevertheless the scheme, though complex and difficult, is neither incoherent nor insane, as at first sight it may seem. On the contrary, it is a highly systematic and skilful presentment of a cosmic theory which for centuries dominated scientific thought.

As an explanation of the complexity of existence which thinkers of all ages have sought to bring within the range of some simple formula, this theory of the essential similarity of macrocosm and microcosm held in the Middle Ages, during the Renaissance, and even into quite modern times, a position comparable to that of the theory of evolution in our own age. If at times it passed into folly and fantasy, it should be remembered that it also fulfilled a high purpose. It gave a meaning to the facts of nature and a formula to the naturalist, it unified philosophic systems, it exercised the ingenuity of theologians, and gave a convenient framework to prophecy, while it seemed to illumine history and to provide a key and meaning to life itself. Even now it is not perhaps wholly devoid of message, but as a phenomenon in the history of human thought, a theory which appealed to such diverse scientific writers as Seneca, Albertus Magnus, Paracelsus, Gilbert, Harvey, Boyle, and Leibnitz, is surely worthy of attention.

In essaying to interpret the views of our authoress on this difficult subject, we rely mainly on the text of the **Liber Divinorum Operum,** supplemented by the beautiful illuminations of that work which adorn the Lucca MS. The book opens with a truly remarkable vision:

> 'I saw a fair human form and the countenance thereof was of such beauty and brightness that it had been easier to gaze upon the sun. The head thereof was girt with a golden circlet through which appeared another face as of an aged man. From the neck of the figure on either side sprang a pinion which swept upward above the circlet and joined its fellow on high. And where on the right the wing turned upward, was portrayed an eagle's head with eyes of flame, wherein appeared as in a mirror the lightning of the angels, while from a man's head in the other wing the lightning of the stars did radiate. From either shoulder another wing reached to the knees. The figure was robed in brightness as of the sun, while the hands held a lamb shining with light. Beneath, the feet trampled a horrible black monster of revolting shape, upon the right ear of which a writhing serpent fixed itself.'[43]

The image declares its identity in words reminiscent of the Wisdom literature or of passages in the hermetic writings, but which seem in fact to be partly borrowed from Bernard Sylvestris.

> 'I am that supreme and fiery force that sends forth all the sparks of life. Death hath no part in me, yet do I allot it, wherefore I am girt about with wisdom as with wings. I am that living and fiery essence of the divine substance that glows in the beauty of the fields. I shine in the water, I burn in the sun and the moon and the stars. Mine is that mysterious force of the invisible wind. I sustain the breath of all living. I breathe in the verdure and in the flowers, and when the waters flow like living things, it is I. I formed those columns that support the whole earth. . . . I am the force that lies hid in the winds, from me they take their source, and as a man may move because he breathes so doth a fire burn but by

my blast. All these live because I am in them and am of their life. I am wisdom. Mine is the blast of the thundered word by which all things were made. I permeate all things that they may not die. I am life.'[44]

Hildegard thus supposes that the whole universe is permeated by a single living spirit, the figure of the vision. This spirit of the macrocosm, the *Nous* or 'world spirit' of the hermetic and Neoplatonic literature, the impersonated *Nature,* as we may perhaps render it, is in its turn controlled by the Godhead that pervades the form and is represented rising from its vertex as a second human face. Nature, the spirit of the cosmic order, controls and holds in subjection the hideous monster, the principle of death and dissolution, the *Hyle* or primordial matter of the Neoplatonists, whose chaotic and anarchic force would shatter and destroy this fair world unless fettered by a higher power.

With the details of the visionary figure we need not delay,[45] but we pass to the description of the structure of the macrocosm itself, to which the second vision is devoted. Here appears the same figure of the macrocosmic spirit. But now the head and feet only are visible, and the arms are outstretched to enclose the disk of the universe which conceals the body. Although the macrocosm now described is considerably altered from Hildegard's original scheme of the universe, she yet declares, 'I saw in the bosom of the form the appearance of a disk of like sort to that which twenty-eight years before I had seen in the third vision, set forth in my book of *Scivias*'.[46] The zones of this disk are then described. They are from without inwards:

(*a*) The *lucidus ignis,* containing the three outer planets, the sixteen principal fixed stars, and the south wind.

(*b*) The *ignis niger,* containing the sun, the north wind, and the materials of thunder, lightning, and hail.

(*c*) The *purus aether,* containing the west wind, the moon, the two inner planets, and certain fixed stars.

(*d*) The *aer aquosus,* containing the east wind.

(*e*) The *fortis et albus lucidusque aer,* where certain other fixed stars are placed.

(*f*) The *aer tenuis,* or atmosphere, in the outer part of which is the zone of the clouds.

From all these objects, from the spheres of the elements, from the sun, moon, and other planets, from the four winds each with their two collaterals, from the fixed stars, and from the clouds, descend influences, indicated by lines, towards the figure of the macrocosm.

The microcosm is then introduced.

'And again I heard the voice from heaven saying, "God, who created all things, wrought also man in his own image and similitude, and in him he traced [*signavit*] all created things, and he held him in such love that he destined him for the place from which the fallen angel had been cast."'[47]

The various characters of the winds are expounded in a set of curious passages in which the doctrine of the macrocosm and microcosm is further mystically elaborated. An endeavour is made to attribute to the winds derived from the different quarters of heaven qualities associated with a number of animals.[48] The conception is illustrated and made comprehensible by the miniatures in the Lucca MS.

'In the middle of the disk [of the universe] there appeared the form of a man, the crown of whose head and the soles of whose feet extended to the *fortis et albus lucidusque aer,* and his hands were outstretched right and left to the same circle. . . . Towards these parts was an appearance as of four heads; a leopard, a wolf, a lion, and a bear. Above the head of the figure in the zone of the *purus aether,* I saw the head of the leopard emitting a blast from its mouth, and on the right side of the mouth the blast, curving itself somewhat backwards, was formed into a crab's head . . . with two chelae; while on the left side of the mouth a blast similarly curved ended in a stag's head. From the mouth of the crab's head, another blast went to the middle of the space between the leopard and the lion; and from the stag's head a similar blast to the middle of the space between the leopard and the bear . . . and all the heads were breathing towards the figure of the man. Under his feet in the *aer aquosus* there appeared as it were the head of a wolf, sending forth to the right a blast extending to the middle of the half space between its head and that of the bear, where it assumed the form of the stag's head; and from the stag's mouth there came, as it were, another breath which ended in the middle line. From the left of the wolf's mouth arose a breath which went to the midst of the half space between the wolf and the lion, where was depicted another crab's head . . . from whose mouth another breath ended in the same middle line. . . . And the breath of all the heads extended sideways from one to another. . . . Moreover on the right hand of the figure in the *lucidus ignis,* from the head of the lion, issued a breath which passed laterally on the right into a serpent's head and on the left into a lamb's head . . . similarly on the figure's left in the *ignis niger* there issued a breath from the bear's head ending on its right in the head of [another] lamb, and on its left in another serpent's head. . . . And above the head of the figure the seven planets were ranged in order,

three in the *lucidus ignis,* one projecting into the *ignis niger* and three into the *purus aether.* . . . And in the circumference of the circle of the *lucidus ignis* there appeared the sixteen principal stars, four in each quadrant between the heads. . . . Also the *purus aether* and the *fortis et albus lucidusque aer* seemed to be full of stars which sent forth their rays towards the clouds, whence . . . tongues like rivers descended to the disk and towards the figure, which was thus surrounded and influenced by these signs.'[49]

The third vision is devoted to an account of the human body, the microcosm, with a comparison of its organs to the parts of the macrocosmic scheme, together with a detailed account of the effects of the heavenly bodies on the humours in man, the whole brought into a strongly theological setting. . . .

The fourth vision explains the influence of the heavenly bodies and of the superior elements on the power of nature as exhibited on the surface of the earth. It is illustrated by a charming miniature in the Lucca MS.

'I saw that the upper fiery firmament was stirred, so that as it were ashes were cast therefrom to earth, and they produced rashes and ulcers in men and animals and fruits.'. . .

'Then I saw that from the *ignis niger* certain vapours (*nebulae*) descended, which withered the verdure and dried up the moisture of the fields. The *purus aether,* however, resisted these ashes and vapours, seeking to hold back these plagues.'. . .

'And looking again I saw that from the *fortis et albus lucidusque aer* certain other clouds reached the earth and infected men and beasts with sore pestilence, so that they were subjected to many ills even to the death, but the *aer aquosus* opposed that influence so that they were not hurt beyond measure.'. . .

'Again I saw that the moisture in the *aer tenuis* was as it were boiling above the surface of the earth, awakening the force of the earth and making fruits to grow.'. . .[50]

The main outline of the *Liber Divinorum Operum* is, we believe, borrowed from the work of Bernard Sylvestris of Tours, *De mundi universitate libri duo sive megacosmus et microcosmus.*[51] In this composition by a teacher at the cathedral school of Chartres,[52] the gods and goddesses of the classical pantheon flit across the stage, for all the world as though the writer were a pagan, and the work might be thought to be the last one from which our pious authoress would borrow. The *De mundi universitate* is alternately in prose and verse and betrays an acquaintance with the classics very rare at its date. 'The rhythm of the hexameters is clearly that of Lucan, while the vocabulary is mainly of Ovid.'[53] The mythology is founded mainly on the *Timaeus*. The eternal *seminaria* of created things are mentioned, and it has been conjectured that the work exhibits traces of the influence of Lucretius,[54] but the general line of thought is clearly related to Neoplatonic literature. Thus the *anima universalis* of Neoplatonic writings can be identified with the *Nous* or *Noys* of Bernard. This principle is contrasted with primordial matter or *Hyle*. The parallel character of the **Liber Divinorum Operum** and the *De mundi universitate* can be illustrated by a few extracts from the latter. It will be seen that although the general setting is changed, yet Hildegard's figure of the spirit of the macrocosm is to be identified with Bernard's *Noys. Hyle,* on the other hand, becomes in Hildegard's plan the monstrous form, the emblem of brute matter, on which the spirit of the universe tramples.

> 'In huius operis primo libro qui Megacosmus dicitur, id est maior mundus, Natura ad Noym, id est Dei providentiam, de primae materiae, id est hyles, confusione querimoniam quasi cum lacrimis agit et ut mundus pulchrius petit. Noys igitur eius mota precibus petitioni libenter annuit et ita quatuor elementa ab invicem seiungit. Novem ierarchias angelorum in coelo ponit. stellas in firmamento figit. signa disponit. sub signis orbes septem planetarum currere facit. quatuor ventos cardinales sibi invicem opponit. Sequitur genesis animantium et terrae situs medius. . . .

> 'In secundo libro qui Microcosmus dicitur, id est minor mundus, Noys ad Naturam loquitur et de mundi expolitione gloriatur et in operis sui completione se hominem plasmaturam pollicetur. Iubet igitur Uraniam, quae siderum regina est, et Physin, quae rerum omnium est peritissima, sollicite perquirat. Natura protinus iubenti obsequitur et per caelestes circulos Uraniam quaeritans eam sideribus inhiantem reperit. eiusque itineris causa praecognita se operis et itineris comitem Urania pollicetur. . . . Subitoque ibi Noys affuit suoque velle eis ostenso trinas speculationes tribus assignando tribuit & ad hominis plasmationem eas impellit. Physis igitur de quatuor elementorum reliquiis hominem format et a capite incipiens membratim operando opus suum in pedibus consummat. . . .

> 'Noys ego scientia et divinae voluntatis arbitraria ad dispositionem rerum, quem ad modum de consensu eius accipio, sic meae administrationis officia circumduco. . . .

> '(Noys) erat fons luminis, seminarium vitae, bonum bonitatis divinae, plenitudo scientiae quae mens altissimi nominatur. Ea igitur noys summi & exsuperantissimi Dei est intellectus et ex eius divinitate nata natura. . . . Erat igitur videre velut in speculo tersiore quicquid generationi quicquid operi Dei secretior destinarat affectus.'[55]

Hildegard's conception of macrocosm and microcosm, which was thus probably borrowed from Bernard

Sylvestris, has analogies also to those well-known figures illustrating the supposed influence of the signs of the zodiac on the different parts of the body.[56] Such figures, with the zodiacal symbols arranged around a figure of Christ, may be seen in certain MSS. anterior to Hildegard,[57] while the influence of the 'Melothesia', to give it the name assigned by Porphyry, has been traced through its period of efflorescence at the Renaissance (Plates XV,[58] XVI,[59] and XVII,[60] compare with Plates VII and VIII) right down to our own age and country, where it still appeals to the ignorant and foolish.[61]

Hildegard often interprets natural events by means of a peculiarly crude form of the doctrine, as when she describes how 'if the excess of waters below are drawn up to the clouds (by the just judgment of God in the requital of sinners), then the moisture from the *aer aquosus* transudes through the *fortis et albus lucidusque aer* as a draught drunk into the urinary bladder; and the same waters descend in an inundation'.[62]

Again, events in the body of man are most naively explained on the basis of the nature of the external world as she has pictured it.

> 'The humours at times rage fiercely as a leopard and again they are softened, going backwards as a crab;[63] or they may show their diversity by leaping and goring as a stag, or they may be as a wolf in their ravening, and yet again they may invade the body of man after the manner of both wolf and crab. Or else they may show forth their strength unceasingly as a lion, or as a serpent they may go now softly, now violently, and at times they may be gentle as a lamb and at times again they may growl as an angered bear, and at times they may partake of the nature of the lamb and of the serpent.'[63]

Having completed her general survey of the macrocosm (Vision II), and having investigated in detail the structure of man's body, the microcosm, in terms of the greater universe (Vision III), and discussed the influence of the heavenly bodies on terrestrial events (Vision IV), Hildegard turns to the internal structure of the terrestrial sphere (Vision V). . . .

Upon the surface of the earth towards the east stands the building which symbolizes the *aedificium* of the church, a favourite conception of our authoress. This church is surmounted by a halo, whence proceed a pair of pinions which extend their shelter over a full half of the earth's circumference. As for the rest of the earth's surface, part is within the wide-opened jaws of a monster, the Destroyer, and the remainder is beneath the surface of the ocean. Within the earth are five parts analogous, as she would have us believe, to the five senses. An eastern clear arc and a western clouded one signify respectively the excellence of the orient where Zion is situated, and the Cimmerian darkness of the occidental regions over which the shadow of the dragon is cast. Centrally is a quadrate area divided into three zones where the qualities of heat and cold and of a third intermediate 'temperateness' (*temperies*) are stored. North and south of this are two areas where purgatory is situate. Each is shaped like a truncated cone and composed also of three sectors. Souls are seen suffering in one sector the torment of flame, in another the torment of water, while in the third or intermediate sector lurk monsters and creeping things which add to the miseries of purgatory or at times come forth to earth's surface to plague mankind. These northern and southern sections exhibit dimly by their identically reversed arrangement the belief in the antipodean inversion of climate, an idea hinted several times in Hildegard's writings, but more definitely illustrated by a figure of Herrade de Landsberg.

Macrocosmic schemes of the type illustrated by the text of Hildegard and by the figures of the Lucca MS. had a great vogue in mediaeval times, and were passed on to later ages. Some passages in Hildegard's work read curiously like Paracelsus (1491-1541),[65] and it is not hard to find a link between these two difficult and mystical writers. Trithemius, the teacher of Paracelsus, was abbot of Sponheim, an important settlement almost within sight of Hildegard's convents on the Rupertsberg and Disibodenberg. Trithemius studied Hildegard's writings with great care and attached much importance to them, so that they may well have influenced his pupil. The influence of mediaeval theories of the relation of macrocosm and microcosm is encountered among numerous Renaissance writers besides Paracelsus, and is presented to us, for instance, by such a cautious, balanced, and scientifically-minded humanist as Fracastor. But as the years went on, the difficulty in applying the details of the theory became ever greater and greater. Facts were strained and mutilated more and more to make them fit the Procrustean bed of an outworn theory, which at length became untenable when the heliocentric system of Copernicus and Galileo replaced the geocentric and anthropocentric systems of an earlier age. The idea of a close parallelism between the structure of man and of the wider universe was gradually abandoned by the scientific, while among the unscientific it degenerated and became little better than an insane obsession. As such it appears in the ingenious ravings of the English follower of Paracelsus, the Rosicrucian, Robert Fludd, who reproduced, often with fidelity, the systems which had some novelty five centuries before his time. As a similar fantastic obsession this once fruitful hypothesis still occasionally appears even in modern works of learning and industry.[66]

Notes

[1] An exception must be made for the *lingua ignota*, which is presumably hers. The absence of Germanisms in her other writings may be partly due to the work of an editor. See the *Vita* by Theodoric, Migne, col. 101. Also the birth scene . . . is perhaps adapted from a German folk-tale.

[2] Johannes Trithemius, *Chronicon insigne Monasterii Hirsaugensis, Ordinis St. Benedicti,* Basel, 1559, p. 174.

[3] Migne, col. 384.

[4] It is not enough to suppose with some of her biographers that the visions were dictated by Hildegard and were latinized by a secretary. The visions imply a good deal of study and considerable book-learning. Among many reasons for believing that she had a very serviceable knowledge of Latin are the following:

(*a*) She was well acquainted with the Biblical writings and quotes them aptly and frequently.

(*b*) She was regarded by her contemporaries as an authority on scriptural interpretation and on Church discipline, and was frequently consulted by them on these subjects.

(*c*) She pleaded in person before clerical tribunals.

(*d*) One of the least remarkable and most credible of her 'miracles', the expounding of certain letters found upon an altar-cloth (Migne, col. 121), depends entirely on a knowledge of Latin.

(*e*) In the *Liber divinorum operum* (Migne, col. 922) she writes 'firmamentum *celum* nominavit quoniam omnia *excellit*', a derivation taken from Isidore and incomprehensible to one ignorant of Latin. There are many other passages in her works in which the sense depends on the Latin usage of a word.

(*f*) No mention of this ignorance is made by Guibert in the short sketch of her life that he wrote almost immediately after her death (1180; see Pitra, p. 407). On the contrary, he suggests that she had been an industrious student.

(*g*) The *Liber divinorum operum* may especially be pointed out among her works as betraying a very considerable degree of learning. Notably her elaborate doctrine of the macrocosm and microcosm must have involved extensive reading.

The general question of Hildegard's knowledge of Latin has also been discussed by Pitra and by Albert Battandier in the *Revue des questions historiques,* vol. xxxiii, p. 395, Paris, 1883.

[5] See chapter viii.

[6] It is, however, just possible that she had consulted the astrological work that had been translated from the Arabic by Hermann the Dalmatian for Bernard Sylvestris, and is represented in the Bodleian MSS. Digby 46 and Ashmole 304.

[7] See Baldassare Boncompagni, *Della vita e delle opere di Gherardo Cremonese, Traduttore del secolo duodecimo, e di Gherardo di Sabbionetta, Astronomo del secolo decimoterzo*, Rome, 1851; also K. Sudhoff, 'Die kurze "Vita" und das Verzeichnis der Arbeiten Gerhards von Cremona, von seinen Schülern und Studiengenossen kurz nach dem Tode des Meisters (1187) zu Toledo verabfasst', in *Archiv für Geschichte der Medizin*, Bd. viii, p. 73, November 1914.

[8] Another translation of the *Almagest* was made in Sicily in 1160, direct from the Greek. See C. H. Haskins and D. P. Lockwood, 'The Sicilian Translators of the Twelfth Century and the First Latin Version of Ptolemy's *Almagest*', in *Harvard Studies in Classical Philology*, xi. 75, Cambridge, Mass., 1910. It is wholly improbable that Hildegard had access to this rendering, which is only known from a single MS. of the fourteenth century.

[9] De Renzi, *Collectio Salernitana*, vol. i, p. 485, and vol. v, p. 50.

[10] De Renzi, i. 486 and 495; v. 51 and 70.

[11] De Renzi, i. 446; v. 3.

[12] De Renzi, i. 485-6; v. 50-2.

[13] *Scivias*, Migne, col. 403, and *Liber Divinorum Operum*, Migne, col. 868 and elsewhere.

[14] *Scivias*, Migne, col. 404, and throughout the *Liber Divinorum Operum*.

[15] Pitra, pp. 8, 114-16, 156, and 216.

[16] The work of Bernard Sylvestris has been printed by C. S. Barach and J. Wrobel, Innsbruck, 1876. His identity, his sources, and his views are discussed by Charles Jourdain, *Dissertation sur l'état de la philosophie naturelle . . . pendant la première moitié du XIIᵉ siècle*; by A. Clerval, *Les Ecoles de Chartres au Moyen Âge*, Paris, 1895, p. 259, &c.; by R. L. Poole, *Illustrations of the History of Mediaeval Thought*, London, 1884, p. 116, &c.; and by J. E. Sandys, *History of Classical Scholarship*, Cambridge, 1903, vol. i, p. 513, &c.

[17] The works of Hugh of St. Victor are published in Migne, *Patrologia Latina*, clxxv-clxxvii.

[18] The Kalonymos family furnished prominent examples.

[19] Charles Singer, 'Allegorical Representation of the Synagogue, in a Twelfth-Century Illuminated MS. of Hildegard of Bingen', *Jewish Quarterly Review*, new series, vol. v, p. 268, Philadelphia, 1915. For further evidence of Hildegard's acquaintance with the Jews see Pitra, p. 216; and Migne, cols. 967 and 1020-36.

[20] Pitra, p. 51 et seq.

[21] Catello de Vivo, *La Visione di Alberico, ristampata, tradotta e comparata con la Divina Commedia*, Ariano, 1899. For a comparison of Dante's visions and those of Hildegard see Albert Battandier in the *Revue des questions historiques*, vol. xxxiii, p. 422, Paris, 1883.

[22] Reprinted in Migne, vol. 195.

[23] Herrade de Landsberg, *Hortus Deliciarum*, by A. Straub and G. Keller, Strasbourg, 1901, with two supplements.

[24] For sphericity of earth see especially Migne, cols. 868 and 903.

[25] In her later *Liber Divinorum Simplicis Hominis* this method of orientation is varied both in the text and also in the Lucca illustrations.

[26] Migne, col. 906.

[27] Migne, cols. 903-4.

[28] See H. Osborn Taylor, *The Mediaeval Mind*, vol. i, p. 472, London, 1911.

[29] Migne, cols. 904-6.

[30] H. Osborn Taylor, *The Mediaeval Mind*, i. 468, 471; ii. 569. See also A. Battandier, *Revue des questions historiques*, vol. xxxiii, p. 422, Paris, 1883.

[31] The *Meteorologica* had been translated about 1150 by Aristippus, the minister of William the Bad of Sicily. The version of Aristippus passed quickly into circulation (Valentine Rose, 'Die Lücke im Diogenes Laërtus und der alte Übersetzer' in *Hermes*, i. 376, Berlin, 1866), but hardly soon enough for Hildegard's *Scivias*, which was completed about 1150. It is, of course, possible that the references to the *ignis niger* are later interpolations, but this is very unlikely in view of the way in which she speaks of this vision in the *Liber Divinorum Operum*.

[32] Migne, cols. 789-91.

[33] Migne, col. 389.

[34] Plate XII *a*. The elements are represented in their original order undisturbed by the Fall. Uppermost is

the *purus aether* or *aer lucidus* containing the stars and representing the element *air* in Hildegard's cosmic system. Next comes *water*. Below, and to the left, is a dark mass separating into tongues, one of which is formed into a serpent's head. These tongues are flames of *fire*. Below, and to the right, are plants and flowers emblematical of *earth*. The serpent, the enemy, vomits over a cloud of stars (signifying the fallen angels) that are borne downward by the falling Adam. In the four corners of the miniature the symbols of the elements are again displayed.

[35] Plate XIII. Above, in a circle, sits the Heavenly Judge. He is flanked on either side by groups of angels bearing the cross and other symbols. The lower circle exhibits the final destruction of the elemental Universe. The four winds and their collaterals are here subjecting the elements to the crucible heat of their combined blasts. Strewn among the elements can be seen men, plants, and animals. Between the circles is an angel sounding the last trump, and holding the recording roll of good and evil deeds. He faces the throng of the righteous who are rising from their bones, while he turns his back on the weeping crowd of those doomed to torment. Below these latter crouches Satan, now enchained.

[36] Plate XII *b*. In the highest circle is the Trinity flanked to the left by the Virgin and to the right by the Baptist, with Cherubim below. In the middle circle are two groups, the Saints above and the Prophets and Apostles below. In the lowest circle are the elements, now re-arranged in their eternal harmony; uppermost of these is the *purus aether* now separated from the *aer lucidus* and containing the stars; on either side are light-coloured flame-like processes representing the *air*; below the aether is *water,* indicated by a zone of undulating lines; then comes the *earth* symbolized, as usual, by a group of plants. Below and to the side of *earth* are dark-coloured flames of fire, now controlled and confined to this lowest rung.

[37] Migne, col. 791.

[38] See Ernest Wickersheimer, 'Figures médico-astrologiques des neuvième, dixième et onzième siècles', in the *Transactions of the Seventeenth International Congress of Medicine, Section XXIII, History of Medicine'*, p. 313, London, 1913.

[39] Migne, cols. 403-14.

[40] Migne, col. 751.

[41] Migne, col. 791.

[42] The *Quaestio de Aqua et Terra* is doubtless a genuine, albeit the least pleasing, production of the great poet. The genuineness is established by Vincenzo Balgi in his edition, Modena, 1907.

[43] Migne, col. 741.

[44] Migne, col. 743.

[45] It is outside our purpose to attempt a full elucidation of Hildegard's allegory. The eagle in the right wing signifies the power of divine grace, while the human head in the left wing indicates the powers of the natural man. To the bosom of the figure is clasped the Lamb of God.

[46] Migne, col. 751.

[47] Migne, col. 744.

[48] *Liber Divinorum Operum,* part i, visions 2 and 3.

[49] Migne, cols. 752-5.

[50] Migne, col. 807.

[51] The work is printed by C.S. Barach and J. Wrobel, Innsbruck, 1876. The writers, however, confuse Bernard Sylvestris of Tours with his somewhat older contemporary, Bernard of Chartres.

[52] A. Clerval, *Les Écoles de Chartres au Moyen Âge,* Paris, 1895.

[53] J. E. Sandys, *History of Classical Scholarship,* Cambridge, 1903, vol. i, p. 515.

[54] R. Lane Poole, *Illustrations of the History of Mediaeval Thought in the Departments of Theology and Ecclesiastical Politics,* Oxford, 1884, pp. 118, 219.

[55] Barach and Wrobel, *loc. cit.,* pp. 5-6, 9 and 13.

[56] For a general consideration of these figures see K. Sudhoff, *Archiv für Geschichte der Medizin,* i. 157, 219; ii. 84.

[57] E. Wickersheimer, 'Figures médico-astrologiques des neuvième, dixième et onzième siècles', *Transactions of the Seventeenth International Congress of Medicine, Section XXIII, History of Medicine,* p. 313, London, 1913.

[58] The MS. from which Plate XV is taken (*Paris, Bibl. nat., Latin* 7028) is entitled *Scholium de duodecim zodiaci signis et de ventis*. It was once the property of St. Hilaire the Great of Poitiers. The legend above our figure reads, 'Secundum philosophorum deliramenta notantur duodecim signa ita ab ariete incipiamus'. The relation of the signs to the parts of the body is different in this eleventh-century MS. from that which was widely accepted in the astrology of the thirteenth and fourteenth centuries as illustrated in Plate XVI.

[59] The MS. from which Plate XVI is taken (*Paris, Bibl. nat., Latin* 11229) was written about the end of the fourteenth century. It has been described by K. Sudhoff, *Arch. f. Gesch. d. Med.,* ii. 84, Leipzig, 1910. The relation of the central figure to the signs of the zodiac in this plate bears a manifest resemblance to the relation of the central figure to the beasts' heads in Plate VII. The lines which cross and recross the figure in Plate VII are analogous also to the lines of influence of Plate XVI. The verse above the figure in Plate XVI is taken from the *Flos medicinae scholae Salerni*; cp. de Renzi, loc. cit., i. 486. This Melothesia and that of the next figure is identical with that propounded in Manilius, ii. 453 (edition of H. W. Garrod, Oxford, 1911).

[60] Plate XVII is from an early German block book. It exhibits a scheme closely parallel to Plate VII. The universe in Plate XVII is represented as a series of concentric spheres, *earth* innermost, followed by *water, air,* and *fire.* In the outermost zone hover the angels who have replaced the beast's head of Hildegard's scheme. The whole world is embraced by the figure of the Almighty, much as in Plate VII.

[61] See E. Wickersheimer, 'La médecine astrologique dans les almanachs populaires du XXe siècle', *Bulletin de la Société française d'histoire de la médecine,* X (1911), pp. 26-39.

[62] Migne, col. 757. This phrase is reproduced in a mediaeval Irish version of the work of Messahalah. See Maura Power, *An Irish Astronomical Text,* Irish Text Society, London, 1912.

[63] The word *cancer* is here used, but the crab goes sideways, not backwards. By *cancer* Hildegard, who had never seen the sea, probably means the crayfish, an animal fairly common in the Rhine basin. It is the head of a crayfish or lobster that is figured in the miniatures of the vision of the macrocosm in the Lucca MS., and a similar organism frequently serves for the sign Cancer in the mediaeval zodiacal medical figures, as in Plate XV of this essay.

[64] Migne, cols. 3, 791-2.

[65] An illustration of this parallelism between Paracelsus and Hildegard is afforded by certain passages in the *Labyrinthus medicorum errantium* and the *Scivias,* lib. i, vis. 4. Especially compare p. 279 et seq. of Huser's edition of the *Opera,* Strasbourg, 1603, with Migne, col. 428.

[66] A good example is furnished by a work of Isaac Myer, *Qabbalah. The philosophical writings of Solomon ben Yehudah ibn Gebirol or Avicebron and their connection with the Hebrew Qabbalah and Sepher ha-Zohar,* Philadelphia, 1888.

Peter Dronke (essay date 1984)

SOURCE: Peter Dronke, "Hildegard of Bingen," in *Women Writers of the Middle Ages,* Cambridge University Press, 1984, pp. 144-201.

[*In the following excerpt, Dronke draws upon "the twelve principal autobiographic passages that are still preserved in Hildegard's* Vita *in the form in which she set them down," in order to discuss the genesis of Hildegard's visionary capacities, the gradual public acceptance of her prophetic voice, and her political sensibility as an abess.*]

I

Hildegard of Bingen still confronts us, after eight centuries, as an overpowering, electrifying presence—and in many ways an enigmatic one. Compared with what earlier and later women writers have left us, the volume of her work is vast. In its range that work is unique. In the Middle Ages only Avicenna is in some ways comparable: cosmology, ethics, medicine and mystical poetry were among the fields conquered by both the eleventh-century Persian master and the twelfth-century 'Rhenish sibyl'. [1] In more recent centuries, Goethe—who saw and was astonished by the illuminated *Scivias* manuscript in Wiesbaden [2]—shows perhaps most affinity to that combination of poetic, scientific and mystic impulses, that freedom with images and ideas, which characterized Hildegard.

To sketch the ways in which Hildegard understood herself and the world around her, we have in a sense too many materials, and of too diverse kinds, at our disposal. The finest studies of her work in the past have given primacy to her trilogy of allegorical visions. [3] Here instead I shall focus first on the twelve principal autobiographic passages that are still preserved in Hildegard's *Vita* in the form in which she set them down. To complement these, certain moments in which Hildegard's personality emerges vividly in her letters will be chosen, with special stress on letters that are not yet published. At the same time, to convey something of Hildegard's wider outlook, I shall turn to the work known as *Causae et curae.* Even though this (surviving imperfectly in a unique manuscript) is only a fragment of what was conceived as a larger synthesis, a book of 'the subtleties of the natures of diverse creatures', [4] it can reveal certain things about Hildegard's way of looking with more immediacy than can the visionary works. Historians of science (Thorndike, Singer and others) [5] have quarried in *Causae et curae* for curious physical notions; the 'autobiographic' element in the work has never been discussed or even surmised.

Born in the Rhineland in 1098, Hildegard was the last of ten children of a noble family. The first extensive autobiographic note cited in the *Vita* tells something of her childhood, and of the way she found her vocation and won through to recognition:[6]

Wisdom teaches in the light of love, and bids me tell how I was brought into this my gift of vision . . . 'Hear these words, human creature, and tell them not according to yourself but according to me, and, taught by me, speak of yourself like this.—In my first formation, when in my mother's womb God raised me up with the breath of life, he fixed this vision in my soul. For, in the eleven hundredth year after Christ's incarnation, the teaching of the apostles and the burning justice which he had set in Christians and spiritual people began to grow sluggish and irresolute. In that period I was born, and my parents, amid sighs, vowed me to God. And in the third year of my life I saw so great a brightness that my soul trembled; yet because of my infant condition I could express nothing of it. But in my eighth year I was offered to God, given over to a spiritual way of life, and till my fifteenth I saw many things, speaking of a number of them in a simple way, so that those who heard me wondered from where they might have come or from whom they might be.

Then I too grew amazed at myself, that whenever I saw these things deep in my soul I still retained outer sight, and that I heard this said of no other human being. And, as best I could, I concealed the vision I saw in my soul. I was ignorant of much in the outer world, because of the frequent illness that I suffered, from the time of my mother's milk right up to now: it wore my body out and made my powers fail.

Exhausted by all this, I asked a nurse of mine if she saw anything save external objects. 'Nothing', she answered, for she saw none of those others. Then, seized with great fear, I did not dare reveal it to anyone; yet nonetheless, speaking or composing, I used to make many affirmations about future events, and when I was fully perfused by this vision I would say many things that were unfathomable (*aliena*) to whose who listened. But if the force of the vision—in which I made an exhibition of myself more childish than befitted my age—subsided a little, I blushed profusely and often wept, and many times I should gladly have kept silent, had I been allowed. And still, because of the fear I had of other people, I did not tell anyone *how* I saw. But a certain high-born woman, to whom I had been entrusted for education, noted this and disclosed it to a monk whom she knew.

. . . After her death, I kept seeing in this way till my fortieth year. Then in that same vision I was forced by a great pressure (*pressura*) of pains to manifest what I had seen and heard. But I was very much afraid, and blushed to utter what I had so long kept silent. However, at that time my veins and marrow became full of that strength which I had always lacked in my infancy and youth.

I intimated this to a monk who was my *magister* . . . Astonished, he bade me write these things down secretly, till he could see what they were and what their source might be. Then, realizing that they came from God, he indicated this to his abbot, and from that time on he worked at this [writing down] with me, with great eagerness.

In that same [experience of] vision I understood the writings of the prophets, the Gospels, the works of other holy men, and those of certain philosophers, without any human instruction, and I expounded certain things based on these, though I scarcely had literary understanding, inasmuch as a woman who was not learned had been my teacher. But I also brought forth songs with their melody, in praise of God and the saints, without being taught by anyone, and I sang them too, even though I had never learnt either musical notation or any kind of singing.

When these occurrences were brought up and discussed at an audience in Mainz Cathedral, everyone said they stemmed from God, and from that gift of prophecy which the prophets of old had proclaimed. Then my writings were brought to Pope Eugene, when he was in Trier. With joy he had them read out in the presence of many people, and read them for himself, and, with great trust in God's grace, sending me his blessing with a letter, he bade me commit whatever I saw or heard in my vision to writing, more comprehensively than hitherto.'

Because of her abnormal gift, Hildegard saw herself as called—notwithstanding all her inner fears and uncertainties—to the rôle of prophet. That, late in life, she felt impelled to tell of herself and her visionary experience, she sees as a summons made to her by Sapientia—the beautiful womanly divine emanation celebrated in the 'Sapiential' books in the Old Testament.[7] She senses that it is not merely her own personal testimony, but Sapientia speaking through her. The prophet sees herself as timid in her own right, daring insofar as she is Sapientia's mouthpiece. This, more than anything else, underlies the blend of diffidence and assurance in Hildegard's account of her rôle. She was born providentially, at a critical moment of Christian world-history. This could easily sound overweening, yet Hildegard is convinced that Sapientia bids her affirm it. She had been aware of her 'talent', her *visio,* from earliest childhood, and it remained with her for the whole of her life.

Hildegard uses *visio* to designate three related things: her peculiar faculty or capacity of vision; her experience of this faculty; and the content of her experience, all that she sees in her *visio.* Her mode of vision is most unusual: she sees 'in the soul' while still fully exercising, and remaining aware, of, the powers of normal perception.

Richard of St Victor, the mystic from Scotland who was Hildegard's contemporary, in his commentary on the Apocalypse of John distinguished four kinds of vision:[8] two outer and two inner, the first two being physical, the others spiritual. The least of the four, physical sight (1), contains no hidden significance; but a second kind of bodily vision, though physical, also contains a force of hidden meaning (2). It was in this mode, for instance, that Moses beheld the burning bush (Exodus 3: 2-4). Of the two modes of spiritual vision, one is that of the eyes of the heart, when the human spirit, illuminated by the Holy Ghost, is led through the likenesses of visible things, and through images presented as figures and signs, to the knowledge of invisible ones (3). This is what Dionysius had called symbolic vision. The second, which Dionysius had called anagogic vision, occurs when the human spirit, through inner aspiration, is raised to the contemplation of the celestial without the mediation of any visible figures (4).

Hildegard's *visio* is clearly of Richard's third kind rather than his fourth. Throughout her visionary trilogy she sees, with an inner eye, images presented as figures and signs. And these lead her to understanding of a spiritual kind: mostly in that she is enlightened by the divine voice she hears in her *visio,* which explains to her the figural or allegoric meaning of the images she beholds. What is exceptional in Hildegard, and what she herself felt to be unique, is that this mode of vision was for her absolutely concurrent with physical sight. There was not the least suspension of her normal faculties: her insights had nothing to do with dream or daydream or trance or hallucination or *extasis* (a word that she, like a number of twelfth-century writers, uses only in a pejorative sense). What Hildegard wants to stress is that, with all that she saw in her soul, she remained physically lucid throughout.

At the same time her *visio* was, she felt, linked in a mysterious way with her recurrent bodily afflictions. When, after describing both her *visio* and her ravaging illness, Hildegard begins the next sentence 'Exhausted by all this . . . (*His valde fatigata . . .*)', it is not clear whether she means, exhausted by illness or exhausted by her *visio*. The ambiguity may even be deliberate: the gift or blessing of *visio* may also have been so great a strain that it was at the same time the chief source of her sickness. (Conversely, the sickness may have been a necessary condition of the *visio*.) Singer, analysing various passages in which Hildegard describes both her symptoms and her mode of vision, as well as some components of the *Scivias* visions themselves—the falling stars, the concentric luminous circles, the many evocations of dazzling or blinding lights—concluded that Hildegard suffered from frequent

migraine or 'scintillating scotoma'.[9] A diagnosis of this kind can indeed be accepted, even if Singer in his formulation did not sufficiently distinguish between the pathological basis of the visions and the distinctive intellectual qualities of what Hildegard said about them. Hildegard did not simply suffer such disturbances: she made something imaginatively and spiritually fecund out of them.

The next lines in Hildegard's notes display something of the same mixture of fear and pride as Hrotsvitha had shown. She is aware of a gift that sets her apart, a gift that in her case even allows her to foretell future events; at the same time she is afraid of staking any claims, and of making herself seem presumptuous or ridiculous. Where with Hrotsvitha it was perhaps no more than a normal bashfulness, together with partly true, partly affected, modesty, with Hildegard it seems to have been an intense, even morbid, fear of the outer world—a world which, she acutely observes, her constant illnesses had made her less capable of coping with in the ways that ordinary people could.

Like Hrotsvitha again, Hildegard is in a kind of limbo of unease till she and her gift are approved and accepted by the 'greater', masculine world. Till then, the temptation to hide or dissemble or abandon their talent was acute in both. The first step in confidence for each of them is with a loved woman teacher, an abbess of high birth—Gerberga in Hrotsvitha's case, Jutta of Sponheim in Hildegard's. Through the teachers, a few men come to know about the young prodigies; but it is only much later that the inner pressure not to remain concealed gains the ascendant in them. Hildegard's *pressura* to reveal her visions was accompanied by an exultant sense of physical strength, such as she had never known in her long years of ailment. The monk in whom she confided, Volmar—after satisfying himself that here was no case of hubris or of demonic delusion—gladly became, with his abbot's permission, her helper and secretary.[10]

The nature and extent of Volmar's help has been much discussed. In his fundamental study Herwegen argued, with detailed reference to the sources, that while Hildegard welcomed the grammatical and syntactic improvements Volmar could furnish, she allowed no changes in vocabulary or content: however strange her wording and imagery could be, they had to remain intact, because given to her prophetically. I believe Herwegen's conclusions are still broadly valid: only with Hildegard's last major work, the ***Liber divinorum operum,*** and some of the very late writings, is the textual situation more complex.[11] Hildegard claimed her prophetic gift as the direct source not only of what she wrote but also of her intuitive mastery of the Scriptures and of theological and philosophic works: she could penetrate their difficulties readily, even though her schooling had been quite rudimentary, her command of Latin had remained in many ways uncertain, and she had had no specialist training in philosophy or theology. In the same way her gift of musical composition and performance was intuitive, not dependent on the study of written music or of singing.[12]

In her fortieth year, then, Hildegard felt an irresistible *pressura* to keep her gifts hidden no longer. We may conjecture that the fact that the previous year, 1136, the sisters on the Disibodenberg had elected Hildegard as their abbess, to succeed her beloved former teacher Jutta, filled her with greater confidence than she had known before; then for the first time she felt a surge of health. The decade 1137-47 saw her progressive acceptance in the more powerful male world around her—first in the ambience of the archbishop of Mainz, then in that of the pope himself, just as Hrotsvitha's progress was (as I argued) from writing, at first chiefly for her own satisfaction, in an aristocratic community of learned women, to finding acceptance in the more grandly aspiring world of the Ottonian court.

The synod of Trier—November 1147 to February 1148—saw the papal ratification of Hildegard's visionary writing, and implicitly of the prophetic rôle which impelled her to write. Earlier in 1147, on that same journey through northern Europe, Pope Eugene had given his approval to another profoundly original work—the *Cosmographia* of Bernard Silvestris.[13] That both the *Cosmographia* and **Scivias** (the second still 'work in progress', not completed till 1151) were given the blessing of this pope is of special importance in terms of twelfth-century intellectual history. Two writers who showed such daring in their cosmological conceptions and formulations could so easily, had it not been for Pope Eugene, have been persecuted, the works called in question and condemned by council or synod, as happened with Abelard, William of Conches, or Gilbert of Poitiers. St Bernard, who was active in the attempts to condemn these three, had himself in 1147 been approached by Hildegard for encouragement in the completing of **Scivias,** and had approved her task (though in a brief, and one must admit somewhat perfunctory, letter);[14] he was also among those present when Pope Eugene declared himself for Hildegard at Trier. The following year another Frenchman, Odo of Paris, who had likewise been at Trier, wrote to Hildegard praising the originality of her songs, and asking her whether, through her *visio,* she could pronounce on the correctness or otherwise of one of the central theses of Gilbert of Poitiers, which was about to be discussed at Gilbert's hearing at the Council of Reims: were God's 'fatherhood' and 'godhead' identical with God?[15] That is, Odo credited Hildegard with a means of judging different from and superior to normal methods of metaphysical enquiry.

From 1147 onwards Hildegard, her prophetic rôle endorsed, is often appealed to for counsel, and often volunteers it, among the secular and religious leaders of her day. Her correspondents include three popes (Anastasius IV and Hadrian IV as well as Eugene III), monarchs (Conrad III, Frederick Barbarossa, Henry II of England, Eleanor of Aquitaine, and the Byzantine Empress Irene), as well as a host of lesser dignitaries. She undertakes preaching journeys, addressing sermons to monks in their abbeys, to bishops and clergy at their synods, as well as to the laity in towns. She attempts to exorcize. In a word, as prophet Hildegard assumed without serious opposition many high sacerdotal functions which in general the Church had seen, and continued to see, as male prerogatives. Always she distinguishes between herself in her own right, the 'poor little womanly figure (*paupercula feminea forma)*', and what the divine voice, or the living light, expresses through her. When she admonishes, warns, or castigates, it is always in the name of that light and that voice, not in her own.

Thus she is able to write Emperor Frederick both a letter holding up to him a mirror of princely conduct, and later (probably in 1164, when for the second time Frederick set up his own anti-pope) a ferocious warning: he is behaving 'childishly, like one whose mode of life is insane (*velut parvulum et velut insane viventem)*'.[16] She explains the nature of the prophet's task beautifully in a letter to Elisabeth of Schönau, whose own visions were of an ecstatic kind. Here Hildegard expresses herself gently, yet her words carry a hint of reproachful admonition:

> Those who long to perfect the works of God . . . should leave heavenly things to him who is heavenly; for they are exiles, ignorant of the celestial, only singing the hiddenness of God, in the same way as a trumpet only brings forth sounds but does not cause them: another must blow into it, for the sound to emerge. So too I, lying low in pusillanimity of fear, at times resound a little, like a small trumpet-note from the living brightness.[17]

The tension that this inner duality entailed showed itself physically in the ever-recurring migraines and related ailments; then, in the years 1150-1, the tension was exacerbated by two events in which Hildegard was certain she had received prophetic knowledge of God's will, but where keen human resistance was shown. In 1150 it was a question of fighting for the independence of her community—of allowing the sisters to move some 30 kilometres away from the Disibodenberg, to the Rupertsberg on the Rhine. Here, after bitter opposition from the Disibodenberg monks, on grounds of prestige and finance as well as of personal attachment, Hildegard at last had her way. The following year she was faced with the desire for independence of Richardis, the nun whom she loved best. There, despite impassioned appeals to archbishops, to members of Richardis' high-born family, and even to Pope Eugene, Hildegard failed.

II

Her own reflections on the two events, which survive in the *Vita,* deserve to be quoted:[18]

> At one time, because of a dimming of my eyes, I could see no light; I was weighed down in body by such a weight that I could not get up, but lay there assailed by the most intense pains. I suffered in this way because I had not divulged the vision I had been shown, that with my girls (*cum puellis meis*) I should move from the Disibodenberg, where I had been vowed to God, to another place. I was afflicted till I named the place where I am now. At once I regained my sight and had things easier, though I still did not recover fully from my sickness. But my abbot, and the monks and the populace in that province, when they realized what the move implied—that we wanted to go from fertile fields and vineyards and the loveliness of that spot to parched places where there were no amenities—were all amazed. And they intrigued so that this should not come about: they were determined to oppose us. What is more, they said I was deluded by some vain fantasy. When I heard this, my heart was crushed, and my body and veins dried up. Then, lying in bed for many days, I heard a mighty voice forbidding me to utter or to write anything more in that place about my vision.
>
> Then a noble marchioness, who was known to us, approached the archbishop of Mainz and laid all this before him and before other wise counsellors. They said that no place could be hallowed except through good deeds, so that it seemed right that we should go ahead. And thus, by the archbishop's permission, with a vast escort of our kinsfolk and of other men, in reverence of God we came to the Rupertsberg. Then the ancient deceiver put me to the ordeal of great mockery, in that many people said: 'What's all this—so many hidden truths revealed to this foolish, unlearned woman, even though there are many brave and wise men around? Surely this will come to nothing!' For many people wondered whether my revelation stemmed from God, or from the parchedness (*inaquositas*) of aerial spirits, that often seduced human beings.
>
> So I stayed in that place with twenty girls of noble and wealthy parentage, and we found no habitation or inhabitant there, save for one old man and his wife and children. Such great misfortunes and such pressure of toil befell me, it was as if a stormcloud covered the sun—so that, sighing and weeping copiously, I said: 'Oh, oh, God confounds no one who trusts in him!' Then God showed me his grace again, as when the clouds recede and the sun bursts forth, or when a mother offers her weeping child milk, restoring its joy after tears.
>
> Then in true vision I saw that these tribulations had come to me according to the exemplar of Moses, for when he led the children of Israel from Egypt through the Red Sea into the desert, they, murmuring against God, caused great affliction to Moses too, even though God lit them on their way with wondrous signs. So God let me be oppressed in some measure by the common people, by my relatives, and by some of the women who had remained with me, when they lacked essential things (except inasmuch as, through God's grace, they were given to us as alms). For just as the children of Israel plagued Moses, so these people, shaking their heads over me, said: 'What good is it for well-born and wealthy girls to pass from a place where they lacked nothing into such penury?' But we were waiting for the grace of God, who had shown us this spot, to come to our aid.
>
> After the pressure of such grief, he rained that bounty upon us. For many, who had previously despised us and called us a parched useless thing, came from every side to help us, filling us with blessings. And many rich people buried their dead on our land, with due honour . . .
>
> Nonetheless, God did not want me to remain steadily in complete security: this he had shown me since infancy in all my concerns, sending me no carefree joy as regards this life, through which my mind could become overbearing. For when I was writing my book *Scivias,* I deeply cherished a nobly-born young girl, daughter of the marchioness I mentioned, just as Paul cherished Timothy. She had bound herself to me in loving friendship in every way, and showed compassion for my illnesses, till I had finished the book. But then, because of her family's distinction, she hankered after an appointment of more repute: she wanted to be named abbess of some splendid church. She pursued this not for the sake of God but for worldly honour. When she had left me, going to another region far away from us, she soon afterwards lost her life and the renown of her appointment.
>
> Some other noble girls, too, acted in similar fashion, separating themselves from me. Some of them later lived such irresponsible lives that many people said, their actions showed that they sinned against the Holy Spirit, and against the person who spoke from out of the Spirit. But I and those who loved me wondered why such great persecution came upon me, and why God did not bring me comfort, since I did not wish to persevere in sins but longed to perfect good works with his help. Amid all this I completed my book *Scivias,* as God willed.

Nearly thirty years before Hildegard's move to the Rupertsberg, Abelard had confronted problems which were in many aspects similar, and which he sketches in his *Historia calamitatum* in ways that are often close to Hildegard's.[19] Abbot Adam of Saint-Denis was as reluctant to let Abelard free himself from the great royal monastery as Abbot Kuno was to release Hildegard from the Disibodenberg. Abelard, like Hildegard, achieved release only after encountering various intrigues, by appealing to high authority—to the bishop of Meaux and the king of France—as Hildegard appealed to the archbishop of Mainz and the marchioness of Stade. The place in which he won freedom is described, like hers, as full of physical hardship: at the barren site that was to become Abelard's foundation, the Paraclete, the students who followed him, 'leaving spacious dwellings, built themselves small huts; instead of living on delicate foods, they ate wild herbs and coarse bread; instead of soft beds they used thatch and straw'. And later, when the Paraclete was made into a refuge for Heloise and her nuns, Abelard expresses the same sense as Hildegard of a miraculous change for the better, a sudden advent of wealth and plenty where before there was want:

> Heloise and her nuns at first endured a life of privation there—for a time they were desolate—but in a short while the gaze of divine mercy gave them comfort . . . and made people all around merciful and helpful to them. And God knows, their earthly commodities were multiplied more in one year, I think, than I could have achieved in a hundred, had I stayed.[20]

Nonetheless, neither Abelard nor Hildegard won complete inner security. He suffered the disloyalties and slanders (and even violence) of the monks at his new abbey, Saint-Gildas; Hildegard too was beset by what she took to be disloyalty among her community—those who complained of the discomforts of the new settlement, those who left it for a less demanding life; most of all she was overcome by the departure of her much-loved Richardis, a defection to which Hildegard attributes only unworthy motives. And just as Abelard tells laconically of the abbot of Saint-Denis, who had refused his plea for permanent release, 'Departing in such obstinacy, he died a few days later', so too Hildegard mentions Richardis' sudden early death as if it had been a consequence of her stubbornness. It is not crude and ferocious way in which, in the seventh century, St Valerius branded those who opposed his will to live in solitude—saying for instance of Bishop Isidore of Asturias, who tried to get the saint to assume some public responsibility at the Council of Toledo:

> . . . through the true judgement of almighty God, he suddenly fell into the pool which he had opened as a trap for me. It left me unharmed, while endless hell swallowed him.[21]

Still, in Abelard's words as in Hildegard's, the sense that God's judgment showed itself in their favour, after their own wish had been thwarted, seems implicit.

And yet Hildegard's account has an element relating to her particular situation that is different from Abelard's. She is a woman, and she claims to have received prophetic illumination: she is disbelieved and mocked on both counts. So too in one of Hildegard's lyrical sequences for St Ursula: she pictures Ursula shouting out her longing to race through the heavens and join the divine Sun, and causing scandal by her mystical utterances—

> so that men said:
> 'What simple, girlish ignorance!
> She does not know what she is saying.'[22]

This detail—which has no parallel in the hagiographic sources about Ursula—suggests that the sequence, which may indeed have been composed in the very years of the events which caused Hildegard such turmoil, contains a personal projection, that Hildegard sees this saint in a special way as *figura* and aspiration for herself.

Yet she is again like Abelard in that she continually applies parallels from Old Testament characters to her own destiny. She leads her little band to the Rupertsberg in the way Moses led the Israelites to the wilderness, and is grumbled at as Moses was. In the next note 'in scripto suo', the exemplars continue. Now her struggle is for administrative and financial independence for her new foundation. On account of this, she says, she suffered hostility like Joshua, she was envied like Joseph by his brothers; and as God came to Joshua's and Joseph's aid, so did he to hers. The details of the conflict are recorded not in the *Vita* but near the beginning of a didactic letter, explaining the Athanasian Creed to her daughters on the Rupertsberg. She fought the monks, she there tells, not only on the question of property, but on that of keeping with them the monk Volmar, who had long been her provost and secretary, and who strictly should have remained in his own cloister. The Disibodenberg monks, even after they had been made to let Hildegard and her twenty sisters move, were not happy to see the disappearance of the endowments which these women (all from prominent families) had brought with them to the monastery; nor did they wish to lose one of their ablest confrères:[23]

> At God's behest I made my way back to the mountain of blessed Disibodus, from where, with permission, I had seceded. And I made my petition in the presence of all those living in the cloister: that our site, and the domains donated with that site, should no longer be tied to them . . .

> And in accordance with what I perceived in my true vision, I said to the Father Abbot: 'The serene light says: You shall be father to our

provost, and father of the salvation of the souls of the daughters of my mystic garden.[24] But their alms do not belong to you or to your brothers—your cloister should be a refuge for these women. If you are determined to go on with your perverse proposals, raging against us, you will be like the Amalekites, and like Antiochus, of whom it was written that he despoiled the Temple of the Lord.[25] If some of you, unworthy ones, said to yourselves: Let's take some of their freeholds away—then I WHO AM[26] say: You are the worst of robbers. And if you try to take away the shepherd of spiritual medicine [i.e. Provost Volmar], then again I say, you are sons of Belial, and in this do not look to the justice of God. So that same justice will destroy you.'

> And when I, poor little creature (*paupercula forma*), had with these words petitioned the abbot and his confrères for the freehold of the site and domains of my daughters, they all granted it to me, entering the transfer in a codex.

In the same way as the Rupertsberg, Abelard's Paraclete, when it was made over to women through his gift, had to have its independence officially secured: a papal *privilegium* (1131) confirmed in perpetuity for Heloise and her nuns the possession of all property connected with the foundation.

III

On the Disibodenberg, Hildegard launched not so much a petition (though she calls it that) as a fulmination. Even more in her other ordeal at this time, the loss of Richardis, where in the end she did not get her way, we sense that Hildegard could use her prophetic persona savagely and overbearingly. In her first letter about this, where she appeals to the marchioness, mother of Richardis and grandmother of Adelheid (who likewise wanted to leave the Rupertsberg and accept a more prominent appointment as an abbess), there is as yet no attempt to legislate in the name of the God of Moses, only a sense of human anguish—quickly followed, however, by a vehement conviction of being in the right:[27]

> I beseech you and urge you not to trouble my soul so deeply that you bring bitter tears to my eyes and wound my heart with dire wounds, on account of my most loving daughters Richardis and Adelheid. I see them now glowing in the dawn and graced with pearls of virtues. So take care lest by your will, your advice and connivance, their senses and their souls be moved away from the sublimity of that grace. For the position of abbess, that you desire for them, is surely, surely, surely not compatible with God (*certe, certe, certe non est cum deo*), or with the salvation of their souls.

Nonetheless, the two girls accepted nomination as abbesses. With Adelheid, there is no record of further

resistance by Hildegard; but she did not give Richardis leave to take up her new task. When the archbishop of Mainz wrote to Hildegard demanding (with even a hint of threat) that she now yield and release Richardis, she answered, claiming to speak with the voice of God, in unbridled denunciation of the archbishop himself. By insisting on this office for Richardis, he shows he is nothing but a simoniac:

> The lucid fountain who is not deceitful but is just says: the reasons that have been alleged for the appointment of this girl are unavailing in the sight of God, because I, the high and deep and encompassing one, who am a piercing light, did not lay down or choose those reasons: they were perpetrated in the conniving audacity of ignorant hearts . . . The spirit of God, full of zeal, says: pastors, lament and mourn at this time, because you do not know what you do, when you squander offices, whose source is God, for financial gain and to please the foolishness of wicked men, who have no fear of God. Then your malicious curses and threatening words must not be heeded . . .

> Arise, because your days are short, and remember that Nebuchadnezzar fell and that his crown perished. And many others fell who rashly raised themselves up to heaven. Ah, you ember, why do you not grow red with shame at flying up when you should be fading?[28]

For Hildegard, losing Richardis meant losing her close collaborator and losing the disciple whom she admired most and to whom she was most deeply attached. Was it simply arrogant possessiveness that impelled her to speak as prophet here, so as to try and overthrow the archbishop's decision? Her broader invective, against clergy motivated by financial gain, implies that there had been something irregular about Richardis' election. This could perhaps be corroborated by considering that the marchioness' grand-daughter, Adelheid, was at almost the same date (1152) elected abbess of the illustrious foundation Gandersheim, making this move at a time when she was probably still of school-girl age and certainly too young to have taken her monastic vows on the Rupertsberg. This suggests that those who elected Adelheid—and possibly those who elected Richardis, too—may have been influenced less by the suitability of the two girls than by a hope of rich endowments from the von Stade family in return for these elections. (Adelheid's mother had married exaltedly three times, and had been Queen of Denmark.)

With Richardis, however, the matter is more complex: Hildegard in the *Vita* passage intimates that Richardis herself was eager for a position that she felt befitted her high worldly rank. Possibly the primitive conditions on the Rupertsberg, in the first year after the move, irked her, possibly she came to feel oppressed by Hildegard's dominance—many contributing elements can be surmised, though none proved.

Hildegard's conviction, which comes out so strongly in the letter to the marchioness, that any acceptance of such dignities for reasons other than idealistic ones is evil and imperils the soul, sounds wholly genuine, however much her own impassioned obduracy may have played a part in her seeing it that way. She next appealed to Richardis' brother, Archbishop Hartwig, whose diocese, Bremen, included his sister's new abbey:

> Dear friend, I greatly cherish your soul, more than your family. Now hear me, prostrate in tears and misfortune before your feet, for my soul is deeply sad, because a horrible man (*horribilis homo*) has overthrown my advice and will.

Here Hildegard seems to accuse even her beloved Richardis of having deliberately bought her office:

> If one of restless mind seeks preferment, longing to be master, striving lustfully for power rather than looking to the will of God, such a one is a marauding wolf in person . . . That is simony.

Yet a moment later the chief blame is laid on Abbot Kuno of the Disibodenberg:

> Thus it was not necessary for our abbot to predetermine a holy soul, bedazed in sense and ignorant, into these actions and into such irresponsibility of mental blindness. If our daughter had remained at peace, God would have prepared her for the intention of his glory. So I beg you . . . send my beloved daughter back to me! For I shan't ignore an election that stems from God, nor contradict her, wherever it may be . . . I ask it, so that I may be consoled through her, and she through me. What God has commanded I do not oppose. May God give you blessing from the dew of heaven, and may all the choirs of angels bless you, if you hear me, God's handmaiden, and accomplish God's will in this issue.[29]

Hildegard's accusations, taken together, are somewhat confusing. At times they are levelled at Richardis herself, at times against her family, at others against the abbot of the Disibodenberg or the archbishop of Mainz. In a word, Hildegard felt there was a conspiracy against her. And quite possibly this was no mere persecution-fantasy. The von Stade family clearly had a whole network of influential connections in the Church throughout Germany. Yet they would scarcely have taken advantage of these had they not been prompted by Richardis' own desire to leave. Hildegard, unwilling to accept this, in her doting attachment, made an exhibition of herself in a way she never did (though she had feared to) in her early visions.

In her letter to Hartwig, once more, Hildegard does not claim outright to be speaking as God's mouthpiece. And yet she is never less than certain that she knows the will of God; doing God's will and doing her will are seen as identical. There is a frightening hint of megalomania here. It does not seem to have escaped Pope Eugene, to whom Hildegard wrote in a last attempt to quash Richardis' abbacy. The text of her appeal to him does not survive, but Eugene's answer,[30] while full of praise for Hildegard, 'so kindled by the fire of divine love', also contains a hint of warning: it is those who are great who often greatly fall. 'Reflect then, my daughter, because that serpent of old who cast the first man out of paradise longs to destroy the great, such as Job . . .' Then, almost as if it were an afterthought, he turns to her petition, and he evades it: only if there were no adequate scope for practising the Benedictine Rule in Richardis' new abbey, Bassum, should she be returned to Hildegard. (As Bassum was at that moment a more renowned Benedictine foundation than the Rupertsberg, this was a wholly hypothetical alternative.) The archbishop of Mainz was to judge whether Bassum was monastically suitable. This was in effect to confirm his earlier decision against Hildegard.

It is a token of Hildegard's greatness that, faced with this defeat, she not only tried to resign herself to it but to find fruitful meaning in it. Thus she wrote, 'to the maiden Richardis':

> 1 Daughter, hear me, your mother in the spirit, saying to you: My grief rises up. Grief kills the great trust and solace that I found in a human being. From now on I shall say: 'It is good to set one's hope in the Lord, better than to set it in the world's mighty ones.' That is, man ought to look to the one on high, the living one, quite unshaded by any love or feeble trust such as the dark sublunary air offers for a brief time. One who beholds God thus raises the eyes like an eagle to the sun. And because of this one should not look to a high personage, who fails as flowers fall.
>
> 2 I fell short of this, because of love for a noble person. Now I tell you, whenever I have sinned in this way, God has made that sin clear to me in some experiences of anguish or of pain—and this has now happened on account of you, as you yourself know.
>
> 3 Now, again, I say: Woe is me, your mother, woe is me, daughter—why have you abandoned me like an orphan? I loved the nobility of your conduct, your wisdom and chastity, your soul and the whole of your life, so much that many said: What are you doing?
>
> 4 Now let all who have a sorrow like my sorrow mourn with me—all who have ever, in the love of God, had such high love in heart and mind for a

human being as I for you—for one snatched away from them in a single moment, as you were from me.

5 But may the angel of God precede you, and the son of God protect you, and his mother guard you. Be mindful of your poor mother Hildegard, that your happiness may not fail.

The language Hildegard uses in this letter is both intimate and heavy with biblical echoes. These can heighten, but also modify, what she is saying; they make the letter suprapersonal as well as personal. Both aspects are vital to what is essentially a harsh confrontation between transcendent love and the love of the heart.

The opening words, 'Daughter, hear me (*Audi me, filia*)', echo a verse in Psalm 44 that, by its continuation—which will have been present to Richardis' mind as to Hildegard's—suggests an implicit claim greater than Hildegard spells out:

Daughter, hear me and see, and incline your
　　ear,
and forget your people and your father's
　　house—
then the King will desire your glorious beauty
　　. . .

That is, Hildegard by her choice of opening suggests it is only by heeding her and turning her back on the world of her own family that Richardis will become a bride of the heavenly King. So too she does not address Richardis as an equal, an abbess like herself: she is still 'the maiden', the spiritual daughter, who must listen to her mother. Yet what the mother now brings forth is not a command but a *planctus*. She expresses her sense of betrayal citing the words of Psalm 117:9 ('Bonum est sperare in Domino quam sperare in principibus'), which contrast the steadfastness of God's love with the fickleness of human hopes. All human attachments, Hildegard concludes, are by their nature mutable, and should be surmounted in singleminded contemplation of the changeless one. Isaiah (40: 7-8) contrasts the human lot—to wither like a flower—with the word of God, which remains forever. Yet the echo from the Epistle of James (1:11) is perhaps even more pertinent here, James who says of a rich person, 'the flower falls, the beauty of its aspect has perished'.

From meditation on the two kinds of attachment (1), Hildegard passes to introspection (2). All that drew her to Richardis was of necessity transitory, and her clinging to that transitoriness was the source of her suffering: it carried its own nemesis within. And yet this second 'movement', of changed awareness (*anagnorisis*), is also parallel with the third, which is outbreak of renewed lament. The closeness of the two

impulses is reflected in the parallelism of wording ('Nunc tibi dico . . . Nunc iterum dico'). In the complaint that follows (3), bibical echoes again evoke the love of God in contrast to human love. But the connotations pull in two directions: the words 'why have you abandoned me (*quare me dereliquisti*)' are the Psalmist's anguished reproach of God (Psalm 21:2), yet here they are capped by the words 'like an orphan (*sicut orphanam*)', recalling the moment in John (13:18) when Christ promises his disciples that, after leaving them to go back to the Father, 'I shall not abandon you like orphans—I shall come to you.'

Amid her grieving Hildegard claims the human loftiness of the love she felt—and a moment later acknowledges that, long before herself, others had perceived this was a hopeless attachment. This leads into a final threnody (4), summoning fellow-mourners, in the words of Jeremiah's lamentation (1: 12):

Oh all of you who pass by the wayside,
　　take heed and see if there is a sorrow like my
　　　　sorrow . . .

In Jeremiah the words are spoken by a feminine projection, Jerusalem. The context there has many reverberations that enrich the letter: the *domina* of peoples has become like a widow . . . there is none to solace her among all her dear ones . . . she has sinned and therefore has become unstable . . . moaning and turning away . . . she has been cast down violently, having no comforter'. And yet there is perhaps an even greater audacity in Hildegard's echo of Jeremiah, for in the medieval Good Friday liturgy the words were seen as spoken not by Jerusalem but figurally by Christ in the Passion.

At the close (5), lament resolves itself in calm and loving valediction. Here Hildegard brings together the thought of Christ's mother and of herself, the 'wretched mother' of Richardis. Now, parted from her unhappy former spiritual mother, Richardis shall have a greater, heavenly mother to watch over her. Yet (again the term that springs to mind is from the Aristoelian dynamic of tragedy) a *peripeteia* has been accomplished: Hildegard has moved from the confident opening summons, 'hear me, your mother in the spirit (*matrem tuam in spiritu*)', to a dejected close— 'be mindful of your poor mother (*esto memor misere matris tue*)'. At the same time the last words—'that your happiness may not fail (*ut non deficiat felicitas tua*)'—suggest that, even if no human attachment can or should endure, this should not exempt anyone from lovingly remembering one's fellow-being 'in the love of God'.

After Richardis' sudden death her brother Hartwig wrote again to Hildegard, telling her that at the end, weeping, with all her heart she longed to return:

So I ask you with all my power, if I am worthy to ask, that you love her as much as she loved you. And if she seems to have failed in any way—since this was due to me, not to her—that at least you consider the tears she shed for having left your convent, tears that many people witnessed. And if death had not prevented her, she would have come to you—the permission had only just been given.[31]

Hildegard answers this letter with a superb flight of magnanimity, sublimation and forgiveness:

Full divine love (*plena caritas*) was in my soul towards her, for in the mightiest vision the living light taught me to love her (*ipsam amare*). Listen: God kept her so jealously that worldly delight could not embrace her: she fought against it, even though she rose like a flower in the beauty and glory and symphony of this world . . .

So my soul has great confidence in her, though the world loved her beautiful looks and her prudence, while she lived in the body. But God loved her more. Thus God did not wish to give his beloved to a rival lover, that is, to the world . . .

So I also expel from my heart that pain you caused me regarding this my daughter.[32]

Hildegard here uses of Richardis a kind of hyperbole more familiar in the love-poetry of the following century. Thus in the *Vita Nuova,* after Beatrice's death, Dante claims 'it was only her great benignity' that took her from the world: 'a sweet desire came to [God] to summon so great a perfection: he made her come to him, from here below, because he saw that this wretched life was unworthy of so noble a creature'.[33] So too, even before her death, an angel in the divine intellect cries out to have Beatrice in 'heaven, which has no defect save for not having her: heaven begs her of its Lord'.[34] Dante also, like Hildegard, echoed Jeremiah's lamenting words to express grief in the dimension of human love: 'Oh you who pass along the road of Love, attend and see if there is any sorrow heavy as mine.'[35] There is a touching incongruity in Hildegard's allusion to Richardis' prudence—she who in life had accused Richardis so vehemently of mental blindness (*obcecatio mentis*), in her longing for independence. Yet if this letter suggests that, at however great an inner cost, Hildegard had arrived at a comprehending acceptance of the young woman who had wanted to carve out her own life rather than remain a disciple, there is the troubling consideration that the succinct and unsympathetic note preserved in the *Vita* represents Hildegard's later reflections. She made these notes probably after the *Liber divinorum operum* (completed 1173/4), which is their last point of reference. Even if some notes had been complied intermittently in earlier years, it is unlikely that any were set down as early as Richardis'

death (29 October 1152). It seems as though, later in her life, it was what had rankled then with Hildegard that came once more to plague her thoughts.

IV

In the next autobiographic note in the *Vita,* Hildegard, describing her recurring illnesses, speaks of 'aerial torments' that pervaded her body, drying up the veins with their blood, the flesh with its humoral juice (*livor*), the marrow with the bones. An 'aerial fire' was burning in her womb. She lay motionless on a coarse cloth (*cilicium*) on the ground, and all gathered round her, convinced she was about to die. Hildegard believed it was 'aerial spirits' who were causing these afflictions. At the same time she heard a good angel, one of Michael's host, inviting her to die and so regain heaven. He summons her in language akin to that of the invitations in the Song of Songs; yet whilst there the beloved bride is called dove (*columba*), Hildegard (who dares to gaze at the divine Sun, like the eagle in the bestiary tradition) is called—or sees herself as—*aquila:* 'Ah, ah my eagle, why do you sleep in knowledge? Rise from your doubt, you are known! Oh gem full of splendour, every eagle shall behold you. The world shall mourn, but heavenly life shall rejoice. And so, in the dawn, fly up to the sun! Rise, rise, come eat and drink!' Again the closest parallel in imaginative situation is the one already cited from the *Vita Nuova*—the angel calling to Beatrice to join the heavenly throng. And just as God answers in Dante's canzone, so here the angelic host answers the first angel, declaring that heaven has not yet sanctioned this hope.

Malignant aerial spirits, Hildegard saw in this *visio,* also attacked some of her noble daughters in the convent, and meshed them in a net of vanities. When she tried to recall them to a holier life, some, who looked at her with fierce eyes (*torvis luminibus me aspicientes*),[36] also slandered her in secret, saying that the form of monastic life she wanted to impose was intolerable. Other sisters took Hildegard's part, she relates, as Daniel took Susanna's, and in the midst of these conflicts God revealed her second visionary work, the *Liber vitae meritorum,* and allowed her to complete it (1158-63).

At the close of this *Liber,* Hildegard not only sets forth once more, with eloquent images, her awareness of her prophetic task, but she adds a curse on any future person who might add to or cut away any word she has written—a curse that, in Christian Latin, Gregory of Tours had been the first to call down upon later generations.[37] As with Gregory, the integrity and inviolability of her written text is of supreme importance to Hildegard—but with her this is grounded specifically in her sense that throughout writing she has been God's instrument: of herself she writes:

She lives and does not live, she perceives the things formed of dust and does not perceive them, and utters God's miracles not of herself but being touched by them, even as a string touched by a lutanist emits a sound not of itself but by his touch . . . Therefore, if anyone of his own accord perversely add anything to these writings that goes beyond their clear intent, he deserves to be exposed to the punishments here described; or if anyone perversely remove any passage from them, he deserves to be banned from the joys that are here shown.[38]

Then, in the elaborate, mysterious vision that next follows in the *Vita,* this awareness of her own work as an entity with its unique claims extends (I would argue) to an intimation of the qualities of her life and work as a whole.—

In vision I saw three towers, by means of which Wisdom opened certain hidden things up for me. The first tower had three rooms. In the first room were nobly-born girls together with some others, who in burning love listened to God's words coming from my mouth—they had a kind of ceaseless hunger for that. In the second were some steadfast and wise women, who embraced God's truth in their hearts and words, saying 'Oh, how long will this remain with us?' They never wearied of that. In the third room were brave armed men from the common people, who, advancing ardently towards us, were led to marvel at the miracles of the first two rooms, and loved them with great longing. They came forward frequently, in the way that common people seek the protection of a prince, to guard them against their enemies, in a firm and mighty tower.

In the second tower there were also three rooms. Two of them had become arid in dryness, and that dryness took the form of a dense fog. And those who were in these rooms said with one voice: 'What are these things, and from where, which that woman utters as if they were from God? It's hard for us to live differently from our forefathers or the people of our time. So let's turn to those who know us, since we cannot persevere in anything else.' Thus they turned back to the common people—they were of no use in this tower, or in the first . . . But in the third room of this tower were common people who, with many kinds of love, cherished the words of God that I brought forth from my true vision, and supported me in my tribulations, even as the publicans clung to Christ.

The third tower had three ramparts. The first was wooden, the second decked with flashing stones, the third was a hedge. But a further building was hidden from me in my vision, so that I learnt nothing about it at the time. Yet in the true light I heard that the future writing which will be set down concerning it will be mightier and more excellent than the preceding ones.

The structuring of a vision by telling of diverse buildings and parts of buildings, of people who welcome a divine message in diverse ways and others who reject it, was something Hildegard had learnt from the second-century prophetic treatise *Pastor Hermas.*[39] But where Hermas explains most details in allegoric terms, and Hildegard often follows him in this technique, here she makes no attempt at interpreting her vision: all is left enigmatic. And yet her meticulous differentiation of details is unlikely to be arbitrary invention. The whole mode of presentation suggests that an allegorical meaning was intended, but is missing (at least among the autobiographic notes that have survived), though it is also possible that Hildegard at the time of receiving this *visio* was not yet fully conscious of its precise further significance. No interpretation, to my knowledge, has ever been proposed. The one I would suggest—though very tentatively—takes its cue from the close of the vision. The building which is still hidden from Hildegard, but which—she hears—will stimulate writing mightier and more excellent than the others, would seem to be a glimmering intuition of her last major work, *Liber divinorum operum.* This is indeed grander in design than her other visionary writings and could be called her masterpiece. If this hypothesis is correct, it indicates some possible interpretations for the earlier part of the vision of the towers. The first tower, with its three rooms, could then stand symbolically for *Scivias,* with its three books. Her words reach her fellow-nuns, younger and older, in the first two rooms, but also go out to the populace, to those among them who acknowledge Hildegard as prophet and are ready to see her as their *princeps.* Does the linking of the common people with the third room perhaps imply that it was especially the third book of *Scivias,* in particular the lyrical and dialogued parts near the close, which ordinary people could come to love (even without knowing Latin), in the form of songs in the *Symphonia* and of dramatic action in the *Ordo Virtutum?*—that it was principally these which brought the unlearned to admire Hildegard and all she stood for?

The next tower would presumably refer in some way to the *Liber vitae meritorum.* That two of its three rooms are arid and filled with fog could then perhaps reflect that in this work, with its wide-ranging images of vices and virtues, the chief emphasis—till near the close—is on evil and sin, and the penalties for these, rather than on the joyous rewards. Yet here there is no exact correspondence of rooms with books: the *Liber vitae meritorum,* at least in the form in which it survives in all the earliest manuscripts, is divided into six books, not three, hence the specific interpretation must remain open. The same holds of the third tower, with its three ramparts. Yet this tower could well be an image for Hildegard's scientific treatise, the *Subtilitates naturarum diversarum creaturarum.* This comprehended both the so-called *Causae et curae* and

Physica—texts that originally belonged to a work which, according to Hildegard's explicit testimony, formed a single, larger whole.[40] In particular, three parts of the **Physica**—the books on trees, on precious stones, and on plants—might correspond to the triple rampart—wooden, gemmed, and hedged—of this tower.

The conviction that her greatest work was still to come increases in the next 'showing' preserved in Hildegard's *Vita*. This is remarkable in being the only time she describes a vision accompanied by loss of normal consciousness. Her note about the three towers, and the fourth, still unfinished, edifice, continues:

> At last in the time that followed I saw a mystic and wondrous vision, such that all my womb was convulsed and my body's sensory powers were extinguished, because my knowledge was transmuted into another mode, as if I no longer knew myself. And from God's inspiration as it were drops of gentle rain splashed into the knowledge of my soul.

She compares this moment to the one in which St John received the inspiration 'In the beginning was the Word . . .' Reflecting on the nature of that Word, 'sucking its revelation' as John had done ('revelationem suxit'), leads her to see the complementarity of human and divine:

> Man, with every creature, is a handiwork of God. But man is also the worker (*operarius*) of divinity, and the shading (*obumbratio*) of the mysteries of divine being.

The vision showed Hildegard how to explain the Prologue of John: 'And I saw that this explanation had to be the beginning of another piece of writing, which had not yet been manifested, in which many investigations of the creations of the divine mystery would have to be pursued.' This is now an unequivocal forward reference to the **Liber divinorum operum,** where the first book has as its climax an interpretation of the Prologue of John.[41]

V

The visionary insight into how to interpret John's Prologue, which came to Hildegard about 1167, was followed by another half-year of mortal sickness, first brought on—she writes—by the blowing of the south wind (*de flatu australis venti*), that 'Föhn' which even in present-day Germany is still seen as a source of malaises of every kind, physical and psychological. It is during this sickness that she hears of Sigewize, a young noblewoman living on the lower Rhine, who is being assailed by a demon. Hildegard was reflecting on and longing to know (*cogitante et scire volente*) the exact way in which a demon can affect human beings. In her vision she sees that it cannot 'enter' a person (*non intrat*); yet she believes it can envelop and shadow

humans 'with a smoke of darkness (*fumo nigredinis*)'. That is, it can besiege or 'obsess' a person (*obsidere*), though there is no question of demonic 'possession (*possessio*)'.[42] God tolerates the demons' causing various disasters in the world: they can vomit up a plague (*pestilentiam evomunt*), they can cause floods and wars and hostilities and evils among mankind. Their effects, in short, can be material and immaterial: their dark smoke, it would seem, has baleful results very similar to those widely attributed to the 'Föhn'.

Hildegard is asked to help Sigewize, because the demon (speaking, the context suggests, with the young woman's voice), had cried out that only a certain *vetula* on the upper Rhine could do so. The ironic reference is elaborated by Theodoric, author of the third book of the *Vita,* which also includes Hildegard's own notes on the episode: according to Theodoric, the *vetula* is named, derisively, not Hildegardis but Scrumpilgardis ('Wrinklegard'). It seems prudent, however, to discount any details given by Theodoric that are not corroborated in Hildegard's own words, for he, concerned to attribute miraculous powers to her, such as she herself never claimed, embellishes his account with many details that patently derive from a less-than-scrupulous hagiographic tradition. What emerges from Hildegard's account is that, after her initial refusal, on grounds of being too unwell, she tried to cure the young woman by devising an elaborate mimetic scenario for her—an *ordo* in many ways comparable to her play, **Ordo Virtutum**—to drive the demon away. A good part of the text of this eloquent and ingenious attempt at shock-therapy survives.[43] Nonetheless, Hildegard makes clear that it had only a passing effect on the patient, not a durable one. So the abbot of Brauweiler, where the scenario had been performed, pleaded with Hildegard to receive Sigewize and try to help her in person.[44] Though she and the Rupertsberg nuns were terrified at the prospect ('multum exterrite fuimus'), they accepted her, and weeks of communal prayer and ascetic practices resulted, first in a physical spasm, then in Sigewize's gradual convalescence ('de die in diem', P.L. 197, 183 A). It is noteworthy that, though Theodoric's part of the *Vita* is packed with fantasizing miracle-tales, Hildegard herself pretends to nothing beyond having assisted the woman's cure by means of prayer, and by letting the demon 'express himself' through her: we might say, she helped Sigewize's recovery by allowing her to voice openly all her religious fixations and woes, and even her 'demonic' rage, when Hildegard argued against some of her utterances.

The last two autobiographic notes preserved in the *Vita* take us to the period 1170-4. Another grievous illness followed the liberation (*liberatio*) of Sigewize. In it, Hildegard sees 'evil spirits mocking my sickness, cackling at it, saying "Hah, she will die, and her friends will weep, those with whom she confounds us!" Yet I did not see the departure of my soul towards being. I suffered this sickness more than forty days and nights.'

In her vision it was shown to her that she was obliged to undertake another voyage as preacher. 'As long as I neglected these journeys that God commanded me to make, for fear of people, the pains in my body increased. They did not cease till I obeyed—as happened to Jonah, who was fiercely afflicted till he bent himself to obedience.'

For her assent, she was rewarded in her *visio* with the consolation of 'the fairest and most loving man' (*pulcherrimus et amantissimus vir*—the identification with Christ is not made explicit),

> . . . such that the look of him perfused all my womb with a balmlike perfume. Then I exulted with great and immeasurable joy, and longed to go on gazing forever. And he commanded those who afflicted me to depart from me, saying: 'Away, I do not want you to torment her any more!' They, departing with great howls, cried out: 'Woe that we ever came here, as we leave confounded!' At once, at the man's words, the sickness that had troubled me, like waters stirred to a flood by tempestuous winds, left me, and I recovered strength.

Hildegard was now well enough, too, to fulfil a request of her former monastery, that she write the life of Disibodus, its patron saint. The same renewed health, she concludes, enabled her to write—that is, complete—the **Liber divinorum operum** (1173/4). For personal testimonies about the last years of her life we must resort to letters.

This last pair of showings has been invested with new kinds of literary stylization. It would seem that Hildegard, refusing here as always to demarcate material and immaterial phenomena, interprets all her illnesses in retrospect as attacks from demons—just as, in early Christian tradition, the nocturnal afflictions and temptations that beset the mind had been both bad dreams and phantoms of the night (*somnia / et noctium phantasmata*). [45] Instinctively, when she gives her demons words, Hildegard resorts to a lower or comic register of speech, including the vernacular exclamations of disgust and disappointment, 'Wach!' and 'Ach!' (So too in Hrotsvitha's writings, evil, about to be confounded, always showed itself as comic and grotesque.) At the same time, Hildegard does not let this lowering of tone affect the central experience: implicitly, with 'forty days and nights', she compares her sickness with Christ's time in the wilderness; explicitly, her dolorous resistance and hard-won obedience to a divine command are likened to Jonah's; and the evocation of the solace of 'the most loving man' relies on the language of the Song of Songs.

VI

Tengswindis, *magistra* of a foundation of canonesses on the Rhine, wrote Hildegard a letter that was both an (overtly polite) enquiry and a challenge. [46] The fame of Hildegard's holy life and wondrous visionary gift, she says, had reached her; yet rumours of a more disquieting kind had also come. Was it true that on festive days Hildegard's nuns wore rings, veils, and tiaras studded with symbolic images? 'We believe you wear all these for love of the heavenly Bridegroom, even though it is right for women (*mulieres*) to adorn themselves modestly.'

Besides, Tengswindis is amazed that Hildegard admits into her fellowship only women who are of high birth. 'Still, we know you are doing this on some reasonable ground (*rationabili causa*), not unaware that in the earliest Church (*in primitiva ecclesia*) the Lord chose fishermen, the lowly and the poor.' She reminds Hildegard of the words of St Peter ('God is no respecter of persons') and of St Paul ('not many who are mighty, not many who are nobly born . . .').

The blandness with which Tengswindis supposes unimpeachable motives behind Hildegard's two innovations becomes, I believe, more palpably ironic near the close, in a request for further illumination:

> Such novelty in your practice incomparably excels the minutes measure of our littleness, and arouses no small wonderment (*admiratio*) in us. Thus we, so exiguous (*tantillule*), rejoicing inwardly at your advances, have resolved to send our letter to your holiness, [47] beseeching humbly and most devoutly—so that our religious observance may be enhanced by the authority of such a one—that your dignity do not disdain to write back to us in the near future.

In her reply, [48] Hildegard begins by distinguishing between the rôles of married woman and virgin. The first should not flaunt herself: since the Fall, woman has been exposed to danger, precisely because she is so beautiful a divine creation:

> The form of woman flashed and radiated in the primordial root . . . both by being an artifact of the finger of God and by her own sublime beauty. Oh how wondrous a being you are, you who laid your foundations in the sun and who have conquered the earth!

Over against this hymn to womanhood Hildegard sets St Paul's notion of woman's submission to her husband in modesty and fidelity. Woman has known winter—she cannot rise proudly in the flower of perpetual spring; she must not demand the exaltation of a tiara or gold, 'except at the wish of her husband, so that, in harmonious measure, she may give him delight'.

The *virgo,* by contrast, can still, even after the Fall, lay claim to that never-fading spring: 'She remains in the simplicity and beautiful integrity of paradise.' It is right for her, 'by licence and by revelation in the mystic breath of God's finger', to have bridal splendour.

Hildegard's answer to the second point, the 'élitism' of her convent, deserves close attention. It is God who holds the 'scrutiny (*scrutinium*)' of diverse classes,[49] 'so that the lesser order does not mount above the higher, as did Satan and the first man'. What farmer would put oxen, asses, sheep and goats in a single enclosure?—they would all scatter. So there must be differentiation among people, 'lest those of diverse estates, herded into the same flock, scatter themselves in the pride of self-assertion and the ignominy of being different . . . tearing one another with hate, when the higher rank sets upon the lower and the lower mounts above the higher.' God ranked his angels in nine hierarchies—and he loves them all.

Hildegard is convinced that this view is based on a correct assessment of human limitations, that it is 're-alistic', and that such realism on earth has its sanction in heaven: 'For it is good that man should not catch hold of a mountain, which he cannot move, but rather should stay in a valley, learning gradually what he can master. These things are said by the living brightness, not by man.'

The eleventh and twelfth centuries, as Georges Duby has shown in an admirable recent book, saw the philo-sophic and political elaboration of a myth of classes, of *les trois ordres,* in Christian Europe.[50] Yet Tengswindis in her letter was clearly, in terms of the original Christian message, right. By her allusions to the Christ of the Gospels, and to Peter and Paul, she succinctly showed that the myth of classes was not compatible with *primitiva ecclesia.* Hildegard's analo-gies, in effect, rest on a fallacy: for there are different *species* of animals (and, to the theologian, of angels), but not of human beings.

That Hildegard claims her fallacy, and all else she says in her reply to Tengswindis, as the word of God (the letter opens with the words, 'The living fountain says . . .'), is not perhaps a particular act of hubris, but the obverse of her frequent admission that in her own right, without the sense of divinity speaking to her and through her, she would not dare pronounce on any-thing. Here she has deluded herself into thinking that the political myth of the ruling class of her day is a divine truth: deluded in the sense that she imagines this myth to be consistent with the teachings of Christ, about which in principle she has no doubts whatever, but which she had not consulted on this point. She is here in full accord with the dominant social beliefs of her class and time (just as, from the twelfth century to the fourteenth, we know of only the fewest people

who believed, or argued, that crusading was an activ-ity irreconcilable with Christ's teachings). Is it anach-ronistic to say that Hildegard could and should have done better? I think not: both because of the amount that *is* freshly and daringly thought out in the course of her writings, and even more, because of the very existence of Tengswindis' letter.

We know almost nothing else about Tengswindis.[51] What is perhaps most surprising is that her letter ema-nated not from a regular convent but from a founda-tion for canonesses—as these were almost invariably, by their statutes, aristocratic communities, founded and maintained by the greatest families of the empire. It was rare indeed for nunneries to be so exclusive. Yet Tengswindis' assured and witty, well-documented plea for human equality in a Christian society comes out of precisely such an enclave of privilege.

The highly-wrought diadems worn by the women on the Rupertsberg also aroused the curiosity of the ar-dent Walloon monk, Guibert of Gembloux (1124/5-1213/14), who began as Hildegard's far-off admirer and became her last intimate friend. As a complete stranger he wrote her two letters full of excited rever-ence and full of questions. Does she dictate her visions in Latin or in German? Does she forget them after they are written down? Does her understanding of Scripture come through literary instruction or sheer inspiration? Does she see her visions during sleep, in the form of dreams, or awake, in ecstasy (*excessus mentis*)? (He seems not to reckon with any other possibility.) What is the exact meaning of the title of her book, *Scivias*? Has she written other books as well? And what about those tiaras? Are they due to a divine revelation, rather than to a taste for finery?[52]

After two such letters, Hildegard wrote a long answer, one that so overwhelmed Guibert that he moved heaven and earth—or better, bent every conventual regulation—to be able to emigrate to the Rupertsberg and spend the rest of his days in Hildegard's company. This he enjoyed for just over two years—from June 1177, till her death (17 September 1179). As Hildegard's and Guibert's mother-tongues were very different, all their conversations must have been in Latin.

The letter of Hildegard's that prompted Guibert to seek his life with her contains some of her most explicit and most beautiful self-revelations. It was to a stranger, though one whose devotedness she sensed in his let-ters, that she revealed for the first—and only—time that her vision comprised two modes, one of which was far rarer, more intense and more blissful than the other. She defines her experience in comparison with that of St Paul and St John: they 'mounted in soul and drained the cup of wisdom from God: holding them-selves to be nothing, they have become heaven's pil-lars'. The contrast with herself seems all too apparent:

Then how could it be that I, poor little creature, should not know myself? God works where he wills—to the glory of his name, not that of earthbound man. But I am always filled with a trembling fear, as I do not know for certain of any single capacity in me. Yet I stretch out my hands to God, so that, like a feather which lacks all weight and strength and flies through the wind, I may be borne up by him. And I cannot [see] perfectly the things that I see in my bodily condition and in my invisible soul—for in these two man is defective.

Since my infancy, however, when I was not yet strong in my bones and nerves and veins, I have always seen this vision in my soul, even till now, when I am more than seventy years old. And as God wills, in this vision my spirit mounts upwards, into the height of the firmament and into changing air, and dilates itself among different nations, even though they are in far-off regions and places remote from me. And because I see these things in such a manner, for this reason I also behold them in changing forms of clouds and other created things. But I hear them not with my physical ears, nor with my heart's thoughts, nor do I perceive them by bringing any of my five senses to bear—but only in my soul, my physical eyes open, so that I never suffer their failing in loss of consciousness (*extasis*); no, I see these things wakefully, day and night. And I am constantly oppressed by illnesses, and so enmeshed in intense pains that they threaten to bring on my death; but so far God has stayed me.

The brightness that I see is not spatial, yet it is far, far more lucent than a cloud that envelops the sun. I cannot contemplate height or length or breadth in it;[53] and I call it 'the shadow of the living brightness'. And as sun, moon and stars appear [mirrored] in water, so Scriptures, discourses, virtues, and some works of men take form for me and are reflected radiant in this brightness.

Whatever I have seen or learnt in this vision, I retain the memory of it for a long time, in such a way that, because I have at some time seen and heard it, I can remember it; and I see, hear and know simultaneously, and learn what I know as if in a moment. But what I do not see I do not know, for I am not learned. And the things I write are those I see and hear through the vision, nor do I set down words other than those that I hear; I utter them in unpolished Latin, just as I hear them through the vision, for in it I am not taught to write as philosophers write. And the words I see and hear through the vision are not like words that come from human lips, but like a sparkling flame and a cloud moved in pure air. Moreover, I cannot know the form of this brightness in any way, just as I cannot gaze completely at the sphere of the sun.

And in that same brightness I sometimes, not often, see another light, which I call 'the living light'; when and how I see it, I cannot express; and for the time I do see it, all sadness and all anguish is taken from me, so that then I have the air of an innocent young girl and not of a little old woman.

Yet because of the constant illness that I suffer, I at times weary of expressing the words and the visions that are shown me; nonetheless, when my soul, tasting, sees those things, I am transformed to act so differently that, as I said, I consign all pain and affliction to oblivion. And what I see and hear in the vision then, my soul drains as from a fountain— yet the fountain stays full and never drainable.

But my soul at no time lacks the brightness called 'shadow of the living brightness'. I see it as if I were gazing at a starless firmament within a lucent cloud. And there I see the things I often declare, and those which I give as answers to the people who ask me, from out of the blaze of the living light.[54]

It was in my vision, also, that I saw that my first book of visions should be called *Scivias* ['Know-ways'], because it was made known by way of the living brightness, not drawn from other teaching. As for [your question about] tiaras: I saw that all the ranks of the Church have bright emblems in accord with the heavenly brightness, yet virginity has no bright emblem—nothing but a black veil and an image of the cross. So I saw that this would be the emblem of virginity: that a virgin's head would be covered with a white veil, because of the radiant-white robe that human beings had in paradise, and lost. On her head would be a circlet (*rota*) with three colours conjoined into one—an image of the Trinity—and four roundels attached: the one on the forehead showing the lamb of God, that on the right a cherub, that on the left an angel, and on the back a human being—all these inclining towards the [figure of the] Trinity. This emblem, granted to me, will proclaim blessings to God,[55] because he had clothed the first man in radiant brightness.

As in the letter to Tengswindis, Hildegard alludes to the notion (common in early Patristic thought)[56] that virginity is a continuing image on earth of the paradisal state. But her development of this here shows that she invests the notion with high 'courtly' significance. If her community of virgins can be an image of paradise, if even on earth they are queens of the divine Bride-groom, then they must manifest joy as a permanent quality of their being. Troubadours had spoken of joy in just this way, as a necessary condition of the true chivalric lover. In Hildegard's counterpart fantasy in the divine sphere, the black veil, suggestive of the servant-girl (*ancilla*), is replaced by the joyous white one, and by the tiara that betokens a *domina*. The imagery on the tiara itself reveals that her maidenly élite displays a convergence of the human, the angelic, and the divine. It is from the standpoint of this spiritualized courtly joy, also, that the cultivation on the Rupertsberg of lyric drama, vocal and (as we shall see) instrumental music becomes fully comprehensible. In one of her last and profoundest letters Hildegard explains music as man's attempt to recapture the lost paradise.[57]

The radiant, half-celestial woman, whom Hildegard longs to see incarnate in the women around her, appears also in some of the allegorical contexts that she creates. Thus for instance in a letter to Werner of Kirchheim, the head of a community whom Hildegard addressed in 1170, in the course of her last preaching journey, she makes an original fusion of feminine images from *Pastor Hermas* and Boethius' *Consolatio Philosophiae*:[58]

> Lying long in my bed of sickness, in the 1170th year of the Lord's incarnation, I saw—awake in body and spirit—a most beautiful image of womanly form, most peerless in gentleness, most dear in her delights. Her beauty was so great that the human mind could not fathom it, and her height reached from earth as far as heaven. Her face shone with the greates radiance, and her eye gazed heavenward. She was dressed in the purest white silk, and enfolded by a cloak studded with precious gems— emerald, sapphire and pearls; her sandals were of onyx. Yet her face was covered in dust, her dress was torn on the right side, her cloak had lost its elegant beauty and her sandlas were muddied. And she cried out . . . 'The foxes have their lairs, and the birds of the sky their nests, but I have no helper or consoler, no staff on which to lean or be supported by.'

The allegory Hildegard unfolds shows that, as in *Pastor Hermas,* this woman, who is both radiant with youth and (as the last words cited imply) weak with age, is Ecclesia. At the same time, like Philosophia at the opening of Boethius' *Consolatio,* her height reaches to heaven, and her dress is torn. Though so beautiful, Ecclesia has been maltreated and humiliated—not by false philosophers, as in Boethius, but here, as we soon learn, by unworthy priests.

Yet there is another such image in Hildegard's letters where womanly perfection and beauty, both in face and dress, remain untarnished. It is Hildegard's vision of heavenly Love (*Caritas*). Love, for Hildegard, is a girl (*puella*) with dazzling brightness streaming from her face; her cloak is whiter than snow and brighter than stars—and this cloak has no need of gems; her shoes are gold—not dark as onyx, like Ecclesia's. She holds the sun and moon, and embraces them; she has a sapphire image of a human being on her breast. 'And all creation called this girl *domina*'.[59]

In the letter, the allegory unfolded from this vision is about creation and redemption; the details become as

tradition-bound as those with Ecclesia had been. It is when we see these images in relation not only to their allegories but to that image of the bride of God which Hildegard wanted to embody in her disciples, that certain aspects of her thought cohere in an unexpected way. In paradise, the first woman was created— Hildegard tells us in *Causae et curae*—as the embodiment of the love that Adam felt. Eve, that is, was initially, in her paradisal state, the glorious *puella* whom Hildegard describes in her vision. And insofar as the virgin brides on the Rupertsberg could still re-enact that paradisal state, they could manifest something of the splendour of this *puella*. That, probably, is also why Hildegard (in the wake of Gregory of Nyssa, Scotus Eriugena and others[60]) decided that the paradisal love was so sublime that it was free of any carnal element. She who wrote so openly about women's sexuality in the context of medicine nonetheless retained an asexual concept of love in her ideal realm. Implicitly this tended to Manichaean fantasy—for it would follow that it was the sensual aspect of love which rendered it unparadisal and tainted. I shall return to this problem below (VII).

Hildegard was the first of the women mystics who personified Love as a consummately beautiful womanly apparition. It is probably not through her direct influence that 'Lady Love' (*Minne, Amour*) becomes a protagonist in the writings of Mechthild, Hadewijch, and Marguerite Porete in the following century: there we must reckon with the convergence of diverse impulses—especially from vernacular personifications of human love, from the 'Sapiential' books of the Old Testament, and from Boethius. What Hildegard shows, however, is the extraordinary imaginative potential that was latent in a certain allegorical tradition. Even if her descriptions of Caritas and Ecclesia turn into elaborately constructed explications, they begin in something that she sees; and in telling what she sees, Hildegard informs these images with a vivacity that gives them momentarily the compelling power of myths. She does not disclose the identity of her figures at first: she captivates by infusing a sense of mystery in the descriptions. The allegoresis that nearly always (except in her lyrics) follows, roots the images again in a more conventional exegetic past. Thus in the allegorizing letters (as also in the one to Tengswindis) divergent and indeed contradictory impulses, towards unpredictable and towards predictable insights, can be traced in Hildegard's outlook.

Notes

[1] This is not to suggest that Hildegard knew any of the early Latin translations of Avicenna's writings: while some might have begun to circulate before the completion of her *Liber divinorum operum* (1173/4), we have absolutely no evidence that she had seen them.

[2] *Goethes Werke* (Weimar 1887-1918) XXXIV.I, 'Kunst und Alterthum am Rhein und Main', p. 102: 'Ein altes Manuscript, die Visionen der heiligen Hildegard enthaltend, ist merkwürding.' It seems less likely that Goethe was referring to the 'Riesenkodex' (Wiesbaden 2), though this also contains the whole of Hildegard's visionary writings; it has no illuminations, however, and could be called 'merkwürding' only by virtue of its size and the chain attached to it.

[3] See especially H. Liebeschütz, *Das allegorische Weltbild*; B. Widmer, *Heilsordnung*.

[4] This is Hildegard's title for it in her Prologue to *LVM* (Pitra p. 7).

[5] L. Thorndike, *A History* II 124-54; C. Singer, *From Magic* pp. 199-239.

[6] In this chapter, unless a footnote gives another reference, all texts are edited afresh below, pp. 231-64. The order of editing generally corresponds to that in the discussion. Surrounding passages of Latin, not translated here, are often also given.

The unusual aspects of Hildegard's style present a translator with many problems. The translations in this chapter are intended, among other things, to show how I construe the more problematic passages, and how I gauge the tone of the writing.

[7] See esp. Prov. 8: 22ff; Wisd. 7-8; Ecclus. 1. I have given further documentation in *JWCI* XLIII (1980) 20ff and n 19.

[8] *In Apoc.* I I (P. L. 196, 686ff).

[9] Pp. 230-4. Other visual abnormalities connected with migraine have recently been related to Hildegard's visions by F. Clifford Rose and M. Gawel, *Migraine: The Facts* (Oxford 1981) pp. 2-6: in particular, they mention the interruption of the visual field 'by shiny lines, arranged like constellations, a phenomenon known as fortification spectra, because of its resemblance to a castellated fort'; with this they compare Hildegard's 'ramparts of the heavenly city' (p. 6).

[10] *Das Leben* p. 151 n 10.

[11] Herwegen, 'Collaborateurs', *passim*. The Gent MS of *LDO*, however, contains both what was completed at the time of Volmar's death (1173), and copied either by his own hand or at his supervision, and at the same time a number of additions and corrections—substantial as well as stylistic—which are in another hand, and for which (as Hildegard's Epilogue (Herwegen pp. 308-9) tells) Abbot Ludwing of Trier and Hildegard's nephew Wescelinus were in some sense responsible. This was finely analysed by A. Derolez,

Essays . . . Lieftinck II 23-33. In a subsequent essay, however, Derolez goes further:

> Hildegarde écrivait-elle elle-même et la tâche des collaborateurs se limitait-elle, comme on l'a cru, à 'employer la lime' et à corriger les fautes d'orthographe et de grammaire dues à sa connaissance défectueuse du latin? Les conclusions de notre étude précédente nous obligent à répondre négativement, et ceci à l'encontre des affirmations de l'auteur elle-même. ('Deux notes' p. 291).

This inference seems to go beyond the codicological evidence: it is possible to attribute stylistic changes to Ludwing and Wescelinus and still allow that all *substantial* changes and additions were inserted at Hildegard's dictation, or copied from notes she had made on wax tablets. Again, this does not rule out that the substantial changes and additions may also in their turn have been revised *stylistically* by the two clerics.

[12] I have discussed this further in 'Problemata', sect. III ('Sources').

[13] Ed. P. Dronke (Leiden 1978) p. 2.

[14] Ed. *Echtheit* p. 107.

[15] P.L. 197, 351f.

[16] For the texts of the Barbarossa letters, and excellent historical discussion, see *Echtheit* pp. 124-31.

[17] P.L. 197, 217f.

[18] The rubrics of a number of these autobiographic passages in the Berlin MS read 'Visio secunda', 'Visio tercia', etc. Those in the *Riesenkodex*—in the form 'De secunda visione', 'De tercia visione . . .'—are mistranslated by Führkötter (*Das Leben* pp. 76ff): 'De secunda visione' does not mean 'Aus der zweiten Schau' but rather 'Über die zweite Schau'. That is, Hildegard is not giving extracts from visions, but giving an account of them.

[19] *HC* 982ff (I am not, of course, suggesting that Hildegard knew Abelard's autobiographic letter).

[20] *Ibid.* 1321ff.

[21] P.L. 87, 415.

[22] Text and melody in my *Poetic Individuality* pp. 209-19; discussion *ibid.* pp. 160-5.

[23] P.L. 197, 1065ff.

[24] The expression—'Pater . . . salutis animarum mysticae plantationis filiarum mearum'—shows Hildegard's

characteristic fondness for constructions with several genitives dependent on one another.

[25] Cf. 1 Macc. 1.

[26] Cf. Exod. 3: 14.

[27] This letter, and Hildegard's letter to Richardis (translated and analysed below), are admirably edited and set in historical context in *Echtheit* pp. 131-41. Scriptural references are given there *ad loc.* Cf. also *Briefwechsel* pp. 94ff.

[28] P.L. 197, 156f ('conviventi audacia', 156 D, should probably read 'conniventi').

[29] Cf. F. Haug, 'Epistolae S. Hildegardis' pp. 60f.

[30] Ed. *Echtheit* pp. 117f.

[31] P.L. 197, 162. The wording, 'venisset', probably implies a visit rather than a permanent renunciation of her position, as Führkötter's translation—'zurückgekehrt' (*Briefwechsel* p. 99)—might suggest.

[32] *Ibid.* 163.

[33] *V.N.* XXXI.

[34] *Ibid.* XIX.

[35] *Ibid.* VII.

[36] Hildegard normally uses *oculi,* not *lumina,* for 'eyes'. The classical ring of her phrase here may be Boethian, or perhaps Ovidian: Philosophia addresses Boethius (*Cons.* 1 pr. 1) 'commota paulisper ac torvis inflammata luminibus'. In the *Metamorphoses,* Minerva is the 'torvi dea bellica luminis' (II 752), and Medusa has 'torva . . . lumina' (V 241); Hercules 'lumine torvo / spectat' (IX 27f); and Arachne looks with fierce eyes at the disguised goddess Pallas: 'aspicit hanc torvis' (VI 34). While it is certain that Hildegard knew the *Consolatio,* and it has not hitherto been suggested that she knew Ovid's *Metamorphoses,* the Ovidian expressions, which include 'spectat' and 'aspicit', are suggestive; a comparison of cosmological language in *Metam.* 1 and in Hildegard's *LDO* might be rewarding and might yield further results.

[37] *Hist. Franc.* X 31.

[38] R 201vb; Berlin Theol. Fol. 727 (=J) 116vab (cf. Pitra p. 244):

> . . . vivit et non vivit, cinerosa sentit et non sentit, ac [*et* J] miracula dei non per se, sed per illa tacta profert, quemadmodum chorda, per cytharedam tacta, sonum non per se, sed per tactum illius reddit.

Et hec vera sunt, et qui verus est ea sic manifestari veraciter voluit. Quapropter si quis super eminentem mentem scripturarum, et proprietatis sue, aliquid eis in contrarietate addiderit, penis hic descriptis subiacere dignus est; aut si quis aliquid ab eis per contrarietatem abstulerit, dignus est ut a gaudiis hic ostensis deleatur.

[39] On Hildegard and Hermas, see esp. Liebeschütz pp. 51-6; P. Dronke, 'Arbor Caritatis' pp. 221-31.

[40] Cf. *Echtheit* pp. 19f.

[41] On the revisions of this passage, traceable in the Gent codex, see Derolez, *Essays . . . Lieftinck* II 23-33.

[42] Cf. 'Problemata' p. 118 and n 64. The annotator of Hildegard's writings in Migne (P.L. 197, 123 n 50) takes pains to stress that Hildegard's view here is unorthodox, 'not congruent with the opinion of theologians'. Her attempt at a materialist interpretation of the demonic effect was too 'modern', we might say, for nineteenth-century theology.

[43] I have published it for the first time in 'Problemata' pp. 127-9 (with discussion *ibid.* pp. 118-22).

[44] The letter is preserved with Hildegard's correspondence, P.L. 197, 280-2.

[45] 'Te lucis ante terminum' st. 2 (ed. A. S. Walpole, *Early Latin Hymns* (Cambridge 1922) p. 299). On the question of the literal or allegorical perception of these phantoms in the Middle Ages, see the acute observations of J. Huizinga, *Über die Verknüpfung des Poetischen mit dem Theologischen bei Alanus de Insulis* (Koninklijke Akad., Amsterdam 1932) pp. 82-91 (with special reference to Hildegard, *ibid.* pp. 87ff).

[46] P.L. 197, 336-7.

[47] Compare Erwin Panofsky's perceptive comments on the modes in which Bernard of Clairvaux and Suger of Saint-Denis addressed each other (including *vestra Magnitudo* and *Sanctitas vestra*), and on the kinds of personal tension and disagreement that underlay the use of such extravagant formulae (Abbot Suger, *On the Abbey Church of St. Denis and its Art Treasures,* ed. and tr. E. Panofsky (Princeton ²1979) pp. 10f).

[48] P.L. 197, 337-8.

[49] The text is corrupt at this point in Migne (338 A): 'Deus etiam habet scrutinium, scrutationes in omni persona . . .' Corr. 'scrutinium scrutationis'?

[50] *Les trois ordres.*

[51] According to *Briefwechsel* p. 204, she is attested in a document of 1152. The date of her letter cannot be ascertained, but it may well be of the same period— late in Hildegard's life—as Guibert's first two letters (1175): when Hildegard describes to Guibert the way she received detailed instructions about costumes in a vision (see below, pp. 169, 253), it does not sound as though she means a vision experienced in the remote past. Thus the unusual modes of dress may have been introduced relatively late on the Rupertsberg—in the 1170s rather than the 1150s—at a time when the foundation, so poor at the start, had acquired enough wealth to afford queen-like diadems for a whole community. There is a particular aptness in these diadems: just as Hildegard herself had spiritual vision at the same time as natural vision, so her diadems are symbolic and at the same time real.

[52] Guibert's two letters are printed in Pitra, pp. 328-31, 378-9. Hildegard's reply is printed, in a more complete version than Pitra's (pp. 331-4), below, pp. 250-6.

[53] For earlier uses of this Pauline expression (cf. Eph. 3: 18) in medieval thought, see E. Jeauneau, *RTAM* 45 (1978) 118-28.

[54] That is, Hildegard sees the answers in the *umbra,* but knows that their source is in the more rarely glimpsed blaze of light beyond the *umbra.*

[55] 'Hoc datum signum deum benedicet': this use of acc. with *benedicere* has good biblical precedent—in the Vulgate, 'benedicere deum' is found particularly in the Book of Tobias.

[56] See especially J. Bugge, *Virginitas.*

[57] See Section X below.

[58] P.L. 197, 269; cf. *Pastor Hermas* Vis. II 4; III 10-13; Boethius, *Cons.* 1 pr. 1. Hildegard knew Boethius' text so well that she could recreate moments from it freely; the importance of the contents of the *Consolatio* for her cosmological thought would also repay detailed study.

[59] P.L. 197, 192 D—193 A. I have given a corrected text (based on R, fol. 343r*b*), with translation, in *Medieval Latin* I 67f.

[60] Cf. E. Jeauneau, 'La division des sexes chez Grégoire de Nysse et chez Jean Scot Erigène', in *Eriugena: Studien zu seinen Quellen,* ed. W. Beierwaltes (Heidelberg 1980) pp. 33-54.

Barbara Newman (essay date 1987)

SOURCE: Barbara Newman, "A Poor Little Female," in *Sister of Wisdom: St. Hildegard's Theology of the Feminine,* University of California Press, 1987, pp. 1-41.

[*In the following excerpt, which has been revised and updated by the author, Newman articulates Hildegard's worldview as depicted in the three books of her trilogy, describes her unique and obscure writing style and the nature of her extensive correspondence, and comments on her influence on the intellectual development of her protégée, Elisabeth of Schönau.*]

Hildegard's visionary oeuvre—rich, opaque, and unwieldy—is a phenomenon unique in twelfth-century letters; yet at the same time her books provide a compendium of contemporary thought. In the *Scivias* her emphasis is doctrinal; in the **Book of Life's Merits,** ethical; in the **Book of Divine Works,** scientific. But despite their differences in content, the three volumes of the trilogy bear one unmistakable impress. Hildegard's is a world in which neither the distinctions of the schoolmen, nor the negations of the apophatic doctors, nor the raptures of the nuptial mystics have any place; yet no less than theirs, it is a world instinct with order, mystery, and flaming love. Her universe rings with the most intricate and inviolate harmonies, yet seethes with the strife of relentlessly warring forces. Things above answer to things below: the eyes of cherubim mirror the faces of saints, and the children of Eve shine like stars in heaven. Soul, body, and cosmos interact in patterns as dynamic as they are eccentric. And the living Light irradiates all—yet even at the heart of the cosmic dance, the power of darkness has its place, if only to lie prostrate beneath the feet of Love. The fragile soul, graced with the fateful knowledge of good and evil, torn by celestial yearnings yet prey to infernal promptings, makes its precarious way through the world under the guidance of Church and Empire, free at every moment to rebel or to obey.

In the **Scivias,** or **Know the Ways [of God],** Hildegard's most famous work, the play of "visionary forms dramatic" shapes a comprehensive guide to Christian doctrine. Despite its outlandish imagery, in substance the book is not far removed from Hugh of St. Victor's summa, *On the Sacraments of the Christian Faith,* written only a decade or two earlier (c. 1134). Like Hugh, though less systematically, Hildegard ranged over the themes of divine majesty, the Trinity, creation, the fall of Lucifer and of Adam, the stages of salvation history, the Church and its sacraments, the Last Judgment and the world to come. She lingered long over the subjects of priesthood, the Eucharist, and marriage—all doctrines openly rejected by the Cathars; and she returned time and again to two of her favorite themes, the centrality of the Incarnation and the necessity of spiritual combat. In the third and longest portion, she described a vast architectonic structure that represents the "edifice of salvation"—the City of God, or the Church in the fullness of its divine and human reality.

Within the walls of this allegorical city dwell a host of women, the *Virtutes,* whose dress, attributes, speeches, and gestures express meaning down to the least detail. Although these Virtues may appear to be conventional figures in the tradition of Prudentius's *Psychomachia,*[1] they actually have a far deeper significance. For every virtue, Hildegard wrote, is in truth "a luminous sphere from God gleaming in the work of man"[2]—not a personified moral quality, but a numinous force that appears in human form only because it empowers human action. The seer's German translators correctly render *Virtutes* as *Kräfte,* not *Tugenden,* for the Virtues' moral significance is secondary to their divine, ontological power. Like Christ and the Church, the Virtues have a dual nature; they indicate, first, divine grace and, second, human cooperation. Through them Hildegard conveyed her profound conception of synergy—salvation as the joint effort of God and humanity. (As we shall see, their feminine form is no mere accident of grammar.) The *Scivias* ends with an apocalyptic section, a cycle of hymns in honor of the blessed, and a morality play—by far the oldest example of this genre—in which the Virtues help a penitent soul to resist diabolic wiles and find salvation.[3]

For students of medieval art, the *Scivias* is of particular interest because of the striking illuminated manuscript prepared at Hildegard's own scriptorium, perhaps on the basis of her sketches, around 1165 (Wiesbaden, Hessische Landesbibliothek, Hs. 1).[4] This manuscript was ill-advisedly taken to Dresden for safekeeping during World War II and has been missing since 1945. Fortunately, however, the nuns of Eibingen had prepared a handwritten and hand-painted facsimile during the late 1920s, and it is from this copy (Eibingen, Abtei St. Hildegard, Cod. 1) that the illustrations are best known today. The Rupertsberg *Scivias* paintings are unique, stylistically remote from the work of contemporary manuscript painters. Some in fact are reminiscent of early woodcuts. They have all the freshness of naïf art, and, like Hildegard's prose, they atone for a certain lack of finesse by their startling energy and originality. Although standard iconographic motifs can be recognized in them, they occur in unusual combinations, and many of the images are so eccentric that it is reasonable to posit a close working relationship between the visionary and the unknown artist—possibly one of Hildegard's nuns.

The *Book of Life's Merits,* the second volume of her trilogy, is organized around a single visionary figure. Hildegard here envisioned God in the form of a winged man (*vir*), whose head and shoulders rise into the pure ether. From his shoulders to his thighs, he is wrapped in a shining cloud; from thighs to knees, enveloped in the air of this world; from knees to calves, immersed

in the earth; and his feet rest in the waters of the abyss. From the breath of his mouth issue three clouds—one flaming, one stormy, and one luminous—representing three orders of blessed spirits. This colossal figure surveys and sustains the cosmos, which unfolds around him, filling it with a boundless vitality. He is called *vir,* the seer explained, because from him proceed all strength (*vis*) and all things that live (*vivunt*). The eternity of God, which he embodies, "is a fire . . . not a hidden fire, or a silent fire, but an active fire" that animates the world.[5] This divine immanence will be the major theme of the *Book of Divine Works.* But in the present book, Hildegard was content to let the grandeur of God highlight the sins of men and women, which form her principal subject.

The book is carefully structured. In each of the first five parts, a brief vision of the Cosmic Man introduces a dialogue in which a group of Vices advertise their wickedness, only to be confounded by the corresponding Virtues. Unlike the Virtues, the Vices do not present their traditional feminine forms; rather, they are grotesques whose elements—part male, part female, and part bestial—reveal their moral deformity. Hardness of Heart, for example, is a dense cloud of smoke with no human features but a pair of great, black eyes, fixed on the darkness; Witchcraft has the head of a wolf, the body of a dog, and the tail of a lion; Self-Pity is a leper who wears nothing but leaves and beats his breast as he speaks.[6] After each set of dialogues, Hildegard gave an exegesis of her vision, interspersed with Biblical glosses and theological commentary; explained the appearance of each Vice allegorically; and concluded by presenting the pains that Vice would merit in purgatory, together with penances the sinner might do here and now to avoid them. In the sixth and last part of the book, she added brief descriptions of heaven and hell to complement this long *Purgatorio.*

The *Book of Divine Works,* or *On the Activity of God,* at once the most systematic and the most digressive of Hildegard's books, presents a teeming moralized cosmos in which anything may symbolize anything else. After an overpowering vision of divine Love as the author and vital force of creation, Hildegard recounted nine cosmological visions, which convey a mathematically precise yet intensely dynamic model of the world, superimposed on the human form divine and on the City of God envisioned in the *Scivias.* Once again, a versatile technique of allegoresis supplies links between the most disparate phenomena. Some of her interpretations are fairly conventional, as when she compared the sixteen principal stars to the doctors of the Church. Their number represents the ten commandments plus the six ages of the world, or the four corners of the earth times the four holy fears, or the eight beatitudes multiplied by the two forms of charity.[7] Other readings are more abstruse. In one section Hildegard worked out an elaborate set of correlations between months of the year, parts of the body, ages of life, and passions of the soul. Some of these, quaint though they seem, display a lively feeling for the depths of experience hidden in everyday life. The month of November, for example, is correlated with the knees, the age of senility or second childhood, and the pangs of remorse.

> An old man, for fear of the chill, folds his limbs to warm himself by the fire, because he is naturally cold. Even so this month, which is cold every day and lacks the jollity of summer, is like the knees that a man bends in sorrow, remembering his beginnings—when with folded knees he sat like a captive in his mother's womb.[8]

What sustains this phantasmagoria of symbols? Although its wealth of detail can seem turgid, its ordering principles are few and cohesive. First, Hildegard, in typical twelfth-century fashion, saw the world as a divine milieu in which every being is both a sign of the Creator's plenitude and a potential instrument for his action. Her outlook was profoundly theocentric. Second, within this divine milieu, the human being holds the place of honor as the image of God. And in the third place, because the most important activity in life is the salvation of the soul, the cosmos is to be read as one vast and complicated moral lesson. So at the heart of her book Hildegard set two long Biblical commentaries, one on the prologue of St. John's Gospel and one on the first chapter of Genesis. The Gospel text rightly precedes, for only the Word-made-flesh can interpret the creative Word uttered by God in the beginning. That same Word now addresses the believing soul from every nook and cranny of creation, as in the celebrated verse of Alan of Lille:

> Omnis mundi creatura
> Quasi liber et pictura
> Nobis est et speculum.[9]

For Hildegard, therefore, the moral interpretation of the east wind, the eyebrows, or the creation of fish was no decorative fancy, but mattered as much as the phenomena themselves; for all creatures were fabricated for man (*homo*), the body for the soul, and the soul for the glory of God.

Even the angels exult in the good works of the saints, because man is the consummate work of God, fashioned from the four elements to receive the splendor that was Lucifer's before he fell. While the angels were created as spiritual beings alone—pure instruments of praise—the human being is destined for both praise and work, possessing an earthen body as well as a fiery spirit. What is more, he is the very garment of the incarnate Word, the creature in whom God vested himself to display his royal majesty.[10] Yet this exalted view of human dignity is balanced—or undercut—by a dualism that goes so far as to claim that the sinful body

can defile the pure soul even against its will. In a passage dealing with infants, Hildegard maintained that the newborn soul is pure as Adam in Paradise until the age of weaning, when the child's body and bones grow stronger. Then the teething baby wails in pain over the loss of its primal joy, because the soul, "oppressed against its nature, has been overcome by the body living in sin."[11] Thus, Hildegard oscillated between a joyful affirmation of the world and the body, and a melancholy horror of the flesh—and its master, the devil. This anthropological tension is deeply rooted and ubiquitous in her works. Often, as we shall see, it takes the form of a dichotomy between a bold and affirmative use of sexual symbolism and a largely negative view of sexual practice.

In the last visions of the *Book of Divine Works,* Hildegard turned from cosmology to history, ranging with equal assurance over past, present, and future. A panegyric on the Apostles leads to a critique of the contemporary Church, which in turn ushers in a passage of apocalyptic prophecy. Her views on the Antichrist are beside my purpose, but it is worth noting that, although her trilogy as a whole found few readers in her own age or any other, her prophecies held the interest of many generations.[12] John of Salisbury, in the seer's lifetime, asked Girardus Pucelle to scour her books for revelations about the papal schism and the unhappy fate of Rome.[13] In 1220, forty years after Hildegard's death, the Cistercian prior Gebeno of Eberbach compiled an anthology of her prophetic and apocalyptic writings. This influential text, entitled *Pentachronon* or *Mirror of Future Times,* survives in well over a hundred manuscripts—as compared with eleven for the *Scivias* and four for the *Book of Divine Works.*[14]

The reason for this lack of readership is not obscure. Gebeno himself, one of Hildegard's admirers, had to admit in his preface that "most people dislike and shrink from reading St. Hildegard's books, because she speaks obscurely and in an unusual style—not understanding that this is a proof of true prophecy."[15] The saint's Renaissance eulogist, Trithemius of Sponheim, echoed Gebeno's opinion and ascribed the obscurity of Hildegard's style to her inspiration; "no mortal can understand" her works, he maintained, "unless his soul has in truth been inwardly reformed to God's likeness."[16] But even a devout reader must face difficulties other than those inherent in the matter. For Hildegard, despite her encyclopedic knowledge, never mastered Latin grammar well enough to write without a secretary to correct her cases and tenses.[17] Even with such assistance, her style suffers from redundancies, awkward constructions, and baffling neologisms; and her ideas often stretched her limited vocabulary to the breaking point.

Yet although the seer was self-conscious about her "unpolished" style, she seems to have cherished it as a mark that her inspiration must be divine because she herself scarcely knew how to write. When Guibert of Gembloux, with his humanistic love of eloquence, succeeded Volmar and Gottfried as her secretary, he and the abbess had a heated argument over the question of style. Hildegard first commended the nuns who took her dictation, as well as her "only beloved son of pious memory, Volmar," for contenting themselves with her *ipsissima verba* in all simplicity. Guibert, however, proposed the classic Augustinian argument that even wisdom needs the seasoning of eloquence: "inept" and "inharmonious" writing repels readers, but a becoming style moves and inspires them. Whether St. Hildegard was genuinely persuaded or merely desperate, she finally conceded:

> When you correct [the *Life of St. Martin*] and the other works, in the emending of which your love kindly supports my deficiency, you should keep to this rule: that adding, subtracting, and changing nothing, you apply your skill only to make corrections where the order or the rules of correct Latin are violated. Or if you prefer—and this is something I have conceded in this letter beyond my normal practice—you need not hesitate to clothe the whole sequence of the vision in a more becoming garment of speech, preserving the true sense in every part. For even as foods nourishing in themselves do not appeal to the appetite unless they are seasoned somehow, so writings, although full of salutary advice, displease ears accustomed to an urbane style if they are not recommended by some color of eloquence.[18]

This letter was written by Guibert in Hildegard's persona, and we may suspect that the eager monk exaggerated his own victory. Nevertheless, the *Life of St. Martin* as "corrected" by his eloquence can scarcely be recognized as Hildegard's. Purists can at least rejoice that their collaboration began only after the seer's major works were completed.

Yet despite its obscurity, Hildegard's style has a fascination of its own. As Peter Dronke has observed, "it is a highly individual language, at times awkward and at times unclear; the adjectives can be repetitious and limited in range, the interjections excessive. It is the language not of a polished twelfth-century humanist but of someone whose unique powers of poetic vision confronted her more than once with the limits of poetic expression."[19] Although Dronke was writing of the seer's verse, his comments apply just as well to her prose works. For despite her defective Latin, Hildegard could be a remarkably "poetic" stylist. It is not only that her writings are governed by symbolic rather than logical thought—a distinguishing feature of monastic vis-à-vis scholastic theology.[20] Even in the context of twelfth-century symbolics, Hildegard had no peer in her kaleidoscopic array of metaphors, her figures within figures, her synesthetic language. In the midst of a

routine bit of exegesis, she would suddenly convey some new insight with an arresting turn of phrase, or use a familiar typological image in a wholly new sense. Expressive flashes of alliteration punctuate otherwise plodding texts. At times a passage will rise to a pitch of lyric intensity, almost to incantation, then as quickly return to bare expository prose.

One of the most distinctive features of her style is the contrast between her visions themselves—described in meticulous detail—and the far longer glosses furnished by a "voice from heaven." Christel Meier has noted that Hildegard's visions are sometimes incoherent on the literal plane because their component parts are related, not to each other but directly to the thing signified.[21] Hence the images do not immediately evoke the desired interpretation, as in conventional iconography; they require glossing by the celestial voice and the visionary forms themselves. All that is elusive and tantalizing in the visions takes on a fixed, unalterable sense in the interpretations, as the evocative freedom of ambiguity hardens into the sharp precision of allegory.[22] Hildegard is one of the rare medieval authors who can be cited both as a textbook example of allegoresis and as a precursor of the Symbolist poets. And she is certainly the only twelfth-century writer to have composed hymns and sequences in free verse. Dronke has cited the liturgical cycle of Notker as a source of her inspiration,[23] but although Hildegard may have taken his cyclic form as a model, her own compositions bear little resemblance to the classic sequence. Her unrhymed, unmetrical songs, wholly unpredictable as to line division, length, and stanzaic pattern, follow the rhythms of thought alone. Their content belongs to the twelfth century, but their form anticipates the twentieth.

From a literary standpoint, the only authors who left an unmistakable mark on Hildegard's style are the Biblical prophets.[24] Like them she appealed to direct experience ("And I saw . . . and I heard"); like them she expressed her awe and terror before the Presence; like them she used metaphor and parable, attempting when all else failed to express the inexpressible with qualifiers (*velut, quasi, forma, imago, similitudo*). Like Ezekiel she gave the precise date of her calling.

> Now it came to pass in the thirtieth year, in the fourth month, on the fifth day of the month, when I was in the midst of the captives by the river Chobar, the heavens were opened, and I saw the visions of God.
>
> (Ezek. 1:1)

> It came to pass in the one thousand one hundred forty-first year of the Incarnation of God's Son Jesus Christ, when I was forty-two years and seven months old, that the heavens were opened.[25]

Like Jeremiah she did not trust herself to speak, but opened her mouth only by the command and power of God.

> Then I said, "Ah, Lord God! Behold, I do not know how to speak, for I am only a youth." But the Lord said to me, "Do not say, 'I am only a youth'; for to all to whom I send you you shall go, and whatever I command you you shall speak."
>
> (Jer. 1:6-7)

> But because you are timid in speaking and simple in expounding and unlearned in writing these things, tell and write them not in accord with human speech, or the understanding of human invention, or the will of human composition, but in accord with what you see and hear in the heavens above, in the marvels of God. . . .

> And again I heard a voice from heaven saying to me: "Cry out, therefore, and write thus."

Another aspect of Hildegard's prophetic style is her frequent, sometimes disconcerting change of grammatical persons. The voice from heaven often speaks in the divine first person; locutions like "My Son, Jesus Christ" indicate that God the Father is speaking through the seer. Without warning, however, the narration will suddenly shift from the first person to the third, as prophecy subsides into exposition. But even when Hildegard spoke in her own persona, she ascribed her words to the celestial exegete, whose voice thus interprets and governs the entire visionary opus. It is significant that, apart from her lyrics, she scarcely ever addressed God in the second person; her writings are proclamation, not prayer.

Hildegard's style, then, clearly proclaims her prophetic self-awareness. Her correspondents, too, compared her to the Biblical prophets—from Deborah, Olda, Hannah, and Elizabeth to Balaam's ass.[26] And, like the great seers of the Old Testament, she sought by all possible means to bring the people of God to repentance. To that end she used both threats of catastrophe and promises of grace, conveyed in graphic and often startling imagery. Exempla from Scripture, symbols from the world of nature, and prophecies of things to come could serve her equally well as vehicles for the critique of abuses, coupled with the call to renewed moral and spiritual zeal.

Typical of Hildegard's prophetic style is the sermon she preached in Trier on the feast of Pentecost, 1160.[27] It begins with a typical protestation of modesty: "I, a poor little figure without health or strength or courage or learning, myself subject to masters, have heard these words addressed to the prelates and clergy of Trier, from the mystical light of the true vision." In the peroration that follows, Hildegard laments that because

prelates neglect to "sound the trumpet of justice," the four quarters of the earth are darkened: in the east the dawn of good works is extinguished, in the south the ardor of virtue is chilled, and in the west the twilight of mercy yields to midnight blackness. But from the north, the figurative realm of Satan, comes a hissing wind of pride, infidelity, and neglect of God.

This grandiloquent imagery sounds vague enough; but, reading between the lines, one can find more specific complaints. In the first place, the prophet opposed excessive clerical wealth: prelates, she said, shall find that the breadth of their estates has forged constraints for their souls. Their easy living has turned virile courage into feminine weakness, which has no strength to fight because man is naturally the head; and this effeminate age began "with a certain tyrant," the source of all the Church's present woes. This "tyrant" is probably Henry IV, whom Hildegard vilified for his conflict with the reformed papacy. But her implicit message is clear: the German bishops, all too ready to accept imperial election and control, have become emasculated and lost the courage to oppose a now-schismatic emperor. After a long digression on the heroes of salvation history—meant to underscore the difference between obeying God and obeying men—Hildegard threatened a lax and worldly Church with the fate that it deserved.

> But now the law is neglected among the spiritual people, who scorn to do and teach what is good. And the masters and prelates sleep, while justice is abandoned. Hence I heard this voice from heaven saying: O daughter of Sion, the crown will tumble from your head, the far-flung pallium of your riches will be drawn in and confined to a narrow measure, and you will be banished from region to region. Many cities and monasteries shall be dispersed by the powerful. And princes will say: Let us take from them the iniquity that turns the whole world upside down among them.

The prophecy continues: because of their injustice and conspicuous wealth, priests will be persecuted and the Church purified. "Virile times" will return with warfare, by the judgment of God, and afterward there will be a renascence of prophecy, learning, and reverence. Even secular people will be converted by the example of their superiors to a holy way of life. Finally, the Antichrist will arise, but God will crush him as a craftsman smashes the useless works in his shop.

At the end of her sermon, Hildegard returned to her most pressing message. Once, in a vision, she saw the city of Trier aglow with Pentecostal fire so that its streets glistened like gold; but now it is so defiled that fiery vengeance from its enemies will fall upon it, unless the city repents like Nineveh in the days of the prophet Jonah. A medieval chronicler might easily see Hildegard's prophecy confirmed by the internecine warfare, the growing breach between Frederick Barbarossa and the German clergy, and the confiscation of church lands that resulted from the continuing papal schism. But even the political message, like the apocalyptic and the visionary language, remains subordinate to the overriding ethical demand. "Repentance" here entails, but is not limited to, restoration of the proper authority and autonomy of the German bishops. It also requires absolute fidelity to the Word of God as set forth in Scripture, tradition, and—not least—the seer's own prophetic writings. This breadth of intention may be one reason why Hildegard was often deliberately vague about names and events, although she did not hesitate to take sides in current affairs. Like the Biblical prophets, she preferred to veil her advice in symbolic language that could apply to a wide range of situations.

In addition to preaching and apocalyptic, Hildegard's prophetic activity extended to the private sphere. Of her many correspondents, the priests and monastics—by far the majority—wrote to ask her for prayers, counsel, and revelations concerning their personal and communal lives. Her answers, dictated "by the living Light," present a miscellany of visions and teachings, often of very general import. But sometimes the questions are more specific: Should I resign my abbacy or persevere? How can we monks correct our fraternal bickering? Are our relics genuine? How can we exorcise a woman obsessed by devils? Should we receive the erring brother who wants to return? And laypeople asked: Are my kinsmen suffering in purgatory? Will my husband recover from his illness? Should I take my inheritance case before the emperor? Hildegard did not always answer such questions: sometimes she explained that God had not shown her everything, or that it was better for the writer not to know. But in trying to reconstruct her daily life and work, we must not forget the constant stream of messengers and pilgrims who honored and sometimes plagued her with these requests. And while we cannot survey the whole of her correspondence, we can imagine her as a woman among women by looking at three letters to persons of widely differing rank: an abbess, an empress, and an afflicted matron.

Much of Hildegard's activity was directed toward monastic reform. We may take her letter to Sophia, abbess of Altwick, as typical both of contemporary monastic problems and of the seer's characteristic imagery in writing of women. Sophia, like so many twelfth-century superiors, yearned to lay down the burden of pastoral care, which weighed heavily upon her, in exchange for an eremitic life "in the solitude of some little cell."[28] But to the seer, this seemingly pious wish was a snare and a delusion.

> O daughter born of the side of man, and figure formed in the building of God: why do you languish so that your mind shifts like clouds in a storm, now shining like the light and now darkened? . . . You say, "I want to rest and seek a place where my heart can have a nest, so that my soul may rest there." Daughter, before God it is useless for you to cast off your burden and abandon the flock of God, while you have a light to illumine it so that you can lead it to pasture. Now restrain yourself, lest your mind blaze in that sweetness which greatly harms you in the vicissitudes of worldly life.

In the lure of the hermitage, Hildegard saw only a spurious and irresponsible pietism. Far better is the onerous but necessary care of souls in fidelity to a vow once taken. With but one exception, she gave the same counsel to all the abbots and abbesses who raised this question—although in each case she claimed to have a special revelation for her correspondent.[29] Collectively, then, the letters express an aspect of Hildegard's concern for effective and vigilant pastoral care at all levels, while her imagery varied with each correspondent's personal need. In this letter to Sophia, she began by comparing the abbess to Eve, then figuratively to Ecclesia—the "new Eve" taken from the side of Christ, the new Adam, to be God's living temple. The greeting reinforces Hildegard's explicit message on the symbolic level: it is by fulfilling her appointed task of leadership in the Church that Abbess Sophia will also live out her feminine role as a figura of it.

In her dealings with the secular powers, Hildegard was not always as harsh as she was with Frederick. One of her letters, addressed to "Bertha, queen of the Greeks"—otherwise Irene, wife of the Byzantine Emperor Manuel Comnenus—was apparently written to console the German-born empress for her failure to bear a son.[30] Hildegard greeted the empress respectfully, but with the authority that befits a prophet.

> The breath of the Spirit of God says: . . . By a stream that rises from a rock in the East the filth of other waters is cleansed, for it runs swiftly and is more useful than other waters, because there is no corruption in it. So it is with those to whom God grants a day of prosperity and a glowing dawn of honor, and whom the north wind does not oppress with the rough blast of hostile foes. Therefore look to him who has touched you, who seeks a burnt offering from your heart and the keeping of his commandments. Sigh to him, therefore, and may he give you the joy of offspring as you desire, and as you petition him in your need. For the living eye regards you and wishes to have you, and you shall live forever.

We do not know whether Bertha had asked Hildegard especially to pray she would bear a son, and the saint made no rash promise. What is noteworthy in Hildegard's letter, beyond the usual exhortation to trust God, is her analogy between the queen's noble status and the mountain stream, which purifies the land because it flows from the heights. The powerful whom God has exalted to prosperity and honor should likewise set an example of gratitude and virtue for the realm. But, while admonishing the empress and promising the salvation of her soul, Hildegard refused to prophesy her earthly future.

The seer stressed this limitation of her fortune-telling abilities when writing to a woman of much humbler rank, one Sibyl of Lausanne.[31] This matron's circumstances are not clear from Hildegard's two surviving letters to her, but she seems to have been bereaved by a complicated family tragedy. Hildegard called her a "daughter of the woods," so perhaps she had tried to adopt the life of a recluse. Whatever the woman's predicament, Hildegard carefully delimited the role she herself was able to play in it.

> Sibyl, handiwork of God's finger, amend your unstable way of life, and do not exert yourself in mental agitation. You cannot excuse yourself by this means, for God discerns everything. But God does not bid me to explain his judgments upon you, but rather to pray for you, because certain people are now watching out for revenge on account of what your parents did. For sometimes God stretches out his lash even to the third and fourth generations. Yet trust in the Lord that he may deliver you from the sword of your enemies, even though your daughter has been seized by them.
>
> I, however, speak more about the salvation of souls than about the fates of men, so I often say nothing about these things. For the Holy Spirit pours out not revelation to confound people's crimes, but just judgment. Now may God set you in the field of life that you may live forever.[32]

Hildegard's private epistles, compared with her public sermons, reveal that she felt more confident in predicting events on a grand scale than in foretelling individual fates. To her friend Sibyl she gave no more than the pious counsel, consolation, and prayers that any Christian might offer, although she still wrote with an assured authority. Yet in a second letter to this woman, she displayed another and more spectacular charism.

This time, the hapless Sibyl had been suffering from an issue of blood, like the sick woman described in Mark 5:25-34. In the name of the visionary Light, Hildegard proposed a cure.

> Place your trust in God. But around your chest and your navel set these words, in the name of him who orders all things rightly: "In the blood of Adam death arose; in the blood of Christ death was restrained. In that same blood of Christ I command you, blood, to cease your flowing."[33]

This charm, like many others in her ***Book of Simple Medicine,*** lies on the borderline between sacraments (in the broadest sense) and sympathetic magic. According to Hildegard's *Vita,* the remedy worked;[34] it is but one of many miraculous cures ascribed to her. Oddly enough, however, her medical books are unique among her writings in that they make no claim to any prophetic or visionary inspiration. The fact that she wrote them on her own initiative, so to speak, suggests that although she took a strong interest in medicine, she considered this aspect of her work less authoritative than her spiritual and ethical teaching. Nevertheless, there can be no doubt that her flair for unconventional healings, like her vivid apocalyptic and her audacious preaching tours, fired the imagination of her peers. Sensational gifts, after all, attract even pious attention more readily than serious calls to a devout and holy life. So Hildegard's renown as a creature blessed among women rested, for Guibert and other saint-watchers throughout the empire, on acts and claims more mysterious than the zeal of her teaching. Above all, it rested on her famed experience as a "seer of the living Light."

THEOLOGY AND THE PROBLEM OF FEMININE AUTHORITY

Hildegard's visions not only supplied her with a message; they also assured an audience for it. Were it not for the visions, she would never have preached or written at all, and she even maintained—echoing a theme as old as Moses—that in spite of them she was hardly eager to prophesy. But it is no less true that, had she not claimed her gift as a mark of divine authority, no one would have listened to her. Many have suggested that, in an age when the Apostle's command that "no woman is to teach or have authority over men" (I Tim. 2:12) was rigorously enforced, it was only through visions that a religious or intellectual woman could gain a hearing. This is not to say that such visions were necessarily rooted in the desire for authority; but the visionary could not help knowing that, although men might perhaps heed a divinely inspired woman, they would have little patience with a mere presumptuous female.

This awareness can explain some of the vehemence with which Hildegard insisted on her inspiration, even to the point of claiming verbal inerrancy. In her *Vita* she told how, at the time of her move to the Rupertsberg, many asked "why so many mysteries should be revealed to a foolish and uneducated woman, when there are many powerful and learned men," and some people wondered whether she had been seduced by evil spirits.[35] Even some of her own nuns rejected her and refused to move to the new foundation. Although only one letter attacking Hildegard is extant, she referred in several places to her detractors. Some resented the severity, others the novelty of her monastic discipline; some questioned her pretensions to divine wisdom; and many must have been appalled at conduct unbecoming to her sex, for she remarked in one place that "now, to the scandal of men, women are prophesying."[36] The more vulnerable she knew herself to be, the more emphatically she needed to proclaim that it was not she but the Holy Spirit who spoke. To that end, only the certitude that she was transcribing exact dictation from the living Light could suffice both for herself and for her readers.

The problem of feminine authority was no less troubling for Hildegard herself than for her auditors, since she partially shared her culture's notions of female inferiority. No matter how strong her sense of the grace that animated her, she suffered from an almost equal sense of her own implausibility as a vessel. No doubt, as she struggled to overcome this diffidence, the aristocratic ease born of rank and privilege helped her more than she realized. But, in order to come to terms with her God-given authority, she needed to reconcile it with her gender in a strictly theological fashion. Two complementary means to this end—two strategies of validation, as it were—lay at hand. In the first place, Hildegard took her strongest stand on what seemed to be her worst disability—"feminine frailty." Because the power of God is perfected in weakness, because the humblest shall be the most exalted, human impotence could become the sign and prelude of divine empowerment.[37] In Hildegard's eyes this negative capability compensated for her meager schooling and her poor health as well as for her gender. Her second mode of validation was more oblique, less conscious and deliberate: It lay in accentuating the feminine aspects of the divine. But these two strategies, apparently so opposed, are not unrelated. To see the feminine as a species of incapacity and frailty, yet also as a numinous and salvific dimension of the divine nature: herein lies the characteristic strain of what I have called Hildegard's "theology of the feminine."

Before examining her visions in detail, it will be useful to see how these two themes were worked out, on a much smaller scale, by a woman closely associated with Hildegard. Her protégée Elisabeth, a young nun at the monastery of Schönau near Bingen, modeled herself from an early age on the seer across the Rhine. In 1152—five years after Hildegard was vindicated by Pope Eugenius III and one year after she published the *Scivias*—the younger nun's visions began. According to her brother, editor, and staunchest supporter, Ekbert of Schönau, the twenty-three-year-old Elisabeth "was visited by the Lord and his hand was with her, doing in her the most marvelous and memorable deeds in accord with his ancient mercies. Indeed, it was given to her to experience ecstasy and to see visions of the secrets of the Lord, which are hidden from mortals' eyes."[38]

Temperamentally, Elisabeth resembled Hildegard in many ways: she shared the older woman's physical frailty, her sensitivity to spiritual impressions of all kinds, and her need for public authentication to overcome initial self-doubt. Just as Hildegard had written in her uncertainty to Bernard, the outstanding saint of the age, so Elisabeth wrote to Hildegard—and, like the abbot of Clairvaux, the abbess of Bingen knew how to console her young protégée while warning her to remain humble. In a characteristic and revealing image, Hildegard told Elisabeth to be like a trumpet, which resounds not by its own effort but by the breath of another.[39] In fact the analogy fit Elisabeth better than Hildegard herself, for the younger woman lacked her admired mother's independence and originality. Many of her visions were inspired by the queries of Ekbert and other patrons, and often they echo Hildegard's in content, imagery, and style.[40]

By 1158 the author of the *Annales Palidenses* found it natural to link the two visionary nuns in a single notice: "In these days also God displayed the signs of his power in the frail sex, that is, in his two handmaidens Hildegard on the Rupertsberg near Bingen and Elisabeth in Schönau, whom he filled with the spirit of prophecy and to whom, through the Gospel, he revealed many kinds of visions, which are extant in writing."[41] The chronicler's reference to "the frail sex" shows once again that contemporaries could not overlook the issue of gender, whether they found in it occasion for praise or for blame. No less than Hildegard, Elisabeth felt this liability keenly. While she was still in doubt about publishing her visions, she feared that some people would dismiss them as satanic delusions or mere feminine fancies (*muliebria figmenta*).[42] And when, like Hildegard, she felt herself called to prophetic preaching, she needed assurance that God would help her fulfill what she felt to be a masculine role. Hence the angel of the Lord commanded her, "Arise, . . . and stand upon your feet, and I will speak with you; and fear not, for I am with you all the days of your life. Play the man (*viriliter age*) and let your heart take courage."[43]

In one sense, Elisabeth's path should have been easier than Hildegard's simply because the older nun could provide a model for her. Her *Book of the Ways of God* (1156) obviously takes its title, though not its subject matter, from the *Scivias*. Elisabeth gracefully acknowledged this debt in her vision of a pavilion filled with books that, an angel tells her, have yet to be revealed before the Day of Judgment. The angel shows Elisabeth her own volume, still unwritten, with the words: "'This is the *Book of the Ways of God,* which is to be revealed through you after you have visited Sister Hildegard and heard her.' And indeed," Elisabeth added, "so the prophecy began to be fulfilled as soon as I had returned from seeing her."[44] Like Hildegard, too, Elisabeth wrote a treatise against the Cathars[45] and a collection of hortatory epistles to religious. Her best-selling book on St. Ursula fostered the cult of that same legendary saint to whom Hildegard wrote some of her most powerful lyrics. Elisabeth could also trust her patron to support her in the face of difficulties. For instance, when Elisabeth felt herself in jeopardy because someone had been circulating a spurious prophecy in her name, and because various disasters she had predicted did not come to pass, she could write to Hildegard in confidence that the abbess of Bingen would clear her name.[46]

On the other hand, the older visionary had sources of security that her protégée lacked. First, from a secular standpoint, she could count on support from a powerful circle of friends, relatives, and churchmen—including St. Bernard, the archbishop of Mainz, and the pope. Elisabeth had only her devoted brother. Second, Hildegard seems to have had fewer doubts about the authenticity of her call, although she did fear its consequences. Elisabeth began more hesitantly still. Not only did she endure sickness and short-term paralysis, like Hildegard; she also suffered from profound depression, anorexia, suicidal temptations, and demonic apparitions, which alternated for a long time with her more wholesome visions. Whereas Hildegard stressed that her visions seldom interfered with her normal functioning, Elisabeth experienced hers in ecstasy, usually accompanied by agony. This state of inner turmoil gradually subsided, and, as the visionary became more confident, her writings became more objective—less concerned with her personal sufferings and more closely connected with the liturgical year, the needs of her community, and the theological interests of her friends. Her later works thus reflect not only Hildegard's influence but also the successful resolution of her early conflicts. The conflicts themselves, however, were worked out in her initial *Book of Visions,* where the problem of feminine authority emerges as a persistent theme. Elisabeth's ways of coming to terms with her prophetic role, through the instruction and consolation received in her visions, can serve as a preview of Hildegard's more sustained and ample development of this same problematic.

One obvious reply to detractors was available in the Old Testament, whence exempla of feminine courage had been drawn from time out of mind. Elisabeth did not hesitate to invoke the great mothers of Israel:

> People are scandalized that in these days the Lord deigns to magnify his great mercy in the frail sex. But why doesn't it cross their minds that a similar thing happened in the days of our fathers when, while men were given to indolence, holy women were filled with the Spirit of God so that they could prophesy, energetically govern the people of God, and even win glorious victories over Israel's enemies? I speak of women like Hilda, Deborah, Judith, Jael, and the like.[47]

In the seer's reference to "men . . . given to indolence" we can again recognize Hildegard's complaint about "effeminate times," which justify feminine leaders.

Further support for the notion of empowered women comes from the visions themselves. It is not surprising that Elisabeth, in her distress, should receive comfort from the Virgin; but it is more striking that she should see Mary dressed like a priest, standing beside the altar vested in a chasuble and a glorious crown.[48] In another vision Elisabeth beheld the apocalyptic woman clothed with the sun, who turned out to be neither Mary nor the Church but "the sacred humanity of the Lord Jesus" weeping over the iniquity of the world.[49] Elisabeth's brother was upset by this identification, so at his bidding she asked her next heavenly visitor "why the Savior's humanity was shown to me in the guise of a virgin and not in the form of a man." She received a conventional answer, namely that this vision could refer to the Virgin Mary as well as to Christ. But the initial interpretation was not withdrawn. To Elisabeth's inspired imagination, it appeared that if Christ is both divine and human he must also be female as well as male. Both these visions obliquely validate the seer's authority through and despite her sex. In one of them a woman appears in a powerful male role, and in the other Christ himself appears as a woman.[50]

In a different vein, the *Book of Visions* closes with a text even more reminiscent of Hildegard. Elisabeth had seen Nebuchadnezzar's vision (Dan. 2:31-33) of a great statue with a head of gold, chest of silver, belly of bronze, legs of iron, and feet of clay; and she interpreted this image as the apocalyptic Christ. The feet of clay in her vision represented Christ's human body and soul, and she wanted to know why these were so frail while the iron and bronze, symbolizing the Church, were so strong. The answer she received is this: "all the virtue and strength of the Church grew out of the Savior's weakness, which he incurred through the flesh. The weakness of God is stronger than men. This was well demonstrated by a figure in the first parents, when the vigor of bone was taken from Adam that Eve might be made; that the woman might be confirmed whence the man was made infirm" (*inde firmaretur mulier, unde infirmatus est vir*).[51] Here Elisabeth, like Hildegard, associated the paradox of saving weakness with the reversal of normal gender roles, whereby men become weak and women strong. Earlier she had seen Christ's humanity in the guise of a woman; now that same humanity is represented by the fragile feet of clay, which, paradoxically, confer strength on the woman Ecclesia.

It was through reflection on the humanity of Christ, considered in its multifarious richness, that Elisabeth came to accept both feminine weakness and feminine strength. Her theology of the feminine, like Hildegard's, has its roots in the charismatic woman's need for authentication in a mistrustful world. But both visionaries finally transcended that need. Hildegard, blending the high traditions of Wisdom theology with received ideas about women and weakness, was able to achieve a distinctive, tense, and highly energized interpretation of the Christian faith.

Notes

[1] See Adolf Katzenellenbogen, *Allegories of the Virtues and Vices in Mediaeval Art,* trans. A. J. Crick (London, 1939).

[2] *Scivias* III.3.3, ed. Adelgundis Führkötter and Angela Carlevaris, Corpus Christianorum: Continuatio Mediaevalis [CCCM] 43-43a (Turnhout, 1978): 375.

[3] A fuller version of this play, the *Ordo virtutum,* exists independently of the *Scivias* and may be related to Hildegard's *Symphonia.* See "The Text of the *Ordo Virtutum,*" ed. Peter Dronke, in *Poetic Individuality in the Middle Ages* (Oxford, 1970): 180-92. There is a performance edition with music edited by Audrey Davidson, *The* Ordo Virtutum *of Hildegard of Bingen* (Kalamazoo, 1985).

[4] On this manuscript see Louis Baillet, *Les Miniatures du* Scivias *de Sainte Hildegarde* (Paris, 1911); Hans Fegers, "Die Bilder im *Scivias* der Hildegard von Bingen," *Das Werk des Künstlers* 1 (1939): 109-45; and Christel Meier, "Zum Verhältnis von Text und Illustration im überlieferten Werk Hildegards von Bingen," in *Hildegard von Bingen, 1179-1979: Festschrift zum 800. Todestag der Heiligen,* ed. Anton Brück (Mainz, 1979): 159-69. The paintings are reproduced in color in the CCCM edition of the *Scivias.*

[5] *Liber vite meritorium* [LVM] I.20 and I.25, ed. Angela Carlevaris, CCCM 90 (Turnhout, 1995): 21, 23..

[6] LVM I.6, p. 15 (Obduratio); V.5, p. 222 (Maleficium); II.10, p. 80 (Infelicitas).

[7] *Liber divinorum operum* [LDO] I.2.42, ed. Albert Derolez and Peter Dronke, CCCM 92 (Turnhout, 1996): 108-09. This work is also known as *De operatione Dei* [*On the Activity of God*].

[8] LDO I.4.98, pp. 240-41.

[9] The whole created world is like a book, a picture, and a mirror for us. Alan of Lille, *Rhythmus alter,* ed. J.-P. Migne, Patrologia latina [PL] 210: 579a.

[10] LDO I.4.105, p. 249.

[11] LDO I.4.42, p. 177.

[12] Charles Czarski, *The Prophecies of St. Hildegard of Bingen* (Ph.D. Diss., University of Kentucky, 1983); H. D. Rauh, "Hildegard von Bingen," in *Das Bild des Antichrist im Mittelalter: Von Tyconius zum deutschen Symbolismus* (Munich, 1973): 474-527; Kathryn Kerby-Fulton, "Hildegard of Bingen and Antimendicant Propaganda," *Traditio* 43 (1987): 386-99.

[13] Visiones et oracula beatae illius et celeberrimae Hildegardis, quae apud vos sunt [mittite]. Quae mihi ex eo commendata est et venerabilis, quod eam dominus Eugenius specialis charitatis affectu familiarius amplectebatur. Explorate etiam et rescribite, an ei sit de fine huius schismatis aliquid revelatum. Praedixit enim in diebus papae Eugenii, quod non esset, nisi extremis diebus, pacem et gratiam in Urbe habiturus. PL 199: 220c. On this subject Hildegard remarked, "De schismate Ecclesie non iubet me Dominus loqui, sed gladium suum uibrat et arcum suum tendit." Ep. 197 in *Hildegardis Bingensis Epistolarium,* ed. Lieven Van Acker, CCCM 91-91a (Turnhout, 1991-1993): 449.

[14] Fragments of Gebeno's work appear in J.-B. Pitra, ed., *Analecta Sanctae Hildegardis* (Monte Cassino, 1882): 483-88, under the title *Speculum futurorum temporum.* The complete text has never been edited.

[15] Gebeno of Ebernach, *Speculum* Prologus 3, Pitra 484-85.

[16] Trithemius of Sponheim, *Chronicon Hirsaugiense ad 1149,* in *Opera historica,* ed. Marquard Freher (Frankfurt, 1601; rpt. 1966): 132.

[17] See Ildefons Herwegen, "Les collaborateurs de Ste. Hildegarde," *Revue bénédictine* 21 (1904): 192-203, 302-15, 381-403; Marianna Schrader and Adelgundis Führkötter, *Die Echtheit des Schrifttums der hl. Hildegard von Bingen* (Cologne, 1956): 143-53.

[18] Guibert of Gembloux, Ep. 29.25-27, Pitra 431-33. For Guibert's argument cf. Augustine, *De doctrina christiana* IV.3 and IV.26, Corpus christianorum: series latina [CCSL] 32, pp. 117, 134-35.

[19] Dronke, *Poetic Individuality* 178-79.

[20] For this distinction see Jean Leclercq, *The Love of Learning and the Desire for God,* trans. Catherine Misrahi (New York, 1961): 233-86. Two good introductions to twelfth-century symbolics are M.-D. Chenu, *Nature, Man, and Society in the Twelfth Century,* trans. Jerome Taylor and L. K. Little (Chicago, 1968); and M.-M. Davy, *Initiation à la symbolique romane, XIIe siècle* (Paris, 1964).

[21] Christel Meier, "Zwei Modelle von Allegorie im 12. Jahrhundert: Das allegorische Verfahren Hildegards von Bingen und Alans von Lille," in Walter Haug, ed.,

Formen und Funktionen der Allegorie (Stuttgart, 1979): 78.

[22] Kent Kraft has compared the shifting imagery of the visions with the commentary, which "spans them out and freezes them, 'frame by frame,' as it were." *The Eye Sees More than the Heart Knows: The Visionary Cosmology of Hildegard of Bingen* (Ph.D. Diss., University of Wisconsin, 1977): 104.

[23] Dronke, *Poetic Individuality* 157; Peter Dronke, "Problemata Hildegardiana," *Mittellateinisches Jahrbuch* 16 (1981): 116-17.

[24] Cf. Adelgundis Führkötter, introduction to *Scivias* xviii.

[25] This passage and the next are from *Scivias*, Protestificatio, 3-6.

[26] Epp. 75 (PL 197:297c); 6 (157c); 92 (313a).

[27] This sermon is published as Ep. 223r in Van Acker, CCCM 91a, pp. 490-96.

[28] Ep. 50r in Van Acker, CCCM 91, pp. 122-23. On twelfth-century ambivalence and antagonism toward the abbatial role see Pierre Salmon, *The Abbot in Monastic Tradition*, trans. Claire Lavoie (Washington, 1972): 95-99; and Caroline Walker Bynum, *Jesus as Mother: Studies in the Spirituality of the High Middle Ages* (Berkeley, 1982): 154-59.

[29] For similar advice cf. Epp. 32, 33, 37, 42, 44, 66, 70, 74, 77, 78, 86, 101, 108, and 112 in PL 197; and Epp. 39, 57, 61, 63, 76, 83, 89, 98, 118, 137, 138, 151, and 159 in Pitra.

[30] Bertha of Sulzbach, sister-in-law of Conrad III, married Manuel Comnenus in 1146 and bore one daughter. See Ep. 81, Pitra 542.

[31] Or "Sibylla trans Alpes" as in the ms heading of Ep. 36, Pitra 521.

[32] Ep. 125, Pitra 560-61. This same letter, with the proper name and the reference to Sibyl's daughter deleted, appears as Ep. 88 in PL 197: 309d-10a, where it is addressed to the provost of a monastery in Koblenz. The editor has conflated Hildegard's letter to Sibyl with another to Bertha, a matron of Fulda (Ep. 43, Pitra 526). As Schrader and Führkötter have pointed out (*Echtheit* 160-71), the so-called Riesenkodex (Wiesbaden, Hess. Landesbibliothek Hs.2), from which most of the letters in Migne's collection are taken, often falsifies the addresses of otherwise authentic letters in order to exalt the rank of Hildegard's correspondents.

[33] Ep. 36, Pitra 521.

[34] *Vita S. Hildegardis* 3.10, ed. Monika Klaes, CCCM 126 (Turnhout, 1993): 51.

[35] *Vita* 2.5, p. 28.

[36] Heinrich Schipperges, ed., "Ein unveröffentlichtes Hildegard Fragment" IV.28, *Sudhoffs Archiv für Geschichte der Medizin* 40 (1956): 71. Cf. *Vita* 2.6, p. 30, and Ep. 52 from Tenxwindis of Andernach, in Van Acker, CCCM 91, pp. 125-27, a searching critique offered in ironically courteous terms.

[37] Cf. Barbara Newman, "Divine Power Made Perfect in Weakness: St. Hildegard on the Frail Sex," in L. Thomas Shank and John Nichols, eds., *Peaceweavers*, vol. 2 of *Medieval Religious Women* (Kalamazoo, 1987): 103-22.

[38] Elisabeth of Schönau, *Liber visionum* I.1, in F. W. E. Roth, ed., *Die Visionen der heiligen Elisabeth und die Schriften der Äbte Ekbert and Emecho von Schönau* (Brünn, 1884): 1. On Elisabeth see Kurt Köster, "Das visionäre Werk Elisabeths von Schönau: Studien zur Entstehung, Überlieferung und Wirkung in der mittelalterlichen Welt," *Archiv für mittelrheinische Kirchengeschichte* 4 (1952): 79-119; Josef Loos, "Hildegard von Bingen und Elisabeth von Schönau," *Festchrift*, ed. Brück, 263-72; Anne Clark, *Elisabeth of Schönau: A Twelfth-Century Visionary* (Philadelphia, 1992).

[39] Ep. 201r in Van Acker, CCCM 91a, pp. 456-57. See Kathryn Kerby-Fulton and Dyan Elliott, "Self-Image and the Visionary Role in Two Letters from the Correspondence of Elizabeth of Schönau and Hildegard of Bingen," *Vox Benedictina* 2 (1985): 204-23.

[40] The mountain, city, and column described in the *Liber visionum* are particularly reminiscent of *Scivias*, Book III, and the stylized dialogues between the prophet and God or his angel also recall Hildegard.

[41] *Annales Palidenses* ad 1158, in Monumenta Germaniae Historica: Scriptores, vol. 16, p. 90.

[42] Elisabeth, *Liber visionum* I.1 in Roth, *Visionen der heiligen Elisabeth* 1.

[43] Elisabeth, *Liber visionum* I.67 in Roth, *Visionen der heiligen Elisabeth* 32. Cf. Ezek. 2:1, Matt. 28:20, Ps. 26:14.

[44] Elisabeth of Schönau, *Liber viarum Dei* 6 in Roth, *Visionen der heiligen Elisabeth* 91.

[45] See Raoul Manselli, "Amicizia spirituale ed azione pastorale nella Germania del seculo XII: Ildegarda di Bingen, Elisabetta ed Ecberto di Schönau contro l'eresia

catara," *Studi e materiali di storia delle religioni* 38 (1967), fasc. 1-2: 302-13.

[46] Ep. 45, PL 197: 214d-16d. The passage in which Elisabeth styled herself "magistra sororum quae in Schonaugia sunt" is an interpolation.

[47] Elisabeth, *Liber visionum* II.1 in Roth, *Visionen der heiligen Elisabeth* 40. Cf. St. Ambrose on Deborah: "In order to enthuse the souls of women, a woman judged, a woman decided, a woman prophesied, a woman triumphed and, in the midst of the fighting troops, taught men the art of war under feminine command. In the mystery, however, the struggle of faith is the Church's victory." *De viduis* 8. 49-50, PL 16: 362-63.

[48] Elisabeth, *Liber visionum* 1.6 in Roth, *Visionen der heiligen Elisabeth* 6. The vision probably derives from the iconography of Mary in priestly vestments as a personification of the Church. See Ilene Forsyth, *The Throne of Wisdom: Wood Sculptures of the Madonna in Romanesque France* (Princeton, 1972): 23-24 and figs. 112-21.

[49] Elisabeth, *Liber visionum* III.4 in Roth, *Visionen der heiligen Elisabeth* 60-61.

[50] Cf. Gertrud Jaron Lewis, "Christus als Frau: Eine Vision Elisabeths von Schönau," *Jahrbuch für Internationale Germanistik* 15 (1983): 70-80. On the femininity of Jesus, an important minor theme in twelfth-century writers, see the title essay and references in Bynum, *Jesus as Mother.*

[51] Elisabeth, *Liber visionum* III.31 in Roth, *Visionen der heiligen Elisabeth* 87.

Barbara J. Newman (essay date 1990)

SOURCE: Barbara J. Newman, in an introduction to *Hildegard of Bingen: Scivias,* translated by Mother Columba Hart and Jane Bishop, Paulist Press, 1990, pp. 9-53.

[*In the following excerpt, from her introduction to a translation of Hildegard's* Scivias, *Newman discusses "the essentially prophetic character of Hildegard's spirituality": the "blend of renunciation with privilege" which characterized the abbess's leadership, and the nature of Hildegard's apocalyptic message.*]

Although Hildegard is frequently classified as a mystic, she may be more precisely identified as a visionary and prophet. Classical definitions of mysticism stress the union of the soul with God and the whole system of ascetic and contemplative disciplines that aim to facilitate that union. But Hildegard, while she certainly

had a powerful sense of the divine presence, did not follow the unitive way. "Prayer" to her meant primarily petition and liturgical praise, while "the love of God" meant reverence, loyalty and obedience to his commands. In the rare texts where she portrays herself as a partner in dialogue with God, she is not the enamored bride longing for divine union, as in St. Bernard's *Sermons on the Song of Songs,* but the fragile and woefully inadequate mortal—"ashes of ashes, and filth of filth"—trembling before the great commission she has received. Like Moses "stuttering and slow of speech," and like Isaiah "of unclean lips," she offers the prophet's classic response to a calling she has not chosen, yet cannot do other than obey.

The essentially prophetic character of Hildegard's spirituality explains the startling lack of interest in her own subjectivity. In spite of her unusual inner experiences, she recorded only as much as she had to reveal in order to authenticate her works. Thus only at the beginning and end of each book does she describe its genesis in visions; elsewhere the emphasis rests firmly on the content, and still more on the meaning, of the things seen. Moreover, her autobiographical prefaces and endings tend to focus as much on the seer's disabilities (her femaleness, poor health and lack of education) as they do on her revelations. These disclaimers, far from representing a simple "modesty topos," also serve the aim of authentication; they are meant to persuade readers that, because the author is not "wise according to worldly standards," her weakness and foolishness have been empowered by God alone.[1]

Hildegard's prophetic self-awareness pervades all her writings except for her scientific works, and accounts for many of their stylistic features as well as their characteristically objective or outer-directed teaching. Because she saw herself as the voice of another, not as a speaker in her own right, she often seems disturbingly unaware of the human element in her writings. Not only does she lapse easily from speaking about God in the third person, as preacher, to speaking *for* him in the first person, as prophet; she also claims direct verbal inspiration for her entire opus and threatens terrible divine vengeance on anyone who dares to add, delete or alter a word. This instrumental view of her activity also required her to deny any education beyond "simple reading," although she was already well-acquainted with the Church Fathers and standard biblical commentaries when she wrote the *Scivias,* and by the end of her life was a woman of remarkably wide culture. Her posture as a simple, unlearned person was not intended to deceive; aside from reinforcing her prophetic persona, it constitutes an implicit critique of the learned clerics whose negligence, she believed, had necessitated her mission.

Hildegard never went beyond her limited and stylized self-disclosures to reveal more of her inner life until she was in her seventies, and even then she did so only at the request of hagiographically inclined admirers. For her first biographer, Gottfried, she wrote or dictated a valuable autobiographical memoir; and for the adoring Guibert she supplied this celebrated and oft-quoted account of her "mode of seeing":

> In this vision my soul, as God would have it, rises up high into the vault of heaven and into the changing sky and spreads itself out among different peoples, although they are far away from me in distant lands and places. And because I see them this way in my soul, I observe them in accord with the shifting of clouds and other created things. I do not hear them with my outward ears, nor do I perceive them by the thoughts of my own heart or by any combination of my five senses, but in my soul alone, while my outward eyes are open. So I have never fallen prey to ecstasy in the visions, but I see them wide awake, day and night. . . . The light that I see thus is not spatial, but it is far, far brighter than a cloud that carries the sun. I can measure neither height, nor length, nor breadth in it; and I call it "the reflection of the living Light." And as the sun, the moon, and the stars appear in water, so writings, sermons, virtues, and certain human actions take form for me and gleam within it.
>
> Now whatever I have seen or learned in this vision remains in my memory for a long time, so that, when I have seen and heard it, I remember; and I see, hear, and know all at once, and as if in an instant I learn what I know. But what I do not see, I do not know, for I am not educated. . . . And the words in this vision are not like words uttered by a human mouth, but like a shimmering flame, or a cloud floating in a clear sky.
>
> Moreover, I can no more recognize the form of this light than I can gaze directly on the sphere of the sun. Sometimes—but not often—I see within this light another light, which I call "the living Light." And I cannot describe when and how I see it, but while I see it all sorrow and anguish leave me, so that then I feel like a simple girl instead of an old woman.[2]

This is not the kind of experience that could be taught or learned. Readers might be reminded of Augustine's theory of illumination, which was probably familiar to Hildegard, or of the variant form of Neoplatonic light-mysticism that reached medieval Europe through Pseudo-Dionysius. A still closer parallel can be found in the experiences of Simeon the New Theologian and the Byzantine hesychasts, who sought by means of spiritual exercises to attain purity of heart and thus behold the uncreated light of Mount Tabor. Hildegard could not possibly have known this latter tradition, however; and as we have seen, she made no effort to cultivate or promulgate her special mode of seeing. Nor did she theologize about her visionary experience *per se.*

Aside from the dynamics of prophetic inspiration, Hildegard's spirituality is best understood through the ecclesiastical roles she played: Benedictine abbess, Gregorian reformer and apocalyptic preacher. As mistress of the Rupertsberg, she was indeed a Benedictine to the core. The *Scivias* opens with a vision of two thoroughly monastic virtues, Fear of the Lord and Poverty of Spirit; one has eyes on every side, and the other is inundated with the glory of God, indicating that only the humble possess true vision. Throughout Hildegard's works, but especially in the *Scivias,* the foundational virtues are humility, obedience and discretion, which, like Benedict, she called "the mother of virtues." In governing her community and advising her fellow superiors, she advocated a middle way between laxity and self-indulgence on the one hand and excessive abstinence on the other. She placed a premium on unity, and her teaching is pervaded with classical monastic themes: spiritual warfare, knowledge of good and evil, the conflict between soul and body, the acquisition of virtues, the special merit of chastity. Monks and virgins, in her view, were "new planets" which first appeared in the heavens at Christ's nativity;[3] she never doubted that they formed an elite corps among Christians and, if they persevered in their vows, would receive a special reward.

Although she herself was raised by a recluse, Hildegard was not particularly sympathetic to the eremitic life. A number of abbots and abbesses sought her counsel because they longed to lay down the burden of governing and work out their salvation in a hermit's cell; she always replied that this was a temptation to be resisted.[4] In fact, Hildegard's originality in so many fields should not obscure the fact that she represented a rather old-fashioned type of monasticism. Her reaction to the newer currents is neatly epitomized in her quarrel with the abbess Tengswich of Andernach, sister of the canonical reformer Richard of Springiersbach.[5] Richard and Tengswich were pioneers in the movement for apostolic poverty, and Tengswich had criticized Hildegard sharply (under the veil of ironic praise) because the abbess of Bingen accepted only noble girls in her convent. What is more, she allowed them to wear jewelry when they received communion. In a spirited reply Hildegard defended the principle of class discrimination: One would not put beasts of different species in the same stall, and even angels had their hierarchy. As for wearing jewels, it was perfectly acceptable for the brides of Christ to dress like noble ladies because, as virgins, they were exempt from the rule of female subordination that required matrons to wear veils and lay aside their elegant attire. This blend of renunciation with privilege continues the long tradition of high-born abbesses, who gave up the titles and secular powers of nobility while retaining its influence, prestige and corporate wealth.

As a reformer Hildegard belongs squarely within the Gregorian camp. In fact, as Jeffrey Russell wrote of Gregory VII himself, her life "is proof that a burning spirit can dwell within a breast committed to order."[6] *Ordo* is indeed a key word in the *Scivias*. Hildegard did not call for radical change of social or ecclesiastical structures; it was the abuse of authority, not the nature of it, that she opposed. Her ideal was a Christendom wherein the secular power would be firmly subordinate to the spiritual, princes and prelates would rule with vigilance and justice, and subjects and layfolk would offer prompt obedience. Yet because her message was largely directed to those in power, and particularly to the ecclesiastical hierarchy, she concerned herself far more with the negligence of clerics and the arrogance of rulers than with the sins of subjects. Three issues that particularly concerned her were clerical celibacy, simony and the subservience of prelates to the secular power—a burning question in Barbarossa's Germany where the bishops were virtually ministers of state. All of these issues, of course, continued the eleventh-century struggle of the reformed papacy against what it perceived as lay encroachments on the dignity of the church.

In addition, Hildegard was zealous for orthodoxy and thus deeply troubled by the hierarchy's failure to offer any effective resistance to the Cathars, who were making numerous converts even as she composed the *Scivias* and had infiltrated the Rhineland by the 1160s. Their alarming success may account for the space she devoted to the sacraments of marriage and the eucharist, which were particularly reviled by these dualistic sectarians. In her most vehement and memorable preaching the abbess highlighted purity of doctrine along with sexual purity, both of which could be symbolized by the powerful image of the virgin Ecclesia. Hildegard not only personified Mother Church in this ancient symbol; in a sense, she impersonated her, making herself a mouthpiece for the pure but continuously imperilled bride of Christ.[7] In short, she placed her zeal for reform at the service of an essentially clerical vision of the church and a hierarchical vision of society. For her there could be no conflict between the spirit of prophecy and the spirit of order.

Hildegard's apocalyptic preaching must be understood in its proper context.[8] As she was not a radical reformer, neither was she a millenarian; she did not envisage an imminent Second Coming or look forward to a golden age of the Spirit. Rather, her apocalyptic message is closely akin to that of the Old Testament prophets. She shared their perception that divine judgment inevitably follows on human sin, and especially on the sins of rulers. If the princes of the church did not renounce their greed, fornication, oppression and negligence, they would be punished by the loss not only of their wealth and power, but even of the dignity they had signally abused. The perpetrators of this vengeance would be princes and people, not because Hildegard believed that kings were superior to prelates or that laypeople had a right to choose their own priests, but because she saw that the secular power could serve as God's scourge to punish his faithless people, just as the Assyrians of old had been allowed to punish Israel. Apocalyptic imagery coupled with the preaching of reform carries the same message that Jonah brought to the Ninevites: If the preaching is obeyed, it is just possible that the prophesied disasters will be averted.

But there is another dimension to Hildegard's apocalyptic. Like all prophets she was deeply concerned with history, and in both the *Scivias* and the *Liber divinorum operum* she surveyed the course of salvation history from beginning to end, from the creation to the final judgment.[9] In order to understand the present it was necessary to consider the past—the successive dispensations of grace before the birth of Christ—as well as the future, in which his work of salvation would at last be fulfilled. Hildegard's vision of the end, as set forth in *Scivias* III.11-12, entails a grim succession of evils that most come to pass before the judgment. As elaborated in the *Liber divinorum operum,* however, her scenario for the last times represents neither a gradual improvement nor a progressive deterioration in the state of the world. On the contrary, history is now seen as "one thing after another"; ages of justice and injustice, each with its own deformations or reforms, would alternate until the coming of Antichrist. Hildegard did not presume to say when he would arrive, but she did frequently speak of her own era as an "effeminate age," which had succeeded the virginal epoch of paradise and the masculine epoch of the apostles and would in turn cede to still worse times. In one passage she even suggested that this effeminate age, signalled by the advent of feminine prophets, began around the time of her own birth.[10] But as a rule, the succession of periods is not dated even in the flexible and teasing manner that is typical of apocalyptic. Later generations could and did interpret the prophecies as they pleased, inserting themselves into the sequence wherever they chose.[11]

Notes

[1] Barbara Newman, "Hildegard of Bingen: Visions and Validation," *Church History* 54 (1985), pp. 163-75; Christel Meier, "Prophetentum als literarische Existenz: Hildegard von Bingen," in *Deutsche Literatur von Frauen* I, ed. Gisela Brinker-Gabler (Munich, 1988) pp. 76-87.

[2] Epistle to Guibert of Gembloux, Pitra, 332-33.

[3] Letter to the monks of St. Disibod, Pitra, 354.

[4] See Epistles 32, 33, 37, 42, 44, 66, 70, 74, 77, 78, 86, 100, 101, 108, and 112 in PL 197; Sabina Flanagan, "Hildegard of Bingen as Prophet: The Evidence of her Contemporaries," *Tjurunga* 32 (1987): 16-45.

[5] Alfred Haverkamp, "Tenxwind von Andernach und Hildegard von Bingen: Zwei 'Weltanschauungen' in der Mitte des 12. Jahrhunderts," in *Institutionen, Kultur und Gesellschaft im Mittelalter: Festschrift Für Josef Fleckenstein,* ed. Lutz Fenske, Werner Rösener and Thomas Zotz (Sigmaringen, 1984): 515-48.

[6] Jeffrey Russell, *A History of Medieval Christianity: Prophecy and Order* (Arlington Heights, 1968), p. 123.

[7] Barbara Newman, *Sister of Wisdom: St. Hildegard's Theology of the Feminine* (Berkeley, 1987), chap. 6.

[8] See Charles Czarski, *The Prophecies of St. Hildegard of Bingen,* diss., University of Kentucky, 1983; Kathryn Kerby-Fulton, *The Voice of Honest Indignation: Reformist Apocalypticism and Piers Plowman* (Cambridge, 1989), chap. 1.

[9] Elisabeth Gössmann, "Zyklisches und Lineares Geschichtsbewusstsein im Mittelalter: Hildegard von Bingen, Johannes von Salisbury and Andere," in *L'Homme et son univers au moyen âge,* 2 ed. Christian Wénin (Louvain, 1986), pp. 882-92.

[10] *Vita* 2.16, PL 197: 102cd. Cf. PL 197: 167b, 185c, 254cd, 1005ab.

[11] Cf. Robert Lerner, "Medieval Prophecy and Religious Dissent," *Past & Present* 72 (1976): 3-24.

Frances Beer (essay date 1992)

SOURCE: Frances Beer, "Hildegard of Bingen," in *Women and Mystical Experience in the Middle Ages,* The Boydell Press, 1992, pp. 15-55.

[*In the following essay, Beer provides a historical context for Hildegard's poetic and intellectual achievements, discussing the nature of life in twelfth-century Benedictine monasteries and convents and the increased credibility of the church as a moral force during this time. The critic then discusses Hildegard's life as an administrator, noting her challenges to the policies of several authoritative male figures, her "effective imperviousness to the potent medieval tradition of antifeminism," and her fundamental concern with spiritual growth.*]

Hildegard of Bingen, born at Bemersheim in 1098, was a figure for whom superlatives seem inadequate. Peter Dronke, for example, author of the major biographical work on Hildegard, resorts to adjectives such as 'over-powering' and 'electrifying', while Matthew Fox, one of her most ardent contemporary admirers, places her among 'the greatest intellectuals of the West'; praising her as a 'woman of genius', instigator of the flowering of German mysticism, Rufus Jones had earlier written that she possessed the 'visionary power and moral passion of the Hebrew prophets'.[1] Her prodigious creative output includes a mystical trilogy for which justifiably she is now best known: ***Scivias, The Book of Life's Merits,*** and ***The Book of Divine Works***. But she also composed medical/scientific treatises, poetry, music, a full-length morality play, and a magnificent series of illustrations intended to clarify and make more accessible her visions. In addition, she was an eminently successful administrator, conducted preaching tours up and down the Rhine, and carried on a voluminous correspondence with key religious and political figures of her day. Before turning to her visionary works, it is worth having a detailed look at her extraordinary life; this is made possible by the fact that we have a Latin *Vita,* substantially of her own composition, as well as many of the letters that she wrote in her capacity as administrator and spiritual advisor.[2]

By her own account, she started to have visions in her infancy; in their earliest manifestation, these took the form of a light of awesome brightness, and they continued on a regular basis throughout her early years. As she describes it, she was uncertain, even fearful of these experiences as a child. She neither knew what to make of them, nor what others would think of her if they knew; so in predictable childlike fashion she tended to keep them to herself. As a child she was also frequently ill, and it seems likely that the two phenomena were linked. Leaving her feelings of anxiety and isolation aside, the very effort involved in keeping visions of such great intensity bottled up would almost inevitably result in headaches and other psychosomatic symptoms. Still, to turn it around, as some have, and argue that the illness caused the visions seems to reflect the limits of our imagination, not of hers.[3] She attributed these painful bouts of illness, which continued throughout her life, to 'aerial torments' which she described as drying up her veins and flesh—even the very marrow of her bones. They seem to have been particularly acute when she was facing some frustration or some undone work. In the Preface to *Scivias* she remarks that she refused to write down her visions until she 'became sick, pressed down by the scourge of God'; and a persistent bout of illness in her 70s ended with a vision of a most loving—'amantissimus'—man who exorcized the tormenting demons, after which she was able to complete the ***Book of Divine Works***.

When Hildegard was seven she was placed by her parents in a monastery named for its founder, the Celtic saint Disibodus, under the tutelage of a noblewoman, Jutta, the *magistra* who was later to become the abbess.[4] Perhaps they made this decision because she was the tenth child in the family, which, however aristocratic, may have been running out of dowries adequate to ensure a proper alliance. It seems possible that she would already have distinguished herself as an unusual child: high-strung, keenly intelligent, plagued by recurrent illness, uncannily able to foretell coming events. In any case her parents referred to her as their 'tithe' to God. She seems to have taken to monastic life naturally and with great success: when Jutta died some years later in 1136, Hildegard, by then 38, was the unanimous choice of the nuns to replace her as abbess. Other details reveal the extent of her personal devotion to her community: she and her sisters invented a secret language, to be used in front of strangers, for which she wrote the glossary; she composed a cycle of hymns—words and music—to be sung within the convent by the nuns; her play, **Ordo Virtutum,** was initially composed for their use.

The Disibodenberg was a Benedictine monastery in the Rhine valley, of which only ruins now remain. As such it would have been a self-sufficient community, protected by high walls, within which would have been found gardens and orchards, bakehouse and granary, dormitory, dining hall, kitchen, pantry, guest houses—and, most important, church and cloister, the 'heart of the monastery'.[5] At the time of Hildegard's arrival in 1106 it was 400 years old, but the abbey's female unit—originally a hermitage—had only recently been added. Other young women, attracted by Jutta's reputation for holiness, placed themselves under her direction, and the number of nuns soon grew to eighteen. These tended to be from aristocratic families, usually bringing some money with them as a kind of dowry when they entered the convent. Limited as their education may have been in comparison with what was offered the men, it was much better than any alternatives outside the cloister; indeed, convents at this time were a haven for any woman who was at all intellectually inclined. Hildegard's education included some Latin, the Scriptures and service books, possibly some music—though in her **Vita** she claims to have composed her songs without having had any musical training. But she also was an avid reader and seemed to have had access to a range of texts: she was familiar enough with Boethius' *Consolation of Philosophy* to quote from it freely; her mystical works show a pronounced Neoplatonic influence, though the source for this material is uncertain; her knowledge of the Scriptures was exhaustive, and their influence pervades her writing.

During the monastic revival of the eleventh and twelfth centuries, double houses—monasteries enclosing both men and women—were not unusual, though by the thirteenth century they had for the most part been phased out. Although the actual buildings housing the nuns and monks were separated by distance and interposing structures, the communities were jurisdictionally

one unit, living under the same rule. There were many obvious advantages from the women's point of view; most of the major abbeys had communities for nuns, who were thus able to participate actively in the reform movement, satisfying their interest in both asceticism and study. But of course what happened, as long as men and women were enclosed together, was that the men were seen as superior; authority rested with the abbots, and the women tended to look to the monks for instruction and leadership. However, after she became abbess, Hildegard chose to move her community of nuns to a new location, at Rupertsberg. She was perhaps eccentric in her desire for independence, but her decision was evidently the right one, as her community grew and flourished after its secession.

The purpose of a monastic community's self-sufficiency was to avoid the distractions and entanglements, not to mention the corruption, of the outer world. Within the double houses rules of claustration differed, and were stricter for women than for men, the underlying assumption being that the women were more susceptible to temptation. In the strictest cases the rule was evidently so restrictive that women were only allowed to leave to be taken to the cemetery. But in both England and Germany claustration tended to be less firmly enforced; women could take part in pilgrimages, visit and be visited by their families. As an administrator Hildegard would have had even more freedom than usual. In other words, she had the advantages of the structure and security provided by her community without being immobilized; she travelled extensively in both Germany and France, visiting and preaching at numerous monastic communities along the way.[6]

The Benedictine schedule, which was minutely regulated, was based upon two central ideals: labour and communality. Personal property and privacy were supposedly non-existent (monastics were to 'claim no dominion even over their own bodies or wills'); meals, prayer, work all were all done together.[7]

Labour was to occupy a specific number of hours each day (St Benedict originally specified six); for the women in Hildegard's monastery this would have involved traditional work such as spinning and weaving: while the particular purpose of manual labour was to imitate the lives of the Apostles, it was also seen as an essential antidote to idleness, the great danger for any enclosed religious. Occasionally the nuns were occupied in copying manuscripts. Hildegard herself was employed in nursing when at the Disibodenberg, but later, at Rupertsberg, her group was noted for its work in manuscript illumination, of which Hildegard's own masterpieces are an outstanding example.[8]

Days for the Benedictines were organized around periods of communal prayer, which took place at three-hour intervals, even during the night. The *Rule* spelled out in meticulous detail which psalms should be sung at what hours, and on which days, and this order was strictly followed. Details ranging from the discipline of a disobedient member to the appropriate quantities of bread and wine to be consumed at dinner were also spelled out. Thus, clearly, the sense of order, stability, and dependable routine was an important part of the Benedictine life, probably a central reason for the survival of the monastic tradition during the chaotic period following the fall of the Roman Empire.[9] The commitment to study, considered an essential part of daily life, not only meant that the Benedictine houses were frequently responsible for rescuing classical knowledge that had been threatened with extinction during the preceding centuries, but also that the individual members of the community were provided with the opportunity for a rich intellectual life; there was 'great scope for local talent and learning'.[10]

It is not surprising that Hildegard would have been satisfied with this life; for someone who had been buffeted by spiritual and physical extremes since earliest childhood, the security and regularity of the Benedictine system would have been profoundly reassuring. The discipline too must have been welcome, providing the structure necessary to develop the confidence and personal strength upon which she would so frequently have to rely in her later career. And for someone as extraordinarily intelligent as Hildegard, who, as a woman, might otherwise have had no access to formal education, the scholarly opportunities would have been irresistible.

Hildegard seems to have been born in the right place at the right time, in a number of ways. A new spiritual emphasis within the Benedictine movement, originally inspired by St Anselm in the previous century, served to make her monastic environment particularly appropriate for her. To the letter of the *Rule,* which had tended to limit itself to questions of structure and discipline, Anselm brought a new dimension. He wrote of the ideal of spiritual development, of inner growth—of what could be described as a new kind of enclosure, within the mind, that would further insulate the soul from the confusions of the world and allow it to be closer to God. His emphasis was not in conflict with the old *Rule,* which had assumed that the personal relationship between God and the soul would progress naturally if the requisite humility and obedience were adhered to. But Anselm's contribution spoke much more explicitly of an intense, personal relationship with God, opening the way for an increased emphasis on individual meditation and, eventually, the visionary experience.[11] Dedicated as Hildegard was to the order and stability of the Benedictine life, this added element must, as it gave validity to her visions, have made it even more appealing. The progress by which she came to confess to others her inner visions was gradual, but

in the meantime her personal tranquility must have been greatly increased by this assurance.

St Anselm's innovations were foreshadowings of the twelfth-century renaissance, which is perhaps too often described in glowing generalities, but which nonetheless does seem to have been a period of remarkable spiritual and literary flowering, of renewed optimism, confidence in the individual, and emphasis on love. Generally this was a period of enormous expansion and influence for the reformed monasteries; the spirit of inquiry and intellectual growth was guided by renewed confidence in Christian faith and ideals, by a new respect for the intensity of the personal religious experience to be found in the monastic life. The church as a moral force gained enormous credibility.[12]

The tenth century had been a period of consolidation for medieval Germany: pagans to the east had been quelled or converted, to the west the kingdom of Burgundy annexed. The German emperor was considered to be the leader of the Western world, and he had absolute control over the church, its lands and officials. But in the next century, during Hildegard's lifetime, this control faltered. Religious leaders felt that lay control was inappropriate, that the superiority of church over state ought to be entrenched. Pope Gregory VII (1073-85) had greatly enhanced the papal image and actual power, and supporters of papal supremacy now urged increased power for all members of the church.[13]

In the middle of the twelfth century, however, the church's newly won credibility was jeopardized by a papal schism, and there was widespread ecclesiastical squabbling within Germany; here again Hildegard was very much in the right place. Deeply troubled by this pervasive instability, she spoke out fearlessly and her voice emerged as that of a serious and greatly respected social reformer. She believed that it was the responsibility of the church to act as 'regenerator to society', that the cure for social ills was 'more active faith, a higher standard of moral conduct'.[14] The king, Frederick Barbarossa (1152-1190), was a strong ruler, who endeavoured to keep the German church under his control; here he fell out with Hildegard, since they supported different candidates for the papacy. Acting as God's mouthpiece, she wrote him a letter expressing fierce condemnation of his stand, blaming him for perpetuating the schism, warning him in apocalyptic language of his error and of the punishment to come: 'Woe, woe upon the evildoing of the unjust who scorn me! Hear this, king, if you would live—else my sword will pierce through you!'

Frederick was not the only powerbroker to be challenged by Hildegard. She also admonished the archbishop of Mainz, predicting his imminent fall (her prophecy here, as was often the case, came true:

Heinrich was soon deposed and exiled).[15] Certain as she was that she was speaking for God, she did not euphemize no matter how powerful the antagonist. It is perhaps surprising that as a woman she could criticize her antagonists so unreservedly without fear of reprisal (not that this would have deterred her); her evident immunity arose at least in part from the fact of her visionary writings having been given the papal seal of approval, by Eugenius III, at the synod of Trier in 1147—he recognized her *Scivias* as being divinely inspired and encouraged her to continue recording her visions as they came to her.[16]

Hildegard was not one to let obstacles stand in the way of her iron will and passionate sense of purpose; so if circumstances did not favour her cause, she tried to ignore them. One of the most remarkable of her characteristics is what appears to be an effective imperviousness to the potent medieval tradition of antifeminism. The classical idea of woman as defective male was augmented by the Middle Ages' view of her as moral cripple: if Eve had not disobeyed, we would all still be in the Garden of Eden. Disobedience was Eve's worst sin, but only one of many. Her defective reason was passed along, with the result that all her daughters were also more prone to vice. Hildegard's French contemporary, Andreas the Chaplain, articulated a particularly comprehensive, and enthusiastic, view of female weakness:

> according to the nature of [her] sex . . . every woman is by nature a miser, . . . she is also envious and a slanderer of other women, greedy, a slave to her belly, inconstant, fickle in her speech, disobedient and impatient of restraint, spotted with the sin of pride . . . , a liar, a drunkard, a babbler, no keeper of secrets, too much given to wantonness, prone to every evil, and never loving any man in her heart.[17]

Andreas was, of course, echoing ideas that had been promoted by the Church Fathers (whose works, incidentally, were read aloud at mealtimes in Benedictine houses). John Chrysostom's view—'the woman taught once, and ruined all . . . The sex is weak and fickle . . . The whole female race transgressed'—echoes Tertullian's question: 'Do you not know that you are Eve? . . . God's sentence still hangs over all your sex and his punishment weighs down upon you . . . '. Women were 'at once repulsive and fatally attractive': life the corner of the dress, observes Jerome, and you will find the tip of the tail. For men, perhaps the obvious solution was to avoid their corrupting presence entirely; for women, the only really safe virtue was chastity; such was their nature that if they actually tried to do anything, they could not help but sin.[18]

An exchange of letters between Hildegard and a Rhineland *magistra* shows how liberated Hildegard could be from this depressing idea of woman's baseness. She had been chided by a fellow administrator, Tenxwind of Andernach, for allowing her nuns to dress up on holidays: not only did they don white gowns and veils, but they adorned their heads with tiaras. In justifying her policy, Hildegard (who was not given to admitting that she was wrong) argued that as virgins, her sisters were untainted by the Fall; retaining 'the simplicity and beautiful integrity of paradise', they were permitted 'bridal splendour'.[19] (*Scivias* portrays a chorus of virgins similarly 'adorned with gold and gems. Some of these had their heads veiled in white, adorned with a gold circlet', signifying that 'they all shine before God more brightly than the sun does on earth; . . . and so are adorned beautifully with the highest wisdom'.)[20]

Hildegard's imagery, if not her policy, is in this case comfortably traditional, as the use of the explicitly nuptial metaphor to describe the relationship between the virgin soul and Christ went back at least as far as the third century.[21] Hildegard is ultimately drawing upon the triumphant description of the New Jerusalem as found in the *Revelation* of St John the Divine (VII, 4 ff.; XIV, 1 ff.), by implication placing her sisters in the blessed, white-robed company which accompanies the Lamb in the heavenly city. And this is the same image that was to be so beautifully elaborated two centuries later by the fourteenth-century *Pearl*-poet at the culmination of his vision, when the bereaved dreamer sees his lost daughter amongst the heavenly company:

> This noble city of rich emprise
> Had suddenly a full array
> Of virgins all in the same guise
> As did my blessed one display,
> And all were crowned in the same way,
> Adorned in pearl and raiment white.
>
> (Þis noble cite of ryche enpresse
> Watȝ sodaynly ful wythouten sommoun
> Of such vergyneȝ in þe same gyse
> Þat watȝ my blysful anvnder croun
> & coronde wern alle of þe same fasoun
> Depaynt in perleȝ & wedeȝ qwyte . . .)[22]

Hildegard might be said to have taken liberties with the apocalyptic material in several ways: however imminent she may have thought it to be, the day of judgement had yet to arrive; her sisters were still very much alive and well; and the decision as to who will finally comprise the chosen company in the heavenly city was not hers to make. Yet it is difficult not to rejoice in Hildegard's courageous defiance of the gloomy, antifeminist tradition by which she was surrounded. Her view of her community of women was confident, proud, joyful: they were a splendid company, worthy to honour God on the special holy days with their beauty rather than their penitence; they were not so morally fragile that the donning of lovely garments as an expression of love for their Creator would tempt them to vanity.

In many other ways Hildegard projects a rare confidence in women's power; there is no sense that she equates strength in women with danger, nor does she see a powerful 'good' woman as a second-best man. Her visionary treatises are peopled—even sustained— by majestic female figures. Synagogue, for example, is 'mother of the incarnation of the Word of God', a tall woman who carries in her lap and arms the Old Testament prophets—'in her heart stood Abraham and in her breast Moses'.[23] Ecclesia, wearing a gem-studded dress and sandals of onyx, gazes heavenward with a radiant face. The 'puella' Caritas, Hildegard's representation of heavenly love, with golden sandals and 'a cloak whiter than snow, brighter than the stars', embraces the sun and the moon.[24]

Hildegard's confidence in women's potential for positive power made her community, even at the Disibodenberg, a uniquely exciting place for religious women to be. As her reputation spread, she attracted more followers; the growing ranks, along with the longing for a fuller independence, seemed to point to expansion. Then in 1148 she received a heavenly command to undertake this move, and establish an independent convent at Rupertsberg, near Bingen.[25] The Benedictine enshrinement of obedience might have been a major obstacle at this point, for as the abbot was God's representative, utter obedience was owed him; and when Hildegard made this proposal to Kuno, her abbot, he rejected it categorically. The presence of Hildegard and her group at the Disibodenberg was desirable for a number of reasons (not the least of which were her fame and the nun's dowries), and, further, he felt that the proposed location was unpromising (evidently the site was arid and deserted). On learning that Kuno opposed her decision, Hildegard's response was hardly that of the docile handmaid: she assumed a rock-like rigidity from which she could not be moved, and lay 'tanquam saxea rupes'—like a rock made of stone—until the stymied abbot finally surrendered and granted her permission.

However much divine aid Hildegard may have received in achieving this state of petrification—she describes herself as having been struck down as with an illness—it is to be assumed that her own fierce will was also a considerable asset. She was sure she would be following God's command in making the move, and this certainty overrode Kuno's temporal authority. She saw herself as comparable to Moses leading his people towards the promised land; when Kuno resisted her efforts, she did not hesitate to compare him and his followers to the wicked Amalekites, foes of the Israelites in the desert and 'from generation to generation' thereafter (*Exodus,* XVII, 8-16). The move to Rupertsberg, when it finally took place in 1150, was felicitous; the convent expanded to include some fifty women—it even had running water!—and was enriched by the decision of various wealthy families to bury their dead within its grounds. Its success was such that Hildegard s200equently set up a second house across the river at Eibingen to which she regularly travelled by boat.

Generally we have no information as to Hildegard's private friendships, but she did have a 'favourite' nun, Richardis von Stade, who seems to have been a sort of personal secretary, and to whom she was particularly attached. However, through the influence of Richardis' brother, the archbishop Hartwig, her friend was offered a prestigious position as abbess at another convent. Hildegard, believing that Richardis' motivation for accepting promotion was based on ambition, tried every means to dissuade her. In her correspondence with Hartwig she was more than liberal with her insults, comparing him to the proud Nebuchadnezzar— punished by God for his presumption by being driven mad—and a 'simoniac', one of that despised species of sinners who traded in ecclesiastical offices, and who were consigned by Dante to the eighth circle of hell. She even appealed to Pope Eugenius in her attempt to block the appointment. But neither insult nor entreaty sufficed to keep her friend with her. Richardis departed; and although she eventually regretted her decision, she became ill before she was able to rejoin Hildegard, and died in 1152. This sad loss is an isolated instance of the failure of Hildegard's will, but she was able to accept it because of her belief that God needed Richardis more than she did; and she even wrote an eloquent letter of consolation to Hartwig.[26]

A final episode, more than 25 years later, shows Hildegard (by now an octogenarian) still in full possession of her great courage and independence. She had agreed to allow a nobleman to be buried in the convent cemetery, which was in itself hardly unusual; the catch was that he was generally thought to have died excommunicate. However, Hildegard knew that he had been given the last rites before his death, and had herself received a divine command to permit the burial. Her superiors ordered that the body be exhumed; Hildegard's response was to make the sign of the cross over the grave with her staff, and obscure the outline of the grave so that no one would be able to disturb it. As punishment for this defiance, the entire community was excommunicated. This was a terrible privation, as mass could not be performed nor communion taken; perhaps most painful of all for the sisters was the prohibition against singing. At length Hildegard appealed to a higher ecclesiastical authority, who arranged for the interdict to be lifted. The stalemate was thus resolved, but not because of Hildegard's capitulation; again, as God's agent, she evidently did not consider this to be an option—nothing 'would let her conscience be crushed by clerical legalism'.[27]

These characteristic anecdotes have to do with Hildegard's active life as an administrator, which was certainly of major importance to her. But far more vital was her inner spiritual existence, the sphere of her visionary life. As we know, she had been subject to intense spiritual experiences from earliest childhood; uncertain as to their significance, worried that others would think her abnormal or presumptuous, she kept them largely to herself. However, shortly after she was elected abbess, in 1140, 'when I was forty-two years and seven months old', a dramatic change occurred. As she reports in **Scivias,** 'a fiery light of exceeding brilliance came and permeated my whole brain, and inflamed my whole heart and my whole breast, not like a burning but like a warming flame, as the sun warms anything its rays touch'; a celestial voice instructed her to 'say and write what you see and hear . . . as you see and hear them on high in the heavenly places in the wonders of God.'[28] Hildegard says that, subsequently, she had the power to understand the meaning of 'the psaltery, . . . the evangelists and the volumes of the Old and New Testament'.

From this point on, although she continues to refer to herself as 'paupercula feminea forma'—a poor little figure of a woman—Hildegard's actions seem to indicate that her self-doubt has been dispelled to a significant degree. She now sees herself as the mouthpiece of God, and her role in the process of salvation—for as much of the world as she can manage to reach—is proportionately evident. Despite this new confidence, and an abiding desire to have things her own way, Hildegard's concern is never for herself: whether she is writing hymns, or books on medicine, or mystical treatises, her aim is always to share with those around her, to enhance their spiritual elevation; her generosity is prodigious.

Hildegard's transcendence of self-doubt may have been facilitated by the acquisition of a new model, the prophetic Old Testament figure of Sapientia: 'The wisdom that grants discernment is crying aloud . . . There she stands, on some high vantage-point by the public way . . . or at the city's approach . . . making proclamation. To every man, high and low, her voice calls: Here is better counsel for the simpleton; O foolish hearts, take warning! I have matters of high moment to unfold . . . A tongue that speaks truth, lips that scorn impiety; here all is sound doctrine' (*Proverbs* VIII, 1-8). Such an identification is what we would by now expect: Hildegard selects for emulation an impressive, active figure of authority—one who avers that 'the Lord made me his when first he went about his work, . . . before his creation began' (*Proverbs* VIII, 22)—as the most effective means, herself, of becoming God's adjutant and working his will. Another important biblical figure with whom she identifies—undeterred by sexual difference—is St John the Divine, who was similarly commanded to 'Write down thy vision of what now is, and what must befall thereafter' (*Revelation*, I, 19). . . . Hildegard's use of apocalyptic imagery in her writings is pervasive; indeed, her kind of prophetic work has been said to be 'largely founded on the Apcalypse.'[29]

After hearing the command of the celestial voice, her obligation to write was imperative. As Hildegard was insistent that her words, as they came directly from God, not be altered at all, she was fortunate in finding a scribe, Volmar, who faithfully recorded every detail of her account, and who stayed with her throughout most of her life. In an illustration from the **Book of Divine Works,** Volmar can be seen in the act of transcription, as Hildegard receives her divine inspiration. Hildegard seems to be recording her revelation directly onto a set of wax tablets; from these Volmar may later have made his permanent copy. Any temptation to attribute a measure of Hildegard's eloquence to Volmar's intervention is dispelled by a letter that she composed after his death, which shows the sophistication of what must be her own prose style: 'she uses rhetoric, figures of speech, complex and fluent sentences with ease'.[30]

Notes

[1] See Peter Dronke, *Women Writers of the Middle Ages* (Cambridge, 1984), pp. 144-201; Hildegard of Bingen, *Book of Divine Works with Letters and Songs,* ed, Matthew Fox, (Santa Fe, New Mexico, 1987), pp. ix-xix; Rufus Jones, *The Flowering of Mysticism* (1939, repr. New York, 1971), pp. 43-44.

[2] For the *Vita* and letters see *Hildegardis abbatissae Opera omnia* in *Patrologiae cursus completus, Ser. Latina* 197, 91-140, ed. J.-P. Migne (Paris, 1882).

[3] C. Singer (*From Magic to Science,* New York, 1958) and O. Sacks (*Migraine: Understanding a Common Disorder,* Berkeley, 1985) explore the connection between Hildegard's afflictions and migraine headaches.

[4] For discussions of Hildegard's life see, in addition to Dronke (*op. cit.*), Lena Eckenstein, *Women Under Monasticism* (Cambridge, 1896), Dom Philibert Schmitz, *Histoire de l'Ordre de Saint-Benoît,* 'Les Moniales', tome VII (Maredsous, 1956), Kent Kraft's essay in *Medieval Women Writers,* ed. Katharina M. Wilson (Athens, Georgia, 1984), *Sister of Wisdom: St. Hildegard's Theology of the Feminine,* Barbara Newman (Berkeley and Los Angeles, 1987), Fox's introduction in *Book of Divine Works* (*op. cit.*).

[5] Lowrie J. Daly, *Benedictine Monasticism, Its Formation and Development Through the 12th Century* (New York, 1965), p. 196. For further information on the Benedictine monastic tradition, see also Cuthbert Butler, *Benedictine Monachism,* 2nd ed. (London, 1924), Schmitz (*op. cit.*), *The Rule of St. Benedict,* trans. and

intro. by Cardinal Gasquet (New York, 1966), *The Rule of St. Benedict,* ed. Timothy Fry, O.S.B. (Collegeville, Minnesota, 1980).

[6] Schmitz *(op. cit.),* tome VII, p. 235. See also Jane Tibbetts Schulenburg, 'Strict Active Enclosure and its Effects on the Female Monastic Experience', in *Distant Echoes,* ed. J.A. Nichols and L. T. Shank (Kalamazoo, Michigan, 1984).

[7] See Gasquet *(op. cit).* This model was based on the ideal set down in the *Acts of the Apostles* (IV, 31ff.): 'And when they had prayed . . . they were all filled with the Holy Ghost . . . And the multitude of them that believed were of one heart and of one soul; . . . they had all things in common'.

[8] According to Schmitz *(op. cit.),* tome VII, p. 271, 'la miniature' was widely practised in the German houses, 'notamment . . . à l'entourage de Hildegard'.

[9] Praised both for its brevity and its broadness of vision, Benedict's *Rule* has been described as the 'most complete and masterful synthesis of monastic tradition' (Fry, *op. cit.,* p. 90).

[10] R.W. Southern, *The Making of the Middle Ages* (New Haven and London, 1961), p. 185.

[11] See Southern *(op. cit.),* p. 226 and ff.

[12] See, for example, Joseph R. Strayer, *Western Europe in the Middle Ages* (New York, 1955), pp. 91 ff., and Southern *(op. cit.), passim.*

[13] See Josef Fleckenstein, trans. Bernard S. Smith, *Early Medieval Germany* (New York, 1978), pp. 190 ff.; cf. also J.B. Gillingham, *The Kingdom of Germany in the High Middle Ages (900-1200)* (London, 1971), and Alfred Haverkamp, trans. H. Braun and R. Mortimer, *Medieval Germany (1056-1273)* (London, 1990).

[14] Eckenstein *(op. cit.),* pp. 256 ff.

[15] Eckenstein, Dronke and others discuss this incident. Hildegard's reputation as a prophet led to her being nicknamed 'the Rhenish sybil', and lasted into the sixteenth century. She would regularly be cited, along with famous prophetic figures such as the Sybils, St Bridget, Joachim, and Gamaleon, when true authority was sought, or when a particular judgment (e.g. for or against a particular ruler) was desired (see Marjorie Reeves, *The Influence of Prophecy in the Later Middle Ages,* Oxford, 1969).

[16] St Bernard, with whom Hildegard corresponded, had been similarly impressed, and himself asked that she pray for him and his community: 'Wherefore I entreat and humbly pray that you would make remembrance of me before God and of those who are joined with me in spiritual society. I trust that you are united to God in the Spirit'. (*Life and Works of St. Bernard,* ed. Dom John Mabillon, vol. 2, p. 915).

[17] Andreas Capellanus, *The Art of Courtly Love,* trans. John Jay Parry (New York, 1969), p. 201.

[18] See O'Faolain and Martines *(op. cit.),* pp. 129 ff. for the Chrysostom and Tertullian quotes. For a discussion of St Jerome and the ideal of chastity see Ann McMillan's introduction to her translation of the *Legend of Good Women* (Houston, Texas, 1987); also Eileen Power's 'The Position of Women' in *The Legacy of the Middle Ages* (ed. G.C. Crump and E.F. Jacob, Oxford, 1926, pp. 401 ff.), in which she discusses the growth of the parallel ideas of woman as temptress, and of chastity as the definition of female virtue and honour.

[19] Dronke *(op. cit.),* p. 166. Hildegard was also criticized by Tenxwind for her exclusion of non-noble women from her convent. She defended her position with citations from the Old Testament and by upholding the traditional type of the 'noble saint'. Thus Tenxwind and Hildegard held opposing views of God: the former's 'pauper Christus' *vs.* Hildegard's '*rex potentissimus . . .* to whom one owes dread and honour' (see Haverkamp, *op. cit.,* p. 191).

[20] Hildegard of Bingen, *Scivias,* II, 5, 7, p. 205; The Classics of Western Spirituality Series, trans. Mother Columba Hart and Jane Bishop, with an introduction by Barbara Newman (New York and Mahwah, 1990); cf. also *Scivias,* trans. Bruce Hozeski (Santa Fe, New Mexico, 1986). The complex role of virginity in the Christian tradition is well analyzed by John Bugge in *Virginitas: An Essay on the History of a Medieval Idea* (The Hague, 1975): humans were meant by nature to be asexual—this was their prelapsarian condition. Sexuality was the result of the Fall, before which life in Eden was comparable to that of angels; virginity could represent, and was an attempt to recreate, the angelic life on earth. Thus the souls of virgins, whether male or female, could be seen as belonging to a higher rank than others, however virtuous those others may have been. See also Newman *(op. cit.),* pp. 221-2.

[21] See Bugge *(op. cit.),* pp. 61 ff., who notes that as early as the fourth century the rite of consecration for Christian female virgins was similar to the nuptial ceremony.

[22] *The Pearl,* trans. Sara de Ford (Northbrook, Illinois, 1967), p. 93. It should be pointed out that the gender of St John's apocalyptic company is not specified, while that of the *Pearl*-poet seems undeniably feminine. As the figure of Christ came, in the course of the Middle Ages, to be seen in more explicitly human terms, the

nuptial image of the Bride/soul's union with him-as-Bridegroom tended to be applied more narrowly to female virgins (see Bugge, *op. cit.,* p. 66).

[23] *Scivias* (Hart and Bishop), I, 5, p. 133.

[24] See Dronke *(op. cit.),* pp. 170 ff.; he notes that Hildegard was 'the first of the women mystics to personify love as a beautiful woman'.

[25] See Hildegard's *Vita (op. cit.) PL* 197.96b-97a. Cf. Kent Kraft, in Wilson *(op. cit.),* pp. 110-11, and Dronke *(op. cit.),* pp. 150 ff.

[26] See Dronke *(op. cit.),* pp. 150 ff. and Newman *(op. cit.),* pp. 222 ff.

[27] Dronke here compares Hildegard's resolution to that of Antigone, defying the unjust decree of Creon. He also quotes her directly on the question of whether she should bow to the ecclesiastical authorities: 'I saw in my soul that if we followed their command and exposed the corpse, such an expulsion would threaten our home with great danger, like a vast blackness—it would envelop like a dark cloud that looms before tempests and thunderstorms . . . [We did not want to] seem to injure Christ's sacraments . . . , yet, so as not to be wholly disobedient, we have till now ceased singing the songs of divine praise, in accordance with the interdict, and have abstained from partaking of the body of the Lord' *(op. cit.),* pp. 195 ff.

[28] *Scivias* (Hart and Bishop), 'Declaration', pp. 59-61; also Eckenstein *(op. cit.),* p. 264.

[29] Eckenstein *(op. cit.),* p. 260.

[30] Dronke *(op. cit.),* p. 195.

Samuel Lyndon Gladden (essay date 1993)

SOURCE: Samuel Lyndon Gladden, "Hildegard's Awakening: A Self-Portrait of Disruptive Excess," in *Representations of the Middle Ages*, edited by Bonnie Wheeler, Academia Press, 1993, pp. 217-33.

[*In the following essay, Gladden challenges the notion (promoted by Hildegard herself) that Hildegard was a passive agent of God's will whose writings merely record divine truth as it was imparted to her. Gladden argues that "Hildegard's role as an active, subjective editor of God's message becomes clear" and attempts to demonstrate that Hildegard "knowingly and willfully encodes a feminine voice in the midst of what appears to be the message of an obviously male-identified God."*]

The twelfth-century German mystic Hildegard of Bingen is perhaps best known for her extraordinary relationship with God, a relationship which apparently enabled Hildegard to communicate directly the voice and words of God to humans. Appearing to Hildegard in a series of visions, God made clear his desire that the holy woman communicate all which she saw and heard and, further, that she refrain from offering any sort of interference—whether that interference take the form of interpretation, explanation, or intentional editing—so that God's message might be delivered intact, so to speak, without the taint of mortal desire. *Scivias,* a text written between 1141 and 1151 and which has become one of Hildegard's most celebrated works, is a document whose words describe Hildegard's visions and whose illuminations provide a sort of window into what Hildegard saw when she received these visions.[1] In the 'Declaration' which opens *Scivias,* Hildegard describes a moment Fox refers to as her 'awakening,' and the illumination corresponding to this moment Fox entitles Hildegard's 'Self-Portrait'.[2] It is this moment of awakening which interests me, and it is the correspondence between the text describing this vision and the illumination itself upon which I will focus in arguing that Hildegard's awakening—a moment almost always read without question as an instance of absolute passivity, of the absence of subjectivity, of, in short, what many might call 'true' femininity—is actually a moment in which Hildegard knowingly and willfully encodes a feminine voice in the midst of what appears to be the message of an obviously male-identified God.

Recent attention to the life and work of Hildegard of Bingen has frequently subscribed to a feminist agenda. The importance of Newman's *Sister of Wisdom* in the context of such concerns cannot be underestimated; that text does much to explore the ramifications of Hildegard's theology for women, specifically for women trapped in patriarchal social and religious systems. One recent discussion of Hildegard in terms of sex, gender, and feminist theory is Allen's 'Hildegard of Bingen's Philosophy of Sex Identity', which draws on the mystic's text *Causae et curae* to describe what Allen refers to as Hildegard's 'phenomenology' of sex identity.[3] Allen describes Hildegard's notion of four distinct kinds of men and women, and she emphasizes Hildegard's insistence that sex identity is a primary means of self-identification which is not altered by death: Hildegard claims in *Scivias* that 'all the people rose up with their members whole, with their bodies whole, and with their own sex'.[4] Allen proves convincingly that 'Hildegard . . . argued that the soul was fully integrated with the body' and that the mystic 'seems to have reached continually toward a balanced view of sex identity which would avoid both the devaluation of the body found in Platonic tradition *and the devaluation of the female* found in Aristotelian tradition'.[5]

In another recent feminist reading of Hildegard of Bingen Newman argues that 'to account for the exceptional claims of a woman like Hildegard, we need to consider both the dynamics of mystical illumination per se and its refraction through the cultural and psychological prism of gender'.[6] Newman identifies three specific goals which Hildegard's visions allowed her to realize: 'a direct experience of God, a source of unmediated truth, *and a form of public validation*'.[7] Newman makes clear that Hildegard was aware of the potential for controversy surrounding a female visionary in a patriarchal age; she quotes Hildegard as remarking that 'now, to the scandal of men, women are prophesying'.[8] Newman assesses the ultimate importance of Hildegard's visions and concludes that, in addition to serving as a medium of divine inspiration, these remarkable experiences stood as 'a source of *vindication* against real or potential opponents'.[9] Finally, Newman acknowledges the almost-clichéd 'I am not worthy' stance of 'poor little female' mystics and concludes that 'many of their visions obliquely sanctioned a role reversal by presenting men as negligent or weak, women as prophetic or powerful, and aspects of God as feminine'.[10]

But the power and significance of the feminine is certainly not a new concern in scholarship relating to Hildegard of Bingen. Indeed, Hildegard may rightfully be called an early proponent of women's rights, and her direct refusals to conform to masculine authority are well-documented. With the spread of Hildegard's fame as a visionary—which attracted the approval of pope Eugenius III, who read parts of the then-incomplete *Scivias* to the prelates at the synod at Trier in 1147-8—the mystic and her female followers expressed a desire to leave the cramped quarters of St Disibod and to establish their own exclusively-female holy community at Rupertsberg, near Bingen.[11] The monks of St Disibod refused to allow Hildegard such freedom, in part because her fame ensured their monastery a certain amount of economic stability. Hildegard became gravely ill and claimed she had been stricken down by God in order that the monks might recognize her desire as divinely authorized; in fact, her body became so inexplicably heavy that the monks could not physically lift her from her sickbed. Finally, they granted her leave to establish her own community at Rupertsberg.

Many years later, this community was again the focus of the harsh disapproval of the church—read, of male—authority. The year before she died, Hildegard and her monastery were placed under interdict because Hildegard had allowed the body of an excommunicate to be buried on the grounds.[12] Church authority demanded the exhumation and relocation of the body; Hildegard refused, saying the deceased had confessed his sins before death. To prevent her sisters from caving in to (male) authority, Hildegard went to the cem-

etery herself and removed all signs marking the place of burial. Under this interdiction, her monastery was denied the pleasure of worshipping through music, a kind of text Hildegard felt was particularly inseparable from the language of spirituality.[13] Hildegard admonished church authority by writing that 'those who choose to silence music . . . will go to a place where they will be "without the company of the angelic songs of praises in heaven"'.[14] Further, she attacked the archbishop of Mainz, saying to him that 'the spirit of God, full of zeal, says: pastors, lament and mourn at this time, because you do not know what you do, when you squander offices, whose source is God, for financial gain and to please the foolishness of wicked men, who have no fear of God'.[15] Before Hildegard's death, the interdict was finally removed, but, perhaps as a result of her stern refusals to bow to what she seems to have perceived as misguided (male) authority, repeated attempts to canonize her have failed.[16]

In her preface to the Paulist Press edition of *Scivias,* Bynum insists that not only are Hildegard's visions political, but, like all of Hildegard's work, they are also unique in their attention to female bodily phenomena, such as menstrual cramps and feminine sexuality.[17] Further, it should be noted that Hildegard was an early gynecologist and produced a text on the subject, *Causae et curae,* as a supplement to her 'major scientific and medical encyclopedia, *Nine Books on the Subtleties of Different Kinds of Creatures*'.[18] In contextualizing *Scivias* within the canon of medieval mystic literature, Bynum asks the following question: 'Did medieval women speak with their own voices and out of their own experience, or is their work merely the inscription of the misogynist and patriarchal values of the dominant religious tradition?'[19] Later, Bynum asks whether 'phrases such as Hildegard's repeated assertion of female inferiority [can] really be accepted as women's own, even when penned or dictated by the woman herself?'.[20] Bynum's answer is persuasive: she notes that female writing may often be shaped by fear and may serve both as a passive service *for* others *and* as 'audacious self-integration',[21] that is, a bold assertion of the feminine subject into a text seemingly directed by and for masculine empowerment.

In assessing these complaints of weakness and inability which pervade Hildegard's texts, one must not neglect the history of writings by other male and female mystics and prophets who make similar protestations. Such positions of weakness, humility, shame, and unworthiness may be called 'feminine' because they imply oppression, but males may occupy these 'feminine' positions as well as females. Consider, for example, the story of Jeremiah:

> Then the word of the Lord came unto me, saying, 'Before I formed thee in the belly I knew thee; and before thou camest forth out of the womb I sanctified

thee, and I ordained thee a prophet unto the nations.'
Then said I, 'Ah, Lord God! behold, I cannot speak:
for I am a child.' . . . Then the Lord put forth his
hand, and touched my mouth. And the Lord said
unto me, 'Behold, I have put my words in thy
mouth.'[22]

Clearly, postures of utter submissiveness, of the inability to speak of one's own accord, of complete passivity and unworthiness, are ones frequently occupied by
individuals claiming to act as messengers of God. Thus
Hildegard's unworthiness, her passivity, is consistent
with the 'feminine' nature of a long line of prophets
and mystics who came before and after her.

Newman argues that Hildegard's theological message—
specifically, the text of *Scivias*—was both endorsed
and protected by men.[23] Further, she suggests,
'[Hildegard's] posture as a simple, unlearned person
was not intended to deceive; aside from reinforcing
her prophetic persona, it constitutes an implicit critique of the learned clerics whose negligence,
[Hildegard] believed, had necessitated her mission'.[24]
In other words, Hildegard assumed the position of an
unworthy woman because she felt the supposedly
worthy males of the church had failed to communicate
effectively, fully, and truthfully, the message of God.
In her assessment of the historical reception of *Scivias,*
Newman makes clear that what she calls 'more virile'—that is, more patriarchal—ages denied Hildegard's
authorship or contribution to the text completely, thus
effectively erasing not only the importance of
Hildegard's participation in the material production of
this document but also her crucial contribution to the
production of its meaning; these 'more virile' ages have
celebrated in her place the one incorrectly perceived to
be the *only* author of *Scivias*—God.[25] Newman's own
assessment of the reception of this text—she says, 'If
Hildegard had been a male theologian, her *Scivias*
would have been considered one of the most important
early medieval *summas'*—again makes clear two key
points about the treatment of this early feminine text
by a patriarchal culture: first, that *Scivias* is a document whose first-person narrative specifically denies
the intervention of a subjective, feminine voice in its
authorship; second, that the reception of *Scivias* by
generations of readers has perpetuated this erasure of
a feminine voice amidst its seemingly masculine—that
is, its God-centered—message.[26]

Newman's argument in *Sister of Wisdom* is particularly relevant to my own assessment of the subversive
agenda of Hildegard's supposed 'lowly woman' status.
First, female powerlessness in Hildegard's work is not
necessarily negative; Newman reminds us that the
'power through powerlessness' agenda is commonly
encouraged by Christianity.[27] Newman also indicates
that Hildegard's notion of female inferiority is not
meant to undercut her own understanding of, and

emphasis on, the sexual nature of God; Hildegard
maintained that God was half-masculine and half-femi-
nine and that these halves remained in perfect balance,
neither one becoming more important or more dominant than the other.[28] Finally, Newman provides another example of female 'power through powerlessness' in the case of Catherine of Siena who 'was told
[by her confessor] that she need not wear male garb
because God could use her, precisely as a woman, in
order to shame unworthy men'.[29] I would add to this
that God's 'use' of Catherine of Siena—in itself interesting in light of feminism's concern with the politics
of power—is dependent upon the patriarchal culture in
which Catherine lived. That is, her ability to 'shame'
men arose from a social condition in which females
always already signified less than males; if a woman
such as Catherine of Siena was able to shame men,
then this was a double shame, because it involved an
'unnatural' violation of a gender hierarchy in which
man was presumed always to be *better* than woman.

The contemporary French philosopher, linguist, psychoanalyst, and feminist theorist Irigaray[30] makes explicit some of the implicit claims of Hildegard: 'I am
trying . . . to go back through the masculine imaginary,
to interpret the way it has reduced [women] to silence,
to muteness or mimicry, and I am attempting, from
that startingpoint and at the same time, to (re)discover
a possible space for the feminine imaginary'.[31] Irigaray
offers a set of questions with which all her work
grapples: She asks, 'How can [women] free themselves
from their expropriation within patriarchal culture?
What questions should they address to its discourse? .
. . How can they "put" these questions so that they will
not be once more "repressed", "censured"? But also
how can they already speak (as) women?'[32] She offers
this possibility: 'by going back through the dominant
discourse. By interrogating men's [supposed] "mastery". By speaking to women. And among women. [But]
can this speaking (as) woman be written? How?'[33]

Irigaray suggests that there is only one 'path' through
which feminine enunciation can take place, the one
she says has been 'historically assigned to the feminine: that of *mimicry*'.[34] Mimesis, a concept Irigaray
co-opts from Plato, may be defined as 'an attempt [first]
to avoid adopting the position of the male subject and
thus perpetuating it; and . . . [second] to avoid recapture within the parameters of a metaphysical system in
which the place of/for the feminine is marked out in
advance'.[35] More simply, mimesis is a process by which
a feminine voice willfully enters into a phallocentric
or patriarchal system of discourse and uses that system
ironically, subverting the discourse and forcing it to
work against itself. During mimicry, the speaking
woman deliberately assumes the feminine style and
posture assigned to her within phallocentric discourse—
that is, the position of a passive, insignificant medium
through whom a masculine message may be transmit-

ted—and, by so doing, the speaking woman uncovers 'the mechanisms by which [phallocentric discourse] exploits her'.[36] Irigaray explains that mimesis 'convert[s] a form of subordination into an affirmation' of feminine subjectivity and thereby enables the feminine to 'thwart' the masculine, phallocentric discourse which it only *pretends* to repeat without censure.[37] Mimesis in the concept of spirituality or religion may result in what Irigaray refers to as a moment of 'disruptive excess', an instance during which a supposedly 'divine' message is exploited by a singular, subjective feminine voice.[38] Instances of disruptive excess confound language and push to the limit the inability of discourse to encapsulate and to convey specific meaning. One might liken an instance of disruptive excess to the proverbial cup which runneth over; disruptive excess may be described as an overflowing of sensory perception, a heightening of physical, mental, and spiritual sensations beyond the descriptive powers of any system of language or discourse which attempts to capture it. Each person involved in such an experience—the prophetic seer as well as those who hear, read, or otherwise re-experience the vision of the seer—is disrupted in the sense that he or she is left to try to make sense of a moment which can never fully be explained. Disruptive excess enables some sort of ecstatic opening in meaning, and this opening immediately disrupts meaning because it can never be made to 'mean' any single, definable thing; meaning is opened, disrupted, and cannot be closed, be made to make 'sense', in such moments of overflow.

Although Newman acknowledges that all of Hildegard's work is 'colored subtly but pervasively by her feminine self-awareness', she implies that such self-awareness is always negative; Newman argues that what she calls Hildegard's 'autobiographical prefaces and endings' focus on feminine weakness and inability and prove beyond a doubt that Hildegard is, indeed, *not* wise and, further, the 'her weakness and foolishness have been empowered by God alone'.[39] But Bynum reads Hildegard's confessions of inability and weakness as ironic: She suggests that 'the low-keyed irony with which Hildegard remainded corrupt clerics that God had been forced to choose an inferior mouthpiece because *they* had fallen so low . . . [has] hardly seemed to all recent interpreters an internalizing of misogyny'.[40]

Irigaray's critique of Freud reminds us that the 'proper' course of action for a female in a patriarchal system is willful sublimation, or the letting go of individual desire.[41] One of the forms common to feminine sublimation is shame; clearly, Hildegard, at least on the surface, appears to be, like Margery Kempe or Julian of Norwich, ashamed of her own inferiority in comparison to the message of the masculine God for whom she claims to speak.[42] Yet even under the rule of patriarchy, there is a means of momentary escape from feminine sublimation: Irigaray contends that a specifi-

cally feminine desire—an undeniably feminine existence—can indeed be experienced and expressed in dreams or in other forms of altered consciousness.[43] Clearly, Hildegard's visions remove her from the world in which she lives, and, obviously, these visions may be said to have been experienced in some sort of ecstatic state of altered consciousness.

Newman and Fox both provide evidence that Hildegard's awakening was experienced during a period of extreme illness. Hildegard describes her condition prior to the awakening as one that left her 'without voice, frustrated, [and] physically sick'.[44] Fox maintains that 'in the name of humility *she made herself sick*';[45] Hildegard herself admitted, 'not in stubbornness but in humility, *I refused to write* for so long that *I felt pressed down* under the whip of God into a bed of sickness'.[46] During her illness, God appeared to her and commanded her to write the visions he revealed. Hildegard recounts beginning this task, saying, 'I put my hand to writing. Once I did this, a deep and profound exposition of books came over me!'[47] It is clear that the usually obvious binary relationship between active and passive elements is, here, much more complicated. It is Hildegard's own action, her explicit *refusal* to communicate her visions to the world, that leads to a temporary experience of passivity—of illness—but which ultimately concludes in another period of activity, the writing of the text of *Scivias* and the beginning of her long literary career. Had Hildegard never asserted her own will, had she not initially refused to write these visions, only then might these visions have truly remained without the 'taint' of a feminine voice; however, it is clear that the act of inscription resulted not directly from God's command that Hildegard write but, more significantly, only after Hildegard firmly refused to be so manipulated.[48]

Hildegard explains her reasons for refusing God's explicit command that she write: 'But I, though I saw and heard these things, *refused to write* for a long time *through doubt and bad opinion and the diversity of human words*. . . .'[49] Hildegard's refusal to write is not only an assertion of her own will over God's, but it is an ironic assertion, for it is made indirectly by way of her continual insistence on her own weakness and inability. Yet in contemplating the act of inscription, Hildegard's role as an active, subjective editor of God's message becomes clear: in the explanation for her own delay in writing, Hildegard addresses an important concern of current literary theory: the inability of language to encapsulate thought. Further, her refusal to write becomes the first step in Hildegard's process not merely of editing but also of co-authoring God's message. It is Hildegard who decides which words to use in communicating God's message, and it is she who first inscribes this message into language.

It is true that at the end of the description of her calling, Hildegard reminds her readers that she is not responsible for the message of *Scivias*. She insists that, 'I spoke and wrote these things not by the invention of my heart or that of any other person, but as by the secret mysteries of God I heard and received them in the heavenly places'.[50] On a level of literal meaning, this sentence is an explicit, first-person denial of any claims to authorship or intervention in the text. But this claim is ironic; in fact, it is perhaps the most clear example of Irigarian mimicry in the canon of Hildegard's writing. The fact that her seemingly sincere denial of authorship comes at the end of this vision, after we have already heard the voice of God insisting that Hildegard's contribution to the meaning of the text is insignificant, indicates that, for the reader of *Scivias,* the true voice of authority is Hildegard's. Why else would Hildegard feel the need to make this first-person intrusion at the last possible second in the narrative? Even though God appears to have the last word, so to speak, in the 'Declaration', His words are quoted—appropriated, taken—by Hildegard: 'And again I heard a voice from Heaven saying to me, "Cry out therefore, and write thus!"'[51] The significance of the last sentence lies only secondarily in God's command; the primary function of this sentence is to bolster Hildegard's own position as the ultimate textual authority. 'I spoke, I wrote, I heard' emerges as Hildegard's litany throughout this 'Declaration', and the words of God she recounts are, in my view, merely the skeleton, the footnotes, upon which Hildegard composes the body of *her* vision(s). Obviously, Hildegard's intention in denying authorial intervention is to remind the reader—one could be even stronger and say to *convince* the reader—that she has nothing to do with authorship or with the construction of meaning in this text. But in this very protestation, Hildegard reveals herself as the 'true' author of *Scivias,* the holder of textual authority.

When she was 'in the forty-third year of [her] earthly course', Hildegard heard the voice of God commanding her thus:

> O fragile human, ashes of ashes, and filth of filth!
> . . . since you are timid in speaking, and simple in expounding, and untaught in writing . . . speak and write these things . . . that you see and hear. And write them not by yourself or any other human being, but by the will of Him Who knows, sees, and disposes all things in the secrets of His mysteries.[52]

Two years earlier, Hildegard had experienced a vision which enabled her to understand religious texts and which she took as a sign that her visions were, in fact, legitimate and were not merely ecstatic hallucinations. The illumination of this vision may be shown visually to corroborate my argument that Hildegard's awakening constitutes a moment of disruptive excess, an instance in which a supposedly masculine, divine message is intruded upon by a feminine voice.[53]

Hildegard's awakening is the moment at which this mystic became 'a recipient of the Pentecostal fire'.[54] The monk on the right is Hildegard's secretary, Volmar, who transcribed into grammatically-correct Latin the text of the visions Hildegard dictated to him.[55] Fox notes that the pillars on the left and right of this illumination contain the stick figures of a male and female figure, and he suggests these be read in terms of the Hopi corn man and woman who symbolize fertility and germination.[56] Although this reading is undeniably anachronistic, it does remind us of a set of concerns appropriate to Hildegard's agenda—fertility, germination, and human reproduction. Recall, for example, Bynum's claim in the preface to *Scivias* that all of Hildegard's work is unique in its attention to feminine bodily phenomena.[57] But the imagery of such phenomena is much more explicit in this illumination than mere outlines of stick figures which may or may not represent the Hopi corn man and woman.[58]

I suggest that we regard this illumination not only as an illustration of awakening but also as a representation of birth. Hildegard sits in a near-fetal position—knees drawn up toward midsection, right arm folded inward—and she is enclosed within an arched opening. The pentecostal fire at her head, the fire of inspiration, is blood-red. What we are witnessing is birth. The arched opening is, perhaps, a vagina. The fire at Hildegard's head may symbolize the painful, bloody tearing of the maternal body during birth; one might even go so far as to say that the fire is actually connected to the arched wall around Hildegard's head and, therefore, that it truly suggests the first moment of the painful serration of the lips of the vagina during childbirth.[59] The columns on the left and right of the illumination, the so-called 'corn' man and woman columns, may be regarded as the drawn-up knees of the birthing mother, and the turrets above these columns are clearly representative of breasts. Thus we are looking at a painting that bears a striking resemblance to a birthing mother squatting, her knees drawn up toward her breasts.[60]

It is necessary to acknowledge and to make clear two important facts in light of my reading of this illumination. Late in life, Hildegard admitted that she had been receiving visions long before God commanded her to write: 'From my early childhood, before my bones, nerves, and veins were fully strengthened, I have always seen this vision in my soul, even to the present time, when I am more than seventy years old'.[61] Further, when she was three years old, Hildegard experienced a vision of dazzling light which, at the time, she was too young to understand or to describe.[62] But even more significant in the context of this paper is Hildegard's recollection of her very first vision, a vision she insisted was experienced in her mother's womb. She recounted, 'In my first formation, when in my mother's womb God raised me up with the breath of life, he fixed this vision in my soul'.[63] Hildegard's account of receiving God's vision while in the womb provides a contemporaneous source that corroborates my reading derived from late twentieth-century feminist theory.

The head of the monk Volmar is the only other object penetrating the space of this vaginal arch. Volmar's head is extended unnaturally from his shoulders. Thus, we may be seeing a metaphorical representation of erection, an erection which extends into the arched area and further reminds us that this rounded space is vaginal. Further, the fact that the body of Volmar is excluded from this arched area may be read in terms of Irigaray's notion of mimesis. Hildegard seems to be penning the message of God, a message from the holder of masculine authority—God—to men, the perpetuators of masculine empowerment. But the space of inscription, the vaginal arch through which Hildegard is birthed by the pentecostal fire, is a space which cannot be completely accessed by a male, and this only-partial access is symbolized by the head-only intrusion of Volmar. Mimesis occurs when a speaking/writing woman *appears* to buy into a phallocentric system of discourse but actually uses phallocentric discourse to deliver a pro-feminine message and, thus, to marginalize from her own meaning the phallus which discourse 'normally' privileges and empowers. Hildegard—a female—is the only one who has complete access to the message/the pentecostal fire/the bloody birth of the awakening; Volmar—a male—can experience this same phenomenon vicariously and then only through the account which Hildegard chooses to reveal to him, thus his depiction here as enjoying only partial access to the (vaginal) chamber of divine inspiration.

Finally, let us consider this illumination's depiction of inscription. Having been awakened by the pentecostal fire, having been born from an undeniably maternal body, Hildegard, a woman, takes up a writing instrument. Drawing on Jacques Derrida's familiar claim, this stylus/pen may be read as a symbol of the penis, the phallus, and, by extension, of male empowerment. Hildegard uses—that is, she mimes—the function of this pen/stylus, and she is thus able to encode her version of what she perceives as truth onto a tablet. Finally, this tablet echoes the arched shape of the vaginal enclosure through which Hildegard is being awakened or born. Thus we are witnessing the birth of a female visionary who has access to what is supposedly a masculine message and who uses a masculine instrument—that is, the pen, or the act of writing itself—to encode the message back into a feminine medium, a text full of words whose meanings, by Hildegard's own admission, are so diverse that they are misleading.[64] This illumination makes clear that Hildegard's moment of awakening and its accompanying 'Self-Portrait' constitute a moment of disruptive excess, for the masculine, divine message it claims to convey is undeniably undercut by mimesis.

Notes

[1] [Hildegard of Bingen,] *Scivias,* [trans Mother Columbia Hart and Jane Bishop, preface Caroline Walker Bynum, intro Barbara J. Newman, *The Classics of Western Spirituality: A Library of the Great Spiritual Masters*] (Paulist Press, New York 1990).

[2] Illuminations of Hildegard of Bingen, ed and commentary Matthew Fox (Bear, Santa Fe 1985) p 26. For a thorough history of the text and illuminations of *Scivias,* see Barbara Newman, *Sister of Wisdom: St. Hildegard's Theory of the Feminine* (University of California Press, Berkeley 1987) p 17.

[3] Prudence Allen, RSM, 'Hildegard of Bingen's Philosophy of Sex Identity,' *Thought* 64 (Sept 1989) pp 231-41.

[4] Quoted Allen p 235.

[5] Allen pp 234, 240, emphasis added.

[6] Barbara Newman, 'Hildegard of Bingen: Visions and Validation,' *Church History* 54 (June 1985) pp 163-75.

[7] Newman, 'Visions' p 164, emphasis added.

[8] 'Ein unveröffentlichtes Hildegard Fragment, 4.28', ed Heinrich Schipperges, *Sudhoffs Archiv für Geschichte der Medizin* 40 (1956) p 71, quoted and trans Newman, 'Visions' p 171.

[9] Newman, 'Visions' p 175, emphasis added.

[10] Newman, 'Visions' p 175.

[11] Newman, *Sister of Wisdom* p 9; Fox p 8.

[12] Newman, *Sister of Wisdom* 14; Fox p 8.

[13] Fox pp 8-9. One must also keep in mind when considering the importance of music to Hildegard's notion of spirituality that she wrote music and maintained that the music she composed had been revealed to her by God in visions. This music, which Hildegard insisted sounded exactly like the music of heaven, was somewhat of a departure from contemporary musical style; before Hildegard's intervention, music consisted of chants. Hildegard, essentially, invented melody, the 'jumping' between individual notes of more than the half-step or whole-step characteristic of the chant style.

[14] Quoted Fox p 9.

[15] Peter Dronke, *Women Writers of the Middle Ages* (Cambridge University Press, Cambridge/New York 1984) p 145.

[16] Fox p 9. Newman, *Sister of Wisdom* pp 3-4, discusses Hildegard's position as a woman trapped in a paradoxically effeminate yet phallocentric age in which men in general have failed to carry out their obligations to God. Newman (pp 241-2) also relates Hildegard's own vision of Ecclesia, the female spirit who embodies the feminine aspects of God and Christianity. Hildegard's fascinating account of this incident further emphasizes the degree to which her male contemporaries persisted in rejecting the role of the feminine in Christianity.

[17] Bynum pp 2-3.

[18] *Subtilitatum diversarum naturarum creaturarum libri novem*, ed Charles Daremberg and F.A. Reuss, *PL* 197 cols 1117-1352; *Causae et curae*, ed Paul Kaiser (Leipzig 1903), cited Newman, *Sister of Wisdom* p 10.

[19] Bynum p 3.

[20] Bynum p 4.

[21] Bynum pp 3-4.

[22] Jer. 1.4-6, 9.

[23] Newman, *Scivias* p 13. For more on Hildegard's acceptance and validation by her male contemporaries, see Newman, *Sister of Wisdom* p 2.

[24] Newman, *Scivias* p 18.

[25] Newman, *Scivias* p 47.

[26] Newman, *Scivias* p 23. Newman also provides additional evidence for the unfavorable treatment of texts written by women: 'In 1220, forty years after Hildegard's death, the Cistercian prior Gebeno of Eberbach compiled an anthology of [Hildegard's] prophetic and apocalyptic writings. This influential text, entitled *Pentachronon or Mirror of Future Times*, survives in well over a hundred manuscripts—as compared with eleven for the Scivias and four for [another of Hildegard's texts], *On the Activity of God*,' *Sister of Wisdom* p 22.

[27] Newman, *Sister of Wisdom* p 248.

[28] Newman, *Sister of Wisdom* p 255.

[29] See *ASB* April, 3 p 884; Newman, *Sister of Wisdom* p 256.

[30] It is purely coincidental that just as Hildegard of Bingen invoked the anger of the monks of St Disibod when she expressed a desire to break from their monastery, so Irigaray was expelled from the department of psychoanalytics at Vincennes as a result of her groundbreaking doctoral dissertation, *Speculum of the Other Woman* (1974), which questioned male authority in all of western culture and, even more significantly, expressed considerable contempt for many of the theories of the 'god' of psychoanalysis, Sigmund Freud. Again, it is merely coincidental that the title of an anthology of Hildegard's prophecies compiled in 1220 by a male editor, *Speculum futurorum temporum*, bears a similarity to the title of Irigaray's controversial dissertation.

[31] Luce Irigaray, *This Sex Which Is Not One*, trans Catherine Porter (Cornell University Press, Ithaca 1985) p 164.

[32] Irigaray p 119.

[33] Irigaray p 119.

[34] Irigaray p 76.

[35] Irigaray p 8, emphasis added.

[36] Catherine Porter, 'Notes on Selected Terms,' Irigaray p 220.

[37] Irigaray p 76.

[38] Irigaray p 76.

[39] *Scivias* pp 45, 17. It is not particularly surprising that Newman would take this stance in accepting Hildegard's status as a weak and foolish being. In fact, Newman suffers from an apparently troublesome relationship with regard to the validation of any aspect of the feminine beyond that which is biologically specific. For instance (and regrettably), Newman lists what she calls the 'two positive attributes' of femininity—virginity and maternity,' *Sister of Wisdom* p 239.

[40] Bynum p 5.

[41] Irigaray p 125. Luce Irigaray, 'The Blind Spot of an Old Dream of Symmetry,' *Speculum of the Other Woman*, trans Gillian C. Gill (Cornell University Press, Ithaca 1985) pp 11-129.

[42] But again, this 'I am not worthy' stance adopted by so many females in the Christian tradition must be read in terms of the Christian insistence that there is great 'power through powerlessness.'

[43] Irigaray p 125.

[44] Fox p 27.

[45] Fox p 27, emphasis added.

[46] Fox p 27, emphasis added.

[47] Fox p 27.

[48] Newman denies that Hildegard's visions were experienced in states of ecstasy but provides evidence that they did occur during instances of great suffering and illness (*Sister of Wisdom* pp 6, 39). Although Newman insists that these visions 'seldom interfered with [Hildegard's] normal functioning,' she does acknowledge that the mystic's senses were often confused or distorted during these experiences. Hildegard herself indicates that '[her] soul *tastes* and sees them,' that her soul literally '*drinks* them in . . .': *Epistola* 2 in *Analecta Sanctae Hildegardis*, ed J.-B. Pitra, *Analecta Sacra*, 8 (Monte Cassino 1882) pp 332-3, quoted and trans Newman, *Sister of Wisdom* p 7, emphasis added. Newman elsewhere adds that in 1917 an attempt was made by 'the historian of science' Charles Singer to diagnose Hildegard as suffering from ' "scintillating scotoma," a form of migraine characterized by hallucinations of flashing, circling, or fermenting points of light.' Newman largely discounts this notion, commenting that '[s]uch a diagnosis may be correct; but unlike Singer, we must avoid the reductionist error of assuming that a physiological cause (or better, correlative) of the visions excludes the possibility of any higher inspiration' ('Visions' p 167).

[49] *Sed ego, quamuis haec uiderem et audirem, tamen propter dubietatem et malam opinionem et propter diuersitatem uerborum hominum . . . scribere recusaui . . . H[ildegardis] S[civias],* ed Adelgundis Führkotter, CCCM 42 'Protestificatio' lines 79-82 (p 5); *Scivias*, 'Declaration' p 60.

[50] *Et dixi et scripsi haec non secundum adinuentionem cordis mei aut ullius hominis, sed ut ea in caelestibus vidi, audiui et percepi per secreta mysteria Dei*, HS, 'Protestificatio' lines 94-6 (p 6); *Scivias*, 'Declaration' p 61.

[51] *Et iterum audiui uocem de caelo mihi dicentem: 'Clama ergo et scribe sic'*, HS, 'Protestificatio' lines 98-9 (p 6); *Scivias*, 'Declaration' p 61.

[52] *O homo fragilis, et cinis cineris, et putredo putredinis . . . . quia timida es ad loquendum et simplex ad exponendum et indocta ad scribendum ea . . . . . dic ea quae uides et audis; et scribe ea non secundum te nec secundum alium hominem, sed secundum uoluntatem scientis, uidentis et disponentis omnia in secretis mysteriorum suorum*, HS, 'Protestificatio' lines 9-21 (p 3); Scivias, 'Declaration' p 59.

[53] My reading of the illumination of Hildegard's awakening will draw harsh criticism from those opposed to Freudian psychoanalytic criticism. It is not my intention to insist that my reading of this painting is the only one possible, nor do I wish to imply that this reading is necessarily the best or even the most appropriate one. Yet, as made clear above, recent scholarship on Hildegard of Bingen has often taken a feminist slant, and I am certain that my reading of Hildegard's 'Self-Portrait' at least reminds us of the importance of the female body, of gynecology, of reproduction and germination, so crucial to many of Hildegard's texts. My reading of this 'Self-Portrait' in no way anticipates the intentions of its original artist, whether that artist be Hildegard, someone working under Hildegard's direction, or someone completely unknown to Hildegard. Yet applying current methods to texts which preceded them is not without precedent, even in the realm of religion; take, for example, the carbon-dating and radioactive imaging of the Shroud of Turin. Although neither *Scivias* nor Hildegard's 'Self-Portrait' directly address gynecological issues, the significance to Hildegard of such concerns may certainly be validated by her other works.

[54] Fox p 28.

[55] Fox p 29. Let me make clear that my reading of this illumination is not meant to discount the significance of Volmar in the life and work of Hildegard of Bingen. On the contrary, Volmar was more than just Hildegard's scribe. He and Hildegard enjoyed a close and meaningful friendship in as much as such closeness was possible given their religious devotion.

[56] Fox p 29.

[57] Bynum p 43.

[58] Of the function of the feminine in Hildegard's theology and on the role of the feminine as a sort of intermediary between humankind and God, Newman notes that 'the feminine is that in God which binds itself most intimately with the human race' (*Sister of Wisdom* p 250). Clearly, Hildegard's awakening is a moment in which she—a mortal—is bound, joined, with God. Further, Newman acknowledges that '[w]here the feminine presides, God stoops to humanity and humanity aspires to God' (p 45).

[59] One might also comment on the significance of the number of fingers/tongues/flames in the pentecostal fire: there are five. This number, of course, corresponds to the number of fingers on the hand, thus suggesting that this is the hand of God reaching toward Hildegard. Further, five is the number of books comprising the Pentateuch, the first five books of the Bible. Five is also the number of bodily senses or, as they were called

in Hildegard's time, 'wits.' Further, five is the number of joys and sorrows and glories of Mary in the rosary.

[60] Indeed, I argue that the Hildegard of the image resembles a birthing mother lying on her back with her feet in stirrups. Having established some sort of authority for discussing Hildegard's vision in terms of womb imagery, I am more than ready to admit that my own reading of this illumination as a birthing mother in stirrups is anachronistic; during Hildegard's lifetime, women gave birth by squatting, a position which, by the way, Hildegard herself assumes in this illumination. I suggest that my reading of Hildegard's 'Self-Portrait' be considered metaphorically: it reminds us that what we are witnessing here is some kind of *representation* of birth. Chapter two of Newman's *Sister of Wisdom*, 'The Feminine Divine' (pp 42-88), provides a lengthy and important discussion about the place and significance of the feminine in the divine nature of God. Newman indicates that one of the names by which Christ is to be known, 'Wisdom,' is feminine in its etymological origin, and she indicates that the theme of Wisdom—and, therefore, the role of Christ—is not infrequently depicted in religious texts and iconography 'as bride, *mother,* and queen' (p 46, emphasis added). Thus my reading of Hildegard's 'Self-Portrait' may not be as subversive as it at first seems. Yes, God is the Father, but, in the form of Christ, God may also be the Mother. Recall Newman's suggestion that were God to be without a feminine nature, he or she would remain unable to 'stoop to humanity.'

[61] *Epistola* 2, Pitra, *Analecta* pp 332-3, quoted and trans, Newman, *Sister of Wisdom* p 6.

[62] *Epistola* 2, Pitra, *Analecta* pp 332-3, quoted and trans, Newman, *Sister of Wisdom* p 7.

[63] *In prima formatione mea, cum deus in utero matris mee spiraculo vite suscitavit me, visionem istam infixit anime mee'* Hildegard of Bingen, *Vita,* Berlin MS Staatsbibl. Lat. Qu. 674, fol 6vb, quoted and trans Dronke pp 145, 231.

[64] Recall that Hildegard's explanation for her initial refusal to write the things which God revealed to her arose from 'doubt and bad faith and *the diversity of human words'* (*Scivias,* 'Declaration' p 60, emphasis added).

FURTHER READING

Biography

Eckenstein, Lina. "St. Hildegard of Bingen and St. Elisabeth of Schonau." In *Woman under Monasticism: Chapters on Saint-Lore and Convent Life Between A.D. 500 and A.D. 1500*, pp. 256-85. Cambridge at the University Press, 1896.

> Provides an overview of Hildegard's life and career and examines the religious and political context of twelfth-century Germany.

Flanagan, Sabina. *Hildegard of Bingen, 1098-1179: A Visionary Life.* London: Routledge, 1989, 230 p.

> Presents a comprehensive introduction to Hildegard's life and work, maintaining that Hildegard's written works "not only surpassed those of most of her male contemporaries in the range of their subject matter . . . but also outshone them in visionary beauty and intellectual power."

Criticism

Baumgardt, David. "The Concept of Mysticism: Analysis of a Letter Written by Hildegard of Bingen to Guibert of Gembloux." *The Review of Religion* XII, No. 3 (March 1948): 277-86.

> Examination of Hildegard's description of her mystical experiences in her 1171 letter to the monk Guibert of Gembloux.

Dronke, Peter. "Hildegard of Bingen as Poetess and Dramatist." In *Poetic Individuality in the Middle Ages: New Departures in Poetry 1000-1150*, pp. 150-79. Oxford at the Clarendon Press, 1970.

> Introduces Hildegard's poetic and dramatic oeuvre, particularly the *Symphonia* and the *Ordo Virtutum*, which, Dronke argues, achieves "a visionary concentration and an evocative and associative richness that set it apart from nearly all other religious poetry of its age."

———. "The Composition of Hildegard of Bingen's *Symphonia*." *Sacris Erudiri* 19-20, Nos. 1-20 (1969-1971): 380-92.

> Argues that Hildegard's song cycle was conceived and designed as a lyrical whole.

Gossman, Elisabeth. "Hildegard of Bingen." In *A History of Women Philosophers, Vol. II: Medieval, Renaissance and Enlightenment Women Philosophers A.D. 500-1600*, pp. 27-65. Dordrecht: Kluwer Academic Publishers, 1989.

> Maintains that "within her visionary experience, [Hildegard] comes to a philosophical-theological view of the world which displays original traits and sometimes emphasizes polemical aspects, but, in addition, raises many unanswered questions about the influences affecting a twelfth-century Benedictine woman's view of the world and of mankind."

Newman, Barbara. "Hildegard of Bingen: Visions and Validation." *Church History* 54, No. 2 (June 1985): 163-75.

> Discusses Hildegard as both a visionary and a prophet, maintaining that her visionary gift conferred three interrelated benefits: "a direct experience of God, a

source of unmediated truth, and a form of public validation."

Nolan, Edward Peter. "Hildegard of Bingen and the *Via Affirmativa*." In his *Cry Out and Write: A Feminine Poetics of Revelation*, pp. 46-135. New York: Continuum, 1994.

    Analyzes Hildegard's visionary works, with particular attention to the *Scivias*, the *Liber Vitae Meritorum*, and the *Liber Divinorum Operum*.

Additional coverage of Hildegard's life and career is contained in the following source published by Gale Research: *Dictionary of Literary Biography,* **Vol. 148.**

Petrarch

1304-1374

(Born Francesco Petracco; changed to Petrarca; also referred to as Francis Petrarch) Italian poet, philosopher, and biographer.

INTRODUCTION

One of the most prominent and influential poets in world literature, Petrarch is a major figure in humanist philosophy and the early Italian Renaissance. Through his *Canzoniere* (begun 1330s), a collection of poems expressing his unrequited love for a woman named Laura, he popularized the Italian, or Petrarchan, sonnet and influenced poets throughout Europe with his imagery, themes, and diction for more than three hundred years.

Biographical Information

Born in Arezzo, Italy, in 1304, Petrarch was the eldest son of a notary who had been banished from Florence two years earlier for his political activities. In 1312 the family moved to Avignon, France, where Petrarch's father established a successful law practice. Petrarch was privately educated by tutors, and in 1316 he began studying civil law in Montpellier. While there Petrarch's habit of spending his allowance on the works of classical poets led his father on one occasion to burn Petrarch's library except for copies of works by Vergil and Cicero. Around this time Petrarch's mother died, and he composed his earliest known poem as a tribute to her. Petrarch and his younger brother, Gherardo, who later became a monk, entered law school in Bologna, Italy, in 1320, where—except for interruptions caused by student riots—they remained until the death of their father in 1326. After abandoning his legal studies and exhausting his inheritance, Petrarch settled in Avignon and took the minor orders necessary to pursue an ecclesiastical career. While attending services on Good Friday, 1327, Petrarch purportedly saw and fell in love with a woman he called Laura. For the remainder of his life Petrarch wrote lyrics about his unrequited love for her, initially gathering them in a volume around 1336 and revising and expanding the collection thereafter. In 1330 Petrarch became a private chaplain to Cardinal Giovanni Colonna and remained in the service of the Colonna family for almost twenty years. During this time he composed or revised most of his major works, traveled on diplomatic missions, and maintained extensive correspondence with friends, scholars, and nobility throughout

Europe. Because his works were widely distributed, Petrarch's passion for Laura and his talents as a lyric poet became well known and admired. In 1340 Petrarch received simultaneous invitations to be poet laureate in Paris and in Rome; after some deliberation he accepted the invitation to Rome. On Easter Sunday in 1341 an elaborate ceremony was held in the Palace of the Senate on Capitoline Hill to coronate Petrarch as poet laureate of Rome; the last ceremony of this magnitude is thought to have been held more than a thousand years earlier. Over the next three decades Petrarch continued to travel widely on diplomatic missions and personal business while continuing his literary endeavors. In 1370 he settled in the village of Arqua, Italy, and focused much of his efforts on revising and collecting his earlier works. Petrarch died on July 18, 1374.

Major Works

Although best known for his Italian poetry—*Trionfi* (*The Triumphs*; begun 1338) and *Rerum vulgarium fragmenta* (*Canzoniere*)—Petrarch composed most of his writings in Latin. His major poetic works include the *Africa* (begun 1338-39), *The Triumphs,* and *Canzoniere.* The *Africa* is an epic poem in Latin hexameter celebrating the victory of the Roman general Scipio Africanus over the Carthaginian general Hannibal in the Second Punic War. During the Renaissance, Petrarch's most popular work was *The Triumphs,* a long allegorical poem in six parts—Love, Chastity, Death, Fame, Time, and Eternity—that portrayed the spiritual journey of the soul from the temporal world to eternity. Written in Italian *terza rima* verse, *The Triumphs* was particularly esteemed for its encyclopedic catalogs of famous persons, its visionary outlook, concern with worldly vanities, and emphasis on salvation through God. Petrarch called his most lasting poetic work *Rerum vulgarium fragmenta* ("Fragments in the Vernacular"), but since his time this work has been variously referred to as the *Rime, Rime sparse, Rhymes,* and, most commonly, the *Canzoniere.* In its final form the *Canzoniere* consists of 366 poems: 317 sonnets, 29 canzone, 9 sestinas, 7 ballads, and 4 madrigals. The collection is divided into two parts; the first section contains 266 poems—the majority of which focus on Laura during her lifetime, with some political, moral, and miscellaneous poems interspersed, while the poems in the second section of the *Canzoniere* are reminiscences about Laura after her death. Throughout the *Canzoniere* the narrator reflects upon his passion for Laura, the suffering caused by his unrequited love, and his efforts to free himself from his desire. The final poem of the *Canzoniere* closes with a plea to the Virgin Mary to end the narrator's heartache. While Laura's existence and identity remain uncertain, critics have observed that she has served as the epitome of feminine virtue and beauty for generations of poets. Petrarch's major prose works include *De viris illustribus* (*On Illustrious Men;* begun 1337); *Secretum* (*Petrarch's Secret;* begun 1342-43); *De otio religioso* (*On Religious Idleness;* 1345-47); and *De remediis utriusque fortunae* (*Remedies for Fortune Fair and Foul;* begun 1353). *On Illustrious Men* is a collection of biographies covering such famous Romans as Romulus, Cincinnatus, and Scipio. *Petrarch's Secret* consists of three dialogues in which Augustine, who personifies the religious ideal, scolds Petrarch for failing to achieve the ideal. Dedicated to the Carthusian religious order, of which Petrarch's brother Gherardo was a member, *On Religious Idleness* examines the benefits of the religious life, particularly the ability to resist temptation. *Remedies for Fortune Fair and Foul* discusses the proper way to live and die under varied circumstances. Petrarch characterizes life as difficult and fraught with troubles and argues that human weakness springs from our abandonment of virtue. Stressing Christian values, self-examination, and individual responsibility, *Remedies for Fortune Fair and Foul* was immensely popular during the early Renaissance.

Critical Reception

Petrarch is credited with popularizing—but not inventing—the Italian sonnet, a poetic form with an octet rhyming in the pattern *abbaabba* and a sestet that usually follows the pattern *cdecde.* His works in this form are generally regarded as his most significant contribution to literature, and numerous critics have credited Petrarch with reviving traditional poetic forms. Commentators have noted the relationship between form and meaning in his poetry, his use of complex syntax, and his imagery. Scholars have also frequently discussed the theme of tension between the body and spirit in Petrarch's works, his extensive use of classical mythology, his celebration of statesmen and leaders from the classical period, and his contributions to humanist philosophy, particularly his efforts to reconcile Christian and pagan ideals. As Christopher Kleinhenz observed, "The 317 sonnets that provide the form and essence of the poetic *corpus* of the *Canzoniere* are without doubt one of the finest literary legacies ever bequeathed to mankind. In their attempts to define the excellence of the Petrarchan sonnet, critics praise it for its precision and compactness, for its graceful symmetry and vibrant musicality, and for its noble sentiments and intimate tones."

PRINCIPAL WORKS

*Rerum familiarium libra [Books on Personal Matters] (letters) 1325-1366

†Rerum vulgarium fragmenta [Canzoniere] (poetry) begun 1330s

De viris illustribus [On Illustrious Men] (biographies) begun 1337

Africa (unfinished epic poem) begun 1338-1339

Trionfi [The Triumphs] (unfinished poem) begun 1338

Secretum [Petrarch's Secret] (dialogues) begun 1342-1343

Rerum memorandarum libri [Books on Matters to Be Remembered] (prose) begun 1342-1343

Psalmi poemitentiales [Penitential Psalms] (poetry) begun 1342-1343

De otio religioso [On Religious Idleness] (essay) 1345-1347

Bucolicum carmen [Bucolic Song] (poetry) begun 1345-1347

De vita solitaria [On the Solitary Life] (essay) 1345-1347

Liber sine nomine [Petrarch's Book without a Name] (letters) 1351-1353

De remediis utriusque fortunae [Remedies for Fortune Fair and Foul] (dialogues) begun 1353

Epistolae seniles [Letters of Old Age] (letters) 1361-1374

De sui ipsius et multorum ignorantia [On His Own Ignorance and That of Many Others] (essay) 1367

Letters from Petrarch [translated by Morris Bishop]
(letters) 1966

*Petrarch's Lyric Poems: The "Rime Sparse" and Other
Lyrics* [translated by Robert M. Durling] (poetry)
1976

Rime Disperse [translated by Joseph A. Barber] (poetry) 1991

*These letters are also collectively known as the *Familiares.*
†This work is also known as the *Rhymes, Rime,* and *Rime sparse.*

CRITICISM

Ugo Foscolo (essay date 1823)

SOURCE: Ugo Foscolo, "A Parallel between Dante
and Petrarach," in *Essays on Petrarch*, John Murray,
1823, pp. 163-208.

[*In the following essay, Foscolo, a renowed Italian poet,
compares the poetry and philosophy of Dante and Petrarch.*]

L'UN DISPOSTO A PATIRE E L'ALTRO A FARE.
DANTE, PURG. C. XXV.

The excess of erudition in the age of Leo the Tenth,
carried the refinements of criticism so far as even to
prefer elegance of taste to boldness of genius. The
laws of the Italian language were thus deduced, and
the models of poetry selected exclusively from the
works of Petrarch; who being then proclaimed superior to Dante, the sentence remained, until our times,
unreversed. Petrarch himself mingles Dante indiscriminately with others eclipsed by his own fame—

> Ma ben ti prego, che in la terza spera,
> Guitton saluti, e Messer Cino, e Dante,
> Franceschin nostro, e tutta quella shiera.

> Così or quinci, or quindi rimirando
> Vidi in una fiorita e verde piaggia
> Gente che d'Amor givan ragionando.

> Ecco Dante, e Beatrice: ecco Selvaggia,
> Ecco Cin da Pistoja; Guitton d' Arezzo;
> Ecco i due Guidi che già furo in prezzo;
> Onesto Bolognese, e i Siciliani.
> —Trionf. c.4.

Salute, I pray thee, in the sphere of love,
  Guitton, my master Cino, Dante too,
Our Franceschin, all that blest band
  above.—

Thus while my gazing eyes around me rove,
  I saw upon a slope of flowery green

Many that held their sweet discourse of
  love:
  Here Dante and his Beatrice, there were
  seen
Selvaggia and Cino of Pistoia; there
Guitton the Aretine; and the high-priz'd pair,
  The Guidi; and Onesto these among,
  And all the masters of Sicilian song.
                                MILMAN

Boccacio, discouraged by the reputation of these two
great masters, determined to burn his own poetry.
Petrarch diverted him from this purpose, writing with
a tone of humility somewhat inconsistent with the
character of a man who was not naturally a hypocrite. "You are a philosopher and a christian," says
he, "and yet you are discontented with yourself for
not being an illustrious poet! Since *another* has occupied the *first* place, be satisfied with the *second,*
and I will take the *third.*"[1]—Boccacio, perceiving the
irony and the allusion, sent Dante's poem to Petrarch,
and intreated that "he would not disdain to read the
work of a great man, from whom exile and death,
while he was still in the vigour of life, had snatched
the laurel."[2]—"Read it, I conjure you; your genius
reaches to the heavens, and your glory extends beyond the earth: but reflect that Dante is our fellow-
citizen; that he has shewn all the force of our language; that his life was unfortunate; that he undertook and suffered every thing for glory; and that he
is still pursued by calumny, and by envy, in the grave.
If you praise him, you will do honour to him—you
will do honour to yourself—you will do honour to
Italy, of which you are the greatest glory and the
only hope."

Petrarch, in his answer, is angry that he can be considered jealous of the celebrity of a poet "whose language is coarse, though his conceptions are lofty"—
"You must hold him in veneration and in gratitude, as
the first light of your education, whilst I never saw
him but once, at a distance, or rather he was pointed
out to me, while I was still in my childhood. He was
exiled on the same day with my father, who submitted
to his misfortunes, and devoted himself solely to the
care of his children. The other, on the contrary, resisted, followed the path which he had chosen, thought
only of glory, and neglected every thing else. If he
were still alive, and if his character were as congenial
to mine as his genius is, he would not have a better
friend than me."[3]—This letter lengthened out by contradictions, ambiguities, and indirect apologies, points
out the individual by circumlocutions, as if the name
was withheld through caution or through awe. Some
maintain that Dante is not referred to;[4] but the authentic list[5] still existing, of the Florentines banished on the
27th of January 1302, contains the names of Dante
and the father of Petrarch, and that of no other individual to whom it is possible to apply any one of the

circumstances mentioned in the letter, whilst each, and the whole of them, apply strictly to Dante.

These two founders of Italian literature, were gifted with a very different genius, pursued different plans, established two different languages and schools of poetry, and have exercised till the present time a very different influence. Instead of selecting, as Petrarch does, the most elegant and melodious words and phrases, Dante often creates a new language, and summons all the various dialects of Italy to furnish him with combinations that might represent, not only the sublime and beautiful, but even the commonest scenes of nature; all the wild conceptions of his fancy; the most abstract theories of philosophy, and the most abstract mysteries of religion. A simple idea, a vulgar idiom, takes a different colour and a different spirit from their pen. The conflict of opposite purposes *thrills in the heart* of Petrarch, and *battles in the brain* of Dante—

> Nè sì nè no nel cor dentro mi suona.—Petr.
> Che sì e no nel capo mi tenzona.—Dante.
> At war 'twixt will and will not.—Shakspeare.

Tasso expressed it with that dignity from which he never departs—

> In gran tempesta di pensieri ondeggia.

Yet not only does this betray an imitation of the *magno curarum fluctuat œstu* of Virgil; but Tasso, by dreading the energy of the idiom *sì e no,* lost, as he does too often, the graceful effect produced by ennobling a vulgar phrase—an artifice which, however, in the pastoral of Aminta he has most successfully employed. His notion of epic style ws so refined, that while he regarded Dante "as the greatest poet of Italy," he often asserted, "had he not sacrificed dignity and elegance, he would have been the first of the world."—No doubt Dante sometimes sacrificed even decorum and perspicuity; but it was always to impart more fidelity to his pictures, or more depth to his reflections. He says to himself—

> Parla, e sie breve e arguto.—
> Speak; and be brief, be subtile in thy words.

He says to his reader—

> Or ti riman, lettor, sovra 'l tuo banco,
> Dietro pensando a ciò, che is preliba,
> S' esser vuoi lieto assai prima, che stanco.
> *Messo t' ho innanzi; omai per te ti ciba.*

> Now rest thee, reader, on thy bench, and muse
> Anticipative of the feast to come;

So shall delight make thee not feel thy toil.
Lo! I have set before thee; for thyself Feed now.

CARY'S TRANSL.

As to their versification, Petrarch attained the main object of erotic poetry; which is, to produce a constant musical flow in strains inspired by the sweetest of human passions. Dante's harmony is less melodious, but is frequently the result of more powerful art—

> S' i' avessi le rime e aspre e chiocce,
> Come si converebbe al tristo buco,
> Sovra 'l qual pontan tutte l'altre rocce,
> I' premerei di mio concetto il suco
> Più pienamente: ma perch' i' non l'abbo,
> Non senza tema a dicer mi conduco:
> Che non è impresa da pigliare a gabbo,
> Descriver fondo a tutto l'universo,
> Nè da lingua, che chiami mamma o babbo.
> Ma quelle donne ajutino 'l mio verso,
> Ch' ajutaro Anfione a chiuder Tebe,
> Sì che dal fatto il dir non sia diverso.

> Oh! had I rough hoarse thunder in my verse,
> To match this gulph of woe on all sides round
> O'erbrow'd by rocks, then dreadfully should roar
> The mighty torrent of my song: such powers
> I boast not; but with shuddering awe attempt
> The solemn theme. The world's extremest depth
> Requires no infant babbling, but the choir
> Of tuneful virgins to assist my strain,
> By whose symphonious aid Amphion raised
> The Theban walls,—but truth shall guide my tongue.

N. HOWARD'S TRANSL.

Here the poet evidently hints that to give colour and strength to ideas by the sound of words, is one of the necessary requisites of the art. The six first lines are made rough by a succession of consonants. But when he describes a quite different subject, the words are more flowing with vowels—

> O anime affannate,
> Venite a noi parlar, s'altri nol niega.
> Quali colombe dal desio chiamate,
> Con l' ali aperte e ferme al dolce nido,
> Volan per l'aer dal voler portate.

> "O wearied spirits! come, and hold discourse

With us, if by none else restrain'd." As
    doves
By fond desire invited, on wide wings
And firm, to their sweet nest returning
    home,
Cleave the air, wafted by their will along.
                      CARY'S TRANSL.

This translator frequently contravenes the position of his author, who, chiefly depending upon the effect of his versification, says, that "nothing harmonized by musical enchainment, can be transmuted from one tongue into another, without destroying all its sweetness and harmony."[6]—The plan of Dante's poem required that he should pass from picture to picture, from passion to passion. He varies the tone in the different scenes of his journey as rapidly as the crowd of spectres flitted before his eyes; and he adapts the syllables and the cadences of each line, in such an artful manner as to give energy, by the change of his numbers, to those images which he intended to represent. For in the most harmonious lines, there is no poetry, whenever they fail to excite that glow of rapture, that exquisite thrill of delight, which arises from the easy and simultaneous agitation of all our faculties—this the poet achieves by powerful use of imagery.

Images in poetry work upon the mind according to the process of nature herself;—first, they gain upon our senses—then, touch the heart—afterwards strike our imagination—and ultimately they imprint themselves upon our memory, and call forth the exertion of our reason, which consists mainly in the examination and comparison of our sensations. This process, indeed, goes on so rapidly as to be hardly perceived; yet all the gradations of it are visible to those who have the power of reflecting upon the operations of their own minds. Thoughts are in themselves only the raw material: they assume one form or another; they receive more or less brilliancy and warmth, more or less novelty and richness, according to the genius of the writer. It is by compressing them in an assemblage of melodious sounds, of warm feelings, of luminous metaphors, and of deep reasoning, that poets transform, into living and eloquent images, many ideas that lie dark and dumb in our mind; and it is by the magic presence of poetical images, that we are suddenly and at once taught to feel, to imagine, to reason, and to meditate, with all the gratification, and with none of the pain, which commonly attends every mental exertion. The notion, "that memory and the art of writing preserve all human knowledge"—the notion, "that hope forsakes not man even on the brink of the grave, and that the expectations of the dying man are still kept alive by the prospect of a life hereafter"—are truths most easy of comprehension, for they are forced upon us by every day's experience. Still the abstract terms in which every general

maxim must inevitably be involved, are incapable of creating the simultaneous excitement by which all our faculties mutually aid each other: as when the poet addresses MEMORY—.

Ages and climes remote to thee impart
What charms in Genius, and refines in Art;
Thee, in whose hands the keys of Science
    dwell,
The pensive portress of her holy cell;
Whose constant vigils chase the chilling
    damp,
Oblivion steals upon her vestal lamp—
              PLEASURES OF MEMORY.

With the metaphysical expressions of *Genius, Art, Science,* are interwoven objects proper to affect the senses, so that the reader sees the maxim set before him as in a picture.—By means of images only, poets can claim the merit of originality; for by the multiplied combination of very few notions, they produce novelty and form groupes, which, though differing in design and character, all exhibit the same truth. The following Italian passage on Memory has not the slightest resemblance to the English lines; yet the diversity lies only in the varied combination of images—"The Muses sit by the tomb, and when Time's icy wing sweeps away alike the marble, and the dust of man, with their song they cheer the desert waste, and harmony overcomes the silence of a thousand generations"—

Siedon le Muse su le tombe, e quando
Il Tempo con sue fredde ali vi spazza
I marmi e l'ossa, quelle Dee fan lieti
Di lor canto i deserti, e l'armonia
Vince di mille e mille anni il silenzio.

And what could be said of our expectations of immortality, which is not all contained and unfolded in this invocation to HOPE?

Thou, undismay'd, shalt o'er the ruin smile,
And light thy torch at Nature's funeral pile.
              PLEASURES OF HOPE.

Petrarch's images seem to be exquisitely finished by a very delicate pencil: they delight the eye rather by their colouring than by their forms. Those of Dante are the bold and prominent figures of an *alto rilievo,* which, it seems, we might almost touch, and of which the imagination readily supplies those parts that are hidden from the view. The commonplace thought of the vanity of human renown is thus expressed by Petrarch—

O cicchi, il tanto affaticar che giova?
Tutti tornate alla gran madre antica,
E il vostro nome appena si ritrova.

O blind of intellect! of what avail
Are your long toils in this sublunar vale?
Tell, ye benighted souls! what gains accrue
From the sad task, which ceaseless ye
    pursue?
Ye soon must mingle with the dust ye tread;
And scarce your name upon a stone be
    read.

BOYD'S TRANSL.

and by Dante,

> La vostra nominanza è color d'erba,
> Che viene e va; e quei la discolora
> Per cui vien fuori della terra acerba.

> Your mortal fame is like the grass whose
>   hue
> Doth come and go; by the same sun
>   decay'd,
> From which it life, and health, and freshness
>   drew.

MERIVALE.

The three lines of Petrarch have the great merit of being more spirited, and of conveying more readily the image of the earth swallowing up the bodies and names of all men; but those of Dante, in spite of their stern profundity, have the still greater merit of leading us on to ideas to which we should not ourselves have reached. Whilst he reminds us, that time, which is necessary for the consummation of all human glory, ultimately destroys it, the changing colour of grass presents the revolutions of ages, as the natural occurrence of a few moments. It is by mentioning "the great periods of time" that an old English poet has lessened this very idea which he intended to magnify—

> I know that all beneath the moon decays;
> And what by mortals in this world is
>   brought,
> In time's great periods shall return to
>   nought.
> I know that all the muse's heavenly lays,
> With toil of sprite which are so dearly
>   bought,
> As idle sounds, of few or none are sought,
>   That there is nothing lighter than mere
>   praise.

DRUMMOND OF HAWTHORNDEN

Again, instead of the agency of time, Dante employs the agency of the sun; because, conveying to us a less metaphysical idea, and being an object more palpable to the senses, it abounds with more glorious and evident images, and fills us with greater wonder and admiration. Its application is more logical also, since every notion which we have of time, consists in the measure of it, which is afforded by the periodical revolutions of the sun.

With respect to the different pleasure these two poets afford, it has been already remarked, that Petrarch calls forth the sweetest sympathies, and awakens the deepest emotions, of the heart: and whether they be of a sad, or of a lively cast, we eagerly wish for them, because, the more they agitate us, the more strongly they quicken our consciousness of existence. Still, as we are perpetually striving against pain, and hurried on in the constant pursuit of pleasure, our hearts would sink under their own agitations, were they abandoned by the dreams of imagination, with which we are providentially gifted to enlarge our stock of happiness, and to gild with bright illusions the sad realities of life. Great writers alone can so control the imagination, as to make it incapable of distinguishing these illusions from the reality. If, in a poem, the ideal and fanciful predominate, we may indeed be surprised for a moment, but can never be brought to feel for objects which either have no existence, or are too far removed from our common nature—and on the other hand, if poetry dwell too much on realities, we soon grow weary; for we see them wherever we turn; they sadden each minute of our existence; they disgust us ever, because we know them even to satiety:—again, if reality and fiction be not intimately blended into one whole, they mutually oppose and destroy one another. Petrarch does not afford many instances of so happy a combination of truth with fiction, as when he describes Laura's features immediately after expiring—

> Pallida no, ma più che neve bianca—
> Parea posar come persona stanca.

> Quasi un dolce dormir ne' suoi begli
>   occhi,
> Sendo lo spirto già da lei diviso—
> Morte bella parea nel suo bel viso.

> No earthy hue her pallid cheek display'd,
> But the pure snow—
> Like one recumbent from her toils she lay,
> Losing in sleep the labours of the day—
> And from her parting soul an heavenly
>   trace
> Seem'd yet to play upon her lifeless face,
> Where death enamour'd sate, and smiled
>   with angel grace.

BOYD'S TRANSL.

Had the translator kept closer in the last line to the original words, "Death seemed beautiful on the lovely features of Laura," he would have conveyed a higher and yet more credible notion of her beauty, and insensibly changed, into an agreeable sensation, the horror with which we regard a corpse. But "Death sitting enamour'd in Laura's face," exhibits no distinct image, unless it be that of the allegorical form of Death transmuted into an angel sitting upon the face of a woman—which affords a striking exemplification of the absurdities arising from the unskilful mixture of truth with fiction.

Petrarch often surrounds the reality with ideal decorations so luxuriantly, that while we gaze at his images they disappear—

> Obscured and lost in flood of golden light.
> ROGERS.

And the poet by whom this line is suggested, justly remarks—that "True taste is an excellent economist, and delights in producing great effects by small means." Dante selects the beauties that lie scattered throughout created Nature, and embodies them in one single subject. The artists who combined in the Apollo of Belvidere, and the Venus de' Medicis, the various beauties observed in different individuals, produced forms, which, though strictly human, have an air of perfection not to be met with upon the earth: however, when contemplating them, we are led insensibly to indulge in the illusion, that mankind may possess such heavenly beauty—

> Stiamo, Amor, a veder la gloria nostra,
> Cose sopra natura altere e nove:
> Vedi ben quanta in lei dolcezza piove;
> Vedi lume che 'l cielo in terra mostra;
>   Vedi quant' arte indora, e imperla, e innostra
> L'abito eletto, e mai non visto altrove,
> Che dolcemente i piedi, e gli occhi move
> Per questa di bei colli ombrosa chiostra.
>   L'erbetta verde, e i fior di color mille
> Sparsi sotto quell' elce antiqua e negra,
> Pregan pur che 'l bel pie' li prema o tocchi;
>   E 'l ciel di vaghe e lucide faville
> S'accende intorno, e'n vista si rallegra
> D'esser fatto seren da sì begli occhi.

> Here stand we, Love, our glory to behold—
>   How, passing nature, lovely, high, and rare!
>   Behold! what showers of sweetness falling there!
> What floods of light by heav'n to earth unroll'd!
> How shine her robes, in purple, pearls, and gold
>   So richly wrought, with skill beyond compare!
>   How glance her feet!—her beaming eyes how fair
> Through the dark cloister which these hills enfold!
> The verdant turf, and flowers of thousand

> hues
> Beneath yon oak's old canopy of state,
> Spring round her feet to pay their amorous duty.
> The heavens, in joyful reverence, cannot choose
> But light up all their fires, to celebrate
> Her praise, whose presence charms their awful beauty.
> MERIVALE.

This description makes us long to find such a woman in the world; but while we admire the poet, and envy him the bliss of his amorous transports, we cannot but perceive that the flowers "that courted the tread of her foot," the sky "that grew more beautiful in her presence," the atmosphere "that borrowed new splendour from her eyes," are mere visions which tempt us to embark with him in the pursuit of an unattainable chimæra. We are induced to think, that Laura must have been endowed with more than human loveliness, since she was able to kindle her lover's imagination to such a degree of enthusiasm, as to cause him to adopt such fantastic illusions, and we conceive the extremity of his passion; but cannot share his amorous ecstasies for a beauty which we never beheld and never shall behold.

On the contrary, the beautiful maiden seen afar off by Dante, in a landscape of the terrestrial paradise, instead of appearing an imaginary being, seems to unite in herself all the attractions which are found in those lovely creatures we sometimes meet, whom we grieve to lose sight of, and to whom fancy is perpetually recurring—the poet's picture recals the original more distinctly to our memory, and enshrines it in our imagination—

> Una donna soletta, che si gia
> Cantando ed isciegliendo fior da fiore,
> Ond' era pinta tutta la sua via.
>   Deh bella donna, ch' a' raggi d'amore
> Ti scaldi, s'io vo'credere a' sembianti,
> Che soglion' esser testimon del cuore,
>   Vengati voglia di trarreti avanti,
> Diss'io a lei, verso questa riviera,
> Tanto ch'io possa intender che tu canti.—
>   Come si volge con le piante strette
> A terra, e intra sè, donna che balli,
> E piede innanzi piede a pena mette,
>   Volsesi 'n su' yermigli ed in su' gialli
> Fioretti, verso me, non altrimenti,
> Che vergine, che gli occhi onesti avvalli;
>   E fece i prieghi miei esser contenti,
> Sì appressando sè, che 'l dolce suono
> Veniva a me co' suoi intendimenti.

> I beheld
> A lady all alone, who, singing, went,

And culling flower from flower, wherewith
  her way
Was all o'er painted. "Lady beautiful!
Thou, who (if looks, that use to speak the
  heart,
Are worthy of our trust) with love's own
  beam
Dost warm thee," thus to her my speech, I
  fram'd;
"Ah! please thee hither tow'rds the
  streamlet bend
Thy steps so near, that I may list thy
  song."—
    As when a lady, turning in the dance,
Doth foot it featly, and advances scarce
One step before the other to the ground;
Over the yellow and vermillion flowers
Thus turn'd she at my suit, most maiden-
  like,
Veiling her sober eyes: and came so near,
That I distinctly caught the dulcet sound.

                        Cary's Transl.

Such is the amazing power with which Dante mingles the realities of nature with ideal accessories, that he creates an illusion which no subsequent reflection is able to dissipate. All that grace and beauty, that warmth and light of love, that vivacity and cheerfulness of youth, that hallowed modesty of a virgin, which we observe, though separately and intermixed with defects, in different persons, are here concentrated into one alone; whilst her song, her dance, and her gathering of flowers, give life, and charm, and motion, to the picture.—To judge fairly between these two poets, it appears, that Petrarch excels in awakening the heart to a deep feeling of its existence; and Dante, in leading the imagination to add to the interest and novelty of nature. Probably a genius never existed, that enjoyed these two powers at once in a pre-eminent degree.

Having both worked upon plans suited to their respective talents, the result has been two kinds of poetry, productive of opposite moral effects. Petrarch makes us see every thing through the medium of one predominant passion, habituates us to indulge in those propensities which by keeping the heart in perpetual disquietude, paralize intellectual exertion—entice us into a morbid indulgence of our feelings, and withdraw us from active life. Dante, like all primitive poets, is the historian of the manners of his age, the prophet of his country, and the painter of mankind; and calls into action all the faculties of our soul to reflect on all the vicissitudes of the world. He describes all passions, all actions—the charm and the horror of the most different scenes. He places men in the despair of Hell, in the hope of Purgatory, and in the blessedness of Paradise. He observes them in youth, in manhood, and in old age. He has brought together those of both sexes, of

all religions, of all occupations, of different nations, and ages; yet he never takes them in masses—he always presents them as individuals; speaks to every one of them, studies their words, and watches their countenances.—"I found," says he, in a letter to Can della Scala, "the original of my Hell, in the earth we inhabit." While describing the realms of death, he catches at every opportunity to bring us back to the occupations and affections of the living world. Perceiving the sun about to quit our hemisphere, he breaks out into—

    Era già l'ora, che volge'l desio
  A'naviganti, e intenerisce il core
  Lo dì, ch'han detto a'dolci amici Addio;
    E che lo nuovo peregrin d'amore
  Punge, se ode squilla di lotano,
  Che paja'l giorno pianger, che si muore.

  'Twas now the hour when fond desire
    renews
    To him who wanders o'er the pathless
      main,
  Raising unbidden tears, the last adieus
    Of tender friends, whom fancy shapes
      again;
  When the late parted pilgrim thrills with
    thought
    Of his lov'd home, if o'er the distant
      plain,
  Perchance, his ears the village chimes have
    caught,
    Seeming to mourn the close of dying day.

                        Merivale.

There is a passage very like this in Apollonius Rhodius, whose many beauties, so admired in the imitations of Virgil, are seldom sought for in the original.—

  Night then brought darkness o'er the
    earth: at sea
  The mariners their eyes from shipboard
    raised,
  Fix'd on the star Orion, and the Bear.
  The traveller, and the keeper of the gate,
  Rock'd with desire of sleep; and slumber
    now
  Fell heavy on some mother, who had wept
  Her children in the grave.

                        Elton's Transl.

By digressions similar to this, introduced without apparent art or effort, Dante interests us for all mankind; whilst Petrarch, being interested only about himself, alludes to men at sea at eventide, only to excite greater compassion for his own sufferings—

  E i naviganti in qualche chiusa valle
  Gettan le membra, poi che'l sol s'asconde,

Sul duro legno e sotto l'aspre gonne:
Ma io; perchè s' attuffi in mezzo l'onde,
E lassi Ispagna dietro alle sue spalle,
E Granata e Marocco e le Colonne,
E gli uomini e le donne
E'l mondo, e gli animali
Acquetino i lor mali,
Fine non pongo al mio ostinato affanno:
E duolmi ch'ogni giorno arroge al danno;
Ch' i' son già pur crescendo in questa
   voglia
Ben presso al decim' anno,
Nè poss' indovinar chi me ne scioglia.

And in some shelter'd bay, at evening's
   close,
The mariners their rude coats round them
   fold,
Stretch'd on the rugged plank in deep
   repose:
But I, though Phœbus sink into the main
And leave Granada wrapt in night, with
   Spain,
Morocco, and the Pillars famed of old,
Though all of human kind
And every creature blest
All hush their ills to rest,
No end to my unceasing sorrows find;
And still the sad account swells day by
   day;
For since these thoughts on my lorn spirit
   prey,
I see the tenth year roll,
Nor hope of freedom springs in my
   desponding soul.

                     LADY DACRE.

Hence Petrarch's poetry wraps us in an idle melancholy, in the softest and sweetest visions, in the error of depending upon others' affection, and leads us vainly to run after perfect happiness, until we plunge headlong into that despair which ensues,

   When Hope has fled affrighted from thy
      face,
   And giant Sorrow fills the empty place.

Still those who meet with this fate are comparatively very few, while far the greater number only learn from sentimental reading how to work more successfully upon impassioned minds, or to spread over vice a thicker cloak of hypocrisy. The number of Petrarch's imitators in Italy may be ascribed to the example of those Church dignitaries and learned men, who, to justify their commerce with the other sex, borrowed the language of Platonic love from his poetry. It is also admirably calculated for a Jesuits' college, since it inspires devotion, mysticism, and retirement, and enervates the minds of youth. But since the late revo-

lutions have stirred up other passions, and a different system of education has been established, Petrarch's followers have rapidly diminished; and those of Dante have written poems more suited to rouse the public spirit of Italy. Dante applied his poetry to the vicissitudes of his own time, when liberty was making her dying struggle against tyranny; and he descended to the tomb with the last heroes of the middle age. Petrarch lived amongst those who prepared the inglorious heritage of servitude for the next fifteen generations.

It was about the decline of Dante's life that the constitutions of the Italian States underwent a total and almost universal change, in consequence of which a new character was suddenly assumed by men, manners, literature, and religion. It was then that the Popes and Emperors, by residing out of Italy, abandoned her to factions, which having fought for independence or for power, continued to tear themselves to pieces through animosity, until they reduced their country to such a state of exhaustion, as to make it an easy prey to demagogues, to despots, and to foreigners. The Guelphs were no longer sanctioned by the Church, in their struggle for popular rights against the feudatories of the empire. The Ghibellines no longer allied themselves to the Emperors to preserve their privileges as great proprietors. Florence, and other small republics, after extirpating their nobles, were governed by merchants, who, having neither ancestors to imitate, nor generosity of sentiment, nor a military education, carried on their intestine feuds by calumny and confiscation. Afraid of a domestic dictatorship, they opposed their external enemies by foreign leaders of mercenary troops, often composed of adventurers and vagabonds from every country, who plundered friends and foes alike, exasperated the discords, and polluted the morals, of the nation. French princes reigned at Naples; and to extend their influence over the south of Italy, destroyed the very shadow of the imperial authority there, by stimulating the Guelphs to all the extravagances of democracy. Meanwhile the nobles who upheld the Ghibelline faction in the north of Italy, being possessed of the wealth and strength of the country, continued to wage incessant civil wars, until they, with their towns and their vassals, were all subjected to the military sway of the victorious leaders, who were often murdered by their own soldiers, and oftener by the heirs apparent of their power. Venice alone, being surrounded by the sea, and consequently exempted from the danger of invasion, and from the necessity of confiding her armies to a single patrician, enjoyed an established form of government. Nevertheless, to preserve and extend her colonies and her commerce, she carried on, in the Mediterranean, a destructive contest with other maritime cities. The Genoese having lost their principal fleet, bartered their liberties with the tyrants of Lombardy, in exchange for assistance. They were thus enabled to gratify their hatred, and defeat the Venetians, who to repeat their attacks exhausted their resources; and both states now fought less for interest, than revenge. It was then that Petrarch's exhortations to peace were so haughtily answered by the Doge Andrea Dandolo.[7] Thus the Italians, though then the arbiters of the seas, weakened themselves to such a degree, by their blind animosities, that, in the ensuing century, Columbus was compelled to beg the aid of foreign princes, to open that path of navigation which has since utterly destroyed the commercial grandeur of Italy.

Meanwhile the Popes and Cardinals, vigilantly watched at Avignon, were sometimes the forced, and often the voluntary, abettors of French policy. The German Princes, beginning to despise the Papal excommunication, refused either to elect Emperors patronized by the Holy See, or to lead forth their subjects to the conquest of the Holy Land, a device, by which from the beginning of the twelfth to the end of the thirteenth century, all the armies of Europe had actually been at the disposal of the Popes. The wild and enterprising fanaticism of religion having thus ceased with the crusades, dwindled into a gloomy and suspicious superstition: new articles of belief brought from the east, gave birth to new Christian sects: the circulation of the classics, the diffusion of a taste for Greek metaphysics, and the Aristotelian materialism, spread through Europe by the writings of Averroes, induced some of Dante's and Petrarch's contemporaries to doubt even the existence of God.[8] It was then deemed expedient to maintain both the authority of the Gospel, and the temporal influence of the Church, by the arbitrary and mysterious laws of the Holy Inquisition. Several of the Popes who filled the chair of St. Peter during the life of Dante, had been originally friars of the order of St. Dominick, the founder of that tribunal; and their successors, in the age of Petrarch, were prelates of France, either corrupted by luxury, or devoted to the interest of their country. The terror which had been propagated by the Dominicans, was followed by the sale of indulgences, and the celebration of the jubilees, instituted about this time by Boniface VIII. As the sovereign pontiffs were no longer allowed to employ in political projects the riches which they derived from their religious ascendancy, ambition yielded to covetousness; and they compounded their declining right of bestowing crowns for subsidies to maintain a luxurious court, and to leave behind them a genealogy of wealthy heirs. The people, though exasperated by oppression, and eager for insurrection, were disunited, and not enlightened enough to bring about a lasting revolution. They revolted only to overturn their ancient laws, to change their masters, and to yield to a more arbitrary government. The monarchs, opposed by an ungovernable aristocracy, were unable to raise armies sufficient to establish their power at home, and their conquests abroad. States were aggrandized more by craft than by bravery; and their rulers became less violent, and more treacherous. The

hardy crimes of the barbarous ages, gave place, by degrees, to the insidious vices of civilization. The cultivation of classical literature improved the general taste, and added to the stores of erudition; but at the same time, it enervated the boldness and originality of natural talent: and those who might have been inimitable writers in their maternal language, were satisfied to waste their powers in being the imitators of the Latins. Authors ceased to take any part in passing events, and remained distant spectators of them. Some detailed to their fellow-citizens the past glory, and warned them of the approaching ruin, of their country; and others repaid their patrons with flattery: for it was precisely in the fourteenth century that tyrannical governments began to teach their successors the policy of retaining men of letters in their pay to deceive the world. Such is the concise history of Italy, during the fifty-three years which elapsed from the death of Dante to the death of Petrarch.

Their endeavours to bring their country under the government of one sovereign, and to abolish the Pope's temporal power, forms the only point of resemblance between these two characters. Fortune seemed to have conspired with nature, in order to separate them by an irreconcilable diversity. Dante went through a more regular course of studies, and at a time when Aristotle and Thomas Aquinas reigned alone in universities. Their stern method and maxims taught him to write only after long meditation—to keep in view "a great practical end, which is that of human life"[9]—and to pursue it steadily with a predetermined plan. Poetical ornaments seem constantly employed by Dante, only to throw a light upon his subjects; and he never allows his fancy to violate the laws which he had previously imposed upon his own genius—

> L'ingegno affreno,
> Perchè non corra che virtù nol guidi.
>   —INFERNO.
> Più non mi lascia gire il fren dell'arte.
>   —PURG.

> I rein and curb
> The powers of nature in me, lest they run
> Where virtue guide not—
>   Mine art
> With warning bridle checks me.—
>   CARY'S TRANSL.

The study of the classics, and the growing enthusiasm for Platonic speculations which Petrarch defended against the Aristotelians,[10] coincided with his natural inclination, and formed his mind on the works of Cicero, Seneca, and St. Augustin. He caught their desultory manner, their ornamented diction, even when handling subjects the most unpoetical; and, above all, their mixture of individual feelings with the universal principles of philosophy and religion. His pen followed the incessant restlessness of his soul: every subject allured his thoughts, and seldom were all his thoughts devoted to one alone. Thus being more eager to undertake, than persevering to complete, the great number of his unfinished manuscripts at last impressed him with the idea, that the result of industry would be little more than that of absolute idleness.[11]—Dante avows that in his youth, he was sinking beneath a long and almost unconquerable despondence; and complains of that stillness of mind which enchains the faculties without destroying them.[12] But his mind, in recovering its elasticity, never desisted until it had attained its pursuit; and no human power or interest could divert him from his meditations.[13]

The intellect of both could only act in unison with the organic and unalterable emotions of their hearts. Dante's fire was more deeply concentrated; it could burn with one passion only at a time: and if Boccacio does not overcharge the picture, Dante, during several months after the death of Beatrice, had the feelings and appearance of a savage.[14] Petrarch was agitated at the same time by different passions: they roused, but they also counteracted, each other; and his fire was rather flashing than burning—expanding itself as it were from a soul unable to bear all its warmth, and yet anxious to attract through it the attention of every eye. Vanity made Petrarch ever eager and ever afraid of the opinion even of those individuals over whom he felt his natural superiority.—Pride was the prominent characteristic of Dante. He was pleased with his sufferings, as the means of exerting his fortitude,—and with his imperfections, as the necessary attendants of extraordinary qualities,—and with the consciousness of his internal worth, because it enabled him to look down with scorn upon other men and their opinions—

> Che ti fa ciò che quivi si pispiglia?—
> Lascia dir le genti;
> Sta come torre ferma che non crolla
> Giammai la cima per soffiar de'venti.

> How
> Imports it thee what thing is whisper'd
> here?—
> To their babblings leave
> The crowd; be as a tower that firmly set,
> Shakes not its top for any blast that blows.
> Cary's Transl.

The power of despising, which many boast, which very few really possess, and with which Dante was uncommonly gifted by nature, afforded him the highest delight of which a lofty mind is susceptible—

> Lo collo poi con le braccia mi cinse,
> Baciommi in volto, e disse: Alma sdegnosa!
> Benedetta colei che in te s'incinse.

> Then with his arms my neck
> Encircling, kiss'd my cheek and spake: O
> soul
> Justly disdainful! blest was she in whom
> Thou was conceived.
> Cary's Transl.

Dante's haughty demeanour towards the princes whose protection he solicited, was that of a republican by birth, an aristocrat by party, a statesman, and a warrior, who, after having lived in affluence and dignity, was proscribed in his thirty-seventh year, compelled to wander from town to town "as the man who stripping his visage of all shame, plants himself in the public way, and stretching out his hand, trembles through every vein."—"I will say no more: I know that my words are dark; but my countrymen shall help thee soon to a comment on the text, *To tremble through every vein*."[15]—Petrarch, born in exile, and brought up, according to his own confession, in indigence,[16] and as the intended servant of a court, was year after year enriched by the great, till enabled to decline new favours, he alluded to it with the complacency inevitable to all those who, whether by chance, or industry, or merit, have escaped from penury and humiliation.

Being formed to love, Petrarch courted the good-will of others, sighed for more friendship than human selfishness is willing to allow, and lowered himself in the eyes, and possibly in the affections, of the persons most devoted to him. His disappointments in this respect often embittered his soul, and extorted from him the confession, "that he feared those whom he loved."[17] His enemies knowing that, if he readily gave vent to his anger, he was still more ready to forget injuries, found fair game for ridicule[18] in his passionate temper, and provoked him to commit himself even in his old age with apologies.[19]—Dante, on the contrary, was one of those rare individuals who are above the reach of ridicule, and whose natural dignity is enhanced, even by the blows of malignity. In his friends he inspired less commiseration than awe; in his enemies, fear and hatred—but never contempt. His wrath was inexorable; with him vengeance was not only a natural impulse but a duty:[20] and he enjoyed the certainty of that slow but everlasting revenge which "his wrath brooded over in secret silence"—

> Fa dolce l'ira sua nel suo secreto—
> Taci e lascia volger gli anni:
> Sì ch'io non posso dir se non che pianto
> Giusto verrà di retro a'vostri danni.

> Let the destined years come round:
> Nor may I tell thee more, save that the meed
> Of sorrow well-deserved, shall quit your
> wrongs.
> Cary's Transl.

One would easily imagine his portrait from these lines:

> Egli non ci diceva alcuna cosa:
> Ma lasciavane gir, solo guardando,
> A guisa di Leon, quando si posa.

> He spoke not aught, but let us onward
> pass,
> Eyeing us as a Lion on his watch.
>   CARY'S TRANSL.

As Petrarch without love would probably never have become a great poet—so had it not been for injustice and persecution which kindled his indignation, Dante, perhaps, would never have persevered to complete—

> Il poema sacro,
> A cui han posto mano e cielo e terra,
> Sì che mi ha fatto per molti anni macro.

> The sacred poem, that hath made
> Both heaven and earth copartners in its toil,
> And with lean abstinence, through many a
> year,
> Faded my brow.
>   CARY'S TRANSL.

The gratification of knowing and asserting the truth, and of being able to make it resound even from their graves, is so keen as to outbalance all the vexations to which the life of men of genius is generally doomed, not so much by the coldness and envy of mankind, as by the burning passions of their own hearts. This sentiment was a more abundant source of comfort to Dante than to Petrarch—

> Mentre ch'i' era a Virgilio congiunto,
> Su per lo monte, che l'anime cura,
> E discendendo nel mondo defunto,
> Dette mi fur di mia vita futura
> Parole gravi; avvegnach'io mi senta
> Ben tetragono a i colpi di ventura.—

> Ben veggio, Padre mio, sì come sprona
> Lo tempo verso me, per colpo darmi
> Tal, ch'è più grave a chi più s'abbandona:
> Perchè di previdenza è buon ch'io
> m'armi.—

> O sacrosante Vergini! se fami,
> Freddi, o vigilie, mai per voi soffersi,
> Cagion mi sprona ch'io mercè ne chiami.
> Or convien ch'Elicona per me versi
> Ed Urania m'ajuti col suo coro
> Forti cose a pensar mettere in versi.—
> E s'io al vero son timido amico,
> Temo di perder vita tra coloro,
> Che questo tempo chiameranno antico.

> I, the whilst I scal'd
> With Virgil, the soul-purifying mount,
> And visited the nether world of woe,
> Touching my future destiny have heard
> Words grievous, though I feel me on all
> sides
> Well squar'd to fortune's blows.—

> My father! well I mark how time spurs on
> Toward me, ready to inflict the blow,
> Which falls most heavily on him who most
> Abandoneth himself. Therefore 'tis good
> I should forecast.—

> O ye thrice holy Virgins! for your sakes
> If e'er I suffer'd hunger, cold, and watching,
> Occasion calls on me to crave your bounty.
> Now through my breast let Helicon his
> stream
> Pour copious, and Urania with her choir
> Arise to aid me; while the verse unfolds
> Things, that do almost mock the grasp of
> thought.—

> And, if I am a timid friend to truth,
> I fear my life may perish among those
> To whom these days shall be of ancient
> date.
>   CARY'S TRANSL.

And from a letter of Dante lately discovered,[21] it appears that about the year 1316, his friends succeeded in obtaining his restoration to his country and his possessions, on condition that he compounded with his calumniators, avowed himself guilty, and asked pardon of commonwealth. The following was his answer on the occasion, to one of his kinsmen, whom he calls 'Father,' because, perhaps, he was an ecclesiastic; or, more probably, because he was older than the poet.

"From your letter, which I received with due respect and affection, I observe how much you have at heart my restoration to my country. I am bound to you the more gratefully, since an exile rarely finds a friend. But, after mature consideration, I must, by my answer, disappoint the wishes of some little minds; and I confide in the judgment to which your impartiality and prudence will lead you. Your nephew and mine has written to me, what indeed had been mentioned by many other friends, that, by a decree concerning the exiles, I am allowed to return to Florence, provided I pay a certain sum of money, and submit to the humiliation of asking and receiving absolution; wherein, father, I see two propositions that are ridiculous and impertinent. I speak of the impertinence of those who mention such conditions to me; for, in your letter, dictated by judgment and discretion, there is no such thing. Is such an invitation to return to his country glorious for Dante, after suffering in banishment almost fifteen years? Is it thus, then, they would recompence innocence which all the world knows, and the labour and fatigue of unremitting study? Far from the man who is familiar with philosophy, be the senseless baseness of a heart of earth, that could act like a little sciolist, and imitate the infamy of some others, by offering himself up as it were in chains. Far from the man who cries aloud for justice, be this compromise, for money, with his persecutors. No, father, this is not the way that shall lead me back to my country. But I shall return with hasty steps, if you or any other can open me a way that shall not derogate from the fame and honour of Dante; but if by no such way Florence can be entered, then Florence I will never enter. What! shall I not every where enjoy the sight of the sun and stars? and may I not seek and contemplate, in every corner of the earth under the canopy of heaven, consoling and delightful truth, without first rendering myself inglorious, nay infamous, to the people and republic of Florence? Bread, I hope, will not fail me."—Yet he continued to experience,

> How salt the savour is of others' bread,
> How hard the passage to descend and climb
> By others' stairs.
>
> CARY'S TRANSL.

His countrymen persecuted even his memory; he was excommunicated after death by the Pope, and his remains were threatened to be disinterred and burnt, and their ashes scattered to the wind.[22] Petrarch closed his life with the reputation of a saint, for whom Heaven performed miracles;[23] and the Venetian Senate made a law against those who purloined his bones, and sold them as relics.[24]

Indeed we might imagine that Petrarch by faithfully and generously discharging all the social duties towards every body about him, and by constantly endeavouring to subdue his passions, was esteemed virtuous and felt happy. Virtuous he was; but he was more unhappy than Dante, who never betrayed that restlessness and perplexity of soul which lowered Petrarch in his own estimation, and made him exclaim in his last days, "In my youth I despised all the world but myself; in my manhood I despised myself; now I despise both the world and myself."[25] Had they lived in habits of intercourse, Dante would have possessed over his competitor that superiority, which all men, who act from predetermined and unalterable resolutions, have over those who yield to variable and momentary impulses.—Petrarch might have said, with Dante—

> Conscienza m'assicura
> La buona compagnia, che l'uom
> francheggia
> Sotto l'usbergo del sentirsi pura.

> Conscience makes me firm,
> The boon companion who her strong breast-
> plate
> Buckles on him who feels no guilt within,
> And bids him on and fear not.
>
> CARY'S TRANSL.

But his ardent aspirations after moral perfection, and the despair of attaining it, made Petrarch look forward "with trembling hope" to the day that should summon him to the presence of an inexorable Judge. Dante believed, that by his sufferings on earth he atoned for the errors of humanity—that

> So wide arms
> Hath goodness infinite, that it receives
> All who turn to it.

> Ma la bontà divina ha sì gran braccia
> Che prende ciò che si rivolge a lei—

and he seems to address Heaven in the attitude of a worshipper rather than a suppliant. Being convinced "that Man is then truly happy when he freely exercises all his energies,"[26] Dante walked through the world with an assured step "keeping his vigils"—

> So that, nor night nor slumber with close
> stealth
> Convey'd from him a single step in all
> The goings on of time.
>
> CARY'S TRANSL.

He collected the opinions, the follies, the vicissitudes, the miseries and the passions that agitate mankind, and left behind him a monument, which while it humbles us by the representation of our own wretchedness, should make us glory that we partake of the same nature with such a man; and encourage us to make the best use of our fleeting existence. Petrarch was led by a wisdom rather contemplative than active, to think that our toils and exertions in behalf of mankind far exceed any benefit they derive from them; that each step after all but brings us nearer to the grave; that death is the best boon of Providence, and the world to come our only secure dwelling-place. He therefore faltered on through life with the conviction, "that a weariness and disgust of every thing were naturally inherent in his soul"[27]—and thus he paid the price of those favours, which nature, fortune, and the world, had heaped upon him, without the alloy even of ordinary reverses.

Notes

[1] Senil. Lib. 5. Ep. 2. et 3.

[2] Nec tibi sit durum versus vidisse poetæ
Exsulis.—

[3] Petr. Epist. edit. Ginevr. an. 1601. p. 445.

[4] TIRABOSCHI, Storia della Let. Ital. vol. 9. lib. 3. cap. 2. sect, 10.

[5] MURATORI, Script. Rer. Ital. vol. 10. p. 501.

[6] DANTE, *Convito.*

[7] Essay on the Char. of Petr. Sect. IV.

[8] Guido Cavalcanti alcuna volta speculando, molto astratto dagli uomini diveniva; e perciò che egli alquanto teneva della opinione degli Epicurj, si diceva tra la gente volgare che queste sue speculazioni eran solo in cercare se trovar si potesse che Iddio non fosse. BOCCACIO, Giorn. vi. Nov. 9.—See also DANTE, Inf. cant. 10., and Petrarch, Senil. lib. 5. ep. 3.

[9] DANTE, Convito.

[10] This is the main object of his treatise, *De sui ipsius et multorum ignorantiâ.*

[11] *Quicquid ferè opusculorum mihi excidit quæ tàm multa fuerunt, ut usque ad hanc œtatem, me exercent, ac fatigent: fuit enim mihi ut corpus, sic ingenium magis pollens dexteritate, quam viribus. Itaque multa mihi facilia cogitatu, quæ executione difficilia prœtermisi.*—Epist. ad Posterit.

[12] Dante, Vita nuova.

[13] POGGIO,—DANTE, Purg. cant. xvii.

[14] Egli era già, sì per lo lagrimare e sì per l'afflizione, che al cuore sentiva dentro, e sì per non aver di sè alcuna cura di fuori, divenuto quasi una cosa salvatica a riguardare, magro, barbuto, e quasi tutto trasformato da quello, che avanti esser soleva; in tanto che'l suo aspetto non che negli amici, ma eziandio in ciascun altro a forza di sè metteva compassione.—BOCCACIO, Vita di Dante.

[15] Purgat. cant. xi. towards the end.

[16] *Honestis parentibus, fortuna (ut verum fatear) ad inopiam vergente, natus sum.*—Epist. ad Post.

[17] Senil. Lib. 13. Ep. 7.

[18] *Indignantissimi animi, sed offensarum obliviosissimi—ira mihi persœpe nocuit, aliis nunquam.*—Epist. ad Post.

[19] AGOSTINI, Scritt. Venez. vol. 1. p. 5.

[20] *Che bell' onor s'acquista in far vendetta.* DANTE, Convito.—See also, Inferno, cant. xxix. vers. 31-36.

[21] APPENDIX, No. VI.

[22] BARTOLUS, *Lex de rejudicandis reis,* ad cod. 1.

[23] *Ea res . . . miraculo ostendit divinum illum spiritum Deo familiarissimum.*—VILLANI, Vit. Petr. sul fine.

[24] TOMASINI, Petrarcha Redivivus, pag. 30.

[25] Senil. Lib. 13. Ep. 7.

[26] *Humanum genus, potissimè liberum, optimè se habet.*—DANTE de Monarchia.

[27] *Cum omnium rerum fastidium atque odium naturaliter in animo meo insitum ferre non possim.*—Epist. ad Post.

Littell's Living Age (essay date 1878)

SOURCE: "Petrarch," in *Littell's Living Age,* Vol. XXIV, No. 1802, December, 1878, pp. 771-87.

[*In the review below, the anonymous critic remarks on Henry Reeve's* Petrarch *(1878) and discusses Petrarch's contribution to the Italian Renaissance as a humanist and poetic stylist.*]

The true position of Petrarch in the history of modern culture has recently been better understood, owing to a renewed and careful examination of his Latin works in prose and verse. Not very long ago he lived upon the lips of all educated people as the lover of Laura, the poet of the **canzoniere,** the hermit of Vaucluse, the founder of a school of sentimental sonneteers called Petrarchisti. This fame of Italy's first lyrist still belongs to Petrarch, and remains perhaps his highest title to immortality, seeing that the work of the artist outlives the memory of services rendered to civilization by the pioneer of learning. Yet we now know that Petrarch's poetry exhausted but a small portion of his intellectual energy, and was included in a vaster and far more universally important life-task. What he did for the modern world was not merely to bequeath to his Italian imitators masterpieces of lyrical art unrivalled for perfection of workmanship, but to open out for Europe a new sphere of mental activity. Petrarch is the founder of humanism, the man of genius who, standing within the threshold of the Middle Ages, surveyed the kingdom of the modern spirit, and by his own inexhaustible industry in the field of study determined the future of the Renaissance. He not only divined but, so to speak, created an ideal of culture essentially different from that which satisfied the mediæval world. By bringing the men of his own generation once more into sympathetic relation with antiquity, he gave a decisive impulse to that great European movement which restored freedom, self-consciousness, and the faculty of progress to the human intellect. To assert that without Petrarch this new direction could not have been taken by the nations at the close of the Middle Ages would be hazardous. The warm reception which he met with in his lifetime and the extraordinary activity of his immediate successors prove that the age itself was ripe for a momentous change. Yet it is none the less certain that Petrarch did actually stamp his spirit on the time, and that the Renaissance continued to be what he first made it. He was in fact the hero of the humanistic struggle; and so far-reaching were the interests controlled by him in this his world-historical capacity, that his achievement as an Italian lyrist seems by comparison insignificant.

It is Mr. Reeve's merit, while writing for the public rather than for scholars, to have kept this point of view before him. Petrarch, he says, "foresaw in a large and liberal spirit a new phase of European culture, a revival of the studies and the arts which constitute the chief glory and dignity of man;" and there are some fine lines in his "Africa," in which he predicts the advancement of knowledge as he discerned it from afar:—

> To thee, perchance, if lengthened days are
> given,
> A better age shall mark the grace of
> Heaven;
> Not always shall this deadly sloth endure;
> Our sons shall live in days more bright and
> pure;
> Then with fresh shoots our Helicon shall
> glow;
> Then the fresh laurel spread its sacred
> bough;
> Then the high intellect and docile mind
> Shall renovate the studies of mankind,
> The love of beauty and the cause of truth
> From ancient sources draw eternal youth.

With reference to Mr. Reeve's life of the poet-scholar it may be briefly said that none of the more interesting or important topics of Petrarch's biography have been omitted, and that the chief questions relating to his literary productions have been touched upon. The little book is clearly the product of long-continued studies and close familiarity with the subject; it is, moreover, marked by unvarying moderation and good taste. Those who have no leisure for studying the more comprehensive biographies of De Sade and Koerting, or for quarrying for themselves in the rich mine of Signor Fracassetti's edition of the poet's letters, will find it a serviceable guide. One general criticism must here be added. Mr. Reeve is not always particularly happy in the choice of his translations. He quotes, for example, not without approval,

Macgregor's version of the *canzone* to Rienzi, which renders the opening lines by this inconceivable clumsiness of phrase:—

> Spirit heroic! who with fire divine
> Kindlest those limbs, awhile which pilgrim
> hold
> On earth a chieftain, gracious, wise, and
> bold.

It might also be parenthetically questioned why he prefers to call the river Sorgues, which in Italian is Sorga, by its Latin name of Sorgia. But these are matters of detail. The book itself is sound. Taking this volume of "Foreign Classics for English Readers" in our hand, we shall traverse a portion of the ground over, which Mr. Reeve has passed, using such opportunities as offer themselves for expressing disagreement upon minor points with his conclusions.

The materials for a comprehensive life of Petrarch are afforded in rich abundance by his letters, collected by himself and prepared for publication under his own eye. Petrarch was an indefatigable epistolographer, carrying on a lively correspondence with his private friends, and also addressing the dignitaries of his age upon topics of public importance. Self-conscious and self-occupied, he loved to pour himself out on paper to a sympathetic audience, indulging his egotism in written monologues, and finding nothing that concerned himself too trivial for regard. His letters have, therefore, a first-rate biographical importance. They not only yield precise information concerning the chief affairs of his life; but they are also valuable for the illustration of his character, modes of feeling, and personal habits. The most interesting of the series is addressed to posterity, and is nothing less than the fragment of an autobiography begun in the poet's old age. Of this remarkable document Mr. Reeve has printed a translation into English. Next in importance to the letters rank the epistles and eclogues in Latin verse and the Italian poems; while apart from all other materials, as furnishing a full confession of Petrarch's passions, weaknesses, and impulses, stand the dialogues upon the "Contempt of the World." The preoccupation with self which led Petrarch to the production of so many autobiographical works, marks him out as a man of the modern rather than the mediæval age. He was not content to remain the member of a class, or to conform his opinions to authorized standards, but strove at all costs to realize his own particular type. This impulse was not exactly egotism, nor yet vanity; though Petrarch had a good share of both qualities. It proceeded from a conviction that personality is infinitely precious as the central fact and force of human nature. The Machiavellian doctrine of self-conscious character and self-dependent *virtù*, so vitally important in the Renaissance, was anticipated by the poet-scholar of Vaucluse, who believed, moreover, that high conditions of culture can only be attained by the free evolution and interaction of self-developed intellects. Nature, besides, had formed him for introspection, gifting him with the sensibilities that distinguish men like Rousseau. Subjectivity was the main feature of his genius, as a poet, as an essayist, as a thinker, as a social being. By surrendering himself to this control, and by finding fit scope for this temperament, he emancipated himself from the conditions of the Middle Ages, which had kept men cooped in guilds, castes, cloisters. Determined to be the best that God had made him, to form himself according to his ideal of excellence, he divested his mind of superstition and pedantry, refused such offices of worldly importance as might have hampered him in his development, and sought his comrades among the great men of antiquity, who, like himself, had lived for the perfection of their own ideal.

After the materials afforded to the biographer by Petrarch's own works, may be placed, but at a vast distance below them, the documents furnished by the Abbé de Sade in his bulky "Life." These chiefly concern Laura, and go to prove that she was a lady of noble birth, married to Hugh de Sade, and the mother of eleven children. It would hardly be necessary to refer to these papers, unless Mr. Reeve had expressed a too unqualified reliance on their authority. He says, "These facts are attested beyond all doubt by documents in the archives of the De Sade family." Yet it is still an open question, in the absence of the deeds which the abbé professed to have copied and printed, whether he was not either the fabricator of a historical romance very flattering to his family vanity, or else the dupe of some earlier impostor. It is true that he submitted the supposed originals to certain burghers of Avignon, who pronounced them genuine; but we may remember with what avidity Barrett and Burgon of Bristol swallowed Chatterton's forgeries about the same period: nor, even were we convinced of the abbé's trustworthiness, is there much beyond an old tradition at Avignon to justify the identification of Petrarch's Laura with his Laure de Sade. Mr. Reeve is therefore hardly warranted in asserting that it is "useless to follow the speculations which have been published as to the person of Laura, and, indeed, as to her existence."

Petrarch was born at the moment when the old order of mediævalism had begun to break up in Italy, but not before the main ideas of that age had been expressed in an epic which remains one of the three or four monumental poems of the world. Between the date 1302, when Dante and Petrarch's father were exiled on one day from Florence, and when Petrarch himself was born at Arezzo, and the year 1321, when Dante died, and when the younger poet was prosecuting his early studies in Montpellier, the "Divine Comedy" had

been composed, and the mighty age of which it was the final product had already passed away. The papacy had been transferred from Rome to Avignon. The emperors had proved their inability to settle the Italian question. Italy herself, exhausted by the conflicts which succeeded to the first strong growth of freedom in her communes, had become a prey to factions. The age of the despots had begun. A new race was being formed, in whom the primitive Italian virtues of warlike independence, of profound religious feeling, and of vigorous patriotism were destined to yield to the languor of indifference beneath a tyrant's sceptre, to half-humorous cynicism, and to egotistic party strife. At the same time a new ideal was arising for the nation, an ideal of art and culture, an enthusiasm for beauty, and a passion for the ancient world. The Italians, deprived of their liberty, thwarted in their development as a nation, and depraved by the easygoing immorality of the rich *bourgeoisie,* intent on only money-getting and enjoyment, were at this momentous crisis of their fortunes on the point of giving to the modern world what now is known as humanism, and had already entered on that career of art which was so fruitful of masterpieces in painting, sculpture, and architecture. The allegories, visions, ecstasies, legends, myths, and mysteries of the Middle Ages had lost their primitive vitality. If handled at all by poets or prose-writers, they had become fanciful or frigid forms of literature, at one time borrowing the colors of secular romance, at another sinking into the rigidity of ossified conventionality. Wearied with the effort of the past, but still young, and with a language as yet but in its infancy, the Italians sought a new and different source of intellectual vitality. They found this in the Roman classics, to whom, as to their own authentic ancestors, they turned with the enthusiasm of discoverers, the piety of neophytes.

For Dante the Middle Age still lived, and its stern spirit, ere it passed away, was breathed into his poem. Petrarch, though he retained a strong tincture of mediævalism, belonged to the new period: and this is the reason why, though far inferior in force of character and grasp of thought to Dante, his immediate influence was so much greater. For the free growth of his genius, and for the special work he had to do, it was fortunate for Petrarch that he was born and lived an exile. This circumstance disengaged him from the concerns of civic life and from the strife of the republics. It left him at liberty to pursue his own internal evolution unchecked. It enabled him to survey the world from the standpoint of his study, and to judge its affairs with the impartiality of a philosophical critic. Without a city, without a home, without a family, without any function but the literary, absorbed in solitary musings at Vaucluse, or accepted as a petted guest by the Italian princes, he nowhere came in contact with the blunt realities of life. He was therefore able to work out his ideal; and visionary as that ideal seems to us in many of its details, it controlled the future with a force that no application of his personal powers to the practical affairs of life could have engendered.

Another circumstance of no little weight in the formation of Petrarch for his destined life-work was his education at Avignon. When his father settled there in 1313, the boy of eleven years had already acquired his mother-tongue at Arezzo, Incisa, and Pisa. Nothing therefore was lost for the future poet of the *canzoniere* in regard to purity of diction. But Avignon was a far more favorable place of training for the humanistic student than any Tuscan town could have been. It was the only cosmopolitan city of that time. A fief of Provence, and owning King Robert of Naples for its sovereign, it was now inhabited by the popes, who swayed Christendom from their palace on the hill above the Rhone. All roads, it is said, lead to Rome; but this proverb in the first half of the fourteenth century might with more propriety have been applied to Avignon. The business of the Catholic Church had to be transacted here; and this brought men of mark together from all quarters of the globe. Petrarch therefore grew up in a society more mingled than could have been found elsewhere at the time in Europe; and since he was destined to be the apostle of the new culture, he had the opportunity of forming a cosmopolitan and universal conception of its scope. His own attitude towards the papal court was not a little peculiar. Though he could boast of being favored by five popes, though he lived on intimate relations with high dignitaries of the Church, though he was frequently pressed to accept the office of apostolic secretary, though he owed his pecuniary independence to numerous small benefices conferred upon him by the pontiffs whom he served, and though he undertook the duties of ambassador at their request, he was unsparing both in prose and verse of the abuse he showered upon them. No fiercer satire of the papal court exists than is contained in the *"Epistolæ sine Titulo."* It was not that Petrarch was other than an obedient son of the Church: but he could not endure to see the chiefs of Christendom neglecting their high duties to Rome. He thought that if they would but return to the seat of St. Peter, a golden age would begin; and thus his residence in Avignon intensified that idealization of Rome which was the cardinal point of his enthusiasm.

Next in importance to his exile from Provence and his education at Avignon, must be reckoned Petrarch's numerous journeys. His biographers have no slight difficulty in following him from place to place. Besides visiting the most important cities of Italy, he travelled through France and the Low Countries, saw the Rhine, crossed the Alps to Prague, and touched the shores of Spain. No sooner is he established in Vaucluse than we find him projecting a flight to Naples or to Rome. His residence at Parma is interrupted by return flights to Avignon. He settles for a while at Milan; then transfers his library to Venice; next makes Padua his home; then goes on pilgrimage to the Eternal City. The one thing that seems fixed in his biography is change. How highly Petrarch valued freedom of movement, may be gathered from his refusal to accept any office which would have bound him to one spot. Thus he persistently rejected the advances of the popes who offered him the post of secretary; and when Boccaccio brought him the invitation to occupy a professorial chair at Florence in 1351, even this proposal, so flattering to his vanity as an exile and a scholar, was declined with thanks. He knew that he must ripen and possess himself in disengagement from all local ties; for the student belongs to the world, and his internal independence demands a corresponding liberty of action. At the same time there is no doubt that he loved a restless life for its own sake; and he expressly tells us that many of his journeys were undertaken in the vain hope of casting off his passion for Laura, in the unaccomplished effort to break the chains of an internal discontent. The effect of so much movement on himself was still further to develop his cosmopolitan ideal of humanism. He was also flung back by contrast on his inner self, and while he made acquaintance with all the men worth knowing among his contemporaries, he remained a solitary in the midst of multifarious societies. Fame came to him upon his travels, and some of his excursions resembled royal progresses rather than the expeditions of a simple priest. In this way he enhanced the dignity of the humanist's vocation. He may be called the first and by far the most illustrious of those poet-scholars who fitted restlessly from town to town in the Renaissance, ever athirst for glory, and scattering the seeds of knowledge where they went.

When we seek to analyze the ideal of life formed by Petrarch in exile, at Avignon, in the solitary valley of Vaucluse, and in the courts of Europe, we shall be led to consider him from several general points of view— as a scholar, as a politician, as a philosopher, as a poet, and lastly as the man who, living still within the Middle Ages, was first clearly conscious of a modern personality. The discussion of these topics will also serve as well as any other method to bring the complex qualities of one of the most strangely blended characters the world has ever known into sufficient prominence.

It is a mistake to suppose that, though Greek was lost to western Europe, the Latin classics were unknown in the Middle Ages. A fair proportion of both poets and prose-writers are quoted by men of encyclopædic learning like John of Salisbury, Vincent of Beauvais, and Brunetto Latini. But the capacity for understanding them was in abeyance, and their custody had fallen into the hands of men who were antagonistic to their spirit. Between Christianity and paganism there could be no permanent truce. Moreover, the visionary enthusiasms of the cloister and crusade were diametrically opposed to the positive precision of the classic genius. The intellectual strength of the Middle Ages lay not in science or in art, but in a vivid quickening of the spiritual imagination. Their learning was a compilation of detached, ill-comprehended fragments. Their theology, as represented in the *"Summa,"* resembled a vast structure of Cyclopean masonary—block placed on block of roughhewn inorganic travertine, solidified and weighty with the force of dogma. Their philosophy started from narrow data of authority, and occupied its energies in the proof or disproof of certain assumed formulæ. It was inevitable that mediæval scholarship should regard the classical literatures as something alien to itself and should fail to appropriate them. The mediæval mind was no less incapable of sympathizing with their æsthetic and scientific freedom than the legendary mathematician, who asked what the "Paradise Lost" proved, was unable to take the point of view required by poetry. Its utter misapprehension of the subject-matter of these studies was expressed in the legends which made Virgil a magician and turned the gods of Hellas into devils. Nor were the most learned men free from such radically false conceptions, such palpable and incurable "lies in the soul," poisoning the very source of erudition, and converting their industry into a childish trifling with the puppets of blindfold fancy. The very fact that, while Greek was a living language in the east and in the south of Italy, it should have been abandoned by the students of the north and west, proves the indifference to literature for its own sake and the apathy with regard to human learning that prevailed in Europe. Had not Latin been the language of the Church, the language of civilized communication, it is certain that the great authors of Rome would have fallen into the same oblivion as those of Athens. An accident of social and ecclesiastical necessity preserved them. Yet none the less did they need to be rediscovered when the time came for a true comprehension of their subject-matter to revive. What Petrarch did for scholarship was to restore the lost faculty of intelligence by placing himself and his generation in a genial relation of sympathy to the Latin authors. He first treated the Romans as men of like nature with ourselves. For him the works of Virgil and Cicero, Livy and Horace, were canonical books—not precisely on a par with the Bible, because the matter they handled had a less vital relation to the eternal concerns of humanity—but still possessing an authority akin to that of inspiration, and demanding no less stringent study than the Christian sacred literature.

The dualism of the papacy and the empire, which had struck such deep roots in mediæval politics, repeated itself in Petrarch's theory of human knowledge. Just as the pope was the sun, the emperor the moon of the mediæval social system, so, with Petrarch, Christ and the Church shed the light of day upon his conscience, while the great men of antiquity were luminaries of a secondary splendor, by no means to be excluded from the heaven of human thought. This is the true meaning of his so-called humanism. It was this which made him search indefatigably for MSS., which prompted him to found public libraries and collect coins, and which impelled him to gather up and live again in his own intellectual experience whatever had been thought and done by the heroes of the Roman world. At its beginning, humanism was a religion rather than a science. Its moral force was less derived from the head than from the heart. It was an outgoing of sympathy and love and yearning towards the past, not a movement of sober curiosity. Petrarch made the classic authors his familiar friends and confidants. His epistles to Cicero, Seneca, and Varro are but fragments of a long-sustained internal colloquy, detached by a literary caprice and offered to the public as a specimen of his habitual mood. Unlike Machiavelli, after a day passed among the boon companions of a village inn, Petrarch had no need to cast aside his vulgar raiment on the threshold of his study, and assume a courtly garb before he entered the august society of the illustrious dead. He had wrought himself into such complete sympathy with the objects of his admiration, that he was always with them. They were more real to him than the men around him. He tells Augustine or Cicero more about his inner self than he communicates to the living friends whom he called Lælius and Socrates and Simonides. These men, of whom we know almost nothing, served Petrarch as the audience of his self-engrossed monologues; but they were separated from him by the spirit of the Middle Ages. He held converse with them, and presumably loved them; but he recognized a difference of intellectual breed which removed them to a greater distance than the lapse of years dividing him from antiquity. Only those friends of Petrarch's who were animated by an instinct for humanism, kindred in nature and equal in intensity to his own, emerge from the shadow-world and stand before us in his correspondence as clearly as his comrades of the Roman age. Cola di Rienzo and Boccaccio have this privilege. The rest are formless, vague, devoid of substance. . . .

When we enquire into the range of Petrarch's knowledge, we find that he had by no means more than belonged to the mediæval students in general. It was not the extent, but the intensity of his erudition, not the matter, but the spirit of his scholarship, not its quantity, but its quality, that placed him at an immeasurable distance of superiority above his predecessors. He had so far appropriated Virgil and Seneca, with the larger portions of Cicero and Livy, as to find some difficulty in avoiding verbal reproductions of their works. Had he so willed, he might have expressed himself in a cento of their prose and verse. Horace and Ovid, Juvenal and Persius, Terence, Lucan, Statius, Ausonius, and Claudian, were among his favorite poets. It is possible that he had read Lucretius, and he twice refers somewhat vaguely to Catullus: but Propertius and Tibullus seem to have been unknown to him, while he makes but scanty use of Martial and Plautus. Valerius Flaccus and Silius Italicus he never saw: else it is improbable that he would have chosen Scipio Africanus for the hero of his Latin epic. With Apuieius he was partially acquainted; but there seems good reason to suppose that he had never read the "Golden Ass," though he alludes to it. He knew Macrobius, Aulus Gellius, Solinus, Hyginus, and Pomponius Mela in part, if not completely; for it must be remembered, in reading this lengthy list of authors, that the MSS. were imperfect and full of errors. What Poggio tells us about his finding Quintilian at St. Gallen, proves that the discovery of a good codex was almost equal to the resuscitation of a forgotten author. Cæsar, Sallust, Suetonius, Florus, Justin, Curtius, Vopiscus, Ælius Lampridius, Spartian, together with the anecdotes of Valerius Maximus and the universal history of Orosius, were among the authors he studied and epitomized while composing his great work on "Famous Men." Tacitus was unfortunately unknown to him; and he possessed Quintilian only in a mutilated copy. It may also be regarded as a special calamity that he was unacquainted with the letters of the younger Pliny, though he possessed the natural histories of the elder. The style of these letters would have supplied Petrarch with a better model than Seneca's rhetorical epistles; and he could have assimilated it more easily than that of Cicero, partly because it is itself less idiomatic, and partly because the poet of Vaucluse would have recognized a vivid bond of intellectual sympathy between himself and the humane and tranquil dilettante of Como. As it was, Petrarch's letters bear the stamp of Seneca, Augustine, and the Middle Ages. He found the MS. of Cicero too late (at Verona in 1345) to profit by its study. And here we must express a total disagreement with a passage of Mr. Reeve's "Petrarch," where he says: "But though the style of Cicero was, no doubt, his model, he attained rather to the epistolary than to the philosophical diction of that great master." It is true that on the next page Mr. Reeve appears to contradict this statement by the following admission: "As his knowledge of the Ciceronian epistles was not attained till Petrarch had passed his fortieth year, it may be concluded that his own epistolary style was formed before he knew them." The fact is here correctly given. There is no trace of Cicero's diction, at once epigrammatic and easy, in Petrarch's letters; but in his philosophical treatises, though these reveal the paramount influence of Seneca, St. Augustine, and Lactantius, we occasionally detect an aiming at Cicero's oratorical cadences. The variety of matter handled in his letters, the rapid transition from description to dissertation, their masterly portraits of men, the pleasant wit and caustic humor that relieve the graver passages, the unaffected friendliness of their familiar discourse, the earnest enthusiasm of their political and philosophical digressions, the animation and the movement that carry the reader on as through an ever-shifting, ever-changing scene, render this great mass of correspondence not only valuable for the historian but delightful to the general reader. The scholar will detect a less than classic elegance in their diction, and the student will desire less generality of treatment on some personal topics. But both will admit that neither the ear for rhythm nor the quick intelligence which Petrarch recognized among his choicest literary gifts, had failed him in their composition.

It was Petrarch's merit, while absorbing the Roman classics and the Latin fathers, to have aimed consistently at a style that should express his own originality, and be no mere copy of however eminent a master's. The ruling consciousness of self, which formed so prominent a feature of his moral character, lying at the root of his vanity and conditioning his genius as a poet, here decided his literary development. He would be no man's ape—not even the ape of Cicero or Virgil. Come good, come bad, he meant to be himself. With this end in view, he forced himself to deal with the most formidable stylistic difficulties, and to find utterance in a practically dying language for thoughts and feelings that were modern. In this respect he contrasted favorably with his Italian followers, and proved that his conception of humanism was loftier than that of Ciceronian Bembo, or Virgilian Vida. They cut their matter down to the requirements of an artificially assimilated standard. He made the idiom bend to his needs, and preferred that purity of form should suffer, rather than that the substance to be expressed should be curtailed. It may indeed be said with truth that Erasmus, at the close of the fifteenth century, returned to the path trodden by Petrarch in the first half of the fourteenth, which had been abandoned by a set of timid and subservient purists on the quest of an impossible ideal.

Petrarch knew no Greek, yet he divined its importance, and made every effort in his power to learn it, if we except the supreme effort of going to the fount of Greek in Constantinople. His opportunities at Avignon were few; and he obtained no hold upon the language. What the subsequent history of Italian scholarship would have been, if Petrarch had but ventured on that journey to Byzantium which Filelfo and Guarino took with such immediate profit, or if by any other means he had acquired the key to Greek literature, it is now impossible to say. The weak side of the Renaissance was that it depended mainly upon Latin: and this explains in no small measure its philosophical superficiality, its tendency to lifeless rhetoric, its stylistic insipidity, the timidity and artificiality that stamp its literary products with the note of mediocrity. It was the echo of an echo, the silver age of a culture which had its own golden age in the Hellenic past: and all that it achieved in close relation to antiquity was consequently third-rate. Whether Petrarch, if he had known Greek, could have resisted the powerful bias which drew Italians back to Rome rather than to Athens, and whether, if he had overcome this tendency himself, he could have had the force to dye the humanism of the Renaissance with Hellenic instead of Latin colors, are questions that cannot by their very nature be decided. But none the less may we regret that tardy and partial impregnation of the modern mind by the Greek spirit which, had it but come earlier and in fuller measure, might have given the world a new birth of Athens instead of Rome. At the moment when humanism was a religion, the Italians absorbed the Latin genius; but now that scholarship has passed into the scientific stage, we are directed to Hellas with an unassimilative curiosity. As regards Petrarch's own knowledge of Greek authors, it may be briefly stated that he possessed MSS. of Homer and some dialogues of Plato. But he lamented that they were dumb for him while he was deaf. He read the "Iliad" in the pitiful Latin version dictated to Boccaccio by Pilatus; and the doctrines of Plato were known to him only in the meagre abstract of Apuleius, in Cicero, and in the works of St. Augustine.

Rome lay near to the Italians on their emergence from the Middle Ages. They were not a new nation, like the French or Germans; but were conscious that once, not very long ago, and separated from them only by a space of dream-existence, their ancestors through Rome had ruled the habitable world. Therefore Florence clung to her traditions of Catiline; the soldiers on watch at Modena told tales of Hector; Padua was proud of Antenor, and Como of the Plinies; Mantua sang hymns to Virgil; Naples pointed out his tomb; Sulmo rejoiced in Ovid, and Tivoli remembered Horace. The newly-formed Italian people, the people who had fought the wars of independence and had founded the communes, were essentially Roman. In no merely sentimental sense, but as a fact of plain historical survival, what still remained of Rome was indefeasibly their own. The *plebs* of the Italian cities was of Roman blood. Their municipal constitution, in the form and name at least, was Roman. Yet this great memory was but dimly descried through the mist of legends and romance, till Petrarch seized upon it and called his fellow-countrymen to recognize their birthright. His letter describing the impression made upon him by the ruins of Rome, dated with pride from the Capitol upon the Ides of March, his epistles to Varro and Cicero, and his burning appeals to each succeeding pope that he should end the Babylonian captivity and place a crown upon the brows of the world's mistress, prove with what a passion of anticipation he forecast the time when Rome should once more be the seat of empire. In the field of scholarship his enthusiasm was destined to be fruitful. The spirit of Roman art and

literature arose from the grave to sway a golden period in the history of human civilization. But in the sphere of politics it remained impotent, idealistic, fanciful.

As a politician, Petrarch continued to the end an incurable idealist. The very conditions of expatriation and pilgrimage, which rendered him so powerful as the leader of the humanistic movement, loosened his grasp upon the realities of political life. We see this on every occasion of his attempting to play a part in the practical business of the world. In his mission from the papal court to Naples, after the accession of Queen Joan, and in his representation of the Visconti at Venice toward the close of her long struggle with Genoa, he was unsuccessful, mainly because he thought that affairs of State could be decided upon moral principles, and because he assumed the tone of an oratorical pedagogue. It was only when the rhetorician's art was needed for a magnificent display, as in his embassy from the Visconti to the French court upon the delivery of John the Good from captivity, in his speech to the conquered people of Novara, and in his ceremonial address to Charles IV. at Prague, that he justified the confidence which had been placed in him. He never saw the world as it was, but as he wished it. And what he wished, was the imposible resuscitation of the Roman commonwealth. Rome was destined, he believed, to be the centre of the globe again as it had been before. With a thoroughly unpractical conception of the very conditions of the problem, he at one time called upon the popes to re-establish themselves in the Eternal City; at another he besought the emperor to make it his headquarters, and to finish by this simple act the anarchy of Italy; at a third, when Rienzi for a moment evoked the pale shadow of the republic from the ruins of the Campagna, he hailed in him the inaugurator of a new and better age. It was nothing to Petrarch that these three solutions were discordant; that pope, emperor, and commonwealth could not simultaneously exist at Rome. Whatever seemed to reflect lustre on the Rome of his romantic vision satisfied him. Indifferent to the claims of gratitude in the past, careless of consequences in the future, he published letters which denounced his old friends and patrons, the Colonna family, as barbarous intruders in the sacred city. Even his humanity forsook him. He burned to play the Brutus, and bade Rienzi to strike and spare not. By the same heated utterances, penetrated, it is true, with the spirit of a sincere patriotism and piety to Rome, he risked the hatred of the papal see. Nor was it until Rienzi had foamed himself away in the madness of vanity that Petrarch awoke from his wild dream. He awoke indeed, but he never relinquished the hope that, if not by this man or that policy, at least by some other Messiah, and upon a different foundation, Rome might still be restored to her primeval splendor. It would seem as though the great ones of the earth estimated his enthusiasm at its real value, and allowed him to pass free as a chartered lunatic; for, much as he said and wrote about the republic, he never seriously imperilled his consideration at the papal court, nor did he interrupt his friendly relations with the petty princes whom he so vehemently denounced as traitors to the Italian people. There was a strange confusion in his mind between his admiration for the ancient Roman commonwealth, which he had imbibed from Livy and which inspired his **"Africa,"** and his mediæval worship of the mixed papal and imperial idea. To Dante's theory of monarchy he added a purely literary enthusiasm for the *populus Romanus.* Yet Petrarch was no real friend of the people, as he found it, and as alone it could exist in the new age. His friendship for Azzo da Correggio and Luchino Visconti, for the tyrants of Padua, Verona, and Parma, and for King Robert of Sicily, prove that, though in theory he desired some phantom of republican government, in practice he accommodated himself to the worst forms of despotism. Democracy formed no portion of his creed; and his plan of Roman government, submitted to the consideration of Clement VI. in 1351, simply consisted of a scheme for placing power in the hands of the Roman burghers to the exclusion of the great Teutonic families. He was possessed with scholarly *hauteur* and literary aristocracy; and if he could not have a senate in Rome, with Scipios and Gracchi perorating before popes and emperors in some impossible chimera of mixed government, he did not care how cities suffered or how princes ground their people into dust. His apathetic attitude toward Jacopo da Bussolari's revolution in Pavia, and his sermon to the Novaresi on obedience, would be enough to prove this, if his whole life at Milan, Parma, and Padua were not conclusive testimony.

The main fault of Petrarch's treatises on politics is that they are too didactic. They do not touch the points at issue, but lose themselves in semi-ethical and superficially rhetorical discourses. Thus he prepared the way for those orators of the Renaissance who thought it enough to adorn their subject with moral sentences and learned citations, neglecting the matter of dispute and flooding their audience with conventional sermons. The same fault may be found with his philosophical writings, although a nobler spirit appears in them and a more sturdy grasp upon the realities of life. It was his misfortune to be cast exclusively upon the Roman eclectics—Cicero, Seneca, and Lactantius— for his training in moral science. His ignorance of Greek deprived him of the opportunity of studying any complete system, while his temperament rendered him incapable of absorbing and reconstructing the stoicism of the later Latin writers. According to his view, orthodoxy was the true philosophy; nor did he ever grasp the notion that in the scientific impulse there is an element of search and criticism perilous to Christian dogmatism. It need scarcely be said that he was a good churchman, though of a type less monumentally

severe than Dante. Early in life he took orders; and here it may be observed that Mr. Reeve is possibly wrong in supposing he was never ordained priest. The point seems proved by his own declaration that he was in the habit of saying mass;[1] and though his life was not irreproachable from a moral point of view, he never pretended that in this respect his conduct had not fallen short of sacerdotal duty.

St. Augustine, whose mental attitude as an orthodox philosopher was similar to his own, became the author of his predilection. Few moments in the history of thought are more interesting than the meeting of that last Roman, already merging his antique individuality in the abyss of theological mysticism, with Petrarch, the first modern to emerge from that contemplative eclipse and reassert the rights of human personality. Between them rolled the river of the Middle Ages, which had almost proved the Lethe of learning; but Petrarch stretched his hand across it, and found in the author of the *"Civitas Dei"* a friend and comrade. The exquisite sensibility of Augustine, his fervid language, the combat between his passions and his piety, his self-analysis, and final conquest over all that checks the soul's flight heavenward, drew Petrarch to him with irresistible attraction. The poet of Vaucluse recognized in him a kindred nature. The "Confessions" were his Werther, his Rousseau, his cherished gospel of tenderness, "running over with a fount of tears." But, more than this, Augustine pointed him the path that he should tread; and though Petrarch could not tread it firmly, though he bitterly avowed that love, restlessness, vanity, thirst for earthly fame, coldness, causeless melancholy, and divided impulse, kept him close to earth, when he would fain have flown aloft to God, yet the communion with this sterner but still sympathetic nature formed his deepest consolation. Those who wish to study Petrarch's very self must seek it in the book he called his **Secretum,** the dialogues with St. Augustine upon the contempt of the world. Between Augustine's own "Confessions" and this masterpiece of self-description, the human intellect had produced nothing of the same kind, if we except Dante's exquisite but comparatively restricted *"Vita Nuova."* With a master hand Petrarch touches the secret springs of his character in these dialogues, lays his finger upon his hidden wounds, and traces the failures and achievements of his life to their true sources. No more consummate piece of self-conscious analysis has ever been penned. It is inspired with an artistic interest in the subject for its own sake; and though the tone is grave, because Petrarch was sincerely religious, there is no obvious aiming at edification. In this intense sense of personality, this delight in the internal world revealed by introspection, it differs widely from mediæval manuals of devotion, from the *"Imitatio Christi,"* for example, which is not the delineation of a man but of a class.

The ***De Contemptu Mundi*** is the most important of Petrarch's quasi-philosophical works, chiefly, perhaps, because it was not written with a would-be scientific purpose. Together with a very few books of a similar description, gathered from all literatures ancient and modern, it remains as a fruitful mine for the inductive moralist. His treatise, ***De Remediis utriusque Fortunœ*** though bulkier, has less value. It consists of sentences and commonplaces upon the good and evil things of life, and how to deal with them, very often acute, and not seldom humorous, and written in a fluent style, that must have made them infinitely charming to the fourteenth century of arid composition. Petrarch had the art of literary gossip; and he displayed it not only in his letters, but also in such studied works as this The essay ***De Vitâ Solitariâ*** has a greater personal interest. Petrarch unfolds in it his theory of the right uses to be made of solitude, and shows how intellectual activity can best be carried on in close communion with nature. What he preached he had fully proved by practice at Vaucluse and Selvapiana. His recluse is no hermit or mediæval monk. He does not retire to the desert, or the woods, or to the cloister; but he lives a life of rational study and sustained communion with himself in the midst of nature's beauties. These he enjoys with placidity and passion, mingled in a wise enthusiasm, till, living thus alone, he finds his true self, enters into the possession of his own mental kingdom, and needs no external support of class interests, official dignities, or work among his fellow-men to buoy him up. There is a profoundly modern tone in this essay. Petrarch describes in it an intellectual egotist, devoted to self-culture, and bent on being sufficient to himself. It is, in fact, the ideal of Goethe, anticipated by four centuries, and colored with a curious blending of piety and paganism peculiar to Petrarch. The ***De Vitâ Solitariâ*** might be styled the panegyric of the wilderness, from a humanistic point of view. . . . [What] Petrarch did was to restate a classic theory of life, which had been merged in the asceticism of the cloister. He did so, without doubt, unconsciously; for Menander was a closed book to him. In harsh contrast is the companion essay on the leisure of the religious, ***De Otio Religiosorum,*** composed by Petrarch after a visit to his brother Gherardo in his cloister near Marseilles. The fascination which, in spite of humanism, the Middle Ages still exerted over Petrarch, may be seen in every line of this apparent palinode. If we examine the two discourses side by side, we are almost driven to the conclusion that his command of rhetoric induced their author to treat two discordant aspects of the same theme with something like cynical indifference. Yet this was not the case. In each discourse Petrarch is sincere; for the mediæval and humanistic ideals, irreconcilable and mutually exclusive, found their meeting-point in him. Their conflict caused his spiritual restlessness, and it was the effort of his life to bring them into equilibrium. At one time the humanist, athirst for glory, bent on self-effectuation, forensic, eloquent, enjoying life, devoting his solitary hours to culture, and communing in spirit with the orators of ancient Rome, was uppermost. At another the ascetic, renouncing the world, absorbing himself in mystic contemplation, fixing all his thoughts on death and on the life beyond the grave, assumed supremacy. In his youth and early manhood the former prevailed. After the year 1348, the year of Laura's death, the year of the great plague, which swept away his friends and changed the aspect of society, the latter gained a permanently growing ascendency. But it may be safely said that both impulses co-existed in him till the day of his own death in 1374. A common ground for both was found in the strong love of seclusion which formed one of his chief characteristics, driving him from time to time away from towns and friends into the country houses he possessed at Vaucluse, near Parma, near Milan, and at Arquà. A singular scheme, communicated in 1348 to his friends Mainardo Accursio and Luca Cristiano, for establishing a kind of humanistic convent, of which the members should be devoted to study as well as to religious exercises, shows that Petrarch even meditated a practical fusion of the scholarly and monastic modes of life.

Petrarch was neither a systematic theologian nor a systematic philosopher. He was an orthodox essayist on moral themes, biassed by a leaning towards pagan antiquity. Far more valuable than any of his ethical dissertations was his large and liberal view of human knowledge; and in this general sense he rightly deserves the title of philosopher. Mere repetitions of prescribed formulæ, reproductions of a master's *ipse dixit,* and scholastic reiterations of authorized doctrines, whether in theology or in philosophy, moved his bitterest scorn. He held that everything was worthless which a man had not assimilated and lived into by actual experience, so as to reconstruct it with the force of his own personality. This point of view was eminently precious in an age of formalism. His antipathy to law, in like manner, did not spring from any loathing of a subject redolent with antiquity and consecrated by the genius of Rome. He only despised the peddling sophistries and narrow arts of those who practised it. His polemic against the physicians, condensed into four ponderous invectives, was likewise based upon their false pretensions to science and their senseless empiricism. In every sphere of human activity he demanded that men should possess real knowledge, and be conscious of its limitations. When he entered into the lists against the Averrhoists, his weightiest argument was founded on the fact that they piqued themselves upon their erudition in the matter of stones, plants, and animals, while they neglected the true concerns of man, and all that may affect his destinies for weal or woe. He dreaded a debasement of human culture by Averrhoistic materialism hardly less than an injury to religion from Averrhoistic atheism. A steady preference of the spirit to the letter, and a firm grasp of the maxim that "the proper study of mankind is man," formed the pith and substance of his intellectual creed. It was here that his humanism and his philosophy joined hands. Nor can we regard the revival of learning in Italy without regretting that the humanists diverged so signally from the path prescribed for them in this respect by their great leader. They copied his faults of vanity and rhetoric. They exaggerated his admiration of Cicero and Virgil into a servile cult. They adhered to Latin authors and Latin canons of taste, when they might have carried on his work into the region of Greek metaphysics. But they lost his large conception of human learning, and gave themselves to puerilities which Petrarch would have been the first to denounce. Thus the true strength of Petrarch's spirit failed to sustain his disciples; while his foibles and shortcomings were perpetuated. In particular it may be affirmed that the Renaissance in Italy produced no philosophy worth notice until the dawn of modern science appeared in Telesio and Campanella, and in the splendid lunes of visionary Bruno.

In his general theory of poetry Petrarch did not free himself from mediæval conceptions, however much his practice may have placed him first upon the list of modern lyrists. He held that the poet and the orator were nearly equal in dignity, though he inclined to assigning a superiority to the latter. This estimate of the two chief species of impassioned eloquence, which we are accustomed to regard as separate and rarely combined in the same person, was probably due to the then prevalent opinion that poets must be learned—an opinion based upon the difficulty of study, and the belief that the unapproachable masterpieces of the ancients had been produced by scientific industry. With the same high sense of the literary function which marked his conception of humanism, he demanded that both orator and poet should instruct and elevate as well as please. The content of the work of art was no matter of indifference to Petrarch; and though he was the most consummate artist of Italian verse, the doctrine of art for art's sake found no favor in his eyes. It may, indeed, be said that he overstepped the mark, and confounded the poet with the prophet or the preacher, retaining a portion of that half-religious awe with which the students of the Middle Ages, unable to understand Virgil, and wonder-smitten by his greatness, had contemplated the author of the "Æneid." It was, he thought, the poet's duty to set forth truth under the veil of fiction, partly in order to enhance the pleasure of the reader and attract him by the rarity of the conceit, and partly to wrap his precious doctrine from the coarse unlettered world. This view of the necessary connection between poetry and allegory dates as far back as Lactantius, from whose "Institutions" Petrarch borrowed the groundwork of his own exposition. That it was shared by the early Florentine lyrists, especially by Dante and Guido Cavalcanti, is well-

known. It reappears in the diploma presented to Petrarch upon the occasion of his coronation. It pervades Boccaccio's critical treatises, and it lives on with diminished energy until the age of Tasso, who supplied a key to the moral doctrine of his *Gerusalemme Liberata.* Genius, however, works by instinct far less than by precept; and the best portions of Petrarch's poetry are free from this æsthetic heresy. We find allegory pure and simple, it is true, in his Latin eclogues, while the *concetti* of the Italian lyrics, where he plays upon the name of Laura, reveal the same taint. In the *Trionfi* allegorical machinery is used with high art for the legitimate presentation of a solemn pageant; so that we need not quarrel with it here. The Latin epistles are comparatively free from the disease, while the "**Africa**" is an epic of the lamp, modelled upon Virgil, and vitiated less by allegory than by an incurable want of constitutional vitality. It is the artificial copy of a poem which itself was artificial, and is therefore thrice removed from the truth of nature. What must be said about Petrarch's Latin poetry may be briefly stated. It has the same merits and the same defects as his prose. That is to say, he studiously strove at being original while he imitated; and, paradoxical as this may seem, he was not unsuccessful. His verse is his own; but it is often rough, and almost always tedious, deformed by frequent defects of rhythm, and very rarely rising into poetry except in some sonorous bursts of declamation. The lament for King Robert at the end of the "Africa," with its fine prophecy of the Renaissance, and a fervid address to Italy, written on the heights of Mont Genèvre in 1353 upon the occasion of his crossing the Alps, to return to Avignon no more,[2] might be cited as two favorable specimens. But when we speak of Petrarch as a poet, we do not think of these scholastic lucubrations. We think of the *canzoniere,* for the sake of which the lover of Madonna Laura is crowned second in the great triumvirate of the *trecento* by the acclaim of his whole nation.

Petrarch the author of the *Rime in Vita e Morte di Madonna Laura,* seems at first sight a very different being from Petrarch the humanist. There is a famous passage in the *De Remediis utriusque Fortunæ,* where the lyrist of chivalrous love pours such contempt on women as his friend Boccaccio might have envied when he wrote the satire of "Corbaccio." In the *Secretum,* again, he describes his own passion as a torment from which he had vainly striven to emancipate himself by solitude, by journeys, by distractions, and by obstinate studies. In fact, he never alludes to the great love of his life without a strange mixture of tenderness and sore regret. That Laura was a real woman, and that Petrarch's worship of her was unfeigned; that he adored her with the senses and the heart as well as with the head; but that this love was at the same time more a mood of the imagination, a delicate disease, a cherished wound, to which he constantly recurred as the most sensitive and lively well-spring of poetic fancy, than a downright and impulsive passion, may be clearly seen in the whole series of his poems and his autobiographical confessions. Laura was a married woman; for he calls her *mulier*. She treated him with the courtesy of a somewhat distant acquaintance, who was aware of his homage and was flattered by it. But they enjoyed no intimacy, and it may be questioned whether, if Petrarch could by any accident have made her his own, the fruition of her love would not have been a serious interruption to the happiness of his life. He first saw her in the Church of St. Claire, at Avignon, on the 6th of April, 1327. She passed from this world on the 6th of April, 1348. These two dates are the two turning-points of Petrarch's life. The interval of twenty-one years, when Laura trod the earth, and her lover in all his wanderings paid his orisons to her at morning, evening, and noonday, and passed his nights in dreams of that fair form which never might be his, was the storm and stress period of his checkered career. There is an old Greek proverb that "to desire the impossible is a malady of the soul." With this malady in its most incurable form the poet was stricken; and, instead of seeking cure, he nursed his sickness and delighted in the discord of his soul. From that discord he wrought the harmonies of his sonnets and *canzoni*. That malady made him the poet of all men who have found in their emotions a dreamland more wonderful and pregnant with delight than in the world which we call real. After Laura's death his love was tranquillized to a sublimer music. The element of discord had passed out of it; and just because its object was now physically unattainable, it grew in purity and power. The sensual alloy which, however spiritualized, had never ceased to disturb his soul, was purged from his still vivid passion. Laura in heaven looked down upon him from her station amid the saints; and her poet could indulge the dream that now at last she pitied him, that she was waiting for him with angelic eyes of love, and telling him to lose no time, but set his feet upon the stairs that led to God and her. The romance finds its ultimate apotheosis in that transcendent passage of the **Trionfo della Morte**, which describes her death and his own vision. Throughout the whole course of this labyrinthine love-lament, sustained for forty years on those few notes so subtly modulated, from the first sonnet on his *"primo giovenile errore"* to the last line of her farewell, *"Tu stara' in terra senza me gran tempo,"* Laura grows in vividness before us. She only becomes a real woman in death, because she was for Petrarch always an ideal, and in the ideal world beyond the tomb he is more sure of her than when "the fair veil" of flesh was drawn between her and his yearning.

No love-poetry of the ancient world offers any analogue to the *canzoniere*. Nor has it a real parallel in the Provençal verse from which it sprang. What distinguishes it, is the transition from a mediæval to a modern mood, the passage from Cino and Guido to Werther and Rousseau. Its tenacity and idealism belong to the chivalrous age. Its preoccupation with emotion as a given subject-matter and its infinite subtlety of self-analysis place it at the front of modern literature. Among the northern nations chivalrous love was treated as a motive for epic poetry in the Arthurian romances. It afterwards found lyrical expression among the poets of Provence. From them it passed to Italy, first appearing among the Lombard troubadours, who still used the *langue d'oc,* and next in Sicily at Frederick's court, where the earliest specimens of genuine Italian verse were fashioned. Guido Guinicelli further developed the sonnet, and built the lofty rhymes of the *canzone* at Bologna. By this time Italian literature was fully started; and the traditions of Provençal poetry had been both assimilated and transcended. From Guido's hands the singers of Florence took the motive up, and gave it a new turn of deeper allegory and more philosophic meaning. The *canzoni* of Dante and Guido Cavalcanti were no mere poems of passion, however elevated. Love supplied the form and language; but there lurked a hidden esoteric meaning. It is true that in the "*Vita Nuova*" Dante found at once the most delicate and the most poetically perfect form for the expression of an unsophisticated feeling. Beatrice was here a woman, seen from far and worshipped, but worshipped with a natural ardor. He was not, however, contented to rest upon this point; nor had he any opportunity of becoming properly acquainted with the object of his adoration in her lifetime. In the "*Convito,*" she had already been idealized as Philosophy, and in the "Divine Comedy" she is transfigured as Theology. Death, by separating her from him, rendered Beatrice's apotheosis conceivable; and Dante may be said to have rediscovered the Platonic mystery, whereby love is an initiation into the secrets of the spiritual world. It was the intuition of a sublime nature into the essence of pure impersonal enthusiasm for beauty, an exaltation of woman similar to that attempted afterwards by Shelley in "*Epipsychidion,*" which pervades the poetry of Michelangelo, and which forms a definite portion of the Positivistic creed. Yet there remained an ineradicable unsubstantiality in this point of view, when tested by the common facts of human feeling. The Dantesque idealism was too far removed from the sphere of ordinary experience to take firm hold upon the modern intellect. In proportion as Beatrice personified abstractions, she ceased to be a woman; nor was it possible, except by losing hold of the individual, to regard her as a symbol of the universal. Plato in the "*Symposium*" had met this difficulty, by saying that the lover, having reached the beatific vision, must renounce the love by which he had been led to it. A different solution, in harmony with the spirit of their age and their religion was offered by the *trecentisti*. Their transmutation of the simpler elements of chivalrous love into something mystical and complex, where the form of the worshipped lady transcends the sphere of experience, and her spirit is identified with the lover's profoundest thoughts and highest aspirations, was a natural process in mediæval Florence. The Tuscan intellect was too virile and sternly strung at that epoch to be satisfied with amorous rhymes. The mediæval theory of æsthetics demanded allegory, and imposed upon the poet erudition; nor was it easy for the singer of that period to command his own immediate emotions, with a firm grasp upon their relation to the world around him, or to use them for the purposes of conscious art. He found it more proper to express a philosophic content under the accepted form of erotic poetry than to paint the personality of the woman he loved with natural precision. Between the mysticism of a sublime but visionary adoration on the one side, and the sensualities of vulgar passion or the decencies of married life upon the other, there lay for him no intermediate artistic region. The Italian genius, in the Middle Ages, created no feminine ideal analogous in the reality of womanhood to Gudrun or Chriemhild, Guinevere or Iseult: and when it left the high region of symbolism, it descended almost without modulation to the prose of common life. Guido Cavalcanti is in this respect instructive. We find in his poetry the two tendencies separated and represented with equal power, not harmonized as in the case of Dante's allegory. His *canzoni* dealt with intellectual abstractions. His *ballate* gave artistic form to feelings stirred by incidents of everyday experience. The former were destined to be left behind, together with the theological scholasticism of the Middle Ages. The latter lived on through Boccaccio to Poliziano and the poets of the sixteenth century. Still we can fix one moment of transition from the transcendental philosophy of love to the positive romance of the "Decameron." Guided by his master, Cino da Pistoja, the least metaphysical and clearest of his immediate predecessors, Petrarch found the right artistic *via media;* and perhaps we may attribute something to that double education which placed him between the influences of the Tuscan lyrists and the troubadours of his adopted country. At any rate he returned from the allegories of the Florentine poets to the simplicity of chivalrous emotion; but he treated the original motive with a greater richness and a more idealizing delicacy than his Provençal predecessors. The marvellous instruments of the Italian sonnet and *canzone* were in his hands, and he knew how to draw from them a purer if not a grander melody than either Guido or Dante. The best work of the Florentines required a commentary; and the structure of their verse, like its content, was scientific rather than artistic. Petrarch could publish his *canzoniere* without explanatory notes. He had laid bare his heart to the world, and every man who had a heart might understand his language. Between the subject-matter and the verbal expression there lay no intervening veil of mystic meaning. The form had become correspondingly more clear and perfect, more harmonious in its proportions, more immediate in musical

effects. In a word, Petrarch was the first to open a region where art might be free, and to find for the heart's language utterance direct and limpid.

This was his great achievement. The forms he used were not new. The subject-matter he handled was given to him. But he brought both form and subject closer to the truth, exercising at the same time an art which had hitherto been unconceived in subtlety, and which has never since been equalled. If Dante was the first great poet, Petrarch was the first true artist of Italian literature. It was, however, impossible that Petrarch should overleap at one bound all the barriers of the Middle Ages. His Laura has still something of the earlier ideality adhering to her. She stands midway between the Beatrice of Dante and the women of Boccaccio. She is not so much a woman with a character and personality, as woman in the general, *la femme,* personified and made the object of a poet's reveries. Though every detail of her physical perfections, with the single and striking exception of her nose, is carefully recorded, it is not easy to form a definite picture even of her face and shape. Of her inner nature we hear only the vaguest generalities. She sits like a lovely model in the midst of a beautiful landscape, like one of Burne Jones's women, who incarnate a mood of feeling while they lack the fulness of personality. The thought of her pervades the valley of Vaucluse; the perfume of her memory is in the air we breathe. But if we met her, we should find it hard to recognize her; and if she spoke, we should not understand that it was Laura. Petrarch had no objective faculty. Just as he failed to bring Laura vividly before us, until she had by death become a part of his own spiritual substance, so he failed to depict things as he saw them. The pictures etched in three or four lines of the **Purgatorio** may be sought for vainly in his *rime.* That his love of nature was intense, there is no doubt. The solitary of Vaucluse, the pilgrim of Mont Ventoux, had reached a point of sensibility to natural scenery far in advance of his age. But when he came to express this passion for beauty, he was satisfied with giving the most perfect form to the emotion stirred in his own subjectivity. Instead of scenes, he delineates the moods suggested by them. He makes the streams and cliffs and meadows of Vaucluse his confidants. He does not lose himself in contemplation of the natural object, though we feel that this self found its freest breathing-space, its most delightful company, in the society of hill and vale. He never cares to paint a landscape, but contents himself with such delicate touches and such cunning combinations of words as may suggest a charm in the external world. At this point the humanist, preoccupied with man as his main subject, meets the poet in Petrarch. What is lost, too, in the precision of delineation, is gained in universality. The *canzoniere* reminds us of no single spot; wherever there are clear, fresh rills and hanging mountains, the lover walks with Petrarch by his side.

If the poet's dominant subjectivity weakened his grasp upon external things, it made him supreme in self-portraiture. Every mood of passion is caught and fixed forever in his verse. The most evanescent shades of feeling are delicately set upon the exquisite picture. Each string of love's many-chorded lyre is touched with a masterly hand. The fluctuations of hope, despair, surprise; the "yea and nay twinned in a single breath;" the struggle of conflicting aspirations in a heart drawn now to God and now to earth; the quiet resting-places of content; the recrudescence of the ancient smart; the peace of absence, when longing is luxury; the agony of presence, adding fire to fire,—all this is rendered with a force so striking, in a style so monumental, that the *canzoniere* may still be called the "introduction to the book of love." Thus, when Petrarch's own self was the object, his hand was firm; his art failed not in modelling the image into roundness. Dante brought the universe into his poem. But "the soul of man, too, is an universe;" and of this inner microcosm Petrarch was the poet. It remained for Boccaccio, the third in the supreme triumvirate, to treat of common life with art no less consummate. From Beatrice through Laura to the Fiammetta; from the "Divine Comedy" through the *canzoniere* to the "Decameron;" from the world beyond the grave through the world of feeling to the world in which we play our puppet parts; from the mystic *terza rima,* through the stately lyric stanzas, to Protean prose. Such was the rapid movement of Italian art within the brief space of some fifty years. We cannot wonder that when Boccaccio died, the source of inspiration seemed to fail. Heaven and hell, the sanctuaries of the soul, and the garden of our earth, had all been traversed. Well might Sacchetti exclaim:—

> Sonati sono i corni
> D' ogni parte a ricolta:
> La stagione è rivolta:
> Se tornerà non so, ma credo tardi.

Hitherto we have spoken only of Petrarch's love-verses. There is a short section of the *canzoniere* devoted to poems on various arguments, which presents him in another light. The oratorical impulse was only second to the subjective in his genius; and three *canzoni,* addressed to Giacomo Colonna, to Rienzi, and to the Princess of Italy, display the pleader's eloquence in its most perfect lustre. If the *Rime in Vita e Morte di Madonna Laura* bequeathed to the Italians models of meditative poetry, these *canzoni* taught them how classical form might be given to hortatory lyrics on subjects of national interest. There was a wail, an outcry in their passionate strophes, which went on gathering volume as the centuries rolled over Italy, until at last, in her final servitude beneath the feet of Spanish Austria, they seemed less poems than authentic prophecies. The Italians inherited from their Roman ancestors a strong forensic bias. What the forum was for the ancients, the *piazza* became for them. To follow out the intricacies of this thought would require more time and space than we can spare. It must be enough to remark that in their literature at large there is a powerful declamatory element. It impairs their philosophical writing, and helps to give an air of superficiality to their poetry. They lack what the Germans call *Innigkeit,* and the French *intimité.* What will not bear recitation in the market-place, what does not go at once home without difficulty to the average intelligence of the crowd, must be excluded from their art. It is rarely that we catch an undertone piercing the splendid resonances of their verse, or that we surprise a singer hidden in the cloud of thought, pouring his song forth as the night-bird sings to ease her soul in solitude. Such being, roughly speaking, the chief bent of the Italians, it followed that Petrarch's rhetorical *canzoni* had a better and more fruitful influence than his meditative poems on their literature. The Petrarchisti of chivalrous passion attenuated his feeling without realizing it in their own lives, and imitated his style without attaining to his mastery of form, until the one lost all vitality and the other became barren mannerism. But from time to time, as in Filicaja's sonnet or Leopardi's "Ode to Italy," we catch the true ring of his passionate *"Italia mia!"*

It will be understood that what has been said in the foregoing paragraph, about the rhetorical bias of the Italians, is only generally applicable. Their greatest artists and poets—Dante, Petrarch, Signorelli, Michelangelo, Tintoretto, Leopardi—have combined the forensic qualities of the Latins with the *Innigkeit* of the Teutons, just as, from the opposite point of view, we find a similar combination in Germans like Goethe, and in the French intellect at large. Petrarch's preoccupation with self so far balanced the oratorical impulse that, while the latter found its scope in his prose works, by far the larger portion of his poems gave expression to the former.

By right of his self-consciousness and thirst for glory, Petrarch was a modern man, fashioned by contact with antiquity. But dwelling as he did within the threshold of the Middle Ages, he had to pay the penalty of this emancipation from their intellectual conditions. After all is said, the final characteristic of Petrarch is the state of spiritual flux in which he lived. His love of Laura seemed to him an error and a sin, because it clashed with an ascetic impulse that had never been completely blunted. In his **"Hymn to the Virgin,"** he spoke of this passion as the Medusa which had turned his purer self to stone:—

> Medusa e l'error mio m'han fatto un sasso
> D'umor vano stillante.

Yet he knew that this same passion had been the cause of his most permanent achievements in the sphere of art. Laura's name was confounded with the laurel wreath, for which he strove, and which he wore with pride upon the Capitol. Even here a new contradiction in his nature revealed itself. Thirsting as he did for fame, he judged this appetite ungodly. The only immortality to be desired by the true Christian was a life beyond this earth. While he expressed a contempt for the world inspired by sympathy with monasticism, he enjoyed each mundane pleasure with the fine taste of an intellectual epicure. Solitude was his ideal, and in solitude he planned his most considerable literary masterpieces: but he frequented the courts of princes, made himself their mouthpiece, and delighted in the parade of a magnificent society. Humanism, which was destined to bring forth a kind of neo-paganism in Italy, had its source in him; and no scholar was more enthusiastic for the heroes of the antique age. But even while he gave his suffrage to the "starry youth" of Scipio, he was reminded that the saints of the Thebaid had wreathed their brows with the palms of a still more splendid victory. He worshipped Laura with a chivalrous devotion; but he lived, according to the custom of his time and his profession, with a concubine who bore him two children. No poet exalted the cult of woman to a higher level; but no monk expressed a bitterer hostility against the sex. He could not choose between the spirit and the flesh, or utter the firm "I will" of acceptance or renunciation upon either side. The genius of Rome and the genius of Nazareth strove in him for mastery. At one time he was fain to ape the antique patriot; at another he affected the monastic saint. He pretended to despise celebrity and mourned the vanity of worldly honors; yet he was greedy of distinction. His correspondence reveals the intrigues with which he sought the poet's laurel, pulling wires at Rome and Paris, in order that he might have the choice of being either crowned upon the Capitol or else before the most august society of learned men in Europe. At the same time, when fame had found him, when he stood forth as the acknowledged hero of culture, he complained that the distractions of renown withdrew him from the service of religion and his soul. He claimed to have disengaged himself from the shackles of personal vanity. Yet a foolish word dropped by some young men in Padua against his learning, made him take up cudgels in his failing years, and engage in a gladiatorial combat for the maintenance of his repute. He was clamorous for the freedom of the *populus Romanus,* and importunate in his assertion of Italian independence. Yet he stooped to flatter kings in letters of almost more than Byzantine adulation, and lent his authority to the infamies of Lombard despotism. It would be easy enough, but wearful, to lengthen out this list of Petrarch's inner contradictions. The malady engendered by them—that incurable *acedia,* that atonic melancholy, which he ascribed to St. Augustine—made him the prototype of an age which had in it, and which still has, a thousand unreconciled antagonisms. Hamlet and Faust, Werther

and René, Childe Harold and Dipsychus, find their ancestor in Petrarch; and it is this which constitutes his chief claim on the sympathies of the modern world. He too has left us a noble example of the method whereby the inevitable discords of an awakened consciousness may be resolved in a superior harmony. Through all his struggles he remained true to the one ideal of intellectual activity, and the very conflict saved him from stagnation. His energies were never for one moment prostrated, nor was his hope extinguished. He labored steadily for the completion of that human synthesis, embracing the traditions of antiquity and Christianity, which, as though by instinct, he felt to be the necessary condition of a European revival. It may be confidently asserted that if his immediate successors had continued his work in the spirit of their leader, the Renaissance would have brought forth nobler fruits.

We are told that the faces of dying persons sometimes reproduce the features of their youth, and the memory of old men reverts to the events of boyhood. Thus Petrarch at the close of life survived the struggles of his manhood, and returned with single-hearted impulse to the *alma mater* of his youth. From the year 1348 forward, he approximated more and more to the mediæval type of character, without losing his zeal for liberal studies. The coming age, which he inaugurated, faded from his vision, and the mystic past resumed its empire. Yet, as a scholar, he never ceased to be industrious. One of his last works was the translation into Latin of Boccaccio's "Griselda;" and on the morning after his unwitnessed death, his servant found him bowed upon his books. But Petrarch was not sustained in age and sickness by a forecast of the culture he had labored to create. The consolations of religion, the piety of the cloister, soothed his soul; and he who had been the Erasmus of his century, passed from it in the attitude of an Augustinian monk.

At Arquà they still show the house where Petrarch spent his last years, the little study where he worked, the chair in which he sat, the desk at which he wrote. From those soft-swelling undulations of the Euganean hills, hoary with olives, rich with fig and vine, the Lombard plain breaks away toward Venice and the Adriatic. The air is light; the prospect is immense; there is a sound of waters hurrying by. In front of the church-door, below the house, and close beside the rushing stream, stands the massive coffer of Verona marble where his ashes rest. No inscription is needed. The fame of Petrarch broods on Arquà like the canopy of heaven. For one who has dwelt long in company with his vexed, steadfast spirit—so divine in aspiration, so human in tenderness, and so like ourselves in its divided impulses—there is something inexpressibly solemn to stand beside this sepulchre, and review the five centuries through which the glory he desired has lived and grown. Few men capable of comprehending his real greatness, while there standing, will not envy him the peace he found upon the end of life, and pause to wonder when that harmony will be achieved between the wisdom of this world and the things of God which Petrarch, through all contradictions, clung to and in death accomplished.

Notes

[1] See Koerting, *"Petrarca's Leben und Werke,"* p. 51.

[2] Ep. Poet Lat., iii. 24.

Henry Dwight Sedgwick (essay date 1904)

SOURCE: Henry Dwight Sedgwick, "Francis Petrarch, 1304-1904," in *The Atlantic Monthly*, Vol. XCIV, No. LXI, July, 1904, pp. 60-9.

[*In the excerpt below, Sedgwick celebrates the six hundreth anniversary of Petrarch's birth with a laudatory survey of the poet's life and literary importance.*]

Six hundred years ago, on the 20th of July, 1304, a little Florentine baby was born into exile in a house on Via dell' Orto in Arezzo, whither his father, banished from Florence, had fled. Civil war between Ghibelline and Guelf raged everywhere, mingled with ambitions of nobles and jealousies of cities, with local wrongs and chance enmities. Exiles found no rest; within the year the baby was suspended from a stick, like a papoose, and carried to Incisa in the Valdarno; and before he was a lad his family had wandered to Pisa, and on to Avignon, lately become the city of the papal court. Thence the boy was sent to school at Carpentras, some fifteen miles away.

His father, Ser Petracco—the fastidious son softened these burgher syllables to Petrarca—was a notary, but like a true Florentine wishing his son to fly higher in the world than he, determined to make him a doctor of law, a student and expounder of Pandects; but by some eccentricity of nature, the sons of notaries become addicted to letters, and the boy Francis was already elbow deep in the Latin classics. Discovering this, Ser Petracco, following the foolish precedents of foolish fathers, seized the precious books and burned them all, except one volume of Cicero and one of Virgil, which he spared out of compassion for the poor boy's tears. Petracco did this from the best of paternal intentions, for he himself was *amantissimus Ciceronis;* but fathers are born unto folly as the sparks fly upward. From Carpentras Francis was sent to the university at Montpellier, a mere lycée as it were, and then at the age of nineteen to the great university of Bologna.

Here, after ten years of exile, Francis's sensitive heart beat hard for his country. The other Italian students might deem themselves Venetians, Milanese, Pisans, Neapolitans, but from the first moment of his coming, he, the exile, felt that he was not a Florentine, but an Italian. This feeling he drank deep in the pleasant city of Bologna, with its Roman traditions and its Italian charm. Those were the years before the great church of San Petronio frowned across the Piazza Maggiore, before the Palace Bevilacqua inclosed the most enchanting of courtyards, before the never-ending arcades protected the just and the unjust from sun and rain; but there was the dungeon palace of the Podestà, where Enzio, poet and king, had for twenty-two years watched his youth go down into the grave; there were the wicked towers, the Asinella, the Garisenda, and an hundred more; and, no doubt, Petrarch used to stop and watch the troop of doves parade and wheel through the air, flinging their shadows on loggia and piazza, flashing them across the narrow streets, as they mounted, stooped, whirled, and encircled the grim, gray towers with their purple and green, for a moment seeming to hang like a wreath, only the more suddenly to swoop down to his feet and pick the corn he had strewn. The city had the charm of Italy, but the university, without hall, dormitory, or lecture room, bare as the poorest student of things corporeal, was greater and more interesting than the city,—*imperium majus in imperio minore.* There were congregated thousands of students, men and lads from Gaul, Picardy, Burgundy, Poitou, Touraine, Maine, Normandy, Catalonia, Provence, Hungary, Germany, Spain, Poland, Bohemia, England, and from every province and city in Italy; a strange world, immensely democratic, yet enwrapped in the great imperial traditions. It was a university devoted to Roman law, and every gloss on Roman law preached the glory of the Roman Empire. There were other intellectual interests at the university,—the canon law, philosophy, medicine, astrology,—and, more stimulating than they, the contact of youth with youth, of enthusiasm with enthusiasm, in that time of life when young men are so many princes entering into their own; but the great Justinian code was the life of the university, and encouraged in Petrarch an admiration and veneration for Rome equal to his love for Italy. He attended lectures diligently, but his heart inclined neither to gloss nor to Corpus Juris. The very beginnings of those copious outpourings of comment and explanation, which flowed from the lips of professors eager "to prove that they were *artists,*" as one grumbler said, must have chilled him. Nevertheless, he went regularly to his professor's room, and scribbled with his stylus, while the learned man in bad Latin waded in: *"Primo dividendo literam, casum ponendo et literalia explanando; secundo loco signabo contraria et solvam, tertio loco, etc. . . . Prima pars potest subdividi in tres particulas,"* etc., in *saecula saeculorum.* Petrarch's thoughts surely wandered away to the sonnets written to Selvaggia la bella by the famous jurist, Ser Guittoncino de' Sinibuldi, more familiarly known to the undergraduates and to posterity as Cino da Pistoia; or perhaps to the verses of Bologna's native poets, to Onesto or to Guido Guinicelli,—

> Al cor gentil ripara sempre Amore
> Come a la selva augello in la verdura.

Or perhaps he thought of his own great compatriot, whose *Commedia,* recited by butchers, fullers, and tavern-keepers, he himself did not read, half aristocratically, half for fear of becoming subservient to the mighty master.

Out of the classroom, no doubt he was a very elegant young gentleman, singing Provençal madrigals under palace windows, or in less proper neighborhoods shouting out,

> Lauriger Horatius, quam vixisti bene,

in the wild company of stroller students. But, though the livery of his youth may have been somewhat gay, at least to the sober eye of his later years, and though the Corpus Juris may have been neglected, Cicero, Virgil, Horace, Ovid, and Seneca were not. Out of reach of the notarial arm, he plunged into what classic literature he could get.

Petrarch stayed three years at the university, and returned to Avignon on the death of his father (1326). His mother died soon afterward. Here he led the life of a fashionable young man much concerned with the brushing of his hair, the cut of his cloak, the fit of his shoes, and the whiteness of his linen, as he says in a letter written in grayer years; but these backward glances of age often cast too vivid a color on the follies of youth, for age has its hypocrisies, and loves to moralize on the deceitfulness of ephemeral pleasures. Certainly he continued his classical studies with diligence, and soon became celebrated as a scholar. On his father's death he had frankly abandoned the law, and, as his patrimony had been stolen by his father's executors, it was necessary for him to take steps toward gaining a livelihood. The church was the natural resource for educated men, especially as there were many livings and sinecures set apart for the support of scholars; animated by some hope of stipend, he took deacon's orders. This step did not necessitate strictness of living. Francis was a charming young man, cultivated, clever, agreeable, brimming with interest in life, learned beyond his years, and adorned by the natural grace of Tuscan manners, which had been bettered by his breeding; his company was sought by men of position and distinction, and he naturally felt that he had but entered into his lawful inheritance. Society, however, was to him but a secondary interest; his heart, still fancy free, beat to Cicero's periods

and Virgil's hexameters. Thus life passed in the easy, luxurious, windy city, until he was nearly twenty-three. Then, on an April morning in Holy Week, the lovely April of Provence, fresh with flowers and the breath of spring, he walked through the narrow streets of Avignon and entered the cold, gray aisles of the church of St. Clare; there he beheld the golden hair and the beautiful eyes that he was never to forget. As the vision moved, hers was no mortal's step, but an angel's, and her voice murmuring the prayers was more than human; the religious light, the solemn music, the high-aspiring arches, the sacredness of the place, transfigured her, or she transfigured them, and always afterwards, save once or twice when the dust of earth rebelled, whenever he thought of that golden head he bent his own in reverence.

History has not revealed who she was. The poet guarded her in the privacy of his art, and all the curiosity of six hundred years has not made sure of more than he has told. There are always guessers; in the eighteenth century the garrulous, indefatigable, agreeable, self-important Abbé de Sade put forward three stout volumes full of evidences and appendices to prove that Laura was the wife of his own ancestor, Ugo de Sade, and mother of eleven children; thus contradicting himself with a dozen reasons. Many critics, wise, spectacled, lean or maybe fat, with *aiblins nae temptations* to leave their books for the frivolous study of love, adopt this theory. Other surmises have had their partisans, among them the theory of pure poetical fancy. Let us hear what Petrarch has told us of her:—

> I bless the spot, the time, the hour
> When my eyes looked so high.—

Her eyes were beautiful, her brow serene, her smile, her laugh, her speech, sweet and gentle, her voice like an angel's, her hands thin, white, and lovely, her arms grace itself, her movements sweetly high-bred; and her beautiful young body, fit temple for her soul, was the home of refinement, of courtesy, of Love himself; her three chief excellencies were her milk-white neck, the roses of her cheeks, and her golden hair, loved by the wind,—but one might as well count the stars as her perfections. Her dress was charming, too; she wore a gown of green, or of cramoisie, or sometimes one inclining to deep blue, to drab, or to some dark indistinguishable color,—all were lovely.

Petrarch used to wander in the woods eager to avoid all mankind, lest his face should betray his inward struggle; there he repeated his own sonnets till mountain, hill, wood, and river knew his inmost thoughts. Everywhere the beautiful eyes haunted him, hid everything but themselves, cloaked in their own splendor mountains, rivers, lakes, the blue Mediterranean. A thousand times he felt impelled to offer her his heart, but she would not suffer him, and after she perceived his too fervent inclination, she wore a veil over her starry eyes and golden hair, and when he gazed at her she put her hand before her face, and even for a time banished him from her company. On one ineffaceable day, as he sat thinking of love, his lady passed; he rose with pale face and reverent gesture to do her honor; but no sooner did she see him than she flushed in anger, and with a brief word walked on. He shrank within himself. But in the earlier days, before his speech or his face had betrayed him, she used to speak to him words that scarcely have had their like in all the world, and she used to honor him with her salutation, such as angels give when they meet, and fired his heart with a passion for heaven.

Everything that had come near her, or touched her, made him tremble; her glove,—

> Candido, leggiadretto, e caro guanto,—

her veil, which a little shepherdess washed at a mountain brook; the portrait, painted (as if in heaven) by Simone Martini; the south window of her house; the stone seat on which she used to sit; every spot on which her shadow had fallen or her foot had trod. Thus in melodious sonnets he berhymed her.

Some years after he first saw her, he wrote a poem in Latin rhymes in which he says: "Especially dear to me is a most illustrious lady, known by her virtue and her birth. My poems have published her fame and spread it abroad. My thoughts always revert to her; always with renewed pangs of love she troubles me. I do not think she will ever be shaken in her lordship over me. Not by coquetry, but by her native charm and beauty has she bound me." Then he describes his efforts to throw off her yoke; how he had traveled north and south, to mountain and to sea, always in vain. Even in the pathless woods, whither he has fled to avoid her, no bush bent in the wind but he saw her lithe figure, no oak stood firm but he saw her immobile, no brooks but reflected her face; he saw her pictured in the clouds, in the empty air, and on the flinty rock.

In December, 1336, he wrote to his friend Giacomo Colonna: "But you, like an everlasting tease, follow me up and say that I have invented the name of Laura, because that which I like to talk of and that which makes other people talk of me is all one, and that the only *Laura* [Laurel] in my heart is that which bestows honor upon poets, for my studies show that to be the top of my desire; but that the other Laura, whose beauty I say has made me prisoner, is the creature of my fancy, that my verses are make-believe, and my sighs imaginary. Would to Heaven that your jests had hit the Truth, and that my love were a joke, and not the madness that it is. But believe me, not without great labor does a man succeed in simulation for a long time, and to labor without any advantage that others may deem you mad, would be the maddest of madnesses. . . . *Time wounds and Time cures;* and against Laura, who you say is imaginary, perhaps that other imaginary friend of mine, St. Augustine, will help me."

Later still, perhaps fifteen years after that scene in the church of St. Clare, Petrarch wrote a book, entitled **Concerning Contempt for the World**, in the form of a dialogue between St. Augustine and himself. The saint is his conscience, and they talk together. I can but give the substance of one dialogue:—

St. Augustine. Is not loving mere folly?

Petrarch. According to the object loved. Love is the noblest or the basest of all passions. To love a worthless woman is a great misfortune; to love a good woman is the top of happiness.

St. Aug. (Bringing the conversation to Laura.) The love of woman is surely folly.

Pet. There are bad women; but a gulf yawns between them and Laura. Her mind, knowing nothing of earthly cares, burns for heaven. In her face (if there be any truth anywhere) shines the glory of divine beauty; her behaviors are the pattern of perfect modesty. Neither her voice, nor the light of her eyes, resembles any mortal thing, and her bearing is more than human.

St. Aug. Think what it will be when you come to die. Remember how it was when she nearly died.

Pet. God let me die first! The memory of her illness makes me cold. I thought to lose the noblest part of my soul.

St. Aug. Turn from her; she has already lost much of her beauty.

Pet. I loved her body less than her soul. Her manners surpass the ways of earth, and her example shows how the dwellers in heaven live. If she die first I shall love her virtue, which cannot die.

St. Aug. But you cannot gainsay that the most noble things are sometimes vilely loved.

Pet. If you could but see my love! It is not less fair than her face. In it there has been nothing base or shameful, nor anything blameworthy except its greatness. One thing I cannot pass in silence,—whatever little I am become, I am because of her; nor should I have ever attained to whatever name or fame I have, if any, had she not, by inspiring me with a most noble affection, watered and tended the tiny seeds of virtue which nature planted in me. She plucked my young mind away from every shameful thing, and dragged it back as with a hook, and bade it look upward to the heights. It is certain that love undergoes a change to conform to the beloved. No backbiter was ever found so base to touch her name with his cur's tooth, or to dare say that there was any fault to find in her; and I do not say in what she did, but even in the turn of her words. They who leave nothing untouched left her in admiration and veneration. It is small wonder therefore, if she, so famous in good repute, made me long for a fairer fame, and smoothed the rude labors by which I sought it. While a young man I desired nothing but only to please her, who alone pleased me; now you bid me forget or love her less, who set me apart from vulgar fellowship.

St. Aug. Filling your heart with love of the creature, you shut yourself off from the love of the Creator,—and that is the road to death.

Pet. Not her body, but her soul I love; the years have faded her cheeks, but her soul has become more beautiful, and my love has likewise increased.

St. Aug. Are you making fun of me? If her soul dwelt in a hideous, knotty body, would it please you as much?

Pet. (Quoting Ovid.) Her soul with her body I loved.

Step by step, however, St. Augustine led him to confess and tell that in the beginning he had not been free from earthly desires, and had striven to gratify them, but that Laura had remained firm against flattery and prayers, and that now he rendered thanks unto her. Lord Byron says: "It is satisfactory to think that the love of Petrarch was not platonic."

There is also on the first leaf of his copy of Virgil a note in his handwriting of the first time he saw her and of her death, and he adds: "To write these lines in bitter memory of this event, and in the place where they will most often meet my eyes, has in it somewhat of a cruel sweetness, lest I forget that nothing more ought in this life to please me, and this by the grace of God need not be difficult to one who thinks strenuously and manfully of the idle cares, the empty hopes, and the unexpected end of the years that are gone."

Such was Laura; not the allegorical Beatrice of Dante, nor the conventional beauty of the troubadours, but still ideal and beautiful, the first real woman in poetry since the Greeks.

Petrarch's renown is so enduring because he is the first master of letters in Europe since the death of Cicero. He was by no means the first modern master of art, even if we pass by Gothic and Moorish art; for in painting, Giotto, in sculpture, Niccola Pisano, in architecture, Arnolfo del Cambio, were a generation ahead of him; in poetry, Dante, born nearly forty years before, was immeasurably greater than he, but Petrarch was the first to make letters as letters the work of his life, and the first to hold the faith that literature is as great a factor in civilization as politics or theology. He was a professional man of letters, and became the first of the great tyrants of European literature; he is more important than his successors,—Erasmus, Voltaire, Goethe,—in that he stands at the threshold of modern literature, while it was hesitating which way to turn, while Latin still was the only known classic literature, and national literatures had not yet got out of their leading strings. In contemporary literature what was there? In France, Froissart was a baby; in England, Langland a little boy, Chaucer not born; in Germany and in Spain, only an encyclopædia knows. The *Roman de la Rose,* setting Dante aside, is the one remembered work of letters that existed when Petrarch wrote his sonnets. For the third time in history Italy was about to take her place at the head of Europe, and Petrarch, representing her intellectual life, set his seal on unformed literatures, and stamped an ideal impression.

Poetry is the attempt by man to carry on the divine labor of creation, and make this world more habitable; poets take mere words, and fashion a habitation, whither, when the world of sense grows chill, we may betake ourselves and breathe a richer atmosphere. In another aspect poetry is merely the arrangement of words in a certain order; it is a matter of empirical psychology. Poets are practical psychologists, measuring sensations by measures finer than men yet use in laboratories; and in mastery of the fuller knowledge of this psychology Petrarch is perhaps unrivaled. Hundreds of thousands of men have loved as dearly as he; thousands have thought greater thoughts than he, and many poets, English poets at least, have had a nobler instrument; but he had the skill to put his words into the right order, and when we read them we forget everything except love.

The charm of his verses made him famous from the very beginning. Well it might, for his sonnet differs from other sonnets as the song of the bird differs from that of a singing master; the soft Italian syllables unburden all their rapture in the fourteen lines, then close their lips, for they have finished. Italian words are made to be strung in a sonnet. Italian verses rhyme, as if they were lovers—Hero and Leander—calling across the gap between line and line; they melt away in sensuous vowels, they echo melodious in *l's* and *m's* and *r's.*

Perhaps the least objectionable way to deliver a lecture on the Petrarchan sonnet will be to show by example how impossible it is to transport this union of sound and sense across the fatal gap between the *lingua di si* and the *tongue of yes*. I choose the best translation I can readily lay hands upon, out of an attractive little book entitled *Sonnets of Petrarch,* translated by Thomas Wentworth Higginson, which has Italian sounds on pages to the left and English to the right.

> Qual donna attende a gloriosa fama
> Di senno, di valor, di cortesia,
> Miri fiso negli occhi a quella mia
> Nemica, che mia donna il mondo chiama.
> Come s'acquista onor, come Dio s'ama,
> Com' è giunta onestà con leggiadria,
> Ivi s' impara; e qual è dritta via
> Di gir al Ciel, che lei aspetta e brama.

> Doth any maiden seek the glorious fame
> Of chastity, of strength, of courtesy?
> Gaze in the eyes of that sweet enemy
> Whom all the world doth as my lady name!
> How honor grows, and pure devotion's
>   flame,
> How truth is joined with graceful dignity,
> There thou mayst learn, and what the path
>   may be,
> To that high heaven which doth her spirit
>   claim.

To begin the lecture with the first time of the sonnet, in the Italian married women are not excluded from gazing at Madonna Laura, nor, in the second line, does *senno* shrink to *chastity,* nor *valor* to *strength,* even if the *cortesia* of the Italians can be frozen into the *courtesy* of us Americans. The fourth line, *Whom all the world doth as my lady name!* sounds a little like the language of hard-put sonneteers, whereas *che mia donna il mondo chiama* would be said with a bow, hand on heart, from the foot of the Alps to the Strait of Messina. *Come Dio s' ama* and *pure devotion's flame* mark the difference between a religion and our American Sunday-go-to-meeting-isms. *Com' è giunta onestà con leggiadria*—most delightful of meetings! *Onestà,* shy dignity of maidenhood, sweet innocence of motherhood, such as looks out from Raphael's Madonnas; *leggiadria,* the gay, girlish motion of comely youth, the grace of the leaping fawn, the sentiment in Botticelli; how did these most charming of feminine graces meet? At what Golden Gate? Are they corporeal or angelic? How, how and where? "How truth is joined with graceful dignity" is the proper junction of two respectable dames,—a sight that arouses very moderate exhilaration. In the last line of the octave, the Italian heaven, in a heavenly way, waits for Laura, *aspetta e brama*; the English heaven, instinct with Common Law, serving, as it were, a writ from the King's Bench, *claims* her.

We are forced to the conclusion that sense and sound are fatally imprisoned in the Petrarchan sonnet, and must stay there forever; they are stored where time doth not corrupt them, neither can translators break in and steal. But from the days of Wyatt and Surrey to those of Colonel Higginson, men who love poetry have felt ever renewing temptations to translate Petrarch, and to carry home the moonbeams that lie so lovely on water.

The union of sound and sense is very nearly perfect in Petrarch,—he used to test and try and substitute until all the words fell into their true order,—and as this perfection was not of a kind to require special knowledge in order to be enjoyed, his poetry, accredited and sustained by his great reputation as a scholar, quickly passed from mouth to mouth, and so set its seal on the nascent literature of Europe.

His poetry asserted this dogma, that in the only real world, the world of ideas, woman and the love of woman are noble and beautiful. From this central dogma of the idealistic faith proceed the derivative dogmas, that all life, all things great and little, are noble and beautiful. This is the mission of poetry,—to see life as a divine work, to be the priestess of a perpetual revelation, in all things to behold the beauty of God. This is the continuation by man of the divine work of creation, for the Lord rested after six days of labor, before His work was complete, and entrusted the fulfillment of the everlasting task to poets. Petrarch has done his duty. What is Laura? Her corporeal existence has become a myth, but she is a thing of beauty and a joy forever, because Petrarch saw her with the eyes of love and faith. This idealism uplifted all modern literature and constitutes Petrarch's greatness, and not that scholastic excellence by which, according to Mr. John Addington Symonds, he "foresaw a whole new phase of European culture,"—melancholy prospect. The Petrarchan view is set forth in the familiar sonnet of Michelangelo, which says that within the shapeless marble lies beauty imprisoned. So it is with all things: within our rude, rough, shapeless, unpolished selves lies imprisoned something that awaits the liberating eye and hand of faith and love.

There was a second very memorable day in Petrarch's life, the 8th of April, 1341. On that day, in the palace of the Roman Senate on the top of the Capitoline Hill, he received the poet's crown of laurel, bestowed in the name of the Senate and the People of Rome.

This ceremony was the outward recognition of a new force in Europe; arms and theology were making room for literature, for the voice of men of peace. There, on the axis of European history, on the Capitol of the City of Rome, pitiably shrunk to an arena for Pope, Emperor, noble, and burgher to play at gladiators, yet still splendid with unequalled renown, a poet, the head of the new estate, was crowned at a time when popes had fled to receive the tiara elsewhere, and emperors were forced to fight their way step by step to the Vatican. Letters were honored indeed, but it was Petrarch who had convinced the world that literature was worthy of honor, and for his sake the honor had been given.

As we look back over six hundred years, with Petrarch's life before our eyes, it is easy for us to see that he, the prince of living poets and the foremost scholar of Europe, was worthy to be the gonfaloniere of the new guild; but how did the cultivated world of 1340 know this? How did it choose this young man, ruddy, and withal of a beautiful countenance, and goodly to look at, to be its king? Petrarch was thirty-six years old; he had written some eighty sonnets, a dozen canzoni, and a few metrical epistles; and these few contributions to literature, excepting what he may afterwards have judged not worth keeping, were all, and there was no printing to spread them abroad. How did the vague new feeling, that literature ought to be publicly recognized as a force in civilization, manage to select him as its standard bearer, and crown him on the Capitol? The answer is that Petrarch himself hoisted the flag, and the world of letters rallied round him. Even by that time he had come into personal acquaintance with a large part of the cultivated world, and everybody he met was charmed by his beauty, his grace, his gifts in conversation, his high morality, his sweet character, as well as by his rare scholarship and his unequalled poetry. First Bologna brought him into familiar fellowship with men who in later life became persons of consequence; afterwards Avignon served him in a similar way. Avignon he never liked; he complained of its dirty streets, where nasty pigs, snarling dogs, noisy carts, four-horse coaches, filthy beggars, gaping foreigners, isolent revelers, and rowdy crowds made walking intolerable. Worse than these was the fundamental sin of harboring popes who ought to go back to Rome, the Holy City. But Avignon returned good for evil. It was the cosmopolitan city of Europe; for Rome without the papal court was but a little bickering town, and Paris was not what it became when the intellectual sceptre of Europe passed from Italy to France. The main current of European life still flowed in the old channel dug by the ideas that acknowledged Pope and Emperor as the two heads of the civilized world; and by Petrarch's time the popes had thrust the emperors into the second place, and had thereby become the most important personages in Europe; where the pope lived, there was the head of ecclesiastical affairs, and the centre of political intrigue. The pope sent legates and nuncios to every court in Christendom, and received ambassadors in return; to him came archbishops, bishops, abbots, heads of monastic orders, princes, and even kings. In this dirty city the papal court lived in ease and luxury,—the cardinals would not go back to Rome, Petrarch said, because they could not bear to leave the Burgundian wines;—all was reminiscent of the old Provençal civi-

lization. A careless, sensual life, these high priests of Christendom led, accompanied by a refinement in manners not common elsewhere. Avignon was a city to which everybody went; it was easier to go there than to Rome, and immeasurably pleasanter to a man lacking belligerent tastes. The papal dinner parties, if nothing else, would have attracted good society from the Ebro to the Elbe. Wonderful were the dishes, glorious the wines of Roccella, of Bielna, of Sanporciano, noble those from Rhineland and from Greece, quisite the old Vernaccia; all flowed *abbondantissimamente*. This high living Petrarch in later days denounced like Habakkuk, but the dinners added lustre to the papal court, and helped his career. Avignon was the natural place to look for a poet laureate, because such a poet must not only be excellent, but he must be known, he must not live away from the main thoroughfare of European life,—not far from its dinner-tables.

At Avignon Petrarch saw everybody, not merely because of his personal charm and gifts for conversation, but as the honored inmate of the Colonna household. This family played a great part in Petrarch's life, particularly on that eventful Easter in 1341. The Colonnas had a European importance, because their strongholds in the city of Rome enabled them to block either pope or emperor in that great move in the game of European politics,—the imperial coronation in Rome. In their palace (report still points out the spot), of which he became an inmate, Petrarch met everybody of consequence who came to Avignon.

Moreover, Petrarch was a Florentine,—the fifth essence in nature, as Boniface VIII said,—and Florentine merchants, notaries, envoys, were spread over Western Europe, and when traveling through Avignon naturally met their attractive fellow citizen. Two of these wandering Florentines were closely concerned with Petrarch's coronation. Roberto de' Bardi, chancellor of the University of Paris, procured him an invitation to be crowned poet laureate there, and Fra Dionigi, for a time professor of philosophy and theology, brought him to the notice of King Robert of Naples, who, patron of philosophy and letters, obtained the crown for him in Rome.

Though these were the reasons that brought Petrarch before the eyes of cultivated Europe, yet Petrarch was worthy to be their cynosure. He was not a mere lover of the classics, a worshiper of the long dead, he was conversant with the moderns as well; he was known from Durham to Messina as a scholar, a poet, a writer of letters, a man of philosophic mind; in truth, by his tongue and pen, by his "rethorique swete" he gave a great upward push to literature, lifting it from a beggarly condition to a great estate in the realm of thought.

Petrarch's life after his coronation was one perpetual recurrence of social successes. The Pope invited him to be a papal secretary, the King of France extended the hospitality of Paris to him, the Emperor bade him to Prague, the Visconti wanted him at Milan, the Scaligeri at Verona, the Correggi at Parma, the Carraresi at Padua, the Lord High Seneschal at Naples; the Florentines asked him to accept a chair in their new university, Venice offered him a house. This social renown was the fulcrum by which, pressing the lever of classical enthusiasm, he stirred the world and budged mediæval ideas from their places.

His immediate influence on his contemporaries was as a classical scholar, as a lover of the wisdom, the beauty, the greatness of the long past. It is this aspect of his career that has impressed Mr. Symonds and the German scholars with so deep a dint; scholars themselves, they admire him as a man of like passions with themselves, they look back at the revival of learning, at the updigging of classic culture, and they regard Petrarch as we regard Christopher Columbus, and do appropriate homage to his memory. That aspect of Petrarch's career naturally obtrudes itself on students; but those of us who are indifferent to the *fanfares* of historic importance may disregard that, and take leave of Petrarch in our own way.

He was a mixture of the good comrade and the anchorite, pushing neither quality to excess. He was fond of talking, and when he could help, never dined alone; but he was also fond of seclusion. Nothing he liked better than to wander along the banks of the Sorgue and dream of Laura, of poetry, of life, of things old and new. He built a house in Vaucluse, the beautiful valley, shut off from Avignon and the whole outer world of lower things, where, from a blue basin within a great cave, the Sorgue breaks out in noisy cataract; there he lived, rich in books, eating black bread, fruits, and the little fishes that he caught himself. His companions were but three,—his dog, and an old couple; the man, gardener, librarian, valet; the woman, farmer, cook, and washerwoman. He loved to stroll about the fields, even long after dark; and sometimes in the middle of the night he would get up, say his prayers, and wander forth in the moonlight, thinking of the beautiful things in heaven and earth. Vaucluse, "loveliest place out of Italy," was his favorite resort; he lived there many years, and thither he loved to return, to meditate in quiet. Even when domiciled by fate in a city, he desired country things; in Milan he rejoiced in dwelling *fuori le mura;* in Parma he grew choice fruits in his garden. In Arquà—

> The mountain-village where his latter days
> Went down the vale of years—

he lived in a little house, built by himself, surrounded by vines and olive trees. Here he had horses, for he was too infirm to walk, several servants to minister to him and to the many guests who came eager to see

him, four or five copyists copying Latin manuscripts, and an old priest, who used to accompany him on his long drives to the church in Padua, where Petrarch as canon had sundry duties. There, among the Euganean hills, his thoughts turned to death. He was found at the last, so report says, his head bent over his book as if he had paused in the reading. Many mourned him. Among the chief was Giovanni Boccaccio, who is never more charming nor more amiable than in the filial demonstrations of his simple admiration for Petrarch.

Petrarch was good and kind and industrious, always hard at work upon those things which seemed to him important,—the discovery and dissemination of classical knowledge; and, moreover, he had continuously with him a sense of a presence which transcends our measures, and this he used to express in mediæval phrases, that nevertheless still satisfy here and there a backward heart. "Philosophy is to love wisdom; true wisdom is Jesus Christ. Let us read historians, poets, philosophers, but let us always have in our hearts the gospel of Jesus Christ, in which abide true wisdom and true happiness."

Annie Russell Marble (essay date 1904)

SOURCE: Annie Russell Marble, "Petrarch" and "Modern Echoes of Petrarch," in *The Dial*, Chicago, Vol. XXXVI, No. 434, July 16, 1904, pp. 27-9, 29-31.

[*In the essay below, Marble discusses Petrarch's influence on poetry from the Renaissance to the present.*]

In the summer of 1304, the exiled Ghibellines, including in their number the greatest of Italian poets, made their headquarters in the Tuscan town of Arezzo, whence they vainly sought to effect a return to their beloved Florence, which had cast them forth with contumely. One of these exiles, expelled from Florence on the same day with Dante something more than two years earlier, was a scholar and politician of some consequence named Petracco; and to him there was born, on the 20th of July, the child destined to a fame among Italian poets second only to that of his father's friend and fellow-exile. The personal relations which thus link the names of Dante and Petrarch did not, however, operate to shape the two poets in anything like the same mould; and the chief instruction offered by setting them side by side is found in the marked contrast between their temperament, their outlook, and their ideals. The main point of contrast is, of course, to be found in the fact that Dante was the incarnation of the mediæval spirit, while Petrarch had in some dim sense the vision of the world to come 'and all the wonder that should be'; the thoughts and the emotions of Dante were held in the strait-jacket of scholasticism, while those of Petrarch were working themselves free from that hampering confinement; while Dante's ideal of the future took the utopian form of the universal dual monarchy of Papacy and Empire, the words of Petrarch, declaring that

"L'antico valore
Nell' italici cor non e 'ancor morto,'

made his voice the first of those to be raised in prophecy of the very practical ideal of a united Italy. In a word, the temper of Dante, for all his deep tenderness and spiritual exaltation, was that of the schoolman; that of Petrarch, on the other hand, for all the mistaken direction of his aims, was that of the humanist.

It has recently been suggested, in a semi-humorous way, that American contributions toward the erection of a monument at Arezzo might most appropriately be made by such of our fellow-countrymen as had ventured to practice the art of sonnet-writing. Certainly, if all of those thus designated should respond to the appeal, abundant means would be forthcoming, no matter how modest the individual offerings. The sonnets of Petrarch have had a multitudinous progeny, not all of whom have done credit to their progenitor, and many a modern maiden has been the recipient of a form of tribute which might never have been thought of had it not been for the sonnets addressed to Madonna Laura six hundred years ago. The *Canzoniere* of Petrarch, that 'epitomised encyclopædia of passion,' as Dr. Garnett calls it, is so precious a jewel among the world's poetical possessions that it predisposes us to a kindly indulgence of the feeblest of Petrarch's modern followers. The **'Africa'** upon which the poet set his hopes of enduring fame has gone the way of all artificial epics, and of all mediæval attempts to keep Latin alive as the medium of literary expression; but the odes, and the sonnets, and the *trionfi*, written in the despised vulgar tongue, have taken on with the succeeding centuries a more assured immortality. Of the influence of Petrarch upon the poetry of later ages, something is said in the special article which we print elsewhere; we wish to devote our own brief remarks to the humanist rather than to the poet, to the forerunner of the revival of learning rather than to the singer of his own joys and sorrows.

The Alpinists claim Petrarch as the first of their number by virtue of his famous ascent of Mont Ventoux. We doubt, however, if they can read with proper sympathy the letter in which the expedition is described. The modern mountain-climber is not likely to sit down in the first convenient valley and say to himself, 'What thou hast repeatedly experienced to-day in the ascent of this mountain, happens to thee, as to many, in the journey toward the blessed life,' and then to indulge in a long retrospective survey of his career. Nor is he apt, after having reached his summit, to take St. Augustine's 'Confessions' from his pocket and pon-

der over its message. In Petrarch's case the effect was startling, for he hit upon the following passage: 'And men go about to wonder at the heights of the mountains, and the mighty waves of the sea, and the wide sweep of rivers, and the circuit of the ocean, and the revolution of the stars, but themselves they consider not.' Whereupon, he says: 'I was abashed, and . . . closed the book, angry with myself that I should still be admiring earthly things who might long ago have learned from even the pagan philosophers that nothing is wonderful but the soul, which, when great itself, finds nothing great outside itself.' From that moment, the panorama of hill-tops and clouds and skies meant no more to him than the view of Lake Leman had meant to Bernard of Clairvaux. 'Then, in truth, I was satisfied that I had seen enough of the mountain. I turned my inward eye upon myself, and from that time not a syllable fell from my lips until we reached the bottom again.'

But Petrarch could hardly have been expected to climb his mountain in the modern spirit; the significant thing is that he did such a thing at all. 'My only motive was the wish to see what so great an elevation had to offer,' is his simple prefatory statement. But we, knowing in how many things his thought groped unconsciously toward the future, may be pardoned for finding this exploit in a certain sense symbolical, or at least highly suggestive of what we can now see to have been his relations to the development of culture. He cherished the past,—none more fondly than he,—but he never took the view that the sum of all possible culture had been made up by the ancients, leaving nothing for the coming ages to add. He knew not what those ages might bring forth; but he had a wistful sense of their possibilities, which amounted almost to prescience.

The analysis of Petrarch's humanism reveals a number of distinct elements. He not only climbed the mountain, but he also travelled far and wide, because he was genuinely curious about the world of nature and of men, and took a wholesome interest in things and affairs. He read the classical authors, not to find in them texts for disputation, but for the purposes of culture as we understand the term, and with a passionate enthusiasm for their beauty. He collected a library of some two hundred manuscript volumes, not for the reputation of owning them, but because they were for him the very bread and wine of the intellectual life. He even planned to bequeath his books to Venice for the general good, thus conceiving the modern idea of the public library. He wrote the most delightful letters to his friends, following the example of Pliny and Cicero, and he wrote them with an eye to their preservation for future generations. He even wrote a fragmentary autobiography; and, what is particularly noteworthy, he made it largely a record of his inner life, of his intellectual and emotional experiences. The course of his speculation was singularly self-determined; he rejected the narrow educational ideals of his age, and made free to find flaws in the teaching of Aristotle,—not, indeed, calling him 'that accursed heathen,' as Luther was to do two centuries later, but flatly refusing to recognize his authority as pontifical.

All these matters, as well as others unmentioned, bring Petrarch into closer touch with the modern world than any of his contemporaries. Carducci makes him the intellectual arbiter of his age, as Erasmus and Voltaire were the intellectual arbiters of theirs; but that strictly historical fact appeals to us less directly than the fresh and sympathetic quality of his work. Those who would like to come into close contact with Petrarch the humanist, as distinguished from Petrarch the poet, will do well to read the volume of selections admirably translated and edited by Professors Robinson and Rolfe. The English reader could have no better introduction than this to the man and his writings. The poems, of course, need no such introduction. There have been over four hundred editions of them in Italian alone, besides countless translations into numerous tongues. And of their author, now in his grave six hundred years less the three score and ten of his life, let our closing words be those of the contemporary who thus described his end: 'Francesco Petrarca, the mirror of our century, after completing a vast array of volumes, on reaching his seventy-first year closed his last day in his library. He was found leaning over a book as if sleeping, so that his death was not at first suspected by his household.'

. . . . .

Each century brings new proof of the permanence of Petrarch's influence and the charm of his poetry. As Italy celebrates, on the 20th of July, the six-hundredth anniversary of his birth, she challenges the world to name a literary hero who has won more sympathetic homage from cultured men and women of every age. Research during the last century has disclosed few new facts in Petrarch's life; but knowledge of his work, both as humanist and poet, has been widely disseminated. Earlier studies, by Abbe de Sade, Foscolo, Ginguene, and Sismondi, have been translated and appreciated. In Italy and France many biographic and critical treatises have appeared; there have also been a few significant volumes by English and American scholars, from the biography by the poet Campbell in 1843 to more recent studies by Mr. Symonds, Mr. Reeve, and the collaborated work of Professors James Harvey Robinson and H. W. Rolfe. Other popular sketches, both in book and magazine form, have testified to the increasing interest in the romantic phases of Petrarch's life. More illuminative, both of the man and the poet, have been the translations of his sonnets, canzone, and letters, by such modern scholars as Hartley Coleridge, Walter Savage Landor, Mr. Richard

Garnett, and Colonel T. W. Higginson. Indirect evidences of his literary influence abound. The Victorian poets and their successors made frequent allusions to him, and their works bear impress of his mode and spirit.

No one would claim Petrarch as one of the world's greatest poets. But the duration of his popularity, and the acknowledged and indirect imitations of his style, give evidence of the progressive quality of his influence. As the lover and sonneteer of Laura, as the patriot-friend of Rienzi and Colonna, as the enthusiast for pure classicism in an age of mental lethargy and pedantry, he merits the remembrance which has never waned from his day to our own. Without loss of his prestige as a scholar, he has won more general recognition as an amatory lyrist, combining the best elements of chivalrous worship for women with the conflicting passions of a modern lover. In the more than three hundred sonnets, and the scores of canzone and sestinas, celebrating the charms and reserve of his mistress, photographing the lover's struggles of heart and conscience, Petrarch has accomplished a work of poetic art more memorable than his cultural reforms. There is an ever-new fascination in his revelations of this fourteenth-century woman, with her soft dark eyes, her golden hair, her alluring voice, and her reposeful beauty of face and presence. Midway between the spiritual Beatrice and the sensual Fiametta, she is a humanized creation of rare charm. Whether she was in truth, as later authorities aver, the wife of Hugo de Sade and the mother of nine children, or only the personification of a poet's vision, she is essentially real yet ideal,—the mistress of feudal days, with the dominant traits of modern womanhood of a loftier type arousing in her lover's heart a conflict between reverence and yearning.

While the last century has given attention chiefly to the love-poetry of Petrarch, it has not overlooked his qualities as a leader both in affairs and in letters. His Latin essays in available form for the modern scholar, his voluminous correspondence carefully edited and largely translated, afford distinct signs of the directive force which he wielded in his own age. Undoubtedly the time was ripe for his influence; but such consideration does not minimize his service. Inferior to Dante as a poet, and separated from him by less than a generation, he was eminently modern in spirit and mode, while Dante was the last noble exponent of mediaevalism. With all his breadth of insight, Petrarch was more than a scholar and a poet; he was the first true Italian patriot-prophet. With vanity and a proneness to servility, he possessed deep-rooted aspirations for political reform, in which are found many of the later tenets of patriotism. In his diplomatic missions, in consultation with Pope and Doge, even in his ardent hope and disappointment in Rienzi, Petrarch was an idealist tempered by practical wisdom. Like Mazzini, his great compatriot of five hundred years later, Petrarch saw in his vision a free and united Italy, though it was his belief that this should come through a revival of Roman standards. For Petrarch, whose father had suffered exile from Florence, there was no specific city-allegiance; he was a patriot, not a partisan, well called by Mr. Symonds 'a freeman of the City of the Spirit.'

Passages in his letters reveal the hidden ethical motives of the man. His honesty, his hatred of deceit in any form, are often reiterated. In the confession of his unabating passion for work, he seems strangely akin to our modern day. The wish expressed to Boccaccio, that death might find him reading or writing, was fulfilled with unexpected literalness. From the letters covering the period between 1326 and 1374, Mr. Lohse selected, translated, and published in London, in 1901, certain 'Thoughts' that well disclose Petrarch's moral and literary traits. Keen insight into humanity and into the fundamental truths of life are interwoven with intimate hints of personal experiences. A few pertinent epigrams have special force,—as 'Nothing can succeed in definance of nature (Bk. IV: Letter 16); 'Idleness alone causes us to disbelieve in our own powers' (Bk. XXI: Letter 10); 'Humble and earnest research is always the first step toward knowledge' (Letters of Old Age; Bk. IV: Letter 5).

Modern scholarship has not only found new meanings in Petrarch, but it has shown greater discrimination in the study of his literary forms. Leigh Hunt's *Book of the Sonnet,* in the middle of the nineteenth century, emphasized for English readers the perfection of Petrarch's verse and its many adaptations. To Mrs. Shelley he wrote, in general tribute, 'Petrarch and Boccaccio and Dante are the morning and noon and night of the great Italian day; or, rather, Dante and Petrarch and Boccaccio are the night and morning and noon.—"And the evening and the morning were the first day."' (Dowden's *Life of Shelley,* II., 220.) To Leigh Hunt we are indebted for one of the most musical translations of Petrarch's '**Ode to Vaucluse.**' Hunt caught the playful spirit of the verse, and delicately portrayed the vision of Laura amid a shower of blossoms. Passing by occasional tributes to Petrarch in prose and verse, by Samuel Rogers, Barry Cornwall, Lord Houghton, Lord Hammer, and other English scholars, one is reminded of the more significant allusions by that coterie of poets to whom Italy was not alone a goal of pilgrimage but a place of long and happy sojourn. In 1813, Byron, in disgust at his own inability in sonnet form, had written: 'They are the most puling, petrifying, stupidly platonic compositions. I detest the Petrarch so much that I would not be the man even to have obtained his Laura, which the metaphysical, whining dotard never could.' In *Don Juan* he interpolated a characteristic sneer,—

'Think you if Laura had been Petrarch's wife,
He would have written sonnets all his life?'

When, however, chance brought Byron to the Euganean hills, he found himself moved to a more sympathetic note toward Petrarch and his adjacent home. In a somewhat skeptical mood, he paid his first visit to Arqua in 1817. He confessed that he was 'moved to turn aside in a second visit,' and two years later he urged the poet Moore 'to spare a day or two to go with me to Arqua; I should like to visit that tomb with you,—a pair of poetical pilgrims,—eh, Tom, what say you?' All are familiar with his commemoration of 'the soft, quiet hamlet at Vaucluse' in 'Childe Harold' (IV: xxx).

Shelley had been under the spell of Petrarch's influence before he came to Italy, when, in 1813, he joined his friend Hogg, and read the Italian poets in company with Mrs. Boinville and her sentimental daughter Cornelia Turner. Shelley's earlier interest was revived under these close associations, and in his 'Defense of Poetry' he spoke warmly of Petrarch, 'whose verses are as spells which unseal the inmost enchanted fountains of the delight which is in the grief of love. It is impossible to feel them without becoming a portion of that beauty which we contemplate.' Vaucluse became a pilgrim-shrine to the Brownings, from that first romantic scene pictured by Mrs. Jamieson, as well as by Mrs. Browning, when the poet-lovers 'sate upon two stones in the midst of the fountain which in its dark prison of rocks flashes and roars and testifies to the memory of Petrarch.' In their Italian studies, the Brownings found Dante and Camoens more stimulating than Petrarch, though one recalls significant references to the latter in 'Apparent Failure,' 'The Ring and the Book,' and 'The Vision of Poets,' such as,

'And Petrarch pale,
From whose brain-lighted heart were thrown
A thousand thoughts beneath the sun,
Each lucid with the name of One.'

For the most pronounced reflection of Petrarch's influence, one turns to Landor. At the outset, he challenges all English writers who have transformed his hero's name. 'For I pretend to no vernacular familiarity with a person of his distinction, and should almost be as ready to abbreviate Francesco into Frank as Petrarca into Petrarch.' The idea of 'The Pentameron' may be traced to the letter sent by Petrarch to Boccaccio after the latter had given him a copy of Dante and asked for a more sympathetic reading of the earlier master. That Petrarch recognized the mental superiority of Dante cannot be questioned; but he confessed that he was repelled by two causes,—the severe adherence to mediaeval standards, and a persistent memory of one glance, when he was eight years old, at the cold and rigorous face of Dante. Two other reasons for this indifference are suggested in Landor's dialogue: first, Petrarch's youthful fear lest by reading Dante he should become a mere imitator; and, second, an objection to Dante's persistent use of the Italian rather than the Latin text for his lofty poetic vision. The natures of these great poets were too antithetical to be in accord,—leaving out all suggestions of Petrarch's vanity; and Landor has well delineated what Disraeli called 'Petrarch's caustic smile on Dante.' To Landor, the character of Petrarch was thus unfolded: 'Unsuspicious, generous, ardent in study, in liberty, in love, with a self-complacency which in less men would be vanity, but arising in him from the general admiration of a noble presence, from his place in the interior of a heart which no other could approach or merit, and from the homage of all who held the principalities of Learning in every part of Europe.'

The early studies and translations of Petrarch's sonnets by Lord Morley, Major MacGregor, Lord Surrey, Lady Dacre, and Susan Wollaston, are still valuable to the modern reader. During the last three decades, several volumes of translations and anthologies have extended general study of the Petrarchan sonnet,—notably the anthologies by Samuel Waddington, William Sharp, Dr. Richard Garnett, and the scientific treatise on the sonnet by Mr. Charles Tomlinson. In his recent volume of sonnets from Dante, Petrarch, and Camoens, Dr. Garnett has shown skill and poetic insight in his renderings of more than sixty Petrarchan sonnets. Especially fine are the thirty-ninth, with the poet's benediction upon Laura; the eightieth, on Vaucluse; and the second of the later memorial sonnets after the passing of Laura and his friend Colonna. Dr. Garnett has prefaced the translations by an original sonnet of tribute, closely following his model in structure and effective play upon the words Laura and Laurel:

> 'Laurel in right of Laura thou didst claim,
> Which wreath Apollo with his bay
> enwound;
> Nature with flower and wit with diamond
> crowned;
> Thine were the wind, the dawn, the star, the
> flame.'

Of American translators, none have rendered more scholarly and sympathetic sonnets by Petrarch and Camoens than Colonel Higginson. Some of these were included in his earlier volume of verse, *The Afternoon Landscape;* and with them have been incorporated a few new translations in the exquisite volume of this memorial year, *Fifteen Sonnets of Petrarch.* Here also is reproduced the essay published in *The Atlantic* many years ago, 'Sunshine and Petrarch,' in which the earlier sonnets were imbedded. The elusive memory of Laura's beauty, and the vacuity of mind after her death, have been retold with perfect sympathy in sonnet 251, 'Gli occhi di ch' io parlai.'

> 'Dead is the source of all my amorous
> strain,
> Dry is the channel of my thoughts outworn,
> And my sad heart can sound but notes of
> pain.'

Deft in portrayal of the lighter fancies, Colonel Higginson has been even more successful in the deeper revelations of the spirit. With earnest grace he has interpreted the three hundred and twenty-third sonnet, the exaltation of Laura's womanliness and its admonition to maidenhood of all ages,—'Qual donna atende a gloriosa fama.'

> 'Doth any maiden seek the glorious fame
> Of chastity, of strength, of courtesy?
> Gaze in the eyes of that sweet enemy
> Whom all the world doth as my lady name!
> How honor grows and pure devotion's
> flame,
> How truth is joined with graceful dignity,
> There thou may'st learn, and what the path
> may be
> To that high heaven which doth her spirit
> claim;
> There learn that speech beyond all poet's
> skill,
> And sacred silence, and those holy ways
> Unutterable, untold by human heart.
> But the infinite beauty that all eyes doth fill,
> This none can learn; because its lovely rays
> Are given by God's pure grace, and not by
> art.'

Though Petrarch's sonnets and songs can never be placed in the very first rank among world-poetry, yet there is an unwaning charm in the life and verse of this man of warm passion, of strenuous ambition for himself and the modern world. Refreshing the mind of his own age with draughts from the spring of classic letters, he speaks a message as pertinent today as when it issued from his romantic valley retreat, or was listened to by his flatterers at the Venetian court.

Nathan Haskell Dole (essay date 1908)

SOURCE: Nathan Haskell Dole, "Lyric Poetry and Petrarca," in *A Teacher of Dante and Other Studies in Italian Literature*, Moffat, Yard & Company, 1908, pp. 89-141.

[*In the following excerpt, Dole provides an overview of Petrarch's life, focusing on the poet's adoration for Laura and the poetry he dedicated to her.*]

In passing from Dante to Petrarca we come into another world. Dante closes an era: he is the Titan of

Italian poetry; with him the mediæval is summed up forever.

Petrarca is as modern as Chaucer. Just as in midsummer, sometimes, a few days of genuine spring weather seem to stray like summer birds from their exile in the South, as if impatient to be at home once more, so we find simultaneously in England and Italy these two modern men centuries ahead of their day. How gay, unsentimental, free from morbidness, from provincialism is Dan Chaucer! He was of humble origin, the name signifying shoemaker, and yet he rose to be courted by kings and emperors and one of his descendants just missed inheriting the throne of England.

So Petrarca, as is proved by the name, which means Little Peter or Peterkin, sprang from the common people. His father was Ser Petracco di Ser Parenza—unable even to boast a family name—and when he was driven from Florence by that miserable squabble between the two factions that were always tearing the vitals of the city, he carried away with him on that January day in 1302 only a small part of the possessions which he had accumulated as a jurist.

The misfortune which befell Italy had been prognosticated. In September, 1301, a comet flamed in the western sky and twice that year Saturn and Mars had been in conjunction in the sign of the Lion which was the astrological symbol of Italy. Those of us who place some reliance on astrological prophecies, looking back, may perhaps see in that comet a sign of the coming poet, who should, more than any other, influence the world of letters.

Ser Patracco took refuge in Arezzo, a city of Tuscany, and found on the so-called Garden Street a house, as the poet says, *haud sane ampla seu magnifica, sed qualis exsulem decuisset*—"not indeed magnificent but suitable for an exile."

On Monday, July 20th, almost at the very hour when the Bianchi were making their last fruitless effort to regain the ascendancy, Francesco di Petracco was born. Here on the fifteenth of June, 1800, so nearly five exact centuries later, Napoleon, about to fight "Marengo's bloody battle," paused to grant, out of honour to Petrarca's memory, amnesty to its inhabitants.

Petrarca's life lies before us with remarkable clearness. Hundreds of letters give us an almost complete autobiography; but it has been charged against him that he was ashamed of his humble birth. He tells us little about his father's family. We know that his great-grandfather Ser Garzo, a man of considerable native wisdom, though uneducated, lived at Incisa a few miles from Florence and died at the age of 104 on his birthday, in the very room where he had been born.

Of Petrarca's mother nothing is known and the Italian biographers are still struggling over the unsolved problem—whether her name was Eletta, as seems to be indicated in his poem on her death, where he calls her *Electa Dei tam nomine quam re*—in that case making her a member of the well-known family of Cino Canigiani; or Nicolosa, daughter of Vanni Cini Sizoli, or whether she was Petracco's second wife or whether she was only sixteen when she gave birth to her famous son Francesco—Cecco as they called him. When he was six months old he went with his mother to Incisa and on the way as they crossed the Arno the horse of the servant who was carrying him stumbled and the baby was almost drowned.

At Incisa he spent the first six or seven years of his life and it is generally believed that he there acquired that perfect Tuscan speech which did him and his country such honour. The house where he dwelt is still shown, though badly ruined, and it bears an inscription to the effect that here the great poet first uttered the sweet sounds of his mother tongue. In 1312 Petracco assembled his family in Pisa but perhaps found it impossible to support them there. Like many other banished Florentines he hoped for better fortunes in France and accordingly took his family to Avignon.

The Pope, Clement V., was wandering about France—at Bordeaux, Lyons, Poitiers, Montpellier and Avignon, and in October, 1316, his successor, John XXII. established the Papal Court definitely at Avignon. Hither Petracco came in 1313 and a second time the son nearly lost his life in a shipwreck near Marseilles. Avignon, on the left bank of the Rhone, was a part of Provence and at this time Provence was the patrimony of King Robert of Naples: here the king had his court from 1318 until 1324.

The influences to which Petrarca must have submitted in this transplantation should not be disregarded. Although he detested Avignon itself with its narrow streets and vile odours, yet it was the home of Provençal song and must have given him his first leaning to poetry.

Little in the way of anecdote can be told of his childhood. An astrologer prophesied that he would win the favour of almost all the princes of his day, and this was fulfilled. Also he himself relates in one of his letters how his father showed him the picture of a double-bodied boy with twin heads, four hands and other curious prototypal anticipations of the Siamese twins, that had been born in Florence and lived two or three weeks. He relates that his father gave his ear a sharp twitch that he might the better remember the marvel.

Expenses were high in Avignon and Petracco established his family at Carpentras, the capital of a little province where were mineral-springs and a quiet easy life. Here Petrarca lived four years and first enjoyed regular schooling at the hands of a scholar named Convennole or Convenevole who had a school there. This Convennole is believed by some to be the author of a portentous Latin poem of very mediocre value. He was in perpetual pecuniary difficulties and Petrarca's father often assisted him, but the man played him a very mean trick. In later years Petrarca himself came to his aid but his generosity was likewise most shabbily acquitted: he took two priceless manuscripts by Cicero and disposed of them. The books must have been destroyed, for no trace of them was ever found and thus were lost Cicero's *Libri de Gloria.*

Nevertheless, when Convennole died at Prato in 1340 or 1344 his fellow-citizens placed a poet's laurel crown on his tomb and Petrarca offered to write his epitaph.

The progress which Petrarca made in his studies was not remarkable and it is to be deeply regretted that a more liberally cultured scholar had not directed his training. A large part of Petrarca's works is in Latin but he never acquired a perfect style, such as Erasmus was able to wield. His Latin is mediæval: he himself discovered Cicero's Epistles but it was too late in life to modify his habits. Only his inherent genius enabled him to invest his Latin Letters with a perennial charm. Certainly his correspondence with Boccaccio is one of the most precious possessions of literature and it is one of the strange anomalies of life that it so long has remained a sealed book to English readers.

Petrarca's principal playmate and friend in Convennole's school was Guido Settimo who became Archbishop of Genoa, their friendship enduring more than fifty years. With the future archbishop the future poet made his first visit to the source of the Sorgue at Vaucluse or *Val chiusa,* the Shut-in Valley which he was to immortalise.

From Carpentras Petrarca was sent to the high school at Montpellier with the idea of fitting him for his father's profession of the law. Here he spent four years but what he studied, or what his experiences were, is wholly unknown, or at least wholly a matter of conjecture mixed with imagination. One single anecdote of this time is preserved in Petrarca's correspondence. His father, thinking that general literature was too much drawing his son's attention away from the law, came unexpectedly to Montpellier, and making a thorough search for his books succeeded in finding them, carefully hidden though they had been, and flung them into the fire; moved, however, by his son's bitter tears he allowed him to rescue a copy of Vergil and Cicero's "Rhetoric."

From Montpellier he went to Bologna in 1323 with his brother Gherardo and here again he neglected the lec-

tures on civic law to the advantage of what are called "the humanities." He also enjoyed the gaieties of a student's life and in his later days liked to recall them, especially as Bologna was at this time free from the disturbances that elsewhere were racking the Italian cities. The gates of the town were not closed till late at night, so secure felt the inhabitants, and the students had free course. With one of his instructors Petrarca made a visit to Venice and here also he found the highest tide of prosperity. Soon both cities were doomed to vail their glories.

Among his many friends at Bologna was Giacomo Colonna who afterwards became Bishop of Lombes and gave him a home.

Petracco died in 1326, leaving his family in deep poverty, and the two sons returned to Avignon. Petrarca's only legacy was a manuscript of Cicero. With this, the profession of the law, none too enticing to him in any circumstances, seemed to be out of the question and as the Church offered greater inducements and especially as his friend Colonna was already on the road to high preferment, he decided to adopt this profession.

On the sixth of April, 1327, almost a year after his father's death and not long after the probable death of his mother, Petrarca saw in the church of Santa Chiara at Avignon for the first time the lady whom he celebrated under the name of Laura.

Who was she?

This question has been a puzzle for two centuries and seems to offer no chance of satisfactory solution. Opinions have varied in the widest way. Some scholars have argued that the lady who inspired Petrarca's muse to such lofty flights of song was only a creature of his imagination; others, including Körting, give a certain amount of credence to the ingenious though somewhat sophisticated evidence of the clever Abbé de Sade, who elaborately argued that she was the daughter of Audibert de Noves and that she was born in 1307, that she was wedded to Hugh de Sade, the Abbé's ancestor, and bore him eleven children. A tomb at Avignon was opened in 1533 and in the coffin were found a medal and a sonnet. The sonnet was supposed to be Petrarca's though it was hardly worthy of his fame. On the medal were the initials "M. L. M. I." which were interpreted to mean *Madonna Laura morta iacit*—"Here lies the body of Madonna Laura."

This discovery was in accordance with an old tradition that Laura was a De Sade. The Abbé Costaing of Pusignan believed that she was Laura des Beaux, the daughter of the Seigneur de Vaucluse Adhemar de Cavaillon, on her mother's side descended from the house of Orange and that she lived with her relatives on her estates of Galas on the hills overlooking the valley, and that she died not of the plague but of a consumption.

There is no phase of this famous passion that has not been made the subject of an essay or a poem.

Was she a widow or a maiden or the mother of a patriarchal family? Was Petrarca's description of her beauty based on the reality or is it an ideal figment of his imagination? Was she a heartless coquette as was believed by Macaulay? Would Petrarca have written a fuller and more perfect book of songs had she been perfectly complacent? So the learned Professor Zendrini argues. Was Laura an ambitious woman caring for nothing but her own praise and cold to Petrarca not by reason of virtue but because of her insensibility?

A hundred similar questions arise, and how idle they are! Only one of them we may answer and that in the poet's own words. Some one of his friends had evidently suggested that his complaints were imaginary and his Laura a being of air, as the name implies. He answered as follows:

"What dost thou mean by saying that I have invented the specious name of L'Aura as if I wished to have something to talk about; that Laura is in reality nothing but a poetic fiction of my mind to which long and unremitting study proves that I have been aspiring; but that of this breathing Laura by whose form and beauty I seem to be a captive taken is all manufactured, verses fictitious, sighs simulated? Would that in this respect thou wert jesting in earnest! Would that it were *simulatio* and not *furor*. But believe me, no one without great effort can long use simulations but to struggle vainly to appear mad is the height of madness [*summa insania*]. Moreover while we may succeed in counterfeiting illness by our actions, we can not imitate pallor"—*tibi pallor tibi labor meus notus est.*

There are several passages in Petrarca's Latin writings where he makes it evident that Laura was an actual person. One is in the treatise concerning Scorn of this World in which he represents himself at the instigation of Truth, who appears to him in the form of a stately virgin, as holding a three days' conversation with his beloved instructor Saint Augustine. In the third dialogue Saint Augustine points out that Petrarca is held in the chains of two passions which keep him from the true contemplation of life and of death: these are love and Glory. Augustine expresses his surprise that a man of Petrarca's talent should spend so large a part of his life in praise of an earthly love; and he predicts that the time will come when he will feel ashamed of himself and of this passion.

Petrarca replies that he has already, even during her life time, written a sonnet on her approaching death,

having seen her once beautiful body exhausted by illnesses and frequent—*what?* Here is one of the mysteries; in the manuscript the word is, as usual, contracted and reads *ptbus,* which De Sade thinks stands for *partubus*—frequent child-bearing; while other manuscripts have the word spelled out:—*pertubationibus.* If she was the mother of eleven children, De Sade would seem to have reason on his side.

Petrarca goes on to assure Saint Augustine that in his Laura he had worshipped not the mortal body but the immortal soul and that even if she should die before he did, he would still love her virtue and her spirit. Saint Augustine objects that though she be perfect as a goddess, yet even that which is most beautiful may be loved shamefully—*turpiter;* but Petrarca asseverates the purity of his passion and declares that in nothing but its impetuosity was he guilty before her: that she was the source and origin of all his glory; she had nurtured the feeble germ of virtue in his breast; she was the mirror of perfection and love has the power to transmute the lover into the standard of the object loved.

But Saint Augustine is not satisfied: he points out the danger of deception and thinks that the fact that he has loved his love so exclusively has caused him to scorn other human beings and human interests. Earthly love has turned Petrarca from the heavenly and into the straight road to death.

In the course of the conversation Saint Augustine brings Petrarca to confess that he has carried next his heart a portrait of his Laura and that even the laurel wreath is dear to him only because it brings the echo of her name. And when Petrarca asks Saint Augustine what he can do to be saved from such a dangerous passion, the Saint recommends change of scene.

"Alas," replies the poet, "in vain have I wandered West and North, far and long, even to the shores of the Deep, and like the wounded stag carried my wound with me wherever I went." Augustine recommends Italy and here occurs his justly famed magnificent eulogium of that beauteous land. This leads naturally to the other chain—glory.

The second passage occurs in a poetic epistle to Giacomo Colonna, written probably in August 1337, two days after returning to Avignon after a long journey:

"Beloved beyond measure is a woman known by her virtue and her ancient lineage—*sanguine vetusto.* And my songs have given her glory and spread her fame far and wide. Ever does my heart turn back to her and with renewed pangs of love she overcomes me nor does it seem likely that she will ever renounce her conquest."

She had conquered him he says not by any arts of coquetry but by the rare beauty of her form. After enduring the chain for ten years, after wasting to a shadow and becoming another man, the fever of love so penetrating the very marrow of his bones that he could hardly drag one leg after another and he yearned for death, suddenly he determined to strike for freedom and shake off the yoke. God gave him strength to win the battle; but even then the mistress of his heart pursued him as if he were an escaped slave.

"I fly," he says, "I wander over the whole circle of the world, I dare to plough the stormy billows of the Adriatic and the Tyrrhene seas and I entrust my life, rescued from the toils of love, to a tossing vessel: for why should I, wearied by the torments of the soul, and sick of life, fear a premature death? I turn my steps toward the West and behold the lofty summits of the Pyrenees from my couch in the sunny grass. I behold the ocean from where the weary God of Day, after his long journey, dips his chariot of fire in the Hesperian flood and where looking up to Atlas turned to stone at sight of Medusa, he causes the steep mountain precipices to throw long shadows, and hides the moors with hastening shades of night. Hence I turn to the North and Boreas, and, lonely, wander through those lands that are filled with the harsh accents of barbarians' tongues, where the gloomy waves of the British sea splash with changeful foam the shores of half-known coasts and where the icy soil denies obedience to the friendly plough and keeps the vinestock alien to the hills. Little by little as I journeyed, the billows of my passion grew calm: pain, wrath and fear began to vanish; now and then peaceful slumber closed my eyelids moist with tears, and an unaccustomed smile played over my face; and already in my recollection with less of threat and less of authority arose the image of my deserted love."

Alas, he goes on, he was deceived; he thought he might disregard the sting of passion; the wound was not healed, the anguish was not allayed. He returned, but no sooner was he within the walls of the beloved city than his breast was again laden with the burden of cares. And then follows that superb description not dimmed even in the Latin in which it is couched:

"The sailor fears not with such terror the reefs as he sails through the night, as I now fear my love's face and her heart-stirring words, her head crowned with golden tresses and her snowy neck encircled with a chain and her eyes dealing sweet death."

Even in the secluded vale of Vaucluse he finds no relief: Useless to bewail the vanished years. Waking he sees her and at night her image seems to come through the triple-locked doors of his chamber at midnight and claim him as her slave. Then before the morning paints with crimson the eastern sky, he arises and leaves the

house and wanders over mountain and through forest, ever on the watch to see if she is not there.

"Oft," he says, "when I think I am alone in the pathless woods, the bushes waving in the breeze present her figure and I see her face in the bole of the lonely oak; her image rises from the waters of the spring; I seem to see her in the clouds, in the empty air and even in the adamantine stone."

To the celebration of this love he consecrates 291 sonnets, twenty-four *canzoni,* nine *sestini,* seven *ballata* and four madrigals, besides the semi-epic poem written in *terza rima* like the "Divina Commedia." In these sonnets—which are curious in this respect that they are not a sequence, they mark no progression: they are like a placid lake, not a river—Petrarca celebrates his love in every way. Every little event inspires a poem. Once he sees her about to cross a stream and the removal of her white shoes and red stockings leads to a sonnet. Her beauty is ever the thought in his mind: both in Italian and Latin he tells us:

> *Una donna più bella che 'l sole,*
> *forman parem non ulla videbunt saecula—*

"A woman lovelier than the sun, whose form no century will ever see equalled."

And again of her gait and voice:

> *non era l'andar suo cosa mortale,*
> *ma d'angelica forma e le parole*
> *sonavan altro che pur voce umana—*

"Her gait was not a mortal thing but of an angelic form and her words sounded different from any human voice:"

> *cuius nec vox nec oculorum vigor*
> *nec incessus hominem repraesentat.*

A few of the lovely passages—which alas! even in a paraphrase must lose much of their charm—must furnish a hint of the richness of this collection of poems which Guiseppe Jacopo Ferrazzi calls the bible of poets and which is by most critics considered "the most perfect monument of love-poetry among modern nations."

Her name, he says in the fifth sonnet, which is devoted to an elaborate pun upon it—Laure-ta and Laure—was written on his heart by love. He sends her some fruit in spring and the thought that the sun has ripened it causes him to call her "a sun among women"—*tra le donne un sole*—which shedding the rays of her bright eyes upon him wakes into life the thoughts, acts and words of love. But he concludes sadly that though spring may shine on earth again there will never be spring again for him. Most beautiful is the beginning of the second *canzone*

Verdi panni, sanguini, oscuri o persi—

excellently translated by Miss Louise Winslow Kidder:

Green robes, blood-coloured, dark or reddish
   black
Or golden hair in shining tresses heaped,
Ne'er clothed a woman beautiful as she
Who robs me of my will, and with herself
Allures me from the path of liberty,
So that no other servitude less grave
Do I endure.

In this *canzone* there are eight stanzas of seven lines each and a sort of coda of two lines, there being only seven rhymes in the whole poem. In the sestine are no rhymes, but each stanza of six lines has the same word endings. In the third *canzone* he speaks of her beautiful soft eyes which carry the keys to his sweet thoughts:

Que' begli occhi soavi
Che portaron le chiavi
De' miei dolci pensier.

And further on he speaks of the golden tresses which should make the sun full of deep envy and her beautiful calm look—*bel guardo sereno*—where the rays of Love are so warm, and still recalling her graces, her white delicate hands and lovely arms—

le man bianchi sottili
e le braccia gentili.

All very well translated by Macgregor:

The soft hands, snowy charm,
The finely rounded arm,
The winning way, by turns, that quiet scorn.

He renders the lines

I dolci sdegni alteramente umili
e 'l bel giovenil petto
torre d'alto intelletto

Chaste anger, proud humility adorn
The fair young breast that shrined
Intellect pure and high.

Wotton translates the lines:

L'oro e le perle e i fior vermigli e i
   bianchi
Che 'l verno devria far languidi e secchi:

Those golden tresses, teeth of pearly white,
Those cheeks' fair roses blooming to decay.

But it very well illustrates the danger one runs in reading translations: the gold and pearls and red and white flowers are the adornments which Laura wears and which are reflected in the mirror against which he complains because in seeing herself reflected there she cares more for herself than for him.

Particularly beautiful is the sonnet in which he blesses all the circumstances of his passion:

Benedetto sia'l giorno, e 'l mese e 'l anno
   E la stagione e 'l tempo e l 'ora e 'l
      punto
   E 'l bel paese e 'l loco ov' io fui giunto
Da duo begli occhi.

This translated literally reads:

"Blest be the day and the month and the year and the season and the time and the hour and the instant and the fair country and the place where I was captured by two lovely eyes that enchained me fast." And the sonnet proceeds: "And blest be the first sweet inquietude [*affanno*] that I felt at being joined with love, and the bow and arrows whereby I was wounded and the wounds that came into my heart. Blest be the voices which calling out the name of my lady, I scattered; and the sighs and the desire; and blest be all the writings whereby I won my fame and my thought which is wholly of her, so that no other has a share in it."

After eleven years of *perduti giorni,* since that "fierce passion's strong entanglement" (as Dacre translates the line) he calls upon the Father of Heaven to vouchsafe unto him power to turn to a different life and to finer achievements

ad altra vita ed a più belle imprese.

But still the charm holds: even if he would forget her the sight of the green laurel-tree brings her so vividly before him that amid the oaks and pines on the shore of the Tuscan sea where the waves broken by the winds complain, he falls as it were dead; even after fourteen years have passed he still sings her golden locks flowing in mazy ringlets to the breeze—*capelli d'oro a l'aura sparsi.*

Leigh Hunt has a good translation of the *canzone* to the Fountain of Vaucluse beginning: *Chiare, fresche e dolci acque—*

Clear, fresh and dulcet streams
Which the fair shape who seems
To me sole woman haunted at noon-tide.

Fair bough, so gently fit
(I sigh to think of it)
Which lent a pillar to her lovely side
And turf and flowers bright-eyed
O'er which her folded gown
Flowed like an angel's down,
Give ear, give ear with one consenting
To my last words, my last and my
    lamenting.

Of Petrarca's later life there are a thousand fascinating details to be found in his letters: his travels, friendships, with all the great men of his day, his relations with popes and prelates, princes and emperors, his clever intrigues to obtain the poet's laurel crown, his studies, his efforts to collect the first private library of modern times, his residences, as for instance in the Magician's house at Selva Piana, or at Venice at the house of Arrigo Molin, from one of the turrets of which he used to watch the ships, or again on the beautiful Euganean Hills.

Nor must we forget his cat which, as Tasoni says, still unburied—*un' insepolta gatta*—"conquers in glory the tombs of haughty kings." A whole chapter should be devoted to his beautiful friendship with Boccaccio and how one of his last works was to translate into Latin the story of the Patient Griselda which Chaucer put into verse.

A few cardinal dates will serve on which to hang the more important events of the latter half of his life: In 1339 he began his Latin poem **"Africa,"** the hero of which was Scipio: it waited more than half a millennium to be published. The next two years he was busy with his growing glory and waiting to be crowned at the Capitol.

After several years' residence at Parma he was made canon and in 1348 while residing at Verona came the sad news of Laura's death. Henceforth his sonnets, though retrospective and often inspired by memory of her beauty become an ascending scale until in the "Trionfi" they rival the more spiritualised poems of Dante, Laura being personified as Chastity triumphant.

In 1350 he was appointed archdeacon of Parma and the following year the Florentines decreed the restoration of his property, but when he refused to live there they confiscated it again. In 1360 he was sent as an ambassador to King Jean of France and then settled in Venice, where he lived another decade and then retired to Arqua among the Euganean Hills, where, in 1374, on the eighteenth of July, he was found dead at his table. A magnificent funeral was decreed in his honour as became so great an ornament to Italy. In 1873 his tomb was opened. His skull and bones were at first intact but on exposure to the air speedily fell to dust.

This great man becomes even greater on close study: he is chiefly known as the author of love-poems which in a dissolute age are absolutely pure and in such perfect Italian that the taste of the most refined and exacting would change scarcely a word. Although these graceful *lavorietti* composed of equal parts of serenity, brightness of touch and absolute perfection of imagery, are so spontaneous in Italian and so impossible to translate into English—wilting (as has been well said by an Italian scholar) when transferred into alien soil—yet all poets who know Italian have tried their hand at them. The latest attempt, by a California lady who published her version[1] in London, is sheer paraphrase: the simplicity and directness of the original appear in an extraordinarily imaginative overlaying of filagree and arabesque. A word or a hint is enlarged to an elaborate comparison; a thousand poetic images and conceits which Petrarca never dreamed of are introduced, and yet the work has been widely heralded as a masterpiece of translation. It was certainly inspired by Petrarca, but if one compares the version with the original, the enormous gulf between them will become at once apparent.

They were turned into Polish by Ian Grotkowski as early as 1465. Spanish, German and French poets—all have drunk at the fountain of this Parnassus. In 1520 there was a Petrarca Academy at Venice. Ioost van Vondel, the greatest of the classic Dutch poets and the master of Milton, made a pilgrimage to Arqua and set Petrarca above all other poets. Boccaccio in 1374 two hundred years earlier had predicted that Arqua, a village scarcely known even in Padua, would rise famous in the whole world: men in days to come would make pilgrimages to it. His prediction was amply verified.

There are at least two score commentaries on Petrarca's Italian poems which he himself regretted and repented having written. According to Crescenbini there were more than six hundred sonnetteers in the sixteenth century all imitating Petrarca: no less than twelve at once in Venice. Marco Foscarini prepared for the press the *Rime* of sixty Venetian gentlemen, all disciples of Laura's lover.

On the fifth centenary of his birth, prizes being offered, more than six hundred responses in French and Provençal were submitted.

But he was not merely a poet, he was also great as an orator, as a scholar, as a philosopher. The more we study his career the more we must marvel at its richness in accomplishment. Ugo Foscolo calls him the restorer of letters. He was the promoter of classic literature. "For us and for all Europe," says Carducci, "Petrarca was above all the recreator of glorious antiquity and the leader who through the desert of the Middle Ages freed our people from the slavery of barbarous peoples."

Professor Domenico Berti calls him at once poet, historian, philosopher, scholar and cultivator of the fine arts and speaks of his fine, exquisite, full, robust genius and his noble soul.

He was also the prophet of United Italy. When Cola di Rienzi engaged in his great but futile struggle to restore to Rome her ancient liberty Petrarca actively sympathised with him and wrote to him one of his noblest *canzoni* beginning

> *Spirto gentil che quelli membra reggi,*

and that which begins *"Italia mia"* praised by all critics and commentators and called the Marseillaise of Italy, as fresh and animated and full of sparkling enthusiasm to-day as if written only yesterday. It may be read in Lady Dacre's spirited version. No wonder the Austrian authorities, when they were making their desperate efforts to keep Italy dismembered and enslaved, forbade its use in the gymnasia, for it well might kindle generous souls to patriotic hatred of tyranny.

Notes

[1] "Madonna Laura." Agnes Tobin, 1907.

Theodor E. Mommsen (essay date 1946)

SOURCE: Theodor E. Mommsen, "An Introduction to Petrarch's Sonnets and Songs," in *Medieval and Renaissance Studies*, edited by Eugene F. Rice, Jr., Cornell, 1959, pp. 73-100.

[*In the following essay, Mommsen contrasts the critiques of Petrarch's poetry offered by his peers with those of subsequent generations, arguing that during Petrarch's lifetime he was valued for his classical style, while later scholars praised his originality.*]

Petrarch presents in his life and work a most interesting example of a complete mutation in literary fame. For there exists in critical annals a very marked and curious contrast between his reputation among his contemporaries and in subsequent periods.

In the popular imagination of today his name is indissolubly linked with that of Laura,

> "La bella giovenetta ch'ora è donna."
>   (*Rime* No. 127)

This tradition reaches back many centuries; in fact it had originated shortly after his death. To the majority of the generations of his admirers, Petrarch has been primarily the lover of Laura and the author of the

Rime, the sonnets and songs which he began in his youth and in which he never tired of singing of his love. Among Italians and non-Italians the image and fame of that Petrarch are just as much alive today as they were vivid towards the end of the fourteenth century when Geoffrey Chaucer glorified him in the *Canterbury Tales:*

> "Frauceys Petrak, the lauriat poete,
> Highte this clerk, whose rethorike sweete
> Enlumyned at Ytaille of poetrie."

Through the mastery of language in his Italian poetry Petrarch not only made an everlasting contribution to world literature, but also rendered a very specific service to the development and moulding of the language of his own country. Since the Renaissance literary historians have referred to him as "the father of the Italian language," a title which he shares with the two other great Florentines of the fourteenth century, Dante and Boccaccio.

By later generations Petrarch was considered an initiator in still another respect. Through the influence of the **Rime** he became the originator of a whole school of poetry, that of the "Petrarchists," which appeared soon after his death both inside and outside Italy. He had brought his favourite form of expression, the sonnet, to such a classical perfection that for centuries to come he remained the admired and widely imitated model of many poets who endeavoured to write in the same pattern. For the Elizabethan period witness the statement made in 1593 by Gabriel Harvey in his *Pierces Supererogation:* "All the noblest Italian, French, and Spanish poets have in their several veins Petrarchized; and it is no dishonour for the daintiest or divinest muse to be his scholar, whom the amiablest invention and beautifullest elocution acknowledge their master." Among these Petrarchists of the Renaissance we find Sir Thomas Wyatt and the Earl of Surrey in England, the group of the *Pléiade* with their leader Ronsard in France.

In marked contrast to the judgment of posterity, Petrarch's own generation, however, found his principal merit in his Latin writings, not in his Italian poetry.

This contemporary estimate is most clearly shown by the fact that it was the authorship of the Latin epic *Africa* and not that of the **Rime** which brought Petrarch, in 1341, at the age of thirty-seven, the famous crown of the poet laureateship on the Roman Capitol. According to the tradition of the fourteenth century, in antiquity this ceremony had symbolized the greatest tribute which could be given to a living poet. To Petrarch's contemporaries no one was deemed more worthy of this ancient honour than he who seemed to re-embody the classical ideal. Through the conscious imitation of the *Aeneid* and the *Eclogues* in his own **Africa** and **Carmen Bucolicum** he appeared to have become a second Vergil. Moreover his numerous treatises dealing with problems of moral philosophy and especially the content and style of his hundreds of widely circulated letters placed him in juxtaposition with Cicero. And as King Robert the Wise of Naples asked Petrarch for the dedication of the **Africa** to himself, so the German Emperor Charles IV requested later on the same honour for Petrarch's main historical work, the collection of Roman biographies entitled **De viris illustribus,** in which Petrarch recounted the lives and deeds of the great political and military leaders of ancient Rome in order to inspire his readers to similar accomplishments.

Throughout all these various Latin writings Petrarch pursued the same purpose: he wished to teach his Italian contemporaries not to regard the great Roman statesmen and writers as figures of a dead past, but to look upon them as living models for the present and as harbingers of the future. The Italians alone, not "barbarians" like the French or Germans, Petrarch asserted, had a legitimate claim to the Latin inheritance. In the acceptance of this Roman legacy Petrarch saw an instrument of spiritual unity for his fellow-countrymen. With this motive he devoted many of his Latin poems, treatises, and letters to the task of awakening the consciousness of this legacy in the hearts and minds of the Italians of his day.

In this sense, then, Petrarch again stands at the beginning of a very important evolution in Italian culture, the great movement known as "the Revival of Antiquity" or "Humanism." He was destined to direct and stimulate these new ideas in many significant ways, as for instance through his zealous effort to write in a "pure," i.e., classical, Latin style, through his tireless and often extremely successful search for ancient manuscripts, and through his gift for textual emendation. In contrast to many of the later humanists, this "father of Humanism" did not, however, study Latin primarily from an antiquarian point of view, since for him this language was the medium through which the greatest aesthetic, intellectual, and political tradition ever created had found its timeless expression. It was as the voice of this tradition that Petrarch was most admired and revered in his lifetime. This reputation of Petrarch within his own generation has been well characterized in Jakob Burckhardt's *Civilization of the Renaissance in Italy:* "Petrarch, who lives in the memory of most people of today chiefly as a great Italian poet, owed his fame among his contemporaries far more to the fact that he was a kind of living representative of Antiquity."

In view of the fact that there exists such a divergence of opinion in the evaluation of the main aspects of Petrarch's lifework and such variety in the judgments rendered by his own generation and by posterity, it seems worth asking what conceptions Petrarch had concerning himself and his work. It is quite easy to find an answer to this question. For Petrarch was fully conscious of the fact that his life and work represented a unique and interesting phenomenon. Thus he says in the first sonnet of his **Rime:**

> ". . . I have seen enough that in this land
> To the whole people like a tale I seem."

When Petrarch wrote these lines in the proem to the collection of his **Rime,** he had reached the summit of his fame. He could rightly assume that to Italian and non-Italian eye-witnesses his accomplishments and his rise to glory would appear "like a tale." Naturally he wished this "tale" to be perpetuated accurately beyond the memory of his contemporaries, and consequently around the year 1351 he wrote a letter which he addressed explicitly "To Posterity." Later he included this epistle, in a revised form, in the first collection of his letters called the **Familiares,** and thus made sure that the letter would actually come down to future generations.

The stated purpose of this letter is to tell posterity "what sort of man I was and what was the fate of my works." There is no better account of the main events during the first part of Petrarch's life than that given by himself in this "**Letter to Posterity**."

He introduces himself with a description of his outward appearance: "In my early days my bodily frame was of no great strength, but of great activity. I cannot boast of extreme comeliness, but only such as in my greener years would be pleasing. My complexion was lively, between fair and dark, my eyes sparkling, my sight very keen for a long time until it failed me unexpectedly after my sixtieth year, so that to my disgust I had to have recourse to glasses."

After this portrait of himself he begins the tale of his life: "I was but a mortal mannikin like yourself, with an origin neither very high nor very low. . . . I was of honourable parents, both natives of Florence but living in exile on a scanty fortune which was, to tell the truth, verging upon poverty. During this exile I was born at Arezzo, in the year of Christ 1304 of this present age, at dawn on Monday the 20th of July. . . . The first year of my life, or rather part of it, I spent at Arezzo where I first saw the light; the six following years, after my mother had been recalled from exile, at Incisa, an estate of my father's about fourteen miles from Florence. My eighth year I passed at Pisa, my ninth and following years in Transalpine Gaul on the left bank of the Rhone. The name of the city is Avignon, where the Roman Pontiff holds, and has long held, the Church of Christ in a shameful exile. . . . There then, on the banks of that most windy of rivers, I passed my boyhood under my parents' care, and, later, all my early manhood under my own vain fancies—not, however, without long intervals of absence. For during this time I spent four whole years at Carpentras, a small town not far east of Avignon; and in these two places I learnt a smattering of Grammar, Dialectic and Rhetoric suited to my age—as much, I mean, as is generally learnt in schools—and how little that is, dear reader, you know well enough. Then I went to Montpellier to study Law, where I spent four more years; and then three years at Bologna where I heard the whole Corpus of Civil Law, and was thought by many to be a youth of great promise if I would only persevere in what I had taken up. However, I abandoned that study altogether as soon as my parents abandoned the care of me; not because I did not respect the authority of Law, which is doubtless great and full of that Roman Antiquity in which I delight, but because it is degraded by the villainy of those who practise it. And so I revolted at learning thoroughly that what I would not turn to dishonourable, and could scarcely turn to honourable, uses; for such rectitude, if I had tried it, would have been laid to ignorance. Accordingly, in my twenty-second year (1326) I returned to Avignon—my exile home, where I had lived from the close of my childhood, for habit is second nature."

Petrarch continues to relate that there in Avignon he gained the friendship and patronage of many distinguished men. Among these patrons he mentions particularly some members of the great Roman family of Colonna who resided at that time at the papal court. He does not tell that after his renunciation of law he took minor orders which entitled him to receive ecclesiastical prebends without becoming a priest. He had now become "a worthy clerk," as Chaucer calls him in the prologue to *The Clerk's Tale*.

During that period, Petrarch's account goes on, "a youthful longing impelled me to travel through France and Germany; and though other causes were feigned to recommend my going to my superiors, yet the real reason was an eager enthusiasm to see the world. On that journey I first saw Paris; and I took delight in finding out the truth or falsehood of what I had heard about that city. Having returned thence, I went to Rome, which from my infancy I had ardently desired to see. And there I so venerated Stefano Colonna, the noble-minded father of that family, who was like one of the ancient heroes, and I was so kindly received by him in return, that you could scarcely have detected a difference between me and one of his own sons."

On his return from Rome, in 1337, Petrarch decided to establish himself in Vaucluse. According to the **"Letter to Posterity"** these were his reasons: "I could not overcome my natural ingrained repugnance to

Avignon, that most wearisome of cities. Therefore I looked about for some bypath of retreat as a harbour of refuge. And I found a narrow valley, delightful and secluded, called Vaucluse (fifteen miles from Avignon), where the Sorgues, king of all fountains, takes its rise. Charmed with the sweetness of the spot, I betook myself thither with my books. It would be a long story if I were to go on to relate what I did there during many, many years. Suffice it to say that nearly every one of my works was either accomplished or begun or conceived there; and these works have been so numerous that they exercise and weary me to this day."

Now Petrarch's tale comes to the supreme moment of his life, his coronation as poet laureate: "While I was spinning out my leisure in Vaucluse, on one and the same day, strange to relate, letters reached me both from the Senate of the city of Rome and from the Chancellor of the University of Paris, bringing me rival invitations to accept the laurel crown of poetry—the former at Rome, the latter at Paris. In my youthful pride at such an honour, thinking I must be worthy of it as such eminent men so thought me, but weighing their verdict instead of my own merit, I yet hesitated for a while which invitation to accept. And on this point I asked by letter for the advice of Cardinal Giovanni Colonna. He was so near that although I had written late in the day, I received his answer the next morning before nine o'clock. In accordance with his advice I decided for the dignity of the city of Rome as superior to all others, and my two replies to him applauding that advice are still extant. I set out accordingly, and though, like all young men, I was a very partial judge of my own works, I still blushed to accept the verdict upon myself even of those who had invited me. Yet no doubt they would not have done so if they had not judged me worthy of the honour so offered. I determined, therefore, first to visit Naples, and appear before that distinguished king and philosopher, Robert—as illustrious in literature as in station, the only king of our time who was a friend of learning and of virtue alike—to see what judgment he would pass upon me. I still wonder at his flattering estimate of me and the kindly welcome that he gave me; and you, reader, if you knew of it, would wonder no less. On hearing of the reason of my coming, he was marvelously delighted, and considered that my youthful confidence in him—perhaps, too, the honour that I was seeking—might be a source of glory to himself, since I had chosen him of all men as the only competent judge in such case. Need I say more? After numberless conversations on various matters, I showed him that epic of mine, the **Africa**, with which he was so delighted that he begged me as a great favour to dedicate it to him—a request which I certainly could not refuse, nor did I wish to do so. At length he fixed a day for my visit and kept me from noon to evening. And since the time proved too short for the press of subjects, he did the same on the following two days. After having fully probed my ignorance for three days, he adjudged me worthy of the laurel crown. His wish was to bestow it upon me at Naples, and he earnestly begged me to consent. But my love of Rome prevailed over even the reverend importunity of so great a king. Therefore, when he saw that my resolution was inflexible, he gave me messengers and letters to the Roman Senate in which he declared his judgment of me in flattering terms. This royal estimate was then, indeed, in accord with that of many others, and especially with my own. Today, however, I cannot approve his verdict, though it agreed with that of myself and others. Affection for me and interest in my youth had more weight with him than consideration of the facts. So I arrived at Rome, and unworthy as I was, yet with confident reliance on such a verdict, I gained the poetic laurel while still a raw scholar with great applause from those of the Romans who could be present at the ceremony. On this subject, too, there are letters of mine, both in verse and in prose."

In the retrospective view of the **"Letter to Posterity"** Petrarch concludes the account of this event with a rather disillusioned comment: "This laurel gained for me no knowledge, but rather much envy, but that also is too long a story to be told here."

It may be true that in the full maturity of his age Petrarch sincerely regretted his early desire for "empty glory" and his "youthful audacity" in accepting the honour of the coronation. But there is no doubt that at the time of the event itself he drew a deep inspiration for his work from his public and official acclaim as "a great poet and historian." He himself tells in the **"Letter to Posterity"** why it was that after his departure from Rome he resolved to finish his Latin epic *Africa* which he always considered his greatest title to fame: "I was mindful of the honour I had just received and anxious that it should not seem to be conferred on one who was unworthy of it. And so one day when, during a visit to the mountains, I had chanced upon the wood called Selvapiana across the river Enza on the confines of Reggio, I was fired by the beauty of the place and turned my pen to my interrupted poem, the *Africa*. Finding my enthusiasm, which had seemed quite dead, rekindled, I wrote a little that very day and some on each successive day until I returned to Parma. There . . . in a short time I brought the work to a conclusion, toiling at it with a zeal that amazes me today." And in the last book of the *Africa* he did not hesitate to insert, in the form of a prophecy, an account of his coronation, "such as Rome has not seen for a thousand years."

While it is thus certain that Petrarch's greatest Latin poem owed its completion to the stimulus of the laurel crown, we might digress here for a moment from the account of the **"Letter to Posterity,"** to point out

that it seems at least probable that Petrarch's greatest Italian poem, the canzone **"Italia mia,"** was conceived under the same inspiration.[2] This fervent appeal for Italian unity is addressed to the Italian princes.

> "In whose hands Fortune has put the rein
> Of the beautiful places. . . . "
> 　　　　　　　　　　　　　(*Rime* No. 128)

It is significant that Petrarch, a poet, not a man of politics, makes himself the mouthpiece of all his fellow countrymen when he reminds the rulers of Italy of their common inheritance of "the gentle Latin blood" and implores them not to call in "barbaric" mercenaries from abroad and not "to ruin the loveliest country of the earth." He places his hopes for the unification and pacification of contemporary Italy in the revival of the ancient *virtus Romana:*

> "Virtue will fight and soon the debt be paid:
> For the old gallantry
> In the Italian hearts is not yet dead."

It is interesting to recall that Machiavelli concludes his *Prince* with "an exhortation to liberate Italy from the barbarians," and that he ends this final chapter with the quotation of those very verses of Petrarch.

There seems to be hardly any other moment in Petrarch's life in which he could feel better entitled to utter such an exhortation than that period following his coronation when he had been acknowledged symbolically not only as the greatest living poet of Italy, but also as the resuscitator of the spirit of ancient grandeur. It is by this spirit that **"Italia mia"** is inspired. In this canzone Petrarch created a poem which, because of its leitmotiv of national unity, might rightly be called the first Italian anthem. But beyond that he distinguished these verses by an intensity of feeling so powerful that all his readers, regardless of their national origin, then found it and have since found it a timeless expression of their sentiments towards their native country:

> "Is not this the dear soil for which I pined?
> Is not this my own nest
> Where I was nourished and was given life?
> Is not this the dear land in which we trust,
> Mother loving and kind
> Who shelters parents, brother, sister, wife?"

It is most significant that for the first time in the history of the western world patriotic feeling had found articulate expression in poetry and had come to consciousness in a man who had grown up and lived in exile and who, therefore, could more clearly perceive the idea of supreme unity which was hidden to the resident citizens through their very entanglement in local rivalry and disunity.

The "tale" of Petrarch's life had reached its climax on the Capitoline in the spring of 1341 and during the period of the greatest productivity of his poetical genius. From the artistic point of view it appears logical, then, that in his **"Letter to Posterity"** Petrarch deals only very briefly with the events during the ten years following his coronation and that he breaks off his account rather abruptly with the year 1351, never to take it up again. For everything he had to narrate concerning the second half of his life would have seemed anticlimactic in comparison with the story of his dramatic rise during the first half. Even more, the account would have necessarily become a record of Petrarch's increasing pessimism and feeling of personal frustration and disillusionment. The hopes which he continued to have for the pacification and unification of Italy were destined to remain unfulfilled, whether he was to place them on the Italian princes or on the Roman Tribune of the People, Cola di Rienzo, or on the German Emperor Charles IV. The fervent exhortations which he addressed to successive popes, admonishing them to return from Avignon to Rome, met with little or no response. To his passionate feelings against Avignon as the seat of the Frenchified papal court he gave frequent expression in both his Latin and Italian writings, as for instance in the *Rime* (No. 138), where he denounces the hated city as:

> "Fountain of sorrow, dwelling of revolts,
> The school of errors, place of heresy,
> Once Rome, now Babylon wicked and false,
> For which the world suffers in infamy."

The nearness of hateful Avignon poisoned even Petrarch's love for Vaucluse, where since 1337 he had so often sought refuge from the turmoil of the world and found inward peace and stimulation for his work. Thus in 1353 Petrarch decided to bring to an end his sojourn of more than forty years in southern France and to go back to Italy.

It was an outwardly restless life Petrarch spent during his remaining years in northern Italy. He did not choose to take up permanent residence in any one place, not even in his native Florence, where he had been offered, at the instigation of his friend and admirer Boccaccio, a professorship at the university. The Italian princes, among them the powerful Visconti family in Milan, as well as the patrician rulers of Venice, considered it a great honour when the poet accepted their hospitality. Petrarch's democratic and republican friends deplored the close relationship into which the herald of the grandeur of the Roman Republic seemed to have entered with the "tyrants" of his age. Petrarch defied these complaints, for he never considered himself the servant of any prince or the tool of any interest contrary to his own convictions. Free from all obligations of office, in complete independence, he lived solely for his literary work and for the cause of the revival of the eternal standards and universal values of classical antiquity.

If we can trust an old report, death overcame Petrarch in the midst of his studies late at night on July 18, 1374, while he was working in the library of his country house in Arquà near Padua.

An examination of Petrarch's literary opera shows that in the most complete edition, that of the year 1554, the various Latin works and letters occupy almost twenty times as much space as the Italian poetry, the *Rime* and the *Trionfi*. Thus Petrarch's Latin writings do not merely outweigh those in the vernacular in actual volume, but they seem also to have had definite preponderance in the mind and judgment of the author himself. For in the **"Letter to Posterity"** he speaks in some detail about most of the Latin works which he had written or begun by that time, but he does not mention specifically the collection of his Italian *Rime*. That this omission was not simply accidental becomes evident from the following passage in the same epistle: "My mind was rather well balanced than acute; and while adapted to all good and wholesome studies, its special bent was towards moral philosophy and poetry. But the latter I neglected, as time went on, because of the delight I took in sacred literature. In this I found a hidden sweetness, though at one time I had despised it, so that I came to use poetry only as an accomplishment. I devoted myself singly, amid a crowd of subjects, to a knowledge of Antiquity; for this age of ours I have always found distasteful, so that, had it not been for the love of those dear to me, I should have preferred to have been born in any other."

This passage leaves no doubt as to which part of his work Petrarch himself considered most important. From his own point of view the judgment of his contemporaries certainly was right and that of later generations wrong. He himself desired to be renowned, above all else, for his "single devotion to the knowledge of Antiquity," and not for his Italian poetry.

The fact that Petrarch gave his personal preference to his humanistic endeavours and accomplishments ought not, however, to compel us to believe that he actually meant to disavow his Italian writings altogether. It is true that in a letter written two years before his death, he called his poems in the vernacular "little trifles" and "juvenile fooleries" and expressed the wish that "they might be unknown to the whole world and even to myself if that could be." But notwithstanding this wish for their obliteration, Petrarch, from the record of his work, actually took the greatest personal care in preserving and editing these very same poems. When in mid-life he decided to collect his "scattered rhymes" (*Rime* No. 1) in one volume, he never ceased working over them throughout the rest of his days, striving to bring them to what he considered the point of perfection.

The clearest evidence of the painstaking effort Petrarch made in this task of polishing his verse is manifestly shown by the great number of corrections and marginal notes in his working copy of the *Rime* which is preserved today in the Vatican Library. A few examples may suffice to illustrate this point. On the margin of the sonnet **"Non fûr ma' Giove"** (*Rime* No. 155) Petrarch remarks: "Note that I had once in mind to change the order of the four stanzas so that the first quatrain and the first terzina would have become second and vice versa. But I gave the idea up because of the sound of the beginning and the end. For (in the case of a change) the fuller sound would have been in the middle and the hollower sound at the beginning and at the end; this, however, is against the laws of rhetoric."

Another marginal note (to *Rime* No. 199) gives an interesting glimpse into Petrarch's working habits: "In 1368," he jots down, "on Friday, August the 19th, sleepless for a long time during the first watch of the night, I at last got up and came by chance upon this very old poem, composed twenty-five years ago." That Petrarch gave a great deal of thought to determining which of his earlier poems were worthy of inclusion in his final collection is well demonstrated by the following note at the end of the sonnet **"Voglia mi sprona"** (*Rime* No. 211): "Amazing. This poem was once crossed out by me and condemned. Now, by chance reading it again after a lapse of many years, I have acquitted it and copied it and put it in the right place. Shortly afterwards, however, on the 27th, in the evening, I made some changes in the final lines, and now I shall have finished with it."

Within the limited compass of this essay it is impossible to go into the intricate problems involving the chronology, the variant forms and arrangements of Petrarch's collection of sonnets and songs. It will be sufficient to state that despite his solemn declarations to the contrary Petrarch never, even during his old age, lost his interest in his "juvenile fooleries" but continued editing and re-editing them to the last. He worked on them until his sense of artistry was truly satisfied. There is tangible evidence of his own critical approval in the frequent recurrence of the word *placet* on the margins of his working copy. And if there is a legitimate suspicion that Petrarch was not quite candid in the denial of his personal interest in his Italian poems, the same doubt can assail our acceptance of the sincerity of his wish that "they might be unknown to the whole world." For he knew very well from the study of his beloved antiquity that glory depends solely on true distinction in whatever field of activity an individual might choose. In his own incessant striving after perfection he must, therefore, have been greatly inspired and impelled by the desire for approval of these poems by readers in his own era as well as in coming centuries.

In the final collection of his verse Petrarch included three hundred and sixty-six poems. Of this number, three hundred and seventeen were written as sonnets, twenty-nine as *canzoni*, nine as *sestine*, seven as *ballate*, and four as madrigals. The collection has no definite title but is known in Italian simply by the generic names of **Canzoniere** or **Rime**, or somewhat more specifically, **Rime Sparse**. For in contrast to Dante, who assembled his poems to Beatrice in a book named by himself *La Vita Nuova*, Petrarch never chose a precise name for his collected poems but was content to call them rather vaguely **Rerum vulgarium fragmenta**, "Fragments," or better "Pieces of matters written in the vernacular." This absence of a concrete title does not seem to be wholly fortuitous. For again in contrast to Dante's *Vita Nuova*, Petrarch's **Rime** do not form an organic unit but are in truth "scattered rhymes," as Petrarch calls them himself in the proem to the collection. The content of most of the longer poems is political, religious, or moral in nature whereas the theme of the overwhelming majority of the sonnets is Petrarch's love for Laura. The author did not arrange his poems according to their poetical form nor apparently did he attempt to divide the long series of the love sonnets to Laura into definite "sequences," although there are to be found certain groups of poems which are more closely interrelated than others.

Some of Petrarch's most beautiful verse is contained in his *canzoni*, as for instance in **"Spirto gentil,"** **"Italia mia,"** or **"Vergine bella."** But it was especially in the sonnet that his genius found the most adequate mode of expression. Petrarch did not invent the form of the sonnet. It had appeared long before his time and flourished greatly in the school of poets writing in the "dolce stil novo," which reached its climax with Dante. He surpassed, however, all his predecessors in the fashion in which he perfected the traditional form and filled it with a content at once richer and more variegated than ever before. The brevity of the fourteen lines actually permits no more than the expression of one idea or one mood or one emotion. These perceptions and feelings, however, are not allowed to remain vague and fleeting but are submitted to the discipline of rigid form. As no other poet before and only few after him, Petrarch, in many of his sonnets, succeeded in striking this delicate balance of form and content and in establishing a true harmony of feeling and thinking. As the unsurpassed master of the love sonnet of his day Petrarch became, as has been shown before, the model of innumerable sonneteers, in Italy as well as abroad, who were fully conscious of their discipleship and even proud of their denomination as "Petrarchists."

In creating the glory of the Italian sonnet Petrarch can lay claim to still another distinction, the tone colour which is one of the most outstanding characteristics of his Italian poetry. In this connection it is worth noting that the Italian terms *sonetto* and *canzone* are derived from the words for "sound" and "song." This derivation tells us very clearly that poems written in these particular two forms were meant to be intoned and that consequently their authors needed musical as well as literary talent. Petrarch in full measure possessed the gifts of the musician. His contemporary biographer, the Florentine Filippo Villani, states: "He played the lyre admirably. His voice was sonorous and overflowing with charm and sweetness." Among the few personal possessions which Petrarch deemed worthy of specific mention in his last will there appears "my good lyre."

In the working copy of his *Rime* we find the following note to one of his sonnets: "I must make these two verses over again, singing them (*cantando*), and I must transpose them.—3 o'clock in the morning, October the 19th." No better testimony than this intimate self-reminder can be found to illustrate both the importance which Petrarch attributed to the musical qualities of his verse and the method which he used to test these qualities. Whoever reads his sonnets and songs aloud in their rich Italian will immediately be impressed by their melodiousness and will readily agree with Filippo Villani who says: "His rhythms flow so sweetly that not even the gravest people can withstand their declamation and sound." Some of Petrarch's most beautiful verse, the poems in honour of the Virgin, were set to music by the greatest composer of the Italian Renaissance, Palestrina, in his *Madrigali Spirituali.*

The theme of the overwhelming majority of Petrarch's *Rime* is his love for Laura. This fact has led many editors since the sixteenth century to divide the collection up into two parts, the first containing the poems written "In vita di Madonna Laura," the second one consisting of those "In morte di Madonna Laura," beginning with the moving lamentation of the sonnet "Oimè il bel viso" (*Rime* No. 267). Although this division cannot be directly traced back to Petrarch himself there is no doubt that the main theme of the sonnets is Petrarch's love for Laura "in life and in death."

Who was Laura? With this question we come to that problem which more than almost any other has attracted the attention of scholars working on Petrarch and has, to an even greater degree, challenged and fascinated the popular imagination.

The crux of the problem is that Petrarch himself, both in his *Rime* and in his Latin writings, chose to give only very few details of a concrete nature concerning Laura and her personal circumstances. This discretion

on the part of Petrarch in regard to the central figure in his life becomes particularly manifest in his "**Letter to Posterity.**" For although in this epistle he speaks of a good many of his close friends in some detail, he condenses all he has to say about the person presumably nearest to his heart in one sentence: "In my youth I suffered from an attachment of the keenest kind, but constant to one, and honourable; and I should have suffered longer, had not death—bitter indeed, but useful—extinguished the flame as it was beginning to subside." The marked restraint and the curious detachment make it very evident that in this autobiographical record written for the perusal of later generations Petrarch was resolved to gloss over the crucial importance of Laura in his life, just as he attempted, in the same document, to belittle the significance and the value of those *Rime* whose principal theme was his love for Laura.

When not thinking of himself in the light of posterity but writing solely for his own record, Petrarch had a good deal more to say about Laura. It was his habit to make notes on the most intimate details of his personal life in the most cherished book of his library, on the fly-leaf of his manuscript of Vergil's works. There appears the following entry: "Laura, illustrious by her own virtues and long celebrated in my poems, first appeared to my eyes in the earliest period of my manhood, on the sixth day of April, anno Domini 1327, in the Church of St. Claire, at the morning hour. And in the same city at the same hour of the same day in the same month of April, but in the year 1348, that light was withdrawn from our day, while I was by chance at Verona, ignorant—alas!—of my fate. The unhappy tidings reached me at Parma in a letter from my friend Louis on the morning of May the 19th in the same year. Her chaste and lovely body was laid in the Church of the Franciscans on the very day of her death at evening. Her soul, however, I am persuaded—as Seneca says of Africanus—has returned to heaven whence it came. I have felt a kind of bitter sweetness in writing this, as a memorial of a painful matter—especially in this place which often comes under my eyes—so that I may reflect that no pleasures remain for me in this life, and that I may be warned by constantly looking at these words and by the thought of the rapid flight of years that it is high time to flee from the world. This, by God's preventing grace, will be easy to me when I keenly and manfully consider the empty, superfluous hopes of the past, and the unforeseen issue."

Neither in this most intimate record nor anywhere else does Petrarch say who Laura actually was. In truth, he kept this secret so well that apparently even among his closest friends the suspicion arose that "Laura" was merely a fictitious name for an imaginary love and that the word stood not so much for the name of a real person as for Petrarch's dearest goal in life, the "laurel," symbol of the poet's fame. Indeed Petrarch himself liked to play upon the similarity between the name of Laura and the Latin and Italian words for laurel. Against the charge of feigned love Petrarch defended himself in a letter written in 1336 to his intimate friend Giacomo Colonna, Bishop of Lombez, as follows: "You actually say that I have invented the name of 'Laura' in order to have some one to talk about, and in order to set people talking about me, but that, in reality, I have no 'Laura' in mind, except that poetical laurel to which I have aspired, as my long and unwearied toil bears witness; and as to this breathing 'laurel,' with whose beauty I seem to be charmed, all that is 'made up'—the songs feigned, the sighs pretended. On this point would that your jests were true! Would that it were a pretense, and not a madness! But, credit me, it takes much trouble to keep up a pretense for long; while to spend useless toil in order to appear mad would be the height of madness. Besides, though by acting we can feign sickness when we are well, we cannot feign actual pallor. You know well both my pallor and my weariness; and so I fear you are making sport of my disease by that Socratic diversion called 'irony,' in which even Socrates must yield the palm to you."

This letter is a convincing proof of the genuineness of Petrarch's love, but it is again noteworthy that even in this self-defense he did not design to reveal the identity of the actual Laura. As the result of Petrarch's silence concerning the real circumstances of Laura's life there arose soon and frew and flourished throughout the centuries almost to the present a Laura-Legend which was an interesting composite of romantic and fanciful imagination, pseudo-scholarly research, and half-truth. It would lead into too many bypaths to follow the story of this legend. May it suffice to say that according to modern scholarship it seems likely that the "historical" Laura was the daughter of a Provençal nobleman, Audibert de Noves, that she was married to Hugues de Sade, and that Petrarch probably met her for the first time about two years after her marriage.

That the object of Petrarch's love was a married woman and the mother of several children was a hypothesis that ran contrary to the popular and sentimental romanticization of the two lovers and their relationship, and for that reason this thesis was long and bitterly contested. But actually the "real" Laura does not matter at all. For whatever the facts of her life might have been, they do not provide us with any "background" for a better understanding of the collection of the *Rime* in the form in which Petrarch wanted them to endure. If he had not burnt many of his earlier poems, as he did according to his own statement, the picture would perhaps be quite different. But his final collection does not present a narrative pattern or sequence, and all attempts have completely failed to crystallize an account of a romance out of the *Rime*.

Everything the more curious need know for the understanding of the nature of Petrarch's relationship with Laura, he himself has told in the self-analysis of his book called the *Secretum,* which he composed in the form of a dialogue between himself and St. Augustine as his father confessor. He started writing this work in 1342 while Laura was still alive and finished it a few years after her death. Therein he states: "Whatever little I am, I have become through her. For if I possess any name and fame at all, I should never have obtained them unless she had cared with her most noble affection for the sparse seeds of virtues planted in my bosom by Nature." Laura's mind, Petrarch says, "does not know earthly cares but burns with heavenly desires. Her appearance truly radiates beams of divine beauty. Her morals are an example of perfect uprightness. Neither her voice nor the force of her eyes nor her gait are those of an ordinary human being." Petrarch asserts emphatically that he had "always loved her soul more than her body," though he has to admit that, under the compulsion of love and youth, "occasionally I wished something dishonourable."

But the purity of the relationship was saved by Laura, for "not moved by any entreaties nor conquered by any flatteries, she protected her womanly honour and remained impregnable and firm in spite of her youth and mine and in spite of many and various other things which ought to have bowed the spirit of even the most adamant. This strength of character of the woman recalled seemly conduct to the mind of the man. The model of her excellence stood before me so that in my own strife for chastity I lacked neither her example nor her reproach. And when finally she saw me break the bridle and fall (this is obviously a reference to a love affair with another woman), she left me rather than follow my course."

Eventually Petrarch succeeded in conquering himself, for in the dialogue he assures St. Augustine: "Now I know what I want and wish, and my unstable mind has become firm. She, on her part, has always been steadfast and has always stayed one and the same. The better I understand her womanly constancy, the more I admire it. If once I was grieved by her unyielding resolution, I am now full of joy over it and thankful." It was for spiritual reasons that Petrarch felt a sense of profound gratitude towards Laura, as he makes clear both in the *Secretum* and in the moving lines of thanksgiving in one of his later sonnets:

"I thank her soul and her holy device
That with her face and her sweet anger's
   bolts
Bid me in burning think of my salvation."
                                                     (*Rime* No. 289)

The autobiographical account in the *Secretum* provides the most valuable clue to the right understanding of Petrarch's conception of Laura's image and his relationship with her, as they are reflected in the *Rime*. For a clear comprehension of the passages quoted it should be remembered that they do not represent simply a personal record but are set forth in the solemn form of an imaginary dialogue with Petrarch's spiritual guide and conscience, St. Augustine. In this dialogue, which has an almost confessional character, Petrarch naturally felt bound to reveal himself fully and frankly, even if this meant his candid admission of aberrations from the right path of acting and feeling. It is purely incidental that he has satisfied our curiosity about certain external details of his relationship with Laura.

On the other hand, it is most significant that he depicted this relationship as one in which were linked together two beings who belonged to two entirely different spheres and therefore acted in an entirely different fashion. Whereas he himself was an ordinary human being with all of man's passions and desires, Laura was above earthly cares and burnt solely with heavenly desires. Whereas his own personality and sentiments underwent many radical changes, she remained always one and the same. The climax of this love was reached when Petrarch, inspired by the example of Laura's perfection, masters himself and his desires and begins, under her guidance, to strive for the salvation of his soul.

What Petrarch has recounted in the prose of his *Secretum* as his personal confession to St. Augustine, he has expressed in the lyrics of his *Rime* to all.

> ". . . who hear in scattered rhymes the sound
> Of that wailing with which I fed my heart."
> *(Rime No. 1)*

For in the *Rime* he gives us the rapture of love in which there is only one subject, the man, who alone speaks and feels, acts and changes, while the woman is but the mute and passive object of this love, an ideal and therefore immutable being.

This ideal object of his love was, however, not imaginary or fictitious. As if to refute any doubt as to the existence of a "real" Laura, Petrarch makes repeatedly very specific chronological statements in the *Rime* themselves concerning the dates of his first meeting with Laura and of her death. Petrarch obviously had very good reasons for such an inclusion of dates into his verse, for his musical ear must have protested against these attempts at fitting bare figures into a rigid metre.

In other ways, too, Petrarch tries to assure his readers of Laura's reality. He describes her appearance, her golden hair and her fair eyes, or he pictures her in the beauty of nature, "walking on the green grass, pressing the flowers like a living girl." But all these descriptions are rather limited in range, for her beauty and charm are beyond the power of the poet's pen, as he himself confesses:

> ". . . I still seem to pass
> Over your beauty in my rhyme . . .
> But the burden I find crushes my frame
> The work cannot be polished by my file.
> And my talent which knows its strength and style
> In this attempt becomes frozen and lame."
> *(Rime No. 20)*

Petrarch is aware that he will be criticized for his endeavour to enshrine her above others in his song and that the temper of his praise will be considered false, but he cannot accept such criticism. For he knows that no matter what he says he will never be able to express his thoughts in verse as well as he feels them enclosed in his breast (*Rime* No. 95).

Eventually Laura assumes an ideal nature such as is disclosed in one of the sonnets in words which are almost identical with the quoted passage from the *Secretum*:

> "In what part of the sky, in what idea
> Was the example from which Nature wrought
> That charming lovely face wherein she sought
> To show her power in the upper sphere?"
> *(Rime No. 159)*

This conception of Laura as the sublime ideal, expressed in terms strongly reminiscent of Platonic thought, shows most clearly the transformation which the picture of the "real" Laura had undergone in the poet's mind: she has become the image of the concept of the beautiful, and we might add from the reading of other poems in the *Rime,* the embodiment, too, of good and the right. The ultimate transfiguration of Laura is attained in one of the later sonnets where his

> ". . . inner eye
> Sees her soar up and with the angels fly
> At the feet of our own eternal Lord."
> *(Rime No. 345)*

While Laura is thus elevated into "the upper sphere," Petrarch himself remains earthbound. The object of his love is an ideal, but his feelings for his beloved are human. From the time when, at the age of twenty-three, he met Laura first in the church in Avignon, to her death twenty-one years later, and from that time to his own death, this was the focusing passion of his life:

"I have never been weary of this love,
My lady, nor shall be while last my years."

(*Rime* No. 82)

Petrarch runs the whole gamut of emotions and passions of a lover, from the highest elation to the deepest despair. In this full scale only one note is missing which in ordinary love would naturally mark the supreme moment: the exaltation of physical consummation. That the love for Laura, by its very nature, was denied fulfillment in the common sense, has to be understood as the mode to which the whole tone of Petrarch's sonnets and songs is pitched. For above all the *Rime* sing of the sad and woeful beauty of love, of the longing for the unattainable, of the rebellion against denial, of the inward laceration of the lover and of his melancholic resignation. In the *Rime* all these moods of a lover have found their timeless representation. And the very fact that the figure of Laura is so idealized has made it possible for many readers of these sonnets and songs to see in the image of Laura the picture of their own beloved and to hear in the verse of the poet the expression of their own thoughts and the echoes of their own love.

While in the exalted conception of his beloved Petrarch was still bound by the tradition of the love poetry of the Provençal troubadours and the Italian poets of the "dolce stil novo," in the representation of himself and of his own humanity he was guided by a very different source of inspiration, the model of Latin poetry of classical times. There is hardly one poem in the *Rime* which does not show more or less definite traces of this influence as to form and content, figures of speech and comparisons, symbols and allegories. Petrarch went wholeheartedly (and with full consciousness of his debt) to school to the great Roman poets. And what he learned there he absorbed so completely that even in imitating he succeeded for the most part in creating something new. The splendour and richness of the *Rime* were to a large extent based on his lifelong devotion to the scholarly study of antiquity. Thus the accomplishments of Petrarch the sonneteer presuppose the research of Petrarch the humanist.

Petrarch once strikingly compares himself to the statue of Janus: like the double-faced Roman god he feels himself to be looking both backward and forward. This, his own comparison, characterizes well Petrarch's personal outlook on life. For often and with profound yearning he looked back to the glory of ancient Rome and drew from its grandeur the deepest inspiration for his work. He regarded the whole epoch of a thousand years, extending from the fall of the Roman Empire to his own days, as a period of "darkness." But throughout his life he hoped that the "revival" of the past

would put an end to the process of decline and would usher in a new and better era. This ardent hope for the future Petrarch has voiced in the canzone "**Italia mia**" and in many other pieces, but nowhere more impressively than in that work which he himself considered as his greatest, the *Africa*. At the very end of this epic he addresses his own poem as follows: "My fate is to live amid varied and confusing storms. But for you perhaps, if, as I hope and wish, you will live long after me, there will follow a better age. This sleep of forgetfulness will not last forever. When the darkness has been dispersed, our descendants can come again in the former pure radiance."

Posterity may accept Petrarch's own judgment and may agree that the figure of Janus truly symbolizes his position in history. His outlook on the world indeed included views of two different ages. Yet to posterity his choice of the image of Janus might seem a simplification. He had, it would seem, more than the two aspects of the Roman god. Witness one of the most famous incidents in his life, the ascent of Mont Ventoux near Vaucluse, which he undertook in 1336, at the age of thirty-two. In a letter written under the immediate impression of this experience Petrarch relates how he decided to climb this mountain, "induced by the sole desire of seeing the remarkable height of the place." As a student of classical authors he knows of similar undertakings in antiquity and thus, in imitation of an ancient model, he does what no man during the Middle Ages had done, he scales a mountain with the sole motive of satisfying his curiosity. He describes in great detail the difficulties which he and his brother, his only companion, found on their way. Despite the warnings which the pair received from an old shepherd, they continue their strenuous ascent and finally reach the summit. What Petrarch sees and feels on that momentous occasion, he endeavours to express in the following sentences: "First of all, braced by the nip of the keen air and the extent of the view, I stood as dazed. I looked back; the clouds were beneath my feet. And now the stories of Athos and Olympus seem less incredible to me, as I behold on a mountain of lesser fame what I had heard and read of them. I turn my eye's glance in the direction of Italy, whither my heart most inclines. . . . I confess I sighed for the skies of Italy, which I looked upon with my mind rather than with my eyes, and an irrepressible longing seized me to behold my friend and my country."

But while he was thus gazing at the beauty of the panorama of the Alps, "a new thought" suddenly possessed him which drew him from the sight of the external world towards a consideration of himself and his past life. He thinks of Laura, saying: "What I used to love, I love no longer—nay, I lie, I do love, but with more restraint, more moderately, more regretfully." He continues: "While I marveled at these things in turn, now recognizing some earthly object, now lifting my soul upwards as my body had been, I thought of looking at the book of Augustine's *Confessions* . . . which I always have with me. I opened the little volume, of handy size but of infinite charm, in order to read whatever met my eye. . . . I call God to witness, and my listener too, that these were the words on which my eyes fell: 'Men go abroad to admire the heights of mountains, and the mighty billows, and the long-winding courses of rivers, the compass of the ocean, and the courses of the stars—and themselves they neglect.' I confess I was amazed; and begging my brother, who was eager to hear more, not to trouble me, I closed the book, indignant with myself that at that very moment I was admiring earthly things—I, who ought to have learnt long ago from even heathen philosophers that there is nothing admirable but the soul—in itself so great that nothing can be great beside it. Then, indeed, content with what I had seen from the mountain, I turned my eyes inward upon myself, and from that moment none heard me say a word till we reached the bottom."

By this narrative of the ascent of Mont Ventoux Petrarch revealed himself in the whole complexity of his personality and in the diversity of his thoughts, feelings, and interests. He was the man of a new age who set out to discover the beauty of the world and relive an experience forgotten for long centuries. He was the humanist who wanted not merely to devote himself to an antiquarian study of the arts and letters, the history and philosophy of Roman days, but who desired to revive the past in the present and for the future by re-enacting what the ancients had done. He was the Italian patriot whose inner eye beheld the unity and splendour of his native country. He was the lover of Laura who was still torn in his human feelings but was beginning to conquer himself. Yet at the end he found himself bound by the traditions of medieval Christianity in which he had been brought up and which he always revered in the person and work of his great guide, St. Augustine. Thus at the culminating point of his new experience Petrarch closed his eyes to the external world and turned to the spiritual problems of his soul.

All these manifold facets of Petrarch, which the account of his impressions on the peak of Mont Ventoux illumines in a most dramatic fashion, have found their expression in the *Rime*. The essential nature remains, but the colours are much more variegated and the pattern as a whole is infinitely richer. Only the most striking parallel may be pointed out. As the story of the mountain climbing ends with spiritual reflections stimulated by the reading of St. Augustine's *Confessions,* so the collection of love poetry concludes with a devout prayer to the Virgin Mary:

"Recommend me to your Son, to the real
Man and the real God,

That Heaven's nod be my ghost's peaceful
seal."

Petrarch lived in an era which in the history of western civilization marks the beginning of the turn from the medieval to the modern age. Petrarch's personal views and his literary work reflect fully the transitional character of his period. For if there are characteristic medieval features to be found in Petrarch, there are also just as many traits which point to a venture into a world of new ideas. Thus the English biographer of Petrarch, Edward H. R. Tatham, rightly names him "the first modern man of letters." It is Petrarch's interest in man and in the problems of human nature that makes him "modern" and differentiates him from medieval writers. All of Petrarch's works, whether they were written in verse or in prose, in Italian or in Latin, have as their main theme the spiritual and intellectual, the emotional and artistic aspects of man's life.

But Petrarch was not only concerned with "man" in general, but was also deeply engrossed in the phenomenon of man as an individual being, as he saw him in the history of the past or as a living actor on the contemporary stage. And above all Petrarch was interested in himself and in the phenomenon of his own individuality.

"In the Middle Ages," writes Jakob Burckhardt, "both sides of human consciousness—that which was turned within as that which was turned without—lay dreaming or half awake beneath a common veil. This veil was woven of faith, illusion, and childish prepossession through which the world and history were seen clad in a strange hue." Petrarch was among the first to tear this veil away by striving for a full understanding of his own individuality through continuous self-analysis and selfportrayal, as illustrated by the "**Letter to Posterity**" or the *Secretum* or, above all, the *Rime*. In this sense Petrarch may be called the founder of modern humanism.

Notes

[1] I should like to thank my friend George W. Freiday, Jr., for his many valuable suggestions and for his constructive criticism.

The quotations from the "Letter to Posterity" and the letter describing Petrarch's ascension of Mont Ventoux are from the translations by Edward H. R. Tatham in *Francesco Petrarca. The First Modern Man of Letters; His Life and Correspondence (1304-1347).* 2 vols. 1925/26. The Sheldon Press, London.

[2] [See Theodor E. Mommsen, "The Date of Petrarch's Canzone *Italia Mia*," *Speculum*, XIV (1939), 28-37. Mommsen argues that "Italia mia" was certainly composed "before the year 1347" and probably composed

in the years 1341-1342, in the months following Petrarch's coronation as poet laureate on April 8, 1341.]

Thomas P. Roche, Jr. (essay date 1974)

SOURCE: Thomas P. Roche, Jr., "The Calendrical Structure of Petrarch's *Canzoniere*," in *Studies in Philology*, Vol. LXXI, No. 2, April, 1974, pp. 152-72.

[*In the essay below, Roche argues that Petrarch consciously utilized Renaissance concepts of numerology in the structuring of the* Canzoniere.]

The purpose of this essay is to argue that the ordering of the three hundred and sixty-six poems in Petrarch's *Canzoniere* is numerologically oriented and that one of the main structures in this ordering is a calendrical framework that places the *Canzoniere* unequivocally in the context of fourteenth-century Christian morality. Without even referring to recent studies about numerological composition in English poetry of the Renaissance or to the overwhelming evidence of Biblical commentaries from earliest times through the seventeenth century,[1] we have the figure of Dante, whose numerological structuring of *La Vita Nuova* and *La Divina Commedia* has never been called into question. Behind Dante are the Platonic and Pythagorean theories of the mathematical basis of the universe. From the time of Plato's *Timaeus* and later of Boethius' *Arithmetic* (both works used as text books throughout the Middle Ages and the Renaissance) men learned that God had created the world in number, weight, and measure, and these philosophical texts for the Christian reader merely corroborated the evidence from the Book of Wisdom: "Omnia in mensura et numero et pondere disposuisti" (*Liber Sapientiae,* XI: 21). By incorporating numerical proportions into his poems, a poet would be eliciting relations already existent in the world and thereby enhancing his poem and making it more "real."

In such a world Petrarch clearly saw beyond mere coincidence when he insists that his first sight of Laura was the same hour and day and month as that of her death:

> Laurea, illustrious for her own virtues and long celebrated in my poems, first appeared to my eyes about the time of my early manhood (*sub primum adolescentie mee tempus*) in the year of the Lord 1327 on the sixth day of the month of April, in the church of St. Clare in Avignon, in the morning (*hora matutina*); and in the same city, in the same month of April, on the same sixth day, at the same first hour, in the year 1348, her light was withdrawn from this light, when I by chance was then at Verona, alas, unaware of my fate. Moreover, the unhappy news reached me through a letter of my Ludovico in the same year, in the month of

May, the nineteenth day early. That most chaste and most beautiful body was placed in the church of the Franciscans on the very day of her death at vespers. . . .[2]

In a world governed by number, one might well begin to believe that a conspiratorial Providence had been numbering her days. I do not want my last punning remark to be taken too lightly, for there is evidence that this kind of numbering of days was familiar to Petrarch. He writes about his grandfather, Ser Garzo, who predicted the hour of his death and having reached the ripe age of one hundred four, when the predicted hour came, lay down quoting the Psalmist: "I will lay me down in peace and sleep" and died. Also Petrarch's earliest surviving poem, written when he was fourteen or fifteen, is thirty-eight Latin hexameters on the death of his mother. She was thirty-eight years old.

I do not want to stress these more lugubrious aspects of numerology, but we have grown away from the belief in Providence and the patterning of human life so far and in so many ways that we can hardly think ourselves into a time when men believed in a God of Love, Who promised that good would eventually emerge from evil, Who proved His Providence in the book of His Revelation and in the trials of His Chosen People, and from Whom the living would expect no less. A man could derive emotional comfort from the power of number to rationalize loss or to memorialize the departed creature through the very same power used by God to create in number, weight, and measure.

For the reasons just indicated and for others that I will develop later I cannot accept the late Professor Wilkins' assumptions about the structuring of the *Canzoniere:*

> Miss Phelps has shown that within each of the two parts [of the *Canzoniere*] the poems are as a whole arranged with great artistic care upon three principles: (1) the maintenance of a generally but not strictly chronological order; (2) the securing of variety in form; and (3) the securing of variety in content. In accordance with the second and third principles, for instance, *canzoni* are so placed as to prevent the existence of long series of sonnets, and political poems are so placed as to prevent the existence of long series of love poems.[3]

I do not find these assumptions convincing as aesthetic principles. Like the outmoded theory of "comic relief" in Renaissance tragedy they do not take into account the extraordinary intellectual analogies that exist between the various poetic forms and topics that constitute the completed *Canzoniere,* and they fail to see the real and valid relation between the love poems and the political poems.[4] Even more to the point, these assumptions do not begin to probe the complexity of

Petrarch's innovation, discussed by Wilkins later in his book:

> Of the 366 poems of the *Canzoniere,* 29 are *canzoni,* nine are *sestine,* seven are ballate, four are *madrigali,* and 317 are sonnets. In the *Canzoniere* these forms are not kept separate, but are so mingled as to afford a pleasing variety. *In view of the consistent practice of the separation of canzoni and sonnets in MS collections of pre-Petrarchan lyrics, Petrarch's procedure in mingling canzoni and sonnets is clearly seen to constitute a notable poetic innovation.*[5]

Wilkins' magisterial studies of the *Canzoniere,* for which I have nothing but admiration, are primarily genetic; they quite rightly emphasize the "making" of the sequence and of necessity do not concern themselves with the *completed* work. Without denying the validity of Wilkins' researches (in fact, using them to test the validity of my own assumptions) I want to examine the evidence of structural patterns in the *Canzoniere* to see what they tell us about the meaning of the sequence and about Petrarch's innovation of mingling canzoni and sonnets.

Let us take the simple example of the four madrigali, all occurring in the first part of the sequence. They are numbers 52, 54, 106 and 121. We know that 121 (*Or vedi, Amor*) was a late addition in Petrarch's manuscript and that it replaced the ten line ballata *Donna mi vene,* which appeared in most of the early manuscripts and even some of the early printed texts.[6] Is it mere coincidence that the number of the first two (52 and 54) add up to the number of the third (106) and that canzone 53 contains 106 lines? Perhaps. But if we look at the alternation of forms in the two segments 38-54 and 105-121, we may see a reason why Petrarch replaced the ballata with that fourth madrigale.

38-49	12 sonnets	105	1 canzone
50	1 canzone	106	1 madrigale
51	1 sonnet	107-118	12 sonnets
52	1 madrigale	119	1 canzone
53	1 canzone	120	1 sonnet
54	1 madrigale	121	1 madrigale

The formal pattern of 38-49 is repeated in 107-118, and the admittedly short pattern of 53-54 is repeated in 105-106, the two patterns being reversed. The facts that these two segments form a pattern embracing all four madrigali and that the groups of twelve sonnets are the only two in the *Canzoniere* suggest that the pattern I am describing may have been intentional. It

would seem all the more likely in that 55-63 is another formal pattern of ballate and sonnets.

55	1 ballata
56-58	3 sonnets
59	1 ballata
60-62	3 sonnets
63	1 ballata

My suggestion about the pattern of the madrigali becomes even more probable if we consider the integration of that pattern with the grouping of the first seventeen canzoni. Only five times in the entire sequence does Petrarch group canzoni together: 28-29, 70-73, 125-129, 206-207, 359-360. The first three groups are respectively two, four, and five canzoni. If we consider the placement of the first seventeen canzoni, we will *almost* see the simple process of adding one more canzone to each succeeding group.

Canzone 1	23	1
Canzoni 2-3	28-29	2
Canzoni 7-10	70-73	4
Canzoni 13-17	125-129	5

The pattern is broken by canzoni 4-6 (37, 50, 53) and canzoni 11-12 (105-119), all but one of which is part of the pattern of the madrigali, but we should note that the missing group of three canzoni is in fact supplied by 37, 50, and 53, which cannot be grouped *together* if the madrigali pattern is to be maintained. The same line of reasoning will explain the apparent intrusion of canzoni 11 and 12 (105 and 119) into the simple additive grouping of canzoni. It should also be pointed out that the largest group of canzoni (125-129) is followed by the one hundredth sonnet, a fact that Petrarch himself noted in his manuscript.[7]

Structural symmetries are not the only use made of numerological composition. The first canzone in the sequence is number 23. The first canzone of Part II is number 264, and it is the twenty-first canzone of the sequence. Are we to ignore the facts that Petrarch was 23 when he first saw Laura and that she died 21 years later after he first fell in love with her? I think not, but I do not want to argue at this point about the meaning to attach to this numerological order or about the difficulties arising from the fact that 264 was probably written before Laura's death in 1348. I simply want to suggest the probability of a more patterned structure in the *completed* sequence.

And we need not confine ourselves to merely formal patterns; verbal repetitions also help to define the structure. The first poem in Part II and the last sonnet have remarkably similar first lines that are meant to recall each other:

I' vo pensando, e nel penser m'assale (264)
I' vo piangendo i miei passati tempi (365)

A more complicated verbal structuring occurs in the segment 70-81.

70-73	4 canzoni
74-79	6 sonnets
80	1 sestina
81-104	24 sonnets

The group of four canzoni, as I have already mentioned, is the second longest grouping of canzoni in the sequence. Number 70, which is also the seventh canzone, is a poem of five ten-line stanzas, the last line of each being the first line from poems by Arnaut Daniel, Guido Cavalcanti, Dante, Cino da Pistoia, with the exception of the last stanza where Petrarch quotes the first line of his own 23, the first canzone in the sequence. Numbers 71-73 are the justly famed "Tre Sorelle" canzoni, so called from the *comiato* of 72:

> Canzon, l'una sorella è poco inanzi,
> E l'altra sento in quel medesmo albergo
> Apparechiarsi; ond'io piú carta vergo.

Each of these poems has the same stanza and rhyme scheme. The underlined words in the *comiato* of 73 are picked up and used as the first line of 74, the first of that six sonnet segment:

> Canzone, i'sento *gia stancar* la penna
> Del lungo e dolce ragionar co llei,
> Ma non di parlar meco i *pensier* mei. (73)

> *Io* son *giá stanco* de *pensar* si come
> I miei pensier in voi stanchi non sono. . . .
>   (74)

Virtually the same line is picked up once more as the first line of the very next block of sonnets: "Io son sí stanco sotto 'l fascio antico . . ." (81).

There are many more isolated instances of formal structuring in the *Canzoniere,* but I do not want to discuss them before establishing the basic calendrical structure. Suffice it to say that my proof of this structure will be based on just such formal considerations as we have been discussing.

It is well known that the *Canzoniere* consists of 366 poems, divided into two parts, poems 1-263, called *In vita di Laura,* and poems 264-366, called *In morte di Laura,* since they deal with the time after her death. Furthermore, there can be no question that Petrarch wanted the major division of the *Canzoniere* to occur at 264.[8] Both the evidence from MS 3195 and Wilkins' definitive studies of the accretions to both parts of the sequence (see chart in Wilkins, *Making,* p. 194) prove that Petrarch had this division in mind as early as 1347.[9] Nevertheless, there is a genuine problem here

since the division, presumably to mark the death of Laura, occurred at least one year before her death. Wilkins summary of the problem is worth quoting in full:

> Those who have been troubled by the division have thought of it from the point of view of the reader rather than from the point of view of the creating poet; and have assumed that the division was made *after Petrarch knew of the death of Laura.* And indeed, if the division had been made after Petrarch had that knowledge, his decision to begin Part II with 264 rather than with 267 [first poem to announce the death] would have been extraordinary. *But this consideration in itself suffices to indicate that the decision to begin Part II with 264 was made before Petrarch knew of the death of Laura.* If this fact is realized, the making of the division at this point is no longer difficult to understand. 264 is—as it has been called in a previous section of this chapter—a very great and distinctive *canzone,* expressive of the fundamental conflict in Petrarch's inner life and of a desired reorientation. The *canzone* was probably written in 1347; it is highly probable that it was Petrarch's intense experience in the writing of this poem that led him, during the composition of the poem or very soon afterward, to decide to use it to mark a major division in the *Canzoniere.* In any case, the decision, once made, was too firmly fixed in Petrarch's mind to be altered even by the death of Laura.[10]

This seems to me an astonishing conclusion. A man who spends a lifetime memorializing the life and death of a woman in poetry, who divides his sequence *in vita* and *in morte,* does not ignore one of the two major events of that lifetime in favor of one poem, no matter how intense the experience of writing it, *unless there is some poetic priority.* The implications of Wilkins' final statement diminish the importance of Laura both for Petrarch's life and for his poetry in ways that cannot be supported either by the text or by his prose statements.

Petrarch insists again and again that he first saw Laura on the sixth of April 1327 and that she died on the sixth of April 1348. We have already quoted the memorial inscription in his copy of Virgil, and he is no less insistent in the *Canzoniere:*

> Mille trecento ventisette, apunto
> Su l'ora prima, il dí sesto d'aprile
> Nel laberinto intrai; né veggio ond'èsca.
>   (211.11-14)

And again,

> Sai che 'n mille trecento quarantotto,
> Il dí sesto d'aprile, in l'ora prima,
> Del corpo uscío quell'anima beata.
>   (336.11-14)[11]

There is no reason to dispute Petrarch's facts, although the remarkable coincidence of his first sight of her and of her death need not even be true historically. The dates are part of the meaning of the myth he created for himself. On the basis of evidence from the 1336 letter to Giacomo Colonna, from the third book of the *Secretum,* from the *Letter to Posterity,* from the memorial inscription in his Virgil, one can say with certainty that Petrarch is telling us that he fell in love with a woman.[12] We can date the occurrence and place it, but we can say very little more. Who is she? What was her name? What was her situation? Questions of this sort we cannot answer from life records, and this has driven critics to the fiction of the *Canzoniere* to find out the facts, with the result that those supremely metaphorical poems have been squeezed and drained of their vitality to produce biographical fact. This will not work; this is not proof. Laura has a reality that comes from Petrarch's statements and from the poems, but this reality does not require the actuality of existence to make it real. If one is a Christian, one does not have to see the actual Jerusalem to know what the real Jerusalem is. That city has been built *aere perennius* in the minds of generations of men through words that defy actuality and the temporal and posit a reality undisturbed by actuality because essential. Laura may have existed. Laura may not have existed. Neither one of these possibilities will affect the reality of the myth that Petrarch created. In the passages refered to above, Petrarch seems to indicate the actual existence of Laura, but this actual existence is always subsumed into the greater myth of fourteenth century Christianity, as is evident in the conclusion of the memorial in his Virgil:

> But her soul has, I am persuaded, returned to the heaven whence it came, as Seneca says of Scipio Africanus. As a memorial, afflicting yet mixed with a certain bitter sweetness, I have decided to make this record in this place of all places, which often falls under my eyes, that I may reflect that there can be no more pleasure for me in this life, and that, now that the chief bond is broken, I may be warned by frequently looking at these words that it is time to flee from Babylon. This, by God's grace, will be easy for me when I think courageously and manfully of the past's vain concerns and empty hopes and unexpected outcomes.[13]

If Petrarch could accommodate his love and his loss to this Augustinian Christian view, then we too as critics should be able to do as much.

Nevertheless, underlying most of the discussions of the problem of the division of the *Canzoniere* are the assumptions that Laura actually existed and that she actually died on the sixth of April 1348, and these assumptions force the critics to consider the division

at 264 as a real problem. If one is starkly logical about the problem, either Laura existed as a woman or she is a symbolic fiction, either the 1327-1348 dates are real, or one or both of them are fictions. If Laura and the dates are real, then there is an indecorum in not starting Part II with 267 because the structure of the sequence does not follow the facts. If, on the other hand, Laura and the dates are fictions, then the indecorum is reduced to a mere bumbling ineptitude in naming the two parts, because Petrarch could have changed at will the dictates of his fictive world. Neither one of these explanations is satisfactory—nor even binding on the poems.

A third possibility exists: Laura was an actual woman, and Petrarch is writing fiction about her. If we now make the assumption that this fiction depended on a plan for ordering the poems, we will escape the problem that Wilkins' genetic approach imposes on him. What could be so "firmly fixed" in Petrarch's mind except some plan, some intellectual program, that would encompass the events of his experience? Let us start with the assumption that Petrarch did have such a plan when he began the *Canzoniere,* that this plan became fixed when in 1347 he decided that 264 would begin the second part, that this plan could accommodate even the unexpected death of Laura, and that this plan found its completion in the writing of MS 3195 over the next twenty-six years. This plan, I am suggesting, is the use of a calendrical structure to order the poems, and it is evident only in the completed MS 3195.

If we return now to Petrarch's insistence that he first saw Laura on the sixth of April 1327, we find another instance where a strictly biographical approach to the poems lands us in difficulty. On the evidence of poem 3 (*Era il giorno*) commentators connect this sixth of April date with Good Friday, but then quickly accuse Petrarch of inaccuracy because the sixth of April 1327 was the Monday of Holy Week and not Good Friday. Nonetheless, we need doubt neither Petrarch's memory nor his calendar. As Carlo Calcaterra has brilliantly shown, Petrarch was not speaking of the annual liturgical celebration of Christ's crucifixion, he was speaking in terms of absolute time, and his scholarly sources told him that Christ was actually crucified on the sixth of April.[14] If the April sixth date of Petrarch's first sight of Laura actually occurred, a man of Petrarch's learning could not have avoided relating this date to other occurrences on the *feria sexta.* According to some traditions, as Calcaterra has shown, on the sixth day man was created, and on the sixth he fell, and on the sixth Christ's death redeemed that fall.[15] Petrarch would have us believe that this same sixth of April was equally important in his life: on the sixth of April 1327 he first saw Laura; on the sixth of April 1338 he first was inspired to write the *Africa;*[16] on the sixth of April 1348 Laura died.

The implications of all these sixes leads me to discuss one more April sixth, which I feel is of equal importance to our reading of the *Canzoniere* as the 1327 and 1348 dates. Good Friday fell on the sixth of April only four times during the fourteenth century—1319, 1330, 1341, and 1352. The third of these—1341—is a most important part of the myth Petrarch was constructing for himself.

On the morning of the first day of September 1340 Petrarch received from the Roman Senate an invitation to be crowned laureate, and on the afternoon of that very same day he received another such invitation from the chancellor of the University of Paris.[17] He chose Rome and asked for the sponsorship of King Robert of Naples, for which purpose he travelled to Naples, reaching there sometime in February 1341. Petrarch was duly examined by King Robert as to his eligibility for this honor and satisfied the requirements. King Robert wanted the ceremony to be performed at Naples, but Petrarch requested that his coronation take place in the Senatorial Palace on the Capitoline in Rome. The request was granted, and armed with a "robe of honor" from King Robert, Petrarch set out for Rome, arriving there probably on the sixth of April. On Easter Sunday, the eighth of April 1341, Petrarch received the triple crown of *poeta laureatus* from the hands of Orso dell'Anguillara and after the ceremony proceeded to St. Peter's where he placed his crown on the altar.[18]

We do not know whether Petrarch chose this precise date, but it is entirely possible that he was most particular about this most spectacular event in his life. Not since antiquity had a poet been crowned in Rome, and only two other laureations had occurred anywhere since antiquity.[19] Could Petrarch *not* have seen some relation among all these April sixth dates, each one of which was a turning point in his life? At any rate that is the assumption I shall make, and it is an assumption that has profound implications for our understanding of the structure of the *Canzoniere.*

We are now in a position to discuss the calendrical structure of the *Canzoniere,* and my hypothesis will, among other things, offer a better reason for Petrarch's dividing the sequence at 264 and will place the whole sequence in that Christian context, without which the poems can only be poorly understood. The hypothesis is quite simple: if we number each poem with a day of the year, beginning with the sixth of April, we will find that when we reach 264 we have also reached the twenty-fifth of December, Christmas Day. In short, I am suggesting that the division of the *Canzoniere* is based on two of the three most important events in the Christian calendar. Part I, dealing with the inception and growth of his love, begins with the death of Christ; Part II, dealing with the death of his love, begins with the birth of Christ.[20]

Instead of seeing Petrarch's grieving love as a kind of formalized autobiography, a reading of the sequence fiercely refuted by the *Secretum,* one might better view it as part and parcel of a fourteenth-century Christian outlook. There is an esthetic distance between Petrarch the lover and Petrarch the poet. It seems to me that Petrarch the poet is saying that he has conceived a passion for Laura that is essentially selfish, that is not the *vera amicitia* of the philosophers, as at least one of the early commentators agrees.[21] Petrarch indulges his longings without success, until he learns that Laura has died, when—deprived of the physical object of his desires—he learns to love her truly for her virtues by the end of the sequence. It is thoroughly medieval: subtly intellectualized and probing deep into the nature of man's desires, whether these be for a woman or for glory. The burden of the third book of the *Secretum,* to which Petrarch gives assent, is that he is still bound by the two golden chains of love and glory, which keep him from the proper love of God, and this subject, it will be recalled, is the major subject of poem 264. The inception of his love on the day that Christ died counterpoints the old Augustinian distinction between *caritas* and *cupiditas,* a point made over and over again by the early commentators.[22] Beginning Part II of the sequence on the anniversary of the birth of Christ proclaims as well the possibility of rejuvenation and a truer understanding of both earthly and heavenly love. Petrarch did not have to change his plan for the division of his sequence when Laura's death occurred in 1348 because her death simply enriched the metaphorical significance of the basic opposition of *caritas* and *cupiditas:* death of Christ—birth of love for Laura; birth of Christ—death of Laura. And that is why Petrarch did not alter his decision to begin Part II with 264.

To test my hypothesis about the Good Friday-Christmas dating of 1 and 264, let us consider other times of the Church year as possible structural devices. This can best be done by considering the placement of nonsonnets in the sequence (i.e., canzoni, sestine, ballate, and madrigali). There are eleven nonsonnets in Part II, and they are by my calculations associated with the following dates:

264	Canzone	25 December
268	Canzone	29 December
270	Canzone	31 December
323	Canzone	22 February
324	Ballata	23 February
325	Canzone	24 February
331	Canzone	1 March
332	Sestina	2 March
359	Canzone	29 March
360	Canzone	30 March
366	Canzone	5 April

Let us begin with 270 since we have already made a case for 264; and 268 is clearly a meditation on the death of Laura announced in the preceding poem. Poem 271 begins a segment of 52 sonnets. The date I attach to 271 is January first, New Year's Day, and I would like to suggest that symbolically those 52 sonnets *form* a year of mourning. This block of sonnets, the second longest in the sequence, is followed by the three non-sonnets 323-325, another structural break introducing the last forty poems of the sequence. I cannot believe that it is mere coincidence that 326 is associated with 25 February, which was the date of Ash Wednesday in 1327. The last forty poems *form* a symbolical forty days of Lent, leading up to 366, that great hymn to the virgin, which is associated with 5 April, which in 1327 was Palm Sunday, the day of Christ's triumphal entry into Jerusalem.

Within that forty-poem segment there are two significant formal breaks: 331-332 and 359-360. Number 331 is associated with the first of March, an alternative beginning of the year, and it is followed by a sestina and 26 sonnets, or a half-year cycle matching the 52 sonnets from 271-322. Number 359 is associated with 29 March, which was Passion Sunday in 1327, the beginning of Passiontide.

Now it may be objected that I have not accounted for all the non-sonnets in Part II, as indeed I have not. The reasons for this neglect are two-fold. One, not all the formal breaks are to be explained by the calendrical form. Two, I have simplified the scheme I believe Petrarch was using. Thus far I have pointed out only those correspondences that would have occurred in 1327. But as I have suggested earlier, Petrarch had in mind at least two other years in which the sixth of April was important: 1342, the year of his coronation, and 1348, the year of Laura's death. These three years are counterpointed against one another to complicate the formal breaks in the sequence. In the following chart I will try to show how this counterpointing is sometimes significant and sometimes not.

Date	Number	Form	1327	1341	1348
21 Feb.	322	sonnet		Ash Wed.	
22 Feb.	323	*canzone*			
23 Feb.	324	*ballata*			
24 Feb.	325	*canzone*			
25 Feb.	326	sonnet	Ash Wed.		
26 Feb.	327	sonnet			
27 Feb.	328	sonnet			
28 Feb.	329	sonnet			
29 Feb.	330	sonnet			

xxxxxxxxxxxxxxxxxxxxxxxx

Date	Number	Form	1327	1341	1348
1 March	331	*canzone*			New Year
2 March	332	*sestina*			
3 March	333	sonnet			
4 March	334	sonnet			
5 March	335	sonnet			Ash Wed.

It must first be pointed out that of the three years in question only 1348 was a leap year, a reason for the ***Canzoniere***'s having 366 poems rather than 365. It will be seen from the chart that the two Ash Wednesdays of 1327 and 1341 frame, as it were, the three non-sonnets 323-325. It will also be seen that the late Ash Wednesday of 1348 does not participate in the formal structure.

A similar use of the three years can be demonstrated in the first two formal breaks of the sequence.

Date	Number	Form	1327	1341	1348
6 April	1	sonnet		Good Friday	
7 April	2	sonnet			
8 April	3	sonnet		Easter	
9 April	4	sonnet			
10 April	5	sonnet			
11 April	6	sonnet			
12 April	7	sonnet			
13 April	8	sonnet			
14 April	9	sonnet			
15 April	10	sonnet	Good Friday		
16 April	11	*ballata*			
17 April	12	sonnet	Easter		
18 April	13	sonnet			Good Friday
19 April	14	*ballata*			
20 April	15	sonnet			Easter

No one has ever advanced a reason for Petrarch's making 11 and 14 ballate, but it would not be out of the question to suppose that there is a change in form at these points to call attention to the occurrences of Good Friday and Easter in 1327 and 1348, dates which frame the ballate as the two Ash Wednesdays framed 323-325.

Another use of the liturgical calendar is Advent, the little Lent, the season of preparation for Christmas. Again, a chart will help.

Date	Number	Form	1327	1341	1348
27 Nov.	236	sonnet			
28 Nov.	237	*sestina*			
29 Nov.	238	sonnet	Advent		
30 Nov.	239	*sestina*		Advent	
1 Dec.	240	sonnet			
2 Dec.	241	sonnet			Advent
3 Dec.	242	sonnet			

The two sestine frame the Advent of 1327, and the other two years, so close, are not used in the formal structure.

One final example may help to clarify the reasons why Petrarch sometimes uses more than one date and sometimes does not. We began our discussion of the formal structure of the **Canzoniere** with what I called the "simple example" of the madrigali pattern, 38-54 and 105-121, in which I tried to show that there was a formal symmetry that obtained between the two segments containing the four madrigali and also how this symmetry was integrated with the arrangement of the first seventeen canzoni. This pattern is, I believe, also integrated into the calendrical structure of the sequence for the feasts of the Ascension and Pentecost.

Date	Number	Form	1327	1341	1348
17 May	42	sonnet		Ascension	
18 May	43	sonnet			
19 May	44	sonnet			
20 May	45	sonnet			
21 May	46	sonnet		Ascension	
22 May	47	sonnet			
23 May	48	sonnet			
24 May	49	sonnet			
25 May	50	*Canzone*			
26 May	51	sonnet			
27 May	52	*madrigale*		Pentecost	
28 May	53	*Canzone*			
29 May	54	*madrigale*			Ascension
30 May	55	*ballata*			
31 May	56	sonnet		Pentecost	
1 June	57	sonnet			
2 June	58	sonnet			
3 June	59	*ballata*			
4 June	60	sonnet			
5 June	61	sonnet			
6 June	62	sonnet			
7 June	63	*ballata*			
8 June	64	sonnet			Pentecost

It will be seen from the chart that 52-55, which is the longest group of non-sonnets of various forms in the sequence, begins with the Pentecost of 1341 and that the segment of three ballate separated by groups of three sonnets is signalized after the first and third ballate (56 and 64) by the Pentecosts of 1327 and 1348. The occurrence of the Ascension dates with 42 and 46 seems to me insignificant, although the coincidence of 54 with the Ascension of 1348 may have a significance of which I am still unaware. What is of importance in this segment is that it is the first time that there is some verbal hint about the correlation between the poem and the date. Poem 53, the canzone that comes between the first two madrigali, whose number of lines adds up to the total of the two surrounding numbers (52 and 54) and is matched by the number of the third madrigale (106), comes immedi-

ately after the poem associated with the Pentecost of 1341 and begins with a phrase never fully explained by the commentators, "Spirto gentil." What is this Spirit if not the Holy Spirit That rules the members of Christ's church on earth and tries to guide the restoration of the ancient seat of that church in Rome through the agency of Cola di Rienzo?[23]

> Spirto gentil, che quelle membra reggi
> dentro a le qua' peregrinando alberga
> un signor valoroso, accorto et saggio,
> poi che se' giunto a l'onorato verga
> colla qual Roma et suoi erranti correggi
> et la richiami al suo antiquo viaggio
> io parlo a te, però ch'altrove un raggio
> non veggio di vertú, ch'al mondo è spenta,
> né trovo chi di mal far si vergogni.
>
> (53.1-9)

In conclusion, one must say that the calendrical framework will not explain all the formal breaks in the sequence, nor will it assist (with the possible exception of 54) in the reading of individual poems. Nevertheless, it must be conceded that the probability of mere coincidence of poem and day is offset by the large number of parallels (approximately 85 percent of the non-sonnets) that adds a new dimension to our reading of the **Canzoniere,** and that this new dimension sets the **Canzoniere** firmly in the context of fourteenth-century Christian morality. The Good Friday-Christmas division of the **Canzoniere** sets up a pattern of parallels between the two parts. In Part I the two ballate (11 and 14) are meant to emphasize the Good Friday-Easter dates of 1327 and 1348. Part I ends with the two sestine (237 and 239) emphasizing the beginning of Advent followed by 24 sonnets in preparation for Christmas. In Part II 270 sets up the segment of 52 sonnets beginning on the first of January, which leads to the non-sonnet group 323-325, framed by the two counterpointed Ash Wednesdays of 1327 and 1341, which leads us into that symbolical Lent of the last forty poems, a parallel to the Advent segment of Part I. Thus the beginnings and the ends of each part would seem to be formally structured around four major events in the Christian year: Good Friday, Advent, Christmas, and Lent. Against this annual cycle Petrarch counterpoints the agony of his earthly love and his growing awareness of the disparity between it and the heavenly love he ultimately sought.

Notes

[1] See especially Alastair Fowler, *Spenser and the Numbers of Time* (London, 1964) and *Triumphal Forms: Structural Patterns in Elizabethan Poetry* (Cambridge, 1970); *Silent Poetry: Essays in Numerological Analysis,* ed. Alastair Fowler (London, 1970); Christopher Butler, *Number Symbolism* (London, 1970). For the

earlier period see the admirable summary study of Edmund Reiss, "Number Symbolism and Medieval Literature," *Medievalia et Humanistica,* n.s. I (1970), 161-74.

[2] Inscription in Petrarch's *Virgil* now in the Ambrosiana in Milano. It is reprinted in Carducci and Ferrari, *Le Rime* (Firenze, 1899), p. 370: "Laurea, propriis virtutibus et meis longum celebrata carminibus, primum oculis meis apparuit sub primum adolescentie mee tempus, anno Domini M° IIJ° XXVIJ° die VJ° mensis aprilis, in ecclesia sancte Clare Avinoni, hora matutina; et in eadem civitate, eodem mense aprilis, eodem die sexto, eadem hora prima, anno autem M° IIJ° XLVIIJ°, ab hac luce lux illa subtracta est, cum ego forte tunc Verone essem, heu! fati mei nescius. Rumor autem infelix per litteras Ludovici mei me Parme repperit anno eodem, mense maio, die XIX° mane. Corpus illud castissimum ac pulcerrimum in loco Fratrum minorum repositum est ipso die mortis ad vesperas. . . ." A slightly different translation from mine appears in Morris Bishop, *Petrarch and His World* (Bloomington, 1963), p. 62.

[3] Ernest Hatch Wilkins, *Life of Petrarch* (Chicago, 1961), pp. 2, 5.

[4] Ernest Hatch Wilkins, *The Making of the "Canzoniere" and Other Petrarchan Studies* (Roma, 1951), p. 93, hereafter cited as Wilkins, *Making.* Ruth Shepard Phelps, *The Earlier and Later Forms of Petrarch's Canzoniere* (Chicago, 1925).

[5] See in particular Aldo S. Bernardo, *Petrarch, Scipio, and the "Africa"* (Baltimore, 1962), Chapter IV, "Scipio vs. Laura," pp. 47-71.

[6] Wilkins, *Making,* p. 266.

[7] Wilkins, *Making,* p. 120.

[8] The division of the *Canzoniere* at 264 is evident in Petrarch's manuscript, MS 3195, from the facts that (1) there are some blank sheets left between poem 263 and 264 and (2) only poem 1 and poem 264 have elaborate initials. We know further that Petrarch was consciously aware of placing poems in some order because he left some blank spaces in MS 3195, which were later filled in by a different hand and in a different ink. This system of transferring poems to specific places in MS 3195 is corroborated by another Vatican manuscript, MS 3196, entirely in Petrarch's hand, which was apparently one of his workbooks. In this manuscript he often makes a carefully dated notation that he has finally transcribed this poem *in ordine* in MS 3195. We know also that Petrarch was consciously aware of the placement of the various kinds of poems he included because he has placed a C opposite the one hundredth sonnet, a CL opposite the one hundred

fiftieth, a CC opposite the two hundredth and so forth (for the misnumbering of later sonnets see Wilkins, *Making,* p. 122). One might also point out that 183, the midpoint of the entire sequence, is also the one hundred fiftieth sonnet. Or we could point to the regular occurrence of groups of six sonnets in conjunction with a sestina: 30 with 31-36, 74-79 with 80, 136-141 with 142 and 143-148, 208-213 with 214.

[9] One such small formal structuring appears even if we accept Wilkins' and Miss Phelps's assumption about a roughly chronological ordering of the poems. Of the self-dating poems (30, 50, 62, 79, 101, 107, 118, 122, 145, 212, 221, 266, 271, 278, 364) all are sonnets except for the first two. Number 30, a sestina, is the seventh non-sonnet in the sequence and contains the phrase "oggi ha sett'anni," the seventh anniversary of his first sight of Laura. Number 50, the fifth canzone and the ninth non-sonnet of the sequence, contains the phrase "ben presso al decim'anno." Counting a poem both as canzone and non-sonnet may seem like double-dealing, but the fifteenth and sixteenth century editors sometimes discriminated among the various non-sonnet forms in numbering and sometimes labelled all non-sonnets "canzoni." For our purposes it is entirely justifiable to call a poem a "sestina" in calculating one formal structure and to count it merely as a non-sonnet in calculating another formal structure because, as I intend to show, the various structures overlap.

[10] Wilkins, *Making,* p. 193.

[11] See also *Triumph of Death,* 1. 133 and *Canzoniere,* 325. 13.

[12] The letter to Colonna is *Fam.* II. 9 and is translated and abridged in Morris Bishop, *Letters from Petrarch* (Bloomington, 1966), pp. 29-33. The *Secretum* was translated by William H. Draper as *Petrarch's Secret* (London, 1911). The *Letter to Posterity* was translated by Morris Bishop, *Letters from Petrarch,* pp. 5-12, but see esp. p. 6. The Latin texts with Italian translations can be found in *Francesco Petrarca Prose,* ed. Martellotti, Ricci, *et al.* (Milano, n.d.).

[13] Translated by Morris Bishop, *Petrarch and His World,* pp. 62-3. The Latin text as cited in Carducci is: "animam quidem eius, ut de Africano ait Seneca, in celum, unde erat, rediisse mihi persuadeo. Hec autem ad acerbam rei memoriam amara quadam dulcedine scribere visum est hoc potissimum loco qui sepe sub oculis meis redit, ut scilicet cogitem nihil esse quod amplius mihi placeat in hac vita, et, effracto maiori laqueo, tempus esse de Babilone fugiendi, crebra horum inspectione ac fugacissime etatis existimatione, commonear: quod, previa Dei gratia, facile erit, preteriti temporis curas supervacuas, spes inanes et inexpectos exitus acriter ac viriliter cogitanti" (p. 370).

[14] Carlo Calcaterra, *La "Data Fatale" nel Canzoniere e nei Trionfi del Petrarca* (Torino, 1926). Reprinted in *Nella Selva del Petrarca* (Bologna, 1942).

[15] Calcaterra, p. 30.

[16] The commentators make the same mistake about the inception of the *Africa* as they do about the April date in *Canzoniere*. Morris Bishop, *Letters*, p. 8, translates the day as Good Friday, but the Latin in *Posteritati* is "sexta feria": "sexta quadam feria maioris hebdomade" (p. 12). It should also be pointed out that in 1338 the sixth of April was the Monday of Holy Week and not Good Friday, exactly as in 1327.

[17] The letter is *Fam.* IV. 4 and is translated by Bishop, *Letters*, pp. 51-2. See the account in Bishop, *Petrarch and His World*, pp. 160-71 and Wilkins, *Life*, pp. 24-9, but note that Wilkins erroneously reverses the order of arrival of the two invitations.

[18] See references in preceding note and Wilkins, *Making "The Coronation of Petrarch,"* pp. 9-69. Petrarch's oration is translated by Wilkins, *PMLA*, LXVIII (1953), 1241-50.

[19] Albertino Mussato had been crowned in his native Pavia in 1315, and Dante had been crowned posthumously.

[20] The Good Friday-Christmas division of the *Canzoniere* was first pointed out by Angel Andrea Zottoli, "Il numero solare nell'ordinamento dei 'Rerum vulgarium fragmenta,'" *La Cultura*, VII (1928), 337-48. Zottoli's argument is radically different from the one presented here. I am indebted to him only for the coincidence of Christmas and 264.

[21] Antonio da Tempo in his commentary on poem 1. His commentary was often reprinted following the commentary of Filelfo, e.g., the edition of Venice 1503.

[22] The early commentaries have not been studied with sufficient attention to their impact on directing the reader's response to the poems, but see Bernard Weinberg, "The *Sposizione* of Petrarch in the Early Cinquecento," *Romance Philology*, XIII (1960), 374-86. I am at present at work on a study of the fifteenth and sixteenth century commentaries and academy lectures as a guide to understanding the reading habits of the Renaissance.

[23] A useful discussion of the difficulties of this opening passage may be found in the notes of Chiorboli's edition of the *Canzoniere* (Milano, 1924).

Francis X. Murphy (essay date 1974)

SOURCE: Francis X. Murphy, "Petrarch and the Christian Philosophy," in *Francesco Petrarca: Citizen of the World*, edited by Aldo S. Bernardo, State University of New York Press, 1980, pp. 223-47.

[*In the excerpt below, Murphy examines Petrarch's humanism and argues that he was a "genuine Christian philosopher."*]

During the month of February, 1325, Francesco Petrarca purchased a manuscript of the *De civitate dei* of St. Augustine for 12 florins from the executors of Cinthius, a cantor of Tours. The budding poet was twenty-one, and on leave in Avignon from his legal studies in Bologna. This information is contained in a note in his own hand on the manuscript, and represents what is probably the earliest of Petrarch's preserved autographs. As such, it is also the first of a long series of annotations that supply an avid posterity with authentic biographical detail, in contrast to the frequently ambiguous if not contrived information he wove into his poems and prose compositions.[1]

The acquisition of the *De civitate* did not immediately affect Petrarch's literary tastes or student mores. He confesses that it was only when he joined the household of the Colonna in the 1330s that he began to take an interest in the sacred scriptures and the literary productions of the Christian authors.[2]

On his definitive return from Bologna, in 1326, Petrarch and his brother Gerard had taken residence in Avignon and engaged in the frivolous pastimes that prevailed among officials and supernumeraries who flocked to the papal court. Nevertheless, almost from the moment of his arrival, Petrarch became part of the literary scene and the commerce in manuscripts and codices encouraged by the pontifical court's largesse. One of his first accomplishments was a critical edition of the first, third and fourth decades of Livy that had been handed down in separate fascicles by the Middle Ages.[3]

Meanwhile, on Good Friday, April 6th, 1327, Petrarch had experienced the fatal encounter with Laura in the Church of Santa Chiara in Avignon, a fact faithfully recorded on his Virgil manuscript. About this time, too, he had taken minor orders in the Church, apparently to obtain a livelihood in the household of the Colonnas. His assumption of clerical status entailed the daily recitation of the divine office—*laudes Cristo diuturnas*—that he acknowledges he performed with little enthusiasm until his conversion, years later.

Inspired with love for the *litterae humaniores* by Convenevole da Prato, his early preceptor in grammar and rhetoric, Petrarch found himself impelled toward the achievement of greatness through the pursuit of classical studies. Despite his complaints about the corruption prevalent in the papal court, it was there he encountered kindred spirits in the pursuit of learning. Of these, the Dominican historian, Giovanni Colonna played an important role, Eight of the **Epistolae rerum familiarium** are addressed to this learned friar.[4]

Colonna wrote a *De viris illustribus* in which he presented examples of virtue to encourage readers to better their lives. This was, of course, the traditional purpose of ancient historical writing. St. Jerome's work of the same name was his model. But his immediate inspiration is to be found in John of Salisbury's prescription for the Christian humanist: "the cult of virtue fostered by eloquence through the use of letters"—*licterarum usus.*[5] The relationship of Petrarch's **De viris** to Colonna's has not been completely unraveled. Both authors paraphrase ancient historians—Colonna, Valerius Maximus; Petrarch, Livy—as they announce their intention to exemplify virtuous deeds. But by a curious twist, Colonna chose learned men as his *viri illustres,*—Plato, Cicero, Paul, Origen, Augustine—while Petrarch concentrated on upright men of action. Colonna compiled a list of some 300 writers for whom he furnished biographical and bibliographical information. Petrarch selected 36 pre-Christian heroes for whom he provided extensive, moralizing lives. This singular interest in moral greatness pervades all his major compositions. It dictates his philosophical interests; and is the criterion he employs in his rejection of the philosophers and theologians of his own day whom he accuses then of cultivating the knowledge of virtue with no intention of achieving its practice.[6]

In 1333 Petrarch journeyed to Paris, then on to Flanders and Germany at the expense of Cardinal Giovanni Colonna. On this voyage, he enjoyed the hospitality of the Hermits of St. Austin with many of whom—Dionigi da Borgo San Sepulcro, Bartolomeo da Urbino, Jean Coci, and Bonaventura da Perargo—he remained on intimate terms all through life. To this period belong the earliest of his *rimes* as well as a Metrical Epistle (1.2) directed to pope Benedict XII calling on the pontiff to return with the papacy to Rome. To it likewise must be traced his introduction to Augustine and the first stirrings of his interest in the Christian philosophy.[7]

Somewhere in the course of 1333, the Austin monk and teacher, Dionigi da Borgo San Sepulcro, gave Petrarch a pocket-sized copy of St. Augustine's *Confessions* together with a fatherly admonition regarding his way of life. Petrarch carried the little book with him through the length and breadth of Europe, including the scaling of Mt. Ventoux, and a near drowning in the bay of Nice.[8] Dionigi, the learned Augustinian churchman, had taught at the University of Paris, and was a noted commentator on the writings of Aristotle

particularly his *Politics* and *Rhetoric.* These were works foreign to Petrarch's tastes, although, later in controversy, the poet boasts that he had read all of Aristotle's moral compositions and listened to not a few others.[9] While he does not mention Dionigi's productions,—which is strange since Petrarch seems to have modelled his **Rerum memorandarum libri** on the *Facta et dicta memorabilia* of Valerius Maximus for which the Austin friar had written an extensive commentary—Petrarch looked on him as his spiritual father and literary mentor, and addressed to him one of his most famous **Epistolae,** the account of the ascent of Mt. Ventoux.[10]

Petrarch traced his active interest in the Christian literature to his reading of Augustine's *Confessions,* and in particular to the passage where Augustine describes his discovery of philosophy through his encounter with Cicero's *Hortensius* and the change it wrought in his intellectual development. Petrarch is not entirely uninfluenced by the Augustinian self-relevation in his own literary inventiveness, when he confesses that previously, with juvenile if not demoniac insolence, he had looked upon the Christian authors as barbaric, of little consequence in comparison with the secular literature. The *Confessions* changed his perspective, While they did not lead him to dismiss his early vices—would that I could forgo them even at this age! he wrote much later—they did give him a new literary and moral insight.[11]

In 1335, Petrarch purchased Augustine's *De vera religione* and on a blank leaf of the codex inscribed the first known catalogue of his literary possessions, some fifty titles with an obvious concentration on the works of Cicero. In a sort of coda to this list, he recorded his four Christian acquistions, all Augustinian works: the *De civitate dei,* the *Confessions,* the *Soliloquies* and a *De deo orando.* It was only two years latter, apparently on his first sojourn in Rome, that he began to expand his collection of Christian manuscripts.

On March 6, 1337 in Rome, he purchased the *Homilies on the Gospels* of St. Gregory the Great; and on the sixteenth of that month, Augustine's *Enarrationes in Psalmos.* The latter codex contained the bishop of Hippo's sermons on the last fifty Psalms of the Davidic psalter, and is copiously annotated with Petrarchan glosses. Much later, Boccaccio was to give him a complete copy of the *Enarrationes* in a large unwieldly codex that Petrarch treasured despite its bulk and difficulty in handling.[12] Petrarch's meditative activity recorded in the annotations on these manuscripts indicate clearly that it is to this period of his life—in his early 30s—that should be traced the first serious stirrings of a deeper religious self-consciouness. A gloss on the *De vera religione* dated the first of June 1335, and another of July 10, 1338, contain prayers composed apparently under the influence of the *So-*

liloquies, in which Petrarch expresses the sentiments of a soul in pain, desirous of living virtuously, but weighed down by worldly cares. The second of these prayers is found in other manuscripts marked with the rubric *"oratio cotidiana."* Among the earliest of the annotations on his first copy of the *Enarrationes* is a meditation on examining one's conscience and a prayer of religious repentence. Thus by 1338, Petrarch had undergone a considerable change of religious sentiment.[13]

In the **Canzoniere** there is no direct record of Petrarch's passion for Laura during the first six years that followed their fatal encounter. The earliest intimation of his enslavement is recorded in his Sestina II (xxx) where he says, that, if his figures are correct, his sighs go back exactly seven years. Thus on April 6, 1334, his love for Laura was still alive and strong. Nevertheless, in the Epistle to Dionigi da Borgo San Sepolcro, presumably of April 26, 1336, ten years to the day since he departed Bologna, there is the admission that for the past three years he had desired to liberate himself from the cruelty of this unrequited love. But in the **Canzone IV** of 1337, Petrarch depicts the poet ensconced in his amorous desires during a whole decade. This was the year of his journey to Rome where, besides the awakening of an intense national sentiment, he felt a further stirring toward liberation. There, the coeval Sonnet depicts a struggle between his love for Laura and his fear for his eternal salvation.

On his return from Rome, Petrarch fled Avignon for Vaucluse, and there he made the first "collected edition" of his *rimes.* In his second Madrigal, the poet acknowledges the perils to which his life is exposed and speaks of changing direction "toward midday," apparently close to age thirty-five, that was considered the middle of life by the ancients. Finally in the haunting sonnet, **Padre del Ciel,** Petrarch addressed a prayer to God to save him "today," in the eleventh year of his amorous passion, thus Good Friday, April 10, 1338. "Rammenta lor come oggi fusti in croce." One does not expect consistency of a poet, particularly one suffering from the pangs of excruciating love unfulfilled. But the evidence embodied in the Lauran poetry would seem to supplement the indications in his manuscript glosses. In the late 1330s Petrarch was involved in a war within himself to shift his spiritual orientation.[14]

Petrarch's first trip to Rome with its antiquarian and bibliophilic delights occurred a year after his account of the Ascent of Mt. Ventoux in which he gives the impression of being deeply imbued with the Augustinian *Weltschmerz,* an excellent possibility if he had mastered the writings of Augustine then in his possession. But Petrarch's confusing literary habits, particularly the frequent reworking of his texts, his predilec-

tion for inventing **Epistolae** and his habit of inserting newly discovered classic as well as patristic quotations in his polished writings long after their original composition, gives one pause in accepting at face value the Epistle to Dionigi with its earliest recording of a poet's Alpinist adventure. This in turn introduces doubt when dealing with the chronological and biographical material in his other, obviously contrived literary accomplishments, as has been the painful experience of Petrarchan scholars over the past six centuries. The suspicions that surround the factual information contained internally in the first book of the **Epistolae rerum familiarium** in particular render the information on the manuscripts, and possibly also the Lauran chronology, of considerable importance in tracing the history of his relation with the Christian philosophy. Petrarch's literary habits are part of the machinery of an extremely deep and diversified mind. He said explicitly that he did not write for the vulgar crowd, but was busy about intricate phases of human knowledge (*De vita sol., prol*). In this sense he is a man and a philosopher unique for his time.[15]

In his own estimation Petrarch is a moral philosopher and a poet.[16] But while a convinced Christian and a pundit with strong moral convictions, he has little direct contact with the thinkers and theologians of his own times. Though his universe was still the closed classical world of antiquity, he was not a medieval poet or theologian as was Dante. Nor was he the libertarian scholar and litterateur found in a Poggio Bracciolini or a Laurentius Valla of the following century. Despite his involvement in the political happenings of his age as diplomat and counsellor, not infrequently travelling on ambassadorial tasks to Paris, to Prague, to Venice and to Naples, and his proffering of unsolicited advice to tyrants, kings and popes, he displays no interest in the development of political theory going on under his very eyes.

Petrarch seems to have ignored the ideological struggle between the papacy and the rising national states, and simply gives no consideration to the polemical writings of William of Ockham, Marsiglio of Padua, John of Paris, or James of Viterbo, or any of the pamphleteers on both sides of the vast quarrel between the papacy and the national monarchies for control of the disordered world in which he lived. He wants the emperor or the king to force the issue, and make the pope resume his proper station as spiritual lord of the universe. When Cola di Rienzi attempts to restore peace and order to the eternal City, Petrarch encourages him with high sounding, patriotic advice. But he seemingly has no interest in the theories of his contemporaries who are seeking to rearrange the constitutional structure of his worldly habitation.[17]

On the other hand he is fully conscious of factors involved in the political arena such as the habits and characteristics of individual peoples and nations. he quotes the Emperor Frederick II, *germanus origine, italus conversatione,* when he warns that the Italians should be dealt with benevolently by their rulers. They can easily be led to repentance, and to respect for authority. With the Germans, by contrast, he says, leniency is an occasion for insolence, and mercy is looked upon as weakness. The Italians should be treated with civility; by no means with familiarity. For no people are quicker to seize the opportunity to search out the vices of others, and while themselves living as a Sardanapalus, to render judgment with the severity of a Fabricius or a Cato. The German can be dealt with familiarly. In this case, familiarity does not breed contempt, but a mutual, affectionate appreciation.[18]

Despite his unbridled criticism of the papacy, it must be stated at once that Petrarch was a believing Christian—a Catholic as he himself frequently asserts in the course of his **Invective On His Own Ignorance and That Of Many Others**. In the third book of the **Secretum,** Augustine questions him regarding the piety of his youth. "Do you remember how great was your fear of God at that time? How much you thought of death? How strong was your religious affection? How great was your love of goodness?" And Francesco replies: "I do indeed remember; and I deplore the fact that with my progress in years, my virtues have diminished." In later life, Petrarch insists that he had fasted on bread and water every Friday from his youth.[19]

Despite his acknowledged moral lapses, or perhaps in consequence of the compunction he felt over his spiritual weaknesses, his faith is unquestioning. It was nourished by his youthful training; his daily recitation of his prayers—the *oratio cotidiana* of his manuscript glosses; the psalms and readings that constituted the divine office, which, in later life, he arose during the night to recite; and his familiarity with both the Austin monks and the Augustinian corpus, particularly the *Confessions* and the *De vera religione*. It is also evident in the support for Christian beliefs that he is constantly turning up in the pagan authors, particularly Plato, Cicero, Seneca, and guardedly Aristotle.[20]

Petrarch's intent differed considerably from that attributed to him by modern, mainly nineteenth century scholars who saw him throwing off the yoke of religious obscurantism by his insistence on his right to an unfettered judgement, and establishing himself as a precursor to the Protestant revolt, if not the age of the Enlightenment. Petrarch's total engagement is quite the contrary; it is to amalgamate the ancient wisdom of his pagan poets and orators with the Christian creed within the framework of the Church that was simply a normal inescapable part of his consciousness.[21]

In a contrary vein, Étienne Gilson deals with him too harshly in his *Unity of Philosophical Experience* where the ebullient historian of medieval philosophy brackets Petrarch between Nicholas of Autrecourt and Erasmus as responsible for giving the *coup de grâce* to the perennial philosophy of the thirteenth century, scholastic renaissance. He accuses Petrarch of having thereby destroyed the possibility of an authentic theological revival in his own and later ages.[22]

The accusation is interesting. For in fact Petrarch had no use for the Christian philosophers of his day, and was equally hostile to the theologians, holding them responsible for the very same ideological crime of which Gilson accuses him. Petrarch excoriates his contemporaries for debilitating the traditional theology. Not only does he not reflect the thinking of his generation, but he even avoids mentioning their names. Actually, he makes specific reference to a few great men of the previous century when, in a polemic jibe at a Gallic critic in his **Invective Against One Who Criticized Italy,** he names Bonaventure, Thomas Aquinas, Peter the Lombard, and James of Viterbo—all Italians—as the only competent teachers the university of Paris ever had.[23]

Petrarch's judgment on the culture of his day was devastating. He blames the decadence on the multiplication of teachers and scribblers, intent on monetary gain rather than wisdom. He claims, not without reason, that much of the older theology had been perverted by dialectics, and that philosophy was being destroyed by the vain pursuit of logic if not of sophistry. Once there were professors worthy of the name of theologians, he explains with indignation. But now in their insolence they attempt to subject God to the laws of their feeble intellects; and so describe the intricacies of the workings of nature that you would think they had just come from heaven where they had been present at the councils of the Almighty.

Behind this decadence Petrarch saw the shadow of Averroes and the spectre of Aristotle. The latter, as the source of the new knowledge regarding the nature of things, had been quickly thrust into the position of an oracle whose *ipse dixit* drove Petrarch literally into a rage. The cult of Averroes found a home among the medieval doctors who, with Pietro d'Abano (d. 1313) and the school of Padua cultivated a naturalistic materialism. Petrarch accused the Averroists of teaching that the created universe was eternal, without beginning or end, thus denying creation and the final judgment; maintaining that the human soul enjoyed immortality as a component of the world soul, thus denying the resurrection; and of cultivating astrology to the detriment of man's free will. In many of his longer letters and philosophical works, Petrarch conducts a recurring assault on these heresies.

As a Christian given to philosophizing, Petrarch was concerned with attacks on monotheism, and particularly on the Catholic creed with its belief in one God, creator of heaven and earth, and judge of the living and the dead. In his apologetic moods, he is ambiguous in his judgements on Aristotle, at times appealing to his authority, at others blaming the fell state of theology on the Stagirite's influence; but he does know that the Latin style in which Aristotle had come down to him was faulty: *qualis est nobis, non admodum delectari* (as we have him, he is hardly pleasing). In the end, Augustine is his theologian, and Cicero his philosopher. But when he finds his Cicero once more discussing the gods, after speaking so eloquently of the Supreme Being, Petrarch chides him: "*Heu, mi Cicero, quid ais? Tam cito Dei unius et tui ipsius oblivisceris?*" (Alas my Cicero, what are you saying? Have you so quickly forgotten the one God and your own nature?)[24]

In his old age, the poet-scholar contemplated writing a refutation of Averroes, "who raves against Christ his Lord and the Catholic faith." But he had to entrust the task to a youthful friend, the Florentine Austin friar, Louis Marsilius. Petrarch advises the young monk—to whom, in view of his failing eyesight and impending death, Petrarch gave his precious copy of the *Confessions,* restoring it to the Augustinian patrimony whence he had received it—to delve deeply into the second book of Augustine's *De doctrina christiana.* There the bishop of Hippo had dealt with the distinction, newly resuscitated by the Averroists, that limited knowledge to the domain of philosophy and granted to theology only the sphere of belief and opinion.

Augustine had insisted on the convergence of all knowledge, both religious and profane, since the totality of what man can know is a gift of the creator. In this framework, Petrarch described the genuine theologian as one who should know many things beyond the realm of faith, indeed if possible, almost everything. Certainly as God, to whom all things are subject is one, so the knowledge of God must be one, under which all things have their proper place.[25]

It is to Augustine that Petrarch owes his own knowledge of theology; and though he made no claim to be other than a "moral philosopher and a poet," the evidence of his theological awareness is clear enough in his later, polemical writings as well as in the first book of the *De vita solitaria,* where he deals with man's knowledge of the presence of God in the world. In an eloquent passage not far removed from the dialectical method he pretended to despise, Petrarch outlines the creative presence of God to the one seeking him, for all practical purposes as if he were a professional theologian engaged in preaching. He sets out his thesis, introduces proof from scripture, then draws his conclusion, applying it immediately to the pragmatic order where his true interest lies. Commenting on an

Epicurean maxim, "Always behave as if Epicurus were watching you," Petrarch remarks that it is the advice of a sage, despite the bad reputation that Epicurus has for some of his ideas. Nevertheless the Christian is not in need of such counselling since he lives continually in the presence of Christ who as God is everywhere, and of his guardian angel assigned to every individual.

How then explain the fact that the believing Christian is not ashamed to do evil? Here Petrarch introduces the testimony of Cicero. He does not discount the witness of Augustine's *De vera religione,* but seeks the concurrent wisdom of a stranger who certainly did not know Christ. To Cicero he attributes the observation that most people are incapable of seeing anything with the mind; they see only what is placed before their eyes. It takes a supreme effort to turn the mind from sense knowledge, and to force one's thinking out of its accustomed ways. Hence the sinner, though a believer, easily ignores the presence of Christ.[26]

Toward the end of this section of the *De vita solitaria,* Petrarch speaks of the possibility that a human being, still bound to the earth, might hear the chanting of the angelic choirs, and see things that on returning within himself, he could not describe. This passage is of considerable interest in that it does not reflect the poet's normal approach to preternatural phenomena. Referring to the stigmata of St. Francis, for example, he shows a reverent but reserved interest. While he venerates the saint's down-to-earth simplicity, he does not over-praise his poverty, and withholds judgment regarding the miracles attributed to him. In his reference to mystical experience, he is ambiguous: he does believe in heavenly immortality; but his true preoccupation is with the immortality he hopes to have engineered in this world. With Cicero he feels, *non omnis moriar.* . . .

In his reference to mystical experience, in the *De vita,* Petrarch seems to reflect the verses of Dante's *Paradiso,* where the Florentine poet spoke of "having seen things that he neither know how to, or could repeat, on returning from there above."

> e vidi cose che ridire
> Né sa né può chi lassù discende
>
> (1, 5-6)

Here, as in the Triumphs of Death and Eternity, Petrarch is influenced by his near contemporary, Dante, an indebtedness he is reluctant to acknowledge. In fact, he was chided by Boccaccio for his neglect of his fellow poet. Petrarch's answer in a long letter, acknowledges the justice of the accusation. He says however that, as he has also cultivated the vernacular poetry, he did not want to be accused of imitation or plagiarism resulting from coincidences that could occur if he read other poets. It is a lame excuse; but it helps explain Petrarch's failure to reflect the massive theological vision that was Dante's.[27]

Gilson has demonstrated that Petrarch did not see himself as the first renaissance man. His perspective was far short of the historical consciousness of a Flavio Biondo (1388 to 1463) who seemingly first selected the period of A.D. 410 to 1440 as the age between antiquity and modernity to which, in 1518, the designation *media aetas* was applied.

Petrarch does speak of himself as "situated on the confines of two peoples, looking at once backward and forward—*velut in confinio duorum populorum constitutus ac simul ante retroque prospiciens (Rerum memor.* 1, 2). The phrase has been interpreted as signifying the Petrarchan consciousness of initiating a new age. But in the context, the meaning is significantly different. Petrarch is complaining about the neglect of ancient learning by his contemporaries. he says they are handing on nothing to posterity. Thus future ages will be blissfully ignorant of the past and thus without complaint. In their complacency they will resemble antiquity, but for a totally different reason. Antiquity had no right to complain since it possessed a plenitude of learning.[28]

Petrarch's ideal was not to reproduce the past as will be the aim of the ages coming after him. His intention was to discover and preserve what still existed, and in this he gave the lie to his own gloomy prediction—*si ut auguror res eunt*—"if things go as I seem to think they will." In his determination to resurrect the learning of the past he turned his attention to the early Fathers of the Church, particularly after settling in Milan in 1353, where he had access to the manuscript treasures in the library of the Church of St. Ambrose. Scattered through his writings are a large number of patristic references, but they are largely illustrative or anecdotal, seldom doctrinal. With Augustine it is different. Petrarch has absorbed much of the master's thought, citing the *De Trinitate* as well as the earlier books that he had in his possession, and using Augustine as part of his intellectual armory. There are definite traces of Augustinian thought, particularly of the *De civitate dei,* in Petrarch's heroic poem, **Africa,** as Calcaterra has demonstrated.[29] Here, and though less obviously, in the **De viris illustribus,** the author's basic themes of Roman virtue and eternal destiny have an evident Augustinian tinge. These works were begun in 1338, soon after Petrarch's awakening to the deeper aspects of the Christian philosophy. It is likewise to Augustine that Petrarch turns for the solution of a problem that bothered him in his later writings concerning his utilization of the pagan learning. In this he was a medieval man, echoing unwittingly Chrétien de Troyes: "The Christians are right, and the pagans are wrong."[30]

Augustine had used the allegory of the Jews despoiling the Egyptians of their treasures before the Exodus; and Petrarch cites this principle in justification of his own inveterate steeping in the pagan classics. He is also well aware of St. Jerome's difficulty in his preoccupation with the secular learning, applyng to himself the accusation hurled at Jerome in a dream: *Mentiris; ciceronianus es, non es christianus*—"You lie; you are a ciceronian, you are not a Christian".[31] He seems to think that Jerome made a great effort to avoid the pagan authors thereafter, missing the full import of the accusation made by Rufinus of Aquileia who charged Jerome with continually parading his Maro, his Tullius, his Flaccus like smoke before his readers' eyes, that he might appear learned and of great erudition! Petrarch seems equally unaware of Jerome's own solution. With the cry regarding his well-stocked memory—"having dyed the wool once purple, what washing could make it clean," Jerome resorted to the passage in Deuteronomy (21. 10-13) where the pious Jew was justified in marryng a captive, gentile woman if first he shaved her head and eyebrows and clipped her nails. Having rid her of vanity and superstition, says this supreme misogynist, he could then retain what was useful.[32]

Among the other early churchmen, Petrarch is fairly well acquainted with Ambrose of Milan whose *De officis ministrorum* he recognizes as a christianized version of Cicero's *De officiis.* Petrarch possessed several manuscripts of the bishop of Milan's sermons, particularly his *De penitentia,* and his funerary orations for his brother Satyrus. Petrarch admires him for the part he played in the conversion of Augustine, although he is well aware of the long itinerary that brought Augustine to Christ along the path of the platonists and neo-platonists.

Petrarch is equally familiar with Lactantius' *Institutes* praising the author's ciceronian style; and he employs the names of Cyprian, Rufinus, Benedict, Pope Gregory I and Isidore of Seville, though of the latter's *Etymologies* he says, "I seldom use them." He was not enamored of the early Christian poets from Prudentius and Paulinus of Nola to Prosper of Aquitaine and Sedulius. Likewise but for a few anecdotes, the Greek fathers were merely names: Origen, Athanasius, Eusebius of Caesarea, Basil and Gregory of Nazianzen. Petrarch signals John Chrysostom for special mention. But though he read and annotated a considerable number of Latin texts of the Fathers, this is the extent of his patristic learning.[33]

In the second book of the **De vita solitaria,** where he praises the wisdom of the saints and sages who had escaped from the world to take refuge in solitude, Petrarch cites a great variety of real and legendary Christian heroes. For the most part he has been delving in the *Lausiac History* of Palladius, the Eusebian-

Jerome *Chronicle,* the *Dialogues* of Gregory the Great, and the *Golden Legend* of James of Voragine.[34]

Of the churchmen between Gregory I (604) and Peter the Lombard, Petrarch took little notice. He did possess a copy of Abelard's *Historia calamitatum* and shows considerable sympathy for its victim. But he confesses that he did not know enough of Abelard's other writing to judge concerning his reputation as a heretic. The literature on the *De contemptu mundi* beginning with Peter Damian and including Bernard of Clairvaux and Pope Innocent III seems to have influenced Petrarch's **De remediis utriusque fortune**. While he does not mention John of Salisbury directly, much of his detail in attacking the dialecticians comes very close to being modelled on, if not drawn, from, the *Polycraticus.*[35]

Among Petrarch's annotated manuscripts are a number of twelfth century authors such as Richard and Hugh of St. Victor, Berengarius of Poitiers, the *Gesta* of Innocent III, Stephen of Tornai, and Albertus Magnus; but there is little indication that these works entered deeply into Petrarch's thought. Pierre Courcelle contrasts Petrarch's reaction in reading the *Confessions* to that of Ailred of Rielvaulx, attributing to the highly spiritual minded monk a much deeper penetration into the depths of Augustine's thought. He assesses Petrarch's interest as more literary and philosophical. But Courcelle thus seems to miss the full significance of Petrarch's **Secretum** in which the fictional Augustine of the dialogue is the real Petrarch, who displays an acute understanding of the spiritual analysis engaged in by the author of the *Confessions.*[36] At the same time, Petrarch aims at supplying an ideal of the Christian way of life better suited to the spiritual needs of his contemporaries—the rising class of merchants and officials—a *docta pietas*—differing from the ascetic and monastic demands of the medieval spirituality. The **Secretum** is not modelled directly on the *Confessions;* it is much closer in inspiration to the *Soliloquies.* With the real Augustine's actual conversion, there was a total turning from the world of everyday affairs. Petrarch was determined to remain in the world and still achieve spiritual well-being. This is the message of his search for easier, divergent paths in contrast to his brother's direct mounting in the ascent of Mt. Ventoux; and in this respect, the *Epistola to Dionigi da Borgo San Sepolcro* is very close in time and content to the **Secretum**.[37]

Complicating enormously the problem posed by Petrarch's attitude toward the Christian philosophers is the startling probability, raised once more by Billanovich that the first section of the **Epistolae rerum familiarium** is a literary creation having no direct connection with the time and place in which they were supposedly composed. I must confess that in a recent rereading of the Petrarchan corpus, the possible significance of the closing line of the Epistle to Bishop Giacomo Colonna, *Hoc saltem oro, ne finxisse me fingas*—this at least I ask, do not imagine that I have imagined this—struck me with impelling force. The whole letter deals with the accusations that Petrarch has deceived his public—that he has simply imagined his own Augustinian devotion, imagined the very existence of Laura, and imagined the unfulfilled promise to make the journey to Rome. In view of these accusations acknowledged by Petrarch himself, to have the discussion close suddenly with that alliterative, but brassy phrase, *ne finxisse me fingas* raises the spectre of a subtle Petrarchan joke—an *epystola iocosa* as he refers to the letter he had apparently received from his episcopal patron and to which this letter is the answer.

Attributing his patron's ironic accusations to his urbanity, he asks the bishop how far he intends to go with his joking. "You indicate," he says, "that many have gathered great opinions about me because of my fictitious creations." And it is in this connection that he brings up once again the legitimacy of using the pagan poets and philosophers. There arises a suspicion of a close relation between this *Epistola* and the **Secretum,** lending substance to the possibility that it is of much later composition than it purports to be. While Morris Bishop and Ernest Hatch Wilkins simply dismiss this notion, Billanovich takes it for demonstrated.[38]

A starker suspicion stalks the chronological claim and the provenience of the *Epistola to Dionigi da Brogo San Sepolcra*. There can be little doubt that the details of the scaling of Mt. Ventoux are an allegorical description of the difference between his brother's sudden withdrawal from the world to join the Carthusians upon the death of his beloved, and Petrarch's dilatory search for compromises on his divagating path to the summit of spirituality. Nor can the sudden change to morose silence when his eyes fell on the passage from Augustine, admonishing men for seeking pleasures in contemplating the skies and travelling the seas, but neglecting their own interior selves, be understood outside the context of the meditations that form the substance of the dialogue in the **Secretum**.

What seems most likely is that during the decade of 1340 Petrarch found himself gradually impelled to follow the Augustinian pattern first in his intellectual pursuits, then in his gradual retreat from the sins of the flesh that had resulted in his fathering two illegitimate children, for all his insistence in his literary compositions that the praise of virtue was useless if one did not strive to live virtuously. There is sufficient evidence that during the Jubilee year of 1350, on his pilgrimage to Rome, he made a definite commitment to a virtuous life. Writing to reassure his brother Gerard, he says that he had received sacramental absolution after revealing the festering sores of his hidden sins to his confessor and that he intended to do so habitually for the future.[39]

There is no direct reference to this personal experience in the *Secretum,* but the dialogue is the fruit of Petrarch's far-ranging meditation of his inner psychological structure and awareness. It is a sort of spiritual metaphysics, not distinguishing between the *id* and the *superego* of Freudian analysis, but pursuing the Augustinian uncovering of the soul's inner recesses.

The *Secretum* is a dialogue between Augustine as the master and his pupil Francesco. While contrived to allow the author to play a double role, the discussion is much less artificial than that of the *De remediis utriusque fortune.* The latter is still within the medieval tradition. The *Secretum* breaks through that barrier and verges toward a new creation. It is a realistic production of Petrarch the humanist who has not merely absorbed the classic learning but has amalgated the Stoic ethic with the Christian consciousness of man's inner liberation in response to the message of salvation. As such it exhibits Petrarch's mastery of the dialectical machinery he deplored so bitterly in the professional philosophers and theologians, but which he turns to good use in his own psychic and spiritual introspection.

The central message of the *Secretum* is the need to strip the soul of its mundane wrappings—the layers of self-deceit that prevent the individual's autorealization and final freedom. This notion is of Stoic origin, of course, and had been developed at length by Seneca, a fact of which Petrarch is fully aware. But Augustine had advanced the analysis by introducing Platonic elements in a Christian perspective. In the *De civitate dei* Petrarch discovered a basic Augustinian postulate. It is not the corruption of the body that weighs down the soul and is therefore the cause of sin. It is rather sinfulness in the soul that renders the body corruptible and thus engenders the punishment of original sin. This distinction is based on the fact that the will can induce man to deceive himself by finding satisfactions in terrestrial and therefore transitory pleasures.

By its very nature the soul cannot be satisfied with finite pleasures. It is in search of the absolute. But on this earth it is subject to the buffeting of vain desires and foolish ambitions due to the contrariety of human wilfulness. But the will is not geared to evil; it seeks only the good. It is in the psyche that the difficultly exists; in the dark corridor between the intellect's searching for light, in order to understand, and the will's impulse to love even when it is exposed only to the appearances of goodness. Thus the problem faced by the individual is to free himself of the encirclement of vices, primarily for Petrarch, pride, avarice, lust and acedia, to discover the soul's pristine beauty.[40]

In the *Secretum* Francesco is assured that his soul was originally well endowed by heaven; but that it has degenerated from its former beauty due to the contagion that surrounds the body. The soul has become so torpid that it forgets its origin and its eternal creator. Nevertheless, the sudden discovery of a great truth through an instant intuition can illuminate the abyss of the soul where the will resides, and awaken it to a consciousness of its potential as a responsible agent, exercising true freedom in the love of which it is capable.

Petrarch's dramatic reaction to the reading of the passage from the *Confessions* on Mt. Ventoux would seem to have been an experience of this kind. He is plunged into stunned silence at the rebuke he received in the unexpected admonition from his spiritual guide, Augustine. Then as he arrives at the inn, he experiences the sudden release that results in a powerful creative effort. Petrarch gives the impression that this beautifully contrived *Epistola,* with its enmeshed themes, polished literary expression, and nuanced psychological revelations was the work of an hour or two of leisure while his retainers were preparing dinner, and after a strenuous, day-long mountain climb. Even granting that the learned allusions and literary citations were inserted later, it is a bit too much to expect the reader to accept this as a straight-forward record of a day's experiences. It is a psychological document, and as such in close affinity with the *Secretum* both in time and subject matter.[41]

Petrarch reaches a climax in his argument in the third book of the *Secretum* when Augustine catechizes Francesco in regard to his love for Laura. At first Francesco protests violently that his affection for this most noble of God's creatures was wholly without self-interest and therefore pure. Under cross-examination, however, he admits that it was in consequence of his contact with Laura that his passions finally got the best of him, and that instead of leading him to the practice of virtue, his lady love had first reproved and then abandoned him.

Augustine takes advantage of this admission to pound home his point. Francesco's original contention that he desired to achieve the love of God through the love of one of God's creatures was blasphemous. It was the obverse of the proper order. God is to be loved in and for himself; and his creatures are to be loved in God. In the second book, Petrarch has supplied the perspective for this contention by confronting human love with its two possibilities. It can serve as a source of sin, or as an occasion for redemption. The origin of human perversity is not in love, but in the human spirit that is capable of confounding its values and thus its loves.[42] The remedy is not to be sought in knowledge as such, nor in flight from the body. Seneca witnesses to the latter truth.

As to knowledge, in his *Invective Against the Doctor of Medicine,* Petrarch says explicitly that he would certainly blame himself for not having read all the medical books if he could see that their therapeutic devices had made these men either better or more learned, or even only healthier of body. But since he could find no such improvement either in the exterior or interior man, he thanks his good fortune that he had been spared this reading, which might have brought him to the same miserable state in which he finds the men of medicine.

In a highly rhetorical passage of his *De otio religioso,* Petrarch reveals the extent of his admiration for Augustine. He calls him a noble soul, endowed with divine ingenuity who lacked neither the light to search out the falsehoods of the enemy, nor the power to strengthen the minds of his friends. In what appears to be a direct reference to the technique he employs in his *Secretum,* Petrarch says Augustine's questions and responses are fully worthy of one who battles for the faith and performs as an athlete of the truth. He refers to the *De civitate dei* as Augustine's standard bearer.[43]

The significance of the *Secretum* is that it is not a meditation in the medieval sense of the term—a dwelling on the miseries of life worsened by one's sinfulness, with a morbid preoccupation with death, and a longing for liberation from earthly cares. The *Secretum* does dwell on these themes, and rings all the cadences of the *De contemptu mundi* with both Augustinian desperation and Bernardian ruthlessness. But it rises to a new experience. Petrarch faces death with the studied indifference of the Stoic and the Christian. But his intention in so doing is not to arrive at the atrium of paradisial joy here on earth. That hope is afar, in the *al di là.* His desire is rather to penetrate to the unfathomable depths of his inner being to find the basis for man's *intimations of immortality* and his potential for eternal bliss. He finds that in this life, man can only reach convalescence, a balance between the tensions of spiritual and bodily maladies over against the possibility of perfect health.[44]

One objective of the *Secretum* was to offset the Occamistic dualism that separated the natural world from the divinity, theology from philosophy, and that grounded religious conviction not on a rational theodicy but on a direct contact of the soul with its creator. In this effort, Occamism reflected a renewal of the Augustinian search for illumination. But it perverted this effort when it turned to the logicism of the later scholastics. By its rejection of a metaphysical foundation for man's spiritual beliefs, it tended to destroy the function of religion as a bridge between man's worldly and transcendant aspirations.

Petrarch tried to find a way between what he considered the excesses on both sides. His was not a return to the ordered scholasticism of a Thomas Aquinas, or even to Bonaventure who was closer to the authentic Augustinian tradition. It is rather an attempt to utilize the psychological experiences of which he was conscious in a very personal fashion to create a spirituality closer to the need of his immediate contemporaries. In so doing Petrarch ran counter to both the structured theology of the schools, and to the superficial dialectics of the new pseudo-aristotelianism.

In Augustine, Petrarch had found the final security he sought for his employment of the classic authors whom he did not want to consider pagans. He says repeatedly that if Plato or Cicero or even Caesar had known Christ and his teachings, they would certainly have embraced the true faith. He believes that these men were models of upright reasonableness whom he does not blush to use as counsellors and guides for the well-being of the faith and moral teaching. If Augustine had not thought the same of them, he could never have written his great *De civitate dei!*[45]

In Petrarch's *Egloga I,* there is a long discussion on the relation of poetry to morality where Petrarch insists that in his eyes poetry is a theology of man—*de hominibus.* The distinction between the poet and the religious thinker arises from the direct object and the form of their meditations, not from a difference in moral obligations. He thus justifies his own vocation and his employment of the muses. There is a commentary on this *Egloga* with its definition of poetry in his *Epistola familiaris* (X. 4).

Toward the close of the *Secretum,* Petrarch has Francesco exclaim: "I believe that not even God can make me embrace eternity, or the heavens and the earth. For me human glory suffices; for this I long, and as a mortal, I have no desire but for mortal things." This outburst leads Augustine to his final correction in which he summarises his message regarding the meaning to be given to life, and the criterion for judging the world in its proper existence. While secular things have a limited and transitory value, they are not to be despised as man adheres to his proper self, gathering together the scattered fragments of his mind, and remains within himself diligently.[46] This is the essence of Petrarch's moral philosophy, and as such his justification as a Christian and a poet.

In his letters written in old age, Petrarch looks toward death benevolently. He confides to Pandolfo Malatesta that his life is most insecure, since he has been struck down by illness four times in the course of the past year. But he is in a gentle mood, as he intimates with true Christian indifference, that he would like to be discovered in death with his head resting on the Psalter of David, the poet of his advanced years, and presumably, we hope, with his Virgil at his side. *"Et certe jam tempus est,"* he remarks, *"non expedit ad fastidium vivere; ad satietatem sufficit."* (And indeed it is now time. For it is not good to live beyond one's time; it is enough to live unto satiety.)[47] (Sen. XXII, 8).

In the Petrarchan humanism, man's humanity is not to be despised, just as it is not to be made the final purpose of his existence. Petrarch prescribes the completion of the whole man, soul and body, insisting on the integral interaction of all his faculties, mind, will and senses. It is in his achievement as an analytic therapist of the soul, and as such, a true moralist, that he deserves the designation of a genuine Christian philosopher, rather than the Gilsonian accusation that he was a forerunner of the breakdown of the Christian culture.

Petrarch's *Weltanschauung* or *ubicazione* was not that of the structured scholastic whose systematic vision of the world was tied to the closed cosmos of his daily experience. Petrarch was a man born out of due time who, by penetrating into the depths of the spirit within him, broke the bonds of intellectual limitation posed by the decadence of the Christian aristotelianism. He thus predated the Copernican revolution, not in its actual discovery of the immensity of the material universe, but in redimensioning man's relation to space and time, under the shadow of eternity—*sub specie eternitatis.* Petrarch might not have been fully at home in our contemporary world, but at least he would have understood the problems of the spirit troubling modern man. If this be not true philosophy, what is?

Notes

[1] Pietro P. Gerosa, *Umanesimo cristiano del Petrarca* (Turin, 1966), 37-81. *Cf.* Pierre de Nolhac, *Pétrarque et l'humanisme,* 2 v. (2nd ed. Paris, 1907; new Printing, Turin, 1959) II, ch. IX.

[2] *Epist. Sen.* XVI, I (*Senilium rerum libri* XVII in *Opera omnia,* Basel, 1581); see Gerosa, *op. cit.,* 115, n. 67.

[3] G. Billanovich, *"Petrarca e i classici,"* in U. Bosco, ed., *Studi Petrarcheschi* 7 (Bologna, 1961), 21-34.

[4] W. Braxton Ross, "Giovanni Colonna, Historian at Avignon," *Speculum,* 45 (1970), 533-545.

[5] Ioannes Saresberiensis, *Policraticus* (ed. C. J. Webb, Oxford, 1909) prol., 12; cf. W. Braxton Ross, 539.

[6] *De sui ipsius et multorum ignorantia* in Francesco Petrarca, *Prose* (ed. G. Martellotti, et al. *La Letteratura Italiana: Storia e testi,* VII, Milan, Naples, 1955), 746-48; cf. "Note critiche," *ibid.,* 1163-66.

[7] *Epist. posteritati,* ed. *Prose, op. cit.,* 10-14.

[8] *Epist. Sen.* XV, 7, *Prose,* 1132-34.

[9] *De Ignorantia, Prose,* 744; cf. R. Arbesmann, *Der Augustiner-Ermitenordern und der Beginn der humanistischen Bewegung* (Wurzburg, 1965), 16-36.

[10] *Epist. fam.* IV, I, *Prose,* 830-844.

[11] *Epist. Sen.* VIII, 6. Cf. Gerosa, *op. cit.,* 49.

[12] Cf. Gerosa, *op. cit.,* 336-337, nn. 72-75.

[13] *Epist. Sen.* XII, 2. See. L. Delisle, *"Notice sur un livre annoté par Pétrarque",* in *Notices et extraits des mss. de la Bibliothèque Nationale,* XXXV, 2 (Paris, 1897). Cf. Gerosa, *op. cit.* 48-49, n. 15.

[14] See E. Gilson, *Pétrarque et sa Muse* (Oxford, 1946); n. 1.

[15] See G. Billanovich, *Petrarca letterato. I. Lo scrittoio del Petrarca* (Rome, 1947), 47-49; N. Iliescu, *Il Canzoniere petrarchesco e Sant' Agostino* (Rome, 1962), 38-42.

[16] *Epist. Poster.:* "ad omne bonum et salubre apto sed ad moralem precipue philosophiam et ad poeticam prono . . ."

[17] Cf. J. H. Robinson and W. Rolfe, *Petrarch the First Modern Man* (New York, 1898); P. Piur, *Petrarca Buch ohne Namen und die papstliche Kurie* (Hall, 1925); M. Bishop, *Petrarch and His World* (Indiana U. Press, 1963), 305-319.

[18] *Epist. Sen.* I, I, *Prose,* 1036. See G. A. Levi, *Classicismo e neoclassicismo* in *Questioni e problemi di storia letteraria italiana,* 824-831.

[19] *Secretum* III, *Prose,* 150.

[20] *Epist. Sen.* XII, 2; Gerosa, *op. cit.,* 279-316.

[21] Cf. L. Geiger, *Petrarca* (tr. D. Cossila, Milan, 1877); *Rinascimento e Umanesimo in Italia e Germania* (Milan, 1891); G. Voigt, *Il risorgimento dell'antichità classica* (Florence, 1889). Cf. V. Bonetti-Brunelli, *Le origini italiane della scuola umanistica* (Milan, 1919).

[22] E. Gilson, *The Unity of Philosophical Experience* (New York, 1937), 102-105.

[23] Cf. Gerosa, *op. cit.,* 181 and n. 1; "Note critiche," *Prose,* 1177.

[24] *De remediis,* 1, 46; on Averroes, see *De Ignorantia, Prose,* 750-52; on Cicero, cf. Gerosa, *op. cit.,* 284-288; *De Ignorantia, Prose,* 726.

[25] *Epist. Sen.* XV, 6; cf. Gerosa, *op. cit.,* 365-66, and n. 29.

[26] *De vita sol.* I, *Prose,* 348-350.

[27] *Epist. fam.* xxi, 15, *Prose,* 1002-1014.

[28] E. Gibson, "Notes sur deux lettres de Pétrarque" in *Studi Petrarcheschi* 7, 42-50.

[29] C. Calcaterra, "S. Agostino nelle opere di Dante e del Petrarca," in *S. Agostino,* (Milan, 1931); P. Gerosa, *op. cit.,* 50-52, n. 21.

[30] See Gerosa, *op. cit.,* 166-179.

[31] Jer. *Epist. xxii,* 30; Cf. *De ignorantia, Prose,* 758; *Epist. fam.* II, 9, *Prose,* 820.

[32] Cf. F. Murphy, *Rufinus of Aquileia* (Washington, 1945), 8-13; 64-66.

[33] Cf. Gerosa, *op. cit.,* 161-66.

[34] *De vita sol., Prose,* 436-454.

[35] Gerosa, *op. cit.,* 180-224.

[36] P. Courcelle, "Un humaniste épris de Confessions: Pétrarque" in *Les Confessions de Saint-Augustin dans la tradition littéraire* (Paris, 1963), 339-351; but see, Gerosa, *op. cit.* and F. Tateo, *Dialogo interiore e polemica ideologica nel "Secretum" del Petrarca* (Florence, 1965), 36-37, n. I.

[37] *Epist. fam.* IV, 1, *Prose,* 830-843.

[38] *Epist. fam.* 11, 9, *Prose,* 816-827. Cf. G. Billanovich, *Lo scrittoio del Petrarca,* 190-198; M. Bishop, *Petrarch and His World,* 381; E. H. Wilkins, *Life of Petrarch* (Chicago, 1961).

[39] *Epist. Sen,* VIII, 1: "Iam a multis annis sed perfectius post Iubileum, a quo septimus decimus annus hic est (1367) sic me adhuc viridem pestis illa deseruit. Scit me Christus liberator meus verum loqui. *Epist. fam.* X, 5: "abditas scelerum meorum sordes, que funesta segnitie longoque silentio putruerunt, in apertum manibus salutifere confessionis elicui . . . idque saepius facere . . ." Cf. Gerosa, *op. cit.,* 112-114.

[40] *Secretum* in *Prose,* 22-215; See F. Tateo, *op. cit.;* Gerosa, *op. cit.,* 82-119.

[41] See Billanovich, *Lo scrittoio del Petrarca,* 192-195 for the temporal affinity.

[42] *Secretum* III, *Prose,* 136-148; see Tateo, *op. cit.,* 62-66.

[43] *De otio religioso,* ed. G. Rotondi, (Vatican City, 1958) I, 18: Et Augustinus in eo libro quem sepe hodie in testimonium arcesso, *e.g., De vera religione,* cap. 65.

[44] *Secretum* III, *Prose,* 166: "Non curandum sanamdumque sed preparandum dixi animum." Tateo, *op. cit.,* 65-67 points out the relationship between this sector and the *Canzone* CCCLX of the *Rime.*

[45] *Epist. fam.* II, 9, *Prose,* 820.

[46] *Secretum* III, *Prose,* 214: "sparsa fragmenta recolligam moraborque mecum sedulo."

[47] *Epist. Sen.* XIII, 8. Much earlier, in his *Vergine bella,* Petrarch had deplored the

> Mortal bellezza, atti et parole m'anno
> Tutta ingombrata l'alma.
> Vergine sacra et alma,
> Non tardar, ch'i' son forse a l'ultimo anno.

(Mortal beauty, its words and deeds have totally overburdened my soul. O Virgin, pure and hodly, do not delay, for I may be in my ultimate year.).

Concetta Carestia Greenfield (essay date 1975)

SOURCE: Concetta Carestia Greenfield, "The Poetics of Francis Petrarch," in *Francis Petrarch, Six Centuries Later: A Symposium,* edited by Aldo Scaglione, University of North Carolina Press and The Newberry Library, 1975, pp. 213-22.

[*In the following essay, Greenfield examines Petrarch's poetics as it relates to Platonism, Aristotelianism, and the legitimacy of pagan literature from the classical period. Greenfield concludes that Petrarch's poetics was "an elaboration of the rhetorical and Platonic tradition against the new Aristotelianism."*]

Poetry for Petrarch was the catalyst for a humanist awakening, the symbol of a renewed consciousness. Salutati and Boccaccio looked back to Petrarch and Dante as the ones who opened the way for the return of the Muses to Italy. Indeed, if the word Humanism referred to a reawakening centering around the consciousness-expanding power of poetry, Petrarch would certainly be its primary innovator.[1] Completely original in his poetry, he developed in his poetics some of the themes introduced by his Paduan predecessor Albertino Mussato. Petrarch's discussion of poetics was tightly bound up with the major issues of the thirteenth-century intellectual tradition, namely: 1) the conflict in poetics between a humanist-patristic tradition of Platonic inspiration and the new Aristotelianism based on all the translations of Aristotle's *Organon;* and 2) the debate over the legitimacy of classical pagan literature for the Christians. The significance to poetics of the latter debate was to raise questions about the nature of poetical and biblical metaphor, and about the place of poetry within the system of the sciences. These issues colored Petrarch's entire life in addition to his intellectual output. For this reason scholars have devoted considerable attention to his biography, the stages of which reflect the progress of these conflicts of the time.[2]

Petrarch spread the Platonic spirit of Cicero and St. Augustine in Florence. On one occasion he even made a gift of St. Augustine's *Confessiones* to the Augustinian monk Luigi Marsili. Under Petrarch's influence, the medieval Platonic heritage remained the center of the Cenacolo of Santo Spirito in which Marsili and, later, Coluccio Salutati participated.[3] When in Padua, he strenuously fought the dehumanizing Aristotelian trend prevailing at the University of Padua in the Faculties of Law and Medicine. A result and expression of this opposition is his ***Invectivae contra medicum.***[4] Finally, in France, as Pierre de Nolhac suggests,[5] he came into contact with many classical manuscripts at the Library of the Sorbonne and experienced the heritage of the School of Chartres. French Humanism played an important role in the development of Italian Humanism through the influence of such representatives of the School of Chartres as John of Salisbury, Bernard Silvestris, and Fulbert of Chartres on Petrarch, Boccaccio, and Salutati. The major feature Petrarch inherited from the School of Chartres and transmitted to Italian Humanism was an insistence on the reconciliation of classical poetry with Christianity. This doctrine was based on the Augustinian philosophical argument in the *De doctrina christiana* concerning the Egyptian gold appropriated by the Jews, and on the practical argument of Cassiodorus' *De ordine,* which suggests that grammar, comprising poetry and history in the Middle Ages, was the first of the liberal arts and was necessary for an understanding of Scripture.

While accepting the idea that the liberal arts are necessary to an adequate understanding of Scripture, Petrarch disengages poetry from its ancillary role to grammar, and defines it as an autonomous science, including the traditional disciplines of the patristic and classical heritage and devoid of the anti-classical and technical spirit of the Aristotelian theology and philosophy. Petrarch's main statements on poetical theory are contained in the ***Invectivae contra medicum***[6] and in letters among his ***Familiares*** and ***Seniles.*** Book III of the ***Invectivae*** specifically concerns poetics. Its tone is that of a defense, this time not against a Dominican, but against a *medicus.* The *medicus* represents the scholastic approach characteristic of fourteenth-century law, medicine, and theology.

Concurring with Augustine,[7] Petrarch attributes the popularity of dialectic to the decadence of the *humanae litterae.* After the invasion of dialectic, the humanism of the church fathers gave way to speculative commentaries; philosophy and theology became matters of captious argumentation or subtle intellectual games. Thus, the Arab translations of the books of the *Organon* made possible the flow of late medieval dialectic into the body of logic then prevailing at the universities. The mania for syllogism, a cumbersome way of reasoning, became the subject of the debate.[8] According to Petrarch, this disease spread and entrenched itself particularly in England's school of Occam and in Italy's Averroistic University of Padua, most noticeably in its Faculty of Medicine. Petrarch complains in a letter of the accusations against poetry directed to him by a Sicilian dialectician.[9] He notes that this pestilence seems to be peculiar to islands, for in addition to the legions of British dialecticians and logicians, a new horde seems to be arising in Sicily. This is the third pack of monsters to have invaded the poor island of Sicily, their predecessors being the Cyclops and the tyrants. Petrarch goes on to say that these dialecticians are anti-Christian, since their naturalistic beliefs stem from the Arab commentators on Aristotle, rather than from Aristotle himself. To Averroism as a pseudo-science, to dialectic as a pseudo-philosophy, he opposes humanist wisdom, the subordination of the intellectual sphere to the moral one.

Petrarch's emphasis on moral philosophy led him not to a metaphysical but to a practical kind of wisdom, much like the philosophy of *bene vivendi* developed by Cicero in his *Tusculan disputations.* The Thomist negation of the cognitive value of poetry is itself to be discounted in view of poetry's esthetic and moral impact, according to Petrarch. In this issue Petrarch sided with the Franciscans, heirs of the Platonic-Augustinian tradition by virtue of its coincidence with their basic spiritualism.

The Aristotelian doctor who makes his charges against poetry is addressed by Petrarch as "Ypocras et Aristoteles secundus,"[10] by which Petrarch means someone who is versed in naturalistic science and syllogism. The first charge of the *medicus* is based on the premise that what is not necessary is not worthy and noble. Petrarch, however, undoes the logic of the syllogism. If necessity argues true nobility, the farmer and the carpenter are truly noble and the ass and the cock are nobler than the lion and the eagle. So necessity does not always imply nobility. In fact, the contrary is sometimes true, since it is obvious that the eagle is no less noble than the cock, although it is less necessary than the cock. The fact that the art of medicine is more necessary makes it only an *ars mechanica.* How does the doctor dare to proclaim himself a follower of Aristotle if he ignores the basic distinction made in the *Metaphysics* (983a 10-11) between the productive and theoretical arts? With this distinction Aristotle locates the *artes mechanicae* among the productive arts. On the other hand, Aristotle holds the theoretical arts in higher esteem because they pursue knowledge for its own sake rather than for utilitarian goals. Since goals are proper to the *artes necessariae* or *artes mechanicae,* they are less noble and the syllogism of the doctor turns out to be incorrect even in Aristotelian terms.

Continuing in this vein, Petrarch argues that the doctor should understand the limits of his trade, insofar as its nobility is concerned, from the fact that there are many doctors but only a few poets. As Horace said, "neither men nor the gods, nor the booksellers allowed the poets to be mediocre" (*Ars Poetica* 372-3), and it is for this reason that they are few and good. Poetry's gratuity is the mark of its superiority; its lack of necessity makes it a theoretical art, hence more worthy than medicine.

The doctor had subsequently argued that since medicine cures the body and helps people to live better, it is on the same level as ethics and poetry. But Petrarch counters by observing that medicine is directed to the cure of the body and is, therefore, at the service of the body. In the same way the liberal arts, as they aim at the benefit of the soul, are at the service of the soul. Now since the soul clearly leads the body and stands above it, it follows that the liberal arts lead and are above the arts which aim to cure the body. Nor should the doctor think, continues Petrarch, that poetry is not a liberal art simply because it is not mentioned in the traditional division of the arts. It is true that poetry is not mentioned by Hugh of St. Victor in his *Libri septem eruditionis,* where he says that the liberal arts include grammar, rhetoric, dialectic, arithmetic, music, geometry, and astronomy, distinguishing them from the *artes mechanicae* including *lanificium, armatura, navigatio, agricultura, venatio, medicina,* and *treatricum.* But poetry goes without mention here because, along with history, it is included in grammar, the leading art. Nobody would deny the existence of philosophy simply because it is not mentioned among the seven liberal arts, and since grammar subsumes poetry, Petrarch concludes that the place of poetry among the liberal arts is so obvious as to have been taken for granted.

In the next point of controversy, the doctor argues that a science is *firma et impermutabilis,* while poetry is a matter of variable meters and words and is, therefore, not a science. Petrarch counters that the doctor should inquire what this variation means before excluding poetry from the sciences, for what changes is words, while the things remain "upon which the sciences are founded."[11] Science, too, uses words which change according to historical periods, yet it is not

judged wholly on the words it uses. Poetry is a science "firm and immutable," as is obvious from the fact that its exercise lends eternity to the poet. It gives the poet a glory which Petrarch's *Secretum* identifies with the particular achievement of the poet in society: through his poetry the poet survives beyond his bodily death. Since poetry transcends the finite barriers of the human life span, it has no time limits and assures the survival of worthwhile human endeavour. Poetry sets itself against the transitoriness of other human values, as a means to eternity. Being eternal, then, its laws remain the same from antiquity to modern times. Hence poetry is a science.

Another accusation made by the doctor is that poets are the enemies of religion: "What do you think of Ambrose, Augustine, Jerome, Cyprian, the martyr Victorinus, Lactantius and all the other Christian writers," asks Petrarch, "since you accuse the poets of being enemies of religion?"[12] He adds that poets have always been concerned with divine matters, and many of them have defended the existence of a unique God. On the other hand, doctors have not become any healthier for reading the treatise of Galen and the Greek treatises based on a naturalistic approach. Furthermore, the doctor seems to ignore the opinion of the philosopher Aristotle, of whom he proclaims himself a follower. In *Metaphysics* 983b 29 Aristotle calls the poets "theologians," since these ancient poets were striving for an understanding of God even more than the philosophers were. Privately, poets believed there was only one God, although the people in those times were uncultured and incapable of understanding concepts of monotheism. Homer thus presented them with images that they could grasp, images of many gods who, in a fashion similar to men, committed crimes and fought with one another. In this way, Homer indicated that since a multiplicity of gods led them to disputes much as it does with man, there must be some sort of supreme being to inspire harmony.

Poetry is theology for Petrarch as well. In the *Familiares* (10.4), he writes: "Poetics is not very different from theology. Are you amazed? Actually I could easily say that theology is that form of poetics concerning itself with the godhead. Christ is described now as a lion, now as a worm, and is this not a form of poetry? It would be a long matter to enumerate all the other similar images which can be found in Scripture."[13] Considering their relationship further, Petrarch says that poetry and theology are identified not only because the ancient poets were theologians, but also because poets and theologians shared a figurative language whose main element is the metaphor. This language was invented by the ancient poet-theologians: in their desire to understand the first causes, struck by the worth and nobility of these generative principles, they built temples and established ministers and a cult to celebrate them. In order to pray and implore the divinity, they had to create a language more noble than the colloquial one, suitable to address the divinity, so they invented poetry. This is a particular form of speaking and writing involving *numerus,* which confers *suavitas.*[14] This form was called poetry, and the people who used is were called poets. Since it was born out of the need to communicate and address the divinity properly, it is a divine form of speech shared by Scripture; however, while poetry and theology have a common means of expression, their subject-matter remains different. For theology always speaks of true facts and presents true gods, while poetry has often portrayed fictional events and false gods. Except for this difference in subject matter, then, poetry and theology basically involve the same literary forms. So there is a tradition which emphasizes the literary quality of Scripture and notices the poetical language used in such works as Jerome's *Breviary,* St. Augustine's *Enarrationes in Psalmos,* and Cassiodorus' Exposition in his *Psalterium.* St. Augustine himself saw David as a poet, and interpreted the Psalms allegorically. Petrarch provides an allegorical interpretation of his *Bucolics* in much the same vein as St. Augustine had done with the Psalms (*Fam.* 10.4; 10.3).

The *suavitas* of the poetical language, its allegorical veil, the doctor counters, is a form of obscurity which, just as it creates wonders, deceives the reader. Petrarch, however, defends the obscurity of poetical allegory, likening it to that of Scriptural allegory.[15] Following the Augustinian argument, he says that the divine word must be obscure, for it is the expression of an inconceivable power, access to which must be rendered difficult to make its understanding pleasing and wondrous. Similarly, poetry uses allegory to signify things not easily understood in a way which stimulates the intelligence of the reader to understand them. Thus, with the allegorical *sermo ornatus* the poet creates wonders, as Horace also noted; the creation of wonder is a main characteristic of poetry. So *veritas* is hidden under the ornamentation of allegory. And beauty resides both in this cortex and in the *veritas* hidden by the cortex, because content and form complement one another. The cortex creates in the reader a sense correlative to the *veritas,* as St. Augustine found in Scripture; Petrarch extends this power to poetry.

It bears noting here that although Petrarch is moved to emphasize that both form and content must be given proper care, it is the *stylus* or *sermo ornatus,* as he calls it, which must be particularly cultivated by the poet. Petrarch's notion of style is a very complex one, as it involves not only poetics but the "expression" of all the *humanae litterae.* It is strictly related to the concept of imitation. In the ***Familiares*** 1.8 he says: "Like the bees, who do not regurgitate the flowers as they find them but combine to make wax and honey, . . . so words and style should be our own although composed out of many. . . . Some are like

silk worms, which spin everything out of themselves. Let us, however, peruse the books of the wise."[16] The invitation here is to read carefully the form of expression of the classical writers and to retain their spirit, *from which all things follow,* not simply to copy them: "Like a father and a son whose features and dimensions are different yet have in common what the painters call 'air.' Do not copy words and expressions, but inspire the general 'air.'"[17] "Mix the old with the new."[18] Imitation is then intended as an invitation to be alert to the general "air," i.e., to the spirit or style of the ancient writers.

While the Thomist movement and even some famous Christian writers de-emphasize form and style, often seeing them as a useless adjunct, Petrarch conceives of style as an integral part of content, by virtue of its formative power over content. Later Petrarch clearly felt a conflict between his attachment to form and the disregard of it by famous Christian writers, whom he otherwise admired:

> I loved Cicero, I admit, and I loved Virgil; . . . similarly I loved, of the Greeks, Plato and Homer. . . . But now I must think of more serious matters. My care is more for salvation than for noble language. I used to read what gave me pleasure, now I read what may be profitable. . . . Now my orators shall be Ambrose, Augustine, Jerome, Gregory; my philosopher shall be Paul, my poet David. . . . But although I put the Christian writers first, I do not reject the others. I seem to love both groups at once, provided that I consciously distinguish between those I prefer for style and those I prefer for content.[19]

The doctor's final objection concerns a passage in Boethius' *De consolatione Philosophiae* (1.1.8). Boethius narrates that at his deathbed the poetical Muses came to comfort him, but Philosophy sent the "scenicas meretriculas" away and wished for the presence of her muses ("meae Musae"). Following Priscian's grammatical reasoning, the doctor tries to establish that the "meae" refers to philosophical Muses rather than to poetical Muses in general. Petrarch laughs at the internal contradiction inherent in the doctor's argument, for it seeks to undermine the existence of poetry by borrowing explanations from the field of grammar. In his turn, Petrarch argues that the Muses have always been muses of poetry. By calling them "meae," the personification of Philosophy means that the Muses, in general, are close to her, for philosophers have frequently dealt with poetics, as Aristotle's *Poetics* proves. Actually, Lady Philosophy in Boethius differentiates between the theatrical and other kinds of poetry, which Petrarch uses as evidence that theatrical poetry has too often deviated from the path of truth. But this is not a fault peculiar to poetry. All good things have an impure side, just as oil has dregs and philosophy has Epicurus. In fact, philosophy, like poetry, has been accused of impurity. In Book VIII of the *Confessiones* (2.3), St. Augustine writes that the books of the philosophers are filled with deceptions and lies; yet by this he does not mean to condemn philosophy, for in the same book he extensively praises Platonic philosophy. He condemns only that branch of philosophy which by the use of limited rational syllogisms claims to arrive at unconditional truths. The impure part of poetry comes from the dramatic poets condemned by Plato in the *Republic* (398a and 606-607) because the theater had become unworthy of the majesty of the gods. But epic poets like Homer and Virgil have never written drama. Thus, the condemnation should not be extended to them.

To sum up Petrarch's poetics, we find it an elaboration of the rhetorical and Platonic tradition against the new Aristotelianism. He mentions Thomas Aquinas only once, but opposition to a technical, dehumanized theology, philosophy, and poetry runs through his entire work. For Petrarch, poetry is a theoretical art because it makes use of grammar and all the other liberal arts. What raises poetry above grammar and the other liberal arts is the poetical language it shares with the Bible. This language has divine origins because it was invented to speak about the gods. Furthermore, it serves as a vehicle for divine revelation, not only on account of its content and origins, but because with its allegorical form of expression it has the air of divine truth, from which every truth proceeds. With its language, then, poetry holds to the spirit of things, and the *stylus ornatus* is the specific characteristic of poetry which gives it a formative power unsurpassed by any other art. In addition, poetry immortalizes the poet through posterity, a theme dear to Petrarch's sonnets in the **Canzoniere**. For insofar as the poet avails himself of the classical poets, imbuing their style with the spirit of his own times, his poetry will come to have enduring force.

Petrarch's poetics is particularly influenced by Platonism.[20] In Book VIII of St. Augustine's *De civitate Dei,* he read about the superiority of Platonism to all other philosophies. And in the work of St. Augustine, Petrarch found much correspondence with Christian Fathers.[21] He knew Plato, too, through Macrobius' *Somnium Scipionis.* He knew Chalcidius' version of the *Timaeus* and Apuleius' *De Platone et eius dogmate.*[22] In addition to this indirect tradition, the School of Chartres handed down to him the ideal of a reconciliation of paganism and Christianity, of classical humanist wisdom and the newly rediscovered Aristotle.[23] The direct influence of John of Salisbury of the School of Chartres on Petrarch has been recently pointed out by Paolo Gerosa.[24] Like John of Salisbury in the *Metalogicon,* Petrarch considers logic a science of persuasion involving basically moral criteria and directed toward practical aims. All this is not to say that Petrarch did not recognize Aristotle's sci-

entific acuity. Petrarch, however, calls Aristotle a student of Plato: "Aristotle, a disciple of Plato, was a man of great intelligence and eloquence; though not comparable to Plato, nevertheless he easily surpasses quite a few."[25] Petrarch's Platonism is of extreme importance, for he is the transmitter of the Platonic heritage in poetics to the Florentine humanists. This tradition was not transmitted without influence from medieval thinkers; Gerosa's investigation of Petrarch's sources indicates that the medieval heritage was his firm cultural background, while he emphasized the classical sources as a "discovery."[26] Thus, his poetics reflect that humanist tradition which, issuing from the classical and Platonic tradition, became crystallized in the system of St. Augustine. This tradition was transmitted to the Renaissance by such early humanists as Mussato, Petrarch, Boccaccio, and Salutati.

Notes

[1] B. L. Ullman, *Studies in the Italian Renaissance* (Rome, 1955), pp. 11-40, supports the idea that early humanist reawakening means reawakening of poetry.

[2] E. H. Tatham, *Francesco Petrarca: The First Man of Letters,* 2 vols. (London, 1925-26); E. H. Wilkins, *Life of Petrarch* (Chicago, 1961).

[3] E. Garin, *La letteratura degli umanisti,* in *Storia della letteratura italiana* (1966), III, 7, sees as symbolic of this heritage the gift of the *Confessiones* made by Petrarch to the humanist Augustinian monk Luigi Marsili, who revamped the Augustinian spirit in the Florentine circle. Petrarch sides with the Franciscans, i.e., the Augustinian Platonic tradition, against the Dominicans who, in the middle of the thirteenth century, following Albertus Magnus and St. Thomas, abandoned that tradition. Platonic idealism corresponded to the spiritualism of the Franciscan order, while Aristotelian intellectualism corresponded to the rationalism of the Dominicans. Hence a continuous polemic between the two schools of thought.

[4] For a discussion of this cultural climate, see G. Toffanin, *Storia dell'Umanesimo* (Bologna, 1933), p. 13, and *Il secolo di Roma* (Bologna, 1942); U. Bosco, "Il Petrarca e l'umanesimo filologico," *Giorn. Stor. della lett. It.,* 120 (1943), 65.

[5] Pierre de Nolhac, *Pétrarque et l'Humanisme* (Paris, 1907), I, 39.

[6] *Invectivae* in *Francisci Petrarchae Opera Omnia* (Basel, 1581). For the text with an Italian translation see P. G. Ricci's edition in Francesco Petrarca, *Prose,* ed. G. Martellotti et al. (Milan, 1955).

[7] *De doctrina christiana* 4.1; 2.50.

[8] *Secretum* 1.1 in *Prose,* p. 52. "Ista quidem dyalecticorum garrulitas nullum finem habitura, et diffinitionum huiuscemodi compendiis scatet et immortalium litigiorum materia gloriatur; plerumque autem, quid ipsum vere sit quod loquuntur, ignorant."

[9] *Familiares* 1.7. See the critical ed. by Rossi-Bosco, 4 vols. (Firenze, 1933-42). Cf., among others, P. O. Kristeller, *Renaissance Thought II* (New York, 1965), pp. 111-118.

[10] *Invectivae* in *Prose,* p. 648.

[11] *Invectivae* in *Prose,* p. 648: "In quibus scientiae fundatae sunt."

[12] *Invectivae* in *Prose,* p. 648. "Quid de Ambrosio, Augustino et Ieronimo, quid de Cypriano, Victorinoque martire, quid de Lactantio ceterisque Catholicis scriptoribus sentias?"

[13] The Latin text with an Italian translation appears in E. Garin, *Il pensiero pedagogico dell'Umanesimo* (Firenze, 1958), p. 32. "Miraris? parum abest quin dicam theologiam poeticam esse de Deo: Cristum modo leonem modo agnum modo vermem dici, quid nisi poeticum est? mille talia in Scripturis Sacris invenies que persequi longum est."

[14] Garin, *Il pens. ped.,* p. 32. "Id quadam non vulgari forma, sed artificiosa et exquisita et nova fieri oportet." See also Isidore's *Etymologiae* 8.7, 1.3; Suetonius, *De poetis* 2; and Boccaccio's *Gen. Deor.* 14.7.

[15] *Invectivae* in *Prose,* pp. 669-70. "Quid sermo ipse divinus, quem etsi valde oderis, tamen aperte calumniari propter metum incendii non audebis? Quam in multis obscurus atque perplexus est. Cum prolatus sit ab eo Spiritu Sancto. . . ."

[16] Garin, *Il pens. ped.,* p. 31. "Apes in inventionibus imitandas, que flores, non quales acceperint, referunt, sed ceras ac mella mirifica quadam permixtione conficiunt. . . . Illud affirmo: elegantioris esse solertie, ut, apium imitatores, nostris verbis quamvis aliorum hominum sententias proferamus. . . . Rursus nec huius stilum aut illius, sed unum nostrum conflatum ex pluribus habeamus; felicius quidem, non apium more passim sparsa colligere, sed quorundam haud multo maiorum verminum exemplo, quorum ex visceribus sericum prodit, ex se ipso sapere potius et loqui, dummodo et sensus gravis ac verus et sermo esset ornatus. . . . Perscrutemur doctorum hominum libros."

[17] *Familiares* 22.19; English translation in Morris Bishop, *Letters from Petrarch* (Bloomington and London, 1966), p. 198.

[18] *Seniles* 2.3 in Garin, *Il pens. ped.,* p. 38: "Veteribus nova permisce."

[19] *Fam.* 22.10 in Bishop, p. 191.

[20] P. P. Gerosa, *Umanesimo cristiano del Petrarca* (Torino, 1966), p. 246.

[21] *De Remediis* 11.119; *Fam.* 22.5.

[22] Giovanni Gentile, "Le traduzioni medievali di Platone e Francesco Petrarca," *Studi sul Rinascimento* (Firenze, 1936); Roberto Weiss, *Il primo secolo dell'Umanesimo* (Roma, 1949).

[23] Pierre de Nolhac, ch. ix.

[24] Gerosa, p. 248.

[25] *Rerum memorandarum* 1.26. "Aristoteles, Platonis discipulus, vir excellentis ingenii et eloquii, Platoni quidem impar, sed multa facile superans."

[26] Gerosa, p. 258, lists all the medieval thinkers who, like the rings of a long chain, connect St. Augustine to Petrarch.

Robert M. Durling (essay date 1976)

SOURCE: Robert M. Durling, in an introduction to *Petrarch's Lyric Poems: The Rime Sparse and Other Lyrics,* edited and translated by Robert M. Durling, Cambridge, Mass.: Harvard University Press, 1976, pp. 1-33.

[*In the essay below, Durling provides a thematic and stylistic analysis of the* Rime sparse.]

Ser Petracco (or, as he sometimes spelled it, Petrarcha) of Florence was exiled from his native city in 1301, at the same time as his friend Dante Alighieri; but his later life was much more prosperous than Dante's. Along with many other Italians he eventually moved to Avignon, the new seat of the papacy, where he became one of the most successful members of the legal profession, thanks partly to the patronage of powerful Italian clergymen. His eldest son, Francesco, who had been born in Arezzo on July 20, 1304, was eight when the family moved to Provence; with his mother and brother Francesco lived near Avignon, in Carpentras. Francesco was given every educational advantage. As a boy he had a distinguished tutor, the grammarian Convenevole da Prato, and as a young man he was maintained for ten years as a law student at two of the foremost universities of the day, first Montpellier and then Bologna.

After Ser Petracco's death in 1326, Francesco and his brother, Gherardo, returned to Avignon, now the most cosmopolitan cultural center in Europe, and lived for a time as wealthy young men about town. Whether the two squandered their considerable inheritance or whether they were swindled by their father's executors and their own servants, as Francesco later related, or both, it eventually became necessary for them to seek some means of support. The idea of practicing law seems to have been repugnant to Francesco from the outset; he decided to take the path of clerical preferment, which would allow him the leisure to continue his studies, and at some time he probably took minor orders so that he could legally hold benefices.

Already a great classical scholar in his early twenties, Francesco came to the attention of a powerful Roman family, the Colonnas, and in 1330 he formally entered the service of Cardinal Giovanni Colonna as a private chaplain (this may have meant no more than that he occasionally sang prayer services in the chapel), remaining more or less loosely under the family's patronage until 1347-48. From 1330 on Petrarch lived essentially in a scholarly semiretirement guaranteed for him by his connections with the great, carrying on a voluminous correspondence with learned and princely friends all over Europe, and frequently indulging his love of travel. Thanks to the patronage of the Colonnas and other prominent friends, he was able to accumulate benefices (most of them in Italy) that assured him a modest financial independence. Although throughout his life he willingly served on special diplomatic missions for popes and other rulers, he repeatedly refused preferments—for instance as a bishop or as papal secretary—that would have meant the end of his devotion to study.

Between 1326 and 1337 Petrarch lived mainly in Avignon; in 1337 he moved to the wild, romantic source of the Sorgue River at the fountain of Vaucluse, twenty miles east of Avignon. The 1340s brought momentous events in Petrarch's life. On Easter Sunday, 1341, Petrarch's celebrated coronation as poet laureate took place on the Capitol in Rome; skillfully dramatized by Petrarch, this event added considerable luster to his fame, especially in Italy, and led to his spending increasing amounts of time there. Petrarch's coronation oration, in form a sermon on a text from Virgil's *Georgics,* calls for a rebirth of classical wisdom and poetry and develops in some detail the idea of the laurel as symbolic of poetry and literary immortality.

In 1342 Gherardo became a Carthusian monk after the death of his beloved, and except for brief visits to Montreux in 1347 and 1353, Petrarch never saw him again. Petrarch's daughter, Francesca, was born in 1342 (his son, Giovanni, had been born in 1337); she lived with him until the end of his life. It is not known who the mother of these illegitimate children was. In 1345 Petrarch made his most notable philological dis-

covery, that of the manuscript of Cicero's letters to Atticus, Quintus, and Brutus, in the library of the cathedral of Verona; these were the models for his collections of his own letters. In 1347 Cola di Rienzo's attempt to revive the Roman Republic at first evoked Petrarch's sympathy. His feelings changed, however, as it became increasingly antipatrician and several members of the Colonna family were killed in bloody uprisings. In 1347 the Black Death appeared in Sicily and began to make its way up the peninsula; during 1348 and 1349 Petrarch lost to it a number of friends and relations, including Cardinal Giovanni Colonna, the poet Sennuccio del Bene, so frequently addressed in the *Rime sparse,* and, he tells us, his beloved Laura.

In October 1350 Petrarch visited Florence for the first time (while on a pilgrimage to Rome) and there made acquantance with his devoted admirer, Giovanni Boccaccio, beginning a friendship that lasted until Petrarch's death. To what extent Petrarch's much-debated religious conversion took place in the late 1330s, in the late 1340s, or in the early 1350s will probably never be determined fully. There is no doubt, however, that after 1350 he rewrote much of his earlier work and composed poems and letters with fictitiously early dates.

In 1353 Petrarch left Provence for good, accepting first the patronage of the Visconti in Milan, who were emerging as the most powerful dynasty in Italy. Boccaccio and other Florentine republicans were scandalized by this apparent condoning of what they regarded as tyranny. Petrarch maintained that he had complete independence, but it seems clear that the Visconti were able to take advantage of his prestige as an ambassador by manipulating his vanity. In 1361 Petrarch left Milan, perhaps because of the increasing gravity of the plague there (his son died of it that year), and gravitated toward the Venetian sphere of influence, while continuing to maintain friendly relations with the Visconti. After long periods of residence in Venice, Pavia, and Padua, he retired in 1370 to a modest house (still standing, though much altered) that he built on land given him by Francesco da Carrara, lord of Padua, at Arquà in the Euganean Hills, where he lived until his death on the night of July 18, 1374.

Boccaccio once accused Petrarch of having spent his life with princes, and the charge has considerable weight in spite of Petrarch's reply that it was the princes who had sought him and that he had preserved his independence. His friends were princes, prelates, and their servants. His identification with privilege was unquestioning, and his quietism amounted to tacit consent in the political arrangements of the day. It can be claimed for him that he did not seek political power for himself (although he does seem to have cherished the hope that Clement VI would make him a cardinal, which may help explain his strange mixture of adulation and denunciation of that pontiff), that when he was manipulated it was because he was naive, and that he actively sought to promote Christian virtue (including the ideal of crusade against the Moslems) and to prevent war among the Christians. But he set a style of ambiguous relation of humanist to prince that in the later Renaissance was to degenerate into subservience.

The glory of the Italian communes was a thing of the past, and it was inevitable that in a society increasingly dominated by princely courts Petrarch's effort to create a secular role for the man of letters should be aristocratic in orientation. After 1350 both Petrarch and Boccaccio threw the weight of their influence on the side of aristocratic culture in Latin; their audience was learned and international, not peninsular, let alone municipal. But both are beloved for the other side of their genius and for their writings in Italian.

To immortalize Laura is an avowed purpose of the *Rime sparse,* as of the *Trionfi* and many verse epistles and eclogues in Latin. We do not know who she was, however, or even whether she really existed. One of Petrarch's closest friends, Giacomo Colonna, seems to have doubted that she was anything but a symbol and a pretext for poetry. At the other extreme are the sixteenth-century commentators who, like Vellutello, imagined a biographical basis for each poem, or the abbé de Sade, who in the eighteenth century discovered what he thought was archival evidence for Laura's being an ancestress of his who died in 1348. Outside of the poetry, however, evidence is slight. Petrarch answered Giacomo Colonna's charges in a letter, asserting that Laura was only too real, his passion all too unfeigned. But the letter by itself is very inconclusive evidence, since it was clearly written for publication (at least in the limited sense of circulation among the poet's friends and wealthy patrons) and since it serves just as much to call Laura's reality into question as to prove it.

More interesting are the references to Laura in Petrarch's *Secretum,* probably first written around 1342 and revised after Laura's death. Although the *Secretum* is as dominated by Petrarch's reflexive irony as any of the works intended for publication, he never published it, and there is no evidence that he ever intended to. This dialogue between Francesco and his spiritual mentor, Saint Augustine of Hippo, imagined as taking place in the presence of Truth, consists of the saint's efforts—sometimes resisted, often successful—to bring his charge to the realization of his sinfulness and of the inadequacy of his earlier efforts to change. The first two books analyze Francesco's preference for a state of sinfulness and measure his varying subjection to each of the seven capital vices. In the third book, Augustine singles out what he regards as the two

greatest obstacles to Francesco's repentance—his "virtuous" love for Laura and his immoderate desire for glory. Francesco argues heatedly against the saint's critique, but he is outmaneuvered by Augustine to the point of acknowledging that his love for Laura must have a basis in sensuality, since he would not have fallen in love with an equally virtuous woman in an ugly body. At one point, in a passage that was probably added in revision, the saint points out that one must expect a woman "worn out with frequent childbearing" to have limited life expectancy. The precision of this indication, in a work presumably not intended for publication (and in none of Petrarch's Italian or Latin poetry or other published works is there any reference to Laura's being married or having children), may be regarded as strong evidence of her existence.

Another piece of evidence is furnished by a note on the flyleaf of Petrarch's copy of Virgil. Throughout his life, Petrarch used the flyleaves of various books for personal notes (lists of his favorite books, gardening enterprises, and so forth). On the flyleaf of his Virgil—a magnificent codex apparently commissioned by Petrarch and his father, stolen at some time but recovered in 1347, when Petrarch commissioned a frontispiece by his friend the famous painter Simone Martini—Petrarch wrote obituaries of relatives and friends. One of the notes refers to Laura.

> Laura, illustrious through her own virtues, and long famed through my verses, first appeared to my eyes in my youth, in the year of our Lord 1327, on the sixth day of April, in the church of St. Clare in Avignon, at matins; and in the same city, also on the sixth day of April, at the same first hour, but in the year 1348, the light of her life was withdrawn from the light of day, while I, as it chanced, was in Verona, unaware of my fate. The sad tidings reached me in Parma, in the same year, on the morning of the 19th day of May, in a letter from my Ludovicus. Her chaste and lovely form was laid to rest at vesper time, on the same day on which she died, in the burial place of the Brothers Minor. I am persuaded that her soul returned to the heaven from which it came, as Seneca says of Africanus. I have thought to write this, in bitter memory, yet with a certain bitter sweetness, here in this place that is often before my eyes, so that I may be admonished, by the sight of these words and by the consideration of the swift flight of time, that there is nothing in this life in which I should find pleasure; and that it is time, now that the strongest tie is broken, to flee from Babylon; and this, by the prevenient grace of God, should be easy for me, if I meditate deeply and manfully on the futile cares, the empty hopes, and the unforeseen events of my past years. (Translated by E. H. Wilkins, in his *Life of Petrarch* [Chicago: University of Chicago Press, 1961], p. 77)

This note suggests some of the respects in which the *Rime sparse* are an expression of genuinely held attitudes—the sense of the connection between grief and *contemptus mundi,* of the liability of earthly existence, of the passage of time—all amply substantiated in Petrarch's repeated experience of bereavement. It suggests also some insights into the indirection, not to say evasiveness, of the *Rime sparse.*

For the *Rime sparse* avoid the factual. There is no mention of Laura's being a married woman (if such she was) or having children, just as there is no mention of Petrarch's two illegitimate children or their mother. There is no mention of Saint Clare's Church—in fact, there is no mention of any encounter with Laura taking place indoors (the inference is possible in several cases, but not imposed by the text). The *Rime sparse* transpose all "events" to the level of recollection and reflection, bring them into a zone where the dividing line between fact, illusion, and fiction is obscured. This is partly a literary elegance, partly a serious theme—again, the line is hard to draw. Not one external event involving Laura is related in a literal, straightforward, factual manner. Did he actually see her bathing naked in the Sorgue? Did he first see her in Avignon and then later fall in love with her in Vaucluse? That is possible, but for the purposes of the *Rime sparse* it is assumed that the first encounter and the decisive encounter are the same. Furthermore, April 6, 1327, was not Good Friday; it was the historical anniversary of the Crucifixion, as its date was calculated in Petrarch's day. But poem 3 says he fell in love amid "the common grief," which clearly implies the liturgical date. (The solution would seem to be that he did not expect the reader to remember the difference.) As Aldo S. Bernardo and Bortolo Martinelli have recently pointed out, April 6, 1348, the date of Laura's death, was Easter Sunday. The coincidence of the two anniversaries comes to involve both the penitential implication for the lover and the assurance of Laura's salvation.

The figure of Laura emerges in the *Rime sparse* with a concrete vividness, rich with at least implied incident, quite different from the hieratically stylized or philosophically abstract manner of the dolce stil or the *Vita nuova,* justifying De Sanctis formula that in comparison with Dante, Petrarch brought woman down from Heaven to earth. Still, Laura herself is not the central focus of the poetry. Her psychology remains transcendent, mysterious (perhaps even miraculous, but that is evaded), the subject of conjecture and bewilderment except at moments represented as virtually total spiritual communion. Rather it is the psychology of the lover that is the central theme of the book.

Although Petrarch was accustomed in later life to disparage poetry in the vernacular, he lavished intense if intermittent care on his own over more than forty years. It does not consitute a large proportion of his entire literary output—some 10,000 lines of Italian verse (the *Rime sparse,* the *Trionfi,* the uncollected poems, a few fragments), as opposed to thousands of pages of verse and prose in Latin—but it has been accepted as his greatest achievement. He apparently began writing the poems that were to form the *Rime sparse* in the early 1330s; perhaps by 1335 he had decided to make a collection; by the mid-1350s most of the 366 poems had been drafted. Working papers of various kinds, from first drafts to fair copies, have come down to us for sixty-five poems and for several of the *Trionfi* in the Vatican Library's codex Vat. Lat. 3196. Many of these papers have dated marginal notations, and on their basis the great Petrarchan scholar Ernest Hatch Wilkins built a series of hypotheses about the development of the collection. The first version of the collection that actually survives is a preliminary, incomplete one that Petrarch allowed to circulate in 1359. It is found in a manuscript (the Vatican's Chigi L. V. 176) that includes an anthology of poems by Dante and others, and an important version of Boccaccio's life of Dante; it is now generally thought to have been transcribed by Boccaccio himself. This version of the *Rime sparse* consists of 215 poems (1-120, "Donna mi vene," 122-156, 159-165, 169-173, 184-185, 178, 176-177, 189, 264-304; in that order).

In 1366 Petrarch began intensive work on a definitive version of the *Rime sparse.* He replaced **"Donna mi vene"** with 121, drastically revised the order of poems after 156, and added 151 other poems, many of which he revised just before they were transcribed into his definitive copy. Abandoned by his copyist late in 1366, Petrarch continued to revise, transcribe, and rearrange the poems well into the last year of his life. The definitive manuscript of the *Rime sparse,* Petrarch's own copy, is the Vatican's codex Vat. Lat. 3195; poems 121, 179, 191-263, and 319-366 are in Petrarch's handwriting. Wilkins inferred reliable dates of transcription into Vat. Lat. 3195 from notations in Vat. Lat. 3196, from variations in the handwriting and ink of Vat. Lat. 3195, and from fairly detailed knowledge of Petrarch's whereabouts from 1366 on. Some time after the transcription had been completed in 1374, Petrarch renumbered the last thirty poems, thereby sharpening the focus of the conclusion. The final version of the *Rime sparse* is the basis of this edition.

Both the Chigi version and the post-1366 versions (Petrarch allowed several copies to be made from Vat. Lat. 3195 while it was in progress) have two parts, often referred to, somewhat inappropriately, as poems *in vita* and *in morte.* The second begins with the great canzone of inner debate, **"I' vo pensando"** (264). In Vat. Lat. 3195 the division between the two parts is indicated by an elaborate initial for poem 264 and by the presence of seven blank pages before it; whether

Petrarch meant to add more poems there has been debated.

In the Chigi version and in manuscripts deriving from it, in Vat. Lat. 3196, and in Vat. Lat. 3195 it is possible to trace the process of revision of individual poems, in some cases from the first draft through several versions to the final one. Some of these materials have been assembled by Carl Appel and Angelo Romanò in their editions of Vat. Lat. 3196, but there has been no reliable codification of all the variant readings, and a truly critical edition of the *Rime sparse* is still awaited.

Petrarch's themes are traditional, his treatment of them profoundly original. From Propertius, Ovid, the troubadors, the *Roman de la rose,* the Sicilians, the dolce stil novo, Dante, Cino da Pistoia there comes to him a repertory of situations, technical vocabulary, images, structures. Love at first sight, obsessive yearning and lovesickness, frustration, love as parallel to feudal service; the lady as ideally beautiful, ideally virtuous, miraculous, beloved in Heaven, and destined to early death; love as virtue, love as idolatry, love as sensuality; the god of love with his arrows, fires, whips, chains; war within the self-hope, fear, joy, sorrow. Conceits, wit, urbane cleverness; disputations and scholastic precision; allegory, personification; wooing, exhortation, outcry; praise, blame; self-examination, self-accusation, self-defense; repentance and the farewell to love. These elements of the world of the *Rime sparse* all exist in the tradition. Petrarch's originality lies in the intensity with which he develops and explores them, in the rich, profoundly personal synthesis of divergent poetic traditions, in the idea of the collection itself.

Although Petrarch's wide familiarity with troubador poetry is evident on every page of the *Rime sparse,* the way in which he assimilated and made use of its influence—at all levels—was shaped by the example of Dante. The study of Provençal poetry, in particular the poems of Arnaut Daniel, had had a profound effect on Dante, provoking (around 1296) a series of radical experiments, the *rime petrose* (stony rhymes), so called because the central theme is the hard, unyielding cruelty of the lady. The way Petrarch learned to adapt to his own purposes what he found in the *rime petrose* was a key moment in the clarification of his attitude toward both the *Vita nuova* and the *Commedia.* . . .

One of Petrarch's greatest originalities lies in the idea of the collection itself. C. S. Lewis once wrote that Petrarch invented the sonnet sequence by omitting the prose narrative found in the *Vita nuova,* and it ought to be kept in mind that, as Wilkins established, before the *Rime sparse* it was the custom to keep different metrical forms separated, in different sections of manuscripts. (The Verona manuscript of Catullus sepa-

rates short poems in lyric meters from long poems in lyric and other meters and from poems in elegiacs; Italian manuscripts regularly separate sonnets, ballate, canzoni; the same principle applies in Provençal collections.) The *Rime sparse* are arranged *as if* they are in chronological order, and most modern opinion holds that they are in fact more or less, and with certain notable exceptions, in the order of composition. But this cannot be determined with much reliability, since the anniversary poems, which used to be thought of as anchors of the "real" chronology, could have been written years later or even years earlier, and we have evidence in Vat. Lat. 3196 that a number of the poems of the first part were written long after 1348. The work presents a *fictional* chronology that should not be confused with a real one, and the ordering of the poems derives from artistic principles.

As a collection the *Rime sparse* have a number of models. Some are classical: Horace's *Odes,* Virgil's *Eclogues,* Propertius' and Ovid's elegies are collected in works that form composites, made up of separate units arranged in complex, obliquely symmetrical patterns. In the *Vita nuova,* the retrospective prose narrative explains the circumstances of composition of the poems and provides some technical commentary; the assumption is that the poems express the most intimate experience of the poet, the meaning of which becomes apparent only later, not at the time of writing. This becomes an important principle in the *Rime sparse*: the meaning of experience is qualified in retrospect, and the passage of time becomes a structural principle as well as a major theme. It is discernible both in the recurrence of the anniversaries and in the succession of separate poems. Presented as if the products of distinct occasions, the poems are arranged as if deposited by the passage of time. Omitting the prose narrative means that there is no mediation between poems, that the reader must supply the narrative and psychological inferences. Successive poems often may or may not have been written on the same day (in the fictional chronology). The passage of time may cast altogether new light on earlier poems, as the second anniversary poem (62) does on the first one (30), or as Laura's death does on the whole first part.

The *Vita nuova* provided another structural principle for the *Rime sparse*. It has thirty-one poems in the following order: ten sonnets or short poems, *one canzone,* four sonnets, *one canzone* (prophetic of Beatrice's death), four sonnets or short poems, *one canzone,* ten sonnets or short poems. Petrarch derived from this arrangement the idea of placing canzoni and groups of canzoni as structural nodes or pillars at varying intervals among the short poems. The arrangement of the second part of the *Rime sparse* is a particularly clear allusion to the symmetry of the *Vita nuova:* it has *three groups* of canzoni, separated by long stretches of sonnets, standing at the beginning

(264, 268, 270), the middle (323, 325, 331, 332), and at the end (359, 360, 366); the first group of sonnets is exactly twice as long as the second, but the midpoint of the second part falls in poem 331. Laura's death is announced in poem 267, which gives exactly one hundred poems from there to the end.

Wilkins accepted Ruth S. Phelps' view that the poems added in the post-Chigi versions were less carefully arranged than those in the Chigi version. It is increasingly clear that this view was based on utterly inadequate criteria and is untenable. Rather what emerges from recent studies is that Petrarch's notion of what he was seeking to achieve in the arrangement of the poems grew clearer as he neared the end of his work on them. His renumbering of the last thirty poems is a striking instance.

Petrarch was less an inventor of new forms than an untiring explorer of the possibilities of existing forms. More than anyone before him, he demonstrated the remarkable range of the sonnet; he developed a new flexibility, sinuousness, and variety in the canzone; he made the sestina peculiarly his own. Some discussion of forms here is vital to an understanding of the interrelation for him of form and the other aspects of poetry.

The formal principle of the sonnet is closely related to that of the Italian canzone stanza. The Italian sonnet consists of two parts (octave and sestet) theoretically governed by a different "melody"; its divisions are marked by the rhymes, which do not overlap between the two parts. The rhythmical, formal contrast between the parts is between double-duple movement (2 x 4 lines, four appearances each of two rhymes) and double-triple (2 x 3 lines, two appearances each of three rhymes, or vice versa). Petrarch explores the possibilities of symmetry and contrast among the parts of the sonnet with endless ingenuity, and the self-conscious technical mastery is integral to his expressiveness. It is commonly said that the Petrarchan sonnet presents a situation, event, image, or generalization in the octave and in the sestet a reflection, result, or application. Many do follow such a scheme, but the range of possibilities is broad, and it is characteristic of Petrarch to capitalize, in the sestet, on the division between first and second tercet—to introduce a qualification or reversal, often epigrammatically coming to focus in the very last line. I shall discuss one example in order to suggest some of the subtlety of what may seem to modern readers merely formal or cerebral.

An extreme case of Petrarch's artificiality, the fifth poem in the **Rime sparse,** puns on the meaning of each syllable of Laura's name (Laurette, adapted to high style in a Latinate form, Laureta). In the octave, after a pair of introductory lines, each of the three syllables receives two lines of comment:

Quando io movo i sospiri a chiamar voi
e 'l nome che nel cor mi scrisse Amore,
LAU-dando s'incomincia udir di fore
il suon de' primi dolci accenti suoi;

vostro stato RE-al che 'ncontro poi
raddoppia a l'alta impresa il mio valore;
ma "TA-ci!" grida il fin, "ché farle onore
è d'altri omeri soma che da' tuoi."

                                                  (5.1-8)

When I move my sighs to call you and the name that Love wrote on my heart, the sound of its first sweet accents is heard without in LAU-ds.

Your RE-gal state, which I meet next, redoubles my strength for the high enterprise; but "TA-lk no more!" cries the ending, "for to do her honor is a burden for other shoulders than yours."

The regularity of the pattern (two lines per syllable) is connected with the idea of slow pronunciation of the name. What is said about each syllable, in addition to being a pun (though that is not strictly true in the case of the first, since according to traditional etymology *laurus* was derived from *laudare,* to praise), also plays on the position of the syllable in the name: praise, he says, *begins* with the first syllable; next, the energy is *redoubled;* and the ending calls for *silence.* Even more: the position of the syllables in the lines corresponds to their position in the name—beginning, middle, and—but just when the structure is becoming mechanical, the urgency of anxiety brings the third syllable back to the beginning of the line.

In the sestet the positioning of the syllables is different. The first two appear immediately and together, while the third is delayed until the last line of the poem (thus the promise of the octave is obliquely fulfilled):

Cosi LAU-dare et RE-verire insegna
la voce stessa, pur ch' altri vi chiami,
o d'ogni reverenza et d'onor degna;

se non che forse Apollo si disdegna
ch'a parlar de' suoi sempre verdi rami
lingua mor-TA-l presuntuosa vegna.

                                                  (5.9-14)

Thus the word itself teaches LAU-d and RE-verence, whenever anyone calls you, O Lady worthy of all reverence and honor; except that perhaps Apollo is incensed that any mor-TA-l tongue should come presumptuous to speak of his eternally green boughs.

The first tercet sets up a neat chiastic relation between line 9 and line 11; it leads up to *degna* as establishing the explanation of the strange efficacy of the name. *Degna* is thus the hinge of the sestet; juxtaposed with it is the forbidding and enigmatic *disdegna,* and the last lines bring in a more serious anxiety than the finitude of the poet's gifts—the finitude of his existence itself. The silence of line 7 is now connected with the idea of death.

Is this merely precious, trivial play? What is the relation between the urbane, witty, complimentary surface and the recurrence of the anxiety, a recurrence dictated by the last syllable of the name, inherent in the formal "perfection" itself? The last word of the poem, *vegna,* may seem a curiously weak one in view of the emphasis on the last syllable of the name. But that emphasis in fact gives it a relief, and it is to be connected with line 12 of the next poem: "a morte mi trasporta; / sol per *venir* al lauro"—to *speak* the name is itself to reenact the myth of Apollo and Daphne. That Petrarch found this an interesting poem may be inferred from his giving it such a prominent place at the beginning of the **Rime sparse:** it is the first poem that refers to the myth of Apollo and Daphne.

Brief mention will suffice for the other short forms Petrarch uses. The term *madrigal* has no precise formal meaning. All of Petrarch's (52, 54, 106, 121) are experiments in three-line groups (their schemes are, respectively, *A B A, B C B, C C; A B A, C B C, D E D E; A B C, A B C, D D; A B B, A C C, C D D*). The principle of *ballata* form is that after an initial statement of a *ritornello* (a melodic unit that recurred, originally, thus a rhyme scheme, not a refrain) one or more stanzas follow, each of which ends with the ritornello; the first rhyme(s) of these later ritornellos must be attached to the rhymes of the individual stanzas, and the last rhyme repeats the last rhyme of the original ritornello, thus (11): *A B B A* (ritornello), *C D E D C E, E F F A* (stanza). When there is more than one stanza, each starts afresh. Most of Petrarch's ballate have only one stanza; two (55 and 59) have two stanzas.

The longest poems in the **Rime sparse** are canzoni, a form in which Petrarch's greatness as a poet reaches its fullest expression. In both the Provençal and the Italian type, a canzone consists of several stanzas of identical form, the form being devised by the poet: he is free to make the stanza as short or as long as he pleases (Petrarch's shortest stanza is seven lines long; his longest, twenty), to arrange the rhymes as he pleases, and to mix long and short lines as he pleases. (Petrarch's long lines are always the normal Italian eleven-syllable line, corresponding to iambic pentameter; his short lines all have seven syllables.) The canzone usually ends with a *commiato* or *congedo* (farewell) that repeats the scheme of the last few lines of the stanza.

It is integral to Petrarch's cult of technical refinement that (except for the sestinas) he devises a new stanza for each new canzone. There are two exceptions to this rule, each involving successive poems. One is the sequence of three canzoni in praise of Laura's eyes (71-73), all in the same stanza form. The other is the pair 125 and 126, discussed below. As one might expect, the interplay in the **Rime sparse** of the different stanza forms and different lengths of poems is carefully planned.

Most of Petrarch's canzoni are of the Italian type, in which the stanza has two "melodies," two rhyme schemes that are separate, except that the first line of the second part rhymes with the last line of the first part. As Dante had pointed out, either or both the parts of the Italian canzone stanza could be symmetrically subdivisible (into two or three parts) or not. Petrarch's stanzas are always divisible in the first part, indivisible in the second. Here is a stanza in which there is a clear division of sense between the first and second parts:

In quella parte dove Amor mi sprona	A
conven ch' io volga le dogliose rime	B
che son seguaci de la mente afflitta	C
quai fien ultime, lasso, et qua' fien prime?	B
Collui che del mio mal meco mi ragiona	A
mi lascia in dubbio, sì confuso ditta.	C
Ma pur quanto la storia trovo scritta	C
in mezzo 'l cor che sì spesso rincorro	D
parlando an triegua et al dolor soccorro.	D
Dico che perch' io miri	e
mille cose diverse attento et fisco,	F
sol una donna veggio e 'l suo bel viso.	F
	(127.1-14)

Like the overwhelming majority of Petrarch's stanzas, this one has a first part of six lines; most rhyme like this one, some rhyme *A B C A B C.* Second, most of the stanzas end, like this one, with a *rima baciata* (two consecutively rhymed lines). Third, in almost all his stanzas, as here, the second part begins with some variant of *C D E E D,* and the longer ones even repeat it (the second part of poem 23 is *C D E e D F G H H G F F I I*). In other words, in Petrarch's usage, the two parts of the stanza tend to be "melodically" related in a way similar to the two parts of the sonnet: in the first part of the canzone stanza the double-triple rhythm, similar to the sestet of the sonnet, governs; in the second part, within the basic asymmetrical indivisibility, there is usually a recurrent sense of double rhythm in the groups of four lines and in the paired lines.

Petrarch used the Provençal type of stanza, which has no division, much less frequently, and in such poems as 70 and 206 there is still a strong feeling for division. The stanza of 135 is a hybrid:

Qual più diversa et nova	a
cosa fu mai in qualche strania clima,	B
quella, se ben s'estima,	b
più mi rasembra: a tal son giunto, Amore.	C
Là onde il dì ven fore	c
vola un augel che sol, senza consorte,	D
di volontaria morte	d
rinasce et tutto a viver si rinova.	A
Così sol si ritrova	a
lo mio voler, et così in su la cima	B
ed' suoi alti pensieri al sol si volve,	E
et così si risolve,	e
et così torna al suo stato di prima;	B
arde et more et riprende i nervi suoi	F
et vive poi con la fenice a prova. (f) A	

(135.1-15)

This stanza has a symmetrically divided first part and seems to move into the ordinary division with line 9; instead it reintroduces both the *a* and *B* rhymes. Thus *a* and *B* occur at the very beginning of the stanza; *A, a,* and *B* at the center; and *B* and *A* at the end. The connection with the theme is clear: the form is renewing itself, finding itself again (lines 8 and 9), ending with its beginning (line 15), in a cycle like that of the phoenix.

The sestina, which was probably invented by Arnaut Daniel, is technically a canzone with undivided stanza, of a type that Arnaut particularly cultivated—one in which rhymes do not occur within stanzas but only between them (*canso a coblas dissolutas*—poems 29 and 70 are of this type) and in which the same rhymes are used throughout the poem (*coblas unissonans*— 29 is an example). More than half of Arnaut's poems are of this difficult type. The sestina has two further refinements: instead of rhymes, entire rhyme-words are repeated, and the order of the rhyme-words is changed according to a fixed rule, called *retrogradatio cruciformis* (cruciform retrograde motion): *a B C D E F, f A E B D C,* and so forth. This procedure would in a seventh stanza bring back the original order; instead Arnaut closes the poem with a three-line envoi in which each line ends with *two* of the rhyme-words. Arnaut's sestina, "Lo ferm voler q'el cor m'entra," is a brilliant poem in which the technical daring is the tense victory of an expressiveness combining obsession, warmth of intimacy, angry frustration, and ironic self-awareness.

Dante's sestina, "Al poco giorno e al gran cerchio d'ombra," is an important part of the *petrose* group. . . . Both Dante's and Arnaut's sestinas are almost by definition unique—one would be surprised to see either poet repeat the form, devised and conquered in an individualized act of expression. Dante—who had changed Arnaut's form by making all six lines the same length—went on to invent an even more elaborate and difficult form, sometimes called a double

sestina, though it is not properly a sestina at all ("Amor, tu vedi ben" . . .). The *rime petrose* are consciously *microcosmic;* "Io son venuto" is based on (1) a parallelism between the cycles governing the cosmos and the cycles governing the life of the self; (2) the traditional parallelism between the realms of nature and the parts of the human body. The sestina is a particularly clear example of a cyclical form expressing the embeddedness of human experience in time.

Petrarch assimilated, codified, and diluted the intensities of Dante's sestina and the other *rime petrose* in order to fit them into his own poetic universe. That he wrote nine sestinas (or ten, if you count 332 as two) is indicative of the process. His theme is not the victorious ascent out of time, though the number six has in the *Rime sparse* an importance analogous to that of the number three in the *Commedia*. As medieval readers knew, God created the world in six days, and on the sixth day (Friday) He created man. According to many medieval authorities, including Dante, man fell on Friday also; and Christ redeemed man on a Friday. Six was, then, the number of the created world, of man's earthly existence, of man's excess, and of time. Seven, corresponding to the day God rested, and eight, corresponding to Easter, were the numbers of eternity, of life beyond the world and beyond time. In Petrarch's sestinas the recurrence of the six rhyme-words expresses the soul's obsession with its inability to transcend time. The rhyme-words recur cyclically but with changing meanings, and the form reflects the nature of the mutable world, governed by cycles in which all things change but recur: *omnia mutantur, nil interit* (*Metamorphoses* 15.165). The *commiati* of Petrarch's sestinas, furthermore, usually have a function related to the figural significance of the number seven: they allude to the intensity of contemplation (30), to conversion (42, 214), to death (22, 332), to the end of time (22). It is not accidental that the vast majority of Petrarch's canzone stanzas have a first part of six lines. Petrarch made the number six peculiarly his own, as can be seen also in the number of poems in the entire *Rime sparse,* 366 (6 x 60 + 6), probably a solar number (the number of days in a leap year), and in the importance assumed by that anniversay of anniversaries, *feria sexta aprilis:* the sixth day of the fourth month. Recent studies suggest that numerological principles also govern the arrangement of the *Rime sparse* to a hitherto unsuspected degree.

The theme of the first sight of Laura derives much of its importance from the fact that Petrarch accepts the traditional conception of love as an obsession with the mental image of the lady, imposed on the fantasy at the moment of falling in love. For the image to take effect, the force with which its arrow reaches the heart must derive from both a special sensuous intensity and a predisposition to love in the observer. Under the right conditions, just as in perception the mind—the imagination—assumes the form of a lady as mental image, so the will assumes her form as its goal; when the two coincide, the image of the lady is always before the mind's eye, the will always moves toward her. So mind and will cooperate to inflame each other. Here is Andreas Capellanus' description of the typical process of amorous meditation:

> only from the reflection of the mind upon what it sees does this passion come. For when a man sees some woman fit for love and shaped according to his taste, he begins at once to lust after her in his heart; then the more he thinks about her the more he burns with love until he comes to a fuller meditation. Presently he begins to think about the fashioning of the woman and to differentiate her limbs, to think about what she does, and to pry into the secrets of her body, and he desires to put each part of it to the fullest use. Then after he has come to this complete meditation, love cannot hold the reins, but he proceeds at once to action . . . This inborn passion comes, therefore, from seeing and meditating. Not every kind of meditation can be the cause of love, an excessive one is required (*immoderata cogitatio*); for a restrained thought does not, as a rule, return to the mind, and so love cannot arise from it. (*The Art of Courtly Love,* trans. J. J. Parry [New York: Columbia University Press, 1941], pp. 28-29)

Andreas is describing the process of a natural love that proceeds to a natural goal, but Petrarch's subject is the possibility of a sublimated, virtuous love, and the different forms of his fantasies are expressions of the conflict inherent in sublimation. Insofar as his love is a form of sexual desire, it consists in sexual fantasies, but these are seldom of the explicit kind Andreas describes. The most nearly explicit ones emerge almost against the lover's will, either when he is off his guard or when his obsession has reached a particularly intense phase (as in 22 or 237). A major theme is the way the lover's meditation on the lady's virtue and on her virtuous influence paradoxically leads to the emergence of the sensual basis of his love. A clear instance is poem 37, closely related to Dante's *canzone montanina,* "Amor, da che convien pur ch' io mi doglia." . . . The subject of both poems is the destructiveness of the obsession with the lady's image as the lover deliberately evokes it. Dante states the theme directly (lines 16-28); Petrarch's poem enacts the principle dramatically: it is the very composition of the poem, a self-pitying meditation on his absence from Laura, that instead of consoling him causes the image to emerge to consciousness and makes his suffering worse. Just before the midpoint of the poem, he states his realization that, since it is in his power not to prolong the process, the composition of the poem is a perversity (lines 49ff). As he describes the psychological mechanism of this self-indulgence he simultaneously enacts

it, and thus the activity of introspective poetic composition results in the emergence to dominance—both in his consciousness and in the poem—of an image of Laura that becomes gradually more sensuous. The poem ends with the cycle completed, with the failure of hope all the more exacerbated.

The fullest exploration of the self-destructiveness of this process is in poems 71-73, where the desire to praise the beauty of Laura's eyes and their power to guide him to virtue is shown dramatically to lead into an uncontrollable negative spiral. He is led to say what he does not wish to say—that he is unhappy—and the poem culminates in a thinly veiled sexual fantasy:

> così vedess' io fiso
> come Amor dolcemente gli governa
> sol un giorno da presso
> senza volger giamai rota superna,
> né pensasse d'altrui né di me stesso,
> e 'l batter gli occhi miei non fosse spesso!
>   (73.70-75)

Might I see thus fixedly how Love sweetly governs them, only one day, up close, without any supernal wheel ever turning, nor think of any other nor of myself, and the blinking of my eyes not be frequent!

There are two kinds of expression in the *Rime sparse* of the fantasy of sexual fulfillment. The direct form avoids sensuous particularity (for example, poem 22); the indirect form, as here, is veiled, but the link with poems 22 and 237 is provided by the optative past subjunctive. Even more important is the presence behind all these passages of the fantasy of fulfillment in Dante's "Così nel mio parlar voglio esser aspro," lines 53-78. . . . Dante's fantasy asserts the passage of time as constitutive of a prolonged sexual encounter, but Petrarch calls for time to stand still. Petrarch's model is the Beatific Vision of God; the more sensuous the content, the greater the tendency to assimilate the fantasy toward the safe religious category of contemplation. The stasis Petrarch desires is both an intensification of the fantasy and an evasion of the idea of activity. This critical tension between contemplative form and sexual content is a major theme of the *Rime sparse,* and not least in the second part.

Petrarch's exploration of the experience of love thus derives considerable depth from his use of Augustinian psychology and metaphysics. The most important Augustinian concepts underlying his analysis are (1) the power and deceptiveness of the images of desire; (2) the instability of man's nature, fluctuating among inconsistent desires and multiple loves, spiraling downward toward nonbeing unless upheld, integrated (*collected,* to use the Augustinian term favored by Petrarch) by grace; (3) the opposition of eternity and time (eternity represents fullness of being, unchanging stability; time represents succession, change, instability).

Petrarch represents the experience of love in terms of these oppositions, but he does not resolve them unambiguously, as Augustine does. In the Augustinian view, sexual desire is love directed outward and downward toward mutable lesser goods; it is doomed to frustration and subjects the soul to its own *habitus ad nihilum*, its tendency toward nothingness. In this view sexuality is not a source of integration but of disorder, and the Augustinian answer to it is denial. The ***Rime sparse*** do demonstrate the lover's subjection to the fluctuating instability of his will, as in the juxtaposition of contradictory poems represented as written on the same day, often an anniversary (poems 60-63, for example). Caught in the inconsistency of his desires, wandering in the labyrinth of his illusions, the lover is only intermittently capable of identifying the erotic source of even his most sacrosanct fantasies. Laura's death does not solve the problem; rather it frees his fantasy all the more, and he imagines her coming down from Heaven to sit on his bed in all her beauty (359), a kind of fantasy earlier identified as dangerous nonsense (345). The lover must pray for grace to heal the split in his will and clear the clouds from his understanding. But the unambiguous experience of grace never comes, and the ***Rime sparse*** end not with victory achieved or assured but with the longest and most poignant of the many prayers for help.

Although Petrarch's pessimism accepts the Augustinian critique of love of the mutable, the other pole of his ambivalence asserts its value. Two of the longest canzoni (264 and 360), placed at the beginning and near the end of the second part, dramatize the impossibility of simple judgments about love; they are closely related to the debates of book 3 of the ***Secretum***. For the experience of love makes possible the only integration the lover does in fact achieve, however temporary or imperfect it may be. Absence is an experience of scattering, presence one of synthesis; the image of Laura in the memory is a principle of integration. This can be seen with particular clarity in the central group of canzoni in the first part, 125-129, most of them explorations of different aspects of the dominance in his fantasy of the image of Laura.

Poems 125 and 126, which form a unit, show clearly the identity in Petrarch's mind of the problematics of poetry and love, both seen in terms of Augustinian categories. In 125 the intensity of the poet's frustration has created a split between the inner poignancy of his feelings and his capacity to express them. If he could express them adequately he would surely win her love, he says, but his frustration has so accumulated with time that he has become blocked even from the kind of outpouring of feeling that formerly gave him relief though it did not succeed in winning her

love (stanzas 1-3). There may seem to be a characteristic Petrarchan paradox in these beautiful verses discussing the poet's inability to write beautiful verses. The paradox has a point, for it focuses the problem of the relation of outer and inner, of form and content: it is resolved by the poem's being dramatic, of *representing* the simultaneity of love and poetic inspiration as *in process*.

The initial situation in 125 is one of impasse, split, alienation, resulting from the fact that Laura, the source of integration and inspiration, is absent. The block can only be broken by an upsurge of energy that will free the sources of feeling and resynthesize the existential situation, reunite inner and outer. A way must be found to make Laura present, and it will consist in eliciting the full power of her image. At the moment there seems no way to accomplish this.

In the fourth stanza the focus of attention is the setting of the meditation (we are meant to identify it as Vaucluse), and the gesture of addressing the landscape is represented as a defeated renunciation of direct address of Laura. Actually this is a first step toward evocation of her presence, but it begins as a demonstration of her absence. The lover's eye interrogates the scene, running discursively over it for the signs of her former presence. The poem ends on a note of provisional satisfaction afforded by imagining her "scattered footprints," which evoke the memory of disconnected moments—not synthesized—of the experience of the first day. In this, poem 125 is recapitulating and gathering up a series of scattered recollections that began around poem 85, and includes especially 90, 100, 108, 112, 116 (all sonnets).

In poem 126 the lover's meditation continues the despairing indulgence in alienation: he imagines his death and hopes to be buried here; after his death, Laura will return to seek him, but he will be dust, and she will weep for him. Here the mixture of despair and displaced wish fulfillment—a low point in terms of any real future but for that very reason safe for fantasy, disinterested and therefore laden with affect—triggers the release called out for in 125, and the image of the first day abruptly emerges with a greater intensity than in any other poem of the book.

This release has a magical intensity partly because its stanza form is identical with that of 125 except that the last line of each stanza has eleven syllables instead of seven, a difference that is stunningly effective in suggesting the overcoming of the halting inhibition of 125. The difference between the two poems is signalized also at the beginning of 126 by the prominence given the image of water (never directly mentioned in 125) and of Laura's body. Poem 126 begins where 125 leaves off, with a discursive interrogation of the place: it looks back to the unsynthesized past, then to the blocked, defeated present, then to the transcendent—and useless—future (in which Laura will interrogate the place); finally comes the ecstatic image, and the synthesis reintegrates both the lover's sense of Laura and the poet's evocative power.

The image itself (stanzas 4 and 5) derives its categories from the Beatific Vision. It is a suspended moment, its immobility evoked by the motion of the falling flowers, Laura's nimbus or glory. It is a contemplative rapture that is utterly engrossing, from which the lover can no more turn away than the blessed can from God. The rain of flowers is a direct reference to the appearance of Beatrice in *Purgatorio* 30:

> Tutti dicean, *'Benedictus qui venis!'*
>   e, fior gittando di sopra e d'intorno,
>   *'Manibus o date lilia plenis!*
> . . . . .
> Così dentro una nuvola di fiori,
>   che dalle mani angeliche saliva
>   e ricadeva in giù dentro e di fuori,
> Sovra candido vel cinta d'uliva,
>   donna m'apparve, sotto verde manto
>   vestita di color di fiamma viva.
>   (*Purgatorio* 30.19-21, 28-33)

All were saying, "Blessed is he who comes" and, throwing flowers above and around, "O give lilies with full hands!" . . . So within a cloud of flowers that rose up from the angles' hands and fell back again within and without, girt with an olive branch over her white veil a lady appeared to me, under a green mantle clothed in the color of living flame.

Petrarch's flowers are natural flowers, expressive of the culminating but transitory moment of the springtime, as opposed to angelic flowers; Laura is sitting, not standing like Beatrice; the flowers touch Laura, falling first on her lap, while Beatrice is within the cloud and there is no mention of the flowers' touching her. Dante will eventually cross the river and see Beatrice unveil herself: for him the moment is a circumscribed, provisional goal soon to be transcended; for Petrarch it is almost mythic *original* synthesis that is a goal in itself. The release, in 126, is both sublimated and orgasmic, and consciously so. The sowing of seed is displaced from the lover to the tree; the lover may not acknowledge the wish, and the tree contains and isolates Laura, protects both lover and poet, and permits the symbolic release, the moment of grace.

A major emphasis of the last stanza of the poem is the difference between the image of Laura treasured in the lover's mind and the "true image," from which the lover says he was "divided." By definition the memory has been transfigured by desire. It is an image from the distant past—eighteen years back, according to

the fictional chronology (see 120). To what extent is it an accurate memory even of his own experience, to what extent refashioned? The question hovers over the vision: the incessant falling of the flowers is the sign both of the present urgency and of the passage of time—the barrier that separates the present from the unrecoverable past. Thus in the *Rime sparse* memory is reevocation and resynthesis, it must be constantly renewed. The recurrences of space and time—revisiting of the consecrated place, commemoration of the recurrent anniversary (a kind of secularization of the Christian year), a new interest in the milestones of experience, personal anniversaries, memorials—express also the anxiety of a reflexiveness clearly aware of the willed, even arbitrary, element in each of its self-assertions.

Poems 125 and 126, then, provide a model of the Petrarchan-Augustinian dialectic of dispersal and reintegration that governs the entire *Rime sparse*. As the fullest evocation of the original synthesis, the climax of 126—emerging from the alienation of 125 (and the sonnets)—provides essential support to the three other canzoni in this central group. The appearance of 125-129 as a group (in violation of chronological order and geographical logic) is an enactment of relative psychological integration around the image of Laura; it is also an important formal node, a poetic integration, of the book. That **"Italia mia,"** Petrarch's most important patriotic poem, is part of this group is not accidental: surrounded by the great love canzoni, with which it has many structural and poetic similarities, it is meant to be related to the critical psychological insights of these poems. The dialectic of 129, where the ascent of the mountain is accompanied by increasing awareness of the lover's actual situation, culminates in a measurement of distance which brings release because of the sense of exalted clarity. Poem 127, a rich exploration of the theme "all things remind me of Laura," gradually intensifies the nature images to the superb effect of stanza 5, where the static image of roses in a vase indoors is suddenly given life in the image of the wind moving across a meadow. But that intense—if indirect—evocation of the *imago* is not the culmination of the poem, for in the sixth stanza the summation suddenly brings to the fore the theoretical models on which the poem has been based.

>   Ad una ad una annoverar le stelle
> e 'n picciol vetro chiuder tutte l'acque
> forse credea, quando in sì poca carta
> novo penser di ricontar mi nacque
> *in quante parti* il fior de l'altre belle
> *stando in se stessa à la sua luce sparta,*
>   *a ciò che mai da lei non mi diparta;*
> né farò io, *et se pur talor fuggo,*
> *in cielo e 'n terra m'à racchiuso i passi.*
>   (127. 85-93)

Perhaps I thought I could count the stars one by one and enclose the sea in a little glass when the strange idea came to me to tell in so few pages *in how many places* the flower of all beauties, *remaining in herself, has scattered her light in order that I may never depart from her;* nor shall I, and *if at times I flee, in Heaven and earth she has circumscribed my steps.*

The idea of a supreme source of beauty which though transcendent fills all things with its omnipresence, which cannot be escaped by any flight, mirrors the relation of God to the universe and to the human soul, as described in the Wisdom of Solomon 7:26-27 and Psalm 138:2-13, passages repeatedly echoed by Augustine in the *Confessions* (see especially 1.2-4, 7.16-19, 10.33-38), not to speak of Dante in the opening lines of the *Paradiso.*

The remarkably original and innovative structure of the *Rime sparse,* with its mixture of symmetries and looseness, with its structural pillars—groups of canzoni where what is scattered among the short poems is gathered and brought to fuller development—this form reflects the provisional, even threatened nature of the integration of experience possible for natural man. Perfect integration of a life or a book comes only when the mutable and imperfect is caught up into eternity. That ultimate gathering, that binding of the scattered leaves, comes only on the anagogical Sabbath. The force of Dante's claim to have the *Commedia* stand as a perfectly integrated poem rests, as Dante understood, in its claim to derive from God, the ultimate unifier of all things:

Nel suo profondo vidi che s'interna,
legato con amore in un volume,
ciò che per l'universo si squaderna.
                    (*Paradiso* 33.85-87)

In its depths I saw internalize itself, bound with love in one volume, what through the universe is scattered unbound.

This is the point of Petrarch's title for his collection, *Rerum vulgarium fragmenta* (Fragments of vernacular poetry), for which the Italian is given in the first poem: "rime sparse" (scattered rhymes). This may well be the first use of the term *fragment* to describe a kind of work of art. There is, however, a scriptural precedent in the story of the miracle of the loaves and fishes (John 6:12), where Jesus says "Colligite fragmenta quae supersunt ne pereant" (Collect the fragments that remain lest they perish). Bede and Alcuin interpreted the words as referring to the gathering together in exegesis of the prophecies and allegories scattered through the Bible. For Petrarch the term expresses the intensely self-critical awareness that all integration of selves and texts is relative, temporary,

threatened. They flow into multiplicity at the touch of time, their inconsistencies juxtaposed as the successive traces of a subject who dissolves and leaves only words behind.

Metamorphosis is, then, a dominant idea in the *Rime sparse.* It is seen in the psychological instability of the lover, the ontological insufficiency of human nature, in time, in death. It is an idea that governs the relation of the poems to their sources or to the broader tradition: they transform it. It governs the relation of the individual poems, themes, motifs, forms, even individual words, to each other. Ovid is omnipresent. The first and basic metamorphosis in the *Rime sparse* reenacts the myth of Apollo and Daphne: when the lover catches up with the object of his pursuit, she has turned into the laurel tree. It is merely the change of a letter that turns *Laura* into *lauro* (laurel), and since Petrarch did not have the apostrophe as part of his punctuation, but simply ran elided words together, there was for him hardly an orthographic distinction between *Laura* and *l'aura* (breeze) or *lauro* and *l'auro* (gold). The deployment of these various kinds of metamorphosis is so ingenious that many critics have been blinded to the poetic seriousness that lies behind them.

Transformation into the laurel is a figure of sublimation, in which desire accepts an object other than its natural one; instead of Laura, the lover gets (or becomes, it amounts to the same thing) the laurel of poetic achievement and glory. The longest poem in the *Rime Sparse* is the canzone **"Nel dolce tempo de la prima etade"** (23), which a marginal note in Vat. Lat. 3196 calls "one of my earliest" ("est de primis inventionibus meis"). In a highly artificial, elaborately rhetorical style, the poem narrates the "events" of the lover's experience as reenactments of six Ovidian myths of metamorphosis. He falls in love with Laura and turns into a laurel tree like Daphne; because his overreaching hope, like Phaeton, was struck down by a thunderbolt, he turns into a swan and mourns like Cygnus; because, misled by deceptive appearances, he spoke of his love after having been forbidden, he turns to stone, like Battus; because all his pleading for mercy is to no avail, he turns to a fountain of tears, like Byblis; though mercifully restored to his own shape, he begs for mercy once more and therefore is divided into stone and a wandering voice, like Echo; finally, one day while out hunting, when the sun is hottest, he stands gazing at Laura naked in a fountain, whereupon she sprinkles his face with water, like Diana, and he is transformed into a fleeing deer, like Actaeon.

The theme of the poem is the incomprehensible changeability of the self in love, which is so violent as to call its very identity into question. The myths succeed one another in a brilliant, surrealistic superimposition of images. There is a baffling coexistence of abrupt, radical instability and of permanence and cyclicality. It is obvious that the myths were not chosen at random, and Petrarch expects the reader to know Ovid and to be alert to subtle changes. None of the myths is reenacted in its entirety or without some significant change. Petrarch's lover completes three times a cycle that takes him through falling in love, hoping and wooing, being rejected and rebuked, and finally (Cygnus, Byblis, Echo) lamenting and writing poetry. Poem 23 ends with the Actaeon myth for many reasons: it is the most violent episode in **"Nel dolce tempo"**; it is the least metaphorical, the least disguised; it allows the fullest emergence of sexual affect and acknowledges most fully the fear resulting from a sense of taboo. Furthermore, it is significant that Petrarch ends the series of transformations with one that is in process: he is still in flight.

> ch' i' senti' trarmi de la propria imago
> et in un cervo solitario et vago
> di selva in selva ratto mi trasformo
> et ancor de' miei can fuggo lo stormo.
>
> (23. 157-160)

> for *I felt myself drawn from my own image* and into a solitary wandering stage from wood to wood quickly *I am transformed* and still I flee the belling of my hounds.

"Ch' i' senti' trarmi de la propria imago" echoes the words describing the first transformation into the laurel (lines 41-45); the unusual turn of phrase of the second two lines quoted here is richly ambiguous, the shift in tenses startling.

What Petrarch has *omitted* from Ovid's myths is also part of the meaning of the poem. He has left out Daphne's sexual fear and her flight from Apollo. In Ovid's account of Actaeon, as the dogs begin to tear Actaeon to pieces he tries to call them by name, to reveal his identity; but, since he is now a stag, that is impossible, and all he can do is weep. In Ovid the myths (with the exception of that of Battus, which Petrarch skillfully adapts) are about frustrated love, about loss and refusal. With the exception of the Battus myth they take place near a body of water into which at least one of the characters gazes. With the exception of the Daphne myth they involve characters who are punished for something they have seen. All of them concern frustrated—or even disastrous—speech or writing, and in each case the speech involves deception or confusion or some question about the identity of one of the protagonists.

As Petrarch saw, the myth of Actaeon is an inversion of the myth of Daphne. In one, it is the beloved who flees, in the other the lover. In one, the end result is speech: poetry and fame; in the other, silence. In one,

there is evergreen eternizing; in the other, dismemberment. Daphne, as she runs, looks into the water and becomes a tree, takes root; Actaeon, who is standing still, branches into a stag, grows hooves, flees, sees his reflection and flees the more. These extremes are also connected in the myth of Orpheus, who was able to move rocks and trees and tame beasts; he both recalled Eurydice from death and was dismembered after losing her again (Virgil, *Georgics* 4.522: "discerptum latos iuvenem sparsere per agros"—tearing the youth apart, they scattered him across the wide fields). By beginning and ending **"Nel dolce tempo"** with Daphne and Actaeon, Petrarch paired myths that are related to the deepest preoccupations of the *Rime sparse:* dismemberment or scattering versus integration; poetic immortality versus death; the creation of poetry as an expression of the impossibility of speech resulting from sexual fear.

Thus the myths of Daphne and Actaeon are intimately connected with Petrarch's other great mythic symbol, the Medusa (Ovid's account is in *Metamorphoses* 4.617ff), whose sight turns men to stone—indeed, into marble statues, something like works of art. Traditionally, the Medusa had been variously interpreted: as a symbol of the fear that blinds the mind (Fulgentius), of lust (*Ovide moralisé*), of the power of memory (Fulgentius). Dante's *rime petrose* are based on the idea of a young woman whose heart is hard as stone; she is a "stone that speaks and has sensation as if it were a woman." This lady is associated with the influence of the cold planet, Saturn, and with the freezing of all nature in the depths of winter. If her cruelty continues long enough, she will turn the lover into a marble statue; in other words, she will be a Medusa for him, an implicit though never stated reference. A celebrated incident in the *Inferno* has Dante, outside the gates of Dis, threatened with the sight of the Medusa and only saved by turning away and covering his eyes. The interpretation of the passage is debatable; clearly the threat of despair—a fear that blinds the soul to God's mercy and deprives it of hope—is involved. Whether, as John Freccero has recently argued, a rejection by Dante of the *petrose* is also implied, there is no doubt that Petrarch did connect the *petrose* with the traditional interpretations of that his countless allusions to the *petrose* are to be connected with his references to the Medusa. The Medusan tranformation most frequently alluded to is that of Atlas. Petrarch combines references to Ovid's account with allusions to Virgil's description (*Aeneid* 4.246-251), a projection of Aeneas' immobile fixation on Dido, as in 366.111-112, where the dripping tears are suggested by the rivers in Virgil's anthropomorphic description. Petrarch's allusions to the Medusa are often implicit, as in poem 129, where they are related to the themes of memory and writing; the parallels with 125 and 126 are perhaps more obvious than the equally important connection with the myths of Daphne and Actaeon:

I' l'ò più volte (or chi fia che mi 'l
　creda?)
ne l'acqua chiara et sopra l'erba verde
veduto viva, et nel troncon d'un faggio
　e'n bianca nube, sì fatta che Leda
avria ben detto che sua figlia perde
come stella che 'l sol copre col raggio;
　et quanto in più selvaggio
loco mi trovo e'n più deserto lido,
tanto più bella il mio pensier l'adombra.
Poi quando il vero sgombra
quel dolce error, pur lì medesmo assido
me freddo, pietra morta in pietra viva,
in guisa d'uom che pensi et pianga et
　scriva.

(129.40-52)

I have many times (now who will believe me?)
seen her alive in the clear water and on the green
grass and in the trunk of a beech tree

　　and in a white cloud, so beautiful that Leda
would have said that her daughter faded like a
star covered by the sun's ray;

　　and in whatever wildest place and most
deserted shore I find myself, so much the more
beautiful does my thought shadow her forth.
Then, when the truth dispels that sweet deception,
right there in the same place I sit down, cold, a
dead stone on the living rock, like a man who
thinks and weeps and writes.

It is not merely the idea of petrifaction that establishes
the connection with the *rime petrose* and the Medusa,
it is such phrases as "sopra l'erba verde" (compare **"Al
poco giorno e al gran cerchio d'ombra,"** lines 28,
39), "stella che 'l sol copre col raggio" (**"Io son venuto
al punto de la rota,"** lines 5-6); "quando il vero sgombra
/ quel dolce error" (**"Io son venuto,"** lines 10-11);
"pur lì medesmo assido / me freddo, pietra morta in
pietra viva" (**"Amor, tu vedi ben che questa donna,"**
lines 33-34, 57; **"Al poco giorno,"** line 34). The central
idea of the passage, that meditation on Laura's image is
in tension with the wildness of the surroundings, is
related to the situation of **"Io son venuto,"** just as the
theme of the projection of the image of the lady onto
the external world is related to **"Amor, tu vedi ben
che questa donna,"** lines 40-43:

per che ne li occhi sì bella mi luce
quando la miro, ch'io la veggio in petra,
e po' in ogni altro ov' io volga mia luce.

so beautiful into my eyes she shines
when I gaze on her, that I see her in stones
and in everything else, wherever I turn my
　sight.

The lover is fascinated with the complexity of his own
psychological processes; the image that turns him to

stone in the *Rime sparse* is a projection of them onto
the outside world. The idea that the lover's fixated
gaze on the beloved turns him into a statue is emphasized in Ovid's account of Narcissus, who stares at
his image in the pool:

. . . vultuque immotus eodem
haeret, ut a Pario formatum marmore signum.
　　(*Metamorphoses* 3.418-419)

he stares unmoving on that one face, like a statue
formed of Parian marble.

This is an ultimate form of the Medusa, a perception
that hovers over the *Rime sparse,* that endlessly polished mirror of the poet's soul. The charge of a
fundamental narcissism in the collection (as in
Petrarch's entire output) would be only partially answered by the undeniable intensity of his self-criti-
cism. He rather tends to avoid making explicit the
presence of Narcissus in the mythic networks he
weaves. But the two extremes of poem 23, Daphne
and Actaeon, like the other myths in the poem,
converage on and point toward the figure of Narcissus: at the midpoint of 23 there is a curious breakdown and a decision to omit certain things (the break
occurs exactly at line 89, in the midst of the Battus
passage, where the lover is turned to stone), and
soon after he recounts how he has reenacted the
myth of Echo. But Echo, after all, wasted away because of her love for Narcissus, and the implicit
connection (Petrarch = Echo means Laura = Narcissus; if Laura's image = Narcissus' image, Petrarch =
Narcissus) is both established and evaded. In the
working papers of poem 23 there is evidence that
completing the poem was difficult for Petrarch. On
the recto of leaf 11 of Vat. Lat. 3196 lines 1-89 are
written in a book hand as a fair copy; on the verso
of leaf 11 are lines 90-169, in a cursive hand as a
working draft. The verso has seven major instances
of revision; the recto has two. The marginal notes
indicate that work on the poem continued over a
number of years. It may well be that the sensitivity
of the nexus Battus-Medusa-Narcissus-Echo (in a
poem beginning with Daphne and ending with
Actaeon) caused Petrarch's difficulty.

In any case, the myths constantly blend into one another, and Petrarch expects us to bring a detailed
knowledge of them to his poems. Poem 23 is echoed
and balanced by poem 323, which describes six em-
blematic visions of Laura's death—a deer with a human face is killed by dogs, a ship sinks suddenly, a
laurel is struck by lightning, the phoenix dies, a fountain is swallowed up by the earth, a lady is bitten in
the heel by a snake—all instances of abrupt mutability.
These myths and their order are related to those of
poem 23. Poem 323 begins with an emblem similar to
Actaeon, has the laurel at the center, and ends with a

more realistic though not less symbolic emblem (the death of Eurydice), in which, as in the last myth of 23, the pathos is allowed to come through less masked. Each of the major emblems for Laura thus at some time or other also stands for the lover, and vice versa. If Laura is the laurel, the lover turns into a laurel; if she is the beautiful deer he is hunting, he is an Actaeon (and, again, in 323 she is torn by dogs); if he becomes a fountain of tears, she is a fountain of inspiration (but is it Narcissus' pool?); if like Echo he becomes merely a voice, she dies, and he is left to imagine her voice in dreams. The myths are constantly being transformed.

To see one's experience in terms of myth is to see in the myth the possibility of the kind of allegorical meaning that was called tropological. Petrarch knew and used freely the traditional allegorical interpretations of the Ovidian myths. But he dissociated them from clear-cut moral judgments, and in this he was closer to the Dante of the *petrose* than of the *Commedia*. To say that falling in love and becoming a love poet is a transformation into a laurel tree involves the sense that the channeling of the vital energy of frustrated love into the sublimated, eternizing mode of poetry has consequences not fully subject to conscious choice or to moral judgment. For Petrarch the perfection of literary form, which exists polished and unchanging on the page in a kind of eternity, is achieved only at the cost of the poet's natural life. His vitality must be metamorphosed into words, and this process is profoundly ambiguous. If on the one hand Petrarch subscribes to—even in a sense almost singlehandedly founds—the humanistic cult of literary immortality and glory, on the other hand he has an acute awareness that writing poetry involves a kind of death. This recognition has something very modern about it; it gives a measure of the distance that separates Petrarch from Dante, who gambled recklessly on the authority his poem would have as a total integration. Petrarch is always calling attention to the psychologically relative, even suspect, origin of individual poems and thus of writing itself. His hope is that ultimately the great theme of praise will redeem even the egotism of the celebrant.

Charles Trinkaus (essay date 1979)

SOURCE: Charles Trinkaus, "Petrarch and Classical Philosophy," in *The Poet as Philosopher: Petrarch and the Formation of Renaissance Consciousness*, Yale University Press, 1979, pp. 1-26.

[*In the following excerpt, Trinkaus examines Petrarch's contributions as a philosopher and argues that his "conception of ancient philosophy was shaped by his sensibilities as a poet."*]

Petrarch's knowledge of ancient thought was amazingly extensive. Yet how he incorporated this knowl-

edge into his own philosophy is not entirely clear. De Nolhac and Sabbadini laid the foundations for our efforts to reconstruct Petrarch's classical humanism, and Billanovich, Pellegrin, and Wilkins, with major assistance from such scholars of the previous generation as Rossi and Bosco, have come close to completing the edifice.[1] But scholars continue to differ on the questions of what ideas Petrarch drew from his knowledge of ancient philosophies, and how, to what degree, and when he made use of his readings.[2]

Petrarch identified himself at various times as a poet, a historian, a rhetorician, and a moral philosopher.[3] His awareness of the classical philosophical heritage was formed by his responses to it in all of these roles. Yet the way in which his conception of ancient philosophy was shaped by his sensibilities as a poet is of special interest. It is likely that Petrarch understood classical philosophy better through Vergil and Horace than through the philosophers he came to know, which suggests that his grasp of ancient philosophy was more characteristically that of a poet than that of a historian. It also suggests that it was possibly through the medium of his poetic understanding of ancient thought that he was incited to conceive and fulfill the roles of both rhetorician and moral philosopher.

Petrarch's kind of poetry had a special relationship to the new mode of philosophical consciousness that was emerging in the Renaissance to which he made so important a contribution. Aristotle, in explaining his famous claim that poetry is more philosophical than history, said that the philosophical character of poetry may be seen in the universal nature of its statements, "whereas those of history are singulars."[4] We must recognize the universality of Petrarch's poetry. Yet we must recognize its subjectivity as well. His use of emotional experience, the recreation in emotion of that experience, and the imagined prolongation and projection of it in the **Canzoniere** underline the difference between his poetry and the kind Aristotle discussed. It is not enough to say that Petrarch's verse was lyric, and hence more personal, whereas Aristotle was referring to epic and dramatic, and thus more objectified poetry. Petrarch's great achievement was that he realized poetic objectivity through the medium of subjective experience.

To say that Petrarch thought philosophically as a poet is not to minimize his importance as a philosopher but to point out his unique mode of thinking. Petrarch's work, whether poetic, historical, or philosophical, is of critical importance as the first major manifestation of the great transformation from the objective mode of classical thought and perception to the subjective Renaissance and modern modes.[5] While many questions remain concerning the character and the extent of such a shift in the basic conceptions of Western art and thought, Petrarch gave a powerful impulse to the movement toward subjectivity.

Under this large assumption about the differences in basic patterns of thought and perception in the ancient and modern worlds, Petrarch's manifold contradictions seem to fall neatly into place. But it is far too neat. It is like saying that we are all romantics in our modern retrospective classicism, since we regard antiquity through the screen of our own affections and imaginations, imitating it and idealizing it because of our own needs and motivations. We view it as at once distant and highly relevant, a historical perspective that Petrarch helped to shape. This insight, stressed by Panofsky, is true in a sense, but it threatens to dissolve amidst our own subjectivity. Not all of modern thought and perception is subjective; otherwise we could not make claims to science or to scholarly understanding. Even Petrarch helped develop the "objective" study of antiquity. On the other hand, not all ancient thought and perception was substantive and objectivistic. Important aspects of it, and especially much of what attracted Petrarch, pointed the way toward more modern modalities.[6]

[Petrarch's] inclination was to value philosophy primarily for its contribution to the strengthening of human virtue. The tendency of contemporary scholasticism was to regard discussions of substantive questions in theology as of limited viability and, almost by default, to move toward the exegetical and pastoral. Petrarch expressed great suspicion regarding both the emphasis on dialectical analysis and the interest in Aristotelian natural philosophy of his contemporaries. He seems, however, to have had a rather scanty knowledge of medieval philosophy. He was certainly not very sympathetic to the possibility that the vogue for dialectic in fourteenth-century scholastic thought might have represented a parallel development to his desire to consider philosophical thought as humanly centered and motivated.[7] Petrarch also seems not to have been aware of those fourteenth-century contributions to natural philosophy that represented experimental departures, however limited, from an all-determining Aristotelian physical framework. It is Petrarch's knowledge of ancient philosophy, however, that is my main concern here.

The philosophical thought of the ancient Greeks and Romans is an enormous, highly diverse body of material. It is now known only through those texts that survived in medieval manuscripts or have been recovered from papyri in the past century. These texts are supplemented by descriptive accounts by other ancient authors and modern collections of scattered quotations from ancient, early Christian, Syriac, Arabic, Jewish, and Byzantine writers. It is tempting to make use of modern scholarship and historical sophistication to give a single characterization to this diverse

mass (as Cranz has so suggestively done; see note 5). But this is clearly a risky undertaking. Some portions of ancient philosophy are rather well known, possibly even understood by modern historians and philosophers. But others, even when reported to be of the greatest importance in antiquity, are unknown, or hardly known. A further element of complication is that ancient philosophical writings contain much that is religious, magical, scientific, literary, critical, and rhetorical, while ancient writings in these other disciplines also contain much that is philosophical.

Ancient philosophy as it is presently known includes the partially understood pre-Socratic speculators concerned with the cosmos and the "nature" of things— the *physici*. Also identified are the equally poorly understood teachers of political discourse whom we call, by their own designation, the *sophistes*. Some Sophists claimed inspiration from contemporary Greek tragedy and traced their ancestry through the poetic tradition back as far as Homer and Hesiod. They were not only admirers of tragedy; their ideas are reflected in Euripides and mocked in Aristophanes. The *physici* preceded and were contemporary with the Sophists, some of whom had studied under and been influenced by them. The *physici,* conventionally divided into Ionians and Eleatics, seem to have followed our loose distinction between empiricists and metaphysicians, though this seems to dissolve in almost every instance thought to be adequately understood. The Sophists seem to have drawn from both the empirical and metaphysical traditions of the pre-Socratics.

Petrarch, of course, knew far less about either the *physici* or the Sophists than do modern scholars. For the most part, he scattered references through his works and his correspondence to sayings or anecdotes of an early Greek or other ancient thinker which helped to reinforce or exemplify his point rhetorically. Of the pre-Socratics, Petrarch devotes greatest attention to Pythagoras and Heraclitus. Pythagoras he knows only as a sage, moral reformer, and orator, but he cites him frequently because of his great reputation for wisdom in the later ancient sources with which Petrarch was familiar.[8] He knows something of Heraclitus's ideas from Seneca and therefore as the Stoics had interpreted him for their own purposes, but he used these ideas more substantively. He cites Heraclitus twice to assert the chaotic and fluctuating character of the world of human experience under the domination of fortune, once at the beginning of book 2 of the *De remediis* and again at the beginning of book 2 of his *De otio religioso*.[9] Valerius Maximus's *Factorum et dictorum memorabilium libri* was a major source for the anecdotes and sayings of others. The writings of Cicero, Seneca, Aulus Gellius, and Macrobius also served him well.

Petrarch hardly seems to have known of the Sophists except as enemies of Socrates and Plato, mentioning

Gorgias's great age[10] and quoting Protagoras as Pythagoras (though significantly).[11] The name "Sophist" he reserves for the scholastic dialecticians and natural philosphers of his day, the twisters of truth and vendors of learning. Socrates was admired by the humanists principally for the emphasis he placed on man and for his self-knowledge, education, and morality. The modern dispute about whether Socrates must also be seen as a Sophist or as Plato portrays him, their archenemy, had little meaning for the Renaissance humanists.[12]

Petrarch, however, is surprisingly uninterested in Socrates, even considering the paucity of his available knowledge. With all his yearning to know Plato, he seems to have seriously studied only the Calcidius partial translation of the *Timaeus,* though he also possessed a copy of the Henricus Aristippus translation of the *Phaedo* (BN. lat. 6567A).[13] For his scattered anecdotal references to Socrates, Petrarch resorts to Valerius Maximus, Cicero, and Apuleius's *De deo Socratis,* slender pickings to be sure. There is little expression in Petrarch of the strenuous admiration that Salutati and other humanists showed for Socrates. The crucial and much quoted statement from Cicero's *Tusculan Disputations*[14]—"But Socrates was the first who brought down philosophy from the heavens and, snatched from the stars, forced it to live on earth among men and to deal with morals and the affairs of men"—was curiously cited in a letter to Gerardo as an example of how philosophers ridiculed each other. He refers to Aristotle's ridicule, cited in Cicero's *De officiis,*[15] of Isocrates (misreading the name as "Socrates") for his mercenary behavior.

It might seem that Petrarch's affirmations of the importance of moral philosophy would have made him more responsive to Socrates. His admiration of Cicero would seemingly have led him to note Cicero's addition to the passage just cited from the *Tusculans:* "I have principally adhered to that (sect) which, in my opinion, Socrates himself followed: and argue so as to conceal my own opinions, while I deliver others from their errors, and so discover what has the greatest appearance of probability in every question . . ." Petrarch only rarely refers to the passage in the *Academica*[16] where Socrates is asserted to have been the first to discuss moral philosophy and to have affirmed "nothing himself but to refute others, to assert that he knows nothing except the fact of his own ignorance." Toward the end of *On His Own Ignorance* he does cite Socrates' "This one thing I know, that I know nothing," and adds to it Arcesilas's saying that "even this knowing nothing cannot be known" (both passages are apparently drawn from the *Academica*), but his purpose is to reject or ridicule this attitude along with a general condemnation of philosophy. "A glorious philosophy, this, that either

confesses ignorance or precludes even the knowledge of this ignorance."[17]

Nonetheless the general influence of Socrates on this work cannot be excluded. Though different in tone and method from the *Dialogues,* Petrarch built it around the ironic stance of his own acknowledged ignorance and the unacknowledged ignorance of many others. This stance he might well have borrowed from Socrates. He at least understood the rhetorical impact of this posture, although he had not been able to read Plato's *Apology* and did not indicate his Socratic model. Yet he used this ploy to draw conclusions similar to those that Plato perhaps intended for Socrates' defense. It is one of several examples where Petrarch employs classical models in order to assert or discover his own cultural identity through an act of role playing.

Petrarch wrote four comments on Socrates in his *Rerum memorandarum libri* which show him to have been aware early in his philosophical career of the chief anecdotes about Socrates and his reputation. Under the rubric **"On Leisure and Solitude"**[18] he briefly cites the anecdote from Cicero's *De senectute*[19] about Socrates as an old man learning to play the lyre. In the next rubric, **"On Study and Learning,"** he repeats the topos of Socrates having brought learning down to earth and turned it from the dimensions of the heavens to the interior of the human heart. "Beginning to treat of the diseases and motions of the soul and of their remedies and the virtues, he was the *primus artifex* of moral philosophy, and as Valerius said, *'vite magister optimus'*."[20] Skipping the third, his fourth item under **"On Oracles"** is equally brief. He narrates from Cicero's *De divinatione* Socrates' advice to Xenophon to join the expedition of Cyrus and his adjunct that this was a human counsel and that in the case of more obscure matters he should consult the oracle. However, Petrarch misread "Epicurus" for Cyrus and proceeded to berate Socrates for being an Epicurean. "But how much better you were and of how much sounder counsel than he to whom you sent your disciple, except in this one matter that he seemed to you the best and most advisable [leader]."[21] Apart from the extraordinary anachronism, one may wonder how Socrates could possibly have seemed an influence in the direction of Epicurus to Petrarch.

His major discussion of Socrates in the *Rerum memorandarum libri* was under **"On Wisdom,"** cataloguing sayings of the wise. Though it may not eliminate a suspicion that Petrarch was somewhat lukewarm in his admiration of Socrates because of his seeming scepticism, Petrarch lays forth his amplification of Valerius Maximus's essentially moralistic and Stoic version. He starts with the Socratic advice to seek nothing from the gods except what truly benefits us and expands the sparse treatment of this theme by his source into a favorite review of all the evils of a

Christian's false desires. But he uses as his model not Socrates but the tenth *Satire* of Juvenal.[22] He seems here to have copied his own earlier letter (*Le familiari,* 4.2 and Gamma) which uses the Juvenal passage as well as Cicero and Seneca. Other moral anecdotes or sayings of Socrates are added, drawn from Seneca's *Ad Lucillium,* Aulus Gellius, and Valerius Maximus.

It is difficult to account for Petrarch's rather conventional and not particularly enthusiastic treatment of Socrates. There are undoubtedly other references I have not cited, but those I have cited show his knowledge to have been thirdhand, deriving from Plato or Xenophon through Cicero or Seneca. But perhaps the main reason for Petrarch's lack of enthusiasm is that essentially he knows the sceptical Socrates of his Latin sources and not the religious philosopher embedded in Plato's *Dialogues.*

With Plato himself it was quite different.[23] Petrarch possessed the medieval Latin Plato—Calcidius's partial translation of the *Timaeus,*[24] Henricus Aristippus's translation of the *Phaedo,* and probably the latter's *Meno.*[25] He owned a large Greek manuscript of some of Plato's works which he hoped to be able to read after he had learned Greek, but this enterprise ended with the premature departure of Barlaam of Calabria. A list of its contents reveals what he could have known had he been able to read Greek: the *Clitophon,* the *Republic,* the *Timaeus,* the *Critias,* the *Minos,* the *Laws,* the *Phaedrus, Letters.* In addition it contained *Diffinitiones Platonis, Confabulationes Platonis, Demodocus de consilio, Critias de Divitiis,* and *Axiochus de morte.*[26] In his ***De ignorantia*** Petrarch refers to this manuscript to indicate the extensiveness of Plato's writings, disdained by his young critics as "one or two small little books." Petrarch says with his usual numerical looseness, "I have sixteen or more of Plato's books at home, of which I do not know whether they have heard the names." He also says that if they come to his house, "these literate men will see not only several Greek writings but also some which are translated into Latin all of which they have never seen elsewhere."[27] It is questionable whether Petrarch possessed some new Latin translations of works of Plato other than the medieval three.

Petrarch's comments on Plato in ***De ignorantia*** and the ***Rerum memorandarum libri*** show great admiration. How much did he actually know of Plato's philosophic doctrines? References to his copy of the *Phaedo* are rare. Identifiable references usually come from Cicero's *Tusculan Disputations.*[28] His knowledge of metempsychosis is not specifically related to the *Phaedo.* Comments on the divisions of the soul are based on those attributed to Plato by Cicero. In the ***Secretum*** "Augustinus" alludes to Plato's statement of the progression of desire from sensual to heavenly in the *Symposium* (which Petrarch could not have read).

But this alludes also to St. Augustine's discussion in the *Confessions.*[29] **"Augustinus"** also cites Plato more directly: "For what else does the celestial doctrine of Plato admonish except that the soul should be pushed away from the lusts of the body, and their images eradicated so that purely and rapidly it may arise toward a deeper vision of the secrets of divinity, to which contemplation of one's own mortality is rightly attached?" This is an authentic echo of the *Phaedo,* and "Franciscus" at this point acknowledges that he has begun to read Plato, but the loss of his tutor in Greek has interrupted him.[30] In the *Secretum* **"Augustinus"** quotes the *Phaedrus,* not read by Petrarch: the poet "beats in vain on the doors of poetry if he is in his right mind."[31] This is certainly a commonplace in many Latin sources.

Petrarch mentions the doctrine of ideas, which he must have known from Cicero's *Tusculans* and elsewhere, in the ***De vita solitaria.*** But it is based on another source of medieval and early Renaissance Platonism, Macrobius's *In somnium Scipionis.*[32] Plotinus, rather than Plato, is cited, and the hierarchy of the virtues is set forth—political, purgative, purged (acquired in solitude), and the fourth and highest, "archetypal," or "exemplary." "Hence the [Platonists] hold that the three other kinds of human virtue originate as though from some eternal exemplar, just as the name itself indicates; or, as Plato would say, from the ideas of the virtues which, like the ideas of other things, he placed in the mind of God."[33] Despite his professed yearning to know Plato, Petrarch makes little use of the *Phaedo* on the questions that interested him most. He infrequently repeats even the commonplaces widely disseminated in Latin sources concerning the teachings of Plato.

Petrarch's most extensive statement about Plato runs for five pages in book 1, chapter 25, of his ***Rerum memorandarum libri,*** under the rubric **"On Study and Learning."**[34] He sketches Plato's life, drawing principally on Apuleius's *De Platone et eius dogmate,* with additions from Cicero and Macrobius. Again following Apuleius, Petrarch summarizes Plato's teachings. It turns out to be a catalogue of topics (discussed at greater length by Apuleius): matter, ideas, the world, the soul, nature, time, the wandering stars, animals, providence, fate, demons, fortune, the parts of the soul and the bodily domicile, the senses, the shape of the human body and the arrangement of its parts, the division of goods, virtues, the three kinds of minds, the three causes for seeking the good, pleasure, labor, friendship and enmity, degraded love, the three loves, the species of human faults, the condition, customs, and death of the sage, the commonwealth, and the republic, its customs and best laws. In Apuleius, he says, the reader will find all these matters treated in succinct brevity and not at all unpleasantly.[35] It suggests the medieval taste for encyclopedic epitomes and the compilation of rhetorical *loci communes.*

Petrarch's more pressing concern is to show Plato's compatibility with Christianity. Unlike Aristotle, Plato taught the creation, not the eternity, of the world (though in this Apuleius seems to differ from Cicero). Petrarch hoped here to cite only secular authors, but finds he cannot and switches to St. Augustine. A question arose that was to surface again with Ficino, Pico, and the other Renaissance Platonists: How did Plato arrive at his anticipations of Christianity, and should he, rather than Christ, be given credit for these doctrines? Petrarch cites Augustine's *De doctrina Christiana* (2.28.43) to the effect that Plato was a contemporary of the prophet Jeremiah and had learned of at least the pre-Christian truths of the Hebrews on his journey to Egypt. But then he cites Augustine's own correction of this tale in *De civitate Dei* (8.1 1), where he asserts that Plato and Jeremiah were not contemporaries and that Plato also lived before the Septuagint translation of the Old Testament had been made. Hence these truths must have been made manifest by God to Plato, as St. Paul argued in Romans 1:19. Thus Plato is made the equivalent of the Renaissance Platonists' *priscus theologus,* or else he discovered these truths by colloquy with someone versed in Hebrew letters. Except on the question of the incarnation, Petrarch advises a reading of Augustine's *Confessions* to see the extent of the parity between Plato and Christianity.[36] Petrarch asserts that as had been said of Carneades, for Plato there was but a single end for both philosophizing and living. This seems to have been basic to Petrarch's conception of philosophy.[37]

Petrarch perhaps most eloquently praises Plato in the *De ignorantia*. It is a rhetorical statement that does not enter into the substance of either the philosophy of Plato or of Aristotle, whom he is denouncing. Plato has been called the prince of philosophy. By whom? Cicero, Vergil, Pliny, Plotinus, Apuleius, Macrobius, Porphyry, Censorinus, Josephus, Ambrose, Augustine, Jerome, and others. Who denies this glory to him? Only Averroës. But there is also the question of weight as well as numbers. Here, too, Plato excels. "I would state without hesitation that in my opinion the difference between them is like that between two persons of whom one is praised by princes and nobles, the other by the entire mass of the common people. Plato is praised by the greater men, Aristotle by the bigger crowd; and both deserve to be praised by great men as well as by many, even by all men." Both came far in natural and human matters, but the Platonists rose higher in divine, and Plato came nearer to our goal. Hence the Greeks today call Plato divine and Aristotle "demonious."[38] Petrarch then cites the large number of books written by Plato, attested by his own Greek manuscript.

The situation with Aristotle is very different. Petrarch seems to have known both the *Nicomachean Ethics*

and the *Rhetoric* fairly well, judging by the nature of his citations of them. Only one Aristotle manuscript, however, can be identified as Petrarch's own, an *Ethica* with commentaries (BN lat. 6458, with scarce annotations). This led De Nolhac to comment, "But the manuscript at least establishes, for reasons that we have said, that Petrarch studied Aristotle but little."[39] It is not certain that this is true. Petrarch at least seems to have read Aristotle and used him for a commonplace book, as he did certain Latin authors. Nor does the manuscript show the kind of overt hostility to Aristotle in the use of his sayings that other passages on him have led us to expect.

This essentially rhetorical use of Aristotle for purposes of argumentation can be seen in *Le familiari* and the *Invective contra medicum*. A key statement in the *Ethics* (1103 B 28) is that "we are inquiring not in order to know what virtue is, but in order to become good." This would seem to have found much favor with Petrarch, and he affirms it as applying to himself. Petrarch denies that Aristotle actually observes this criterion in his great polemic against Aristotle and Aristotelians, the *De ignorantia*.[40] Twice he uses Aristotle's advice that faults of one extreme must be corrected by leaning to the other, "as people do in straightening sticks that are bent" (1109 B 4-7). He does this once in admonishing the four cardinals on how to reform the contemporary Romans, and once in fictitiously admonishing Julius Caesar.[41] Aristotle, discussing deliberation as an intellectual virtue, points out that the end of the investigation is the discovery of the beginning or the first cause: "What is last in the order of analysis seems to be first in the order of becoming" (1112 B 23-24). Petrarch in a brief note to a close friend uses this statement merely to suggest that he has finally got around to writing. Just as it pleases the philosophers, he who is first in deliberating is last in performing—certainly a loose proverbializing of an originally serious philosophical point.[42]

Petrarch suggests to a friend that the day of birth may be worse than the day of death, as the one brings sorrows and the other joys. "But lest we should depart from the opinions of the vulgar—from whom, nevertheless, if we should progress toward salvation, how far we must part—it is said that death is to be feared, and that most widely repeated saying of Aristotle is heard, 'death is the ultimate of terrible things.'" Aristotle was discussing courage (1115 A 27), and death is the greatest of the terrible things a man must face. But Petrarch adds, twisting Aristotle's meaning, "He, himself, also deliberately wished to call it, not the greatest but the last." There follows a long list of heroic ancient deaths and misfortunes to show, no doubt, how terrible is this world.[43]

Petrarch turns another citation from the *Ethics* to his advantage in the *Invective contra medicum*. His basic argument is that medicine is less honorable than poetry because it is more necessary, and thus it is comparable to agriculture. To make his point he cites Aristotle's discussion of justice, where an equality of exchange between two mutually needy persons, each of whom has something the other wishes, must take place: "For it is not two doctors that associate for exchange, but a doctor and a farmer" (1113 A 17-78). Petrarch says, "I do not wish to insult you that I place you and farmers together, Aristotle does the same. . . . I believe that on account of reverence for Aristotle you have allowed this to be suffered in silence."[44]

In our final example, Petrarch seems to have applied the *Nicomachean Ethics* to a more comparable argument. In **Le familiari** 8.3, he is discussing the relative advantages of places to live. "The crowd thinks even philosophers and poets are hard and stony, but in this as in so many things they are mistaken, for they also are of flesh, they retain humanity, they abandon pleasures. Moreover, it is a certain measure of necessity, whether philosophic or poetic, which it is suspected they pass by. 'Nature,' as Aristotle says, 'is not sufficient by itself for speculation but also needs a sound body, and food, and the other means of existence.'"[45] So also says Aristotle in his discussion of the greater happiness of the life of contemplation (1178 B 34-35).

Petrarch cites the *Metaphysics* several times, though entirely from book 1. Twice he interprets Aristotle as saying that the first theologians were poets, because this fits the notion of *theologia poetica* he is promoting in competition with scholastic theology. In the **Invective** the reference (to *Metaph.* 983 B 28) is vague: "Certainly the first theologians among the pagans were poets as the greatest of the philosophers and the authority of the saints confirm."[46] In the well-known letter to Gerardo analyzing his own eclogue as a form of theology, Petrarch first refers to the use of allegory in Scripture as poetry and suggests that the pagan poets do the same—that is, mean God and divine matters when they speak of gods and heroes—"whence also we read in Aristotle that the first poets were theologians."[47] Aristotle, no doubt thinking of Homer, says, "Some think that even the ancients who lived long before the present generation, and first framed accounts of the gods, had a similar view of nature (to Thales'); for they made Ocean and Tethys the parents of creation. . . ." But as E. R. Curtius pointed out, Aristotle is trying to discuss the origins of natural philosophy and not theology.[48] In the **Invective** Petrarch refers to his medical opponent's criticism that even Aristotle reprehended the poets for their arrogance which aroused the envy of the gods. This, at least, seems to be the argument he refers to. But Petrarch's answer is equally vague because, he says, he does not have the *Metaphysics* with him at Vaucluse. Petrarch does not find it agreeable to scold the poets for their liberty of speech or to excuse the envy of the gods,

but he assumes his enemy does not cite this passage any more accurately than he does others.[49] Aristotle, of course, argues that the gods cannot be jealous of philosophers, as the poets suggest, since to engage in the study of metaphysics is divine and honorable because it deals with divine matters.

Whether he had his *Metaphysics* at Vaucluse when writing his **Invective** or not, Petrarch certainly knew this passage. He refers at least twice to its concluding line: "All the sciences are more necessary than this but none is better." This is a basic argument of his invective, that medicine is not of greater dignity than poetry (or philosophy) because it is more necessary, but that the reverse is true. The less the necessity the greater the nobility and dignity of an art or a science. He pursues the same argument in **Le familiari** (1.12), which according to Billanovich was apparently composed not long before the **Invective** of 1353,[50] and in which he refutes the fictitious old dialectician who argued that Petrarch's art, by which Petrarch guesses he means poetry, is the least necessary of all. This Petrarch gladly admits, for poetry is written for delight and beauty, not out of necessity. His opponent's argument makes all the most sordid, necessary things the most noble. As he would have it, "Philosophy and all the other arts which in any way make life happy, civilized and beautiful, if they confer nothing to the necessities of the vulgar, they are ignoble. O new and exotic doctrine unknown also to him whose name they celebrate, Aristotle! For he said: 'Necessariores quidem omnes, dignior vero nulla.'"[51] He is equally sharp toward his medical opponent: "Impudent idiot, you always have Aristotle in your mouth. . . . He certainly did not approve of your little conclusion where he said 'All others indeed more necessary, none, indeed, more worthy! I do not indicate the place, for it is a most famous place, and to a famous Aristotelian!'"[52]

Clearly, Petrarch uses Aristotle for essentially rhetorical, not philosophical, purposes. Yet he agrees with a basic philosophical attitude of Aristotle's—the superiority of the liberal arts, particularly philosophy and poetry, over the mechanical. This is specifically illustrated in the principle of the inverse ratio of necessity and nobility. Petrarch also knows and uses the *Rhetoric*, sometimes disagreeing with Aristotle's assertions. He draws on the discussions in books 2 and 3 of the emotions to which the orator appeals and of the problem of style. Petrarch particularly chides his medical foe, who professes to understand rhetoric and poetry, for his ignorance of Aristotle's *Rhetoric, Poetics,* and *De poetis*.[53] The latter two Petrarch obviously knew of but could not have seen.

Petrarch's statements against Aristotle in **De ignorantia** may now be placed in better perspective. It is not so much Aristotle but the cult of Aristotle that he is attacking. All pagan philosophers are to be condemned equally for their non-Christian statements, made from ignorance. Aristotle is neither better nor worse than Plato in this respect. Petrarch revealingly says of his young friends that they "are so captivated by their love for the mere name 'Aristotle' that they call it a sacrilege to pronounce any opinion which differs from his on any matter." Petrarch's so-called "ignorance" may be due to his inadvertent differences from Aristotle, or to the problem of stating the same view with different words. "The majority of the ignorant lot cling to words . . . and believe that a matter cannot be better said and cannot be phrased otherwise: so great is the destitution of their intellect or of their speech, by which their conceptions are expressed."[54] Petrarch adds (as he did in his entry on Aristotle under **"On Eloquence"** in his ***Rerum memorandarum libri***) that he cannot understand how Aristotle has such a bad style when Cicero had praised its sweetness. Not knowing that Cicero refers to Aristotle's dialogues, he thinks the poor quality of the translations into Latin has destroyed Aristotle's style. His contemporary Aristotelians, "whereas they can in no way be similar to Aristotle himself of whom they are always speaking, attempt to render him similar to themselves, saying that he, as a man who sought after the highest matters, was contemptuous of any eloquence, as if no splendor of speech can dwell in high matters, when on the contrary a high style is most fitting to a sublime science."[55]

The ***De ignorantia*** makes clear Petrarch's preference for "our Latin writers"—Cicero, Seneca, and Horace—who have "the words that sting and set afire and urge toward love of virtue and hatred of vice."[56] Despite his interest, albeit wavering, in the Greek philosophers, Petrarch fundamentally prefers the Latin tradition. He is basically concerned with rhetoric and not philosophy as we and the ancients know it.

It is impossible to review in detail the enormous influence and use in his writings of the works of the two Latins who had any claim to be called philosophers—Cicero and Seneca. In Umberto Bosco's magnificent (though still not entirely complete) index to *Le familiari,* Petrarch's citations of Cicero far exceed those of any other writer.[57] The *Tusculan Disputations* is the most cited single work of Cicero. Petrarch's interest in this work and in Seneca (and there is a marked predominance of citations from the *Epistulae ad Lucilium*) shows his concentration on consolatory Stoicism. Roman Stoicism, although differing significantly in the two versions presented by Cicero and Seneca, retains the common hortatory emphasis on the classical goal of moral autonomy. This, it seems, was central for Petrarch.

The most important idea Petrarch got from classical philosophy was the notion of pyschic and moral self-

sufficiency. He could have drawn equivalent ideas from Plato's image of Socrates but did not, either through unwillingness or inability. He surely encountered the notion in the *Nicomachean Ethics,* but it was here entangled with the more mundane aim of securing a sufficiency of external goods to ensure the virtuous man's performance of his moral and civic duties. Cicero's exposition of Panaetius's views in the *De officiis* and of Posidonius's (presumably) in the *De natura deorum* set the problem in the same framework. Hence Petrarch's lesser use of these works. Significantly, in **On His Own Ignorance,** he discusses the *De natura deorum,* particularly Balbus's exposition of Stoicism. But rightly unsure of how much of these views to attribute to Cicero, Petrarch plays up the emphasis on Providence. He fails to find in it the magnificent paean to the rational powers of man that had once so appealed to Lactantius and would again to Giannozzo Manetti.[58]

As Petrarch does not see this concern for moral autonomy as necessarily a pagan position opposing the Christian doctrines of grace and justification, he comfortably engages in a series of role identifications or philosophical experimentations. It is here that the claim that Petrarch engages in philosophy as a poet finds its principal basis. His doctrine of imitation—that one should penetrate to the essence of a model and then benefit from it in a totally original and autonomous way—is familiar. In his invectives and his letters he sought to emulate but not ape Cicero and thought that even in his retirement and love of solitude he was following Cicero's example of composing his moral treatises in his country retreats. With Seneca the role playing becomes even more explicit, in Petrarch's conception of himself as a lay counselor and moral adviser, particularly through his letters and in his use of the pseudo-Senecan *De remediis fortuitarum* as a model for his own ***De remediis utriusque fortunae.*** He explicitly played the role of St. Augustine in the ***Secretum,*** but in this work it is "Franciscus" who plays the part of St. Augustine, while "Augustinus" is developed as a kind of Christian Seneca. Seneca is even more central to the ***De vita solitaria*** than the directly attributed citations indicate, as passage after passage echoes the letters and moral dialogues of the Latin sage. I have already suggested that although the evidence is not explicit, his ironic plea of ignorance in ***De ignorantia*** can be conceived as analogous to Socrates' profession that he was wisest of all because he knew nothing.[59]

It is particularly in connection with the ***Secretum*** and the ***De remediis*** that the question of Petrarch's concept of moral autonomy needs to be discussed. Klaus Heitmann in his study of the ***De remediis*** and in subsequent articles on the ***Secretum*** is deeply concerned with his seeming lack of discrimination between Stoicism and Aristotelianism and even sometimes Christianity, though he strongly affirms Petrarch's ultimate Christian orthodoxy.[60] So also notes Bobbio in her study of Seneca and Petrarch.[61] Yet Petrarch in his personal experience of *accidia* or despair and in his sense of its omnipresence in his contemporaries turned to the elaboration of a theology of *sola gratia*—salvation by grace alone.[62] Time and again he repudiates the classical notion, particularly as it is stated by Cicero, that man's virtuousness is in his own hands, whereas we must thank the gods, or fortune, or providence for our material well-being. Petrarch could not be more emphatic in repudiating virtue as the sole or the supreme goal in life. He does, however, see a link between the attainment of moral autonomy in this life and the desire, faith in, and hope for the grace that can lift the Christian out of his condition of despair and grant him the necessary justification for salvation. It is the role of the writer, the poet, the philosopher, the moral counselor, the rhetor to assist the ordinary man by exposition and exhortation to detach himself from his alienating and self destructive involvement in the affairs of the world.

Reason (*Ratio*) in the **De remediis** counsels *Dolor* and *Superbia* to find their own moral center when bad or good fortune leads them to succumb emotionally with elation or fear to the uncontrollable flow of events as they impinge upon each individual. The self-integrating attitude he urges is a psychological, emotional, and moral detachment but not a withdrawal. Only the man who achieves this moral autonomy can even enter into the economy of grace and salvation.

Seneca, too, understood that the formal rigidities of Stoic doctrine were inapplicable to case after case of actual life. Like other Stoic moralists, he devised a casuistry that would alleviate the strictness of the code. In Seneca, there is a rhetorical convergence with Aristotle's more principled stress on the need for external goods. Petrarch could easily follow the example of Seneca rhetorically, as he could follow Cicero in his Academic affirmation that a rigid philosophical or moral rule was not essential.

Thus Petrarch, with all the inadequacies and defects of his knowledge of classical philosophy, managed to intuit and to adapt to the needs of his own religion and age perhaps antiquity's greatest moral insight—the ideal of selfsufficiency or *autarkeia*. In a syncretic way, Petrarch was able to unify opposing schools of philosophy, and even Sophists, rhetors and philosophers, through the writings of Cicero and Seneca. With the models of St. Augustine and St. Jerome before him, he could see how Platonism, Stoicism, and Ciceronian rhetoric could be drawn upon to serve and clarify the Christian goal of salvation. Like Augustine, he was aware of the differences between pagan and Christian doctrine and alert to the dangers of a failure to discriminate. But with his deep appreciation and understanding of this central insight drawn from classical moral philosophy, he was able to adapt, transform, and apply it to the new moral and religious situation of the later Middle Ages. Petrarch himself thus became a paradigm for posterity and thereby guided the transformation of late medieval culture into that of the Renaissance.

If Petrarch through his poetry "became a spiritual individual and recognized himself as such" (Burckhardt), he tried to persuade others to do so through his letters and treatises based on classical moral philosophy. In this way the poet became a philosopher and sought to make his own subjective insights universal. Through establishing the centrality of his own and every other man's subjectivity, he laid the basis for much of modern philosophy and spirituality—except for modern natural science, which has grown out of the great rival of Petrarch's world view, late medieval natural philosophy. The poet describing what the human condition *might be* becomes the philosopher making subjective statements concerning individuals that simultaneously acquire the nature of universals. And this is what Petrarch meant when he thought of himself as a *poeta theologicus*.

Notes

[1] I refer here to the names of some of the greatest Petrarch scholars. For full references to the works of these authors, see List of Works Cited. To the names of Nolhac, Sabbadini, Rossi, Bosco, Billanovich, Pellegrin, and Wilkins, there should certainly be added Guido Martellotti and B. L. Ullman. See under "Petrarca" and "Studies."

[2] Cf. the following, which concern Petrarch's "inconsistencies": Klaus Heitmann, "Augustins Lehre," "L'insegnamento agostiniano," and *Fortuna und Virtus;* Hans Baron, "The Evolution of Petrarch's Thought," "Petrarch's *Secretum,"* and "Petrarch: His Inner Struggles"; Jerrold E. Seigel, *Rhetoric and Philosophy,* chap. 2, "Ideals of Eloquence and Silence in Petrarch." I have tried to resolve some of the dilemmas in "Petrarch: Man between Despair and Grace," chap. 1 of *Image.*

[3] Cf. P. O. Kristeller, "Il Petrarca, l'umanesimo e la scolastica."

[4] *Poetica,* 1451a-b. (Bywater trans.)

[5] More than twenty years ago, Leo Spitzer showed how the Latin verse of Pontano and Poliziano broke out of the mold of antiquity, unable to dispel the personal lyric quality so freely evident in their Italian poems, despite their classicizing aims and conscious imitations. See his "Latin Renaissance Poetry." Edward Cranz has more recently stressed a similar transformation of the philosophical perceptions of antiquity

and early Christianity in the High and late Middle Ages, and specifically in Petrarch; see "Cusanus" and "1100 A.D." Professor Cranz is currently preparing a major study of this theme which is briefly summarized in these papers.

[6] A good antidote to the objectivistic stereotype of the classical mentality is the comprehensive survey of Rodolfo Mondolfo, *La Comprensione del soggetto.* For Petrarch's contribution to the scholarly study of antiquity, see Billanovich, "Petrarch and the Textual Tradition of Livy," and Roberto Weiss, *Renaissance Discovery,* 30-38. For Panofsky's thesis concerning the Renaissance view of antiquity, see *Renaissance and Renascences,* 108-13 and passim.

[7] The use of dialectic seems to have been resorted to by many thinkers to compensate for their loss of confidence in the reliability of metaphysical speculation. They, as the humanists after them, sought to make precise statements about the relationship of thought to perception and language rather than sweeping assertions about what, in their view, could be known only vaguely.

[8] He scatters twelve references to anecdotes and sayings through *Le familiari.* There are two entries on Pythagoras in his *Rer. mem.;* they closely follow Justin, *Epitome;* Cicero, *Tusc.* 5. 3-4, and *De inven.* 2.1.

[9] Cf. *Image,* 49, 195-96, 343 nn. 103-05, 400 n. 38; *De rem.* in *Op. om.,* 121-25; *De otio,* 59-60. Cf. Seneca, *Epist.,* 58. 23.

[10] *Rer. fam.,* 6. 3. 17.

[11] Nachod, 125. Cf. *Image,* 50.

[12] Ancient historians have recently given greater recognition to the Sophists. They are frequently designated as the founders of ancient humanism or of the humanist tradition. Whether the rather scanty knowledge of and interest in the Sophists on the part of Renaissance humanists can be accounted for is not of present concern. But there is no doubt that the humanists followed Cicero in considering Socrates as the true founder of their own tradition. What they would have thought of the Sophists if they had possessed or known of Cicero's lost translation of Plato's *Protagoras* cannot be said. See Werner Jaeger, *Paideia,* vol. 1, book 2, chap. 3, "The Sophists"; W. K. C. Guthrie, *Greek Philosophy,* vol. 3, part 1, "The World of the Sophists"; Mario Untersteiner, *The Sophists.* On Renaissance humanists and the Sophists, see my "Protagoras in the Renaissance."

[13] Pellegrin, *La bibliothèque,* 105, lists no. 148 of the 1426 inventory of the Visconti-Sforza Library (*Phedon Platonis*) as Paris, BN. lat. 6567A. Cf. L. Minio-Paluello, "Il Fedone latino," 107-13. De Nolhac, *Pétrarque et l'humanisme,* 2, 141 and n. 3, expresses surprise that Petrarch had not made greater use of the *Phaedo.* But see L. Minio-Paluello on Petrarch's marginalia to BN. lat. 6567A. He suggests (113) that Petrarch may have read this work only in his final years.

[14] *Tusc.,* 5.4.

[15] *Rer. fam.,* 10.5.15; *De offic.,* 1.1.

[16] *Acad.,* 1.4.15.

[17] *De ignor.,* Nachod, 126.

[18] *Rer. mem.,* 1.9. (Unless lines and pages are specified, numbers refer to book and section.)

[19] *De sen.,* 8.26.

[20] *Rer. mem.,* 1.27.

[21] Ibid., 4.22; Cic. *De divin.,* 1.54.

[22] *Rer. mem.,* 3.71.

[23] One might say with De Nolhac (1.9) that "the need to oppose a name to that of Aristotle, as much as the study of Cicero and St. Augustine, caused Petrarch to grasp the importance of Plato."

[24] Paris BN. lat. 6280. See De Nolhac, 2.141; Pellegrin, 98. It is no. 121 of the 1426 inventory of the Visconti-Sforza Library.

[25] See note 13.

[26] De Nolhac (2.133-40, 313) discusses this manuscript and Petrarch's efforts to learn Greek in order to read it. Pellegrin lists it (98) as no. 120 of the 1426 inventory and as no. 463 of the 1459 inventory (310). She suggests in n. 2 that because of similarity of contents, it may well be Paris BN grec 1807, which came from Catherine de Médicis.

[27] *Prose,* 756; Nachod, 112-13.

[28] *Tusc.,* 1.30; *Rer. fam.,* 3.18.5 (1.139); 4.3.6 (1.165).

[29] *Prose,* 46; *Confess.,* 10.6.

[30] *Prose,* 98-100.

[31] Ibid., 174; *Phaedrus* 245 A.

[32] *In somn. Scip.,* 1.8; *Prose,* 340-42.

[33] *Prose,* 342.

[34] *Rer. mem.,* 1.25, pp. 26-31.

[35] Ibid., 1.25, lines 78-94.

[36] Ibid., lines 99-157.

[37] Ibid., lines 158-69.

[38] *Prose,* 750-54; Nachod, 107-11.

[39] 2:152. De Nolhac discusses Petrarch's knowledge of Aristotle on 147-52. Pellegrin (115) identifies this manuscript as (293) no. 190 of the 1426 inventory and as no. 78 of the 1459 inventory (293).

[40] *Prose* 744-46; Nachod, 103-04.

[41] *Rer. fam.,* 11.16.35, and 23.2.42.

[42] Ibid., 11.4.1.

[43] Ibid., 3. 10. 7.

[44] *Contra med.,* 3.328-35.

[45] *Rer. fam.,* 2.159.

[46] *Contra mem.,* 3.448-49.

[47] *Rer. fam.,* 10.4.2 (2.301).

[48] *European Literature,* 217-18.

[49] *Contra med.,* 3.490-97.

[50] *Petrarca letterato,* 1:49-50.

[51] *Rer. fam.,* 1.12.4-5.

[52] *Contra med.,* 3.100-06.

[53] Ibid., 2.270-81;3.173-86.

[54] *Prose,* 742-44; Nachod, 102.

[55] *Rer. mem.,* 2.31, pp. 64-66, lines 37-43.

[56] *Prose,* 744-46; Nachod, 102.

[57] Citations to Cicero run to six and a half columns. The Bible and Vergil run for four and three and a third; Seneca runs for two and a third. Horace gets one and two-thirds, and Augustine one and a half. All other classical authors run for less than a column, the historians claiming a certain prominence, rightly enough, as the source for his *exempla.* Of the philosophers Plato is given two-thirds of a column and Aristotle and Socrates each one half. Cicero, Vergil, Seneca, Horace, and St. Augustine are, then, his most cited classical authors, with Cicero massively dominating. Cf. B. L. Ullman, "Petrarch's Favorite Books," *Studies,* 117-37.

[58] *Prose,* 726-40; Nachod, 79-100.

[59] Cf. the important comments on Petrarch's role playing of the various careers he assigned himself in Thomas M. Greene, "The Flexibility of the Self," 246-49, especially 248. Greene has also written the most profound study (in my judgment) of Petrarch's theory and practice of *imitation,* "Petrarch and the Humanist Hermeneutic."

[60] See note 2.

[61] Aurelia Bobbio, *Seneca e la formazione spirituale e culturale del Petrarca.*

[62] *Image,* 35-41.

Mariann Sanders Regan (essay date 1982)

SOURCE: Mariann Sanders Regan, "Petrarch," in *Love Words: The Self and the Text in Medieval and Renaissance Poetry,* Cornell, 1982, pp. 184-222.

[*In the following excerpt, Regan focuses on themes of love and self-examination in her reading of the* Rime sparse.]

> et perché 'l mio martir non giunga a riva,
> mille volte il dì moro et mille nasco,
> tanto da la salute mia son lunge.[1]

We cannot intuit *Lover infans* in Petrarch's *Canzoniere* so easily or directly as we can in the lyrics by Dante and Arnaut Daniel. For through the metaphoric language of fusion, an illumined dyad sustains Daniel's poems, and a central presencing event rests at the heart of Dante's poetry; by contrast, in none of Petrarch's various works do *Poet* and *Lover* move harmoniously, in continual metaphors of fusion, toward some central *arrheton,* Rather, in these poems *Poet* and *Lover* join in more difficult, defensive verbal efforts, as though in reaction to an inadequate or finally unavailable Source. This "as though"—this pervasive sense of untrustworthy central Source and conflicted central *infans*—may serve as our beginning intuition for Petrarch's poetry. The lyrics of the *Canzoniere* may be understood as works of self-texturing appropriate to this uncertain ontological center.

In all of Petrarch's works, final values are never quite final. Final judgments can be postponed, or retracted. When Reason receives the Poet-Lover's appeal for justice late in the *Canzoniere,* she replies that she needs more time to make up her mind (360. 157).

Augustine, who often seems the winner in the debates of the *Secretum,* does not really have the last word. Laura is all but obliterated in the palinode, "Vergine bella" (366), but she is there again at the close of the *Trionfo dell'Eternità,* with those who possess immortal beauty and eternal fame. Perhaps such shifting purposes argue an uneasy ontology for these poems, an inability to fix Source and goal, an inherent restlessness. We recall how the Petrarch of the letters perceived his "wandering life" to have begun at birth:

> But I was conceived in exile and born in exile. I cost my mother such labor and struggle that for a long time the midwives and physicians thought her dead. Thus I began to know danger even before I was born, and I crossed the threshold of life under the loom of death. . . . I was removed [from Arezzo] in my seventh month and borne all over Tuscany by a certain sturdy youth; as Metabus did Camilla, he wrapped me in a linen cloth suspended from a knotty stick, to protect my tender body from contact. In fording the Arno, his horse fell, and in trying to save his precious burden he nearly lost his own life in the raging stream.

> After the wanderings in Tuscany we went to Pisa. I was removed from there in my seventh year and transported by sea to France. We were shipwrecked by the winter storms not far from Marseilles, and I was nearly carried off again on the threshold of my young life. . . . Thenceforward, certainly, I have hardly had a chance to stand still and get my breath.[2]

As a young boy, he says, he sensed as "true and almost present" those passages from classical authors about the mutability of life and "time's irrecoverability" (*Fam.* XXIV. 1, p. 201). He was barely in his teens when his mother died, and during those same years his father threw Petrarch's cherished library of classical books into the fire.[3] The Petrarch of the letters would see such incidents as further evidence that "there is no resting-place for me," that he must lie exhausted on the bed of this life (*Fam.* XV. 4, p. 135). He was forever unable or reluctant to find a permanent residence, as though a final sense of belonging, or home, eluded him. For to be by one's very nature deracinated, or homeless, is to lack that definite imagination, that crucial *absent presence,* at one's psychic center: it is not a question of geography, but of how surely one possesses an intrapsychic representation of self-as-Source, toward which one internally is always directed, always "traveling." Without this sure imagination, in Petrarchan texturing, one can hardly even *conceive* of arriving home. Source becomes entirely contingent, a central ground that may always be pulled away. And indeed no ground seems to be truly secure in these letters; even though Gherardo has reached spiritual harbor in a Carthusian monastery, Petrarch neverthe-

less sends him exhortations to piety, as well as a reading list (*Fam.* X. 3, p. 100). No metaphors of suckling infants belong to this texturing; rather, one exists as though wrapped in a linen cloth and suspended from a knotty stick.

We sense in Petrarch's *Canzoniere* and in his other works a central *infans* moved by the full force of both those original contradictory motions, the dread of Void as well as the longing for Source. It is as though this Poet-Lover lives in the interchange of death and birth: "mille volte il dì moro et mille nasco." For the evocations of Source here are centrally threatened, and any Source that might be intuited from these pages seems to be always already departing. For instance, Laura is typically a shadow, an elusive *ombra,* even in her surest representations. Whereas the *donna* of Donte's *nove rime* approaches and brings life with her gaze, making her presence felt, it is of Laura's essence to vanish, to be summoned only with weeping and imaginative effort. And so *in morte:* Laura as salvific vision, *guida al cielo,* simply does not work as well as Dante's Beatrice. Her eyes do not show the Poet-Lover "la via ch'al ciel conduce" (the way that leads to heaven, 72. 3), despite all intentions. Instead of guiding him step by step to a consummate "fulgore," Laura repeatedly appears and disappears from his bedside: her tender counsel is intermittent, ephemeral—as her memory has always been. And her presence is swept away in the last poems where she becomes merely "tale" (one, 366. 92).

Moreover, except for those tenuous nightly visitations, the Poet-Lover of the *Canzoniere* receives no grace, no responsive, infinite Maternal Source, no presencing or represencing to strengthen his repentance and hope for *salute.* Neither Laura's arms nor God's arms reach down to him in his lifelong wanderings; neither Laura's face nor God's face approaches to bring him definitive rest. One might ask, as Lucia asks Beatrice at the start of the *Inferno,* do you not hear his cries? Such repentant moments as "Padre del Ciel" (62) and "I' vo pensando" (264) move on unanswered, and the Virgin's exhorted presence subtends the final poem silently. The Poet-Lover's final prayers move full cricle to the first poem in the sequence, where *pietà* and *perdono* are left to the reader in an unresolvable appeal. This first poem presents the whole sequence as an endless purgatorial chain, but without final absolution and remission of sins. There is no context that assures a sympathetic audience: it is Laura's role not to listen, of course (223), but there is no sense through the verbal texture that God and the Virgin Mary are listening, either. The poems revolve essentially alone, filling the silences left by their own failing pleas. For in Petrarchan texturing, such Dantean echoes as "il ver tacito" (the silent truth, 309) do not really allay the fear that there may be no truth, no trusted listening figure, in the silence. The pilgrim of the *Commedia* can experience nourishing silences, long gazes that lead to the final eternal gazing—but the *Canzoniere* does not evoke such a "silent terminal point"[4] to engender and direct the words. The Poet-Lover must himself fill the silences, while no responsive presences arrive to lead him home. He calls Laura's name into a Void:

> . . . onde con gravi accenti
> è ancor chi chiami, et non è chi responda.
> [318]

(. . . whence there is one who calls out with heavy accents, but there is no one to answer.)

The silence that is death shares the maternity of these poems.

In response and reaction to an untrustworthy central Source and a fully conflicted central *infans, Poet* and *Lover* meet in difficult textures, where often pain and solitude seem elaborated almost purposefully, willfully, self-consciously, dramatically. Or, one might say, defensively. For through several intricate verbal means that resemble defenses, *Poet* and *Lover* join as though to guard uncertain Source, or even to reclaim Source from all uncertainty. Like many defensive efforts, these do not work very well, but the efforts remain to mark Petrarchan texturing. In the cause of these defenses, whole human presences seem deliberately distanced from these poems, while at the same time parts of cherished presences seem to be assimilated, possessed in words. Moreover, the Poet-Lover works hard to turn against himself, in distinctive representations of *amant martyr,* so that the rages of incompleted mourning are deflected away from Source and into the verbal texture. Source remains uncertain, but finally, through the verbal negations and deviations of these pervasive defenses, *Poet* takes on weight—becoming perhaps strong enough to subsume, nourish, and compensate *Lover* for the centrally inadequate Source that provoked the defenses in the first place. Strengthened by *Poet,* the Poet-Lover may come to love self, his own being-in-words, almost as he would have loved a securely evoked Source. The expectations and problems of this self-love may lead us to the final self-consciousness of the *Canzoniere,* the Petrarchan "lifelong condition"[5] that we all in some measure share with these poems as equivalent selves.

It may seem paradoxical that *Poet* and *Lover* would move together in purposeful defense to *distance* important presences from these poems, since intimations of a departing Source can be centrally threatening to the self. But such distancing can allow a crucial, saving measure of defensive control against a Maternal Source felt to be untrustworthy. For if that Source seems by its nature to vanish, the self can defensively take as its own the act of distancing, in order the

more surely to circumscribe and hold the imagination of Source, *absent presence,* internalized "ideal object." The self contrives its own "optimal distance" from Source, defensively appropriating its own boundaries. And on the other hand, if Source seems by its nature to be overbearing or overpresencing, such managed distancing can be all the more a saving grace, can allow the self to exist in division. For there are some indications in Petrarchan texts that their evoked always-departing Source may operate, on a deeper level of defense, to screen the opposite evocation: an all-engulfing Source. And in this case, the self through the defense of primal envy would tend to devalue and distance important presences, lest they become entirely overwhelming. Thus ultimately, at some evocative level past the signifiers, that central untrustworthy Source in Petrarchan textures may be too near as well as too far, engulfing as well as abandoning, and these two untrustworthy "imagos" may be always oscillating in mutual reaction to each other. From such a conflicted "core" *infans,* the self would surely move to impose its own distances.

For instance, in an early canzone of the *Canzoniere,* **"Una donna più bella"** (119), the figure of Glory may suggest a Source both too far away and too near, and some ambivalence may inform the Poet-Lover's reception of her. When she leaves, she winds the garland of laurel around his temples as though to soften her departure: "'Non temer ch' i' mi allontani" (Do not be afraid that I am going away, 119. 102-5). Formulating this distance from her, the laureled self is discovered; Petrarch is crowned as poet laureate. On the other hand, when several lines earlier, after she presences him with her gaze (88-90), she tells him, "ciascuna di noi due [Virtue and Glory] nacque immortale" (each of us was born immortal, 119. 92), she seems intent to overwhelm him, to provoke his despair.

> "Miseri, a voi che vale?
> Me' v'era che da noi fosse il defetto"
> [93-94]

("Wretches, what does it avail you? It would be better for you that we did not exist.")

Her exclamation here is like the proverb near the close of the *Trionfo del Tempo:* blessed is he who is not born. For he wanes in comparison with her; he can hope at best, through Glory, to live a long time (14-15), but she is overbearingly immortal.

These allusions to literary fame, and to an age without Virtue or Glory, recall certain similar passages in the letters, mixed evocations of abandonment and engulfment by Source, with appropriate defensive distancing. For in the letters also, Petrarch suggests that none of his contemporaries are worthy of Glory, or indeed worth reading, and that for this reason "I exert all my mental powers to flee contemporaries and seek out the men of the past" (*Fam.* VI. 4, p. 68). Bergin offers a more defensive cause for this flight—that Petrarch might have found true rivals among his contemporaries, especially those in Florence. Perhaps the Petrarch of the letters would like to hold his literary sources at a comfortable distance, to devalue those that are not already distanced by time. Such devaluing and distancing could manifest a primal envy of Source, an anxiety of influence. And as for those writers already safely distanced by time, not to mention by language and culture, he could continue to lament their irrevocable departure, taking them—from a distance—to heart. Petrarch, unable to read Greek, could clasp a volume of Homer to his bosom and sigh, "'O great man, how gladly would I hear you speak!'" (*Fam.* XVIII. 2, p. 153). Yet by contrast he could not bring himself to hold so close a copy of Dante's works: "I was strangely indifferent to this one book, which was new and easily procurable. . . . I was afraid that if I should immerse myself in his words, or in those of any other man, I might unwillingly or unconsciously become an imitator. (At that age one is so malleable, so prone to admire everything!)" (*Fam.* XXI. 15, pp. 178-79). Thus even while he carefully explains why he could never hate or envy Dante, the Petrarch of this letter is busy with primal defensive texturing, minimizing Dante's achievements and setting himself at a distance, clearly apart, lest he be immersed, shaped, overborne by a contemporary literary presence.

Perhaps the same defensive patterns inform Petrarch's tendency to avoid close or intimate associations, as well as fixed duties or responsibilities. As Bergin says, "with an art more instinctive than calculated, he managed to keep himself ultimately uncommitted." For example, when he was offered a Papal secretaryship in Avignon, he contrived to disqualify himself.[6] He believed that his own father had been prevented from rising "high in the scholarly world" by the burdens of a job and family (*Sen.* XVI. 1, p. 292), and perhaps in consequence he avoided both; yet he also claims that his ability to reject long hopes—a "natural weakness, or natural soundness"—has saved him "from marriage and from others of life's troubles" (*Fam.* XXIV. 1, p. 201). One leaves, perhaps, before one can be either engulfed or abandoned. And the Petrarch of the letters refuses not only job and family but also a permanent home: he keeps up his travels and changes residence almost incessantly, never becoming definitively "at home," not even in his favorite Vaucluse. He will not belong to a community of close friends, although he several times professes his desire to do so, as when he writes to Guido Sette, "You must know that I never look at pleasant places without recalling my own country home and the friends with whom, God willing, I should most gladly pass there the remnants of my brief life" (*Fam.* XVII. 5, p. 152). He

will not choose any city, such as Florence, upon which he might have some claim as "home." His life has often been called a "voluntary exile," and contrasted with Dante's involuntary exile. He cannot explain his "wanderings," which bring him by his own account more trouble than profit, except to say: "If I should be asked why then I do not stand still, I can only respond . . . I don't know why" (*Sen.* IX. 2, p. 260). Perhaps this continual interchange, along with the yearning for the solitary life, helps to preserve the circumference of the self: one keeps home and friends at a safer distance this way, and all evocations of dangerous Source in balance. When Petrarch invites a friend to live with him, he assures him, as he would probably himself like to be assured: "Don't think I am proposing to shackle you, or that you would be confined to a single house" (*Fam.* VIII. 5, p. 71).

The letters may provide a clarifying context, then, for the defensive texturing of the **Canzoniere,** where *Poet* and *Lover* join to distance all intact human presences from the words. After that "primiero assalto" (first assault, 2), Laura is dramatized only as a vanishing presence, so that the Poet-Lover seldom risks encountering her; moreover, few other whole presences—such as, for instance, the consoling ladies of Dante's "Donna pietosa"—are summoned by these poems. Only the distant invocations of apostrophe really belong to these lyrics; even substantial personifications, such as Glory (119) or Reason (360), are exceptional here. Safe from presencing or represencing events, the Poet-Lover can reflect upon his elusive *l'aura.* As Budel says of this distance willingly sought, "in the final analysis, he did not want what he seemed to want."[7] As he wanders "Solo e pensoso" in "i più deserti campi" (Alone and filled with care . . . [in] the most deserted fields, 35), he resembles the Poet-Lover of Arnaut's "En cest sonet," intent to create himself "en desert.". . . For at this perpetual distance, he seems to invoke Laura's *absent presence* almost at will, while the landscapes (unlike Dante's) yield their inherent significance to serve as a backdrop for his well-controlled intimations of Source:

> Ove porge ombra un pino alto od un colle
> talor m'arresto, et pur nel primo sasso
> disegno co la mente il suo bel viso.
>
> [129. 27-29]

> (Where a tall pine or a hillside extends shade,
> there I sometimes stop, and in the first stone I see
> I portray her lovely face with my mind.)

Because she is not there, he can take charge almost entirely of her image, its appearance and disappearance: he "designs" her. And he nourishes himself with this kind of "error," keeps himself symbiotically alive through this *absent presence* he has worked through distancing to create (129. 37-39; 127. 102-6). Perhaps such brief but distinctive metaphors of fusion, *Lover* with *Poet,* are enabled by the defensive distancing.

For he will distance her in time as well as in space. He envisions a future "benedetto giorno" (blessed day, 126. 31) when she would weep at his graveside, and he ranges "ne la memoria" (in memory, 41) to design a spellbinding image:

> Così carco d'oblio
> il divin portamento
> e 'l volto e le parole e 'l dolce riso
>   m'aveano, et sì diviso
> da l'imagine vera,
> ch' i' dicea sospirando:
> "Qui come venn' io o quando?"
> credendo esser in ciel, non là dov' era.
>   [126. 56-63]

(Her divine bearing and her face and her words and her sweet smile had so laden me with forgetfulness

and so divided me from the true image, that I was sighing: "How did I come here and when?" thinking I was in Heaven, not there where I was.)

Here again is the language of fusion: Poet-Lover and poem seem almost to disappear into a carefully removed, imaged Presence. He creates his own trance, fixing and directing his memory until it can "mirar lei et obliar me stesso" (look at her and forget myself, 129. 35). Even so, it is a self-conscious trance, where the Poet-Lover in "obsessive" memory[8] still circumscribes and measures his own self-forgetfulness. These textures of fusion are well guarded.

Perhaps the Poet-Lover of the **Canzoniere** even tries to appropriate Laura's death for his own defensive purposes, another act of distancing. His efforts have perhaps caused some readers to believe (probably erroneously) that when Petrarch noted Laura's death in the margin of his Virgil, he was simply tailoring a fiction. After all, when Laura has been removed by death, the Poet-Lover can be even surer of her image. He can summon her presence closer now in the poetry: Laura *in morte,* more than *in vita,* will console, advise, linger a while, and even profess her love. Of course, she is never by any means so direct and immediate a presence as Beatrice. But still, the poems continue to grow in the space cleared by her death: just as the Poet-Lover can *in vita* design her face against a tree or rock, he can mourn both bitterly and sweetly in the landscape that she has abandoned forever:

> et quanto in più selvaggio
> loco mi trovo e 'n più deserto lido,
> tanto più bella il mio pensier l'adombra.
>   [129. 46-48]

(and in whatever wildest place and most deserted shore I find myself, so much the more beautiful does my though shadow her forth.)

In the letters, Petrarch writes to "Socrates" of his reaction to the news that two of his friends have been murdered by brigands: "I feel something fatal, horrible, and yet pleasurable to my mind. Assuredly there is a certain sweetness in mourning . . ." (*Fam.* VIII. 9, p. 76). He was planning to spend the rest of his life with these friends, he says, living together in a single house; but now that they are removed, he will "feed and torture" himself with mourning. And so the Poet-Lover of the **Canzoniere** continues for many years to call Laura's name, for the most part unrewarded—and unencumbered—by her answers. Thus in this defensive texturing *Poet* rises in significance over *Lover,* as words born in solitude and memory come to seem more important than the longing for the present lady.

Even while *Poet* and *Lover* move to distance whole presences, and especially to hold Laura removed in time and space, they move also to bring worded parts of Laura's presence into the body of the poem. It is as though a sensed untrustworthy Source—too near and too far, engulfing and abandoning—provokes these complementary defensive efforts to draw away from the whole and yet possess the parts. The poems seem to incorporate concrete fragments of Source, worded "part objects" of the unwordable "ideal object," with items taken from Laura and her surroundings. The Poet-Lover works to have her in his own terms, so to speak, to control the poem's genesis by devouring and holding *absent presence* in words that can neither engulf nor abandon the body of the poem. *Poet* and *Lover* join in synecdoche, metonymy, symbol or emblem, and phonic texturing to gather these nourishing fragments.

Any simple, whole, direct representations of Laura as *donna* are soon lost beneath the loving enumerations of her separate beauties, her *belle membra,* her attributes. Most frequent in this collection are her eyes (*begli occhi*), her face (*bel viso*), and her blonde hair (*chiome bionde* or *capei d'oro*); but the poems linger also over her arms (*braccia*), side (*fianco*), feet (*piede*), limbs (*membra*), cheeks (*guancie*), even her hands and fingers, "bella man" and "diti schietti soavi" (199). Cherished parts seem indispensable to these poems: synecdochic presences become habitual substitutes for whole presences, and part-objects are as insistently desired as Source. "Each part of her has the significance of her entire person."[9] In Petrarchan texturing, the distanced whole and the appropriated parts together seem to allow that solid imagination of fusion upon which the self must spin; they provide the equivalent of Dantean "presencing" to define and direct these lyrics. For this Poet-Lover, however long he continues, never can continue long *in vita* or *in morte* without returning to the naming of parts; even the Virgin Mary is praised for her "belli occhi" (366. 22).

The spectrum between synecdoche and metonymy in these poems is a long and full one, so that fragments of Laura accumulate here as in a dream-work to displace the affective charge of her presence among a rich panorama of cathected items, part-presences. She is a glance, a smile, a bearing, sweet whispers, words, angelic singing, an inventory of "mortal bellezza, atti et parole" (mortal beauty, acts, and words, 366. 85). She is a veil, a gown, a white glove; she is *l'auro,* the gold that binds her hair, as well as *l'aura,* the breeze that plays with her hair—even the paronomasia is metonymic. For she is here through whatever she touches, through any reality once contiguous: she becomes her footprints upon the grass, as the "sì bel piede" (so beautiful a foot) becomes "be' vestigi sparsi" (lovely footprints, 125. 53, 60); she can be known only through "quest' erba sì" (this grass, 126. 65). Time is ignored by this contiguity—as when in the ***Trionfo dell'Eternità*** the speaker exclaims, Happy is the stone that covers her fair face! This touching need not even be quite physical, for she becomes the quality of the air through which her glance has penetrated:

> Ovunque gli occhi volgo
> trovo un dolce sereno
> pensando: "Qui percosse il vago lume."
> [125. 66-68]

(Wherever I turn my eyes, I find a sweet brightness, thinking: "Here fell the bright light of her eyes.")

This Poet-Lover also manages to turn the moment of the original meeting into an enumeration of time and space, as items *near* Laura which he can savor one by one: the hour, the instant, the countryside, the place . . . (61). And of course, metonymy in this texture can move almost imperceptibly toward symbol, when Laura becomes also the parts of the natural landscape that call her to mind. Mountain by mountain, with water, grass, cloud, rock, the naming of parts continues, though displaced from her body: "in tante parti et sì bella la veggio" (in so many places and so beautiful I see her, 129. 38). The Poet-Lover in "Chiare fresche et dolci acque" (126) summons a gently melancholy sequence, part for part: *acque* (waters) for *membra* (limbs), *gentil ramo* (gentle branch) for *bel fianco* (lovely side), *erba et fior* (grass and flowers) for *gonna* (garment) and *seno* (breast), *aere sacro sereno* (sacred bright air) for those *begli occhi*. It seems as though this list can never be completed, can never constitute a whole. And even when the Poet-Lover designs the final vignette of Laura here, to move himself toward his own trance, the poem still holds her only through parts, through lovely branches, falling flowers, blonde braids like burnished gold and pearls. This kind of effort to make her present brings her there only in treasured synecdoche, metonymy, symbol, *l'auro:* the whole has been scattered into *rime sparse.*

With this texturing of Laura as part-Presence, metaphor is usually not the language of fusion, the inspired evocation of wordless Source—as metaphor can be in the texts of Daniel or Dante. Instead, metaphor and symbol and emblem here often seem merely to extend the uses of synecdoche and metonymy: unsignifiable presences are regularly assumed to become solid objects rendered by concrete, recurring words, *cose in rima.* The reader comes to expect metamorphosis by metonymy; the lady under a green laurel becomes virtually a lady-*lauro,* and the weeping Poet-Lover becomes the stone upon which he sits. In appropriated parts of Ovid, the Poet-Lover becomes a laurel, a swan, a stone, a fountain of tears, a voice, a stag like Acteon (23); emblems of Laura's death, in the corresponding canzone *in morte,* include a deer, a ship, a laurel, a phoenix, a fountain, and a lady like Eurydice (323). For these poems work to transform presences, and ultimately to transform Source, into emblems, into words. All presences, and infinite Presence, are presumed there by contiguity, all but *in* the word, in this closely metonymic texture; it is a kind of verbal metamorphosis. And the Daphne myth suits this defensive texture well: in the tree, the fleeing lady is both forever distanced and yet still entirely available. For in these poems *words* or *parts* of the laurel can be brought close, appropriated by synecdoche: *fronde, rami, legno, scorza, ombra* (leaves, branches, wood, bark, shade). Thus the laurel as metonymic symbol yields in turn its own nourishing parts. Like Apollo, this Poet-Lover can take those "sacra fronde" (holy leaves, 34) to himself, or receive the laurel garland from Glory, and thus he guards himself against untrustworthy source. He can distance *l'aura* while he yet assimilates *l'auro,* valued part-presences. Perhaps in this way also *l'ombra,* always on the verge of disappearance or dispersion, can be held in words as a reality almost tangible, sweet and sensual, to feed and generate these poems as selves.

> seguirò l'ombra di quel dolce lauro
> [30. 16]

(I shall follow the shadow of that sweet laurel)

> Poi quando il vero sgombra
> quel dolce error . . .
> [129. 49-50]

(Then, when the truth dispels that sweet deception . . .)

> L'arbor gentil che forte amai molt'anni
> (mentre i bei rami non m'ebber a sdegno)

fiorir faceva il mio debile ingegno
a la sua ombra . . .

[60]

(The noble tree that I have strongly loved for
many years, while its lovely branches did not
disdain me, made my weak wit flower in its
shade . . .)

The metonymic use of *ombra* can belong in these
poems to suggestions of sexual union, as when the
end-words of the sestina **"Non à tanti animali"** (237)
seem to be repeated and savored as dark, delectable
part-objects: *piaggia, notte, luna, sera, onde, boschi*
(rain, night, moon, evening, waves, woods.) For *ombra*
is often gathered into the poems with night and
evening, in sensual dream-wish: when the Poet-Lover
sees the stars "dopo notturna pioggia" (after nocturnal
rain), he remembers her eyes "quali io gli vidi a l'ombra
d'un bel velo" (such as I saw them in the shadow of
a lovely veil, 127. 57, 62).

Through repeating and savoring, *Poet* and *Lover* also
join to bring Laura's presence into the poem phoni-
cally, so that sounds work as part-presences. In the
Secretum "Augustine" accuses "Petrarch" of being in
love with Laura's *name,* and even apart from the
multifold paronomasia, the naming of Laura seems itself
satisfying, an activity to be relished: "L'aura che 'l
verde lauro et l'aureo crine / soavemente sospirando
move" (246). Sometimes in his lists of cherished parts
the Poet-Lover seems to include this very naming,
"qualche dolce mio detto" (some sweet saying of mine,
70. 17), as when he adds to a catalogue of natural
beauties "dir d'amore in stili alti et ornati" (poems of
love in high and ornate style) and "dolce cantare oneste
donne et belle" (sweet singing of virtuous and beautiful ladies, 312), or as when he blesses, along with all
the "parts" of their first meeting, "le voci tante" (the
many words) that he has scattered in calling her name
(61). Her sweet presence seems almost to be ritualis-
tically incorporated, ingested again and again with liquid consonants and open-throated vowels: *l'aura, lauro,
l'ombra, l'ambra, l'aureo, l'aurora, l'oro, l'auro,
laureta.* Or the words themselves can become her
hair, spread with the *l*'s and *s*'s into delicate, enticing
strands:

L'aura soave al sole spiega et vibra
l'auro ch' Amor di sua man fila et tesse;
là da' belli occhi et de le chiome stesse
lega 'l cor lasso e i lievi spirti cribra.

[198]

(The soft breeze spreads and waves in the sun
the gold that Love spins and weaves with his
own hands; there with her lovely eyes and with
those very locks he binds my weary heart and
winnows my light spirits.)

In the course of this sonnet he takes her presence into
his marrow and blood, while his mind reels with the
sweetness, "di tanto dolcezza," that has been swallowed with the words—*as* the words, perhaps—into
the poem. These are words more than *pexa,* for the
very syllables seem delectable: whereas in "Ne li occhi"
the words seem to efface themselves before that nameless *donna,* in Petrarch's poems the words themselves
become substantial, upstaging the whole human presence. The words themselves attract and overwhelm:
"'l dir m'infiamma e pugne . . . mi struggo al suon de
le parole" (speaking inflames me and pricks me on . . .
I melt in the sound of the words, 73. 10-14). The
words seem not to let the light of Presence through,
but to rest in themselves.

Thus *Poet* and *Lover* join in paronomasia, synecdoche, metonymy, symbol, emblem, and phonic texturing to assimilate nourishing part-presences, worded
fragments of Laura's presence, into the Poet-Lover or
poem as equivalent self. These part-presences effectively serve as that "image of the lady" which, as
Robert Durling points out in his reading of **"Giovene
donna"** (30), seems to become more rigid and more
metallic as the Petrarchan lover meditates upon it; these
metonymic part-presences, rather than the whole Presence, provide in Petrarchan texture the Aristotelian
internalized phantasm of the lady, the impression
stamped upon the wax of the lover's soul. The image
of the lady hardens into "l'idolo mio scolpito in vivo
lauro" (my idol carved in living laurel, 30. 27) because
the *parts* so harden, as Durling points out—the branches
diamond, the hair gold, the eyes topaz. Furthermore,
we might ask exactly *how* the Poet-Lover's "psychological fixation"[10] upon these internalized, imagined parts
brings about their hardening, for "hard" images are
curiously textured in the **Canzoniere**. Not only is the
lady hard, "lei che come un ghiaccio stassi" (she . . .
who now stands like ice, 125. 11), leaving an unanswered flame within him, but he also is hard as though
in response:

e d'intorno al mio cor pensier gelati
fatto avean quasi adamantino smalto

[23. 24-25]

(and around my heart frozen thoughts had made
almost an adamantine hardness)

He seems to absorb, ingest, take on her hardness: here
are Medusa and victim, of course, or in psycho-onto-
logical terms here is a darker version of that original
scene of infant spellcasting—unyielding Source becomes frozen self. For Source, however fatally hard,
still must be taken in to the vital center of self; we
recall the combined responses of mimesis and revenge
in Dante's *petrose.* Thus "hard" or "concrete" images
come to suggest not only her Medusa gaze, rejecting
and petrifying him (197), but also his response in

kind, inevitably mimetic of her or joined to her some-how: he is "hard" because he is ice or marble or stone; but his need for her is also unyielding, as when Time binds him in the "più saldi nodi" (tighter knots, 196) of her hair, or when "il giogo et le catene e i ceppi" (the yoke and the chains and the shackles, 89) entrap him, oppress him. For these chains are also treasures, and belong by metonymy to those cherished parts of Source that the poems so eagerly incorporate, those diamond branches, that "oro forbito e perle" (burnished gold and pearls, 126. 48). By this route the Poet-Lover also becomes "hard" in the strength with which he holds these part-presences, and that hardness becomes displaced upon the parts themselves: her name becomes as solid as marble (104). All these associations of "hard" images, and more, are involved with the Poet-Lover's "fixation" as he contemplates the part-images of the lady. She becomes a part-presence both concrete and vital, "hard" both in her treatment of him and in his intense appropriation of her: "questa viva petra" (this living stone, 50. 78). And he is "pietra morta in pietra viva" (a dead stone on the living rock, 129. 51), in the semblance of a man who thinks and weeps and writes; he takes on her fatal hardness in mimetic response, clinging to her for life even as she deprives him of life. It is as though at his central being, at the pri-mary term of the metaphor here, he is "pietra," like her.

Thus in these complex senses, the Poet-Lover's "con-templation," his motion toward Source, works to harden the partimages of the beloved. Moreover, *Poet* and *Lover* move defensively in these words toward yet another kind of "hardening." For one might describe the vocabulary of the **Canzoniere,** made of small groups of frequently recurring words, as "hard"—refined, restricted, well fixed. The Poet-Lover's metonymic tenacity affects not only the worded fragments of Laura's presence but also the words for his own suffering: *pensieri, sospiri, dolor, occhi molli, danni, giogo, vita acerba* (thoughts, sighs, grief, soft eyes, pain, yoke, bitter life). He seems to hold to limited sets of words, with little variation: this is hardly a *vario stile* in vocabulary. In a way the repetitive vocabulary seems almost to encrust these poems with the con-ventional, the familiar—so that an unusual image would seem intrusive. Bergin notes that the imagery of these poems is "personal," not remaining distinct or "objec-tive" or sharply visual, like Dante's imagery; rather, "with Petrarch the image is absorbed and devoured, and it is precisely this emotional solidarity that the poet seeks."[11] Through images made ever more famil-iar, both Laura and Poet-Lover become constant, pos-sessed in "solidarity." And when in some poems the metonymic vocabulary becomes both substance and audience, as in **"Chiare, fresche et dolci acque"** (126), the "solidarity" between Poet-Lover and image becomes all the more intense. Poet-Lover becomes a

being-in-words defensively, with a vengeance. For in these poems *Poet* and *Lover* do not move in *infans* receptivity, open to the wordless influence of Laura or other whole human presences. In Dante's poems the path to Source, ultimate "fulgore," is clear despite all *orribile lingue,* so that the language is cosmically di-verse, but there is little such "negative capability" in Petrarch's poems. It is as though in Petrarchan tex-ture Source had become treacherous, perhaps both too far and too near, so that individual words are not free to roam and generate worded differences; rather, words seem almost to be circumscribed, taken as part-presences, repeatedly devoured. Through this kind of rigidity, worded part-presences are firmly held, as though in place of a central *absent presence,* and again *Poet* comes to seem more important than *Lover.*

Even the religious language of the **Canzoniere** does not usually work as the metaphoric language of fu-sion, but is instead textured with this fixed vocabu-lary. For usually in the repentance sequences the words themselves remain constant while the references shift from secular to Christian,[12] so that even as the Poet-Lover professes change he is holding stubbornly to the language, the words resisting almost all diversity: the unusual "croce" or "miserere" (62) in such in-stances becomes the exception that proves the rule. And more generally, the very repetition of certain clus-ters of religious terms establishes them as part of the "hardened," carefully possessed vocabulary: *salute, benedetto, beata, miracolo, meraviglia, paradiso, divina* (salvation, holy, blessed, miracle, wonder, para-dise, divine). And through further allusions, Christian ceremony and ritual are appropriated, and the "com-mune dolor" (universal woe) brought to the service of "miei quai" (my misfortunes), in religious terms that are savored as insistently as any others (3). These terms can fill out items of synecdoche, as when her voice is "chiara, soave, angelica, divina" (clear, soft, angelic, divine, 167). They can consecrate metonymic presences:

> Qual miracolo è quel, quando tra l'erba
> quasi un fior siede.
>
> [160]

(What a miracle it is, when on the grass she sits like a flower!)

> Benedetto sia 'l giorno e 'l mese et l'anno
>
> [61]

(Blessed be the day and the month and the year . . .)

But even when these poems approach the language of fusion, as when the Poet-Lover exclaims, "Costei per fermo nacque in paradiso!" (She was surely born in Paradise! 126. 55), the "blessing" of the Christian words does not seem to enable the words to reach past themselves. The religious terms are, instead, included with the hair, the pearls, the grass, the flowers, the voice—with the treasured metonymic parts, so worded and so named, signifiers as Signified, *Poet* over *Lover*.

> guerra è 'l mio stato
>
> [164]

> (war is my state)

Thus in Petrarchan texturing, whole presences are distanced while part-presences are hoarded in words. *Poet* and *Lover* move together in these complementary defenses, and in their difficulties the individuating *Poet* emerges; the poem, as a being-in-words, rises to distinction. But there is still further defensive texturing in these poems—intricate *amant martyr* representations through which the distinctive Petrarchan "voice" emerges even more clearly. Here *Poet* and *Lover* move in continuing, subtle displacements to deflect negative impulses from the problematic Source of the poems; by contrast, in Dante's works with their secure presencing events, primal rages seem to be diverted simply, as with a single clean stroke, to the walled compartments of the *petrose* and the *Inferno*.

Thus in the **Canzoniere** aggression appears displaced or transmuted into that wearying and interminable sorrow, *dolore, pena,* that will mark the Petrarchan lover through several generations of love poetry. In his use of Ovid, this Poet-Lover does not include Daphne's sexual fear, and he does not follow the story of Acteon through to his dismemberment:[13] in these poems, one turns from rage and passion, in painful flight. Of course, he is reluctant to rail at the beloved;[14] what is more, he slights the representations of Laura as "cruel," and instead turns his attentions to his own afflicted image, *amant martyr.* For in this verbal texture, the presences and personifications that always wound the speaker seem perhaps less important than the pain of the blows:

> Voglia mi sprona, Amor mi guida et scorge,
> Piacer mi tira, Usanza mi trasporta;
>
> [211]

> (Desire spurs me, Love guides and escorts me,
> Pleasure draws me, Habit carries me away;)

Here and elsewhere, as in the canzone "**I' vo pensando**" (264), the active, angry verbs become the speaker's continuing pain, passively endured. Potential rage or invective is turned away from Laura as Source, and becomes woven into the vocabulary of his martyrdom: *martiri, sospiri, piaghe, mal, duol, pena, dolore, affanno, danno, tristi, duri, miseri, amare, paura, sconsolato, dispietata.* That is, war becomes this Poet-Lover's state of being, and he can thereby avoid actively waging war.

Thus as *amant martyr,* this Poet-Lover turns against himself centrally, from the beginning of the sequence, to emphasize his swift and lasting departure in time from Laura's presence. Unlike Dante's speaker, he does not linger in the universal moment of presencing; he moves immediately *de via,* away from that briefly invoked "luogo e tempo" (time and place, 2) to reflection upon the moment, and within a very few poems this moment must be called upon from the past. In this way he avoids making Laura's cruelty the target of his invective. For it is Time that here becomes cruel and implacable, that carries the ever-vanishing Source of these poems all the more surely away. And indeed, Time in its merciless turning, *volgendo,* could eventually scatter that first moment entirely:

> Quand' io mi volgo indietro a mirar gli anni
> ch' ànno fuggendo i miei penseri sparsi,
> et spento 'l foco ove agghiacciando io arsi,
>
> [298]

> (When I turn back to gaze at the years that fleeing
> have scattered all my thoughts, and put out the
> fire where I freezing burned . . .)

Time, as the agent of the Poet-Lover's martyrdom, renders him helpless, himself absorbing the possible anger toward the elusive beloved, and thus guarding that problematic Source from aggression. For not only does he typically receive the weight of the transitive verbs: even more frequently, the intransitive verbs governed by the speaker seem to have absorbed the wearing of time: "piango et ragiono" (I weep and speak, 1), "vegghio, penso, ardo, piango" (I am awake, I think, I burn, I weep, 164), "vo mesurando" (I go measuring, 35), "I' vo pensando" (I go thinking, 264. 1), "Là 've cantando andai di te molt'anni / or, come vedi, vo di te piangendo" (Where I went singing of you many years, now, as you see, I go weeping for you, 282).[15] In these present tenses and present gerunds, the entropic force of time acts upon him: these are verbs of habitual endurance, always bearing the implicit threat of full dissolution and absence. With these verbs, time takes the speaker ever further from that first moment, and the painful moments of increasing distance are stretched out as though upon a rack of time. He addresses Laura in one of the earlier poems:

> . . . i' vi discovrirò de' miei martiri
> qua' sono stati gli anni, e i giorni, et l'ore;
>
> [12]

> (I shall disclose to you what have been the years
> and the days and the hours of my sufferings;)

For moments are the elements of his martyrdom—in the recurring present tenses, a war of attrition continues to be his present state.

There are some momentary truces in this war, of course. Several defenses appear to cancel each other: even while time threatens to dissolve the memory of Laura's presence, the defensive distancing allows the Poet-Lover to re-create, elaborate, even improve that memory in moments of *pace*. There is such "breve conforto" (brief solace, 14) in the solitude canzoni, and also when Laura returns *in morte*. In these cases his endurance seems almost to have earned a renewal, a recovery of presencing, for she appears unmarked by time, "qual io la vidi in su l'età fiorita" ("just as I saw her in her flowering, 336), and the visions bring him "pace" (126. 55), "soccorso" (help, 283), "tregua" (a truce, 285). But these truces are also subject to time, and indeed time will remove these peaceful illusions:

> . . . se l'error durasse, altro non cheggio.
>
> [129. 39]

(. . . if the deception should last, I ask for no more.)

> i' come uom ch' erra et poi più dritto estima
> dico a la mente mia: "Tu se' 'ngannata. . . ."
>
> [336]

(I, like one who errs and then esteems more justly, say to my mind: "You are deceived. . . .")

Eventually these poems always turn time back against themselves: the cherished memories, like the original moment, yield to the sweep of time. Dante's *Commedia* moves steadily toward definitive represencing, but Petrarch's *Canzoniere* is carried away from all represencing scenes. Even though Petrarch in his daily routine fought time like Rabelais' Gargantua, reading while he shaved or ate, and writing in the middle of the night (*Fam.* XXI. 12, pp. 174-75), he still could acknowledge to Guido Sette, "there is no standing still for man here below; there is nothing but continual flow and down-slipping and at the end the collapse of all" (*Fam.* XIX. 16, p. 161). "La vita fugge et non s'arresta un'ora" (Life flees and does not stop an hour, 272). There is really no contest in time's war against the self. Time wears away the Poet-Lover, continues to dissolve presencing and represencing scenes: the laurels become oaks and elms (363), and the *morte* poems reiterate their own fatigue: "Omai son stanco" (Now I am weary, 364). The vaunted moral or religious progress must at best coexist with time's war against all central meaning for this self-in-words. The verbs here appear to have absorbed the rages of primal separation, so that Time in ongoing present tenses keeps drawing the poems toward their own Void, their own unpresenced final appeals.

Moreover, in the *amant martyr* texturing of these poems, it is not only Time that is turned against the self. The very moment of Presence, such as it is, is turned against the self also, in the elaborated pain of the experience and the memory. In this way also, the Poet-Lover exists in a state of war from the first few sonnets, with the military language of the enamorment as "'l colpo mortal" (the fatal blow) or "primiero assalto" (the first assault, 2) or the time "quando i' fui preso" (when I was taken, 3). Thus far we have only an echo of some of the textures, perhaps, of Dante or Cavalcanti; but Petrarch's Poet-Lover continues insistently to turn the violence of these metaphors upon himself, appropriating the language of *colpo, piaghe, giogo, ancide, pena,* and taking these words of the pain, as it were, to the heart of the poems. He becomes inseparable from this pain. In this way he manages usually, though certainly not always, to deflect his rage from Laura; it is the moment, the day, the experience that is cruel, "crudo" (298), and not her. But there may be also a *causa sui* wish defensively textured in this continuing self-affliction. Especially if Source is felt to be untrustworthy—engulfing or abandoning (or both)—the self moves in defense to take charge of, to "write," its own conflicted presencing scene. Thus the self intensifies and receives its own rage toward a Source "too near" or "too far," and perhaps thereby comes to earn a remembered sweetness; the self can design its own nourishing scene of Presence, its own conflated suffering and reward. Indeed, in the *Canzoniere* that first moment is not really *dolce;* its sweetness is largely conjured by memory, as though partly in response to the emphatic pain.

Perhaps other defenses are involved here, too. But in any case, surely the complex, defensive representations of the enamorment serve to establish and focus the oxymoronic texture of the *Canzoniere*.[16] For that first "blow" sets up a radical ambivalence that lasts throughout the sequence, so that no luminous meeting in the light of the lamp, no pure drinking of *spiriti* with the eyes, is ever quite possible in this texture. Evocations of that first moment are virtually always conflicted, scrupulously including pain; the memory can burden him as well as give him rest. Time renews "le prime piaghe sì dolci profonde" (the first deep sweet wounds, 196); the speaker will bless his wounds (61); anniversaries recall a "per me sempre dolce Giorno et crudo" (Day to me always sweet and cruel, 298), a "dolce amaro / colpo" (sweet bitter blow, 296). And this central ambivalence underlies the rich ambivalences of the sequence, where *Poet* and *Lover* move together in the oxymorons, antitheses, and paradoxes—the pain with the joy, the bitter with the sweet—that have come to mark the poetry as "Petrarchan." The love that ensnares him is "l'onesta pregion" (the worthy prison, 296), both a promise and a threat: "Amor, con quanto sforzo oggi mi vince!" (Love, with what power today you vanquish me! 85). For in this oxymoronic texturing, the state of war continues. Laura's eyes can emanate a sweet and nourishing light that keeps him alive (71. 76-82), but they can also dazzle or burn him, or wound him (195), or turn his heart to marble (197). Laura makes him feel "dolcezze amare et empie" (sweetness . . . bitter and cruel, 210), and one can "take in" her presence only through paradox:

> Così sol d'una chiara fonte viva
> move 'l dolce et l'amaro ond' io mi pasco.
>
> [164]

(Thus from one clear living fountain alone spring the sweet and the bitter on which I feed;)

He would die content of "tal piaga" (such a wound) and live in "tal nodo" (such a bond, 296); she brings life and death at once, and death itself is made sustaining, "bel morir" (beautiful death, 278).

Besides these familiar phrases, there are other textures of ambivalence in these poems, also growing from their centrally ambivalent moment. For even "dolce ne la memoria," the interludes of *pace* are so slight that they are virtually oxymoronic, disappearing almost at once back into the prevailing *guerra*. Paradoxically, even these sustaining memories need expression in negative language:

> Da indi in qua mi piace
> quest'erba sì ch'altrove non ò pace.
>
> [126. 64-65]

(From then on this grass has pleased me so that elsewhere I have no peace.)

> pur mentr' io veggio lei, nulla mi noce.
>
> [284]

(As long as I see her, nothing pains me.)

> né trovo in questa vita altro soccorso;
>
> [283]

(Nor do I find any other help in this life.)

After all, "dolce giogo" (sweet yoke) is a characteristic oxymoron for his memory itself; his heart is nourished by sighs (1). And of course, the central ambivalence will at times seem to govern the very construction of the sonnets, binding sonnet divisions that would separately express "dolce" or "amaro"; often the Petrarchan *volta* between octave and sestet seems to be thus formulated. And there are other variations: in one *morte* sonnet, for example, the first eleven lines savor Vaucluse in its natural beauty, while the last

tercet knows the grief of Laura's death (303). More broadly, the ambivalence informs the alternating hope and despair in the *morte* poems: now he is dazzled by Laura's return as a vision, radiant yet familiar (282; 284); and now he despairs of writing when he realizes that her *belle membra* are all "poca polvere . . . che nulla sente" (a bit of dust that feels nothing, 292). And of course, the periodic and final poems of repentance add an overriding ambivalence. Now he blesses that first moment (61), and now he rejects it, a "dispietato giogo" (pitiless yoke) no longer sweet (62). Reinforced by the **Secretum,** this has been the ambivalence most striking to readers of Petrarch's works. Recently, Aldo Bernardo speaks of the "irreconcilability of Petrarch's haunting polarities," his vacillation between Laura as "myth" and Laura as "living Christian witness."[17] It is as though the Poet-Lover wishes to write a new Source for himself, when he senses that the presencing event he has helped to design is inadequate, after all, and finite.

Thus *Poet* rises to prominence in these *amant martyr* representations, in which both Time and the "premiero assalto" are turned against the Poet-Lover. For these poems are *defined* as *rime sparse* partly by their war with Time. The speaker is adamant about including the weight, the pain, the dissolution that Time brings. "Cure me, and I shall be stronger, but my bed will be no smoother and softer" (**Fam.** XV. 4, p. 135). After all, the motions of *Poet* are served through this defensive texturing, for this Poet-Lover "chi pianse sempre" (who weeps eternally) finds immortality among the blessed precisely through his unending pain, his ongoing passive defeat before Time.[18] By suffering endlessly, he gains endless distinction. Moreover, the oxymoronic texture, established perhaps by that first ambivalent moment, works even further to individuate the Petrarchan "voice." For the tropes of antithesis, oxymoron, and paradox are perhaps those most clearly visible to Petrarch's long line of imitators.[19] We can see the introduction of this texture even in the first sonnet: the Poet-Lover names his own style as the "vario stile in ch'io piango et ragiono / fra le vane speranze e 'l van dolore" (varied style in which I weep and speak between vain hopes and vain sorrow). There are many ways of interpreting the stylistic variety of the **Canzoniere,** of course. But on the most basic level, "vario" is defined by these very lines, as ranging between hope and despair.[20] In this sense the self is "varied," or endlessly vacillating, between the polarities of the oxymorons and antitheses, with no further range or progress possible: "né per mille rivolte ancor son mosso" (nor for a thousand turnings about have I yet moved, 118). And the "van" of the first sonnet surely gestures toward that ultimate defensive ambivalence, rejecting that original moment entirely. For even the interludes of repentance, along with those intermittent protestations of moral progress and those late evocations of Dantean *luce,*[21] can be read in the contexts of this vacillation. The path here is almost always "rivolte," not Dante's steady journeying. This self is less centrally secure than the Gherardo who proceeds straight to the top of Mont Ventoux; but for that very reason, the wandering route of "error," more fully informed by *Poet,* makes this self more distinctive. Thus John Freccero can speak of "real literary strength from fictionalized moral flaws."[22] And thus Petrarch can almost proudly apply to himself a sentence from one of Plautus' plays: "'I beat everybody in torturability of soul'" (*Fam.* IX. 4, p. 83).

There are other strengths for *Poet* in this antithetical texturing. For through the established habits of oxymorons, antitheses, paradoxes, and contradictions, these beings-in-words become self-generating, in a sense inexhaustible. Through these devices the language comes to feed on its own negations: there must be a pain counterpoint to every pleasure, and each antithetical pair seems to breed further pairs. The sequences of paradoxes (132; 134) gather energy as they continue, as though they could go on forever; they are brought only arbitrarily and temporarily to a graceful close, "In questo stato son, Donna, per vui" (In this state am I, Lady, on account of you, 134). In this texturing the eternity lost at that ambivalent presencing is reclaimed, in a sense, in the very interminability of the tropes. This Poet-Lover, being-in-words, can resonate between *speranza* and *dolore* essentially forever; these poems are sustained, born a thousand times a day, by their very lack of rest or repose, their incessant deaths. Thus certainly the last sequence of "conversion" poems, or any other announced closure, would seem inherently unsuitable here. But it is fitting that *pace* would be the last word for these warring antitheses.

> Benedette le voci tante ch'io
> chiamando il nome de mia donna ò sparte,
> [61]

(Blessed be the many words I have scattered calling the name of my lady.)

As *Poet* and *Lover* move through these complex defensive textures, the words themselves rise to importance, and the Poet-Lover is clearly distinguished as a being-in-words. *Poet* emerges as a strong individuating motion in the negations and deviations of these defensive verbal devices—the savored parts of metonymy and synecdoche; the intensified, melancholy distancing of whole presences; the unending oxymorons, antitheses, and verbs of endurance. This *Poet* motion, in its unusual pervasiveness and strength, seems in several ways to answer that endemic longing, *Lover infans:* that is, the poems come in large measure to serve as their own Source, to work as "substitute" Source. These poems seem to offer their own worded beings to themselves in the place of unwordable Source,

designing themselves in a negative mimesis to possess the qualities *lacked* by the elusive, untrustworthy Source intuited at their center.

Some of these qualities we have seen achieved through the defensive texturing itself, which works with *Poet* to make these poems inexhaustible and self-generating, secure, closely held, unique, full of treasured ideal parts. But the poems also imitate ideal Source through some further texturings where *Poet* and *Lover* cooperate: individually, the poems become unified wholes that are sweetly, musically, coenesthetically nourishing. They may also become timeless, permanent "ideal objects" that are places of infinite repose. In these ways the "ben colto lauro" (well-tended laurel, 30.36) replaces Laura; the self feeds its own longing; the poems become themselves that wholly present *donna* or Source that they do not receive into their texture. In Kohut's terms, perhaps, secondary narcissism absorbs the charge of primary narcissism, and the poems, with a "constant and conscious egocentricity,"[23] usurp for themselves the place of Source. Thus Freccero is right about the poems' "self-contained dynamism" and "auto-reflexive" thematic,[24] in this sense: these are not *nove rime,* where Source shines through effaced words; rather, these words, in all their opacity and dense music, seem designed to be poetic selves-as-Source.

Petrarch in the letters seems to know that a literary text could work like a maternal presence, arousing and fulfilling expectations at the coenesthetic level of deep sensibility, until the text becomes an integrated and satisfying whole, allowing one to "coenesthetically fantasize" primal identification with Source. For he speaks of his study of Cicero in early childhood:

> At that age I could really understand nothing, but a certain sweetness and sonority so captured me that any other book I read or heard read seemed to me to give off a graceless, discordant sound. I must admit that this was not a very juvenile judgment, if one may call judgment what was not based on reason. But certainly it is remarkable that while I didn't understand anything, I already felt exactly what I feel today, when after all I do understand something, little though it be. That love for Cicero increased day by day, and my father, amazed, encouraged my immature propensity through paternal affection. And I, dodging no labor that might aid my purpose, breaking the rind began to savor the taste of the fruit, and couldn't be restrained from my study. I was ready to forego all other pleasures to seek out everywhere the books of Cicero. [*Fam.* XVI. 1, pp. 292-93]

Whatever this "certain sweetness and sonority" that marks Cicero as a literary presence, it seems to be more profound than mere "understanding," and more lasting—it seems perhaps to reside even at that "level of deep sensibility" posited by Spitz.[25] Perhaps Petrarch, having thus been rapt with the sweetness of another's wit, sought himself in the *Canzoniere* to devise poems that could likewise be capturing presences; perhaps he refers partly to this captivating sweetness when he insists that he wants any reader, while reading, to be "entirely mine" (*Fam.* XIII. 5, p. 115).[26] But whatever the reason, the poems have a lulling, maternal *sound*. Even while the poems defensively distance whole presences and rigidly possess worded parts, they *sound* sweetly nourishing. To this end, the coherence and affective energy of each individual *Canzoniere* poem inheres in an elaborate, tightly woven "interstitial web" in which logical, causal, and syntactic patterns merge and are overlaid with rhythmic and phonic equivalences. Thus Durling notes that **"Giovene donna"** (30), with its "sense of balance, cyclical recurrence, and progressive intensification and enlargement," outdoes its predecessor, Dante's "Al poco giorno."[27] Similarly, Bergin points out that Petrarch, both in syntax and in the stanzaic patterns that seem to flow so easily from syntax, achieved a unity and integrity markedly greater than that of his predecessors who wrote in the medieval pattern of coordinate clauses. For over and above his rhetorical and prosodic virtuosity, Petrarch typically devises a clear statement, straightforward in syntax and diction, "united and musically set forth."[28]

These poems can be aural presences, with a "certain sweetness and sonority" enhanced by the syntactic unity and balance—presences that address *Lover infans* on that primal level explained by Spitz, of "rhythm, tempo, duration, pitch, tone, resonance, clang." And on this aural or phonic level most of the poems are quintessentially sweet, a consoling and nourishing music. One might apply to these poems as constructions of sound the same adjectives that cluster around the *donna* of Dante's *nove rime: soave, piano, umile, dolce.* Or their sound might remind one of Laura in her *morte* visitations, as she speaks "col dolce mormorar pietoso et basso" (with . . . sweet, low, pitying murmur, 286). Granted, in several poems after Laura's death, the Poet-Lover undergoes harsher texturing, *roche rime* (332, 32), for as he explains,

non posso, et non ò più sì dolce lima,
rime aspre et fosche far soavi et chiare.

[293]

(I cannot—and I no longer have so sweet a file—
make harsh, dark rhymes into sweet, bright ones.)

But the uses of the rougher consonant groups seem to be, on the whole, short-lived; in sound, this highly selective vocabulary resembles Dante's *pexa* words. As in the sweet, incorporative naming of Laura, the resulting aural presence of the poem seems indeed maternal—*soave, chiare, dolce.*

Chiare fresche et dolci acque . . .

[126]

Quel rosigniuol che sì soave piagne . . .

[311]

Soleano i miei penser soavemente . . .

[295]

Quando io v'odo parlar sì dolcemente . . .

[143]

We come as readers to rest in "confident expectation" of this lulling voice, the voice of poem as substitute Source, and the *music* of the individual poem can serve in a way to override or reward the painful negations and deviations of the defensive texturing, somewhat as the sweetness of the memory rewards the Poet-Lover for suffering its "blows."

Ma ben veggio or sì come al popol tutto
favola fui gran tempo, onde sovente
di me medesmo meco mi vergogno;

et del mio vaneggiar vergogna è 'l frutto,
e 'l pentersi, e 'l conoscer chiaramente
che quanto piace al mondo è breve sogno.

[1]

(But now I see well how for a long time I was the talk of the crowd, for which often I am ashamed of myself within; and of my raving, shame is the fruit, and repentance, and the clear knowledge that whatever pleases in the world is a brief dream.)

In this "sweet, low, pitying murmur" of the introductory sonnet, we are told that everything that follows will record only a brief dream, worthy of nothing but shame and repentance. And yet we are enticed to read on even by sound alone—for example, by the dolorous o's and mournful m's of this beautifully weeping voice. For weeping is sweet in the *Canzoniere,* so that sighs, as this first sonnet also tells us, can themselves be nourishing, and the sighs of these poems are indeed easy to "drink in" with the ear. In the margin of his Virgil, Petrarch writes that he records Laura's death with a certain "bitter sweetness,"[29] and when he writes of the death of two good friends, he confesses, "Assuredly there is a certain sweetness in mourning; on this theme I am unhappy enough to feed and torture myself and find pleasure for days at a time" (*Fam.* VIII. 9, p. 76). This is not a simple masochism, here or in the lyrics of the *Canzoniere*: *Poet* and *Lover* move in defensive textures that convert rage to pain, and then nevertheless, as though in answer to conflicted *Lover infans,* the pain is made sweet, musical. The poems are rocked with their own intonations, fed with their own sweetness, as they revolve alone in time.

These poems themselves become the significant maternal presences, ultimate systems of equivalences rewarding all "confident expectations," and perhaps therefore the poems are less than successful in assembling Laura as a whole presence. For as we have seen, the evocations of Laura *in vita* tend to be lists of her treasured parts, and often the poems *in morte* continue this cataloguing in the *ubi sunt* tradition (282; 292; 299). For the Poet-Lover is not trying, finally, to evoke Laura as Source, unwordable Presence; the presence of Laura is not ultimately the point here, though it may indeed seem to be. The poem is mimetic of ideal Source while it holds Laura distant. For this is a texture of complex verbal defenses, not Dante's texture of primal receptivity. Dante's pilgrim can hold up the very syllables of Beatrice's name, BE and ICE, as diaphanous to the light of Source (see *Par.* vii. 13-15), whereas Petrarch's Poet-Lover seeds his own octave and sestet with the syllables of Laura's name, weaving LAU, RE, and TA into his own carefully formed syntactic unit: "Quando . . . poi . . . Così . . . se non che . . ." (5). The tribute to the lady or her name is lost to, or indeed becomes, the wordplay itself, the opaque music of syntax and sound.[30] It is his own presence he is assembling from these fragments of her name, just as throughout the lyrics it is his own presence he assembles from all the synecdochic and metonymic parts of Laura. The poem is the distinctive and recognizable presence; Laura remains a shadow, *l'ombra* or *l'aura,* cast by the worded fragments of her.

One wonders whether perhaps this Poet-Lover treats his literary sources in the same way, assimilating them in fragments in order to reconstitute them as himself. He does specify that only a deeply hidden resemblance to the parent literary work should be observable in the child, the successor (**Fam.** XXIII. 19. pp. 198-99); and his oral, incorporative metaphors for this process of making new works from old tend to stress a total assimilation by the new text as self:

> . . . I have read Virgil, Horace, Livy, Cicero, not once but a thousand times, not hastily but in repose, and I have pondered them with all the powers of my mind. I ate in the morning what I would digest in the evening; I swallowed as a boy what I would ruminate upon as a man. These writings I have so thoroughly absorbed and fixed, not only in my memory but in my very marrow, these have become so much a part of myself, that even though I should never read them again they would cling in my spirit. . . . It has cost me great labor to distinguish my sources. [**Fam.** XXII. 2, pp. 182-83]

Those who read poetry, "sweet to the taste," should feed on it and absorb it, not just "taste the Pierian honey with their tongue's tip" (**Fam.** XIII. 7, p. 120).

Sometimes the features of Petrarch's sources seem almost deliberately recognizable, as with the entire quoted lines from predecessors in the love lyric (70), or perhaps more subtly with such Dantean fragments in the *morte* poems as "l'alma, che tanta luce non sostene" (my soul, who cannot bear so much light, 284), or "la mia debile vista" (my weak sight, 339), or "l'occhio interno" (my internal eye, 345), or even "vera beatrice" (366. 52). But usually this Poet-Lover knows how to devour and digest literary presences thoroughly. Thomas Greene demonstrates that Petrarch aims to produce texts that must be deeply sub-read, and Adelia Noferi discusses Petrarch's style as a blending of the styles of Cicero, Augustine, and Seneca.[31]

There is another sense in which these poems take on the qualities of ideal Source—in the continual application of the *lauro* emblem to the poems themselves. In this way, the poems as selves reclaim the eternity so doubtful in that elusive central Source. For as *lauro,* the poems themselves become the desired lady, taking one step further a familiar use of emblems in these poems: "Each of the major emblems for Laura thus at some time or other also stands for the lover, and vice versa."[32]

This mimetic effort is not like the straightforward construction of ideal Source in the poems' music; rather, involved here are several defenses—negations and deviations. For as *lauro,* the poems become the whole presence of the lady forever distanced, and they become thereby an emblem of the Poet-Lover's own unassuageable and ongoing pain. Moreover, by calling themselves *lauro* the poems imply that they are evergreen, permanent, even petrified—and they are all the more permanent for including the "hardness" of the lady, the rejection and the distancing. Those branches are "sempre verdi" (eternally green, 5) partly because the lady-*lauro* never yields, indeed is immobilized in her refusal. Eternal desire, as the Gnostics knew, is at least eternal. In this way the poems as *lauro* become their own treasured part-presences, their own laurel leaves or crown; they "crown [themselves] with the symbol of [their] defeat."[33] This sonnet addressed to Apollo even makes for itself a conclusive laurel crown, in those shading arms:

> sì vedrem poi per meraviglia inseme
> seder la donna nostra sopra l'erba
> et far de la sue braccia a se stessa ombra.
>
> [34]

> (Thus we shall then together see a marvel—our lady sitting on the grass and with her arms making a shade for herself.)

Finally, the poems as *lauro* try to weave into themselves a receptive future audience, moving further to assure their own eternity. These efforts, like other defenses here, are not felt as secure; but at least, in this understanding of *lauro* both self and Source are intended to live together forever. Petrarch wrote in an early Latin lament on his mother's death, "Vivimus pariter, pariter memorabimur ambo."[34] And in the emblem of *lauro,* the Poet-Lover and Laura are verbally fused: thus in this one opaque word *Poet* and *Lover* try to accomplish a fusion that they rarely join to evoke beyond the words. Moreover, the invocation of a sympathetic public helps to confirm these poems as places of infinite repose, to bestow *lauro* upon these poems as *lauro.* For an audience can work as Source . . . , whether it be the masses with their "windy applause" that Petrarch scorned when Dante earned it, or only a circle of initiate readers and lovers, such as those invoked for the **Canzoniere.** From the first "Voi," those textured listening presences allow a chance of pity and pardon, and they encourage the Poet-Lover's hope: "i' spero / farmi immortal" (I hope to become immortal, 71. 95-96). Laura, God, and the Virgin Mary are possible audiences, too, but they hardly care for the poems as *lauro;* it is with their future readers that the poems make their largest effort, to texture their own "stade du miroir" and reclaim themselves from the void.

> ma ricogliendo le sue sparte fronde
> dietro le vo pur così passo passo,
>
> [333]

(but . . . gathering up her scattered leaves, I still follow after her step by step.)

Thus in the music of single poems, and in the application of the term *lauro,* these poems are made as beings-in-words that resemble ideal Source—to answer *Lover infans,* their own central longing. Nevertheless, as a group the poems remain *rime sparse, rerum vulgarium fragmenta,* as though there is not a strong enough sense of Maternal Source in these texts to integrate them beyond the level of the individual poem. For it is positive maternal affect that organizes the self's ability to organize, and that allows to texts their coherence, affective energy, and intentionality. These poems as a book are *fragmenta* in response to their uncertain ontological center.

For example, the poems are episodic, and on the whole they are arranged with no felt integration moment to moment; they are joined to each other by only the slightest of narrative threads. No immediately evident design, chronological or otherwise, governs the poems. Bergin has said of the **Trionfi** and of all Petrarch's longer works that they are composed of fragments, very loosely united, and that this "basic flaw derives from a constitutional incapacity of Petrarch to handle the grand design" for "the synthesizing resolution eluded Petrarch."[35] Those who have found patterns in the

Canzoniere have had to work hard to do so, as though any real integration in the sequence were well hidden. For instance, Ernest Wilkins has carefully traced the various orderings of the poems, exploring rationales for each of them. Bernardo has recently sought to connect the search for form with the development of Laura's image, especially in the *Triumphs;* he stresses the frequent reorderings of the last thirty poems. Thomas Roche has suggested that the Christian liturgical calendar may offer a map for the sequence.[36] By contrast, Freccero sees the episodic nature of the sequence as a self-contained strength: the poems "spatialize time" and are "free of the threat of closure."[37] But even with such an implied rhetorical infinity, *Poet* still threatens *Lover,* for the poems are also "free," in their fragmentation, of those secure organizing affects that could enable integration and closure. As a whole, the sequence hardly forms a densely integrated presence, even though the rich defensive texturing is insistently distinctive, always identifiable as Petrarch. Durling speaks of Petrarch's "intensely self-critical awareness that all integration of selves and texts is relative, temporary, threatened."[38] But the best description of the fragmentary nature of the sequence is Petrarch's own, or his adoption of Dante's metaphor: the leaves of this book are scattered, *rime sparse,* because they have not been well bound with Love. The Poet-Lover must keep toiling, step by step, in the endless task of collecting again all the scattered leaves of *lauro,* self and Source.

Moreover, some of the defensive texturing seems finally to fail, to threaten the intentionality of the sequence, to cut rather too deeply into the **Canzoniere** as self. For instance, time as antagonist seems not only to distinguish this Poet-Lover but also gradually to remove the purpose of his existence. As the sequence endures through twenty-one years "ardendo" (burning) and another ten years "piangendo" (weeping, 364), he tells us ever more often that he is weary, "stanco di viver" (weary of life, 363), and we sense a relaxing of his will to continue in those potentially inexhaustible antitheses, *Poet* without *Lover.* At several points the weight of time, and the grief at Laura's death, seem to usurp for him even his "sense of an ending," to bring this weeping and writing figure to an abrupt close.[39] Also with the experience of Laura's death, the Poet-Lover seems to lose his defensive confidence that he can possess worded parts of Laura's presence. He seems to move beyond his earlier inexpressibility tropes and now fully to acknowledge, at moments, the distance between his worded part-presences and a Presence beyond words. Whatever I spoke or wrote about her, he once says, "fu breve stilla d'infiniti abissi" (was a little drop from infinite depths; 339).[40] As she tells him in her last visionary appearance, she is now a "Spirito ignudo" (naked spirit), inaccessible to mortal words and far above the level of his sweet music, "queste dolci tue fallaci ciance" (these sweet deceptive chatterings of yours, 359. 60, 41).

Even more troubling for the coherence of the sequence are those intermittent repentance poems and the final "conversion" poems, where *Poet* and *Lover* turn against the self centrally, at the presencing moment. Here defensive ambivalence surely jeopardizes the very reason for the existence of poems and Poet-Lover, their entire foundation of affective energy. The poems contend that they should be otherwise created, that they should be "più belle imprese" (more beautiful undertakings, 62). In this thorough self-doubt, Laura becomes an invalid Source, a mistake, and poems that grow from her *absent presence* are likewise invalid:

> . . . i' chiamo il fine per lo gran desire
> di riveder cui non veder fu 'l meglio.
>
> [319]

(. . . I call out for the end in my great desire to see her again whom it would have been better not to have seen at all.)

All the poems of Laura have been a wandering, an error, better never to have been. When in *De Librorum Copia* Joy boasts, "I possess countless books," Reason replies, "And countless errors. . . ."[41] In the last poems even *lauro* disappears:

> terra è quella ond' io ebbi et freddi et caldi,
> spenti son i miei lauri, or querce et olmi.
>
> [363]

(She is dust from whom I took chills and heat; my laurels are faded, are oaks and elms.)

With *lauro* no longer evergreen, Laura ceases to be named: "tale è terra" (366. 92). The Virgin Mary is brought forward as legitimate Source, new ground of the poems' being:

> Vergine, i' sacro et purgo
> al tuo nome et pensieri e 'ngegno et stile,
> la lingua e 'l cor, le lagrime e i sospiri.
>
> [366. 126-28]

(Virgin, I consecrate and cleanse in your name my thought and wit and style, my tongue and heart, my tears and my sighs.)

But this consecration works only for future poems, not for past ones, and now the sequence is over. The whole sequence seems to have been merely a prelude to its palinode: these retractions, if one takes them at all seriously (and many readers have been understandably reluctant to do so), draw all purpose and intentionality from the poems and leave them grounded on full absence. In this sense we have perhaps not liter-

ary strength, but literary weakness, from fictionalized moral flaws. As the first sonnet announces, the poems to follow are to be understood as valueless: raving, "vaneggiar," and cause for repentance, and "giovenile errore." They have taken their being from one who is dust. Who would ask integration or coherence, then, from such fully devalued poems as these?

Perhaps this ultimate turning-against-the-self works as a last, desperate defense—a "splitting" away of almost all the poems as "bad" in order to preserve the ensuing silence after the sequence as "good." That is, the poems seem to annihilate themselves, to renounce their long-held purposes, in order to purify the blank spaces beyond themselves, to conjure the Void as God or true Source. To put it another way, one must renounce all, must be "revolted by physical pleasures and nauseated by unremitting joys," in order to reach "the still, secure harbor of life" (*Fam.* XXI. 13, pp. 175-76). And among these possible joys the Poet-Lover surely includes the formation of the self in words, "queste dolci tue fallaci ciance." For in these defensive textures some would recognize the "Augustinian" Petrarch holding sway over the "Ciceronian." Bergin finds in the *Africa* a "melancholy acknowledgment that nothing in this world is of lasting importance," and in the *De remediis* a "continuous disparagement of life's joys" that seems "to come very close to a negation of the value of life itself and to press the pessimistic attack somewhat beyond the Christian frontiers."[42] If poems and self are fully renounced, then it is all the more likely that God may lie behind the poems, "il ver tacito . . . / ch'ogni stil vince" (that silent truth which surpasses every style, 309), cradling their lamentations.

But if there is this "splitting" defense at work, it too is ultimately a failure. These poems cannot quite bear to throw themselves away. Thus they reclaim themselves from the silence, gathering their scattered leaves and presenting them to the reader: "Voi ch'ascoltate in rime sparse il suono / di quei sospiri" (You who hear in scattered rhymes the sound of those sighs). For these poems, despite all doubts, fall back upon themselves as Source. In this texturing, Eternity is not other than, but merely *più bella* than Laura,[43] and correspondingly the Poet-Lover's Eternity is not other than the painful, defensive response to her in these words. To belong in Eternity, this Poet-Lover must be one "chi pianse sempre."

Notes

[1] *Epigraph* "And that my suffering may not reach an end, a thousand times a day I die and a thousand am born, so distant am I from health."

Quotations from the *Canzoniere* or *Rime sparse* are from *Petrarch's Lyric Poems,* translated and edited by Robert M. Durling (Cambridge: Harvard University Press, 1976), reprinted by permission of Harvard

University Press. In general, I give line numbers only for the canzoni. Translations are Durling's unless otherwise noted.

[2] *Letters from Petrarch,* selected and translated by Morris Bishop (Bloomington: Indiana University Press, 1966), p. 19 (*Fam.* I. 1). All passages from Petrarch's letters, the *Epistolae familiares* (*Fam.*) and the *Epistolae seniles* (*Sen.*), are cited in Bishop's translation.

[3] See Thomas G. Bergin, *Petrarch* (Boston: Twayne, 1970), pp. 38-39.

[4] John Freccero, "The Fig Tree and the Laurel: Petrarch's Poetics," *Diacritics,* 5 (Spring 1975), 35.

[5] Bergin, p. 36.

[6] *Fam.* xiii. 5, pp. 112-15; Bergin, pp. 33, 79.

[7] Oscar Budel, "Illusion Disabused: A Novel Mode in Petrarch's *Canzoniere,*" in *Francis Petrarch, Six Centuries Later: A Symposium,* ed. Aldo Scaglione, NCSRLL, 3 (Chapel Hill: University of North Carolina Press, 1975), p. 150.

[8] Bergin, p. 170.

[9] Freccero, p. 39.

[10] Robert M. Durling, "Petrarch's 'Giovene donna sotto un verde lauro,'" *Modern Language Notes,* 86 (1971), pp. 9-11, 16.

[11] Bergin, p. 178.

[12] See my article "Petrarch's Courtly and Christian Vocabularies: Language in *Canzoniere* 61-63," *Romance Notes,* 15. 3 (1974).

[13] See Robert M. Durling, Introduction to *Petrarch's Lyric Poems,* p. 28.

[14] See Leonard Foster, *The Icy Fire: Five Studies in European Petrarchism* (Cambridge: Cambridge University Press, 1969), p. 14.

[15] Thomas Greene points out that the characteristic verb tense of the *Canzoniere* is the iterative present: *The Light in Troy: Imitation and Deconstruction in Renaissance Poetry* (New Haven: Yale University Press, to be published in 1982). In my comments about Petrarch's poems, I am indebted to Greene's perceptive readings.

[16] Greene has remarked that rhetorical escape from the oxymoronic pattern of these poems can be only momentary.

[17] Aldo S. Bernardo, *Petrarch, Laura, and the Triumphs* (Albany: State University of New York Press, 1974), pp. 201, 63.

[18] *Trionfo dell'Eternità.* line 95.

[19] Foster, p. 74.

[20] William J. Kennedy, in *Rhetorical Norms in Renaissance Literature* (New Haven: Yale University Press, 1978), discusses the rhetorical strategy of the Petrarchan speaker in his first chapter, "The Petrarchan Mode in Lyric Poetry." He says, "By 'vario stile' one may understand the range of tones, moods, and attitudes, that play off one another in balanced patterns of statement and reversal, thesis and antithesis, resolution and dissolution. . . . One could thus characterize the modality of the Petrarchan sonnet by how it involves the reader in the speaker's evolution of thought, feeling, idea, and attitude through multiple statements, shifts, and reversals within a formally limited space of fourteen lines" (pp. 26-28).

[21] See for example poems 61-62, 80-82, 141-42, 277-96, as well as those later poems involving Laura's visitations and the Poet-Lover's "conversion."

[22] Freccero, p. 37.

[23] Bergin, p. 191.

[24] Freccero, pp. 37, 38.

[25] See René A. Spitz, *The First Year of Life* (New York: International Universities Press, 1965), pp. 98, 135-36.

[26] See above, Chap. 1, at n. 59.

[27] Durling, "Petrarch's 'Giovene donna,'" p. 5.

[28] Bergin, pp. 175-76.

[29] Translated by Ernest H. Wilkins, *Life of Petrarch* (Chicago: University of Chicago Press, 1977).

[30] If there is an impulse to reparation here, it is very much the *new* presence that is being put together. See above, Chap 1. n. 60.

[31] Thomas M. Greene, "Petrarch and the Humanist Hermeneutic," in *Italian Literature: Roots and Branches* (New Haven: Yale University Press, 1976), pp. 211-21. Adelia Noferi, *L'esperienza poetica del Petrarca* (Florence: Le Monnier, 1962), pp. 118-49.

[32] Durling, Introduction, p. 32.

[33] Budel, p. 144.

[34] "We two live together; we will be remembered together." This is *Ep. Met.* I. 7, and is quoted in Bergin, p. 39. Bergin specifies that the number of lines in the poem is equal to the number of years in Petrarch's mother's life.

[35] Bergin, pp. 152, 103.

[36] Thomas P. Roche, Jr., "The Calendrical Structure of Petrarch's *Canzoniere*," *Studies in Philology*, 62 (1974), 152-72.

[37] Freccero, p. 39.

[38] Durling, Introduction, p. 26.

[39] According to Ernest H. Wilkins in *The Making of the "Canzoniere"* (Rome: Edizioni di Storia e Letteratura, 1951), Chap. 9, poems 292 and 304 were each at one time designed as final poems for the *Canzoniere*. See Table 1, p. 194.

[40] See my article "The Evolution of the Poet in Petrarch's *Canzoniere*," *Philological Quarterly*, 57 (Winter 1978).

[41] *De Librorum Copia*, in *Petrarch: Four Dialogues for Scholars*, ed. and trans. Conrad H. Rawski (Cleveland: Western Reserve University Press, 1967), p. 35.

[42] Bergin, pp. 114, 131.

[43] See 359. 64; 268. 40-44, *Trionfo dell'Eternità*, 143-45. The final poem of the *Canzoniere* argues that love for the Virgin Mary should be *proportionately* greater than love for Laura (366. 121-23).

Gordon Braden (essay date 1986)

SOURCE: Gordon Braden, "Love and Fame: The Petrarchan Career," in *Pragmatism's Freud: The Moral Disposition of Psychoanalysis*, edited by Joseph K. Smith and William Kerrigan, The Johns Hopkins University Press, 1986, pp. 126-58.

[*In the essay below, Braden bases his discussion of Petrarch's love poetry on Freud's ideas concerning "unconventional object choices."*]

"The most striking distinction between the erotic life of antiquity and our own," Freud ventures in a late footnote to his *Three Essays on the Theory of Sexuality*, "no doubt lies in the fact that the ancients laid the stress upon the instinct itself, whereas we emphasize its object. The ancients glorified the instinct and were prepared on its account to honour even an inferior object; while we despise the instinctual activity in it-

self, and find excuses for it only in the merits of the object" (*S.E.* 7: 149). Those are not equal options; psychoanalysis aligns itself with the ancient wisdom: "Anyone who looks down with contempt upon psychoanalysis from a superior vantage-point should remember how closely the enlarged sexuality of psycho-analysis coincides with the Eros of the divine Plato" (134). Understanding such Eros means undoing a major disposition of our culture: "We have been in the habit of regarding the connection between the sexual instinct and the sexual object as more intimate than it in fact is. . . . It seems probable that the sexual instinct is in the first instance independent of its object; nor is its origin likely to be due to its object's attractions" (147-48). The immediate context here is the question of unconventional object choices, homosexual and other; but the real point is that any successful settlement of our sexual attention is going to be something of an effort, the result of a complicated process that has more to do with us than with the others who satisfy us or let us down—and that it is possible to be more lucid about this than Western culture since the end of antiquity has tended to be.

This chapter argues on behalf of Freud's historical generalization, which I think will take more weight than he asks it to carry; his graph of the course of Western moral thought tracks more than superficial standards of sexual behavior and taste. I end by corroborating, in a widened sense, Freud's alignment of psychoanalysis with the classical emphasis on the instinct over the object. But I also want to argue that the psychoanalytic critique of romantic love has important historical roots in the world that intervenes between the two paganisms, in a Christian moral tradition that is deeply involved in the very literature that I assume is on Freud's mind and that certainly does the most to legitimate the contrast he makes. There is nothing in classical literature comparable to the exaltation of woman that arises with the Troubadours of the Pays d'Oc in the twelfth century and is transmitted from them to the rest of Europe: to northern France and the Trouvères, to Germany and the Minnesänger, and to Italy and the *stilnovisti*. These poets sing, time and again, of the woman who is the decisive event in a man's life, whose arrival divides that life in two ("Incipit uita noua . . ."), who makes all other concerns trivial in comparison. Among the classical poets, Catullus adumbrates such an enthrallment, but he has other things—and other kinds of love—to write about, too. Freud is right to see the elevation of the feminine object into the alpha and omega of masculine desire as in some ways the special mark of postclassical Western culture. Yet the very origins of that hypostatization are also perceptibly troubled about just what is being so rapturously affirmed; some of the founding works of Western European lyric poetry testify to a distressed awareness that Freud might be right about the nature of love as well.

The significant figure, historically and otherwise, is Petrarch (1304-74), the inheritor of Provençal and stilnovist lyric who gives it the shape in which it becomes the dominant form for serious love poetry for the next three centuries. During the general European Renaissance of the fifteenth and sixteenth centuries, it is Petrarchan imitation that trains the lyric poets of the developing vernaculars: imitation Petrarchan in form—the sonnet, which owes its prominence among the wide repertoire of Italian verse forms to Petrarch's example—but also, and more surprisingly, Petrarchan in content. Italian, French, Spanish, English, German poets, and others, will recount, as though on their own experience, a love that in its general outlines and often in specific details mimics that presented in Petrarch's own *Canzoniere,* the sequence of lyrics about his love for the blond woman with black eyes (and eyebrows) whom he calls Laura. He saw her first during morning services in the Church of St. Claire in Avignon, April 6, 1327, and she took over his life:

> I' vidi Amor che' begli occhi volgea
> soave sì ch' ogni altra vista oscura
> da indi in qua m'incominciò apparere. . . .
>
> [I saw Love moving her lovely eyes so gently that every other sight from then on began to seem dark to me. . . .]

(Canzoniere 144.9-11, 1976)

His devotion remained constant and all-consuming; even her death from the plague twenty-one years later—at exactly the same hour and day of the year at which he first saw her—did not loosen her hold on him. Petrarch's inability to think of anything else ramifies through the Renaissance and beyond.

Yet if that becomes the great love story of its time, literary history has some explaining to do as to why it should have become so central. For it is a peculiar story, peculiarly told: a story, for one thing, in which virtually nothing happens. The preceding paraphrase includes almost all the clearly recoverable events, and some of those can be specified only from information available outside the poems. The surviving evidence of Petrarch's intense interest in the order of his 366 poems—there were several states of the collection, with much meticulous rearranging—sorts oddly with the modern impression that the poems could be read in almost any order (as they usually are: even scholars seldom read them straight through). The very point of the sequence's main event—Laura's death, announced in poem 267—is that it changes almost nothing. The situation Petrarch writes about is largely a static one, and at least ostensibly for a simple but important reason: Laura responds with implacable indifference, if not active hostility, to her lover's attention. In the face of this, he can muster few resources; what he most

famously expresses is his despair. The *fin amor* celebrated by Petrarch's predecessors was itself characteristically unconsummated: "the concept of true love was not framed to include success" (Valency 1982, 160). Petrarch's extraordinary elongation of that frustration is echoed in almost all of the *Canzoniere's* Renaissance descendants, a run of masculine bad luck so insistent that it becomes almost a joke, a sign of Petrarchism's monotonous conventionality. But jokes have their reasons; and one may meditate on why the European lyric celebration of the feminine object of desire should begin with several centuries fixated on the unavailability of that object.

Petrarch himself for the most part attributes Laura's unresponsiveness to her virtuousness; tradition assumes (as in Provençal lyric) a husband (perhaps ambiguously referred to in 219), so that she is simply doing what Petrarch himself can admit is the correct thing: "veggio ch' ella / per lo migliore al mio desir contese," "I see it was for the best that she resisted my desire" (1976, 289.5-6). Later Petrarchists will be more willing to attack the woman's behavior as, in the usual accusation, cruelty: "Cruell fayre Love, I justly do complaine, / Of too much rigour, and they heart unkind" (Giles Fletcher the Elder 1964, *Licia* 44.1-2). The claim draws on Renaissance lore about female nature, in which cruelty was often listed as a characteristic flaw. Subtler thoughts on the matter, however, take us into an important area of psychoanalytic theory about erotic development; Freud's own delineation of "the type of female most frequently met with, which is probably the purest and truest one" (*S.E.* 14: 88), is a credible portrait of the Petrarchan mistress: "Women, especially if they grow up with good looks, develop a certain self-contentment which compensates them for the social restrictions that are imposed upon them in their choice of object. Strictly speaking, it is only themselves that such women love with an intensity comparable to that of the man's love for them. Nor does their need lie in the direction of loving, but of being loved" (88-89). What is happening makes sense because it is in fact a reversion to the original disposition of the libido, which in its first stages is invested not in any external presence, male or female, but in the self; and the spectacle of that reversion can be reveting: "The importance of this type of woman for the erotic life of mankind is to be rated very high. Such women have the greatest fascination for men" (89). It is indeed the allure of their selfishness that may be said to exact the spectacular selflessness of their lovers' devotion, and the man's despair in the Petrarchan story overlays a profound congruence: he and his mistress both adore the same thing. Extreme object love is symbiotic with an extreme self-love that is if anything the more powerful force; the anaclitic lover is trained by the narcissistic beloved.

Which is in fact to use Petrarch's own language from one of the few significant reproaches he ever brings himself to make against Laura:

> Il mio adversario in cui veder solete
> gli occhi vostri ch' Amore e 'l Ciel onora
> colle non sue bellezze v'innamora
> più che 'n guisa mortal soavi et liete.
>
> Per consiglio di lui, Donna, m'avete
> scacciato del mio dolce albergo fora;
> miserio esilio! avegna ch' i' non fora
> d'abitar degno ove voi sola siete.
>
> Ma s' io v'era con saldi chiovi fisso,
> non dovea specchio farvi per mio danno
> a voi stessa piacendo aspra et superba.
> Certo, se vi rimembra di Narcisso,
> questo et quel corso ad un termino vanno—
> ben che di sì bel fior sia indegna l'erba.
>
> [My adversary in whom you are wont to see your eyes, which Love and Heaven honor, enamors you with beauties not his but sweet and happy beyond mortal guise. By his counsel, Lady, you have driven me out of my sweet dwelling: miserable exile! even though I may not be worthy to dwell where you alone are. But if I had been nailed there firmly, a mirror should not have made you, because you pleased yourself, harsh and proud to my harm. Certainly, if you remember Narcissus, this and that course lead to one goal—although the grass is unworthy of so lovely a flower.]
>
> (*Canzoniere* 1976, 45)

The flower is of course the narcissus, into which, according to Ovid's *Metamorphoses,* the Greek youth is transformed at his death. The flower's appearance gives a grace to Narcissus's end, but his dying itself is a punishment inflicted by Nemesis for spurning the nymph Echo, who in rejection fades into the phenomenon that carries her name. In Ovid, Narcissus has an early disposition toward his fate—"in tenera tam dura superbia forma," "such harsh pride in that tender form" (1916, 3.354)—but he does not actually look into the fatal pool, does not become a narcissist, until after he has refused to love another. A minor adjustment of cause and effect allows Petrarch to make the myth into a telling version of his own relation to Laura: hypnotized self-absorption paired with tragic anaclisis. And in so doing he indeed gives the classical myth a remarkable approximation of what has become its modern meaning, to sound a sophisticated warning. Laura's indifference is hardly virtue, and worse than mere cruelty to him; it is a self-destructive perversion of her own capacity for love.

Putting it that way only slightly overstates the polemical force of psychoanalysis: "A strong egoism is a protection against falling ill, but in the last resort we must begin to love in order not to fall ill" (Freud *S.E.*

14: 85). Secure object love is an important achievement of psychic health, likely for all its difficulties to be the most fortunate outcome for the individual, while secondary narcissism is a frequent—increasingly frequent—and proper target for therapeutic correction. Rorty . . . reminds us of Freud's larger sense, stated on several occasions, that the mission of psychoanalysis was to attack "the universal narcissism of men, their self-love" (Freud, *S.E.* 17:139). If, as Rorty argues, Freud has not entirely thought through his point here, that is in great part because of the august heritage behind such a stand: at least as much a moral as a scientific heritage, and one that in this regard Freud shares with Petrarch. Petrarch's own accusatory diagnosis of Laura's state draws on the late medieval mythography in which Narcissus's pride, *superbia,* became a matter of special interest: for pride is, in Christian thinking, not a mere character flaw but the most insidious of human sins.[1]

Of all sins, pride is perhaps the cleverest in its disguises; Petrarch's philosophical writings brood on its capacity for, indeed, passing itself off as virtue (e.g., **De remediis utriusque fortunae,** book 1, chap. 10, in Petrarch 1554, 1:14-15). Instructing such wariness is the spirit of Augustine, who identified pride as the primal sin of the fall: "'Pride is the start of every kind of sin' [Ecclesiasticus 10.15]. And what is pride except a longing for a perverse kind of exaltation? For it is a perverse kind of exaltation to abandon the basis on which the mind should be firmly fixed, and to become, as it were, based on oneself, and so remain. This happens when a man is too pleased with himself" (*City of God* 1984, 14.13; see also Green 1949). In its original context, much of Augustine's polemic was aimed at the heroic values of classical pagan culture, a culture that, for all its sensitivity to the dangers of overreaching, was much less severe on self-regard and had no trouble praising *autarceia* as a goal. But the Empire had provided ample evidence of the civic and other dangers of such values, and Augustine spoke for a new ethical dispensation from which classical narcissism was to be uprooted: "The earthly city was created by selflove reaching the point of contempt for God, the Heavenly City by the love of God carried as far as contempt of self" (*City of God* 1984, 14.28). Humility becomes a central standard, and the self's comfort must be understood as depending on something beyond its own borders; under Christian influence, the contrast between self-love and the love of others, Eros and agapê, becomes newly visible as a contrast of profoundly moral urgency.

Petrarch's application of that urgency to the matter of courtship accordingly informs some of the most compelling arguments in the tradition to follow:

> Ach, Freundin, scheu der Götter Rache,
> dass du dir nicht zu sehr gefällst,

dass Amor nicht einst deiner lache,
den du itzt höhnst und spöttlich hältst.
Dass, weil du nichts von mir wilst wissen,
ich nicht mit Echo lasse mich,
und du denn müssest mit Narzissen
selbst lieben und doch hassen dich.

[Ah, darling, avoid the gods' wrath; do not be too
pleased with yourself, do not let Love, whom you
now disdain and treat mockingly, some day laugh at
you. Do not make me lose myself, like Echo, because
you take no notice of me, and so make yourself, like
Narcissus, love yourself and yet hate yourself.]

(*Oden* 5.38.25-32, in Fleming 1965)

Addressing the threat of corrosive pride in the woman's
resistance is not merely a seducer's ploy; it is nowhere more eloquently rendered than in the tradition's
most adroitly Christian sequence:

Ne none so rich or wise, so strong or fayre,
   but fayleth trusting on his owne
      assurance:
   and he that standeth on the hyghest
      stayre
   fals lowest: for on earth nought hath
      enduraunce.
Why then doe ye proud fayre, misdeeme so
   farre,
   that to your selfe ye most assured arre.

(Spenset, *Amoretti* 1926, 58.9-14)

At least as embodied in poetry, however, the moral
stand here comes with an acknowledgment of
narcissism's indelibility; and what is, at best, in the
offing is not a mere humbling of the woman. Other
moral issues are still in play; even contaminated with
pride, resistance to lust is a virtue, and the most sophisticated Petrarchan sequences trace a complicated
response to the strength behind that resistance. The
sonnet of Spenser's just quoted is immediately followed by a twin that praises something very close to
what the first poem seems to attack:

Thrise happie she, that is so well assured
Unto her selfe and setled so in hart:
that nether will for better be allured,
ne feard with worse to any chaunce to
   start

(*Amoretti* 1926, 59.1-4)

And Spenser's sequence is in fact moving toward a happy
ending in marriage that allows us to say just what the telos
of the Petrarchan love story actually is. Petrarch briefly
adumbrates that telos in offering himself as the replacement for Laura's mirror; Spenser expands the hint:

Leave lady in your glasse of christall clene,
   Your goodly selfe for evermore to vew:

and in my selfe, my inward selfe I meane,
   most lively lyke behold your semblant
      trew.
Within my hart, though hardly it can shew
   thing so divine to vew of earthly eye,
   the fayre Idea of your celestiall hew,
   and every part remaines immortally:
And were it not that through your cruelty,
   with sorrow dimmed and deformd it were:
   the goodly ymage of your visnomy,
   clearer then christall would therein appere.
But if your selfe in me ye playne will see,
   remove the cause by which your fayre
      beames darkned be.

(*Amoretti* 1926, 45)

The traditional reproach is there, yet the alternative
being imagined is not a fundamental alteration of the
woman's narcissism, but rather its incorporation into
a cooperative endeavor. The lover's bid to replace the
mirror in the lady's affections involves a promise to
perform the function that his old adversary performs:
she can continue to admire herself in the mirror of his
admiration. This possibility is itself no more than the
fundamental congruence of their situation; the chance
for happiness lies in her capacity to acknowledge it
and to trust her lover to live up to his role in it. That
trust can, as it were, reconcile pride and dependence,
and provide a basis for communion within which her
self-absorption nevertheless has a privileged place.
Milton's Eve follows a similar path. The Petrarchan
drama of selfless devotion, in one of its dimensions, is
actually a testing of the possible arrangements between narcissistic selfhood and the world around it.

The real truth of that proposition, however, takes us
into darker territory, beyond the prospect of any familiar romantic success. If Spenser presents his lady
as a narcissist, he offers Narcissus himself as a figure
for the poet who loves her:

My hungry eyes through greedy covetize,
   still to behold the object of their paine,
   with no contentment can themselves
      suffize:
   but having pine and having not complaine.
For lacking it they cannot lyfe sustayne,
   and having it they gaze on it the more:
   in their amazement lyke *Narcissus* vaine
   whose eyes him starv'd: so plenty makes
      me poore.

(*Amoretti* 1926, 35.1-8; also *Amoretti* 83)

And the tradition of such references is a rich one,
extending back beyond Petrarch:

Come Narcissi, in sua spera mirando,
s'inamorao, per ombra, a la fontana,
veggendo se medesimo pensando

ferissi il core e la sua mente vana,

gittovisi entro, per l'ombria pilgliando,
di quello amore lo prese morte strana;
ed io, vostra bieltate rimembrando,
l'ora ch'io vidi voi, donna sovrana,

inamorato sono sì feramente,
che, poi ch'io volglia non poria partire,
sì m'ha l'amor compreso strettamente.

Tormentami lo giorno e fa languire,
com'a Narcissi parami piagente,
veggendo voi, la morte sofferire.

[As Narcissus, gazing in his mirror, came to love
through the shadow in the fountain, and, seeing
himself in the midst of regretting—his heart and
vain mind smitten—plunged in, to catch the
shadow, and then strange death embraced him
with that love, so I, remembering how beautiful
you were when I saw you, sovereign lady, fall in
love so wildly I could not, though I might want
to, part from you, love holds me in its grip so
tightly. Day torments me, draws off my strength,
and, like Narcissus, to me it looks like pleasure, as
I gaze on you, to suffer death.]
(Chiaro Davanzati, *Sonetti* 26, in Goldin 1973,
276-77[2])

In particular instances one may be less sure than with
the poems about the lady's mirror just how far the
mythic reference is meant to reach; but cumulatively
the examples make too much sense to ignore within a
tradition where the beloved, for all one actually gets to
see of her, might as well not exist.

An ongoing topos in discussion of Petrarchan poets
has been to wonder if the lady in question was, actually, *real;* the questioning began in fact in Petrarch's
own time, with his defensive insistence to Giacomo
Colonna that Laura was not merely a literary character
(*Epistolae familiares,* trans. Bernardo 1975-85, 2.9).
Enlightened criticism has come to insist that the question is irrelevant to an appreciation of the poems themselves, but it is still impressive how systematically
Petrarchan love poems, and especially the *Canzoniere,*
veer away from direct encounter with a substantial
presence. As a character, Laura is not called upon to
do much work. Most of the poems in which she
actually speaks to Petrarch come after her death, in
dreams or visions; what few exchanges we have before that are ambiguous in their status:

Chinava a terra il bel guardo gentile
et tacendo dicea, come a me parve:
"Chi m'allontana il mio fedele amico?"

[She bent to earth her lovely noble glance and in
her silence said, as it seemed to me: "Who sends

away from me my faithful friend?"]
(1976, 123.12-14)

The impression of comparative eventlessness in the
Canzoniere is generated in great part by this overlay
of interpretive subjectivity. Apparent events are seldom followed up; it is possible that this particular
poem is answered not much later when the detec-
tion of Laura's goodwill turns out to be presumptuous:

Quella ch' amare et sofferir ne 'nsegna
e vol che 'l gran desio, l'accesa spene
ragion, vergogna, et reverenza affrene,
di nostro ardir fra se stessa si sdegna.

Onde Amor paventoso fugge al core,
lasciando ogni sua impresa, et piagne et
   trema;
ivi s'asconde et non appar più fore.

[She who teaches us to love and to be patient,
and wishes my great desire, my kindled hope, to
be reined in by reason, shame, and reverence, at
our boldness is angry within herself. Wherefore
Love flees terrified to my heart, abandoning his
every enterprise, and weeps and trembles; there
he hides and no more appears outside.]

(140.5-11)

Yet the rebuke is of a piece with the encouragement:
Laura's anger "fra se stessa" is enough to send the
lover fleeing (inward) in terror. Indeed, we are not
sure his own aggression was anything more than a
nuanced look; elsewhere we hear of his virtual inability to speak in Laura's presence:

Ben, si i' non erro, di pietate un raggio
scorgo fra 'l nubiloso altero ciglio,
che 'n parte rasserena il cor doglioso;

allor raccolgo l'alma, et poi ch' i' aggio
di scovrirle il mio mal preso consiglio,
tanto gli ò a dit che 'ncominciar non oso.

[If I do not err, I do perceive a gleam of pity on
her cloudy, proud brow, which partly clears my
sorrowing heart: then I collect my soul, and, when
I have decided to discover my ills to her, I have
so much to say to her that I dare not begin.]

(169.9-14)

The reality of that gleam of pity remains untested, and
it should not surprise us to be told in the last poem in
the sequence that Laura actually knew nothing of
Petrarch's torment; his conviction that she would have
refused him out of virtue is entangled with the likeli-
hood that she was not even clearly challenged to do
so:

tale è terra et posto à in doglia
lo mio cor, che vivendo in pianto il tenne
et de mille miei mali un non sapea;
et per saperlo pur quel che n'avenne
fora avvenuto, ch' ogni altra sua voglia
era a me morte et a lei fama rea.

[one is now dust and makes my soul grieve who
kept it, while alive, in weeping and of my thousand
sufferings did not know one; and though she had
known them, what happened would still have
happened, for any other desire in her would have
been death to me and dishonor to her.]

(366.92-97³)

It seems a fair guess that the lover's frustration is
actually self-censorship, and that anything he has to
say about his beloved's own state of mind is effectively preempted by his own actions and imaginings.

The general run of poems in the **Canzoniere** do not
essay direct presentation of Laura at all. She shows up
obliquely, sometimes through a fetishized object such
as a veil or—a particularly influential detail—a glove
(Mirollo 1984, 99-159). Most famously, she appears
in the abstracted symbols for parts of her body that
become the conventional decor by which later Petrarchan
verse is most quickly recognized: "La testa or fino, et
calda neve il volto, / ebeno i cigli, et gli occhi eran due
stelle," "Her head was fine gold, her face warm snow,
ebony her eyebrows, and her eyes two stars" (1976,
157.9-10). What is here spelled out is often the merest
shorthand, as such metaphors take on a life of their
own that can make Petrarch's poetry surreal and baffling at first encounter:

L'oro et le perle e i fior vermigli e i bianchi
che 'l verno devria far languidi et secchi
son per me acerbi et velenosi stecchi
ch' io provo per lo petto et per li fianchi.

[The gold and the pearls, and the red and white
flowers that the winter should have made languid
and dry, are for me sharp and poisonous thorns
that I feel along my breast and my sides.]

(46.1-4)

A famous seventeenth-century portrait literalizing such
conventions—the woman's eyes *are* suns, her teeth
are pearls, her breasts *are* globes, with the lines of
longitude visible on them—makes blatant, after long
impatience, a grotesquerie implicit from the start (see
the reproduction in Booth 1977, 453). The motifs do
not converge but scatter into incongruent areas of
metaphorical reference, and do as much to conceal or
replace the woman as to present her. They are verbal
fetishes, displacements of erotic intent away from its
normal object; what they communicate is not the
woman's beauty but the fierceness of the energy that
fixes on it. They are only the appropriate mode of
description for a poetry whose principal business is
the hyperbolic dramatizing of the lover's reaction to
his condition: "O passi sparsi, o pensier vaghi et pronti,
/ o tenace memoria, o fero ardore . . . ," "O scattered
steps, O yearning, ready thoughts, O tenacious memory,
O savage ardor . . ." (161.1-2). The most important
reason for Petrarch's ongoing haziness as to what, if
anything, is actually happening is that his real interest
is in a private intensity of response most memorable
exactly for being able to swamp the lineaments of its
particular occasion. This is not the least of the reasons
for speaking of him as the first modern lyric poet.

Petrarch's response is, of course, primarily one of
distress, yoked to strong feelings of helplessness; yet
the distress has its rewards: "in tale stato / è dolce il
pianto più ch' altri non crede," "in such a state weeping is sweeter than anyone knows" (1976, 130.7-8).
And the most convincing and substantial passages of
relief the **Canzoniere** provides the lover are not the
brief moments when a favorable response is (probably) hallucinated from Laura herself, but come rather
with a deeper plunge into alienation. The poet of incurable love is also the poet of actively sought solitude:

In una valle chiusa d'ogn' intorno,
ch' è refrigerio de' sospir miei lassi,
giunsi sol con Amor, pensoso et tardo;

ivi non donne ma fontane et sassi
et l'imagine trovo di quel giorno
che 'l pensier mio figura ovunque io
    sguardo.

[In a valley closed on all sides, which cools my
weary sighs, I arrived alone with Love, full of
care, and late; there I find not ladies but fountains
and rocks and the image of that day which my
thoughts image forth wherever I may glance.]

(116.9-14)

The cooling of the sighs afforded by such retreat
from the object of desire is not a lessening of desire
but quite the contrary: away from all human interference, that desire can exercise itself with a new freedom and ease, in the image that the mind can project
onto the passive landscape. It is in just this mode that
Petrarch can become his most rapturous:

I' l'ò più volte (or chi fia che mi 'l
    creda?)
ne l'acqua chiara et sopra l'erba verde
veduto viva, et nel troncon d'un faggio
    e 'n bianca nube, sì fatta che Leda
avria ben detto che sua figlia perde
come stella che 'l sol copre col raggio;
    et quanto in più selvaggio

loco mi trovo e 'n più deserto lido,
tanto più bella il mio pensier l'adombra.

[I have many times (now who will believe me?)
seen her alive in the clear water and on the green
grass and in the trunk of a beech tree and in a
white cloud, so beautiful that Leda would have
said that her daughter faded like a star covered
by the sun's ray; and in whatever wildest place
and most deserted shore I find myself, so much
the more beautiful does my thought shadow her
forth.]

(129.40-48)

The woman's very distance (*lontonanza*) enables a
heady sense of power on the lover's part, of the capacity of his own mind to transform or displace external reality. At its most cogently celebratory. Petrarchan
love poetry can seem an exaltation less of the woman
herself—"Whose presence, absence, absence presence
is" (Sidney, *Astrophil and Stella* 60.13)—than of the
poet's own imagination.

An awareness of the deep connection between love
and the imagination is one of Petrarch's most important legacies to the Renaissance. "Love lookes not
with the eye, but with the minde" (Shakespeare, *Midsummer Night's Dream* 1968, 1.1.234); the lover's eye
learns to see what he wants it to see:

if it see the rud'st or gentlest sight,
The most sweet-favor or deformedst
    creature,
The mountaine, or the sea, the day, or
    night:
The Croe, or Dove, it shapes them to your
    feature.
Incapable of more, repleat with you,
My most true minde thus maketh m'eyne
untrue.

(Shakespeare, *Sonnets* 113.9-14,
Q1 emended, see Booth 1977, 374-75)

A major interpretation of Petrarchism is that its experience of frustrated enamorment is, properly
handled, the first step into an autonomous mental
reality. Erotic enlightenment begins when the absence
of the presumed object of desire prompts the lover to
replace it with a more secure one of his own making:
"To escape the torment of this absence and to enjoy
beauty without suffering, the Courtier, aided by reason, must turn his desire entirely away from the
body and to beauty alone . . . and in his imagination
give it a shape distinct from all matter; and thus
make it loving and dear to his soul, and there enjoy
it; and let him keep it with him day and night, in
every time and place, without fear of ever losing it"
(Castiglione 1959, 351). Loving the woman's image
is better than loving the woman herself, on both

practical and ontological grounds; and the effort of
intellectual abstraction so provoked can lead the lover
to the wisdom of a desire wholly independent of
worldly objects, leaving his original beloved far behind: "Among such blessings the lover will find another much greater still, if he will make use of this
love as a step by which to mount to a love far more
sublime . . . he will no longer contemplate the particular beauty of one woman, but that universal beauty
which adorns all bodies; and so, dazzled by this greater
light, he will not concern himself with the lesser, and
burning with a better flame, he will feel little esteem
for what at first he so greatly prized" (352).
Petrarchism, in such theorizing, intersects the arc of
Neoplatonic philosophy, that great Renaissance recovery of "the Eros of the divine Plato" that nurtures
so much of the period's glorification of artistic creativity.

Much of the power of that philosophy lies in its ability
to guarantee that a withdrawal from external reality—
"instead of going outside himself in thought . . . let
him turn within himself, in order to contemplate that
beauty which is seen by the eyes of the mind" (Castiglione
1959, 353)—can in fact give access to the true ground
of that reality: "Just as from the particular beauty of
one body [love] guides the soul to the universal beauty
of all bodies, so in the highest stage of perfection
beauty guides it from the particular intellect to the
universal intellect" (354). What may be mistaken for
self-absorption is in fact the truest route beyond the
self. Extrapolated to those levels, however,
Neoplatonism—to which Petrarch himself had no direct recourse—does not really give us the *Canzoniere*.
Petrarch's own faith in his visions is never more than
poignant:

Ma mentre tener fiso
posso al primo pensier la mente vaga,
et mirar lei e obliar me stesso,
sento Amor sì da presso
che del suo proprio error l'alma s'appaga;
in tante parti et sì bella la veggio
che se l'error durasse, altro non cheggio.

[But as long as I can hold my yearning mind fixed
on the first thought, and look at her and forget
myself, I feel Love so close by that my soul is
satisfied by its own deception; in so many places
and so beautiful I see her, that, if the deception
should last, I ask for no more.]

(1976, 129.33-39)

What the mind holds to is still, in the final analysis, an
error; it can be argued that the true focus of the
Canzoniere is not the erotic vision but its dispersal,
when a less exalted but more realistic version of the
poet's work than Neoplatonism tends to propagate
makes its appearance:

Poi quando il vero sgombra
quel dolce error, pur lì medesmo assido
me freddo, pietra morta in pietra viva,
in guisa d'uom che pensi et pianga et
    scriva.

[Then, when the truth dispels that sweet deception,
right there in the same place I sit down, cold, a
dead stone on the living rock, like a man who
thinks and weeps and writes.]

(129.49-52)

A pun used elsewhere as well encrypts a signature—
"me freddo, pietra": I, Francesco Petrarca—and the
residue of the vision is a return to self in a toughened,
newly frightening form, whose climactic activity is
writing. And for all the torment that Laura seems to
impose on him, Petrarch's most telling anguish comes
with his consideration of what is involved in a poetic
career of the sort he has set for himself.

That anguish is keyed to an even more momentous
pun:

Giovene donna sotto un verde lauro
vidi più bianca et più fredda che neve
non percossa dal sol molti et molt'anni;
e 'l suo parlare e 'l bel viso et le chiome
mi piacquen sì ch' i' l' ò dinanzi agli occhi
ed avrò sempre ov' io sia in poggio o 'n
    riva.

[A youthful lady under a green laurel I saw, whiter
and colder than snow not touched by the sun
many and many years, and her speech and her
lovely face and her locks pleased me so that I
have her before my eyes and shall always have
wherever I am, on slope or shore.]

(1976, 30.1-6)

Laura the woman is never wholly separable from *lauro*,
the laurel, the crown of poetic fame; and Petrarch's
desire for the woman in Avignon grades into the desire
for literary immortality. The mythic version of that transformation gives the ***Canzoniere***—indeed, perhaps the
whole of Petrarch's oeuvre—its master trope:

Apollo, s' ancor vive il bel desio
che t'infiammava a le tesaliche onde,
et se non ài l'amate chiome bionde,
volgendo gli anni, già poste in oblio,

dal pigro gelo et dal tempo aspro et rio
che dura quanto 'l tuo viso s'asconde
difendi or l'onorata et sacra fronde
ove tu prima et poi fu' invescato io.

[Apollo, if the sweet desire is still alive that
inflamed you beside the Thessalian waves, and if

you have not forgotten, with the turning of the
years, those beloved blond locks; against the
slow frost and the harsh and cruel time that lasts
as long as your face in hidden, now defend the
honored and holy leaves where you first and then
I were limed.]

(34.1-8[4])

Among the first of the famous stories in the *Metamorphoses* is that of Apollo's desire for the nymph Daphne,
who by Cupid's design flees from him: "auctaque
forma fuga est," writes Ovid (1916, 1.530), "her beauty
was enhanced by her flight." On appeal to her father,
the river-god Peneus, she is transformed into a laurel
tree, and Apollo finds recompense for his sexual frustration in appropriating her leaves as his special insigne:

"at, quoniam coniunx mea non potes
    esse,
arbor eris certe" dixit "mea! semper
    habebunt
te coma, te citharae, te nostrae, laure,
    pharetrae."

["Since you cannot be my wife, you will certainly
be my tree," he said. "Forever will my hair, my
lyres, my quivers carry you, laurel."]

(557-59)

Ovid goes on to rehearse the classical role of the laurel
as the honor given to victorious Caesars, but the detail
that interests Petrarch is the cithara. For him, Apollo
is preeminently the god of poetry, and the laurel crown
is most important as the one that certifies poetry as a
potential source of public recognition at least as great
as that accorded princes and generals: "Since both
Caesars and poets move toward the same goal, though
by different paths, it is fitting that one and the same
reward be prepared for both, namely, a wreath from
a fragrant tree, symbolizing the fragrance of good
fame and of glory" (Wilkins 1955, 309). So Petrarch
on the most momentous public occasion of his life: his
own receipt of the laurel crown in 1341, on the
Capitoline Hill in Rome, in a ceremony that he himself
had done much to reestablish, after a millennial lapse
("non percossa dal sol molti et molt' anni"), as the
centerpiece of the program that came to be known as
humanism, the revival of classical literary culture as a
field both of study and of new endeavor. Fueling that
program is the promise of a classical style of heroic
recognition—*bona fama et gloria*—achievable in the
process, now by the exercise not merely of physical
and political prowess but of intellectual capability as
well. Opening onto that possibility, the pun in Laura's
name is perhaps the strongest connection between the
dazed obsessiveness of the ***Canzoniere*** and the agora
of normal human business. Frustrated desire and professional success somehow belong together.

Even though (aside from one Mistress Bays in the mid-sixteenth century [Rollins 1966, 1:251-53]) the different names of later Petrarchan ladies cannot supply the same pun, the connection sustains itself throughout the tradition. Adoration of the woman is seldom far from an assertion of the immortalizing powers of the poetry written about her: "Then would I decke her head with glorious bayes, / and fill the world with her victorious prayse" (Spenser, *Amoretti* 1926, 29.13-14). The topos comes with many valences to fit local situations. The most straightforward rationalization for its persistence is that the loved one's resistance shows her worthy of praise (the mythographers take the myth of Daphne primarily as a celebration of virginity), and in this connection the lover's own posture can reach a special purity of selflessness: "No publike Glorie vainely I pursue, / All that I seeke, is to eternize you" (Drayton, *Idea* 1931-41, 47.13-14).

Yet the injection of this theme into the tradition also does more than perhaps anything else to queer such protestations; it is on just this point that the shifty politics of the situation declare themselves most obviously. The beloved ostensibly being immortalized is, in simple historical fact, almost invariably unknown, and even when known is not actually being made famous. Elizabeth Boyle (who?) is not famous; Edmund Spenser is. The author of the last lines quoted is also capable of being, to my mind, more honest:

> though in youth, my Youth untimely
>   perish,
> To keepe Thee from Oblivion and the Grave,
> Ensuing Ages yet my Rimes shall cherish,
> Where I intomb'd, my better part shall save;
> And though this Earthly Body fade and die.
> My Name shall mount upon Eternitie.
>
> (*Idea* 44.9-14)

This is in a sense only fair, indeed an act of psychic health in making the best of a bad situation: the fulfillment sacrificed to the woman's indifference is recuperated in artistic achievement. One may even cheer the hint of revenge (in some writers more than that) in such a maneuver. But the most challenging intimation is the more duplicitous one that Petrarch reports was put to him by Colonna: "That I invented the splendid name of Laura so that it might be not only something for me to speak about but occasion to have others speak of me; that indeed there was no Laura on my mind except perhaps the poetic one for which I have aspired as is attested by my long and untiring studies" (*Epistolae familiares,* trans. Bernardo 1975-85, 2.9). The arrangement here posited in its crudest form fits in subtler ways as well with the poetry before us—"deh, ristate a veder quale è 'l mio male," "ah, stay to see what my suffering is"

(*Canzoniere* 1976, 161.14)—and there are good reasons for thinking professional calculation not merely a compensatory response to erotic failure but its partner and even master from the first. The story of the ego's apparent impoverishment may itself be a strategy for its extraordinary enrichment.

It is accordingly not only or even primarily the Petrarchan mistress who lies open to the charge of *superbia.* Petrarch's Christian heritage is skillfully accusatory toward love such as his, and especially toward the involuted dynamics of the male imagination. An important tradition of late medieval moral thought makes much of the lover's *immoderata cogitatio,* in a way that can be related to deployment of the Narcissus myth in the age's love poetry. Erotic fascination is actually self-fascination, a sophisticated sin of idolatry that threatens to substitute the lover's own fantasizing for proper devotion to the true creator (Robertson 1962, 65-113; Freccero 1975). Petrarch assents to such language—"l'idolo mio scolpito in vivo lauro," "my idol carved in living laurel" (*Canzoniere* 1976, 30.27, on which see Durling 1971)—and adding the cult of literary fame (previously only hinted at; see Valency 1982, 95-96) to the thematics of courtly love gears with the accusation and gives it new power, a condemnatory force that outlasts many more transient aspects of Christian morality. Freud himself . . . felt that force in a quite personal way; unpagan anxiousness over a classical style of personal ambition pushes what little Freud has to say about fame, for all its obvious relevance to the theory of narcissim, into virtually the last of his writings. One may both confirm and extend that theory by listening to Petrarch's articulate fear for the state of his soul, a fear in which the sin of sexual desire is characteristically entangled with the sin of pride.

In his most directly personal work, the Latin prose dialogue ***De secreto conflictu curarum mearum,*** Petrarch invokes the very spirit of Augustine ("that other fiction of mine," as he puts it in the letter to Colonna) to interrogate and accuse him, in a scenario of scathing introspection about "the causes that inflate your mind with pride [*superbis flatibus*]" (1911, 55). The brief opens with *superbia* in some of its most obvious forms: "Will you perchance be taken in by your own good-looking face, and when you behold in the glass your smooth complexion and comely features are you minded to be smitten, entranced, charmed?" (54-55). Petrarch parries such attacks—"I will not deny that in the days of my youth I took some care to trim my head and to adorn my face; but the taste for that kind of thing has gone with my early years" (57)[5]—only to confront subtler diagnoses: "I cannot disguise from you one word in your discourse which to you may seem very humble, but to me seems full of pride and arrogance. . . . To depreciate others is a kind of pride more intolerable than to exalt oneself above one's due measure" (59). And the final chicane, of course, is from Laura to *lauro:* "As for your boasting that it is she who has made you thirst for glory, I pity your delusion, for I will prove to you that of all the burdens of your soul there is none more fatal than this" (124). A lengthy penultimate denunciation of Petrarch's lust leads to a final assault on his other desire: "Ambition still has too much hold on you. You seek too eagerly the praise of men, and to leave behind you an undying name. . . . I greatly fear lest this pursuit of a false immortality of fame may shut for you the way that leads to the true immortality of life" (165-66). "I freely confess it," says Petrarch (166), but the admission gains no purchase on the passion itself: "I am not ignorant that . . . it would be much safer for me to attend only to the care of my soul, to relinquish altogether every bypath and follow the straight path of the way to salvation. But I have not strength to resist that old bent for study altogether" (192). And there the dialogue ends, with a parting shot from Augustine: "uoluntatem impotentiam uocas," "what you call lack of strength is in fact your own doing." In petrarch's own divided understanding, the greatest impediment to his salvation is an insidiously complacent selfishness: "The story of Narcissus has no warning for you" (55).

The point rewards further meditation. Augustine's trajectory of accusation passes through what has, since the nineteenth century, seemed unexpectedly "modern" territory: "You are the victim of a terrible plague of the soul . . . which the moderns call *accidie*" (Petrarch 1911, 84; on the term, see Wenzel 1961). The *uoluptas dolendi* that in the *Canzoniere* is mainly focused on Laura is here abstracted and generalized:

> While other passions attack me only in bouts . . . this one usually has invested me so closely that it clings to and tortures me for whole days and nights together. In such times I take no pleasure in the light of day, I see nothing, I am as one plunged in the darkness of hell itself, and seem to endure death in its most cruel form. But what one may call the climax of the misery is, that I so feed upon my tears and sufferings with a morbid attraction [*atra quadam cum uoluptate*] that I can only be rescued from it by main force and in despite of myself. (84-85).

The cryptic pleasurability of such suffering is one of the marks that for Freud distinguishes melancholia from grief; the nearest thing to an explanation that Petrarch himself can muster is his inability to mourn: "In my case there is no wound old enough for it to have been effaced and forgotten: my sufferings are all quite fresh, and if anything by chance were made better through time, Fortune has so soon redoubled her strokes that the open wound has never been perfectly healed over"

(86-87). It is well within the spirit of the *Secretum* to adduce Freud's thesis that what is at work here is a narcissistic regression of an especially powerful sort, the active withdrawal of libido from an object-choice that was itself probably narcissistically based (Freud *S.E.* 14:249-50). Introjected disaffection with reality is a not altogether paradoxical strategy for denying transience and loss: "By taking flight into the ego love escapes extinction" (257). Petrarch's misery has its links to his drive for self-bestowed immortality.

One may accordingly expect the assertiveness that stirs even as Petrarch catalogues his unhappiness. The blame shifts perceptibly outward from himself to malicious fortune, and *accidia*—which Dante and Chaucer both linked with the sin of wrath[6]—passes into the resentment of unacknowledged virtue: "In the pushing and shameless manners of my time, what place is left for modesty, which men now call slackness or sloth?" (Petrarch 1911, 91). Augustine reminds Petrarch of his frequently professed scorn for popular opinion, and has it reaffirmed: "I care as much for what the crowd thinks of me as I care what I am thought of by the beasts of the field." "Well, then?" "What raises my spleen is that having, of all my contemporaries whom I know, the least exalted ambitions, not one of them has encountered so many difficulties as I have in the accomplishment of my desires" (91). Anyone exercising the second part of the Platonic soul should be on guard against claiming humility as his motivation (Braden 1985, 10 ff.). Augustine responds with some sensible remarks about realistic expectations and the control of anger ("first calm down the tumult of your imagination"— 104), but we may well consider the topic open until the subject of reputation comes up again and Petrarch is brought to acknowledge the actual reach of his ambition: "Now see what perversity is this! You let yourself be charmed with the applause of those whose conduct you abominate" (167-68). That is one of Augustine's most skillful thrusts: in dealing with his audience, the writer can find himself in a posture uncannily similar to that of the Petrarchan mistress toward her admirers.

Had Freud had more to say about fame, he might well have dwelt on the narcissistic convolutions of an artist's involvement with his public. It is certainly not hard to recognize Petrarch's case in psychoanalytically inspired critiques of the modern cult of celebrity: "Studies of personality disorders that occupy the border line between neurosis and psychosis . . depict a type of personality that ought to be immediately recognizable . . . to observers of the contemporary cultural scene: facile at managing the impressions he gives to others, ravenous for admiration but contemptuous of those he manipulates into providing it; unappeasably hungry for emotional experiences with which to fill an inner void; terrified of aging and death" (Lasch 1978, 38). The connection is not merely anachronistic; Petrarch was arguably the first major example of a seductively treacherous kind of literary celebrity. In his later years especially, his fame served him in a very immediate way as his ticket to prestigious but unstable accommodations in a series of northern Italian city-states; and his inner disequilibrium legitimately anticipates fuller experiences of the cost of life lived through a negotiable self-image. (Petrarch left his own polemics against the literary marketplace; their mixture of detachment and involvement is well discussed by Trinkaus 1979, 71-89.) Yet more august problematics loom as well. The isolation within which Petrarch locates himself with his scorn for those on whom he makes his impression manifests something inescapably narcissistic in the career of writing itself: an intersection, if you will, of the myth of Apollo and Daphne with that of Narcissus and Echo.[7] Petrarch's own life and work invite us to reflect on the ways in which the literary enterprise, in particular, works to elide its real audience into one that is in some important dimension a figment of the writer's imagination.

Consider this. A writer, sitting alone, facing a blank sheet of paper, puts on that paper words that are the words of speech but are not being spoken, and translates into silence the gestures of speaking to someone who in all but the most peculiar circumstances is not there, but whose presence the writer nevertheless tries in some form to imagine. Similarly, when that writing is read, the writer ostensibly speaking is, in all but very special situations, not there—though one tends to say writers succeed to the extent that they can nevertheless make us feel their presence. Cutting in two the face-to-face encounter that speech (one assumes) originally developed to serve, the skill of writing traffics at both ends in absent presences; a simulacrum of speech, it diverts language from literal to fictive others whose existence depends on the operations of a solitary's fantasy. Most of the important human connections of Petrarch's life seem to have been so mediated, in an immense epistolary corpus that was itself carefully organized and revised with an eye on eventual publication. Within that corpus Petrarch made no firm distinction between actual and imagined recipients, almost filling one book with Herzog-like letters to Cicero, Seneca, Homer, and the like ("do give my greetings to Orpheus and Linus, Euripides and the others"—*Epistolae familiares,* trans. Bernardo 1975-85, 24.12); a prose autobiographical fragment is in the form of a letter to Posterity. Petrarch was quite attuned to writing as "an unyielding passion" of strange self-sufficiency, indifferent to any external reference: "Incredible as it may seem, I desire to write but I know not about what or to whom to write" (13.7). And on this level we may seek some of the most cogent reasons that Petrarch and his avatars should choose as their great literary theme the otherwise perplexing story of the tongue-tied lover devoted for

years to a distant woman to whom he can barely bring himself to speak, and who scarcely deigns to answer him when he does. It is a story in which utterance fails systematically of its ostensible external goal, to double back on its originator.

Such a course is most overtly dramatized in one of Petrarch's most compelling but difficult poems—the longest of the *Canzoniere,* and at least in appearance the sequence's fullest piece of autobiographical narrative:

> canterò com' io vissi in libertade
> mentre Amor nel mio albergo a sdegno
>   s'ebbe;
>   poi seguirò sì come a lui ne 'ncrebbe
> troppo altamente e che di ciò m'avenne,
> di ch' io son fatto a molta gente esempio.

[I shall sing how then I lived in liberty while Love was scorned in my abode; then I shall pursue how that chagrined him too deeply, and what happened to me for that, by which I have become an example for many people.]

(1976, 23.5-9)

It is also the poem that presents the fullest narrative unfolding of the Laura-laurel pun, in a personalized retelling of Ovid. Yet it is a retelling with a strange twist:

>   sentendo il crudel di ch' io ragiono
> infin allor percossa di suo strale
> non essermi passato oltra la gonna,
> prese in sua scorta una possente Donna
> ver cui poco giamai mi valse o vale
> ingegno o forza o dimandar perdono;
> ei duo mi trasformaro in quel ch' i' sono,
> facendomi d'uom vivo un lauro verde
> che per fredda stagion foglia non perde.

[that cruel one of whom I speak [Love], seeing that as yet no blow of his arrows had gone beyond my garment, took as his patroness a powerful Lady, against whom wit or force or asking pardon has helped or helps me little: those two transformed me into what I am, making me of a living man a green laurel that loses no leaf for all the cold season.]

(32-40)

The lover himself becomes the laurel. His own previous refusal to love mythically identifies him with Daphne to some extent, but Laura does not become identified with Apollo in the process; rather, the lover becomes both pursuer and pursued:

>   Qual mi fec' io quando primier m'accorsi
> de la trasfigurata mia persona,

e i capei vidi far di quella fronde
di che sperato avea già lor corona. . . .

[What I became, when I first grew aware of my
person being transformed and saw my hairs
turning into those leaves which I had formerly
hoped would be my crown. . . .]

(41-44)

The frightening unexpectedness of the result produces
neither the satisfaction nor the resignation that Ovid's
Daphne and Apollo respectively feel. Part of what makes
Petrarch's poem so difficult is that, however catastrophic,
the event is not decisive; the lover is merely beginning a
series of wrenching metamorphoses, adapted with similar dark compression from Ovid. Having undergone the
fate of Daphne, he swerves into the fate of Cygnus:

Né meno ancor m'agghiaccia
l'esser coverto poi di bianche piume
allor che folminato et morto giacque
il mio sperar che tropp' alto montava

· · · · ·

et giamai poi la mia lingua non tacque
mentre poteo del suo cader maligno,
ond' io presi col suon color d'un cigno.

[Nor do I fear less for having been later covered
with white feathers, when thunderstruck and dead
lay my hope that was mounting too high . . . and
from then on my tongue was never silent about
its evil fall, as long as it had power; and I took
on with the sound of a swan its color.]

(1976, 50-53, 58-60)

Presumably this myth figures some subsequent act of
erotic aggression, obscure in the usual Petrarchan
manner. The narrative event is less clear and less
important than its role in intensifying the lover's poetic
vocation: the failure of his presumption has loosed his
tongue, given him his voice. Yet true to its origins, it
is a special kind of voice:

Così lungo l'amate rive andai,
che volendo parlar, cantava sempre,
mercé chiamando con estrania voce;
né mai in sì dolci o in sì soavi tempre
risonar seppi gli amorosi guai
che 'l cor s'umiliasse aspro et feroce.

[Thus I went along the beloved shores, and,
wishing to speak, I sang always, calling for mercy
with a strange voice; nor was I ever able to make
my amorous woes resound in so sweet or soft a
temper that her harsh and ferocious heart was
humbled.]

(Translation changed, 61-66)

Speech, which aims to persuade its addressee, is diverted into song, a use of language that may ravish
with its beauty but makes nothing happen. In the events
that follow, what one can recover most clearly is the
woman's insistence on denying speech its usual purpose:

Questa che col mirar gli animi fura
m'aperse il petto el' cor prese con mano,
dicendo a me: "Di ciò non far parola."
Poi la rividi in altro abito sola,
tal ch' i' non la conobbi, o senso umano!
anzi le dissi 'l ver pien di paura;
ed ella ne l'usata sua figura
tosto tornando fecemi, oimè lasso!
d'un quasi vivo et sbigottito sasso.

[She, who with her glance steals souls, opened
my breast and took my heart with her hand, saying
to me: "Make no word of this." Later I saw her
alone in another garment such that I did not know
her, oh human sense! rather I told her the truth,
full of fear, and she to her accustomed form quickly
returning made me, alas, an almost living and
terrified stone.]

(72-80)

Following the logic of this suppression, the poetic
career becomes literary:

le vive voci m'erano interditte,
ond' io gridai con carta et con incostro:
"Non son mio, no; s' io moro il danno è
    vostro."

[Words spoken aloud were forbidden me; so I
cried out with paper and ink: "I am not my own,
no; if I die, yours is the loss."]

(98-100)

"Interditte" and, in the previous line, "afflitte," take
their rhyme, after a long postponement, from line 92:
"scritte."

The agenda of that last word's appearance itself bears
further thought. To speak in paper and ink is to speak
con estrania voce, with an estranged voice that the
speaker almost does not recognize as his own; the
process of estrangement moves toward a complete
split of speech and speaker:

ancor poi ripregando i nervi et l'ossa
mi volse in dura selce, et così scossa
voce rimasi de l'antiche some,
chiamando Morte et lei sola per nome.

[when I prayed again, she turned my sinews and
bones into hard flint, and thus I remained a voice
shaken from my former burden, calling Death and

only her by name.]

(1976, 137-40)

The voice of his love is simultaneously the voice of death, the inverse of the interdicted *vive voci*. Again, there is an Ovidian text in the background, and perhaps the most readily Petrarchan of Ovid's stories: "tamen haeret amor crescitque dolore repulsae," "though rejected, her love sticks and grows with her grief" (*Metamorphoses* 1916, 3.395). The character in question—about to separate into petrified body and abstracted voice—is Echo; and her appearance points us toward the myth that is conspicuously not used in Petrarch's poem but that, as Durling has shown, is almost there in the recurring motifs of the myths that are: "With the exception of the Battus myth they take place near a body of water into which at least one of the characters gazes. With the exception of the Daphne myth they involve characters who are punished for something they have seen. All of them concern frustrated—or even disastrous—speech or writing, and in each case the speech involves deception or confusion or some question about the identity of one of the protagonists" (Petrarch 1976, 28). There are reasons (31-32) for suspecting that the story of Narcissus is about to come up around line 90, when, after some documentable trouble in the composition, Petrarch changes the subject, so: "più cose ne la mente scritte / vo trapassando," "I pass over many things written in my mind" (92-93). The absent presence written in the mind is credibly the myth that hovers over the whole poem like a guilty secret.

Remembering Narcissus at any rate allows us to track the movement between the poem's opening event and its impendingly violent end:

> I' segui' tanto avanti il mio desire
> ch' un dì, cacciando sì com' io solea,
> mi mossi, e quella fera bella et cruda
> in una fonte ignuda
> si stava, quando 'l sol più forte ardea.
> Io perché d'altra vista non m'appago
> stetti a mirarla, ond' ella ebbe vergogna
> et per farne vendetta o per celarse
> l'acqua nel viso co le man mi sparse.
> Vero dirò; forse e' parrà menzogna:
> ch' i' senti' trarmi de la propria imago
> et in un cervo solitario et vago
> di selva in selva ratto mi trasformo,
> et ancor de' miei can fuggo lo stormo.

[I followed so far my desire that one day, hunting as I was wont, I went forth, and that lovely cruel wild creature was in a spring naked when the sun burned most strongly. I, who am not appeased by any other sight, stood to gaze on her, whence she felt shame and, to take revenge or to hide herself,

sprinkled water in my face with her hand. I shall speak the truth, perhaps it will appear a lie, for I felt myself drawn from my own image and into a solitary wandering stag from wood to wood quickly I am transformed and still I flee the belling of my hounds.]

(1976, 147-60)

The myth—from the same book of the *Metamorphoses* as that of Narcissus—is the story of the hunter Actaeon, who saw the goddess Diana bathing, and in punishment was turned into a stage, to be hunted and torn apart by his own dogs, whom he could not call off:

>   clamare libebat:
> "Actaeon ego sum: dominum cognoscite
>   uestrum!"
> uerba animo desunt; resonat latratibus
>   aether.

[He wanted to cry, "I am Actaeon! Know your master!" His words failed his spirit; the air resounded with barking.]

(3.229-31)

Durling attributes the story's appearance here to Petrarch's perception of it as "an inversion of the myth of Daphne. In one, it is the beloved who flees, in the other, the lover. In one, the end result is speech: poetry and fame; in the other, silence. In one, there is evergreen eternizing; in the other, dismemberment. Daphne, as she runs, looks into the water and becomes a tree, takes root; Actaeon, who is standing still, branches into a stag, grows hooves, flees, sees his reflection and flees the more" (Petrarch 1976, 28-29).

But the linkage is not only one of contrast. The story of Actaeon also parallels that of Daphne in Petrarch's alteration of the latter: at the end of the poem as at the beginning, the lover suddenly, catastrophically, becomes the object of his own pursuit. And if the concluding episode allows Laura to take uniquely unguarded, direct action, her motives are intentionally made uncertain—"per farne vendetta o per celarse"—while the verbs describing the metamorphosis become reflexive—"i' senti' trarmi"—as they move from the narrative past to the definitive present: "mi trasformo." The myth becomes a popular one in the tradition to come (Barkan 1980), where it is often moralized as a cautionary fable about the self-destructiveness of lust: "J'ay pour mes chiens l'ardeur & le jeune âge," "For my dogs I have passion and youth" (Ronsard 1966-70, *Amours* 1.120.7). Within Petrarch's own context, however, it intimates subtler but deeper terrors as a paradigm for the reflexive aggression of narcissistic melancholy; and the roaring that rises toward him at the end—"fuggo lo stormo"—supplies the climax to the trajectory of his estranged new voice. The barking of his hounds, I would argue, is the plaintive song whose development the *canzone* has narrated, returning to its now speechless creator.[8] The terror on the other side of narcissistic beguilement—Freud locates it as the point at which melancholia becomes suicidal (*S.E.* 14:252)—is the experience of one's own self as the other, the outsider. The lover in Petrarch's poem flees from the sound of his own poetic voice, echoing murderously inside the bell jar.

That horrific climax is one of the reaches of Petrarch's moral self-arraignment, its mythic subtlety—I have tried to show—answerable to a coincidence of Christianity and psychoanalysis in their understanding of what the self is up to in its dealings with the world, and of the dangerousness of its way. Yet a final turn still awaits us; Petrarch's poem itself is not over, and what follows is not entirely the obvious conclusion:

> né per nova figura il primo alloro
> seppi lassar, ché pur la sua dolce ombra
> ogni men bel piacer del cor mi sgombra.

> [nor for any new shape could I leave the first laurel, for still its sweet shade turns away from my heart any less beautiful pleasure.]

(1976, 167-69)

The allure of the deadly object is suavely reaffirmed, almost as if the lover had learned nothing at all; we might almost wonder if Petrarch is tacking on a *commiato* written for another, less relentless poem. There is, nevertheless, a continuity of action if not of tone in the sustaining of the present tense, as if to insist on the tenacity of the state to which the lover has come. No mere terror is going to change things. And a further twist to Petrarch's moral thought unfurls in his poem's final disjunction, which has its own meaning within the context of his life and work as a whole. We are led back once more to the standoff at the end of the *Secretum*.

The irresolution there is felt with particular acuteness because of the counterexample provided by Augustine himself: "A deep meditation at last showed me the root of all my misery and made it plain before my eyes. And then my will after that became fully changed, and my weakness also was changed in that same moment to power, and by a marvellous and most blessed alteration I was transformed instantly and made another man, another Augustine altogether" (1911, 19-20). By the standard set in Augustine's *Confessions* (which, he goes on to say, I'm sure you've read) Petrarch's self-scrutiny ought to be leading to a summary transformation of the personality, whereby self-love is replaced by the love of God with a definitiveness answerable to that first, profane enamorment. The *Canzoniere* even-

tually seeks to give appropriate form to such expectations with a renunciation of Laura and a hymn to the Virgin Mary: at last the suitable object, love for which will not be a screen for something base. Such a prospect lodges in the tradition as in some ways the proper end to the story ("Leave me ô Love, which reachest but to dust . . ."—Sidney 1962, *Certain Sonnets* 32.1), and the biographical tradition on Petrarch has sought for a major change of life around the time of the *Secretum*. There are those who claim to have found it (Tatham 1925-26, 2:277ff.). Yet the evidence is inevitably shifty and a bit wishful, subject to varying interpretation; and among the least uncertain facts is that, whatever Petrarch did or did not purge from his soul, the *desiderium gloriae* stayed with him (Baron 1971). In the specifically literary terms with which the *Secretum* finally hardens its conflict, Petrarch's indecisiveness endured almost to the very end; one of the last letters puts by Boccaccio's plea that Petrarch ease up on his studies: "I do hope that death may find me reading or writing, or, if it should so please Christ, in tearful prayer" (*Epistolae seniles,* book 17, epistle 2, in Wilkins 1959, 248). Scholars now find it credible to read Petrarch's story as a "lifelong wait" for a repeatedly deferred Augustinian conversion, colored by "his growing fear, his growing realization that the miracle of will and grace was not to be vouchsafed him" (Greene 1968, 247).

Learning to live with that realization brings hints of a shift in ethical standards. Greene senses a reaching back behind the Christian dispensation: "Insofar as [Petrarch's] psychology came to focus on the soul's instability without any opening to the divine, he recalls not so much Augustine as those pagan moralists who had earlier recognized the volatility of passion" (1968, 247)—who had, in other words, recognized that desire is intractably prior to its object (Greene is thinking specifically of Horace, *Epistolae* 1.1.90ff.). And one may, to at least some extent, place Petrarch as a moralist within what Freud, as described in the opening lines of this chapter, delineated as the pre-Christian dimension of psychoanalysis. We are certainly at the point where the intersection of Freud and Augustine ends; for the psychoanalyst as for the virtuous pagan, the ultimate external object of desire that would unclasp us from our specific individuality does not exist, except in our own imagination. This is not to say that such imagining will not be good for us, even essential; but the narcissistic roots of love are never simply extirpated, and the real comfort and obligation toward which we strive is not transcendence but clearheadedness as to what we are doing. The *Secretum* has occasionally been likened in passing to a series of psychoanalytic sessions, and the analogy can be made fairly specific. Petrarch's positive act is as it were to accept Augustine's diagnosis while avoiding its transcendental imperative, and with that the apparent indecisiveness becomes more clearly a therapeutic achievement. *Voluntatem impotentiam uocas:* as the speakers find their way to the topic of Petrarch's literary career, they move toward a disclosure of the calculation within what had presented itself as mere helplessness, the psychic purpose behind consequences previously disowned. From such a point we would now extrapolate not successful or failed conversion, but a lifelong conversation with the secret logic of an intimate stranger.

Notes

[1] See Petrarch's own austere formulation: "Placere sibi superbire est," "to be pleased with oneself is to be prideful" (*De remediis utriusque fortunae,* book 1, chap. 13, in Petrarch 1554, 1:17). The fullest source on the mythography of Narcissus is Vinge 1967; I have tried to respect her caution about overconflating the mythological character and the psychoanalytic concept, but want to argue here for serious continuity of meaning between the two, at least as mediated by Christian moral interpretation. My general perspective in this regard is close to that of Zweig 1980. Zweig also has some acute things to say on the not quite mastered complexities of the Christian position: in being linked to the promise of individual immortality, the ideal of selfless love is really inseparable from its proclaimed opposite, and keeps nourishing its own heresy. For my own purposes, I take Christianity pretty much at its word, but the deconstructive force of its critique of Petrarchan love potentially rebounds against the religion itself.

[2] I choose an Italian sonnet for effect, but the trope is already well established (and just as startling) among the Troubadours. See Vinge 1967, 66-72; Zweig 1980, 85-99; and, at great length, Goldin 1967.

[3] An alternative conclusion is, to be sure, imagined in Petrarch's *Trionfi,* his other major work in vernacular poetry, where the spirit of Laura informs him that she not only knew of his love but fully returned it, keeping quiet for the good of both their souls (*Triumphus mortis* 2.76 ff., see Bernardo 1974, 123-27). The dream-vision frame keeps the status of this revelation, at least by the standards of the *Canzoniere,* uncertain.

[4] This particular poem originally stood first in the collection. On Petrarch's developing involvement with the story, the fullest discussion is still Calcaterra (1942); see especially 35-87. On Daphne's general mythographic history (and the innovative character of Petrarch's role in it), see Stechow (1965) and Giraud (1968).

[5] Those early years are more fully described in a letter to Petrarch's brother Gherardo: "What should I say about the curling irons and the care we took of our hair? How often did the resulting pain interrupt our sleep" (*Epistolae familiares,* trans. Bernardo 1975-85,

10.3). The claim in the *Secretum* to have outgrown such things has on inspection an odd spin. Petrarch twice identifies himself in this connection with the psychopathic, prematurely gray emperor Domitian (57, 154), and insists that his own fading hair color provides him moral instruction as a *memento mori.* There is good reason to credit Petrarch's obsession with that change, which is a recurring topic in the *Canzoniere*— "Dentro pur foco et for candida neve, / sol con questi pensier, con altre chiome," "Inwardly fire, though outwardly white snow, alone with these thoughts, with changed locks" (30.31-32)—but of course you only stay aware of your hair color if you check the mirror regularly.

[6] Dante, *Inferno* 7.100-26 (on which see Wenzel 1967, 200-2); Chaucer, *The Parson's Tale:* "Envye and Ire maken bitternesse in herte, which bitternesse is mooder of Accidie" (1957, 249).

[7] There are visible if not fully articulated signs of contamination between the two stories in late medieval mythography. Several commentators—including Petrarch's friend Boccaccio—allegorize Echo as *bona fama* (Vinge 1967, 73-76, 102-04); and a twelfth-century French *Narcisse* replaces Echo by "Dané," that is, Daphne (Thiry-Stassin 1978).

[8] Kilmer's translation is felicitous: "I can hear the dogs while I write this" (Petrarch 1981).

Peter Hainsworth (essay date 1988)

SOURCE: Peter Hainsworth, in an introduction to *Petrarch the Poet: An Introduction to the Rerum Vulgarium Fragmenta,* Routledge, 1988, pp. 1-29.

[*In the following essay, Hainsworth focuses on Petrarch's* Rerum vulgarium fragmenta, *which is commonly known as the* Canzoniere *or* Rime sparse. *Hainsworth discusses the context in the which the poems were written and examines Petrarch's concern with humanism and the meaning of poetry.*]

Two languages

Italian literature of the Middle Ages and the Renaissance is composed in the shadow of Latin. The shadow may seem sometimes shorter, sometimes longer, but it is inevitably there, evoking an alternately benign and threatening presence whose roots stretch back into antiquity and whose branches extend across Europe. Latin asserts repeatedly that it has the exclusive right to knowledge and excellence, and continually demands that its authors and authority should be attended to. When it seems most displaced, it infiltrates the less prestigious, less stable language with its words, its turns of phrase, its rhetoric and its standards. If there is such a thing as popular literature, the index of popularity is the distance from Latin. Literature which makes implicit or explicit claims to refinement, let alone to greatness, does so in virtue of its power to assimilate what Latin has to offer and to become like it. Only in the sixteenth century does literary culture in Italy make a general commitment to Italian, and even then the result is symbiosis with Latin rather than its eviction. For earlier writers the two languages are mostly in tension. Even Dante, who declared Italian the nobler language in the *De vulgari eloquentia* and gave an overwhelming demonstration of its power in the *Divina commedia,* was the victor in a battle, not the war.

There were many reasons, some stemming from the *Commedia* itself, others from the linguistic and cultural pressures at work in fourteenth-century Italy, why Dante's example could not be wholeheartedly embraced by the generation that followed him. But one of the prime factors was the emergence of a humanist movement which was intent on the recovery and renewal of Latinity, with, at its centre, the figure who dominated the literary culture of his time. Petrarch wrote with equal seriousness in both Latin and Italian and redrew the lines of demarcation between the two languages. In one way the result was a return to orthodoxy, in another it was a radical revision with implications for both literatures. The effects were immediate, deep, widely felt, and, in the longer term, asymmetrically bi-focal in a way that reflected the actual constitution of Petrarch's work. For a century and more after his death humanism evolved within the perspective defined in his Latin writings, whilst Italian retreated to the literary margins. Then in the sixteenth century his Italian poems, which had always been influential within vernacular literature, were pronounced the supreme examples of modern poetry. They were the paradigms of language, style, and, to a lesser degree, of love, and were to exert a profound influence upon poetry inside and outside Italy. By then the Latin works were already fading from view: henceforth it would be the Italian poems which spoke for Petrarch and defined him. Only since the later nineteenth century has the eclipse been slowly rectified. Gradually it has become evident that the whole of Petrarch is not contained within what he wrote in either language considered in isolation, though it has become equally clear that any composite picture has to take as much account of contrasts and contradictions as of similarities or underlying consistencies.

In themselves neither his bilingualism nor his humanism is surprising. His father, Ser Petracco, was a notary who lived and worked in Florence, though his family was from Incisa, a small town not far from Arezzo. In 1302, a few months after Dante, he too was exiled. He first returned to Incisa and Arezzo, where Petrarch was born in 1304. But in 1312 he moved with his family to Provence, where, like other White Guelphs exiled from Florence, he found work and refuge in the ambit of the Papal Court at Avignon. From now until his definitive departure for Northern Italy in 1353, Provence would be Petrarch's base, though a base which he would frequently leave, more often than not, for lengthy visits to Italy. There were also Italian friends, some of whom at least had an interest in vernacular literature, notably the poet Sennuccio del Bene. But Papal Provence was primarily international and its culture was enthusiastically Latinate, particularly amongst its Italian members. Petrarch's father directed him as a boy towards Virgil and Cicero, and, in the light of his ability in the language and his enthusiasm for classical antiquity, brought him to the notice of the Colonna family, whose centre was Rome but whose members were currently important figures in the Church in Southern France. The Colonna were to be Petrarch's patrons and friends until his support for the revolutionary attempts of Cola di Rienzo to re-create the Roman republic led to a cooling of relations during his last years in Provence. With their own humanist interests, their contacts in both France and Italy, and their sheer political and financial power, they provided a springboard for Petrarch's studies and writings. They also provided material support: Petrarch took minor orders and was granted a canonry at Lombez, where Giacomo Colonna was bishop. Like other livings which he acquired later, the canonry made minimal demands. Petrarch always insisted that his means were modest, though they were sufficient for him to acquire, sometime in the early 1330s, the famous villa at Vaucluse which became his country retreat. With Colonna help and careful manipulation of his own myth, the culminating point of which was his coronation as poet laureate in Rome in 1341, he made himself famous and respected. From his thirties onwards, kings, princes, emperors and popes would correspond with him, or at least receive his letters, would welcome him as the greatest adornment of learning in contemporary Europe, would use him as an ambassador or seek his advice. When he moved to Italy in 1353, he had no difficulty in finding support, first from the Visconti in Milan, then from the Venetian republic, and finally from Francescoda Carrara of Padua, who provided him with the land in Arquà in the Euganean hills where he built the house in which he was to die in 1374.

Petrarch's life was a remarkable achievement in itself, and one accomplished in virtue of his work in Latin, not Italian. It marked the emergence of a new kind of writer. Petrarch was not a member of any university or any other institution, and was not directly in the service of any of his patrons, not even the Colonna, or of any state organisation. Though he was continually negotiating his position and continually threatened by the powers amongst which he moved, he created an independence for himself and for his work which no other intellectual had enjoyed since antiquity. With him high literature established a distance between itself and the vocationalism and institutionalism to which it had been subjected throughout the Middle Ages. Its arbiter was the author, a figure who created himself in and through his writing and who was dignified in his own eyes and those of society for his literary excellence and for no other reason.

At the base of Petrarch's work was textual mastery. As a young man he brought together the surviving decades of Livy, which had been separated from each other throughout the medieval period, and emended the text of accretions and corruptions in a way that presupposed a respect both for classical Latin and for the wishes of the author. He went on to emend, copy and make available other texts, including some which had been lost to the intellectual life of Europe for centuries. One of his early discoveries was Cicero's *Pro Archia*; another, still more important, was the collection of Cicero's letters to Atticus, which he found in the cathedral library of Verona in 1345. These and other texts became part of the largest private library that had existed in Europe since ancient times. Though Petrarch's readings in medieval literature were much more extensive than he cared to admit, the texts he chooses to edit and, even more, those which he values, signal a reaction against literary and intellectual concerns that were dominant in the preceding century. He has no truck with scholastic or Aristotelian thought. In place of speculative metaphysical systems, of scientific, especially medical, investigation, of legal codification, he puts grammar, rhetoric, poetry, history, moral philosophy. Virgil and the other classical poets, Cicero, Seneca, Livy are his authors, not Aristotle, Aquinas, Averroes, let alone the jurists and the decretalists. When he turns to Christian philosophy, it is above all to Augustine, with whose position *vis-à-vis* pagan thought he felt bound at times to identify. In all this there is evident a desire to recover what had been lost in the Middle Ages (though the term, like the term 'humanism', was still to be invented) and to present a historically accurate version of it to the present, or, given the decadence of the present—which episodes such as that of Cola, and lasting sores such as the exile of the Papacy from Rome, made seem all too apparent—to a future that was yet to take shape.

There was little dissociation of sensibility in Petrarch. Knowing was doing. Though the next generation of humanists would easily surpass him, his Latin was more classical than that of any of his contemporaries or medieval predecessors, and made its classical connections evident through a web of allusions, citations, and reformulations or phrases taken from great and not so great authors. At the same time Petrarch insisted on his individuality. None of his works are totally subservient to ancient models, in some cases perhaps inadvertently. His unfinished epic poem, the *Africa,* unreleased in his lifetime apart from one short

passage and the greatest literary flop when it eventually emerged after his death, was less epic than it was discursive and personal. The large collections of letters, principally the *Familiares* and the *Seniles,* which were apparently inspired by his Ciceronian discoveries, were less anecdotal and occasional than measured moral discourses, miniature treatises, self-analyses and self-portraits. But these are only part of a literary production which is amazing in its diversity and abundance. It includes allegorical eclogues, verse epistles, biographies, treatises, polemical defences of humanistic studies and of Petrarch's own position within them, a self-analysis in the form of a dialogue with St Augustine (*Secretum*), and moral dialogues (*De remediis utriusque fortune*), as well as relatively minor pieces such as the oration he delivered on his coronation (*Collatio laureationis*) or the letter addressed to posterity (*Posteritati*).

In that letter, as throughout his writings, Petrarch is primarily concerned with himself, or rather with formulating some version of himself which caters for his continual shifts of perspective on himself and on his work, and for the doubts and contradictions which he never fully resolves. He continually debates the nature of his studies and his writing, exploring their relationship to a truth which his disavowal of metaphysics prevents him from even beginning to express, but which impinges as an absence, or as a matter of faith. In the course of his career he entertains every possibility: he normally dismisses simple restoration of classical glories as something which he foolishly entertained in his youth, but he moves between a humanism which is also Christian, a Christianity which has a humanist colouring, and a Christianity which has nothing to do with the folly of writing. Though he liked to present himself as evolving from a more or less Christian but distinctly humanist poet into a distinctly Christian moral philosopher, the phases blur together. Almost everything we have of Petrarch belongs to his maturity. Although the passage of time and the changes it brings is one of his constant themes, there is a sense in which all his surviving writings are an encyclopaedia which includes as many kinds of writing and as many attitudes to the nature and function of writing as they possibly can, all united not by any reference to some external truth but by a self which is present in all of them, though complete in none, and whose boundaries are determined by the totality of the authorised *oeuvre*.

Much of Petrarch is incomplete or composed of short units in different states of elaboration. Most betokens a state of unease or even of crisis. But the assurance is also striking. However much rewritten, however much they might have been further revised, the fragments and incomplete works are formally and stylistically accomplished. What is more important, the fundamental decisions are unhesitatingly held to. From the beginning there is a rejection of the conceptual and literary practices of the previous generation of Italian writers (especially those of Dante) and a conviction that all matters of intellectual and moral importance should find expression in a renovated form of Latin. What is left to Italian is poetry, and poetry of a particular kind.

Petrarch's work in Italian falls into three parts. Most important are the 366 lyric poems which make up the collection often called the *Canzoniere,* sometimes the *Rime sparse* (from the first line of the first poem), but which Petrarch himself entitled *Rerum vulgarium fragmenta,* literally 'Fragments of vernacular matters': I shall follow Petrarch, at least to some degree, by using the acronym *RVF.* Then there are some poems excluded from the major collection: at least twenty-nine of these *Rime disperse (RD),* as they are conventionally called, are genuine, though there may well be others amongst the vast body of poems attributed to Petrarch between the fourteenth and the sixteenth century. Lastly there are the *Triumphi (Triumphs),* a sequence of six visionary poems which was never quite completed. It is a substantial body of work: the *RVF* alone is larger than the total surviving production of any earlier lyric poet, except perhaps Guittone d'Arezzo, and at least as large as the production of some of his prolific contemporaries. But it is dwarfed by the Latin writings. In the Basle edition of 1554, which is still the only comprehensive, if not quite complete, edition of his works, the Italian poems are crammed into some 78 pages: the Latin writings fill nearly 1,400.

The contrast is not solely of scale. In Latin Petrarch looks to the ancient world, in Italian to the lyric tradition of Tuscany and Provence, and to the love-poetry that had always been at its centre. Though the poems are much more than the expression of passion and at least some turn explicitly away from love, the great majority centre on Petrarch's love for the woman he called Laura, whom he claims to have first seen in 1327 and to have loved from then until long after her death in 1348. Love is largely absent from the Latin works. There are love-poems for Laura amongst the verse epistles (*Epistole metrice):* she is allegorised as the laurel in some of the eclogues (*Bucolicum carmen*); but she becomes a major issue only in the dialogue with Augustine in the *Secretum,* which debates some of the dangers of love in a comparable way to some of the poems. In the self-portrait given in the letter to posterity there is only a cursory dismissal of a passion which, to judge by the Italian poems, obsessed their author from the ages of twenty-three until at least his sixties.

Laura may or may not have existed as an individual. But poetically the obsession was certainly real and long-lasting. Some of the poems in the *RVF* were written in the 1330s or perhaps even earlier, though

Petrarch probably began work on making a collection in the 1340s at the earliest. But it was in his later years that he did most of the work on the composition of the whole, and, in all probability, wrote a considerable number of the individual poems. He gave the arrangement of the collection its final form something less than a year before his death.

His Latin work offers a different picture. By the 1350s he was presenting himself as having abandoned poetry altogether, and, so far as poetry in Latin was concerned, this was true. As for the work on his Italian poetry, he declares that he is merely collecting together youthful trifles: he is now ashamed of them, but they are in demand from friends whom he cannot refuse: he also wishes to protect them from abuse and distortion. But the disparities are comprehensible. Italian poetry, as he conceived and wrote it, was not to be reconciled with humanism in any intellectually coherent fashion, even if humanists and their patrons enjoyed writing and reading it. There could be no justification for indulgence in sexual love, however refined, nor for love-poetry. It was available to the vulgar at large, and, what was perhaps worse, available to women. It had to be judged frivolous, immoral, and, as literature, inferior in every way to what might be written in Latin. Such a poetry might perhaps have been justified if it were allegorical—if, that is, Laura were indeed the laurel, the symbol of glory and poetry, which she became in the *Bucolicum carmen*. But that was a step whose ambiguous possibilities Petrarch explored in the *RVF* without totally committing himself. Instead he risked the absurdity and ridicule of being a man in his fifties and sixties who wrote love-poetry. Contemporaries seem to have been indifferent to this contradiction of the equation between love and youth which goes back to antiquity and which had been particularly strong in Provençal poetry. Petrarch himself was not. For him there had to be some degree of shame in such a display, as the poems themselves indicate. In spite of public appreciation and the protracted work of composition, it was unthinkable that the results could be called poetry: had that been done, they would have entered the same category as the *Aeneid* or the *Africa,* with implications for the possible status of the vernacular generally which Petrarch the humanist was anxious to avoid.

Clearly he was also anxious to orient writing in the two languages in two separate, even opposed directions. That does not mean that what he writes in the one is radically different from what he writes in the other. The very professions of shame, the slighting dismissals as trifles of works on which he spent years, are applied to his Latin writings as well as to the Italian. And the more we look, the more the points of contact proliferate, ranging from turns of phrase, favoured images, direct cross-references to fundamental concerns. If Petrarch writes in Italian of despair, confusion, frustration, that is only a reformulation in the terms of the lyric of much that appears in his Latin works. If he puts at the centre of his Latin works a self who is continually reshaped and re-examined, it is a similar fluctuating and uncertain self which is created and explored in Italian. If he voices and investigates in Latin various contradictory positions *vis-à-vis* the purposes and nature of writing, so in Italian he articulates and examines a series of poetic possibilities, embracing all and settling for none. As in Latin, writing is less a way of making statements about the world or reality than an area in which multiple pathways alternately diverge and cross each other, their contradictions being reconciled (though not annulled) in the writing itself rather than in any point of arrival or final judgment. The difference is one of quality; for Italian, in Petrarch's hands, has the advantage: in a way that he could not quite achieve in Latin, he is able, in the inferior language, to create a style which is consistent whilst constantly varied, which can absorb literature of the past whilst retaining its own identity, which is always beautiful in a convincing, if sometimes bewildering way. There is no disparity of aspiration or literary attention between the Latin and the Italian Petrarch: but the latter presupposes the former in a way that is not true if we invert the terms. As Petrarch's Latin title suggests, the **Rerum vulgarium fragmenta** are the vernacular poems of a humanist.

The Italian context

Though there are important difference of perspective between them, Dante and Petrarch both make historical interpretations of Italian poetry which, taken together, suggest the idea of a poetic tradition running fairly smoothly from the Sicilians, or perhaps even from Provence, through to Petrarch. But in many ways the tradition was, and is, a retrospective construction. In reality continuity was neither automatic nor linear. At any point—and at some more than others—connections with the past had to be affirmed or denied, interferences had to be assimilated or rejected, and the past itself reassessed. There were always risks of rupture or dispersal. In the first half of the fourteenth century they were particularly intense. For Petrarch and his contemporaries, writing poetry in Italian was a quite different enterprise from what it had been in thirteenth-century Tuscany. At the same time the later poetry came into being largely in the shadow of the earlier. Petrarch was able to reshape the past in the light of the contradictory exigencies at work in himself and in fourteenth-century culture generally. His contemporaries often had similar aspirations, but were repeatedly thrown into confusion or confined to epigonal roles.

The tradition was no more than a hundred years old when Petrarch wrote the earliest poems which he included in the *RVF*. It had been initiated, quite abruptly

it seems, by a loose-knit group of administrators, lawyers and notaries connected with the court of the Emperor Frederick II in Sicily and Southern Italy. Perhaps the Emperor himself encouraged, or ordered, the production in an Italian language of a poetry similar in kind and quality to that produced by the minnesinger and troubadours whom he patronised. At all events the Sicilians (as they have been called since at least the time of Petrarch, though not all of them were from Sicily) produced a quite sophisticated love-poetry which owed a great deal to Provençal *fin' amors*. They made the Sicilian language in which they wrote acceptable by giving it a Provençal and, to a lesser extent, a Latin flavour, as well as by importing idioms, images and conventions from the troubadours. So Italian poetry began on the elevated level which it was to maintain up to and beyond Petrarch. It also acquired its fundamental poetic forms—the major form, the canzone, deriving from the Provençal *canso;* the minor one, the sonnet, being an invention of the Sicilians, and probably of the dominant figure amongst them, the notary Giacomo da Lentini.

Sicilian poetry came to an abrupt end when the German power on which it depended was shattered by the French at the battles of Benevento (1265) and Tagliacozzo (1267). But by then it had long penetrated Central Italy. Bologna and the cities of Tuscany were to be the centres in which it developed and to which it was confined until almost exactly the end of the thirteenth century. Broadly speaking, the first phase was one of expansion. It was centred around Guittone d'Arezzo (*c.* 1230-94), who produced the first sizeable body of work in Italian lyric poetry and who was considerably more ambitious than the Sicilians had been, drawing on some of the techniques of the Provencal *trobar clus* and also on the refinements of the *Ars dictaminis*. Guittone also wrote political and moral poetry, eventually denouncing love as carnal and adulterous when he became one of the new lay order of *Frati gaudenti* in the early 1260s. Nor was the expansion simply internal. Canzoni and sonnets in the Sicilian and Guittonian mode proliferated amongst notaries, merchants, bankers in the various Tuscan towns. There may even have been a woman poet, the socalled 'Compiuta Donzella'.

This too was sophisticated poetry, aware of its own conventions and aware of European ideas of literary hierarchy. Overall the Tuscans aimed to be elevated, whether celebrating or denouncing love. But they also made moves in the direction of a more colloquial register in political and occasional verse, whilst in Florence, probably in the 1270s, the antithesis of high poetry suddenly appeared in some of the poems of Rustico Filippi. Vulgar, idiomatic, morally perverse, what is now called *poesia giocosa* was less a questioning of high poetry than its parasitical inversion, written in complete accordance with the accepted rules for low-style poetry.

But the limitations were evident, at least by contemporary standards. The early Tuscans were the voices of a provincial culture which had emerged quite suddenly into literacy as a result of rapid commercial expansion. Their points of reference were principally Sicilian and Provençal poetry and contemporary Latin rhetoric. Though the debates about the nature of love echo scholastic procedures of argument and suggest some acquaintance with contemporary medical and psychological thought, intellectual vitality is largely limited to the manipulation of commonplaces. The practitioners, whether we call them poets or not, were in contemporary parlance *rimatori, dettatori, trovatori,* not *poeti* or *auctores* whose names were to be respected and whose texts were to be commented on or glossed. In a sense their poetry was public property. Though it was certainly literate and, to judge from the evidence, it differed from Provençal poetry in not being directly associated with music, it quickly passed outside its authors' control into anthologies where it was at the mercy of scribal whim and regional variation.

This last problem would continue into Petrarch's time. But in the later years of the century there were major revisions of Tuscan poetic habits. What is now generally called the *dolce stil novo* (though Dante's phrase may well have a different emphasis in its original context in *Purg.* 24. 57) began in Bologna with Guido Guinizzelli (?1230-?1276), whose slender surviving *oeuvre* includes poems in the Guittonian style, but also some others which are conspicuously both more harmonious and more complex intellectually. What Bonagiunta da Lucca, one of his contemporary critics from the old school, considered an excess of Bolognese learning (*Poeti* 2. 481) is especially strong in the famous canzone on the nature of love, *Al cor gentil rempaira sempre Amore.* But it was in Florence in the work of Guido Cavalcanti (c. 1259-1300) that the new style really developed both its characteristic 'sweetness' and its conceptual scope, the latter being formidably displayed in Cavalcanti's philosophical canzone *Donna me prega,* the former being more apparent in his other poems. The new poetry was aimed at a circle of initiates, presupposing an intellectual and literary sophistication far exceeding that demanded by the run of previous poets. In other words with Cavalcanti the modes of high literature began to be reproduced in the vernacular.

It was Dante (1265-1321) who made the claims of the vernacular explicit. In the *Vita nuova* (c. 1294) he gathered together a selection of his youthful poetry and, with the help of a prose commentary, made its coherence evident. Love, reason and vernacular poetry were, he argued, complementary. At this stage he thought poetry in Italian should restrict itself thematically to love, but, since there was as much sense and order in the best vernacular poetry as traditional theory held there to be in the Latin masters, it followed that there was no difference in kind between the *rimatori* and the *poeti* (*VN* 25).

The rest of Dante's work is, amongst other things, a demonstration of the truth of this radical proposition. He had already gone beyond Cavalcanti in the *Vita nuova.* Over the next decade or so he wrote a series of poems which were conceptually more substantial and technically stricter than anything so far written in Italian. Concurrently he supported practice with theory, moving from the relatively restricted claims of his first book to the eventual proclamation of the *De vulgari eloquentia* (1. 1. 4) that 'nobilior est vulgaris' (the vernacular is the nobler language), and that meant that it could deal with the noblest of themes—moral and spiritual well-being, political and military struggle, as well as love.

For all his theoretical pronouncements, all the poetry which Dante had written was just about containable within the confines of the tradition and within traditional ways of seeing the relationship between Latin and the vernacular. The *Divina commedia* was not. It was finished not long before Dante died in Ravenna in 1321. Within ten years it was well known and widely read in Northern and Central Italy. Though one or two dissenters were to be heard, it was quickly recognised that here was a work in Italian which rivalled any work of ancient poetry. It satisfied all criteria for poetic excellence. It showed a complete mastery of rhetoric: it was immensely learned in philosophy, science and theology: and it was rich in moral lessons for its readers' improvement. If it quickly became popular with the people at large, it was also clear that its appealing surface concealed difficult, even arcane truths. Learned commentaries began to appear almost at once. By 1333 there were at least four in existence which have survived (Jacopo di Dante, Graziolo Bambaglioli, il Lana and l'Ottimo), indicating a *de facto* recognition that the text required the same depth of exegesis as, say, the *Aeneid.* The theoretical recognition was voiced most forcefully by Boccaccio. Dante, he proclaimed in his celebratory biography, is a great and glorious *poeta*: his work has the sweetness and beauty which appeals to everyone, including women and young people, but it also has a wealth of deep meaning which first puzzles and then 'refreshes and nourishes serious minds' ('ricrea e pasce gli solenni intelletti': *Opere* 384).

Boccaccio may have been right, but the *Commedia* posed enormous problems for any subsequent poet. Apart from its assault upon linguistic certainties which had been presumed valid for centuries, there was the question of how Italian poetry was to deal with a literary father who seemed simultaneously to have created the poetic language and to have exhausted all its resources. Indeed, if the implications of his poem are taken seriously, he had said everything worth saying. One response was to attempt encyclopaedical poems on the Dantesque model, but with different matter; another, already evident in Dante's friend, the canon lawyer Cino da Pistoia (*c.* 1270-1336/7), was to incorporate phrases, words, images from the *Commedia* into lyric poems of a familiar kind, in Cino's case a generally more subdued *dolce stil novo.*

Both responses are signs that Dante's great synthesis could only collapse. Perhaps it was in any case a more fragile, idiosyncratic creation than it pretended: the attempt to demonstrate the truth of the assumption that everything which existed did somehow cohere could perhaps only convince within the terms of the poem. Outside there were too many disruptive forces. Dante's universalist politics were already outmoded when he was writing. The exile of the Papacy to Avignon, the weakness of successive emperors, the increasing importance of national monarchs, the rise of the new *signorie* in Northern Italy—all these political realities made one of the major struts of his work outmoded except as literature. The republican city-states of Central Italy which had obsessed him were reduced in numbers in the course of the fourteenth century, and the strongest of them, Florence, developed in precisely the direction he wished it not to take. The commercialism which Dante detested was absorbed into a culture which found its image in the human world of the *Decameron.* Philosophically, too, the unity was broken. Dante made a unique fusion of Aristotelian and Neo-Platonic thinking: in the fourteenth century the two divided again, with humanists of the Petrarchan stamp rejecting out of hand all the speculative thought that was fundamental to the *Commedia.* If its commentators are anything to go by, even the poem itself could only be read as a series of episodes or of difficulties whose place in the whole was not to be considered.

Cultural and political fragmentation was linked with geographic dispersal. In the early years of the century lyric poetry spread out of Tuscany to the North, partly, it seems, as a result of the banishment of the White Guelphs from Florence in 1302. According to Boccaccio's biography (*Opere* 338), Dante himself made converts to the cause of poetry in general and vernacular poetry in particular during his last years in Ravenna. Already between 1325 and 1335 Niccolò de' Rossi, a notary in Treviso, assembled an anthology of poems that ran back through Dante and Cavalcanti all the way to goliardic Latin. Niccolò also wrote a great deal of largely old-fashioned lyric verse of his own. His manuscript of his poems, completed probably before 1330, is the earliest example we have of an Italian poet making an 'edition' of his own work (see Brugnolo ed.).

As in the previous century, many poets were notaries, like Niccolò, or merchants. But they were not domi-

nant voices as their Tuscan equivalents had been. There is an immense profusion of fourteenth-century poetry, in which many conflicting tendencies are visible. A major one is the rise of court-poetry, which to all intents and purposes did not exist in thirteenth-century Tuscany. The rule of absolute *signori* meant a return to the situation of the troubadours or even of their *jongleurs,* at least for some of the most important Northern poets. Dante himself had become a dependant of princes, though protected by his prestige against the worst indignities of such a position, in spite of his gloomy comments in *Paradiso* (17. 58-60). Some of his successors, such as Antonio da Ferrara (1315-71/ 4) and Francesco di Vannozzo (*c.* 1340-90?), were less fortunate. Of poor birth, with relatively little education and no material resources, they found themselves continually moving from court to court, looking for support and patronage, and often producing poems at their patrons' requests. As Francesco di Vannozzo put it in one of his poems, 'vo cantando fole / su per le tole altrui / con questo e con colui / per un bicchier di vino' ('I go singing fables / at others' tables / with this fellow and that / for a glass of wine': ed. Medin, p. 248).

In this kind of poetry, and in much written by sober notaries and merchants, the sense of poetry as a means of investigating and articulating serious and complex issues has all but evaporated. So too has the linguistic and stylistic homogeneity of Tuscan poetry, with its strict distinction between styles and its careful cultivation of the high style as the supreme form of poetic expression. Antonio da Tempo, a Paduan who wrote a pedantic treatise on vernacular lyric forms, datable to 1332, said that the Tuscan language was more appropriate to literature ('ad literam sive literaturam') than other idioms, because it was 'magis communis et intelligibilis', that is, because it had more features that were general and hence was more widely understood, though he also allowed that other idioms could be used too (ed. Andrews, p. 99). Other Northern poets would probably have agreed with Antonio, although they did not have the means to act on even this uncertain programme. There was no grammar detailing the rules and forms of Tuscan. In practice Northerners were limited to reworking Tuscan poems and to embedding words and phrases from Dante and the other poets in a language based on their own usage, with *ad libitum* admixtures from Latin. Much is written in a more or less conversational vein, with overtly autobiographical or occasional content (such as the lines from Vannozzo given above). Much too is written expressly to be set to music, especially *madrigali,* which were probably not cultivated by the earlier Tuscan poets, if they existed at all.

Though these developments suggest a resurgence of orality, poetry was also becoming more distinctly literate, as the example of Niccolò de' Rossi shows. Manuscript collections, both of earlier and contemporary poetry proliferate in the course of the century. There were also clear aspirations towards higher styles of writing. Dante, the new learning of humanism and, from at least the middle of the century and perhaps before, Petrarch's own Italian poetry, all had their effects. But the results often flaunt classical learning, or else become heterogeneous mixtures which, by Petrarchan standards, are medieval rather than humanist. Brizio Visconti (d. 1357), the bastard son of Luchino, wrote a canzone on the beauty of his *donna, Mal d'Amor parla chi d'amor non sente* ('He who has no feeling of love speaks ill of love': *Rimatori* 184). Each stanza ends with a comparison to a famous figure: viz. Ovid's Actaeon, St Paul, Apuleius' Psyche, Absalom, the Polyxena of Daretes Phrygius, Virgil's Lavinia, Solomon, Isolde, Aristotle, Polycletus (the sculptor), and St Augustine. Brizio has mixed together the classical, the vernacular, the biblical, in a sequence that has no rationale which I can discover. But he does give his poem more of a structure than this. He described the lady in accordance with the rules for female description laid down in textbooks of poetics: he begins with her hair and works downwards feature by feature until the limits of decency are reached. There is nothing comparable in thirteenth-century poetry, nor will there be in Petrarch, but such curious combinations of haphazard learning and rigid structuring are quite frequent amongst other fourteenth-century poets.

To a large extent it is the context of Northern poetry which is relevant to Petrarch. He composed the *RVF* largely in Northern Italy and it was for Northern *signori* that he made various intermediate versions of the collection. His contacts with contemporary Tuscan poets, other than Boccaccio, belong principally to the earlier phases of his career. The most important of these was probably with Sennuccio del Bene (see section 4 below), though he certainly knew the work of Cino da Pistoia, and may even have known him personally. In any case, whilst Florentines and Tuscans were protected against linguistic heterogeneity to some degree, their poetry shows many of the same tendencies as that of the Northerners. Cino, Sennuccio and others continued to write in the manner of the *stil novo*, though in less exalted vein than their predecessors. There were also Dantesque imitations, classicising poetry of various kinds, and, increasingly as the century went on, homely occasional verse, speaking good sense in colloquial language. The most important Tuscan writer is of course Boccaccio (1313-75), who was a personal friend of Petrarch from 1351 until the end of his life. Before he largely abandoned the vernacular, Boccaccio continually opened up new avenues in prose and verse, principally in the area of narrative, exploiting his large, unsystematic readings in medieval and classical literature to produce a series of works which

combined the two in unprecedented amalgamations. Within the terms of the mercantile culture in which he worked, he, like Petrarch, found a series of solutions, some perhaps more successful than others, to the problem of reconciling different cultural pressures and energies in complex wholes. His surviving lyric poetry is largely occasional, sometimes classicising, sometimes popularising, even casual from a technical point of view.

The story that Boccaccio burnt his poems after seeing Petrarch's may or may not be true, but the letter by Petrarch (*Sen.* 5.2) consoling him for his sense of literary inferiority affirms what will become the dominant perspective on Italian literature of the thirteenth and fourteenth centuries. In whatever order of precedence they are to be arranged, the three authors are Dante, Petrarch and Boccaccio. For the rest there is silence. The historical reality was of course much less clear cut. In the last section of this chapter I shall look briefly at what can be deduced of Petrarch's involvement in the common situation of the poets of his time and at his relations with other poets.

The Rerum vulgarium fragmenta

The *RVF* was a major poetic enterprise beyond the powers of any of Petrarch's contemporaries, none of whom had a comparable experience of literature, or an equivalent critical and historical awareness. It is conditioned throughout by Petrarch's humanism. Though the poems do not flaunt classicism, it is in the light of his work in Latin that he carries through a reassessment of the possibilities of poetry in Italian. Alone of fourteenth-century poets, Petrarch rethinks and remakes the tradition, finding solutions to some of the major problems which poetry faced in his own time, whilst recognising that some of the fundamental ones were, unhappily, intractable, except, perhaps, in the contradictions of which poetry itself is made. At the same time he absorbs into his work the main tendencies evident in his contemporaries, even, when it suited him (or his poetry), drawing directly on their work. For, in spite of his sheer egocentricity and the effacement which he inflicted on them, Petrarch spoke for, not against, other Italian poets of his time.

The foundation of the work was the making of a text. Whilst at least one partly autograph collection (by Niccolò de' Rossi) predates the *RVF*, it is Petrarch's text which is historically significant. Here we have a major author expressly recognising the destruction that his poems were exposed to at the hands of performers to whom he released them (*Fam.* 21. 15 and *Sen.* 5. 3). In the manuscript which he made in the last years of his life Petrarch created a defence against the absorption of his poetry into an oral culture, and also made a humanist resolution of the textual problems of contemporary and preceding poetry generally. He takes control as author of his production, making the same provisions as he makes with any of his Latin works to resist the forces of dispersal and corruption, and presuming implicitly that the poems have the same status as his works in Latin. It is on this act of control and preservation that everything about his poetry depends, from the finest and most subtle of musical effects, to the complexities of the relations between poems. In the fullest sense these are literary poems.

Within the collection the poems are autonomous. Petrarch excludes poems by others and refuses to specify any of the occasions which gave rise to poems, whether these are *tenzoni* with other poets, incidents in his life, or the ups and downs, true or invented, of a peculiarly protracted love-affair. At the same time the autobiographical and occasional character of poetry after Dante is not denied. The *RVF* tells a story, but it does so indirectly in the full recognition that poetic narrative, especially that of lyric poetry, is subject to other pressures, some of which run counter to narrative demands. As well as the partial autobiography which a collection of lyric poems might easily furnish, Petrarch creates a complex interplay between poems, in which narrative possibilities, formal and thematic patterning, and variety (or disorder) compete with each other. On the whole the poems are abstracted from history. When they do display a sense of poetry having an active role to play, it is primarily with reference to some moment in the future which they themselves can only anticipate. . . .

Like his contemporaries Petrarch looks to the past. Unlike them, he makes a serious and lucid recuperation of the central features of the tradition. Although he admits political poems and poems of other kinds, he gives overwhelming priority to love-poetry, almost as if he were following Dante's dictates in the *Vita nuova,* and certainly in accordance with the general practice of thirteenth-century poets. And with the choice of the canonical theme he makes a choice of language and poetic forms which also looks back to the earlier Tuscan lyric. The hybridism and outrageous classicism of his contemporaries, their liking for extended or irregular forms, their conversational tone are all discarded. So too are they: the references, the echoes, the different varieties of metrical organisation are all cast primarily as reassessments of the past, not the present.

All the same there are fundamental modifications. In Italian, as in Latin, Petrarch rejects the scholastic and speculative tendency which had been the strength of later thirteenth-century poetry, and re-forms the style or styles of his predecessors in the light of his own criteria of selfhood, recasting the figure of the *donna* and creating a psychological complexity in poetry for which there were no precedents. He also finds a solution to the problem of Dante. Beatrice is remade as

Laura and questions of transcendental love and transcendental poetry are re-formed in a poetry which is far more sceptical, although unhappily so. The *Commedia* itself is ousted. It becomes the prodigy which it had to be, something quite distinct from lyric poetry, not its point of arrival. In its place there is a reaffirmation of order: the progress of the lyric in Italian ran (as we still tend to think it does) from the Sicilians through the lyric Dante to Petrarch, who in his turn became its culmination. The *RVF* is a representation of the poet's self, but the self represented is also poetic. The changes and fluctuations which the collection represents make up a selective encyclopaedia of Italian poetry, which absorbs and reinterprets the practices of earlier poets, simultaneously casting them as having no greater role than that of being its precursors.

All is accomplished by accepting even more than his contemporaries the cultural dispersal in which they and Petrarch wrote. Earlier poetry in Provencal and Italian reappears in the *RVF* in fragmentory, even pulverised form. So too do fragments from the full range of Petrarch's vast reading. The difference lies in the reconstitution: in the *RVF* there is no literary pastiche, no embedding of literary jewels in drab or uncertain language. Everything is re-formed as an aspect of the self, which is constantly changing but constantly the same, and which finds poetic identity in all the forms it takes, however uncertain it may be about their meaning or status.

The combination of order and disorder, of resolution and indecision, is one of the most disquieting and deep-rooted attractions of the *RVF*. Thematically the poems raise questions about the meaning and scope of poetry which had been voiced by earlier poets (though not, it seems, by other poets of the fourteenth century) and by Petrarch himself in Latin. Simultaneously, they reshape those questions and answer them in some measure, only to discard the answers as provisional, or as only the material of a poetry which can never find a single formulation to embrace its multiple ambiguities. . . . The very stylistic and formal brilliance of the poetry, so evidently not present in the work of his contemporaries, is itself dependent on conflicts and unresolved contrasts, on elements of language which are never rid of their irrational and ambiguous overtones, as much as it is dependent on the creation of lucidly balanced structures. In the course of the Renaissance the *RVF* will become a paradigm of aesthetic achievement in poetry. As we look at the collection now, it betrays constant unease as well as pleasure in the artefacts of which it is made. In some sense it recognises and includes its own negativity, never excluding the aura of death and vanity which surrounds all of Petrarch's work. A combination of the uncombinable, in what may or may not be an integrated whole, is achieved in each poem of the *RVF* and in the totality of the collection, with resonances which extend far beyond the specific personal and cultural crises from which the work historically evolved.

Petrarch's career as an Italian poet

Whilst it is possible to outline the general context from which the *RVF* emerged, the specifics largely elude us. It is hard to speak with any confidence about Petrarch's evolution as a vernacular poet or his personal and literary relations with contemporaries who wrote in Italian. The main collection of poems is at best an ambiguous guide, and other evidence—principally the *Rime disperse (RD)*—is fragmentary and insubstantial. All the same, it is possible to map out a little of the itinerary which Petrarch must have traced, and to explore one or two points of contact with a poetic culture from which he was clearly not so divorced as the *RVF* as a whole seems to suggest.

We do not know when Petrarch began to write Italian poems. His earliest surviving poem is a Latin elegy on the death of his mother written when he was eighteen (*Ep. met.* 1.7), though a letter to his brother Gherardo probably written in 1348 (*Fam.* 10.3) talks disparagingly of love-poems which they wrote during their student days. None of these have survived, if indeed they ever existed. The earliest poems we can identify belong to a group of twenty-five which Petrarch copied out into his rough manuscript in the years 1336-8, forming what Wilkins called a 'reference collection' on the grounds that the poems seem to have been transcribed in no significant order for personal use (1951: 81-92). Eighteen of the poems would eventually enter the *RVF* as 23, 34-6, 41-6, 49, 58, 60, 64, 69, 77, 78, 179. According to a later note, *RVF* 23 (*Nel dolce tempo de la prima etade*) was one of the earliest poems which Petrarch wrote (Romanò 1955: 169. . .). The discarded poems comprise five by Petrarch himself (*RD* 1-5), and two poems by a certain Geri dei Gianfigliazzi and the equally obscure figure of Ser Pietro Dietisalvi, to which two of his own poems were originally replies. In all probability two other excluded poems (*RD* 17 and 18), addressed to Sennuccio del Bene, which were not amongst those transcribed in 1336-8, are also very early.

Taken as a group, these poems are less distinct from much other poetry of their time than are the *RVF* as a whole. Although the poems admitted into the collection are fully integrated, they make a more open display of classical mythology than most of the *RVF*. In the rejected poems myth seems to be used relatively or uncertainly. *Quando talor, da giusta ira commosso* (*RD* 1) uneasily fits the myth of Hercules into a generally Cavalcantian poem: from its first line *Se Febo al primo amor non è bugiardo* (*RD* 5) introduces the myth of Apollo, which is fundamental to much of the *RVF*, in an emphatic conversational register which the

later Petrarch avoids: *Sí come il padre del folle Fetonte* (*RD* 17) strings together one Ovidian myth after another, with an explicit mention of the name Daphne, which is to be excluded from the *RVF*. . . . This poem is also exceptional in apparently making a pun between Laura's name and 'l'ora' (time), and, like one or two other excluded poems (and many poems by other fourteenth-century poets) in being an extended sonnet.

At this stage, or at least in the poems he rejected, Petrarch has not completely established the voice which he will have in the *RVF*. He is also and quite so autonomous. He is willing to write poems on request: *RD* 3 and 4, which are love-poems of a sort, have notes saying that they were written to order, the second note making it plain that the unknown commissioner also told him what matter ('materiam') to put into the poem. At least two other poems were written, if not to order, with the express purpose of furthering his patrons' interests. The sonnet *Vinse Hanibàl* (*RVF* 103), urging Stefano Colonna to press on and destroy the Orsini after his victory over them in 1333, is almost certainly the short piece ('breve quiddam') which, according to a letter on the same theme (*Fam.* 4.3), was composed in the vernacular so that his feelings would be known to the soldiers in Stefano's army. The canzone *Quel c'ha nostra natura in sé più degno* (*RD* 29), written after the bloody recovery of Parma by Azzo da Correggio and his brothers in 1341, makes it plain in its *congedo* that it is intended to celebrate their achievement and to make it known particularly in Tuscany. But perhaps these are exceptional. Taken together, poems to patrons included in the *RVF* suggest a picture, perhaps somewhat idealised, of relations between a great humanist and the powerful. Those to the Colonna, Agapito (58), Stefano (10, 103) and Giovanni (266, 269, 322), like those to Orso dell'Anguillara (38) and Pandolfo Malatesta (104), suggest a shared interest in Roman virtue and in ancient poetry. Here there are no requests for gifts, no indignities, but instead a friendship not so distant in tone from that of Ennius and Scipio in the *Africa*.

The poems from the 1330s also include poetic exchanges (*tenzoni*). It appears that Petrarch was willing to continue taking part in these until well into the 1340s. Two are with friends in humanist circles or on its edges, whose poems (often printed at the end of the *RVF* in Renaissance editions) show that they too can turn a reasonable sonnet. One friend was the schoolmaster Stramazzo da Perugia, mentioned in *Fam.* 14.12 as one of the few men in Italy to know Greek, the other Giovanni Dondi, the Paduan mathematician and astronomer; *RVF* 24 was originally a reply to the first, 244 to the second. But Petrarch's principal poetic correspondents are Sennuccio del Bene and Antonio da Ferrara, two figures who represent quite different trends in fourteenth-century poetry and whose relations with Petrarch are of rather different kinds.

Sennuccio (c. 1275-1349) wrote in the somewhat toned-down version of the *stil novo* which had become common amongst Tuscans in the early part of the fourteenth century, although it is significant, in the light of Petrarch's development, that amongst the small number of his surviving poems are two on the theme of the elderly lover (**Canz.** 9 and 10). He is probably Petrarch's main direct link with poetry of the previous century. The two became friends when Petrarch was quite young. The older poet was exiled from Florence as a result of his involvement with other Whites in Henry VII's siege of the city in 1312. From 1316 to 1326 he was in Avignon, where he too entered humanist circles and was also a protégé of the Colonna. He also made at least one further visit after being allowed to return to Florence. Petrarch addressed seven poems to him which have survived, five of them (the last on his death) being included in the **RVF** (108, 112, 113, 114, 287 . . .), the two classicising poems already mentioned being excluded (**RD** 17 and 18). The poems on both sides have a tone of relaxed intimacy that does not appear elsewhere in the **RVF**, though one of the poems by Sennuccio is written in the name of Giovanni Colonna as a reply to Petrarch's poem to the latter, **Signor mio caro** (**RVF** 266). Petrarch thought enough of his work to mention him, with another friend and minor poet, Franceschino degli Albizzi (who died of the plague in 1348), at the end of his selective survey of Italian poets in the **Triumphus Cupidinis** (4. 37-8), though admittedly in words that suggest personal rather than poetic excellence: 'Senneccio e Franceschin, che fur sí umani, / come ogni uom vide' ('Sennuccio and Franceschino, who were so human, / as every man saw). As always on poetic matters, Petrarch was ruthless but right.

Petrarch's exchanges with Antonio da Ferrara belong to a time when his position as an eminent writer was assured. To a large extent they reflect the differences in prestige and education between the two, but they also show Petrarch stepping outside his familiar persona. Antonio (1315-71/74) was the son of a butcher, an autodidact, and, throughout his life, a second- or third-grade courtier, dependent on the various Northern *signori* for whom he wrote. The acquaintance with Petrarch began in 1343 when a report spread that he had died of an illness in Sicily. Antonio wrote a fullsome canzone of lament and celebration, *I' ho già letto el pianto d'i Troiani* ('I have read in the past the lament of the Trjoans': **Rime** 67a), the first line of which gives a hint of the display of text-book erudition which is to follow, though the canzone ends with a characteristically forthright and modest admonition to the poem to say that it is by 'Antonio Beccar, un da Ferrara, / che poco sa ma volenter impara' ('Antonio Beccari, one from Ferrara, / who knows little,

but learns willingly'). Antonio eventually received a sonnet in return (to become **RVF** 120), in which Petrarch assured him that he was still alive though he had been ill, and disclaimed his worthiness to receive such a tribute. Sooner or later there followed other *tenzoni* (texts in Antonio, **Rime,** 78-82). In the first two Petrarch is surprisingly willing to debate—playfully, no doubt—worn commonplaces about love and hope, and the difference between honourable love and carnal passion, though the authenticity of the second poem (**Rime** 79b) has been doubted, in part because it ends with the statement that he has been in love himself more than twenty-two times. Another *tenzone* is initiated by Petrarch: in a poem beginning 'Antonio cos' ha fatto la tua terra?' (**RD** 15: Antonio, **Rime** 80a) Petrarch says that he has fallen passionately in love with a Ferrarese girl and asks Antonio who she is. In his reply (**Rime** 80b) Antonio regrets that Petrarch has become so enamoured that he has forgotten their friendship, but hopes that the outcome will be that he will stay in Ferrara, so that he can enjoy his company once again. Obviously enough we are a long way here from the serious, complex figure of the **RVF,** though it may just be that the Ferrarese girl is the new love who appears in **RVF** 270 and 271, from which Petrarch is glad to say he is quickly liberated, once again by death.

The *tenzoni* are not all there is to Petrarch's poetic relationship with Antonio. There are three sonnets, one by Antonio (**Rime** 11), one by Petrarch (**RVF** 102), and one attributed to Boccaccio (**Rime** 41) (though its authenticity has been doubted), which rework the same material in almost exactly the same order. The texts of all three are given at the end of this section. The first quattrain of each begins with the example of Caesar concealing his joy at receiving the head of Pompey; the second takes the opposite case of Hannibal concealing his grief when the head of his brother Hasdrubal was sent to him; in the sestet the poet applies the examples to himself, saying that he is obliged to present to the world the image of someone happier than he really is. It is quite possible that the original sonnet was by Antonio. An early biography of Petrarch by Lelio de'Lelii (quoted by Bellucci in her notes to Antonio, **Rime** 11) says that Antonio's sonnet came into his hands, and, feeling that the idea was a good one ('l'invenzione era buona') but that the sound of the verse was inadequate, he wrote another, much better sonnet which followed Antonio 'verse by verse with different and much more ornate words' ('verso per verso con diverse e molto piú ornate parole').

The interdependence of the three poems is not simply a matter of the use they make of classical history or the organisation of their material. They also seem to demonstrate a shared sense of what is poetically desirable. All three are based on antitheses of thought and expression which they attempt to integrate with flowing syntax and imagery to give an impression of ease and yet decorum. Antonio has grave difficulties: hampered by Northern forms ('fazzol', 'pianȝendo', 'soa' etc) which contrast uneasily with the Tuscan of the greater part of the poem, he is also semantically loose (eg 1.3), melodically awkward (eg in the rhyme between the two proper names in 11.6 and 7), uncertain in his Latinisms (eg 'intrinseche' in 1.14) and clumsy in some of his phrases ('la gran testa reverente' in 1.5). His main technique for enriching the texture of his verse is lexical repetition ('testa', 'allegrezza', 'canto', 'celar', etc), which gives the poem an air of old-fashioned rigidity, particularly since some of the repeated items appear at the same point in the line. The sonnet attributed to Boccaccio errs in the contrary direction, that is, towards becoming excessively conversational, even causal. In spite of elevated moments (especially 1.2), it is willing to be dully prosaic (above all 11.6-7), and, like some poems of Boccaccio which certainly are genuine, it can accept a quite imperfect rhyme (1.8). Petrarch alone maintains throughout his poem (certainly not one of his most important) an evenness of register and tone, which is at the same time subtly varied, creating a whole which is complex, musical and apparently effortless. As elsewhere, he appears not so much to depart from the aesthetic implicit in the work of his fellow-poets as to realise their aspirations more successfully.

There is a point in the **RVF** where we can trace the outlines of another victory over the poetically unfortunate Antonio, a victory which also betrays some of the basic dynamics of the collection. I said above that relations between the two poets began with Antonio's canzone of lament on Petrarch's reported death in 1343, in response to which Petrarch wrote the sonnet which was to become **RVF** 120. In the **RVF** there is no hint of the destinatee or of the occasion of the poem, but the issue is not forgotten. This sonnet of self-deprecation is placed immediately after the canzone in which Petrarch presents his coronation of 1341 in allegorical form. A *donna,* representing Glory, appears to Petrarch, and enters into a dialogue with him, in the course of which another *donna* representing Virtue also appears. The dialogue is measured, decorous, raising questions of moral and cultural decline and presenting Petrarch as a lonely and devoted aspirant who is eventually symbolically rewarded with the laurel crown. The contrasts with Antonio's poem are striking: for Antonio had simply packed in allegorical figures and authoritative names ranging from Priscian to the Muses, all of whom he represents as coming to pay tribute to the dead Petrarch. There may or may not be any connection so far as the actual composition of Petrarch's canzone is concerned. But it effectively corrects what Antonio had written, and demonstrates how a celebratory poem might be managed. When it is put together with the following sonnet, Antonio's effacement is complete: the issues of celebration and

modest refusal of celebration are poetically counterposed within the collection. The link with another poet is reduced to an imprecise occasion preceding the second poem: the poems are now internally related and autonomous. Poetry outside the **RVF** has been absorbed and excluded.

It may be that some of Boccaccio's poetry underwent a similar fate. The friendship between the two writers was largely a humanist one, in which Petrarch played the senior role, and Boccaccio that of admiring disciple. In Italian, although there are broad analogies to be drawn between their treatment of the problem of variety and disorder, their paths mostly diverge. However, in some ways Petrarch was willing to be the learner. His principal model for the *Triumphi* is the *Amorosa visione* and he probably drew on other poems for one or two sonnets in the **RVF**. More importantly, Boccaccio's enthusiasm seems to have made him write directly about the issue of Dante in the late 1350s, which he had previously hoped to pass over in silence, and, more important still, to have confirmed the making of the **RVF** as a serious enterprise. So far as the **RVF** are concerned, Boccaccio's shadowy presence is not to be underestimated.

Notes

[*Two languages*] For P's reputation see Bonora (1954), Sozzi (1963), Dionisotti (1974). For general studies on P see Bosco (1961), Noferi (1962), Quaglio (1967), Foster (1984), Mann (1984), and specifically on P's humanism, De Nolhac (1907), Billanovich (1947 and 1965), Trinkaus (1979). For the development of P's thought see also Baron (1968). For P as scholar see also Reynolds and Wilson (1974: 113-17). On P's life see Wilkins (1961). For a survey of recent criticism see Turchi (1978).

[*The Italian context*] For the Sicilians see Folena (1973). For Guittone see Marguéron (1966). For *poesia giocosa* see Marti (1953). For the *dolce stil novo* see Marti (1973), Favati (1975). For the diffusion of the *Divina commedia* see the introduction to Petrocchi ed. (1966). For the general situation in fourteenth-century Italy see Larner (1980). For fourteenth-century poetry see Dionisotti (1967), Tartaro (1971), Balduino (1973), Lanza (1978), Russell (1982). For Niccolò de' Rossi see Brugnolo ed. (1974-7). For music and poetry see Roncaglia (1978). . . .

[*Petrarch's career as an Italian poet*] For Sennuccio see Altamura ed. (1950) and Billanovich (1965). For P and Sennuccio see also Barber (1982). For Antonio da Ferrara and texts of *tenzoni* with P see Bellucci ed. (1972). For P and vernacular Boccaccio see Branca (1981: 300-32). For a discussion of Boccaccio's lyrics see Branca (1981: 250-76).

FURTHER READING
Biography

Wilkins, Ernest H. *Life of Petrarch.* Chicago: Phoenix Books/ University of Chicago Press, 1961, 276 p.
　　Standard biography of Petrarch.

Criticism

Mazzotta, Giuseppe. "Humanism and Monastic Spirituality in Petrarch." *Stanford Literature Review* 5, Nos. 1-2 (1988): 57-74.
　　Discusses Petrarch's ideas on asceticism, secular humanism, and spirituality, focusing on Petrarch's *De vita solitaria* and *De otio religioso* as well as his relationship with his brother Gherardo, who was a monk.

Prier, Raymond. "The Figural Ontology of the Text: Petrarch." In *Interpreting the Italian Renaissance: Literary Perspectives,* edited by Antonio Toscano, pp. 1-8. Stony Brook: Forum Italicum, 1991.
　　Compares the figural poetics of Dante and Petrarch. Prier concludes that "Petrarch experiences a figura within and expresses it in a multiplicity of language on a page that lies without."

Proctor, Robert E. "Petrarch and the Origins of the Humanities." In *Education's Great Amnesia: Reconsidering the Humanities from Petrarch to Freud,* pp. 25-58. Bloomington: Indiana University Press, 1988.
　　Examines Petrarch's ideas on values and the meaning of existence, focusing on his letters and his reading of the ancient Romans.

Shapiro, Marianne. *Hieroglyph of Time: The Petrarchan Sestina.* Minneapolis: University of Minnesota Press, 1980, 254 p.
　　A study of the sestina in the context of European and American poetry which also attempts to reconcile the languages of literary scholarship.

Strozier, Robert M. "Renaissance Humanist Theory: Petrarch and the Sixteenth Century." *Rinascimento* XXVI, second series (1986): 193-229.
　　Argues that a shift in theoretical focus among philosophers occurred between Petrarch's era and that of the humanists of the 1500s.

Waller, Marguerite R. *Petrarch's Poetics and Literary History.* Amherst: University of Massachusetts, 1980, 163 p.
　　Literary-historical study which concerns the "literary inter-relationship inscribed in the Petrarchan texts themselves between a notion of the self and its history or story, an understanding of language which raises problems concerning any and all narrative representations."

Wilkins, Ernest H. "The Evolution of the *Canzoniere* of Petrarch." *Publications of the Modern Language Association of America* LXIII, No. 2 (June 1948): 412-55.
　　Traces Petrarch's revisions of the *Canzoniere* through nine major versions.

————. *Studies in the Life and Works of Petrarch.* Cambridge: Medieval Academy of America, 1955, 324 p.
　　Collects new and revised essays on Petrarch's life and works, including a discussion of the chronology of the *Triumphs* and a survey of Renaissance Petrarchism.

Additional coverage of Petrarch's life and career is contained in the following sources published by Gale Research: *Poetry Criticism,* Vol. 8, and *DISCovering Authors Modules.*

Jalal al-Din Rumi

1207-1273

(Also known as Mowlānā Jalāloddin Rūmī, Jalāluddin Rumi, Jelaluddin Rumi, Jalāl-ud-dīn, Mawlānā, and Mevlevi) Persian poet.

INTRODUCTION

One of the most widely translated figures of Islamic literature, Rumi has been deemed by numerous commentators as the greatest mystical poet of Persia. The *Mathnawi*, his largest body of work, has been compared to the *Koran* and is regarded as one of the masterpieces of religious literature. Rumi belonged to a religious sect of Islam called Sufism, which honored love and devotion to God above all else. Many of Rumi's writings reflect the Sufi doctrine and various dimensions of spiritual life.

Biographical Information

Rumi was born in Balkh (present-day Afghanistan), a center of Islamic study, where his father, Baha Walad, was a renowned scholar and Sufi. When Rumi was twelve years old, his family fled the city fearing the impending invasion of the Mongols. After nine years of travel, they settled in Konya (present-day Turkey). After his father's death in 1231, Rumi was appointed his successor and became a prominent Islamic scholar, well versed in law and theology. He also continued to study the Sufi doctrine under the direction of a disciple of his father. It was not until Rumi met Shams al-Din of Tabriz at the age of thirty-seven, however, that he was spiritually transformed into an ecstatic Sufi who celebrated the mysteries of Divine Love with dancing, music, and poetry. Little is known about Shams except that a great spiritual love existed between the two men. Rumi's disciples were very jealous of Shams. Their abuse and threats of violence forced him to flee on two occasions, and in 1248 Shams disappeared; according to some reports, he was murdered by Rumi's jealous followers. Rumi was devastated by his loss and searched for Shams for many years. He began writing poetry in earnest after Shams's disappearance, and it was during this time that Rumi wrote much of the *Diwan-i Shams-i Tabriz*, a collection of odes dedicated to the memory of Shams. For the rest of his life, Rumi devoted himself to his Sufi disciples, his spiritual practice, and his writing. He was still working on his last and greatest work, the *Mathnawi*, when he died in 1273.

Major Works

Rumi's two major works of poetry are the *Mathnawi* and the *Diwan-i Shams-i Tabriz*. The *Mathnawi* is a collection of six volumes totaling over 25,000 verses which Rumi began around 1260 and continued to work on until his death. Written at the request of his favorite disciple, who was responsible for transcribing Rumi's verses. the *Mathnawi* is a collection of anecdotes and stories drawn from all areas of Islamic wisdom—from the *Koran* to common folktales—which attempts to explain the Sufi way and the various dimensions of spiritual life. The *Diwan*, which was written over a thirty-year time span, is thought to have been started after Shams's arrival in Konya in 1244. Comprising approximately 40,000 verses, it contains poems which focus mainly on various mystical states, such as spiritual intoxication and ecstatic love. Scholars believe that many of the poems in the *Diwan* were composed spontaneously by Rumi while engaged in mystical dancing. Among Rumi's other works are the *Fihi ma Fihi* and the *Majalis-i sab'ah*, both of which include transcriptions of his sermons and conversations. In addition, Rumi's letters have been compiled in the *Makatib*, which contains more than one hundred documents written mainly to the nobility of Konya in order to appeal for help on behalf of his friends and disciples.

Critical Reception

Critical opinion of Rumi has varied. Although many view his *Mathnawi* as second only to the *Koran* as a work of religious literature, others have found it difficult to comprehend. Western readers are often confused by his seemingly unsystematic narratives and find the loose construction of his stories hard to follow. In his own time, Rumi's detractors faulted his anecdotal style and his lack of metaphysical discussions. Generally, however, Rumi was viewed with deep veneration by his contemporaries. Christians, Jews, and Muslims alike attended Rumi's funeral, and centuries after his death he was still being honored by poets, musicians, and artists. Regarding Rumi's lasting influence, R. A. Nicholson concluded: "Familiarity does not always breed disillusion. Today the words I applied to the author of the *Mathnawi* thirty-five years ago, 'the greatest mystical poet of any age,' seem to me no more than just. Where else shall we find such a panorama of universal existence unrolling itself through Time into Eternity?"

PRINCIPAL WORKS

*Majalis-i sab'ah (prose)

*Makatib (letters)
*Fihi ma fihi (prose)
**Diwan-i Shams-i Tabriz (poetry) c. 1244-1273
Mathnawi (6 vols.) (poetry) c. 1260-1273

*The date of composition for these works is unknown.
**This volume contains Rumi's quatrains, or *Ruba'iyat.*

PRINCIPAL ENGLISH TRANSLATIONS

*The Mesnevi of Mevlana Jelalu'd-din Muhammed, er-Rumi...Book of the First (translated by James W. Redhouse) 1881
*Masnavi-i Ma'navi, Spiritual Couplets (translated by E. H. Whinfield) 1887
Selected Poems from the Diwan-i Shams-i Tabriz (translated by R. A. Nicholson) 1898

The Mathnawi of Jalau'ddin Rumi, 8 vols. (translated by R. A. Nicholson) 1925-1940
Tales of Mystic Meaning: Being Selections from the Mathnawi of Jalul-ud-Din Rumi (translated by R. A. Nicholson) 1931
**The Ruba'iyat of Jalal al-Din Rumi (translated by A. J. Arberry) 1949
***Discourses of Rumi (translated by A. J. Arberry) 1961
**Mystical Poems of Rumi: First Selection—Poems 1-200 (translated by A. J. Arberry) 1968
**Mystical Poems of Rumi: Second Selection—Poems 200-400 (translated by A. J. Arberry) 1979

*These works represent translated selections of the *Mathnawi.*
**These works represent translated selections of the *Diwan-i Shams-i Tabriz.*
***This work represents a translated selection of the *Fihi ma fihi.*

CRITICISM

E. H. Whinfield (essay date 1887)

SOURCE: E. H. Whinfield, in an introduction to *Masnavi I Ma'Navi: The Spiritual Couplets of Maulana Jalalu-'d-din Muhammad I Rumi,* edited and translated by E. H. Whinfield, Trubner & Co., 1887, pp. xiii-xxxii.

[*In the excerpt that follows. Whinfield analyzes the influence of the Koran and Sufism on Rumi's* Masnavi, *noting that Rumi took these sources and "fused them into a system by the cardinal principal of 'Love.'"*]

The **Masnavi** is described by the Author in his Arabic Preface as follows:—

> Thus saith the feeble servant, in need of the mercy of God, whose name be extolled, Muhammad, son of Muhammad, son of Husain, of Balkh, of whom may God accept it,—'I have exerted myself to enlarge this book of poetry in rhymed couplets, which contains strange and rare narratives, beautiful sayings, and recondite indications; a path for the devout, and a garden for the pious; short in its expressions, numerous in its applications. . . . It contains the roots of the roots of the roots of the Faith, and treats of the mysteries of Union and sure Knowledge.'[1]

In modern language the **Masnavi** may be called the "Divina Commedia," or the "Paradise Lost" of Islám— a summary of religious thought, a *"Théodicée,"* justifying the way of Allah to man, and a standard of religious feeling. In India it is regarded as a very weighty document of the Faith, second only to the Koran and the Traditions; in Turkey, according to Khaja 'Aini, one of the *'Ulama,* it is esteemed "the amulet of the soul;" and Sir J. Malcolm and Mr. Hughes, in spite of its *Sunni* bias, call it the Bible of Persia.

The central idea of the poem is that the only true basis of spiritual religion is love, and that all seeming faith and piety which do not grow from love profit nothing. And this is illustrated by what Cardinal Newman calls the "Mystical or Sacramental" view of the Universe, *i.e.,* the religious insight which sees in the visible Universe only outward signs of the spiritual realities within it, and especially in human beauty a type of the Divine perfections.[2]

I.

The poet's *data* were the Koran and the Traditions, the speculations of the Scholastic Theologiaus, and lastly, the Mysticism of the Sufis.

To begin with the Koran:—Allah is the Jehovah of the Pentateuch—The One God, the Maker of heaven and earth, the Eternal, the Most High, who sitteth above the heavens (*'arsh*), a Great King above all gods. Of all the Divine attributes that which Muhammad realised most strongly was Power. He pictures Allah as a mighty Oriental Sultan, who at his arbitrary will exalts some to honour, and abases others to disgrace[3]—a God of mercy and of vengeance; of goodness and of severity; very gracious to his faithful servants, but a terrible chastiser of all who offend him. Muhammad had not attained to that sense of the intimate relation between God and the soul,—that recognition of the Fatherhood of God,—which inspires some of the Psalms. His dominant thought is, "How irresistible is the power of God!—how terrible a thing it is to fall into His hands!—and how absolute the need for "fear of God, and for complete resignation to His will."

Muhammad said of himself, "A messenger has only to deliver his message," and his message related to practice, not speculation. He accepted without question the old Judaic view of the Divine Nature and the simple morality of the Patriarchs and of King Solomon. As time went on, men found in the Koran dogmas as to the Divine Nature, as to Predestination, as to the Origin of evil, and so on, but in reality these were only the "after-thoughts of theology." The language of the Koran is popular, and not meant to bear the strain of analysis. Some of its expressions, for instance, seem to make for Predestination, while others are equally strong for Free Will.[4] Two sayings are ascribed to Muhammad which, whether genuine or not, certainly express his general attitude towards speculative questions:—"Think on the mercies of God, not on the Essence of God;" and, "Tarry not with them that discuss Predestination." He had, however, some presentiment of what would come to pass after his death, for he said, "My people shall be divided into three-and-seventy sects, of which all save one shall have their portion in the fire."

It was inevitable that knowledge should widen, and that widened knowledge should breed speculation, for "knowledge is a goad to them that have it." Neither the sinister prediction of the Prophet, nor the trenchant sentence of 'Omar, nor the anathema of the Canonist Ash-Shafi'i could hinder the faithful from philosophising. In the first century of the Flight they were brought into contact with the speculations of the Christian sects, with the theosophy of the Neoplatonists and Gnostics, and with the old Persian learning of Balkh and Khorásán, and by the end of the third century portions of Plato, of Aristotle, "the parent of heresies," and of the Alexandrian commentators had been translated into Arabic. The Mu'tazilites and Mutakallamín at once carried philosophy into divinity, and, in the light of this new learning, debated all the trite topics of theology.

Parallel to this stream of scholasticism there ran another stream of mystical theosophy,—derived in part from Plato, "the Attic Moses," but mainly from Christianity, as presented in the "spiritual Gospel" of St. John, and as expounded by the Christian Platonists and Gnostics. This second stream was Sufiism.

The Dabistan records an opinion that the creed of the Sufis is the same as that of the Platonists (*Ishráqin*),[5] and in the Sufi writings we are constantly confronted by the "fair humanities of old *philosophy*,"—the two worlds of "ideas" and of sensible objects, the One and the Many, the figment of "Not-being," the generation of opposites from opposites, the Alexandrian *gnosis* of the *Logos,* of Ecstasy and of Intuition, and the doctrine of the Phædrus that human beauty is the bridge of communication between the world of sense and the world of ideas, leading man by the stimulus of love to the "Great Ocean of the Beautiful."

The influence of Christianity on Sufiism is more marked still. M. Garcin de Tassy calls Islám "une grande aberration Chrétienne," but he would have been nearer the mark if he had limited this description to Sufiism. In the *Masnavi,* for instance, we not only find notices of the chief events in the Gospel history, but also sentences and phrases which are obviously only free renderings of Gospel texts.[6] The cardinal Sufi terms, "The Truth," "The Way," "Universal Reason" (*Logos*), "Universal Soul" (*Pneuma*), "Grace" (*Faiz*), and "Love," are almost certainly of Christian extraction, and the main Sufi doctrine of eternal life after annihilation (*Baga ba'd ul Fana*) is a reflection, though only a blurred reflection, of the Christian death to sin and life to righteousness.

II.

Such, in brief outline, were the poet's *data,* and he fused them into a system by the cardinal principle of "Love," which is, in fact, no other than the "Love," the "Charity," the "New commandment," the "more excelent way," of St. John and St. Paul.

The substantial identity of the Love (*'Ishq* or *Erós*) of the **Masnavi** with the Love (*Agapé*) of the New Testament is obscured by the figurative language of the poem. Now-a-days we have lost the key to all this symbolism, though it would have been quite intelligible to St. Bernard, St. Theresa, or St. Thomas à Kempís. This sensuous imagery was first used by that fervid Copt Origen, in his commentary on the Song of Songs,—a book which, by the way, the Rabbis were half inclined to exclude from the Canon,—and even Origen himself, in his cooler moments, felt misgivings as to its propriety.[7] Hence we can hardly be surprised at finding modern divines, like Hughes and Tholuck,[8] stoutly denying that Christian "Love of God" has anything in common with the mystical love of the Sufis. But no unbiassed person can read the **Masnavi** without being forced to admit the *intended* identity of the two. And, what is more, we cannot pronounce its sensuous symbolism, however objectionable, to be an unpardonable sin without at the same time condemning our own "Mystical Theology" and uncanonizing not a few of our own saints.

The poet repeats again and again, in language that would almost satisfy Dean Mansel or Mr. Herbert Spencer, that man is utterly unable to form adequate conceptions of the Absolute, and that all symbols derived from the world of sense are more or less misleading;[9] but he justifies their use by the necessities of human thought and by the example of the Koran. And, casting about among sensible objects to find a type of heavenly love, he finds nothing better than earthly love. Beauty "stands upon the threshold of the mystical world," and the phenomena of earthly love, excited by the thrill of human beauty,—the frenzy of Majnun, disclosing to him a beauty in Laila which was hidden from strangers,—the passion of Zulaikha for Yusuf, making her reckless of disgrace,—sublime self-devotion, like that of Heloise to the worthless Abélard,—lifelong reverence, like that paid by Dante to Beatrice,—phenomena such as these seemed to him the most appropriate types of love to God attainable by human faculties.

According to him love is the "astrolabe of heavenly mysteries," the "eye-salve which opens the eyes to spiritual beauty," the touch of emotion which changes the service of slaves into the devotion of children, the key to spiritual knowledge (*ma'rifat* or *gnosis*), and the only true basis of genuine practical religion.

First as to knowledge:—The poet, like St. Paul, condemns the "oppositions of knowledge (*gnosis*) falsely so called,"[10] but at the same time he has a very definite *gnosis* of his own. His main purpose is to display the merciful attributes,—to bring out the Fatherhood of God,—and to explain away the terrible attributes and the mystery of evil. Hence he approaches all speculative questions, not on their metaphysical, but on their ethical side, *i.e.,* through his principle of love. The more a man loves, the deeper he penetrates the purposes of God.

Pious Muslíms are dominated by the same vivid sense of the presence and action of God that inspires the Psalms. God, they say, is all in all, the "Only Real Agent," who is "working every day." We might say in modern language that God is conceived by them as ever renewing all the matter and all the force in the universe. If He withdrew His sustaining presence, the whole would relapse into its original nothingness. Not a leaf sprouts on a tree, not a sparrow falls to the ground, not a thought occurs to the mind, without God's impulsion. And this impulsion is exercised, not in accordance with uniform "laws of nature," but by an arbitrary *fiat* pronounced in each individual case. It is plain that this view of God's action on the world must bring Muslíms face to face with the problem of evil in a vivid way that we Europeans, with our "laws of nature," can hardly realise. On this view it is hard to see how any actions can be done except those which are done, and how therefore man can be justly held responsible for actions so utterly beyond his control.[11] Dean Mansel seems to think it a mark of special heretical pravity to dwell on the problem of evil,[12] but when pious minds are thus brought face to face with it, and realise the awful nature of the question, it is, surely, impossible for them to shirk it.

To this question "knowledge" (*ma'rifat* or *gnosis*) is the poet's answer. And the key to this *gnosis* is love,—such love as guides a lover to divine the cause of his mistress's cruelty, or an affectionate child the reasons of its father's severity. The child of God, reading with the commentary of love the twin Books of Revelation and Reason,—its Father's word and its own feeble sense,—becomes *clairvoyant* through love, and attains to knowledge or *"gnosis"* of God. This *gnosis,* which bears some likeness to that given in the first chapter of St. John, may be summarised as follows:—

God said, "I desired to manifest forth my glory, and I created the worlds in order to manifest it." "The first thing created was Reason" (*'Agl* or *Logos*),[13] first unspoken Thought, then the spoken Word. From the *Logos* proceeded or emanated the "Universal Soul" (*Ján i kull* or *Pneuma*), which, like the *Logos,* contained the fulness of the Godhead,—the sum of all the divine "names," attributes, or "ideas" (*'Ayán i Sabita*).[14] The light of these divine "ideas" then shone upon the darkness of "Not-being," and each atom of Not-being reflected one of them,[15]—heaven and the angels, for instance, reflecting the attributes of mercy, and hell and the devils the terrible attributes.[16] And so on with all the creatures of the visible universe. Last of all came forth the soul of man, which reflected all the attributes, merciful as well as terrible. Man is thus a "Microcosm" or recapitulation of the whole universe. On one side he is luminous with the light of the merciful attributes, but on the other he is black with the darkness of the terrible attributes, also reflected in his essential "Not-being." He is thus "created half to rise and half to fall;" but he, of his own accord, accepted the "deposit" of this double nature, involving power to refuse the evil and choose the good. All the phenomena of the universe, man included, have no real existence of their own, but are every moment renewed by the constant outpouring, through the channel of the *Logos,* of reflections from the One *Noumenon,* and, when the divine purposes are accomplished, the whole phantasmagoria of phenomenal existence will vanish away, and "God will be heir of all."

Thus the "Knower" or Gnostic (*'Arif*) penetrates the divine scheme, and is able to admit the divine Power without impugning the divine Goodness. A skilful painter is of necessity able to paint ugly pictures as well as fair ones. Hence the "Knower" does not, like the Magians, set up over against the good Ormuzd an evil Ahriman to account for the origin of evil, but recognises that God created all things, even including what seems to us evil.[17] But what we call evil has in reality no real existence of its own, being merely, as St. Augustine said, a "negation,"—a departure from the Only Self-existent Being. Here the poet first takes "Not-being" in its literal sense of "Nothing," and then, misled by the old notion that all words must have things answering to them,[18] as Something,—as Nothing in relation to God, but as a very pernicious Something in relation to man. In the next place the poet points out that much of what we call evil is only relative,—what is evil for one being good for another,—nay more, that evil itself is often turned into good for the good. Further, he insists on the probationary design of much so-called evil. As Bishop Butler says, life is a state of probation, and probation involves the existence of evil lusts and pains to prove us. How, the poet asks, could there be self-control without evil passions to be controlled, or patience without the pressure of afflictions to be borne? Much evil, again, is medicinal,—the jail serves as the mosque of the criminal, because it makes him cry to God, just as fasting and discipline are the school of the ill-regulated passions. Lastly, much evil has a punitive purpose. "He who grieves the *Logos* must look for tribulation in the world."

So, again, with the question of "compulsion" or predestination:—God is the "Only Real Agent," and, in

His inscrutable wisdom He undoubtedly fashions some to be vessels of wrath, such as were Iblis, Cain, Nimrod, Pharaoh,[19] and Abu Jahl; but, as we can see only a small part of the divine scheme, we must be wary of judging in these cases. Adam was rebuked for scorning Iblis, and it may be that Iblis will one day be turned again into an angel of light. So it is said that Pharaoh was a doer of God's will equally with Moses, and was wont at night to bewail the "compulsion" which made him oppose that faithful servant of God. But the "Knower," while refusing to judge others, will not be backward in judging himself. He will admit the ability to choose good and refuse evil, which his own consciousness testifies to as existing in himself. He will not, like Iblis, throw the responsibility for his sins upon the Creator, but rather he will cry with Adam, "O Lord, we have blackened our own faces!" Finally, when man's will is altogether identified with God's will, and he finds his chief pleasure in doing God's will, the whole opposition and distinction between "compulsion" and free will is annihilated, just as raindrops falling into oyster-shells become pearls.

Much of the phraseology used by the poet to express his doctrine of the indwelling and inworking of Allah in the universe approaches that used by the Pantheists, and it has become a commonplace of European criticism to say that this Sufi doctrine is mere Pantheism. M. Garcin de Tassy, for instance, has the usual tirade against "ces funestes doctrines." But in reality the two doctrines are entirely distinct.[20] Pantheism "makes everything God except God Himself,"—*i.e.,* explains away a Personal God by identifying Him with the universe. The Sufi poet, on the other hand, makes everything naught except God, and gives life to this dead "Not-being," the universe, by representing it as instinct with the "deeply interfused" presence of the Personal God. And, as we have seen, he is directly at issue with the Pantheists in insisting on the free will of man and his responsibility for his actions.

The key to all this *gnosis,* as already stated, is Love. "The eye sees only what it brings with it to see," and till the inner eye is made *clairvoyant* by love of God, it is blind to the deep things of the Spirit, even as cold-hearted strangers were blind to the charms of Laila. Then comes the question, Does this grace of love come from the lover or the Beloved,—from man or from God? The poet's theory requires the latter; but, like St. Augustine, he is forced to attribute something to the *"opus operantis".* God's grace, he seems to say, is the sole efficient cause of love, and the resultant "inner sense which sees all things as they really are;"[21] but yet a certain pious aspiration is required on man's part to attract the grace. He says man must strive to obtain this grace of love and intuition. He must not rest content with the "hearing of the ear,"[22] or with merely "naming the names of God," but must press on till he gains the "eye of certainty,"—the actual intuition of spiritual realities.

With the "mighty spell" of love the poet conjures away all difficulties. Thus, take the question of the evidences of religion:—There are some minds, illuminated by the "dry light" of reason, which are irresistibly impelled to prove all things. Such a sober and candid mind, for instance, as that of Bishop Butler cannot rest in what seems to it mere "enthusiasm." Bishop Butler, like his master Locke, cannot help proportioning his beliefs to the evidence for them. Even for the glory of God he cannot exaggerate the evidence, and, where he finds only probable evidence, he will not pretend to demonstrable certitude. And it may be noted by the way, that our poet himself does not disdain to use the argument from probability in addressing the worldly, though he insists that his own faith rests on far deeper foundations. In addressing the worldly, however, he says, "Even in your trade you act on probability. You despatch goods by sea at the risk of shipwreck, for if you decline the risk you can gain no livelihood. And so you ought to act with the great venture of faith." But for himself the poet cannot rest on mere probability. He must have "indefectible certitude,"—a firm conviction independent of varying moods and shifting probabilities,—a very "passion of belief." A true lover, he says, is ashamed to demand proofs of his mistress, and prides himself on trusting her in spite of appearances telling against her.[23] He has an evidence in his heart which makes him turn away from all external evidences with disgust. This was just the feeling with which the Evangelical School regarded the "Probabilities" of Butler and the "Evidences" of Paley. And so we read in Cardinal Newman's "Apologia"[24] that Mr. Keble "ascribed the firmness of assent which we give to religious doctrines, not to the probabilities which introduced it, but to the living power of faith and love which accepted it." Just so the *Masnavi* teaches that it is love which generates intuition and belief.[25] Love absorbs a man's whole being and makes him indifferent to the cavils of cold reason; just as Zaid, smarting with the pain of the blow, was unable to attend to the hair-splitting distinctions of his assailant.

Not only is faith generated by love, but, what is more, faith generated by any other motive is worthless. Faith, like that of respectable conformists, growing from mere blind imitation and the contagion of custom, or like that of scholastic theologians, consisting in mere intellectual apprehension and repetition of orthodox dogmas (*Jamá'at*), to say nothing of the faith professed by conscious hypocrites, and by the devils "who believe and tremble,"—all these kinds of faith, summed up by the poet in the general term of "the yoke of custom" (*Taqlíd*), profit nothing. To be of any value faith must be rooted and grounded in love, "the bond of perfectness."[26] The mere external righteousness

generated by "*Taqlíd*,"—the mere matter-of-course adoption of the virtues of the age, the class, the sect,—is compared to a "veil of light" (virtue) which hides the Truth more entirely than the "veil of darkness" (vice). For "self-deluding goodness is of necessity unrepentant," while the avowed sinner is already self-condemned, and so advanced one step on the road to repentance.

Since there are so many kinds of spurious faith current in the world, the pious man must walk warily, and before copying the words and actions of those who seem to be religious, he must test and prove them. Sometimes he will find their professions contradicted by their practice; sometimes, especially in moments of unguarded anger, their "speech will betray them," and show their motive to be *odium theologicum* and not religious love. He must apply a sort of Socratic *elenchus* to their Shibboleths, and see if the root of the matter is in them. Even when he has found a genuine saint he must not run away with the notion that all he has to do is to copy his outward conduct, but he must try to divine his inward motives and ruling principles, and strive earnestly to attain the disciplined affections, the concentrated will, the all-absorbing love of God, which are the characteristics of His true children.

God judges not as men judge, from outward conduct, but looks at the heart, the secret motives, and the "aspiration."[27] Hence the poet holds outward forms and rites to be matters of very minor importance. Islam is the "religion of Abraham"[28] (*minus* the priesthood)—a religion of new moons and fasts, of circumcision, of purifications, of holy war,[29] of precise postures in prayer, which, as Dr. Liddon recently pointed out, are the very postures described in the Psalms.[30] Naturally Muslíms get to rely on these forms too entirely,—to lose the sense of proportion in religious matters,—to fancy that a painful and scrupulous observance of forms will atone for the neglect of the weightier matters of the law,—the essential religious graces summed up by St. Paul under the name of Charity. Hence the poet was led to regard forms, generally speaking, as indifferent. In the parable of Moses and the Shepherd he points out that so long as a worshipper is inspired by love of God the words in which he expresses his devotion are quite immaterial. He says, "Fools exalt the Mosque, and ignore the true temple in the heart." He has even a good word for idolaters who act up to their lights. The old satire of Xenophanes, that if lions had a god they would represent him as a lion, would affect him not at all. He says it is not from any perverse preference that men buy counterfeit gold, but only because it seems to them genuine. Man is not saved by "naming the divine names" with orthodox accuracy,[31] or by worshipping with "fair rites," but by heartfelt love and earnest endeavour to please God. In every nation he who loves God and does His will according to his lights is accepted of Him.

As regards religious practice, it must be borne in mind that the Masnavi is addressed to Sufis, and contains what may be called "counsels of perfection." Those who aimed at the more perfect way, as opposed to the moderate practice of average Muslíms, were first named "Companions," then "Followers" (*Tabá'iún*), and, in the third generation, "Ascetics" or "Devotees" (*Záhid* or *'Abid*).[32] The name "Sufi" was first adopted by one Abu Háshim, a Syrian Ascetic, who died in 150 A.H., and the first convent (*Khánaqáh*) was built in his time at Ramla, in Syria.[33] After that the Tradition "There is no monkery in Islam" was entirely explained away, and there was no limit to the ascetic practices of the Sufis. The austere precepts of the Gospel as to forsaking family and position and wealth for religion's sake took firm hold of these fervid spirits, and were carried out with the same uncompromising ardour as that shown by the early Christian monks. Voluntary poverty, mortification, obedience, and renunciation of the world became the very essence of Sufi practice.

They described the state they sought to attain by these ascetic practices as "self-annihilation" (*faná*),—the death of passions and self-will and self-consciousness, which produces the spiritual resurrection to eternal life (*baqá*).[34] This "ecstasy" (*Hál*), and the raptures (*Zauq* and *Muwájid*) which attended it, were condemned as heresy (*Bid'at*),[35] but continued to be held by the Sufis notwithstanding. The poet says these ecstatic states must be experienced to be understood. The accounts given of them naturally vary. As Jeremy Taylor says, "When they suffer transportation beyond the burden and support of reason, they feel they know not what, and call it what they please."[36] Some describe *faná* as a sort of "thinking away self." Thus Lahiji says it is to "emerge from the limitations of self which veil man's real essence (God)."[37] Imám Ghazzáli describes *faná* as a "prayer of rapture." "In that state man is effaced from self, so that he is conscious neither of his body nor of outward things, nor of inward feelings. He is 'rapt' from all these, journeying first *to* his Lord, and then *in* his Lord; and if the thought that he is effaced from self occurs to him, that is a defect. The highest state is to be effaced from effacement."[38] Shabistari describes it as an approximation to the Light of lights, which blinds the mental eye with excess of light.[39] The poet, pursuing his favourite metaphor of human love, describes the state of "*faná*" as one in which "the flame of everlasting love doth burn ere it transforms,"[40]—utterly consuming "self" ere it quickens the lover with the embrace of "union."

This doctrine of ecstasy is the really mischievous part of the poet's system. Like Ghazzáli,[41] he was aware of its liability to abuse,[42] and for ordinary persons he prescribes a sort of safeguard in the person of the "Spiritual Director" (*Pir*). When, however, he has to deal with what Cardinal Newman calls the "eccentricities of the saints,"—with the excesses of the "*Pirs*" themselves,—his theology blinds his moral judgment, and he does not dare to censure even such outrageous pretensions as those he relates of the saint Bayazid. He goes so far as to say that in the mouth of a saint even infidelity and blasphemy may be true piety.[43] Such are the pitfalls that lie in the road of all who regard religion as something beyond human criticism, and ignore Bishop Butler's *dictum,* that reason cannot abdicate its right of judging obvious immoralities in religious doctrines and persons.

Speaking generally, the poet's view of the saints is not unlike the old Catholic view. He represents them as the special favourites of heaven, endued with miraculous gifts (*Karámát* or *Charismata*).[44] Minds having a very vivid sense of God's presence and action, and a very weak sense, if any at all, of the uniformity of nature, come to regard miracles as almost part of the natural order of things. Hence the more ancient Sufis did not make much account of these miraculous gifts,[45] just as, according to Paley, the early Christian Apologists did not lay much stress on the evidentiary force of miracles.

A very remarkable doctrine is that of unrecognised saints. There are always on earth four thousand persons who are, so to speak, saints without knowing it. These are they who are born with a natural goodness, which lifts them without effort to a point that most labour to reach in vain,—loyal, gentle, unselfish souls, endowed with a natural intuition of good and a natural inclination to pursue it, the stay and comfort of those who enjoy the blessing of their society, and, when they have passed away, perhaps canonized in the hearts of one or two who loved them. Spontaneous goodness of this sort is not to be submitted to rules or forms. The inward inclination, not the outward ordinance, is the source of their goodness. "Against such there is no law." They have a standard of thought and character of their own, quite independent of the praise or blame of "men of externals."[46] Pure gold needs no mint-stamp to give it value.

It is hardly necessary to dwell on the virtues of the "new commandment,"—the love of man to man, which is the necessary complement of the love of man to God. The poet loses no opportunity of insisting on the paramount obligation of compassion, humility, toleration, patience, the peaceful temper,—in fact, all that beauty of holiness summed up by St. Paul under the name of Charity.

Space is wanting to describe others of the poet's doctrines. But attention may be called to his allegorizing method of interpreting the Koran. He held that each word of the Koran, "spiritually understood," had seven senses; and here he outdid Origen, who contented himself with ascribing only three senses to Scripture.[47] Also noteworthy is his view of the evolution of man out of inanimate matter, through the grades of the vegetive and animal souls, up to humanity, and the presage and augury thence derived that this ascending process will not cease at death, but will be carried on, and the "great aspiration of humanity" realised in a yet higher life to come. His doctrine of the final restitution of all who at the last judgment throw themselves unreservedly on the mercy of the Great Judge is also remarkable. This, as well as his doctrine of "Reserve," he probably took from the Christian Platonists.[48] Also noteworthy are his appreciation of the disputes of the Christian sects,[49] and his very unoriental view that woman is not a mere plaything, but a ray of the Deity.

Notes

[1] I avail myself of Mr. Redhouse's translation.

[2] "While men of externals believe that there is nothing in existence but what is visible to sight, interior men hold that much is veiled from outward sight, which can only be seen through a near approach to God and a close communion with His omnipresent Spirit." *Fasúsu'l Hikam.*

[3] Koran iii. 25.

[4] Renan, Averroes, p. 160; Cp. Deutsch, Remains, p. 129.

[5] Dabistan, by Shea and Troyer, iii. p. 281.

[6] *E.g.,* Some of the *"Hadís."*

[7] Bigg's "Christian Platonists of Alexandria," p. 188. Bishop Lightfoot, too, is sometimes staggered by the Patristic use of *Erós* for *Agapé. Ib.,* p. ix.

[8] Hughes' "Notes on Muhammadanism," p. 233; Tholuck, "Blüthensammlung," p. 26. But see "Saufismus," p. 304.

[9] See pp. 5, 31, 263.

[10] I Tim. vi. 20.

[11] Cp. Omar Khayyám, *passim.*

[12] "Gnostic Heresies," p. 11.

[13] Renan, "Averroes," p. 118. Tholuck admits the identity of the *Logos* with' *Agl i kull,* ("Ssufismus," pp. 274, 286), but apparently not that of *Pneuma* with *Jan i kull (Ib.,* p. 233).

[14] Jorjani in Notices et Ext. des MSS., x. 65.

[15] "As the spirit of man becomes voice and voice words, so the Divine Spirit becomes substance, and substance spirits and bodies."—"Dabistan" (Calcutta ed.), p. 479.

[16] See De Sacy, quoted in note to Shea and Troyer's "Dabistan," iii. 256.

[17] Here the poet deserts his usual guides. Neither Plato ("Resp.," ii. p. 380) nor Christians would admit that God is the Author of Evil. The "Evil One" was created originally good.

[18] See p. 52.

[19] See "Dabistan," by Shea and Troyer, iii. 272, note.

[20] Cp. Deutsch, Remains, p. 160.

[21] See p. 324.

[22] Cp. Job xlii. 5: "I heard of Thee by the hearing of the ear, but now mine eye seeth Thee."

[23] Credo quia impossibile.

[24] "Apologia," p. 19.

[25] "Præstat *Amor* supplementum Sensuum defectui."

[26] Col. iii. 14.

[27] See Book VI.—Prologue.

[28] See Koran iii. 89, and Deutsch, Remains, p. 129.

[29] See Deuteronomy, chap. xx.

[30] Psalm xcv. 6.

[31] Jalalu-'d-Din once said that he agreed with all the seventy-three sects. Nafahatu-'l Uns, p. 532.

[32] Qushairi, quoted in "Haji Khalfa," ii. 308.

[33] Nafahatu-'l Uns (Lees' ed.), p. 34. Jami says this convent was built for the Sufis by a Christian nobleman who marvelled at their love for one another.

[34] Possibly they were influenced by the Buddhist "Nirvana."

[35] "Haji Khalfa," ii. 471. "Ibn Khalliqan," i. 365.

[36] Quoted by Vaughan, "Hours with the Mystics," ii. 127.

[37] Gulshan i Raz, p. 8, note. Cp. the passage from Dionysius the Pseudo Areopagite given there from Vaughan, i. 288.

[38] Tholuck "Ssufismus," pp. 4, 105. See Vaughan, ii. 132, on Tauler.

[39] Gulshan i Raz, 1. 120.

[40] From "The Dream of Gerontius."

[41] Sale's Koran, Prelim. Disc., p. 126.

[42] He compares ecstasy to possession by a spirit— possibly an evil spirit. So Wesley said of the transports of religious excitement experienced, by his energumens that "Satan sometimes mimicked the work of Grace." Cp. Virgil's description of the ecstasy of the l'ythian priestess. Æn., vi. 77.

[43] Cp. "Plus nobis profuit ad fidem Thomæ infidelitas quam fides credentium."

[44] And also as objects of semi-adoration (*dulia*).

[45] Ibn Khaldun, quoted in Notices et Ext. des MSS., xii. p. 304.

[46] See pp. 129, 224, 227.

[47] Bigg, "Christian Platonists," p. 136.

[48] *Ibid.,* pp 143, 292.

[49] See p. 13. Mir Khwánd and Shahrastáni (Cureton's ed., p. 173), evidently following some Judaizing Christian authority, make St. Paul the first heresiarch.

Khalifa 'Abdul Hakim (essay date 1933)

SOURCE: Khalifa 'Abdul Hakim, "Love," in *The Metaphysics of Rumi: A Critical and Historical Sketch*, 1933. Reprint by The Institute of Islamic Culture, 1959, pp. 43-61.

[*In the following essay, originally published in 1933, Hakim compares Rumi's "philosophy of love" to the theories of Plato.*]

If there is anything in Rumi's mysticism that defies all attempts at analysis, that is his ecstatic utterances about Love. It is exactly here that theory has so very little in common with life and experience, and the words of Mephistopheles are justified: "Grau . . . ist alle Theorie Und grün des Lebens goldner Baum." If it were concerned only with lyrical fervours and ecstasies, there would no doubt be much that touches our own inner chords and stirs emotions in the soul that are too deep for words. But that is not all that we find in Rumi. He tells us that what he means by Love is indescribable and the attempt to define it is as baffling as to define

life itself. Life as well as love, not in spite of, but on account of their immediacy cannot be defined.[1] He tells us that it is not logic but music[2] that is a partial medium of its expression, and love being paradoxical in its nature, music, that is its vehicle, becomes paradoxical too: "Poison and Antidote at the same time." "Our sweetest songs are those that tell us of saddest thoughts." Love is the greatest mystery of life and music is the garb in which it symbolises itself in the phenomenal realm:

> There is a secret in the melody of the flute which if divulged would upset the scheme of things.

> Who ever saw a poison and antidote like the reed? Who ever saw a sympathiser and a longing lover like the reed?

But the indescribability of the experience does not hinder him from giving to the uninitiated a kind of philosophy of Love. It is just this aspect that we propose to consider. So far as the theories of love are concerned, a part of his arguments and views can be directly traced back to Plato who has had a decisive influence on all mysticism, both Islamic and Christian, by his conception of a supersensuous Reality, as well as Eros as a cosmical power. Rumi's Love as an experience was not a product of any theory; as something intimately personal, it cannot be a subject of criticism. But the conceptual apparatus that he employs to philosophise about love requires to be understood in its historical connections. The contents of *Phaedrus* and *Symposium* that give us most of the theories of Love ever conceived by man were not unknown to the thinkers of Islam. Ibn Sina's (Avicenna) *Fragment on Love*[3] is mostly a reproduction of the dialogues in *Symposium*. Love as a cosmic force and its universal operation in Nature; Love as the movement towards Beauty which being identical with Goodness and Truth represents Perfection and the Highest Idea, and Love as the inherent desire of the individual for immortality; in short, the whole outline of the theory of Life given by Avicenna is a simple repetition of the Platonic theory of Love. The processes of Assimilation, Growth, Reproduction are so many manifestations of Love. All things are moving towards Eternal Beauty and the worth of a thing is proportionate to its realisation of that beauty in itself.

Before coming to that aspect of Rumi's conception of Love where he differs from Plato, let us first pick out from the Mathnav the ideas that run parallel to the conceptions expounded in the dialogues of Plato.

(1) The idea developed in Phaedrus that Love is not utilitarian, Rumi gives us back with the addition that it is the intellect that is utilitarian and that weighs profit and loss before taking a step. Love considering itself

to be an end in itself does not ask 'Why' before it sacrifices. As a divine madness, it is directly opposed to the calculated Love of the sophists.

> How should Reason wend the way of despair?
> 'Tis Love that runs on its head in that direction.
>
> Love is reckless, not Reason: Reason seeks that from which it may get some profit. (vi, 1966-1967).
>
> Neither do they put God to any test, nor do they work at the door of any profit or loss. (vi, 1974).

(2) In the speech of Agathon that precedes the speech of Socrates, we find the view of the young Plato that Love is Love of the Beautiful and the Beautiful alone is worth our love and homage. Rumi repeats the same conception in different words when he says that Perfect and Eternal Beauty belongs to God, and all that is beautiful in the phenomenal world is only a passing reflection of the Eternal Beauty of God and is related to God as sunlight is related to the sun. The beauty of a thing is like the illumination of a wall by the sun; when the sun looks away from it, lo! it is dark again.[4] So our love should not stop short at the beautiful thing whose light is only transient and borrowed, but rise from the phenomenal to the noumenal origin of all beauty. . . .

(3) Love is a principle of Unification and Assimilation. The force of attraction in every atom and one form of life losing itself in another form (Assimilation) and thereby resulting in Growth—all are manifestations of the form of Love.

> If there had not been Love, how should there have been existence? How should bread have attached itself to you and become (assimilated to) you?
>
> The bread became you: through what? Through (your) love and appetite; otherwise, how should the bread have had any access to the (vital) spirit?
>
> Love makes the dead bread into spirit: it makes the spirit that was perishable everlasting. (v, 2012-2014).

(4) That Love as a cosmogonical principle is the origin and beginning of life, an idea that Phaedrus put in the mythological form by saying that Eros belongs to the oldest gods. Love as a principle of the genesis of the world was present in Greek thought even before Plato. Hesiod had taught that in the beginning of all things was Chaos out of which sprang at first Earth and Love,[5] i.e. the dead substratum and the informing principle.

> If there had not been Love, how should there have been existence? How should bread have

attached itself to you and become (assimilated to) you? (v, 2012).

But in spite of all this parallelism of ideas sketched above, there are some important and fundamental differences between Plato and Rumi in their conceptions of the nature and function of Love. Most of the conceptions given above as parallel with Rumi's ideas are the views of the various speakers in the Dialogues that throw light on the different sides of the problem and represent different ways of looking at it. Plato's own views are only those put in the mouth of Socrates and can be summed up as follows:

> (1) Love as a craving after immortality in its various forms through procreation and through intellectual and artistic productions or through heroic deeds.
>
> (2) Love as a movement towards the idea of Perfect Beauty in order to look at it in its purest form in which the soul once looked at it before its connection with matter and sensibility.
>
> (3) Love as a mediator between the two worlds. (An idea taken up and developed by Christian dogma.)

The fundamental difference between the two thinkers can be best understood when we examine the relation of Rationalism with Irrationalism in their respective outlooks on Life. Plato was a rationalist in so far as he believed in the knowability of the ground of Being through theoretical Reason. What he calls Eternal Beauty was nothing but one of the highest Ideas or the attractive side of the picture of Eternal Truth. But in Truth there is nothing individual and personal; so his Highest Idea or his God is impersonal, theoretical Truth that sits in the Ideal Realm unmoved and untouched by its worshippers and admirers. It is something objective and outside the human soul, only to be looked at and admired like a perfect piece of art. Love, which taken by itself is an irrational element, is only a means to an end, which is the realisation of theoretical Truth. So in the end Eros of Plato is nothing but Spinoza's intellectual love of God.

Rumi, in contrast with Plato, is an Irrationalist. In him the position between Reason and Love is reversed. He does not believe in the knowability of the ground of Being through Theoretical Reason. The categories of the Understanding . . . or what he calls the Particular Reason . . . are from their very nature incapable of grasping the ultimate Reality and on account of their discursive and dualistic nature cannot comprehend the Unitary Essence of Existence. Reason for him is a light and a guide but not a goal. As life in its essence is non-intellectual, so the Eternal Beauty that attracts the lover is not the beauty that is the "Effulgence of

Truth." Rumi employs the Platonic terminology for views that are poles apart from Plato. For Plato the word 'Ultrarational' would have been utter nonsense. When reason is identical with the ultimate reality, how can there be anything beyond it? That explains again why the Eros of Plato is theoretically intelligible and the Love . . . of Rumi defies all description. The nature of God and the nature of the human soul are ultrarational; so their deepest and ultimate relation must necessarily be so.[6]

It is a characteristic feature of Rumi's world of thought that his central conception is not Truth or Knowledge of God but Life. It is the organism and its function of Growth and Assimilation that presents to him a picture which explains life more than any system of intellectualistic metaphysics. Love is a paradox in the sense that in it by giving we take and by dying we live. This process of dying to live is represented by organic life. Inorganic matter becomes organic by dying to itself and living a higher life in the plant and so can the plant be exalted into still higher life by dying unto itself and living in the animal. The whole course of evolution is an illustration of the principle of dying to live.

Rumi finds the principle of growth and development through the organic power of assimilation as the highest principle of explanation. Although true to his anti-intellectual metaphysics, he admits the impossibility of explaining the connection and the interaction of body and soul in terms of spatial contact and physical causation, yet he untiringly points to the miraculous power of transformation which we can see everywhere in Nature. Mechanism may try to explain phenomena by the principle of identity of cause and effect, but Mechanism is an extremely partial abstraction from the Real. Reality presents to us nothing but qualitative transformation. Fuel turning into fire and bread turning into life and consciousness point to the incommensurability of the cause and the effect.[7] The 'how' of it may not be intelligible but the fact itself is so evident and incontrovertible that for unsophisticated consciousness it hardly requires any proof. Now Rumi pushes the analogy further and asks us if it is not justifiable to believe that something like the principle that holds good in the evolution from man to matter should hold good further up from man to the all-embracing spiritual organism—God.[8] That is the conclusion to which Rumi's interpretation of Assimilation as a process of love leads him. So here we find a tremendous difference between the Eros of Plato and the '*Ishq* of Rumi; the former leading to the gazing of impersonal intellectual beauty and the latter leading us to be partakers of Infinite Life by becoming living organs in the Life of Life.

Philosophy attempts to find a thread of unity running through the multiplicity of phenomena. This attempt can succeed only partially, because Reason can never overcome the dualism of the subject and the object. In the words of Rumi, "there is a squint in the eye of the intellect," it sees double that which in reality is one. It is intellectual analysis that splits reality into two which it does not know afterwards how to bind again. As a principle of unification, Love stands higher that Reason. Reason differentiates and separates,[9] while Love binds and assimilates the heterogeneous and makes it homogeneous with itself. One cannot help noticing a striking resemblance between Rumi's view of love and the various types of the philosophy of intuition developed in post-Kantian idealism. As his conception of the pure Ego is fundamentally the same as that of Fichte, so his utterances about that ultimate intuition which he calls Love have a marked similarity with the intuition of Schelling and Bergson. Rumi's views about the relation of the intellect to the spring of life within us are an astounding anticipation of the views of Schopenhauer and Bergson—that intellect is only a utilitarian product, an instrument in the hand of "will to live" and hence is incapable of measuring the depths and scanning the nature of our immediate intuition of life.

> Partial (discursive) reason is a denier of Love, though it may give out that it is a confidant.
>
> It is clever and knowing, but it is naught (devoid of self-existence); until the augel has become naught, he is an Ahriman (Devil).
>
> It (partial reason) is our friend in word and deed, (but) when you come to the case of inward feeling (ecstasy), it is naught (of no account). (i, 1982-1984).

Our ultimate intuition is an intuition of identity that transcends all contradictions and all relations and, therefore, from its very nature it is incapable of stepping into the realm of intellect and speech whose nature is dualistic in the sense that, in order to think at all, we must analyse and compare.[10] That is a drawback rooted in the very nature of intellect. Life in its immediacy can only be lived and felt but not described. Analysis of life is a *post mortem* examination of it. Rumi who always calls this immediate intuition as '*Ishq* (considering the connotation which Rumi attaches to the word, 'Love' is a very inadequate and misleading translation of it) expresses in the following verses a longing for a kind of expression that could unveil the nature of this intuition and at the same time tells us as to why it is not communicable:

> Then what is love? The sea of Not-being: then the foot of the intellect is shattered. (iii, 4723).
>
> Would that Being had a tongue, that it might remove the veils from existent beings.

O breath of (phenomenal) existence, whatsoever words thou mayest utter, know that thereby thou hast bound another veil upon it (the mystery).

That utterance and (that) state (of existence) are the bane of spiritual perception; to wash away blood with blood is absurd, absurd. (iii, 4725-4727).

The contrast of love and reason . . . is a popular topic in the Sufi literature. The demands of these two potent factors in the personality of man are felt to be conflicting. This conflict is sometimes expressed as the conflict of law and love . . . and at other times as a contradiction between law and reality . . . and the general tendency in the Sufi doctrine is to assert the Primacy of Love to Law and Reason. Sometimes the contradiction is maintained in all its sharpness by the bold assertion that Love is lawless and Law is loveless. Love is identified with ecstacy that absorbs all distinctions: fidelity and infidelity, good and bad, right and wrong—in short, all values are drowned in it. In weaker natures this doctrine degenerated into antinomianism against which sobriety and healthy commonsense had to protest. Hujwiri[11] says that truth is a synthesis of both these elements and points to the formula of the Islamic faith: "There is no god except Allah and Muhammad is His Prophet" . . . , as an example of this synthesis, the first part as Reality and the second part as Law.

What the Sufis really meant to assert was the primacy and immediacy of the one as compared with the other. What they maintained was that the essence of religion is neither identical with law nor with morals, nor with theoretical reason, nor with the outward form of any positive religion. Their viewpoint was exactly that of Schleiermacher[12] that the essence of religion is neither morals nor theology but a cosmical feeling, an intuition of oneness with the spirit of the Universe. In this respect religion is not immoral or irrational but amoral and non-rational. It does not contradict morals and reason; it is categorically different from them.[13] This indescribable cosmical feeling is exactly the same as the 'Ishq of Rumi. The following quotations from the Mathnavi will verify this statement.

(1) This cosmical feeling has not any particular form as its object:

Do not say that the heart that is bound (conditioned) by (such bodily attributes as)

sadness and laughter is worthy of seeing Thee (as Thou really art). (i, 1791).

Love is higher than these two states of feeling: without spring and without autumn it is (ever) green and fresh. (i, 1794).

Our emotion is not caused by grief and joy, our consciousness is not related to fancy and imagination.

There is another state (of consciousness), which is rare: do not thou disbelieve, for God is very mighty. (i, 1803-1804).

(3) This cosmical feeling is the very essence of religion. . . . A man with this feeling cannot be pronounced irreligious in whatever from he might express his faith.

Whatsoever the man in love (with God) speaks, the scent of love is springing from his mouth into the abode of Love. (i, 2882).

And if he speaks infidelity, it has the scent of (the true) religion, and if he speaks doubtfully, his doubt turns to certainty. (i, 2882).

If he speaks falsehood, it seems (like) the truth. O (fine) falsehood that would adorn (even) the truth l (i, 2886).

Theoretical reason cannot lead to this feeling; one must turn away from logic in order to realise this feeling.

I have tried far-thinking (Providence) intellect; henceforth I will make myself mad. (ii, 2332).

(4) This feeling consumes away all doubts and difficulties raised by man's theoretical and practical interests; it is a source of englightenment not accessible to reason.

His (God's) love is a fire that consumes difficulties; the daylight sweeps away every phantom. (iii, 1136).

It is the Infinite in man which, dissatisfied with the Finite, doubts it and puts questions to it. Seek the answer there where the question emerges, i.e. in this infinite cosmical feeling.

O thou with whom He is pleased, seek the answer from the same quarter from which this question came to thee. (iii, 1137).

Why on this side and on that, like a beggar, O mountain of Belief, art thou seeking the echo? (iii, 1139).

(2) 'Ishq cannot be identified with the psychophysical feeling of pleasure and pain; it is categorically different from them.

The only muzzle for evil suggestions (of doubt)
is Love; else, when has anyone (ever) stopped
(such) temptation? (v, 3230).

The identification of *'Ishq* with this immediate cosmical
intuition reveals the real meaning of a number of utterances in the Sufi literature which otherwise appear
to be irresponsible and extravagant. For instance, the
following verses attributed to Abu'l Khair[14] must be
interpreted in this spirit:

> He whom destiny places among the group of
> lovers becomes free from the mosque and the
> temple. He whose mode of life is annihilation
> and *Faqr* (detachment from the world) has
> neither relation nor belief nor gnosis nor
> religion.[15]

Rumi is never tired telling us that this intuition is neither communicable nor teachable. Morality and reason
may serve as helps to the relisation of it. He marks it
off clearly from science as well as art.

> Science is learnt through words and art is learnt
> through practice, but *Faqr* is awakened by personal
> touch.

As a consequence of seeing in this intuition the real
purpose of religion, he prefers one moment of it to a
thousand years spent sincerely in the service of God.[16]
Religion as revealed in forms and dogmas is not identical with this immediate intuition.[17]

In connection with this problem of the relation of this
intuition to reason, Rumi has interpreted the story of
Adam and Satan as given in the Qur'an. In order to
appreciate Rumi's interpretation, we give a brief sketch
of the story.[18]

"The universe and the angels were long in existence
before the creation of man. When God proposed to
create Adam, He put His proposal before the angels
saying that He wished to create a being who should
represent Him on the earth and act as His Vicegerent.
The angels did not relish the proposal and asserted
their purity and superiority and their incessant praise
and glorification of Him. They objected to the creation
of man because he would be cruel and shed blood on
earth. To refute the angels God established the superiority of Adam by giving him the knowledge of all
things. They acknowledged their ignorance and the
worth of Adam. Having established the dignity of man
on the basis of a type of knowledge that the angels did
not possess, they were asked to pay homage to Adam
by prostrating themselves before him. All the angels
obeyed except Ibl s, the Satan, who refused out of
pride looking down upon Adam as a mean creation of
clay. For this crime against, God and Man, the Satan
was cursed. He fell from his dignified position and

determined to avenge himself on this new creature and
his Creator.

"The Satan misled Adam and Eve into eating the fruit
of the forbidden tree. They acknowledged their sin
and were forgiven and sent down to live on the Earth.
Adam was dignified again, but Satan kept on in his
contempt of man and the consequent revolt against
God."

Now, let us turn to Rumi's interpretation of the story
which partly agrees and partly differs from the Biblical narrative. His views may be summed up as follows:

> (1) Adam of the Qur'an is symbolical of Humanity[19]
> in its original Essence; he is the prototype of man.

> (2) The knowledge given to Adam[20] which put the
> angels to shame and established his superiority
> to them was of an intuitional nature; it had nothing
> in common with intellectual knowledge or theoretical
> reason.

> (3) In the creation of Adam God breathed His own
> Spirit into him that was the source of Adam's
> divinity and dignity and that was the Essence to
> which angels were asked to pay homage.

> (4) Satan, the principle of evil, represents a view
> of life that is incapable of appreciating the divine
> dignity of man.[21]

Intellect working by itself is materialistic and realistic
and is incapable of realising the eternal value of man.
This value lies in the intuition of man's divinity and
infinity which the fallen man is always trying to realise
and reattain.[22]

Satan is the personification of the realistic intellect
while Adam's essence is the love of the Ideal and the
Infinite. Then again Rumi represents Satan as a deter-
minist[23] giving a hint that intellect cannot believe in
freedom; freedom lies in the non-intellectual side of
man. So Satan is the embodiment of the intellect which
is realistic and deterministic, while the intuitional side
of man represents him as an ideal and free being.

Thus it is love allied with the sense of freedom that
Rumi conceives as the essence of man. . . .

Notes

1

> My secret is not far from my plaint, but ear and
> eye lack the light (whereby it should be
> apprehended). Body is not veiled from soul, nor
> soul from body, yet none is permitted to see the
> soul. (i, 7, 8).

2

The reed is the comrade of busy one who has been parted from a friend: its strains pierced our hearts.

Whatsoever I say in exposition and explanation of Love, when I come to Love (itself) I am ashamed of that (explanation).

Although the commentary of the tongue makes (all) clear, yet tongueless love is clearer. (i, 112, 113).

3 This fragment on love forms part of his collected works preserved in the British Museum Library and has been edited by N. A. F. Mehren (Leiden, 1894).

4

That (friendship) was a radiance (cast) upon their wall: the sign (of the sun) went back towards the sun.

On whatsoever thing that radiance may fall, thou becomest in love with that (thing), O brave man.

On whatsoever existent thing thy love (is bestowed), that (thing) is glided with Divine qualities. (iii, 552-554).

5 Compare it with the following:

Had it not been for pure Love's sake, how should I have bestowed an existence on the heavens? (v, 2739).

6

There is a union beyond description or analogy between the Lord of Man and the spirit of Man. (iv, 760)

No created being is unconnected with Him: that connection, O uncle, is indescribable.

Because in the spirit there is no separating and uniting, while (our) thought cannot think except of separating and uniting. (iv, 3695-3696).

How should the intellect find the way to this connection? This intellect is in bondage to separation and union. (iv, 3699).

7

Everything except love is devoured by love: to the beak of love the two worlds are (but) a single grain. (v, 2726).

Again they crushed the bread under their teeth: it became the mind and spirit and understanding of one endowed with reason.

Again, when that spirit became lost in Love, it became (as that which) rejoiceth the sowers after the sowing. (i, 3167-3168).

The delight of (every) kind is certainly in its own kind (congener): the delight of the past, observe, is in its whole. (i, 889).

As (for instance) water and bread, which were not our congeners, became homegeneous with us and increased within us (added to our bulk and strength). (i. 891).

Oh, happy is the man who was freed from himself and united with the existence of a living one! (i, 1535).

8

Love is an (infinite) ocean, on which the heavens are (but) a flake of foam: (they are distraught) like Zalikha in desire for a Joseph.

Know that the wheeling heavens are turned by waves of Love: were it not for Love, the world would be frozen (inanimate).

How would an inorganic thing disappear (by change) into a plant? How would vegetive things sacrifice themselves to become (enclosed with) spirit?

How would the spirit sacrifice itself for the sake of that Breath by the draft whereof a Mary was made pregnant? (v, 3853-3856).

9

That Unity is beyond description and condition: nothing comes into the arena (domain) of speech except duality. (vi, 2034).

10

The substance of the spirit is itself beyond contraries (vi, 63).

11 *Kashf al-Mahjub*, pp. 139-40.

12 *Uber die Religion Reden an die Gehildeten unter ihrer Verächiern*, Deutsche, Bibleotek, Berlin, pp. 1-27.

13

In that quarter where love was increasing (my) pain, Bu Hanifa and Shafi'i gave no instruction. (iii, 3832).

The religion of love is different from all other religions.

Verily, the circumambulation performed by him who beholds the king is above wrath and grace and infidelity and religion. (iv, 2697).

[14] *Abu Sa'id Abu'l Khair,* edited by Mitra, Lahore. About the life of Abu'l Khair see R. A. Nicholson, *Studies in Islamic Mysticism* (Cambridge).

[15] A comparison of these lines with a quatrain of 'Umar Khayyam shows into what utter Nihilism an exaggeration of this standpoint might lead:

> I saw a free Sufi squatting on the ground, who was neither for infidelity nor for Islam, neither for the world nor for religion: truth and reality and law and belief were nothing to him: in the two worlds who is brave like him?

[16]

> A short time (spent) in the company of God's friends is better than sincere religious worship of a hundred years.

[17]

> In that quarter where love was increasing (my) pain, Bu Hanifa and Shafi'i gave no instruction. (iii, 3832).

> Verily, the circumambulation performed by him who beholds the king is above wrath and grace and infidelity and religion. (iv, 2967).

> Not one word (capable of) expressing it has (ever) come into the world, for it is hidden, hidden, hidden. (iv, 2968).

The Mathnavi is full of utterances about the superiority of love to law. The Qur'an emphasised the aspect of law and duty and obedience and the relation of God and man was depicted as the relation of the master to the servant. The Sufi reaction against orthodoxy expressed itself mainly in this revision of values. Rumi conceives of duty and service only as a disguise of love:

> At the time of the Sama' Love's minstrel strikes up this (strain): 'Servitude is chains and lordship headache.' (iii, 4722).

> Servitude and sovereignty are known: loverhood is concealed by these two veils. (iii, 4724).

[18] References to the story in the Qur'an:

> Adam created to rule on earth. (ii. 30).

> Adam is taught the names of all things. (ii. 31).

> Angels ordered to make obeisance to Adam. (ii. 34; vii. II; xv. 28; xvii. 61; xviii. 50; xx. 116; xxxviii. 72).

> Iblis refuses to make obeisance to Adam. (ii. 34; vii. II; xiv. 30; xvii. 61; xviii. 50; xx. 116; xxxviii. 73, 74).

[19]

> The Adam like this whose name I am celebrating, if I praise (him) till the Resurrection, I fall short (of what is due). (i, 1248).

> Adam was the eye of the Eternal light. (ii, 18).

> If outwardly, the *peri* is hidden, (yet) Man is a hundred times more hidden than the *peris*. (iii, 4255).

> Since, in the view of the intelligent, Man is hidden, how (hidden) must be the Adam who is pure (chosen of God) in the unseen world! (iii, 4257).

About the identification of Adam with man in general there is a verse in the Qur'an which, though not directly alluded to by Rumi, may have served him as a scriptural basis for his doctrine:

> And certainly We created you, then We fashioned you, then We said to the angels: Make obeisance to Adam. So they did obeisance except Ibl s. (vii 11).

[20]

> Inasmuch as the eye of Adam saw by means of the pure light, the soul and in most sense of the names became evident to him. (i, 1246).

[21]

> He (Iblis) had knowledge, (but) since he had no religious love, he beheld in Adam nothing but figure of clay. Though you may know (all) the mimitiae of knowledge, O trustworty (scholar) not by that (means) will your two (inward) eyes that discern the invisible be opened. (vi 260-261).

[22]

> He that is blessed and familiar (with spiritual mysteries) knows that intelligence is of Iblis, while love is of Adam. (iv, 1402).

[23] That the Devil, the embodiment of intellect, is at the same time a personification of Determinism as opposed to Freedom represented by Adam, is very ingeniously based by Rumi on certain verses of the Qur'an. Adam as well as Satan committed a sin; the former admitted having committed it out of his own choice and begged for forgiveness but Satan attributed his own sin to God. . . .

Arbery discusses Rumi's opinion of his own poetry:

Rumi affected an astonishing contempt for his own poetry. On one occasion he remarked, "I am affectionate to such a degree that when these friends come to me, for fear that they may be wearied I speak poetry so that they may be occupied with that. Otherwise, what have I to do with poetry? By Allah, I care nothing for poetry, and there is nothing worse in my eyes than that. It has become incumbent upon me, as when a man plunges his hands into tripe and washes it out for the sake of a guest's appetite, because the guest's appetite is for tripe." The poet's modesty, rooted in a puritanical scrupulosity, does not need to affect our judgment. In Rumi we encounter one of the world's greatest poets. In profundity of thought, inventiveness of image, and triumphant mastery of language, he stands out as the supreme genius of Islamic mysticism. He invites and deserves the most attentive and intensive study, by a succession of devoted scholars, whose combined explorations will vastly improve upon our first halting attempt. Future generations, as his poetry becomes wider known and more perfectly understood, will enjoy and applaud with increasing insight and enthusiasm the poems of this wisest, most penetrating, and saintliest of men.

A.J. Arberry, trans., in Mystical Poems of Rumi, *The University of Chicago Press, 1968.*

Reynold A. Nicholson (essay date 1945?)

SOURCE: Reynold A. Nicholson, in an introduction to *Rumi: Poet and Mystic (1207-1275)*, George Allen and Unwin Ltd., 1950, pp. 17-26.

[*In the following excerpt, redrafted by A. J. Arberry and published five years after Nicholson's death, Nicholson discusses the pantheistic themes found in Rumi's* Mathnavi *and praises the poem's "exhilarating sense of largeness and freedom by its disregard for logical cohesion, defiance of conventions, bold use of the language of common life, and abundance of images drawn from homely things and incidents familiar to every one."*]

Rumi's literary output, as stupendous in magnitude as it is sublime in content, consists of the very large collection of mystical odes, perhaps as many as 2,500, which make up the *Diwan-i Shams-i Tabrizi*; the *Mathnawi* in six books of about 25,000 rhyming couplets; and the *Ruba'iyat* or quatrains, of which maybe about 1,600 are authentic.[1] The forms in which he clothes his religious philosophy had been fashioned before him by two great Sufi poets, Sana'i of Ghaznah and Faridu'l-Din 'Attar of Nishapur. Though he makes no secret of his debt to them both, his flight takes a wider range, his materials are richer and more varied, and his method of handling the subject is so original

that it may justly be described as "a new style." It is a style of great subtlety and complexity, hard to analyse; yet its general features are simple and cannot be doubted. In the *Mathnawi,* where it is fully developed, it gives the reader an exhilarating sense of largeness and freedom by its disregard for logical cohesion, defiance of conventions, bold use of the language of common life, and abundance of images drawn from homely things and incidents familiar to every one. The poem resembles a trackless ocean: there are no boundaries; no lines of demarcation between the literal "husk" and the "kernel" of doctrine in which its inner sense is conveyed and copiously expounded. The effortless fusion of text and interpretation shows how completely, in aesthetics as in every other domain, the philosophy of Rumi is inspired by the monistic idea. "The *Mathnawi,*" he says, "is the shop for Unity (*wahdat*); anything that you see there except the One (God) is an idol." Ranging over the battlefield of existence, he finds all its conflicts and discords playing the parts assigned to them in the universal harmony which only mystics can realize.

Sufi pantheism or monism involves the following propositions:

(*a*) There is One Real Being, the Ultimate Ground of all existence. This Reality may be viewed either as God (the Divine Essence) or as the World (phenomena by which the hidden Essence is made manifest).

(*b*) There is no creation in Time. Divine Self-manifestation is a perpetual process. While the *forms* of the universe change and pass and are simultaneously renewed without a moment's intermission, in its *essence* it is co-eternal with God. There never was a time when it did not exist as a whole in His Knowledge.

(*c*) God is both Immanent, in the sense that He appears under the aspect of limitation in all phenomenal forms, and Transcendent, in the sense that He is the Absolute Reality above and beyond every appearance.

(*d*) The Divine Essence is unknowable. God makes His Nature known to us by Names and Attributes which He has revealed in the Koran. Though essentially identical, from our point of view the Divine Attributes are diverse and opposed to each other, and this differentiation constitutes the phenomenal world, without which we could not distinguish good from evil and come to know the Absolute Good. In the sphere of Reality there is no such thing as evil.

(*e*) According to the Holy Tradition, "I created the creatures in order than I might be known," the entire content of God's Knowledge is objectified in the universe and pre-eminently in Man. The Divine Mind, which rules and animates the cosmos as an Indwelling Rational Principle (Logos), displays itself completely in the Perfect Man. The supreme type of the Perfect Man is the pre-existent Reality or Spirit of Muhammad, whose "Light" irradiates the long series of prophets beginning with Adam and, after them, the hierarchy of Muslim saints, who are Muhammad's spiritual heirs. Whether prophet or saint, the Perfect Man has realized his Oneness with God: he is the authentic image and manifestation of God and therefore the final cause of creation, since only through him does God become fully conscious of Himself.

These are some of the themes underlying Rumi's poetry. He is not their original author; they may be regarded as having been gradually evolved by the long succession of Sufi thinkers from the ninth century onwards, then gathered together and finally formulated by the famous Andalusian mystic, Ibnu'l-'Arabi (1165-1240). Ibnu'l-'Arabi has every right to be called the father of Islamic pantheism. He devoted colossal powers of intellect and imagination to constructing a system which, though it lacks order and connexion, covers the whole ground in detail and perhaps, all things considered, is the most imposing monument of mystical speculation the world has ever seen. While it is evident that Rumi borrowed some part of his terminology and ideas from his elder contemporary, who himself travelled in Rum and lies buried in Damascus, the amount of the debt has inevitably been exaggerated by later commentators whose minds are filled with forms of though alien to the *Mathnawi* but familiar to readers of Ibnu'l-'Arabi's *Fususu'l-hikam* ("Bezels of Wisdom") and *al-Futuhatu'l-Makkiyya* ("Meccan Revelations"). The Andalusian always writes with a fixed *philosophical* purpose, which may be defined as the *logical* development of a single all-embracing concept, and much of his thought expresses itself in a dialectic bristling with technicalities. Rumi has no such aim. As E. H. Whinfield said, his mysticism is not "doctrinal" in the Catholic sense but "experimental." He appeals to the heart more than to the head, scorns the logic of the schools, and nowhere does he embody in philosophical language even the elements of a system. The words used by Dante in reference to the *Divine Commedia* would serve excellently as a description of the *Mathnawi*: "the poem belongs to the moral or ethical branch of philosophy, its quality is not speculative but practical, and its ultimate end is to lead into the state of felicity those now enduring the miserable life of man." The *Mathnawi* for the most part shows Rumi as the perfect spiritual guide engaged in making others perfect and furnishing novice and adept alike with matter suitable to their needs. Assuming the general monistic theory to be well known to his readers, he gives them a panoramic view of the Sufi gnosis (direct intuition of God) and kindles their enthusiasm by depicting the rapture of those who "break through to the Oneness" and see all mysteries revealed.[2]

While the *Mathnawi* is generally instructional in character, though it also has entertaining passages, as befits a book intended for the enlightenment of all sorts of disciples, the *Diwan* and, on a much smaller scale, the *Ruba'iyat* are personal and emotional in appeal. Lyrics and quatrains alike have everywhere the authentic ring of spiritual inspiration, while in image, style and language they often approximate very closely to the *Mathnawi*. In some of these poems the mystic's passion is so exuberant, his imagination so overflowing, that we catch glimpses of the very madness of Divine experience. Yet the powerful intellect of Rumi the man never quite capitulates to the enthusiasm of Rumi the mystic; at the last moment there is a sudden drawing-back, a consciousness that certain matters are too secret and too holy to be communicated in words. It is not surprising to read that these poems, chanted (as many of them were doubtless composed) in the spiritual séance of the Mevlevis, roused the hearers to an almost uncontrollable fervour.

In Rumi the Persian mystical genius found its supreme expression. Viewing the vast landscape of Sufi poetry, we see him standing out as a sublime mountain-peak; the many other poets before and after him are but foot-hills in comparison. The influence of his example, his thought and his language is powerfully felt through all the succeeding centuries; every Sufi after him capable of reading Persian has acknowledged his unchallenged leadership. To the West, now slowly realizing the magnitude of his genius, . . . he is fully able to prove a source of inspiration and delight not surpassed by any other poet in the world's literature.

Notes

[1] [This sentence has been added to the author's draft.—A. J. A.]

[2] Here Professor Nicholson's notes end.

Afzal Iqbal (essay date 1956)

SOURCE: Afzal Iqbal, "The Poet as Thinker," in *The Life and Work of Muhammad Jalal-ud-Din Rumi*, revised edition, Institute of Islamic Culture, 1964, pp. 157-85.

[*In the essay below, originally published in 1956, Iqbal examines the message of Rumi's* Mathnavi *and discusses such concepts as the relation between love and intellect, the nature of the self, evolution, determinism and responsibility, knowledge of God, and the Ideal Man.*]

When we talk of Rumi's thought, we should not be taken to mean that he had a systematic and coherent philosophy. His thoughts lie scattered and unconnected like broken threads but a patient effort can weave them into an almost consistent pattern. The point is that we should not approach Rumi's thought in the same spirit as we approach the thought of a systematic thinker.

Another point of difference between Rumi and systematic thinkers is that whereas the latter usually support their contentions with arguments, Rumi generally makes assertions and tries to invest them with power by means of analogies.

As Whinfield points out, the **Mathnavi** is an exposition of 'experimental' mysticism, and not a treatise of 'doctrinal' mysticism. Hence Rumi does not set out all this Sufi gnosis with the logical precision of a systematic thinker but rather assumes it all as known to his readers.[1]

Muslim philosophers used to employ *a priori* reasoning in order to establish the truth of metaphysical dogma. This method, however, does not elicit ready approval from the average individual whose mind is not trained for abstract thinking of a high order. Rumi, therefore, employs analogies in order to drive home a subtle point—analogies from this matter-of-fact, sensible world of ours. Analogy used in poetry often assumes the form of a didactic story; and a didactic story in order to be successful should possess three characteristics: the moral should entice our imagination by its originality, uniqueness and importance; the moral should appear like the 'soul' and the story like the 'body'; and both should be interwoven into each other, and during the perusal of the story the reader should not even think of the moral. It should come as a complete surprise, an original experience.

There are numerous stories in Rumi which aptly illustrate this method. In fact it is the effective employment of this method which has given unique influence and popularity to his **Mathnavi**. For example, here is an interesting story. There was a *muezzin* who had an extremely unpleasant voice. The people of his village offered him a lump sum with the request that he should proceed to Mecca for a pilgrimage. This was obviously a pretext to get rid of him. The *muezzin,* on his way to Mecca, halted in a village. There he went into the mosque and called the faithful to prayers. After a short while, a Zoroastrian came, laden with presents, and asked for the *muezzin.* People were naturally surprised. 'What is it?' they asked. 'What has he done for you that you bring him such valuable presents?' 'I am greatly indebted to him,' said the Zoroastrian, 'he has saved my daughter.' 'How?' came the anxious query, and this is what the Zoroastrian told the curious crowd. 'I have a young and beautiful daughter. Much to my embarrassment, of late she has been showing a growing inclination towards Islam. I tried

my best to dissuade her; all the influential members of my community helped in bringing pressure to bear upon her, but our efforts not withstanding, she persisted in her designs of conversion. Today she heard the *muezzin* call the faithful to prayers; she was so much disgusted with his voice that she has now decided to abandon her plan. This decision has brought me great relief, and it is in recognition of this unique service that I bring these rich presents to the *muezzin.*'

The moral of this story does not seem to be evident. It becomes evident only when Rumi points it out, and administers an effective rebuke to the so-called Mussalmans who are bringing discredit to their religion by their wrong example.

It is by means of such delightful stories that Rumi discusses and analyses profound truths:

> Now hear the outward form of my story,
> But yet separate the grain from the chaff.

A systematic thinker usually has a set of ideas which he either wants primarily to communicate to others or he wants just to express in words. Expression in words may *ipso facto* mean communication to others, but a thinker might only aim at expression and not at communication. It seems that Rumi is certainly not a thinker of this type. He does not primarily aim at communication; he is not thinking of conveying his ideas as such. On the contrary, it seems that Rumi is giving expression to an experience or a series of experiences. There is an enormous difference between giving expression to an experience and giving expression to an idea—and this difference is the difference between Rumi and the systematic thinkers. Our experiences do not follow one another like premises in a syllogism. We can deduce one thought from another but we cannot deduce one experience from another. While reading the **Mathnavi** we find ourselves not in the presence of a mind but in the presence of a personality. Experiences of a personality cannot possess a logical sequence, since logical sequence is a characteristic only of thoughts. Therefore, when thoughts are interwoven with experiences, and it is the expression of experiences which is primarily intended, thoughts have to be scattered and unconnected as they are in Rumi's **Mathnavi**. Any attempt, therefore, to summarise his thought will inevitably damage the spirit of his work.

The nature of Rumi's experience is essentially religious. By religious experience is not meant an experience induced by the observance of a code of taboos and laws, but an experience which owes its being to love; and by love Rumi means 'a cosmic feeling, a spirit of oneness with the Universe.' 'Love,' says Rumi, 'is the remedy of our pride and self-conceit, the physician of all our infirmities. Only he whose garment is rent by love becomes entirely unselfish.' Love, according to him, is the motive force of the universe; it is because of love that everything restlessly travels towards its origin; it is love which animates music and gives a meaning to life. It is in love that the contradictory forces of nature achieve a unique unity. And love is not logic; it eludes reason and analysis and is best understood by experience. It does not ask why before it makes the supreme sacrifice for the Beloved, it jumps into the battlefield regardless of consequences. . . .

> It is love, not reason, which is heedless of
>   consequences,
> Reason pursues that which is of benefit.
> (Love) never puts God to the test,
> Nor does it weigh profit and loss (in its
>   pursuit).

Love is a mighty spell—an enchantment. Reason dare not stand against it. Love puts reason to silence.

> When those Egyptian women sacrificed their
>   reason,[2]
> They penetrated the mansions of Joseph's
>   love;
> The cup-bearer of life bore away their
>   reason,
> They were filled with wisdom of the world
>   without end.
> Joseph's beauty was only an offshoot of
>   God's beauty;
> Be lost, then, in God's beauty more than
>   those women.[3]

The more a man loves, the deeper he penetrates into the divine purpose. 'Love is the "astrolab of heavenly mysteries," the "eye salve" which clears the spiritual eye and makes it clairvoyant.' Rumi compares it to the love of an affectionate child which divines the reasons for its father's severity, and to the love of a lover who finds excuses for the cruelty of his mistress.[4]

Love endures hardships at the hands of the Beloved with pleasure.

> Through love bitter things seem sweet,
> Through love bits of copper are made gold.
> Through love dregs taste like pure wine,
> Through love pains are as healing balms.
> Through love thorns become roses, and
> Through love vinegar becomes sweet wine.
> Through love the stake becomes a throne,
> Through love reverse of fortune seems good
>   fortune.
> Through love a prison seems a rose bower,
> Through love a grate full of ashes seems a
>   garden.

> Through love burning fire is pleasing light.
> Through love the Devil becomes a Houri.
> Through love hard stone becomes soft as
>   butter,
> Through love soft wax becomes hard iron.
> Through love grief is a joy,
> Through love Ghouls turn into angels.
> Through love stings are as honey,
> Through love lions are harmless as mice.
> Through love sickness is health,
> Through love wrath is as mercy.
> Through love the dead rise to life,
> Through love the king becomes a slave.[5]

And true love, he says, is ashamed to demand proofs of his beloved, and prides himself on trusting her in spite of appearances telling against her. 'Not only is faith generated by love, but, what is more, faith generated by any other motive is worthless. Faith, like that of respectable conformists, growing from mere blind imitation and the contagion of customs, or like that of scholastic theologians, consisting in mere intellectual apprehension of orthodox dogmas and all mere mechanical and routine professions of belief,—is summed up by the poet under the general name of the "yoke of custom" (*taqlid*). They only produce the spiritual torpor called by Dante *accidia*. To be of any value, faith must be rooted and grounded in love. The mere external righteousness generated by *taqlid*—the mere matter-of-course adoption of the virtues of the age, the class, the sect,—is compared to a "veil of light" (formal righteousness) which hides the truth more entirely than the "will of darkness" (open sin). For self-deluding goodness is of necessity unrepentant, while the avowed sinner is always self-condemned, and so advanced one step on the road to repentance.'[6] Love is the essence of all religion. It has three important characteristics:

> (1) Any form in which love expresses itself is good—not because it is a particular expression but because it is an expression of love. Forms of love are irrelevant to the nature of religious experience.

> (2) Love is different from feelings of pleasure and pain. It is not regulated by any consideration of reward and punishment.

> (3) Love transcends intellect. We do not live in order to think, we think in order to live.

Rumi admits the utility of the intellect and does not reject it altogether. His emphasis on intuition as against the intellect is explained by the fact that some of his outstanding predecessors had placed an incredible premium on reason. Since the tenth century, those Muslim thinkers who are called 'philosophers' entrusted themselves completely to the guidance of Aristotle. Al-

Farabi, the tenth-century philosopher, was so fanatical in his admiration of Greek thought that he considered it the final word in wisdom. For him Plato and Aristotle were the 'Imams or the highest authority in philosophy.'[7] For Ibn Rushd, 'that fanatical admirer of Aristotelian logic'[8] (born in Cordova 1126), Aristotle is the supremely perfect man, the greatest thinker, the philosopher who was in possession of infallible truth. It was upon Aristotle that his activity was concentrated and it was because of this that he has been assigned the title of 'the commentator' in Canto IV of Dante's *Commedia*.

Neoplatonism, which wielded such tremendous influence on Muslim thinkers, is theistic in teaching a transcendant God, and pantheistic in conceiving everything, down to the lowest matter, as an emanation of God. It is a 'religious idealism';[9] the final goal of the soul is to find rest in the mind of God, and though this is impossible of attainment in this life, man should prepare for it by keeping his mind on God, by freeing himself from the shackles of the senses.

The doctrine of reason emerged for the first time with Kindi. According to him, all knowledge is acquired by reason; that which lies between is either fancy or imagination. The faith in the capacity of the human mind to attain knowledge had become so great that philosophy itself had become dogmatic. Reason had presumptuously arrogated to itself functions which it was not fit to discharge.

The entire system of philosophy which had been built up in the East on Greek foundation was attacked and shattered by Ghazali. He did in the East what Kant did in the West. Both started a crusade against the monopoly of reason in apprehending Reality. Ghazali went a step further and formulated that *Kashf* (intuition) alone is the surest way to Reality. 'How great is the difference between knowing the definition, causes, and conditions of drunkenness and actually being drunk! The drunken man knows nothing about the definition and theory of drunkenness, but he is drunk; while the sober man, knowing the definition and the principles of drunkenness, is not drunk at all.'[10]

It is against this background that we must consider Rumi's overwhelming emphasis on intuition rather than on reason. Rumi gives an important place to knowledge, and makes a clear distinction between 'knowledge' and 'opinion'.

> Knowledge has two wings, Opinion one wing:
> Opinion is defective and curtailed in flight.
> The one-winged bird soon falls headlong;
> then again it flies up some two paces or (a little) more.

> The bird, Opinion, falling and rising, goes on with one wing in hope of (reaching the nest).
> But when he has been delivered from opinion, knowledge shows its face to him that one-winged bird becomes two-winged and spreads two wings.
> After that, he walks erect and straight, not falling flat on his face or ailing.
> He flies aloft with two wings, like Gabriel without opinion and without peradventure and without disputation.[11]

In another place he says that opinion, imagination or *wahm* is the counterfeit of reason and in opposition to it, and though it resembles reason it is not reason. He then defends reason against imagination. 'Reason is the contrary of sensuality: O brave man, do not call reason that which is attached to sensuality. That which is a beggar of sensuality call it imagination.'[12]

But with all this he regards vision as superior to knowledge. 'Knowledge is inferior to certainty but above opinion, know that knowledge is a seeker of certainty, and certainty is a seeker of vision and intuition—Vision is immediately born of certainty, just as fancy is born of opinion.'[13]

Experience shows that truth revealed through pure reason is incapable of bringing that fire of living conviction which personal revelation can bring. That is the reason why pure thought has so little influenced man, while religion has always elevated individuals and transformed whole societies.[14] Even today, 'religion, which in its higher manifestations is neither dogma, nor priesthood, nor ritual, can alone ethically prepare the modern man for the burden of the great responsibility which the advancement of modern science necessarily involves, and restore to him that attitude of faith which makes him capable of winning a personality here and retaining it hereafter. It is only by rising to a fresh vision of his origin and future, his whence and whither, that man will eventually triumph over a society motivated by an inhuman competition, and civilization which has lost its spiritual unity by its inner conflict of religious and political values.'[15]

The apparent belittling of the intellect, it will be clear by now, is only a protest against the gross exaggeration of its role in life. Like Goethe, Rumi looks upon Satan as the embodiment of pure intellect, which, though valuable in itself, is likely to become an instrument of terrible destruction without the guiding hands of love. Satan passionately defends himself in his meeting with Amir Mu'aviya in Vol. II of the *Mathnavi,* and as you read his defence you feel that the sympathetic poet has striven very hard indeed to do justice to his hero. Again, Hallaj, in his dialogues, asserts Satan's superiority to Adam and to Moses, though he raises Muhammad above him. For this Satan, Rumi has a soft corner but he realises that unless his powers are wedded to those of Adam, humanity cannot achieve its full development. Iqbal, the greatest commentator of Rumi, elucidates this point in his famous *Lectures:*

> The modern man with his philosophies of criticism and scientific specialism finds himself in a strange predicament. His Naturalism has given him an unprecedented control over the forces of nature, but has robbed him of faith in his own future. . . . Wholly overshadowed by the results of his intellectual activity, the modern man has ceased to live soulfully, *i.e.,* from within. In the domain of thought, he is living in open conflict with himself; and in the domain of economic and political life he is living in open conflict with others. He finds himself unable to control his ruthless egoism and his infinite gold-hunger which is gradually killing all higher striving in him and bringing him nothing but life-weariness.[16]

Rumi's philosophy is at once a description, and explanation and a justification of his religious experience—where description, explanation and justification should be regarded as different notes combining and merging into a higher unity—Rumi's symphony of Love.

In order to understand Rumi's philosophy,[17] I think, we should begin by understanding what he says about the nature of the self. A spiritualistic philosophy has to start with the nature of the self, for the only thing which we can call spirit and of the existence of which we claim to have an immediate awareness is the self.

Rumi divides Reality into two realsm: the Realm of Spirit and the Realm of Nature. Material objects belong to the realm of nature but soul is the realm of spirit. Soul is one and undifferentiated—the 'that' of all being. It is what Spinoza calls substance and defines as 'that which is in itself and is conceived through itself; in other words, the conception of which does not need the conception of another thing from which it must be formed.' It is a pertinent question to ask here: How does one (Transcendental) Soul differentiate itself into so many (Phenomenal) Souls inhabiting the bodies of different human beings? Rumi, true to himself, gives a characteristically spiritual answer. One and many, he says, are categories of the understanding. Soul is substance and its nature is super-sensual and super-rational. Therefore the popular belief that the soul was created by God is totally false; soul is itself the ultimate reality, how can it be created by something else?[18]

The realm of nature consists of the attributes of the eternal substance. Spinoza defines an attribute as 'that which the intellect perceives of substance as if consti-tuting its essence.' The most important difference between the realm of spirit and the realm of nature is that the former is out of time (since time is a category of the understanding) and the latter is in time. Rumi does not tell us clearly whether time is a mode (as Spinoza thought) or a category of the understanding (as Kant thought). Khalifa Abdul Hakim is of the view that Rumi used it in the latter sense. It is not clear whether time is itself an attribute of substance or it is the category of time which is an attribute of substance. If time itself is an attribute of substance, then it is as much real as substance—a conclusion which contradicts Rumi's assertion that time is a characteristic only of the phenomenal world and not of the ultimate Reality. If, on the other hand, time is a category of the understanding only, then time, as such, can in no sense be an attribute of the substance. This conclusion is quite in accordance with Rumi's utterances about time—but this is certainly a precarious position to hold. Rumi is a firm believer in evolution. But can evolution and the unreality of time go together?

Evolution, according to Rumi, started with matter. But matter is not what it appears to be. Khalifa Abdul Hakim tells us that Rumi does not regard matter as 'independent of mind' and Rumi himself tells us that 'my body is a product of my soul, not my soul a product of my body.' . . . It seems, therefore, that Rumi not only regards matter as having been produced by mind but also as being dependent for its existence on mind. Not only that. He regards mind as independent of matter. The question, how matter, which is an attribute of the soul, can be also a product of the soul is left unanswered by Rumi. The other question, how matter, which is an attribute of the soul, can be dependent for its existence on the soul, without the soul being dependent for its existence on matter, is also left unanswered.

An attribute is as real as the substance. Attributes without substance are as unreal as substance without attributes. We may even go so far as to say that 'the what' without 'the that' is conceivable but not 'the that' without 'the what.'

Matter is the foundation-stone of Evolution. There was 'fire and water as wind and cloud' until the emergence of a new form of existence—the plant life. From plant life emerged animal life which assumed its highest form (so far) in human life. Rumi does not believe that the process of creative evolution has ended with the emergence of man in the existing spatio-temporal order. He has a contagious faith in the unlimited possibilities of man's development.

> I died as mineral and became a plant,
> I died as plant and rose to animal,
> I died as animal and I was man,

Why should I fear? When was I less by
   dying?
Yet once more I shall die as man, to soar
With angels blest; but even from angelhood
I must pass on: all except God doth perish.
When I have sacrificed my angel soul,
I shall become what no mind ever
   conceived.

Life is a passage through a series of deaths[19]—which cannot, however, quench its surging flame! It is open to every individual not only to become a saint but to become a prophet for a nation—a highly shocking assertion for the orthodox yet very much consistent with the thought of Rumi. . . .

Evolution takes place, not as Darwinians thought, by 'mechanical and passive natural selection' but according to the will of the organism to live a higher and fuller life, by assimilating the qualities of the higher organism. 'That a mystic should have shown the way to the scientists and the philosophers, is one of the rarest phenomena in the history of thought. But the mystic neither begins with naturalism nor ends with it. His matter, to start with, is not the matter of the materialists or the Darwinists. It was from the beginning only the outer form of the spirit; it consisted rather of the monads of Leibniz than the atoms of Democritus. Then again Darwin ends with man but Rumi does not stop there. Nor do the mystic and scientist agree about the forces that lead to this evolution. Darwin's doctrine consists of struggle for existence, chance variations and natural selection. . . . With Rumi there is no development by chance variations. For him development consists in the creation of an ever-increasing need for expansion and by assimilation into a higher organism.'[20]

But this conception of evolution suffers from three difficulties. Firstly, how can the new species assimilate the other unless it is already in existence? This difficulty has also been pointed out by Dr. Hakim but he brushes it aside with the remark 'As his [Rumi's] purpose was not scientific so he has neither put nor tried this question.' I am inclined to believe that this conception cuts at the root of the conception of evolution as being creative. If the new species is somehow already in existence, then the whole course of evolution is pre-arranged. Teleology in this sense, as Bergson has pointed out, becomes inverted mechanism.

Secondly, the conception of a definite cyclic order runs counter to the conception of creative evolution. A truly creative organism is one which has infinite possibilities of growth and expansion and none of the forms it assumes can ever be predicted. We cannot say for certain that man in his development will become an angel. For a creative individual the future exists as an open possibility and like a work of art it is unpredictable. No fixed order of events with definite outlines can, therefore, be visualised consistent with the theory of creative evolution.

'Every act of a free Ego creates a new situation and thus offers further opportunities for creative unfolding . . . every moment in the life of Reality is original, giving birth to what is absolutely novel and unforeseeable.'[21] And does not Rumi himself declare:

Every instant I give to the heart a different
   desire,
Every moment I lay upon the heart a
   different brand.
At every dawn I have a new employment.[22]

The third difficulty follows from the second. Rumi admits that evil does not exist for angels and yet he talks of angels as being the next stage in evolution after man. It means that the higher stage of life is bereft of choice and responsibility, two characteristics which constitute the essence of creative individuality.

Everything else, according to Rumi, is controlled by influence outside it; man alone carries his star, his destiny within him.

'Tis wonderful that the spirit is in prison,
   and then, (all that time) the key of the
   prison is in its hand!
That youth (the spirit) is plunged in dung
   from head to foot, (whilst) the flowing
   river is (almost) touching his skirt![23]

This world is a stage where man—the principal actor—continues his experiment in living. In the words of the Qur'an he is the 'trustee of a free personality which he accepted at his own peril.' This freedom is at once most dangerous and most valuable. 'Freedom to choose good involves also the freedom to choose what is opposite of good. That God has taken this risk shows his immense faith in man; it is for man now to justify this faith.'[24]

Free will is as the salt to piety,
Otherwise heaven itself were matter of
   compulsion.
In its revolutions rewards and punishment
   were needless,
For 'tis free will that has merit at the great
   reckoning.
If the whole world were framed to praise
   God,
There would be no merit in praising God.
Place a sword in his hand and remove his
   impotence,
To see if he turns out a warrior or a robber.

Rumi does not believe in the decadent theory of pre-determination which absolves men of their responsibilities and tends to work for the decay and degeneration of nations and individuals. He, however, believes that the universal laws of nature are unalterable. It is predetermined, for example, that if you take a few steps, you will be walking, but the direction in which you walk is certainly a question of your choice; it is entirely left to your discretion and judgment. It is predetermined, for instance, that if you aim a pistol at somebody that person will be mortally wounded. It is now your free choice to select the object—he can be your dear brother, he can be your most deadly enemy.

It is to this extent that Rumi believes in predetermination. He goes thus far and no further. Man is the paragon of existence only because he and he alone has the freedom of choice. For animals lower than man, good and evil do not exist. Therefore the question of their choice does not arise. It is man alone who is confronted by both good and evil. 'Here a world and there a world' says Rumi, 'I am seated on the threshold.'[25]

Man is potentially lower than the brutes and higher than angels.

> Angel and brute man's wondrous leaven
>   compose
> To these including, less than these he
>   grows,
> But if he means the angel, more than those.

Evil indeed plays an extremely important role in the development of man's personality; without it, realisation of values would become impossible. Things are known through their opposites, and had evil remained uncreated divine omnipotence would have been incomplete.

> He is the source of evil, as thou sayest,
> Yet evil hurts Him not. To make the evil
> Denotes in Him perfection. Hear from me
> A parable. The heavenly artist paints
> Beautiful shapes and ugly: in one picture
> The loveliest women in the land of Egypt
> Gazing at youthful Joseph amorously;
> And lo, another scene by the same hand,
> Hell fire and Iblis with his hideous crew:
> Both master-works, created for good ends,
> To show His perfect wisdom as confound
> The sceptics who deny His mastery,
> Could He not evil make, He would lack still;
> Therefore he fashions infidel alike
> And Muslim me, that both my witness bear
> To Him, and worship One ·Almighty Lord.

But why, it may be asked, has God created that to which man has given the name of evil? And since He is the only real Agent, who are we to blame for the

actions that we are caused to commit? It is characteristic of Rumi that he finds the answer to this old riddle not in thought but in feeling, not in theological speculation but in religious experience. We can feel as one what we must think as two. Everything has an opposite by means of which it is manifested; God alone, whose being includes all things, has no opposite, and therefore He remains hidden. Evil is the inevitable condition of Good: out of drakness was created light. From this standpoint it possesses a positive value: it serves the purpose of God, it is relatively good.[26]

Rumi, therefore, welcomes evil as being helpful for the development of man's personality. In fact, the conflict of good and evil is inherent in man and his greatness depends to the extent to which he resolves this conflict.

While Rumi certainly concedes that everything is not good in this world, he refuses steadfastly to adopt an attitude of quietude and renunciation but urges, on the contrary, a relentless war against all forces of evil, which, he believes, man by his very nature is capable of overcoming. Indeed, he would be betraying the very ingredients of his nature by refusing to recognise in evil a golden opportunity to carry his personality a step further on the path of development. The existence of evil has, therefore, a positive contribution to make and the development of a man's personality is reflected proportionately to his success in this struggle. Man is, therefore, not left with any justification to complain on this score, for how could he hope to be the paragon of creation without the presence of evil?

Where there is no enemy, there is no Holy War and the question of success does not arise; where there is not lust, there can be no obedience to the Divine Command. And has not the Holy Qur'an made this position abundantly clear with the declaration 'And for trial will We test you with evil and with good'?[27] Good and evil, therefore, though opposite, must fall within the same whole.[28]

> Moses and Pharaoh are in thy being: thou must seek these two adversaries in thyself. The (process of) generation for Moses is (continuing) till the Resurrection: the Light is not different, (though) the lamp has become different.[29]

Nothing, however, is absolutely evil: what is bad for me may be good for you. And what is more important, evil itself can be turned to good for the righteous. But the soul of goodness in evil can be discerned by love alone.

The freedom of choice, however, is not an end in itself; the end of all freedom is to freely determine to live according to your higher self. So the end of all freedom is self-determination on a higher plane. At the end freedom and determination are identified. Life starts with determinism at the lower plane, develops to the capacity of Free Choice in man, in order to rise to a Higher Determinism again, where man makes a free offer of his freedom.[30] Kant perhaps is the first thinker of the West who believed that it is the innermost self of man that expresses itself in the moral law: the moral law is *his* command, *he* imposes the law upon himself, this is *his* autonomy.

While Satan considers it a servitude of the worst order to serve somebody other than his own self, the loyal angel recognises quite clearly that servitude comes when you serve your own baser self and not when you bow to God's command. Milton has beautifully brought out this point in *Paradise Lost*.[31]

> This is servitude
> To serve th' unwise, or him who hath
>   rebelled
> Against his worshipper, as thine now serve
>   thee,
> Thyself not free, but to thyself enthrall'd.

Man's love of God is God's love of man, and in loving God, man realises his own personality:

> The word 'compulsion' makes me impatient
>   for Love's sake,
> 'Tis only he who loves not that is fettered
>   by 'compulsion.'
> The shining of the moon, not a cloud
> Or if it be 'compulsion' exerted by self-will
>   inciting us to sin.[32]

And again:

> When the predestination of God becomes
>   the pleasure of
> His servant, he (the servant) becomes a
>   willing slave to His decree.
> Not (because of) tasking himself, and not on
>   account of the (future) reward and
>   recompense;
> Nay, his nature has become so goodly
> He does not desire his life for himself nor
>   to the end that
> He may enjoy the life that is found sweet
>   (by others).
> Whatsoever the Eternal Command takes its
>   course, living and dying are on to him.
> He tries for God's sake, not for riches; he
>   dies for
> God's sake, not from fear and pain,
> His faith is (held) for the sake of (doing)
>   His will, not for the sake of Paradise and
>   its trees and streams.
> His abandonment of infidelity is also for

> God's sake, not for fear but he goes into
>   the Fire.
> That disposition of his is like this originally:
>   it is not (acquired by) discipline or by his
>   effort and endeavour.
> He laughs at the moment when he sees the
>   Divine pleasure: to him Destiny is even as
>   a sugared sweetmeat.[33]

And if such a state be called compulsion, it is not 'common compulsion,' as Rumi puts it:

> They possess free will and compulsion
>   besides,
> As in oyster shells raindrops become pearls.
> Outside the shell they are raindrops, great
>   and small;
> Inside they are precious pearls, big and
>   little.
> These men also resemble the musk deer's
>   bag;
> Outside it is blood, but inside pure musk.[34]

To be united with the world-soul is, therefore, the most exhilarating bliss for man.

And mind you, man does not attain this union with perfection by contemplation but by a consistent effort at creating in himself all the attributes of Perfection.

> Whether one be slow or speedy (in movement),
>   he that is a seeker will be a finder.
> Always apply yourself with both hands
>   (with all your mightt) to seeking, for
>   search is an excellent guide on the way.
>   (Though you be) lame and limping and
>   bent in figure and unmannerly, ever creep
>   towards Him and be in quest of Him.[35]

Greatness or smallness are meaningless in themselves. We are great or small because of the greatness or smallness of our ideals and because of the varying strength of faith and determination with which we seek to achieve them. Given love, faith, determination and an effort at consistent search, our frailty and infirmity can move mountains.

> Do not regard the fact that thou art
>   despicable or infirm; look upon thy
>   aspiration, O noble one.
> In whatsoever state thou be, keep
>   searching;
> For this seeking is a blessed motion; this
>   search is a killer of obstacles on the way
>   to God.[36]

Iqbal who freely admits his debt to Rumi amply elucidates this point in a letter to Professor Nicholson. He says, 'Physically as well as spiritually man is a self-contained centre, but he is not yet a complete individual. The greater his distance from God, the lesser his individuality. He who comes nearest to God is the completest person. Not that he is finally absorbed in God. On the other hand, he absorbs God in himself. The true person not only absorbs the world of matter; by mastering it he absorbs God Himself. . . . Life is a forward assimilative movement. It removes all obstructions in its march by assimilating them. Its essence is the continual creation of desires and ideals, and for the purpose of his preservation and expansion it has invented or developed out of itself certain instruments, *e.g.,* senses, intellect, etc., which help in to assimilate obstructions. . . . The ego attains to freedom by the removal of all obstructions in its way. It is partly free, partly determined, and reaches full freedom by approaching the individual who is most free—God.'[37]

Farabi offers an interesting contrast to this attitude. About three centuries before Rumi he declared in vigorously accentuated terms that if a man knew everything that stands in the writings of Aristotle, but did not act in accordance with his knowledge, while another man shaped his conduct in accordance with Aristotle's teachings without being acquainted with it, preference would have to be assigned to the former. Rumi completely reverses the emphasis. For him development does not consist in idle metaphysical speculation. He completely rejects the pseudo-mystic quietism which produces a class of irresponsive dervishes who 'remain unmoved in the midst of sorrow, meets praise and blame with equal effect, and accepts insults, blows, torture and death as mere incidents.'[38]

He also rejects the idea of a closed, predetermined universe which is subject to Nietzsche's gloomy law of 'eternal recurrence.' 'There is nothing more alien to the Quranic world than the idea that the Universe is a temporal working out of a preconceived plan—an already completed product which left the hand of its Maker ages ago and is now lying stretched in space as a dead mass of matter to which time does nothing and consequently is nothing.'[39]

Like Iqbal in our own days, Rumi's entire philosophical thought is an eloquent plea for a life of strenuous activity and endeavour in which the self interests with its material and cultural environment and utilises it, first to realise its rudimentary grouping purpose and later, through the process of creative self-expression, to form greater purposes and attain to new reaches of power. He condemns a life of seclusion, withdrawal and passivity.[40] He is emphatically opposed to those pseudo-mystics, other-worldly idealists, and self-centred aesthetes who would cheerfully ignore the evils, injustices and imperfections of this world, and abandon all active effort in behalf of its reconstruction and seek a cowardly compensation in obliterating their own

selfish interests—intellectual, artistic and spiritual—in seclusion. It is only by flinging ourselves like good crusaders into the struggle that we can fulfil the purpose of our life—not by shunning the struggle on earth because our head is in the clouds.

The motive behind creative evolution is love. It is love which compels matter to become life, and life to become mind. 'The striving for the ideal is love's movement towards beauty which is identical with perfection. Beneath the visible evolution of forms is the force of love which actualises all striving, movement, progress. The determinate matter, dead in itself, assumes by the inner force of love, various forms, and rises higher in the scale of beauty. All things are moving towards the first Beloved—the Eternal Beauty. The worth of a thing is decided by its nearness to, or distance from, this ultimate principle."[41]

Life is a journeying back to God; it proceeds according to a process of evolution. The minerals develop into plants, and plants into animals, animals into man and man into superhuman beings ultimately to reach back the starting point—a glorious interruption of the Qur'anic verses 'God is the beginning and God is the end' and 'To Him do we return.'[42]

Rumi compares the soul to a moaning dove that has lost his mate, to a reed torn from its bed and made into a flute whose plaintive music fills the eye with tears; to a falcon summoned by the fowler's whistle to perch upon his wrist; to snow melting in the sun and mounting as vapour to the sky; to a frenzied camel swiftly plunging in the desert by night, to a caged parrot, and fish on dry land, a pawn that seeks to become a king.[43]

Love, according to Rumi, is the motive force of the universe; it is because of love that everything travels towards its origin. And love is not logic, it eludes reason and analysis, it is best understood by experience. It brings with it not reasoned belief but intense conviction arising from immediate intuition.

How can a man know God? 'Not by senses, for He is immaterial, nor by the intellect, for He is unthinkable. Logic never gets beyond the finite; philosophy sees double; book learning fosters self-conceit and obscures the idea of the truth with clouds of empty words.' Rumi addressing the sceptics asks:

> Do you know a name without a thing
>   answering to it?
> Have you ever plucked a rose from R, O, S, E?
> You name His name; go, seek the reality
>   named by it;
> Look for the moon in the sky, not in the
>   water!
> If you desire to rise above mere names and
>   letters,

Make yourself free from self at one stroke,
Become pure from all attributes of self,
That you may see your own bright essence.
Yea, see in your own heart knowledge of
    the Prophet,
Without book, without tutor, without
    perception.

This knowledge comes by illumination, revelation, inspiration and inward co-operation. Those who have reached the highest degree of perfection—Muhammad topping the list—have not reached it through logical calculation or laborious cogitation. They have discovered the truth and reality by means of an inward and Divine illumination.

For Rumi, revelation is not a historical fact of the past; it is a living reality and it is open to everyone. To those who are sceptical about the possibility of revelation, Rumi puts a pertinent question. Wherefrom, asks he, did the first man learn to dispose of the dead body of his brother? Was it through reason and instructed knowledge or was it through revelation and intuition? . . .

When was grave-digging, which was the
    meanest trade (of all), acquired from
    thought and cunning and meditation?

Reason, in fact, is blind and unimaginative, and argument at best is a weak support. Sense-perception does not carry us far and is certainly no equipment for probing the deep realities of nature.

If any one were to say to the embryo in the
    womb,
'Outside is a world exceedingly well—
A pleasant earth, broad and long, wherein
    are hundred delights and so many things
    to eat,
Mountains and seas and plains, fragrant
    orchards, gardens and sown fields,
A sky very lofty and full of light, sun and
    moon-beams and a hundred stars . . .
Its marvels come not into (are beyond)
    description: why art thou in tribulation in
    this darkness.'[44]

The embryo would be incredulous and would disbelieve it. The proposition would appear to it as a deceit and a delusion because the judgment of the blind has no imagination. The embryo's perception has not seen anything of the kind and its incredulous perception would not therefore be willing to see the Truth. Exactly in the same manner we find ourselves unable to see a world beyond our own 'dark and narrow pit.' And reason can never lead us there—it is intuition, revelation alone which make this discovery possible.

And revelation is nothing but the eternal spirit of man himself.[45] The characteristic of all that is spiritual is its knowledge of its own essential nature. We cannot treat life and consciousness mathematically, scientifically and logically, for how can we depend upon our senses which do not carry us very far? Knowledge is and must remain a vision of reality, a *weltanschauung,* an intuition.

Love alone takes us to the Reality or love; ceaseless effort is necessary.[46] Peace only comes when you identify yourself with the one that stands outside this struggle. An impetus is given to this love by intense, zealous desire; a compelling urge and a wish devoutful. Decadent Sufism had created useless drones and hypocrites. Such passive life is of no use to Rumi. In his world there is no scope for parasites. Rumi's lover cannot afford to be static and ascetic. He is constantly at war—at war with his own baser self, at war with those elements in the world which hinder or prevent his ascent. It is the very fate of man to struggle. Struggling against destiny is the destiny of man. . . .

We have seen that life emanates from matter and mind emanates from life. It seems, however, that though even matter is really spiritual, yet the trend of evolution is only unconsciously felt by it. It is only in man that a full awareness of the trend of evolution is present. We have seen that Rumi explains Evolution by referring to the concept of Assimilation. Man has assimilated into himself all the attributes which belong to the lower species. Thus we may divide man into two parts, viz. one which he has assimilated from the lower species and the other which constitutes its essence—the divine spark in man. This division of man's nature into two parts corresponds exactly to the bifurcation of human nature effected by Kant and now completely discredited by modern psychology. Man is animated by two naturally hostile principles—animality and divinity. It is on the basis of this distinction that Rumi builds up his moral system. A person who obeys his animal self lives the life of a slave determined for him by forces alien to his essential nature. A person on the contrary who complies with the demands of his higher self lives the life of a free man—determined from within. The higher self is the divine spark in man and its realisation makes one the source of infinite power and knowledge. Realisation of the ideal self rids one of the fears and hopes. 'I am the ruling power in both the worlds, here and hereafter; in both the worlds I saw nobody whom I could fear or from whom I could hope to get any favour; I saw only myself.'

One also transcends discursive knowledge and attains to the divine knowledge—which is not sensuous in origin and character. Knowledge is itself a great power—and the ideal man of Rumi purged of fear and anxiety, enriched by the divine knowledge, holds complete sway over the spiritual and material world. . . .

Such a man moves the world according to
   his desire.
According to whose desire the torrents and
   rivers flow, and the stars move in such
   wise as he wills;
And life and Death are his officers, going to
   and from according to his desire.[47]

Such is the 'Man of God,' the perfect man, who
assimilates God himself but does not lose his own
individuality. Such a man eludes all description. . . .

The man of God is drunken without wine,
The man of God is full without meat.
The man of God is distraught and
   bewildered,
The man of God has no food or sleep.
The man of God is a king 'neath dervish-
   cloak,
The man of God is a treasure in a ruin.
The man of God is not of air and earth,
The man of God is not of fire and water.
The man of God is a boundless sea,
The man of God rains pearls without a
   cloud.
The man of God hath hundred moons and
   skies,
The man of God hath hundred suns.
The man of God is made wise by the
   Truth,
The man of God is not learned from book.
The man of God is beyond infidelity and
   religion,
To the man of God right and wrong are
   alike.
The man of God has ridden away from Not-
   being,
The man of God is gloriously attended
The man of God is concealed, Shams-i-Din,
The man of God do thou seek and find![48]

Notes

[1] Whinfield, *Mathnavi,* Introduction, xxxv.

[2] And when they saw him they were amazed at him
and cut their hands' (Quran, xii. 31).

[3] Whinfield, *Mathnavi* p. 260.

[4] Ibid., Introduction, p. xxviii.

[5] Ibid., p. 80.

[6] Ibid., Introduction, pp. xxxii and xxxiii,

[7] De Boer, p. 102.

[8] Ibid., p. 188.

[9] Thilly, *History of Philosophy.*

[10] *Munqidh,* pp. 20-21.

[11] *Mathnavi,* III (Nicholson's Translation), p. 85.

[12] Ibid., IV, p. 399.

[13] Ibid., p. 230.

[14] Iqbal, *Lectures,* p. 170.

[15] Ibid., p. 189.

[16] Ibid., pp. 186-188.

[17] In a way it is wrong to call Rumi's thought a 'philosophy,' for as a saint he is superior to a philosopher.
"The philosopher is in bondage to things perceived by
the intellect; (but) the pure (saint) is he that rides as
a prince on the Intellect of Intellect."

The Intellect of intellect is your kernel, (while)
your intellect is (only) the husk; the belly of
animals is ever seeking husks (*Mathnavi,* III, p.
141).

[18] With the denial of creation, the denial of God as
Creator becomes a logical necessity and Rumi boldly
faces the consequences.

[19]

I have tried it: my death is (i.e. consists) in
   life;
   When I escape from this life, 'tis to
     endure for ever.
   Kill me, kill me, O trusty friends! Lo, in my
     being killed is life on life.
          (*Mathnavi,* Book III, p. 215.)

[20] Khalifa Abdul Hakim, *Metaphysics of Rumi,* pp. 38-
40.

[21] Iqbal, *Lectures,* p. 48.

[22] *Mathnavi,* III, Nicholson's Translation, lines 1639,
1640.

[23] Ibid., IV, Nicholson's Translation, p. 384.

[24] Iqbal, *Lectures,* p. 81.

[25] For further elucidation, see *Mathnavi,* IV,
Nicholson's Translation, pp. 355, 357 and 358.

[26] Nicholson, *Idea of Personality in Sufism,* p. 55. . . .

[27] *The Our'an,* xxi. 36.

Nasr assesses Rumi's place in the Sufi tradition:

Rumi is indeed a major peak in the tradition of Sufism, but like every peak which is related to a mountain chain of which it is a part; Rumi is inextricably linked to the Sufi tradition, to the sacred tradition which as a result of the possession of sacred teachings and the grace [*baraka*] present within its spiritual means was able to produce a saint and poet of this dimension. The appearance of Rumi was not an accidental affair. Rather, he was the flower, albeit an outstanding one, of a tree that was at that time in full bloom. He appeared at a moment when six centuries of Islamic spirituality had already molded a tradition of immense richness. And he lived during a century which was like a return to the spiritual intensity of the moment of the genesis of Islam, a century which produced remarkable saints and sages throughout the Islamic world, from Ibn al-'Arabi, who hailed from Andalusia, to Najm al-Din Kubra from Samarqand. Rumi came at the end of this period of immense spiritual activity and rejuvenation which in fact molded the subsequent spiritual history of the Islamic peoples.

Seyyed Hossein Nasr, in "Rumi and the Sufi Tradition," in The Scholar and the Saint, *edited by Peter J. Chelkowski, New York University Press, 1975.*

---

[28] Iqbal, *Lectures,* p. 118.

[29] Nicholson, Vol. IV. p. 71.

[30] Khalifa Abdul Hakim, *Metaphysics of Rumi.*

[31] *Paradise Lost,* VI. 178-181.

[32] *Mathnavi* (Bulaq ed.), 1, 59.

[33] Nicholson, Vol. IV, pp. 106, 107.

[34] Whinfield, p. 27.

[35] Nicholson, Vol. IV, p. 56.

[36] Ibid., p. 81.

[37] *Secrets of the Self,* pp. xix-xxi.

[38] Nicholson, *Mystics of Islam,* pp. 44-46.

[39] Iqbal, *Lectures,* p. 48.

[40] Sayyidain, *Iqbal's Educational Philosophy,* pp. 46, 60.

[41] Iqbal, *Metaphysics of Persia* pp. 39-41.

[42] Khalifah Abdul Hakim, *Metaphysics of Rumi,* p. 25.

[43] Nicholson, *Mysticism in Islam,* p. 117.

[44] *Mathanvi,* Vol. IV, pp. 7-8.

[45] Ibid., Vol. IV, p. 344.

[46] Ibid., Vol. I, line 976.

[47] Nicholson, Vol. IV, pp. 105-106.

[48] Nicholson's translation, *Divan-i-Shams-i-Tabriz,* pp. 30-31.

A. J. Arberry (essay date 1961)

SOURCE: A. J. Arberry, in an introduction to *Tales from the Masnavi,* George Allen and Unwin Ltd., 1961, pp. 11-20.

[*In this excerpt, Arberry examines the prosody and poetic style of the* Masnavi *and discusses how Rumi was influenced by his predecessors.*]

The use of the parable in religious teaching has of course a very long history, and Rumi broke no new ground when he decided to lighten the weight of his doctrinal exposition by introducing tales and fables to which he gave an allegorical twist. He was especially indebted, as he freely acknowledges in the course of his poem, to two earlier Persian poets, Sana'i of Ghazna and Farid al-Din 'Attar of Nishapur. More will be said presently of these authors, Rumi's immediate models; but they themselves, though original writers within the boundaries of Persian poetical literature, were not original in an absolute sense. Persian authors, many of whom wrote also or exclusively in Arabic particularly during the earlier history of Islam, leaned heavily upon the traditions established in Arabic writing which preceded the origins of classical Persian literature by some three centuries.

First and foremost, there was the Koran itself to serve as a perfect, because a divinely inspired examplar. As I have endeavoured to demonstrate in my *Koran Interpreted,* that 'incoherency' for which the Suras, making up the corpus of Muhammad's revelations, have been frequently criticized is apparent rather than real; the criticism arises from a misconception, a failure to notice the unusual but perfectly valid and sound structural pattern of the composition. In the Koran, incidents from the lives of earlier prophets, told with great artistry, are introduced at intervals and episodically as proofs of the eternal verities being enunciated.

In much the same way, anecdotes from the life of Muhammad himself were recited by lawyers, theologians and pastoral preachers to give chapter and verse for their theoretical expositions of Muslim life and doctrine. In the field of statecraft the 'Mirrors for Princes' tradition, taken over from the Sassanian writings of pre-Islamic Persia, was early on supplemented by Indian animal fables to which veiled political meanings were attached. The *Kalila and Dimna,* translated by the Persian Ibn al-Muqaffa' out of the Pahlavi, itself a version from the original Sanskrit, achieved an immediate and lasting popularity though its unlucky author ended his days young in a furnace.

The first mystics in Islam, or rather those of them who were disposed to propagate Sufi teachings in writing as well as by example, followed the lead set by the preachers. Ibn al-Mubarak, al-Muhasibi and al-Kharraz were competent Traditionists and therefore sprinkled acts and sayings of the Prophet, and of his immediate disciples, through the pages of their ascetic manuals. They themselves, and other mystics of their times, furnished the next generation of Sufi writers with supplementary evidence, their own acts and words, to support the rapidly developing doctrine. Abu Talib al-Makki, al-Kalabadhi, al-Sarraj, al-Qushairi and Hujviri (who was the first to write on Sufism in Persian), leading up to the great Muhammad al-Ghazali, all used the same scheme in their methodical statements: first topic, then citation from the Koran, a Tradition or two of the Prophet, followed by appropriate instances from the lives and works of earlier saints and mystics. Biographies of the Sufi masters, such as were compiled by al-Sulami, Abu Nu 'aim al-Isbahani and al-Ansari (the last in Persian), provided rich and varied materials enabling later theorists to enlarge the range of their illustrations.

Meanwhile the allegory, reminiscent of the 'myths' of Plato and the fables of Aesop, established itself as a dramatic alternative method of demonstration. It seems that here the philosophers were first in the field, notably Avicenna who himself had mystical interests; he would have been preceded by the Christian Hunain ibn Ishaq, translator of Greek philosophical texts, if we may accept as authentic the ascription to him of a version 'made from the Greek' of the romance of Salaman and Absal. Among Avicenna's compositions in this genre was the famous legend of Haiy ibn Yaqzan, afterwards elaborated by the Andalusian Ibn Tufail and thought by some, through the medium of Simon Ockley's English translation, to have influenced Daniel Defoe in his *Robinson Crusoe.* Shihab al-Din al-Suhrawardi al-Maqtul, executed for heresy at Aleppo in 1191—only sixteen years before Rumi was born in distant Balkh—combining philosophy with mysticism wrote Sufi allegories in Persian prose, and was apparently the first author to do so; unless indeed we may apply the word allegory to describe the subtle meditations on mystical love composed by Ahmad al-Ghazali, who died in 1126.

Such in brief are the antecedents to Rumi's antecedents. When Sana'i began writing religious and mystical poetry in the early years of the twelfth century, he found the Persian language prepared for his task by Hujviri and Ansari. His greatest and most famous work, the *Garden of Mystical Truth,* completed in 1131 and dedicated to the Ghaznavid ruler Bahram Shah, is best understood as an adaptation in verse of the by now traditional prose manual of Sufism. The first mystical epic in Persian, it is divided into ten chapters, each chapter being subdivided into sections with illustrative stories. It thus gives the superficial impression of a learned treatise in verse; though its affinity to the established pattern of Persian epic is shown by the lengthy exordia devoted to praising Allah, blessing his Prophet, and flattering the reigning Sultan. Rumi in his **Masnavi** quotes or imitates the *Garden* of Sana'i on no fewer than nine occasions. It should be added that Sana'i, like Rumi after him, composed many odes and lyrics of a mystical character; unlike Rumi, he also wrote a number of shorter mystical epics including one, the *Way of Worshippers,* which opens as an allegory and only in its concluding passages, far too extended, turns into a panegyric.

Farid al-Din 'Attar, whom Rumi met as a boy and whose long life ended in about 1230, improved and expanded greatly on the foundations laid by Sana'i. Judged solely as a poet he was easily his superior; he also possessed a far more penetrating and creative mind, and few more exciting tasks await the student of Persian literature than the methodical exploration, as yet hardly begun, of his voluminous and highly original writings. His best known poem, paraphrased by Edward FitzGerald as *The Bird-Parliament,* has been summarized by Professor H. Ritter, the leading western authority on 'Attar and a scholar of massive and most varied erudition, as a 'grandiose poetic elaboration of the *Risalat al-Tayr* of Muhammad or Ahmad Ghazali. The birds, led by the hoopoe, set out to seek Simurgh, whom they had elected as their king. All but thirty perish on the path on which they have to traverse seven dangerous valleys. The surviving thirty eventually recognize themselves as being the deity (*si murgh—Simurgh*), and then merge in the divine Simurgh.' It is not difficult to apprehend in this elaborate and beautiful allegory, surely among the greatest works of religious literature, the influence of the animal fables of Ibn al-Muqaffa'.

In his *Divine Poem,* . . . 'Attar takes as the framework of his allegory a legend which might have been lifted bodily out of the *Thousand and One Nights.* 'A king asks his six sons what, of all things in the world, they wish for. They wish in turn for the daughter of the fairy king, the art of witchcraft, the magic cup of Djam, the water of life, Solomon's ring, and the elixir.

The royal father tries to draw them away from their worldly desires and to inspire them with higher aims.' The supporting narratives are, like those of *The Bird-Parliament*, told with masterly skill and a great dramatic sense.

For his *Poem of Suffering* Farid al-Din 'Attar drew upon yet another type of folk legend. The story of Muhammad's 'ascension', that miraculous night-journey 'from the Holy Mosque to the Further Mosque' which is hinted at in Sura XVIII of the Koran and was afterwards picturesquely elaborated in the Traditions, had long fascinated Sufi mystics who liked to describe their spiritual raptures in terms of an ascent into heaven. The *Book of Ascension* of al-Qushairi, as yet unprinted, collects together a number of versions of the celestial adventure. In 'Attar's narrative 'a Sufi disciple, in his helplessness and despair, is advised by a *pir* to visit successively all mythical and cosmic beings: angel, throne, writing tablet, stilus, heaven and hell, sun, moon, the four elements, mountain, sea, the three realms of nature, Iblis, the spirits, the prophets, senses, phantasy, mind heart and soul (the self). In the sea of the soul, in his own self, he eventually finds the godhead.' It may be remarked in parenthesis that the modern Indian poet Iqbal employed the same allegory in his last great Persian epic, the *Song Immortal*.

Though Rumi was certainly familiar with the first two of these three poems, and probably had recourse to other epics of 'Attar—and his debt to 'Attar's prose *Biographies of the Saints* is manifest—the work which exercised the most immediate and powerful influence upon him was the *Book of Secrets,* a copy of which 'Attar is said to have presented to him. This poem, unlike most of 'Attar's epics, 'has no framework-story, and repeatedly mentions the gnostic motif of the entanglement of the pre-existing soul in the base material world.' Somewhat similar in design to the *Garden* of Sana'i, the *Book of Secrets* is more methodically planned than the *Masnavi* but falls far short of it in size and scope. Professor Nicholson traced seven borrowings from this poem.

The foregoing are but a few of the very many sources on which Rumi drew for his illustrative stories. Professor Nicholson's very learned annotations on the *Masnavi* trace the lineage of most of the anecdotes, and Professor Furuzanfar of Teheran, the leading Persian authority on Rumi, has published a valuable monograph on this subject. In my *Classical Persian Literature* I have set out the antecedents to the 'Miracle of the Pearls'. . . . That story is a good example of how Rumi expanded on his basic materials; 'The Elephant in the Dark' . . . is a rarer instance of compression. The anecdote is told at considerable length by al-Ghazali in his *Revival of Religious Sciences,* and Sana'i gives an elaborate version of it in his *Garden*. Readers may like to look at E. G. Browne's translation and to compare it with Rumi's brief summary.

Not far from Ghur once stood a city tall
Whose denizens were sightless one and all.
A certain Sultan once, when passing nigh,
Had pitched his camp upon the plain hard by,
Wherein, to prove his splendour, rank, and state,
Was kept an elephant most huge and great.
Then in the townsmen's minds arose desire
To know the nature of this creature dire.
Blind delegates by blind electorate
Were therefore chosen to investigate
The beast, and each, by feeling trunk or limb,
Strove to acquire an image clear of him.
Thus each conceived a visionary whole,
And to the phantom clung with heart and soul.

When to the city they were come again,
The eager townsmen flocked to them amain.
Each one of them—wrong and misguided all—
Was eager his impressions to recall.
Asked to describe the creature's size and shape,
They spoke, while round about them, all agape,
Stamping impatiently, their comrades swarm
To hear about the monster's shape and form.
Now, for his knowledge each inquiring wight
Must trust to touch, being devoid of sight,
So he who'd only felt the creature's ear,
On being asked: 'How doth its heart appear?'
'Mighty and terrible,' at once replied,
'Like to a carpet, hard and flat and wide!'
Then he who on its trunk had laid his hand
Broke in: 'Nay, nay! I better understand!
'Tis like a water-pipe, I tell you true,
Hollow, yet deadly and destructive too';
While he who'd had but leisure to explore
The sturdy limbs which the great beast upbore,
Exclaimed: 'No, no! To all men be it known
'Tis like a column tapered to a cone!'
Each had but known one part, and no man all;
Hence into deadly error each did fall.
No way to know the All man's heart can find:
Can knowledge e'er accompany the blind? . . .

As it is my hope some day to publish a full study of the life, writings and teachings of Rumi, I propose to postpone to that occasion a more extended analysis of the contents, pattern and doctrine of the *Masnavi*. . . . I propose to touch briefly on the prosody and poetic style of this great work, and to explain summarily the method followed in making this translation.

First then as to the prosody: the *Masnavi* is composed throughout—apart from the prose prefaces and headings—in rhyming couplets (which is what its title means) in the metre called *ramal,* the pattern of which consists of three feet, the first two made up of one long syllable, one short, and two longs, the third foot being of one long, one short, one long. . . . This deliberate and somewhat solemn measure, used already by 'Attar in his *Bird-Parliament,* is peculiarly suited to leisurely narrative and lengthy didactic; and Rumi, who in his odes and lyrics proved himself a virtuoso in handling the rarest and most intricate rhythms, controls the more pedestrian metre of the *Masnavi* like the master of melody that he was.

The rhyming couplet had never commended itself as a vehicle of serious poetry to the Arabs, who consequently failed to discover the epic. For the Persians, from Firdausi onwards, the easy flow of poetic discourse essential to epopee was fully secured once the impediment of the Arab monorhyme had been removed. Rhyme then acquired a different function; or perhaps it may rather be said to have resumed its original function as a characteristic feature of elevated or emphatic prose utterance. 'A stitch in time—saves nine'; 'jedes Tierchen—hat sein Plaisirchen': in folk wisdom the rhyme is not meant as an aesthetic embellishment, even less (as in the formal ode of the Arabs and Persians) as a means of displaying linguistic virtuosity. It invests the statement with a kind of magical authority; but being readily contrived in Arabic and Persian, which abound in rhyme, in those languages it carries very little rhetorical weight. It is not a consciously 'poetical' device.

Poets of the 'new style' like Nizami and Khaqani, when they came to employ the rhyming couplet, sought to compensate for its simplicity and informality by loading it with a formidable charge of tropes and figures, and by introducing references so obscure that only the most erudite could fully penetrate their meaning. Rumi for his part, writing not for princes but for the love of God and of his fellow man, was content to eschew artificial ornament almost entirely. The language which he employed was plain and direct, though at times highly idiomatic; this latter feature, which must have appealed immediately to the ordinary folk who heard his verses recited at the nightly 'concerts' of the Mevlevi dervish circle in Konia, presents the modern reader with problems of understanding due not to any original obscurity but to the changes in popular usage which seven centuries have inevitably brought about.

But the major difficulty of interpreting Rumi springs not (as with Nizami and his like) from obscurity of

reference, usually to be cleared up by consulting the relevant specialist textbooks, but from obscurity of a doctrine based largely on experiences in their very nature wellnigh incommunicable. Professor Nicholson put this point very well. 'Oriental interpreters expound the *Masnavi* in terms of the pantheistic system associated with Ibn al-'Arabi. Being convinced that the poem was deeply influenced from that quarter, they hold that it cannot be made intelligible without reference to those ideas. So far I agree, though such a mode of explanation is apt to mislead us unless we remember that Rumi is a poet and mystic, not a philosopher and logician. He has no system, he creates an aesthetic atmosphere which defies analysis. As a rule, we apprehend the main drift and broad sense of his words: the precise and definite meanings assigned to them are a makeshift: we can really do no more than indicate parallel lines of thought, call attention to affinities, and suggest clues. Commentators inevitably turn mystical poetry into intellectual prose. Viewed through this medium, what was a fish swimming in its native element becomes a dry dissected specimen on the laboratory table.' . . .

Robert M. Rehder (essay date 1975)

SOURCE: Robert M. Rehder, "The Style of Jalal al-Din Rumi," in *The Scholar and the Saint: Studies in Commemoration of Abu'l-Rayhan al-Biruni and Jalal al-Din al-Rumi,* edited by Peter J. Chelkowski, New York University Press, 1975, pp. 275-85.

[*Here, Rehder asserts that Rumi must be understood as a poet rather than a philosopher, and claims that "the structures of his poems are the structures of his unconscious phantasies."*]

Any study of the style of a Persian author is a particularly difficult problem at present because the literary criticism of Persian literature is a new and unexplored subject. The old, overall notions of Persian literature can now be seen to be wrong, but we still do not know enough to put anything new in their place. Above all, the need is for detailed studies. The greatest Persian poets, Mawlana included, are almost as unknown as the lesser.

I want to try to describe some of the distinctive qualities of Mawlana's work as they emerge from an analysis of individual poems. I will begin with a single poem:

1 Suratgar naqqa sham har lahzah buti sazam
   V-angah hamah buthara dar pish-i tu bigudazam

2 Sad naqsh bar angizam ba ruh dar amizam
   Chun naqsh i tura binam dar atishash andazam

3 Tu saqi yi khammari ya dushman i hushyari
  Ya ankih kuni viran har khanah kih mi sazam

4 Jan rikhtah shud bar tu amikhtah shud ba tu
  Chun buy i tu darad jan janra halah binvazam

5 Har khun kih z man ruyad ba khak-i tu miguyad
  Ba mihr-i tu hamrangam ba ashq-i tu hambazam

6 Dar khanah-yi ab u gil bi tust kharab in dil
  Ya khanah dar a ay jan ya khanah bipardazam[2]

1 I am a painter, a maker of pictures: every
  moment I form an image
  And when all the images are before you, I
  melt them.
2 I rouse a hundred pictures; I mix them
  with the spirit.
  When I see your picture, I throw them in
  the fire.
3 Are you the wine-merchant's cup-bearer or
  the enemy of caution
  Or the one who ruins every house I build?
4 The soul has been poured over you,
  mixed with you—
  Because the soul possesses your perfume,
  I shall caress the soul.
5 The blood which drops from me upon
  your earth is saying
  I am one colour with your love, I am the
  companion of your passion.
6 In the house of water and mud, without
  you, this heart is rubble.
  Enter the house, O beloved, or I shall
  leave it.

This poem shows us an important fact about the poetry of Mawlana: that he is not a painter of pictures, and it is an especially good poem for this purpose because in it the poet asserts the contrary. What is interesting is that painting pictures as a subject in no way causes the poet to create any. There is nothing in the poem that depends upon looking carefully at any object. There is no interest in shapes, shadows, or colours. This can be called a poem without images. The only observation in it is psychological. Nothing is depicted except the poet's mood.

Curiously, the language suggests more than one art. *Suratgar, naqsh* and *naqqash* are associated with painting, while *buti sazam* and *buthara . . . bigudazam* have connotations of sculpture or metal-working. The mixing of the second bayt does not indicate any particular art. It belongs to painting, perhaps to sculpture, and certainly to the craft of the builder referred to in the third and the sixth bayt (where the builder's mixture of water and mud is mentioned). It is a significant demonstration of Mawlana's interests that once he has begun with it, he does not continue with

the subject and associations of the action of painting.

This absence or paucity of pictures is not a characteristic of the Islamic poetic tradition as a whole. The archaic Arabic poetry is full of carefully observed descriptions and visual metaphors. The famous *muʿallaqah* of Imru }l-Qays is a good example. Similarly, many Persian poems are full of images, such as Farrukhi's beautiful poem on the branding ground of Amir Abu 'l-Muzaffar or Manuchihri's *musammat* on wine-making, *Madar-i may*. There is nothing in Mawlana's work like Manuchihri's portrait of an apple:

> And that apple like a smooth-turned ball of
>   white sugar
> That has been dipped three hundred times
>   in yellow dye,
> On its cheeks some small spots of coral,
> And on its tail a green saddlecloth of
>   emerald hue—
> In its stomach are two or three tiny domed
>   chambers;
> In each sleeps a Negro child, as black as
>   pitch.[3]

Such description is, in general, more likely to be found in a *qasida* than in a *ghazal*, but perhaps it is significant that the edition of the *Kulliyyat-i Divon-i Shams-i Tabrizi* with introductions by Furuzanfar and Dashti has a single section for the *ghazaliyyat* and *qasa'id*, as if Mawlana did not distinguish between the two forms.

The above poem, like so many by Mawlana, seems barely located in the world in which we live. Only a few things are named: *atish, soqi, khanah, khun, khak, ab* and *gil*, but in no case is their appearance described. It is a characteristic of this poem, and a part of its success, that no single point is elaborated at any length. This small number of nouns which refer to physical objects is accompanied by an almost total absence of adjectives, further evidence of how little Mawln n is concerned with looking at the world.

The interest in the poem is in mental events, and its center is the poet's imagination. The activity described is that of conjuring up vague images of the beloved. The lover is in many ways self-absorbed. He looks inwards, not outwards. The focus wavers. It is not so much on the beloved as on the insubstantial and intangible, the *naqqash butha, ruh,* and *jan,* of which the beloved is the most important exemplar. The beloved is faceless and ghostly, without features or even very many characteristics, and, appropriately, the poet threatens to become a ghost himself at the end of the poem.

The poet desires the presence of his love, but the reason for the beloved's absence is not clear. The effect of this is not much altered if we assume the beloved is God. Interestingly, this is neither obviously a religious poem or clearly a love poem. It cannot be positively identified as a poem written for Shams-i Tabrizi (although *mihr* also means sun) and it has no *takhallus* of any kind. At the same time it does not belong definitely to the group of poems addressed both to God and a human lover.

This ambiguity is kept alive by the play on two of the most important words in the poem: *but* and *jan*. *But* is an idol which is worshipped, an image of God forbidden to Moslems, and, by extension, the adored beloved. Similarly, *jan* is both the soul and a term of endearment.

The declaration *Suratgar naqqasham* presents the poet as disobeying the traditional Islamic prohibition against representational art (in Islam the creation of images came to be thought of as the exclusive power of God), and *buti sazam* suggests that he is an infidel. The Qur'an (59.23) refers to God as *al-musawwir*, the shaper, a word derived from the same Arabic root as *suratgar* and which later became an ordinary word for painter (or sculptor) in both Arabic and Persian. Although this Qur'anic passage, . . . *He is God, the creator, the maker, the shaper. The most beautiful names are his,* in its context has nothing to do with art, it appears to have provided the justification for the attack on the painter in the *hadith* literature. The following *hadith* (from the well-known collection of al-Bukhari) is not only representative in its condemnation of painting, but like the first two bayts of the poem, it refers to the painter trying to breathe life into his images: "On the Day of Judgment the punishment of hell will be meted out to the painter, and he will be called to breathe life into the forms that he has fashioned; but he cannot breathe life into anything."[4] Thus, by his statements at the beginning of the poem, the poet puts himself in the place of God the creator and in direct opposition to Islamic tradition. Like Hafiz, but in a very different manner, Mawlana takes pleasure in the outrageous and forbidden. He removes himself not only from the perceptions of the world, but also from its conventions and laws. Moreover, he provides himself with an opportunity for making dramatic assertions. Mawlana enjoys gestures of rebellion, but, in the end, as the above analysis reveals, he does not create a representational art. It is as if unconsciously he obeys the traditional prohibition.

Mawlana's lack of interest in looking carefully at the world in his poems is related, I suggest, to his thinking about it as in a state of flux. This is not simply a philosophical belief. It is a fact of both his conscious and unconscious behaviour as a poet, a fact of his style. The inference to be drawn is that the world being in a state of flux makes it both impossible to observe and not worth apprehending. Everything in this poem, as in so many others in his *Diwan*, is changeable and temporary. The point is made in each bayt in the poem:

(1) Every moment the poet makes a new picture, but they are unsatisfactory and their existence is brief. Melting is a blurring of boundaries, a change of state.

(2) Again there is a multiplicity of undefined images and again they are destroyed. After their initial appearance the poet alters them by mixing them with the spirit.

(3) The question is unanswered. The beloved, who could not be represented or contained in any of the images, is not fixed in a single phrase, but described by three. There is a hint that these images may be the result of the unstable state of drunkenness.

(4) The verb *amikhtan* is used for the second time which draws attention to the fact that the idea of mixing is central to the poem. The poet ceases to be the mixer and his soul becomes the thing mixed. The perfume is incorporated by inhalation. *Rikhtah* with its meanings of poured, infused, cast, melted, scattered, combines most of the actions of the poem.

(5) The poet's blood flows. The spilling of his blood is parallel to the pouring out or infusion of his soul in the previous bayt. The blood combines with the dust as the water with the mud in the following bayt. *Hamrang* and *hamb z* mean sharing and partnership—the merging of differences.

(6) The component parts of the house are emphasized. The heart is broken in pieces. The statement that the beloved ruins every house that the poet builds informs his plea that the beloved enter the house. The final metaphor of change and combination is the poet's declaration that he may change his state and more if his beloved rejects him. Thus, the world of the poem is in motion, coming apart and coming together. All its forms are destroyed or empty or in the process of metamorphosis.

The question that presents itself is what does Mawlana offer in place of the world in which we live. The answer is, I think, the universe of his phantasy. I deliberately do not say *world* because in his poems he talks regularly of the two worlds, our world and the other world of the divine, and sometimes he seems to think that there are an infinite number of worlds. The incredible and the impossible are ordinary in phantasy as they are in Mawlana's poems:

Wherever you set foot, from the earth a
head rises
And for one head, how could anyone wash
his hands of you?[5]

The poems are full of references to heads, especially disembodied heads and decapitations.

When in the road you see a severed head
Which is rolling towards our city square,
Ask it, ask it, the secrets of the heart.[6]

These events can be imagined in the mind's eye, although they cannot be seen in the real world, but the poems are full of events which cannot be visualized:

A hundred thousand sweet apples you may
count in your hand.
If you want them to be one, press them all
together.[7]

or

The world is like a body without a head
without that king.
Fold yourself around such a head like a
turban.[8]

Metaphors such as these show us how far away Mawlana is from any desire for mimesis.

Phantasy is a process of endless change. There are no limits on change in the imagination and anything can become anything else. Mawlana constantly transforms his metaphors. In any given poem one thing may not simply be represented by many different things, but may become many different things—and usually a number of things in a given poem are transformed in this way. If there are several sets of things, each set may be involved in a partially completed story. In the poem *Bar charkh sahargah yiki mah 'iyan shud,* the poet is successively: watching the moon, carried off by the moon, invisible, the soul, a ship, and the sea. The moon appears and seizes the poet like a falcon and receives into itself the nine spheres of heaven. The sea breaks into waves, intellect, and a voice. Its foam becomes anonymous, multitudinous forms dissolve and become spirit in the sea. The events are first of the sky and then of the sea. The poem is what it is not only because of the number of these changes but also because of the abruptness and speed with which they happen (this example is a short poem of nine bayts).[9]

Beyond this, that these transformations can be called abrupt means that they are not fully explained or prepared for in the poem, and that we do not feel immediately their interrelation. This accounts for some of the strangeness and incongruity of Mawlana's work.

Valéry states that the secret of all great minds *"est et ne peut être que dans les relations qu'ils trouvèrent,— qu'ils furent forcés de trouver—entre des choses dont nous échappe la loi de continuité."*[10] One might say that the genius of Mawlana consists of seeing relations between things which are not related in the world and are related only in his unconscious. That is, when he combines and connects in ways that remain strange even after he has pointed them out, he is putting things in relation according to the structures and associations of his unconscious. Every writer does this and every writer does it in a unique way. Mawlana makes, I believe, a deliberate use of incongruous elements in his poetry, but has, at the same time, a special sense of what is congruous in his poems and in any given poem, as there are many possible incongruities which are not found in his poems.

Another way of saying this is that the structures of his poems are the structures of his unconscious phantasies. The poems are reworkings of phantasies and what happens in them happens according to the laws of phantasy. This again is something which is true of all poets, but each person is unique and, therefore, each person does unique work. The uniqueness of Mawlana is in the amount of phantasy not under conscious control that he had made available to himself in his poetry.

The sudden changes in Mawlana's poems also involve changes of subject and changes of tone, the introduction of new matter into the poems, or a change in behaviour to what is happening there. He appears to interrupt himself, with a vocative or a rhetorical question or by speaking directly to the reader or listener. His own voice keeps breaking through whatever metaphorical structure he may have created. It is as if at a certain point he cannot bear the artificiality of poetry or the way in which it separates and hides him from his audience, and he seeks for a moment a closer contact with his audience. This causes him to address his listeners more directly, or to undermine or alter in some way the nature of his communication as a poetic whole, as when he transforms his metaphors or makes them strange or incongruous. Here, I believe, is one of the reasons for the large number of vocatives in his poems and for their placement in individual poems. It is equally significant that he never forsakes poetry. He returns from direct speech to artificiality. He speaks directly but in metaphors. For all their individuality, the poems are conventional, and I think it is especially significant that each poem has a poetic conclusion. At the end he is absorbed more by the demands of the poem as a whole and the desire to speak more directly is not expressed.

The phrases *khamush kardam* or *khamush kun* or variations on them constantly appear in his poems. This is particularly striking in a poet who is so obviously concerned to make himself heard. It is to be noted that this call for silence is usually at the end of a poem if not in the final bayt. I am not certain I agree with Ritter that *khamush* is a *takhallus,* although the functions of these phrases is similar to that of a *takhallus,* and in using them as he does Mawlana reveals his sense of the form of the ghazal and its unity.[11]

It is not the case that these statements show that Mawlana stops short of the ultimate religious experience and refuses to describe what is most sacred to him. He did not believe that there were some aspects of religious experience about which one could not speak. His poems are full of his attempts to imagine union with the absolute. As he wants to see the invisible, he wants to express the ineffable. He only stops talking when he has had his say, and the enormous size of the **Divan** and of the **Masnavi** are proof that he never satisfied his need for self-expression and communication. The command *khamush* is significantly often spoken to the audience. These phrases are usually the sign that the poem is about to end, and they dramatize the poem by pointing to the hush which follows its conclusion, as if pointing out what a difference it makes when the poet stops speaking. In this they seem a call for the poem to continue its existence silently in the minds of the poet and his audience, an attempt to create an unheard echo or reverberation.

Ritter points out that an analysis of Mawlana's thought cannot depend on the commentators of the **Masnavi** who "read into the work the views of their own time or their personal views."[12] Similarly, it is no longer satisfactory to gloss the **Divan** with the *Gulshan-i Raz* as Nicholson does on the assumption that "Sufism has few ideas, but an inexhaustible wealth and variety of illustrations."[13] This is essentially an ahistorical view which appears to ignore the great expanse of space and length of time over which sufism developed, and to deny that sufism is the creation of individuals (each with a unique historical existence), and that many made distinctive and personal contributions to sufism. It does not, I think, follow from the truth of Nicholson's other assumption that "all manifestations of the mystical spirit are fundamentally the same, in so far as each is not modified by its peculiar environment. . . . "[14]

Mawlana, I believe, must be understood as a poet. The thought of a poet cannot be separated from his poems, cannot be arranged and discussed under headings such as: God, nature, man, the soul, or life after death. As his work proves, Mawlana is not a philosopher. He is the author of 5,498 poems, a book of essays (**Fihi ma fihi**), which tend to become stories and which resemble his poems in many ways, and a number of sermons, but not one work of philosophy. This total includes 1,995 poems of two bayts each (the **ruba'i**), but also one poem of around 27,000 bayts (the **Masnavi**).[15] If one assumes that Mawlana lived sixty-six years (1207-1273) and that he began writing poetry when he was twelve, then he composed about 100 poems a year, on the average of one every three or four days. If one accepts the tradition that the bulk of his poems were written after the death of Shams-i Tabrizi (1247) in the last twenty-six years of Mawlana's life—say 5,200 of the 5,498, then that is about 200 poems a year, on the average of one every two or three days.[16] These figures are only approximate, but they demonstrate that this is indeed a life devoted to poetry.

Nicholson is wrong, I belive, when he states that "Sufistic theosophy is the fountainhead of Jalal's inspiration."[17] Mawlana did not try to elaborate or explain a philosophy. He was trying to understand his experience—and work through it—by expressing it. Every poet writes about himself and out of a need for self-expression—somehow the process of writing poems is necessary to him. Poets are rarely philosophers and vice versa. Poetry and philosophy are essentially different modes of thought and activities which involve different psychologies.

Mawlana is not a philosopher because he is satisfied with the truth of his own experience. The person who lives deeply in individual moments, or who is trying to escape from living deeply in individual moments, is rarely a maker of systems. Mawlana is more interested in his experience—the experience of his imagination or the continuous daydream of his conscious mind, not in his experience of the world—than in any abstraction of that experience. He comes back to the same subjects and the same experiences again and again. He never finishes with them. Philosophers and all those who work with abstractions characteristically want to come to a conclusion. Mawlana, like most poets, is absorbed in getting to the end of a poem—and then beginning again. As Nicholson observes he "has no special term to denote the highest hypostasis. His favourite metaphors, referring to Absolute Being, are Sea, Light, Love, Wine, Beauty and Truth."[18] Unorganized diversity such as this is the opposite of systematic work. Abstractions, which are extreme simplifications of experience, might be defined as ways of coming to a conclusion. Abstractions are never stable in Mawlana's poems. They become metaphors. They are personified or take on the forms of the world (such as "the cup of the light of the absolute"), or become involved in stories.[19] The ship of being disappears in the sea of the divine and a visit to eternity is a journey by caravan. The poems of Mawlān are vague and partial stories in which he is the protagonist—often under an assumed name—and the other characters are abstractions and/or metaphors.

The work of art approximates itself. Philosophy is an attempt to approximate something other than itself.

However abstract it may be, it is evidence of a belief in the value of the world. This is truer in the Islamic tradition than in the European where works of philosophy are more often autobiographies and works of art (at least after Descartes). Art is independent; philosophy is dependent. Mawlana's lack of interest in philosophy reveals his scepticism about the value of the world and how deeply rooted is his belief in its transcience.

When one looks at Mawlana's work as a whole, his greatness is that of a great lyric poet and the poems in the **Divan-i Shams-i Tabrizi** are his major achievement. The **Masnavi** has been preferred to the lyrics because of the belief that a long poem is superior to a short poem, the persistent and false notion that major work has to be big (as if the **Divan** were not big enough!), because the unity of the ghazal as a form has not been understood (even Nicholson writes: "If my book were not addressed to students of Persian rather than to lovers of literature, I should have been tempted to imitate Abu Tammam, whose *Hamasa* is a compilation of verses torn from their context. Such a plan is peculiarly favoured by the loose structure of the ghazal, where couplets complete in themselves are strung together in the slightest fashion."), and because most of the scholars who have written about Mawlana have read both the **Divan** and the **Masnavi** for the *ideas,* not as poems.[20] Certainly the **Masnavi** is unique as a record of discursive genius, but one might say of it what Henry James said of *War and Peace* (in his Preface to *The Tragic Muse*) that it is a "large loose baggy monster." I do not want to deny either its importance or its beauty, but to put forward that it is in the **Divan** that Mawlana's best work is to be found. There he appears to be most himself. Each poem is a moment or a unit of thought. It sometimes seems that the poems represent his feelings at their highest pitch and that what we have is an ecstasy of words. The disorder, the continuous metamorphoses, the unsystematic and unexpected connections are integral parts of the whole. The passion is not lost. The poet, with a curious disregard for form, creates his own forms, moving back and forth between the world and the universe of his phantasy. There, after 750 years, we still hear the sound of a living voice.

> Here the world, there the world, I am seated
>   on the threshold.
> On the threshold is that person who is the
>   mute speaker.
> This intimation you have spoken is enough,
>   speak no more, draw back the tongue. . . .

Notes

[1] All the citations from Mawlana in this essay are from the *Kulliyyat-i Divan-i Shams-i Tabrizi* [Kulliyyat], with introductions by Ali Dashti and Badiᶜ al-Zaman Furuzanfar (Tehran, 1345 A.H.S.) and the references are to the number of the poem in this edition (and sometimes also the bayt and misraᶜ). This is poem 1,462.

[2] Jerome W. Clinton, *The Divan of Manuchihri Damghani. A Critical Study* (Minneapolis, 1972), pp. 114-115.

[3] Bukhari, *Le Receuil de traditions mahométans,* L. Krehl and T. W. Juynboll, eds. (Leiden, 1862-1908), vol. II, p. 41 and vol. IV, p. 106, as cited by K. A. Creswell, "The Lawfulness of Painting in Early Islam," *Ars Islamica,* 11-12 (1946), 162, n. 21. Creswell states (p. 161) that the *hadith* literature is "uniformly hostile to all representations of living forms." This attitude hardened, he believes, toward the end of the eighth century. For an extremely interesting discussion of this matter, see Oleg Grabar, *The Formation of Islamic Art* (New Haven, 1973), 75ff.

[4] *Kulliyyat,* 622.2.

[5] *Kulliyyat,* 239.3-4a.

[6] *Kulliyyat,* 1077.8.

[7] *Kulliyyat,* 3055.9.

[8] *Kulliyyat,* 649.

[9] Paul Valéry, "Introduction à la méthode de Léonard de Vinci," *Oeuvres,* Pléiade edition (Paris, 1957), vol. I, p. 1160.

[10] H. Ritter, "Djalal Al-Din Rumi," *The Encyclopaedia of Islam* (New Edition) [NEI], vol. II (1965), p. 395.

[11] Ritter, NEI, vol. II, p. 395.

[12] R. A. Nicholson, *selected Poems from the Divani Shamsi Tabriz* (Cambridge, 1898) [Nicholson], p. viii. The *Gulshan-i Raz* was composed by Shabistari in 717 A.H. (v 'Abbas Iqbal, *Tarikh-i Mughul,* (Tehran, 1341, A.H.S., 545). Mawlana died in 672 A.H.

[13] Nicholson, p. xxx.

[14] These totals are from the *Kulliyyat.* For the size of the *Masnavi,* see J. Rypka, *History of Iranian Literature* (Dordrecht, 1968), 241.

[15] Almost none of Mawlana's poems can be dated. The assumption that he began writing poems when he was twelve is problematical and somewhat arbitrary, but it is perhaps more likely to have been later than earlier, which is the important point for these calculations. There are many stories about him as a child prodigy, but most of them concern his religious experiences

---

Moyne and Barks examine Rumi's short poems:

In the mountains along a creek half-frozen with thick ledges of ice, a friend once handed me an icy drop of dew. I held it close to my eye like a lens. The hemlock and the rhododendron and the creek were suddenly upsidedown above me! The world reversed in a tear.

Rumi's short poems, the quatrains (*Rubaiyat*) have many tones and effects: Some of them quick, joyful whimsies—songs a carload of friends might spin off on a trip.

> Tonight, a singing competition:
>
> Jupiter, the moon, and myself,
> the friends I've been looking for!

Some are finely faceted, abstract statements.

> Being is not what it seems,
> nor non-being. The world's
> existence is not
> in the world.

But most do what the dewdrop did, put vast space where you thought you were standing. Like grief, they flip normal, rational perspective to sudden mystery and clarity. And like short poems from other lineages, they require a lot of emptiness, room to wander, sky, the inward space of patience and longing. They are small doors that somehow *are* the region they open into.

> *John Moyne and Coleman Barks, in* Unseen Rain: Quatrains of Rumi, *Threshold Books, 1986.* and none can be relied upon. That the bulk of the poems may have been composed later, see Nicholson, p. xxiii; Ritter, NEI, vol. II, p. 394.

[16] Nicholson, p. xxxviii.

[17] Nicholson, p. xxxii, n. 2.

[18] *Kulliyyat*, 2389.3a.

[19] Nicholson, p. ix.

Gholam Hosein Yousofi (essay date 1975)

SOURCE: Gholam Hosein Yousofi, "Mawlavi as a Storyteller," in *The Scholar and the Saint: Studies in Commemoration of Abu'l-Rayhan al-Biruni and Jalal al-Din al-Rumi*, edited by Peter J. Chelkowski, New York University Press, 1975, pp. 287-306.

[*In the following essay, Yousofi describes Rumi's storytelling—with its use of dialogue, anecdotes, short and expressive descriptions, creation of characters, and humor—as an art, asserting that he presents "a true picture of human beings and their different characteristics in various instances."*]

Stories have always been attractive to all of mankind. Most people enjoy novels, short stories, plays, scenarios, biographies, etc., in prose as well as in poetry. The authors of stories are, in fact, great discoverers of human character and everybody, particularly the common people, are so impressed by their work. Besides, any idea, including its most subtle points, can be understood better through stories, which make it possible for the readers to comprehend and to conclude the facts easily by themselves. We find many interesting stories particularly in the Old Testament, the Gospels, and the Qur'an. In Islamic studies there are two important branches, both of them based upon religious stories: these are . . . Qur'anic tales and . . . prophets' biographies.

It is not surprising that the Sufis have paid so much attention to stories and have used them to express their ideas in their books. For instance, we find 1885 tales in 'Attar's works.[1] The characters of his stories are mostly typical common people; among them we notice even distraught people whose words contain truth.[2] The Sufis found stories to be the most effective means to impress various groups: the learned, as well as ignorant people; the old as well as the young; men as well as women; Muslims as well as followers of other religions, etc. Besides, important points and social criticism, which they would not have dared to discuss openly in their prejudiced times, could be expressed easily in stories. On this matter Mawlavi writes: . . .

> I said to him, "It is better that the secret of the Friend should be disguised: do thou hearken (to it as implied) in the contents of the tale. . . ."
>
> It is better that the lovers' secret should be told in the talk of others. (II, 11).[3]

. . . . .

In the **Mathnawi** we notice not only the vast domain of Mawlavi's knowledge but also his rich information concerning Islamic narratives, Persian literary and popular tales, folklore, parables, etc. The **Mathnawi** is an interesting collection of fascinating stories among which there are a rather large number of Islamic tales. One aspect of Rumi's talent is the interpretation of Qur'anic verses as well as Muhammad's sayings . . . through stories. For example, in the story of "The two snake-catchers" we read as a conclusion:

Many are the prayers which are loss and
  destruction, and from kindness
the Holy God is not hearing them (II, 229).

The idea behind the verse of the story is the same as in the Qur'an: . . . *Yet peradventure that ye hate a thing while it is good for you, and peradventure that ye love a thing while it is bad for you; God knows, and ye,—ye do not know!*[4]

We may have the same impression when we read the story entitled, "How a lover found his beloved unexpectedly": . . . *Unbeknown (to me), Thou hast created the means: from the gate of Hell Thou hast brought me to Paradise* (IV, 268).

The story of Pharaoh and Moses (IV, 49 ff.) as well as Noah's building of the Ark (IV, 157), and Bilqis's gift from the city of Saba to Solomon (IV, 303 ff.) are all based upon Qur'anic verses.[5] The visit of Muhammad to the sick Companion (II, 332 ff.) is also taken from one of the prophetic narratives.[6]

There are several stories related to the miracles performed by the prophets and the intuitive insight of holy men. But witchcraft, enchantment, or unreasonable fictitious events are rare in the stories of the **Mathnawi**.

Mawlavi does not write stories for the amusement of his readers; rather, his tales are elements by means of which he expresses his mystical ideas. They enable him to simplify and to make comprehensible the most delicate and complicated subjects, such as, for example, determinism and free will. . . .

. . . . .

Many of the stories of the **Mathnawi** were already known and popular among the people or had been written in previous books. But Mawlavi, with his graceful talent, has recreated many of them. A very short tale or a simple ordinary event is a sufficient basis upon which he builds a beautiful story composed of several attractive scenes. Besides, he adapts the stories to his own thoughts and through them makes us aware of his wisdom. Therefore, his adoption and adaption of older stories leads to a literary creation.[7] When we compare some of the stories with their sources, we recognize how skilfully he has developed or changed them. I can mention, for example, "The story of Joseph's guest who brought him the gift of a mirror" (II, 172-174); "The story of an enemy who spat in the face of 'Ali b. Abi-Talib and how 'Ali dropped the sword from his hand" (II, 202 ff.); "How a peasant stroked a lion in the dark, because he thought it was his ox" (II, 247-248); "How the Sufis sold the traveler's ass to pay for the expenses of the mystic dance" (II, 248-252); "The teacher who fancied he

was ill" (IV, 85-90), and "The story of the king's falling in love with a handmaiden." (II, 6-17).[8]

. . . . .

The stories of the **Mathnawi** reveal Mawlavi's deep knowledge of human nature and his psychological understanding. In his tales, he skilfully illuminates the virtues as well as the weak points of human beings in various ways. For example, in one story a grammarian is so proud of his qualifications that he says to a boatman who has not studied grammar, "Half your life is gone to naught," (II, 155); another story shows "How a braggart greased his lips and moustache every morning with the skin of a fat sheep's tail and came amongst his companions, saying, 'I have eaten such and such viands'" (IV, 43-44). There is also an interesting example to show the effect of inculation in people and "How the boys made the teacher imagine that he was ill" (IV, 87). We see elsewhere an avaricious man "whose dog is dying of hunger, while his wallet is full of bread; he is lamenting over the dog and reciting poetry and sobbing and beating his head and face; and yet he grudges the dog a morsel from his wallet" and says: "Bread cannot be obtained (from a traveler) on the road without money, but water from the eyes costs nothing" (VI, 31).

An ascetic "goes about with a lamp in the daytime in the midst of the bazaar" and is searching everywhere for a man and saying: "Where is one who is a man at the moment of anger and at the moment of lust? In search of such a man I am running from street to street" (VI, 174). There is also the "Story of an old woman who depilates and rouges her ugly face" and this is her description: . . .

> Her face was in folds like the surface of a
>   traveler's food-wallet, but there remained in
>   her the passionate desire for a husband.
>
> She was like a cock that crows at the wrong
>   time, a road that leads nowhere, a big fire
>   beneath an empty kettle (VI, 326).

Some stories present the admirable virtues of people, such as: the sincere love of Majnum for Layla (IV, 34); the sacrifice of a mother who abandons her faith to rescue her child from the fire (II, 44); the generosity of 'Ali for an enemy (II, 202 ff.); the benevolence of some people towards others (II, 266-267); and, the deep faith of Bilal whose "master was flogging him by way of correction, with a thorny branch under the blazing sun of the Hijaz," and he remained loyal to Muhammad "because he was so full of the passion of love that there was no room for any care about relieving the pain of the thorns" (VI, 307 ff.).

In many other cases Mawlavi depicts a true picture of human beings and their different characteristics in various instances. While we are enjoying his stories, we gradually become aware of certain subtle points.

. . . . .

Mawlavi's knowledge of mankind is not limited to individuals only; he also depicts the social behavior of people and their relations to one another.

In some stories the importance of compatibility has been described in various aspects. For example, a certain sage sees a crow running about with a stork and he says:

> I marvelled long, and I investigated their
> cause, in order that I might find the clue
> as to what it was that they had in
> common.
>
> When, amazed and bewildered, I approached
> them, then indeed I saw that both of them
> were lame (II, 330).

Birds can symbolize human beings and their relationship with each other.

In another story a "woman whose child crawls to the top of the water-spout and is in danger of falling, beseeches the help of 'Ali Murtaza" and here is 'Ali's response:

> He said, "Take another child up to the roof,
> in order that the boy may see his
> congener,
>
> And come nimbly from the water-spout to
> his congener: congener is ever in love
> with congener."
>
> The woman did so, and when her child saw
> its congener, it turned its face towards it
> with delight
>
> And came from the ridge of the water-spout
> to the roof:
>
>> Know that a congener attracts every
>> congener (IV, 419).

On the contrary, in the "Story of a young gazelle being confined in the donkey stable where the donkey assails the stranger with hostility and mockery," Mawlavi says: "This is a description of the chosen servant of God amongst worldlings and those addicted to passion and sensuality." Then he writes: . . . *Whosoever is left (in company with his opposite, they (who are wise) have deemed that punishment (terrible) as death* (VI, 52).

In another tale a gardener can profit from the weak points of a Sufi, a jurist, and a descendant of 'Ali to isolate them from one another and to drive them out of the garden.

> He said, "I have a hundred arguments
> against these fellows, but they are united,
> and a united party is a source of strength.
>
> I cannot cope singly with three persons,
> so first I will sunder them from one
> another.
>
> I will isolate each one from the others, and
> when each is alone, I will tear out his
> moustache" (II, 333).

There is also a story in which we see two different types of people: a simple-minded peasant whose ram is stolen by cunning thieves. "Not only content with that, they steal his clothes too by means of a trick" (VI, 283-284).

There are other stories about the behavior and reaction of different groups towards one another, such as the complaint of an objector to the Prophet who has appointed "a youth of *Hudhayl* to be commander of an expeditionary force in which there were elders and veteran warriors" and Muhammad's answer:

> Often have I tested his understanding: that
> youth has shown the ripe experience of
> age in handling affairs.
>
> O son, the really old is the old in
> understanding: 'tis not whiteness of the
> hair in the beard and on the head (IV,
> 382-391).

There is the "Story of the tanner who fainted and sickened on smelling otto and musk in the bazaar of the perfumers and how his brother sought to cure him secretly with the smell of dung" (IV, 286, 288). This story shows the effect of accustomed environment. Another story depicts the impression of two children of their own living conditions. The first boy whose father has died comes from a well-to-do family and the second whose name is Juh is a pauper. This is the story:

> A child was crying bitterly and beating his
> head beside his father's coffin,
>
> Saying, "Why, father, where are they taking
> you to press you tight under some earth?
>
> They are taking you to a narrow and
> noisome house: there is no carpet in it,
> nor any mat;
>
> No lamp at night and no bread by day;
> neither smell nor sign of food is there.
>
> No door in good repair, no way to the roof;
> not one neighbor to be your refuge.
>
> Your body, which was kissed by people—
> how should it go into a blind and murky
> house?—
>
> A pitiless house and narrow room, where
> neither your face will be lasting nor your
> color."

In this manner was he enumerating the
qualities of the house, whilst he wrung
tears of blood from his two eyes.

Juhi said to his father, "O worthy sir, by
God they are taking this corpse to our
house."

The father said to Juhi, "Don't be a fool!"
"O papa," said he, "hear the marks of
identity.

These marks which he mentioned one by
one—our house has them all, without
uncertainty or doubt" (II, 383).

Mawlavi describes elsewhere different types of people:
a lover who sacrifices his life for the beloved with
ease and rejoicing (VI, 76); another lover who falls
asleep at the rendezvous with his sweetheart (VI, 290).
We see a Sufi "who has been brought up in ease" and
is not able to participate in the war so the soldiers say
to him: "Fighting is not the business of any faint-heart
who runs away from a specter [hallucination], like a
[flitting] specter" (VI, 224-226). There is "another
sufi who enters the battle-line twenty times for the
purpose of fighting,": "He was wounded, but he ban-
daged the wound which he had received, and once
more advanced to the charge and combat" (VI, 228).

There are also two viziers with the same name, Hasan,
at the same court: the first one is generous and the
second very mean (IV, 336-340).

Some stories present the internal problems of the . . .
monastery among the sufis (II, 403 ff.), and the dispute
between wives and husbands concerning family matters (VI, 356-357, 204 ff.).

The number and the variety of types of people, their
temperaments and their behavior, in Rumi's stories,
show this author's intelligence and awareness concerning the nature and mentality of mankind.

. . . . .

Another important aspect of the **Mathnawi** is its social
criticism. Mawlavi criticizes society and the corruption of different people, such as prejudiced and nar-
row-minded persons, hypocrites, officials, and others.
For example, in one story an eminent man has feigned
to be mad to avoid being appointed qazi of the city (II,
342 ff.). His behavior is an objection to the judicial
system. Mawlavi describes elsewhere a "qazi who falls
a prey to the pleading words and beauty of a fair
woman"; to enjoy her love he forgets his own duty
(VI, 504). There is also "a certain divine who has
collected some old rags and wound them in his turban,
in order that it might become big and look grand when
he comes into the assembly." His deceitfulness is
described in the **Mathnawi** with these words: "The
exterior of the turban was like a robe of paradise, but

it was shameful and ugly within, like the hypocrite"
(IV, 360; see also II, 345).

The following tale depicts the lack of social security
in the community:

A certain man took refuge in a house:
his face was yellow, his lips blue, and his
color had ebbed away.

The master of the house said to him, "Is
it will with you? for your hand is
trembling like that of an old man.

What has happened? Why have you
taken refuge here? How have you lost the
color of your face so entirely?"

The man replied: "Today, they are seizing
asses in the streets." The householder
said: "Since you are not an ass, why are
you troubled at this?"

He answered, "They are very urgent and
furious in taking them; 'twill be no
wonder if they take me too for an ass.

They have put their hands with all their
might to the job of taking asses:
accordingly discrimination has ceased."

Since undiscriminating persons are our
rulers, they carry off the owner of the ass
instead of the ass (VI, 153).

The confrontation of Moses and Pharaoh (IV, 61 ff),
in several stories, is the war between faith and power.
The poverty of a philosopher is another tale which
shows critically the situation of learned men in the
society. This is the description of the sage:

I run about with bare feet and naked body.
If any one will give me a loaf of bread—
thither I go.

From this wisdom and learning and
excellence of mind I have got nothing but
phantasy and headache (II, 387).

Mawlavi depicts a sponger Sufi (II, 248 ff.). He also
criticizes "the beguiling talk of ascetics" and those
"who incontinently devour the property of orphans"
through the "Story of the fowler and the clever bird"
(VI, 282-290).

Mawlana also disapproves of the wrong thinking of
the people who believe in dreams (VI, 490 ff.). He
also describes Sabzavar where no one was named Abu
Bakr because all the inhabitants were Shi'ites, and
Muhammad Khwarazmshah, who took the city by war
said to them: "I will grant you security as soon as ye
produce from this city a man named Abu Bakr and
present him to me" (VI, 53 ff.). Also, in the town of
Kashan "if your name were 'Umar, nobody would sell

you a roll of bread even for a hundred *dangs*" (VI, 436).

The social corruption can be noticed in other cases too, such as the "Story of a Sufi who caught his wife with a strange man" (VI, 281-283), and "How Dalqak (the jester) excused himself when he was asked why he had married a harlot."

> Dalqak replied, "I have already married nine chaste and virtuous women: they became harlots, and I wasted away with grief."

> "I married this harlot without previous acquaintance with her, in order to see how this one also would turn out in the end" (II, 342).

Social criticism is, as I have pointed out, an important part of the stories of the **Mathnawi.**

. . . . .

These tales, as a mirror of society, present a rather good picture of it. They relate, for example, some of the customs, mores, and folklore of the times. Some of these are the tattooing of the figure of animals in blue on people's bodies in Qazvin (II, 163); snake-catching as a job (II, 229; IV, 56); "How the criers of the q   advertised an insolvent round the town" (II, 252); some parts of popular medicine (IV, 286 ff.); tricky watchmen of caravans (VI, 287-288), and how "those who commit the Qur' n to memory placed the peacock feathers, on account of its being prized and acceptable, within the folding of the Holy Book" or "for the sake of stirring the healthful air its feathers were used as fans" (VI, 35).

Several folk tales are also to be found in the **Mathnawi,** such as: "Putting trust in the fawningness and good faith of the bear" . . . (II, 320 ff.) and "The sea-cow that fetches a fabulous pearl . . . (the gem radiating by night as a lamp)—out of the sea, lays it on the meadow, and grazes around it" (VI, 419).

All these folk traits make Mawlavi's stories more natural and vivid.

. . . . .

Mawlavi is an intelligent and gifted poet who can draw an unexpected and delicate conclusion from any simple tale or event. His imagination helps him to make subtle points. For example, in "The story of the greengrocer and the parrot," the parrot's wrong inference leads him to this conclusion concerning the error of those who advocate argument by analogy . . . *Do not measure the actions of holy men by (the analogy of) your-*

self, though shir (lion) and shir (milk) are similar in writing (II, 17-18).

The story of the deaf man who went to visit his sick neighbor leads to a similar conclusion (II, 183-184). Let me give you an example of an ordinary conversation ending in a philosophical and revolutionary idea:

> A certain man came and was cleaving the soil: a fool cried out and could not control himself,
>
> Saying, "wherefore are you ruining this soil and cleaving and scattering it?"
>
> "O fool," said he, "begone, do not interfere with me: recognise the difference of cultivation from devastation.
>
> How should this soil became a rose-garden or cornfield till this soil becomes ugly and ruined?
>
> How should it become orchards and crops and leaves and fruit till its arrangement is turned upside down?"
>
> Whenever they [the builders] put an old building in good repair, do not they first ruin the old one? (IV, 401-402). . . .

Mawlavi's wisdom, sensitivity, and his creative mind enable him to observe important points everywhere. He employs stories beautifully to illustrate his mystical ideas. For instance, here is one interesting story showing the reason for people's diversity of opinions on any matter.

> The elephant was in a dark house: some Hindus had brought it for exhibition.
>
> In order to see it, many people were going, every one, into that darkness.
>
> As seeing it with the eye was impossible, each one was feeling it in the dark with the palm of his hand.
>
> The hand of one fell on its trunk: he said, "This creature is like a water-pipe."
>
> The hand of another touched its ear: to him it appeared to be like a fan.
>
> Since another handled its leg, he said, "I found the elephant's shape to be like a pillar."
>
> Similarly, whenever anyone heard a description of the elephant, he understood it only in respect of the part that he had touched.
>
> On account of the diverse points of view, their statements differed: one man entitled it *"dal,"* another *"alif."*
>
> If there had been a candle in each one's hand, the difference would have gone out of their words (IV, 71-72).

We find the same idea, i.e., the unity of truth, in the story entitled "Four persons who quarrelled about grapes, which were known to each of them by a different name" in four languages (II, 413) or "How dissension and enmity amongst the Ansar were removed by the blessings of the Prophet" (II, 414). These anecdotes remind us of Hafiz's famous verse: . . .

> The wrangle of seventy-two sects,—
>   establish excuse for all—
> When truth, they saw not, the door of fable
>   they beat.[9]

In another story, "Moses takes offence at the ignorant prayer of the shepherd," who says: "Where are Thou, that I may become Thy servant and sew They shoes and comb Thy head?" But a revelation comes to Moses from God: "Thou hast parted My servant from Me. Didst thou come [as a prophet] to unite, or didst thou come to sever?, / I look not at the tongue and the speech; I look at the inward [spirit] and the state [of feeling]" (II, 310-312).

The philosophy that everybody has the right to worship God anywhere in any way or in any language that he knows, represents one of the humanistic aspects of sufism. The Sufis say: . . . the ways to God are an many as human souls (individuals). This freedom of religion should be appreciated particularly when one considers that those were the days when religious prejudice was the main factor in many social problems. It is based upon the same kind of thinking expressed in another of Mawlavi's stories, where the author writes:

> The veracious Bilal in [uttering] the call to prayer used, from ardent feeling, to pronounce *hayya* as *hayya,*
> So that they [some people] said, "O Messenger [of God], this fault is not right [permissible] now when 'tis the beginning of the edifice (of Islam)."
> The Prophet's wrath boiled up, and he gave one or two indications of the hidden favors [which God had bestowed upon Bilal],
> Saying, "O base men, in God's sight the [mispronounced] *hayy* of Bilal is better than a hundred *hays* and *khays* and words and phrases" (IV, 13-14).

These stories present their author as an open-minded man; his thinking places him above all organized religions and creeds.

. . . . .

Besides sufism, there are many philosophical thoughts illuminated in the form of simple tales in the **Mathnawi** such as this pleasant "Story in answer to the Necessitarian" . . . confirming Man's free will . . . :

A certain man was climbing up a tree and vigorously scattering the fruit in the manner of thieves.

The owner of the orchard came along and said to him, "O, rascal, where is your reverence for God? What are you doing?"

He replied, "If a servant of God eat from God's orchard the dates which God has bestowed upon him as a gift,

Why do you vulgarly blame him? Stinginess at the table of the all-Rich Lord!"

"O Aybak," said he, "fetch that rope, that I may give my answer to Bu'l-Hasan (to this fine fellow)."

Then at once he bound him tightly to the tree and thrashed him hard on the back and legs with a cudgel.

He [the thief] cried, "Pray, have some reverence for God! Thou art killing me miserably who am innocent."

He answered, "With God's cudgel this servant of His is soundly beating the back of another servant.

'Tis God's cudgel, and the back and sides belong to Him: I am only the slave and instrument of His command."

He [the thief] said, "O cunning knave, I make a recantation of Necessitarianism: there is free will, there is free will, there is free will!" (VI, 185-186).

. . . . .

Many of the most popular and famous of Mawlavi's proverbially renowned verses belong to some parts of his stories, such as the few following lines: . . .

> Oh, many are the Indians and Turks that speak the same tongue; oh, many the pair of Turks that are as strangers [to each other].

> Therefore the tongue of mutual understanding is different indeed: to be one in heart is better than to be one in tongue (II, 67) . . .

> The religion of Love is apart from all religions: for lovers, the only religion and creed is—God (II, 312). . . .

> I am exceedingly enamoured of His violence and His gentleness: 'tis marvellous that I am in love with both these contraries (II, 86).

. . . . .

Now it is time for me to call your attention to Mawlavi's storytelling as an art. Some of his stories also appear in the famous Persian translation of the *Kalilah-u Dimnah*. If we compare, for example, the story of "The three fishes" (IV, 394-398) and the story of "The fox and the ass' (VI, 140 ff.) with the same tales in the *Kalilah-u Dimnah,* we will notice how beautifully Mawlavi's are written; indeed, they are better than their original version.

This is the story of "The three fishes" symbolizing intelligent, half-intelligent, and foolish men:

> This, O obstinate man, is the story of the lake in which there were three great fishes.
>
> Some fishermen passed beside the lake and saw that concealed prey.
>
> Then they hastened to bring the net: the fishes noticed and became aware of their intention.
>
> The intelligent one resolved to journey, resolved to make the difficult unwelcome journey.
>
> That wary fish made its breast a foot [swam away] and was going from its perilous abode to the sea of light.
>
> That fish departed and took the way to the sea: it took the far way and the vast expanse.
>
> It suffered many afflictions, and in the end it went after all towards safety and welfare.
>
> So when the fishermen brought their net [to the lake], the half-intelligent fish was bitterly grieved thereat,
>
> And said, "Alas, I have lost the opportunity: how did not I accompany that guide?
>
> He hath gone towards the sea and is freed from sorrow: such a good comrade hath been lost to me!
>
> But I will not think of that and will attend to myself: at this present time I will feign to be dead."
>
> He [the fish] died in that manner and threw his belly upwards: the water was carrying him, now alow, now aloft.
>
> Every one of those pursuers [the fishermen] bore great vexation [in his heart], saying, "Alas, the best fish is dead."
>
> Then a worthy fisherman seized him and spat on him and flung him on the ground.
>
> He [the half-intelligent fish], rolling over and over, went secretly into the water; the [entirely] foolish one remained where he was, moving to and fro in agitation.
>
> They cast the net, and he at last remained in the net: foolishness ensconced him in that fire of perdition.

> On the top of the fire, on the surface of a frying-pan, he became the bedfellow of Folloy (IV, 394-398).

Though Mawlavi is not basically a story writer but merely uses anecdotes to illustrate and confirm his ideas, his technique is remarkable. His stories, short or long, are for the most part fascinating, and the reader cannot take his eyes off them before reaching the end.

. . . . .

Some of these stories are very short and illustrate Rumi's skill in making his points in a few verses.[10] Let me give you some examples: . . .

> The Caliph said to Layl : "Art thou she by whom Majin n was distracted and led astray?
>
> Thou art not superior to other fair ones." "Be silent," she replied, "since thou art not Majn n" (II, 25): . . .

> A certain stranger was hastily seeking a house: a friend took him to a house in ruins.
>
> He said [to the stranger], "If this house had a roof, it would be a home for you beside me.
>
> Your family too would be comfortable, if it had another room in it."
>
> "Yes," said he, "it is nice to be beside friends, but my dear soul, one cannot lodge in 'if'" (II, 259-260).

. . . . .

One of the most significant points in a story is the creation of characters. The great number of characters in Mawlavi's stories reminds us of Balzac's works. In the **Mathnawi** we find the prophets, Muhammad's companions, caliphs, kings, viziers, Sufis, tradesmen, middle-and lower-class people historical personages, teachers, students, honest or wicked people, various officials, men, women, boys, and girls. In the **Mathnawi** as in some other mystical works, we find some characters, who were not frequently mentioned previously in Persian literary works, such as minstrels (II, 104; VI, 293), prisoners (II, 252), jesters and harlots (II, 342).

Most of the characters typically act like the shepherd in his prayers and Moses (II, 310-317); the grammarian and the boatman (II, 155); the deaf man and his sick neighbor (II, 183-184); and, the woman whose children never lived long (IV, 191), and others.

Some characters seem very likeable when we read the stories. These are: Muhammad (VI, 323), 'Ali (II, 202 ff.) Luqman (II, 296-301), Hamza, who came to battle without a coat of mail (IV, 192 ff.), the honest man who said to another man: "Consult someone else, for I am your enemy" (IV, 381-382), Bilal (VI, 307 ff.), Ayaz (VI, 111 ff.), and the old harpist (II, 104 ff.).

There are also many fables in the **Mathnawi,** in which the characters are animals or inanimate objects. Some of these are very interesting fables, such as: the story of "The merchant and the parrot which gave him a message for the parrots of India" (II, 85-101); "The wolf and the fox who went to hunt with the lion" (II, 164-170); "The falcon amongst the owls" (II, 279-282); the conversation of the cock and the dog (IV, 186); "The fox and the ass" (vi, 140 ff.): "The jackal that fell into the dyeing-vat and pretended to be a peacock" (IV, 42 ff.); and "The attachment between the mouse and the frog" (VI, 403 ff.).

In some stories, the characters are: a gnat and the wind (IV, 258-260); or even in some parables: peas and the pot (IV, 232-235) or a reed (II, 5). These are personified to symbolize ideas.

. . . . .

Another interesting aspect in Mawlavi's stories is the confrontation of the characters and their dialogues. We notice some beautiful scenes in which the characters stand face to face, such as: 'Umar and the old harpist (II, 104 ff.); Moses and the shepherd (II, 310-317); the caliph 'Umar and the ambassador of Rumi (II, 77 ff.); the teacher, his students, and his wife (IV, 85-90); the harsh-voiced muezzin in the land of infidels (VI, 202 ff.); Dhu'l-Nun and his friends in the madhouse (II, 292-296); the Turk and the tailor (VI, 351-354); and, the king playing chess with Dalqak (VI, 210).

I would like to quote, as an example, one of the shortest scenes: the meeting of an old man with a physician.

> An old man said to a doctor, "I am in torment because of my brain."
>
> The doctor replied, "That weakness of brain is from age." Said the old man, "There are spots of darkness on my eyes."
>
> "It is from age, O ancient Shaykh," said the doctor. "Awful pain comes in my back," said he.
>
> "It is from age, O emaciated Shaykh," said the doctor. "Whatever I eat," said he, "is not digested."
>
> The doctor replied, "Weakness of stomach also is the result of age." Said he, "When I breathe, respiration is hard for me."

> "Yes," he said, "it is asthma; when old age arrives, two hundred diseases come on."
>
> "O fool," he exclaimed, "You have stuck at this: this is all that you have learned of medicine."
>
> Then the doctor said to him, "O sexagenarian, this anger and this choler are also from old age" (II, 382).

There are also many examples of beautifully written dialogues in these stories. I can mention some examples such as: the conversation between the Sufi and the servant of the monastery (II, 230, 250); the countryman and the townsman (IV, 17 ff.); the Arab of the desert and the philosopher (II, 386 ff.); and the deaf man and his neighbor (II, 183-184), etc.

. . . . .

Short and expressive description is another interesting feature in Mawlavi's storytelling. He depicts everything so vividly that the atmosphere of the stories becomes real. In the **Mathnawi,** not only the appearance of the characters, but also their emotional states are beautifully described. That is why we find them to be sensitive and the stories seem full of life. Some examples are: the description of the thirsy man's feeling (II, 282-283); the captives' thoughts (IV, 250); Nasuh's anxiety to be searched (VI, 136-137); the lover's sentiments during the separation (IV, 265); the amativeness (IV, 51); the old harpist's repentance (II, 113); the anger of the lion with the hare (II, 64); the vow made by the dogs every winter (IV, 162); and, the sorrow of the merchant whose parrot died in the cage. This is part of his lament:

> He said, "O beautiful parrot with thy sweet cry, what is this that has happened to thee? Why hast thou become like this?
>
> Oh, alas for my sweet-voiced bird! Oh, alas for my bosom-friend and confidant!
>
> Oh, alas for my melodious bird, the wine of my spirit and my garden and my sweet basil!" (II, 93)

Besides, the description of the scenes and the atmosphere in the stories is attractive. For instance, I can mention Jesus' flight to the top of a mountain to escape from the fools (IV, 144); the mad behavior of Dhu'l-Nun with his friends in the madhouse (II, 296); the fish that feigned to be dead (IV, 397-398); the women's bath (VI, 134-136); and the precipitation of the wife to hide her lover (IV, 282). Mawlavi does not forget any detail to give a complete picture of a scene. The enjoinment of the Sufi to the famulus of the monastery concerning his ass and the situation of the poor ass without fodder all the night (II, 232, 234) are good examples.

Let me give you an example in which Mawlavi describes drunkenness:

> He replied, "Nay, nay, I am the fellow for that wine: I am not content with testing this delight (of which ye speak).
>
> I desire such wine, that, like the jasmine, I may ever be reeling crookedly now that way, now this,
>
> And, having been delivered from all fear and hope, I may be swaying to every side, like the willow,
>
> Swaying to left and right like the willow-bough, which is made to dance all sorts of dances by the wind" (VI, 214-215).

All these factors add fascination to Rumi's stories, and we read them with enthusiasm. The long story of "The countryman and the townsman" (IV, 17-40) is an excellent example; it has several characters, varied scenes, exciting events, and amusing dialogues. We have the same feeling in reading the story of "The teacher and the tricky students" (IV, 85-90) and the story of "The three fishes" (IV, 394-398). In short tales we find more continuity and unity such as the story of "The four Indians who lost their prayers" (II, 378).

. . . . .

Another interesting aspect of the **Mathnawi** is in its humorous stories. Although the **Mathnawi** is, in general, a didactic work, it also contains some humor through which the poet calls our attention to serious points. Some of the above mentioned tales are humorous ones, but let me mention the "Story of the minstrel who began to sing this ode at the banquet of the Turkish Amir:

> 'Art Thou a rose or a lily or a cypress or a moon? I know not. What dost Thou desire from this bewildered one who has lost his heart? I know not'—and how the Turk shouted at him, 'Tell of that which you know?'" (VI, 297).

Other humorous tales are: the "Story of a lover's being engrossed in reading and perusing a love letter in the presence of his beloved, and how the beloved was displeased thereat" (IV, 79); the "Story of the lover who, in hope of the tryst promised to him by his beloved, came at night to the house that she had indicated. He waited there part of the night; then he was overcome by sleep. When his beloved came to fulfill her promise and found him asleep, she filled his lap with walnuts and left him sleeping, saying, 'Thou art a child: take these and play a game of dice'" (VI, 290-291). Also, "How the traveler lost his ass because of the blind imitation of the Sufis" (II, 248-251); "The police inspector and the drunken man" (II, 345); "The

cadi and the wife of Juhi" (VI, 504-510); and, several other tales. To bring a light note to this article I quote one of the short humoristic stories of the **Mathnawi:**

> A certain man killed his mother in wrath, with blows of a dagger and also with blows of his fist.
>
> Some one said to him, "From evil nature you have not borne in mind what is due to motherhood.
>
> Hey, tell me why you killed your mother. What did she do? Pray, tell me, O foul villain!"
>
> He said, "She did a deed that is a disgrace to her; I killed her because that earth [her grave] is her coverer [hides her shame]."
>
> The other said, "O honored sir, kill that one who was her partner in guilt." "Then," he replied, "I should kill a man every day."
>
> That mother of bad character, whose wickedness is in every quarter, is your fleshly soul (II, 261-262).

. . . . .

There are other points concerning Mawlavi's storytelling that I will mention briefly. In the **Mathnawi** we notice several episodes in the course of a story which break up the continuity of the narrative. One such story is "Moses and Pharaoh" in Books III and IV. Mawlavi's imagination is so sensitive that anything can move it to new horizons. This is an important trait of his style which causes the prolixity of his stories. For instance, several similes may describe a single object, or numerous examples may be given to make a single idea comprehensible, or else rather lengthy dialogues appear in some stories.[11]

Some tales are only a conversation or a debate between two or more people through which Mawlavi makes his points. These anecdotes do not have the essential elements of a story. A few other stories have been written twice, such as "The complaint of the mule to the camel" (IV, 98, 458) and "The thirsty man who threw bricks (or walnuts) into the water" (II, 282; IV, 313). Two stories seem incomplete: "The three princes who fell in love with the portrait of the princess of China" (VI, 455 ff.) and "The man who left his property to the laziest of his three sons" (VI, 527 ff.).[12]

Concerning Rumi's stories, I would like also to mention a few critical points which we do not expect to find in the **Mathnawi**. In the story of "The King and the handmaiden," the poisoning of the goldsmith by the physician does not seem convincing though Mawlavi writes: "The slaying of this man was not done on account of hope or fear, cease from thinking evil and disputing" (II, 14-16). In another story the philosopher who says: "With strokes of the spade and with the sharpness of the axe we bring the water up from below," does not deserve to lose his sight even though if he should doubt the practical validity of a Qur'anic verse (II, 305). The cause of earth-quakes explained by Mount Qaf does not seem satisfying (IV, 476). A character who is introduced as "a valiant man" is called "a foolish man", in the same story, because he trusts in the loyalty of a bear (II, 320 ff.).

I bring this article to an end with one of Mawlavi's verses, concerning the **Mathnawi** and its stories: . . .

> O my friends, hearken to this tale: in truth it
> is the very marrow of our inward state (II,
> 6).

Notes

[1] See B. Furuzanfar, *Sharh-i Ahval-u Naqd-u Tahlil-i Athar-i Shaykh Farid al-Din 'Attar-i Nishaburi*, "Biography and Critique of the Works of 'Attar of Nishaburi" (Tehran: Anjuman-i Athar-i Milli, Publication No. 41, 1960), pp. 50-51.

[2] Ibid., pp. 53-57.

[3] This and all subsequent references to the stories of the *Mathnawi* (text or translation) will be given in parentheses (volume and page number). They all concern Nicholson, op. cit.

[4] Quoted from the *Qur'an,* trans. by E. H. Palmer (Oxford: Clarendon Press, 1900), 2 vols., I: 31.

[5] cf. B. Furuzanfar, *Ma'akhidh-i Qisas-u Tamthilat-i Mathnawi*, "The Sources of the Stories and Parables of *"Mathnawi"* (Tehran: University of Tehran, Publication No. 214, 1955), pp. 93-94, 95-96, 115-116, 132. Hereafter cited as *Ma'akhidh*.

[6] Ibid., pp. 66-67.

[7] cf. Ibid., pp. 109, Muhammad Qazvini's statement.

[8] cf. Ibid., pp. 31-32, 37, 49-51, 101, 3-6.

[9] Quoted from *The Divan-i Hafiz,* trans. by Wilberforce Clarke (Calcutta: Government of India Central Printing Office, 1891), 2 vols., I: 408.

[10] cf. M. A. Djamalzadih, *Bang-i Nav,* "Song of the Reed" (Complete Stories and Episodes of *Mathnawi* of Rumi), (Tehran: Book Society of Persia, 1958), pp. XXI-XXII.

[11] cf. Ibid., pp. XIII-XXI.

[12] cf. Ibid., p. 379, n. 3; p. 393, n. 4.

> **Star and Shiva praise Rumi's movement:**
>
> Like the wandering of the soul, or the tireless flight of birds, Rumi's poetry is always moving. It tells of the all-encompassing movement of life: the rising and setting sun, the change of seasons, the turning of the night sky, and the whirling of man which embodies all the movements of heaven and earth. Rumi often composed his poetry while whirling, and the inherent structure of his poetry—the relentless flow of imagery, the inner cadence, and the mantra-like repetition of rhymes—often echoes this whirling motion. There are also subtle movements from one level of meaning to another, and from one perspective to another. Even the state of silence that Rumi refers to so often is not stagnant but filled with ever-new possibilities. Nothing with Rumi can be taken literally: one must always be aware of the meaning behind the meaning, and the veils behind the veils.
>
> *Jonathan Star and Shahram Shiva, in* A Garden Beyond Paradise: The Mystical Poetry of Rumi, *Bantam Books, 1992.*

James Roy King (essay date 1989)

SOURCE: James Roy King, "Narrative Disjunction and Conjunction in Rumi's Mathnawi," in *The Journal of Narrative Technique*, Vol. 19, No. 3, Fall, 1989, pp. 276-86.

[*In the essay below, King studies Rumi's narrative technique and asserts that "the 'meaning' of the* Mathnawi *cannot be separated from the narrative and the peculiar form into which it is cast."*]

The **Mathnawi,** composed during the 13th Century by the Turco-Persian mystic/theologian Jalal ad-Din Rumi, is an enormous poem of 27,500 couplets, regarded by Muslims as second only to the Qur'an in its authority over their lives. In it, Rumi retells some two hundred stories from a wide variety of sources, interweaving them with each other, enriching them with his own searching comments. In his preface, he describes his work as made up of "strange tales and rare sayings and excellent discourses and precious indications,"[1] and at the start of the sixth and last book, he suggests that his couplets are "a Lamp in the darkness of imagination and perplexity and phantasies and doubt and suspicion" (III, 257). Later he asserts that "Every shop has a different [kind of] merchandise: the **Mathnawi** is the shop for [spiritual] poverty" (III, 343). (The reference to a Middle Eastern suq or pazar, with all kinds of goods displayed in seeming disarray, cannot be missed.) Repeated descriptions of this kind suggest that Rumi was fully aware of his function as a poet and storyteller whose purpose was to help the reader elevate his or her spiritual state. To this purpose the unusual narrative method he chose was uniquely suited.

Rumi was certainly not a pioneer in using stories for religious instruction. Jesus of Nazareth, whom Rumi revered profoundly and who was a wandering teacher himself, made use of similar material in his parables. In later centuries Zen Buddhist monks and Hasidic rabbis also employed the teaching tale. But in Medieval Islam there seems to have been some tendency to hold this material in contempt,[2] and Rumi reports considerable criticism of his poem by contemporary readers. Once a "great booby popped his head out of an ass-stable," he says, and declared the *Mathnawi* to be "low . . . it is the story of the Prophet and [consists of] imitation"; the fool delared that it lacked "[theosophical] investigation and the sublime mysteries towards which the saints make their steeds gallop"; that it did not contain "the explanation and definition of every station and stage, so that by means of the wings thereof a man of heart [a mystic] should soar" (II, 237). In response to such criticism, Rumi reminds his readers that like the Qur'an his *Mathnawi* has both an exterior and interior sense. Yet Rumi's critics merit some sympathy, for it still strikes us as bold—this decision of his to try to get at the profoundest and most important truths of his faith— the escape from necessitarianism, the destruction of secondary causes and the bonds of the flesh, trust in God and divine grace, the unity of human experience—through anecdotes which are often very amusing, sometimes even a bit silly. (Rumi himself describes some of his stories as donkey's heads [i.e., scarecrows] "amidst the sugar-plantation"—II, 481 n.) But like the metaphor, the tale can imply, suggest, so much, and in the hands of a great artist stories may become a highly effective vehicle for the most profound spiritual truths.

In form, the *Mathnawi* is unique. The frame tale—a common genre in Middle Eastern literature (witness *Kalila and Dimna, Tutinama,* and *Thousand and One Nights*)—comes to mind, but Rumi's poem does not fit, for there is no larger story into which the tale's reflections are inserted. Better, I think, to describe it as the product of an extended stream of consciousness, in which an idea from the middle or one tale suggests another story, and that story gives rise to a moral reflection or a theological question or to yet another story which takes us back finally to complete the first. Motifs from several stories are called upon to enrich each other, and the most tenuous implications of the main story are pulled and twisted about, several narratives and interpretations thoroughly interwoven with each other. The result is a multi-leveled, multi-pronged examination of some significant area of experience, from many different angles. Narrative thus becomes a kind of probe into other realities, with fingers examining this element and that, finding some-

times nothing, sometimes truths of great importance. "Whither will it [the story] flee . . . ?" (II, 129) Rumi asks boldly—and somewhat helplessly. In another striking image he suggests making a breach in the *Mathnawi,* to let its waters pour out (III, 261). This suggests, among other things, the massive, fortress-like quality of the poem itself: many other works are far more approachable. Perhaps it was in an attempt to help the waters flow that Arberry excerpted the "stories" from the total text and served them up straightforwardly, in two volumes. This reductionist approach yields very clear narratives and beautifully simple morals but it seriously distorts the impact of the difficult original form.

Let us study Rumi's narrative technique by examining the story of the cow, on the surface simple enough, involving a legal judgment and some detective work, though from start to finish it spans over sixty pages in the Nicholson translation. The tale is introduced as an illustration of the injunction—so dear to mystics—that human beings must keep searching: a thought exists in the mind, an image, a goal, and the one who holds it must never falter in his attempt to unfold it fully, to explore all its implications. Everything of value was "at first a quest and a thought" (II, 81).

Once a man prayed that he might have bread without doing any work. He argued that since God had made him lazy, God should support him. Working for one's bread, he felt, was far too fatiguing. So one day, when a cow wandered into his house, he killed it for meat—very quickly, it would seem, and without making any inquiries about its owner. Rumi here pauses to ask for divine aid in discussing the different ways men glorify God, and in considering the mysteries of vengeance and mercy, and the difference between knowledge and opinion. Each issue suggests some unexpected line of reflection to the listener.

One can, for example, relate the knowledge-opinion issue to the man's over-hasty response to the cow, certain assumptions plunging the man into disaster. Or one can recall the earlier position about keeping alive the quest for truth. But this may be forcing the issue unjustifiably: there is an organic structure here that transcends the manipulating intellect. In any case, Rumi digresses now to the story of some schoolboys who, under the leadership of one clever lad, told their teacher how ill he looked. The intellectual abilities of human beings differ, Rumi notes, and even though these boys were young and inexperienced, they were able to overwhelm the imagination of an older person, their teacher, just as the Egyptian Pharoah, his mind turned by the praise of his people, came to believe that he was divine. Imagination can be highly destructive. (We may need to recall here that this long narrative began with a man who suffered from a kind of imagination-problem.) Back now to the teacher, who grew angry with his wife for her lack of sympathy and complained that he had not noticed any illness until his pupils called it to his attention. Here Rumi recalls the familiar story of Zuleika[3] and how the friends she invited to enjoy fruit with her cut their hands with their fruit knives when Joseph entered the room. But they felt no pain, their sensitivities being over-borne by the beauty of the young man. Often we become so involved in a situation that we forget all about our own condition—a theme also relevant to the problem of the schoolmaster. This new motif also enables Rumi to note that the body is a garment which at some point we can forget and discard. Back briefly to the story of the schoolboys (whose unhappy mothers complain to the schoolmaster), and then on to the story of a dervish who made a vow to eat only fruit fallen from trees. Unfortunately, circumstances compelled him to break this vow. Then the dervish fell in with twenty robbers and suffered the amputation of his own hand and foot, when they were captured, before his identity was discovered. But he accepted his suffering as legitimate punishment for his breach of faith, in breaking his vow. Later, he was found weaving baskets: God restored his limbs whenever he sat down to this task, as a way of reminding the dervish that even when he died, God would bring together again the scattered parts of his personality. This bit of *occasionalism* further expands the possible themes of the story of the cow.

But quite a different direction is suggested by a story with which Rumi interrupts the tale of the dervish— a story about a man who asked a goldsmith for scales. I do not have a sieve, said the goldsmith. I want scales, said the man. Yes, I understand: you want to weigh some tiny filings of gold, but you will spill them (because your hand shakes), and you want a sieve— and a broom—to sweep them up. In an instant the goldsmith grasped the entire picture. This motif is not difficult to relate to the theme of the quest, but other themes can be found here too: how the mind is turned by outside influences, the harm wrought by faulty imaginings, the capacity of some individuals to grasp concepts quickly, and the problem of reading accurately the data offered us. The possible permutations of the elements of even these few stories are already enormous.

The issue of amputation (suggested by the story of the dervish) leads Rumi back again to Pharoah and (this time) his magicians, whose hands and feet Pharoah threatened to amputate because he thought their imaginations out of control. Hence Rumi passes to dreams about amputations and the nature of dreams and sleep. (Pharoah, it will be recalled, had dreams which Joseph interpreted; here is one connecting link.) Then, to illustrate a point about vision, Rumi recounts the story of a mule who kept falling down because his

eyesight was clouded. Discussion of the importance of clear vision leads to speculation on the nature of human growth (the coming together of scattered particles), a concept which reminds Rumi of a skillful tailor who could make invisible seams and of a sheikh who did not weep when his sons died because, he said, he was already united to them by spiritual vision. Eventually we reach a long and complex narrative about Daquqi, a man with extraordinary visionary powers, who saved the lives of many, only to be accused of meddling. But Daquqi is urged for the good of mankind to continue his quest, a motif that will soon tie into the determination of the judge, in the cow story, to find the truth, no matter what the cost.

Now, forty-seven pages after the introduction of the story of the cow, Rumi gets back to the theme of gaining one's livelihood without work and the joy of the man who killed the cow that his prayer had been heard. There was, of course, a legal dispute and both parties went to David for a judgment, violent protests being made by the owner of the cow: How can that lazy man's prayers make my property his? What validity can his dreams about the truth of the matter have? Wrangling thus and insulting each other viciously, the two litigants approach David, who hears the case and rather hastily, it seems, subjects the defendant to a series of "loaded" legal questions. The defendant begs David to avoid appearances and seek inner truth through prayer, and David does appear eager to "connect" on some deeper level. As a result, the truth is eventually revealed to him, and he orders the owner of the cow to turn over to the lazy man all his property. Unaware of the basis of this decision, the people cry out against David, who explains that an older crime has come to light: the owner of the cow and his wife had been servants to the grandfather of the defendant, but when that family had grown destitute, they had taken everything, even murdering the grandfather and burying his head. The knife is found beneath a tree, and the owner of the cow is ordered executed with it. All men have an instinctive yearning to see justice done, says Rumi (and, we might add, an instinctive taste for irony), and those who demand justice a little too shrilly (this seems to have been an important clue for David) call attention to themselves and may get more justice than they seek.

This section concludes with a long allegorical interpretation of the story, throughout which, I believe, Rumi is not being true to his own best instincts as poet and seer. Here he abandons his technique of communicating by image/action-clusters and takes refuge in words and seriality. We are told, for example, that the claimants of the cow are the fleshly soul, which can be conquered only by the kind of insight into inner truth that David brings to the situation. But Davids are rare, and not all who pretend to have his powers do indeed possess them! Moreover, it is noted that with the slaying of the murderer the world once again became alive. Such suggestions, though they may point to one kind of meaning, seem thin and vapid by contrast with the rich messages borne along to the intuition by the intertwining narratives. In any case, some 1,100 couplets after he began the tale, Rumi brings it to a conclusion.

Throughout his poem Rumi seems to be quite aware of the problems his readers may have with it—and indeed he invites us to a kind of reader-response criticism of his work. He is conscious that many different kinds of readers may study his poem (I, 409, 419). For certain readers a hundred explanations of a particular story may prove too subtle, and others may misinterpret a story as the result of a long-drawn-out explanation (I, 264). Moreover, Rumi complains that his own narrative is too long, that his purpose has grown obscure, even that madness is overtaking him. And often he expresses distaste for the poetic process: "Let a torrent take away these rhymes and specious words!" he says; "They are skin! They are skin! Fitting only for the brains of poets! . . . Take this poetry and tear it up. . . . meanings transcend words and wind and air."[4]

It is also surprising, in the light of his own willingness to be the flute on which God plays His music (I, 35) and his conviction that he was essentially only a transcriber of material from other worlds, to see him complaining that poetry is as uncontrollable as a sling: one can never be sure in what direction the missile will shoot off or where it will hit (I, 84). Any single image may generate any number of metaphors in a given reader's mind, because we always judge by the analogy of ourselves, in terms of our own contexts.[5] Moreover, inspiration (according to Rumi the capacity to grasp materials from the spiritual world) may flag, for it is a fragile thing, and "it needs a very well illumined eye" to grasp the links between this world and the world of the spirit (I, 273). Little wonder that Rumi felt the need to descend to allegory from time to time.

Behind Rumi's anxiety lest his poem be misunderstood and his generally (I think) misplaced effort to offer some guidance for his readers, lies the Medieval Islamic concept of a world of images or similitudes, *'alam al-Mithal,* whence streams material into the consciousness of individuals able to receive it.[6] Presumably, some of this material is embodied in the stories Rumi tells, and it is to be distinguished from purely fanciful or made-up products of the human imagination. As Rumi observes, "Whither will it [the story] flee, since wisdom has poured [on us] from the clouds of God's bounty?" (II, 129). And elsewhere, "the troops of imagination arrive unwearied from behind the heart's curtain," streaming into our consciousness in "company after company." These pictures, which God is drawing on our minds, become the regulators of the phenomenal world. But while most people see only the outer form of these images, and take that outer form for reality, the saints are able to see beyond externals, thereby gaining knowledge about the World of Non-Existence, the world of unity. The saints thus may be described as "scouts" reaching the "watchtower . . . of Nonexistence" and what they do is comparable to seeing a painting still in the painter's mind.[7]

In his discussion of the World of Similitudes, Henri Corbin emphasizes that it is an "imaginal" not an "imaginary" world, a world made up of images that have, in some important sense, absolute reality. "We are not dealing here with irreality," Corbin insists, but with a world of "autonomous forms and images" not graspable by the senses or by the intellect but by the "imaginative consciousness" or by some imaging power.[8] Marshall Hodgson agrees: the *'alam al-Mithal* is the source of visionary experiences that are in some sense "genuine," not merely subjective fancies, pictures of "ultimately valid, objective facts of life."[9] And a Medieval Sufi describes the *'alam al-Mithal* as a kind of mirror reflecting the contents of both the everyday real world (the world of bodies) and the world of spirits,[10] which has already been referred to as the world of non-existence. This mirror image may also be applied to the stories which Rumi tells in the *Mathnawi.* The existence of this world, which is without limits of any kind, has been affirmed repeatedly by *spirituales* of every age and place (Rahman 415).

The concept of a "world of non-existence" back of the world of similitudes (*Mathnawi* I, 168-9) is critical for any attempt to grasp Rumi's views about poetic inspiration and narrative technique. It suggests that he was responding to pressures and inspiration other than the logical and the lineal. It is, ultimately, what he was trying to get at; it is both a matter of technique and content. The structure of his poem illustrates another mode of being. The world of non-existence has been described as a treasure house from which all things are created,[11] and it suggests fecundity and potentiality, that which continues to manifest itself. While Sir Thomas Browne referred to a very similar "place" as "the deep dark and abysm of time," Rumi turns to images of sleep, the ocean, leaves and trees (Schimmel 78, 87), music, and wine. When we see Rumi's stories and reflections against the background of this very rich concept/reality, we gain a new understanding of what he felt their significance to be and we realize that the thrust of the stories and their source is one and the same thing: if you can move along from story to story, under the guidance of the spirit, you also gain some foothold in that other world. So rich and complex lines of interpretation are opened up, and we draw back from easy allegorizing of the material, as well as from attempts to see Rumi as *just* a storyteller, or *just* a theologian-moralist.

In Rumi (and in al-Arabi before him), this combination of the spiritual/intellectual/conceptual and the physical/material, of form and content, is often symbolized by the figures of Mary and Gabriel and the story of the conception of Jesus.[12] In this great event, Gabriel may be regarded as the notional or intellectual element, the "idea" or "image" of a Jesus in the mind, the abstraction (the "word" which was "in the beginning"); Mary can then be seen as the flesh, the material being, the good soil (I, 104) without which the notion cannot be realized (the logos "became flesh and dwelt among us"). Gabriel "breathes" on Mary and Jesus is conceived. Thus it might be said that the earthly Jesus himself is the supreme product of the imagination, the finest manifestation of the *'alam al-Mithal,* the supreme intermediary (Rahman 419). But in the class to which Jesus belongs we must also place certain stories, certain melodies, scents, dances, faces, the Qur'an—all instances of a very special kind of abstraction or notion being accorded physical form.

The relationship of Gabriel and Mary I have compared to the aesthetic question of the relationship of form to meaning, and Rumi is determined to do justice to both sides of the equation, as I am trying to do in talking about both the narrative of the story and its meaning. Thus Rumi speaks of the exterior journey (made up of speech and action) and the interior journey above the sky (I, 33), and he notes that "Outward acts of kindness bear witness to feelings of love in your heart" (I, 143). So we should say too that the "meaning" of the **Mathnawi** cannot be separated from the narrative and the peculiar form into which it is cast—stories within stories, broken up by prayers, hints, images, proverbs, ejaculations, and intricate reflections. On any given issue, light is shed from many different quarters. Neither the stories alone nor the ideas alone, nor the images alone constitute the work. The particular combination which Rumi has created exists for one purpose alone—to help the reader move within, to escape the phenomenal world, after he/she has gained the kind of strength which it is Mary's role to bring. The stories which Rumi tells are thus of immense importance; they are the very "marrow" of inward states (I, 6). They transcend the elements of which they are formed—words, sentences, episodes—just as their relationship to one another transcends the seeming illogic and confusion of their arrangement.

The problem of bringing the two worlds together engaged Rumi all his life, and his struggle with narrative seems to have been only one attempt to deal with it. Dancing interested him because he saw in it an instrument of both passage and connection, of transcendence and incarnation. The ney or flute, which accompanies the dancing, is valued for its thin, reedy sound, and it became one of Rumi's favorite images for the call of the other world. Clearly, he saw certain of his followers—particularly his beloved scribes—as yet other instruments of this process, as was the act of writing poetry—not the problem of dealing with rhyme and meter, but the more important process of reading off a script unfolding, as it were, from the other world. Thus Rumi speaks of himself, the poet, as a diver after pearls, bringing up from deep beneath the surface of the sea beautiful objects found within the rough oyster, at great risk to himself. He reminds us that Muhammad once described a particularly probing question as "boring the pearl" (I, 356).

One of the first stories Rumi tells deals with this very problem of using physical/material data to probe the spiritual world. It is the story of a king who falls in love with a beautiful woman, marries her, and then has to watch her pine away in sadness. None of his physicians can determine the cause of the woman's sickness, but a dervish offers to help. He encourages the woman to talk about her previous life in a distant city, and as she talks about places and people, he keeps his finger on her pulse, watching the beat increase as they close in on the place where lives the man she loves (I, 12-3). So spirit and body join to create a problem and point the way to its solution.

Rumi recognizes the problems created by the meddlesome intellect for those who would move between the two worlds: the intellect interferes with the flow of images from the other world (I, 83) and resists the often-peculiar (to us) form into which the other world casts its material. Allegorizing is an example of the way the intellect can misdirect. Moreover, the intellect tends to be fascinated by secondary causes—causes other than God (cf. I, 83, and II, 141) and by logical order, and over-intellectualizing often manifests itself in an over-emphasis on the importance of words. Words are thorns in the hedge of the vineyard (I, 95); old words fall short of the new meaning (II, 65); tongueless love is clearest (I, 10); eloquent speech comes as from a sea (I, 265). Through such brilliant metaphors does Rumi express his awareness of the phenomenal world (as represented by words and formulas), at the same time affirming his recognition of the even greater importance of an inner, wordless perception of contact with the realm of the imagination, which, to repeat, is reflected in the peculiar form his narrative takes.

Elsewhere the issue of the meddlesome intellect is put in terms of missing the inner reality because one has become preoccupied with form. A Bedouin takes pure water from the desert to the Caliph in Baghdad as a gift. Most of the courtiers snicker at the man's naivete, but the caliph accepts the gift solemnly and gratefully. "The followers of Form were woven [entangled] in pearls; the followers of Reality had found the Sea of Reality" (I, 148-9; cf. I, 410). And just what is the form of something? Rumi suggest sucking on a confection shaped like a loaf of bread. Will anyone believe it is bread, not candy? (I, 157). A poet's sweetheart complains to him—Why are you thinking about your rhymes now? Why are you missing my presence? (I, 95). And, Rumi advises, a child needs to be given special training in not being satisfied with purely formal, verbal formulations (I, 375). Hence, again, the fundamental importance of stories, which are marvelously vivid, earthy, and concrete, and of the way Rumi intertwines them with other stories, and with his reflections, so as to replicate the precise process through which the reader/thinker/hearer passes, as he moves from the literal story to the world of the imagination and submits himself to the influence of the world of images.

When we confront a document such as the story of the cow, we may be inclined to regret that Rumi too often took his own advice to "sell intellect and talent and buy bewilderment" (II, 65). Rumi seems to be moving in far too many directions and in ways that are most difficult (for the intellect, anyway) to follow. The ending of that story seems to shed very little light on the point that Rumi seems to have intended to illustrate. Rumi's disclaimers and apologies and expressions of distress often seem all too relevant. So we must ask if the peculiar form into which he cast his long poem or (as he might prefer to put it) into which it was cast by his inspiration is justified by the result. Does the theory about the imagination which was so critical to the tradition he worked in stand up? Is there some depth-unity to his poem or to the story of the cow which makes it a genuine work of art? Or is his poem best seen as a compilation of charming stories and one-liners and striking theological assertions? These, of course, are intellectual formulations which scarcely do justice to the workings of the imagination. Chittick, who has assembled a collection of his statements arranged by topic, and Arberry, who has given us two anthologies of his tales, seem to stand at opposite ends of the aesthetic spectrum, one implying that the tales get in the way of the important ideas; the other, that the concepts are less important than the stories.

Let us look again at the story of the cow. One way of approaching it would be to say that Rumi tells the story (as has already been noted) to illustrate the importance of keeping alive the search, any search, no matter how far or how deep it must go. Of course, to say this goes against my argument that in reading Rumi we are not trying to extract discursive meanings from his stories, but rather that story, form, and ideas constitute a whole which we are invited to experience. Better, therefore, to say that the idea of keeping alive the search is one possible way of putting into words

part of what emerges from a series of tales which coalesced in Rumi's mind as he contemplated the story of a slain animal, and schoolboys, and a goldsmith, and Pharoah, and a dervish. But of course the problems created by an over-powerful fancy are also important and can lead us to combine the stories in quite another way. In either case, the act of *putting a theme into words* is not necessarily a desirable or only possible outcome of reading the stories. All that the words do is suggest that the experience we can have with these stories may be related to a larger cluster of experiences open to all of us, experiences that seem to include laziness, dependence upon grace, work, trust in God, the escape from determinism, the power of the imagination, the role of desire as a motivator, the validity of dreams and intuitions, the uncovering of past misdeeds, restitution and justice, patience in suffering, a sense of union with loved ones who are dead, heeding God's voice, contentment. But words will be of little help where participation in such experiences is lacking—particularly a real-life experience of the way these issues are interwoven.

The same point might be made about the metaphors that Rumi offers in this passage, for in their own way they bear into our minds the truths which Rumi wishes to convey, but truths inseparable from pictures—putting on asses a load suitable for horses (81); climbing the sky without a ladder (83); a cow running into a house (83); a one-winged bird falling through the sky (85); the dust of evil imagination (87); staggering as one walks a high wall—even when the wall is quite wide (88); a sick man sweating under coverlets (90); a palsied man trying to weigh gold (92); a bird flying into a snare, eyes wide open (93); a one-handed man weaving a basket (96); invisible seams (99), etc. All— and these are a mere sample of the rich texture of metaphor Rumi gives us—contribute in one way or another to our sense of the strengths and weakness of the human psyche, as it struggles to bring its ideas and dreams into some kind of fruition, a theme that is certainly relevant to the story of David and the theme of the quest.

In trying to understand the interplay of reason and imagination in the **Mathnawi** it may also be helpful to look at the way Rumi moves from section to section of his narrative, his use of the *segue*. The supposition would be that there is some logic here (after all, he is trying to get his reader to follow his narrative) but also something unexpected, since he was dealing with material from *'alam al-Mithal,* with the workings of the spirit, which Jesus compared to wind blowing where it chose. For example, Rumi moves into the story of the cow with the observation that when you have at hand what you seek, the quest is over—otherwise, keep searching. He finds the entry of the cow into the lazy man's house a case of answered prayer, and yet he prays for help with his poem, as he senses the demands of God upon him. This will eventually relate to David's quest for the truth. The movement of Rumi's mind can be followed, but it is tricky. His prayer for aid leads him to a distinction between knowledge and opinion, out of which grows the story of the schoolmaster who was rendered sick by suggestion. Faulty imagination also led Pharoah to believe that he was divine, which leads him back to the schoolmaster and his anger at his wife for not being sympathetic enough. The mothers of the schoolboys visit the master, who notes that until his attention was called to it, he did not realize he was ill. Then on to the story of Zuleika's friends (another Egyptian connection), who were so entranced by Joseph's beauty that they did not realize that their hands were cut, and so to the Platonic concept of the body as a garment to be sloughed off by the soul. This process, of which I have described only a tiny section, may be linked to the free association of stream of consciousness, to make an anachronistic comparison, but Rumi obviously believed that other forces were at work.

In his study of the way we organize our world, *The Order of Things,* Michael Foucault discusses a suggestion of Jorge Luis Borges for a new division of the animal world—into such bizarre divisions as those belonging to the emperor; those embalmed, tame, fabulous; stray dogs; those drawn with a camelhair brush; those that have just broken the water pitcher, etc. Foucault wonders about the impossibility of such an analysis, being particularly fascinated by "the disorder in which fragments of a large number of possible orders glitter separately in the dimension, without law or geometry, of the *heteroclite*. . . ."[13] But such groupings also suggest a kind of order by which the seeming disorder of the **Mathnawi** might also be thought about, a disorder-in-order which is, finally, about all that we have to grasp when we try to talk about the impact of the *'alam al-Mithal* upon Rumi. How can we bring together the story of the cow rushing into the house and the friends of Zuleika, looking at their wounded hands? Daquqi rescuing the shipwrecked sailors and the insistence of the Mu'tazilites that the intellects of people are originally different? A palsied man shaking as he weighs gold and an armless dervish being supplied with hands when he weaves baskets? The pitfalls of opinion and a schoolmaster's rage at his unsympathetic wife? David's discovery of the knife beneath the tree and a bird with one wing crashing out of the sky? A fool's determination not to work and Rumi's need of inspiration?

It would be a task worthy of the imaginations of Borges or Kafka to identify (even with the help of both modern computers and the *'alam al-Mithal*) all the possible ways of putting together the material Rumi has given us. He did not supply all the clues, but through the literary form in which he worked he seems to have pointed the way, to have shown how each motif of each story can resonate in so many different ways with motifs from other stories. For in some way—in many ways perhaps—the badly confused David, and the palsied man with his gold-scales, and the questing Daquqi—all towering figures who possess my imagination so powerfully—lead me by paths I'm not quite certain of to a response to the problems of one man who sought from life a "free ride" and of another whose behavior did not quite resonate appropriately with the wrong that had been done him.

Notes

[1] I, 3. All references are to the three-volume translation by R. A. Nicholson originally published in 1926. London: Luzac, 1977.

[2] See, for example, al-Kisai, *The Tales of the Prophets,* trans. W. M. Thackston, Jr. (Boston: Twayne, 1978), xiv-xv.

[3] The wife of Potiphar, in the Joseph story; see Qur'an XII.

[4] William C. Chittick, *The Sufi Path of Love* (Albany: SUNY Press, 1983), 271.

[5] See, as a case in point, "The Story of a Parrot," I, 17.

[6] See Fazlur Rahman, "Dream, Imagination, and 'Alam al-Mithal," in G. von Grunebaum and Roger Caillois, *The Dream and Human Societies* (Berkeley, University of California Press, 1966), 409.

[7] Chittick, 250-6.

[8] Henry Corbin, "The Visionary Dream and Islamic Spirituality," in von Grunebaum and Caillois, 406-7.

[9] Marshall Hodgson, *The Venture of Islam* (University of Chicago Press, 1974), III, 43.

[10] Quoted by Rahman, in von Grunebaum and Caillois, 419.

[11] Annemarie Schimmel, *The Triumphal Sun* (London: Fine Books, 1978), 228. Prof. Schimmel offers a valuable analysis of image-patterns in Rumi in Chapter 2.

[12] Ibn al-Arabi, *The Bezels of Wisdom,* trans. R. W. J. Austin (London: SPCK, 1980), 174-179.

[13] Michael Foucault, *The Order of Things: An Archeology of the Human Sciences* (New York: Pantheon, 1970), xvii.

John Renard (essay date 1994)

SOURCE: John Renard, in an afterword to *All the King's Falcon's: Rumi on Prophets and Revelation,* State University of New York Press, 1994, pp. 151-58.

[In the following excerpt. Renard discusses the prophetic imagery found in Rumi's writings and examines the function of the prophets and Muhammad as models of the spiritual guide. Please note that the parenthetical references throughout the excerpt and the unmarked references in the notes correspond to Nicholson's translation of the Mathnawi.]

Where the Qur'an employs the prophetic stories chiefly as moral exempla, Rumi the teacher uses the prophets and their stories as a convenient reservoir of familiar and attractive images with which he catches the ear of his listener, and as the come-on with which he entices the prospective buyer into his shop. Leaving himself open to the charge of bait-and-switch merchandizing, what Rumi is really selling is a vision of the relationship of the divine to the human and of a way homeward. Prophets and their deeds thus become metaphorical guideposts and reminders that function somewhat as does Rumi's celebrated reed flute: as a hollow tube capable of hauntingly plaintive song, but only when inspired not with wind but with fire.

One could of course single out dozens of major metaphors and image clusters that Rumi uses to serve his larger religious purposes as viewed from this angle. But Rumi's use of explicitly prophetic imagery, along with his penchant for creating unexpected twists in already familiar tales by overlaying new images on the old, makes that imagery as reliable an index of the poet's thought processes as one can hope for. For sheer frequency of occurrence alone, for example, few classes of image can approach that of prophet metaphors.

In addition, one could read Mawlana's interpretation of prophets and revelation through a number of other filters. A biographical-developmental model, for example, might approach Rumi as a fascinating personality whose own life experiences provide an essential key to his writings. This method might study the imagery chronologically with an eye to possible correspondences between changes in his personal life and variations in his development of prophet imagery. Offering a clue as to what such an approach might turn up, Annemarie Schimmel points out that Joseph's rejection by his envious brothers gave Rumi a way of interpreting both his own relationship to Shams and the bitter jealousy of Rumi's family and friends.[1] One could observe something similar in his views of other prophetic figures as well. Prophets are, from this perspective, in a sense also psychological *topoi,* and

prophetic revelation the larger framework within which Rumi understands all important human relationships.

Another approach might identify Rumi chiefly as a mystical poet, situating his work within the history of Persian mystical literature, or even more broadly, of Islamicate literatures. Such a perspective might highlight the continuity, or lack thereof, in the mystical development of these themes so central to the Islamic tradition as a whole. . . .

A third point of view might identify Mawlana primarily as a deft wordsmith, a literary artist capable of crafting highly specialized uses of different types of imagery for finely nuanced purposes. Such an approach might investigate comparatively variations in the complexity or density of certain kinds of imagery employed in certain contexts. For example, as Fatemeh Keshavarz suggests, when Rumi is speaking directly and clearly about God's dealings with humankind—especially through the Messengers—he tends to use rather simple metaphors, such as those drawn from nature. One needs little or no technical savvy to appreciate them. When he delves into the vagaries of human interrelationships, by contrast, the poet seems to gravitate to more complex images, such as astrological allusions or references to the intricacies of backgammon. One needs a more specialized and often highly technical knowledge of the conceptual system and its rules to catch the drift of the imagery.[2]

Finally, from the perspective of the history of religion or, more narrowly, of Sufism, one might characterize Rumi as an important communicator of specific major religious concepts through his prophetology. A prominent example is that of the function of shaykh or spiritual guide. As we have mentioned in several contexts already, Mawlana does not concern himself with expounding the theory and practice of any particular mystical school, and often uses the technical language of Sufism with less than technical precision. Still the poet clearly regards the role of shaykh as at least generically crucial and as an extension of the prophetic function of guidance from darkness into light. To illustrate how one might look at Rumi's prophet imagery through a lens or filter other than that of a prophet's life story, let us conclude with a brief glimpse, first, at how three prophets not previously discussed function as models of the spiritual guide, and second, at how the same lens reframes our picture of Muhammad in Rumi's writings.

Taking his cue from a hadith that likens the shaykh to a prophet among his people (III:4319, 1774), Rumi often uses the authority of such prophets as Adam, Noah, and David to give added substance to the role of the shaykh. Adam models the prophetic struggle to remain in tune with true knowledge, and to impart that knowledge as a shaykh would. He teaches creation the names and "melodies" of God, the inner truth of things. Because that knowledge was infused from creation in all beings and then gradually forgotten, the role of the prophet shaykh is to reactivate humankind's faulty memory. At the moment of Adam's creation, God sowed *'aql* into the water and clay. In an allusion to the greater jihad, Rumi says that the angelic *'aql* thus paid homage to Adam while the *nafs* of Iblis refused. Iblis won a temporary victory by blocking Adam's inspiration and insight (*wahy* and *nazar*).[3]

Pure light is the source of Adam's *ma'rifa* (intimate knowledge); hence his defeat was only temporary. Rumi plays on the irony of Iblis' inability to discern that light even though he was fashioned from fire. Iblis was too impressed by his own form and its apparent superiority to that of Adam. Angelic *'aql* discerned in Adam the child of earth illumined like the moon by divine rays, and to its own surprise, acknowledged its debt to dust.[4] That light then becomes the thread that binds together in timeless succession all the prophets, Muhammad's Companions, and all the subsequent great mystics (II:905-30).

On the other side of the coin, Adam also models the experience of the *murid*, whom the poet seems to regard as the untutored falcon. Rumi likens Adam's forty-day development to the *murid*'s formation: "It is not surprising that the Sufis made attempts to designate Adam as the first Sufi; for he was forty days 'in seclusion' . . . before God endowed him with spirit: then God put the lamp of reason in his heart and the light of wisdom on his tongue, and he emerged like an illuminated mystic from the retirement during which he was kneaded by the hands of God."[5] Adam's forty tearful years of exile from the garden is likewise compared to the *chilla* from which the seeker emerges as a fully initiated mystical adept; the *safi* (pure) is therefore also *sufi*. Unlike Iblis, who blames God for leading him on, Adam accepts responsibility for his fall and thus models repentance as the first stage on the Path.[6]

Rumi uses the image of taking refuge in Noah's ark as a metaphor for seeking the tutelage of a shaykh. In that context the flood is a metaphor for the greater jihad. Rumi often speaks rather generally in that vein, as in this reference in one of his letters, quoting a hadith: "In the flood of Noah . . . there was no refuge except to turn to Noah. . . . And the Messenger said . . . , 'O Umma, in every age there is a flood and a Noah and a Qutb of that time who is the caliph of the age. The ship of Noah exists in that time and whoever grasps his hem is saved from the flood.' "[7]

Sometimes the poet likens the ark to the intimate knowledge toward which the shaykh assists the seeker: "The tablet of *ma'rifa* is the ark of Noah; the storm will drown whoever does not enter his ship."[8] Though Noah had never read Qushayri's *Risala* or Makki's *Qut al-Qulub,* he possessed all the requisite qualifications of a guide and merits a place in the company of such great mystics as Karkhi, Shibli, and Bayazid.[9] As a type of the mystic, Noah rode heavenward on the Buraq of the Ark (VI:2208). Finally, Rumi makes his most direct and explicit connection with Noah as shaykh. Alluding to a second hadith, in which Muhammad first calls himself the ship in the "flood of time" and then includes his Companions in the image, the poet says, "While you are in the presence of the Shaykh evil is far from you, for night and day you travel in a ship. Life-giving spirit shields you: asleep in the ship, you travel the path."[10]

In one of his lengthiest prophet tales, Rumi has David display his divinely inspired justice and skill in arbitration and discernment that make him an outstanding paradigm of the shaykh. The story uses the theme of animal as *nafs*. A poor man prayed earnestly that God would grant him livelihood without effort. Next day a cow battered down his door and allowed the man to slaughter it. The owner of the cow took the man before David to plead his case. At first the judge sided with the plaintiff. But when the poor man appealed, David reversed his decision after prayerful seclusion, and he ordered the plaintiff to give all his possessions to the defendant.

After this Khizresque action, David revealed to an angry crowd the reason for his decision. He showed the people a tree beneath which the plaintiff had long ago murdered his master. He then ordered the plaintiff executed with the very weapon he had buried beneath that tree. Rumi explains that David is the shaykh whose judgment aids the *murid* to kill the cow of *nafs* with the weapon of intellect. He can then render justice upon the *nafs* (the plaintiff) and secure unearned sustenance for the *murid*. "With the shaykh to help it, the intellect pursues and defeats the lower self; the *nafs* is a dragon with immeasurable strength and cunning; the face of the shaykh is the emerald that plucks out its eye."[11]

Luqman then becomes a model of the *murid* to David's shaykh. The sage watched David at his blacksmith's furnace making chain mail. Luqman was unacquainted with the armorer's art and wanted very much to ask what David was making, but he refrained, telling himself that patience was better. Asking too many questions merely hampers the shaykh's efficiency. David rewards Luqman's virtue with a fine coat of mail, for patience defends against pain (III:1842-54). Luqman's patience as embodied in an ascetical separation from all attractive morsels (*luqma*) teaches seekers to seek the hidden game rather than the game that attracts by appearance only.

Finally, Muhammad naturally strikes the poet as the ideal spiritual guide. Rumi's most extended allusion to Muhammad as shaykh occurs in a story of how the Prophet went to visit one of his sick Companions. Rumi leads up to the story with a long series of interwoven frame like tales, each emphasizing the need for the kind of spiritual insight in which only a shaykh can provide instruction: "if you do not want to lose your head, become a foot, under the tutelage of the discerning Qutb" (II:1984).

In the stories that precede the segments on Muhammad's visitation, the underlying pattern is that one character comes to the aid of another in trouble: the man who woke a person into whose mouth a snake had crawled; the man who rescued a bear from the dragon's mouth and did not recognize the bear for what it was—the *nafs;* and Moses trying to open the people's eyes to the falsehood of the golden calf. In those that come after and/or recur intermittently within the visitation story frame, images of the greater jihad appear and Rumi speaks more explicitly of the role of shaykh and *pir,* Muhammad as shaykh helps the sick man to realize the cause of his malady, and instructs him in the greater jihad. With imagery that recalls the first two stories—of the serpent swallowed and the dragon swallowing the bear—Rumi takes the metaphors a step further by conjuring up the image of how Moses transformed the snake-become-dragon into a potent rod against Pharaoh the *nafs.*

Before bringing the story of Muhammad's visitation to a close, the poet introduces several more stories exemplifying the greater jihad. Finally Muhammad discovers that the man has been praying inappropriately, asking God to inflict upon him now the pain of the next life's possible punishment, so as to let him avoid it hereafter. The Prophet, whom Rumi again likens to Moses leading out of the desert of the first stages of spiritual wayfaring, warns him not to be so arrogant as to think he could bear such a thing. He should ask rather for good and ease both here and hereafter. After concluding that frame sequence, Rumi nevertheless continues the jihad theme, returning to feature Muhammad as shaykh battling the *nafs* symbol called the Mosque of Opposition. The entire complex of stories (II: 1778-3026), in turn, sits between a set of stories of Moses and Jesus as shaykhs and a series, running virtually to the end of the Book, continuing the themes of the role of the shaykh in discernment and spiritual combat.

Various aspects of Muhammad's shaykh-hood emerge from this cycle, especially, but from elsewhere as well. Not only is Muhammad a shaykh, but he is the model for shaykhs. As leader in the greater jihad, Muhammad wields his famous twin-tipped sword, Dhu 'l-Faqar. Rumi uses the sword as metaphor for spiritual maturity: the seeker who submits to spiritual tutelage is transformed from a mere needle into a Dhu 'l-Faqar, thus giving a dervish power to behead his selfhood—Dhu 'l-Faqar, makes the seeker a *faqir.* Rumi often likens the sword to the staff of Moses.[12] The shaykh who has achieved perfection is born of Mustafa and is like a prophet to his people; and Rumi explicitly calls the model *pir a nabi.*[13] . . .

Notes

[1] Annemarie Schimmel, "Yusuf in Mawlana Rumi's Poetry," in Lewisohn, Leonard, ed. *The Legacy of Medieval Persian Sufism,* (London: Khaniqahi Nimatullahi Publications, 1992), 45-59, esp. 47. See also *I am Wind, You are Fire* 118-38, and *Triumphal Sun* 280-89.

[2] Thanks to Fatemeh Keshavarz for these suggestions after reading the manuscript of this book.

[3] VI:153-54, 3134-40, 3193-99; *D* [Rumi's *Diwan,* poem: verse, Furuzanfar's one volume edition.] 2447:2; *R* [Rumi's *Ruba'iyat,* quatrain number, Furuzanfar's edition.] 1590; *F* [Rumi's *Fihi Ma Fihi,* Arberry/ Furuzanfar pages.] 22/10; V:2103ff., 2610.

[4] I:1246-47, 1944-5, 2657-63, 3396ff., 3403; II:17-18, 909-10, 1254, 1353-54; III:3198; V:185, 563-64; *D* 1597:7; 2583:5; 3212:6.

[5] *MDI* [*Mystical Dimensions of Islam,* A. Schimmel.] 16; see also 419.

[6] I:1480-92, 1633-36; II:2507; III:4257; IV:324ff., 363-64, 403-4, 1402, 3413ff.; VI:1216; *D* 280:7; 1203:2; 1905:3; 2041:10; 2608:10/3121:10; *F* 39/27; 53/41; 113/101; *M* [Rumi's *Maktubat,* letter/page number, Jamshidpur edition.] 68/150.

[7] *M* 72/157; IV:3357ff.

[8] *D* 729:3. See also Rumi's prayeRumi128/243.

[9] VI:2652-55; *D* 879:15.

[10] IV:538-41. Additional ark imagery in I:403-4; IV:1414; V:2344; *D* 148:3; 402:13; 539:10; 541:3; 668:9; 729:3; 876:3; 895:2; 935:6; 1020:2; 1250:5; 1301:5/ 1302:5; 1343:4; 1369:6; 1674:5; 1840:2; 1889:14; 2017:4; 2090:2; 2391:6; 2646:4; 2684:4; 2747:3; 2830:7; 3090:3; 3351:9; *R* 159; *M* 22/74.

[11] III: 1450-89, 2306-2569, quoting 2547-48. For literary analysis of the extended tale, see J. R. King, "Narrative Disjunction and Conjunction in Rumi's *Mathnawi," Journal of Narrative Technique* 19:3 (1989): 276-85.

[12] II:2300; IV:3374; V:2506; VI:1522, 2117, 3313; *D* 57:9; 202:10; 235:3; 588:8; 718:19; 871:1; 985:6;

1095:5; 1126:3; 1747:5; 1859:6; 1985:7; 2032:1; 2503:6/
2531.8; 2934:9; 2965:2; 3496:3; *M* 138/264.

[13] I:1950, 1966; II:3101; III:1773-74.

FURTHER READING

Arasteh, A. Reza. *Rumi the Persian: Rebirth in Creativity
and Love.* Lahore, Pakistan: Sh. Muhammad Ashraf
Kashmiri Bazar, 1965, 200 p.
> Examines the process of rebirth and creativity in the
> life of Rumi and attempts to "relate his contribution to
> the theory of personality and the social and individual
> state of well being."

Chittick, William C. *The Sufi Doctrine of Rumi: An
Introduction.* Tehran: Aryamehr University, 1974, 96 p.
> Provides an introduction to Rumi's doctrine and
> attempts to "present plainly and briefly the main points
> of Sufi doctrine as expounded in Rumi's writings."

————. *The Sufi Path of Love: The Spiritual Teachings
of Rumi.* Albany: State University of New York Press,
1983, 433 p.

Divides Rumi's teachings into the three dimensions of
Sufism: knowledge or theory, works or practice, and
attainment to God.

King, James Roy. "Jesus and Joseph in Rumi's *Mathnawi.*"
The Muslim World LXXX, No. 2 (April 1990): 81-95.
> Examines the literary treatment of Jesus and Joseph
> in Rumi's *Mathnawi* and claims that "Rumi
> transcends the limitations of any single view of
> Jesus."

Schimmel, Annemarie. *I Am Wind, You Are Fire: The Life
and Work of Rumi.* Boston: Shambhala, 1992, 214 p.
> A general overview of Rumi's life and works.

————. *The Triumphal Sun: A Study of the Works of
Jalaloddin Rumi.* rev. ed. London: East-West Publications,
1980, 520 p.
> Compares Rumi to his predecessors, 'Attar and Sana'i,
> and discusses the use of imagery and symbolism in
> his writings.

Turkmen, Erkan. "On the First Eighteen Verses of Rumi's
Masnevi." *Islam and the Modern Age* 14, No. 4 (November
1983): 286-98.
> Deciphers the symbols found in the first eighteen
> verses of Rumi's *Masnevi* and finds the verses to be
> interlinked.

CLASSICAL AND MEDIEVAL LITERATURE CRITICISM

INDEXES

Literary Criticism Series
Cumulative Author Index

Literary Criticism Series
Cumulative Topic Index

CMLC Cumulative Nationality Index

CMLC Cumulative Title Index

CMLC Cumulative Critic Index

How to Use This Index

The main references

Calvino, Italo
1923-1985.....CLC 5, 8, 11, 22, 33, 39,
73; SSC 3

list all author entries in the following Gale Literary Criticism series:

BLC = *Black Literature Criticism*
CLC = *Contemporary Literary Criticism*
CLR = *Children's Literature Review*
CMLC = *Classical and Medieval Literature
   Criticism*
DA = *DISCovering Authors*
DAB = *DISCovering Authors: British*
DAC = *DISCovering Authors: Canadian*
DAM = *DISCovering Authors Modules*
   DRAM: Dramatists module
   MST: Most-studied authors module
   MULT: Multicultural authors module
   NOV: Novelists module
   POET: Poets module
   POP: Popular/genre writers module

DC = *Drama Criticism*
HLC = *Hispanic Literature Criticism*
LC = *Literature Criticism from 1400 to 1800*
NCLC = *Nineteenth-Century Literature Criticism*
PC = *Poetry Criticism*
SSC = *Short Story Criticism*
TCLC = *Twentieth-Century Literary Criticism*
WLC = *World Literature Criticism, 1500 to the
   Present*

The cross-references

See also CANR 23; CA 85-88;
   obituary CA 116

list all author entries in the following Gale biographical and literary sources:

AAYA = *Authors & Artists for Young Adults*
AITN = *Authors in the News*
BEST = *Bestsellers*
BW = *Black Writers*
CA = *Contemporary Authors*
CAAS = *Contemporary Authors
   Autobiography Series*
CABS = *Contemporary Authors
   Bibliographical Series*
CANR = *Contemporary Authors New
   Revision Series*
CAP = *Contemporary Authors Permanent
   Series*
CDALB = *Concise Dictionary of American
   Literary Biography*
CDBLB = *Concise Dictionary of British
   Literary Biography*

DLB = *Dictionary of Literary Biography*
DLBD = *Dictionary of Literary Biography
   Documentary Series*
DLBY = *Dictionary of Literary Biography Yearbook*
HW = *Hispanic Writers*
JRDA = *Junior DISCovering Authors*
MAICYA = *Major Authors and Illustrators for
   Children and Young Adults*
MTCW = *Major 20th-Century Writers*
NNAL = *Native North American Literature*
SAAS = *Something about the Author Autobiography
   Series*
SATA = *Something about the Author*
YABC = *Yesterday's Authors of Books for Children*

Literary Criticism Series
Cumulative Author Index

Abasiyanik, Sait Faik 1906-1954
See Sait Faik
See also CA 123

Abbey, Edward 1927-1989 . . . . . **CLC 36, 59**
See also CA 45-48; 128; CANR 2, 41

Abbott, Lee K(ittredge) 1947- . . . . . . **CLC 48**
See also CA 124; CANR 51; DLB 130

Abe, Kobo
1924-1993 . . . . **CLC 8, 22, 53, 81;**
DAM NOV
See also CA 65-68; 140; CANR 24; MTCW

Abelard, Peter c. 1079-c. 1142 . . . **CMLC 11**
See also DLB 115

Abell, Kjeld 1901-1961 . . . . **CLC 15**
See also CA 111

Abish, Walter 1931- . . . . **CLC 22**
See also CA 101; CANR 37; DLB 130

Abrahams, Peter (Henry) 1919- . . . . . **CLC 4**
See also BW 1; CA 57-60; CANR 26;
DLB 117; MTCW

Abrams, M(eyer) H(oward) 1912- . . . **CLC 24**
See also CA 57-60; CANR 13, 33; DLB 67

Abse, Dannie
1923- . . . **CLC 7, 29; DAB; DAM POET**
See also CA 53-56; CAAS 1; CANR 4, 46;
DLB 27

Achebe, (Albert) Chinua(lumogu)
1930- . . . . . **CLC 1, 3, 5, 7, 11, 26, 51, 75;**
BLC; DA; DAB; DAC; DAM MST,
MULT, NOV; WLC
See also AAYA 15; BW 2; CA 1-4R;
CANR 6, 26, 47; CLR 20; DLB 117;
MAICYA; MTCW; SATA 40;
SATA-Brief 38

Acker, Kathy 1948- . . . . **CLC 45**
See also CA 117; 122; CANR 55

Ackroyd, Peter 1949- . . . . **CLC 34, 52**
See also CA 123; 127; CANR 51; DLB 155;
INT 127

Acorn, Milton 1923- . . . . **CLC 15; DAC**
See also CA 103; DLB 53; INT 103

Adamov, Arthur
1908-1970 . . . . **CLC 4, 25; DAM DRAM**
See also CA 17-18; 25-28R; CAP 2; MTCW

Adams, Alice (Boyd)
1926- . . . . **CLC 6, 13, 46; SSC 24**
See also CA 81-84; CANR 26, 53;
DLBY 86; INT CANR-26; MTCW

Adams, Andy 1859-1935 . . . . **TCLC 56**
See also YABC 1

Adams, Douglas (Noel)
1952- . . . . **CLC 27, 60; DAM POP**
See also AAYA 4; BEST 89:3; CA 106;
CANR 34; DLBY 83; JRDA

Adams, Francis 1862-1893 . . . . **NCLC 33**

Adams, Henry (Brooks)
1838-1918 . . . . . . **TCLC 4, 52; DA; DAB;**
DAC; DAM MST
See also CA 104; 133; DLB 12, 47

Adams, Richard (George)
1920- . . . . **CLC 4, 5, 18; DAM NOV**
See also AAYA 16; AITN 1, 2; CA 49-52;
CANR 3, 35; CLR 20; JRDA; MAICYA;
MTCW; SATA 7, 69

Adamson, Joy(-Friederike Victoria)
1910-1980 . . . . **CLC 17**
See also CA 69-72; 93-96; CANR 22;
MTCW; SATA 11; SATA-Obit 22

Adcock, Fleur 1934- . . . . **CLC 41**
See also CA 25-28R; CAAS 23; CANR 11,
34; DLB 40

Addams, Charles (Samuel)
1912-1988 . . . . **CLC 30**
See also CA 61-64; 126; CANR 12

Addison, Joseph 1672-1719 . . . . **LC 18**
See also CDBLB 1660-1789; DLB 101

Adler, Alfred (F.) 1870-1937 . . . . . . **TCLC 61**
See also CA 119

Adler, C(arole) S(chwerdtfeger)
1932- . . . . **CLC 35**
See also AAYA 4; CA 89-92; CANR 19,
40; JRDA; MAICYA; SAAS 15;
SATA 26, 63

Adler, Renata 1938- . . . . **CLC 8, 31**
See also CA 49-52; CANR 5, 22, 52;
MTCW

Ady, Endre 1877-1919 . . . . **TCLC 11**
See also CA 107

Aeschylus
525B.C.-456B.C. . . . . **CMLC 11; DA;**
DAB; DAC; DAM DRAM, MST

Afton, Effie
See Harper, Frances Ellen Watkins

Agapida, Fray Antonio
See Irving, Washington

Agee, James (Rufus)
1909-1955 . . . . **TCLC 1, 19; DAM NOV**
See also AITN 1; CA 108; 148;
CDALB 1941-1968; DLB 2, 26, 152

Aghill, Gordon
See Silverberg, Robert

Agnon, S(hmuel) Y(osef Halevi)
1888-1970 . . . . **CLC 4, 8, 14**
See also CA 17-18; 25-28R; CAP 2; MTCW

Agrippa von Nettesheim, Henry Cornelius
1486-1535 . . . . **LC 27**

Aherne, Owen
See Cassill, R(onald) V(erlin)

Ai 1947- . . . . **CLC 4, 14, 69**
See also CA 85-88; CAAS 13; DLB 120

Aickman, Robert (Fordyce)
1914-1981 . . . . **CLC 57**
See also CA 5-8R; CANR 3

Aiken, Conrad (Potter)
1889-1973 . . . . **CLC 1, 3, 5, 10, 52;**
DAM NOV, POET; SSC 9
See also CA 5-8R; 45-48; CANR 4;
CDALB 1929-1941; DLB 9, 45, 102;
MTCW; SATA 3, 30

Aiken, Joan (Delano) 1924- . . . . **CLC 35**
See also AAYA 1; CA 9-12R; CANR 4, 23,
34; CLR 1, 19; DLB 161; JRDA;
MAICYA; MTCW; SAAS 1; SATA 2,
30, 73

Ainsworth, William Harrison
1805-1882 . . . . **NCLC 13**
See also DLB 21; SATA 24

Aitmatov, Chingiz (Torekulovich)
1928- . . . . **CLC 71**
See also CA 103; CANR 38; MTCW;
SATA 56

Akers, Floyd
See Baum, L(yman) Frank

Akhmadulina, Bella Akhatovna
1937- . . . . **CLC 53; DAM POET**
See also CA 65-68

Akhmatova, Anna
1888-1966 . . . . **CLC 11, 25, 64;**
DAM POET; PC 2
See also CA 19-20; 25-28R; CANR 35;
CAP 1; MTCW

Aksakov, Sergei Timofeyvich
1791-1859 . . . . **NCLC 2**

Aksenov, Vassily
See Aksyonov, Vassily (Pavlovich)

Aksyonov, Vassily (Pavlovich)
1932- . . . . **CLC 22, 37**
See also CA 53-56; CANR 12, 48

Akutagawa, Ryunosuke
1892-1927 . . . . **TCLC 16**
See also CA 117; 154

Alain 1868-1951 . . . . **TCLC 41**

Alain-Fournier . . . . **TCLC 6**
See also Fournier, Henri Alban
See also DLB 65

Alarcon, Pedro Antonio de
1833-1891 . . . . **NCLC 1**

Alas (y Urena), Leopoldo (Enrique Garcia)
1852-1901 . . . . **TCLC 29**
See also CA 113; 131; HW

Albee, Edward (Franklin III)
1928- . . . . . . **CLC 1, 2, 3, 5, 9, 11, 13, 25,**
53, 86; DA; DAB; DAC; DAM DRAM,
MST; WLC
See also AITN 1; CA 5-8R; CABS 3;
CANR 8, 54; CDALB 1941-1968; DLB 7;
INT CANR-8; MTCW

Alberti, Rafael 1902- . . . . **CLC 7**
See also CA 85-88; DLB 108

Albert the Great 1200(?)-1280 . . . . **CMLC 16**
See also DLB 115

Alcala-Galiano, Juan Valera y
See Valera y Alcala-Galiano, Juan

Alcott, Amos Bronson 1799-1888 .. **NCLC 1**
See also DLB 1

Alcott, Louisa May
1832-1888 ..... **NCLC 6, 58; DA; DAB;**
DAC; DAM MST, NOV; WLC
See also CDALB 1865-1917; CLR 1, 38;
DLB 1, 42, 79; DLBD 14; JRDA;
MAICYA; YABC 1

Aldanov, M. A.
See Aldanov, Mark (Alexandrovich)

Aldanov, Mark (Alexandrovich)
1886(?)-1957 .... **TCLC 23**
See also CA 118

Aldington, Richard 1892-1962...... **CLC 49**
See also CA 85-88; CANR 45; DLB 20, 36,
100, 149

Aldiss, Brian W(ilson)
1925- .... **CLC 5, 14, 40; DAM NOV**
See also CA 5-8R; CAAS 2; CANR 5, 28;
DLB 14; MTCW; SATA 34

Alegria, Claribel
1924- .... **CLC 75; DAM MULT**
See also CA 131; CAAS 15; DLB 145; HW

Alegria, Fernando 1918-........... **CLC 57**
See also CA 9-12R; CANR 5, 32; HW

Aleichem, Sholom .... **TCLC 1, 35**
See also Rabinovitch, Sholem

Aleixandre, Vicente
1898-1984 .... **CLC 9, 36; DAM POET;**
PC 15
See also CA 85-88; 114; CANR 26;
DLB 108; HW; MTCW

Alepoudelis, Odysseus
See Elytis, Odysseus

Aleshkovsky, Joseph 1929-
See Aleshkovsky, Yuz
See also CA 121; 128

Aleshkovsky, Yuz .... **CLC 44**
See also Aleshkovsky, Joseph

Alexander, Lloyd (Chudley) 1924- .. **CLC 35**
See also AAYA 1; CA 1-4R; CANR 1, 24,
38, 55; CLR 1, 5; DLB 52; JRDA;
MAICYA; MTCW; SAAS 19; SATA 3,
49, 81

Alexie, Sherman (Joseph, Jr.)
1966- .... **CLC 96; DAM MULT**
See also CA 138; NNAL

Alfau, Felipe 1902-.............. **CLC 66**
See also CA 137

Alger, Horatio, Jr. 1832-1899 ..... **NCLC 8**
See also DLB 42; SATA 16

Algren, Nelson 1909-1981 .... **CLC 4, 10, 33**
See also CA 13-16R; 103; CANR 20;
CDALB 1941-1968; DLB 9; DLBY 81,
82; MTCW

Ali, Ahmed 1910-................ **CLC 69**
See also CA 25-28R; CANR 15, 34

Alighieri, Dante 1265-1321 .... **CMLC 3, 18**

Allan, John B.
See Westlake, Donald E(dwin)

Allen, Edward 1948-.............. **CLC 59**

Allen, Paula Gunn
1939- .... **CLC 84; DAM MULT**
See also CA 112; 143; NNAL

Allen, Roland
See Ayckbourn, Alan

Allen, Sarah A.
See Hopkins, Pauline Elizabeth

Allen, Woody
1935- .... **CLC 16, 52; DAM POP**
See also AAYA 10; CA 33-36R; CANR 27,
38; DLB 44; MTCW

Allende, Isabel
1942- .... **CLC 39, 57, 97; DAM MULT,**
NOV; HLC
See also AAYA 18; CA 125; 130;
CANR 51; DLB 145; HW; INT 130;
MTCW

Alleyn, Ellen
See Rossetti, Christina (Georgina)

Allingham, Margery (Louise)
1904-1966 .... **CLC 19**
See also CA 5-8R; 25-28R; CANR 4;
DLB 77; MTCW

Allingham, William 1824-1889 ... **NCLC 25**
See also DLB 35

Allison, Dorothy E. 1949- .... **CLC 78**
See also CA 140

Allston, Washington 1779-1843.... **NCLC 2**
See also DLB 1

Almedingen, E. M. .... **CLC 12**
See also Almedingen, Martha Edith von
See also SATA 3

Almedingen, Martha Edith von 1898-1971
See Almedingen, E. M.
See also CA 1-4R; CANR 1

Almqvist, Carl Jonas Love
1793-1866 .... **NCLC 42**

Alonso, Damaso 1898-1990 .... **CLC 14**
See also CA 110; 131; 130; DLB 108; HW

Alov
See Gogol, Nikolai (Vasilyevich)

Alta 1942-...................... **CLC 19**
See also CA 57-60

Alter, Robert B(ernard) 1935-...... **CLC 34**
See also CA 49-52; CANR 1, 47

Alther, Lisa 1944-.............. **CLC 7, 41**
See also CA 65-68; CANR 12, 30, 51;
MTCW

Altman, Robert 1925-............. **CLC 16**
See also CA 73-76; CANR 43

Alvarez, A(lfred) 1929-.......... **CLC 5, 13**
See also CA 1-4R; CANR 3, 33; DLB 14,
40

Alvarez, Alejandro Rodriguez 1903-1965
See Casona, Alejandro
See also CA 131; 93-96; HW

Alvarez, Julia 1950-.............. **CLC 93**
See also CA 147

Alvaro, Corrado 1896-1956 .... **TCLC 60**

Amado, Jorge
1912- .... **CLC 13, 40; DAM MULT,**
NOV; HLC
See also CA 77-80; CANR 35; DLB 113;
MTCW

Ambler, Eric 1909-............ **CLC 4, 6, 9**
See also CA 9-12R; CANR 7, 38; DLB 77;
MTCW

Amichai, Yehuda 1924- ...... **CLC 9, 22, 57**
See also CA 85-88; CANR 46; MTCW

Amiel, Henri Frederic 1821-1881 .. **NCLC 4**

Amis, Kingsley (William)
1922-1995 ..... **CLC 1, 2, 3, 5, 8, 13, 40,**
44; DA; DAB; DAC; DAM MST, NOV
See also AITN 2; CA 9-12R; 150; CANR 8,
28, 54; CDBLB 1945-1960; DLB 15, 27,
100, 139; INT CANR-8; MTCW

Amis, Martin (Louis)
1949-................ **CLC 4, 9, 38, 62**
See also BEST 90:3; CA 65-68; CANR 8,
27, 54; DLB 14; INT CANR-27

Ammons, A(rchie) R(andolph)
1926-......... **CLC 2, 3, 5, 8, 9, 25, 57;**
DAM POET; PC 16
See also AITN 1; CA 9-12R; CANR 6, 36,
51; DLB 5, 165; MTCW

Amo, Tauraatua i
See Adams, Henry (Brooks)

Anand, Mulk Raj
1905-......... **CLC 23, 93; DAM NOV**
See also CA 65-68; CANR 32; MTCW

Anatol
See Schnitzler, Arthur

Anaya, Rudolfo A(lfonso)
1937- .... **CLC 23; DAM MULT, NOV;**
HLC
See also CA 45-48; CAAS 4; CANR 1, 32,
51; DLB 82; HW 1; MTCW

Andersen, Hans Christian
1805-1875 .... **NCLC 7; DA; DAB;**
DAC; DAM MST, POP; SSC 6; WLC
See also CLR 6; MAICYA; YABC 1

Anderson, C. Farley
See Mencken, H(enry) L(ouis); Nathan,
George Jean

Anderson, Jessica (Margaret) Queale
.... **CLC 37**
See also CA 9-12R; CANR 4

Anderson, Jon (Victor)
1940- .... **CLC 9; DAM POET**
See also CA 25-28R; CANR 20

Anderson, Lindsay (Gordon)
1923-1994 .... **CLC 20**
See also CA 125; 128; 146

Anderson, Maxwell
1888-1959 ...... **TCLC 2; DAM DRAM**
See also CA 105; 152; DLB 7

Anderson, Poul (William) 1926- .... **CLC 15**
See also AAYA 5; CA 1-4R; CAAS 2;
CANR 2, 15, 34; DLB 8; INT CANR-15;
MTCW; SATA 90; SATA-Brief 39

Anderson, Robert (Woodruff)
1917- .... **CLC 23; DAM DRAM**
See also AITN 1; CA 21-24R; CANR 32;
DLB 7

Anderson, Sherwood
1876-1941 .... **TCLC 1, 10, 24; DA;**
DAB; DAC; DAM MST, NOV; SSC 1;
WLC
See also CA 104; 121; CDALB 1917-1929;
DLB 4, 9, 86; DLBD 1; MTCW

Andier, Pierre
  See Desnos, Robert

Andouard
  See Giraudoux, (Hippolyte) Jean

Andrade, Carlos Drummond de . . . . . . **CLC 18**
  See also Drummond de Andrade, Carlos

Andrade, Mario de   1893-1945 . . . . . **TCLC 43**

Andreae, Johann V(alentin)
  1586-1654 . . . . **LC 32**
  See also DLB 164

Andreas-Salome, Lou   1861-1937 . . . **TCLC 56**
  See also DLB 66

Andrewes, Lancelot   1555-1626 . . . . **LC 5**
  See also DLB 151, 172

Andrews, Cicily Fairfield
  See West, Rebecca

Andrews, Elton V.
  See Pohl, Frederik

Andreyev, Leonid (Nikolaevich)
  1871-1919 . . . . **TCLC 3**
  See also CA 104

Andric, Ivo   1892-1975 . . . . **CLC 8**
  See also CA 81-84; 57-60; CANR 43;
  DLB 147; MTCW

Angelique, Pierre
  See Bataille, Georges

Angell, Roger   1920- . . . . **CLC 26**
  See also CA 57-60; CANR 13, 44; DLB 171

Angelou, Maya
  1928- . . . . **CLC 12, 35, 64, 77; BLC; DA;**
    DAB; DAC; DAM MST, MULT, POET,
                                                   POP
  See also AAYA 7; BW 2; CA 65-68;
  CANR 19, 42; DLB 38; MTCW;
  SATA 49

Annensky, Innokenty Fyodorovich
  1856-1909 . . . . **TCLC 14**
  See also CA 110

Anon, Charles Robert
  See Pessoa, Fernando (Antonio Nogueira)

Anouilh, Jean (Marie Lucien Pierre)
  1910-1987 . . . . . . **CLC 1, 3, 8, 13, 40, 50;**
                                             DAM DRAM
  See also CA 17-20R; 123; CANR 32;
  MTCW

Anthony, Florence
  See Ai

Anthony, John
  See Ciardi, John (Anthony)

Anthony, Peter
  See Shaffer, Anthony (Joshua); Shaffer,
  Peter (Levin)

Anthony, Piers   1934- . . **CLC 35; DAM POP**
  See also AAYA 11; CA 21-24R; CANR 28;
  DLB 8; MTCW; SAAS 22; SATA 84

Antoine, Marc
  See Proust, (Valentin-Louis-George-Eugene-)
  Marcel

Antoninus, Brother
  See Everson, William (Oliver)

Antonioni, Michelangelo   1912- . . . . . **CLC 20**
  See also CA 73-76; CANR 45

Antschel, Paul   1920-1970
  See Celan, Paul
  See also CA 85-88; CANR 33; MTCW

Anwar, Chairil   1922-1949 . . . . **TCLC 22**
  See also CA 121

Apollinaire, Guillaume
  1880-1918 . . . . **TCLC 3, 8, 51;**
                                           DAM POET; PC 7
  See also Kostrowitzki, Wilhelm Apollinaris
  de
  See also CA 152

Appelfeld, Aharon   1932- . . . . **CLC 23, 47**
  See also CA 112; 133

Apple, Max (Isaac)   1941- . . . . **CLC 9, 33**
  See also CA 81-84; CANR 19, 54; DLB 130

Appleman, Philip (Dean)   1926- . . . . . **CLC 51**
  See also CA 13-16R; CAAS 18; CANR 6,
  29

Appleton, Lawrence
  See Lovecraft, H(oward) P(hillips)

Apteryx
  See Eliot, T(homas) S(tearns)

Apuleius, (Lucius Madaurensis)
  125(?)-175(?) . . . . **CMLC 1**

Aquin, Hubert   1929-1977 . . . . **CLC 15**
  See also CA 105; DLB 53

Aragon, Louis
  1897-1982 . . . . . **CLC 3, 22; DAM NOV,**
                                                   POET
  See also CA 69-72; 108; CANR 28;
  DLB 72; MTCW

Arany, Janos   1817-1882 . . . . **NCLC 34**

Arbuthnot, John   1667-1735 . . . . **LC 1**
  See also DLB 101

Archer, Herbert Winslow
  See Mencken, H(enry) L(ouis)

Archer, Jeffrey (Howard)
  1940- . . . . **CLC 28; DAM POP**
  See also AAYA 16; BEST 89:3; CA 77-80;
  CANR 22, 52; INT CANR-22

Archer, Jules   1915- . . . . **CLC 12**
  See also CA 9-12R; CANR 6; SAAS 5;
  SATA 4, 85

Archer, Lee
  See Ellison, Harlan (Jay)

Arden, John
  1930- . . . . . . **CLC 6, 13, 15; DAM DRAM**
  See also CA 13-16R; CAAS 4; CANR 31;
  DLB 13; MTCW

Arenas, Reinaldo
  1943-1990 . . . . . . **CLC 41; DAM MULT;**
                                                     HLC
  See also CA 124; 128; 133; DLB 145; HW

Arendt, Hannah   1906-1975 . . . . . **CLC 66, 98**
  See also CA 17-20R; 61-64; CANR 26;
  MTCW

Aretino, Pietro   1492-1556 . . . . **LC 12**

Arghezi, Tudor . . . . **CLC 80**
  See also Theodorescu, Ion N.

Arguedas, Jose Maria
  1911-1969 . . . . **CLC 10, 18**
  See also CA 89-92; DLB 113; HW

Argueta, Manlio   1936- . . . . **CLC 31**
  See also CA 131; DLB 145; HW

Ariosto, Ludovico   1474-1533 . . . . **LC 6**

Aristides
  See Epstein, Joseph

Aristophanes
  450B.C.-385B.C. . . . . **CMLC 4; DA;**
    DAB; DAC; DAM DRAM, MST; DC 2

Arlt, Roberto (Godofredo Christophersen)
  1900-1942 . . . . . **TCLC 29; DAM MULT;**
                                                     HLC
  See also CA 123; 131; HW

Armah, Ayi Kwei
  1939- . . . . **CLC 5, 33; BLC;**
                                       DAM MULT, POET
  See also BW 1; CA 61-64; CANR 21;
  DLB 117; MTCW

Armatrading, Joan   1950- . . . . **CLC 17**
  See also CA 114

Arnette, Robert
  See Silverberg, Robert

Arnim, Achim von (Ludwig Joachim von
  Arnim)   1781-1831 . . . . **NCLC 5**
  See also DLB 90

Arnim, Bettina von   1785-1859 . . . . **NCLC 38**
  See also DLB 90

Arnold, Matthew
  1822-1888 . . . . . **NCLC 6, 29; DA; DAB;**
    DAC; DAM MST, POET; PC 5; WLC
  See also CDBLB 1832-1890; DLB 32, 57

Arnold, Thomas   1795-1842 . . . . . . **NCLC 18**
  See also DLB 55

Arnow, Harriette (Louisa) Simpson
  1908-1986 . . . . **CLC 2, 7, 18**
  See also CA 9-12R; 118; CANR 14; DLB 6;
  MTCW; SATA 42; SATA-Obit 47

Arp, Hans
  See Arp, Jean

Arp, Jean   1887-1966 . . . . **CLC 5**
  See also CA 81-84; 25-28R; CANR 42

Arrabal
  See Arrabal, Fernando

Arrabal, Fernando   1932- . . . **CLC 2, 9, 18, 58**
  See also CA 9-12R; CANR 15

Arrick, Fran . . . . **CLC 30**
  See also Gaberman, Judie Angell

Artaud, Antonin (Marie Joseph)
  1896-1948 . . . **TCLC 3, 36; DAM DRAM**
  See also CA 104; 149

Arthur, Ruth M(abel)   1905-1979 . . . . **CLC 12**
  See also CA 9-12R; 85-88; CANR 4;
  SATA 7, 26

Artsybashev, Mikhail (Petrovich)
  1878-1927 . . . . **TCLC 31**

Arundel, Honor (Morfydd)
  1919-1973 . . . . **CLC 17**
  See also CA 21-22; 41-44R; CAP 2;
  CLR 35; SATA 4; SATA-Obit 24

Arzner, Dorothy   1897-1979 . . . . **CLC 98**

Asch, Sholem   1880-1957 . . . . **TCLC 3**
  See also CA 105

Ash, Shalom
  See Asch, Sholem

Ashbery, John (Lawrence)
1927- ...... CLC 2, 3, 4, 6, 9, 13, 15, 25,
41, 77; DAM POET
See also CA 5-8R; CANR 9, 37; DLB 5,
165; DLBY 81; INT CANR-9; MTCW

Ashdown, Clifford
See Freeman, R(ichard) Austin

Ashe, Gordon
See Creasey, John

Ashton-Warner, Sylvia (Constance)
1908-1984 .... CLC 19
See also CA 69-72; 112; CANR 29; MTCW

Asimov, Isaac
1920-1992 ..... CLC 1, 3, 9, 19, 26, 76,
92; DAM POP
See also AAYA 13; BEST 90:2; CA 1-4R;
137; CANR 2, 19, 36; CLR 12; DLB 8;
DLBY 92; INT CANR-19; JRDA;
MAICYA; MTCW; SATA 1, 26, 74

Assis, Joaquim Maria Machado de
See Machado de Assis, Joaquim Maria

Astley, Thea (Beatrice May)
1925- .... CLC 41
See also CA 65-68; CANR 11, 43

Aston, James
See White, T(erence) H(anbury)

Asturias, Miguel Angel
1899-1974 .... CLC 3, 8, 13;
DAM MULT, NOV; HLC
See also CA 25-28; 49-52; CANR 32;
CAP 2; DLB 113; HW; MTCW

Atares, Carlos Saura
See Saura (Atares), Carlos

Atheling, William
See Pound, Ezra (Weston Loomis)

Atheling, William, Jr.
See Blish, James (Benjamin)

Atherton, Gertrude (Franklin Horn)
1857-1948 .... TCLC 2
See also CA 104; DLB 9, 78

Atherton, Lucius
See Masters, Edgar Lee

Atkins, Jack
See Harris, Mark

Attaway, William (Alexander)
1911-1986 .... CLC 92; BLC;
DAM MULT
See also BW 2; CA 143; DLB 76

Atticus
See Fleming, Ian (Lancaster)

Atwood, Margaret (Eleanor)
1939- ..... CLC 2, 3, 4, 8, 13, 15, 44,
84; DA; DAB; DAC; DAM MST, NOV,
POET; PC 8; SSC 2; WLC
See also AAYA 12; BEST 89:2; CA 49-52;
CANR 3, 24, 33; DLB 53;
INT CANR-24; MTCW; SATA 50

Aubigny, Pierre d'
See Mencken, H(enry) L(ouis)

Aubin, Penelope 1685-1731(?) .... LC 9
See also DLB 39

Auchincloss, Louis (Stanton)
1917- .... CLC 4, 6, 9, 18, 45;
DAM NOV; SSC 22
See also CA 1-4R; CANR 6, 29, 55; DLB 2;
DLBY 80; INT CANR-29; MTCW

Auden, W(ystan) H(ugh)
1907-1973 ..... CLC 1, 2, 3, 4, 6, 9, 11,
14, 43; DA; DAB; DAC; DAM DRAM,
MST, POET; PC 1; WLC
See also AAYA 18; CA 9-12R; 45-48;
CANR 5; CDBLB 1914-1945; DLB 10,
20; MTCW

Audiberti, Jacques
1900-1965 ...... CLC 38; DAM DRAM
See also CA 25-28R

Audubon, John James
1785-1851 .... NCLC 47

Auel, Jean M(arie)
1936- .... CLC 31; DAM POP
See also AAYA 7; BEST 90:4; CA 103;
CANR 21; INT CANR-21; SATA 91

Auerbach, Erich 1892-1957 ...... TCLC 43
See also CA 118

Augier, Emile 1820-1889 .... NCLC 31

August, John
See De Voto, Bernard (Augustine)

Augustine, St. 354-430 ...... CMLC 6; DAB

Aurelius
See Bourne, Randolph S(illiman)

Aurobindo, Sri 1872-1950 .... TCLC 63

Austen, Jane
1775-1817 ..... NCLC 1, 13, 19, 33, 51;
DA; DAB; DAC; DAM MST, NOV;
WLC
See also AAYA 19; CDBLB 1789-1832;
DLB 116

Auster, Paul 1947- .... CLC 47
See also CA 69-72; CANR 23, 52

Austin, Frank
See Faust, Frederick (Schiller)

Austin, Mary (Hunter)
1868-1934 .... TCLC 25
See also CA 109; DLB 9, 78

Autran Dourado, Waldomiro
See Dourado, (Waldomiro Freitas) Autran

Averroes 1126-1198 .... CMLC 7
See also DLB 115

Avicenna 980-1037 .... CMLC 16
See also DLB 115

Avison, Margaret
1918- .... CLC 2, 4, 97; DAC;
DAM POET
See also CA 17-20R; DLB 53; MTCW

Axton, David
See Koontz, Dean R(ay)

Ayckbourn, Alan
1939- ...... CLC 5, 8, 18, 33, 74; DAB;
DAM DRAM
See also CA 21-24R; CANR 31; DLB 13;
MTCW

Aydy, Catherine
See Tennant, Emma (Christina)

Ayme, Marcel (Andre) 1902-1967 ... CLC 11
See also CA 89-92; CLR 25; DLB 72;
SATA 91

Ayrton, Michael 1921-1975 .... CLC 7
See also CA 5-8R; 61-64; CANR 9, 21

Azorin .... CLC 11
See also Martinez Ruiz, Jose

Azuela, Mariano
1873-1952 ..... TCLC 3; DAM MULT;
HLC
See also CA 104; 131; HW; MTCW

Baastad, Babbis Friis
See Friis-Baastad, Babbis Ellinor

Bab
See Gilbert, W(illiam) S(chwenck)

Babbis, Eleanor
See Friis-Baastad, Babbis Ellinor

Babel, Isaak (Emmanuilovich)
1894-1941(?) ...... TCLC 2, 13; SSC 16
See also CA 104

Babits, Mihaly 1883-1941 .... TCLC 14
See also CA 114

Babur 1483-1530 .... LC 18

Bacchelli, Riccardo 1891-1985 ..... CLC 19
See also CA 29-32R; 117

Bach, Richard (David)
1936- ...... CLC 14; DAM NOV, POP
See also AITN 1; BEST 89:2; CA 9-12R;
CANR 18; MTCW; SATA 13

Bachman, Richard
See King, Stephen (Edwin)

Bachmann, Ingeborg 1926-1973..... CLC 69
See also CA 93-96; 45-48; DLB 85

Bacon, Francis 1561-1626 .... LC 18, 32
See also CDBLB Before 1660; DLB 151

Bacon, Roger 1214(?)-1292 ...... CMLC 14
See also DLB 115

Bacovia, George .... TCLC 24
See also Vasiliu, Gheorghe

Badanes, Jerome 1937- .... CLC 59

Bagehot, Walter 1826-1877 ...... NCLC 10
See also DLB 55

Bagnold, Enid
1889-1981 ...... CLC 25; DAM DRAM
See also CA 5-8R; 103; CANR 5, 40;
DLB 13, 160; MAICYA; SATA 1, 25

Bagritsky, Eduard 1895-1934 ..... TCLC 60

Bagrjana, Elisaveta
See Belcheva, Elisaveta

Bagryana, Elisaveta .... CLC 10
See also Belcheva, Elisaveta
See also DLB 147

Bailey, Paul 1937- .... CLC 45
See also CA 21-24R; CANR 16; DLB 14

Baillie, Joanna 1762-1851 .... NCLC 2
See also DLB 93

Bainbridge, Beryl (Margaret)
1933- .... CLC 4, 5, 8, 10, 14, 18, 22, 62;
DAM NOV
See also CA 21-24R; CANR 24, 55;
DLB 14; MTCW

Baker, Elliott 1922- .... CLC 8
See also CA 45-48; CANR 2

Baker, Jean H. .... TCLC 3, 10
See also Russell, George William

Baker, Nicholson
1957- .... CLC 61; DAM POP
See also CA 135

Baker, Ray Stannard 1870-1946 ... TCLC 47
See also CA 118

Baker, Russell (Wayne) 1925-...... **CLC 31**
See also BEST 89:4; CA 57-60; CANR 11,
41; MTCW

Bakhtin, M.
See Bakhtin, Mikhail Mikhailovich

Bakhtin, M. M.
See Bakhtin, Mikhail Mikhailovich

Bakhtin, Mikhail
See Bakhtin, Mikhail Mikhailovich

Bakhtin, Mikhail Mikhailovich
1895-1975 .... **CLC 83**
See also CA 128; 113

Bakshi, Ralph 1938(?)-........... **CLC 26**
See also CA 112; 138

Bakunin, Mikhail (Alexandrovich)
1814-1876 .... **NCLC 25, 58**

Baldwin, James (Arthur)
1924-1987 ...... **CLC 1, 2, 3, 4, 5, 8, 13,
15, 17, 42, 50, 67, 90; BLC; DA; DAB;
DAC; DAM MST, MULT, NOV, POP;
DC 1; SSC 10; WLC**
See also AAYA 4; BW 1; CA 1-4R; 124;
CABS 1; CANR 3, 24;
CDALB 1941-1968; DLB 2, 7, 33;
DLBY 87; MTCW; SATA 9;
SATA-Obit 54

Ballard, J(ames) G(raham)
1930- .... **CLC 3, 6, 14, 36; DAM NOV,
POP; SSC 1**
See also AAYA 3; CA 5-8R; CANR 15, 39;
DLB 14; MTCW

Balmont, Konstantin (Dmitriyevich)
1867-1943 .... **TCLC 11**
See also CA 109

Balzac, Honore de
1799-1850 .... **NCLC 5, 35, 53; DA;
DAB; DAC; DAM MST, NOV; SSC 5;
WLC**
See also DLB 119

Bambara, Toni Cade
1939-1995 ...... **CLC 19, 88; BLC; DA;
DAC; DAM MST, MULT**
See also AAYA 5; BW 2; CA 29-32R; 150;
CANR 24, 49; DLB 38; MTCW

Bamdad, A.
See Shamlu, Ahmad

Banat, D. R.
See Bradbury, Ray (Douglas)

Bancroft, Laura
See Baum, L(yman) Frank

Banim, John 1798-1842 .... **NCLC 13**
See also DLB 116, 158, 159

Banim, Michael 1796-1874 ...... **NCLC 13**
See also DLB 158, 159

Banks, Iain
See Banks, Iain M(enzies)

Banks, Iain M(enzies) 1954-....... **CLC 34**
See also CA 123; 128; INT 128

Banks, Lynne Reid .... **CLC 23**
See also Reid Banks, Lynne
See also AAYA 6

Banks, Russell 1940- .... **CLC 37, 72**
See also CA 65-68; CAAS 15; CANR 19,
52; DLB 130

Banville, John 1945-.............. **CLC 46**
See also CA 117; 128; DLB 14; INT 128

Banville, Theodore (Faullain) de
1832-1891 .... **NCLC 9**

Baraka, Amiri
1934- .... **CLC 1, 2, 3, 5, 10, 14, 33;
BLC; DA; DAC; DAM MST, MULT,
POET, POP; DC 6; PC 4**
See also Jones, LeRoi
See also BW 2; CA 21-24R; CABS 3;
CANR 27, 38; CDALB 1941-1968;
DLB 5, 7, 16, 38; DLBD 8; MTCW

Barbauld, Anna Laetitia
1743-1825 .... **NCLC 50**
See also DLB 107, 109, 142, 158

Barbellion, W. N. P. .... **TCLC 24**
See also Cummings, Bruce F(rederick)

Barbera, Jack (Vincent) 1945-...... **CLC 44**
See also CA 110; CANR 45

Barbey d'Aurevilly, Jules Amedee
1808-1889 .... **NCLC 1; SSC 17**
See also DLB 119

Barbusse, Henri 1873-1935 .... **TCLC 5**
See also CA 105; 154; DLB 65

Barclay, Bill
See Moorcock, Michael (John)

Barclay, William Ewert
See Moorcock, Michael (John)

Barea, Arturo 1897-1957 .... **TCLC 14**
See also CA 111

Barfoot, Joan 1946-.............. **CLC 18**
See also CA 105

Baring, Maurice 1874-1945 .... **TCLC 8**
See also CA 105; DLB 34

Barker, Clive 1952- ... **CLC 52; DAM POP**
See also AAYA 10; BEST 90:3; CA 121;
129; INT 129; MTCW

Barker, George Granville
1913-1991 ..... **CLC 8, 48; DAM POET**
See also CA 9-12R; 135; CANR 7, 38;
DLB 20; MTCW

Barker, Harley Granville
See Granville-Barker, Harley
See also DLB 10

Barker, Howard 1946-............. **CLC 37**
See also CA 102; DLB 13

Barker, Pat(ricia) 1943-........ **CLC 32, 94**
See also CA 117; 122; CANR 50; INT 122

Barlow, Joel 1754-1812 .... **NCLC 23**
See also DLB 37

Barnard, Mary (Ethel) 1909-....... **CLC 48**
See also CA 21-22; CAP 2

Barnes, Djuna
1892-1982 ... **CLC 3, 4, 8, 11, 29; SSC 3**
See also CA 9-12R; 107; CANR 16, 55;
DLB 4, 9, 45; MTCW

Barnes, Julian (Patrick)
1946- .... **CLC 42; DAB**
See also CA 102; CANR 19, 54; DLBY 93

Barnes, Peter 1931-............. **CLC 5, 56**
See also CA 65-68; CAAS 12; CANR 33,
34; DLB 13; MTCW

Baroja (y Nessi), Pio
1872-1956 .... **TCLC 8; HLC**
See also CA 104

Baron, David
See Pinter, Harold

Baron Corvo
See Rolfe, Frederick (William Serafino
Austin Lewis Mary)

Barondess, Sue K(aufman)
1926-1977 .... **CLC 8**
See also Kaufman, Sue
See also CA 1-4R; 69-72; CANR 1

Baron de Teive
See Pessoa, Fernando (Antonio Nogueira)

Barres, Maurice 1862-1923 .... **TCLC 47**
See also DLB 123

Barreto, Afonso Henrique de Lima
See Lima Barreto, Afonso Henrique de

Barrett, (Roger) Syd 1946- .... **CLC 35**

Barrett, William (Christopher)
1913-1992 .... **CLC 27**
See also CA 13-16R; 139; CANR 11;
INT CANR-11

Barrie, J(ames) M(atthew)
1860-1937 .... **TCLC 2; DAB;
DAM DRAM**
See also CA 104; 136; CDBLB 1890-1914;
CLR 16; DLB 10, 141, 156; MAICYA;
YABC 1

Barrington, Michael
See Moorcock, Michael (John)

Barrol, Grady
See Bograd, Larry

Barry, Mike
See Malzberg, Barry N(athaniel)

Barry, Philip 1896-1949.......... **TCLC 11**
See also CA 109; DLB 7

Bart, Andre Schwarz
See Schwarz-Bart, Andre

Barth, John (Simmons)
1930- ...... **CLC 1, 2, 3, 5, 7, 9, 10, 14,
27, 51, 89; DAM NOV; SSC 10**
See also AITN 1, 2; CA 1-4R; CABS 1;
CANR 5, 23, 49; DLB 2; MTCW

Barthelme, Donald
1931-1989 ...... **CLC 1, 2, 3, 5, 6, 8, 13,
23, 46, 59; DAM NOV; SSC 2**
See also CA 21-24R; 129; CANR 20;
DLB 2; DLBY 80, 89; MTCW; SATA 7;
SATA-Obit 62

Barthelme, Frederick 1943-........ **CLC 36**
See also CA 114; 122; DLBY 85; INT 122

Barthes, Roland (Gerard)
1915-1980 .... **CLC 24, 83**
See also CA 130; 97-100; MTCW

Barzun, Jacques (Martin) 1907-.... **CLC 51**
See also CA 61-64; CANR 22

Bashevis, Isaac
See Singer, Isaac Bashevis

Bashkirtseff, Marie 1859-1884 ... **NCLC 27**

Basho
See Matsuo Basho

Bass, Kingsley B., Jr.
See Bullins, Ed

Bass, Rick 1958-................. **CLC 79**
See also CA 126; CANR 53

Belser, Reimond Karel Maria de 1929-
See Ruyslinck, Ward
See also CA 152

Bely, Andrey .... **TCLC 7; PC 11**
See also Bugayev, Boris Nikolayevich

Benary, Margot
See Benary-Isbert, Margot

Benary-Isbert, Margot 1889-1979 ... **CLC 12**
See also CA 5-8R; 89-92; CANR 4;
CLR 12; MAICYA; SATA 2;
SATA-Obit 21

Benavente (y Martinez), Jacinto
1866-1954 ..... **TCLC 3; DAM DRAM,
MULT**
See also CA 106; 131; HW; MTCW

Benchley, Peter (Bradford)
1940- ..... **CLC 4, 8; DAM NOV, POP**
See also AAYA 14; AITN 2; CA 17-20R;
CANR 12, 35; MTCW; SATA 3, 89

Benchley, Robert (Charles)
1889-1945 .... **TCLC 1, 55**
See also CA 105; 153; DLB 11

Benda, Julien 1867-1956 .... **TCLC 60**
See also CA 120; 154

Benedict, Ruth 1887-1948 .... **TCLC 60**

Benedikt, Michael 1935- .... **CLC 4, 14**
See also CA 13-16R; CANR 7; DLB 5

Benet, Juan 1927-................ **CLC 28**
See also CA 143

Benet, Stephen Vincent
1898-1943 ...... **TCLC 7; DAM POET;
SSC 10**
See also CA 104; 152; DLB 4, 48, 102;
YABC 1

Benet, William Rose
1886-1950 ...... **TCLC 28; DAM POET**
See also CA 118; 152; DLB 45

Benford, Gregory (Albert) 1941-.... **CLC 52**
See also CA 69-72; CANR 12, 24, 49;
DLBY 82

Bengtsson, Frans (Gunnar)
1894-1954 .... **TCLC 48**

Benjamin, David
See Slavitt, David R(ytman)

Benjamin, Lois
See Gould, Lois

Benjamin, Walter 1892-1940 ...... **TCLC 39**

Benn, Gottfried 1886-1956........ **TCLC 3**
See also CA 106; 153; DLB 56

Bennett, Alan
1934- ... **CLC 45, 77; DAB; DAM MST**
See also CA 103; CANR 35, 55; MTCW

Bennett, (Enoch) Arnold
1867-1931 ....**TCLC 5, 20**
See also CA 106; CDBLB 1890-1914;
DLB 10, 34, 98, 135

Bennett, Elizabeth
See Mitchell, Margaret (Munnerlyn)

Bennett, George Harold 1930-
See Bennett, Hal
See also BW 1; CA 97-100

Bennett, Hal .... **CLC 5**
See also Bennett, George Harold
See also DLB 33

Bennett, Jay 1912-.............. **CLC 35**
See also AAYA 10; CA 69-72; CANR 11,
42; JRDA; SAAS 4; SATA 41, 87;
SATA-Brief 27

Bennett, Louise (Simone)
1919- ..... **CLC 28; BLC; DAM MULT**
See also BW 2; CA 151; DLB 117

Benson, E(dward) F(rederic)
1867-1940 .... **TCLC 27**
See also CA 114; DLB 135, 153

Benson, Jackson J. 1930-......... **CLC 34**
See also CA 25-28R; DLB 111

Benson, Sally 1900-1972 .... **CLC 17**
See also CA 19-20; 37-40R; CAP 1;
SATA 1, 35; SATA-Obit 27

Benson, Stella 1892-1933........ **TCLC 17**
See also CA 117; 154; DLB 36, 162

Bentham, Jeremy 1748-1832 ..... **NCLC 38**
See also DLB 107, 158

Bentley, E(dmund) C(lerihew)
1875-1956 .... **TCLC 12**
See also CA 108; DLB 70

Bentley, Eric (Russell) 1916-....... **CLC 24**
See also CA 5-8R; CANR 6; INT CANR-6

Beranger, Pierre Jean de
1780-1857 .... **NCLC 34**

Berdyaev, Nicolas
See Berdyaev, Nikolai (Aleksandrovich)

Berdyaev, Nikolai (Aleksandrovich)
1874-1948 .... **TCLC 67**
See also CA 120

Berendt, John (Lawrence) 1939-.... **CLC 86**
See also CA 146

Berger, Colonel
See Malraux, (Georges-)Andre

Berger, John (Peter) 1926- ...... **CLC 2, 19**
See also CA 81-84; CANR 51; DLB 14

Berger, Melvin H. 1927-.......... **CLC 12**
See also CA 5-8R; CANR 4; CLR 32;
SAAS 2; SATA 5, 88

Berger, Thomas (Louis)
1924-......... **CLC 3, 5, 8, 11, 18, 38;
DAM NOV**
See also CA 1-4R; CANR 5, 28, 51; DLB 2;
DLBY 80; INT CANR-28; MTCW

Bergman, (Ernst) Ingmar
1918- .... **CLC 16, 72**
See also CA 81-84; CANR 33

Bergson, Henri 1859-1941 .... **TCLC 32**

Bergstein, Eleanor 1938-.......... **CLC 4**
See also CA 53-56; CANR 5

Berkoff, Steven 1937-............. **CLC 56**
See also CA 104

Bermant, Chaim (Icyk) 1929- ...... **CLC 40**
See also CA 57-60; CANR 6, 31

Bern, Victoria
See Fisher, M(ary) F(rances) K(ennedy)

Bernanos, (Paul Louis) Georges
1888-1948 .... **TCLC 3**
See also CA 104; 130; DLB 72

Bernard, April 1956- .... **CLC 59**
See also CA 131

Berne, Victoria
See Fisher, M(ary) F(rances) K(ennedy)

Bernhard, Thomas
1931-1989 .... **CLC 3, 32, 61**
See also CA 85-88; 127; CANR 32;
DLB 85, 124; MTCW

Berriault, Gina 1926-............. **CLC 54**
See also CA 116; 129; DLB 130

Berrigan, Daniel 1921-............. **CLC 4**
See also CA 33-36R; CAAS 1; CANR 11,
43; DLB 5

Berrigan, Edmund Joseph Michael, Jr.
1934-1983
See Berrigan, Ted
See also CA 61-64; 110; CANR 14

Berrigan, Ted. .... **CLC 37**
See also Berrigan, Edmund Joseph Michael,
Jr.
See also DLB 5, 169

Berry, Charles Edward Anderson 1931-
See Berry, Chuck
See also CA 115

Berry, Chuck. .... **CLC 17**
See also Berry, Charles Edward Anderson

Berry, Jonas
See Ashbery, John (Lawrence)

Berry, Wendell (Erdman)
1934- .... **CLC 4, 6, 8, 27, 46;
DAM POET**
See also AITN 1; CA 73-76; CANR 50;
DLB 5, 6

Berryman, John
1914-1972 ...... **CLC 1, 2, 3, 4, 6, 8, 10,
13, 25, 62; DAM POET**
See also CA 13-16; 33-36R; CABS 2;
CANR 35; CAP 1; CDALB 1941-1968;
DLB 48; MTCW

Bertolucci, Bernardo 1940- .... **CLC 16**
See also CA 106

Bertrand, Aloysius 1807-1841 .... **NCLC 31**

Bertran de Born c. 1140-1215..... **CMLC 5**

Besant, Annie (Wood) 1847-1933 ... **TCLC 9**
See also CA 105

Bessie, Alvah 1904-1985........... **CLC 23**
See also CA 5-8R; 116; CANR 2; DLB 26

Bethlen, T. D.
See Silverberg, Robert

Beti, Mongo.... **CLC 27; BLC; DAM MULT**
See also Biyidi, Alexandre

Betjeman, John
1906-1984 .... **CLC 2, 6, 10, 34, 43;
DAB; DAM MST, POET**
See also CA 9-12R; 112; CANR 33;
CDBLB 1945-1960; DLB 20; DLBY 84;
MTCW

Bettelheim, Bruno 1903-1990 ...... **CLC 79**
See also CA 81-84; 131; CANR 23; MTCW

Betti, Ugo 1892-1953 .... **TCLC 5**
See also CA 104

Betts, Doris (Waugh) 1932-.... **CLC 3, 6, 28**
See also CA 13-16R; CANR 9; DLBY 82;
INT CANR-9

Bevan, Alistair
See Roberts, Keith (John Kingston)

Bialik, Chaim Nachman
1873-1934 .... **TCLC 25**

Bickerstaff, Isaac
See Swift, Jonathan

Bidart, Frank 1939- . . . . **CLC 33**
See also CA 140

Bienek, Horst 1930- . . . . **CLC 7, 11**
See also CA 73-76; DLB 75

Bierce, Ambrose (Gwinett)
1842-1914(?) . . . . **TCLC 1, 7, 44; DA;**
DAC; DAM MST; SSC 9; WLC
See also CA 104; 139; CDALB 1865-1917;
DLB 11, 12, 23, 71, 74

Biggers, Earl Derr 1884-1933 . . . . . **TCLC 65**
See also CA 108; 153

Billings, Josh
See Shaw, Henry Wheeler

Billington, (Lady) Rachel (Mary)
1942- . . . . **CLC 43**
See also AITN 2; CA 33-36R; CANR 44

Binyon, T(imothy) J(ohn) 1936- . . . . **CLC 34**
See also CA 111; CANR 28

Bioy Casares, Adolfo
1914- . . . . **CLC 4, 8, 13, 88;**
DAM MULT; HLC; SSC 17
See also CA 29-32R; CANR 19, 43;
DLB 113; HW; MTCW

Bird, Cordwainer
See Ellison, Harlan (Jay)

Bird, Robert Montgomery
1806-1854 . . . . **NCLC 1**

Birney, (Alfred) Earle
1904- . . . . **CLC 1, 4, 6, 11; DAC;**
DAM MST, POET
See also CA 1-4R; CANR 5, 20; DLB 88;
MTCW

Bishop, Elizabeth
1911-1979 . . . . . . **CLC 1, 4, 9, 13, 15, 32;**
DA; DAC; DAM MST, POET; PC 3
See also CA 5-8R; 89-92; CABS 2;
CANR 26; CDALB 1968-1988; DLB 5,
169; MTCW; SATA-Obit 24

Bishop, John 1935- . . . . **CLC 10**
See also CA 105

Bissett, Bill 1939- . . . . **CLC 18; PC 14**
See also CA 69-72; CAAS 19; CANR 15;
DLB 53; MTCW

Bitov, Andrei (Georgievich) 1937- . . . **CLC 57**
See also CA 142

Biyidi, Alexandre 1932-
See Beti, Mongo
See also BW 1; CA 114; 124; MTCW

Bjarme, Brynjolf
See Ibsen, Henrik (Johan)

Bjornson, Bjornstjerne (Martinius)
1832-1910 . . . . **TCLC 7, 37**
See also CA 104

Black, Robert
See Holdstock, Robert P.

Blackburn, Paul 1926-1971 . . . . . **CLC 9, 43**
See also CA 81-84; 33-36R; CANR 34;
DLB 16; DLBY 81

Black Elk
1863-1950 . . . . . **TCLC 33; DAM MULT**
See also CA 144; NNAL

Black Hobart
See Sanders, (James) Ed(ward)

Blacklin, Malcolm
See Chambers, Aidan

Blackmore, R(ichard) D(oddridge)
1825-1900 . . . . **TCLC 27**
See also CA 120; DLB 18

Blackmur, R(ichard) P(almer)
1904-1965 . . . . **CLC 2, 24**
See also CA 11-12; 25-28R; CAP 1; DLB 63

Black Tarantula
See Acker, Kathy

Blackwood, Algernon (Henry)
1869-1951 . . . . **TCLC 5**
See also CA 105; 150; DLB 153, 156

Blackwood, Caroline 1931-1996 . . . **CLC 6, 9**
See also CA 85-88; 151; CANR 32;
DLB 14; MTCW

Blade, Alexander
See Hamilton, Edmond; Silverberg, Robert

Blaga, Lucian 1895-1961 . . . . **CLC 75**

Blair, Eric (Arthur) 1903-1950
See Orwell, George
See also CA 104; 132; DA; DAB; DAC;
DAM MST, NOV; MTCW; SATA 29

Blais, Marie-Claire
1939- . . . . **CLC 2, 4, 6, 13, 22; DAC;**
DAM MST
See also CA 21-24R; CAAS 4; CANR 38;
DLB 53; MTCW

Blaise, Clark 1940- . . . . **CLC 29**
See also AITN 2; CA 53-56; CAAS 3;
CANR 5; DLB 53

Blake, Nicholas
See Day Lewis, C(ecil)
See also DLB 77

Blake, William
1757-1827 . . . . **NCLC 13, 37, 57; DA;**
DAB; DAC; DAM MST, POET; PC 12;
WLC
See also CDBLB 1789-1832; DLB 93, 163;
MAICYA; SATA 30

Blake, William J(ames) 1894-1969 . . . **PC 12**
See also CA 5-8R; 25-28R

Blasco Ibanez, Vicente
1867-1928 . . . . **TCLC 12; DAM NOV**
See also CA 110; 131; HW; MTCW

Blatty, William Peter
1928- . . . . **CLC 2; DAM POP**
See also CA 5-8R; CANR 9

Bleeck, Oliver
See Thomas, Ross (Elmore)

Blessing, Lee 1949- . . . . **CLC 54**

Blish, James (Benjamin)
1921-1975 . . . . **CLC 14**
See also CA 1-4R; 57-60; CANR 3; DLB 8;
MTCW; SATA 66

Bliss, Reginald
See Wells, H(erbert) G(eorge)

Blixen, Karen (Christentze Dinesen)
1885-1962
See Dinesen, Isak
See also CA 25-28; CANR 22, 50; CAP 2;
MTCW; SATA 44

Bloch, Robert (Albert) 1917-1994 . . . **CLC 33**
See also CA 5-8R; 146; CAAS 20; CANR 5;
DLB 44; INT CANR-5; SATA 12;
SATA-Obit 82

Blok, Alexander (Alexandrovich)
1880-1921 . . . . **TCLC 5**
See also CA 104

Blom, Jan
See Breytenbach, Breyten

Bloom, Harold 1930- . . . . **CLC 24**
See also CA 13-16R; CANR 39; DLB 67

Bloomfield, Aurelius
See Bourne, Randolph S(illiman)

Blount, Roy (Alton), Jr. 1941- . . . . . **CLC 38**
See also CA 53-56; CANR 10, 28;
INT CANR-28; MTCW

Bloy, Leon 1846-1917 . . . . **TCLC 22**
See also CA 121; DLB 123

Blume, Judy (Sussman)
1938- . . . **CLC 12, 30; DAM NOV, POP**
See also AAYA 3; CA 29-32R; CANR 13,
37; CLR 2, 15; DLB 52; JRDA;
MAICYA; MTCW; SATA 2, 31, 79

Blunden, Edmund (Charles)
1896-1974 . . . . **CLC 2, 56**
See also CA 17-18; 45-48; CANR 54;
CAP 2; DLB 20, 100, 155; MTCW

Bly, Robert (Elwood)
1926- . . . . **CLC 1, 2, 5, 10, 15, 38;**
DAM POET
See also CA 5-8R; CANR 41; DLB 5;
MTCW

Boas, Franz 1858-1942 . . . . **TCLC 56**
See also CA 115

Bobette
See Simenon, Georges (Jacques Christian)

Boccaccio, Giovanni
1313-1375 . . . . **CMLC 13; SSC 10**

Bochco, Steven 1943- . . . . **CLC 35**
See also AAYA 11; CA 124; 138

Bodenheim, Maxwell 1892-1954 . . . **TCLC 44**
See also CA 110; DLB 9, 45

Bodker, Cecil 1927- . . . . **CLC 21**
See also CA 73-76; CANR 13, 44; CLR 23;
MAICYA; SATA 14

Boell, Heinrich (Theodor)
1917-1985 . . . . **CLC 2, 3, 6, 9, 11, 15, 27,**
32, 72; DA; DAB; DAC; DAM MST,
NOV; SSC 23; WLC
See also CA 21-24R; 116; CANR 24;
DLB 69; DLBY 85; MTCW

Boerne, Alfred
See Doeblin, Alfred

Boethius 480(?)-524(?) . . . . **CMLC 15**
See also DLB 115

Bogan, Louise
1897-1970 . . . . **CLC 4, 39, 46, 93;**
DAM POET; PC 12
See also CA 73-76; 25-28R; CANR 33;
DLB 45, 169; MTCW

Bogarde, Dirk . . . . **CLC 19**
See also Van Den Bogarde, Derek Jules
Gaspard Ulric Niven
See also DLB 14

Bogosian, Eric   1953- .... **CLC 45**
See also CA 138

Bograd, Larry   1953-.............. **CLC 35**
See also CA 93-96; SAAS 21; SATA 33, 89

Boiardo, Matteo Maria   1441-1494 .... **LC 6**

Boileau-Despreaux, Nicolas
1636-1711 .... **LC 3**

Bojer, Johan   1872-1959 .... **TCLC 64**

Boland, Eavan (Aisling)
1944- .... **CLC 40, 67; DAM POET**
See also CA 143; DLB 40

Bolt, Lee
See Faust, Frederick (Schiller)

Bolt, Robert (Oxton)
1924-1995 ...... **CLC 14; DAM DRAM**
See also CA 17-20R; 147; CANR 35;
DLB 13; MTCW

Bombet, Louis-Alexandre-Cesar
See Stendhal

Bomkauf
See Kaufman, Bob (Garnell)

Bonaventura .... **NCLC 35**
See also DLB 90

Bond, Edward
1934- ... **CLC 4, 6, 13, 23; DAM DRAM**
See also CA 25-28R; CANR 38; DLB 13;
MTCW

Bonham, Frank   1914-1989........ **CLC 12**
See also AAYA 1; CA 9-12R; CANR 4, 36;
JRDA; MAICYA; SAAS 3; SATA 1, 49;
SATA-Obit 62

Bonnefoy, Yves
1923- ...... **CLC 9, 15, 58; DAM MST,
POET**
See also CA 85-88; CANR 33; MTCW

Bontemps, Arna(ud Wendell)
1902-1973 .... **CLC 1, 18; BLC;
DAM MULT, NOV, POET**
See also BW 1; CA 1-4R; 41-44R; CANR 4,
35; CLR 6; DLB 48, 51; JRDA;
MAICYA; MTCW; SATA 2, 44;
SATA-Obit 24

Booth, Martin   1944-.............. **CLC 13**
See also CA 93-96; CAAS 2

Booth, Philip   1925-.............. **CLC 23**
See also CA 5-8R; CANR 5; DLBY 82

Booth, Wayne C(layson)   1921- ..... **CLC 24**
See also CA 1-4R; CAAS 5; CANR 3, 43;
DLB 67

Borchert, Wolfgang   1921-1947 ..... **TCLC 5**
See also CA 104; DLB 69, 124

Borel, Petrus   1809-1859........ **NCLC 41**

Borges, Jorge Luis
1899-1986 ... **CLC 1, 2, 3, 4, 6, 8, 9, 10,
13, 19, 44, 48, 83; DA; DAB; DAC;
DAM MST, MULT; HLC; SSC 4; WLC**
See also AAYA 19; CA 21-24R; CANR 19,
33; DLB 113; DLBY 86; HW; MTCW

Borowski, Tadeusz   1922-1951 ...... **TCLC 9**
See also CA 106; 154

Borrow, George (Henry)
1803-1881 .... **NCLC 9**
See also DLB 21, 55, 166

Bosman, Herman Charles
1905-1951 .... **TCLC 49**

Bosschere, Jean de   1878(?)-1953... **TCLC 19**
See also CA 115

Boswell, James
1740-1795 ..... **LC 4; DA; DAB; DAC;
DAM MST; WLC**
See also CDBLB 1660-1789; DLB 104, 142

Bottoms, David   1949-............. **CLC 53**
See also CA 105; CANR 22; DLB 120;
DLBY 83

Boucicault, Dion   1820-1890...... **NCLC 41**

Boucolon, Maryse   1937(?)-
See Conde, Maryse
See also CA 110; CANR 30, 53

Bourget, Paul (Charles Joseph)
1852-1935 .... **TCLC 12**
See also CA 107; DLB 123

Bourjaily, Vance (Nye)   1922- .... **CLC 8, 62**
See also CA 1-4R; CAAS 1; CANR 2;
DLB 2, 143

Bourne, Randolph S(illiman)
1886-1918 .... **TCLC 16**
See also CA 117; DLB 63

Bova, Ben(jamin William)   1932-.... **CLC 45**
See also AAYA 16; CA 5-8R; CAAS 18;
CANR 11; CLR 3; DLBY 81;
INT CANR-11; MAICYA; MTCW;
SATA 6, 68

Bowen, Elizabeth (Dorothea Cole)
1899-1973 ...... **CLC 1, 3, 6, 11, 15, 22;
DAM NOV; SSC 3**
See also CA 17-18; 41-44R; CANR 35;
CAP 2; CDBLB 1945-1960; DLB 15, 162;
MTCW

Bowering, George   1935-........ **CLC 15, 47**
See also CA 21-24R; CAAS 16; CANR 10;
DLB 53

Bowering, Marilyn R(uthe)   1949-... **CLC 32**
See also CA 101; CANR 49

Bowers, Edgar   1924- .... **CLC 9**
See also CA 5-8R; CANR 24; DLB 5

Bowie, David .... **CLC 17**
See also Jones, David Robert

Bowles, Jane (Sydney)
1917-1973 .... **CLC 3, 68**
See also CA 19-20; 41-44R; CAP 2

Bowles, Paul (Frederick)
1910- .... **CLC 1, 2, 19, 53; SSC 3**
See also CA 1-4R; CAAS 1; CANR 1, 19,
50; DLB 5, 6; MTCW

Box, Edgar
See Vidal, Gore

Boyd, Nancy
See Millay, Edna St. Vincent

Boyd, William   1952-........ **CLC 28, 53, 70**
See also CA 114; 120; CANR 51

Boyle, Kay
1902-1992 ..... **CLC 1, 5, 19, 58; SSC 5**
See also CA 13-16R; 140; CAAS 1;
CANR 29; DLB 4, 9, 48, 86; DLBY 93;
MTCW

Boyle, Mark
See Kienzle, William X(avier)

Boyle, Patrick   1905-1982......... **CLC 19**
See also CA 127

Boyle, T. C.   1948-
See Boyle, T(homas) Coraghessan

Boyle, T(homas) Coraghessan
1948- ..... **CLC 36, 55, 90; DAM POP;
SSC 16**
See also BEST 90:4; CA 120; CANR 44;
DLBY 86

Boz
See Dickens, Charles (John Huffam)

Brackenridge, Hugh Henry
1748-1816 .... **NCLC 7**
See also DLB 11, 37

Bradbury, Edward P.
See Moorcock, Michael (John)

Bradbury, Malcolm (Stanley)
1932- .... **CLC 32, 61; DAM NOV**
See also CA 1-4R; CANR 1, 33; DLB 14;
MTCW

Bradbury, Ray (Douglas)
1920- ..... **CLC 1, 3, 10, 15, 42, 98; DA;
DAB; DAC; DAM MST, NOV, POP;
WLC**
See also AAYA 15; AITN 1, 2; CA 1-4R;
CANR 2, 30; CDALB 1968-1988; DLB 2,
8; INT CANR-30; MTCW; SATA 11, 64

Bradford, Gamaliel   1863-1932..... **TCLC 36**
See also DLB 17

Bradley, David (Henry, Jr.)
1950- ..... **CLC 23; BLC; DAM MULT**
See also BW 1; CA 104; CANR 26; DLB 33

Bradley, John Ed(mund, Jr.)
1958- .... **CLC 55**
See also CA 139

Bradley, Marion Zimmer
1930- .... **CLC 30; DAM POP**
See also AAYA 9; CA 57-60; CAAS 10;
CANR 7, 31, 51; DLB 8; MTCW;
SATA 90

Bradstreet, Anne
1612(?)-1672 ...... **LC 4, 30; DA; DAC;
DAM MST, POET; PC 10**
See also CDALB 1640-1865; DLB 24

Brady, Joan   1939- .... **CLC 86**
See also CA 141

Bragg, Melvyn   1939- .... **CLC 10**
See also BEST 89:3; CA 57-60; CANR 10,
48; DLB 14

Braine, John (Gerard)
1922-1986 .... **CLC 1, 3, 41**
See also CA 1-4R; 120; CANR 1, 33;
CDBLB 1945-1960; DLB 15; DLBY 86;
MTCW

Brammer, William   1930(?)-1978 .... **CLC 31**
See also CA 77-80

Brancati, Vitaliano   1907-1954..... **TCLC 12**
See also CA 109

Brancato, Robin F(idler)   1936- ..... **CLC 35**
See also AAYA 9; CA 69-72; CANR 11,
45; CLR 32; JRDA; SAAS 9; SATA 23

Brand, Max
See Faust, Frederick (Schiller)

Brand, Millen   1906-1980........... **CLC 7**
See also CA 21-24R; 97-100

Branden, Barbara .... **CLC 44**
See also CA 148

Brown, George Mackay
1921-1996 .... **CLC 5, 48**
See also CA 21-24R; 151; CAAS 6;
CANR 12, 37; DLB 14, 27, 139; MTCW;
SATA 35

Brown, (William) Larry 1951-...... **CLC 73**
See also CA 130; 134; INT 133

Brown, Moses
See Barrett, William (Christopher)

Brown, Rita Mae
1944- ..... **CLC 18, 43, 79; DAM NOV,**
POP
See also CA 45-48; CANR 2, 11, 35;
INT CANR-11; MTCW

Brown, Roderick (Langmere) Haig-
See Haig-Brown, Roderick (Langmere)

Brown, Rosellen 1939-........... **CLC 32**
See also CA 77-80; CAAS 10; CANR 14, 44

Brown, Sterling Allen
1901-1989 .... **CLC 1, 23, 59; BLC;**
DAM MULT, POET
See also BW 1; CA 85-88; 127; CANR 26;
DLB 48, 51, 63; MTCW

Brown, Will
See Ainsworth, William Harrison

Brown, William Wells
1813-1884 .... **NCLC 2; BLC;**
DAM MULT; DC 1
See also DLB 3, 50

Browne, (Clyde) Jackson 1948(?)-... **CLC 21**
See also CA 120

Browning, Elizabeth Barrett
1806-1861 ..... **NCLC 1, 16; DA; DAB;**
DAC; DAM MST, POET; PC 6; WLC
See also CDBLB 1832-1890; DLB 32

Browning, Robert
1812-1889 .... **NCLC 19; DA; DAB;**
DAC; DAM MST, POET; PC 2
See also CDBLB 1832-1890; DLB 32, 163;
YABC 1

Browning, Tod 1882-1962 .... **CLC 16**
See also CA 141; 117

Brownson, Orestes (Augustus)
1803-1876 .... **NCLC 50**

Bruccoli, Matthew J(oseph) 1931- .. **CLC 34**
See also CA 9-12R; CANR 7; DLB 103

Bruce, Lenny.................... **CLC 21**
See also Schneider, Leonard Alfred

Bruin, John
See Brutus, Dennis

Brulard, Henri
See Stendhal

Brulls, Christian
See Simenon, Georges (Jacques Christian)

Brunner, John (Kilian Houston)
1934-1995 ...... **CLC 8, 10; DAM POP**
See also CA 1-4R; 149; CAAS 8; CANR 2,
37; MTCW

Bruno, Giordano 1548-1600........ **LC 27**

Brutus, Dennis
1924- ..... **CLC 43; BLC; DAM MULT,**
POET
See also BW 2; CA 49-52; CAAS 14;
CANR 2, 27, 42; DLB 117

Bryan, C(ourtlandt) D(ixon) B(arnes)
1936-...................... **CLC 29**
See also CA 73-76; CANR 13;
INT CANR-13

Bryan, Michael
See Moore, Brian

Bryant, William Cullen
1794-1878 ..... **NCLC 6, 46; DA; DAB;**
DAC; DAM MST, POET
See also CDALB 1640-1865; DLB 3, 43, 59

Bryusov, Valery Yakovlevich
1873-1924 .... **TCLC 10**
See also CA 107

Buchan, John
1875-1940 .... **TCLC 41; DAB;**
DAM POP
See also CA 108; 145; DLB 34, 70, 156;
YABC 2

Buchanan, George 1506-1582 .... **LC 4**

Buchheim, Lothar-Guenther 1918- ... **CLC 6**
See also CA 85-88

Buchner, (Karl) Georg
1813-1837 .... **NCLC 26**

Buchwald, Art(hur) 1925-........... **CLC 33**
See also AITN 1; CA 5-8R; CANR 21;
MTCW; SATA 10

Buck, Pearl S(ydenstricker)
1892-1973 .... **CLC 7, 11, 18; DA; DAB;**
DAC; DAM MST, NOV
See also AITN 1; CA 1-4R; 41-44R;
CANR 1, 34; DLB 9, 102; MTCW;
SATA 1, 25

Buckler, Ernest
1908-1984 .. **CLC 13; DAC; DAM MST**
See also CA 11-12; 114; CAP 1; DLB 68;
SATA 47

Buckley, Vincent (Thomas)
1925-1988 .... **CLC 57**
See also CA 101

Buckley, William F(rank), Jr.
1925- .... **CLC 7, 18, 37; DAM POP**
See also AITN 1; CA 1-4R; CANR 1, 24,
53; DLB 137; DLBY 80; INT CANR-24;
MTCW

Buechner, (Carl) Frederick
1926- ...... **CLC 2, 4, 6, 9; DAM NOV**
See also CA 13-16R; CANR 11, 39;
DLBY 80; INT CANR-11; MTCW

Buell, John (Edward) 1927-........ **CLC 10**
See also CA 1-4R; DLB 53

Buero Vallejo, Antonio 1916- ... **CLC 15, 46**
See also CA 106; CANR 24, 49; HW;
MTCW

Bufalino, Gesualdo 1920(?)-........ **CLC 74**

Bugayev, Boris Nikolayevich 1880-1934
See Bely, Andrey
See also CA 104

Bukowski, Charles
1920-1994 .... **CLC 2, 5, 9, 41, 82;**
DAM NOV, POET
See also CA 17-20R; 144; CANR 40;
DLB 5, 130, 169; MTCW

Bulgakov, Mikhail (Afanas'evich)
1891-1940 .... **TCLC 2, 16;**
DAM DRAM, NOV; SSC 18
See also CA 105; 152

Bulgya, Alexander Alexandrovich
1901-1956 .... **TCLC 53**
See also Fadeyev, Alexander
See also CA 117

Bullins, Ed
1935- .... **CLC 1, 5, 7; BLC;**
DAM DRAM, MULT; DC 6
See also BW 2; CA 49-52; CAAS 16;
CANR 24, 46; DLB 7, 38; MTCW

Bulwer-Lytton, Edward (George Earle Lytton)
1803-1873 .... **NCLC 1, 45**
See also DLB 21

Bunin, Ivan Alexeyevich
1870-1953 .... **TCLC 6; SSC 5**
See also CA 104

Bunting, Basil
1900-1985 .... **CLC 10, 39, 47;**
DAM POET
See also CA 53-56; 115; CANR 7; DLB 20

Bunuel, Luis
1900-1983 .... **CLC 16, 80;**
DAM MULT; HLC
See also CA 101; 110; CANR 32; HW

Bunyan, John
1628-1688 ...... **LC 4; DA; DAB; DAC;**
DAM MST; WLC
See also CDBLB 1660-1789; DLB 39

Burckhardt, Jacob (Christoph)
1818-1897 .... **NCLC 49**

Burford, Eleanor
See Hibbert, Eleanor Alice Burford

Burgess, Anthony
. **CLC 1, 2, 4, 5, 8, 10, 13, 15, 22, 40, 62,**
81, 94; DAB
See also Wilson, John (Anthony) Burgess
See also AITN 1; CDBLB 1960 to Present;
DLB 14

Burke, Edmund
1729(?)-1797 ...... **LC 7, 36; DA; DAB;**
DAC; DAM MST; WLC
See also DLB 104

Burke, Kenneth (Duva)
1897-1993 .... **CLC 2, 24**
See also CA 5-8R; 143; CANR 39; DLB 45,
63; MTCW

Burke, Leda
See Garnett, David

Burke, Ralph
See Silverberg, Robert

Burke, Thomas 1886-1945 .... **TCLC 63**
See also CA 113

Burney, Fanny 1752-1840 .... **NCLC 12, 54**
See also DLB 39

Burns, Robert 1759-1796 .... **PC 6**
See also CDBLB 1789-1832; DA; DAB;
DAC; DAM MST, POET; DLB 109;
WLC

Burns, Tex
See L'Amour, Louis (Dearborn)

Burnshaw, Stanley 1906-..... **CLC 3, 13, 44**
See also CA 9-12R; DLB 48

Burr, Anne 1937-.................. **CLC 6**
See also CA 25-28R

Burroughs, Edgar Rice
1875-1950 .... **TCLC 2, 32; DAM NOV**
See also AAYA 11; CA 104; 132; DLB 8;
MTCW; SATA 41

Burroughs, William S(eward)
1914- .... **CLC 1, 2, 5, 15, 22, 42, 75;**
DA; DAB; DAC; DAM MST, NOV,
POP; WLC
See also AITN 2; CA 9-12R; CANR 20, 52;
DLB 2, 8, 16, 152; DLBY 81; MTCW

Burton, Richard F. 1821-1890.... **NCLC 42**
See also DLB 55

Busch, Frederick 1941- ... **CLC 7, 10, 18, 47**
See also CA 33-36R; CAAS 1; CANR 45;
DLB 6

Bush, Ronald 1946- .... **CLC 34**
See also CA 136

Bustos, F(rancisco)
See Borges, Jorge Luis

Bustos Domecq, H(onorio)
See Bioy Casares, Adolfo; Borges, Jorge
Luis

Butler, Octavia E(stelle)
1947- ..... **CLC 38; DAM MULT, POP**
See also AAYA 18; BW 2; CA 73-76;
CANR 12, 24, 38; DLB 33; MTCW;
SATA 84

Butler, Robert Olen (Jr.)
1945- .... **CLC 81; DAM POP**
See also CA 112; DLB 173; INT 112

Butler, Samuel 1612-1680 .... **LC 16**
See also DLB 101, 126

Butler, Samuel
1835-1902 ...... **TCLC 1, 33; DA; DAB;**
DAC; DAM MST, NOV; WLC
See also CA 143; CDBLB 1890-1914;
DLB 18, 57, 174

Butler, Walter C.
See Faust, Frederick (Schiller)

Butor, Michel (Marie Francois)
1926- .... **CLC 1, 3, 8, 11, 15**
See also CA 9-12R; CANR 33; DLB 83;
MTCW

Buzo, Alexander (John) 1944- ...... **CLC 61**
See also CA 97-100; CANR 17, 39

Buzzati, Dino 1906-1972 .... **CLC 36**
See also CA 33-36R

Byars, Betsy (Cromer) 1928-....... **CLC 35**
See also AAYA 19; CA 33-36R; CANR 18,
36; CLR 1, 16; DLB 52; INT CANR-18;
JRDA; MAICYA; MTCW; SAAS 1;
SATA 4, 46, 80

Byatt, A(ntonia) S(usan Drabble)
1936- ... **CLC 19, 65; DAM NOV, POP**
See also CA 13-16R; CANR 13, 33, 50;
DLB 14; MTCW

Byrne, David 1952-.............. **CLC 26**
See also CA 127

Byrne, John Keyes 1926-
See Leonard, Hugh
See also CA 102; INT 102

Byron, George Gordon (Noel)
1788-1824 ..... **NCLC 2, 12; DA; DAB;**
DAC; DAM MST, POET; PC 16; WLC
See also CDBLB 1789-1832; DLB 96, 110

Byron, Robert 1905-1941......... **TCLC 67**

C. 3. 3.
See Wilde, Oscar (Fingal O'Flahertie Wills)

Caballero, Fernan 1796-1877..... **NCLC 10**

Cabell, Branch
See Cabell, James Branch

Cabell, James Branch 1879-1958 ... **TCLC 6**
See also CA 105; 152; DLB 9, 78

Cable, George Washington
1844-1925 .... **TCLC 4; SSC 4**
See also CA 104; DLB 12, 74; DLBD 13

Cabral de Melo Neto, Joao
1920- .... **CLC 76; DAM MULT**
See also CA 151

Cabrera Infante, G(uillermo)
1929- ..... **CLC 5, 25, 45; DAM MULT;**
HLC
See also CA 85-88; CANR 29; DLB 113;
HW; MTCW

Cade, Toni
See Bambara, Toni Cade

Cadmus and Harmonia
See Buchan, John

Caedmon fl. 658-680............. **CMLC 7**
See also DLB 146

Caeiro, Alberto
See Pessoa, Fernando (Antonio Nogueira)

Cage, John (Milton, Jr.) 1912- ..... **CLC 41**
See also CA 13-16R; CANR 9;
INT CANR-9

Cain, G.
See Cabrera Infante, G(uillermo)

Cain, Guillermo
See Cabrera Infante, G(uillermo)

Cain, James M(allahan)
1892-1977 .... **CLC 3, 11, 28**
See also AITN 1; CA 17-20R; 73-76;
CANR 8, 34; MTCW

Caine, Mark
See Raphael, Frederic (Michael)

Calasso, Roberto 1941- .... **CLC 81**
See also CA 143

Calderon de la Barca, Pedro
1600-1681 .... **LC 23; DC 3**

Caldwell, Erskine (Preston)
1903-1987 .... **CLC 1, 8, 14, 50, 60;**
DAM NOV; SSC 19
See also AITN 1; CA 1-4R; 121; CAAS 1;
CANR 2, 33; DLB 9, 86; MTCW

Caldwell, (Janet Miriam) Taylor (Holland)
1900-1985 .... **CLC 2, 28, 39;**
DAM NOV, POP
See also CA 5-8R; 116; CANR 5

Calhoun, John Caldwell
1782-1850 .... **NCLC 15**
See also DLB 3

Calisher, Hortense
1911- ..... **CLC 2, 4, 8, 38; DAM NOV;**
SSC 15
See also CA 1-4R; CANR 1, 22; DLB 2;
INT CANR-22; MTCW

Callaghan, Morley Edward
1903-1990 ..... **CLC 3, 14, 41, 65; DAC;**
DAM MST
See also CA 9-12R; 132; CANR 33;
DLB 68; MTCW

Callimachus
c. 305B.C.-c. 240B.C........ **CMLC 18**

Calvino, Italo
1923-1985 ..... **CLC 5, 8, 11, 22, 33, 39,**
73; DAM NOV; SSC 3
See also CA 85-88; 116; CANR 23; MTCW

Cameron, Carey 1952-............ **CLC 59**
See also CA 135

Cameron, Peter 1959-............. **CLC 44**
See also CA 125; CANR 50

Campana, Dino 1885-1932........ **TCLC 20**
See also CA 117; DLB 114

Campanella, Tommaso 1568-1639.... **LC 32**

Campbell, John W(ood, Jr.)
1910-1971 .... **CLC 32**
See also CA 21-22; 29-32R; CANR 34;
CAP 2; DLB 8; MTCW

Campbell, Joseph 1904-1987 .... **CLC 69**
See also AAYA 3; BEST 89:2; CA 1-4R;
124; CANR 3, 28; MTCW

Campbell, Maria 1940-....... **CLC 85; DAC**
See also CA 102; CANR 54; NNAL

Campbell, (John) Ramsey
1946- .... **CLC 42; SSC 19**
See also CA 57-60; CANR 7; INT CANR-7

Campbell, (Ignatius) Roy (Dunnachie)
1901-1957 .... **TCLC 5**
See also CA 104; DLB 20

Campbell, Thomas 1777-1844 .... **NCLC 19**
See also DLB 93; 144

Campbell, Wilfred................. TCLC 9
See also Campbell, William

Campbell, William 1858(?)-1918
See Campbell, Wilfred
See also CA 106; DLB 92

Campion, Jane.................... CLC 95
See also CA 138

Campos, Alvaro de
See Pessoa, Fernando (Antonio Nogueira)

Camus, Albert
1913-1960 .... **CLC 1, 2, 4, 9, 11, 14, 32,**
63, 69; DA; DAB; DAC; DAM DRAM,
MST, NOV; DC 2; SSC 9; WLC
See also CA 89-92; DLB 72; MTCW

Canby, Vincent 1924-............. **CLC 13**
See also CA 81-84

Cancale
See Desnos, Robert

Canetti, Elias
1905-1994 .... **CLC 3, 14, 25, 75, 86**
See also CA 21-24R; 146; CANR 23;
DLB 85, 124; MTCW

Canin, Ethan 1960-............... **CLC 55**
See also CA 131; 135

Cannon, Curt
See Hunter, Evan

Cape, Judith
See Page, P(atricia) K(athleen)

Capek, Karel
1890-1938 ...... **TCLC 6, 37; DA; DAB;**
DAC; DAM DRAM, MST, NOV; DC 1;
WLC
See also CA 104; 140

Capote, Truman
1924-1984 ...... **CLC 1, 3, 8, 13, 19, 34, 38, 58; DA; DAB; DAC; DAM MST, NOV, POP; SSC 2; WLC**
See also CA 5-8R; 113; CANR 18; CDALB 1941-1968; DLB 2; DLBY 80, 84; MTCW; SATA 91

Capra, Frank 1897-1991........... **CLC 16**
See also CA 61-64; 135

Caputo, Philip 1941-.............. **CLC 32**
See also CA 73-76; CANR 40

Card, Orson Scott
1951- ...... **CLC 44, 47, 50; DAM POP**
See also AAYA 11; CA 102; CANR 27, 47; INT CANR-27; MTCW; SATA 83

Cardenal, Ernesto
1925- .... **CLC 31; DAM MULT, POET; HLC**
See also CA 49-52; CANR 2, 32; HW; MTCW

Cardozo, Benjamin N(athan)
1870-1938 .... **TCLC 65**
See also CA 117

Carducci, Giosue 1835-1907...... **TCLC 32**

Carew, Thomas 1595(?)-1640........ **LC 13**
See also DLB 126

Carey, Ernestine Gilbreth 1908-.... **CLC 17**
See also CA 5-8R; SATA 2

Carey, Peter 1943-......... **CLC 40, 55, 96**
See also CA 123; 127; CANR 53; INT 127; MTCW

Carleton, William 1794-1869...... **NCLC 3**
See also DLB 159

Carlisle, Henry (Coffin) 1926-...... **CLC 33**
See also CA 13-16R; CANR 15

Carlsen, Chris
See Holdstock, Robert P.

Carlson, Ron(ald F.) 1947-......... **CLC 54**
See also CA 105; CANR 27

Carlyle, Thomas
1795-1881 .... **NCLC 22; DA; DAB; DAC; DAM MST**
See also CDBLB 1789-1832; DLB 55; 144

Carman, (William) Bliss
1861-1929 .... **TCLC 7; DAC**
See also CA 104; 152; DLB 92

Carnegie, Dale 1888-1955 .... **TCLC 53**

Carossa, Hans 1878-1956........ **TCLC 48**
See also DLB 66

Carpenter, Don(ald Richard)
1931-1995 .... **CLC 41**
See also CA 45-48; 149; CANR 1

Carpentier (y Valmont), Alejo
1904-1980 .... **CLC 8, 11, 38; DAM MULT; HLC**
See also CA 65-68; 97-100; CANR 11; DLB 113; HW

Carr, Caleb 1955(?)-.............. **CLC 86**
See also CA 147

Carr, Emily 1871-1945........... **TCLC 32**
See also DLB 68

Carr, John Dickson 1906-1977 ...... **CLC 3**
See also CA 49-52; 69-72; CANR 3, 33; MTCW

Carr, Philippa
See Hibbert, Eleanor Alice Burford

Carr, Virginia Spencer 1929-....... **CLC 34**
See also CA 61-64; DLB 111

Carrere, Emmanuel 1957- .... **CLC 89**

Carrier, Roch
1937- ... **CLC 13, 78; DAC; DAM MST**
See also CA 130; DLB 53

Carroll, James P. 1943(?)-......... **CLC 38**
See also CA 81-84

Carroll, Jim 1951- .... **CLC 35**
See also AAYA 17; CA 45-48; CANR 42

Carroll, Lewis .... **NCLC 2, 53; WLC**
See also Dodgson, Charles Lutwidge
See also CDBLB 1832-1890; CLR 2, 18; DLB 18, 163; JRDA

Carroll, Paul Vincent 1900-1968.... **CLC 10**
See also CA 9-12R; 25-28R; DLB 10

Carruth, Hayden
1921- .... **CLC 4, 7, 10, 18, 84; PC 10**
See also CA 9-12R; CANR 4, 38; DLB 5, 165; INT CANR-4; MTCW; SATA 47

Carson, Rachel Louise
1907-1964 .... **CLC 71; DAM POP**
See also CA 77-80; CANR 35; MTCW; SATA 23

Carter, Angela (Olive)
1940-1992 ...... **CLC 5, 41, 76; SSC 13**
See also CA 53-56; 136; CANR 12, 36; DLB 14; MTCW; SATA 66; SATA-Obit 70

Carter, Nick
See Smith, Martin Cruz

Carver, Raymond
1938-1988 .... **CLC 22, 36, 53, 55; DAM NOV; SSC 8**
See also CA 33-36R; 126; CANR 17, 34; DLB 130; DLBY 84, 88; MTCW

Cary, Elizabeth, Lady Falkland
1585-1639 .... **LC 30**

Cary, (Arthur) Joyce (Lunel)
1888-1957 .... **TCLC 1, 29**
See also CA 104; CDBLB 1914-1945; DLB 15, 100

Casanova de Seingalt, Giovanni Jacopo
1725-1798 .... **LC 13**

Casares, Adolfo Bioy
See Bioy Casares, Adolfo

Casely-Hayford, J(oseph) E(phraim)
1866-1930 .... **TCLC 24; BLC; DAM MULT**
See also BW 2; CA 123; 152

Casey, John (Dudley) 1939-........ **CLC 59**
See also BEST 90:2; CA 69-72; CANR 23

Casey, Michael 1947-.............. **CLC 2**
See also CA 65-68; DLB 5

Casey, Patrick
See Thurman, Wallace (Henry)

Casey, Warren (Peter) 1935-1988 ... **CLC 12**
See also CA 101; 127; INT 101

Casona, Alejandro .... **CLC 49**
See also Alvarez, Alejandro Rodriguez

Cassavetes, John 1929-1989........ **CLC 20**
See also CA 85-88; 127

Cassill, R(onald) V(erlin) 1919-... **CLC 4, 23**
See also CA 9-12R; CAAS 1; CANR 7, 45; DLB 6

Cassirer, Ernst 1874-1945 .... **TCLC 61**

Cassity, (Allen) Turner 1929- .... **CLC 6, 42**
See also CA 17-20R; CAAS 8; CANR 11; DLB 105

Castaneda, Carlos 1931(?)-......... **CLC 12**
See also CA 25-28R; CANR 32; HW; MTCW

Castedo, Elena 1937- .... **CLC 65**
See also CA 132

Castedo-Ellerman, Elena
See Castedo, Elena

Castellanos, Rosario
1925-1974 ...... **CLC 66; DAM MULT; HLC**
See also CA 131; 53-56; DLB 113; HW

Castelvetro, Lodovico 1505-1571..... **LC 12**

Castiglione, Baldassare 1478-1529 ... **LC 12**

Castle, Robert
See Hamilton, Edmond

Castro, Guillen de 1569-1631........ **LC 19**

Castro, Rosalia de
1837-1885 ...... **NCLC 3; DAM MULT**

Cather, Willa
See Cather, Willa Sibert

Cather, Willa Sibert
1873-1947 .... **TCLC 1, 11, 31; DA; DAB; DAC; DAM MST, NOV; SSC 2; WLC**
See also CA 104; 128; CDALB 1865-1917; DLB 9, 54, 78; DLBD 1; MTCW; SATA 30

Catton, (Charles) Bruce
1899-1978 .... **CLC 35**
See also AITN 1; CA 5-8R; 81-84; CANR 7; DLB 17; SATA 2; SATA-Obit 24

Catullus c. 84B.C.-c. 54B.C. ..... **CMLC 18**

Cauldwell, Frank
See King, Francis (Henry)

Caunitz, William J. 1933-1996 ..... **CLC 34**
See also BEST 89:3; CA 125; 130; 152; INT 130

Causley, Charles (Stanley) 1917-..... **CLC 7**
See also CA 9-12R; CANR 5, 35; CLR 30; DLB 27; MTCW; SATA 3, 66

Caute, David 1936-.... **CLC 29; DAM NOV**
See also CA 1-4R; CAAS 4; CANR 1, 33; DLB 14

Cavafy, C(onstantine) P(eter)
1863-1933 .... **TCLC 2, 7; DAM POET**
See also Kavafis, Konstantinos Petrou
See also CA 148

Cavallo, Evelyn
See Spark, Muriel (Sarah)

Cavanna, Betty .... **CLC 12**
See also Harrison, Elizabeth Cavanna
See also JRDA; MAICYA; SAAS 4; SATA 1, 30

Cavendish, Margaret Lucas
1623-1673 .... **LC 30**
See also DLB 131

Caxton, William 1421(?)-1491(?)..... **LC 17**
See also DLB 170

Cayrol, Jean 1911-............... **CLC 11**
See also CA 89-92; DLB 83

Cela, Camilo Jose
1916-..... **CLC 4, 13, 59; DAM MULT;**
HLC
See also BEST 90:2; CA 21-24R; CAAS 10;
CANR 21, 32; DLBY 89; HW; MTCW

Celan, Paul ...... **CLC 10, 19, 53, 82; PC 10**
See also Antschel, Paul
See also DLB 69

Celine, Louis-Ferdinand
.... **CLC 1, 3, 4, 7, 9, 15, 47**
See also Destouches, Louis-Ferdinand
See also DLB 72

Cellini, Benvenuto 1500-1571 .... **LC 7**

Cendrars, Blaise .... **CLC 18**
See also Sauser-Hall, Frederic

Cernuda (y Bidon), Luis
1902-1963 .... **CLC 54; DAM POET**
See also CA 131; 89-92; DLB 134; HW

Cervantes (Saavedra), Miguel de
1547-1616 .... **LC 6, 23; DA; DAB;**
DAC; DAM MST, NOV; SSC 12; WLC

Cesaire, Aime (Fernand)
1913-............... **CLC 19, 32; BLC;**
DAM MULT, POET
See also BW 2; CA 65-68; CANR 24, 43;
MTCW

Chabon, Michael 1963-........... **CLC 55**
See also CA 139

Chabrol, Claude 1930-............ **CLC 16**
See also CA 110

Challans, Mary 1905-1983
See Renault, Mary
See also CA 81-84; 111; SATA 23;
SATA-Obit 36

Challis, George
See Faust, Frederick (Schiller)

Chambers, Aidan 1934-........... **CLC 35**
See also CA 25-28R; CANR 12, 31; JRDA;
MAICYA; SAAS 12; SATA 1, 69

Chambers, James 1948-
See Cliff, Jimmy
See also CA 124

Chambers, Jessie
See Lawrence, D(avid) H(erbert Richards)

Chambers, Robert W. 1865-1933... **TCLC 41**

Chandler, Raymond (Thornton)
1888-1959 .... **TCLC 1, 7; SSC 23**
See also CA 104; 129; CDALB 1929-1941;
DLBD 6; MTCW

Chang, Jung 1952-............... **CLC 71**
See also CA 142

Channing, William Ellery
1780-1842 .... **NCLC 17**
See also DLB 1, 59

Chaplin, Charles Spencer
1889-1977 .... **CLC 16**
See also Chaplin, Charlie
See also CA 81-84; 73-76

Chaplin, Charlie
See Chaplin, Charles Spencer
See also DLB 44

Chapman, George
1559(?)-1634 ..... **LC 22; DAM DRAM**
See also DLB 62, 121

Chapman, Graham 1941-1989 ...... **CLC 21**
See also Monty Python
See also CA 116; 129; CANR 35

Chapman, John Jay 1862-1933 ..... **TCLC 7**
See also CA 104

Chapman, Lee
See Bradley, Marion Zimmer

Chapman, Walker
See Silverberg, Robert

Chappell, Fred (Davis) 1936-.... **CLC 40, 78**
See also CA 5-8R; CAAS 4; CANR 8, 33;
DLB 6, 105

Char, Rene(-Emile)
1907-1988 .... **CLC 9, 11, 14, 55;**
DAM POET
See also CA 13-16R; 124; CANR 32;
MTCW

Charby, Jay
See Ellison, Harlan (Jay)

Chardin, Pierre Teilhard de
See Teilhard de Chardin, (Marie Joseph)
Pierre

Charles I 1600-1649 .... **LC 13**

Charyn, Jerome 1937-........ **CLC 5, 8, 18**
See also CA 5-8R; CAAS 1; CANR 7;
DLBY 83; MTCW

Chase, Mary (Coyle) 1907-1981 ...... **DC 1**
See also CA 77-80; 105; SATA 17;
SATA-Obit 29

Chase, Mary Ellen 1887-1973....... **CLC 2**
See also CA 13-16; 41-44R; CAP 1;
SATA 10

Chase, Nicholas
See Hyde, Anthony

Chateaubriand, Francois Rene de
1768-1848 .... **NCLC 3**
See also DLB 119

Chatterje, Sarat Chandra 1876-1936(?)
See Chatterji, Saratchandra
See also CA 109

Chatterji, Bankim Chandra
1838-1894 .... **NCLC 19**

Chatterji, Saratchandra .... **TCLC 13**
See also Chatterje, Sarat Chandra

Chatterton, Thomas
1752-1770 .... **LC 3; DAM POET**
See also DLB 109

Chatwin, (Charles) Bruce
1940-1989 .. **CLC 28, 57, 59; DAM POP**
See also AAYA 4; BEST 90:1; CA 85-88;
127

Chaucer, Daniel
See Ford, Ford Madox

Chaucer, Geoffrey
1340(?)-1400 .... **LC 17; DA; DAB;**
DAC; DAM MST, POET
See also CDBLB Before 1660; DLB 146

Chaviaras, Strates 1935-
See Haviaras, Stratis
See also CA 105

Chayefsky, Paddy .... **CLC 23**
See also Chayefsky, Sidney
See also DLB 7, 44; DLBY 81

Chayefsky, Sidney 1923-1981
See Chayefsky, Paddy
See also CA 9-12R; 104; CANR 18;
DAM DRAM

Chedid, Andree 1920-............ **CLC 47**
See also CA 145

Cheever, John
1912-1982 ...... **CLC 3, 7, 8, 11, 15, 25,**
64; DA; DAB; DAC; DAM MST, NOV,
POP; SSC 1; WLC
See also CA 5-8R; 106; CABS 1; CANR 5,
27; CDALB 1941-1968; DLB 2, 102;
DLBY 80, 82; INT CANR-5; MTCW

Cheever, Susan 1943-........... **CLC 18, 48**
See also CA 103; CANR 27, 51; DLBY 82;
INT CANR-27

Chekhonte, Antosha
See Chekhov, Anton (Pavlovich)

Chekhov, Anton (Pavlovich)
1860-1904 ..... **TCLC 3, 10, 31, 55; DA;**
DAB; DAC; DAM DRAM, MST; SSC 2;
WLC
See also CA 104; 124; SATA 90

Chernyshevsky, Nikolay Gavrilovich
1828-1889 .... **NCLC 1**

Cherry, Carolyn Janice 1942-
See Cherryh, C. J.
See also CA 65-68; CANR 10

Cherryh, C. J. .... **CLC 35**
See also Cherry, Carolyn Janice
See also DLBY 80

Chesnutt, Charles W(addell)
1858-1932 .... **TCLC 5, 39; BLC;**
DAM MULT; SSC 7
See also BW 1; CA 106; 125; DLB 12, 50,
78; MTCW

Chester, Alfred 1929(?)-1971....... **CLC 49**
See also CA 33-36R; DLB 130

Chesterton, G(ilbert) K(eith)
1874-1936 .... **TCLC 1, 6, 64;**
DAM NOV, POET; SSC 1
See also CA 104; 132; CDBLB 1914-1945;
DLB 10, 19, 34, 70, 98, 149; MTCW;
SATA 27

Chiang Pin-chin 1904-1986
See Ding Ling
See also CA 118

Ch'ien Chung-shu 1910-........... **CLC 22**
See also CA 130; MTCW

Child, L. Maria
See Child, Lydia Maria

Child, Lydia Maria 1802-1880 .... **NCLC 6**
See also DLB 1, 74; SATA 67

Child, Mrs.
See Child, Lydia Maria

Child, Philip 1898-1978 .... **CLC 19, 68**
See also CA 13-14; CAP 1; SATA 47

Childers, (Robert) Erskine
1870-1922 .... **TCLC 65**
See also CA 113; 153; DLB 70

Childress, Alice
1920-1994 .... **CLC 12, 15, 86, 96; BLC; DAM DRAM, MULT, NOV; DC 4**
See also AAYA 8; BW 2; CA 45-48; 146; CANR 3, 27, 50; CLR 14; DLB 7, 38; JRDA; MAICYA; MTCW; SATA 7, 48, 81

Chislett, (Margaret) Anne 1943- .... **CLC 34**
See also CA 151

Chitty, Thomas Willes 1926- .... **CLC 11**
See also Hinde, Thomas
See also CA 5-8R

Chivers, Thomas Holley
1809-1858 .... **NCLC 49**
See also DLB 3

Chomette, Rene Lucien 1898-1981
See Clair, Rene
See also CA 103

Chopin, Kate
.... **TCLC 5, 14; DA; DAB; SSC 8**
See also Chopin, Katherine
See also CDALB 1865-1917; DLB 12, 78

Chopin, Katherine 1851-1904
See Chopin, Kate
See also CA 104; 122; DAC; DAM MST, NOV

Chretien de Troyes
c. 12th cent. - .... **CMLC 10**

Christie
See Ichikawa, Kon

Christie, Agatha (Mary Clarissa)
1890-1976 ...... **CLC 1, 6, 8, 12, 39, 48; DAB; DAC; DAM NOV**
See also AAYA 9; AITN 1, 2; CA 17-20R; 61-64; CANR 10, 37; CDBLB 1914-1945; DLB 13, 77; MTCW; SATA 36

Christie, (Ann) Philippa
See Pearce, Philippa
See also CA 5-8R; CANR 4

Christine de Pizan 1365(?)-1431(?) .... **LC 9**

Chubb, Elmer
See Masters, Edgar Lee

Chulkov, Mikhail Dmitrievich
1743-1792 .... **LC 2**
See also DLB 150

Churchill, Caryl 1938- ... **CLC 31, 55; DC 5**
See also CA 102; CANR 22, 46; DLB 13; MTCW

Churchill, Charles 1731-1764........ **LC 3**
See also DLB 109

Chute, Carolyn 1947- .... **CLC 39**
See also CA 123

Ciardi, John (Anthony)
1916-1986 .... **CLC 10, 40, 44; DAM POET**
See also CA 5-8R; 118; CAAS 2; CANR 5, 33; CLR 19; DLB 5; DLBY 86; INT CANR-5; MAICYA; MTCW; SATA 1, 65; SATA-Obit 46

Cicero, Marcus Tullius
106B.C.-43B.C............... **CMLC 3**

Cimino, Michael 1943- .... **CLC 16**
See also CA 105

Cioran, E(mil) M. 1911-1995....... **CLC 64**
See also CA 25-28R; 149

Cisneros, Sandra
1954- ..... **CLC 69; DAM MULT; HLC**
See also AAYA 9; CA 131; DLB 122, 152; HW

Cixous, Helene 1937- .... **CLC 92**
See also CA 126; CANR 55; DLB 83; MTCW

Clair, Rene...................... **CLC 20**
See also Chomette, Rene Lucien

Clampitt, Amy 1920-1994 .... **CLC 32**
See also CA 110; 146; CANR 29; DLB 105

Clancy, Thomas L., Jr. 1947-
See Clancy, Tom
See also CA 125; 131; INT 131; MTCW

Clancy, Tom..... **CLC 45; DAM NOV, POP**
See also Clancy, Thomas L., Jr.
See also AAYA 9; BEST 89:1, 90:1

Clare, John
1793-1864 .... **NCLC 9; DAB; DAM POET**
See also DLB 55, 96

Clarin
See Alas (y Urena), Leopoldo (Enrique Garcia)

Clark, Al C.
See Goines, Donald

Clark, (Robert) Brian 1932- .... **CLC 29**
See also CA 41-44R

Clark, Curt
See Westlake, Donald E(dwin)

Clark, Eleanor 1913-1996 .... **CLC 5, 19**
See also CA 9-12R; 151; CANR 41; DLB 6

Clark, J. P.
See Clark, John Pepper
See also DLB 117

Clark, John Pepper
1935- .... **CLC 38; BLC; DAM DRAM, MULT; DC 5**
See also Clark, J. P.
See also BW 1; CA 65-68; CANR 16

Clark, M. R.
See Clark, Mavis Thorpe

Clark, Mavis Thorpe 1909- .... **CLC 12**
See also CA 57-60; CANR 8, 37; CLR 30; MAICYA; SAAS 5; SATA 8, 74

Clark, Walter Van Tilburg
1909-1971 .... **CLC 28**
See also CA 9-12R; 33-36R; DLB 9; SATA 8

Clarke, Arthur C(harles)
1917- .... **CLC 1, 4, 13, 18, 35; DAM POP; SSC 3**
See also AAYA 4; CA 1-4R; CANR 2, 28, 55; JRDA; MAICYA; MTCW; SATA 13, 70

Clarke, Austin
1896-1974 ...... **CLC 6, 9; DAM POET**
See also CA 29-32; 49-52; CAP 2; DLB 10, 20

Clarke, Austin C(hesterfield)
1934- .... **CLC 8, 53; BLC; DAC; DAM MULT**
See also BW 1; CA 25-28R; CAAS 16; CANR 14, 32; DLB 53, 125

Clarke, Gillian 1937- .... **CLC 61**
See also CA 106; DLB 40

Clarke, Marcus (Andrew Hislop)
1846-1881 .... **NCLC 19**

Clarke, Shirley 1925- .... **CLC 16**

Clash, The
See Headon, (Nicky) Topper; Jones, Mick; Simonon, Paul; Strummer, Joe

Claudel, Paul (Louis Charles Marie)
1868-1955 .... **TCLC 2, 10**
See also CA 104

Clavell, James (duMaresq)
1925-1994 .... **CLC 6, 25, 87; DAM NOV, POP**
See also CA 25-28R; 146; CANR 26, 48; MTCW

Cleaver, (Leroy) Eldridge
1935- ..... **CLC 30; BLC; DAM MULT**
See also BW 1; CA 21-24R; CANR 16

Cleese, John (Marwood) 1939- ..... **CLC 21**
See also Monty Python
See also CA 112; 116; CANR 35; MTCW

Cleishbotham, Jebediah
See Scott, Walter

Cleland, John 1710-1789 .... **LC 2**
See also DLB 39

Clemens, Samuel Langhorne 1835-1910
See Twain, Mark
See also CA 104; 135; CDALB 1865-1917; DA; DAB; DAC; DAM MST, NOV; DLB 11, 12, 23, 64, 74; JRDA; MAICYA; YABC 2

Cleophil
See Congreve, William

Clerihew, E.
See Bentley, E(dmund) C(lerihew)

Clerk, N. W.
See Lewis, C(live) S(taples)

Cliff, Jimmy...................... **CLC 21**
See also Chambers, James

Clifton, (Thelma) Lucille
1936- .... **CLC 19, 66; BLC; DAM MULT, POET**
See also BW 2; CA 49-52; CANR 2, 24, 42; CLR 5; DLB 5, 41; MAICYA; MTCW; SATA 20, 69

Clinton, Dirk
See Silverberg, Robert

Clough, Arthur Hugh 1819-1861.. **NCLC 27**
See also DLB 32

Clutha, Janet Paterson Frame 1924-
See Frame, Janet
See also CA 1-4R; CANR 2, 36; MTCW

Clyne, Terence
See Blatty, William Peter

Cobalt, Martin
See Mayne, William (James Carter)

Cobbett, William 1763-1835 ..... **NCLC 49**
See also DLB 43, 107, 158

Coburn, D(onald) L(ee) 1938- ...... **CLC 10**
See also CA 89-92

Cocteau, Jean (Maurice Eugene Clement)
1889-1963 .... **CLC 1, 8, 15, 16, 43; DA; DAB; DAC; DAM DRAM, MST, NOV; WLC**
See also CA 25-28; CANR 40; CAP 2; DLB 65; MTCW

Copeland, Stewart (Armstrong)
1952- .... **CLC 26**

Coppard, A(lfred) E(dgar)
1878-1957 .... **TCLC 5; SSC 21**
See also CA 114; DLB 162; YABC 1

Coppee, Francois 1842-1908 ...... **TCLC 25**

Coppola, Francis Ford 1939- .... **CLC 16**
See also CA 77-80; CANR 40; DLB 44

Corbiere, Tristan 1845-1875 ..... **NCLC 43**

Corcoran, Barbara 1911- .... **CLC 17**
See also AAYA 14; CA 21-24R; CAAS 2;
CANR 11, 28, 48; DLB 52; JRDA;
SAAS 20; SATA 3, 77

Cordelier, Maurice
See Giraudoux, (Hippolyte) Jean

Corelli, Marie 1855-1924 .... **TCLC 51**
See also Mackay, Mary
See also DLB 34, 156

Corman, Cid .... **CLC 9**
See also Corman, Sidney
See also CAAS 2; DLB 5

Corman, Sidney 1924-
See Corman, Cid
See also CA 85-88; CANR 44; DAM POET

Cormier, Robert (Edmund)
1925- .... **CLC 12, 30; DA; DAB; DAC;
DAM MST, NOV**
See also AAYA 3, 19; CA 1-4R; CANR 5,
23; CDALB 1968-1988; CLR 12; DLB 52;
INT CANR-23; JRDA; MAICYA;
MTCW; SATA 10, 45, 83

Corn, Alfred (DeWitt III) 1943- .... **CLC 33**
See also CA 104; CAAS 25; CANR 44;
DLB 120; DLBY 80

Corneille, Pierre
1606-1684 .... **LC 28; DAB; DAM MST**

Cornwell, David (John Moore)
1931- .... **CLC 9, 15; DAM POP**
See also le Carre, John
See also CA 5-8R; CANR 13, 33; MTCW

Corso, (Nunzio) Gregory 1930- ... **CLC 1, 11**
See also CA 5-8R; CANR 41; DLB 5, 16;
MTCW

Cortazar, Julio
1914-1984 ...... **CLC 2, 3, 5, 10, 13, 15,
33, 34, 92; DAM MULT, NOV; HLC;
SSC 7**
See also CA 21-24R; CANR 12, 32;
DLB 113; HW; MTCW

CORTES, HERNAN 1484-1547 ..... **LC 31**

Corwin, Cecil
See Kornbluth, C(yril) M.

Cosic, Dobrica 1921- .... **CLC 14**
See also CA 122; 138

Costain, Thomas B(ertram)
1885-1965 .... **CLC 30**
See also CA 5-8R; 25-28R; DLB 9

Costantini, Humberto
1924(?)-1987 .... **CLC 49**
See also CA 131; 122; HW

Costello, Elvis 1955- .... **CLC 21**

Cotter, Joseph Seamon Sr.
1861-1949 .... **TCLC 28; BLC;
DAM MULT**
See also BW 1; CA 124; DLB 50

Couch, Arthur Thomas Quiller
See Quiller-Couch, Arthur Thomas

Coulton, James
See Hansen, Joseph

Couperus, Louis (Marie Anne)
1863-1923 .... **TCLC 15**
See also CA 115

Coupland, Douglas
1961- .... **CLC 85; DAC; DAM POP**
See also CA 142

Court, Wesli
See Turco, Lewis (Putnam)

Courtenay, Bryce 1933- .... **CLC 59**
See also CA 138

Courtney, Robert
See Ellison, Harlan (Jay)

Cousteau, Jacques-Yves 1910- ...... **CLC 30**
See also CA 65-68; CANR 15; MTCW;
SATA 38

Coward, Noel (Peirce)
1899-1973 .... **CLC 1, 9, 29, 51;
DAM DRAM**
See also AITN 1; CA 17-18; 41-44R;
CANR 35; CAP 2; CDBLB 1914-1945;
DLB 10; MTCW

Cowley, Malcolm 1898-1989 .... **CLC 39**
See also CA 5-8R; 128; CANR 3, 55;
DLB 4, 48; DLBY 81, 89; MTCW

Cowper, William
1731-1800 ...... **NCLC 8; DAM POET**
See also DLB 104, 109

Cox, William Trevor
1928- .... **CLC 9, 14, 71; DAM NOV**
See also Trevor, William
See also CA 9-12R; CANR 4, 37, 55;
DLB 14; INT CANR-37; MTCW

Coyne, P. J.
See Masters, Hilary

Cozzens, James Gould
1903-1978 .... **CLC 1, 4, 11, 92**
See also CA 9-12R; 81-84; CANR 19;
CDALB 1941-1968; DLB 9; DLBD 2;
DLBY 84; MTCW

Crabbe, George 1754-1832 .... **NCLC 26**
See also DLB 93

Craddock, Charles Egbert
See Murfree, Mary Noailles

Craig, A. A.
See Anderson, Poul (William)

Craik, Dinah Maria (Mulock)
1826-1887 .... **NCLC 38**
See also DLB 35, 163; MAICYA; SATA 34

Cram, Ralph Adams 1863-1942 .... **TCLC 45**

Crane, (Harold) Hart
1899-1932 .... **TCLC 2, 5; DA; DAB;
DAC; DAM MST, POET; PC 3; WLC**
See also CA 104; 127; CDALB 1917-1929;
DLB 4, 48; MTCW

Crane, R(onald) S(almon)
1886-1967 .... **CLC 27**
See also CA 85-88; DLB 63

Crane, Stephen (Townley)
1871-1900 ...... **TCLC 11, 17, 32; DA;
DAB; DAC; DAM MST, NOV, POET;
SSC 7; WLC**
See also CA 109; 140; CDALB 1865-1917;
DLB 12, 54, 78; YABC 2

Crase, Douglas 1944- .... **CLC 58**
See also CA 106

Crashaw, Richard 1612(?)-1649 ...... **LC 24**
See also DLB 126

Craven, Margaret
1901-1980 .... **CLC 17; DAC**
See also CA 103

Crawford, F(rancis) Marion
1854-1909 .... **TCLC 10**
See also CA 107; DLB 71

Crawford, Isabella Valancy
1850-1887 .... **NCLC 12**
See also DLB 92

Crayon, Geoffrey
See Irving, Washington

Creasey, John 1908-1973 .... **CLC 11**
See also CA 5-8R; 41-44R; CANR 8;
DLB 77; MTCW

Crebillon, Claude Prosper Jolyot de (fils)
1707-1777 .... **LC 28**

Credo
See Creasey, John

Creeley, Robert (White)
1926- ..... **CLC 1, 2, 4, 8, 11, 15, 36, 78;
DAM POET**
See also CA 1-4R; CAAS 10; CANR 23, 43;
DLB 5, 16, 169; MTCW

Crews, Harry (Eugene)
1935- .... **CLC 6, 23, 49**
See also AITN 1; CA 25-28R; CANR 20;
DLB 6, 143; MTCW

Crichton, (John) Michael
1942- .... **CLC 2, 6, 54, 90; DAM NOV,
POP**
See also AAYA 10; AITN 2; CA 25-28R;
CANR 13, 40, 54; DLBY 81;
INT CANR-13; JRDA; MTCW; SATA 9,
88

Crispin, Edmund .... **CLC 22**
See also Montgomery, (Robert) Bruce
See also DLB 87

Cristofer, Michael
1945(?)- .... **CLC 28; DAM DRAM**
See also CA 110; 152; DLB 7

Croce, Benedetto 1866-1952 ...... **TCLC 37**
See also CA 120

Crockett, David 1786-1836 .... **NCLC 8**
See also DLB 3, 11

Crockett, Davy
See Crockett, David

Crofts, Freeman Wills
1879-1957 .... **TCLC 55**
See also CA 115; DLB 77

Croker, John Wilson 1780-1857 .. **NCLC 10**
See also DLB 110

Crommelynck, Fernand 1885-1970 .. **CLC 75**
See also CA 89-92

Davies, (William) Robertson
　　1913-1995 . . . . . **CLC 2, 7, 13, 25, 42, 75,**
　　　　91; DA; DAB; DAC; DAM MST, NOV,
　　　　　　　　　　　　　　　　　　POP; WLC
　　See also BEST 89:2; CA 33-36R; 150;
　　　CANR 17, 42; DLB 68; INT CANR-17;
　　　MTCW

Davies, W(illiam) H(enry)
　　1871-1940 . . . . **TCLC 5**
　　See also CA 104; DLB 19, 174

Davies, Walter C.
　　See Kornbluth, C(yril) M.

Davis, Angela (Yvonne)
　　1944- . . . . **CLC 77; DAM MULT**
　　See also BW 2; CA 57-60; CANR 10

Davis, B. Lynch
　　See Bioy Casares, Adolfo; Borges, Jorge
　　　Luis

Davis, Gordon
　　See Hunt, E(verette) Howard, (Jr.)

Davis, Harold Lenoir 1896-1960 . . . . **CLC 49**
　　See also CA 89-92; DLB 9

Davis, Rebecca (Blaine) Harding
　　1831-1910 . . . . **TCLC 6**
　　See also CA 104; DLB 74

Davis, Richard Harding
　　1864-1916 . . . . **TCLC 24**
　　See also CA 114; DLB 12, 23, 78, 79;
　　　DLBD 13

Davison, Frank Dalby 1893-1970 . . . **CLC 15**
　　See also CA 116

Davison, Lawrence H.
　　See Lawrence, D(avid) H(erbert Richards)

Davison, Peter (Hubert) 1928- . . . . . **CLC 28**
　　See also CA 9-12R; CAAS 4; CANR 3, 43;
　　　DLB 5

Davys, Mary 1674-1732 . . . . **LC 1**
　　See also DLB 39

Dawson, Fielding 1930- . . . . **CLC 6**
　　See also CA 85-88; DLB 130

Dawson, Peter
　　See Faust, Frederick (Schiller)

Day, Clarence (Shepard, Jr.)
　　1874-1935 . . . . **TCLC 25**
　　See also CA 108; DLB 11

Day, Thomas 1748-1789 . . . . **LC 1**
　　See also DLB 39; YABC 1

Day Lewis, C(ecil)
　　1904-1972 . . . . **CLC 1, 6, 10;**
　　　　　　　　　　　　　　　　DAM POET; PC 11
　　See also Blake, Nicholas
　　See also CA 13-16; 33-36R; CANR 34;
　　　CAP 1; DLB 15, 20; MTCW

Dazai, Osamu . . . . **TCLC 11**
　　See also Tsushima, Shuji

de Andrade, Carlos Drummond
　　See Drummond de Andrade, Carlos

Deane, Norman
　　See Creasey, John

de Beauvoir, Simone (Lucie Ernestine Marie
　　　Bertrand)
　　See Beauvoir, Simone (Lucie Ernestine
　　　Marie Bertrand) de

de Brissac, Malcolm
　　See Dickinson, Peter (Malcolm)

de Chardin, Pierre Teilhard
　　See Teilhard de Chardin, (Marie Joseph)
　　　Pierre

Dee, John 1527-1608 . . . . **LC 20**

Deer, Sandra 1940- . . . . **CLC 45**

De Ferrari, Gabriella 1941- . . . . **CLC 65**
　　See also CA 146

Defoe, Daniel
　　1660(?)-1731 . . . . **LC 1; DA; DAB; DAC;**
　　　　　　　　　　　　DAM MST, NOV; WLC
　　See also CDBLB 1660-1789; DLB 39, 95,
　　　101; JRDA; MAICYA; SATA 22

de Gourmont, Remy(-Marie-Charles)
　　See Gourmont, Remy (-Marie-Charles) de

de Hartog, Jan 1914- . . . . **CLC 19**
　　See also CA 1-4R; CANR 1

de Hostos, E. M.
　　See Hostos (y Bonilla), Eugenio Maria de

de Hostos, Eugenio M.
　　See Hostos (y Bonilla), Eugenio Maria de

Deighton, Len . . . . **CLC 4, 7, 22, 46**
　　See also Deighton, Leonard Cyril
　　See also AAYA 6; BEST 89:2;
　　　CDBLB 1960 to Present; DLB 87

Deighton, Leonard Cyril 1929-
　　See Deighton, Len
　　See also CA 9-12R; CANR 19, 33;
　　　DAM NOV, POP; MTCW

Dekker, Thomas
　　1572(?)-1632 . . . . . **LC 22; DAM DRAM**
　　See also CDBLB Before 1660; DLB 62, 172

Delafield, E. M. 1890-1943 . . . . . . **TCLC 61**
　　See also Dashwood, Edmee Elizabeth
　　　Monica de la Pasture
　　See also DLB 34

de la Mare, Walter (John)
　　1873-1956 . . . . **TCLC 4, 53; DAB; DAC;**
　　　　　　　　　DAM MST, POET; SSC 14; WLC
　　See also CDBLB 1914-1945; CLR 23;
　　　DLB 162; SATA 16

Delaney, Franey
　　See O'Hara, John (Henry)

Delaney, Shelagh
　　1939- . . . . **CLC 29; DAM DRAM**
　　See also CA 17-20R; CANR 30;
　　　CDBLB 1960 to Present; DLB 13;
　　　MTCW

Delany, Mary (Granville Pendarves)
　　1700-1788 . . . . **LC 12**

Delany, Samuel R(ay, Jr.)
　　1942- . . . . **CLC 8, 14, 38; BLC;**
　　　　　　　　　　　　　　　　　　DAM MULT
　　See also BW 2; CA 81-84; CANR 27, 43;
　　　DLB 8, 33; MTCW

De La Ramee, (Marie) Louise 1839-1908
　　See Ouida
　　See also SATA 20

de la Roche, Mazo 1879-1961 . . . . . . **CLC 14**
　　See also CA 85-88; CANR 30; DLB 68;
　　　SATA 64

Delbanco, Nicholas (Franklin)
　　1942- . . . . **CLC 6, 13**
　　See also CA 17-20R; CAAS 2; CANR 29,
　　　55; DLB 6

del Castillo, Michel 1933- . . . . **CLC 38**
　　See also CA 109

Deledda, Grazia (Cosima)
　　1875(?)-1936 . . . . **TCLC 23**
　　See also CA 123

Delibes, Miguel . . . . **CLC 8, 18**
　　See also Delibes Setien, Miguel

Delibes Setien, Miguel 1920-
　　See Delibes, Miguel
　　See also CA 45-48; CANR 1, 32; HW;
　　　MTCW

DeLillo, Don
　　1936- . . . . . **CLC 8, 10, 13, 27, 39, 54, 76;**
　　　　　　　　　　　　　　　　DAM NOV, POP
　　See also BEST 89:1; CA 81-84; CANR 21;
　　　DLB 6, 173; MTCW

de Lisser, H. G.
　　See De Lisser, H(erbert) G(eorge)
　　See also DLB 117

De Lisser, H(erbert) G(eorge)
　　1878-1944 . . . . **TCLC 12**
　　See also de Lisser, H. G.
　　See also BW 2; CA 109; 152

Deloria, Vine (Victor), Jr.
　　1933- . . . . **CLC 21; DAM MULT**
　　See also CA 53-56; CANR 5, 20, 48;
　　　MTCW; NNAL; SATA 21

Del Vecchio, John M(ichael)
　　1947- . . . . **CLC 29**
　　See also CA 110; DLBD 9

de Man, Paul (Adolph Michel)
　　1919-1983 . . . . **CLC 55**
　　See also CA 128; 111; DLB 67; MTCW

De Marinis, Rick 1934- . . . . **CLC 54**
　　See also CA 57-60; CAAS 24; CANR 9, 25,
　　　50

Dembry, R. Emmet
　　See Murfree, Mary Noailles

Demby, William
　　1922- . . . . . **CLC 53; BLC; DAM MULT**
　　See also BW 1; CA 81-84; DLB 33

Demijohn, Thom
　　See Disch, Thomas M(ichael)

de Montherlant, Henry (Milon)
　　See Montherlant, Henry (Milon) de

Demosthenes 384B.C.-322B.C. . . . . **CMLC 13**

de Natale, Francine
　　See Malzberg, Barry N(athaniel)

Denby, Edwin (Orr) 1903-1983 . . . . . **CLC 48**
　　See also CA 138; 110

Denis, Julio
　　See Cortazar, Julio

Denmark, Harrison
　　See Zelazny, Roger (Joseph)

Dennis, John 1658-1734 . . . . **LC 11**
　　See also DLB 101

Dennis, Nigel (Forbes) 1912-1989 . . . . **CLC 8**
　　See also CA 25-28R; 129; DLB 13, 15;
　　　MTCW

De Palma, Brian (Russell) 1940- . . . . **CLC 20**
　　See also CA 109

De Quincey, Thomas 1785-1859 . . . **NCLC 4**
　　See also CDBLB 1789-1832; DLB 110; 144

Deren, Eleanora 1908(?)-1961
See Deren, Maya
See also CA 111

Deren, Maya . . . . **CLC 16**
See also Deren, Eleanora

Derleth, August (William)
1909-1971 . . . . **CLC 31**
See also CA 1-4R; 29-32R; CANR 4;
DLB 9; SATA 5

Der Nister 1884-1950. . . . . **TCLC 56**

de Routisie, Albert
See Aragon, Louis

Derrida, Jacques 1930-. . . . . **CLC 24, 87**
See also CA 124; 127

Derry Down Derry
See Lear, Edward

Dersonnes, Jacques
See Simenon, Georges (Jacques Christian)

Desai, Anita
1937- . . . . **CLC 19, 37, 97; DAB;**
DAM NOV
See also CA 81-84; CANR 33, 53; MTCW;
SATA 63

de Saint-Luc, Jean
See Glassco, John

de Saint Roman, Arnaud
See Aragon, Louis

Descartes, Rene 1596-1650 . . . . . . **LC 20, 35**

De Sica, Vittorio 1901(?)-1974 . . . . . **CLC 20**
See also CA 117

Desnos, Robert 1900-1945. . . . . . . **TCLC 22**
See also CA 121; 151

Destouches, Louis-Ferdinand
1894-1961 . . . . **CLC 9, 15**
See also Celine, Louis-Ferdinand
See also CA 85-88; CANR 28; MTCW

Deutsch, Babette 1895-1982 . . . . **CLC 18**
See also CA 1-4R; 108; CANR 4; DLB 45;
SATA 1; SATA-Obit 33

Devenant, William 1606-1649 . . . . **LC 13**

Devkota, Laxmiprasad
1909-1959 . . . . **TCLC 23**
See also CA 123

De Voto, Bernard (Augustine)
1897-1955 . . . . **TCLC 29**
See also CA 113; DLB 9

De Vries, Peter
1910-1993 . . . . **CLC 1, 2, 3, 7, 10, 28, 46;**
DAM NOV
See also CA 17-20R; 142; CANR 41;
DLB 6; DLBY 82; MTCW

Dexter, John
See Bradley, Marion Zimmer

Dexter, Martin
See Faust, Frederick (Schiller)

Dexter, Pete
1943- . . . . **CLC 34, 55; DAM POP**
See also BEST 89:2; CA 127; 131; INT 131;
MTCW

Diamano, Silmang
See Senghor, Leopold Sedar

Diamond, Neil 1941- . . . . **CLC 30**
See also CA 108

Diaz del Castillo, Bernal 1496-1584 . . **LC 31**

di Bassetto, Corno
See Shaw, George Bernard

Dick, Philip K(indred)
1928-1982 . . . . **CLC 10, 30, 72;**
DAM NOV, POP
See also CA 49-52; 106; CANR 2, 16;
DLB 8; MTCW

Dickens, Charles (John Huffam)
1812-1870 . . . . . . **NCLC 3, 8, 18, 26, 37,**
50; DA; DAB; DAC; DAM MST, NOV;
SSC 17; WLC
See also CDBLB 1832-1890; DLB 21, 55,
70, 159, 166; JRDA; MAICYA; SATA 15

Dickey, James (Lafayette)
1923- . . . . **CLC 1, 2, 4, 7, 10, 15, 47;**
DAM NOV, POET, POP
See also AITN 1, 2; CA 9-12R; CABS 2;
CANR 10, 48; CDALB 1968-1988;
DLB 5; DLBD 7; DLBY 82, 93;
INT CANR-10; MTCW

Dickey, William 1928-1994 . . . . . . **CLC 3, 28**
See also CA 9-12R; 145; CANR 24; DLB 5

Dickinson, Charles 1951-. . . . . **CLC 49**
See also CA 128

Dickinson, Emily (Elizabeth)
1830-1886 . . . . **NCLC 21; DA; DAB;**
DAC; DAM MST, POET; PC 1; WLC
See also CDALB 1865-1917; DLB 1;
SATA 29

Dickinson, Peter (Malcolm)
1927- . . . . **CLC 12, 35**
See also AAYA 9; CA 41-44R; CANR 31;
CLR 29; DLB 87, 161; JRDA; MAICYA;
SATA 5, 62

Dickson, Carr
See Carr, John Dickson

Dickson, Carter
See Carr, John Dickson

Diderot, Denis 1713-1784 . . . . **LC 26**

Didion, Joan
1934- . . **CLC 1, 3, 8, 14, 32; DAM NOV**
See also AITN 1; CA 5-8R; CANR 14, 52;
CDALB 1968-1988; DLB 2, 173;
DLBY 81, 86; MTCW

Dietrich, Robert
See Hunt, E(verette) Howard, (Jr.)

Dillard, Annie
1945- . . . . **CLC 9, 60; DAM NOV**
See also AAYA 6; CA 49-52; CANR 3, 43;
DLBY 80; MTCW; SATA 10

Dillard, R(ichard) H(enry) W(ilde)
1937- . . . . **CLC 5**
See also CA 21-24R; CAAS 7; CANR 10;
DLB 5

Dillon, Eilis 1920-1994. . . . . **CLC 17**
See also CA 9-12R; 147; CAAS 3; CANR 4,
38; CLR 26; MAICYA; SATA 2, 74;
SATA-Obit 83

Dimont, Penelope
See Mortimer, Penelope (Ruth)

Dinesen, Isak. . . . . **CLC 10, 29, 95; SSC 7**
See also Blixen, Karen (Christentze
Dinesen)

Ding Ling. . . . . **CLC 68**
See also Chiang Pin-chin

Disch, Thomas M(ichael) 1940-. . . **CLC 7, 36**
See also AAYA 17; CA 21-24R; CAAS 4;
CANR 17, 36, 54; CLR 18; DLB 8;
MAICYA; MTCW; SAAS 15; SATA 54

Disch, Tom
See Disch, Thomas M(ichael)

d'Isly, Georges
See Simenon, Georges (Jacques Christian)

Disraeli, Benjamin 1804-1881 . . **NCLC 2, 39**
See also DLB 21, 55

Ditcum, Steve
See Crumb, R(obert)

Dixon, Paige
See Corcoran, Barbara

Dixon, Stephen 1936-. . . . . **CLC 52; SSC 16**
See also CA 89-92; CANR 17, 40, 54;
DLB 130

Dobell, Sydney Thompson
1824-1874 . . . . **NCLC 43**
See also DLB 32

Doblin, Alfred . . . . **TCLC 13**
See also Doeblin, Alfred

Dobrolyubov, Nikolai Alexandrovich
1836-1861 . . . . **NCLC 5**

Dobyns, Stephen 1941-. . . . . **CLC 37**
See also CA 45-48; CANR 2, 18

Doctorow, E(dgar) L(aurence)
1931- . . . . . **CLC 6, 11, 15, 18, 37, 44, 65;**
DAM NOV, POP
See also AITN 2; BEST 89:3; CA 45-48;
CANR 2, 33, 51; CDALB 1968-1988;
DLB 2, 28, 173; DLBY 80; MTCW

Dodgson, Charles Lutwidge 1832-1898
See Carroll, Lewis
See also CLR 2; DA; DAB; DAC;
DAM MST, NOV, POET; MAICYA;
YABC 2

Dodson, Owen (Vincent)
1914-1983 . . . . **CLC 79; BLC;**
DAM MULT
See also BW 1; CA 65-68; 110; CANR 24;
DLB 76

Doeblin, Alfred 1878-1957. . . . . **TCLC 13**
See also Doblin, Alfred
See also CA 110; 141; DLB 66

Doerr, Harriet 1910- . . . . **CLC 34**
See also CA 117; 122; CANR 47; INT 122

Domecq, H(onorio) Bustos
See Bioy Casares, Adolfo; Borges, Jorge
Luis

Domini, Rey
See Lorde, Audre (Geraldine)

Dominique
See Proust, (Valentin-Louis-George-Eugene-)
Marcel

Don, A
See Stephen, Leslie

Donaldson, Stephen R.
1947- . . . . **CLC 46; DAM POP**
See also CA 89-92; CANR 13, 55;
INT CANR-13

Donleavy, J(ames) P(atrick)
1926- . . . . **CLC 1, 4, 6, 10, 45**
See also AITN 2; CA 9-12R; CANR 24, 49;
DLB 6, 173; INT CANR-24; MTCW

Donne, John
1572-1631 . . . . . . LC 10, 24; DA; DAB;
DAC; DAM MST, POET; PC 1
See also CDBLB Before 1660; DLB 121,
151

Donnell, David 1939(?)- . . . . CLC 34

Donoghue, P. S.
See Hunt, E(verette) Howard, (Jr.)

Donoso (Yanez), Jose
1924- . . . . CLC 4, 8, 11, 32;
DAM MULT; HLC
See also CA 81-84; CANR 32; DLB 113;
HW; MTCW

Donovan, John 1928-1992 . . . . CLC 35
See also CA 97-100; 137; CLR 3;
MAICYA; SATA 72; SATA-Brief 29

Don Roberto
See Cunninghame Graham, R(obert)
B(ontine)

Doolittle, Hilda
1886-1961 . . . . . CLC 3, 8, 14, 31, 34, 73;
DA; DAC; DAM MST, POET; PC 5;
WLC
See also H. D.
See also CA 97-100; CANR 35; DLB 4, 45;
MTCW

Dorfman, Ariel
1942- . . . . CLC 48, 77; DAM MULT;
HLC
See also CA 124; 130; HW; INT 130

Dorn, Edward (Merton) 1929-. . . CLC 10, 18
See also CA 93-96; CANR 42; DLB 5;
INT 93-96

Dorsan, Luc
See Simenon, Georges (Jacques Christian)

Dorsange, Jean
See Simenon, Georges (Jacques Christian)

Dos Passos, John (Roderigo)
1896-1970 . . . . . . CLC 1, 4, 8, 11, 15, 25,
34, 82; DA; DAB; DAC; DAM MST,
NOV; WLC
See also CA 1-4R; 29-32R; CANR 3;
CDALB 1929-1941; DLB 4, 9; DLBD 1;
MTCW

Dossage, Jean
See Simenon, Georges (Jacques Christian)

Dostoevsky, Fedor Mikhailovich
1821-1881 . . . . . . NCLC 2, 7, 21, 33, 43;
DA; DAB; DAC; DAM MST, NOV;
SSC 2; WLC

Doughty, Charles M(ontagu)
1843-1926 . . . . TCLC 27
See also CA 115; DLB 19, 57, 174

Douglas, Ellen . . . . CLC 73
See also Haxton, Josephine Ayres;
Williamson, Ellen Douglas

Douglas, Gavin 1475(?)-1522 . . . . LC 20

Douglas, Keith 1920-1944 . . . . TCLC 40
See also DLB 27

Douglas, Leonard
See Bradbury, Ray (Douglas)

Douglas, Michael
See Crichton, (John) Michael

Douglass, Frederick
1817(?)-1895 . . . . NCLC 7, 55; BLC; DA;
DAC; DAM MST, MULT; WLC
See also CDALB 1640-1865; DLB 1, 43, 50,
79; SATA 29

Dourado, (Waldomiro Freitas) Autran
1926- . . . . CLC 23, 60
See also CA 25-28R; CANR 34

Dourado, Waldomiro Autran
See Dourado, (Waldomiro Freitas) Autran

Dove, Rita (Frances)
1952- . . . . CLC 50, 81; DAM MULT,
POET; PC 6
See also BW 2; CA 109; CAAS 19;
CANR 27, 42; DLB 120

Dowell, Coleman 1925-1985 . . . . CLC 60
See also CA 25-28R; 117; CANR 10;
DLB 130

Dowson, Ernest (Christopher)
1867-1900 . . . . TCLC 4
See also CA 105; 150; DLB 19, 135

Doyle, A. Conan
See Doyle, Arthur Conan

Doyle, Arthur Conan
1859-1930 . . . . TCLC 7; DA; DAB;
DAC; DAM MST, NOV; SSC 12; WLC
See also AAYA 14; CA 104; 122;
CDBLB 1890-1914; DLB 18, 70, 156;
MTCW; SATA 24

Doyle, Conan
See Doyle, Arthur Conan

Doyle, John
See Graves, Robert (von Ranke)

Doyle, Roddy 1958(?)- . . . . CLC 81
See also AAYA 14; CA 143

Doyle, Sir A. Conan
See Doyle, Arthur Conan

Doyle, Sir Arthur Conan
See Doyle, Arthur Conan

Dr. A
See Asimov, Isaac; Silverstein, Alvin

Drabble, Margaret
1939- . . . . CLC 2, 3, 5, 8, 10, 22, 53;
DAB; DAC; DAM MST, NOV, POP
See also CA 13-16R; CANR 18, 35;
CDBLB 1960 to Present; DLB 14, 155;
MTCW; SATA 48

Drapier, M. B.
See Swift, Jonathan

Drayham, James
See Mencken, H(enry) L(ouis)

Drayton, Michael 1563-1631 . . . . LC 8

Dreadstone, Carl
See Campbell, (John) Ramsey

Dreiser, Theodore (Herman Albert)
1871-1945 . . . . . . TCLC 10, 18, 35; DA;
DAC; DAM MST, NOV; WLC
See also CA 106; 132; CDALB 1865-1917;
DLB 9, 12, 102, 137; DLBD 1; MTCW

Drexler, Rosalyn 1926- . . . . CLC 2, 6
See also CA 81-84

Dreyer, Carl Theodor 1889-1968. . . . CLC 16
See also CA 116

Drieu la Rochelle, Pierre(-Eugene)
1893-1945 . . . . TCLC 21
See also CA 117; DLB 72

Drinkwater, John 1882-1937 . . . . . . TCLC 57
See also CA 109; 149; DLB 10, 19, 149

Drop Shot
See Cable, George Washington

Droste-Hulshoff, Annette Freiin von
1797-1848 . . . . NCLC 3
See also DLB 133

Drummond, Walter
See Silverberg, Robert

Drummond, William Henry
1854-1907 . . . . TCLC 25
See also DLB 92

Drummond de Andrade, Carlos
1902-1987 . . . . CLC 18
See also Andrade, Carlos Drummond de
See also CA 132; 123

Drury, Allen (Stuart) 1918- . . . . CLC 37
See also CA 57-60; CANR 18, 52;
INT CANR-18

Dryden, John
1631-1700 . . . . LC 3, 21; DA; DAB;
DAC; DAM DRAM, MST, POET;
DC 3; WLC
See also CDBLB 1660-1789; DLB 80, 101,
131

Duberman, Martin 1930- . . . . CLC 8
See also CA 1-4R; CANR 2

Dubie, Norman (Evans) 1945- . . . . . . CLC 36
See also CA 69-72; CANR 12; DLB 120

Du Bois, W(illiam) E(dward) B(urghardt)
1868-1963 . . . . CLC 1, 2, 13, 64, 96;
BLC; DA; DAC; DAM MST, MULT,
NOV; WLC
See also BW 1; CA 85-88; CANR 34;
CDALB 1865-1917; DLB 47, 50, 91;
MTCW; SATA 42

Dubus, Andre
1936- . . . . CLC 13, 36, 97; SSC 15
See also CA 21-24R; CANR 17; DLB 130;
INT CANR-17

Duca Minimo
See D'Annunzio, Gabriele

Ducharme, Rejean 1941- . . . . CLC 74
See also DLB 60

Duclos, Charles Pinot 1704-1772 . . . . . LC 1

Dudek, Louis 1918- . . . . CLC 11, 19
See also CA 45-48; CAAS 14; CANR 1;
DLB 88

Duerrenmatt, Friedrich
1921-1990 . . . . . . CLC 1, 4, 8, 11, 15, 43;
DAM DRAM
See also CA 17-20R; CANR 33; DLB 69,
124; MTCW

Duffy, Bruce (?)- . . . . CLC 50

Duffy, Maureen 1933- . . . . CLC 37
See also CA 25-28R; CANR 33; DLB 14;
MTCW

Dugan, Alan 1923- . . . . CLC 2, 6
See also CA 81-84; DLB 5

du Gard, Roger Martin
See Martin du Gard, Roger

Eichendorff, Joseph Freiherr von
   1788-1857 .... NCLC 8
   See also DLB 90

Eigner, Larry .... CLC 9
   See also Eigner, Laurence (Joel)
   See also CAAS 23; DLB 5

Eigner, Laurence (Joel) 1927-1996
   See Eigner, Larry
   See also CA 9-12R; 151; CANR 6

Einstein, Albert 1879-1955 .... TCLC 65
   See also CA 121; 133; MTCW

Eiseley, Loren Corey 1907-1977 ..... CLC 7
   See also AAYA 5; CA 1-4R; 73-76;
   CANR 6

Eisenstadt, Jill 1963- .... CLC 50
   See also CA 140

Eisenstein, Sergei (Mikhailovich)
   1898-1948 .... TCLC 57
   See also CA 114; 149

Eisner, Simon
   See Kornbluth, C(yril) M.

Ekeloef, (Bengt) Gunnar
   1907-1968 .... CLC 27; DAM POET
   See also CA 123; 25-28R

Ekelof, (Bengt) Gunnar
   See Ekeloef, (Bengt) Gunnar

Ekwensi, C. O. D.
   See Ekwensi, Cyprian (Odiatu Duaka)

Ekwensi, Cyprian (Odiatu Duaka)
   1921- ...... CLC 4; BLC; DAM MULT
   See also BW 2; CA 29-32R; CANR 18, 42;
   DLB 117; MTCW; SATA 66

Elaine .... TCLC 18
   See also Leverson, Ada

El Crummo
   See Crumb, R(obert)

Elia
   See Lamb, Charles

Eliade, Mircea 1907-1986 .... CLC 19
   See also CA 65-68; 119; CANR 30; MTCW

Eliot, A. D.
   See Jewett, (Theodora) Sarah Orne

Eliot, Alice
   See Jewett, (Theodora) Sarah Orne

Eliot, Dan
   See Silverberg, Robert

Eliot, George
   1819-1880 ..... NCLC 4, 13, 23, 41, 49;
   DA; DAB; DAC; DAM MST, NOV;
   WLC
   See also CDBLB 1832-1890; DLB 21, 35, 55

Eliot, John 1604-1690 .... LC 5
   See also DLB 24

Eliot, T(homas) S(tearns)
   1888-1965 ..... CLC 1, 2, 3, 6, 9, 10, 13,
   15, 24, 34, 41, 55, 57; DA; DAB; DAC;
   DAM DRAM, MST, POET; PC 5;
   WLC 2
   See also CA 5-8R; 25-28R; CANR 41;
   CDALB 1929-1941; DLB 7, 10, 45, 63;
   DLBY 88; MTCW

Elizabeth 1866-1941 .... TCLC 41

Elkin, Stanley L(awrence)
   1930-1995 ...... CLC 4, 6, 9, 14, 27, 51,
   91; DAM NOV, POP; SSC 12
   See also CA 9-12R; 148; CANR 8, 46;
   DLB 2, 28; DLBY 80; INT CANR-8;
   MTCW

Elledge, Scott .... CLC 34

Elliot, Don
   See Silverberg, Robert

Elliott, Don
   See Silverberg, Robert

Elliott, George P(aul) 1918-1980 ..... CLC 2
   See also CA 1-4R; 97-100; CANR 2

Elliott, Janice 1931- .... CLC 47
   See also CA 13-16R; CANR 8, 29; DLB 14

Elliott, Sumner Locke 1917-1991 ... CLC 38
   See also CA 5-8R; 134; CANR 2, 21

Elliott, William
   See Bradbury, Ray (Douglas)

Ellis, A. E. .... CLC 7

Ellis, Alice Thomas .... CLC 40
   See also Haycraft, Anna

Ellis, Bret Easton
   1964- .... CLC 39, 71; DAM POP
   See also AAYA 2; CA 118; 123; CANR 51;
   INT 123

Ellis, (Henry) Havelock
   1859-1939 .... TCLC 14
   See also CA 109

Ellis, Landon
   See Ellison, Harlan (Jay)

Ellis, Trey 1962- .... CLC 55
   See also CA 146

Ellison, Harlan (Jay)
   1934- ...... CLC 1, 13, 42; DAM POP;
   SSC 14
   See also CA 5-8R; CANR 5, 46; DLB 8;
   INT CANR-5; MTCW

Ellison, Ralph (Waldo)
   1914-1994 .... CLC 1, 3, 11, 54, 86;
   BLC; DA; DAB; DAC; DAM MST,
   MULT, NOV; WLC
   See also AAYA 19; BW 1; CA 9-12R; 145;
   CANR 24, 53; CDALB 1941-1968;
   DLB 2, 76; DLBY 94; MTCW

Ellmann, Lucy (Elizabeth) 1956- .... CLC 61
   See also CA 128

Ellmann, Richard (David)
   1918-1987 .... CLC 50
   See also BEST 89:2; CA 1-4R; 122;
   CANR 2, 28; DLB 103; DLBY 87;
   MTCW

Elman, Richard 1934- .... CLC 19
   See also CA 17-20R; CAAS 3; CANR 47

Elron
   See Hubbard, L(afayette) Ron(ald)

Eluard, Paul .... TCLC 7, 41
   See also Grindel, Eugene

Elyot, Sir Thomas 1490(?)-1546 ..... LC 11

Elytis, Odysseus
   1911-1996 .... CLC 15, 49; DAM POET
   See also CA 102; 151; MTCW

Emecheta, (Florence Onye) Buchi
   1944- .. CLC 14, 48; BLC; DAM MULT
   See also BW 2; CA 81-84; CANR 27;
   DLB 117; MTCW; SATA 66

Emerson, Ralph Waldo
   1803-1882 ..... NCLC 1, 38; DA; DAB;
   DAC; DAM MST, POET; WLC
   See also CDALB 1640-1865; DLB 1, 59, 73

Eminescu, Mihail 1850-1889 ..... NCLC 33

Empson, William
   1906-1984 .... CLC 3, 8, 19, 33, 34
   See also CA 17-20R; 112; CANR 31;
   DLB 20; MTCW

Enchi Fumiko (Ueda) 1905-1986 .... CLC 31
   See also CA 129; 121

Ende, Michael (Andreas Helmuth)
   1929-1995 .... CLC 31
   See also CA 118; 124; 149; CANR 36;
   CLR 14; DLB 75; MAICYA; SATA 61;
   SATA-Brief 42; SATA-Obit 86

Endo, Shusaku
   1923-1996 .... CLC 7, 14, 19, 54;
   DAM NOV
   See also CA 29-32R; 153; CANR 21, 54;
   MTCW

Engel, Marian 1933-1985 .... CLC 36
   See also CA 25-28R; CANR 12; DLB 53;
   INT CANR-12

Engelhardt, Frederick
   See Hubbard, L(afayette) Ron(ald)

Enright, D(ennis) J(oseph)
   1920- .... CLC 4, 8, 31
   See also CA 1-4R; CANR 1, 42; DLB 27;
   SATA 25

Enzensberger, Hans Magnus
   1929- .... CLC 43
   See also CA 116; 119

Ephron, Nora 1941- .... CLC 17, 31
   See also AITN 2; CA 65-68; CANR 12, 39

Epsilon
   See Betjeman, John

Epstein, Daniel Mark 1948- .... CLC 7
   See also CA 49-52; CANR 2, 53

Epstein, Jacob 1956- .... CLC 19
   See also CA 114

Epstein, Joseph 1937- .... CLC 39
   See also CA 112; 119; CANR 50

Epstein, Leslie 1938- .... CLC 27
   See also CA 73-76; CAAS 12; CANR 23

Equiano, Olaudah
   1745(?)-1797 .... LC 16; BLC;
   DAM MULT
   See also DLB 37, 50

Erasmus, Desiderius 1469(?)-1536 .... LC 16

Erdman, Paul E(mil) 1932- .... CLC 25
   See also AITN 1; CA 61-64; CANR 13, 43

Erdrich, Louise
   1954- .... CLC 39, 54; DAM MULT,
   NOV, POP
   See also AAYA 10; BEST 89:1; CA 114;
   CANR 41; DLB 152; MTCW; NNAL

Erenburg, Ilya (Grigoryevich)
   See Ehrenburg, Ilya (Grigoryevich)

Erickson, Stephen Michael   1950-
See Erickson, Steve
See also CA 129

Erickson, Steve . . . . CLC 64
See also Erickson, Stephen Michael

Ericson, Walter
See Fast, Howard (Melvin)

Eriksson, Buntel
See Bergman, (Ernst) Ingmar

Ernaux, Annie   1940- . . . . CLC 88
See also CA 147

Eschenbach, Wolfram von
See Wolfram von Eschenbach

Eseki, Bruno
See Mphahlele, Ezekiel

Esenin, Sergei (Alexandrovich)
1895-1925 . . . . TCLC 4
See also CA 104

Eshleman, Clayton   1935- . . . . CLC 7
See also CA 33-36R; CAAS 6; DLB 5

Espriella, Don Manuel Alvarez
See Southey, Robert

Espriu, Salvador   1913-1985 . . . . CLC 9
See also CA 154; 115; DLB 134

Espronceda, Jose de   1808-1842 . . . NCLC 39

Esse, James
See Stephens, James

Esterbrook, Tom
See Hubbard, L(afayette) Ron(ald)

Estleman, Loren D.
1952- . . . . . . CLC 48; DAM NOV, POP
See also CA 85-88; CANR 27;
INT CANR-27; MTCW

Eugenides, Jeffrey   1960(?)- . . . . CLC 81
See also CA 144

Euripides   c. 485B.C.-406B.C. . . . . DC 4
See also DA; DAB; DAC; DAM DRAM,
MST

Evan, Evin
See Faust, Frederick (Schiller)

Evans, Evan
See Faust, Frederick (Schiller)

Evans, Marian
See Eliot, George

Evans, Mary Ann
See Eliot, George

Evarts, Esther
See Benson, Sally

Everett, Percival L.   1956- . . . . CLC 57
See also BW 2; CA 129

Everson, R(onald) G(ilmour)
1903- . . . . CLC 27
See also CA 17-20R; DLB 88

Everson, William (Oliver)
1912-1994 . . . . CLC 1, 5, 14
See also CA 9-12R; 145; CANR 20; DLB 5,
16; MTCW

Evtushenko, Evgenii Aleksandrovich
See Yevtushenko, Yevgeny (Alexandrovich)

Ewart, Gavin (Buchanan)
1916-1995 . . . . CLC 13, 46
See also CA 89-92; 150; CANR 17, 46;
DLB 40; MTCW

Ewers, Hanns Heinz   1871-1943 . . . TCLC 12
See also CA 109; 149

Ewing, Frederick R.
See Sturgeon, Theodore (Hamilton)

Exley, Frederick (Earl)
1929-1992 . . . . CLC 6, 11
See also AITN 2; CA 81-84; 138; DLB 143;
DLBY 81

Eynhardt, Guillermo
See Quiroga, Horacio (Sylvestre)

Ezekiel, Nissim   1924- . . . . CLC 61
See also CA 61-64

Ezekiel, Tish O'Dowd   1943- . . . . CLC 34
See also CA 129

Fadeyev, A.
See Bulgya, Alexander Alexandrovich

Fadeyev, Alexander . . . . TCLC 53
See also Bulgya, Alexander Alexandrovich

Fagen, Donald   1948- . . . . CLC 26

Fainzilberg, Ilya Arnoldovich   1897-1937
See Ilf, Ilya
See also CA 120

Fair, Ronald L.   1932- . . . . CLC 18
See also BW 1; CA 69-72; CANR 25;
DLB 33

Fairbairns, Zoe (Ann)   1948- . . . . CLC 32
See also CA 103; CANR 21

Falco, Gian
See Papini, Giovanni

Falconer, James
See Kirkup, James

Falconer, Kenneth
See Kornbluth, C(yril) M.

Falkland, Samuel
See Heijermans, Herman

Fallaci, Oriana   1930- . . . . CLC 11
See also CA 77-80; CANR 15; MTCW

Faludy, George   1913- . . . . CLC 42
See also CA 21-24R

Faludy, Gyoergy
See Faludy, George

Fanon, Frantz
1925-1961 . . . . CLC 74; BLC;
DAM MULT
See also BW 1; CA 116; 89-92

Fanshawe, Ann   1625-1680 . . . . LC 11

Fante, John (Thomas)   1911-1983 . . . CLC 60
See also CA 69-72; 109; CANR 23;
DLB 130; DLBY 83

Farah, Nuruddin
1945- . . . . . CLC 53; BLC; DAM MULT
See also BW 2; CA 106; DLB 125

Fargue, Leon-Paul   1876(?)-1947 . . . TCLC 11
See also CA 109

Farigoule, Louis
See Romains, Jules

Farina, Richard   1936(?)-1966 . . . . CLC 9
See also CA 81-84; 25-28R

Farley, Walter (Lorimer)
1915-1989 . . . . CLC 17
See also CA 17-20R; CANR 8, 29; DLB 22;
JRDA; MAICYA; SATA 2, 43

Farmer, Philip Jose   1918- . . . . CLC 1, 19
See also CA 1-4R; CANR 4, 35; DLB 8;
MTCW

Farquhar, George
1677-1707 . . . . LC 21; DAM DRAM
See also DLB 84

Farrell, J(ames) G(ordon)
1935-1979 . . . . CLC 6
See also CA 73-76; 89-92; CANR 36;
DLB 14; MTCW

Farrell, James T(homas)
1904-1979 . . . . CLC 1, 4, 8, 11, 66
See also CA 5-8R; 89-92; CANR 9; DLB 4,
9, 86; DLBD 2; MTCW

Farren, Richard J.
See Betjeman, John

Farren, Richard M.
See Betjeman, John

Fassbinder, Rainer Werner
1946-1982 . . . . CLC 20
See also CA 93-96; 106; CANR 31

Fast, Howard (Melvin)
1914- . . . . CLC 23; DAM NOV
See also AAYA 16; CA 1-4R; CAAS 18;
CANR 1, 33, 54; DLB 9; INT CANR-33;
SATA 7

Faulcon, Robert
See Holdstock, Robert P.

Faulkner, William (Cuthbert)
1897-1962 . . . . . CLC 1, 3, 6, 8, 9, 11, 14,
18, 28, 52, 68; DA; DAB; DAC;
DAM MST, NOV; SSC 1; WLC
See also AAYA 7; CA 81-84; CANR 33;
CDALB 1929-1941; DLB 9, 11, 44, 102;
DLBD 2; DLBY 86; MTCW

Fauset, Jessie Redmon
1884(?)-1961 . . . . CLC 19, 54; BLC;
DAM MULT
See also BW 1; CA 109; DLB 51

Faust, Frederick (Schiller)
1892-1944(?) . . . . . TCLC 49; DAM POP
See also CA 108; 152

Faust, Irvin   1924- . . . . CLC 8
See also CA 33-36R; CANR 28; DLB 2, 28;
DLBY 80

Fawkes, Guy
See Benchley, Robert (Charles)

Fearing, Kenneth (Flexner)
1902-1961 . . . . CLC 51
See also CA 93-96; DLB 9

Fecamps, Elise
See Creasey, John

Federman, Raymond   1928- . . . . . . CLC 6, 47
See also CA 17-20R; CAAS 8; CANR 10,
43; DLBY 80

Federspiel, J(uerg) F.   1931- . . . . CLC 42
See also CA 146

Feiffer, Jules (Ralph)
1929- . . . . . . CLC 2, 8, 64; DAM DRAM
See also AAYA 3; CA 17-20R; CANR 30;
DLB 7, 44; INT CANR-30; MTCW;
SATA 8, 61

Feige, Hermann Albert Otto Maximilian
See Traven, B.

Feinberg, David B.   1956-1994 . . . . . . CLC 59
See also CA 135; 147

Feinstein, Elaine 1930-. . . . . **CLC 36**
See also CA 69-72; CAAS 1; CANR 31;
DLB 14, 40; MTCW

Feldman, Irving (Mordecai) 1928-. . . . **CLC 7**
See also CA 1-4R; CANR 1; DLB 169

Fellini, Federico 1920-1993 . . . . . **CLC 16, 85**
See also CA 65-68; 143; CANR 33

Felsen, Henry Gregor 1916- . . . . **CLC 17**
See also CA 1-4R; CANR 1; SAAS 2;
SATA 1

Fenton, James Martin 1949- . . . . **CLC 32**
See also CA 102; DLB 40

Ferber, Edna 1887-1968. . . . . . . **CLC 18, 93**
See also AITN 1; CA 5-8R; 25-28R; DLB 9,
28, 86; MTCW; SATA 7

Ferguson, Helen
See Kavan, Anna

Ferguson, Samuel 1810-1886. . . . . **NCLC 33**
See also DLB 32

Fergusson, Robert 1750-1774 . . . . **LC 29**
See also DLB 109

Ferling, Lawrence
See Ferlinghetti, Lawrence (Monsanto)

Ferlinghetti, Lawrence (Monsanto)
1919(?)-. . . . . **CLC 2, 6, 10, 27;**
DAM POET; PC 1
See also CA 5-8R; CANR 3, 41;
CDALB 1941-1968; DLB 5, 16; MTCW

Fernandez, Vicente Garcia Huidobro
See Huidobro Fernandez, Vicente Garcia

Ferrer, Gabriel (Francisco Victor) Miro
See Miro (Ferrer), Gabriel (Francisco
Victor)

Ferrier, Susan (Edmonstone)
1782-1854 . . . . **NCLC 8**
See also DLB 116

Ferrigno, Robert 1948(?)-. . . . . **CLC 65**
See also CA 140

Ferron, Jacques 1921-1985 . . . **CLC 94; DAC**
See also CA 117; 129; DLB 60

Feuchtwanger, Lion 1884-1958 . . . . . **TCLC 3**
See also CA 104; DLB 66

Feuillet, Octave 1821-1890 . . . . . . **NCLC 45**

Feydeau, Georges (Leon Jules Marie)
1862-1921 . . . . . **TCLC 22; DAM DRAM**
See also CA 113; 152

Ficino, Marsilio 1433-1499 . . . . **LC 12**

Fiedeler, Hans
See Doeblin, Alfred

Fiedler, Leslie A(aron)
1917- . . . . **CLC 4, 13, 24**
See also CA 9-12R; CANR 7; DLB 28, 67;
MTCW

Field, Andrew 1938-. . . . . **CLC 44**
See also CA 97-100; CANR 25

Field, Eugene 1850-1895 . . . . **NCLC 3**
See also DLB 23, 42, 140; DLBD 13;
MAICYA; SATA 16

Field, Gans T.
See Wellman, Manly Wade

Field, Michael . . . . **TCLC 43**

Field, Peter
See Hobson, Laura Z(ametkin)

Fielding, Henry
1707-1754 . . . . . . **LC 1; DA; DAB; DAC;**
DAM DRAM, MST, NOV; WLC
See also CDBLB 1660-1789; DLB 39, 84,
101

Fielding, Sarah 1710-1768 . . . . **LC 1**
See also DLB 39

Fierstein, Harvey (Forbes)
1954- . . . . . **CLC 33; DAM DRAM, POP**
See also CA 123; 129

Figes, Eva 1932-. . . . . **CLC 31**
See also CA 53-56; CANR 4, 44; DLB 14

Finch, Robert (Duer Claydon)
1900- . . . . **CLC 18**
See also CA 57-60; CANR 9, 24, 49;
DLB 88

Findley, Timothy
1930- . . . . . . **CLC 27; DAC; DAM MST**
See also CA 25-28R; CANR 12, 42;
DLB 53

Fink, William
See Mencken, H(enry) L(ouis)

Firbank, Louis 1942-
See Reed, Lou
See also CA 117

Firbank, (Arthur Annesley) Ronald
1886-1926 . . . . **TCLC 1**
See also CA 104; DLB 36

Fisher, M(ary) F(rances) K(ennedy)
1908-1992 . . . . **CLC 76, 87**
See also CA 77-80; 138; CANR 44

Fisher, Roy 1930-. . . . . **CLC 25**
See also CA 81-84; CAAS 10; CANR 16;
DLB 40

Fisher, Rudolph
1897-1934 . . . . **TCLC 11; BLC;**
DAM MULT
See also BW 1; CA 107; 124; DLB 51, 102

Fisher, Vardis (Alvero) 1895-1968. . . . **CLC 7**
See also CA 5-8R; 25-28R; DLB 9

Fiske, Tarleton
See Bloch, Robert (Albert)

Fitch, Clarke
See Sinclair, Upton (Beall)

Fitch, John IV
See Cormier, Robert (Edmund)

Fitzgerald, Captain Hugh
See Baum, L(yman) Frank

FitzGerald, Edward 1809-1883 . . . . **NCLC 9**
See also DLB 32

Fitzgerald, F(rancis) Scott (Key)
1896-1940 . . . . . . **TCLC 1, 6, 14, 28, 55;**
DA; DAB; DAC; DAM MST, NOV;
SSC 6; WLC
See also AITN 1; CA 110; 123;
CDALB 1917-1929; DLB 4, 9, 86;
DLBD 1; DLBY 81; MTCW

Fitzgerald, Penelope 1916-. . . **CLC 19, 51, 61**
See also CA 85-88; CAAS 10; DLB 14

Fitzgerald, Robert (Stuart)
1910-1985 . . . . **CLC 39**
See also CA 1-4R; 114; CANR 1; DLBY 80

FitzGerald, Robert D(avid)
1902-1987 . . . . **CLC 19**
See also CA 17-20R

Fitzgerald, Zelda (Sayre)
1900-1948 . . . . **TCLC 52**
See also CA 117; 126; DLBY 84

Flanagan, Thomas (James Bonner)
1923- . . . . **CLC 25, 52**
See also CA 108; CANR 55; DLBY 80;
INT 108; MTCW

Flaubert, Gustave
1821-1880 . . . . **NCLC 2, 10, 19; DA;**
DAB; DAC; DAM MST, NOV; SSC 11;
WLC
See also DLB 119

Flecker, Herman Elroy
See Flecker, (Herman) James Elroy

Flecker, (Herman) James Elroy
1884-1915 . . . . **TCLC 43**
See also CA 109; 150; DLB 10, 19

Fleming, Ian (Lancaster)
1908-1964 . . . . **CLC 3, 30; DAM POP**
See also CA 5-8R; CDBLB 1945-1960;
DLB 87; MTCW; SATA 9

Fleming, Thomas (James) 1927- . . . . **CLC 37**
See also CA 5-8R; CANR 10;
INT CANR-10; SATA 8

Fletcher, John 1579-1625. . . . . . **LC 33; DC 6**
See also CDBLB Before 1660; DLB 58

Fletcher, John Gould 1886-1950 . . . **TCLC 35**
See also CA 107; DLB 4, 45

Fleur, Paul
See Pohl, Frederik

Flooglebuckle, Al
See Spiegelman, Art

Flying Officer X
See Bates, H(erbert) E(rnest)

Fo, Dario 1926-. . . . . **CLC 32; DAM DRAM**
See also CA 116; 128; MTCW

Fogarty, Jonathan Titulescu Esq.
See Farrell, James T(homas)

Folke, Will
See Bloch, Robert (Albert)

Follett, Ken(neth Martin)
1949- . . . . **CLC 18; DAM NOV, POP**
See also AAYA 6; BEST 89:4; CA 81-84;
CANR 13, 33, 54; DLB 87; DLBY 81;
INT CANR-33; MTCW

Fontane, Theodor 1819-1898 . . . . . **NCLC 26**
See also DLB 129

Foote, Horton
1916- . . . . **CLC 51, 91; DAM DRAM**
See also CA 73-76; CANR 34, 51; DLB 26;
INT CANR-34

Foote, Shelby
1916- . . . . **CLC 75; DAM NOV, POP**
See also CA 5-8R; CANR 3, 45; DLB 2, 17

Forbes, Esther 1891-1967. . . . . **CLC 12**
See also AAYA 17; CA 13-14; 25-28R;
CAP 1; CLR 27; DLB 22; JRDA;
MAICYA; SATA 2

Forche, Carolyn (Louise)
1950- . . . . **CLC 25, 83, 86; DAM POET;**
PC 10
See also CA 109; 117; CANR 50; DLB 5;
INT 117

Ford, Elbur
See Hibbert, Eleanor Alice Burford

Ford, Ford Madox
1873-1939 .... **TCLC 1, 15, 39, 57;**
DAM NOV
See also CA 104; 132; CDBLB 1914-1945;
DLB 162; MTCW

Ford, John 1895-1973............. **CLC 16**
See also CA 45-48

Ford, Richard 1944-.............. **CLC 46**
See also CA 69-72; CANR 11, 47

Ford, Webster
See Masters, Edgar Lee

Foreman, Richard 1937-........... **CLC 50**
See also CA 65-68; CANR 32

Forester, C(ecil) S(cott)
1899-1966 .... **CLC 35**
See also CA 73-76; 25-28R; SATA 13

Forez
See Mauriac, Francois (Charles)

Forman, James Douglas 1932-..... **CLC 21**
See also AAYA 17; CA 9-12R; CANR 4,
19, 42; JRDA; MAICYA; SATA 8, 70

Fornes, Maria Irene 1930-...... **CLC 39, 61**
See also CA 25-28R; CANR 28; DLB 7;
HW; INT CANR-28; MTCW

Forrest, Leon 1937- .... **CLC 4**
See also BW 2; CA 89-92; CAAS 7;
CANR 25, 52; DLB 33

Forster, E(dward) M(organ)
1879-1970 ..... **CLC 1, 2, 3, 4, 9, 10, 13,**
15, 22, 45, 77; DA; DAB; DAC;
DAM MST, NOV; WLC
See also AAYA 2; CA 13-14; 25-28R;
CANR 45; CAP 1; CDBLB 1914-1945;
DLB 34, 98, 162; DLBD 10; MTCW;
SATA 57

Forster, John 1812-1876 .... **NCLC 11**
See also DLB 144

Forsyth, Frederick
1938- .. **CLC 2, 5, 36; DAM NOV, POP**
See also BEST 89:4; CA 85-88; CANR 38;
DLB 87; MTCW

Forten, Charlotte L. .... **TCLC 16; BLC**
See Grimke, Charlotte L(ottie) Forten
See also DLB 50

Foscolo, Ugo 1778-1827.......... **NCLC 8**

Fosse, Bob .... **CLC 20**
See also Fosse, Robert Louis

Fosse, Robert Louis 1927-1987
See Fosse, Bob
See also CA 110; 123

Foster, Stephen Collins
1826-1864 .... **NCLC 26**

Foucault, Michel
1926-1984 .... **CLC 31, 34, 69**
See also CA 105; 113; CANR 34; MTCW

Fouque, Friedrich (Heinrich Karl) de la Motte
1777-1843 .... **NCLC 2**
See also DLB 90

Fourier, Charles 1772-1837 ...... **NCLC 51**

Fournier, Henri Alban 1886-1914
See Alain-Fournier
See also CA 104

Fournier, Pierre 1916-............ **CLC 11**
See also Gascar, Pierre
See also CA 89-92; CANR 16, 40

Fowles, John
1926- ...... **CLC 1, 2, 3, 4, 6, 9, 10, 15,**
33, 87; DAB; DAC; DAM MST
See also CA 5-8R; CANR 25; CDBLB 1960
to Present; DLB 14, 139; MTCW;
SATA 22

Fox, Paula 1923-............... **CLC 2, 8**
See also AAYA 3; CA 73-76; CANR 20,
36; CLR 1; DLB 52; JRDA; MAICYA;
MTCW; SATA 17, 60

Fox, William Price (Jr.) 1926- ..... **CLC 22**
See also CA 17-20R; CAAS 19; CANR 11;
DLB 2; DLBY 81

Foxe, John 1516(?)-1587 .... **LC 14**

Frame, Janet
1924- .... **CLC 2, 3, 6, 22, 66, 96**
See also Clutha, Janet Paterson Frame

France, Anatole .... **TCLC 9**
See also Thibault, Jacques Anatole Francois
See also DLB 123

Francis, Claude 19(?)- .... **CLC 50**

Francis, Dick
1920- .... **CLC 2, 22, 42; DAM POP**
See also AAYA 5; BEST 89:3; CA 5-8R;
CANR 9, 42; CDBLB 1960 to Present;
DLB 87; INT CANR-9; MTCW

Francis, Robert (Churchill)
1901-1987 .... **CLC 15**
See also CA 1-4R; 123; CANR 1

Frank, Anne(lies Marie)
1929-1945 .... **TCLC 17; DA; DAB;**
DAC; DAM MST; WLC
See also AAYA 12; CA 113; 133; MTCW;
SATA 87; SATA-Brief 42

Frank, Elizabeth 1945-............ **CLC 39**
See also CA 121; 126; INT 126

Frankl, Viktor E(mil) 1905-........ **CLC 93**
See also CA 65-68

Franklin, Benjamin
See Hasek, Jaroslav (Matej Frantisek)

Franklin, Benjamin
1706-1790 ..... **LC 25; DA; DAB; DAC;**
DAM MST
See also CDALB 1640-1865; DLB 24, 43,
73

Franklin, (Stella Maraia Sarah) Miles
1879-1954 .... **TCLC 7**
See also CA 104

Fraser, (Lady) Antonia (Pakenham)
1932- .... **CLC 32**
See also CA 85-88; CANR 44; MTCW;
SATA-Brief 32

Fraser, George MacDonald 1925-.... **CLC 7**
See also CA 45-48; CANR 2, 48

Fraser, Sylvia 1935-.............. **CLC 64**
See also CA 45-48; CANR 1, 16

Frayn, Michael
1933-............... **CLC 3, 7, 31, 47;**
DAM DRAM, NOV
See also CA 5-8R; CANR 30; DLB 13, 14;
MTCW

Fraze, Candida (Merrill) 1945-..... **CLC 50**
See also CA 126

Frazer, J(ames) G(eorge)
1854-1941 .... **TCLC 32**
See also CA 118

Frazer, Robert Caine
See Creasey, John

Frazer, Sir James George
See Frazer, J(ames) G(eorge)

Frazier, Ian 1951-................ **CLC 46**
See also CA 130; CANR 54

Frederic, Harold 1856-1898...... **NCLC 10**
See also DLB 12, 23; DLBD 13

Frederick, John
See Faust, Frederick (Schiller)

Frederick the Great 1712-1786 ...... **LC 14**

Fredro, Aleksander 1793-1876..... **NCLC 8**

Freeling, Nicolas 1927- .... **CLC 38**
See also CA 49-52; CAAS 12; CANR 1, 17,
50; DLB 87

Freeman, Douglas Southall
1886-1953 .... **TCLC 11**
See also CA 109; DLB 17

Freeman, Judith 1946-............ **CLC 55**
See also CA 148

Freeman, Mary Eleanor Wilkins
1852-1930 .... **TCLC 9; SSC 1**
See also CA 106; DLB 12, 78

Freeman, R(ichard) Austin
1862-1943 .... **TCLC 21**
See also CA 113; DLB 70

French, Albert 1943- .... **CLC 86**

French, Marilyn
1929-................. **CLC 10, 18, 60;**
DAM DRAM, NOV, POP
See also CA 69-72; CANR 3, 31;
INT CANR-31; MTCW

French, Paul
See Asimov, Isaac

Freneau, Philip Morin 1752-1832 .. **NCLC 1**
See also DLB 37, 43

Freud, Sigmund 1856-1939 .... **TCLC 52**
See also CA 115; 133; MTCW

Friedan, Betty (Naomi) 1921-...... **CLC 74**
See also CA 65-68; CANR 18, 45; MTCW

Friedlander, Saul 1932-........... **CLC 90**
See also CA 117; 130

Friedman, B(ernard) H(arper)
1926- .... **CLC 7**
See also CA 1-4R; CANR 3, 48

Friedman, Bruce Jay 1930-.... **CLC 3, 5, 56**
See also CA 9-12R; CANR 25, 52; DLB 2,
28; INT CANR-25

Friel, Brian 1929-........... **CLC 5, 42, 59**
See also CA 21-24R; CANR 33; DLB 13;
MTCW

Friis-Baastad, Babbis Ellinor
1921-1970 .... **CLC 12**
See also CA 17-20R; 134; SATA 7

Frisch, Max (Rudolf)
1911-1991 ..... **CLC 3, 9, 14, 18, 32, 44;**
DAM DRAM, NOV
See also CA 85-88; 134; CANR 32;
DLB 69, 124; MTCW

Fromentin, Eugene (Samuel Auguste)
1820-1876 .... **NCLC 10**
See also DLB 123

Frost, Frederick
See Faust, Frederick (Schiller)

Frost, Robert (Lee)
1874-1963 .... CLC 1, 3, 4, 9, 10, 13, 15,
26, 34, 44; DA; DAB; DAC; DAM MST,
POET; PC 1; WLC
See also CA 89-92; CANR 33;
CDALB 1917-1929; DLB 54; DLBD 7;
MTCW; SATA 14

Froude, James Anthony
1818-1894 .... NCLC 43
See also DLB 18, 57, 144

Froy, Herald
See Waterhouse, Keith (Spencer)

Fry, Christopher
1907- ..... CLC 2, 10, 14; DAM DRAM
See also CA 17-20R; CAAS 23; CANR 9,
30; DLB 13; MTCW; SATA 66

Frye, (Herman) Northrop
1912-1991 .... CLC 24, 70
See also CA 5-8R; 133; CANR 8, 37;
DLB 67, 68; MTCW

Fuchs, Daniel 1909-1993 .... CLC 8, 22
See also CA 81-84; 142; CAAS 5;
CANR 40; DLB 9, 26, 28; DLBY 93

Fuchs, Daniel 1934- .... CLC 34
See also CA 37-40R; CANR 14, 48

Fuentes, Carlos
1928- ...... CLC 3, 8, 10, 13, 22, 41, 60;
DA; DAB; DAC; DAM MST, MULT,
NOV; HLC; SSC 24; WLC
See also AAYA 4; AITN 2; CA 69-72;
CANR 10, 32; DLB 113; HW; MTCW

Fuentes, Gregorio Lopez y
See Lopez y Fuentes, Gregorio

Fugard, (Harold) Athol
1932- .... CLC 5, 9, 14, 25, 40, 80;
DAM DRAM; DC 3
See also AAYA 17; CA 85-88; CANR 32,
54; MTCW

Fugard, Sheila 1932- .... CLC 48
See also CA 125

Fuller, Charles (H., Jr.)
1939- .... CLC 25; BLC; DAM DRAM,
MULT; DC 1
See also BW 2; CA 108; 112; DLB 38;
INT 112; MTCW

Fuller, John (Leopold) 1937-....... CLC 62
See also CA 21-24R; CANR 9, 44; DLB 40

Fuller, Margaret .... NCLC 5, 50
See also Ossoli, Sarah Margaret (Fuller
marchesa d')

Fuller, Roy (Broadbent)
1912-1991 .... CLC 4, 28
See also CA 5-8R; 135; CAAS 10;
CANR 53; DLB 15, 20; SATA 87

Fulton, Alice 1952-.............. CLC 52
See also CA 116

Furphy, Joseph 1843-1912........ TCLC 25

Fussell, Paul 1924-.............. CLC 74
See also BEST 90:1; CA 17-20R; CANR 8,
21, 35; INT CANR-21; MTCW

Futabatei, Shimei 1864-1909 ...... TCLC 44

Futrelle, Jacques 1875-1912 ...... TCLC 19
See also CA 113

Gaboriau, Emile 1835-1873 ...... NCLC 14

Gadda, Carlo Emilio 1893-1973 .... CLC 11
See also CA 89-92

Gaddis, William
1922- ..... CLC 1, 3, 6, 8, 10, 19, 43, 86
See also CA 17-20R; CANR 21, 48; DLB 2;
MTCW

Gage, Walter
See Inge, William (Motter)

Gaines, Ernest J(ames)
1933- .... CLC 3, 11, 18, 86; BLC;
DAM MULT
See also AAYA 18; AITN 1; BW 2;
CA 9-12R; CANR 6, 24, 42;
CDALB 1968-1988; DLB 2, 33, 152;
DLBY 80; MTCW; SATA 86

Gaitskill, Mary 1954-............. CLC 69
See also CA 128

Galdos, Benito Perez
See Perez Galdos, Benito

Gale, Zona
1874-1938 ...... TCLC 7; DAM DRAM
See also CA 105; 153; DLB 9, 78

Galeano, Eduardo (Hughes) 1940-... CLC 72
See also CA 29-32R; CANR 13, 32; HW

Galiano, Juan Valera y Alcala
See Valera y Alcala-Galiano, Juan

Gallagher, Tess
1943- .. CLC 18, 63; DAM POET; PC 9
See also CA 106; DLB 120

Gallant, Mavis
1922- .... CLC 7, 18, 38; DAC;
DAM MST; SSC 5
See also CA 69-72; CANR 29; DLB 53;
MTCW

Gallant, Roy A(rthur) 1924- .... CLC 17
See also CA 5-8R; CANR 4, 29, 54;
CLR 30; MAICYA; SATA 4, 68

Gallico, Paul (William) 1897-1976 ... CLC 2
See also AITN 1; CA 5-8R; 69-72;
CANR 23; DLB 9, 171; MAICYA;
SATA 13

Gallo, Max Louis 1932-........... CLC 95
See also CA 85-88

Gallois, Lucien
See Desnos, Robert

Gallup, Ralph
See Whitemore, Hugh (John)

Galsworthy, John
1867-1933 ...... TCLC 1, 45; DA; DAB;
DAC; DAM DRAM, MST, NOV;
SSC 22; WLC 2
See also CA 104; 141; CDBLB 1890-1914;
DLB 10, 34, 98, 162

Galt, John 1779-1839........... NCLC 1
See also DLB 99, 116, 159

Galvin, James 1951-.............. CLC 38
See also CA 108; CANR 26

Gamboa, Federico 1864-1939...... TCLC 36

Gandhi, M. K.
See Gandhi, Mohandas Karamchand

Gandhi, Mahatma
See Gandhi, Mohandas Karamchand

Gandhi, Mohandas Karamchand
1869-1948 ..... TCLC 59; DAM MULT
See also CA 121; 132; MTCW

Gann, Ernest Kellogg 1910-1991.... CLC 23
See also AITN 1; CA 1-4R; 136; CANR 1

Garcia, Cristina 1958- .... CLC 76
See also CA 141

Garcia Lorca, Federico
1898-1936 ... TCLC 1, 7, 49; DA; DAB;
DAC; DAM DRAM, MST, MULT,
POET; DC 2; HLC; PC 3; WLC
See also CA 104; 131; DLB 108; HW;
MTCW

Garcia Marquez, Gabriel (Jose)
1928- .... CLC 2, 3, 8, 10, 15, 27, 47, 55,
68; DA; DAB; DAC; DAM MST,
MULT, NOV, POP; HLC; SSC 8; WLC
See also AAYA 3; BEST 89:1, 90:4;
CA 33-36R; CANR 10, 28, 50; DLB 113;
HW; MTCW

Gard, Janice
See Latham, Jean Lee

Gard, Roger Martin du
See Martin du Gard, Roger

Gardam, Jane 1928-.............. CLC 43
See also CA 49-52; CANR 2, 18, 33, 54;
CLR 12; DLB 14, 161; MAICYA;
MTCW; SAAS 9; SATA 39, 76;
SATA-Brief 28

Gardner, Herb(ert) 1934-.......... CLC 44
See also CA 149

Gardner, John (Champlin), Jr.
1933-1982 ..... CLC 2, 3, 5, 7, 8, 10, 18,
28, 34; DAM NOV, POP; SSC 7
See also AITN 1; CA 65-68; 107;
CANR 33; DLB 2; DLBY 82; MTCW;
SATA 40; SATA-Obit 31

Gardner, John (Edmund)
1926- .... CLC 30; DAM POP
See also CA 103; CANR 15; MTCW

Gardner, Miriam
See Bradley, Marion Zimmer

Gardner, Noel
See Kuttner, Henry

Gardons, S. S.
See Snodgrass, W(illiam) D(e Witt)

Garfield, Leon 1921-1996.......... CLC 12
See also AAYA 8; CA 17-20R; 152;
CANR 38, 41; CLR 21; DLB 161; JRDA;
MAICYA; SATA 1, 32, 76;
SATA-Obit 90

Garland, (Hannibal) Hamlin
1860-1940 .... TCLC 3; SSC 18
See also CA 104; DLB 12, 71, 78

Garneau, (Hector de) Saint-Denys
1912-1943 .... TCLC 13
See also CA 111; DLB 88

Garner, Alan
1934- .... CLC 17; DAB; DAM POP
See also AAYA 18; CA 73-76; CANR 15;
CLR 20; DLB 161; MAICYA; MTCW;
SATA 18, 69

Garner, Hugh 1913-1979 .... CLC 13
See also CA 69-72; CANR 31; DLB 68

Garnett, David 1892-1981 .... CLC 3
See also CA 5-8R; 103; CANR 17; DLB 34

Garos, Stephanie
See Katz, Steve

Garrett, George (Palmer)
1929- .... CLC **3, 11, 51**
See also CA 1-4R; CAAS 5; CANR 1, 42;
DLB 2, 5, 130, 152; DLBY 83

Garrick, David
1717-1779 ...... LC **15; DAM DRAM**
See also DLB 84

Garrigue, Jean 1914-1972 .... CLC **2, 8**
See also CA 5-8R; 37-40R; CANR 20

Garrison, Frederick
See Sinclair, Upton (Beall)

Garth, Will
See Hamilton, Edmond; Kuttner, Henry

Garvey, Marcus (Moziah, Jr.)
1887-1940 .... TCLC **41; BLC;**
DAM MULT
See also BW 1; CA 120; 124

Gary, Romain .... CLC **25**
See Kacew, Romain
See also DLB 83

Gascar, Pierre .... CLC **11**
See also Fournier, Pierre

Gascoyne, David (Emery) 1916- .... CLC **45**
See also CA 65-68; CANR 10, 28, 54;
DLB 20; MTCW

Gaskell, Elizabeth Cleghorn
1810-1865 .. NCLC **5; DAB; DAM MST**
See also CDBLB 1832-1890; DLB 21, 144,
159

Gass, William H(oward)
1924- ... CLC **1, 2, 8, 11, 15, 39; SSC 12**
See also CA 17-20R; CANR 30; DLB 2;
MTCW

Gasset, Jose Ortega y
See Ortega y Gasset, Jose

Gates, Henry Louis, Jr.
1950- .... CLC **65; DAM MULT**
See also BW 2; CA 109; CANR 25, 53;
DLB 67

Gautier, Theophile
1811-1872 ...... NCLC **1; DAM POET;**
SSC 20
See also DLB 119

Gawsworth, John
See Bates, H(erbert) E(rnest)

Gay, Oliver
See Gogarty, Oliver St. John

Gaye, Marvin (Penze) 1939-1984 ... CLC **26**
See also CA 112

Gebler, Carlo (Ernest) 1954- .... CLC **39**
See also CA 119; 133

Gee, Maggie (Mary) 1948- .... CLC **57**
See also CA 130

Gee, Maurice (Gough) 1931- .... CLC **29**
See also CA 97-100; SATA 46

Gelbart, Larry (Simon) 1923- ... CLC **21, 61**
See also CA 73-76; CANR 45

Gelber, Jack 1932- .... CLC **1, 6, 14, 79**
See also CA 1-4R; CANR 2; DLB 7

Gellhorn, Martha (Ellis) 1908- .. CLC **14, 60**
See also CA 77-80; CANR 44; DLBY 82

Genet, Jean
1910-1986 ...... CLC **1, 2, 5, 10, 14, 44,**
46; DAM DRAM
See also CA 13-16R; CANR 18; DLB 72;
DLBY 86; MTCW

Gent, Peter 1942- .... CLC **29**
See also AITN 1; CA 89-92; DLBY 82

Gentlewoman in New England, A
See Bradstreet, Anne

Gentlewoman in Those Parts, A
See Bradstreet, Anne

George, Jean Craighead 1919- ...... CLC **35**
See also AAYA 8; CA 5-8R; CANR 25;
CLR 1; DLB 52; JRDA; MAICYA;
SATA 2, 68

George, Stefan (Anton)
1868-1933 .... TCLC **2, 14**
See also CA 104

Georges, Georges Martin
See Simenon, Georges (Jacques Christian)

Gerhardi, William Alexander
See Gerhardie, William Alexander

Gerhardie, William Alexander
1895-1977 .... CLC **5**
See also CA 25-28R; 73-76; CANR 18;
DLB 36

Gerstler, Amy 1956- .... CLC **70**
See also CA 146

Gertler, T. .... CLC **34**
See also CA 116; 121; INT 121

gfgg .... CLC **XvXzc**

Ghalib .... NCLC **39**
See also Ghalib, Hsadullah Khan

Ghalib, Hsadullah Khan 1797-1869
See Ghalib
See also DAM POET

Ghelderode, Michel de
1898-1962 .... CLC **6, 11; DAM DRAM**
See also CA 85-88; CANR 40

Ghiselin, Brewster 1903- .... CLC **23**
See also CA 13-16R; CAAS 10; CANR 13

Ghose, Zulfikar 1935- .... CLC **42**
See also CA 65-68

Ghosh, Amitav 1956- .... CLC **44**
See also CA 147

Giacosa, Giuseppe 1847-1906 ...... TCLC **7**
See also CA 104

Gibb, Lee
See Waterhouse, Keith (Spencer)

Gibbon, Lewis Grassic .... TCLC **4**
See also Mitchell, James Leslie

Gibbons, Kaye
1960- .... CLC **50, 88; DAM POP**
See also CA 151

Gibran, Kahlil
1883-1931 .... TCLC **1, 9; DAM POET,**
POP; PC 9
See also CA 104; 150

Gibran, Khalil
See Gibran, Kahlil

Gibson, William
1914- .... CLC **23; DA; DAB; DAC;**
DAM DRAM, MST
See also CA 9-12R; CANR 9, 42; DLB 7;
SATA 66

Gibson, William (Ford)
1948- .... CLC **39, 63; DAM POP**
See also AAYA 12; CA 126; 133; CANR 52

Gide, Andre (Paul Guillaume)
1869-1951 .... TCLC **5, 12, 36; DA;**
DAB; DAC; DAM MST, NOV; SSC 13;
WLC
See also CA 104; 124; DLB 65; MTCW

Gifford, Barry (Colby) 1946- .... CLC **34**
See also CA 65-68; CANR 9, 30, 40

Gilbert, W(illiam) S(chwenck)
1836-1911 ..... TCLC **3; DAM DRAM,**
POET
See also CA 104; SATA 36

Gilbreth, Frank B., Jr. 1911- .... CLC **17**
See also CA 9-12R; SATA 2

Gilchrist, Ellen
1935- .... CLC **34, 48; DAM POP;**
SSC 14
See also CA 113; 116; CANR 41; DLB 130;
MTCW

Giles, Molly 1942- .... CLC **39**
See also CA 126

Gill, Patrick
See Creasey, John

Gilliam, Terry (Vance) 1940- ...... CLC **21**
See Monty Python
See also AAYA 19; CA 108; 113;
CANR 35; INT 113

Gillian, Jerry
See Gilliam, Terry (Vance)

Gilliatt, Penelope (Ann Douglass)
1932-1993 .... CLC **2, 10, 13, 53**
See also AITN 2; CA 13-16R; 141;
CANR 49; DLB 14

Gilman, Charlotte (Anna) Perkins (Stetson)
1860-1935 .... TCLC **9, 37; SSC 13**
See also CA 106; 150

Gilmour, David 1949- .... CLC **35**
See also CA 138, 147

Gilpin, William 1724-1804 .... NCLC **30**

Gilray, J. D.
See Mencken, H(enry) L(ouis)

Gilroy, Frank D(aniel) 1925- .... CLC **2**
See also CA 81-84; CANR 32; DLB 7

Ginsberg, Allen
1926- ...... CLC **1, 2, 3, 4, 6, 13, 36, 69;**
DA; DAB; DAC; DAM MST, POET;
PC 4; WLC 3
See also AITN 1; CA 1-4R; CANR 2, 41;
CDALB 1941-1968; DLB 5, 16, 169;
MTCW

Ginzburg, Natalia
1916-1991 .... CLC **5, 11, 54, 70**
See also CA 85-88; 135; CANR 33; MTCW

Giono, Jean 1895-1970 .... CLC **4, 11**
See also CA 45-48; 29-32R; CANR 2, 35;
DLB 72; MTCW

Giovanni, Nikki
    1943- . . . . . . **CLC 2, 4, 19, 64; BLC; DA;
    DAB; DAC; DAM MST, MULT, POET**
    See also AITN 1; BW 2; CA 29-32R;
    CAAS 6; CANR 18, 41; CLR 6; DLB 5,
    41; INT CANR-18; MAICYA; MTCW;
    SATA 24

Giovene, Andrea 1904- . . . . **CLC 7**
    See also CA 85-88

Gippius, Zinaida (Nikolayevna) 1869-1945
    See Hippius, Zinaida
    See also CA 106

Giraudoux, (Hippolyte) Jean
    1882-1944 . . . . **TCLC 2, 7; DAM DRAM**
    See also CA 104; DLB 65

Gironella, Jose Maria 1917- . . . . **CLC 11**
    See also CA 101

Gissing, George (Robert)
    1857-1903 . . . . **TCLC 3, 24, 47**
    See also CA 105; DLB 18, 135

Giurlani, Aldo
    See Palazzeschi, Aldo

Gladkov, Fyodor (Vasilyevich)
    1883-1958 . . . . **TCLC 27**

Glanville, Brian (Lester) 1931- . . . . . . **CLC 6**
    See also CA 5-8R; CAAS 9; CANR 3;
    DLB 15, 139; SATA 42

Glasgow, Ellen (Anderson Gholson)
    1873(?)-1945 . . . . **TCLC 2, 7**
    See also CA 104; DLB 9, 12

Glaspell, Susan 1882(?)-1948 . . . . . . **TCLC 55**
    See also CA 110; 154; DLB 7, 9, 78;
    YABC 2

Glassco, John 1909-1981 . . . . **CLC 9**
    See also CA 13-16R; 102; CANR 15;
    DLB 68

Glasscock, Amnesia
    See Steinbeck, John (Ernst)

Glasser, Ronald J. 1940(?)- . . . . **CLC 37**

Glassman, Joyce
    See Johnson, Joyce

Glendinning, Victoria 1937- . . . . **CLC 50**
    See also CA 120; 127; DLB 155

Glissant, Edouard
    1928- . . . . **CLC 10, 68; DAM MULT**
    See also CA 153

Gloag, Julian 1930- . . . . **CLC 40**
    See also AITN 1; CA 65-68; CANR 10

Glowacki, Aleksander
    See Prus, Boleslaw

Gluck, Louise (Elisabeth)
    1943- . . . . **CLC 7, 22, 44, 81;
    DAM POET; PC 16**
    See also CA 33-36R; CANR 40; DLB 5

Gobineau, Joseph Arthur (Comte) de
    1816-1882 . . . . **NCLC 17**
    See also DLB 123

Godard, Jean-Luc 1930- . . . . **CLC 20**
    See also CA 93-96

Godden, (Margaret) Rumer 1907- . . . **CLC 53**
    See also AAYA 6; CA 5-8R; CANR 4, 27,
    36, 55; CLR 20; DLB 161; MAICYA;
    SAAS 12; SATA 3, 36

Godoy Alcayaga, Lucila 1889-1957
    See Mistral, Gabriela
    See also BW 2; CA 104; 131; DAM MULT;
    HW; MTCW

Godwin, Gail (Kathleen)
    1937- . . . . **CLC 5, 8, 22, 31, 69;
    DAM POP**
    See also CA 29-32R; CANR 15, 43; DLB 6;
    INT CANR-15; MTCW

Godwin, William 1756-1836 . . . . . . **NCLC 14**
    See also CDBLB 1789-1832; DLB 39, 104,
    142, 158, 163

Goethe, Johann Wolfgang von
    1749-1832 . . . . **NCLC 4, 22, 34; DA;
    DAB; DAC; DAM DRAM, MST,
    POET; PC 5; WLC 3**
    See also DLB 94

Gogarty, Oliver St. John
    1878-1957 . . . . **TCLC 15**
    See also CA 109; 150; DLB 15, 19

Gogol, Nikolai (Vasilyevich)
    1809-1852 . . . . **NCLC 5, 15, 31; DA;
    DAB; DAC; DAM DRAM, MST; DC 1;
    SSC 4; WLC**

Goines, Donald
    1937(?)-1974 . . . . **CLC 80; BLC;
    DAM MULT, POP**
    See also AITN 1; BW 1; CA 124; 114;
    DLB 33

Gold, Herbert 1924- . . . . **CLC 4, 7, 14, 42**
    See also CA 9-12R; CANR 17, 45; DLB 2;
    DLBY 81

Goldbarth, Albert 1948- . . . . **CLC 5, 38**
    See also CA 53-56; CANR 6, 40; DLB 120

Goldberg, Anatol 1910-1982 . . . . **CLC 34**
    See also CA 131; 117

Goldemberg, Isaac 1945- . . . . **CLC 52**
    See also CA 69-72; CAAS 12; CANR 11,
    32; HW

Golding, William (Gerald)
    1911-1993 . . . . **CLC 1, 2, 3, 8, 10, 17, 27,
    58, 81; DA; DAB; DAC; DAM MST,
    NOV; WLC**
    See also AAYA 5; CA 5-8R; 141;
    CANR 13, 33, 54; CDBLB 1945-1960;
    DLB 15, 100; MTCW

Goldman, Emma 1869-1940 . . . . . . **TCLC 13**
    See also CA 110; 150

Goldman, Francisco 1955- . . . . **CLC 76**

Goldman, William (W.) 1931- . . . . **CLC 1, 48**
    See also CA 9-12R; CANR 29; DLB 44

Goldmann, Lucien 1913-1970 . . . . . . **CLC 24**
    See also CA 25-28; CAP 2

Goldoni, Carlo
    1707-1793 . . . . **LC 4; DAM DRAM**

Goldsberry, Steven 1949- . . . . **CLC 34**
    See also CA 131

Goldsmith, Oliver
    1728-1774 . . . . . . **LC 2; DA; DAB; DAC;
    DAM DRAM, MST, NOV, POET;
    WLC**
    See also CDBLB 1660-1789; DLB 39, 89,
    104, 109, 142; SATA 26

Goldsmith, Peter
    See Priestley, J(ohn) B(oynton)

Gombrowicz, Witold
    1904-1969 . . . . **CLC 4, 7, 11, 49;
    DAM DRAM**
    See also CA 19-20; 25-28R; CAP 2

Gomez de la Serna, Ramon
    1888-1963 . . . . **CLC 9**
    See also CA 153; 116; HW

Goncharov, Ivan Alexandrovich
    1812-1891 . . . . **NCLC 1**

Goncourt, Edmond (Louis Antoine Huot) de
    1822-1896 . . . . **NCLC 7**
    See also DLB 123

Goncourt, Jules (Alfred Huot) de
    1830-1870 . . . . **NCLC 7**
    See also DLB 123

Gontier, Fernande 19(?)- . . . . **CLC 50**

Goodman, Paul 1911-1972 . . . . **CLC 1, 2, 4, 7**
    See also CA 19-20; 37-40R; CANR 34;
    CAP 2; DLB 130; MTCW

Gordimer, Nadine
    1923- . . . . **CLC 3, 5, 7, 10, 18, 33, 51, 70;
    DA; DAB; DAC; DAM MST, NOV;
    SSC 17**
    See also CA 5-8R; CANR 3, 28;
    INT CANR-28; MTCW

Gordon, Adam Lindsay
    1833-1870 . . . . **NCLC 21**

Gordon, Caroline
    1895-1981 . . . **CLC 6, 13, 29, 83; SSC 15**
    See also CA 11-12; 103; CANR 36; CAP 1;
    DLB 4, 9, 102; DLBY 81; MTCW

Gordon, Charles William 1860-1937
    See Connor, Ralph
    See also CA 109

Gordon, Mary (Catherine)
    1949- . . . . **CLC 13, 22**
    See also CA 102; CANR 44; DLB 6;
    DLBY 81; INT 102; MTCW

Gordon, Sol 1923- . . . . **CLC 26**
    See also CA 53-56; CANR 4; SATA 11

Gordone, Charles
    1925-1995 . . . . . **CLC 1, 4; DAM DRAM**
    See also BW 1; CA 93-96; 150; CANR 55;
    DLB 7; INT 93-96; MTCW

Gorenko, Anna Andreevna
    See Akhmatova, Anna

Gorky, Maxim . . . . **TCLC 8; DAB; WLC**
    See also Peshkov, Alexei Maximovich

Goryan, Sirak
    See Saroyan, William

Gosse, Edmund (William)
    1849-1928 . . . . **TCLC 28**
    See also CA 117; DLB 57, 144

Gotlieb, Phyllis Fay (Bloom)
    1926- . . . . **CLC 18**
    See also CA 13-16R; CANR 7; DLB 88

Gottesman, S. D.
    See Kornbluth, C(yril) M.; Pohl, Frederik

Gottfried von Strassburg
    fl. c. 1210- . . . . **CMLC 10**
    See also DLB 138

Gould, Lois . . . . **CLC 4, 10**
    See also CA 77-80; CANR 29; MTCW

Gourmont, Remy (-Marie-Charles) de
1858-1915 . . . . TCLC **17**
See also CA 109; 150

Govier, Katherine 1948- . . . . CLC **51**
See also CA 101; CANR 18, 40

Goyen, (Charles) William
1915-1983 . . . . CLC **5, 8, 14, 40**
See also AITN 2; CA 5-8R; 110; CANR 6;
DLB 2; DLBY 83; INT CANR-6

Goytisolo, Juan
1931- . . . . . CLC **5, 10, 23; DAM MULT;**
HLC
See also CA 85-88; CANR 32; HW; MTCW

Gozzano, Guido 1883-1916 . . . . PC **10**
See also CA 154; DLB 114

Gozzi, (Conte) Carlo 1720-1806 . . NCLC **23**

Grabbe, Christian Dietrich
1801-1836 . . . . NCLC **2**
See also DLB 133

Grace, Patricia 1937- . . . . CLC **56**

Gracian y Morales, Baltasar
1601-1658 . . . . LC **15**

Gracq, Julien . . . . CLC **11, 48**
See also Poirier, Louis
See also DLB 83

Grade, Chaim 1910-1982 . . . . CLC **10**
See also CA 93-96; 107

Graduate of Oxford, A
See Ruskin, John

Graham, John
See Phillips, David Graham

Graham, Jorie 1951- . . . . CLC **48**
See also CA 111; DLB 120

Graham, R(obert) B(ontine) Cunninghame
See Cunninghame Graham, R(obert)
B(ontine)
See also DLB 98, 135, 174

Graham, Robert
See Haldeman, Joe (William)

Graham, Tom
See Lewis, (Harry) Sinclair

Graham, W(illiam) S(ydney)
1918-1986 . . . . CLC **29**
See also CA 73-76; 118; DLB 20

Graham, Winston (Mawdsley)
1910- . . . . CLC **23**
See also CA 49-52; CANR 2, 22, 45;
DLB 77

Grahame, Kenneth
1859-1932 . . . . TCLC **64; DAB**
See also CA 108; 136; CLR 5; DLB 34, 141;
MAICYA; YABC 1

Grant, Skeeter
See Spiegelman, Art

Granville-Barker, Harley
1877-1946 . . . . . . TCLC **2; DAM DRAM**
See also Barker, Harley Granville
See also CA 104

Grass, Guenter (Wilhelm)
1927- . . . . . CLC **1, 2, 4, 6, 11, 15, 22, 32,**
49, 88; DA; DAB; DAC; DAM MST,
NOV; WLC
See also CA 13-16R; CANR 20; DLB 75,
124; MTCW

Gratton, Thomas
See Hulme, T(homas) E(rnest)

Grau, Shirley Ann
1929- . . . . CLC **4, 9; SSC 15**
See also CA 89-92; CANR 22; DLB 2;
INT CANR-22; MTCW

Gravel, Fern
See Hall, James Norman

Graver, Elizabeth 1964- . . . . CLC **70**
See also CA 135

Graves, Richard Perceval 1945- . . . . CLC **44**
See also CA 65-68; CANR 9, 26, 51

Graves, Robert (von Ranke)
1895-1985 . . . . . . CLC **1, 2, 6, 11, 39, 44,**
45; DAB; DAC; DAM MST, POET;
PC 6
See also CA 5-8R; 117; CANR 5, 36;
CDBLB 1914-1945; DLB 20, 100;
DLBY 85; MTCW; SATA 45

Graves, Valerie
See Bradley, Marion Zimmer

Gray, Alasdair (James) 1934- . . . . . . CLC **41**
See also CA 126; CANR 47; INT 126;
MTCW

Gray, Amlin 1946- . . . . CLC **29**
See also CA 138

Gray, Francine du Plessix
1930- . . . . CLC **22; DAM NOV**
See also BEST 90:3; CA 61-64; CAAS 2;
CANR 11, 33; INT CANR-11; MTCW

Gray, John (Henry) 1866-1934 . . . . TCLC **19**
See also CA 119

Gray, Simon (James Holliday)
1936- . . . . CLC **9, 14, 36**
See also AITN 1; CA 21-24R; CAAS 3;
CANR 32; DLB 13; MTCW

Gray, Spalding 1941- . . CLC **49; DAM POP**
See also CA 128

Gray, Thomas
1716-1771 . . . . . . LC **4; DA; DAB; DAC;**
DAM MST; PC 2; WLC
See also CDBLB 1660-1789; DLB 109

Grayson, David
See Baker, Ray Stannard

Grayson, Richard (A.) 1951- . . . . CLC **38**
See also CA 85-88; CANR 14, 31

Greeley, Andrew M(oran)
1928- . . . . CLC **28; DAM POP**
See also CA 5-8R; CAAS 7; CANR 7, 43;
MTCW

Green, Anna Katharine
1846-1935 . . . . TCLC **63**
See also CA 112

Green, Brian
See Card, Orson Scott

Green, Hannah
See Greenberg, Joanne (Goldenberg)

Green, Hannah . . . . CLC **3**
See also CA 73-76

Green, Henry 1905-1973 . . . . . CLC **2, 13, 97**
See also Yorke, Henry Vincent
See also DLB 15

Green, Julian (Hartridge) 1900-
See Green, Julien
See also CA 21-24R; CANR 33; DLB 4, 72;
MTCW

Green, Julien . . . . CLC **3, 11, 77**
See also Green, Julian (Hartridge)

Green, Paul (Eliot)
1894-1981 . . . . . . CLC **25; DAM DRAM**
See also AITN 1; CA 5-8R; 103; CANR 3;
DLB 7, 9; DLBY 81

Greenberg, Ivan 1908-1973
See Rahv, Philip
See also CA 85-88

Greenberg, Joanne (Goldenberg)
1932- . . . . CLC **7, 30**
See also AAYA 12; CA 5-8R; CANR 14,
32; SATA 25

Greenberg, Richard 1959(?)- . . . . CLC **57**
See also CA 138

Greene, Bette 1934- . . . . CLC **30**
See also AAYA 7; CA 53-56; CANR 4;
CLR 2; JRDA; MAICYA; SAAS 16;
SATA 8

Greene, Gael . . . . CLC **8**
See also CA 13-16R; CANR 10

Greene, Graham
1904-1991 . . . . CLC **1, 3, 6, 9, 14, 18, 27,**
37, 70, 72; DA; DAB; DAC; DAM MST,
NOV; WLC
See also AITN 2; CA 13-16R; 133;
CANR 35; CDBLB 1945-1960; DLB 13,
15, 77, 100, 162; DLBY 91; MTCW;
SATA 20

Greer, Richard
See Silverberg, Robert

Gregor, Arthur 1923- . . . . CLC **9**
See also CA 25-28R; CAAS 10; CANR 11;
SATA 36

Gregor, Lee
See Pohl, Frederik

Gregory, Isabella Augusta (Persse)
1852-1932 . . . . TCLC **1**
See also CA 104; DLB 10

Gregory, J. Dennis
See Williams, John A(lfred)

Grendon, Stephen
See Derleth, August (William)

Grenville, Kate 1950- . . . . CLC **61**
See also CA 118; CANR 53

Grenville, Pelham
See Wodehouse, P(elham) G(renville)

Greve, Felix Paul (Berthold Friedrich)
1879-1948
See Grove, Frederick Philip
See also CA 104; 141; DAC; DAM MST

Grey, Zane
1872-1939 . . . . TCLC **6; DAM POP**
See also CA 104; 132; DLB 9; MTCW

Grieg, (Johan) Nordahl (Brun)
1902-1943 . . . . TCLC **10**
See also CA 107

Grieve, C(hristopher) M(urray)
1892-1978 . . . . CLC **11, 19; DAM POET**
See also MacDiarmid, Hugh; Pteleon
See also CA 5-8R; 85-88; CANR 33;
MTCW

Haley, Alex(ander Murray Palmer)
1921-1992 .... **CLC 8, 12, 76; BLC; DA;
DAB; DAC; DAM MST, MULT, POP**
See also BW 2; CA 77-80; 136; DLB 38;
MTCW

Haliburton, Thomas Chandler
1796-1865 .... **NCLC 15**
See also DLB 11, 99

Hall, Donald (Andrew, Jr.)
1928- .. **CLC 1, 13, 37, 59; DAM POET**
See also CA 5-8R; CAAS 7; CANR 2, 44;
DLB 5; SATA 23

Hall, Frederic Sauser
See Sauser-Hall, Frederic

Hall, James
See Kuttner, Henry

Hall, James Norman 1887-1951 ... **TCLC 23**
See also CA 123; SATA 21

Hall, (Marguerite) Radclyffe
1886-1943 .... **TCLC 12**
See also CA 110; 150

Hall, Rodney 1935- .... **CLC 51**
See also CA 109

Halleck, Fitz-Greene 1790-1867 .. **NCLC 47**
See also DLB 3

Halliday, Michael
See Creasey, John

Halpern, Daniel 1945- .... **CLC 14**
See also CA 33-36R

Hamburger, Michael (Peter Leopold)
1924- .... **CLC 5, 14**
See also CA 5-8R; CAAS 4; CANR 2, 47;
DLB 27

Hamill, Pete 1935- .... **CLC 10**
See also CA 25-28R; CANR 18

Hamilton, Alexander
1755(?)-1804 .... **NCLC 49**
See also DLB 37

Hamilton, Clive
See Lewis, C(live) S(taples)

Hamilton, Edmond 1904-1977....... **CLC 1**
See also CA 1-4R; CANR 3; DLB 8

Hamilton, Eugene (Jacob) Lee
See Lee-Hamilton, Eugene (Jacob)

Hamilton, Franklin
See Silverberg, Robert

Hamilton, Gail
See Corcoran, Barbara

Hamilton, Mollie
See Kaye, M(ary) M(argaret)

Hamilton, (Anthony Walter) Patrick
1904-1962 .... **CLC 51**
See also CA 113; DLB 10

Hamilton, Virginia
1936- .... **CLC 26; DAM MULT**
See also AAYA 2; BW 2; CA 25-28R;
CANR 20, 37; CLR 1, 11, 40; DLB 33,
52; INT CANR-20; JRDA; MAICYA;
MTCW; SATA 4, 56, 79

Hammett, (Samuel) Dashiell
1894-1961 .... **CLC 3, 5, 10, 19, 47;
SSC 17**
See also AITN 1; CA 81-84; CANR 42;
CDALB 1929-1941; DLBD 6; MTCW

Hammon, Jupiter
1711(?)-1800(?) .... **NCLC 5; BLC;
DAM MULT, POET; PC 16**
See also DLB 31, 50

Hammond, Keith
See Kuttner, Henry

Hamner, Earl (Henry), Jr. 1923- ... **CLC 12**
See also AITN 2; CA 73-76; DLB 6

Hampton, Christopher (James)
1946- .... **CLC 4**
See also CA 25-28R; DLB 13; MTCW

Hamsun, Knut .... **TCLC 2, 14, 49**
See also Pedersen, Knut

Handke, Peter
1942- .... **CLC 5, 8, 10, 15, 38;
DAM DRAM, NOV**
See also CA 77-80; CANR 33; DLB 85,
124; MTCW

Hanley, James 1901-1985 ... **CLC 3, 5, 8, 13**
See also CA 73-76; 117; CANR 36; MTCW

Hannah, Barry 1942-....... **CLC 23, 38, 90**
See also CA 108; 110; CANR 43; DLB 6;
INT 110; MTCW

Hannon, Ezra
See Hunter, Evan

Hansberry, Lorraine (Vivian)
1930-1965 ...... **CLC 17, 62; BLC; DA;
DAB; DAC; DAM DRAM, MST,
MULT; DC 2**
See also BW 1; CA 109; 25-28R; CABS 3;
CDALB 1941-1968; DLB 7, 38; MTCW

Hansen, Joseph 1923-............. **CLC 38**
See also CA 29-32R; CAAS 17; CANR 16,
44; INT CANR-16

Hansen, Martin A. 1909-1955..... **TCLC 32**

Hanson, Kenneth O(stlin) 1922- .... **CLC 13**
See also CA 53-56; CANR 7

Hardwick, Elizabeth
1916- .... **CLC 13; DAM NOV**
See also CA 5-8R; CANR 3, 32; DLB 6;
MTCW

Hardy, Thomas
1840-1928 ...... **TCLC 4, 10, 18, 32, 48,
53; DA; DAB; DAC; DAM MST, NOV,
POET; PC 8; SSC 2; WLC**
See also CA 104; 123; CDBLB 1890-1914;
DLB 18, 19, 135; MTCW

Hare, David 1947- .... **CLC 29, 58**
See also CA 97-100; CANR 39; DLB 13;
MTCW

Harford, Henry
See Hudson, W(illiam) H(enry)

Hargrave, Leonie
See Disch, Thomas M(ichael)

Harjo, Joy 1951- ... **CLC 83; DAM MULT**
See also CA 114; CANR 35; DLB 120;
NNAL

Harlan, Louis R(udolph) 1922-..... **CLC 34**
See also CA 21-24R; CANR 25, 55

Harling, Robert 1951(?)- .... **CLC 53**
See also CA 147

Harmon, William (Ruth) 1938-..... **CLC 38**
See also CA 33-36R; CANR 14, 32, 35;
SATA 65

Harper, F. E. W.
See Harper, Frances Ellen Watkins

Harper, Frances E. W.
See Harper, Frances Ellen Watkins

Harper, Frances E. Watkins
See Harper, Frances Ellen Watkins

Harper, Frances Ellen
See Harper, Frances Ellen Watkins

Harper, Frances Ellen Watkins
1825-1911 .... **TCLC 14; BLC;
DAM MULT, POET**
See also BW 1; CA 111; 125; DLB 50

Harper, Michael S(teven) 1938- .. **CLC 7, 22**
See also BW 1; CA 33-36R; CANR 24;
DLB 41

Harper, Mrs. F. E. W.
See Harper, Frances Ellen Watkins

Harris, Christie (Lucy) Irwin
1907- .... **CLC 12**
See also CA 5-8R; CANR 6; DLB 88;
JRDA; MAICYA; SAAS 10; SATA 6, 74

Harris, Frank 1856-1931........ **TCLC 24**
See also CA 109; 150; DLB 156

Harris, George Washington
1814-1869 .... **NCLC 23**
See also DLB 3, 11

Harris, Joel Chandler
1848-1908 .... **TCLC 2; SSC 19**
See also CA 104; 137; DLB 11, 23, 42, 78,
91; MAICYA; YABC 1

Harris, John (Wyndham Parkes Lucas)
Beynon 1903-1969
See Wyndham, John
See also CA 102; 89-92

Harris, MacDonald................. **CLC 9**
See also Heiney, Donald (William)

Harris, Mark 1922- .... **CLC 19**
See also CA 5-8R; CAAS 3; CANR 2, 55;
DLB 2; DLBY 80

Harris, (Theodore) Wilson 1921-.... **CLC 25**
See also BW 2; CA 65-68; CAAS 16;
CANR 11, 27; DLB 117; MTCW

Harrison, Elizabeth Cavanna 1909-
See Cavanna, Betty
See also CA 9-12R; CANR 6, 27

Harrison, Harry (Max) 1925-...... **CLC 42**
See also CA 1-4R; CANR 5, 21; DLB 8;
SATA 4

Harrison, James (Thomas)
1937- .... **CLC 6, 14, 33, 66; SSC 19**
See also CA 13-16R; CANR 8, 51;
DLBY 82; INT CANR-8

Harrison, Jim
See Harrison, James (Thomas)

Harrison, Kathryn 1961-.......... **CLC 70**
See also CA 144

Harrison, Tony 1937-............. **CLC 43**
See also CA 65-68; CANR 44; DLB 40;
MTCW

Harriss, Will(ard Irvin) 1922-...... **CLC 34**
See also CA 111

Harson, Sley
See Ellison, Harlan (Jay)

Hart, Ellis
See Ellison, Harlan (Jay)

Hart, Josephine
1942(?)- . . . . CLC 70; DAM POP
See also CA 138

Hart, Moss
1904-1961 . . . . . CLC 66; DAM DRAM
See also CA 109; 89-92; DLB 7

Harte, (Francis) Bret(t)
1836(?)-1902 . . . . TCLC 1, 25; DA; DAC;
DAM MST; SSC 8; WLC
See also CA 104; 140; CDALB 1865-1917;
DLB 12, 64, 74, 79; SATA 26

Hartley, L(eslie) P(oles)
1895-1972 . . . . CLC 2, 22
See also CA 45-48; 37-40R; CANR 33;
DLB 15, 139; MTCW

Hartman, Geoffrey H. 1929- . . . . CLC 27
See also CA 117; 125; DLB 67

Hartmann von Aue
c. 1160-c. 1205 . . . . CMLC 15
See also DLB 138

Hartmann von Aue 1170-1210. . . . CMLC 15

Haruf, Kent 1943- . . . . CLC 34
See also CA 149

Harwood, Ronald
1934- . . . . CLC 32; DAM DRAM, MST
See also CA 1-4R; CANR 4, 55; DLB 13

Hasek, Jaroslav (Matej Frantisek)
1883-1923 . . . . TCLC 4
See also CA 104; 129; MTCW

Hass, Robert 1941- . . . . . CLC 18, 39; PC 16
See also CA 111; CANR 30, 50; DLB 105

Hastings, Hudson
See Kuttner, Henry

Hastings, Selina . . . . CLC 44

Hatteras, Amelia
See Mencken, H(enry) L(ouis)

Hatteras, Owen . . . . TCLC 18
See also Mencken, H(enry) L(ouis); Nathan,
George Jean

Hauptmann, Gerhart (Johann Robert)
1862-1946 . . . . . . TCLC 4; DAM DRAM
See also CA 104; 153; DLB 66, 118

Havel, Vaclav
1936- . . . . CLC 25, 58, 65;
DAM DRAM; DC 6
See also CA 104; CANR 36; MTCW

Haviaras, Stratis . . . . CLC 33
See also Chaviaras, Strates

Hawes, Stephen 1475(?)-1523(?) . . . . . LC 17

Hawkes, John (Clendennin Burne, Jr.)
1925- . . . . . . CLC 1, 2, 3, 4, 7, 9, 14, 15,
27, 49
See also CA 1-4R; CANR 2, 47; DLB 2, 7;
DLBY 80; MTCW

Hawking, S. W.
See Hawking, Stephen W(illiam)

Hawking, Stephen W(illiam)
1942- . . . . CLC 63
See also AAYA 13; BEST 89:1; CA 126;
129; CANR 48

Hawthorne, Julian 1846-1934 . . . . . TCLC 25

Hawthorne, Nathaniel
1804-1864 . . . . . . NCLC 39; DA; DAB;
DAC; DAM MST, NOV; SSC 3; WLC
See also AAYA 18; CDALB 1640-1865;
DLB 1, 74; YABC 2

Haxton, Josephine Ayres 1921-
See Douglas, Ellen
See also CA 115; CANR 41

Hayaseca y Eizaguirre, Jorge
See Echegaray (y Eizaguirre), Jose (Maria
Waldo)

Hayashi Fumiko 1904-1951 . . . . TCLC 27

Haycraft, Anna
See Ellis, Alice Thomas
See also CA 122

Hayden, Robert E(arl)
1913-1980 . . . . . . CLC 5, 9, 14, 37; BLC;
DA; DAC; DAM MST, MULT, POET;
PC 6
See also BW 1; CA 69-72; 97-100; CABS 2;
CANR 24; CDALB 1941-1968; DLB 5,
76; MTCW; SATA 19; SATA-Obit 26

Hayford, J(oseph) E(phraim) Casely
See Casely-Hayford, J(oseph) E(phraim)

Hayman, Ronald 1932- . . . . CLC 44
See also CA 25-28R; CANR 18, 50;
DLB 155

Haywood, Eliza (Fowler)
1693(?)-1756 . . . . LC 1

Hazlitt, William 1778-1830 . . . . . . NCLC 29
See also DLB 110, 158

Hazzard, Shirley 1931- . . . . CLC 18
See also CA 9-12R; CANR 4; DLBY 82;
MTCW

Head, Bessie
1937-1986 . . . . CLC 25, 67; BLC;
DAM MULT
See also BW 2; CA 29-32R; 119; CANR 25;
DLB 117; MTCW

Headon, (Nicky) Topper 1956(?)- . . . CLC 30

Heaney, Seamus (Justin)
1939- . . . . . . CLC 5, 7, 14, 25, 37, 74, 91;
DAB; DAM POET
See also CA 85-88; CANR 25, 48;
CDBLB 1960 to Present; DLB 40;
DLBY 95; MTCW

Hearn, (Patricio) Lafcadio (Tessima Carlos)
1850-1904 . . . . TCLC 9
See also CA 105; DLB 12, 78

Hearne, Vicki 1946- . . . . CLC 56
See also CA 139

Hearon, Shelby 1931- . . . . CLC 63
See also AITN 2; CA 25-28R; CANR 18,
48

Heat-Moon, William Least . . . . CLC 29
See also Trogdon, William (Lewis)
See also AAYA 9

Hebbel, Friedrich
1813-1863 . . . . NCLC 43; DAM DRAM
See also DLB 129

Hebert, Anne
1916- . . . . CLC 4, 13, 29; DAC;
DAM MST, POET
See also CA 85-88; DLB 68; MTCW

Hecht, Anthony (Evan)
1923- . . . . . . CLC 8, 13, 19; DAM POET
See also CA 9-12R; CANR 6; DLB 5, 169

Hecht, Ben 1894-1964 . . . . CLC 8
See also CA 85-88; DLB 7, 9, 25, 26, 28, 86

Hedayat, Sadeq 1903-1951 . . . . TCLC 21
See also CA 120

Hegel, Georg Wilhelm Friedrich
1770-1831 . . . . NCLC 46
See also DLB 90

Heidegger, Martin 1889-1976 . . . . . . CLC 24
See also CA 81-84; 65-68; CANR 34;
MTCW

Heidenstam, (Carl Gustaf) Verner von
1859-1940 . . . . TCLC 5
See also CA 104

Heifner, Jack 1946- . . . . CLC 11
See also CA 105; CANR 47

Heijermans, Herman 1864-1924 . . . TCLC 24
See also CA 123

Heilbrun, Carolyn G(old) 1926- . . . . . CLC 25
See also CA 45-48; CANR 1, 28

Heine, Heinrich 1797-1856 . . . . NCLC 4, 54
See also DLB 90

Heinemann, Larry (Curtiss) 1944- . . CLC 50
See also CA 110; CAAS 21; CANR 31;
DLBD 9; INT CANR-31

Heiney, Donald (William) 1921-1993
See Harris, MacDonald
See also CA 1-4R; 142; CANR 3

Heinlein, Robert A(nson)
1907-1988 . . . . . . CLC 1, 3, 8, 14, 26, 55;
DAM POP
See also AAYA 17; CA 1-4R; 125;
CANR 1, 20, 53; DLB 8; JRDA;
MAICYA; MTCW; SATA 9, 69;
SATA-Obit 56

Helforth, John
See Doolittle, Hilda

Hellenhofferu, Vojtech Kapristian z
See Hasek, Jaroslav (Matej Frantisek)

Heller, Joseph
1923- . . . . CLC 1, 3, 5, 8, 11, 36, 63; DA;
DAB; DAC; DAM MST, NOV, POP;
WLC
See also AITN 1; CA 5-8R; CABS 1;
CANR 8, 42; DLB 2, 28; DLBY 80;
INT CANR-8; MTCW

Hellman, Lillian (Florence)
1906-1984 . . . . . . CLC 2, 4, 8, 14, 18, 34,
44, 52; DAM DRAM; DC 1
See also AITN 1, 2; CA 13-16R; 112;
CANR 33; DLB 7; DLBY 84; MTCW

Helprin, Mark
1947- . . . . CLC 7, 10, 22, 32;
DAM NOV, POP
See also CA 81-84; CANR 47; DLBY 85;
MTCW

Helvetius, Claude-Adrien
1715-1771 . . . . LC 26

Helyar, Jane Penelope Josephine 1933-
See Poole, Josephine
See also CA 21-24R; CANR 10, 26;
SATA 82

Hemans, Felicia 1793-1835 . . . . . . NCLC 29
See also DLB 96

Hemingway, Ernest (Miller)
1899-1961 .... CLC 1, 3, 6, 8, 10, 13, 19,
30, 34, 39, 41, 44, 50, 61, 80; DA; DAB;
DAC; DAM MST, NOV; SSC 1; WLC
See also AAYA 19; CA 77-80; CANR 34;
CDALB 1917-1929; DLB 4, 9, 102;
DLBD 1; DLBY 81, 87; MTCW

Hempel, Amy 1951- .... CLC 39
See also CA 118; 137

Henderson, F. C.
See Mencken, H(enry) L(ouis)

Henderson, Sylvia
See Ashton-Warner, Sylvia (Constance)

Henley, Beth .... CLC 23; DC 6
See also Henley, Elizabeth Becker
See also CABS 3; DLBY 86

Henley, Elizabeth Becker 1952-
See Henley, Beth
See also CA 107; CANR 32; DAM DRAM,
MST; MTCW

Henley, William Ernest
1849-1903 .... TCLC 8
See also CA 105; DLB 19

Hennissart, Martha
See Lathen, Emma
See also CA 85-88

Henry, O. .... TCLC 1, 19; SSC 5; WLC
See also Porter, William Sydney

Henry, Patrick 1736-1799 .... LC 25

Henryson, Robert 1430(?)-1506(?). ... LC 20
See also DLB 146

Henry VIII 1491-1547 .... LC 10

Henschke, Alfred
See Klabund

Hentoff, Nat(han Irving) 1925- ..... CLC 26
See also AAYA 4; CA 1-4R; CAAS 6;
CANR 5, 25; CLR 1; INT CANR-25;
JRDA; MAICYA; SATA 42, 69;
SATA-Brief 27

Heppenstall, (John) Rayner
1911-1981 .... CLC 10
See also CA 1-4R; 103; CANR 29

Herbert, Frank (Patrick)
1920-1986 ...... CLC 12, 23, 35, 44, 85;
DAM POP
See also CA 53-56; 118; CANR 5, 43;
DLB 8; INT CANR-5; MTCW; SATA 9,
37; SATA-Obit 47

Herbert, George
1593-1633 .... LC 24; DAB;
DAM POET; PC 4
See also CDBLB Before 1660; DLB 126

Herbert, Zbigniew
1924- .... CLC 9, 43; DAM POET
See also CA 89-92; CANR 36; MTCW

Herbst, Josephine (Frey)
1897-1969 .... CLC 34
See also CA 5-8R; 25-28R; DLB 9

Hergesheimer, Joseph
1880-1954 .... TCLC 11
See also CA 109; DLB 102, 9

Herlihy, James Leo 1927-1993 ...... CLC 6
See also CA 1-4R; 143; CANR 2

Hermogenes fl. c. 175- .... CMLC 6

Hernandez, Jose 1834-1886 ...... NCLC 17

Herodotus c. 484B.C.-429B.C. .... CMLC 17

Herrick, Robert
1591-1674 ..... LC 13; DA; DAB; DAC;
DAM MST, POP; PC 9
See also DLB 126

Herring, Guilles
See Somerville, Edith

Herriot, James
1916-1995 .... CLC 12; DAM POP
See also Wight, James Alfred
See also AAYA 1; CA 148; CANR 40;
SATA 86

Herrmann, Dorothy 1941- .... CLC 44
See also CA 107

Herrmann, Taffy
See Herrmann, Dorothy

Hersey, John (Richard)
1914-1993 .... CLC 1, 2, 7, 9, 40, 81, 97;
DAM POP
See also CA 17-20R; 140; CANR 33;
DLB 6; MTCW; SATA 25;
SATA-Obit 76

Herzen, Aleksandr Ivanovich
1812-1870 .... NCLC 10

Herzl, Theodor 1860-1904 .... TCLC 36

Herzog, Werner 1942- .... CLC 16
See also CA 89-92

Hesiod c. 8th cent. B.C.- .... CMLC 5

Hesse, Hermann
1877-1962 .... CLC 1, 2, 3, 6, 11, 17, 25,
69; DA; DAB; DAC; DAM MST, NOV;
SSC 9; WLC
See also CA 17-18; CAP 2; DLB 66;
MTCW; SATA 50

Hewes, Cady
See De Voto, Bernard (Augustine)

Heyen, William 1940- .... CLC 13, 18
See also CA 33-36R; CAAS 9; DLB 5

Heyerdahl, Thor 1914- .... CLC 26
See also CA 5-8R; CANR 5, 22; MTCW;
SATA 2, 52

Heym, Georg (Theodor Franz Arthur)
1887-1912 .... TCLC 9
See also CA 106

Heym, Stefan 1913- .... CLC 41
See also CA 9-12R; CANR 4; DLB 69

Heyse, Paul (Johann Ludwig von)
1830-1914 .... TCLC 8
See also CA 104; DLB 129

Heyward, (Edwin) DuBose
1885-1940 .... TCLC 59
See also CA 108; DLB 7, 9, 45; SATA 21

Hibbert, Eleanor Alice Burford
1906-1993 .... CLC 7; DAM POP
See also BEST 90:4; CA 17-20R; 140;
CANR 9, 28; SATA 2; SATA-Obit 74

Hichens, Robert S. 1864-1950 ..... TCLC 64
See also DLB 153

Higgins, George V(incent)
1939- .... CLC 4, 7, 10, 18
See also CA 77-80; CAAS 5; CANR 17, 51;
DLB 2; DLBY 81; INT CANR-17;
MTCW

Higginson, Thomas Wentworth
1823-1911 .... TCLC 36
See also DLB 1, 64

Highet, Helen
See MacInnes, Helen (Clark)

Highsmith, (Mary) Patricia
1921-1995 .... CLC 2, 4, 14, 42;
DAM NOV, POP
See also CA 1-4R; 147; CANR 1, 20, 48;
MTCW

Highwater, Jamake (Mamake)
1942(?)- .... CLC 12
See also AAYA 7; CA 65-68; CAAS 7;
CANR 10, 34; CLR 17; DLB 52;
DLBY 85; JRDA; MAICYA; SATA 32,
69; SATA-Brief 30

Highway, Tomson
1951- ..... CLC 92; DAC; DAM MULT
See also CA 151; NNAL

Higuchi, Ichiyo 1872-1896 ...... NCLC 49

Hijuelos, Oscar
1951- .... CLC 65; DAM MULT, POP;
HLC
See also BEST 90:1; CA 123; CANR 50;
DLB 145; HW

Hikmet, Nazim 1902(?)-1963 .... CLC 40
See also CA 141; 93-96

Hildesheimer, Wolfgang
1916-1991 .... CLC 49
See also CA 101; 135; DLB 69, 124

Hill, Geoffrey (William)
1932- .... CLC 5, 8, 18, 45; DAM POET
See also CA 81-84; CANR 21;
CDBLB 1960 to Present; DLB 40;
MTCW

Hill, George Roy 1921- .... CLC 26
See also CA 110; 122

Hill, John
See Koontz, Dean R(ay)

Hill, Susan (Elizabeth)
1942- .. CLC 4; DAB; DAM MST, NOV
See also CA 33-36R; CANR 29; DLB 14,
139; MTCW

Hillerman, Tony
1925- .... CLC 62; DAM POP
See also AAYA 6; BEST 89:1; CA 29-32R;
CANR 21, 42; SATA 6

Hillesum, Etty 1914-1943 .... TCLC 49
See also CA 137

Hilliard, Noel (Harvey) 1929- ...... CLC 15
See also CA 9-12R; CANR 7

Hillis, Rick 1956- .... CLC 66
See also CA 134

Hilton, James 1900-1954 .... TCLC 21
See also CA 108; DLB 34, 77; SATA 34

Himes, Chester (Bomar)
1909-1984 .... CLC 2, 4, 7, 18, 58; BLC;
DAM MULT
See also BW 2; CA 25-28R; 114; CANR 22;
DLB 2, 76, 143; MTCW

Hinde, Thomas .... CLC 6, 11
See also Chitty, Thomas Willes

Hindin, Nathan
See Bloch, Robert (Albert)

Hine, (William) Daryl   1936- . . . .   CLC 15
See also CA 1-4R; CAAS 15; CANR 1, 20;
DLB 60

Hinkson, Katharine Tynan
See Tynan, Katharine

Hinton, S(usan) E(loise)
1950- . . . . CLC 30; DA; DAB; DAC;
DAM MST, NOV
See also AAYA 2; CA 81-84; CANR 32;
CLR 3, 23; JRDA; MAICYA; MTCW;
SATA 19, 58

Hippius, Zinaida . . . .   TCLC 9
See also Gippius, Zinaida (Nikolayevna)

Hiraoka, Kimitake   1925-1970
See Mishima, Yukio
See also CA 97-100; 29-32R; DAM DRAM;
MTCW

Hirsch, E(ric) D(onald), Jr.   1928- . . .   CLC 79
See also CA 25-28R; CANR 27, 51;
DLB 67; INT CANR-27; MTCW

Hirsch, Edward   1950- . . . .   CLC 31, 50
See also CA 104; CANR 20, 42; DLB 120

Hitchcock, Alfred (Joseph)
1899-1980 . . . .   CLC 16
See also CA 97-100; SATA 27;
SATA-Obit 24

Hitler, Adolf   1889-1945 . . . .   TCLC 53
See also CA 117; 147

Hoagland, Edward   1932- . . . .   CLC 28
See also CA 1-4R; CANR 2, 31; DLB 6;
SATA 51

Hoban, Russell (Conwell)
1925- . . . .   CLC 7, 25; DAM NOV
See also CA 5-8R; CANR 23, 37; CLR 3;
DLB 52; MAICYA; MTCW; SATA 1,
40, 78

Hobbes, Thomas   1588-1679 . . . .   LC 36
See also DLB 151

Hobbs, Perry
See Blackmur, R(ichard) P(almer)

Hobson, Laura Z(ametkin)
1900-1986 . . . .   CLC 7, 25
See also CA 17-20R; 118; CANR 55;
DLB 28; SATA 52

Hochhuth, Rolf
1931- . . . . .   CLC 4, 11, 18; DAM DRAM
See also CA 5-8R; CANR 33; DLB 124;
MTCW

Hochman, Sandra   1936- . . . .   CLC 3, 8
See also CA 5-8R; DLB 5

Hochwaelder, Fritz
1911-1986 . . . . . .   CLC 36; DAM DRAM
See also CA 29-32R; 120; CANR 42;
MTCW

Hochwalder, Fritz
See Hochwaelder, Fritz

Hocking, Mary (Eunice)   1921- . . . . .   CLC 13
See also CA 101; CANR 18, 40

Hodgins, Jack   1938- . . . .   CLC 23
See also CA 93-96; DLB 60

Hodgson, William Hope
1877(?)-1918 . . . .   TCLC 13
See also CA 111; DLB 70, 153, 156

Hoeg, Peter   1957- . . . .   CLC 95
See also CA 151

Hoffman, Alice
1952- . . . .   CLC 51; DAM NOV
See also CA 77-80; CANR 34; MTCW

Hoffman, Daniel (Gerard)
1923- . . . .   CLC 6, 13, 23
See also CA 1-4R; CANR 4; DLB 5

Hoffman, Stanley   1944- . . . .   CLC 5
See also CA 77-80

Hoffman, William M(oses)   1939- . . .   CLC 40
See also CA 57-60; CANR 11

Hoffmann, E(rnst) T(heodor) A(madeus)
1776-1822 . . . .   NCLC 2; SSC 13
See also DLB 90; SATA 27

Hofmann, Gert   1931- . . . .   CLC 54
See also CA 128

Hofmannsthal, Hugo von
1874-1929 . . . .   TCLC 11; DAM DRAM;
DC 4
See also CA 106; 153; DLB 81, 118

Hogan, Linda
1947- . . . .   CLC 73; DAM MULT
See also CA 120; CANR 45; NNAL

Hogarth, Charles
See Creasey, John

Hogarth, Emmett
See Polonsky, Abraham (Lincoln)

Hogg, James   1770-1835 . . . .   NCLC 4
See also DLB 93, 116, 159

Holbach, Paul Henri Thiry Baron
1723-1789 . . . .   LC 14

Holberg, Ludvig   1684-1754 . . . .   LC 6

Holden, Ursula   1921- . . . .   CLC 18
See also CA 101; CAAS 8; CANR 22

Holderlin, (Johann Christian) Friedrich
1770-1843 . . . .   NCLC 16; PC 4

Holdstock, Robert
See Holdstock, Robert P.

Holdstock, Robert P.   1948- . . . .   CLC 39
See also CA 131

Holland, Isabelle   1920- . . . .   CLC 21
See also AAYA 11; CA 21-24R; CANR 10,
25, 47; JRDA; MAICYA; SATA 8, 70

Holland, Marcus
See Caldwell, (Janet Miriam) Taylor
(Holland)

Hollander, John   1929- . . . . . .   CLC 2, 5, 8, 14
See also CA 1-4R; CANR 1, 52; DLB 5;
SATA 13

Hollander, Paul
See Silverberg, Robert

Holleran, Andrew   1943(?)- . . . .   CLC 38
See also CA 144

Hollinghurst, Alan   1954- . . . .   CLC 55, 91
See also CA 114

Hollis, Jim
See Summers, Hollis (Spurgeon, Jr.)

Holly, Buddy   1936-1959 . . . .   TCLC 65

Holmes, John
See Souster, (Holmes) Raymond

Holmes, John Clellon   1926-1988 . . . .   CLC 56
See also CA 9-12R; 125; CANR 4; DLB 16

Holmes, Oliver Wendell
1809-1894 . . . .   NCLC 14
See also CDALB 1640-1865; DLB 1;
SATA 34

Holmes, Raymond
See Souster, (Holmes) Raymond

Holt, Victoria
See Hibbert, Eleanor Alice Burford

Holub, Miroslav   1923- . . . .   CLC 4
See also CA 21-24R; CANR 10

Homer
c. 8th cent. B.C.- . . . . .   CMLC 1, 16; DA;
DAB; DAC; DAM MST, POET

Honig, Edwin   1919- . . . .   CLC 33
See also CA 5-8R; CAAS 8; CANR 4, 45;
DLB 5

Hood, Hugh (John Blagdon)
1928- . . . .   CLC 15, 28
See also CA 49-52; CAAS 17; CANR 1, 33;
DLB 53

Hood, Thomas   1799-1845 . . . .   NCLC 16
See also DLB 96

Hooker, (Peter) Jeremy   1941- . . . . . .   CLC 43
See also CA 77-80; CANR 22; DLB 40

hooks, bell . . . .   CLC 94
See also Watkins, Gloria

Hope, A(lec) D(erwent)   1907- . . . .   CLC 3, 51
See also CA 21-24R; CANR 33; MTCW

Hope, Brian
See Creasey, John

Hope, Christopher (David Tully)
1944- . . . .   CLC 52
See also CA 106; CANR 47; SATA 62

Hopkins, Gerard Manley
1844-1889 . . . .   NCLC 17; DA; DAB;
DAC; DAM MST, POET; PC 15; WLC
See also CDBLB 1890-1914; DLB 35, 57

Hopkins, John (Richard)   1931- . . . . . .   CLC 4
See also CA 85-88

Hopkins, Pauline Elizabeth
1859-1930 . . . .   TCLC 28; BLC;
DAM MULT
See also BW 2; CA 141; DLB 50

Hopkinson, Francis   1737-1791 . . . . . .   LC 25
See also DLB 31

Hopley-Woolrich, Cornell George   1903-1968
See Woolrich, Cornell
See also CA 13-14; CAP 1

Horatio
See Proust, (Valentin-Louis-George-Eugene-)
Marcel

Horgan, Paul (George Vincent O'Shaughnessy)
1903-1995 . . . . . .   CLC 9, 53; DAM NOV
See also CA 13-16R; 147; CANR 9, 35;
DLB 102; DLBY 85; INT CANR-9;
MTCW; SATA 13; SATA-Obit 84

Horn, Peter
See Kuttner, Henry

Hornem, Horace Esq.
See Byron, George Gordon (Noel)

Hornung, E(rnest) W(illiam)
1866-1921 . . . .   TCLC 59
See also CA 108; DLB 70

Hustvedt, Siri 1955-............. **CLC 76**
See also CA 137

Hutten, Ulrich von 1488-1523....... **LC 16**

Huxley, Aldous (Leonard)
1894-1963 ..... **CLC 1, 3, 4, 5, 8, 11, 18,**
35, 79; DA; DAB; DAC; DAM MST,
NOV; WLC
See also AAYA 11; CA 85-88; CANR 44;
CDBLB 1914-1945; DLB 36, 100, 162;
MTCW; SATA 63

Huysmans, Charles Marie Georges
1848-1907
See Huysmans, Joris-Karl
See also CA 104

Huysmans, Joris-Karl.............. TCLC 7
See also Huysmans, Charles Marie Georges
See also DLB 123

Hwang, David Henry
1957-.... **CLC 55; DAM DRAM; DC 4**
See also CA 127; 132; INT 132

Hyde, Anthony 1946-............ **CLC 42**
See also CA 136

Hyde, Margaret O(ldroyd) 1917-... **CLC 21**
See also CA 1-4R; CANR 1, 36; CLR 23;
JRDA; MAICYA; SAAS 8; SATA 1, 42,
76

Hynes, James 1956(?)-........... **CLC 65**

Ian, Janis 1951-................. **CLC 21**
See also CA 105

Ibanez, Vicente Blasco
See Blasco Ibanez, Vicente

Ibarguengoitia, Jorge 1928-1983.... **CLC 37**
See also CA 124; 113; HW

Ibsen, Henrik (Johan)
1828-1906....... **TCLC 2, 8, 16, 37, 52;**
DA; DAB; DAC; DAM DRAM, MST;
DC 2; WLC
See also CA 104; 141

Ibuse Masuji 1898-1993........... **CLC 22**
See also CA 127; 141

Ichikawa, Kon 1915-............. **CLC 20**
See also CA 121

Idle, Eric 1943-................. **CLC 21**
See also Monty Python
See also CA 116; CANR 35

Ignatow, David 1914-...... **CLC 4, 7, 14, 40**
See also CA 9-12R; CAAS 3; CANR 31;
DLB 5

Ihimaera, Witi 1944- .... **CLC 46**
See also CA 77-80

Ilf, Ilya........................ TCLC 21
See also Fainzilberg, Ilya Arnoldovich

Illyes, Gyula 1902-1983............ **PC 16**
See also CA 114; 109

Immermann, Karl (Lebrecht)
1796-1840 .... **NCLC 4, 49**
See also DLB 133

Inclan, Ramon (Maria) del Valle
See Valle-Inclan, Ramon (Maria) del

Infante, G(uillermo) Cabrera
See Cabrera Infante, G(uillermo)

Ingalls, Rachel (Holmes) 1940-..... **CLC 42**
See also CA 123; 127

Ingamells, Rex 1913-1955........ **TCLC 35**

Inge, William (Motter)
1913-1973 .. **CLC 1, 8, 19; DAM DRAM**
See also CA 9-12R; CDALB 1941-1968;
DLB 7; MTCW

Ingelow, Jean 1820-1897........ **NCLC 39**
See also DLB 35, 163; SATA 33

Ingram, Willis J.
See Harris, Mark

Innaurato, Albert (F.) 1948(?)- .. **CLC 21, 60**
See also CA 115; 122; INT 122

Innes, Michael
See Stewart, J(ohn) I(nnes) M(ackintosh)

Ionesco, Eugene
1909-1994 .... **CLC 1, 4, 6, 9, 11, 15, 41,**
86; DA; DAB; DAC; DAM DRAM,
MST; WLC
See also CA 9-12R; 144; CANR 55;
MTCW; SATA 7; SATA-Obit 79

Iqbal, Muhammad 1873-1938 ..... **TCLC 28**

Ireland, Patrick
See O'Doherty, Brian

Iron, Ralph
See Schreiner, Olive (Emilie Albertina)

Irving, John (Winslow)
1942-..... **CLC 13, 23, 38; DAM NOV,**
POP
See also AAYA 8; BEST 89:3; CA 25-28R;
CANR 28; DLB 6; DLBY 82; MTCW

Irving, Washington
1783-1859 ..... **NCLC 2, 19; DA; DAB;**
DAM MST; SSC 2; WLC
See also CDALB 1640-1865; DLB 3, 11, 30,
59, 73, 74; YABC 2

Irwin, P. K.
See Page, P(atricia) K(athleen)

Isaacs, Susan 1943- ... **CLC 32; DAM POP**
See also BEST 89:1; CA 89-92; CANR 20,
41; INT CANR-20; MTCW

Isherwood, Christopher (William Bradshaw)
1904-1986 .... **CLC 1, 9, 11, 14, 44;**
DAM DRAM, NOV
See also CA 13-16R; 117; CANR 35;
DLB 15; DLBY 86; MTCW

Ishiguro, Kazuo
1954- ...... **CLC 27, 56, 59; DAM NOV**
See also BEST 90:2; CA 120; CANR 49;
MTCW

Ishikawa, Hakuhin
See Ishikawa, Takuboku

Ishikawa, Takuboku
1886(?)-1912 .... **TCLC 15;**
DAM POET; PC 10
See also CA 113; 153

Iskander, Fazil 1929-............ **CLC 47**
See also CA 102

Isler, Alan .... **CLC 91**

Ivan IV 1530-1584 .... **LC 17**

Ivanov, Vyacheslav Ivanovich
1866-1949 .... **TCLC 33**
See also CA 122

Ivask, Ivar Vidrik 1927-1992....... **CLC 14**
See also CA 37-40R; 139; CANR 24

Ives, Morgan
See Bradley, Marion Zimmer

J. R. S.
See Gogarty, Oliver St. John

Jabran, Kahlil
See Gibran, Kahlil

Jabran, Khalil
See Gibran, Kahlil

Jackson, Daniel
See Wingrove, David (John)

Jackson, Jesse 1908-1983 .... **CLC 12**
See also BW 1; CA 25-28R; 109; CANR 27;
CLR 28; MAICYA; SATA 2, 29;
SATA-Obit 48

Jackson, Laura (Riding) 1901-1991
See Riding, Laura
See also CA 65-68; 135; CANR 28; DLB 48

Jackson, Sam
See Trumbo, Dalton

Jackson, Sara
See Wingrove, David (John)

Jackson, Shirley
1919-1965 .... **CLC 11, 60, 87; DA;**
DAC; DAM MST; SSC 9; WLC
See also AAYA 9; CA 1-4R; 25-28R;
CANR 4, 52; CDALB 1941-1968; DLB 6;
SATA 2

Jacob, (Cyprien-)Max 1876-1944 ... **TCLC 6**
See also CA 104

Jacobs, Jim 1942-................ **CLC 12**
See also CA 97-100; INT 97-100

Jacobs, W(illiam) W(ymark)
1863-1943 .... **TCLC 22**
See also CA 121; DLB 135

Jacobsen, Jens Peter 1847-1885 .. **NCLC 34**

Jacobsen, Josephine 1908-......... **CLC 48**
See also CA 33-36R; CAAS 18; CANR 23,
48

Jacobson, Dan 1929- .... **CLC 4, 14**
See also CA 1-4R; CANR 2, 25; DLB 14;
MTCW

Jacqueline
See Carpentier (y Valmont), Alejo

Jagger, Mick 1944-............... **CLC 17**

Jakes, John (William)
1932-.... **CLC 29; DAM NOV, POP**
See also BEST 89:4; CA 57-60; CANR 10,
43; DLBY 83; INT CANR-10; MTCW;
SATA 62

Jalal al-Din Rumi 1297-1373..... **CMLC 20**

James, Andrew
See Kirkup, James

James, C(yril) L(ionel) R(obert)
1901-1989 .... **CLC 33**
See also BW 2; CA 117; 125; 128; DLB 125;
MTCW

James, Daniel (Lewis) 1911-1988
See Santiago, Danny
See also CA 125

James, Dynely
See Mayne, William (James Carter)

James, Henry Sr. 1811-1882..... **NCLC 53**

Jones, Gayl
1949- .... **CLC 6, 9; BLC; DAM MULT**
See also BW 2; CA 77-80; CANR 27;
DLB 33; MTCW

Jones, James 1921-1977.... **CLC 1, 3, 10, 39**
See also AITN 1, 2; CA 1-4R; 69-72;
CANR 6; DLB 2, 143; MTCW

Jones, John J.
See Lovecraft, H(oward) P(hillips)

Jones, LeRoi .... **CLC 1, 2, 3, 5, 10, 14**
See also Baraka, Amiri

Jones, Louis B. .... **CLC 65**
See also CA 141

Jones, Madison (Percy, Jr.) 1925- ... **CLC 4**
See also CA 13-16R; CAAS 11; CANR 7,
54; DLB 152

Jones, Mervyn 1922- .... **CLC 10, 52**
See also CA 45-48; CAAS 5; CANR 1;
MTCW

Jones, Mick 1956(?)- .... **CLC 30**

Jones, Nettie (Pearl) 1941- .... **CLC 34**
See also BW 2; CA 137; CAAS 20

Jones, Preston 1936-1979 .... **CLC 10**
See also CA 73-76; 89-92; DLB 7

Jones, Robert F(rancis) 1934- .... **CLC 7**
See also CA 49-52; CANR 2

Jones, Rod 1953- .... **CLC 50**
See also CA 128

Jones, Terence Graham Parry
1942- .... **CLC 21**
See also Jones, Terry; Monty Python
See also CA 112; 116; CANR 35; INT 116

Jones, Terry
See Jones, Terence Graham Parry
See also SATA 67; SATA-Brief 51

Jones, Thom 1945(?)- .... **CLC 81**

Jong, Erica
1942- .... **CLC 4, 6, 8, 18, 83;**
DAM NOV, POP
See also AITN 1; BEST 90:2; CA 73-76;
CANR 26, 52; DLB 2, 5, 28, 152;
INT CANR-26; MTCW

Jonson, Ben(jamin)
1572(?)-1637 ...... **LC 6, 33; DA; DAB;**
DAC; DAM DRAM, MST, POET;
DC 4; WLC
See also CDBLB Before 1660; DLB 62, 121

Jordan, June
1936- ..... **CLC 5, 11, 23; DAM MULT,**
POET
See also AAYA 2; BW 2; CA 33-36R;
CANR 25; CLR 10; DLB 38; MAICYA;
MTCW; SATA 4

Jordan, Pat(rick M.) 1941- .... **CLC 37**
See also CA 33-36R

Jorgensen, Ivar
See Ellison, Harlan (Jay)

Jorgenson, Ivar
See Silverberg, Robert

Josephus, Flavius c. 37-100 ...... **CMLC 13**

Josipovici, Gabriel 1940- .... **CLC 6, 43**
See also CA 37-40R; CAAS 8; CANR 47;
DLB 14

Joubert, Joseph 1754-1824 .... **NCLC 9**

Jouve, Pierre Jean 1887-1976 ...... **CLC 47**
See also CA 65-68

Joyce, James (Augustine Aloysius)
1882-1941 .... **TCLC 3, 8, 16, 35, 52;**
DA; DAB; DAC; DAM MST, NOV,
POET; SSC 3; WLC
See also CA 104; 126; CDBLB 1914-1945;
DLB 10, 19, 36, 162; MTCW

Jozsef, Attila 1905-1937......... **TCLC 22**
See also CA 116

Juana Ines de la Cruz 1651(?)-1695 ... **LC 5**

Judd, Cyril
See Kornbluth, C(yril) M.; Pohl, Frederik

Julian of Norwich 1342(?)-1416(?) .... **LC 6**
See also DLB 146

Juniper, Alex
See Hospital, Janette Turner

Junius
See Luxemburg, Rosa

Just, Ward (Swift) 1935- .... **CLC 4, 27**
See also CA 25-28R; CANR 32;
INT CANR-32

Justice, Donald (Rodney)
1925- .... **CLC 6, 19; DAM POET**
See also CA 5-8R; CANR 26, 54;
DLBY 83; INT CANR-26

Juvenal c. 55-c. 127 .... **CMLC 8**

Juvenis
See Bourne, Randolph S(illiman)

Kacew, Romain 1914-1980
See Gary, Romain
See also CA 108; 102

Kadare, Ismail 1936- .... **CLC 52**

Kadohata, Cynthia................. **CLC 59**
See also CA 140

Kafka, Franz
1883-1924 .... **TCLC 2, 6, 13, 29, 47, 53;**
DA; DAB; DAC; DAM MST, NOV;
SSC 5; WLC
See also CA 105; 126; DLB 81; MTCW

Kahanovitsch, Pinkhes
See Der Nister

Kahn, Roger 1927-............... **CLC 30**
See also CA 25-28R; CANR 44; DLB 171;
SATA 37

Kain, Saul
See Sassoon, Siegfried (Lorraine)

Kaiser, Georg 1878-1945 .... **TCLC 9**
See also CA 106; DLB 124

Kaletski, Alexander 1946- .... **CLC 39**
See also CA 118; 143

Kalidasa fl. c. 400- .... **CMLC 9**

Kallman, Chester (Simon)
1921-1975 .... **CLC 2**
See also CA 45-48; 53-56; CANR 3

Kaminsky, Melvin 1926-
See Brooks, Mel
See also CA 65-68; CANR 16

Kaminsky, Stuart M(elvin) 1934- ... **CLC 59**
See also CA 73-76; CANR 29, 53

Kane, Francis
See Robbins, Harold

Kane, Paul
See Simon, Paul (Frederick)

Kane, Wilson
See Bloch, Robert (Albert)

Kanin, Garson 1912-.............. **CLC 22**
See also AITN 1; CA 5-8R; CANR 7;
DLB 7

Kaniuk, Yoram 1930-............. **CLC 19**
See also CA 134

Kant, Immanuel 1724-1804 ...... **NCLC 27**
See also DLB 94

Kantor, MacKinlay 1904-1977 ...... **CLC 7**
See also CA 61-64; 73-76; DLB 9, 102

Kaplan, David Michael 1946- ...... **CLC 50**

Kaplan, James 1951- .... **CLC 59**
See also CA 135

Karageorge, Michael
See Anderson, Poul (William)

Karamzin, Nikolai Mikhailovich
1766-1826 .... **NCLC 3**
See also DLB 150

Karapanou, Margarita 1946-....... **CLC 13**
See also CA 101

Karinthy, Frigyes 1887-1938...... **TCLC 47**

Karl, Frederick R(obert) 1927- ..... **CLC 34**
See also CA 5-8R; CANR 3, 44

Kastel, Warren
See Silverberg, Robert

Kataev, Evgeny Petrovich 1903-1942
See Petrov, Evgeny
See also CA 120

Kataphusin
See Ruskin, John

Katz, Steve 1935-................. **CLC 47**
See also CA 25-28R; CAAS 14; CANR 12;
DLBY 83

Kauffman, Janet 1945-............. **CLC 42**
See also CA 117; CANR 43; DLBY 86

Kaufman, Bob (Garnell)
1925-1986 .... **CLC 49**
See also BW 1; CA 41-44R; 118; CANR 22;
DLB 16, 41

Kaufman, George S.
1889-1961 ...... **CLC 38; DAM DRAM**
See also CA 108; 93-96; DLB 7; INT 108

Kaufman, Sue .... **CLC 3, 8**
See also Barondess, Sue K(aufman)

Kavafis, Konstantinos Petrou 1863-1933
See Cavafy, C(onstantine) P(eter)
See also CA 104

Kavan, Anna 1901-1968...... **CLC 5, 13, 82**
See also CA 5-8R; CANR 6; MTCW

Kavanagh, Dan
See Barnes, Julian (Patrick)

Kavanagh, Patrick (Joseph)
1904-1967 .... **CLC 22**
See also CA 123; 25-28R; DLB 15, 20;
MTCW

Kawabata, Yasunari
1899-1972 .... **CLC 2, 5, 9, 18;**
DAM MULT; SSC 17
See also CA 93-96; 33-36R

Kaye, M(ary) M(argaret) 1909-..... **CLC 28**
See also CA 89-92; CANR 24; MTCW;
SATA 62

King, Martin Luther, Jr.
　　1929-1968 .... CLC 83; BLC; DA; DAB;
　　　　　　　　　　　DAC; DAM MST, MULT
　　See also BW 2; CA 25-28; CANR 27, 44;
　　CAP 2; MTCW; SATA 14

King, Stephen (Edwin)
　　1947- .... CLC 12, 26, 37, 61;
　　　　　　　　　　　DAM NOV, POP; SSC 17
　　See also AAYA 1, 17; BEST 90:1;
　　CA 61-64; CANR 1, 30, 52; DLB 143;
　　DLBY 80; JRDA; MTCW; SATA 9, 55

King, Steve
　　See King, Stephen (Edwin)

King, Thomas
　　1943- ..... CLC 89; DAC; DAM MULT
　　See also CA 144; NNAL

Kingman, Lee...................... CLC 17
　　See also Natti, (Mary) Lee
　　See also SAAS 3; SATA 1, 67

Kingsley, Charles 1819-1875 ..... NCLC 35
　　See also DLB 21, 32, 163; YABC 2

Kingsley, Sidney 1906-1995 .... CLC 44
　　See also CA 85-88; 147; DLB 7

Kingsolver, Barbara
　　1955- .... CLC 55, 81; DAM POP
　　See also AAYA 15; CA 129; 134; INT 134

Kingston, Maxine (Ting Ting) Hong
　　1940- .... CLC 12, 19, 58; DAM MULT,
　　　　　　　　　　　　　　　NOV
　　See also AAYA 8; CA 69-72; CANR 13,
　　38; DLB 173; DLBY 80; INT CANR-13;
　　MTCW; SATA 53

Kinnell, Galway
　　1927- .... CLC 1, 2, 3, 5, 13, 29
　　See also CA 9-12R; CANR 10, 34; DLB 5;
　　DLBY 87; INT CANR-34; MTCW

Kinsella, Thomas 1928- .... CLC 4, 19
　　See also CA 17-20R; CANR 15; DLB 27;
　　MTCW

Kinsella, W(illiam) P(atrick)
　　1935- .... CLC 27, 43; DAC;
　　　　　　　　　　　DAM NOV, POP
　　See also AAYA 7; CA 97-100; CAAS 7;
　　CANR 21, 35; INT CANR-21; MTCW

Kipling, (Joseph) Rudyard
　　1865-1936 ...... TCLC 8, 17; DA; DAB;
　　　　　　DAC; DAM MST, POET; PC 3; SSC 5;
　　　　　　　　　　　　　　　WLC
　　See also CA 105; 120; CANR 33;
　　CDBLB 1890-1914; CLR 39; DLB 19, 34,
　　141, 156; MAICYA; MTCW; YABC 2

Kirkup, James 1918- .... CLC 1
　　See also CA 1-4R; CAAS 4; CANR 2;
　　DLB 27; SATA 12

Kirkwood, James 1930(?)-1989 ...... CLC 9
　　See also AITN 2; CA 1-4R; 128; CANR 6,
　　40

Kirshner, Sidney
　　See Kingsley, Sidney

Kis, Danilo 1935-1989 .... CLC 57
　　See also CA 109; 118; 129; MTCW

Kivi, Aleksis 1834-1872 .... NCLC 30

Kizer, Carolyn (Ashley)
　　1925- ..... CLC 15, 39, 80; DAM POET
　　See also CA 65-68; CAAS 5; CANR 24;
　　DLB 5, 169

Klabund 1890-1928 .... TCLC 44
　　See also DLB 66

Klappert, Peter 1942- .... CLC 57
　　See also CA 33-36R; DLB 5

Klein, A(braham) M(oses)
　　1909-1972 .... CLC 19; DAB; DAC;
　　　　　　　　　　　DAM MST
　　See also CA 101; 37-40R; DLB 68

Klein, Norma 1938-1989 .... CLC 30
　　See also AAYA 2; CA 41-44R; 128;
　　CANR 15, 37; CLR 2, 19;
　　INT CANR-15; JRDA; MAICYA;
　　SAAS 1; SATA 7, 57

Klein, T(heodore) E(ibon) D(onald)
　　1947- .... CLC 34
　　See also CA 119; CANR 44

Kleist, Heinrich von
　　1777-1811 .... NCLC 2, 37;
　　　　　　　　　　　DAM DRAM; SSC 22
　　See also DLB 90

Klima, Ivan 1931- ..... CLC 56; DAM NOV
　　See also CA 25-28R; CANR 17, 50

Klimentov, Andrei Platonovich 1899-1951
　　See Platonov, Andrei
　　See also CA 108

Klinger, Friedrich Maximilian von
　　1752-1831 .... NCLC 1
　　See also DLB 94

Klopstock, Friedrich Gottlieb
　　1724-1803 .... NCLC 11
　　See also DLB 97

Knebel, Fletcher 1911-1993 .... CLC 14
　　See also AITN 1; CA 1-4R; 140; CAAS 3;
　　CANR 1, 36; SATA 36; SATA-Obit 75

Knickerbocker, Diedrich
　　See Irving, Washington

Knight, Etheridge
　　1931-1991 .... CLC 40; BLC;
　　　　　　　　　　　DAM POET; PC 14
　　See also BW 1; CA 21-24R; 133; CANR 23;
　　DLB 41

Knight, Sarah Kemble 1666-1727 ..... LC 7
　　See also DLB 24

Knister, Raymond 1899-1932 ...... TCLC 56
　　See also DLB 68

Knowles, John
　　1926- ...... CLC 1, 4, 10, 26; DA; DAC;
　　　　　　　　　　　DAM MST, NOV
　　See also AAYA 10; CA 17-20R; CANR 40;
　　CDALB 1968-1988; DLB 6; MTCW;
　　SATA 8, 89

Knox, Calvin M.
　　See Silverberg, Robert

Knye, Cassandra
　　See Disch, Thomas M(ichael)

Koch, C(hristopher) J(ohn) 1932- ... CLC 42
　　See also CA 127

Koch, Christopher
　　See Koch, C(hristopher) J(ohn)

Koch, Kenneth
　　1925- .... CLC 5, 8, 44; DAM POET
　　See also CA 1-4R; CANR 6, 36; DLB 5;
　　INT CANR-36; SATA 65

Kochanowski, Jan 1530-1584 .... LC 10

Kock, Charles Paul de
　　1794-1871 .... NCLC 16

Koda Shigeyuki 1867-1947
　　See Rohan, Koda
　　See also CA 121

Koestler, Arthur
　　1905-1983 .... CLC 1, 3, 6, 8, 15, 33
　　See also CA 1-4R; 109; CANR 1, 33;
　　CDBLB 1945-1960; DLBY 83; MTCW

Kogawa, Joy Nozomi
　　1935- ...... CLC 78; DAC; DAM MST,
　　　　　　　　　　　　　　　MULT
　　See also CA 101; CANR 19

Kohout, Pavel 1928- .... CLC 13
　　See also CA 45-48; CANR 3

Koizumi, Yakumo
　　See Hearn, (Patricio) Lafcadio (Tessima
　　Carlos)

Kolmar, Gertrud 1894-1943 ...... TCLC 40

Komunyakaa, Yusef 1947- ...... CLC 86, 94
　　See also CA 147; DLB 120

Konrad, George
　　See Konrad, Gyoergy

Konrad, Gyoergy 1933- ...... CLC 4, 10, 73
　　See also CA 85-88

Konwicki, Tadeusz 1926- ..... CLC 8, 28, 54
　　See also CA 101; CAAS 9; CANR 39;
　　MTCW

Koontz, Dean R(ay)
　　1945- ...... CLC 78; DAM NOV, POP
　　See also AAYA 9; BEST 89:3, 90:2;
　　CA 108; CANR 19, 36, 52; MTCW

Kopit, Arthur (Lee)
　　1937- ..... CLC 1, 18, 33; DAM DRAM
　　See also AITN 1; CA 81-84; CABS 3;
　　DLB 7; MTCW

Kops, Bernard 1926- .... CLC 4
　　See also CA 5-8R; DLB 13

Kornbluth, C(yril) M. 1923-1958.... TCLC 8
　　See also CA 105; DLB 8

Korolenko, V. G.
　　See Korolenko, Vladimir Galaktionovich

Korolenko, Vladimir
　　See Korolenko, Vladimir Galaktionovich

Korolenko, Vladimir G.
　　See Korolenko, Vladimir Galaktionovich

Korolenko, Vladimir Galaktionovich
　　1853-1921 .... TCLC 22
　　See also CA 121

Korzybski, Alfred (Habdank Skarbek)
　　1879-1950 .... TCLC 61
　　See also CA 123

Kosinski, Jerzy (Nikodem)
　　1933-1991 .... CLC 1, 2, 3, 6, 10, 15, 53,
　　　　　　　　　　　70; DAM NOV
　　See also CA 17-20R; 134; CANR 9, 46;
　　DLB 2; DLBY 82; MTCW

Kostelanetz, Richard (Cory) 1940- .. CLC 28
　　See also CA 13-16R; CAAS 8; CANR 38

Kostrowitzki, Wilhelm Apollinaris de
　　1880-1918
　　See Apollinaire, Guillaume
　　See also CA 104

Kotlowitz, Robert 1924- .... CLC 4
　　See also CA 33-36R; CANR 36

Landon, Letitia Elizabeth
　　1802-1838 . . . . **NCLC 15**
　　See also DLB 96

Landor, Walter Savage
　　1775-1864 . . . . **NCLC 14**
　　See also DLB 93, 107

Landwirth, Heinz　1927-
　　See Lind, Jakov
　　See also CA 9-12R; CANR 7

Lane, Patrick
　　1939- . . . . **CLC 25; DAM POET**
　　See also CA 97-100; CANR 54; DLB 53;
　　　INT 97-100

Lang, Andrew　1844-1912 . . . . **TCLC 16**
　　See also CA 114; 137; DLB 98, 141;
　　　MAICYA; SATA 16

Lang, Fritz　1890-1976 . . . . **CLC 20**
　　See also CA 77-80; 69-72; CANR 30

Lange, John
　　See Crichton, (John) Michael

Langer, Elinor　1939- . . . . **CLC 34**
　　See also CA 121

Langland, William
　　1330(?)-1400(?) . . . . . . **LC 19; DA; DAB;**
　　　　　　　　　　　　DAC; DAM MST, POET
　　See also DLB 146

Langstaff, Launcelot
　　See Irving, Washington

Lanier, Sidney
　　1842-1881 . . . . . . **NCLC 6; DAM POET**
　　See also DLB 64; DLBD 13; MAICYA;
　　　SATA 18

Lanyer, Aemilia　1569-1645 . . . . . . **LC 10, 30**
　　See also DLB 121

Lao Tzu . . . . **CMLC 7**

Lapine, James (Elliot)　1949- . . . . **CLC 39**
　　See also CA 123; 130; CANR 54; INT 130

Larbaud, Valery (Nicolas)
　　1881-1957 . . . . **TCLC 9**
　　See also CA 106; 152

Lardner, Ring
　　See Lardner, Ring(gold) W(ilmer)

Lardner, Ring W., Jr.
　　See Lardner, Ring(gold) W(ilmer)

Lardner, Ring(gold) W(ilmer)
　　1885-1933 . . . . **TCLC 2, 14**
　　See also CA 104; 131; CDALB 1917-1929;
　　　DLB 11, 25, 86; MTCW

Laredo, Betty
　　See Codrescu, Andrei

Larkin, Maia
　　See Wojciechowska, Maia (Teresa)

Larkin, Philip (Arthur)
　　1922-1985 . . . . **CLC 3, 5, 8, 9, 13, 18, 33,**
　　　　　　　　　　39, 64; DAB; DAM MST, POET
　　See also CA 5-8R; 117; CANR 24;
　　　CDBLB 1960 to Present; DLB 27;
　　　MTCW

Larra (y Sanchez de Castro), Mariano Jose de
　　1809-1837 . . . . **NCLC 17**

Larsen, Eric　1941- . . . . **CLC 55**
　　See also CA 132

Larsen, Nella
　　1891-1964 . . . . **CLC 37; BLC;**
　　　　　　　　　　　　　　　　　DAM MULT
　　See also BW 1; CA 125; DLB 51

Larson, Charles R(aymond)　1938-. . . **CLC 31**
　　See also CA 53-56; CANR 4

Las Casas, Bartolome de　1474-1566 . . **LC 31**

Lasker-Schueler, Else　1869-1945 . . **TCLC 57**
　　See also DLB 66, 124

Latham, Jean Lee　1902-. . . . . **CLC 12**
　　See also AITN 1; CA 5-8R; CANR 7;
　　　MAICYA; SATA 2, 68

Latham, Mavis
　　See Clark, Mavis Thorpe

Lathen, Emma . . . . **CLC 2**
　　See also Hennissart, Martha; Latsis, Mary
　　　J(ane)

Lathrop, Francis
　　See Leiber, Fritz (Reuter, Jr.)

Latsis, Mary J(ane)
　　See Lathen, Emma
　　See also CA 85-88

Lattimore, Richmond (Alexander)
　　1906-1984 . . . . **CLC 3**
　　See also CA 1-4R; 112; CANR 1

Laughlin, James　1914- . . . . **CLC 49**
　　See also CA 21-24R; CAAS 22; CANR 9,
　　　47; DLB 48

Laurence, (Jean) Margaret (Wemyss)
　　1926-1987 . . . . **CLC 3, 6, 13, 50, 62;**
　　　　　　　　　　　　　DAC; DAM MST; SSC 7
　　See also CA 5-8R; 121; CANR 33; DLB 53;
　　　MTCW; SATA-Obit 50

Laurent, Antoine　1952- . . . . **CLC 50**

Lauscher, Hermann
　　See Hesse, Hermann

Lautreamont, Comte de
　　1846-1870 . . . . **NCLC 12; SSC 14**

Laverty, Donald
　　See Blish, James (Benjamin)

Lavin, Mary　1912-1996 . . **CLC 4, 18; SSC 4**
　　See also CA 9-12R; 151; CANR 33;
　　　DLB 15; MTCW

Lavond, Paul Dennis
　　See Kornbluth, C(yril) M.; Pohl, Frederik

Lawler, Raymond Evenor　1922- . . . . **CLC 58**
　　See also CA 103

Lawrence, D(avid) H(erbert Richards)
　　1885-1930 . . . . **TCLC 2, 9, 16, 33, 48, 61;**
　　　　　　　　　DA; DAB; DAC; DAM MST, NOV,
　　　　　　　　　　　　　POET; SSC 4, 19; WLC
　　See also CA 104; 121; CDBLB 1914-1945;
　　　DLB 10, 19, 36, 98, 162; MTCW

Lawrence, T(homas) E(dward)
　　1888-1935 . . . . **TCLC 18**
　　See also Dale, Colin
　　See also CA 115

Lawrence of Arabia
　　See Lawrence, T(homas) E(dward)

Lawson, Henry (Archibald Hertzberg)
　　1867-1922 . . . . **TCLC 27; SSC 18**
　　See also CA 120

Lawton, Dennis
　　See Faust, Frederick (Schiller)

Laxness, Halldor . . . . **CLC 25**
　　See also Gudjonsson, Halldor Kiljan

Layamon　fl. c. 1200-. . . . . **CMLC 10**
　　See also DLB 146

Laye, Camara
　　1928-1980 . . . . **CLC 4, 38; BLC;**
　　　　　　　　　　　　　　　　　DAM MULT
　　See also BW 1; CA 85-88; 97-100;
　　　CANR 25; MTCW

Layton, Irving (Peter)
　　1912- . . . . **CLC 2, 15; DAC; DAM MST,**
　　　　　　　　　　　　　　　　　　　　　POET
　　See also CA 1-4R; CANR 2, 33, 43;
　　　DLB 88; MTCW

Lazarus, Emma　1849-1887 . . . . **NCLC 8**

Lazarus, Felix
　　See Cable, George Washington

Lazarus, Henry
　　See Slavitt, David R(ytman)

Lea, Joan
　　See Neufeld, John (Arthur)

Leacock, Stephen (Butler)
　　1869-1944 . . **TCLC 2; DAC; DAM MST**
　　See also CA 104; 141; DLB 92

Lear, Edward　1812-1888 . . . . **NCLC 3**
　　See also CLR 1; DLB 32, 163, 166;
　　　MAICYA; SATA 18

Lear, Norman (Milton)　1922- . . . . . . **CLC 12**
　　See also CA 73-76

Leavis, F(rank) R(aymond)
　　1895-1978 . . . . **CLC 24**
　　See also CA 21-24R; 77-80; CANR 44;
　　　MTCW

Leavitt, David　1961-. . . **CLC 34; DAM POP**
　　See also CA 116; 122; CANR 50; DLB 130;
　　　INT 122

Leblanc, Maurice (Marie Emile)
　　1864-1941 . . . . **TCLC 49**
　　See also CA 110

Lebowitz, Fran(ces Ann)
　　1951(?)-. . . . . **CLC 11, 36**
　　See also CA 81-84; CANR 14;
　　　INT CANR-14; MTCW

Lebrecht, Peter
　　See Tieck, (Johann) Ludwig

le Carre, John . . . . **CLC 3, 5, 9, 15, 28**
　　See also Cornwell, David (John Moore)
　　See also BEST 89:4; CDBLB 1960 to
　　　Present; DLB 87

Le Clezio, J(ean) M(arie) G(ustave)
　　1940- . . . . **CLC 31**
　　See also CA 116; 128; DLB 83

Leconte de Lisle, Charles-Marie-Rene
　　1818-1894 . . . . **NCLC 29**

Le Coq, Monsieur
　　See Simenon, Georges (Jacques Christian)

Leduc, Violette　1907-1972 . . . . **CLC 22**
　　See also CA 13-14; 33-36R; CAP 1

Ledwidge, Francis　1887(?)-1917 . . . **TCLC 23**
　　See also CA 123; DLB 20

Lee, Andrea
　　1953- . . . . . **CLC 36; BLC; DAM MULT**
　　See also BW 1; CA 125

Lee, Andrew
　　See Auchincloss, Louis (Stanton)

Levine, Norman 1924- . . . . **CLC 54**
See also CA 73-76; CAAS 23; CANR 14;
DLB 88

Levine, Philip
1928- . . . . **CLC 2, 4, 5, 9, 14, 33;**
DAM POET
See also CA 9-12R; CANR 9, 37, 52;
DLB 5

Levinson, Deirdre 1931- . . . . **CLC 49**
See also CA 73-76

Levi-Strauss, Claude 1908- . . . . **CLC 38**
See also CA 1-4R; CANR 6, 32; MTCW

Levitin, Sonia (Wolff) 1934- . . . . **CLC 17**
See also AAYA 13; CA 29-32R; CANR 14,
32; JRDA; MAICYA; SAAS 2; SATA 4,
68

Levon, O. U.
See Kesey, Ken (Elton)

Lewes, George Henry
1817-1878 . . . . **NCLC 25**
See also DLB 55, 144

Lewis, Alun 1915-1944 . . . . **TCLC 3**
See also CA 104; DLB 20, 162

Lewis, C. Day
See Day Lewis, C(ecil)

Lewis, C(live) S(taples)
1898-1963 . . . . . **CLC 1, 3, 6, 14, 27; DA;**
DAB; DAC; DAM MST, NOV, POP;
WLC
See also AAYA 3; CA 81-84; CANR 33;
CDBLB 1945-1960; CLR 3, 27; DLB 15,
100, 160; JRDA; MAICYA; MTCW;
SATA 13

Lewis, Janet 1899- . . . . **CLC 41**
See also Winters, Janet Lewis
See also CA 9-12R; CANR 29; CAP 1;
DLBY 87

Lewis, Matthew Gregory
1775-1818 . . . . **NCLC 11**
See also DLB 39, 158

Lewis, (Harry) Sinclair
1885-1951 . . . . . **TCLC 4, 13, 23, 39; DA;**
DAB; DAC; DAM MST, NOV; WLC
See also CA 104; 133; CDALB 1917-1929;
DLB 9, 102; DLBD 1; MTCW

Lewis, (Percy) Wyndham
1884(?)-1957 . . . . **TCLC 2, 9**
See also CA 104; DLB 15

Lewisohn, Ludwig 1883-1955 . . . . . . **TCLC 19**
See also CA 107; DLB 4, 9, 28, 102

Leyner, Mark 1956- . . . . **CLC 92**
See also CA 110; CANR 28, 53

Lezama Lima, Jose
1910-1976 . . . . **CLC 4, 10; DAM MULT**
See also CA 77-80; DLB 113; HW

L'Heureux, John (Clarke) 1934- . . . . **CLC 52**
See also CA 13-16R; CANR 23, 45

Liddell, C. H.
See Kuttner, Henry

Lie, Jonas (Lauritz Idemil)
1833-1908(?) . . . . **TCLC 5**
See also CA 115

Lieber, Joel 1937-1971 . . . . **CLC 6**
See also CA 73-76; 29-32R

Lieber, Stanley Martin
See Lee, Stan

Lieberman, Laurence (James)
1935- . . . . **CLC 4, 36**
See also CA 17-20R; CANR 8, 36

Lieksman, Anders
See Haavikko, Paavo Juhani

Li Fei-kan 1904-
See Pa Chin
See also CA 105

Lifton, Robert Jay 1926- . . . . **CLC 67**
See also CA 17-20R; CANR 27;
INT CANR-27; SATA 66

Lightfoot, Gordon 1938- . . . . **CLC 26**
See also CA 109

Lightman, Alan P. 1948- . . . . **CLC 81**
See also CA 141

Ligotti, Thomas (Robert)
1953- . . . . **CLC 44; SSC 16**
See also CA 123; CANR 49

Li Ho 791-817 . . . . **PC 13**

Liliencron, (Friedrich Adolf Axel) Detlev von
1844-1909 . . . . **TCLC 18**
See also CA 117

Lilly, William 1602-1681 . . . . **LC 27**

Lima, Jose Lezama
See Lezama Lima, Jose

Lima Barreto, Afonso Henrique de
1881-1922 . . . . **TCLC 23**
See also CA 117

Limonov, Edward 1944- . . . . **CLC 67**
See also CA 137

Lin, Frank
See Atherton, Gertrude (Franklin Horn)

Lincoln, Abraham 1809-1865 . . . . . **NCLC 18**

Lind, Jakov . . . . **CLC 1, 2, 4, 27, 82**
See also Landwirth, Heinz
See also CAAS 4

Lindbergh, Anne (Spencer) Morrow
1906- . . . . **CLC 82; DAM NOV**
See also CA 17-20R; CANR 16; MTCW;
SATA 33

Lindsay, David 1878-1945 . . . . **TCLC 15**
See also CA 113

Lindsay, (Nicholas) Vachel
1879-1931 . . . . **TCLC 17; DA; DAC;**
DAM MST, POET; WLC
See also CA 114; 135; CDALB 1865-1917;
DLB 54; SATA 40

Linke-Poot
See Doeblin, Alfred

Linney, Romulus 1930- . . . . **CLC 51**
See also CA 1-4R; CANR 40, 44

Linton, Eliza Lynn 1822-1898 . . . . **NCLC 41**
See also DLB 18

Li Po 701-763 . . . . **CMLC 2**

Lipsius, Justus 1547-1606 . . . . **LC 16**

Lipsyte, Robert (Michael)
1938- . . . . **CLC 21; DA; DAC;**
DAM MST, NOV
See also AAYA 7; CA 17-20R; CANR 8;
CLR 23; JRDA; MAICYA; SATA 5, 68

Lish, Gordon (Jay) 1934- . . **CLC 45; SSC 18**
See also CA 113; 117; DLB 130; INT 117

Lispector, Clarice 1925-1977 . . . . **CLC 43**
See also CA 139; 116; DLB 113

Littell, Robert 1935(?)- . . . . **CLC 42**
See also CA 109; 112

Little, Malcolm 1925-1965
See Malcolm X
See also BW 1; CA 125; 111; DA; DAB;
DAC; DAM MST, MULT; MTCW

Littlewit, Humphrey Gent.
See Lovecraft, H(oward) P(hillips)

Litwos
See Sienkiewicz, Henryk (Adam Alexander
Pius)

Liu E 1857-1909 . . . . **TCLC 15**
See also CA 115

Lively, Penelope (Margaret)
1933- . . . . **CLC 32, 50; DAM NOV**
See also CA 41-44R; CANR 29; CLR 7;
DLB 14, 161; JRDA; MAICYA; MTCW;
SATA 7, 60

Livesay, Dorothy (Kathleen)
1909- . . . . **CLC 4, 15, 79; DAC;**
DAM MST, POET
See also AITN 2; CA 25-28R; CAAS 8;
CANR 36; DLB 68; MTCW

Livy c. 59B.C.-c. 17 . . . . **CMLC 11**

Lizardi, Jose Joaquin Fernandez de
1776-1827 . . . . **NCLC 30**

Llewellyn, Richard
See Llewellyn Lloyd, Richard Dafydd
Vivian
See also DLB 15

Llewellyn Lloyd, Richard Dafydd Vivian
1906-1983 . . . . **CLC 7, 80**
See also Llewellyn, Richard
See also CA 53-56; 111; CANR 7;
SATA 11; SATA-Obit 37

Llosa, (Jorge) Mario (Pedro) Vargas
See Vargas Llosa, (Jorge) Mario (Pedro)

Lloyd Webber, Andrew 1948-
See Webber, Andrew Lloyd
See also AAYA 1; CA 116; 149;
DAM DRAM; SATA 56

Llull, Ramon c. 1235-c. 1316 . . . . . **CMLC 12**

Locke, Alain (Le Roy)
1886-1954 . . . . **TCLC 43**
See also BW 1; CA 106; 124; DLB 51

Locke, John 1632-1704 . . . . **LC 7, 35**
See also DLB 101

Locke-Elliott, Sumner
See Elliott, Sumner Locke

Lockhart, John Gibson
1794-1854 . . . . **NCLC 6**
See also DLB 110, 116, 144

Lodge, David (John)
1935- . . . . **CLC 36; DAM POP**
See also BEST 90:1; CA 17-20R; CANR 19,
53; DLB 14; INT CANR-19; MTCW

Loennbohm, Armas Eino Leopold 1878-1926
See Leino, Eino
See also CA 123

Loewinsohn, Ron(ald William)
1937- . . . . **CLC 52**
See also CA 25-28R

Logan, Jake
See Smith, Martin Cruz

Logan, John (Burton) 1923-1987..... **CLC 5**
See also CA 77-80; 124; CANR 45; DLB 5

Lo Kuan-chung 1330(?)-1400(?)...... **LC 12**

Lombard, Nap
See Johnson, Pamela Hansford

London, Jack.. **TCLC 9, 15, 39; SSC 4; WLC**
See also London, John Griffith
See also AAYA 13; AITN 2;
CDALB 1865-1917; DLB 8, 12, 78;
SATA 18

London, John Griffith 1876-1916
See London, Jack
See also CA 110; 119; DA; DAB; DAC;
DAM MST, NOV; JRDA; MAICYA;
MTCW

Long, Emmett
See Leonard, Elmore (John, Jr.)

Longbaugh, Harry
See Goldman, William (W.)

Longfellow, Henry Wadsworth
1807-1882..... **NCLC 2, 45; DA; DAB;**
DAC; DAM MST, POET
See also CDALB 1640-1865; DLB 1, 59;
SATA 19

Longley, Michael 1939-........... **CLC 29**
See also CA 102; DLB 40

Longus fl. c. 2nd cent. -.......... **CMLC 7**

Longway, A. Hugh
See Lang, Andrew

Lonnrot, Elias 1802-1884....... **NCLC 53**

Lopate, Phillip 1943-............. **CLC 29**
See also CA 97-100; DLBY 80; INT 97-100

Lopez Portillo (y Pacheco), Jose
1920-....................... **CLC 46**
See also CA 129; HW

Lopez y Fuentes, Gregorio
1897(?)-1966................. **CLC 32**
See also CA 131; HW

Lorca, Federico Garcia
See Garcia Lorca, Federico

Lord, Bette Bao 1938-........... **CLC 23**
See also BEST 90:3; CA 107; CANR 41;
INT 107; SATA 58

Lord Auch
See Bataille, Georges

Lord Byron
See Byron, George Gordon (Noel)

Lorde, Audre (Geraldine)
1934-1992......... **CLC 18, 71; BLC;**
DAM MULT, POET; PC 12
See also BW 1; CA 25-28R; 142; CANR 16,
26, 46; DLB 41; MTCW

Lord Jeffrey
See Jeffrey, Francis

Lorenzini, Carlo 1826-1890
See Collodi, Carlo
See also MAICYA; SATA 29

Lorenzo, Heberto Padilla
See Padilla (Lorenzo), Heberto

Loris
See Hofmannsthal, Hugo von

Loti, Pierre .... **TCLC 11**
See also Viaud, (Louis Marie) Julien
See also DLB 123

Louie, David Wong 1954-......... **CLC 70**
See also CA 139

Louis, Father M.
See Merton, Thomas

Lovecraft, H(oward) P(hillips)
1890-1937.... **TCLC 4, 22; DAM POP;**
SSC 3
See also AAYA 14; CA 104; 133; MTCW

Lovelace, Earl 1935-............ **CLC 51**
See also BW 2; CA 77-80; CANR 41;
DLB 125; MTCW

Lovelace, Richard 1618-1657....... **LC 24**
See also DLB 131

Lowell, Amy
1874-1925.... **TCLC 1, 8; DAM POET;**
PC 13
See also CA 104; 151; DLB 54, 140

Lowell, James Russell 1819-1891.. **NCLC 2**
See also CDALB 1640-1865; DLB 1, 11, 64,
79

Lowell, Robert (Traill Spence, Jr.)
1917-1977... **CLC 1, 2, 3, 4, 5, 8, 9, 11,**
15, 37; DA; DAB; DAC; DAM MST,
NOV; PC 3; WLC
See also CA 9-12R; 73-76; CABS 2;
CANR 26; DLB 5, 169; MTCW

Lowndes, Marie Adelaide (Belloc)
1868-1947 .... **TCLC 12**
See also CA 107; DLB 70

Lowry, (Clarence) Malcolm
1909-1957 ....**TCLC 6, 40**
See also CA 105; 131; CDBLB 1945-1960;
DLB 15; MTCW

Lowry, Mina Gertrude 1882-1966
See Loy, Mina
See also CA 113

Loxsmith, John
See Brunner, John (Kilian Houston)

Loy, Mina .... **CLC 28; DAM POET; PC 16**
See also Lowry, Mina Gertrude
See also DLB 4, 54

Loyson-Bridet
See Schwob, (Mayer Andre) Marcel

Lucas, Craig 1951-............. **CLC 64**
See also CA 137

Lucas, George 1944-............. **CLC 16**
See also AAYA 1; CA 77-80; CANR 30;
SATA 56

Lucas, Hans
See Godard, Jean-Luc

Lucas, Victoria
See Plath, Sylvia

Ludlam, Charles 1943-1987..... **CLC 46, 50**
See also CA 85-88; 122

Ludlum, Robert
1927-... **CLC 22, 43; DAM NOV, POP**
See also AAYA 10; BEST 89:1, 90:3;
CA 33-36R; CANR 25, 41; DLBY 82;
MTCW

Ludwig, Ken.................... **CLC 60**

Ludwig, Otto 1813-1865.......... **NCLC 4**
See also DLB 129

Lugones, Leopoldo 1874-1938..... **TCLC 15**
See also CA 116; 131; HW

Lu Hsun 1881-1936 ...... **TCLC 3; SSC 20**
See also Shu-Jen, Chou

Lukacs, George .... **CLC 24**
See also Lukacs, Gyorgy (Szegeny von)

Lukacs, Gyorgy (Szegeny von) 1885-1971
See Lukacs, George
See also CA 101; 29-32R

Luke, Peter (Ambrose Cyprian)
1919-1995 .... **CLC 38**
See also CA 81-84; 147; DLB 13

Lunar, Dennis
See Mungo, Raymond

Lurie, Alison 1926-........ **CLC 4, 5, 18, 39**
See also CA 1-4R; CANR 2, 17, 50; DLB 2;
MTCW; SATA 46

Lustig, Arnost 1926-............. **CLC 56**
See also AAYA 3; CA 69-72; CANR 47;
SATA 56

Luther, Martin 1483-1546........... **LC 9**

Luxemburg, Rosa 1870(?)-1919.... **TCLC 63**
See also CA 118

Luzi, Mario 1914-................ **CLC 13**
See also CA 61-64; CANR 9; DLB 128

L'Ymagier
See Gourmont, Remy (-Marie-Charles) de

Lynch, B. Suarez
See Bioy Casares, Adolfo; Borges, Jorge
Luis

Lynch, David (K.) 1946-........... **CLC 66**
See also CA 124; 129

Lynch, James
See Andreyev, Leonid (Nikolaevich)

Lynch Davis, B.
See Bioy Casares, Adolfo; Borges, Jorge
Luis

Lyndsay, Sir David 1490-1555 ...... **LC 20**

Lynn, Kenneth S(chuyler) 1923-.... **CLC 50**
See also CA 1-4R; CANR 3, 27

Lynx
See West, Rebecca

Lyons, Marcus
See Blish, James (Benjamin)

Lyre, Pinchbeck
See Sassoon, Siegfried (Lorraine)

Lytle, Andrew (Nelson) 1902-1995.. **CLC 22**
See also CA 9-12R; 150; DLB 6; DLBY 95

Lyttelton, George 1709-1773........ **LC 10**

Maas, Peter 1929- .... **CLC 29**
See also CA 93-96; INT 93-96

Macaulay, Rose 1881-1958..... **TCLC 7, 44**
See also CA 104; DLB 36

Macaulay, Thomas Babington
1800-1859 .... **NCLC 42**
See also CDBLB 1832-1890; DLB 32, 55

MacBeth, George (Mann)
1932-1992..................... **CLC 2, 5, 9**
See also CA 25-28R; 136; DLB 40; MTCW;
SATA 4; SATA-Obit 70

MacCaig, Norman (Alexander)
1910- ..... **CLC 36; DAB; DAM POET**
See also CA 9-12R; CANR 3, 34; DLB 27

MacCarthy, (Sir Charles Otto) Desmond
1877-1952 .... TCLC 36

MacDiarmid, Hugh
.... CLC 2, 4, 11, 19, 63; PC 9
See also Grieve, C(hristopher) M(urray)
See also CDBLB 1945-1960; DLB 20

MacDonald, Anson
See Heinlein, Robert A(nson)

Macdonald, Cynthia 1928- ...... CLC 13, 19
See also CA 49-52; CANR 4, 44; DLB 105

MacDonald, George 1824-1905 ..... TCLC 9
See also CA 106; 137; DLB 18, 163;
MAICYA; SATA 33

Macdonald, John
See Millar, Kenneth

MacDonald, John D(ann)
1916-1986 .... CLC 3, 27, 44;
DAM NOV, POP
See also CA 1-4R; 121; CANR 1, 19;
DLB 8; DLBY 86; MTCW

Macdonald, John Ross
See Millar, Kenneth

Macdonald, Ross ..... CLC 1, 2, 3, 14, 34, 41
See also Millar, Kenneth
See also DLBD 6

MacDougal, John
See Blish, James (Benjamin)

MacEwen, Gwendolyn (Margaret)
1941-1987 .... CLC 13, 55
See also CA 9-12R; 124; CANR 7, 22;
DLB 53; SATA 50; SATA-Obit 55

Macha, Karel Hynek 1810-1846 .. NCLC 46

Machado (y Ruiz), Antonio
1875-1939 .... TCLC 3
See also CA 104; DLB 108

Machado de Assis, Joaquim Maria
1839-1908 ..... TCLC 10; BLC; SSC 24
See also CA 107; 153

Machen, Arthur .... TCLC 4; SSC 20
See also Jones, Arthur Llewellyn
See also DLB 36, 156

Machiavelli, Niccolo
1469-1527 .... LC 8, 36; DA; DAB;
DAC; DAM MST

MacInnes, Colin 1914-1976 ...... CLC 4, 23
See also CA 69-72; 65-68; CANR 21;
DLB 14; MTCW

MacInnes, Helen (Clark)
1907-1985 ..... CLC 27, 39; DAM POP
See also CA 1-4R; 117; CANR 1, 28;
DLB 87; MTCW; SATA 22;
SATA-Obit 44

Mackay, Mary 1855-1924
See Corelli, Marie
See also CA 118

Mackenzie, Compton (Edward Montague)
1883-1972 .... CLC 18
See also CA 21-22; 37-40R; CAP 2;
DLB 34, 100

Mackenzie, Henry 1745-1831 .... NCLC 41
See also DLB 39

Mackintosh, Elizabeth 1896(?)-1952
See Tey, Josephine
See also CA 110

MacLaren, James
See Grieve, C(hristopher) M(urray)

Mac Laverty, Bernard 1942- ...... CLC 31
See also CA 116; 118; CANR 43; INT 118

MacLean, Alistair (Stuart)
1922-1987 .... CLC 3, 13, 50, 63;
DAM POP
See also CA 57-60; 121; CANR 28; MTCW;
SATA 23; SATA-Obit 50

Maclean, Norman (Fitzroy)
1902-1990 .... CLC 78; DAM POP;
SSC 13
See also CA 102; 132; CANR 49

MacLeish, Archibald
1892-1982 .... CLC 3, 8, 14, 68;
DAM POET
See also CA 9-12R; 106; CANR 33; DLB 4,
7, 45; DLBY 82; MTCW

MacLennan, (John) Hugh
1907-1990 .... CLC 2, 14, 92; DAC;
DAM MST
See also CA 5-8R; 142; CANR 33; DLB 68;
MTCW

MacLeod, Alistair
1936- ...... CLC 56; DAC; DAM MST
See also CA 123; DLB 60

MacNeice, (Frederick) Louis
1907-1963 ...... CLC 1, 4, 10, 53; DAB;
DAM POET
See also CA 85-88; DLB 10, 20; MTCW

MacNeill, Dand
See Fraser, George MacDonald

Macpherson, James 1736-1796 ...... LC 29
See also DLB 109

Macpherson, (Jean) Jay 1931- ...... CLC 14
See also CA 5-8R; DLB 53

MacShane, Frank 1927- .... CLC 39
See also CA 9-12R; CANR 3, 33; DLB 111

Macumber, Mari
See Sandoz, Mari(e Susette)

Madach, Imre 1823-1864 .... NCLC 19

Madden, (Jerry) David 1933- .... CLC 5, 15
See also CA 1-4R; CAAS 3; CANR 4, 45;
DLB 6; MTCW

Maddern, Al(an)
See Ellison, Harlan (Jay)

Madhubuti, Haki R.
1942- .... CLC 6, 73; BLC;
DAM MULT, POET; PC 5
See also Lee, Don L.
See also BW 2; CA 73-76; CANR 24, 51;
DLB 5, 41; DLBD 8

Maepenn, Hugh
See Kuttner, Henry

Maepenn, K. H.
See Kuttner, Henry

Maeterlinck, Maurice
1862-1949 ...... TCLC 3; DAM DRAM
See also CA 104; 136; SATA 66

Maginn, William 1794-1842 .... NCLC 8
See also DLB 110, 159

Mahapatra, Jayanta
1928- .... CLC 33; DAM MULT
See also CA 73-76; CAAS 9; CANR 15, 33

Mahfouz, Naguib (Abdel Aziz Al-Sabilgi)
1911(?)-
See Mahfuz, Najib
See also BEST 89:2; CA 128; CANR 55;
DAM NOV; MTCW

Mahfuz, Najib .... CLC 52, 55
See also Mahfouz, Naguib (Abdel Aziz
Al-Sabilgi)
See also DLBY 88

Mahon, Derek 1941- .... CLC 27
See also CA 113; 128; DLB 40

Mailer, Norman
1923- ...... CLC 1, 2, 3, 4, 5, 8, 11, 14,
28, 39, 74; DA; DAB; DAC; DAM MST,
NOV, POP
See also AITN 2; CA 9-12R; CABS 1;
CANR 28; CDALB 1968-1988; DLB 2,
16, 28; DLBD 3; DLBY 80, 83; MTCW

Maillet, Antonine 1929- ...... CLC 54; DAC
See also CA 115; 120; CANR 46; DLB 60;
INT 120

Mais, Roger 1905-1955 .... TCLC 8
See also BW 1; CA 105; 124; DLB 125;
MTCW

Maistre, Joseph de 1753-1821 .... NCLC 37

Maitland, Frederic 1850-1906 ..... TCLC 65

Maitland, Sara (Louise) 1950- ...... CLC 49
See also CA 69-72; CANR 13

Major, Clarence
1936- .... CLC 3, 19, 48; BLC;
DAM MULT
See also BW 2; CA 21-24R; CAAS 6;
CANR 13, 25, 53; DLB 33

Major, Kevin (Gerald)
1949- .... CLC 26; DAC
See also AAYA 16; CA 97-100; CANR 21,
38; CLR 11; DLB 60; INT CANR-21;
JRDA; MAICYA; SATA 32, 82

Maki, James
See Ozu, Yasujiro

Malabaila, Damiano
See Levi, Primo

Malamud, Bernard
1914-1986 ...... CLC 1, 2, 3, 5, 8, 9, 11,
18, 27, 44, 78, 85; DA; DAB; DAC;
DAM MST, NOV, POP; SSC 15; WLC
See also AAYA 16; CA 5-8R; 118; CABS 1;
CANR 28; CDALB 1941-1968; DLB 2,
28, 152; DLBY 80, 86; MTCW

Malaparte, Curzio 1898-1957 ..... TCLC 52

Malcolm, Dan
See Silverberg, Robert

Malcolm X .... CLC 82; BLC
See also Little, Malcolm

Malherbe, Francois de 1555-1628 ..... LC 5

Mallarme, Stephane
1842-1898 .... NCLC 4, 41;
DAM POET; PC 4

Mallet-Joris, Francoise 1930- ...... CLC 11
See also CA 65-68; CANR 17; DLB 83

Malley, Ern
See McAuley, James Phillip

Mallowan, Agatha Christie
See Christie, Agatha (Mary Clarissa)

Martines, Julia
　　See O'Faolain, Julia

Martinez, Jacinto Benavente y
　　See Benavente (y Martinez), Jacinto

Martinez Ruiz, Jose 1873-1967
　　See Azorin; Ruiz, Jose Martinez
　　See also CA 93-96; HW

Martinez Sierra, Gregorio
　　1881-1947 .... TCLC 6
　　See also CA 115

Martinez Sierra, Maria (de la O'LeJarraga)
　　1874-1974 .... TCLC 6
　　See also CA 115

Martinsen, Martin
　　See Follett, Ken(neth Martin)

Martinson, Harry (Edmund)
　　1904-1978 .... CLC 14
　　See also CA 77-80; CANR 34

Marut, Ret
　　See Traven, B.

Marut, Robert
　　See Traven, B.

Marvell, Andrew
　　1621-1678 ...... LC 4; DA; DAB; DAC;
　　　　　　DAM MST, POET; PC 10; WLC
　　See also CDBLB 1660-1789; DLB 131

Marx, Karl (Heinrich)
　　1818-1883 .... NCLC 17
　　See also DLB 129

Masaoka Shiki.................. TCLC 18
　　See also Masaoka Tsunenori

Masaoka Tsunenori 1867-1902
　　See Masaoka Shiki
　　See also CA 117

Masefield, John (Edward)
　　1878-1967 .... CLC 11, 47; DAM POET
　　See also CA 19-20; 25-28R; CANR 33;
　　CAP 2; CDBLB 1890-1914; DLB 10, 19,
　　153, 160; MTCW; SATA 19

Maso, Carole 19(?)- .... CLC 44

Mason, Bobbie Ann
　　1940- .... CLC 28, 43, 82; SSC 4
　　See also AAYA 5; CA 53-56; CANR 11,
　　31; DLB 173; DLBY 87; INT CANR-31;
　　MTCW

Mason, Ernst
　　See Pohl, Frederik

Mason, Lee W.
　　See Malzberg, Barry N(athaniel)

Mason, Nick 1945- .... CLC 35

Mason, Tally
　　See Derleth, August (William)

Mass, William
　　See Gibson, William

Masters, Edgar Lee
　　1868-1950 ...... TCLC 2, 25; DA; DAC;
　　　　　　DAM MST, POET; PC 1
　　See also CA 104; 133; CDALB 1865-1917;
　　DLB 54; MTCW

Masters, Hilary 1928- .... CLC 48
　　See also CA 25-28R; CANR 13, 47

Mastrosimone, William 19(?)- ...... CLC 36

Mathe, Albert
　　See Camus, Albert

Matheson, Richard Burton 1926- ... CLC 37
　　See also CA 97-100; DLB 8, 44; INT 97-100

Mathews, Harry 1930- .... CLC 6, 52
　　See also CA 21-24R; CAAS 6; CANR 18,
　　40

Mathews, John Joseph
　　1894-1979 ...... CLC 84; DAM MULT
　　See also CA 19-20; 142; CANR 45; CAP 2;
　　NNAL

Mathias, Roland (Glyn) 1915- ...... CLC 45
　　See also CA 97-100; CANR 19, 41; DLB 27

Matsuo Basho 1644-1694 .... PC 3
　　See also DAM POET

Mattheson, Rodney
　　See Creasey, John

Matthews, Greg 1949- .... CLC 45
　　See also CA 135

Matthews, William 1942- .... CLC 40
　　See also CA 29-32R; CAAS 18; CANR 12;
　　DLB 5

Matthias, John (Edward) 1941- ...... CLC 9
　　See also CA 33-36R

Matthiessen, Peter
　　1927- .... CLC 5, 7, 11, 32, 64;
　　　　　　　　　　　　　DAM NOV
　　See also AAYA 6; BEST 90:4; CA 9-12R;
　　CANR 21, 50; DLB 6, 173; MTCW;
　　SATA 27

Maturin, Charles Robert
　　1780(?)-1824 .... NCLC 6

Matute (Ausejo), Ana Maria
　　1925- .... CLC 11
　　See also CA 89-92; MTCW

Maugham, W. S.
　　See Maugham, W(illiam) Somerset

Maugham, W(illiam) Somerset
　　1874-1965 .... CLC 1, 11, 15, 67, 93;
　　　　DA; DAB; DAC; DAM DRAM, MST,
　　　　　　　　　NOV; SSC 8; WLC
　　See also CA 5-8R; 25-28R; CANR 40;
　　CDBLB 1914-1945; DLB 10, 36, 77, 100,
　　162; MTCW; SATA 54

Maugham, William Somerset
　　See Maugham, W(illiam) Somerset

Maupassant, (Henri Rene Albert) Guy de
　　1850-1893 ..... NCLC 1, 42; DA; DAB;
　　　　　　DAC; DAM MST; SSC 1; WLC
　　See also DLB 123

Maupin, Armistead
　　1944- .... CLC 95; DAM POP
　　See also CA 125; 130; INT 130

Maurhut, Richard
　　See Traven, B.

Mauriac, Claude 1914-1996 .... CLC 9
　　See also CA 89-92; 152; DLB 83

Mauriac, Francois (Charles)
　　1885-1970 .... CLC 4, 9, 56; SSC 24
　　See also CA 25-28; CAP 2; DLB 65;
　　MTCW

Mavor, Osborne Henry 1888-1951
　　See Bridie, James
　　See also CA 104

Maxwell, William (Keepers, Jr.)
　　1908- .... CLC 19
　　See also CA 93-96; CANR 54; DLBY 80;
　　INT 93-96

May, Elaine 1932- .... CLC 16
　　See also CA 124; 142; DLB 44

Mayakovski, Vladimir (Vladimirovich)
　　1893-1930 .... TCLC 4, 18
　　See also CA 104

Mayhew, Henry 1812-1887 ...... NCLC 31
　　See also DLB 18, 55

Mayle, Peter 1939(?)- .... CLC 89
　　See also CA 139

Maynard, Joyce 1953- .... CLC 23
　　See also CA 111; 129

Mayne, William (James Carter)
　　1928- .... CLC 12
　　See also CA 9-12R; CANR 37; CLR 25;
　　JRDA; MAICYA; SAAS 11; SATA 6, 68

Mayo, Jim
　　See L'Amour, Louis (Dearborn)

Maysles, Albert 1926- .... CLC 16
　　See also CA 29-32R

Maysles, David 1932- .... CLC 16

Mazer, Norma Fox 1931- .... CLC 26
　　See also AAYA 5; CA 69-72; CANR 12,
　　32; CLR 23; JRDA; MAICYA; SAAS 1;
　　SATA 24, 67

Mazzini, Guiseppe 1805-1872 .... NCLC 34

McAuley, James Phillip
　　1917-1976 .... CLC 45
　　See also CA 97-100

McBain, Ed
　　See Hunter, Evan

McBrien, William Augustine
　　1930- .... CLC 44
　　See also CA 107

McCaffrey, Anne (Inez)
　　1926- ...... CLC 17; DAM NOV, POP
　　See also AAYA 6; AITN 2; BEST 89:2;
　　CA 25-28R; CANR 15, 35, 55; DLB 8;
　　JRDA; MAICYA; MTCW; SAAS 11;
　　SATA 8, 70

McCall, Nathan 1955(?)- .... CLC 86
　　See also CA 146

McCann, Arthur
　　See Campbell, John W(ood, Jr.)

McCann, Edson
　　See Pohl, Frederik

McCarthy, Charles, Jr. 1933-
　　See McCarthy, Cormac
　　See also CANR 42; DAM POP

McCarthy, Cormac 1933- ..... CLC 4, 57, 59
　　See also McCarthy, Charles, Jr.
　　See also DLB 6, 143

McCarthy, Mary (Therese)
　　1912-1989 ...... CLC 1, 3, 5, 14, 24, 39,
　　　　　　　　　　　　59; SSC 24
　　See also CA 5-8R; 129; CANR 16, 50;
　　DLB 2; DLBY 81; INT CANR-16;
　　MTCW

McCartney, (James) Paul
　　1942- .... CLC 12, 35
　　See also CA 146

Merezhkovsky, Dmitry Sergeyevich
1865-1941 .... TCLC 29

Merimee, Prosper
1803-1870 .... NCLC 6; SSC 7
See also DLB 119

Merkin, Daphne 1954-............ CLC 44
See also CA 123

Merlin, Arthur
See Blish, James (Benjamin)

Merrill, James (Ingram)
1926-1995 .... CLC 2, 3, 6, 8, 13, 18, 34,
91; DAM POET
See also CA 13-16R; 147; CANR 10, 49;
DLB 5, 165; DLBY 85; INT CANR-10;
MTCW

Merriman, Alex
See Silverberg, Robert

Merritt, E. B.
See Waddington, Miriam

Merton, Thomas
1915-1968 .. CLC 1, 3, 11, 34, 83; PC 10
See also CA 5-8R; 25-28R; CANR 22, 53;
DLB 48; DLBY 81; MTCW

Merwin, W(illiam) S(tanley)
1927-...... CLC 1, 2, 3, 5, 8, 13, 18, 45,
88; DAM POET
See also CA 13-16R; CANR 15, 51; DLB 5,
169; INT CANR-15; MTCW

Metcalf, John 1938-.............. CLC 37
See also CA 113; DLB 60

Metcalf, Suzanne
See Baum, L(yman) Frank

Mew, Charlotte (Mary)
1870-1928 .... TCLC 8
See also CA 105; DLB 19, 135

Mewshaw, Michael 1943-.......... CLC 9
See also CA 53-56; CANR 7, 47; DLBY 80

Meyer, June
See Jordan, June

Meyer, Lynn
See Slavitt, David R(ytman)

Meyer-Meyrink, Gustav 1868-1932
See Meyrink, Gustav
See also CA 117

Meyers, Jeffrey 1939- .... CLC 39
See also CA 73-76; CANR 54; DLB 111

Meynell, Alice (Christina Gertrude Thompson)
1847-1922 .... TCLC 6
See also CA 104; DLB 19, 98

Meyrink, Gustav .... TCLC 21
See also Meyer-Meyrink, Gustav
See also DLB 81

Michaels, Leonard
1933-............ CLC 6, 25; SSC 16
See also CA 61-64; CANR 21; DLB 130;
MTCW

Michaux, Henri 1899-1984 ..... CLC 8, 19
See also CA 85-88; 114

Michelangelo 1475-1564............ LC 12

Michelet, Jules 1798-1874...... NCLC 31

Michener, James A(lbert)
1907(?)-.......... CLC 1, 5, 11, 29, 60;
DAM NOV, POP
See also AITN 1; BEST 90:1; CA 5-8R;
CANR 21, 45; DLB 6; MTCW

Mickiewicz, Adam 1798-1855 ..... NCLC 3

Middleton, Christopher 1926-...... CLC 13
See also CA 13-16R; CANR 29, 54;
DLB 40

Middleton, Richard (Barham)
1882-1911 .... TCLC 56
See also DLB 156

Middleton, Stanley 1919-........ CLC 7, 38
See also CA 25-28R; CAAS 23; CANR 21,
46; DLB 14

Middleton, Thomas
1580-1627 .... LC 33; DAM DRAM,
MST; DC 5
See also DLB 58

Migueis, Jose Rodrigues 1901-..... CLC 10

Mikszath, Kalman 1847-1910 ..... TCLC 31

Miles, Josephine (Louise)
1911-1985 .... CLC 1, 2, 14, 34, 39;
DAM POET
See also CA 1-4R; 116; CANR 2, 55;
DLB 48

Militant
See Sandburg, Carl (August)

Mill, John Stuart 1806-1873 .. NCLC 11, 58
See also CDBLB 1832-1890; DLB 55

Millar, Kenneth
1915-1983 .... CLC 14; DAM POP
See also Macdonald, Ross
See also CA 9-12R; 110; CANR 16; DLB 2;
DLBD 6; DLBY 83; MTCW

Millay, E. Vincent
See Millay, Edna St. Vincent

Millay, Edna St. Vincent
1892-1950 ...... TCLC 4, 49; DA; DAB;
DAC; DAM MST, POET; PC 6
See also CA 104; 130; CDALB 1917-1929;
DLB 45; MTCW

Miller, Arthur
1915- .... CLC 1, 2, 6, 10, 15, 26, 47, 78;
DA; DAB; DAC; DAM DRAM, MST;
DC 1; WLC
See also AAYA 15; AITN 1; CA 1-4R;
CABS 3; CANR 2, 30, 54;
CDALB 1941-1968; DLB 7; MTCW

Miller, Henry (Valentine)
1891-1980 .... CLC 1, 2, 4, 9, 14, 43, 84;
DA; DAB; DAC; DAM MST, NOV;
WLC
See also CA 9-12R; 97-100; CANR 33;
CDALB 1929-1941; DLB 4, 9; DLBY 80;
MTCW

Miller, Jason 1939(?)- .... CLC 2
See also AITN 1; CA 73-76; DLB 7

Miller, Sue 1943-..... CLC 44; DAM POP
See also BEST 90:3; CA 139; DLB 143

Miller, Walter M(ichael, Jr.)
1923-..................... CLC 4, 30
See also CA 85-88; DLB 8

Millett, Kate 1934-................ CLC 67
See also AITN 1; CA 73-76; CANR 32, 53;
MTCW

Millhauser, Steven 1943-....... CLC 21, 54
See also CA 110; 111; DLB 2; INT 111

Millin, Sarah Gertrude 1889-1968 .. CLC 49
See also CA 102; 93-96

Milne, A(lan) A(lexander)
1882-1956 .... TCLC 6; DAB; DAC;
DAM MST
See also CA 104; 133; CLR 1, 26; DLB 10,
77, 100, 160; MAICYA; MTCW;
YABC 1

Milner, Ron(ald)
1938- ..... CLC 56; BLC; DAM MULT
See also AITN 1; BW 1; CA 73-76;
CANR 24; DLB 38; MTCW

Milosz, Czeslaw
1911- .... CLC 5, 11, 22, 31, 56, 82;
DAM MST, POET; PC 8
See also CA 81-84; CANR 23, 51; MTCW

Milton, John
1608-1674 ...... LC 9; DA; DAB; DAC;
DAM MST, POET; WLC
See also CDBLB 1660-1789; DLB 131, 151

Min, Anchee 1957-............... CLC 86
See also CA 146

Minehaha, Cornelius
See Wedekind, (Benjamin) Frank(lin)

Miner, Valerie 1947- .... CLC 40
See also CA 97-100

Minimo, Duca
See D'Annunzio, Gabriele

Minot, Susan 1956- .... CLC 44
See also CA 134

Minus, Ed 1938-................. CLC 39

Miranda, Javier
See Bioy Casares, Adolfo

Mirbeau, Octave 1848-1917....... TCLC 55
See also DLB 123

Miro (Ferrer), Gabriel (Francisco Victor)
1879-1930 .... TCLC 5
See also CA 104

Mishima, Yukio
.... CLC 2, 4, 6, 9, 27; DC 1; SSC 4
See also Hiraoka, Kimitake

Mistral, Frederic 1830-1914 ...... TCLC 51
See also CA 122

Mistral, Gabriela............ TCLC 2; HLC
See also Godoy Alcayaga, Lucila

Mistry, Rohinton 1952-...... CLC 71; DAC
See also CA 141

Mitchell, Clyde
See Ellison, Harlan (Jay); Silverberg, Robert

Mitchell, James Leslie 1901-1935
See Gibbon, Lewis Grassic
See also CA 104; DLB 15

Mitchell, Joni 1943-.............. CLC 12
See also CA 112

Mitchell, Joseph (Quincy)
1908-1996 .... CLC 98
See also CA 77-80; 152

Mitchell, Margaret (Munnerlyn)
1900-1949 ...... TCLC 11; DAM NOV,
POP
See also CA 109; 125; CANR 55; DLB 9;
MTCW

Mitchell, Peggy
See Mitchell, Margaret (Munnerlyn)

Mitchell, S(ilas) Weir 1829-1914 .. TCLC 36

Morris, William 1834-1896 . . . . **NCLC 4**
See also CDBLB 1832-1890; DLB 18, 35,
57, 156

Morris, Wright 1910-. . . **CLC 1, 3, 7, 18, 37**
See also CA 9-12R; CANR 21; DLB 2;
DLBY 81; MTCW

Morrison, Chloe Anthony Wofford
See Morrison, Toni

Morrison, James Douglas 1943-1971
See Morrison, Jim
See also CA 73-76; CANR 40

Morrison, Jim . . . . **CLC 17**
See also Morrison, James Douglas

Morrison, Toni
1931- . . . . **CLC 4, 10, 22, 55, 81, 87;**
BLC; DA; DAB; DAC; DAM MST,
MULT, NOV, POP
See also AAYA 1; BW 2; CA 29-32R;
CANR 27, 42; CDALB 1968-1988;
DLB 6, 33, 143; DLBY 81; MTCW;
SATA 57

Morrison, Van 1945- . . . . **CLC 21**
See also CA 116

Mortimer, John (Clifford)
1923- . . . . . . **CLC 28, 43; DAM DRAM,**
POP
See also CA 13-16R; CANR 21;
CDBLB 1960 to Present; DLB 13;
INT CANR-21; MTCW

Mortimer, Penelope (Ruth) 1918-. . . . **CLC 5**
See also CA 57-60; CANR 45

Morton, Anthony
See Creasey, John

Mosher, Howard Frank 1943-. . . . . . **CLC 62**
See also CA 139

Mosley, Nicholas 1923-. . . . . **CLC 43, 70**
See also CA 69-72; CANR 41; DLB 14

Mosley, Walter
1952- . . . . . **CLC 97; DAM MULT, POP**
See also AAYA 17; BW 2; CA 142

Moss, Howard
1922-1987 . . . . **CLC 7, 14, 45, 50;**
DAM POET
See also CA 1-4R; 123; CANR 1, 44;
DLB 5

Mossgiel, Rab
See Burns, Robert

Motion, Andrew (Peter) 1952-. . . . . . **CLC 47**
See also CA 146; DLB 40

Motley, Willard (Francis)
1909-1965 . . . . **CLC 18**
See also BW 1; CA 117; 106; DLB 76, 143

Motoori, Norinaga 1730-1801 . . . . **NCLC 45**

Mott, Michael (Charles Alston)
1930- . . . . **CLC 15, 34**
See also CA 5-8R; CAAS 7; CANR 7, 29

Mountain Wolf Woman
1884-1960 . . . . **CLC 92**
See also CA 144; NNAL

Moure, Erin 1955- . . . . **CLC 88**
See also CA 113; DLB 60

Mowat, Farley (McGill)
1921- . . . . . . **CLC 26; DAC; DAM MST**
See also AAYA 1; CA 1-4R; CANR 4, 24,
42; CLR 20; DLB 68; INT CANAR-24;
JRDA; MAICYA; MTCW; SATA 3, 55

Moyers, Bill 1934-. . . . . **CLC 74**
See also AITN 2; CA 61-64; CANR 31, 52

Mphahlele, Es'kia
See Mphahlele, Ezekiel
See also DLB 125

Mphahlele, Ezekiel
1919- . . . . . **CLC 25; BLC; DAM MULT**
See also Mphahlele, Es'kia
See also BW 2; CA 81-84; CANR 26

Mqhayi, S(amuel) E(dward) K(rune Loliwe)
1875-1945 . . . . **TCLC 25; BLC;**
DAM MULT
See also CA 153

Mrozek, Slawomir 1930-. . . . . **CLC 3, 13**
See also CA 13-16R; CAAS 10; CANR 29;
MTCW

Mrs. Belloc-Lowndes
See Lowndes, Marie Adelaide (Belloc)

Mtwa, Percy (?)-. . . . . **CLC 47**

Mueller, Lisel 1924-. . . . . **CLC 13, 51**
See also CA 93-96; DLB 105

Muir, Edwin 1887-1959 . . . . **TCLC 2**
See also CA 104; DLB 20, 100

Muir, John 1838-1914 . . . . **TCLC 28**

Mujica Lainez, Manuel
1910-1984 . . . . **CLC 31**
See also Lainez, Manuel Mujica
See also CA 81-84; 112; CANR 32; HW

Mukherjee, Bharati
1940- . . . . **CLC 53; DAM NOV**
See also BEST 89:2; CA 107; CANR 45;
DLB 60; MTCW

Muldoon, Paul
1951- . . . . **CLC 32, 72; DAM POET**
See also CA 113; 129; CANR 52; DLB 40;
INT 129

Mulisch, Harry 1927-. . . . . **CLC 42**
See also CA 9-12R; CANR 6, 26

Mull, Martin 1943-. . . . . **CLC 17**
See also CA 105

Mulock, Dinah Maria
See Craik, Dinah Maria (Mulock)

Munford, Robert 1737(?)-1783 . . . . **LC 5**
See also DLB 31

Mungo, Raymond 1946-. . . . . **CLC 72**
See also CA 49-52; CANR 2

Munro, Alice
1931- . . . . . . **CLC 6, 10, 19, 50, 95; DAC;**
DAM MST, NOV; SSC 3
See also AITN 2; CA 33-36R; CANR 33,
53; DLB 53; MTCW; SATA 29

Munro, H(ector) H(ugh) 1870-1916
See Saki
See also CA 104; 130; CDBLB 1890-1914;
DA; DAB; DAC; DAM MST, NOV;
DLB 34, 162; MTCW; WLC

Murasaki, Lady. . . . . **CMLC 1**

Murdoch, (Jean) Iris
1919- . . . . . . **CLC 1, 2, 3, 4, 6, 8, 11, 15,**
22, 31, 51; DAB; DAC; DAM MST,
NOV
See also CA 13-16R; CANR 8, 43;
CDBLB 1960 to Present; DLB 14;
INT CANR-8; MTCW

Murfree, Mary Noailles
1850-1922 . . . . **SSC 22**
See also CA 122; DLB 12, 74

Murnau, Friedrich Wilhelm
See Plumpe, Friedrich Wilhelm

Murphy, Richard 1927-. . . . . **CLC 41**
See also CA 29-32R; DLB 40

Murphy, Sylvia 1937-. . . . . **CLC 34**
See also CA 121

Murphy, Thomas (Bernard) 1935-. . . **CLC 51**
See also CA 101

Murray, Albert L. 1916- . . . . **CLC 73**
See also BW 2; CA 49-52; CANR 26, 52;
DLB 38

Murray, Les(lie) A(llan)
1938- . . . . **CLC 40; DAM POET**
See also CA 21-24R; CANR 11, 27

Murry, J. Middleton
See Murry, John Middleton

Murry, John Middleton
1889-1957 . . . . **TCLC 16**
See also CA 118; DLB 149

Musgrave, Susan 1951- . . . . **CLC 13, 54**
See also CA 69-72; CANR 45

Musil, Robert (Edler von)
1880-1942 . . . . **TCLC 12; SSC 18**
See also CA 109; CANR 55; DLB 81, 124

Muske, Carol 1945- . . . . **CLC 90**
See also Muske-Dukes, Carol (Anne)

Muske-Dukes, Carol (Anne) 1945-
See Muske, Carol
See also CA 65-68; CANR 32

Musset, (Louis Charles) Alfred de
1810-1857 . . . . **NCLC 7**

My Brother's Brother
See Chekhov, Anton (Pavlovich)

Myers, L. H. 1881-1944. . . . . **TCLC 59**
See also DLB 15

Myers, Walter Dean
1937- . . . . . **CLC 35; BLC; DAM MULT,**
NOV
See also AAYA 4; BW 2; CA 33-36R;
CANR 20, 42; CLR 4, 16, 35; DLB 33;
INT CANR-20; JRDA; MAICYA;
SAAS 2; SATA 41, 71; SATA-Brief 27

Myers, Walter M.
See Myers, Walter Dean

Myles, Symon
See Follett, Ken(neth Martin)

Nabokov, Vladimir (Vladimirovich)
1899-1977 . . . . . **CLC 1, 2, 3, 6, 8, 11, 15,**
23, 44, 46, 64; DA; DAB; DAC;
DAM MST, NOV; SSC 11; WLC
See also CA 5-8R; 69-72; CANR 20;
CDALB 1941-1968; DLB 2; DLBD 3;
DLBY 80, 91; MTCW

Nagai Kafu. **TCLC 51**
See also Nagai Sokichi

Nagai Sokichi 1879-1959
See Nagai Kafu
See also CA 117

Nagy, Laszlo 1925-1978............ **CLC 7**
See also CA 129; 112

Naipaul, Shiva(dhar Srinivasa)
1945-1985 ..... **CLC 32, 39; DAM NOV**
See also CA 110; 112; 116; CANR 33;
DLB 157; DLBY 85; MTCW

Naipaul, V(idiadhar) S(urajprasad)
1932- .... **CLC 4, 7, 9, 13, 18, 37; DAB;**
DAC; DAM MST, NOV
See also CA 1-4R; CANR 1, 33, 51;
CDBLB 1960 to Present; DLB 125;
DLBY 85; MTCW

Nakos, Lilika 1899(?)-............ **CLC 29**

Narayan, R(asipuram) K(rishnaswami)
1906- .... **CLC 7, 28, 47; DAM NOV**
See also CA 81-84; CANR 33; MTCW;
SATA 62

Nash, (Frediric) Ogden
1902-1971 .... **CLC 23; DAM POET**
See also CA 13-14; 29-32R; CANR 34;
CAP 1; DLB 11; MAICYA; MTCW;
SATA 2, 46

Nathan, Daniel
See Dannay, Frederic

Nathan, George Jean 1882-1958 ... **TCLC 18**
See also Hatteras, Owen
See also CA 114; DLB 137

Natsume, Kinnosuke 1867-1916
See Natsume, Soseki
See also CA 104

Natsume, Soseki .... **TCLC 2, 10**
See also Natsume, Kinnosuke

Natti, (Mary) Lee 1919-
See Kingman, Lee
See also CA 5-8R; CANR 2

Naylor, Gloria
1950- ..... **CLC 28, 52; BLC; DA; DAC;**
DAM MST, MULT, NOV, POP
See also AAYA 6; BW 2; CA 107;
CANR 27, 51; DLB 173; MTCW

Neihardt, John Gneisenau
1881-1973 .... **CLC 32**
See also CA 13-14; CAP 1; DLB 9, 54

Nekrasov, Nikolai Alekseevich
1821-1878 .... **NCLC 11**

Nelligan, Emile 1879-1941....... **TCLC 14**
See also CA 114; DLB 92

Nelson, Willie 1933-.............. **CLC 17**
See also CA 107

Nemerov, Howard (Stanley)
1920-1991 .... **CLC 2, 6, 9, 36;**
DAM POET
See also CA 1-4R; 134; CABS 2; CANR 1,
27, 53; DLB 5, 6; DLBY 83;
INT CANR-27; MTCW

Neruda, Pablo
1904-1973 ..... **CLC 1, 2, 5, 7, 9, 28, 62;**
DA; DAB; DAC; DAM MST, MULT,
POET; HLC; PC 4; WLC
See also CA 19-20; 45-48; CAP 2; HW;
MTCW

Nerval, Gerard de
1808-1855 ..... **NCLC 1; PC 13; SSC 18**

Nervo, (Jose) Amado (Ruiz de)
1870-1919 .... **TCLC 11**
See also CA 109; 131; HW

Nessi, Pio Baroja y
See Baroja (y Nessi), Pio

Nestroy, Johann 1801-1862...... **NCLC 42**
See also DLB 133

Neufeld, John (Arthur) 1938- ...... **CLC 17**
See also AAYA 11; CA 25-28R; CANR 11,
37; MAICYA; SAAS 3; SATA 6, 81

Neville, Emily Cheney 1919-....... **CLC 12**
See also CA 5-8R; CANR 3, 37; JRDA;
MAICYA; SAAS 2; SATA 1

Newbound, Bernard Slade 1930-
See Slade, Bernard
See also CA 81-84; CANR 49;
DAM DRAM

Newby, P(ercy) H(oward)
1918- .... **CLC 2, 13; DAM NOV**
See also CA 5-8R; CANR 32; DLB 15;
MTCW

Newlove, Donald 1928- .... **CLC 6**
See also CA 29-32R; CANR 25

Newlove, John (Herbert) 1938-..... **CLC 14**
See also CA 21-24R; CANR 9, 25

Newman, Charles 1938-.......... **CLC 2, 8**
See also CA 21-24R

Newman, Edwin (Harold) 1919- .... **CLC 14**
See also AITN 1; CA 69-72; CANR 5

Newman, John Henry
1801-1890 .... **NCLC 38**
See also DLB 18, 32, 55

Newton, Suzanne 1936- .... **CLC 35**
See also CA 41-44R; CANR 14; JRDA;
SATA 5, 77

Nexo, Martin Andersen
1869-1954 .... **TCLC 43**

Nezval, Vitezslav 1900-1958 ...... **TCLC 44**
See also CA 123

Ng, Fae Myenne 1957(?)-.......... **CLC 81**
See also CA 146

Ngema, Mbongeni 1955- .... **CLC 57**
See also BW 2; CA 143

Ngugi, James T(hiong'o)........ **CLC 3, 7, 13**
See also Ngugi wa Thiong'o

Ngugi wa Thiong'o
1938- ..... **CLC 36; BLC; DAM MULT,**
NOV
See also Ngugi, James T(hiong'o)
See also BW 2; CA 81-84; CANR 27;
DLB 125; MTCW

Nichol, B(arrie) P(hillip)
1944-1988 .... **CLC 18**
See also CA 53-56; DLB 53; SATA 66

Nichols, John (Treadwell) 1940-.... **CLC 38**
See also CA 9-12R; CAAS 2; CANR 6;
DLBY 82

Nichols, Leigh
See Koontz, Dean R(ay)

Nichols, Peter (Richard)
1927- .... **CLC 5, 36, 65**
See also CA 104; CANR 33; DLB 13;
MTCW

Nicolas, F. R. E.
See Freeling, Nicolas

Niedecker, Lorine
1903-1970 .... **CLC 10, 42; DAM POET**
See also CA 25-28; CAP 2; DLB 48

Nietzsche, Friedrich (Wilhelm)
1844-1900 .... **TCLC 10, 18, 55**
See also CA 107; 121; DLB 129

Nievo, Ippolito 1831-1861 .... **NCLC 22**

Nightingale, Anne Redmon 1943-
See Redmon, Anne
See also CA 103

Nik. T. O.
See Annensky, Innokenty Fyodorovich

Nin, Anais
1903-1977 ...... **CLC 1, 4, 8, 11, 14, 60;**
DAM NOV, POP; SSC 10
See also AITN 2; CA 13-16R; 69-72;
CANR 22, 53; DLB 2, 4, 152; MTCW

Nishiwaki, Junzaburo 1894-1982 .... **PC 15**
See also CA 107

Nissenson, Hugh 1933-........... **CLC 4, 9**
See also CA 17-20R; CANR 27; DLB 28

Niven, Larry .... **CLC 8**
See also Niven, Laurence Van Cott
See also DLB 8

Niven, Laurence Van Cott 1938-
See Niven, Larry
See also CA 21-24R; CAAS 12; CANR 14,
44; DAM POP; MTCW

Nixon, Agnes Eckhardt 1927-...... **CLC 21**
See also CA 110

Nizan, Paul 1905-1940.......... **TCLC 40**
See also DLB 72

Nkosi, Lewis
1936- ..... **CLC 45; BLC; DAM MULT**
See also BW 1; CA 65-68; CANR 27;
DLB 157

Nodier, (Jean) Charles (Emmanuel)
1780-1844 .... **NCLC 19**
See also DLB 119

Nolan, Christopher 1965-.......... **CLC 58**
See also CA 111

Noon, Jeff 1957-................. **CLC 91**
See also CA 148

Norden, Charles
See Durrell, Lawrence (George)

Nordhoff, Charles (Bernard)
1887-1947 .... **TCLC 23**
See also CA 108; DLB 9; SATA 23

Norfolk, Lawrence 1963-.......... **CLC 76**
See also CA 144

Norman, Marsha
1947- .... **CLC 28; DAM DRAM**
See also CA 105; CABS 3; CANR 41;
DLBY 84

Norris, Benjamin Franklin, Jr.
1870-1902 .... **TCLC 24**
See also Norris, Frank
See also CA 110

Norris, Frank
See Norris, Benjamin Franklin, Jr.
See also CDALB 1865-1917; DLB 12, 71

Norris, Leslie 1921-.............. **CLC 14**
See also CA 11-12; CANR 14; CAP 1;
DLB 27

North, Andrew
See Norton, Andre

North, Anthony
See Koontz, Dean R(ay)

North, Captain George
See Stevenson, Robert Louis (Balfour)

North, Milou
See Erdrich, Louise

Northrup, B. A.
See Hubbard, L(afayette) Ron(ald)

North Staffs
See Hulme, T(homas) E(rnest)

Norton, Alice Mary
See Norton, Andre
See also MAICYA; SATA 1, 43

Norton, Andre 1912- .... **CLC 12**
See also Norton, Alice Mary
See also AAYA 14; CA 1-4R; CANR 2, 31;
DLB 8, 52; JRDA; MTCW; SATA 91

Norton, Caroline 1808-1877...... **NCLC 47**
See also DLB 21, 159

Norway, Nevil Shute 1899-1960
See Shute, Nevil
See also CA 102; 93-96

Norwid, Cyprian Kamil
1821-1883 .... **NCLC 17**

Nosille, Nabrah
See Ellison, Harlan (Jay)

Nossack, Hans Erich 1901-1978 ..... **CLC 6**
See also CA 93-96; 85-88; DLB 69

Nostradamus 1503-1566............ **LC 27**

Nosu, Chuji
See Ozu, Yasujiro

Notenburg, Eleanora (Genrikhovna) von
See Guro, Elena

Nova, Craig 1945-.............. **CLC 7, 31**
See also CA 45-48; CANR 2, 53

Novak, Joseph
See Kosinski, Jerzy (Nikodem)

Novalis 1772-1801 .... **NCLC 13**
See also DLB 90

Nowlan, Alden (Albert)
1933-1983 .. **CLC 15; DAC; DAM MST**
See also CA 9-12R; CANR 5; DLB 53

Noyes, Alfred 1880-1958 .... **TCLC 7**
See also CA 104; DLB 20

Nunn, Kem 19(?)-................ **CLC 34**

Nye, Robert
1939- .... **CLC 13, 42; DAM NOV**
See also CA 33-36R; CANR 29; DLB 14;
MTCW; SATA 6

Nyro, Laura 1947- .... **CLC 17**

Oates, Joyce Carol
1938- ...... **CLC 1, 2, 3, 6, 9, 11, 15, 19,
33, 52; DA; DAB; DAC; DAM MST,
NOV, POP; SSC 6; WLC**
See also AAYA 15; AITN 1; BEST 89:2;
CA 5-8R; CANR 25, 45;
CDALB 1968-1988; DLB 2, 5, 130;
DLBY 81; INT CANR-25; MTCW

O'Brien, Darcy 1939-............. **CLC 11**
See also CA 21-24R; CANR 8

O'Brien, E. G.
See Clarke, Arthur C(harles)

O'Brien, Edna
1936- .... **CLC 3, 5, 8, 13, 36, 65;
DAM NOV; SSC 10**
See also CA 1-4R; CANR 6, 41;
CDBLB 1960 to Present; DLB 14;
MTCW

O'Brien, Fitz-James 1828-1862... **NCLC 21**
See also DLB 74

O'Brien, Flann....... CLC 1, 4, 5, 7, 10, 47
See also O Nuallain, Brian

O'Brien, Richard 1942-.......... **CLC 17**
See also CA 124

O'Brien, Tim
1946- .... **CLC 7, 19, 40; DAM POP**
See also AAYA 16; CA 85-88; CANR 40;
DLB 152; DLBD 9; DLBY 80

Obstfelder, Sigbjoern 1866-1900... **TCLC 23**
See also CA 123

O'Casey, Sean
1880-1964 ...... **CLC 1, 5, 9, 11, 15, 88;
DAB; DAC; DAM DRAM, MST**
See also CA 89-92; CDBLB 1914-1945;
DLB 10; MTCW

O'Cathasaigh, Sean
See O'Casey, Sean

Ochs, Phil 1940-1976............. **CLC 17**
See also CA 65-68

O'Connor, Edwin (Greene)
1918-1968 .... **CLC 14**
See also CA 93-96; 25-28R

O'Connor, (Mary) Flannery
1925-1964 .... **CLC 1, 2, 3, 6, 10, 13, 15,
21, 66; DA; DAB; DAC; DAM MST,
NOV; SSC 1, 23; WLC**
See also AAYA 7; CA 1-4R; CANR 3, 41;
CDALB 1941-1968; DLB 2, 152;
DLBD 12; DLBY 80; MTCW

O'Connor, Frank........... CLC 23; SSC 5
See also O'Donovan, Michael John
See also DLB 162

O'Dell, Scott 1898-1989........... **CLC 30**
See also AAYA 3; CA 61-64; 129;
CANR 12, 30; CLR 1, 16; DLB 52;
JRDA; MAICYA; SATA 12, 60

Odets, Clifford
1906-1963 .... **CLC 2, 28, 98;
DAM DRAM; DC 6**
See also CA 85-88; DLB 7, 26; MTCW

O'Doherty, Brian 1934-........... **CLC 76**
See also CA 105

O'Donnell, K. M.
See Malzberg, Barry N(athaniel)

O'Donnell, Lawrence
See Kuttner, Henry

O'Donovan, Michael John
1903-1966 .... **CLC 14**
See also O'Connor, Frank
See also CA 93-96

Oe, Kenzaburo
1935- ..... **CLC 10, 36, 86; DAM NOV;
SSC 20**
See also CA 97-100; CANR 36, 50;
DLBY 94; MTCW

O'Faolain, Julia 1932-....... **CLC 6, 19, 47**
See also CA 81-84; CAAS 2; CANR 12;
DLB 14; MTCW

O'Faolain, Sean
1900-1991 .... **CLC 1, 7, 14, 32, 70;
SSC 13**
See also CA 61-64; 134; CANR 12;
DLB 15, 162; MTCW

O'Flaherty, Liam
1896-1984 .... **CLC 5, 34; SSC 6**
See also CA 101; 113; CANR 35; DLB 36,
162; DLBY 84; MTCW

Ogilvy, Gavin
See Barrie, J(ames) M(atthew)

O'Grady, Standish James
1846-1928 .... **TCLC 5**
See also CA 104

O'Grady, Timothy 1951- .... **CLC 59**
See also CA 138

O'Hara, Frank
1926-1966 .... **CLC 2, 5, 13, 78;
DAM POET**
See also CA 9-12R; 25-28R; CANR 33;
DLB 5, 16; MTCW

O'Hara, John (Henry)
1905-1970 .... **CLC 1, 2, 3, 6, 11, 42;
DAM NOV; SSC 15**
See also CA 5-8R; 25-28R; CANR 31;
CDALB 1929-1941; DLB 9, 86; DLBD 2;
MTCW

O Hehir, Diana 1922- .... **CLC 41**
See also CA 93-96

Okigbo, Christopher (Ifenayichukwu)
1932-1967 .... **CLC 25, 84; BLC;
DAM MULT, POET; PC 7**
See also BW 1; CA 77-80; DLB 125;
MTCW

Okri, Ben 1959- .... **CLC 87**
See also BW 2; CA 130; 138; DLB 157;
INT 138

Olds, Sharon
1942- ..... **CLC 32, 39, 85; DAM POET**
See also CA 101; CANR 18, 41; DLB 120

Oldstyle, Jonathan
See Irving, Washington

Olesha, Yuri (Karlovich)
1899-1960 .... **CLC 8**
See also CA 85-88

Oliphant, Laurence
1829(?)-1888 .... **NCLC 47**
See also DLB 18, 166

Oliphant, Margaret (Oliphant Wilson)
1828-1897 .... **NCLC 11**
See also DLB 18, 159

Oliver, Mary 1935-........ **CLC 19, 34, 98**
See also CA 21-24R; CANR 9, 43; DLB 5

Olivier, Laurence (Kerr)
1907-1989 .... **CLC 20**
See also CA 111; 150; 129

Olsen, Tillie
1913- ..... **CLC 4, 13; DA; DAB; DAC;
DAM MST; SSC 11**
See also CA 1-4R; CANR 1, 43; DLB 28;
DLBY 80; MTCW

Olson, Charles (John)
1910-1970 ..... **CLC 1, 2, 5, 6, 9, 11, 29;
DAM POET**
See also CA 13-16; 25-28R; CABS 2;
CANR 35; CAP 1; DLB 5, 16; MTCW

Olson, Toby 1937- . . . . **CLC 28**
See also CA 65-68; CANR 9, 31

Olyesha, Yuri
See Olesha, Yuri (Karlovich)

Ondaatje, (Philip) Michael
1943- . . . . **CLC 14, 29, 51, 76; DAB;**
DAC; DAM MST
See also CA 77-80; CANR 42; DLB 60

Oneal, Elizabeth 1934-
See Oneal, Zibby
See also CA 106; CANR 28; MAICYA;
SATA 30, 82

Oneal, Zibby . . . . **CLC 30**
See also Oneal, Elizabeth
See also AAYA 5; CLR 13; JRDA

O'Neill, Eugene (Gladstone)
1888-1953 . . . . . . **TCLC 1, 6, 27, 49; DA;**
DAB; DAC; DAM DRAM, MST; WLC
See also AITN 1; CA 110; 132;
CDALB 1929-1941; DLB 7; MTCW

Onetti, Juan Carlos
1909-1994 . . . . **CLC 7, 10; DAM MULT,**
NOV; SSC 23
See also CA 85-88; 145; CANR 32;
DLB 113; HW; MTCW

O Nuallain, Brian 1911-1966
See O'Brien, Flann
See also CA 21-22; 25-28R; CAP 2

Oppen, George 1908-1984 . . . . **CLC 7, 13, 34**
See also CA 13-16R; 113; CANR 8; DLB 5,
165

Oppenheim, E(dward) Phillips
1866-1946 . . . . **TCLC 45**
See also CA 111; DLB 70

Origen c. 185-c. 254 . . . . **CMLC 19**

Orlovitz, Gil 1918-1973 . . . . **CLC 22**
See also CA 77-80; 45-48; DLB 2, 5

Orris
See Ingelow, Jean

Ortega y Gasset, Jose
1883-1955 . . . . . **TCLC 9; DAM MULT;**
HLC
See also CA 106; 130; HW; MTCW

Ortese, Anna Maria 1914- . . . . **CLC 89**

Ortiz, Simon J(oseph)
1941- . . . . **CLC 45; DAM MULT, POET**
See also CA 134; DLB 120; NNAL

Orton, Joe . . . . **CLC 4, 13, 43; DC 3**
See also Orton, John Kingsley
See also CDBLB 1960 to Present; DLB 13

Orton, John Kingsley 1933-1967
See Orton, Joe
See also CA 85-88; CANR 35;
DAM DRAM; MTCW

Orwell, George
. . . . . **TCLC 2, 6, 15, 31, 51; DAB; WLC**
See also Blair, Eric (Arthur)
See also CDBLB 1945-1960; DLB 15, 98

Osborne, David
See Silverberg, Robert

Osborne, George
See Silverberg, Robert

Osborne, John (James)
1929-1994 . . . . . **CLC 1, 2, 5, 11, 45; DA;**
DAB; DAC; DAM DRAM, MST; WLC
See also CA 13-16R; 147; CANR 21;
CDBLB 1945-1960; DLB 13; MTCW

Osborne, Lawrence 1958- . . . . **CLC 50**

Oshima, Nagisa 1932- . . . . **CLC 20**
See also CA 116; 121

Oskison, John Milton
1874-1947 . . . . . **TCLC 35; DAM MULT**
See also CA 144; NNAL

Ossoli, Sarah Margaret (Fuller marchesa d')
1810-1850
See Fuller, Margaret
See also SATA 25

Ostrovsky, Alexander
1823-1886 . . . . **NCLC 30, 57**

Otero, Blas de 1916-1979 . . . . **CLC 11**
See also CA 89-92; DLB 134

Otto, Whitney 1955- . . . . **CLC 70**
See also CA 140

Ouida . . . . **TCLC 43**
See also De La Ramee, (Marie) Louise
See also DLB 18, 156

Ousmane, Sembene 1923- . . . . **CLC 66; BLC**
See also BW 1; CA 117; 125; MTCW

Ovid
43B.C.-18(?) . . . **CMLC 7; DAM POET;**
PC 2

Owen, Hugh
See Faust, Frederick (Schiller)

Owen, Wilfred (Edward Salter)
1893-1918 . . . . . . **TCLC 5, 27; DA; DAB;**
DAC; DAM MST, POET; WLC
See also CA 104; 141; CDBLB 1914-1945;
DLB 20

Owens, Rochelle 1936- . . . . **CLC 8**
See also CA 17-20R; CAAS 2; CANR 39

Oz, Amos
1939- . . . . **CLC 5, 8, 11, 27, 33, 54;**
DAM NOV
See also CA 53-56; CANR 27, 47; MTCW

Ozick, Cynthia
1928- . . . . **CLC 3, 7, 28, 62; DAM NOV,**
POP; SSC 15
See also BEST 90:1; CA 17-20R; CANR 23;
DLB 28, 152; DLBY 82; INT CANR-23;
MTCW

Ozu, Yasujiro 1903-1963 . . . . **CLC 16**
See also CA 112

Pacheco, C.
See Pessoa, Fernando (Antonio Nogueira)

Pa Chin . . . . **CLC 18**
See also Li Fei-kan

Pack, Robert 1929- . . . . **CLC 13**
See also CA 1-4R; CANR 3, 44; DLB 5

Padgett, Lewis
See Kuttner, Henry

Padilla (Lorenzo), Heberto 1932- . . . **CLC 38**
See also AITN 1; CA 123; 131; HW

Page, Jimmy 1944- . . . . **CLC 12**

Page, Louise 1955- . . . . **CLC 40**
See also CA 140

Page, P(atricia) K(athleen)
1916- . . . . **CLC 7, 18; DAC; DAM MST;**
PC 12
See also CA 53-56; CANR 4, 22; DLB 68;
MTCW

Page, Thomas Nelson 1853-1922 . . . . **SSC 23**
See also CA 118; DLB 12, 78; DLBD 13

Paget, Violet 1856-1935
See Lee, Vernon
See also CA 104

Paget-Lowe, Henry
See Lovecraft, H(oward) P(hillips)

Paglia, Camille (Anna) 1947- . . . . **CLC 68**
See also CA 140

Paige, Richard
See Koontz, Dean R(ay)

Pakenham, Antonia
See Fraser, (Lady) Antonia (Pakenham)

Palamas, Kostes 1859-1943 . . . . **TCLC 5**
See also CA 105

Palazzeschi, Aldo 1885-1974 . . . . **CLC 11**
See also CA 89-92; 53-56; DLB 114

Paley, Grace
1922- . . . . **CLC 4, 6, 37; DAM POP;**
SSC 8
See also CA 25-28R; CANR 13, 46;
DLB 28; INT CANR-13; MTCW

Palin, Michael (Edward) 1943- . . . . . **CLC 21**
See also Monty Python
See also CA 107; CANR 35; SATA 67

Palliser, Charles 1947- . . . . **CLC 65**
See also CA 136

Palma, Ricardo 1833-1919 . . . . **TCLC 29**

Pancake, Breece Dexter 1952-1979
See Pancake, Breece D'J
See also CA 123; 109

Pancake, Breece D'J . . . . **CLC 29**
See also Pancake, Breece Dexter
See also DLB 130

Panko, Rudy
See Gogol, Nikolai (Vasilyevich)

Papadiamantis, Alexandros
1851-1911 . . . . **TCLC 29**

Papadiamantopoulos, Johannes 1856-1910
See Moreas, Jean
See also CA 117

Papini, Giovanni 1881-1956 . . . . **TCLC 22**
See also CA 121

Paracelsus 1493-1541 . . . . **LC 14**

Parasol, Peter
See Stevens, Wallace

Parfenie, Maria
See Codrescu, Andrei

Parini, Jay (Lee) 1948- . . . . **CLC 54**
See also CA 97-100; CAAS 16; CANR 32

Park, Jordan
See Kornbluth, C(yril) M.; Pohl, Frederik

Parker, Bert
See Ellison, Harlan (Jay)

Parker, Dorothy (Rothschild)
1893-1967 . . . . **CLC 15, 68;**
DAM POET; SSC 2
See also CA 19-20; 25-28R; CAP 2;
DLB 11, 45, 86; MTCW

Parker, Robert B(rown)
1932- ...... CLC 27; DAM NOV, POP
See also BEST 89:4; CA 49-52; CANR 1, 26, 52; INT CANR-26; MTCW

Parkin, Frank 1940-............. CLC 43
See also CA 147

Parkman, Francis, Jr.
1823-1893 .... NCLC 12
See also DLB 1, 30

Parks, Gordon (Alexander Buchanan)
1912- ... CLC 1, 16; BLC; DAM MULT
See also AITN 2; BW 2; CA 41-44R;
CANR 26; DLB 33; SATA 8

Parnell, Thomas 1679-1718 .... LC 3
See also DLB 94

Parra, Nicanor
1914- ...... CLC 2; DAM MULT; HLC
See also CA 85-88; CANR 32; HW; MTCW

Parrish, Mary Frances
See Fisher, M(ary) F(rances) K(ennedy)

Parson
See Coleridge, Samuel Taylor

Parson Lot
See Kingsley, Charles

Partridge, Anthony
See Oppenheim, E(dward) Phillips

Pascal, Blaise 1623-1662 .... LC 35

Pascoli, Giovanni 1855-1912 ...... TCLC 45

Pasolini, Pier Paolo
1922-1975 .... CLC 20, 37
See also CA 93-96; 61-64; DLB 128;
MTCW

Pasquini
See Silone, Ignazio

Pastan, Linda (Olenik)
1932- .... CLC 27; DAM POET
See also CA 61-64; CANR 18, 40; DLB 5

Pasternak, Boris (Leonidovich)
1890-1960 ...... CLC 7, 10, 18, 63; DA;
DAB; DAC; DAM MST, NOV, POET;
PC 6; WLC
See also CA 127; 116; MTCW

Patchen, Kenneth
1911-1972 ... CLC 1, 2, 18; DAM POET
See also CA 1-4R; 33-36R; CANR 3, 35;
DLB 16, 48; MTCW

Pater, Walter (Horatio)
1839-1894 .... NCLC 7
See also CDBLB 1832-1890; DLB 57, 156

Paterson, A(ndrew) B(arton)
1864-1941 .... TCLC 32

Paterson, Katherine (Womeldorf)
1932- .... CLC 12, 30
See also AAYA 1; CA 21-24R; CANR 28;
CLR 7; DLB 52; JRDA; MAICYA;
MTCW; SATA 13, 53

Patmore, Coventry Kersey Dighton
1823-1896 .... NCLC 9
See also DLB 35, 98

Paton, Alan (Stewart)
1903-1988 ...... CLC 4, 10, 25, 55; DA;
DAB; DAC; DAM MST, NOV; WLC
See also CA 13-16; 125; CANR 22; CAP 1;
MTCW; SATA 11; SATA-Obit 56

Paton Walsh, Gillian 1937-
See Walsh, Jill Paton
See also CANR 38; JRDA; MAICYA;
SAAS 3; SATA 4, 72

Paulding, James Kirke 1778-1860.. NCLC 2
See also DLB 3, 59, 74

Paulin, Thomas Neilson 1949-
See Paulin, Tom
See also CA 123; 128

Paulin, Tom .... CLC 37
See also Paulin, Thomas Neilson
See also DLB 40

Paustovsky, Konstantin (Georgievich)
1892-1968 .... CLC 40
See also CA 93-96; 25-28R

Pavese, Cesare
1908-1950 ..... TCLC 3; PC 13; SSC 19
See also CA 104; DLB 128

Pavic, Milorad 1929-............. CLC 60
See also CA 136

Payne, Alan
See Jakes, John (William)

Paz, Gil
See Lugones, Leopoldo

Paz, Octavio
1914- .... CLC 3, 4, 6, 10, 19, 51, 65;
DA; DAB; DAC; DAM MST, MULT,
POET; HLC; PC 1; WLC
See also CA 73-76; CANR 32; DLBY 90;
HW; MTCW

p'Bitek, Okot
1931-1982 .... CLC 96; BLC;
DAM MULT
See also BW 2; CA 124; 107; DLB 125;
MTCW

Peacock, Molly 1947-............. CLC 60
See also CA 103; CAAS 21; CANR 52;
DLB 120

Peacock, Thomas Love
1785-1866 .... NCLC 22
See also DLB 96, 116

Peake, Mervyn 1911-1968 ...... CLC 7, 54
See also CA 5-8R; 25-28R; CANR 3;
DLB 15, 160; MTCW; SATA 23

Pearce, Philippa .... CLC 21
See also Christie, (Ann) Philippa
See also CLR 9; DLB 161; MAICYA;
SATA 1, 67

Pearl, Eric
See Elman, Richard

Pearson, T(homas) R(eid) 1956- .... CLC 39
See also CA 120; 130; INT 130

Peck, Dale 1967-................. CLC 81
See also CA 146

Peck, John 1941-................. CLC 3
See also CA 49-52; CANR 3

Peck, Richard (Wayne) 1934-...... CLC 21
See also AAYA 1; CA 85-88; CANR 19,
38; CLR 15; INT CANR-19; JRDA;
MAICYA; SAAS 2; SATA 18, 55

Peck, Robert Newton
1928- .. CLC 17; DA; DAC; DAM MST
See also AAYA 3; CA 81-84; CANR 31;
JRDA; MAICYA; SAAS 1; SATA 21, 62

Peckinpah, (David) Sam(uel)
1925-1984 .... CLC 20
See also CA 109; 114

Pedersen, Knut 1859-1952
See Hamsun, Knut
See also CA 104; 119; MTCW

Peeslake, Gaffer
See Durrell, Lawrence (George)

Peguy, Charles Pierre
1873-1914 .... TCLC 10
See also CA 107

Pena, Ramon del Valle y
See Valle-Inclan, Ramon (Maria) del

Pendennis, Arthur Esquir
See Thackeray, William Makepeace

Penn, William 1644-1718.......... LC 25
See also DLB 24

Pepys, Samuel
1633-1703 ..... LC 11; DA; DAB; DAC;
DAM MST; WLC
See also CDBLB 1660-1789; DLB 101

Percy, Walker
1916-1990 .... CLC 2, 3, 6, 8, 14, 18, 47,
65; DAM NOV, POP
See also CA 1-4R; 131; CANR 1, 23;
DLB 2; DLBY 80, 90; MTCW

Perec, Georges 1936-1982 .... CLC 56
See also CA 141; DLB 83

Pereda (y Sanchez de Porrua), Jose Maria de
1833-1906 .... TCLC 16
See also CA 117

Pereda y Porrua, Jose Maria de
See Pereda (y Sanchez de Porrua), Jose
Maria de

Peregoy, George Weems
See Mencken, H(enry) L(ouis)

Perelman, S(idney) J(oseph)
1904-1979 ...... CLC 3, 5, 9, 15, 23, 44,
49; DAM DRAM
See also AITN 1, 2; CA 73-76; 89-92;
CANR 18; DLB 11, 44; MTCW

Peret, Benjamin 1899-1959 .... TCLC 20
See also CA 117

Peretz, Isaac Loeb 1851(?)-1915... TCLC 16
See also CA 109

Peretz, Yitzhok Leibush
See Peretz, Isaac Loeb

Perez Galdos, Benito 1843-1920... TCLC 27
See also CA 125; 153; HW

Perrault, Charles 1628-1703 .... LC 2
See also MAICYA; SATA 25

Perry, Brighton
See Sherwood, Robert E(mmet)

Perse, St.-John .... CLC 4, 11, 46
See also Leger, (Marie-Rene Auguste) Alexis
Saint-Leger

Perutz, Leo 1882-1957.......... TCLC 60
See also DLB 81

Peseenz, Tulio F.
See Lopez y Fuentes, Gregorio

Pesetsky, Bette 1932-............. CLC 28
See also CA 133; DLB 130

Police, The
See Copeland, Stewart (Armstrong);
Summers, Andrew James; Sumner,
Gordon Matthew

Polidori, John William
1795-1821 . . . . NCLC 51
See also DLB 116

Pollitt, Katha 1949- . . . . CLC 28
See also CA 120; 122; MTCW

Pollock, (Mary) Sharon
1936- . . . . CLC 50; DAC; DAM DRAM,
MST
See also CA 141; DLB 60

Polo, Marco 1254-1324 . . . . CMLC 15

Polonsky, Abraham (Lincoln)
1910- . . . . CLC 92
See also CA 104; DLB 26; INT 104

Polybius c. 200B.C.-c. 118B.C. . . . . CMLC 17

Pomerance, Bernard
1940- . . . . CLC 13; DAM DRAM
See also CA 101; CANR 49

Ponge, Francis (Jean Gaston Alfred)
1899-1988 . . . . . CLC 6, 18; DAM POET
See also CA 85-88; 126; CANR 40

Pontoppidan, Henrik 1857-1943 . . . TCLC 29

Poole, Josephine . . . . CLC 17
See also Helyar, Jane Penelope Josephine
See also SAAS 2; SATA 5

Popa, Vasko 1922-1991 . . . . CLC 19
See also CA 112; 148

Pope, Alexander
1688-1744 . . . . . . LC 3; DA; DAB; DAC;
DAM MST, POET; WLC
See also CDBLB 1660-1789; DLB 95, 101

Porter, Connie (Rose) 1959(?)- . . . . . CLC 70
See also BW 2; CA 142; SATA 81

Porter, Gene(va Grace) Stratton
1863(?)-1924 . . . . TCLC 21
See also CA 112

Porter, Katherine Anne
1890-1980 . . . . . . CLC 1, 3, 7, 10, 13, 15,
27; DA; DAB; DAC; DAM MST, NOV;
SSC 4
See also AITN 2; CA 1-4R; 101; CANR 1;
DLB 4, 9, 102; DLBD 12; DLBY 80;
MTCW; SATA 39; SATA-Obit 23

Porter, Peter (Neville Frederick)
1929- . . . . CLC 5, 13, 33
See also CA 85-88; DLB 40

Porter, William Sydney 1862-1910
See Henry, O.
See also CA 104; 131; CDALB 1865-1917;
DA; DAB; DAC; DAM MST; DLB 12,
78, 79; MTCW; YABC 2

Portillo (y Pacheco), Jose Lopez
See Lopez Portillo (y Pacheco), Jose

Post, Melville Davisson
1869-1930 . . . . TCLC 39
See also CA 110

Potok, Chaim
1929- . . . . CLC 2, 7, 14, 26; DAM NOV
See also AAYA 15; AITN 1, 2; CA 17-20R;
CANR 19, 35; DLB 28, 152;
INT CANR-19; MTCW; SATA 33

Potter, Beatrice
See Webb, (Martha) Beatrice (Potter)
See also MAICYA

Potter, Dennis (Christopher George)
1935-1994 . . . . CLC 58, 86
See also CA 107; 145; CANR 33; MTCW

Pound, Ezra (Weston Loomis)
1885-1972 . . . . . . CLC 1, 2, 3, 4, 5, 7, 10,
13, 18, 34, 48, 50; DA; DAB; DAC;
DAM MST, POET; PC 4; WLC
See also CA 5-8R; 37-40R; CANR 40;
CDALB 1917-1929; DLB 4, 45, 63;
MTCW

Povod, Reinaldo 1959-1994 . . . . CLC 44
See also CA 136; 146

Powell, Adam Clayton, Jr.
1908-1972 . . . . CLC 89; BLC;
DAM MULT
See also BW 1; CA 102; 33-36R

Powell, Anthony (Dymoke)
1905- . . . . CLC 1, 3, 7, 9, 10, 31
See also CA 1-4R; CANR 1, 32;
CDBLB 1945-1960; DLB 15; MTCW

Powell, Dawn 1897-1965 . . . . CLC 66
See also CA 5-8R

Powell, Padgett 1952- . . . . CLC 34
See also CA 126

Power, Susan . . . . CLC 91

Powers, J(ames) F(arl)
1917- . . . . CLC 1, 4, 8, 57; SSC 4
See also CA 1-4R; CANR 2; DLB 130;
MTCW

Powers, John J(ames) 1945-
See Powers, John R.
See also CA 69-72

Powers, John R. . . . . CLC 66
See also Powers, John J(ames)

Powers, Richard (S.) 1957- . . . . CLC 93
See also CA 148

Pownall, David 1938- . . . . CLC 10
See also CA 89-92; CAAS 18; CANR 49;
DLB 14

Powys, John Cowper
1872-1963 . . . . CLC 7, 9, 15, 46
See also CA 85-88; DLB 15; MTCW

Powys, T(heodore) F(rancis)
1875-1953 . . . . TCLC 9
See also CA 106; DLB 36, 162

Prager, Emily 1952- . . . . CLC 56

Pratt, E(dwin) J(ohn)
1883(?)-1964 . . . . CLC 19; DAC;
DAM POET
See also CA 141; 93-96; DLB 92

Premchand . . . . TCLC 21
See also Srivastava, Dhanpat Rai

Preussler, Otfried 1923- . . . . CLC 17
See also CA 77-80; SATA 24

Prevert, Jacques (Henri Marie)
1900-1977 . . . . CLC 15
See also CA 77-80; 69-72; CANR 29;
MTCW; SATA-Obit 30

Prevost, Abbe (Antoine Francois)
1697-1763 . . . . LC 1

Price, (Edward) Reynolds
1933- . . . . CLC 3, 6, 13, 43, 50, 63;
DAM NOV; SSC 22
See also CA 1-4R; CANR 1, 37; DLB 2;
INT CANR-37

Price, Richard 1949- . . . . CLC 6, 12
See also CA 49-52; CANR 3; DLBY 81

Prichard, Katharine Susannah
1883-1969 . . . . CLC 46
See also CA 11-12; CANR 33; CAP 1;
MTCW; SATA 66

Priestley, J(ohn) B(oynton)
1894-1984 . . . . CLC 2, 5, 9, 34;
DAM DRAM, NOV
See also CA 9-12R; 113; CANR 33;
CDBLB 1914-1945; DLB 10, 34, 77, 100,
139; DLBY 84; MTCW

Prince 1958(?)- . . . . CLC 35

Prince, F(rank) T(empleton) 1912- . . CLC 22
See also CA 101; CANR 43; DLB 20

Prince Kropotkin
See Kropotkin, Peter (Aleksieevich)

Prior, Matthew 1664-1721 . . . . LC 4
See also DLB 95

Pritchard, William H(arrison)
1932- . . . . CLC 34
See also CA 65-68; CANR 23; DLB 111

Pritchett, V(ictor) S(awdon)
1900- . . . . CLC 5, 13, 15, 41;
DAM NOV; SSC 14
See also CA 61-64; CANR 31; DLB 15,
139; MTCW

Private 19022
See Manning, Frederic

Probst, Mark 1925- . . . . CLC 59
See also CA 130

Prokosch, Frederic 1908-1989 . . . . CLC 4, 48
See also CA 73-76; 128; DLB 48

Prophet, The
See Dreiser, Theodore (Herman Albert)

Prose, Francine 1947- . . . . CLC 45
See also CA 109; 112; CANR 46

Proudhon
See Cunha, Euclides (Rodrigues Pimenta) da

Proulx, E. Annie 1935- . . . . CLC 81

Proust, (Valentin-Louis-George-Eugene-)
Marcel
1871-1922 . . . . TCLC 7, 13, 33; DA;
DAB; DAC; DAM MST, NOV; WLC
See also CA 104; 120; DLB 65; MTCW

Prowler, Harley
See Masters, Edgar Lee

Prus, Boleslaw 1845-1912 . . . . TCLC 48

Pryor, Richard (Franklin Lenox Thomas)
1940- . . . . CLC 26
See also CA 122

Przybyszewski, Stanislaw
1868-1927 . . . . TCLC 36
See also DLB 66

Pteleon
See Grieve, C(hristopher) M(urray)
See also DAM POET

Puckett, Lute
See Masters, Edgar Lee

Puig, Manuel
1932-1990 . . . . **CLC 3, 5, 10, 28, 65;**
DAM MULT; HLC
See also CA 45-48; CANR 2, 32; DLB 113;
HW; MTCW

Purdy, Al(fred Wellington)
1918- . . . . **CLC 3, 6, 14, 50; DAC;**
DAM MST, POET
See also CA 81-84; CAAS 17; CANR 42;
DLB 88

Purdy, James (Amos)
1923- . . . . **CLC 2, 4, 10, 28, 52**
See also CA 33-36R; CAAS 1; CANR 19,
51; DLB 2; INT CANR-19; MTCW

Pure, Simon
See Swinnerton, Frank Arthur

Pushkin, Alexander (Sergeyevich)
1799-1837 . . . . . **NCLC 3, 27; DA; DAB;**
DAC; DAM DRAM, MST, POET;
PC 10; WLC
See also SATA 61

P'u Sung-ling 1640-1715 . . . . **LC 3**

Putnam, Arthur Lee
See Alger, Horatio, Jr.

Puzo, Mario
1920- . . . . . **CLC 1, 2, 6, 36; DAM NOV,**
POP
See also CA 65-68; CANR 4, 42; DLB 6;
MTCW

Pygge, Edward
See Barnes, Julian (Patrick)

Pym, Barbara (Mary Crampton)
1913-1980 . . . . **CLC 13, 19, 37**
See also CA 13-14; 97-100; CANR 13, 34;
CAP 1; DLB 14; DLBY 87; MTCW

Pynchon, Thomas (Ruggles, Jr.)
1937- . . . . . **CLC 2, 3, 6, 9, 11, 18, 33, 62,**
72; DA; DAB; DAC; DAM MST, NOV,
POP; SSC 14; WLC
See also BEST 90:2; CA 17-20R; CANR 22,
46; DLB 2, 173; MTCW

Qian Zhongshu
See Ch'ien Chung-shu

Qroll
See Dagerman, Stig (Halvard)

Quarrington, Paul (Lewis) 1953- . . . . **CLC 65**
See also CA 129

Quasimodo, Salvatore 1901-1968 . . . **CLC 10**
See also CA 13-16; 25-28R; CAP 1;
DLB 114; MTCW

Quay, Stephen 1947- . . . . **CLC 95**

Quay, The Brothers
See Quay, Stephen; Quay, Timothy

Quay, Timothy 1947- . . . . **CLC 95**

Queen, Ellery . . . . **CLC 3, 11**
See also Dannay, Frederic; Davidson,
Avram; Lee, Manfred B(ennington);
Marlowe, Stephen; Sturgeon, Theodore
(Hamilton); Vance, John Holbrook

Queen, Ellery, Jr.
See Dannay, Frederic; Lee, Manfred
B(ennington)

Queneau, Raymond
1903-1976 . . . . **CLC 2, 5, 10, 42**
See also CA 77-80; 69-72; CANR 32;
DLB 72; MTCW

Quevedo, Francisco de 1580-1645 . . . . **LC 23**

Quiller-Couch, Arthur Thomas
1863-1944 . . . . **TCLC 53**
See also CA 118; DLB 135, 153

Quin, Ann (Marie) 1936-1973 . . . . **CLC 6**
See also CA 9-12R; 45-48; DLB 14

Quinn, Martin
See Smith, Martin Cruz

Quinn, Peter 1947- . . . . **CLC 91**

Quinn, Simon
See Smith, Martin Cruz

Quiroga, Horacio (Sylvestre)
1878-1937 . . . . . **TCLC 20; DAM MULT;**
HLC
See also CA 117; 131; HW; MTCW

Quoirez, Francoise 1935- . . . . **CLC 9**
See also Sagan, Francoise
See also CA 49-52; CANR 6, 39; MTCW

Raabe, Wilhelm 1831-1910 . . . . **TCLC 45**
See also DLB 129

Rabe, David (William)
1940- . . . . . . **CLC 4, 8, 33; DAM DRAM**
See also CA 85-88; CABS 3; DLB 7

Rabelais, Francois
1483-1553 . . . . . . **LC 5; DA; DAB; DAC;**
DAM MST; WLC

Rabinovitch, Sholem 1859-1916
See Aleichem, Sholom
See also CA 104

Rachilde 1860-1953 . . . . **TCLC 67**
See also DLB 123

Racine, Jean
1639-1699 . . . . **LC 28; DAB; DAM MST**

Radcliffe, Ann (Ward)
1764-1823 . . . . **NCLC 6, 55**
See also DLB 39

Radiguet, Raymond 1903-1923 . . . . **TCLC 29**
See also DLB 65

Radnoti, Miklos 1909-1944 . . . . **TCLC 16**
See also CA 118

Rado, James 1939- . . . . **CLC 17**
See also CA 105

Radvanyi, Netty 1900-1983
See Seghers, Anna
See also CA 85-88; 110

Rae, Ben
See Griffiths, Trevor

Raeburn, John (Hay) 1941- . . . . **CLC 34**
See also CA 57-60

Ragni, Gerome 1942-1991 . . . . **CLC 17**
See also CA 105; 134

Rahv, Philip 1908-1973 . . . . **CLC 24**
See also Greenberg, Ivan
See also DLB 137

Raine, Craig 1944- . . . . **CLC 32**
See also CA 108; CANR 29, 51; DLB 40

Raine, Kathleen (Jessie) 1908- . . . **CLC 7, 45**
See also CA 85-88; CANR 46; DLB 20;
MTCW

Rainis, Janis 1865-1929 . . . . **TCLC 29**

Rakosi, Carl . . . . **CLC 47**
See also Rawley, Callman
See also CAAS 5

Raleigh, Richard
See Lovecraft, H(oward) P(hillips)

Raleigh, Sir Walter 1554(?)-1618 . . . . **LC 31**
See also CDBLB Before 1660; DLB 172

Rallentando, H. P.
See Sayers, Dorothy L(eigh)

Ramal, Walter
See de la Mare, Walter (John)

Ramon, Juan
See Jimenez (Mantecon), Juan Ramon

Ramos, Graciliano 1892-1953 . . . . . **TCLC 32**

Rampersad, Arnold 1941- . . . . **CLC 44**
See also BW 2; CA 127; 133; DLB 111;
INT 133

Rampling, Anne
See Rice, Anne

Ramsay, Allan 1684(?)-1758 . . . . **LC 29**
See also DLB 95

Ramuz, Charles-Ferdinand
1878-1947 . . . . **TCLC 33**

Rand, Ayn
1905-1982 . . . . . . **CLC 3, 30, 44, 79; DA;**
DAC; DAM MST, NOV, POP; WLC
See also AAYA 10; CA 13-16R; 105;
CANR 27; MTCW

Randall, Dudley (Felker)
1914- . . . . . . **CLC 1; BLC; DAM MULT**
See also BW 1; CA 25-28R; CANR 23;
DLB 41

Randall, Robert
See Silverberg, Robert

Ranger, Ken
See Creasey, John

Ransom, John Crowe
1888-1974 . . . . **CLC 2, 4, 5, 11, 24;**
DAM POET
See also CA 5-8R; 49-52; CANR 6, 34;
DLB 45, 63; MTCW

Rao, Raja 1909- . . . **CLC 25, 56; DAM NOV**
See also CA 73-76; CANR 51; MTCW

Raphael, Frederic (Michael)
1931- . . . . **CLC 2, 14**
See also CA 1-4R; CANR 1; DLB 14

Ratcliffe, James P.
See Mencken, H(enry) L(ouis)

Rathbone, Julian 1935- . . . . **CLC 41**
See also CA 101; CANR 34

Rattigan, Terence (Mervyn)
1911-1977 . . . . **CLC 7; DAM DRAM**
See also CA 85-88; 73-76;
CDBLB 1945-1960; DLB 13; MTCW

Ratushinskaya, Irina 1954- . . . . **CLC 54**
See also CA 129

Raven, Simon (Arthur Noel)
1927- . . . . **CLC 14**
See also CA 81-84

Rawley, Callman 1903-
See Rakosi, Carl
See also CA 21-24R; CANR 12, 32

Rawlings, Marjorie Kinnan
1896-1953 . . . . **TCLC 4**
See also CA 104; 137; DLB 9, 22, 102;
JRDA; MAICYA; YABC 1

Rosa, Joao Guimaraes 1908-1967 . . . **CLC 23**
See also CA 89-92; DLB 113

Rose, Wendy
1948- . . . . **CLC 85; DAM MULT; PC 13**
See also CA 53-56; CANR 5, 51; NNAL;
SATA 12

Rosen, Richard (Dean) 1949- . . . . **CLC 39**
See also CA 77-80; INT CANR-30

Rosenberg, Isaac 1890-1918 . . . . . . **TCLC 12**
See also CA 107; DLB 20

Rosenblatt, Joe . . . . **CLC 15**
See also Rosenblatt, Joseph

Rosenblatt, Joseph 1933-
See Rosenblatt, Joe
See also CA 89-92; INT 89-92

Rosenfeld, Samuel 1896-1963
See Tzara, Tristan
See also CA 89-92

Rosenstock, Sami
See Tzara, Tristan

Rosenstock, Samuel
See Tzara, Tristan

Rosenthal, M(acha) L(ouis)
1917-1996 . . . . **CLC 28**
See also CA 1-4R; 152; CAAS 6; CANR 4,
51; DLB 5; SATA 59

Ross, Barnaby
See Dannay, Frederic

Ross, Bernard L.
See Follett, Ken(neth Martin)

Ross, J. H.
See Lawrence, T(homas) E(dward)

Ross, Martin
See Martin, Violet Florence
See also DLB 135

Ross, (James) Sinclair
1908- . . . . . . **CLC 13; DAC; DAM MST;
SSC 24**
See also CA 73-76; DLB 88

Rossetti, Christina (Georgina)
1830-1894 . . . . . **NCLC 2, 50; DA; DAB;
DAC; DAM MST, POET; PC 7; WLC**
See also DLB 35, 163; MAICYA; SATA 20

Rossetti, Dante Gabriel
1828-1882 . . . . **NCLC 4; DA; DAB;
DAC; DAM MST, POET; WLC**
See also CDBLB 1832-1890; DLB 35

Rossner, Judith (Perelman)
1935- . . . . **CLC 6, 9, 29**
See also AITN 2; BEST 90:3; CA 17-20R;
CANR 18, 51; DLB 6; INT CANR-18;
MTCW

Rostand, Edmond (Eugene Alexis)
1868-1918 . . . . . **TCLC 6, 37; DA; DAB;
DAC; DAM DRAM, MST**
See also CA 104; 126; MTCW

Roth, Henry 1906-1995 . . . . . . **CLC 2, 6, 11**
See also CA 11-12; 149; CANR 38; CAP 1;
DLB 28; MTCW

Roth, Joseph 1894-1939 . . . . **TCLC 33**
See also DLB 85

Roth, Philip (Milton)
1933- . . . . . . **CLC 1, 2, 3, 4, 6, 9, 15, 22,
31, 47, 66, 86; DA; DAB; DAC;
DAM MST, NOV, POP; WLC**
See also BEST 90:3; CA 1-4R; CANR 1, 22,
36, 55; CDALB 1968-1988; DLB 2, 28,
173; DLBY 82; MTCW

Rothenberg, Jerome 1931- . . . . **CLC 6, 57**
See also CA 45-48; CANR 1; DLB 5

Roumain, Jacques (Jean Baptiste)
1907-1944 . . . . **TCLC 19; BLC;
DAM MULT**
See also BW 1; CA 117; 125

Rourke, Constance (Mayfield)
1885-1941 . . . . **TCLC 12**
See also CA 107; YABC 1

Rousseau, Jean-Baptiste 1671-1741 . . . **LC 9**

Rousseau, Jean-Jacques
1712-1778 . . . . **LC 14, 36; DA; DAB;
DAC; DAM MST; WLC**

Roussel, Raymond 1877-1933 . . . . . **TCLC 20**
See also CA 117

Rovit, Earl (Herbert) 1927- . . . . **CLC 7**
See also CA 5-8R; CANR 12

Rowe, Nicholas 1674-1718 . . . . **LC 8**
See also DLB 84

Rowley, Ames Dorrance
See Lovecraft, H(oward) P(hillips)

Rowson, Susanna Haswell
1762(?)-1824 . . . . **NCLC 5**
See also DLB 37

Roy, Gabrielle
1909-1983 . . . . **CLC 10, 14; DAB; DAC;
DAM MST**
See also CA 53-56; 110; CANR 5; DLB 68;
MTCW

Rozewicz, Tadeusz
1921- . . . . **CLC 9, 23; DAM POET**
See also CA 108; CANR 36; MTCW

Ruark, Gibbons 1941- . . . . **CLC 3**
See also CA 33-36R; CAAS 23; CANR 14,
31; DLB 120

Rubens, Bernice (Ruth) 1923- . . . **CLC 19, 31**
See also CA 25-28R; CANR 33; DLB 14;
MTCW

Rubin, Harold
See Robbins, Harold

Rudkin, (James) David 1936- . . . . . . **CLC 14**
See also CA 89-92; DLB 13

Rudnik, Raphael 1933- . . . . **CLC 7**
See also CA 29-32R

Ruffian, M.
See Hasek, Jaroslav (Matej Frantisek)

Ruiz, Jose Martinez . . . . **CLC 11**
See also Martinez Ruiz, Jose

Rukeyser, Muriel
1913-1980 . . . . **CLC 6, 10, 15, 27;
DAM POET; PC 12**
See also CA 5-8R; 93-96; CANR 26;
DLB 48; MTCW; SATA-Obit 22

Rule, Jane (Vance) 1931- . . . . **CLC 27**
See also CA 25-28R; CAAS 18; CANR 12;
DLB 60

Rulfo, Juan
1918-1986 . . . . **CLC 8, 80; DAM MULT;
HLC**
See also CA 85-88; 118; CANR 26;
DLB 113; HW; MTCW

Runeberg, Johan 1804-1877 . . . . . . **NCLC 41**

Runyon, (Alfred) Damon
1884(?)-1946 . . . . **TCLC 10**
See also CA 107; DLB 11, 86, 171

Rush, Norman 1933- . . . . **CLC 44**
See also CA 121; 126; INT 126

Rushdie, (Ahmed) Salman
1947- . . . . . **CLC 23, 31, 55; DAB; DAC;
DAM MST, NOV, POP**
See also BEST 89:3; CA 108; 111;
CANR 33; INT 111; MTCW

Rushforth, Peter (Scott) 1945- . . . . . **CLC 19**
See also CA 101

Ruskin, John 1819-1900 . . . . **TCLC 63**
See also CA 114; 129; CDBLB 1832-1890;
DLB 55, 163; SATA 24

Russ, Joanna 1937- . . . . **CLC 15**
See also CA 25-28R; CANR 11, 31; DLB 8;
MTCW

Russell, George William 1867-1935
See Baker, Jean H.
See also CA 104; 153; CDBLB 1890-1914;
DAM POET

Russell, (Henry) Ken(neth Alfred)
1927- . . . . **CLC 16**
See also CA 105

Russell, Willy 1947- . . . . **CLC 60**

Rutherford, Mark . . . . **TCLC 25**
See also White, William Hale
See also DLB 18

Ruyslinck, Ward 1929- . . . . **CLC 14**
See also Belser, Reimond Karel Maria de

Ryan, Cornelius (John) 1920-1974 . . . **CLC 7**
See also CA 69-72; 53-56; CANR 38

Ryan, Michael 1946- . . . . **CLC 65**
See also CA 49-52; DLBY 82

Rybakov, Anatoli (Naumovich)
1911- . . . . **CLC 23, 53**
See also CA 126; 135; SATA 79

Ryder, Jonathan
See Ludlum, Robert

Ryga, George
1932-1987 . . **CLC 14; DAC; DAM MST**
See also CA 101; 124; CANR 43; DLB 60

S. S.
See Sassoon, Siegfried (Lorraine)

Saba, Umberto 1883-1957 . . . . **TCLC 33**
See also CA 144; DLB 114

Sabatini, Rafael 1875-1950 . . . . **TCLC 47**

Sabato, Ernesto (R.)
1911- . . . . **CLC 10, 23; DAM MULT;
HLC**
See also CA 97-100; CANR 32; DLB 145;
HW; MTCW

Sacastru, Martin
See Bioy Casares, Adolfo

Sacher-Masoch, Leopold von
1836(?)-1895 . . . . **NCLC 31**

Sachs, Marilyn (Stickle) 1927- ..... **CLC 35**
See also AAYA 2; CA 17-20R; CANR 13,
47; CLR 2; JRDA; MAICYA; SAAS 2;
SATA 3, 68

Sachs, Nelly 1891-1970 .... **CLC 14, 98**
See also CA 17-18; 25-28R; CAP 2

Sackler, Howard (Oliver)
1929-1982 .... **CLC 14**
See also CA 61-64; 108; CANR 30; DLB 7

Sacks, Oliver (Wolf) 1933- .... **CLC 67**
See also CA 53-56; CANR 28, 50;
INT CANR-28; MTCW

Sade, Donatien Alphonse Francois Comte
1740-1814 .... **NCLC 47**

Sadoff, Ira 1945-................. **CLC 9**
See also CA 53-56; CANR 5, 21; DLB 120

Saetone
See Camus, Albert

Safire, William 1929- .... **CLC 10**
See also CA 17-20R; CANR 31, 54

Sagan, Carl (Edward) 1934-........ **CLC 30**
See also AAYA 2; CA 25-28R; CANR 11,
36; MTCW; SATA 58

Sagan, Francoise .... **CLC 3, 6, 9, 17, 36**
See also Quoirez, Francoise
See also DLB 83

Sahgal, Nayantara (Pandit) 1927-... **CLC 41**
See also CA 9-12R; CANR 11

Saint, H(arry) F. 1941- .... **CLC 50**
See also CA 127

St. Aubin de Teran, Lisa 1953-
See Teran, Lisa St. Aubin de
See also CA 118; 126; INT 126

Sainte-Beuve, Charles Augustin
1804-1869 .... **NCLC 5**

Saint-Exupery, Antoine (Jean Baptiste Marie
Roger) de
1900-1944 .... **TCLC 2, 56; DAM NOV;
WLC**
See also CA 108; 132; CLR 10; DLB 72;
MAICYA; MTCW; SATA 20

St. John, David
See Hunt, E(verette) Howard, (Jr.)

Saint-John Perse
See Leger, (Marie-Rene Auguste) Alexis
Saint-Leger

Saintsbury, George (Edward Bateman)
1845-1933 .... **TCLC 31**
See also DLB 57, 149

Sait Faik .... **TCLC 23**
See also Abasiyanik, Sait Faik

Saki .... **TCLC 3; SSC 12**
See also Munro, H(ector) H(ugh)

Sala, George Augustus .... **NCLC 46**

Salama, Hannu 1936-............. **CLC 18**

Salamanca, J(ack) R(ichard)
1922- .... **CLC 4, 15**
See also CA 25-28R

Sale, J. Kirkpatrick
See Sale, Kirkpatrick

Sale, Kirkpatrick 1937- .... **CLC 68**
See also CA 13-16R; CANR 10

Salinas, Luis Omar
1937- ..... **CLC 90; DAM MULT; HLC**
See also CA 131; DLB 82; HW

Salinas (y Serrano), Pedro
1891(?)-1951 .... **TCLC 17**
See also CA 117; DLB 134

Salinger, J(erome) D(avid)
1919- ...... **CLC 1, 3, 8, 12, 55, 56; DA;
DAB; DAC; DAM MST, NOV, POP;
SSC 2; WLC**
See also AAYA 2; CA 5-8R; CANR 39;
CDALB 1941-1968; CLR 18; DLB 2, 102,
173; MAICYA; MTCW; SATA 67

Salisbury, John
See Caute, David

Salter, James 1925- .... **CLC 7, 52, 59**
See also CA 73-76; DLB 130

Saltus, Edgar (Everton)
1855-1921 .... **TCLC 8**
See also CA 105

Saltykov, Mikhail Evgrafovich
1826-1889 .... **NCLC 16**

Samarakis, Antonis 1919- .... **CLC 5**
See also CA 25-28R; CAAS 16; CANR 36

Sanchez, Florencio 1875-1910..... **TCLC 37**
See also CA 153; HW

Sanchez, Luis Rafael 1936-........ **CLC 23**
See also CA 128; DLB 145; HW

Sanchez, Sonia
1934- ...... **CLC 5; BLC; DAM MULT;
PC 9**
See also BW 2; CA 33-36R; CANR 24, 49;
CLR 18; DLB 41; DLBD 8; MAICYA;
MTCW; SATA 22

Sand, George
1804-1876 .... **NCLC 2, 42, 57; DA;
DAB; DAC; DAM MST, NOV; WLC**
See also DLB 119

Sandburg, Carl (August)
1878-1967 .... **CLC 1, 4, 10, 15, 35; DA;
DAB; DAC; DAM MST, POET; PC 2;
WLC**
See also CA 5-8R; 25-28R; CANR 35;
CDALB 1865-1917; DLB 17, 54;
MAICYA; MTCW; SATA 8

Sandburg, Charles
See Sandburg, Carl (August)

Sandburg, Charles A.
See Sandburg, Carl (August)

Sanders, (James) Ed(ward) 1939- ... **CLC 53**
See also CA 13-16R; CAAS 21; CANR 13,
44; DLB 16

Sanders, Lawrence
1920- .... **CLC 41; DAM POP**
See also BEST 89:4; CA 81-84; CANR 33;
MTCW

Sanders, Noah
See Blount, Roy (Alton), Jr.

Sanders, Winston P.
See Anderson, Poul (William)

Sandoz, Mari(e Susette)
1896-1966 .... **CLC 28**
See also CA 1-4R; 25-28R; CANR 17;
DLB 9; MTCW; SATA 5

Saner, Reg(inald Anthony) 1931- .... **CLC 9**
See also CA 65-68

Sannazaro, Jacopo 1456(?)-1530...... **LC 8**

Sansom, William
1912-1976 ...... **CLC 2, 6; DAM NOV;
SSC 21**
See also CA 5-8R; 65-68; CANR 42;
DLB 139; MTCW

Santayana, George 1863-1952..... **TCLC 40**
See also CA 115; DLB 54, 71; DLBD 13

Santiago, Danny .... **CLC 33**
See also James, Daniel (Lewis)
See also DLB 122

Santmyer, Helen Hoover
1895-1986 .... **CLC 33**
See also CA 1-4R; 118; CANR 15, 33;
DLBY 84; MTCW

Santos, Bienvenido N(uqui)
1911-1996 ...... **CLC 22; DAM MULT**
See also CA 101; 151; CANR 19, 46

Sapper .... **TCLC 44**
See also McNeile, Herman Cyril

Sappho
fl. 6th cent. B.C.- .... **CMLC 3;
DAM POET; PC 5**

Sarduy, Severo 1937-1993....... **CLC 6, 97**
See also CA 89-92; 142; DLB 113; HW

Sargeson, Frank 1903-1982 .... **CLC 31**
See also CA 25-28R; 106; CANR 38

Sarmiento, Felix Ruben Garcia
See Dario, Ruben

Saroyan, William
1908-1981 ..... **CLC 1, 8, 10, 29, 34, 56;
DA; DAB; DAC; DAM DRAM, MST,
NOV; SSC 21; WLC**
See also CA 5-8R; 103; CANR 30; DLB 7,
9, 86; DLBY 81; MTCW; SATA 23;
SATA-Obit 24

Sarraute, Nathalie
1900- .... **CLC 1, 2, 4, 8, 10, 31, 80**
See also CA 9-12R; CANR 23; DLB 83;
MTCW

Sarton, (Eleanor) May
1912-1995 .... **CLC 4, 14, 49, 91;
DAM POET**
See also CA 1-4R; 149; CANR 1, 34, 55;
DLB 48; DLBY 81; INT CANR-34;
MTCW; SATA 36; SATA-Obit 86

Sartre, Jean-Paul
1905-1980 .... **CLC 1, 4, 7, 9, 13, 18, 24,
44, 50, 52; DA; DAB; DAC;
DAM DRAM, MST, NOV; DC 3; WLC**
See also CA 9-12R; 97-100; CANR 21;
DLB 72; MTCW

Sassoon, Siegfried (Lorraine)
1886-1967 .... **CLC 36; DAB;
DAM MST, NOV, POET; PC 12**
See also CA 104; 25-28R; CANR 36;
DLB 20; MTCW

Satterfield, Charles
See Pohl, Frederik

Saul, John (W. III)
1942- ...... **CLC 46; DAM NOV, POP**
See also AAYA 10; BEST 90:4; CA 81-84;
CANR 16, 40

Saunders, Caleb
See Heinlein, Robert A(nson)

Saura (Atares), Carlos 1932-....... **CLC 20**
See also CA 114; 131; HW

Sauser-Hall, Frederic 1887-1961.... **CLC 18**
See also Cendrars, Blaise
See also CA 102; 93-96; CANR 36; MTCW

Saussure, Ferdinand de
1857-1913 .... **TCLC 49**

Savage, Catharine
See Brosman, Catharine Savage

Savage, Thomas 1915- .... **CLC 40**
See also CA 126; 132; CAAS 15; INT 132

Savan, Glenn 19(?)- .... **CLC 50**

Sayers, Dorothy L(eigh)
1893-1957 ..... **TCLC 2, 15; DAM POP**
See also CA 104; 119; CDBLB 1914-1945;
DLB 10, 36, 77, 100; MTCW

Sayers, Valerie 1952-............. **CLC 50**
See also CA 134

Sayles, John (Thomas)
1950- .... **CLC 7, 10, 14**
See also CA 57-60; CANR 41; DLB 44

Scammell, Michael .... **CLC 34**

Scannell, Vernon 1922- .... **CLC 49**
See also CA 5-8R; CANR 8, 24; DLB 27;
SATA 59

Scarlett, Susan
See Streatfeild, (Mary) Noel

Schaeffer, Susan Fromberg
1941- .... **CLC 6, 11, 22**
See also CA 49-52; CANR 18; DLB 28;
MTCW; SATA 22

Schary, Jill
See Robinson, Jill

Schell, Jonathan 1943-............ **CLC 35**
See also CA 73-76; CANR 12

Schelling, Friedrich Wilhelm Joseph von
1775-1854 .... **NCLC 30**
See also DLB 90

Schendel, Arthur van 1874-1946 ... **TCLC 56**

Scherer, Jean-Marie Maurice 1920-
See Rohmer, Eric
See also CA 110

Schevill, James (Erwin) 1920-....... **CLC 7**
See also CA 5-8R; CAAS 12

Schiller, Friedrich
1759-1805 .... **NCLC 39; DAM DRAM**
See also DLB 94

Schisgal, Murray (Joseph) 1926-..... **CLC 6**
See also CA 21-24R; CANR 48

Schlee, Ann 1934-.............. **CLC 35**
See also CA 101; CANR 29; SATA 44;
SATA-Brief 36

Schlegel, August Wilhelm von
1767-1845 .... **NCLC 15**
See also DLB 94

Schlegel, Friedrich 1772-1829 .... **NCLC 45**
See also DLB 90

Schlegel, Johann Elias (von)
1719(?)-1749 .... **LC 5**

Schlesinger, Arthur M(eier), Jr.
1917- .... **CLC 84**
See also AITN 1; CA 1-4R; CANR 1, 28;
DLB 17; INT CANR-28; MTCW;
SATA 61

Schmidt, Arno (Otto) 1914-1979.... **CLC 56**
See also CA 128; 109; DLB 69

Schmitz, Aron Hector 1861-1928
See Svevo, Italo
See also CA 104; 122; MTCW

Schnackenberg, Gjertrud 1953-..... **CLC 40**
See also CA 116; DLB 120

Schneider, Leonard Alfred 1925-1966
See Bruce, Lenny
See also CA 89-92

Schnitzler, Arthur
1862-1931 .... **TCLC 4; SSC 15**
See also CA 104; DLB 81, 118

Schopenhauer, Arthur
1788-1860 .... **NCLC 51**
See also DLB 90

Schor, Sandra (M.) 1932(?)-1990 ... **CLC 65**
See also CA 132

Schorer, Mark 1908-1977 .... **CLC 9**
See also CA 5-8R; 73-76; CANR 7;
DLB 103

Schrader, Paul (Joseph) 1946-...... **CLC 26**
See also CA 37-40R; CANR 41; DLB 44

Schreiner, Olive (Emilie Albertina)
1855-1920 .... **TCLC 9**
See also CA 105; DLB 18, 156

Schulberg, Budd (Wilson)
1914- .... **CLC 7, 48**
See also CA 25-28R; CANR 19; DLB 6, 26,
28; DLBY 81

Schulz, Bruno
1892-1942 .... **TCLC 5, 51; SSC 13**
See also CA 115; 123

Schulz, Charles M(onroe) 1922- .... **CLC 12**
See also CA 9-12R; CANR 6;
INT CANR-6; SATA 10

Schumacher, E(rnst) F(riedrich)
1911-1977 .... **CLC 80**
See also CA 81-84; 73-76; CANR 34

Schuyler, James Marcus
1923-1991 ..... **CLC 5, 23; DAM POET**
See also CA 101; 134; DLB 5, 169; INT 101

Schwartz, Delmore (David)
1913-1966 ... **CLC 2, 4, 10, 45, 87; PC 8**
See also CA 17-18; 25-28R; CANR 35;
CAP 2; DLB 28, 48; MTCW

Schwartz, Ernst
See Ozu, Yasujiro

Schwartz, John Burnham 1965- .... **CLC 59**
See also CA 132

Schwartz, Lynne Sharon 1939-..... **CLC 31**
See also CA 103; CANR 44

Schwartz, Muriel A.
See Eliot, T(homas) S(tearns)

Schwarz-Bart, Andre 1928-....... **CLC 2, 4**
See also CA 89-92

Schwarz-Bart, Simone 1938-........ **CLC 7**
See also BW 2; CA 97-100

Schwob, (Mayer Andre) Marcel
1867-1905 .... **TCLC 20**
See also CA 117; DLB 123

Sciascia, Leonardo
1921-1989 .... **CLC 8, 9, 41**
See also CA 85-88; 130; CANR 35; MTCW

Scoppettone, Sandra 1936-........ **CLC 26**
See also AAYA 11; CA 5-8R; CANR 41;
SATA 9

Scorsese, Martin 1942- .... **CLC 20, 89**
See also CA 110; 114; CANR 46

Scotland, Jay
See Jakes, John (William)

Scott, Duncan Campbell
1862-1947 .... **TCLC 6; DAC**
See also CA 104; 153; DLB 92

Scott, Evelyn 1893-1963........... **CLC 43**
See also CA 104; 112; DLB 9, 48

Scott, F(rancis) R(eginald)
1899-1985 .... **CLC 22**
See also CA 101; 114; DLB 88; INT 101

Scott, Frank
See Scott, F(rancis) R(eginald)

Scott, Joanna 1960-.............. **CLC 50**
See also CA 126; CANR 53

Scott, Paul (Mark) 1920-1978.... **CLC 9, 60**
See also CA 81-84; 77-80; CANR 33;
DLB 14; MTCW

Scott, Walter
1771-1832 .... **NCLC 15; DA; DAB;**
DAC; DAM MST, NOV, POET; PC 13;
WLC
See also CDBLB 1789-1832; DLB 93, 107,
116, 144, 159; YABC 2

Scribe, (Augustin) Eugene
1791-1861 .... **NCLC 16; DAM DRAM;**
DC 5

Scrum, R.
See Crumb, R(obert)

Scudery, Madeleine de 1607-1701..... **LC 2**

Scum
See Crumb, R(obert)

Scumbag, Little Bobby
See Crumb, R(obert)

Seabrook, John
See Hubbard, L(afayette) Ron(ald)

Sealy, I. Allan 1951- .... **CLC 55**

Search, Alexander
See Pessoa, Fernando (Antonio Nogueira)

Sebastian, Lee
See Silverberg, Robert

Sebastian Owl
See Thompson, Hunter S(tockton)

Sebestyen, Ouida 1924-........... **CLC 30**
See also AAYA 8; CA 107; CANR 40;
CLR 17; JRDA; MAICYA; SAAS 10;
SATA 39

Secundus, H. Scriblerus
See Fielding, Henry

Sedges, John
See Buck, Pearl S(ydenstricker)

Sedgwick, Catharine Maria
1789-1867 .... **NCLC 19**
See also DLB 1, 74

Seelye, John 1931-................ **CLC 7**

Seferiades, Giorgos Stylianou 1900-1971
See Seferis, George
See also CA 5-8R; 33-36R; CANR 5, 36;
MTCW

Strummer, Joe   1953(?)- . . . . CLC 30

Stuart, Don A.
  See Campbell, John W(ood, Jr.)

Stuart, Ian
  See MacLean, Alistair (Stuart)

Stuart, Jesse (Hilton)
    1906-1984 . . . . CLC 1, 8, 11, 14, 34
  See also CA 5-8R; 112; CANR 31; DLB 9,
    48, 102; DLBY 84; SATA 2;
    SATA-Obit 36

Sturgeon, Theodore (Hamilton)
    1918-1985 . . . . CLC 22, 39
  See Queen, Ellery
  See also CA 81-84; 116; CANR 32; DLB 8;
    DLBY 85; MTCW

Sturges, Preston   1898-1959 . . . . TCLC 48
  See also CA 114; 149; DLB 26

Styron, William
    1925- . . . . CLC 1, 3, 5, 11, 15, 60;
                             DAM NOV, POP
  See also BEST 90:4; CA 5-8R; CANR 6, 33;
    CDALB 1968-1988; DLB 2, 143;
    DLBY 80; INT CANR-6; MTCW

Suarez Lynch, B.
  See Bioy Casares, Adolfo; Borges, Jorge
    Luis

Su Chien   1884-1918
  See Su Man-shu
  See also CA 123

Suckow, Ruth   1892-1960 . . . . SSC 18
  See also CA 113; DLB 9, 102

Sudermann, Hermann   1857-1928 . . TCLC 15
  See also CA 107; DLB 118

Sue, Eugene   1804-1857 . . . . NCLC 1
  See also DLB 119

Sueskind, Patrick   1949- . . . . CLC 44
  See also Suskind, Patrick

Sukenick, Ronald   1932- . . . . . CLC 3, 4, 6, 48
  See also CA 25-28R; CAAS 8; CANR 32;
    DLB 173; DLBY 81

Suknaski, Andrew   1942- . . . . CLC 19
  See also CA 101; DLB 53

Sullivan, Vernon
  See Vian, Boris

Sully Prudhomme   1839-1907 . . . . . . TCLC 31

Su Man-shu . . . . TCLC 24
  See also Su Chien

Summerforest, Ivy B.
  See Kirkup, James

Summers, Andrew James   1942- . . . . . CLC 26

Summers, Andy
  See Summers, Andrew James

Summers, Hollis (Spurgeon, Jr.)
    1916- . . . . CLC 10
  See also CA 5-8R; CANR 3; DLB 6

Summers, (Alphonsus Joseph-Mary Augustus)
    Montague   1880-1948 . . . . TCLC 16
  See also CA 118

Sumner, Gordon Matthew   1951- . . . . CLC 26

Surtees, Robert Smith
    1803-1864 . . . . NCLC 14
  See also DLB 21

Susann, Jacqueline   1921-1974 . . . . CLC 3
  See also AITN 1; CA 65-68; 53-56; MTCW

Su Shih   1036-1101 . . . . CMLC 15

Suskind, Patrick
  See Sueskind, Patrick
  See also CA 145

Sutcliff, Rosemary
    1920-1992 . . . . CLC 26; DAB; DAC;
                             DAM MST, POP
  See also AAYA 10; CA 5-8R; 139;
    CANR 37; CLR 1, 37; JRDA; MAICYA;
    SATA 6, 44, 78; SATA-Obit 73

Sutro, Alfred   1863-1933 . . . . TCLC 6
  See also CA 105; DLB 10

Sutton, Henry
  See Slavitt, David R(ytman)

Svevo, Italo . . . . TCLC 2, 35
  See also Schmitz, Aron Hector

Swados, Elizabeth (A.)   1951- . . . . CLC 12
  See also CA 97-100; CANR 49; INT 97-100

Swados, Harvey   1920-1972 . . . . CLC 5
  See also CA 5-8R; 37-40R; CANR 6;
    DLB 2

Swan, Gladys   1934- . . . . CLC 69
  See also CA 101; CANR 17, 39

Swarthout, Glendon (Fred)
    1918-1992 . . . . CLC 35
  See also CA 1-4R; 139; CANR 1, 47;
    SATA 26

Sweet, Sarah C.
  See Jewett, (Theodora) Sarah Orne

Swenson, May
    1919-1989 . . . . CLC 4, 14, 61; DA; DAB;
                     DAC; DAM MST, POET; PC 14
  See also CA 5-8R; 130; CANR 36; DLB 5;
    MTCW; SATA 15

Swift, Augustus
  See Lovecraft, H(oward) P(hillips)

Swift, Graham (Colin)   1949- . . . . CLC 41, 88
  See also CA 117; 122; CANR 46

Swift, Jonathan
    1667-1745 . . . . . . LC 1; DA; DAB; DAC;
                     DAM MST, NOV, POET; PC 9; WLC
  See also CDBLB 1660-1789; DLB 39, 95,
    101; SATA 19

Swinburne, Algernon Charles
    1837-1909 . . . . . . TCLC 8, 36; DA; DAB;
                     DAC; DAM MST, POET; WLC
  See also CA 105; 140; CDBLB 1832-1890;
    DLB 35, 57

Swinfen, Ann . . . . CLC 34

Swinnerton, Frank Arthur
    1884-1982 . . . . CLC 31
  See also CA 108; DLB 34

Swithen, John
  See King, Stephen (Edwin)

Sylvia
  See Ashton-Warner, Sylvia (Constance)

Symmes, Robert Edward
  See Duncan, Robert (Edward)

Symonds, John Addington
    1840-1893 . . . . NCLC 34
  See also DLB 57, 144

Symons, Arthur   1865-1945 . . . . TCLC 11
  See also CA 107; DLB 19, 57, 149

Symons, Julian (Gustave)
    1912-1994 . . . . CLC 2, 14, 32
  See also CA 49-52; 147; CAAS 3; CANR 3,
    33; DLB 87, 155; DLBY 92; MTCW

Synge, (Edmund) J(ohn) M(illington)
    1871-1909 . . . . TCLC 6, 37;
                             DAM DRAM; DC 2
  See also CA 104; 141; CDBLB 1890-1914;
    DLB 10, 19

Syruc, J.
  See Milosz, Czeslaw

Szirtes, George   1948- . . . . CLC 46
  See also CA 109; CANR 27

Tabori, George   1914- . . . . CLC 19
  See also CA 49-52; CANR 4

Tagore, Rabindranath
    1861-1941 . . . . TCLC 3, 53;
                             DAM DRAM, POET; PC 8
  See also CA 104; 120; MTCW

Taine, Hippolyte Adolphe
    1828-1893 . . . . NCLC 15

Talese, Gay   1932- . . . . CLC 37
  See also AITN 1; CA 1-4R; CANR 9;
    INT CANR-9; MTCW

Tallent, Elizabeth (Ann)   1954- . . . . . CLC 45
  See also CA 117; DLB 130

Tally, Ted   1952- . . . . CLC 42
  See also CA 120; 124; INT 124

Tamayo y Baus, Manuel
    1829-1898 . . . . NCLC 1

Tammsaare, A(nton) H(ansen)
    1878-1940 . . . . TCLC 27

Tan, Amy (Ruth)
    1952- . . . . CLC 59; DAM MULT, NOV,
                                         POP
  See also AAYA 9; BEST 89:3; CA 136;
    CANR 54; DLB 173; SATA 75

Tandem, Felix
  See Spitteler, Carl (Friedrich Georg)

Tanizaki, Jun'ichiro
    1886-1965 . . . . . . CLC 8, 14, 28; SSC 21
  See also CA 93-96; 25-28R

Tanner, William
  See Amis, Kingsley (William)

Tao Lao
  See Storni, Alfonsina

Tarassoff, Lev
  See Troyat, Henri

Tarbell, Ida M(inerva)
    1857-1944 . . . . TCLC 40
  See also CA 122; DLB 47

Tarkington, (Newton) Booth
    1869-1946 . . . . TCLC 9
  See also CA 110; 143; DLB 9, 102;
    SATA 17

Tarkovsky, Andrei (Arsenyevich)
    1932-1986 . . . . CLC 75
  See also CA 127

Tartt, Donna   1964(?)- . . . . CLC 76
  See also CA 142

Tasso, Torquato   1544-1595 . . . . LC 5

Tate, (John Orley) Allen
    1899-1979 . . . . CLC 2, 4, 6, 9, 11, 14, 24
  See also CA 5-8R; 85-88; CANR 32;
    DLB 4, 45, 63; MTCW

Tate, Ellalice
See Hibbert, Eleanor Alice Burford

Tate, James (Vincent) 1943- ... **CLC 2, 6, 25**
See also CA 21-24R; CANR 29; DLB 5, 169

Tavel, Ronald 1940-............... **CLC 6**
See also CA 21-24R; CANR 33

Taylor, C(ecil) P(hilip) 1929-1981... **CLC 27**
See also CA 25-28R; 105; CANR 47

Taylor, Edward
1642(?)-1729 .... **LC 11; DA; DAB;**
                        DAC; DAM MST, POET
See also DLB 24

Taylor, Eleanor Ross 1920-......... **CLC 5**
See also CA 81-84

Taylor, Elizabeth 1912-1975 ... **CLC 2, 4, 29**
See also CA 13-16R; CANR 9; DLB 139;
MTCW; SATA 13

Taylor, Henry (Splawn) 1942-...... **CLC 44**
See also CA 33-36R; CAAS 7; CANR 31;
DLB 5

Taylor, Kamala (Purnaiya) 1924-
See Markandaya, Kamala
See also CA 77-80

Taylor, Mildred D................ **CLC 21**
See also AAYA 10; BW 1; CA 85-88;
CANR 25; CLR 9; DLB 52; JRDA;
MAICYA; SAAS 5; SATA 15, 70

Taylor, Peter (Hillsman)
1917-1994 ..... **CLC 1, 4, 18, 37, 44, 50,**
                        71; SSC 10
See also CA 13-16R; 147; CANR 9, 50;
DLBY 81, 94; INT CANR-9; MTCW

Taylor, Robert Lewis 1912-........ **CLC 14**
See also CA 1-4R; CANR 3; SATA 10

Tchekhov, Anton
See Chekhov, Anton (Pavlovich)

Teasdale, Sara 1884-1933.......... **TCLC 4**
See also CA 104; DLB 45; SATA 32

Tegner, Esaias 1782-1846......... **NCLC 2**

Teilhard de Chardin, (Marie Joseph) Pierre
1881-1955 .... **TCLC 9**
See also CA 105

Temple, Ann
See Mortimer, Penelope (Ruth)

Tennant, Emma (Christina)
1937-..................... **CLC 13, 52**
See also CA 65-68; CAAS 9; CANR 10, 38;
DLB 14

Tenneshaw, S. M.
See Silverberg, Robert

Tennyson, Alfred
1809-1892 .... **NCLC 30; DA; DAB;**
                        DAC; DAM MST, POET; PC 6; WLC
See also CDBLB 1832-1890; DLB 32

Teran, Lisa St. Aubin de .... **CLC 36**
See also St. Aubin de Teran, Lisa

Terence 195(?)B.C.-159B.C....... **CMLC 14**

Teresa de Jesus, St. 1515-1582 ..... **LC 18**

Terkel, Louis 1912-
See Terkel, Studs
See also CA 57-60; CANR 18, 45; MTCW

Terkel, Studs .... **CLC 38**
See also Terkel, Louis
See also AITN 1

Terry, C. V.
See Slaughter, Frank G(ill)

Terry, Megan 1932-................ **CLC 19**
See also CA 77-80; CABS 3; CANR 43;
DLB 7

Tertz, Abram
See Sinyavsky, Andrei (Donatevich)

Tesich, Steve 1943(?)-1996...... **CLC 40, 69**
See also CA 105; 152; DLBY 83

Teternikov, Fyodor Kuzmich 1863-1927
See Sologub, Fyodor
See also CA 104

Tevis, Walter 1928-1984 .... **CLC 42**
See also CA 113

Tey, Josephine................... **TCLC 14**
See also Mackintosh, Elizabeth
See also DLB 77

Thackeray, William Makepeace
1811-1863 .... **NCLC 5, 14, 22, 43; DA;**
                        DAB; DAC; DAM MST, NOV; WLC
See also CDBLB 1832-1890; DLB 21, 55,
159, 163; SATA 23

Thakura, Ravindranatha
See Tagore, Rabindranath

Tharoor, Shashi 1956- .... **CLC 70**
See also CA 141

Thelwell, Michael Miles 1939-..... **CLC 22**
See also BW 2; CA 101

Theobald, Lewis, Jr.
See Lovecraft, H(oward) P(hillips)

Theodorescu, Ion N. 1880-1967
See Arghezi, Tudor
See also CA 116

Theriault, Yves
1915-1983 .. **CLC 79; DAC; DAM MST**
See also CA 102; DLB 88

Theroux, Alexander (Louis)
1939-.................... **CLC 2, 25**
See also CA 85-88; CANR 20

Theroux, Paul (Edward)
1941- .... **CLC 5, 8, 11, 15, 28, 46;**
                        DAM POP
See also BEST 89:4; CA 33-36R; CANR 20,
45; DLB 2; MTCW; SATA 44

Thesen, Sharon 1946-............. **CLC 56**

Thevenin, Denis
See Duhamel, Georges

Thibault, Jacques Anatole Francois
1844-1924
See France, Anatole
See also CA 106; 127; DAM NOV; MTCW

Thiele, Colin (Milton) 1920- .... **CLC 17**
See also CA 29-32R; CANR 12, 28, 53;
CLR 27; MAICYA; SAAS 2; SATA 14,
72

Thomas, Audrey (Callahan)
1935- .... **CLC 7, 13, 37; SSC 20**
See also AITN 2; CA 21-24R; CAAS 19;
CANR 36; DLB 60; MTCW

Thomas, D(onald) M(ichael)
1935-................. **CLC 13, 22, 31**
See also CA 61-64; CAAS 11; CANR 17,
45; CDBLB 1960 to Present; DLB 40;
INT CANR-17; MTCW

Thomas, Dylan (Marlais)
1914-1953 ... **TCLC 1, 8, 45; DA; DAB;**
                        DAC; DAM DRAM, MST, POET;
                        PC 2; SSC 3; WLC
See also CA 104; 120; CDBLB 1945-1960;
DLB 13, 20, 139; MTCW; SATA 60

Thomas, (Philip) Edward
1878-1917 ...... **TCLC 10; DAM POET**
See also CA 106; 153; DLB 19

Thomas, Joyce Carol 1938-........ **CLC 35**
See also AAYA 12; BW 2; CA 113; 116;
CANR 48; CLR 19; DLB 33; INT 116;
JRDA; MAICYA; MTCW; SAAS 7;
SATA 40, 78

Thomas, Lewis 1913-1993 .... **CLC 35**
See also CA 85-88; 143; CANR 38; MTCW

Thomas, Paul
See Mann, (Paul) Thomas

Thomas, Piri 1928-............... **CLC 17**
See also CA 73-76; HW

Thomas, R(onald) S(tuart)
1913-............ **CLC 6, 13, 48; DAB;**
                        DAM POET
See also CA 89-92; CAAS 4; CANR 30;
CDBLB 1960 to Present; DLB 27;
MTCW

Thomas, Ross (Elmore) 1926-1995 .. **CLC 39**
See also CA 33-36R; 150; CANR 22

Thompson, Francis Clegg
See Mencken, H(enry) L(ouis)

Thompson, Francis Joseph
1859-1907 .... **TCLC 4**
See also CA 104; CDBLB 1890-1914;
DLB 19

Thompson, Hunter S(tockton)
1939- .... **CLC 9, 17, 40; DAM POP**
See also BEST 89:1; CA 17-20R; CANR 23,
46; MTCW

Thompson, James Myers
See Thompson, Jim (Myers)

Thompson, Jim (Myers)
1906-1977(?) .... **CLC 69**
See also CA 140

Thompson, Judith .... **CLC 39**

Thomson, James
1700-1748 ..... **LC 16, 29; DAM POET**
See also DLB 95

Thomson, James
1834-1882 ..... **NCLC 18; DAM POET**
See also DLB 35

Thoreau, Henry David
1817-1862 ..... **NCLC 7, 21; DA; DAB;**
                        DAC; DAM MST; WLC
See also CDALB 1640-1865; DLB 1

Thornton, Hall
See Silverberg, Robert

Thucydides c. 455B.C.-399B.C.... **CMLC 17**

Thurber, James (Grover)
    1894-1961 .... CLC 5, 11, 25; DA; DAB;
    DAC; DAM DRAM, MST, NOV; SSC 1
    See also CA 73-76; CANR 17, 39;
    CDALB 1929-1941; DLB 4, 11, 22, 102;
    MAICYA; MTCW; SATA 13

Thurman, Wallace (Henry)
    1902-1934 . . . . TCLC 6; BLC;
                                      DAM MULT
    See also BW 1; CA 104; 124; DLB 51

Ticheburn, Cheviot
    See Ainsworth, William Harrison

Tieck, (Johann) Ludwig
    1773-1853 . . . . NCLC 5, 46
    See also DLB 90

Tiger, Derry
    See Ellison, Harlan (Jay)

Tilghman, Christopher 1948(?)-. . . . . CLC 65

Tillinghast, Richard (Williford)
    1940- . . . . CLC 29
    See also CA 29-32R; CAAS 23; CANR 26,
    51

Timrod, Henry 1828-1867 . . . . NCLC 25
    See also DLB 3

Tindall, Gillian 1938- . . . . CLC 7
    See also CA 21-24R; CANR 11

Tiptree, James, Jr. . . . . CLC 48, 50
    See also Sheldon, Alice Hastings Bradley
    See also DLB 8

Titmarsh, Michael Angelo
    See Thackeray, William Makepeace

Tocqueville, Alexis (Charles Henri Maurice
    Clerel Comte) 1805-1859. . . . . NCLC 7

Tolkien, J(ohn) R(onald) R(euel)
    1892-1973 . . . . CLC 1, 2, 3, 8, 12, 38;
                  DA; DAB; DAC; DAM MST, NOV,
                                      POP; WLC
    See also AAYA 10; AITN 1; CA 17-18;
    45-48; CANR 36; CAP 2;
    CDBLB 1914-1945; DLB 15, 160; JRDA;
    MAICYA; MTCW; SATA 2, 32;
    SATA-Obit 24

Toller, Ernst 1893-1939 . . . . TCLC 10
    See also CA 107; DLB 124

Tolson, M. B.
    See Tolson, Melvin B(eaunorus)

Tolson, Melvin B(eaunorus)
    1898(?)-1966 . . . . CLC 36; BLC;
                                DAM MULT, POET
    See also BW 1; CA 124; 89-92; DLB 48, 76

Tolstoi, Aleksei Nikolaevich
    See Tolstoy, Alexey Nikolaevich

Tolstoy, Alexey Nikolaevich
    1882-1945 . . . . TCLC 18
    See also CA 107

Tolstoy, Count Leo
    See Tolstoy, Leo (Nikolaevich)

Tolstoy, Leo (Nikolaevich)
    1828-1910 . . . . . . TCLC 4, 11, 17, 28, 44;
            DA; DAB; DAC; DAM MST, NOV;
                                      SSC 9; WLC
    See also CA 104; 123; SATA 26

Tomasi di Lampedusa, Giuseppe 1896-1957
    See Lampedusa, Giuseppe (Tomasi) di
    See also CA 111

Tomlin, Lily. . . . . CLC 17
    See also Tomlin, Mary Jean

Tomlin, Mary Jean 1939(?)-
    See Tomlin, Lily
    See also CA 117

Tomlinson, (Alfred) Charles
    1927- . . . . CLC 2, 4, 6, 13, 45;
                                      DAM POET
    See also CA 5-8R; CANR 33; DLB 40

Tonson, Jacob
    See Bennett, (Enoch) Arnold

Toole, John Kennedy
    1937-1969 . . . . CLC 19, 64
    See also CA 104; DLBY 81

Toomer, Jean
    1894-1967 . . . . . . CLC 1, 4, 13, 22; BLC;
                          DAM MULT; PC 7; SSC 1
    See also BW 1; CA 85-88;
    CDALB 1917-1929; DLB 45, 51; MTCW

Torley, Luke
    See Blish, James (Benjamin)

Tornimparte, Alessandra
    See Ginzburg, Natalia

Torre, Raoul della
    See Mencken, H(enry) L(ouis)

Torrey, E(dwin) Fuller 1937-. . . . . . . CLC 34
    See also CA 119

Torsvan, Ben Traven
    See Traven, B.

Torsvan, Benno Traven
    See Traven, B.

Torsvan, Berick Traven
    See Traven, B.

Torsvan, Berwick Traven
    See Traven, B.

Torsvan, Bruno Traven
    See Traven, B.

Torsvan, Traven
    See Traven, B.

Tournier, Michel (Edouard)
    1924- . . . . CLC 6, 23, 36, 95
    See also CA 49-52; CANR 3, 36; DLB 83;
    MTCW; SATA 23

Tournimparte, Alessandra
    See Ginzburg, Natalia

Towers, Ivar
    See Kornbluth, C(yril) M.

Towne, Robert (Burton) 1936(?)-. . . . CLC 87
    See also CA 108; DLB 44

Townsend, Sue 1946-. . CLC 61; DAB; DAC
    See also CA 119; 127; INT 127; MTCW;
    SATA 55; SATA-Brief 48

Townshend, Peter (Dennis Blandford)
    1945- . . . . CLC 17, 42
    See also CA 107

Tozzi, Federigo 1883-1920. . . . . . . TCLC 31

Traill, Catharine Parr
    1802-1899 . . . . NCLC 31
    See also DLB 99

Trakl, Georg 1887-1914. . . . . TCLC 5
    See also CA 104

Transtroemer, Tomas (Goesta)
    1931- . . . . CLC 52, 65; DAM POET
    See also CA 117; 129; CAAS 17

Transtromer, Tomas Gosta
    See Transtroemer, Tomas (Goesta)

Traven, B. (?)-1969. . . . . CLC 8, 11
    See also CA 19-20; 25-28R; CAP 2; DLB 9,
    56; MTCW

Treitel, Jonathan 1959- . . . . CLC 70

Tremain, Rose 1943-. . . . . CLC 42
    See also CA 97-100; CANR 44; DLB 14

Tremblay, Michel
    1942- . . . . . . CLC 29; DAC; DAM MST
    See also CA 116; 128; DLB 60; MTCW

Trevanian. . . . . CLC 29
    See also Whitaker, Rod(ney)

Trevor, Glen
    See Hilton, James

Trevor, William
    1928- . . . . . CLC 7, 9, 14, 25, 71; SSC 21
    See also Cox, William Trevor
    See also DLB 14, 139

Trifonov, Yuri (Valentinovich)
    1925-1981 . . . . CLC 45
    See also CA 126; 103; MTCW

Trilling, Lionel 1905-1975 . . . . CLC 9, 11, 24
    See also CA 9-12R; 61-64; CANR 10;
    DLB 28, 63; INT CANR-10; MTCW

Trimball, W. H.
    See Mencken, H(enry) L(ouis)

Tristan
    See Gomez de la Serna, Ramon

Tristram
    See Housman, A(lfred) E(dward)

Trogdon, William (Lewis) 1939-
    See Heat-Moon, William Least
    See also CA 115; 119; CANR 47; INT 119

Trollope, Anthony
    1815-1882 . . . . . NCLC 6, 33; DA; DAB;
                  DAC; DAM MST, NOV; WLC
    See also CDBLB 1832-1890; DLB 21, 57,
    159; SATA 22

Trollope, Frances 1779-1863 . . . . . NCLC 30
    See also DLB 21, 166

Trotsky, Leon 1879-1940. . . . . TCLC 22
    See also CA 118

Trotter (Cockburn), Catharine
    1679-1749 . . . . LC 8
    See also DLB 84

Trout, Kilgore
    See Farmer, Philip Jose

Trow, George W. S. 1943-. . . . . CLC 52
    See also CA 126

Troyat, Henri 1911-. . . . . CLC 23
    See also CA 45-48; CANR 2, 33; MTCW

Trudeau, G(arretson) B(eekman) 1948-
    See Trudeau, Garry B.
    See also CA 81-84; CANR 31; SATA 35

Trudeau, Garry B. . . . . CLC 12
    See also Trudeau, G(arretson) B(eekman)
    See also AAYA 10; AITN 2

Truffaut, Francois 1932-1984. . . . . . . CLC 20
    See also CA 81-84; 113; CANR 34

Trumbo, Dalton 1905-1976 . . . . CLC 19
    See also CA 21-24R; 69-72; CANR 10;
    DLB 26

Trumbull, John 1750-1831 . . . . NCLC 30
See also DLB 31

Trundlett, Helen B.
See Eliot, T(homas) S(tearns)

Tryon, Thomas
1926-1991 . . . . . . CLC 3, 11; DAM POP
See also AITN 1; CA 29-32R; 135;
CANR 32; MTCW

Tryon, Tom
See Tryon, Thomas

Ts'ao Hsueh-ch'in 1715(?)-1763 . . . . . . LC 1

Tsushima, Shuji 1909-1948
See Dazai, Osamu
See also CA 107

Tsvetaeva (Efron), Marina (Ivanovna)
1892-1941 . . . . TCLC 7, 35; PC 14
See also CA 104; 128; MTCW

Tuck, Lily 1938- . . . . CLC 70
See also CA 139

Tu Fu 712-770 . . . . PC 9
See also DAM MULT

Tunis, John R(oberts) 1889-1975 . . . CLC 12
See also CA 61-64; DLB 22, 171; JRDA;
MAICYA; SATA 37; SATA-Brief 30

Tuohy, Frank . . . . CLC 37
See also Tuohy, John Francis
See also DLB 14, 139

Tuohy, John Francis 1925-
See Tuohy, Frank
See also CA 5-8R; CANR 3, 47

Turco, Lewis (Putnam) 1934- . . . CLC 11, 63
See also CA 13-16R; CAAS 22; CANR 24,
51; DLBY 84

Turgenev, Ivan
1818-1883 . . . . NCLC 21; DA; DAB;
DAC; DAM MST, NOV; SSC 7; WLC

Turgot, Anne-Robert-Jacques
1727-1781 . . . . LC 26

Turner, Frederick 1943- . . . . CLC 48
See also CA 73-76; CAAS 10; CANR 12,
30; DLB 40

Tutu, Desmond M(pilo)
1931- . . . . . CLC 80; BLC; DAM MULT
See also BW 1; CA 125

Tutuola, Amos
1920- . . . . CLC 5, 14, 29; BLC;
DAM MULT
See also BW 2; CA 9-12R; CANR 27;
DLB 125; MTCW

Twain, Mark
. . . . . TCLC 6, 12, 19, 36, 48, 59; SSC 6;
WLC
See also Clemens, Samuel Langhorne
See also DLB 11, 12, 23, 64, 74

Tyler, Anne
1941- . . . . CLC 7, 11, 18, 28, 44, 59;
DAM NOV, POP
See also AAYA 18; BEST 89:1; CA 9-12R;
CANR 11, 33, 53; DLB 6, 143; DLBY 82;
MTCW; SATA 7, 90

Tyler, Royall 1757-1826 . . . . NCLC 3
See also DLB 37

Tynan, Katharine 1861-1931 . . . . TCLC 3
See also CA 104; DLB 153

Tyutchev, Fyodor 1803-1873 . . . . . NCLC 34

Tzara, Tristan
1896-1963 . . . . . . CLC 47; DAM POET
See also Rosenfeld, Samuel; Rosenstock,
Sami; Rosenstock, Samuel
See also CA 153

Uhry, Alfred
1936- . . . . . CLC 55; DAM DRAM, POP
See also CA 127; 133; INT 133

Ulf, Haerved
See Strindberg, (Johan) August

Ulf, Harved
See Strindberg, (Johan) August

Ulibarri, Sabine R(eyes)
1919- . . . . CLC 83; DAM MULT
See also CA 131; DLB 82; HW

Unamuno (y Jugo), Miguel de
1864-1936 . . . TCLC 2, 9; DAM MULT,
NOV; HLC; SSC 11
See also CA 104; 131; DLB 108; HW;
MTCW

Undercliffe, Errol
See Campbell, (John) Ramsey

Underwood, Miles
See Glassco, John

Undset, Sigrid
1882-1949 . . . . TCLC 3; DA; DAB;
DAC; DAM MST, NOV; WLC
See also CA 104; 129; MTCW

Ungaretti, Giuseppe
1888-1970 . . . . CLC 7, 11, 15
See also CA 19-20; 25-28R; CAP 2;
DLB 114

Unger, Douglas 1952- . . . . CLC 34
See also CA 130

Unsworth, Barry (Forster) 1930- . . . . CLC 76
See also CA 25-28R; CANR 30, 54

Updike, John (Hoyer)
1932- . . . . . . CLC 1, 2, 3, 5, 7, 9, 13, 15,
23, 34, 43, 70; DA; DAB; DAC;
DAM MST, NOV, POET, POP;
SSC 13; WLC
See also CA 1-4R; CABS 1; CANR 4, 33,
51; CDALB 1968-1988; DLB 2, 5, 143;
DLBD 3; DLBY 80, 82; MTCW

Upshaw, Margaret Mitchell
See Mitchell, Margaret (Munnerlyn)

Upton, Mark
See Sanders, Lawrence

Urdang, Constance (Henriette)
1922- . . . . CLC 47
See also CA 21-24R; CANR 9, 24

Uriel, Henry
See Faust, Frederick (Schiller)

Uris, Leon (Marcus)
1924- . . . . CLC 7, 32; DAM NOV, POP
See also AITN 1, 2; BEST 89:2; CA 1-4R;
CANR 1, 40; MTCW; SATA 49

Urmuz
See Codrescu, Andrei

Urquhart, Jane 1949- . . . . CLC 90; DAC
See also CA 113; CANR 32

Ustinov, Peter (Alexander) 1921- . . . . CLC 1
See also AITN 1; CA 13-16R; CANR 25,
51; DLB 13

Vaculik, Ludvik 1926- . . . . CLC 7
See also CA 53-56

Valdez, Luis (Miguel)
1940- . . . . . CLC 84; DAM MULT; HLC
See also CA 101; CANR 32; DLB 122; HW

Valenzuela, Luisa
1938- . . . CLC 31; DAM MULT; SSC 14
See also CA 101; CANR 32; DLB 113; HW

Valera y Alcala-Galiano, Juan
1824-1905 . . . . TCLC 10
See also CA 106

Valery, (Ambroise) Paul (Toussaint Jules)
1871-1945 . . . . TCLC 4, 15;
DAM POET; PC 9
See also CA 104; 122; MTCW

Valle-Inclan, Ramon (Maria) del
1866-1936 . . . . . TCLC 5; DAM MULT;
HLC
See also CA 106; 153; DLB 134

Vallejo, Antonio Buero
See Buero Vallejo, Antonio

Vallejo, Cesar (Abraham)
1892-1938 . . . . TCLC 3, 56;
DAM MULT; HLC
See also CA 105; 153; HW

Vallette, Marguerite Eymery
See Rachilde

Valle Y Pena, Ramon del
See Valle-Inclan, Ramon (Maria) del

Van Ash, Cay 1918- . . . . CLC 34

Vanbrugh, Sir John
1664-1726 . . . . LC 21; DAM DRAM
See also DLB 80

Van Campen, Karl
See Campbell, John W(ood, Jr.)

Vance, Gerald
See Silverberg, Robert

Vance, Jack . . . . CLC 35
See also Vance, John Holbrook
See also DLB 8

Vance, John Holbrook 1916-
See Queen, Ellery; Vance, Jack
See also CA 29-32R; CANR 17; MTCW

Van Den Bogarde, Derek Jules Gaspard Ulric
Niven 1921-
See Bogarde, Dirk
See also CA 77-80

Vandenburgh, Jane . . . . CLC 59

Vanderhaeghe, Guy 1951- . . . . CLC 41
See also CA 113

van der Post, Laurens (Jan) 1906- . . . CLC 5
See also CA 5-8R; CANR 35

van de Wetering, Janwillem 1931- . . CLC 47
See also CA 49-52; CANR 4

Van Dine, S. S. . . . . TCLC 23
See also Wright, Willard Huntington

Van Doren, Carl (Clinton)
1885-1950 . . . . TCLC 18
See also CA 111

Van Doren, Mark 1894-1972 . . . . . CLC 6, 10
See also CA 1-4R; 37-40R; CANR 3;
DLB 45; MTCW

Wagner, Richard 1813-1883....... NCLC 9
See also DLB 129

Wagner-Martin, Linda 1936-....... CLC 50

Wagoner, David (Russell)
1926-.................... CLC 3, 5, 15
See also CA 1-4R; CAAS 3; CANR 2;
DLB 5; SATA 14

Wah, Fred(erick James) 1939-...... CLC 44
See also CA 107; 141; DLB 60

Wahloo, Per 1926-1975 .... CLC 7
See also CA 61-64

Wahloo, Peter
See Wahloo, Per

Wain, John (Barrington)
1925-1994 .... CLC 2, 11, 15, 46
See also CA 5-8R; 145; CAAS 4; CANR 23,
54; CDBLB 1960 to Present; DLB 15, 27,
139, 155; MTCW

Wajda, Andrzej 1926-............. CLC 16
See also CA 102

Wakefield, Dan 1932-.............. CLC 7
See also CA 21-24R; CAAS 7

Wakoski, Diane
1937-........... CLC 2, 4, 7, 9, 11, 40;
DAM POET; PC 15
See also CA 13-16R; CAAS 1; CANR 9;
DLB 5; INT CANR-9

Wakoski-Sherbell, Diane
See Wakoski, Diane

Walcott, Derek (Alton)
1930-.... CLC 2, 4, 9, 14, 25, 42, 67, 76;
BLC; DAB; DAC; DAM MST, MULT,
POET
See also BW 2; CA 89-92; CANR 26, 47;
DLB 117; DLBY 81; MTCW

Waldman, Anne 1945-.............. CLC 7
See also CA 37-40R; CAAS 17; CANR 34;
DLB 16

Waldo, E. Hunter
See Sturgeon, Theodore (Hamilton)

Waldo, Edward Hamilton
See Sturgeon, Theodore (Hamilton)

Walker, Alice (Malsenior)
1944-....... CLC 5, 6, 9, 19, 27, 46, 58;
BLC; DA; DAB; DAC; DAM MST,
MULT, NOV, POET, POP; SSC 5
See also AAYA 3; BEST 89:4; BW 2;
CA 37-40R; CANR 9, 27, 49;
CDALB 1968-1988; DLB 6, 33, 143;
INT CANR-27; MTCW; SATA 31

Walker, David Harry 1911-1992.... CLC 14
See also CA 1-4R; 137; CANR 1; SATA 8;
SATA-Obit 71

Walker, Edward Joseph 1934-
See Walker, Ted
See also CA 21-24R; CANR 12, 28, 53

Walker, George F.
1947-........ CLC 44, 61; DAB; DAC;
DAM MST
See also CA 103; CANR 21, 43; DLB 60

Walker, Joseph A.
1935-.... CLC 19; DAM DRAM, MST
See also BW 1; CA 89-92; CANR 26;
DLB 38

Walker, Margaret (Abigail)
1915-.... CLC 1, 6; BLC; DAM MULT
See also BW 2; CA 73-76; CANR 26, 54;
DLB 76, 152; MTCW

Walker, Ted..................... CLC 13
See also Walker, Edward Joseph
See also DLB 40

Wallace, David Foster 1962-....... CLC 50
See also CA 132

Wallace, Dexter
See Masters, Edgar Lee

Wallace, (Richard Horatio) Edgar
1875-1932 .... TCLC 57
See also CA 115; DLB 70

Wallace, Irving
1916-1990 ..... CLC 7, 13; DAM NOV,
POP
See also AITN 1; CA 1-4R; 132; CAAS 1;
CANR 1, 27; INT CANR-27; MTCW

Wallant, Edward Lewis
1926-1962 .... CLC 5, 10
See also CA 1-4R; CANR 22; DLB 2, 28,
143; MTCW

Walley, Byron
See Card, Orson Scott

Walpole, Horace 1717-1797......... LC 2
See also DLB 39, 104

Walpole, Hugh (Seymour)
1884-1941 .... TCLC 5
See also CA 104; DLB 34

Walser, Martin 1927-............. CLC 27
See also CA 57-60; CANR 8, 46; DLB 75,
124

Walser, Robert
1878-1956 .... TCLC 18; SSC 20
See also CA 118; DLB 66

Walsh, Jill Paton................ CLC 35
See also Paton Walsh, Gillian
See also AAYA 11; CLR 2; DLB 161;
SAAS 3

Walter, Villiam Christian
See Andersen, Hans Christian

Wambaugh, Joseph (Aloysius, Jr.)
1937-.... CLC 3, 18; DAM NOV, POP
See also AITN 1; BEST 89:3; CA 33-36R;
CANR 42; DLB 6; DLBY 83; MTCW

Ward, Arthur Henry Sarsfield 1883-1959
See Rohmer, Sax
See also CA 108

Ward, Douglas Turner 1930-....... CLC 19
See also BW 1; CA 81-84; CANR 27;
DLB 7, 38

Ward, Mary Augusta
See Ward, Mrs. Humphry

Ward, Mrs. Humphry
1851-1920 .... TCLC 55
See also DLB 18

Ward, Peter
See Faust, Frederick (Schiller)

Warhol, Andy 1928(?)-1987........ CLC 20
See also AAYA 12; BEST 89:4; CA 89-92;
121; CANR 34

Warner, Francis (Robert le Plastrier)
1937-..................... CLC 14
See also CA 53-56; CANR 11

Warner, Marina 1946-............. CLC 59
See also CA 65-68; CANR 21, 55

Warner, Rex (Ernest) 1905-1986.... CLC 45
See also CA 89-92; 119; DLB 15

Warner, Susan (Bogert)
1819-1885 .... NCLC 31
See also DLB 3, 42

Warner, Sylvia (Constance) Ashton
See Ashton-Warner, Sylvia (Constance)

Warner, Sylvia Townsend
1893-1978 .... CLC 7, 19; SSC 23
See also CA 61-64; 77-80; CANR 16;
DLB 34, 139; MTCW

Warren, Mercy Otis 1728-1814... NCLC 13
See also DLB 31

Warren, Robert Penn
1905-1989 .... CLC 1, 4, 6, 8, 10, 13, 18,
39, 53, 59; DA; DAB; DAC; DAM MST,
NOV, POET; SSC 4; WLC
See also AITN 1; CA 13-16R; 129;
CANR 10, 47; CDALB 1968-1988;
DLB 2, 48, 152; DLBY 80, 89;
INT CANR-10; MTCW; SATA 46;
SATA-Obit 63

Warshofsky, Isaac
See Singer, Isaac Bashevis

Warton, Thomas
1728-1790 .... LC 15; DAM POET
See also DLB 104, 109

Waruk, Kona
See Harris, (Theodore) Wilson

Warung, Price 1855-1911........ TCLC 45

Warwick, Jarvis
See Garner, Hugh

Washington, Alex
See Harris, Mark

Washington, Booker T(aliaferro)
1856-1915 .... TCLC 10; BLC;
DAM MULT
See also BW 1; CA 114; 125; SATA 28

Washington, George 1732-1799...... LC 25
See also DLB 31

Wassermann, (Karl) Jakob
1873-1934 .... TCLC 6
See also CA 104; DLB 66

Wasserstein, Wendy
1950-................ CLC 32, 59, 90;
DAM DRAM; DC 4
See also CA 121; 129; CABS 3; CANR 53;
INT 129

Waterhouse, Keith (Spencer)
1929-..................... CLC 47
See also CA 5-8R; CANR 38; DLB 13, 15;
MTCW

Waters, Frank (Joseph)
1902-1995 .... CLC 88
See also CA 5-8R; 149; CAAS 13; CANR 3,
18; DLBY 86

Waters, Roger 1944-.............. CLC 35

Watkins, Frances Ellen
See Harper, Frances Ellen Watkins

Watkins, Gerrold
See Malzberg, Barry N(athaniel)

Watkins, Gloria 1955(?)-
See hooks, bell
See also BW 2; CA 143

Watkins, Paul 1964-.............. **CLC 55**
See also CA 132

Watkins, Vernon Phillips
1906-1967 .... **CLC 43**
See also CA 9-10; 25-28R; CAP 1; DLB 20

Watson, Irving S.
See Mencken, H(enry) L(ouis)

Watson, John H.
See Farmer, Philip Jose

Watson, Richard F.
See Silverberg, Robert

Waugh, Auberon (Alexander) 1939-.. **CLC 7**
See also CA 45-48; CANR 6, 22; DLB 14

Waugh, Evelyn (Arthur St. John)
1903-1966 ...... **CLC 1, 3, 8, 13, 19, 27, 44; DA; DAB; DAC; DAM MST, NOV, POP; WLC**
See also CA 85-88; 25-28R; CANR 22; CDBLB 1914-1945; DLB 15, 162; MTCW

Waugh, Harriet 1944- .... **CLC 6**
See also CA 85-88; CANR 22

Ways, C. R.
See Blount, Roy (Alton), Jr.

Waystaff, Simon
See Swift, Jonathan

Webb, (Martha) Beatrice (Potter)
1858-1943 .... **TCLC 22**
See also Potter, Beatrice
See also CA 117

Webb, Charles (Richard) 1939-...... **CLC 7**
See also CA 25-28R

Webb, James H(enry), Jr. 1946-.... **CLC 22**
See also CA 81-84

Webb, Mary (Gladys Meredith)
1881-1927 .... **TCLC 24**
See also CA 123; DLB 34

Webb, Mrs. Sidney
See Webb, (Martha) Beatrice (Potter)

Webb, Phyllis 1927-.............. **CLC 18**
See also CA 104; CANR 23; DLB 53

Webb, Sidney (James)
1859-1947 .... **TCLC 22**
See also CA 117

Webber, Andrew Lloyd............. **CLC 21**
See also Lloyd Webber, Andrew

Weber, Lenora Mattingly
1895-1971 .... **CLC 12**
See also CA 19-20; 29-32R; CAP 1; SATA 2; SATA-Obit 26

Webster, John
1579(?)-1634(?) ...... **LC 33; DA; DAB; DAC; DAM DRAM, MST; DC 2; WLC**
See also CDBLB Before 1660; DLB 58

Webster, Noah 1758-1843 .... **NCLC 30**

Wedekind, (Benjamin) Frank(lin)
1864-1918 ...... **TCLC 7; DAM DRAM**
See also CA 104; 153; DLB 118

Weidman, Jerome 1913-............ **CLC 7**
See also AITN 2; CA 1-4R; CANR 1; DLB 28

Weil, Simone (Adolphine)
1909-1943 .... **TCLC 23**
See also CA 117

Weinstein, Nathan
See West, Nathanael

Weinstein, Nathan von Wallenstein
See West, Nathanael

Weir, Peter (Lindsay) 1944- .... **CLC 20**
See also CA 113; 123

Weiss, Peter (Ulrich)
1916-1982 .... **CLC 3, 15, 51; DAM DRAM**
See also CA 45-48; 106; CANR 3; DLB 69, 124

Weiss, Theodore (Russell)
1916-.................. **CLC 3, 8, 14**
See also CA 9-12R; CAAS 2; CANR 46; DLB 5

Welch, (Maurice) Denton
1915-1948 .... **TCLC 22**
See also CA 121; 148

Welch, James
1940-..... **CLC 6, 14, 52; DAM MULT, POP**
See also CA 85-88; CANR 42; NNAL

Weldon, Fay
1933-......... **CLC 6, 9, 11, 19, 36, 59; DAM POP**
See also CA 21-24R; CANR 16, 46; CDBLB 1960 to Present; DLB 14; INT CANR-16; MTCW

Wellek, Rene 1903-1995.......... **CLC 28**
See also CA 5-8R; 150; CAAS 7; CANR 8; DLB 63; INT CANR-8

Weller, Michael 1942-......... **CLC 10, 53**
See also CA 85-88

Weller, Paul 1958-............... **CLC 26**

Wellershoff, Dieter 1925-.......... **CLC 46**
See also CA 89-92; CANR 16, 37

Welles, (George) Orson
1915-1985 .... **CLC 20, 80**
See also CA 93-96; 117

Wellman, Mac 1945- .... **CLC 65**

Wellman, Manly Wade 1903-1986 .. **CLC 49**
See also CA 1-4R; 118; CANR 6, 16, 44; SATA 6; SATA-Obit 47

Wells, Carolyn 1869(?)-1942 ...... **TCLC 35**
See also CA 113; DLB 11

Wells, H(erbert) G(eorge)
1866-1946 .... **TCLC 6, 12, 19; DA; DAB; DAC; DAM MST, NOV; SSC 6; WLC**
See also AAYA 18; CA 110; 121; CDBLB 1914-1945; DLB 34, 70, 156; MTCW; SATA 20

Wells, Rosemary 1943-........... **CLC 12**
See also AAYA 13; CA 85-88; CANR 48; CLR 16; MAICYA; SAAS 1; SATA 18, 69

Welty, Eudora
1909- ...... **CLC 1, 2, 5, 14, 22, 33; DA; DAB; DAC; DAM MST, NOV; SSC 1; WLC**
See also CA 9-12R; CABS 1; CANR 32; CDALB 1941-1968; DLB 2, 102, 143; DLBD 12; DLBY 87; MTCW

Wen I-to 1899-1946 .... **TCLC 28**

Wentworth, Robert
See Hamilton, Edmond

Werfel, Franz (V.) 1890-1945 ...... **TCLC 8**
See also CA 104; DLB 81, 124

Wergeland, Henrik Arnold
1808-1845 .... **NCLC 5**

Wersba, Barbara 1932-.......... **CLC 30**
See also AAYA 2; CA 29-32R; CANR 16, 38; CLR 3; DLB 52; JRDA; MAICYA; SAAS 2; SATA 1, 58

Wertmueller, Lina 1928- .... **CLC 16**
See also CA 97-100; CANR 39

Wescott, Glenway 1901-1987....... **CLC 13**
See also CA 13-16R; 121; CANR 23; DLB 4, 9, 102

Wesker, Arnold
1932- .... **CLC 3, 5, 42; DAB; DAM DRAM**
See also CA 1-4R; CAAS 7; CANR 1, 33; CDBLB 1960 to Present; DLB 13; MTCW

Wesley, Richard (Errol) 1945-...... **CLC 7**
See also BW 1; CA 57-60; CANR 27; DLB 38

Wessel, Johan Herman 1742-1785 .... **LC 7**

West, Anthony (Panther)
1914-1987 .... **CLC 50**
See also CA 45-48; 124; CANR 3, 19; DLB 15

West, C. P.
See Wodehouse, P(elham) G(renville)

West, (Mary) Jessamyn
1902-1984 .... **CLC 7, 17**
See also CA 9-12R; 112; CANR 27; DLB 6; DLBY 84; MTCW; SATA-Obit 37

West, Morris L(anglo) 1916-..... **CLC 6, 33**
See also CA 5-8R; CANR 24, 49; MTCW

West, Nathanael
1903-1940 ..... **TCLC 1, 14, 44; SSC 16**
See also CA 104; 125; CDALB 1929-1941; DLB 4, 9, 28; MTCW

West, Owen
See Koontz, Dean R(ay)

West, Paul 1930- .... **CLC 7, 14, 96**
See also CA 13-16R; CAAS 7; CANR 22, 53; DLB 14; INT CANR-22

West, Rebecca 1892-1983 .. **CLC 7, 9, 31, 50**
See also CA 5-8R; 109; CANR 19; DLB 36; DLBY 83; MTCW

Westall, Robert (Atkinson)
1929-1993 .... **CLC 17**
See also AAYA 12; CA 69-72; 141; CANR 18; CLR 13; JRDA; MAICYA; SAAS 2; SATA 23, 69; SATA-Obit 75

Westlake, Donald E(dwin)
1933- .... **CLC 7, 33; DAM POP**
See also CA 17-20R; CAAS 13; CANR 16, 44; INT CANR-16

Westmacott, Mary
See Christie, Agatha (Mary Clarissa)

Weston, Allen
See Norton, Andre

Wetcheek, J. L.
See Feuchtwanger, Lion

Wetering, Janwillem van de
See van de Wetering, Janwillem

Wetherell, Elizabeth
See Warner, Susan (Bogert)

Whale, James 1889-1957 . . . . TCLC 63

Whalen, Philip 1923- . . . . CLC 6, 29
See also CA 9-12R; CANR 5, 39; DLB 16

Wharton, Edith (Newbold Jones)
1862-1937 . . . . . . TCLC 3, 9, 27, 53; DA;
DAB; DAC; DAM MST, NOV; SSC 6;
WLC
See also CA 104; 132; CDALB 1865-1917;
DLB 4, 9, 12, 78; DLBD 13; MTCW

Wharton, James
See Mencken, H(enry) L(ouis)

Wharton, William (a pseudonym)
. . . . CLC 18, 37
See also CA 93-96; DLBY 80; INT 93-96

Wheatley (Peters), Phillis
1754(?)-1784 . . . . LC 3; BLC; DA; DAC;
DAM MST, MULT, POET; PC 3; WLC
See also CDALB 1640-1865; DLB 31, 50

Wheelock, John Hall 1886-1978 . . . . CLC 14
See also CA 13-16R; 77-80; CANR 14;
DLB 45

White, E(lwyn) B(rooks)
1899-1985 . . CLC 10, 34, 39; DAM POP
See also AITN 2; CA 13-16R; 116;
CANR 16, 37; CLR 1, 21; DLB 11, 22;
MAICYA; MTCW; SATA 2, 29;
SATA-Obit 44

White, Edmund (Valentine III)
1940- . . . . CLC 27; DAM POP
See also AAYA 7; CA 45-48; CANR 3, 19,
36; MTCW

White, Patrick (Victor Martindale)
1912-1990 . . CLC 3, 4, 5, 7, 9, 18, 65, 69
See also CA 81-84; 132; CANR 43; MTCW

White, Phyllis Dorothy James 1920-
See James, P. D.
See also CA 21-24R; CANR 17, 43;
DAM POP; MTCW

White, T(erence) H(anbury)
1906-1964 . . . . CLC 30
See also CA 73-76; CANR 37; DLB 160;
JRDA; MAICYA; SATA 12

White, Terence de Vere
1912-1994 . . . . CLC 49
See also CA 49-52; 145; CANR 3

White, Walter F(rancis)
1893-1955 . . . . TCLC 15
See also White, Walter
See also BW 1; CA 115; 124; DLB 51

White, William Hale 1831-1913
See Rutherford, Mark
See also CA 121

Whitehead, E(dward) A(nthony)
1933- . . . . CLC 5
See also CA 65-68

Whitemore, Hugh (John) 1936- . . . . . CLC 37
See also CA 132; INT 132

Whitman, Sarah Helen (Power)
1803-1878 . . . . NCLC 19
See also DLB 1

Whitman, Walt(er)
1819-1892 . . . . . NCLC 4, 31; DA; DAB;
DAC; DAM MST, POET; PC 3; WLC
See also CDALB 1640-1865; DLB 3, 64;
SATA 20

Whitney, Phyllis A(yame)
1903- . . . . CLC 42; DAM POP
See also AITN 2; BEST 90:3; CA 1-4R;
CANR 3, 25, 38; JRDA; MAICYA;
SATA 1, 30

Whittemore, (Edward) Reed (Jr.)
1919- . . . . CLC 4
See also CA 9-12R; CAAS 8; CANR 4;
DLB 5

Whittier, John Greenleaf
1807-1892 . . . . NCLC 8
See also DLB 1

Whittlebot, Hernia
See Coward, Noel (Peirce)

Wicker, Thomas Grey 1926-
See Wicker, Tom
See also CA 65-68; CANR 21, 46

Wicker, Tom . . . . CLC 7
See also Wicker, Thomas Grey

Wideman, John Edgar
1941- . . . . CLC 5, 34, 36, 67; BLC;
DAM MULT
See also BW 2; CA 85-88; CANR 14, 42;
DLB 33, 143

Wiebe, Rudy (Henry)
1934- . . . . CLC 6, 11, 14; DAC;
DAM MST
See also CA 37-40R; CANR 42; DLB 60

Wieland, Christoph Martin
1733-1813 . . . . NCLC 17
See also DLB 97

Wiene, Robert 1881-1938 . . . . TCLC 56

Wieners, John 1934- . . . . CLC 7
See also CA 13-16R; DLB 16

Wiesel, Elie(zer)
1928- . . . . . . CLC 3, 5, 11, 37; DA; DAB;
DAC; DAM MST, NOV
See also AAYA 7; AITN 1; CA 5-8R;
CAAS 4; CANR 8, 40; DLB 83;
DLBY 87; INT CANR-8; MTCW;
SATA 56

Wiggins, Marianne 1947- . . . . CLC 57
See also BEST 89:3; CA 130

Wight, James Alfred 1916-
See Herriot, James
See also CA 77-80; SATA 55;
SATA-Brief 44

Wilbur, Richard (Purdy)
1921- . . . CLC 3, 6, 9, 14, 53; DA; DAB;
DAC; DAM MST, POET
See also CA 1-4R; CABS 2; CANR 2, 29;
DLB 5, 169; INT CANR-29; MTCW;
SATA 9

Wild, Peter 1940- . . . . CLC 14
See also CA 37-40R; DLB 5

Wilde, Oscar (Fingal O'Flahertie Wills)
1854(?)-1900 . . . . TCLC 1, 8, 23, 41; DA;
DAB; DAC; DAM DRAM, MST, NOV;
SSC 11; WLC
See also CA 104; 119; CDBLB 1890-1914;
DLB 10, 19, 34, 57, 141, 156; SATA 24

Wilder, Billy . . . . CLC 20
See also Wilder, Samuel
See also DLB 26

Wilder, Samuel 1906-
See Wilder, Billy
See also CA 89-92

Wilder, Thornton (Niven)
1897-1975 . . . . . . CLC 1, 5, 6, 10, 15, 35,
82; DA; DAB; DAC; DAM DRAM,
MST, NOV; DC 1; WLC
See also AITN 2; CA 13-16R; 61-64;
CANR 40; DLB 4, 7, 9; MTCW

Wilding, Michael 1942- . . . . CLC 73
See also CA 104; CANR 24, 49

Wiley, Richard 1944- . . . . CLC 44
See also CA 121; 129

Wilhelm, Kate . . . . CLC 7
See also Wilhelm, Katie Gertrude
See also CAAS 5; DLB 8; INT CANR-17

Wilhelm, Katie Gertrude 1928-
See Wilhelm, Kate
See also CA 37-40R; CANR 17, 36; MTCW

Wilkins, Mary
See Freeman, Mary Eleanor Wilkins

Willard, Nancy 1936- . . . . CLC 7, 37
See also CA 89-92; CANR 10, 39; CLR 5;
DLB 5, 52; MAICYA; MTCW;
SATA 37, 71; SATA-Brief 30

Williams, C(harles) K(enneth)
1936- . . . . CLC 33, 56; DAM POET
See also CA 37-40R; DLB 5

Williams, Charles
See Collier, James L(incoln)

Williams, Charles (Walter Stansby)
1886-1945 . . . . TCLC 1, 11
See also CA 104; DLB 100, 153

Williams, (George) Emlyn
1905-1987 . . . . . . CLC 15; DAM DRAM
See also CA 104; 123; CANR 36; DLB 10,
77; MTCW

Williams, Hugo 1942- . . . . CLC 42
See also CA 17-20R; CANR 45; DLB 40

Williams, J. Walker
See Wodehouse, P(elham) G(renville)

Williams, John A(lfred)
1925- . . . CLC 5, 13; BLC; DAM MULT
See also BW 2; CA 53-56; CAAS 3;
CANR 6, 26, 51; DLB 2, 33;
INT CANR-6

Williams, Jonathan (Chamberlain)
1929- . . . . CLC 13
See also CA 9-12R; CAAS 12; CANR 8;
DLB 5

Williams, Joy 1944- . . . . CLC 31
See also CA 41-44R; CANR 22, 48

Williams, Norman 1952- . . . . CLC 39
See also CA 118

Williams, Sherley Anne
1944- . . . . . CLC 89; BLC; DAM MULT,
POET
See also BW 2; CA 73-76; CANR 25;
DLB 41; INT CANR-25; SATA 78

Williams, Shirley
See Williams, Sherley Anne

Williams, Tennessee
1911-1983 ..... **CLC 1, 2, 5, 7, 8, 11, 15, 19, 30, 39, 45, 71; DA; DAB; DAC; DAM DRAM, MST; DC 4; WLC**
See also AITN 1, 2; CA 5-8R; 108; CABS 3; CANR 31; CDALB 1941-1968; DLB 7; DLBD 4; DLBY 83; MTCW

Williams, Thomas (Alonzo)
1926-1990 .... **CLC 14**
See also CA 1-4R; 132; CANR 2

Williams, William C.
See Williams, William Carlos

Williams, William Carlos
1883-1963 .... **CLC 1, 2, 5, 9, 13, 22, 42, 67; DA; DAB; DAC; DAM MST, POET; PC 7**
See also CA 89-92; CANR 34; CDALB 1917-1929; DLB 4, 16, 54, 86; MTCW

Williamson, David (Keith) 1942-.... **CLC 56**
See also CA 103; CANR 41

Williamson, Ellen Douglas 1905-1984
See Douglas, Ellen
See also CA 17-20R; 114; CANR 39

Williamson, Jack................... **CLC 29**
See also Williamson, John Stewart
See also CAAS 8; DLB 8

Williamson, John Stewart 1908-
See Williamson, Jack
See also CA 17-20R; CANR 23

Willie, Frederick
See Lovecraft, H(oward) P(hillips)

Willingham, Calder (Baynard, Jr.)
1922-1995 .... **CLC 5, 51**
See also CA 5-8R; 147; CANR 3; DLB 2, 44; MTCW

Willis, Charles
See Clarke, Arthur C(harles)

Willy
See Colette, (Sidonie-Gabrielle)

Willy, Colette
See Colette, (Sidonie-Gabrielle)

Wilson, A(ndrew) N(orman) 1950- .. **CLC 33**
See also CA 112; 122; DLB 14, 155

Wilson, Angus (Frank Johnstone)
1913-1991 .. **CLC 2, 3, 5, 25, 34; SSC 21**
See also CA 5-8R; 134; CANR 21; DLB 15, 139, 155; MTCW

Wilson, August
1945- .... **CLC 39, 50, 63; BLC; DA; DAB; DAC; DAM DRAM, MST, MULT; DC 2**
See also AAYA 16; BW 2; CA 115; 122; CANR 42, 54; MTCW

Wilson, Brian 1942-............. **CLC 12**

Wilson, Colin 1931-............ **CLC 3, 14**
See also CA 1-4R; CAAS 5; CANR 1, 22, 33; DLB 14; MTCW

Wilson, Dirk
See Pohl, Frederik

Wilson, Edmund
1895-1972 .... **CLC 1, 2, 3, 8, 24**
See also CA 1-4R; 37-40R; CANR 1, 46; DLB 63; MTCW

Wilson, Ethel Davis (Bryant)
1888(?)-1980 .... **CLC 13; DAC; DAM POET**
See also CA 102; DLB 68; MTCW

Wilson, John 1785-1854......... **NCLC 5**

Wilson, John (Anthony) Burgess 1917-1993
See Burgess, Anthony
See also CA 1-4R; 143; CANR 2, 46; DAC; DAM NOV; MTCW

Wilson, Lanford
1937- ..... **CLC 7, 14, 36; DAM DRAM**
See also CA 17-20R; CABS 3; CANR 45; DLB 7

Wilson, Robert M. 1944-........ **CLC 7, 9**
See also CA 49-52; CANR 2, 41; MTCW

Wilson, Robert McLiam 1964-..... **CLC 59**
See also CA 132

Wilson, Sloan 1920-.............. **CLC 32**
See also CA 1-4R; CANR 1, 44

Wilson, Snoo 1948-.............. **CLC 33**
See also CA 69-72

Wilson, William S(mith) 1932- ..... **CLC 49**
See also CA 81-84

Winchilsea, Anne (Kingsmill) Finch Counte
1661-1720 .... **LC 3**

Windham, Basil
See Wodehouse, P(elham) G(renville)

Wingrove, David (John) 1954-...... **CLC 68**
See also CA 133

Winters, Janet Lewis .... **CLC 41**
See also Lewis, Janet
See also DLBY 87

Winters, (Arthur) Yvor
1900-1968 .... **CLC 4, 8, 32**
See also CA 11-12; 25-28R; CAP 1; DLB 48; MTCW

Winterson, Jeanette
1959- .... **CLC 64; DAM POP**
See also CA 136

Winthrop, John 1588-1649......... **LC 31**
See also DLB 24, 30

Wiseman, Frederick 1930-........ **CLC 20**

Wister, Owen 1860-1938 .... **TCLC 21**
See also CA 108; DLB 9, 78; SATA 62

Witkacy
See Witkiewicz, Stanislaw Ignacy

Witkiewicz, Stanislaw Ignacy
1885-1939 .... **TCLC 8**
See also CA 105

Wittgenstein, Ludwig (Josef Johann)
1889-1951 .... **TCLC 59**
See also CA 113

Wittig, Monique 1935(?)-.......... **CLC 22**
See also CA 116; 135; DLB 83

Wittlin, Jozef 1896-1976 .... **CLC 25**
See also CA 49-52; 65-68; CANR 3

Wodehouse, P(elham) G(renville)
1881-1975 ... **CLC 1, 2, 5, 10, 22; DAB; DAC; DAM NOV; SSC 2**
See also AITN 2; CA 45-48; 57-60; CANR 3, 33; CDBLB 1914-1945; DLB 34, 162; MTCW; SATA 22

Woiwode, L.
See Woiwode, Larry (Alfred)

Woiwode, Larry (Alfred) 1941-.... **CLC 6, 10**
See also CA 73-76; CANR 16; DLB 6; INT CANR-16

Wojciechowska, Maia (Teresa)
1927- .... **CLC 26**
See also AAYA 8; CA 9-12R; CANR 4, 41; CLR 1; JRDA; MAICYA; SAAS 1; SATA 1, 28, 83

Wolf, Christa 1929- .... **CLC 14, 29, 58**
See also CA 85-88; CANR 45; DLB 75; MTCW

Wolfe, Gene (Rodman)
1931- .... **CLC 25; DAM POP**
See also CA 57-60; CAAS 9; CANR 6, 32; DLB 8

Wolfe, George C. 1954-........... **CLC 49**
See also CA 149

Wolfe, Thomas (Clayton)
1900-1938 .... **TCLC 4, 13, 29, 61; DA; DAB; DAC; DAM MST, NOV; WLC**
See also CA 104; 132; CDALB 1929-1941; DLB 9, 102; DLBD 2; DLBY 85; MTCW

Wolfe, Thomas Kennerly, Jr. 1931-
See Wolfe, Tom
See also CA 13-16R; CANR 9, 33; DAM POP; INT CANR-9; MTCW

Wolfe, Tom .... **CLC 1, 2, 9, 15, 35, 51**
See also Wolfe, Thomas Kennerly, Jr.
See also AAYA 8; AITN 2; BEST 89:1; DLB 152

Wolff, Geoffrey (Ansell) 1937- ..... **CLC 41**
See also CA 29-32R; CANR 29, 43

Wolff, Sonia
See Levitin, Sonia (Wolff)

Wolff, Tobias (Jonathan Ansell)
1945- .... **CLC 39, 64**
See also AAYA 16; BEST 90:2; CA 114; 117; CAAS 22; CANR 54; DLB 130; INT 117

Wolfram von Eschenbach
c. 1170-c. 1220 .... **CMLC 5**
See also DLB 138

Wolitzer, Hilma 1930-............ **CLC 17**
See also CA 65-68; CANR 18, 40; INT CANR-18; SATA 31

Wollstonecraft, Mary 1759-1797...... **LC 5**
See also CDBLB 1789-1832; DLB 39, 104, 158

Wonder, Stevie .... **CLC 12**
See also Morris, Steveland Judkins

Wong, Jade Snow 1922-.......... **CLC 17**
See also CA 109

Woodcott, Keith
See Brunner, John (Kilian Houston)

Woodruff, Robert W.
See Mencken, H(enry) L(ouis)

Woolf, (Adeline) Virginia
1882-1941 .... **TCLC 1, 5, 20, 43, 56; DA; DAB; DAC; DAM MST, NOV; SSC 7; WLC**
See also CA 104; 130; CDBLB 1914-1945; DLB 36, 100, 162; DLBD 10; MTCW

Woollcott, Alexander (Humphreys)
1887-1943 .... **TCLC 5**
See also CA 105; DLB 29

Zhukovsky, Vasily 1783-1852 . . . . **NCLC 35**

Ziegenhagen, Eric . . . . **CLC 55**

Zimmer, Jill Schary
See Robinson, Jill

Zimmerman, Robert
See Dylan, Bob

Zindel, Paul
1936- . . . . . **CLC 6, 26; DA; DAB; DAC;**
DAM DRAM, MST, NOV; DC 5
See also AAYA 2; CA 73-76; CANR 31;
CLR 3; DLB 7, 52; JRDA; MAICYA;
MTCW; SATA 16, 58

Zinov'Ev, A. A.
See Zinoviev, Alexander (Aleksandrovich)

Zinoviev, Alexander (Aleksandrovich)
1922- . . . . **CLC 19**
See also CA 116; 133; CAAS 10

Zoilus
See Lovecraft, H(oward) P(hillips)

Zola, Emile (Edouard Charles Antoine)
1840-1902 . . . . . . **TCLC 1, 6, 21, 41; DA;**
DAB; DAC; DAM MST, NOV; WLC
See also CA 104; 138; DLB 123

Zoline, Pamela 1941- . . . . **CLC 62**

Zorrilla y Moral, Jose 1817-1893 . . **NCLC 6**

Zoshchenko, Mikhail (Mikhailovich)
1895-1958 . . . . **TCLC 15; SSC 15**
See also CA 115

Zuckmayer, Carl 1896-1977 . . . . **CLC 18**
See also CA 69-72; DLB 56, 124

Zuk, Georges
See Skelton, Robin

Zukofsky, Louis
1904-1978 . . . . **CLC 1, 2, 4, 7, 11, 18;**
DAM POET; PC 11
See also CA 9-12R; 77-80; CANR 39;
DLB 5, 165; MTCW

Zweig, Paul 1935-1984 . . . . **CLC 34, 42**
See also CA 85-88; 113

Zweig, Stefan 1881-1942 . . . . **TCLC 17**
See also CA 112; DLB 81, 118

Literary Criticism Series
Cumulative Topic Index

This index lists all topic entries in Gale's *Classical and Medieval Literature Criticism, Contemporary Literary Criticism, Literature Criticism from 1400 to 1800, Nineteenth-Century Literature Criticism,* and *Twentieth-Century Literary Criticism.*

Topic Index

CMLC Cumulative Nationality Index

CMLC Cumulative Title Index

Title Index

Title Index

Title Index

Title Index

CMLC Cumulative Critic Index

Critic Index

Grahn, Judy
Sappho **3**:494

Grane, Leifn
Abelard **11**:25

Granrud, John E.
Cicero, Marcus Tullius **3**:205

Gransden, Antonia
Anglo-Saxon Chronicle **4**:21

Grant, Michael
Aeschylus **11**:175
Apuleius **1**:26
Cicero, Marcus Tullius **3**:285, 291
Josephus, Flavius **13**:240
Livy **11**:367
Ovid **7**:405
Polybius **17**:176
Thucycdides **17**:296

Graves, Robert
Aeneid **9**:394
Apuleius **1**:20
Iliad **1**:361
Menander **9**:236
Terence **14**:341

Gray, Vivienne
Xenophon **17**:371

Gray, V. J.
Xenophon **17**:369

Gray, Wallace
Iliad **1**:405

Grayson, Christopher
Xenophon **17**:346

Green, D. H.
Hartmann von Aue **15**:206
Wolfram von Eschenbach **5**:391

Green, Peter
Juvenal **8**:68
Ovid **7**:419
Sappho **3**:438

Greenberg, Moshe
The Book of Job **14**:196

Greene, Thomas
Aeneid **9**:399

Greenfield, Concetta Carestia
Petrarch **20**:265

Greenfield, Stanley B.
Beowulf **1**:119
The Dream of the Rood **14**:243

Greenwood, Thomas
Albert the Great **16**:17

Gregory, Eileen
Sappho **3**:495

Grene, David
Aeschylus **11**:220
Herodotus **17**:113
Thucydides **17**:280

Grierson, Herbert J. C.
Beowulf **1**:90

Grieve, Patricia E.
Razon de Amor **16**:364

Griffin, Jasper
Iliad **1**:392
Odyssey **16**:304

Grigson, Geoffrey
Sei Shonagon **6**:300

Grimm, Charles
Chretien de Troyes **10**:141

Groden, Suzy Q.
Sappho **3**:436

Groos, Arthur
Wolfram von Eschenbach **5**:423

Grossman, Judith
Arabian Nights **2**:57

Grossvogel, Steven
Boccaccio, Giovanni **13**:114

Grube, G. M. A.
Aristophanes **4**:136
Cicero, Marcus Tullius **3**:258

Gruffydd, W. J.
Mabinogion **9**:159

Grundy, G. B.
Thucydides **17**:268

Grunmann-Gaudet, Minnette
The Song of Roland **1**:248

Guardini, Romano
Augustine, St. **6**:95
The Book of Psalms **4**:414

Guarino, Guido A.
Boccaccio, Giovanni **13**:52

Gudzy, N. K.
The Igor Tale **1**:485

Gunkel, Hermann
The Book of Psalms **4**:379

Gunn, Alan M. F.
Romance of the Rose **8**:402

Guthrie, W. K. C.
Plato **8**:321, 360

Hackett, Jeremiah M. G.
Bacon, Roger **14**:99, 110

Hadas, Moses
Aeschylus **11**:150
Apuleius **1**:23
Aristophanes **4**:121
Hesiod **5**:98
Juvenal **8**:45
Plato **8**:304
Sappho **3**:417
Seneca, Lucius Annaeus **6**:378, 385

Hagg, Tomas
Longus **7**:262

Haight, Elizabeth Hazelton
Apuleius **1**:18

Haines, C. R.
Sappho **3**:397

Hainsworth, Peter
Petrarch **20**:324

Haley, Lucille
Ovid **7**:310

Hall, David L.
Confucius **19**:88

Hallam, Henry
Bacon, Roger **14**:16
Poem of the Cid **4**:225

Hallberg, Peter
Hrafnkel's Saga **2**:124
Njals saga **13**:339

Hallett, Judith P.
Sappho **3**:465

Halleux, Pierre
Hrafnkel's Saga **2**:99, 102

Halverson, John
Beowulf **1**:131

Hamilton, Edith
Aeschylus **11**:128
Aristophanes **4**:109
Sophocles **2**:328
Terence **14**:322

Hamori, Andras
Arabian Nights **2**:51

Handley, E. W.
Menander **9**:243, 276

Hanford, James Holly
Razon de Amor **16**:337

Hanning, Robert
Marie de France **8**:158

Hanson-Smith, Elizabeth
Mabinogion **9**:192

Haraszti, Zoltan
Mandeville, Sir John **19**:113

Hardison, O. B., Jr.
Mystery of Adam **4**:203

Hardy, E. G.
Juvenal **8**:17

Hardy, Lucy
Boccaccio, Giovanni **13**:30

Harris, Charles
Kalidasa **9**:81

Harrison, Ann Tukey
The Song of Roland **1**:261

Harrison, Robert
The Song of Roland **1**:220

Harsh, Philip Whaley
Menander **9**:216

Hart, Henry H.
Polo, Marco **15**:309

Hart, Thomas R.
Poem of the Cid **4**:306

Hartley, L. P.
Murasaki, Lady **1**:422

Hastings, R.
Boccaccio, Giovanni **13**:59

Hatto, A. T.
Gottfried von Strassburg **10**:259
Das Nibelungenlied **12**:194

Havelock, E. A.
Catullus **18**:91

Havelock, Eric A.
Hesiod **5**:111, 150
Iliad **1**:382, 386

Hay, John
Khayyam **11**:261

Haymes, Edward R.
Das Nibelungenlied **12**:244

Headstrom, Birger R.
Boccaccio, Giovanni **13**:35

Hearn, Lafcadio
Khayyam **11**:258

Hegel, G. W. F.
Aristophanes **4**:46
The Book of Job **14**:157
Inferno **3**:12
Plato **8**:225
Sophocles **2**:297

Heidegger, Martin
Plato **8**:295
Sophocles **2**:376

Heidel, Alexander
Epic of Gilgamesh **3**:310

Heine, Heinrich
Bertran de Born **5**:10

Heinemann, Frederik J.
Hrafnkel's Saga **2**:120, 123

Heiserman, Arthur
Apuleius **1**:46
Longus **7**:254
Xenophon **17**:351

Herder, Johann Gottfried von
The Book of Psalms **4**:355
Kalidasa **9**:102

Herington, John
Aeschylus **11**:210

Critic Index

Critic Index

Critic Index

Vivekananda, Swami
Bhagavad Gita **12**:5

Voltaire, François-Marie Arouet
Aeneid **9**:314
Aristophanes **4**:41
The Book of Job **14**:123
Iliad **1**:288

von Fritz, Kurt
Polybius **17**:160

Vossler, Karl
Inferno **3**:51

Wa, Kathleen Johnson
Lao Tzu **7**:196
Vita Nuova **18**:329

Wailes, Stephen L.
Das Nibelungenlied **12**:231

Walbank, F. W.
Polybius **17**:167

Waldock, A. J. A.
Sophocles **2**:368

Waley, Arthur
Confucius **19**:17
Lao Tzu **7**:128
Li Po **2**:137
Murasaki, Lady **1**:421

Walhouse, Moreton J.
Sappho **3**:385

Waliszewski, K.
The Igor Tale **1**:479

Walker, Roger M.
Razon de Amor **16**:346

Walker, Warren S.
Book of Dede Korkut **8**:98

Wallace, David
Boccaccio, Giovanni **13**:87, 94

Walpole, Horace
Arabian Nights **2**:3

Walsh, George B.
Hesiod **5**:166

Walsh, P. G.
Livy **11**:342, 350

Walshe, M. O'C.
Gottfried von Strassburg **10**:274
Das Nibelungenlied **12**:171
Wolfram von Eschenbach **5**:333

Warburton, William
Apuleius **1**:7

Ward, Benedicta
Bede **20**:102

Warmington, B. H.
Seneca, Lucius Annaeus **6**:395

Warton, Joseph
Inferno **3**:6

Watling, E. F.
Seneca, Lucius Annaeus **6**:387

Watson, Burton
Si Shih **15**:391

Webbe, Joseph
Terence **14**:296

Webbe, William
Ovid **7**:290

Webber, Ruth H.
Poem of the Cid **4**:286

Weber, Alfred
Bacon, Roger **14**:20

Webster, T. B. L.
Callimachus **18**:34
Menander **9**:246

Weigand, Hermann J.
Wolfram von Eschenbach **5**:315, 370

Weil, Simone
Iliad **1**:331

Weiler, Royal W.
Kalidasa **9**:113

Weinberg, Julius R.
Averroes **7**:44
Bacon, Roger **14**:94

Weinberg, S. C.
Layamon **10**:360

Weiss, Paul
The Book of Job **14**:157

Welch, Holmes
Lao Tzu **7**:141

Wellek, Rene
Pearl **19**:299

West, M. L.
Pindar **12**:333

Westcott, John Howell
Livy **11**:312

Westermann, Claus
The Book of Psalms **4**:428

Westlake, John S.
Anglo-Saxon Chronicle **4**:4

Weston, Jessie L.
Arthurian Legend **10**:28
Chretien de Troyes **10**:133
Gottfried von Strassburg **10**:247
Wolfram von Eschenbach **5**:300

Wetherbee, Winthrop
Romance of the Rose **8**:422

Wheeler, Arthur Leslie
Cattullus **18**:82

Whewell, William
Bacon, Roger **14**:3

Whibley, Charles
Apuleius **1**:15

Whigham, Peter
Catullus **18**:109

Whinfield, E. H.
Khayyam **11**:255
Rumi, Jalal al-Din **20**:338

Whitehead, Alfred North
Plato **8**:271

Whitelock, Dorothy
Beowulf **1**:101

Whitman, Cedric H.
Aristophanes **4**:133
Iliad **1**:350
Odyssey **16**:254
Sophocles **2**:362

Wicksteed, Philip H.
Inferno **3**:46

Wiersma, S.
Longus **7**:274

Wilhelm, James J.
Bertran de Born **5**:39

Wilhelmsen, Frederick D.
Cicero, Marcus Tullius **3**:274

Wilkinson, L. P.
Ovid **7**:329

Williams, Harry F.
Chretien de Troyes **10**:225

Willson, H. B.
Gottfried von Strassburg **10**:278
Hartmann von Aue **15**:148, 165, 175, 196

Wilson, B. W. J. G.
Cicero, Marcus Tullius **3**:281

Wilson, Edmund
Sophocles **2**:341

Wilson, H. Schutz
Khayyam **11**:238

Wilson, Harry Langford
Juvenal **8**:23

Wilson, R. M.
Layamon **10**:335

Windelband, Wilhelm
Abelard **11**:3
Augustine, St. **6**:11
Averroes **7**:6

Winkler, John J.
Apuleius **1**:47

Winnington-Ingram, R. P.
Aeschylus **11**:206
Sophocles **2**:415

Winternitz, Moriz
Mahabharata **5**:202

Wiseman, T. P.
Catullus **18**:148

Witte, Karl
Inferno **3**:41

Wittgenstein, Ludwig
Augustine, St. **6**:55

Wolf, Carol Jean
The Dream of the Rood **14**:280

Wolff, Hope Nash
Epic of Gilgamesh **3**:328

Wolfram von Eschenbach
Wolfram von Eschenbach **5**:292, 293

Wolpert, Stanley
Mahabharata **5**:281

Wood, Anthony à
Bacon, Roger **14**:3

Woodman, A. J.
Livy **11**:382

Woodruff, F. Winthrop
Bacon, Roger **14**:66

Woodruff, Paul
Plato **8**:364

Woolf, Rosemary
The Dream of the Rood **14**:230

Woolf, Virginia
Aeschylus **11**:126
Murasaki, Lady **1**:418
Sappho **3**:395
Sophocles **2**:326

Wooten, Cecil W.
Demosthenes **13**:189
Hermogenes **6**:202

Wordsworth, William
Arabian Nights **2**:5
Sophocles **2**:304

Wrenn, C. L.
Anglo-Saxon Chronicle **4**:13
Beowulf **1**:107
Cædmon **7**:93

Wright, F. A.
Ovid **7**:304
Sappho **3**:396

Wright, Henry Parks
Juvenal **8**:22

Wright, Thomas
Polo, Marco **15**:261

Critic Index

ISBN 0-7876-1126-3